Marketing
Real People, Real Choices

Eleventh Edition

Michael R. SOLOMON
Saint Joseph's University

Greg W. MARSHALL
Rollins College

Elnora W. STUART
University of South Carolina Upstate

Pearson

Please contact https://support.pearson.com/getsupport/s/ with any queries on this content

Cover Images from Goodboy Picture Company, Getty Images, and fizkes/Shutterstock.

ScoutAutomatedPrintCode

ISBN-10: 0-13-681038-1
ISBN-13: 978-0-13-681038-4

Brief Contents

Contents

PART 3: Develop the Value Proposition for the Customer   274

Preface

MARKETING: REAL PEOPLE, REAL CHOICES

Why did we write this book? We'll answer this question with a simple, yet profound, statement: *Companies don't make decisions. People do.* And those decisions have never been harder than in recent memory, when marketers had to adjust to a worldwide pandemic that challenged many of the choices they needed to make. Professors and students have had to make hard choices, too! We all had to adapt to this "strange new world" together.

But regardless of what changing economic and social conditions may bring, at the end of the day, good marketing is good marketing! That's why "real people, real choices" is our mantra. Too often students read about what *a company* did or didn't do. We've worked with a lot of marketers and their great brands over the years, but we've never "met" a company (whether in lockdown or not). Have you? It's not faceless companies but rather real flesh-and-blood *people*—people like students and their professors—who agonize over important marketing decisions.

These managers (hopefully) applied the marketing lessons they learned both while in school and in the trenches to make the best choices they could. Our focus on "real people, real choices" adds people (yes, *real* ones) to the equation that many marketing textbooks neglect. The real people, real choices focus is reinforced throughout the book by the end-of-chapter cases that require students to evaluate real companies' decisions and make their own recommendations and by the decision-making opportunities in many of the end-of-chapter questions and activities.

Solving Teaching and Learning Challenges

Just like the executives we profile, we know what it's like to be in the trenches. That's because we teach the Principles of Marketing course on a regular basis in both face-to-face and online formats. We understand the challenge of engaging an entire class of students—many of whom are not marketing majors and who come to class with a bit of a chip on their shoulders, like: "Why should I have to take this class if I'm not going into marketing as a career path?" That's why we work hard wherever possible to emphasize the role that marketing plays in a larger context and in real-world organizations (and we encourage you to do so as well).

Real People vignettes feature a variety of real decision makers, from CEOs to brand managers, who confront decisions in their jobs that relate to each chapter. These vignettes help students to understand how marketing plays out in real companies, including Levi Strauss, PepsiCo, AdventHealth, the Philadelphia Phillies, and many others. Each vignette includes a **Here's My Problem** section that presents real options considered by the marketer. Students can then use their critical-thinking skills to determine the best solution to each problem.

It's a revelation to students when they understand that, if nothing else, they definitely will need to market themselves. This textbook was the first to emphasize the notion of "Brand You," and to show students how the concepts they learn in the course apply directly to their own personal marketing plan. Beginning with the 10th edition, we expanded on that idea to offer a complete **Brand You** section in every chapter that discusses how the topic of the chapter, such as research or pricing, plays an important role in developing a personal marketing plan.

4.4

OBJECTIVE
Understand how to
research both online
and offline resources
to search for a job or
internship.

Brand You: Career and Internship Information and Research

Taylor recognizes the importance of a good "fit" with the company and industry where he will work and spend his career. He also knows that he must investigate the culture of companies where he is interviewing. Understanding this, he is set to research different companies and industries in planning his personal brand.

How many times has someone asked you, "What do you want to do when you finish college?" While you may not know the answer to the question now, this is an excellent time to begin finding out more about your options. Yes, you need to find where there are some cool jobs, but at the same time, you also need to explore careers.

Just as a brand manager or a professional salesperson or an online retailer continuously gathers and analyzes information about his/her customers and other important factors relative to the product's success, your success in marketing yourself for a great internship or your dream job requires that you have information. And the more information you have, the better decisions about your marketing strategy you can make. This section can help you to:

- Know how to gather relevant information
- Understand how trends will potentially affect your career
- Identify resources you can use to find companies

A great read—that's how students describe our book. As we've always done, throughout this 11th edition, we deliver content in a conversational, jargon-free, and not overly academic style that students actually enjoy reading (we know, because they tell us). One reason we can do this is because all three authors have extensive experience working in marketing in industry in addition to their academic training and experience, and to this day, all three continue to work with organizations as marketing consultants! That's the secret sauce of what keeps *Real People, Real Choices* so real!

Developing Employability Skills

So, how do we prepare tomorrow's marketer? For one, we know that they will need to be "a numbers person." In the old days, a lot of students majored in marketing because they "weren't good at math," hence avoiding majors like accounting, finance, or economics. That's so 20th century! Increasingly, the marketing field is data driven, and sophisticated analytics are revolutionizing the options organizations have at their fingertips to create, communicate, deliver, and measure value. We're proud to say that with each edition we have continued to lead the field in offering to instructors and students cutting-edge coverage of marketing analytics and metrics. In this edition, we've continued to expand that coverage significantly to show how marketers use the exciting new tools they have available to understand and harness Big Data through marketing analytics as they strive to identify and meet customer needs.

To reinforce this focus throughout the book:

- **Apply Marketing Metrics** exercises at the end of each chapter provide additional opportunities for students to try their hand at applying some of the same metrics that marketers use to help them make good decisions.

- Way back in the 8th edition when quite a few practicing marketers hadn't even heard of Big Data, we were proud to be the first Principles of Marketing textbook to devote **an entire chapter (Chapter 5)** to the emerging and vital topic of marketing analytics and related tools. In this 11th edition, we've greatly expanded that chapter's coverage to include numerous new key terms, many more application examples to connect concepts to practice, and several new tables and figures to further illustrate this fascinating aspect of the emerging world of the "new marketer."

- The name of the game in marketing nowadays is maximizing the success of the customer experience. To do this requires that marketers think and plan more holistically about what makes for a great customer experience, rather than just doing it piecemeal. In this 11th edition, we include a chapter (Chapter 12) that is fully devoted to best practices across the components of the customer's experience with a provider and its offerings.

- One critical area to enhance employability in marketing today is a keen understanding of the role of digital and social media marketing approaches to marketing communication. In today's agency and company environments, often it is digital and social marketing that takes precedence over more "traditional" promotional tools, like television and print advertising. Marketing students need to gain a body of knowledge about these newer approaches from their very first marketing course, and this 11th edition features a heavily revamped and extensive coverage of these important topics (Chapters 13 and 14).

New to This Edition

So far, you've read about a wide variety of new and enhanced features of this 11th edition. Just in case we haven't impressed you enough already, here's a summary list of those and more that make our book stand out as by far the most up-to-date, cutting-edge product in the Marketing Principles market!

- Five of the decision-focused Real People vignettes that open each chapter are new to this edition. The new vignettes feature marketers from: PepsiCo, AdventHealth, Mary Kay, Terra Cycle, and the Philadelphia Phillies.
- Nine (9) new and five (5) extensively updated Marketing in Action cases are included at the end of chapters. The nine new cases feature the problems and opportunities faced by the following exciting, contemporary organizations:
  - StockX
  - P&G
  - Anheuser-Busch InBev
  - ThirdLove
  - Helen of Troy
  - Rent the Runway
  - Lululemon Athletica
  - Nestlé
  - Brud
- 80 new key terms appear throughout the chapters.

For more information on changes in each chapter of this 11th edition, see the chart below.

Chapter-by-Chapter Updates

Chapter 1 Welcome to the World of Marketing: Create and Deliver Value	<ul><li>New discussion of the continuing evolution of marketing, including the very important customer experience, service-dominant logic, and the co-creation of value</li><li>Discussion of disruption in marketing with examples of how product innovations have created disruptions in marketing</li><li>New Marketing in Action Case: Real Choices at StockX</li><li>New key terms added to this chapter:<ul><li>customer experience (CX or CEX)</li><li>service-dominant logic</li><li>customer co-creation</li><li>recommendation engine</li><li>disruptive marketing</li></ul></li></ul>
Chapter 2 Global, Ethical, and Sustainable Marketing	<ul><li>New Real People opening vignette featuring Tom Szaky at TerraCycle</li><li>New discussion of disruption in the global marketplace, including changes in the distribution of wealth, access to education, and improvements in infrastructure, especially media and telecommunications</li><li>Discussion of increasing differences in have and have-not countries as exposed by the COVID-19 pandemic</li><li>Increased coverage of the tariff debate and the U.S.–China trade war</li><li>New key terms added to this chapter:<ul><li>climate change</li><li>consumer xenocentrism</li></ul></li></ul>

Chapter 3 Strategic Market Planning	• New Real People opening vignette featuring Bob Roncska at AdventHealth
	• Stronger linking of the role of organizational strategy to marketing strategy and planning
	• Enhanced explanation and example of the concept of strategic business units
	• New coverage of the meaning and importance of organizational mission, vision, and values, along with clear examples of each
	• Multiple examples and connections between the COVID-19 crisis and its impact on organizational and marketing strategy and planning
	• Additional attention to the need for contingency planning and examining multiple planning scenarios
	• New Marketing in Action Case: Real Choices at P&G
	• New key terms added to this chapter:
	
	   - strategy - strategic pivot
	   - mission - marketing metrics
	   - vision - digital disruption
	   - vision statement - digital vortex
	   - organizational values - contingency planning
	   - nimble organization - scenarios

Chapter 4 Market Research	• Added focus on the importance of confidentiality and anonymity in market research
	• New dialogue on data privacy, data security, and risk management as the issues pertain to marketers
	• Discussion of the concept of using mystery shoppers in market research
	• Update on the Q Score syndicated research process
	• Enhanced coverage of qualitative research, quantitative research, and in-depth interviews
	• Introduction of robocalls and spoofed numbers and their impact on consumers
	• Coverage of the technique of catfishing online
	• New key terms added to this chapter:
	
	   - GIGO - qualitative research
	   - data privacy - quantitative research
	   - confidentiality - in-depth interview
	   - anonymity - survey research
	   - risk management - robocall
	   - data security - spoofed numbers
	   - mystery shoppers - catfish
	   - data analytics

Chapter 5 Marketing Analytics: Welcome to the Era of Data-Driven Insights!	• New Real People opening vignette featuring Josh Barbieri at the Philadelphia Phillies • Major overhaul of this chapter to provide students the most up-to-date treatment of marketing analytics among all Marketing Principles books • This rapidly changing area in marketing required the addition of 26 brand new key terms, which run a gamut of core concepts in analytics • Numerous attractively designed new figures and tables throughout the chapter add enjoyment and clarity to student learning about marketing analytics • Heavily updated treatment of CRM to bring this critical learning topic for students up to state-of-the-field level, including setting SMART goals and establishing key performance indicators (KPIs) and meaningful metrics to assess results • Extended new example of marketing automation, including focus on the sales funnel and lead nurturing • Heavy attention to three key categories of metrics that are central to marketers: marketing metrics, sales metrics, and service metrics

	• A new supplemental section after the main chapter that walks students through calculations of several of these important metrics • New and enhanced discussion of numerous contemporary data-related issues for marketers, such as cyber security, hackers, data breach, edge computing, augmented intelligence, deep learning, deepfake, and blockchain • New key terms added to this chapter: - lead - augmented intelligence - lead nurturing - deep learning - SMART goals - deepfake - user adoption metrics - customer acquisition cost (CAC) - customer perception metrics - sales cycle - business performance metrics - share of wallet - key performance indicators (KPIs) - net promoter score (NPS) - edge computing - return on experience (ROX)
Chapter 6 Understand Consumer and Business Markets	• New discussion of changing consumer values and the resulting trends, including the sharing economy, healthier living, diversity and multiculturalism, and consumers' demand for authenticity • Discussion of what the new normal following the COVID-19 pandemic will likely look like for consumers • New Marketing in Action Case: Real Choices at Anheuser-Busch InBev • New key terms added to this chapter: - HoloLens - data-driven disruptive marketing - flawsome - in-homing - social graph
Chapter 7 Segmentation, Target Marketing, and Positioning	• Attention to the impact of the COVID-19 crisis on segmentation, target marketing, and positioning—particularly in terms of future widespread market fragmentation • Enhanced treatment of a growing issue of oversegmentation by firms • Increased attention to Gen Z—the current up-and-coming group of consumers • Strong and positive treatment of the push toward greater social justice and its relationship to how marketers do segmentation, target marketing, and positioning • New and highly relevant content on gender identity and related issues, including a discussion of gender-bending products • Discussion of the potential impact of the COVID-19 crisis on demographic segmentation in the context of future spending power • The artificial intelligence (AI) discussion from Chapter 5 is continued here, bridging to the concept of "segments of one"—tracking the activity and preferences of a single potential customer and tailoring marketing responses to that unique person • Addition of a discussion about personas, including examples of the concept in action • A helpful new illustration of the concept of perceptual maps, using the U.S. steakhouse market as the example in the graphic • New Marketing in Action Case: Real Choices at ThirdLove • New key terms added to this chapter: - oversegmentation - Me Too movement - gender identity - segment of one - androgyny - personas - gender-bending products

Chapter 8 Product I: Innovation and New Product Development	• New Real People opening vignette featuring Sheryl Adkins-Green at Mary Kay
	• Discussion of the phenomenon during the early days of the COVID-19 crisis of certain products in the fast-moving-consumer-goods (FMCG) category experiencing substantial increases in consumer demand
	• Treatment of geofencing marketing, including an example of how it can be effectively used
	• Greatly increased coverage of design thinking, including its inherent process steps, an approach that continues to migrate into the way marketers develop products
	• Inclusion of a great new Tropicana example of how the brand tackled the tough "awareness stage" of new product adoption by consumers
	• New key term added to this chapter: geofencing marketing
Chapter 9 Product II: Product Strategy, Branding, and Product Management	• More emphasis on product objectives, especially their role in supporting broader marketing objectives and the firm's overall mission
	• New clarifying discussion of the differences between product managers and brand managers
	• Coverage of Anheuser-Busch (A-B) InBev's approach to increasing its product mix by acquiring new beverage products often by acquiring smaller craft breweries
	• A great new explanation of the importance of balance between individual branding approaches and parlaying the family brand, centered on Coca-Cola's experiences
	• Enhanced discussion and examples of cobranding and lifestyle brands
	• A new section sparked by the significant movement toward social justice that began in 2020, highlighting marketing's role in this effort, and particularly exemplifying several legacy brands that committed to rebranding away from prior words and images to ensure they are not hurtful to others
	• New Marketing in Action Case: Real Choices at Helen of Troy
	• New key terms added to this chapter:
	- product objectives
	- lifestyle brands
	- rebranding
Chapter 10 Price: What Is the Value Proposition Worth?	• New section on innovations in payment systems—digital and virtual currencies and updates on cryptocurrencies
	• Discussion of airlines and other firms changing pricing strategies in response to COVID-19's effects on business
	• Discussion of consumer responses to the economic effects of COVID-19, including growth in re-commerce, especially with luxury products
	• Discussion of a possible future cashless society
	• Stories of price gouging during the pandemic
	• New key terms added to this chapter:
	- subscription pricing - collaborative savings and consumption
	- digital wallet - peer-to-peer (P2P), or social lending
	- mobile wallet - rent-to-own
	- buy-now-pay-later (BNPL) - cashless society
	- save-now-buy-later (SNBL)
Chapter 11 Deliver the Goods: Determine the Distribution Strategy	• Additional attention to the option of an "indirect channel" of distribution in which firms sell their products through third parties
	• More emphasis on the malady of copyright infringement in the context of online distribution piracy

	• Coverage of Nike's Triple Double Strategy (2X), the cornerstone of which is the Nike Consumer Experience (NCX), which includes the firm's own direct-to-consumer network, as well as a vastly streamlined slate of wholesale distribution partners
	• Clear connections pointed out between new-age distribution channel approaches and opportunities for people in the "gig economy"
	• Updated discussion of the use of drones in distribution, along with example firms on the forefront of this trend
	• New Marketing in Action Case: Real Choices at Rent the Runway
	• New key term added to this chapter: indirect channel
Chapter 12 Deliver the Customer Experience	• New Real People opening vignette featuring Paula Hopkins at PepsiCo
	• Discussion and examples of the changing customer experience, including customer journey mapping
	• Additional coverage of how the COVID-19 pandemic has affected both online and offline retailers
	• Discussion of changes in technology that have improved distribution
	• New examples of experiential retailing
	• New section on concept stores
	• New Marketing in Action Case: Real Choices at Lululemon Athletica
	• New key terms added to this chapter: - direct-to-consumer (D2C) retail — recommerce - Amazon effect — upcycling - concept stores — dollar and variety stores - flash retailing, or pop-up stores and — extended reality (XR) pop-up retailing — order fulfillment automation
Chapter 13 Promotion I: Planning and Advertising	• New section on how technology is providing opportunities for personalized advertising messages
	• A discussion of how multichannel strategies can be super successful, using *Game of Thrones* first season and final season as examples
	• New discussion on the effects on advertising caused by the COVID-19 pandemic
	• New discussion of the importance of content marketing
	• New content on programmatic advertising used for buying digital advertising
	• New Marketing in Action Case: Real Choices at Nestlé
	• New key terms added to this chapter: - ethical bribe — programmatic advertising, or - interactive agency, or digital agency programmatic ad buying - in-house agency — drip pricing — upfront TV ad pricing
Chapter 14 Promotion II: Social Media Platforms and Other Promotion Elements	• Expanded discussion of social media marketing
	• Expanded discussion of the most important social media platforms for marketers, including Instagram, YouTube, TikTok, Snapchat, and Twitch
	• New discussion of viral marketing with DJ D-Nice's #ClubQuarantine example
	• New discussion of social selling, social commerce, media multitasking (or second screening), cord-cutting, memes, storytelling, and short-form storytelling
	• New coverage of PR activity of corporate activism, or social marketing, and the use of event-management software such as Eventbrite

	• New Marketing in Action Case: Real Choices at Brud
	• New key terms added to this chapter:
	
	  - groundswell
	  - media multitasking, or second screening
	  - cord-cutting
	  - cosplay
	  - Instagram
	  - sponsored posts
	  - YouTube
	  - TikTok
	  - Snapchat
		- Twitch
		- social commerce
		- storytelling
		- short-form storytelling
		- Zoom-bombing
		- social selling
		- corporate activism, or social marketing
		- memes

Instructor Teaching Resources

Please go to www.pearson.com for more information on instructor resources.

Acknowledgements

Thanks for the tremendous support we receive from our Pearson team, including (in alphabetical order) Claudia Fernandes, Julie Jigour, Kristin Ruscetta, and of course our intrepid editor, Lynn Huddon. George Allen at Asbury University, one of the very best case writers in the business, skillfully developed a wide range of new and revised Marketing Decision Cases for the 11th edition and for this we are very grateful. We're also thrilled to introduce two new contributors to this edition: Janée Burkhalter of Saint Joseph's University and Brad Carlson of Saint Louis University. Kudos also go to Chrissy Schreiber and Christian Panier, MBA student GAs at the Crummer Graduate School of Business at Rollins College, who artfully brought their perspectives into the updates for this 11th edition by supplying many new examples and critiquing and suggesting topics and changes from the student point of view—a highly valued perspective to us as authors. Great job all!

REVIEWERS

The guidance and recommendations of the following instructors through their reviews of the 10th edition helped us make better choices in revising the content and features of this new 11th edition of *Marketing: Real People, Real Choices*. We are grateful for their reviews and truly believe that their feedback was indispensable:

William Branson, Phoenix College

W. Peter Cornish, Temple University

Oliver Cruz-Milan, Texas A&M University-Corpus Christi

Randy Hacker, Baylor University

David Kaiser, Temple University

Nick Levandusky, University of Delaware

Lynda P. Walker, Eastern Michigan University

Andrew Thoeni, University of North Florida

EXECUTIVES

In addition to our reviewers, we want to extend our gratitude to the busy executives who gave generously of their time for the Real People, Real Choices opening vignettes throughout the chapters:

Chapter 1: Suzanne McFadden, Comcast

Chapter 2: Tom Szaky, TerraCycle

Chapter 3: Bob Roncska, AdventHealth

Chapter 4: Cindy Bean, Campbell Soup Company

Chapter 5: Josh Barbieri, Philadelphia Phillies

Chapter 6: Dondeena Bradley, WW International

Chapter 7: Jen Sey, Levi Strauss

Chapter 8: Sheryl Adkins-Green, Mary Kay

Chapter 9: Aaron Keller, Capsule

Chapter 10: Imad Khalidi, Auto Europe

Chapter 11: Michael Ford, BDP International

Chapter 12: Paula Hopkins, PepsiCo

Chapter 13: Sara Bamossy, Pitch

Chapter 14: Andrew Mitchell, Brandmovers

About the Authors

Michael R. Solomon, Ph.D., joined the Haub School of Business at Saint Joseph's University in Philadelphia as Professor of Marketing in 2006. From 2007 to 2013, he also held an appointment as Professor of Consumer Behaviour at the University of Manchester in the United Kingdom. From 1995 to 2006, he was the Human Sciences Professor of Consumer Behavior at Auburn University. Before joining Auburn in 1995, he was chairman of the Department of Marketing in the School of Business at Rutgers University, New Brunswick, New Jersey. Professor Solomon's primary research interests include consumer behavior and lifestyle issues; branding strategy; the symbolic aspects of products; the psychology of fashion, decoration, and image; services marketing; and the development of visually oriented online research methodologies. He currently sits on the editorial boards of the *Journal of Consumer Behaviour*, the *Journal for the Advancement of Marketing Education*, the *Journal of Marketing Theory and Practice*, and *Critical Studies in Fashion and Beauty*. In addition to other books, he is also the author of Pearson's text *Consumer Behavior: Buying, Having, and Being*, which is widely used in universities throughout the world. Professor Solomon frequently appears on television and radio shows, such as *The Today Show*, *Good Morning America*, Channel One, the *Wall Street Journal* Radio Network, and National Public Radio to comment on consumer behavior and marketing issues. He also is a regular contributor at Forbes.com.

Greg W. Marshall, Ph.D., is the Charles Harwood Professor of Marketing and Strategy in the Crummer Graduate School of Business at Rollins College in Winter Park, Florida. For three years, he also served as vice president for strategic marketing for Rollins. Before joining Rollins, he was on the faculty of Oklahoma State University, the University of South Florida, and TCU. He also holds a visiting professorship in the Marketing Group at Aston Business School, Birmingham, United Kingdom. Professor Marshall earned a BSBA in marketing and an MBA from the University of Tulsa and a Ph.D. in marketing from Oklahoma State University. His research interests include sales management, marketing management decision making, and intraorganizational relationships. He is editor-in-chief of the *European Journal of Marketing* and former editor of the *Journal of*

Marketing Theory and Practice and the *Journal of Personal Selling & Sales Management.* He currently serves on the editorial boards of the *Journal of the Academy of Marketing Science*, the *Journal of Business Research*, and *Industrial Marketing Management*. Professor Marshall is past president of the American Marketing Association Academic Council and also a former member of the AMA Board of Directors. He is a distinguished fellow and past president of the Academy of Marketing Science, and a distinguished fellow and past president of the Society for Marketing Advances. In 2018 he received the Lifetime Achievement Award from the American Marketing Association Selling and Sales Management Special Interest Group (SIG) and in 2019 he received the Circle of Honor Award from the Direct Selling Education Foundation. His industry experience before entering academe includes product management, field sales management, and retail management positions with firms such as Warner-Lambert, the Mennen Company, and Target Corporation.

Elnora W. Stuart, Ph.D., having most recently served as Professor of Marketing and Associate Dean of the George Dean Johnson, Jr. College of Business and Economics at the University of South Carolina Upstate, is now Distinguished Professor Emerita, University of South Carolina. She continues to teach, consult, and conduct research. Prior to joining USC Upstate in 2008, she was professor of marketing and the BP Egypt Oil Professor of Management Studies at the American University in Cairo, professor of marketing at Winthrop University in Rock Hill, South Carolina, and on the faculty of the University of South Carolina. She has also been a regular visiting professor at Instituto de Empresa in Madrid, Spain and Landshut College of Applied Sciences in Landshut, Germany. She earned a B.A. in theater and speech from the University of North Carolina at Greensboro and both an M.A. in journalism and mass communication and a Ph.D. in marketing from the University of South Carolina. Professor Stuart's research has been published in major academic journals, including the *Journal of Consumer Research*, the *Journal of Advertising*, the *Journal of Business Research*, the *Journal of Public Policy and Marketing*, the *Journal of Promotion Management*, and the *International Journal of Pharmaceutical and Healthcare Marketing*. For over 25 years, she has served as a consultant for numerous businesses and not-for-profit organizations in the United States and in Egypt.

1 Welcome to the World of Marketing

Create and Deliver Value

Suzanne McFadden

Meet Suzanne McFadden

▼ A Decision Maker at Comcast

Suzanne McFadden is Senior Vice President, Customer Experience & Communications at Comcast Cable, a part of Comcast NBCUniversal. Headquartered in Philadelphia, Comcast Cable is one of the nation's largest video, high-speed Internet, and phone providers to residential customers under the XFINITY brand, and it also provides these services to businesses. Additionally, it offers wireless, security, and automation services to residential customers under the XFINITY brand.

Suzanne received a BA in marketing and finance from the University of Delaware. She joined Comcast in 1997 in a field marketing role and gained experience in many aspects of marketing, such as customer acquisition and competitive and operations marketing, to rise through the ranks to land in her current responsibility for the end-to-end customer communications journey, from onboarding through engagement and the entire customer life cycle of Comcast's cable operations.

Suzanne's Info

What I do when I'm not working: Love spending time with family and friends—in particular, travel and food experiences. Also squeeze in time for reading, exercise, and TV watching.

First job out of school: Marketing Coordinator, SportsChannel Philadelphia

Career high: Being involved in the launch of Comcast High-Speed Internet. At the time, early 1997, companies were questioning if this "Internet thing" was really going to pay off—absolutely amazing to see the impact.

A job-related mistake I wish I hadn't made: Never taking a chance early on to move to a different part of the country or the world.

My hero: All of the career women who came before me—I am amazed when I look back at the corporate gender stereotypes of history and realize my success is only possible due to the women who endured inequality to get us where we are today.

My motto to live by: Never burn a bridge. People will often circle back into your life in a personal or professional capacity—make sure things always end on a positive note.

What drives me: In work, it is the competitive nature of the industry. It's fast paced, so you need to stay informed and make quick decisions.

My management style: Partnership and understanding. I make sure I know what motivates and drives my employees to success and work to give them what they need from me—leadership, time, attention, or hands off. It is different for all and that is what leaders must understand.

Don't do this when interviewing with me: Say "I" over and over.

Here's my problem...

Real **People**, Real **Choices**

Comcast has been working hard to improve its customer service and brand reputation. Over the last few years, they put tools in place to measure customer advocacy and satisfaction and provide a real-time feedback loop for employees to report and solve problems in order to help customers. In addition, they continue to innovate their product lines to meet customers' increasing entertainment, communication, and home needs. As a result, they have seen brand perception and customer satisfaction continue to rise.

But because there is now so much choice, customers do not always order the right package and set of services at the time of sale, and because Comcast offers a full 30-day money back guarantee, customers feel empowered to change up their package as they try out their new services.

Research shows that customers' anxiety goes up after they place an order and it stays up until their services are fully installed and activated. If the customer has signed up for a quad-play (Xfinity TV, Internet, Voice and Home Security), there is much to tell the customer about installation and activation. Thus, one of the team's first priorities was to ensure that the first 90 days of a customer's service experience are perfect.

The team identified one simple solution: Stay in touch with customers during the "onboarding" process and put them at ease that all will go well. They took advantage of new communications technologies to maintain this contact. By using platforms like email and SMS (short message service) that allowed them to text their customers, ratings of satisfaction with their service climbed significantly.

Knowing that the first 90 days are not only a learning time but a key time for a customer to "right size" and make sure they ordered the right tiers of services and products, the team wanted to contact customers to point out additional services they might want to add. At the time, the team was sending service emails and texts that educated customers about the products they had. Now they also considered using email to provide customers with more detail about products they might want.

Because Comcast opts-in customers to marketing messages at point of sale, promotional messages are permitted through email. Comcast had to weigh the decision to balance any messages seen as noncritical or promotional with key service messages—too many messages might cause a customer to tune-out all messages but sending none would not aid the customer in understanding what services might be a better fit for their household.

Suzanne and her team considered their options 1·2·3

1 Option
Don't email these customers about anything more than the products they have. Keep up the current practice of service messaging only to show them how to install their cable box, remind them of appointments, tell them when their kit will arrive, and introduce them to the services and features they have. This choice would ensure that customers would not tune out messages due to the noncritical nature of the promotional information. On the other hand, the lack of a promotional email strategy would make it more difficult to help customers "right size" if they realized within the first 90 days they didn't choose the ideal service package for their needs.

2 Option
Add promotional emails to the flow, but keep them distinct from the service emails to ensure that customers don't tune out a service email by thinking it is just a sales message. Use emails to encourage customers to upgrade their services, but clearly label them as promotional, and include information on convenient ways to upgrade. As with any other sales-related email, the customer would be free to ignore the message based upon its subject line or a quick review of the content. This choice would still allow customers to "right size" their cable package if they weren't satisfied with what they had. But there would always be the danger that customers would start to engage less with email from Comcast and perhaps even opt out of emails from the company entirely. That would remove any chance to connect with the customer down the road.

3 Option
Use emails to highlight ways to upgrade service plans as a part of the service email. This strategy would be less intrusive than Option #2, because customers would regard these emails as educational rather than as a pitch to buy more features. Still, it would be possible that customers might try to opt out of these additional emails, negatively impacting the perfect first 90 days Comcast was striving to deliver.

Now, put yourself in Suzanne's shoes. Which option would you choose, and why?

You Choose

Which **Option** would you choose, and **why**?

☐ Option 1   ☐ Option 2   ☐ Option 3

1.1

OBJECTIVE

Explain what marketing is, the marketing mix, what can be marketed, and the value of marketing.

Marketing: What Is It?

Marketing. People either love it or hate it. The crazy part of this is that whether they love it or hate it, most folks really do not understand what marketing really is! How about when a Rihanna concert in Atlanta or Chicago entices fans from Peoria, Illinois, to travel to those cities just to scream in ecstasy alongside the locals? Then there are the pop-up ads on your Facebook page for something you were searching for at Poshmark last week. And of course, there are those emails that fill your inbox from Amazon.com, suggesting products that might entice you to let go of some hard-earned cash. Yes, these are all examples of marketing. And that's just scratching the surface.

You already know a lot about marketing; it's been a part of your life from day one. As one of billions of **consumers** around the globe, you are the ultimate user of a good or service. Every time you purchase or use your car, your clothes, your lunch at the cafeteria (whether an old-school burger or a vegan version), a movie, or a haircut, you are part of the marketing process. In this text, we'll tell you why—and why you should care.

consumer
The ultimate user of a good or service.

Indeed, consumers like you (and your humble authors!) are at the center of all marketing activities. By the way, when we refer to *consumers*, we don't just mean individuals. Organizations—whether a company, government, sorority, or charity—are also consumers.

Here's the key: *Marketing is first and foremost about satisfying consumer needs*. We like to say that the consumer is king (or queen), but it's important not to lose sight of the fact that the seller also has needs—to make a profit, to remain in business, and even to take pride in selling the highest-quality products possible. Products are sold to satisfy both consumers' and marketers' needs; it's a two-way street.

Let's think for a minute about satisfying customer needs. While this is easy enough to understand, it's far more difficult to achieve. Customers face millions of companies offering gazillions of products.

Traditionally, marketing gurus would tell us that all we need to do is to offer consumers a great product at a reasonable price and show them how their lives would be improved if they own it. Voilà! Success and profits!

Today it's a little more difficult. There are literally millions of companies around the globe all vying for the limited demand of consumers. And the customer is exposed to not only traditional marketing activities but also the contacts provided by companies and other consumers who are, like them, online 24/7.

customer experience (CX or CEX)
A customer's overall assessment of every interaction the customer has experienced with a business, from navigating the company website to talking to customer service to the packaging the product arrives in.

So how does one brand succeed? Today, what matters is the **customer experience (CX or CEX)**. CX is the customer's overall assessment of every interaction the customer has experienced with a business from navigating the company website to talking to customer service to the packaging the product arrives in. Today's customer is only going to buy and be loyal to a brand that has always given them positive experiences. Even one bad experience can send customers scurrying to your competitor. We'll talk more about CX and how marketers map the customer's experience later in Chapter 5 and again in Chapter 12.

marketing
Marketing is the activity, set of institutions, and processes for creating, communicating, delivering, and exchanging offerings that have value for customers, clients, partners, and society at large.[1]

When you ask people to define **marketing**, you get many answers. Some people say, "That's all those emails and popups I get on my computer from Amazon and every other online site I know of, trying to get me to buy something from them." Many people say, "Oh, that's simple—TV commercials." Students might answer, "That's a course I have to take before I can get my business degree." Each of these responses has a grain of truth to it, but the official definition of marketing the American Marketing Association adopted in 2013 is as follows:

> Marketing is the activity, set of institutions, and processes for creating, communicating, delivering, and exchanging offerings that have value for customers, clients, partners, and society at large.[2]

The basic idea behind this somewhat complicated definition is that marketing is all about delivering value to everyone whom a transaction affects. That's a long-winded explanation. Let's take it apart to understand exactly what marketing is all about.

"Marketing Is the Activity, Set of Institutions, and Processes . . . "

As we will discuss throughout this text, marketing includes a great number of activities—from top-level market planning by the chief marketing officer (CMO) of a big company to the creation of a Facebook page by your university. The importance organizations assign to marketing activities varies a lot. Top management in some firms is marketing oriented (especially when the chief executive officer, or CEO, comes from the marketing ranks), whereas in other companies marketing is an afterthought. One study shows that over 25 percent of CEOs have either a marketing or a sales background—that makes this information pretty relevant, so stick with us![3]

In the text, we discuss many of the activities of marketing that include:

- Better understanding of customer needs through marketing research
- Selecting the people or organizations in the market that are your best bets for success
- Developing the product
- Pricing the product
- Getting the product to the consumer
- Delivering marketing messages via traditional and online advertising and a host of other activities

We'll also learn about a variety of institutions that help firms create a better marketing program:

- Advertising and other types of agencies that firms work with to create and deliver a variety of marketing communication activities, including traditional advertising, as well as newer digital communications, sales promotions, and research activities

Of course today, there are a number of different categories of agencies. Some of these are:

  - Startup marketing
  - Public relations
  - Advertising
  - Digital marketing
  - Content marketing & SEO
  - Social media marketing[4]
- Marketing research firms, such as Nielsen, that provide data vital to the planning and implementation of successful marketing programs
- The traditional media
- The Internet and social media
- Governments that enforce laws and regulations to make sure marketing occurs in a fair and ethical manner
- Logistics firms that get the product to the consumer most efficiently
- Retailers that interact directly with the final customer

We also talk about some of the processes marketers use in combination with these institutions to satisfy customer needs—the end-all for all marketing activities.

Whether it is a giant global producer of consumer products, such as Procter & Gamble, or a smaller organization, such as Lizard's Thicket, a restaurant business in Columbia, SC, a marketer's decisions affect—and are affected by—the firm's other activities. Marketing managers must work with financial and accounting officers to figure out whether products are profitable, to set marketing budgets, and to determine prices. They must work with people in manufacturing to be sure that the new iPhone is produced on time and in the right quantities for those avid iPhone fans who camp out in front of Apple stores to get their hands on the new model. Marketers also must work with research-and-development specialists to create products that meet consumers' needs. And most important, marketers must maintain their expertise on the ever-changing innovations that occur daily in every aspect of marketing.

Figure 1.1 *Snapshot* | The Marketing Mix

The marketing mix is the marketer's strategic toolbox.

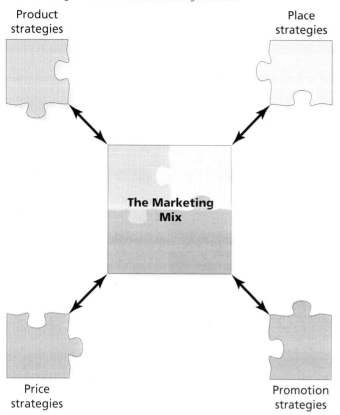

Product strategies

Place strategies

The Marketing Mix

Price strategies

Promotion strategies

marketing mix
A combination of the product itself, the price of the product, the promotional activities that introduce it, and the places where it is made available that together create a desired response among a set of predefined consumers.

four Ps
Product, price, promotion, and place.

product
A tangible good, service, idea, or some combination of these that satisfies consumer or business customer needs through the exchange process; a bundle of attributes including features, functions, benefits, and uses.

promotion
The coordination of a marketer's communication efforts to influence attitudes or behavior.

" . . . for Creating, Communicating, Delivering, and Exchanging . . . ": The Marketing Mix

As we said, marketing is about satisfying needs. To do this, marketers need many tools. The **marketing mix** is the marketer's strategic toolbox. It consists of the tools the organization uses to create a desired response among a set of predefined consumers. These tools include the product itself, the price of the product, the promotional activities (such as advertising and social media marketing) that introduce the product to consumers, and the places where it is available. We commonly refer to the elements of the marketing mix as the **four Ps**: *product, price, promotion,* and *place.*

Although we talk about the four Ps as separate parts of a firm's marketing strategy, in reality, product, price, promotion, and place decisions are interdependent. Decisions about any single one of the four are affected by and affect every other marketing mix decision. For example, what if Superdry (a rapidly growing Japanese apparel company) decides to introduce a leather biker jacket that is higher end than the ones it makes now? If the company uses more expensive materials to make this item, it has to boost the selling price to cover these higher costs; this also signals to consumers that the garment is more upscale. In addition, Superdry would have to create advertising and other promotional strategies to convey a top-quality image. Furthermore, the firm must include high-end retailers like Bergdorf Goodman and Bloomingdale's in its distribution strategy to ensure that shoppers who seek out high-end items will come across the jacket. Thus, all the pieces in the puzzle we call the marketing mix work together. As Figure 1.1 shows, each P is interconnected with each of the other three Ps. This shows us that the activities of each of the four Ps must be coordinated with each of the other three Ps.

We'll examine these components of the marketing mix in detail later in this book. For now, let's briefly look at each of the four Ps to gain some more insight into their role in the marketing mix.

Product

What have you spent your money and time to get recently? A pizza on Friday night, a concert on the weekend, a drone that will take photos from high in the air—maybe even a "wonderful" marketing textbook? These are all products. A **product** can be a good, a service, an idea, a place, a person—whatever a person or organization offers for sale in the exchange. Creating new products is vital to the success and even the life of an organization. The product, one aspect of the marketing mix, includes the design and packaging of a good as well as its physical features and any associated services, such as free delivery.

The product is a combination of many different elements, all of which are important to the product's success. Think about your college education—an expensive product, for sure. You are buying more than the boring lecture in that chemistry class (or the awesome lecture in your marketing class). You are also paying for the health center with a weight room, pool, and a rock-climbing wall; for the classroom building; for the football and basketball teams; and maybe for the bragging rights of graduating from a "Big Ten" school.

Promotion

Although we all are familiar with advertising, **promotion**, also referred to as *marketing communication,* includes many different activities marketers undertake to inform consumers about their products and to encourage potential customers to buy these products. Marketing communication takes the form of personal selling, TV advertising, store coupons, billboards, magazine ads, publicity releases, web pages, social media sites, and a lot more. Today marketers are quickly moving much of their energy and money to devising and implementing digital marketing communications, including mobile marketing, location-based marketing, behavioral digital marketing, and, of course, social media marketing.

Place

Place refers to the availability of the product to the customer at the desired time and location. This P relates to a **channel of distribution**, which is the series of firms or individuals that facilitates the movement of a product from the producer to the final customer. For clothing or electronics, this channel includes local retailers as well as other outlets, such as retail sites on the web that strive to offer the right quantity of products in the right styles at the right time. Place now has expanded past the traditional channel of distribution to consumers renting their homes or cars or RVs to other consumers in the *sharing economy* that we'll talk more about later.

A product is actually a "bundle" of benefits. For some universities, that means that in addition to a great education they offer cool amenities like a rock-climbing wall.

place
The availability of the product to the customer at the desired time and location.

channel of distribution
The series of firms or individuals that facilitates the movement of a product from the producer to the final customer.

price
The assignment of value, or the amount the consumer must exchange to receive the offering.

Price

Price—we all know what price is. It's the amount you have to pay for the pizza, the concert tickets, the tennis racket, and, yes, this book. Price is the assignment of value, or the amount the consumer must exchange to receive the offering. Marketers often turn to price to increase consumers' interest in a product. This happens when they put an item on sale, but in other cases, marketers actually try to sell a product with a higher price than people are used to if they want to communicate that it's high quality or cutting edge. For example, designer clothes and accessories are priced so high that only a few consumers can afford them. Not many of us can afford a Prada Python/Crocodile Arcade-Stripe Frame Satchel Bag priced at $9,600 or a pair of Valentino Rockstud Metallic Leather Mid-Heel Pumps at $1,045. If you can, you probably don't need to take this course!

At the heart of every marketing act—big or small—is something we refer to as an *exchange relationship*. An **exchange** occurs when a person gives something and gets something else in return. The buyer receives an object, service, or idea that satisfies a need, and the seller receives something he or she feels is of equivalent value. Today, most exchanges occur as monetary transactions in which one party surrenders currency (in the form of cash, check, credit card, or even Bitcoin) in return for a good or a service. But there are also other kinds of exchanges. A politician, for example, can agree to work toward certain goals in exchange for your vote, city officials may offer you a cleaner environment if you recycle, and health officials tell you that you can save lives (perhaps your own) if you wash your hands with soap and hot water for 20 seconds.

exchange
The process by which some transfer of value occurs between a buyer and a seller.

For an exchange to occur, at least two people or organizations must be willing to make a trade, and each must have something the other wants. Both parties must agree on the value of the exchange and how it will be carried out. Each party also must be free to accept or reject the other's terms for the exchange. Under these conditions, a knife-wielding robber's offer to "exchange" your money for your life does *not* constitute a valid exchange. In contrast, although someone may complain that a store's prices are "highway robbery," an exchange occurs if he or she still forks over the money to buy something there—even if he or she still grumbles about it weeks later.

To complicate things a bit more, everyone does not always agree on the terms of the exchange. Think, for example, about movie piracy. That's what happens when a new Marvel blockbuster is available on street corners for a few dollars—or free on BitTorrent— before it even opens in theaters.

" . . . Offerings . . . ": What Can We Market?

Is there any limit to what marketers can and will market? Marketing applies to more than just the new iPhone and the Microwavable S'Mores Maker your mother bought you before you came to college.

Some of the best marketers come from the ranks of services companies, such as American Express, or not-for-profit organizations, like Greenpeace. Politicians, athletes, and performers use marketing to their advantage (the Kardashians have figured it out). Ideas such as political systems (democracy, totalitarianism), religion (Christianity, Islam), and art (realism, abstract) also compete for acceptance in a "marketplace." In this text, we'll refer to any good, service, person, place, or idea that we can market as a product, even though what you buy may not take a physical form.

Consumer Goods and Services

consumer goods
The goods individual consumers purchase for personal or family use.

services
Intangible products that are exchanged directly between the producer and the customer.

Consumer goods are the tangible products that individual consumers purchase for personal or family use. **Services** are intangible products that we pay for and use but don't own. In 2017, service transactions contribute 80 percent of the gross domestic product (GDP) in the U.S. and other developed countries.[5] Marketers need to understand the special challenges that arise when they market an intangible service rather than a tangible good.[6] Because both goods and services are products, it's more accurate to say "goods and services" rather than "products and services."

Business-to-Business Goods and Services

business-to-business marketing
The marketing of goods and services from one organization to another.

industrial goods
Goods that individuals or organizations buy for further processing or for their own use when they do business.

Business-to-business marketing is about the exchange of goods and services from one organization to another. Although we usually think of marketing in terms of the piles of consumer goods that beg for our dollars every day, the reality is that businesses and other organizations buy a lot more stuff than consumers do. They purchase these **industrial goods** for further processing or to use in their own business operations. For example, automakers buy tons of steel to use in the manufacturing process. They also buy powerful computer systems to track manufacturing costs and other information essential to operations and much smaller computers to install in their cars to control those neat functions that keep drivers safe and happy.

e-commerce
The buying or selling of goods and services electronically, usually over the Internet.

Similarly, the growth of **e-commerce** isn't just about things people buy for themselves—books, clothing, cars, and so forth—on the Internet. Just like in the offline world, much of the real online action is in the area of business-to-business marketing.

Not-for-Profit Marketing

not-for-profit organizations, or **nongovernmental organizations (NGOs)**
Organizations with charitable, educational, community, and other public service goals that buy goods and services to support their functions and to attract and serve their members.

As we noted previously, you don't have to be a businessperson to use marketing principles. Many **not-for-profit organizations**, or **nongovernmental organizations (NGOs)**, including museums, zoos, and even churches, practice the marketing concept to survive. Local governments adopt marketing techniques to attract new businesses and industries to their counties and cities. Even states are getting into the act: We've known for a long time that I♥NY, but recently Kentucky and Oregon hired advertising agencies to develop statewide branding campaigns. (The official state motto of Oregon is now "Oregon. We love dreamers.")[7]

Idea, Place, and People Marketing

Marketing principles also encourage people to endorse ideas or to change their behaviors in positive ways. Many organizations work hard to "sell" everything from the elimination of racism and gender discrimination to shelter-pet adoption to stopping teen bullying. We are all familiar with tourism marketing that promotes wonderful places with slogans such as "Smile! You are in Spain!" or "Live your myth in Greece."

You may have heard the expression "Stars are made, not born." There's a lot of truth to that. Adele may have a killer voice and Chris Davis may have a red-hot baseball bat, but talent alone doesn't make thousands or even millions of people buy their music or stadium seats. Some of the same principles that go into "creating" a celebrity apply to you. An entertainer—whether Miranda Lambert, Selena Gomez, or Drake—must "package" his or her talents, identify a market that is likely to be interested, and work hard to gain exposure to these potential customers by appearing in the right musical venues.

In the same way, everyday people like you "package" themselves when they create a great social media profile. And this person-marketing perspective is more valid than ever—now that almost everyone can find "15 minutes of fame" on a website or blog or in a YouTube video. We even have a new word—*microcelebrity*—to describe those who are famous not necessarily to millions of people but certainly to hundreds or even thousands who follow their comings and goings on Facebook, Instagram, or Twitter. Whether it's the guy who sang the "Bed Intruder Song," Boxxy, Gary the Goat, "Alex from Target," or even Grumpy Cat, the Internet churns out hundreds of temporarily famous people who probably won't be remembered for long.

The idea of marketing people is especially important to college students like you who are trying to land an internship or a job. In fact, we believe this is so important that we have a section in every chapter of this book called "Brand You." As we go through the marketing process chapter by chapter, we will discuss how you can use marketing strategies to create your unique brand. We will talk about how Brand You can be useful not only for getting a first job but also for enjoying a successful career.

" . . . Value for Customers . . . "

Most successful firms today practice the **marketing concept**—that is, marketers first identify consumer needs and then provide products that satisfy those needs to ensure the firm's long-term profitability. Practicing the marketing concept is, of course, more complex and requires that marketers understand the most basic elements of successful marketing.

These elements—needs, wants, benefits, demand, a market, and a marketplace—are listed and explained in Table 1.1.

---

marketing concept
A management orientation that focuses on identifying and satisfying consumer needs to ensure the organization's long-term profitability.

need
The recognition of any difference between a consumer's actual state and some ideal or desired state.

want
The desire to satisfy needs in specific ways that are culturally and socially influenced.

benefit
The outcome sought by a customer that motivates buying behavior that satisfies a need or want.

demand
Customers' desires for products coupled with the resources needed to obtain them.

market
All the customers and potential customers who share a common need that can be satisfied by a specific product, who have the resources to exchange for it, who are willing to make the exchange, and who have the authority to make the exchange.

marketplace
Any location or medium used to conduct an exchange.

Table 1.1	Value for Customers	
Term	**Definition**	**In Practice**
Need	The recognition of any difference between a consumer's actual state and some ideal or desired state.	If the difference is big enough, the consumer is motivated to take action to satisfy the need. When you're hungry, you buy a snack. If you're not happy with your hair, you get a new hairstyle.
Want	The desire to satisfy needs in specific ways that are culturally and socially influenced.	If two students are hungry, the first student may be a health nut who fantasizes about gulping down a big handful of trail mix, whereas the second person may lust for a greasy cheeseburger and fries. The first student's want is trail mix, whereas the second student's want is fast food (and some antacid for dessert).
Benefit	The outcome sought by a customer that motivates buying behavior that satisfies a need or want.	After several years when sales were down, McDonald's responded to the number-one request of its customers: breakfast all day. The new program attracted lapsed customers back and increased lunch business.[8]
Demand	Customers' desires for products coupled with the resources needed to obtain them.	Demand for a snappy red BMW convertible includes the people who want the car minus those who can't afford to buy or lease one.
Market	All the customers and potential customers who share a common need that can be satisfied by a specific product, who have the resources to exchange for it, who are willing to make the exchange, and who have the authority to make the exchange.	The availability of scholarships, government aid, and loans has increased the market for college education as more students can afford an education.
Marketplace	Any location or medium used to conduct an exchange.	Today the exchange may be face-to-face or through a mail-order catalog, a TV shopping network, an eBay auction, or a phone app.

For example, you may *need* transportation but *want* a new Tesla Model S Performance. The Tesla Model S Performance will not only get you from point A to point B; it will also go from 0 to 60 mph in under 3 seconds. Unfortunately, it's possible that Tesla can't count you in their estimates of *demand* or the size of the *market* for the Model S because, at around $90,000, you can't afford such an expensive car. In that case, you need to check out a different *marketplace*: a used car lot.

Of course, marketplaces continue to evolve. Increasingly consumers, especially younger ones, would rather rent than purchase the products they use. One of the biggest changes is in the domain of car sales, which are plummeting among newer drivers. Innovative start-ups like Zipcar figured out that many people, especially those who live in urban areas, would rather rent a ride by the hour instead of dealing with the hassles of car loans and hunting for parking spots. Now the big guys are testing the waters. BMW now wholly owns the DriveNow electric vehicle car-sharing program and ReachNow, which operates in North American cities.

A second change in the transportation marketplace is ridesharing. Uber, founded in 2009, has become a global phenomenon based on this concept. Uber drivers use their own cars and work when they want to. Average customers prefer Uber to traditional taxis because typically the ride is cleaner. Even business travelers are choosing Uber over rentals and taxis—one study showed that this type of travel made up two-thirds of business expense receipts for ground transportation in 2017. It's clear the business is thriving—Uber gave four billion rides in 2017 alone![9] Lyft, the second largest ride-sharing company, began doing business as Zimride in 2012.

utility
The usefulness or benefit that consumers receive from a product.

Millions of enterprising consumers, in turn, are considering joining the *sharing economy* by renting out their stuff when they aren't using it; they're offering everything from barbecue grills and power tools to Halloween costumes and who knows what else on sites like Zilok in France and Craigslist in the United States. Some analysts refer to this mushrooming trend as *collaborative consumption*.

The sharing economy continues to grow as more and more consumers have the ability and the preference to rent or borrow goods rather than buy their own. The sharing economy is estimated to grow from $14 billion in 2014 to $335 billion by 2025.[10] This estimate is based on the rapid growth of Uber and Airbnb as indicators. We'll talk more about the sharing economy in Chapters 10 and 11.

Marketing Creates Utility

In the beginning of this chapter, we discussed the definition of marketing: "marketing is . . . for delivering value for customers." Value for consumers is the ratio of benefits to cost (as perceived by the customer) that motivates purchase. The benefit is some type of utility of goods and services as delivered by the four Ps. Thus, **utility** refers to the usefulness or benefit customers receive through the product itself, its price, its distribution, and the marketing communications about it. Marketing processes create several different kinds of utility to provide value to consumers:

Rent the Runway is a service started by two recent business school grads. It rents high-end dresses from designers, like Diane von Furstenberg, for about one-tenth of the cost of buying the same garment in a store. A woman can rent a dress for four nights; it's shipped directly to her doorstep, much like a Netflix DVD. The customer returns the dress in a prepaid envelope and the rental price includes the cost of dry cleaning. Place utility at work!

Bryan Bedder/Stringer/Getty Images

- *Form utility* is the benefit marketing provides by transforming raw materials into finished products, as when a dress manufacturer combines silk, thread, and zippers to create a bridesmaid's gown.

- *Place utility* is the benefit marketing provides by making products available when and where customers want them. The most sophisticated evening gown sewn in New York's garment district is of little use to a bridesmaid in Kansas City if it isn't shipped to her in time.

- *Time utility* is the benefit marketing provides by storing products until they are needed. Some women rent their wedding gowns instead of buying them and wearing them only once (they hope!).
- *Possession utility* is the benefit marketing provides by allowing the consumer to own (at a reasonable price), use, and enjoy the product. The bridal store provides access to a range of styles and colors that would not be available to a woman outfitting a bridal party on her own.

As we've seen, marketers provide utility in many ways. Now, let's see how customers and others "take delivery" of this added value.

Value for Clients and Partners

Marketing doesn't just meet the needs of customers—it meets the needs of diverse stakeholders. The term **stakeholders** refers to buyers, sellers, or investors in a company; community residents; and even citizens of the nations where goods and services are made or sold—in other words, any person or organization that has a "stake" in the outcome. Thus, marketing is about satisfying everyone involved in the marketing process.

Value for Society at Large

Is it possible to contribute in a positive way to society and the Earth and still make a good profit for stockholders? Target, one of the nation's largest retailers, seems to think so. The company announced in its 2012 corporate responsibility report that two of its top five priorities are environmental sustainability and responsible sourcing.

Some SOLO products are made of environmentally preferable materials—Green marketing in action.

1.2 *When* Did Marketing Begin? The Evolution of a Concept

OBJECTIVE
Explain the evolution of the marketing concept.

Now that we have an idea of how the marketing process works, let's take a step back and see how this process worked (or didn't work) in "the old days." Although it just sounds like common sense to us, believe it or not, the notion that businesses and other organizations succeed when they satisfy customers' needs actually is a pretty recent idea. Before the 1950s, organizations only needed to make products faster and cheaper to be successful. Let's take a quick look at how the marketing discipline has developed since then. Table 1.2 tells us about a few of the more recent events in this marketing history.

stakeholders
Buyers, sellers, or investors in a company; community residents; and even citizens of the nations where goods and services are made or sold—in other words, any person or organization that has a "stake" in the outcome.

Table 1.2	Marketing's "Greatest Hits"

Year	Marketing Event
1961	Procter & Gamble launches Pampers.
1964	Blue Ribbon Sports (now known as Nike) ships its first shoes.
1971	Cigarette advertising is banned on radio and TV.
1980	Ted Turner creates CNN.
1981	MTV begins.
1985	New Coke is launched; old Coke rebranded as Coca-Cola Classic is brought back 79 days later.
2004	Online sales in the U.S. top $100 billion.
2010	Apple launches the iPad; sells 300,000 of the tablets on the first day and 1 million iPads in 28 days—less than half of the 74 days it took to sell 1 million iPhones. Consumers watch more than 30 billion videos online per month.
2014	Facebook spends $2 billion to buy Oculus Rift, a manufacturer of virtual reality headsets, as it signals the next frontier for social networks.
2016	Microsoft buys LinkedIn for $26.1 billion.
2017	Tax reform makes it less advantageous for U.S. firms to move their operations out of the country, which should be good news for consumers who like "Made in the USA."
2018	Coke introduces new flavored (Feisty Cherry, Twisted Mango, Ginger Lime, and Zesty Blood Orange) versions of Diet Coke in skinny cans.
2020	Zoom comes into its own as the definitive leader in the digital meeting platforms space, quickly leap-frogging over more mature (and initially much larger) rivals Cisco WebEx and Microsoft Teams. Necessity being the mother of invention that it is, Zoom quickly innovated and adapted to enable marketers and salespeople alike to carry on their business and customer relationships on a user-friendly and intuitive platform that is loaded with great features.

Sources: Patricia Sellers, "To Avoid Trampling, Get Ahead of the Mass," *Fortune*, 1994, 201–2, except as noted. Keith Regan, "Report: Online Sales Top $100 Billion," June 1, 2004, http://www.ecommercetimes.com/story/34148.html.

The Production Era

We think about the history of marketing as moving through four distinct eras, summarized in Table 1.3 and briefly described here. Many people say that Henry Ford's Model T changed America forever. From the start in 1908, when the "Tin Lizzie," or "flivver," as the T was known, sold for $575, Ford continued to make improvements in production.

production orientation
A management philosophy that emphasizes the most efficient ways to produce and distribute products.

Ford's focus illustrates a **production orientation**, which works best in a seller's market when demand is greater than supply because it focuses on the most efficient ways to produce and distribute products.

The Sales Era

When product availability exceeds demand in a buyer's market, businesses may engage in the "hard sell," in which salespeople aggressively push their wares. This **selling orientation** means that management views marketing as a sales function, or a way to move products out of warehouses so that inventories don't pile up. The selling orientation gained in popularity a short while after World War II ended and prevailed well into the 1950s. But consumers as a rule don't like to be pushed, and the hard sell gave marketing a bad image.

selling orientation
A managerial view of marketing as a sales function, or a way to move products out of warehouses to reduce inventory.

Companies that still follow a selling orientation tend to be more successful at making one-time sales rather than at building repeat business. We are most likely to find this focus among companies that sell *unsought goods*—products that people don't tend to buy without some prodding. For example, most of us aren't exactly "dying" to shop for cemetery plots, so some encouragement may be necessary to splurge on a final resting place. Even in these categories, however, we still may find that competitors try to stay on top of consumers' evolving needs. That's why we see the rise in popularity of *eco burials* that avoid embalming and encourage cremation and also online funerals that stream images of the loved one on the Internet.

| Table 1.3 | The Evolution of Marketing |

Icon	Era	Description	Example
	Production Era	Consumers have to take whatever is available; marketing plays a relatively insignificant role.	Henry Ford's Model T sold for less than $575 and owned 60 percent of the market.
	Sales Era	When product availability exceeds demand in a buyer's market. Management views marketing as a sales function, or a way to move products out of warehouses so that inventories don't pile up. Businesses engage in the "hard sell," in which salespeople aggressively push their wares.	The selling orientation gained in popularity after World War II when post-war demand had been satisfied and companies needed to sell more.
	Relationship Era	Firms have a customer orientation that satisfies customers' needs and wants.	Organizations research customer needs and develop products to meet the needs of various groups.
	Triple-Bottom-Line Era	Business emphasizes the need to maximize three components: 1. *The financial bottom line* 2. *The social bottom line* 3. *The environmental bottom line*	Companies try to create financial profits for stakeholders, contribute to the communities in which the company operates, and engage in sustainable business practices that minimize damage to the environment or that even improve it.

Vira Honcharenko/Shutterstock · Hit Toon/Shutterstock · marcojavier/DigitalVision Vectors/Getty Image · Inspiring/Shutterstock · stamen al/saefus/Shutterstock · Dana Hudson/Shutterstock

The Relationship Era

Zappos is an online retailer whose company-wide goal is to "WOW" customers. Zappos is one of many firms that have adopted a **customer orientation.**

JetBlue is another firm known for its customer orientation. From its beginning in 2000, JetBlue's goal has been to provide features that delight customers and make flying fun. JetBlue planes offer the most legroom of any economy airline in coach, complimentary high-speed Fly-Fi broadband on every aircraft, free seatback entertainment at every seat, free snacks and soft drinks, hospitality-trained crewmembers offering award-winning service, and affordable fares. During the 20 years of JetBlue's operation, the airline has received 13 J.D. Power annual awards for highest customer satisfaction.[11]

Following the Sales Era, the world's most successful firms began to adopt a customer orientation that provided marketers with a new and important way to outdo the competition—through satisfying customer needs better than the competition. In this, the Relationship Era, companies increasingly concentrated on improving the quality of their products. By the early 1990s, many in the marketing community followed a **total quality management (TQM)** approach, which is a management philosophy that involves all employees from the assembly line onward in continuous product quality improvement. We'll learn more about TQM in Chapter 9.

customer orientation
A business approach that prioritizes the satisfaction of customers' needs and wants.

total quality management (TQM)
A management philosophy that focuses on satisfying customers through empowering employees to be an active part of continuous quality improvement.

The Triple-Bottom-Line Era

More recently, organizations began to wake up to the idea that making monetary profit is important but that there's more to think about than just the financial bottom line. Instead, they began to focus on a **triple-bottom-line orientation**.[12] This new way of looking at business emphasizes the need to maximize not just one, but three components:

triple-bottom-line orientation
A business orientation that looks at financial profits, the community in which the organization operates, and creating sustainable business practices.

1. *The financial bottom line:* Financial profits to stakeholders
2. *The social bottom line:* Contributing to the communities in which the company operates
3. *The environmental bottom line:* Creating sustainable business practices that minimize damage to the environment or that even improve it

One result of this new way of long-term thinking is the **societal marketing concept**. It states that marketers must satisfy customers' needs in ways that also benefit society while they still deliver a profit to the firm. A similar important trend now is for companies to think of ways to design and manufacture products with a focus on **sustainability**, which we define as "meeting present needs without compromising the ability of future generations to meet their needs."[13] This philosophy is often referred to as "doing well by doing good." Many firms, big and small alike, practice sustainability through their efforts that satisfy society's environmental and social needs for a cleaner, safer environment.

societal marketing concept
A management philosophy that marketers must satisfy customers' needs in ways that also benefit society and deliver profit to the firm.

sustainability
A design and manufacturing focus that meets present needs without compromising the ability of future generations to meet their needs.

Bombas is a good example of a company that was founded on the societal marketing concept. Socks are the number one most requested item by people without homes. Bombas, a socially conscious company that got its start on the hit show *Shark Tank*, was determined to help solve that problem. The company donates one pair of socks for every pair purchased—resulting in over 8.6 million pairs of socks going to people without homes around the country.[14]

Sustainability applies to many aspects of doing business, including social and economic practices (e.g., humane working conditions, diplomacy to prevent wars that deplete food supplies, good atmospheric quality, and of course, the protection of lives). One other crucial pillar of sustainability is the environmental impact of the product. **Green marketing** means developing marketing strategies that support environmental stewardship by creating an environmentally founded differential benefit in the minds of consumers. Green marketing is one aspect of a firm's overall commitment to sustainability.

green marketing
A marketing strategy that supports environmental stewardship, thus creating a differential benefit in the minds of consumers.

In addition to building long-term relationships and focusing on social responsibility, triple-bottom-line firms place a much greater focus on **accountability**—measuring just how much value an organization's marketing activities create. This means that marketers at these organizations ask hard questions about the true value of their efforts and their impact on the bottom line. These questions all boil down to the simple acronym of **ROI (return on investment)**, or, specifically for marketing, *ROMI (return on marketing investment)*. Marketers now realize that if they want to assess just how much value they create for the firm, they need to know exactly what they are spending and what the concrete results of their actions are. You will learn more about ROMI in Chapter 3.

accountability
A process of determining just how much value an organization's marketing activities create and their impact on the bottom line.

return on investment (ROI)
The direct financial impact of a firm's expenditure of a resource, such as time or money.

However, it's not always so easy to assess the value of marketing activities. Many times, managers state their marketing objectives using vague phrases like "increase awareness of our product" or "encourage people to eat healthier snacks." These goals are important, but their lack of specificity makes it pretty much impossible for senior management to determine marketing's true impact. Because management may view these efforts as costs rather than investments, marketing activities often are among the first to be cut out of a firm's budget. To win continued support for what they do (and sometimes to keep their jobs), marketers in triple-bottom-line firms do their best to prove to management that they generate measurable value by aligning marketing activities with the firm's overall business objectives.[15] Often triple-bottom-line firms include an accounting of the firm's social bottom line and environmental bottom line as well as the traditional financial bottom line in the Annual Report for shareholders to see.

MillerCoors believes that a critical part of implementing accountability is that finance people respect marketing people for their knowledge and vice versa. The company has made this possible by developing a closer bond between the two groups. The CFO and CMO have adjacent offices and finance people have been dispersed among their marketing counterparts.[16]

What's Next in the Evolution of Marketing?

Although no one can really predict the future, most agree that in the years ahead we will see an acceleration of the most important factors that marketers think about today. These predictions include good content, user-generated content, branded content, Big Data, mobile marketing, the sharing economy, artificial intelligence, and corporate citizenship.[17] Let's briefly dive in and see what these terms mean.

Customers' demand for good content will continue to dominate online marketing. **User-generated content**, or **consumer-generated content**, in which consumers engage in marketing activities such as creating advertisements, will grow and overtake the importance of **branded content**. Branded content has been an important communication strategy for a number of years. It is produced by a brand and may even indicate the brand is the sponsor but still presents itself as something other than an attempt to sell a product. *The Lego Movie* was a great example of branded content. Despite the claims that the movie was not created to sell Legos, the company did have a major say-so in decisions about details of the movie.

The Lego brand is a leader in leveraging user-generated content.

Consumers' use of online reviews, blogs, and social media will require more than ever that brands create a positive image for every customer and in any place that the company touches him or her, whether online or offline. All of this means that branding will increasingly become a two-way conversation, allowing consumers to have a greater voice. Because this increases the ability of marketers to track consumer behavior, they will be able to provide a more personalized brand communication experience.

Firms that do well by doing good will become more important than ever. Customers will continue the current trend of rewarding brands that do good and punishing those that do not. **Corporate citizenship**, or **corporate social responsibility**, refers to a firm's responsibility to the community in which it operates and to society in general. In the future, good corporate citizenship will become a major marketing function.

Big Data is the term marketers use to describe the voluminous data that a business gathers daily. The important thing about Big Data is not how much it is or how it's gathered; it's importance is in how it's used by an organization. Organizations can and should analyze big data in order to gain insights for decision making. Big Data can help an organization:

- Understand why there is a product, pricing, or promotion failure
- Deliver coupons or other sales promotions to individual consumers based on their captured data
- Develop a new product that meets customer needs

We'll do a deeper dive into Big Data in Chapter 5.

Mobile marketing, interacting with consumers via mobile phones, tablets, and wearable screens such as smart watches, will be one of the prime factors in marketing's future. Not only will these small screens allow for more personalized relationships with customers, but the growth of mobile screens in developing countries will exponentially increase the number of potential customers.

As we discussed earlier in this chapter, the *sharing economy* is a term used to describe the peer-to-peer renting and sharing of goods.

user-generated content, or **consumer-generated content**
Marketing content and activities created by consumers and users of a brand such as advertisements, online reviews, blogs, social media, input to new product development, or serving as wholesalers or retailers.

branded content
Marketing communication developed by a brand to provide educational or entertainment value rather than to sell the brand in order to develop a relationship with consumers; may indicate the brand is the sponsor.

corporate citizenship, or **corporate social responsibility**
Refers to a firm's responsibility to the community in which they operate and to society in general.

Artificial intelligence (AI) allows machines to learn from experience and perform human-like tasks. Whether you talk about self-driving cars or creating individual ads, with AI, computers can be trained by processing large amounts of data and finding patterns in the data.

Artificial intelligence (AI) allows marketers, whether online or in a physical store, to provide customers with a satisfactory experience. Many e-commerce marketers expect to increase AI use by 200 percent in the next year as it is fast becoming the only way to reach consumers. AI is no longer complex; rather, it now comes standard with the application marketers buy.

The Internet of Things (IoT) is a network of physical objects that use sensors, software, and connections to exchange and collect data. AI allows machines to learn from experience and perform human-like tasks.

In the future, customers will expect brand organizations to have a *purpose*. A purpose answers the question of why the organization exists and directs all organizational decision making. An organization uses its purpose to create deeper bonds with their customers, to articulate the problems it addresses, to do more for their communities, and to have greater results in the process.[18]

The future of marketing undoubtedly involves *more customers*. It's estimated that around 3 billion consumers from emerging markets will have access to the Internet by 2022. It's also estimated that 20 percent of all retail sales in 2022 will come from buyers who currently reside in those emerging markets.

Marketing communication will continue to evolve and expand. Today, marketers face an *infinite media* market as consumers produce media on their own and make their own rules.

Customer experience (CX or CEX) has become central to marketing. As we said earlier, customers don't buy products anymore. They buy experiences and emotions. Emotional branding is what makes a business stand out. The most successful brands offer customers real experiences and emotions. Disneyland and Coca-Cola sell happiness. Adidas and Nike give you courage to follow your dreams. L'Oréal sells beauty. That's why people buy these brands.

Social media has enabled the development of *influencer marketing*. Today, Internet users trust recommendations from a favorite YouTube creator more than they do marketer-generated messages.[19]

service-dominant logic
A firm's mindset for understanding the exchange process, acknowledging that all firms are service firms and that a firm has more opportunities with the service-dominant logic.

We're shifting from goods-dominant logic to **service-dominant logic**. When we think of a marketing enterprise, we usually think of a producer of goods. This process has been built on a goods-dominant logic that focuses on building, exchanging, and destroying (through use) value. Raw materials, such as iron ore, that are pretty worthless are processed and eventually become an automobile that is sold to a consumer who drives it until it will be sold for a lot less than its initial value or it finally dies and is junked.

Today, we are moving from selling goods to offering services. We need also to move to the service-dominant logic that looks at the exchange of a service rather than value. In the service-dominant logic, the customer becomes the focus, not the value. Services can be looked at as getting a job done for a customer, and they require an interaction between the customer and the service provider.

The service-dominant logic suggests that customers do not buy goods or services. Rather they buy offerings which provide services and create value. If the job we want done is transporting us or others from one place to another, we might buy a car or we might use Uber or Lyft services. We might even pay a subscription fee that enables us to pick a different (or the same) car to drive each day from a service provider with a wide range of options. The advantage of the service-dominant logic is that by focusing on the job to be done, marketers are open to many more opportunities.[20]

customer co-creation
The process when a company and their customers work together to create a product.

Co-creation of value occurs when a company and their customer(s) work together to jointly create a product to suit the customer's needs. Co-creation is a win-win option. Companies have an opportunity to better understand customers' product desires and needs, and customers gain a new appreciation for the firm. Co-creation programs and experiments, while still new, have been adopted by major companies, including IKEA, Coke, Anheuser Busch, Starbucks, Unilever, Lego, and BMW.[21]

1.3 The Value of Marketing and the Marketing of Value

OBJECTIVE

Understand value from the perspectives of customers, producers, and society.

We said that marketing is all about delivering value to everyone who is affected by a transaction. That includes the customer, the seller, and society at large.

How do customers decide how much value they will get from a purchase? One way to look at value is to think of it simply as a ratio of benefits to costs—that is, customers "invest" their precious time and money to do business with a firm, and they expect a certain bundle of benefits in return.

Let's look at value from the different perspectives of the parties that are involved in an exchange: the customers, the sellers, and society.

Value from the Customer's Perspective

Think about something you would like to buy—say, a new pair of shoes. You have narrowed the choice down to several options. Your purchase decision no doubt will be affected by the ratio of costs versus benefits for each type of shoe. When you buy a pair of shoes, you consider the price (and other costs) along with all the other benefits (utilities) that each competing pair of shoes provides you.

Marketers communicate these benefits to the customer in the form of a **value proposition**, which is a marketplace offering that fairly and accurately sums up the value that the customer will realize if he or she purchases the product. The value proposition includes the whole bundle of benefits the firm promises to deliver, not just the benefits of the product itself. For example, although most people probably won't get to their destination sooner if they drive a BMW versus a Mercedes-Benz or Audi, many die-hard loyalists swear by their favorite brand.

value proposition
A marketplace offering that fairly and accurately sums up the value that will be realized if the good or service is purchased.

These archrival brands are largely marketed in terms of their images—meaning the images their respective marketing communication firms have carefully crafted for them with the help of slickly produced commercials, YouTube videos, and millions of dollars. When you buy a shiny new BMW, you do more than choose a car to get you around town; you also make a statement about the type of person you are or wish you were. In addition to providing a luxury ride or superior maintenance services, that statement also is part of the value the product delivers to you. The challenge to the marketer is to create a killer value proposition. A big part of this challenge is to convince customers that this value proposition is superior to others they might choose from competitors.

Value from the Seller's Perspective

We've seen that marketing transactions produce value for buyers, but how do sellers experience value, and how do they decide whether a transaction is valuable? One answer is obvious: They determine whether the exchange is profitable to them. Has it made money for the company's management, its workers, and its shareholders?

That's an important factor, but not the only one. Just as we can't measure the value of an automobile from the consumer's perspective only in terms of basic transportation, value from the seller's perspective can take many forms. For example, in addition to making a buck or two, many firms measure value along other dimensions, such as prestige among rivals or pride in doing what they do well. As we said earlier, online shoe retailer Zappos's top core value is to "deliver WOW

A value proposition is about all the benefits a customer receives from a product, not just the product's physical attributes. In this case Lunchables sells food products, but kids also experience "fun."

Kris Connor/WireImage/Getty Images

Jeep cultivates its loyal drivers with brandfests that include the Jeep Jamboree, Camp Jeep, and Jeep 101.

brandfests
Events that companies host to thank customers for their loyalty.

through service" and JetBlue's is to "delight the customer." Some organizations by definition don't even care about making money, or they may not even be allowed to make money. Not-for-profits like Greenpeace, the Smithsonian Institution, or National Public Radio regard value in terms of their ability to motivate, educate, or delight the public.

In recent years, many firms have transformed the way they do business. They now regard consumers as *partners* in the transaction rather than as passive "victims." That explains why it's becoming more common for companies to host events (sometimes called **brandfests**) to thank customers for their loyalty. For example, Jeep builds strong bonds with its Jeep 4 × 4 owners when it holds several off-road adventure weekends every year. These Jeep Jamborees are where other Jeep owners get to challenge the limits of their 4 × 4s on off-road trails and commune with fellow brand loyalists.[22] Another example of a popular brandfest is the Sam Adams OctoberFest. For those of you who enjoy Octoberfest in your community, you might be interested to know that Octoberfest began in Munich, Germany, when the Crown Prince's wedding was celebrated with a 16-day party and märzen beer.[23]

Jeep's cultivation of its 4 × 4 enthusiasts and Sam Adams' OctoberFest reflect an important lesson the company understands very well: *It is more expensive to attract new customers than it is to retain current ones.* This notion has transformed the way many companies do business, and we'll repeat it several times in this book. However, there is an important exception to the rule: In recent years, companies have been working harder to calculate the true value of their relationships with customers by asking, "How much is this customer *really* worth to us?" Firms recognize that it can be costly in terms of both money and human effort to do whatever it takes to keep some customers loyal to the company. Often these actions pay off, but there are cases in which keeping a customer is a losing proposition.

The concept described above of calculating the *customer lifetime value (CLV)* is very important in marketing. To calculate CLV, companies first estimate the amount the person will spend year after year and then subtract what it will cost to gain the customer and to retain the relationship for the period of years they expect the customer to continue to buy from them. You will read more about CLV and other important metrics later on in Chapter 5.

Provide Value through Competitive Advantage

competitive advantage
A firm's edge over its competitors that allows it to have higher sales, higher profits, and more customers and enjoy greater success year after year.

Firms of all types seek to gain a **competitive advantage**—an edge over their competitors that allows them to have higher sales, higher profits, more customers—in short, to enjoy greater success year after year. In general, a competitive advantage comes from either a *cost advantage* or a *differential advantage*. A firm has a cost advantage when the firm can produce a good or service at a lower cost than competitors and thus charge customers a lower price. A differential advantage means that the firm produces a product that differs significantly from competitors' products and customers see the product as superior.

distinctive competency
A superior capability of a firm in comparison to its direct competitors.

How does a firm go about creating a competitive advantage? The first step is to identify what it does really well. A **distinctive competency** is a firm's capability that is superior to that of its competition. For example, Coca-Cola's success in global markets—Coke commands nearly 50 percent of the world's soft-drink business—is related to its distinctive competencies in distribution and marketing communications. Coke's global distribution system got a jump on the competition during World War II, when Coke partnered with the military to make sure every soldier had access to its soft drink. The military actually paid for the transportation of Coca-Cola and helped the company to build bottling plants to keep the troops happy.[24] Coke's skillful marketing communications program, a second distinctive competency, has contributed to its global success. Coke doesn't just market a beverage; it sells "happiness."

| Table 1.4 | How Firms Achieve a Competitive Advantage with a Distinctive Competency[25] | | |

Company	Distinctive Competency	Differential Benefit	Competitive Advantage
Coca-Cola	Distribution and marketing communications	Convenience and brand awareness for customers all over the world	Other soft drinks are unable to take loyal customers away from Coke. Coca-Cola has more than 50 percent of the world soft-drink market.
Apple	Product quality and design	Easy access to cutting-edge technology	Apple's sales of its Mac computer increased 28.5 percent as the overall market for PCs decreased.
JetBlue Airlines	Customer service	A fun flight without any unpleasant surprises	JetBlue has been ranked first in customer satisfaction by JD Powers for 13 years.
Amazon.com	Fulfillment and distribution	Availability, convenience, ease of access, its customer-friendly services and policies, and an extremely varied selection of products provided through third-party sellers	Fifty-five percent of consumers search Amazon first. Worldwide, it has 6.4 percent of e-commerce and a 20 percent annual growth rate since its founding.
Starbucks	Product quality	Customer satisfaction	Starbucks has just under 33 percent of the market share in its industry.

The second step to develop a competitive advantage is to turn a distinctive competency into a **differential benefit**—value that competitors don't offer and that customers want. Differential benefits set products apart from competitors' products by providing something unique that customers want, that is the competitive advantage. Differential benefits provide reasons for customers to pay a premium for a firm's products and exhibit a strong brand preference. For many years, loyal Apple computer users benefited from superior graphics capability compared to their PC-using counterparts. Later, when PC manufacturers caught up with this competitive advantage, Apple relied on its inventive product designers to create another differential benefit—futuristic-looking computers in a multitude of colors. This competitive advantage even tempted many loyal PC users to take a bite of the Apple (see Table 1.4). Apple's distinctive competency is product design as seen in the futuristic look of its computers. This distinctive competency has been continued in the design of its phones and other products, making them leaders in the markets of the world.

differential benefit
Properties of products that set them apart from competitors' products by providing unique customer benefits.

Add Value through the Value Chain

Many different players—both within and outside a firm—need to work together to create and deliver value to customers. The **value chain** is a useful way to appreciate all the players that work together to create value. This term refers to a series of activities involved in designing, producing, marketing, delivering, and supporting any product. In addition to marketing activities, the value chain includes business functions such as human resource management and technology development.[26]

The value chain concept reminds us that every product starts with raw materials, such as iron ore or crude oil, that are of relatively limited value to the end customer. Each link in the chain has the potential to either add or remove value from the product the customer eventually buys. The successful firm is the one that can perform one or more of these activities better than other firms; this is its distinctive competency and thus provides an opportunity to gain a competitive advantage. The main activities of value chain members include the following:

value chain
A series of activities involved in designing, producing, marketing, delivering, and supporting any product. Each link in the chain has the potential to either add or remove value from the product the customer eventually buys.

- *Inbound logistics:* Bringing in materials or component parts necessary to make the product
- *Operations:* Converting the materials into another form or the final product
- *Outbound logistics:* Shipping out the final product
- *Marketing:* Promoting and selling the final product
- *Service:* Meeting the customer's needs by providing any additional support required

Figure 1.2 *Snapshot* │ Apple's Value Chain

Apple's value chain includes inbound logistics, operations, outbound logistics, marketing and sales, and service.

Inbound Logistics	Operations	Outbound Logistics	Marketing and Sales	Service
• Planar lithium battery (Sony) • Hard drive (Toshiba) • MP3 decoder and controller chip (PortalPlayer) • Flash memory chip (Sharp Electronics Corp.) • Stereo digital-to-analog converter (Wolfson Microelectronics Ltd.) • Firewire interface controller (Texas Instruments)	• Consumer research • New product development team • Engineering and production	• Trucking companies • Wholesalers • Retailers	• Advertising • Social media and other forms of marketing communication • Sales force	• Computer technicians

Source: Based on information from Erik Sherman, "Inside the Apple iPod Design Triumph," May 27, 2006, http://www.designchain.com/coverstory.asp?issue=summer02.

To better understand the value chain, consider a new iPad you buy at your local Apple store. Do you think about all the people and steps involved in designing, producing, and delivering that product to the store? And there are other people who create brand advertising, who conduct consumer research to figure out what people like or dislike about their small tablet, and who make the box it comes in or the packaging that keeps the unit from being damaged in shipment. Without these people, there simply would be no iPad—only a box of raw materials and parts.

As Figure 1.2 shows, all these activities and companies belong to Apple's value chain. This means that Apple must make a lot of decisions. What electronic components will go into its music players? What accessories will it include in the package? What trucking companies, wholesalers, and retailers will deliver the iPods to stores? What service will it provide to customers after the sale? And what marketing strategies will it use? In some cases, members of a value chain will work together to coordinate their activities to be more efficient and thus create a competitive advantage.

We've organized this book around the series of steps in the marketing process. Each of these steps is essential to ensuring that the appropriate value exchange occurs and that both parties to the transaction are satisfied—making it more likely they'll continue to do business in the future. Figure 1.3 shows these steps. Basically, we're going to learn about what marketers do as a product makes its way through the firm's value chain, from obtaining the raw materials and component parts to producing the product to delivery into the customer's hands.

We'll start in Part 1 with a focus on how companies plan for success with global and ethical marketing strategies. In Part 2, we'll see how research and Big Data help marketers understand and meet the different needs of different customers. Then Part 3 takes a look at how firms decide to "position" the product in the marketplace, including choices about what it should look like,

Figure 1.3 *Process* │ Create and Deliver Value

This book is organized around the sequence of steps necessary to ensure that the appropriate value exchange occurs and that both parties to the transaction are satisfied. Each step corresponds to one of the book's four parts.

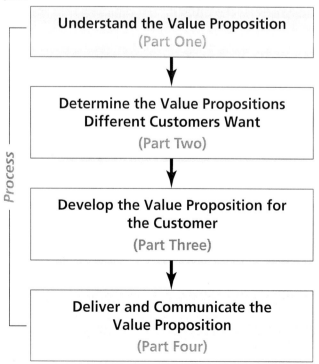

how its value should be communicated to customers, and how much to charge for it. As we reach the end of our marketing journey in Part 4, we'll talk about how the product gets delivered and promoted to consumers.

Consumer-Generated Value: From Audience to Community

As we discussed earlier, one of the most exciting changes in the world of marketing is that everyday people actually *generate* value instead of just buying it; consumers are turning into advertising directors, retailers, and new-product-development consultants. They create their own ads (some flattering, some not) for products and post them on sites like YouTube. They buy and sell merchandise ranging from Beatles memorabilia to washing machines (to body parts, but that's another story) on eBay. They share ideas for new styles with fashion designers, design new advertising, and customize their own unique versions of products on websites. Some even proudly announce the latest stuff they've bought in "**haul videos**" they shoot and post on YouTube (if you don't believe us, just search for "haul videos" and see how many people take the time to do this).

Consumers generate value through social media—creating their own content and sharing it with others. Haul videos allow users to share their shopping "hauls" with their followers.

haul videos
Videos consumers post on YouTube that detail the latest stuff they bought.

These profound changes mean that marketers must adjust their thinking about customers: They need to stop thinking of buyers as a passive audience and start thinking of them as a community that is motivated to participate in both the production and the consumption of what companies sell. They also are part of the brand communication process as they create their own videos, provide product reviews, and participate in blogs. Some examples of this consumer-generated content include:

- Loews Hotels opted to use photos of actual guests in their marketing instead of hiring actors. They began the process by looking through Instagram photos that their guests had already shared. This inspiration turned into the #TravelForReal campaign where they invited real travelers to capture the essence of each hotel. They collected these photos and used them on their website, social media outlets, and more with the tagline "Nobody tells our story better than you."[27]

- Calvin Klein asked its customers to fill in the blank: "I _____ in #MyCalvins." In no time, nearly 200,000 photos had been posted with the hashtag to Instagram. The brand also earned millions of new followers across Facebook, Instagram, and Twitter. Ultimately, they set up a photo gallery that swelled to 4.5 million interactions in four months.[28]

- For a decade, Doritos cashed in on its "Crash the Super Bowl" contest, where fans submitted their best 30-second commercials. The winning commercial (as voted on by fans) was aired during the Super Bowl game, and the winner not only received bragging rights but also took home a cool $1 million.[29]

Consumer-Generated Value: Social Networking

In the 1990s, the Internet (**Web 1.0**) was typified by static content provided by a site's creator. Businesses and institutions permitted little consumer involvement on websites.[30] These commercially and technically based organizations created sites that were crude, simple, and designed to accomplish one specific function. Later, **Web 2.0** offered marketers two-way communication through social networking sites such as Facebook. People wrote blogs and e-commerce expanded.

With the web, consumers create value through *social media*, which are Internet-based platforms that allow users to create their own content and share it with others who access their

Web 1.0
The beginning phase of the Internet that offered static content provided by the owner of the site.

Web 2.0
The second generation of the World Wide Web that incorporated social networking and user interactivity via two-way communication.

REUTERS / Alamy Stock Photo

On the Internet, almost anyone can be a celebrity. Liza Koshy began her career on Vine before starting her YouTube channel, which has more than 17 million subscribers. She has had various acting roles, hosted shows, and won many awards, including a Kids' Choice Award.

social networking platforms
Online platforms that allow a user to represent himself or herself via a profile on a website and provide and receive links to other members of the network to share input about common interests.

recommendation engine
Computer system that has access to customers' former shopping behavior in order to make a recommendation for future purposes.

folksonomy
A classification system that relies on users rather than preestablished systems to sort contents.

wisdom of crowds
Under the right circumstances, groups are smarter than the smartest people in them, meaning that large numbers of consumers can predict successful products.

crowdsourcing
A practice where firms outsource marketing activities (such as selecting an ad) to a community of users.

sites. Social media include, among others, social networks, such as Facebook and Twitter, and product review sites, such as TripAdvisor. On **social networking platforms**, a user posts a profile on a website and he or she provides and receives links to other members of the network to share input about common interests. The odds are that you and most of your classmates checked Snapchat before (or during?) class today.

Social media platforms like this are very hot today; more and more advertisers realize that these sites are a great way to reach an audience that tunes in regularly and enthusiastically to catch up with friends, check out photos of what they did at that outrageous party Saturday night (ouch!), proclaim opinions about political or social issues, or share discoveries of new musical artists.[31] They share several important characteristics:

- They improve as the number of users increases. For example, Amazon's ability to recommend books, movies, concerts, and other items for sale to you, a process that uses AI and **recommendation engines**, is based on what other people with similar interests have bought. The recommendations get better as it tracks more and more people who enter search queries.

- Their currency is eyeballs. Google makes its money by charging advertisers according to the number of people who see their ads after they type in a search term.

- They are version free and in perpetual beta. Unlike static websites or books, content is always a work in progress. Enthusiastic users who serve as volunteer editors constantly update Wikipedia, the online encyclopedia, and "correct" others' errors.

- They categorize entries according to **folksonomy** rather than "taxonomy." In other words, sites rely on users rather than preestablished systems to sort contents. Listeners at Pandora create their own "radio stations" that play songs by artists they choose as well as other similar artists.[32]

This last point highlights a key change in the way some new media companies approach their businesses: Think of it as marketing strategy by committee. The **wisdom of crowds** perspective (from a book by that name) argues that under the right circumstances, groups are smarter than the smartest people in them. If this is true, it implies that large numbers of (nonexpert) consumers can predict successful products.[33] Marketers rely on **crowdsourcing** when they outsource marketing activities to a large group of people, often through a social networking community. For example, Lego offers up its Lego CUUSOO crowdsourcing platform to solicit product and concept ideas from fans. The company periodically reviews the ideas that garner 10,000 supporters to see which ones might merit the chance to become a real Lego product, such as the *Voltron – Defender of the Universe* set, and "winners" earn 1 percent of the profits on net sales.[34] We'll talk more about crowdsourcing in Chapter 13.

Value from Society's Perspective

Every company's activities influence the world around it in ways both good and bad. Therefore, we must also consider how marketing transactions add or subtract value from society. In many ways, we as consumers are at the mercy of marketers, because we trust them to sell us products that are safe and perform as promised. We also trust them to price and distribute these products fairly. Conflicts often arise in business when the pressure to succeed in the marketplace provokes dishonest business practices; the huge failure of major financial services organizations like AIG and Goldman Sachs is a painful case in point.

Companies usually find that stressing ethics and social responsibility also is good business. The Internet and social media mean that consumers communicate about unsafe or faulty products, bad service, or scams. Some find this out the hard way:

The U.S. Environmental Protection Agency accused Volkswagen AG of using software to make 482,000 Volkswagen diesel-powered cars appear cleaner than they were. After first denying the accusation, Volkswagen later admitted to the charge. VW stock lost a third of its value in one day, and the company eventually paid over $15 billion to settle lawsuits.

In a similar FTC finding, Lumos Labs, the maker of the Luminosity brain training program, had to pay $2 million in redress. The company claimed that the Luminosity games helped users perform better in school or work and reduce cognitive deterioration with age without any scientific evidence.[35]

In 2019, Anheuser-Busch InBev was forced to remove "no corn syrup" from its advertising and packaging of Bud Light.[36]

The Dark Side of Marketing and Consumer Behavior

For some—hopefully not many and hopefully not *you* after you read this book—marketing is a four-letter word. Whether intentionally or not, some marketers *do* violate their bond of trust with consumers, and unfortunately the "dark side" of marketing often is the subject of harsh criticism.[37] In some cases, these violations are illegal, such as when a retailer adopts a "bait-and-switch" selling strategy, luring consumers into the store with promises of inexpensive products with the sole intent of getting them to switch to higher-priced goods.

In other cases, marketing practices have detrimental effects on society even though they are not actually illegal. Some alcohol and tobacco companies advertise in neighborhoods where abuse of these products is known to be a big problem. Others sponsor commercials that depict groups of people in an unfavorable light or sell products that encourage antisocial behavior. An online game based on the Columbine High School massacre drew criticism from some who say it trivializes the actions of the two teen killers. We'll talk more about marketing ethics in Chapter 2.

Despite the best efforts of researchers, government regulators, and concerned industry people, sometimes consumers' worst enemies are themselves. We tend to think of ourselves as rational decision makers, calmly doing our best to obtain products and services that will maximize our health and well-being and that of our families and society. In reality, however, our desires, choices, and actions often result in negative consequences to ourselves and the society in which we live. Some of these actions are relatively harmless, but others have more onerous consequences. Some harmful consumer behaviors, such as excessive drinking or cigarette smoking, stem from social pressures, and the cultural value that people place on money encourages activities such as shoplifting or insurance fraud. Exposure to unattainable ideals of beauty and success can create dissatisfaction with the self. Let's briefly review some dimensions of the "dark side" of consumer behavior:

Addictive consumption: **Consumer addiction** is a physiological or psychological dependency on goods or services. These problems, of course, include alcoholism, drug addiction, and cigarettes, and many companies profit from addictive products or by selling solutions. More recently, as we've already seen, many have become concerned about small-screen addiction. Although most people equate addiction with drugs, consumers can use virtually anything to relieve (at least temporarily) some problem or satisfy some need to the point that reliance on it becomes extreme. "Shopaholics" turn to shopping much the way addicted people turn to drugs or alcohol.[38] Numerous treatment centers in China, South Korea, and Taiwan (and now a few in the U.S. also) deal with cases of Internet or small-screen

consumer addiction

A physiological or psychological dependency on goods or services, including alcohol, drugs, cigarettes, shopping, and use of the Internet.

Internet overuse or addiction is a growing problem around the world. The South Korean government is concerned about teens who log a huge amount of hours in Internet "bangs" where they play videogames for hours on end.

Jean Chung/Bloomberg/Getty Images

addiction—some hardcore gamers have become so hooked that they literally forget to eat or drink. There is even a ChapStick Addicts support group with approximately 250 active members![39]

Illegal activities: The cost of crimes that consumers commit against businesses has been estimated at more than $40 billion per year. A survey the McCann-Erickson advertising agency conducted revealed the following tidbits:[40]

- Ninety-one percent of people say they lie regularly. One in three fibs about their weight, one in four fudges their income, and 21 percent lie about their age. Nine percent even lie about their natural hair color.
- Four out of 10 Americans have tried to pad an insurance bill to cover the deductible.
- Nineteen percent say they've snuck into a theater to avoid paying admission.
- More than three out of five people say they've taken credit for making something from scratch when they have done no such thing. According to Pillsbury's CEO, this "behavior is so prevalent that we've named a category after it—speed scratch."

anticonsumption
The deliberate defacement of products.

Anticonsumption: Some types of destructive consumer behavior are **anticonsumption**, when people deliberately deface or otherwise damage products. This practice ranges from relatively mild acts, like spray-painting graffiti on buildings and subways, to serious incidences of product tampering or even the release of computer viruses that can bring large corporations to their knees.

1.4 Marketing as a Process

OBJECTIVE
Explain the basics of market planning.

Our definition of marketing also refers to *processes*. This means that marketing is not a one-shot operation. When it's done right, marketing is a decision process in which marketing managers determine the strategies that will help the firm meet its objectives and then execute those strategies using the tools they have at their disposal. In this section, we'll look at how marketers make business decisions and plan actions and the tools they use to execute their plans. We'll build on this brief overview in Chapter 3.

A big part of the marketing process is *market planning*, where we think carefully and strategically about the "big picture" and where our firm and its products fit within it. The first phase of market planning is to analyze the marketing environment. This means understanding the firm's current strengths and weaknesses by assessing factors that might help or hinder the development and marketing of products. The analysis must also take into account the opportunities and threats the firm will encounter in the marketplace, such as the actions of competitors, cultural and technological changes, and the economy.

Firms (or individuals) that engage in market planning ask questions like these:

- What product benefits will our customers look for in three to five years?
- What capabilities or distinctive competencies does our firm have that set it apart from the competition?
- What additional customer groups might provide important market segments for us in the future?
- How will changes in technology affect our production process, our communication strategy, and our distribution strategy?
- What changes in social and cultural values are occurring now that will impact our market in the next few years?
- How will customers' awareness of environmental issues affect their attitudes toward our manufacturing facilities?
- What legal and regulatory issues may affect our business in both domestic and global markets?

Answers to these and other questions provide the foundation for developing an organization's *marketing plan*. This is a document that describes the marketing environment, outlines the marketing objectives and strategy, and identifies who will be responsible for carrying out each part of the marketing strategy. Marketing plans will be discussed in full detail in Chapter 3—in fact, in that chapter you will learn about the basic layout and content of a marketing plan. A major marketing decision for most organizations is which products to market to which consumers without simultaneously turning off other consumers. Some firms choose to reach as many customers as possible, so they offer their goods or services to a **mass market** that consists of all possible customers in a market regardless of the differences in their specific needs and wants. Market planning then becomes a matter of developing a basic product and a single strategy to reach everyone.

Although this approach can be cost effective, the firm risks losing potential customers to competitors whose marketing plans instead try to meet the needs of specific groups within the market. A **market segment** is a distinct group of customers within a larger market who are similar to one another in some way and whose needs differ from other customers in the larger market. For example, automakers such as Ford, General Motors, and BMW offer different automobiles for different market segments. Depending on its goals and resources, a firm may choose to focus on one or on many segments. A *target market* is the segment(s) on which an organization focuses its marketing plan and toward which it directs its marketing efforts. Marketers develop *positioning* strategies to create a desired perception of the product in consumers' minds in comparison to competitors' brands. We'll learn more about these ideas in Chapter 7.

As marketers plan their strategies for the future, it is good to remember that marketing is not static but has changed greatly, even in your lifetime. And it will continue to change. To be successful, marketers need to be ready for disruptions, see them as opportunities, and respond accordingly.

Disruptive Marketing

In this chapter, we've provided an introduction and an overview of marketing. We dare not finish this chapter, however, without talking about **disruptive marketing**. Many experts believe that disruptive marketing is the only way to stay in business for the long term.

So what is disruptive marketing? Disruptive marketing requires that marketers must first understand the consumer, identifying what is missing in the marketplace to satisfy the customer and stepping outside the box. Disruptive marketing means turning the existing marketing rules upside down, changing how customers think not only of your company and brand but of the industry as a whole. *Harvard Business Review* defined disruptive marketing as "a process whereby a smaller company with fewer resources is able to successfully challenge established incumbent businesses."[41]

Disruptive marketing displaces something that is well established, like filling a need with a totally new product that the existing product was not able to fill. It's about doing something risky and new in marketing your brand. If other brands try to do the same thing, they will be dismissed by the consumer.

Perhaps the best way to understand disruptive marketing is to look at some examples of disruptive marketing, both historical and recent.

Was the first automobile a market disruption? Not really, because early automobiles were very expensive and only a few could afford them. Ford's *Model T*, however, did create a market disruption because it made automobiles affordable for thousands of people. It replaced the horse and buggy, turning an industry on its head.

The Adidas Group recognizes that sustainability is gaining in importance and consumers are willing to pay more for brands which do provide sustainable alternatives to other brands. To this end Adidas introduced the UltraBOOST running shoe made from 11 plastic bottles gathered from the ocean. Reebok, another Adidas Group brand, has developed its

mass market
All possible customers in a market, regardless of the differences in their specific needs and wants.

market segment
A distinct group of customers within a larger market who are similar to one another in some way and whose needs differ from other customers in the larger market.

disruptive marketing
A process whereby marketers, by understanding customer needs and identifying what is missing, step "outside the box" to displace something well established, such as filling a need with a totally new product.

first plant-based sneaker, Forever Floatride GROW, made with castor beans, algae, eucalyptus trees and natural rubber.

Microsoft introduced its new Xbox Adaptive Controller designed to "level the playing field" for all gamers. It is especially designed to meet the needs of gamers with limited mobility.

Stay alert for what disruptive marketing will enter the market next.[42]

1.5 Brand You: A Framework for Managing Your Career

OBJECTIVE

Understand how to increase your chances of getting a great first job and having a successful career by using the marketing process to create a personal brand.

We'd like to introduce you to Taylor. Taylor is an undergraduate business student. Well-meaning people keep asking Taylor what he plans to do when he graduates. Taylor has no idea; it's a bit embarrassing. Taylor is now thinking about his career after graduation and maybe an internship before he graduates. But just thinking isn't getting him there. He knows he needs help.

In his marketing class, he heard about "Brand You" and immediately knew this was exactly what he needs to do. He is happy that he finally has a path that he believes will allow him to have the internship and career he wants.

What is the most important brand you will ever market? It's Brand **YOU**!

If you're one of those people who cringes whenever someone asks, "What do you want to do when you graduate?" . . .

If you're someone who has several ideas about an internship that you might enjoy but aren't sure of any one . . .

Or if you have an idea of what you want to do in your career but have no clue how to get a job in that area . . .

Brand You is for you!

Brand You is a process, using the same tools marketers have used to create Nike and Starbucks and Apple, to create a personal brand. Your brand will help you present yourself to employers as a top candidate when you seek internships and jobs during college.

Developing a great brand doesn't happen overnight. It is a process. In that process, marketers must identify the needs of the target market, create a product that provides value for customers, price it, and deliver compelling messages that convince consumers to try the product. In going through the process, you have the opportunity to discover what makes you unique and what benefits you can offer an employer, your customer.

Starting the *Brand You* Process

The journey of developing your personal brand will help you answer many key questions, such as: Do you know what kind of job you want? Have you thought about the kind of company where you'd enjoy working? Do you know what steps to take to prepare for your field? Have you even thought about your future in terms of a career as opposed to what job you want when you graduate? Reading and working through the marketing strategies for Brand You can lead you to courses that teach the needed skills to increase your value to employers. And, of course, these same marketing strategies will help you succeed whenever you search for work—you'll be able to communicate your value with a clear, dynamic message.

If you think you don't need to create a personal brand because you're not a marketing major, think again. No matter what type of career you want, creating your personal brand will help you manage that career. A personal brand will help you determine who you are and what you want to do. It prepares you to effectively communicate to a prospective employer why he or she should choose you for the job. A personal brand can help distinguish you from other job candidates, whether you're applying for a job in accounting, operations, human resources, sales, or any other area.

Whether you are graduating during a period of economic prosperity or recession, there are always some companies hiring and some good jobs. And new job titles are created every day. Just imagine the new jobs that will appear during the next decade. If you are likely to enter the job market when the economy is down, it is more important than ever that you begin now working to create and market a great Brand You. Although you can't make any assumptions about job retention, you will still have security—the security that comes from being a career activist, security you create by constantly scanning the horizon for new opportunities to add value.

Applying Marketing Concepts to Brand You

Developing a brand identity is only the first step. Once a brand has been created, it needs to be marketed. Here are three ways marketing concepts apply to your own personal brand:

Marketing is about meeting needs. That means that you have to figure out what kind of employer you want to work for and what skills and knowledge are needed for a position with that employer. Jobs exist because employers need people who accomplish tasks and solve problems.

Marketing is about creating utility. The goal of your personal brand is communicating to prospective employers that your skills and knowledge will be useful to them, that is, will meet their needs. To communicate utility, marketers develop a *value proposition*—a statement that sums up the value the customer will realize if he or she buys the product. Brand You will guide you in developing your own personal value proposition tailored to the wants and needs of the employers you're targeting.

Marketing is about exchange relationships. In marketing a good or service, an exchange relationship exists when the marketer exchanges the good or service for some amount of money. Work is the ultimate exchange relationship—you exchange your skills for learning opportunities and compatible work arrangements as well as financial rewards.

Taylor now understands some of the benefits of a personal brand and is ready to start the process. He hopes that through the process he will find answers to questions such as: What kind of job do I want? What kind of company do I want to work for? And too, Taylor knows that to get the great job he wants, he needs to differentiate himself and set himself apart from all the other recent graduates trying to land the same job.

Objective **Summaries** and **Key Terms**

1.1 Objective Summary

Explain what marketing is, the marketing mix, what can be marketed, and the value of marketing.

Marketing is the activity, set of institutions, and processes for creating, communicating, delivering, and exchanging offerings that have value for customers, clients, partners, and society at large. Therefore, marketing is all about delivering value to stakeholders, that is, to everyone who is affected by a transaction.

Organizations that seek to ensure their long-term profitability by identifying and satisfying customers' needs and wants adopt the marketing concept.

The marketing mix includes product, price, place, and promotion. The product is what satisfies customer needs. The price is the assigned value or amount to be exchanged for the product. The place or channel of distribution gets the product to the customer. Promotion is the organization's efforts to persuade customers to buy the product.

Any good, service, or idea that can be marketed is a product, even though what is being sold may not take a physical form. Consumer goods are the tangible products that consumers purchase for personal or family use. Services are intangible products that we pay for and use but never own. Business-to-business goods and services are sold to businesses and other organizations for further processing or for use in their business operations. Not-for-profit organizations, ideas, places, and people can also be marketed.

Marketing provides value for customers when they practice the marketing concept and focus on identifying and satisfying customer needs. Marketing provides form, place, time, and possession utility. In addition, marketing provides value through satisfying the needs of diverse stakeholders, society, and the earth.

Key Terms

consumer
customer experience (CX or CEX)
marketing
marketing mix
four Ps
product
promotion
place
channel of distribution
price
exchange
consumer goods
services
business-to-business marketing
industrial goods
e-commerce
not-for-profit organizations, or nongovernmental
    organizations (NGOs)
marketing concept
need
want
benefit
demand
market
marketplace
utility
stakeholders

1.2 Objective Summary

Explain the evolution of the marketing concept.

Early in the 20th century, firms followed a production orientation in which they focused on the most efficient ways to produce and distribute products. Beginning in the 1930s, some firms adopted a selling orientation that encouraged salespeople to aggressively sell products to customers. In the 1950s, organizations adopted a customer orientation that focused on customer satisfaction. This led to the development of the marketing concept. Today, many firms are moving toward a triple-bottom-line orientation that includes a commitment to quality and value and a concern for both economic and social profit while protecting the environment. The societal marketing concept maintains that marketers must satisfy customers' needs in

ways that also benefit society while still delivering a profit to the firm. Similarly, companies think of ways to design and manufacture products with a focus on *sustainability*, or "doing well by doing good." Experts believe marketing will continue to change with greater use of good content, Big Data, mobile marketing, metrics and accountability, customer interaction, and corporate citizenship.

Key Terms

production orientation
selling orientation
customer orientation
total quality management (TQM)
triple-bottom-line orientation
societal marketing concept
sustainability
green marketing
accountability
return on investment (ROI)
user-generated content, or consumer-generated content
branded content
corporate citizenship, or corporate
    social responsibility
service-dominant logic
customer co-creation

1.3 Objective Summary

Understand value from the perspectives of customers, producers, and society.

Value is the benefits a customer receives from buying a good or service. Marketing communicates these benefits as the value proposition to the customer. For customers, the value proposition includes the whole bundle of benefits the product promises to deliver, not just the benefits of the product itself. Sellers determine value by assessing whether their transactions are profitable, whether they are providing value to stakeholders by creating a competitive advantage, and whether they are providing value through the value chain. Customers generate value when they turn into advertising directors, retailers, and new-product-development consultants, often through social networking using social media. Society receives value from marketing activities when producers stress ethics and social responsibility. Criticisms of both marketing and consumer activities may be valid in a few instances, but most are unfounded.

Key Terms

value proposition
brandfests
competitive advantage
distinctive competency
differential benefit
value chain
haul videos
Web 1.0

Web 2.0
social networking platforms
recommendation engine
folksonomy
wisdom of crowds
crowdsourcing
consumer addiction
anticonsumption

1.4 Objective Summary

Explain the basics of market planning.

The strategic process of market planning begins with an assessment of factors within the organization and in the external environment that could help or hinder the development and marketing of products. On the basis of this analysis, marketers set objectives and develop strategies. Many firms use a target marketing strategy in which they divide the overall market into segments and then target the most attractive one(s). Then they design the marketing mix to gain a competitive position in the target market.

Key Terms

mass market
market segment
disruptive marketing

1.5 Objective Summary

Understand how to increase your chances of getting a great first job and having a successful career by using the marketing process to create a personal brand.

Brand You is a process to create a personal brand that will help you present yourself to employers when you seek an internship as a student or a job when you graduate. Brand You strategies are not just for marketing majors. No matter what type of career you want, a personal brand can set you apart from other job candidates and will help you manage that career.

Three marketing concepts apply to your personal brand:
- Marketing is about meeting needs.
- Marketing is about creating utility.
- Marketing is about exchange relationships.

Chapter **Questions** and **Activities**

Concepts: Test Your Knowledge

1-1. Briefly explain what marketing is.

1-2. List and describe the four Ps of the marketing mix.

1-3. Define the terms *consumer goods, services*, and *industrial goods*. What do we mean by *marketing ideas, people, and places?*

1-4. What is *user-generated content?* What is *branded content?*

1-5. What is *utility?* List, describe, and give an example of the different types of utility.

1-6. Explain the different stages in the evolution of the marketing concept. What is the *triple-bottom-line orientation?*

1-7. Explain how marketers practice the societal marketing concept and sustainability.

1-8. Explain the concept of a *value proposition*.

1-9. Today, marketing is all about the *customer experience (CX)*. Explain CX and some ways firms work to ensure a positive CX.

1-10. Define the terms *distinctive competency, differential benefit, and competitive advantage*. What does it mean for a firm to have a competitive advantage? What gives a firm a competitive advantage?

1-11. What is involved in marketing planning?

Activities: Apply What You've Learned

1-12. *In Class, 10–25 Minutes for Teams* Assume that you are a marketing consultant employed by retail giant

Target, which offers consumers products in a number of brick-and-mortar stores and online. Target wishes to increase its loyal customer base by engaging customers through interaction opportunities on social networks. Develop a list and describe at least 10 specific social network activities that will work together to increase customer engagement.

1-13. *In Class, 10–25 Minutes for Teams* Successful firms have a competitive advantage because they are able to identify distinctive competencies and use these to create differential benefits for their customers. Consider your business school or your university. What distinctive competencies does it have? What differential benefits does it provide for students? What is its competitive advantage? What are your ideas as to how your university could improve its competitive position? Write an outline of your ideas.

1-14. *In Class, 10–25 Minutes for Teams* As college students, you and your friends sometimes discuss the various courses you are taking. Assume you overhear your roommate say to another friend, "Marketing's not important. It's just dumb advertising." The other friend says, "Marketing doesn't really affect people's lives in any way." As a role-playing exercise, present your arguments against these statements to your class.

1-15. *For Further Research (Individual)* Recent reports indicate that consumers, including children and teens, are becoming small-screen addicts. Develop a series of questions to be used in a survey (about 10). Use these to interview at least five of your fellow students about their use of smartphones and tablets. Write up a report on your findings and conclusions.

1-16. *For Further Research (Groups)* Select a global or national company that you are familiar with. Examine the firm's website and other sources of information about the company to determine its competitive advantages. Who are their biggest competitors? What are each of their competitive advantages? Give three suggestions for how the company can market their products or services to feature their advantages and overcome the advantages of the competition.

1-17. *For Further Research (Individual)* One of the items that might be included in the Dark Side of Marketing is advertising that has the potential to encourage discrimination, criminal behavior, and unsafe activities, or to be insensitive or insulting to certain individuals or groups. Go online and search for various articles that discuss and show hundreds of examples of these types of advertising. Develop a report and if possible discuss your findings with your class.

Concepts: Apply Marketing Metrics

The chapter discusses the growing importance of sustainability, and it notes that companies and consumers increasingly consider other costs in addition to financial kinds when they decide what to sell or buy. One of these cost categories is damage to the environment. How can marketers make it easier for shoppers to compute these costs? The answer is more apparent in some product categories than in others. For example, American consumers often are able to compare the power consumption and annual costs of appliances by looking at their EnergyStar™ rating. In other situations, we can assess the *carbon footprint* implications of a product or service; this tells us how much CO_2 our purchase will emit into the atmosphere (e.g., if a person flies from New York to London). The average American is responsible for over 16 metric tons of CO_2 per year![43] A carbon footprint comes from the sum of two parts, the direct, or primary, footprint and the indirect, or secondary, footprint:

- The *primary footprint* is a measure of our direct emissions of CO_2 from the burning of fossil fuels, including domestic energy consumption and transportation (e.g., cars and planes).
- The *secondary footprint* is a measure of the indirect CO_2 emissions from the whole life cycle of products we use, from their manufacture to their eventual breakdown.[44]

Although many of us are more aware today that our consumption choices carry unseen costs, there is still a lot of confusion about the best way to communicate the environmental costs of our actions, and in many cases, consumers aren't motivated to take these issues into account unless the costs impact them directly and in the short term.

1-18. As a consumer, what other metrics would you suggest that might reflect benefits of sustainability initiatives that would motivate you to purchase from one provider or the other?

1-19. Would you buy from a demonstrably more expensive provider just because they exhibited a higher level of commitment to sustainability?

Choices: What Do You Think?

1-20. *Critical Thinking* Journalists, government officials, and consumers have been highly critical of companies for gathering and storing large amounts of data on consumers (i.e., Big Data). Others argue that such practices are essential for firms to provide high-quality, affordable products that satisfy consumers' varied needs. What do you think? Should the government regulate such practices? How can such practices help the consumer? What potential downfalls are there?

1-21. *Ethics* Despite best efforts to ensure product safety, products that pose a danger to consumers sometimes reach the marketplace. At what point should marketers release information about a product's safety to the public? How should marketers be held accountable if their product harms a consumer?

1-22. *Critical Thinking* Organizations are now focusing more on the triple-bottom-line orientation, meaning that firms should focus on maximizing the financial, social, and environmental areas of the business. What should companies do when they realize that two or more of these conflict with one another? Do you think any one of them is more important? Why?

1-23. *Critical Thinking* Many consumers are concerned about their impact on the environment. They demand green products as well as green marketing activities. However, these same consumers often opt not to purchase green products as they are traditionally more expensive than their alternatives. What do you think is driving this decision? How can marketers change their products or the way in which they are marketing them to encourage consumers to increase their purchases of green products? What are some ideas that you have for ways companies can execute green marketing?

1-24. *Critical Thinking* Many would argue that Amazon's competitive advantages include fast delivery and its vast array of product options. Do you think these advantages are sustainable? Who do you think are Amazon's biggest competitors? How are they working to overcome Amazon's advantages?

1-25. *Ethics* The American Psychological Association formally recognizes Internet addiction as a psychological disorder. Should it? Why or why not?

1-26. *Ethics* Crowdsourcing has a lot of upsides—for the company initiating the crowdsourcing. The company gets to generate buzz among its fans as well as generate new product ideas and inventive advertising campaigns for little to no investment. Is there an upside to crowdsourcing for the customer, or are companies exploiting their users?

1-27. *Critical Thinking* The chapter section on the dark side of marketing discusses alcohol and smoking abuse, deceptive or other advertising that can have negative consequences, illegal activities, claiming credit for something someone else has done, and deliberately defacing or damaging goods. Try to think of five additional consumer activities which could also be included in the topic of the "dark side of marketing." Describe each of your five and suggest activities for governments or marketers that would help decrease the problem.

Learn by Doing

The purpose of this miniproject is to develop an understanding of the practice of marketing and the importance of societal marketing and sustainability to different organizations.

1-28. Working as a team with two or three other students, select an organization in your community. It may be a manufacturer, a service provider, a retailer, a not-for-profit organization—almost any organization will do. Then schedule a visit with someone within the organization who is involved in the marketing activities. Arrange for a short visit during which the person can give your group a tour of the facilities and explain the organization's marketing activities.

1-29. Divide the following list of topics among your team and ask each person to be responsible for developing a set of questions to ask during the interview to learn about the company's program:

- What customer segments the company targets.
- How it determines customer needs and wants.
- What products it offers, including features, benefits, and goals for customer satisfaction.
- What its pricing strategies are.
- How it uses interactive content to engage customers.
- How it distributes products and whether it has encountered any problems.
- How it determines whether the needs and wants of customers are being met.
- Explain what marketers mean by the "societal marketing concept" and "sustainability" and ask if these are areas of concern to the organization. If so, how do they address them in their organization's activities? If not, ask if they have any plans to move in this direction in the future and, if so, how.

1-30. Develop a team report of your findings. In each section of the report, share what you learned that is new or surprising to you compared to what you expected.

1-31. Develop a team presentation for your class that summarizes your findings. Conclude your presentation with comments on what your team believes the company was doing that was particularly good and what was not quite so good.

Marketing in Action **Case**   Real Choices at StockX

Are you a *sneakerhead*? If you proudly claim this nickname for collectors of limited-edition athletic shoes, you may be familiar with StockX, the stock market for sneakerheads. The success of this innovative company offers several lessons about *value*, the most fundamental concept in marketing.

Sneakers are big business for retailers. They are also big business for collectors who not only love shoes but also love the dollars others are willing to pay for a pair of sneakers with limited availability. The North American resale market for sneakers and other streetwear has grown to over $2 billion and is expected to reach more than $6 billion by 2025. Notable sales include a pair of Nike Air Max for $40,000 and a 2020 sale of Air Jordans for $560,000—but, of course, those Jordans were actually worn by the basketball phenom.

Air Jordans were the "gateway collectible" that led to addiction for many avid collectors. Among them was StockX founder Josh Luber, a former IBM analyst who founded Campless, a kind of Kelley Blue Book for sneakers. You can find his Ted Talk online in which he passionately made the case for sneakers as an investment and explained the need for a platform that could facilitate the buying and selling of these "commodities"—a "stock market of things." When Quicken Loans billionaire Dan Gilbert learned about Luber's concept, the two joined together to form StockX in 2016.

StockX uses the concepts of a stock exchange that buys and sells shares of publicly traded companies and applies it to the world of product resale. The price a seller is willing to sell for is an "ask"; the price the buyer is willing to pay is a "bid." When these two match up, a transaction occurs automatically. Collectors can track the value of their own "portfolio" via StockX and can see how their shoes and those they are considering purchasing are tracking in value, including a 52-week trend line—a "ticker" for sneakers. Another critical service is the examination of the product by StockX "authenticators." These sneaker experts carefully scrutinize packaging, stitching, even the smell of the shoes to make sure they are the genuine article, not a counterfeit. For their services, StockX collects a 3 percent processing fee plus a transaction fee ranging from 8 to 9.5 percent.

Value is realized by every player in the StockX transaction process. Sellers get access to thousands of eager and able customers for their products and a simple and reliable process for handling the transactions. Buyers have access to useful information to help them assess whether a price is fair, plus they have a way to evaluate the change in value of their investments over time. Novice buyers are put on more of a level playing field with veteran buyers and sellers as the market price information in StockX allows them to assess the scarcity of a particular shoe. Perhaps most important to the purchaser is the authentication process, a feature not available with a private transaction between individuals or via competitor eBay. Even the shoe brands win as the prestige of their products increases through publicity about the prices at which they sell on the exchange. StockX is clearly receiving value too. In 2019, the company reached "unicorn" status, the term for privately held companies valued at $1 billion or more.

StockX is also experimenting with another stock market concept—the initial public offering (IPO). In financial markets, the IPO is used to let the market set a price for shares of a business that is converting from private status to a publicly traded company. StockX is using that idea to allow shoe manufacturers to offer their new styles to the marketplace. In 2019, Adidas offered 333 exclusive pairs of their Campus 80s without a retail price, allowing consumers to set the market price. StockX founder Luber believes these IPOs are the future of e-commerce. He hopes that retailers will treat the StockX platform as a full-fledged distribution channel, allowing users to bid for products through an auction process. Borrowing yet another idea from Wall Street, the company wants to let their customers do an exchange without even taking possession of the goods, facilitating "day trading." According to Luber, the idea behind all of this was simple: "The stock market has been the most efficient form of commerce for 200 years. All we did was copy that, and point it from old commodities, like stocks and bonds and oil and gas, to new commodities, like streetwear and watches and handbags."[45]

Questions for Discussion

1-32. Consider all of the potential stakeholders involved in a StockX transaction, from creation of the shoes to the acquisition by a collector. In what other ways is value created by the StockX service for each of these stakeholders?

1-33. Marketing is also concerned with providing value to society—people not directly involved in the exchange process. In what ways does—or could—StockX provide value to this stakeholder group?

1-34. As you'll learn in Chapter 10, pricing is an important tool available to marketers to signal value and to persuade prospects to make a purchase. In what ways does StockX help and/or hurt a shoe manufacturer's ability to use this important tool?

1-35. Consider StockX's vision for expanding the use of the IPO concept to eliminate the retail price and let consumers decide the market price for a new product. What are the pros and cons of this approach? For what kinds of products would this work and for what kinds of products might it be problematic?

Chapter **Notes**

1. American Marketing Association, "About AMA," www.ama.org/AboutAMA/Pages/Definition-of-Marketing.aspx (accessed May 24, 2018).

2. American Marketing Association, "About AMA," www.ama.org/AboutAMA/Pages/Definition-of-Marketing.aspx (accessed May 24, 2018).

3. Hal Concik, "Study Finds One Quarter of CEOs Have a Marketing or Sales Background," American Marketing Association, February 18, 2017, https://www.ama.org/publications/eNewsletters/Marketing-News-Weekly/Pages/quarter-ceos-have-marketingsales-background.aspx (accessed May 29, 2018).

4. Hailey Friedman, "The Best Marketing Agencies in New York: Top NYC Agencies," Improvado, April 10, 2020, https://improvado.io/blog/best-marketing-agencies-new-york (accessed June 13, 2020).

5. CIA World Factbook, updated June 11, 2020, https://www.cia.gov/library/publications/the-world-factbook/geos/us.html (accessed June 14, 2020).

6. Lee D. Dahringer, "Marketing Services Internationally: Barriers and Management Strategies," Journal of Service Marketing 5 (1991): 5–17.

7. Stuart Elliott, "Introducing Kentucky, the Brand," New York Times, June 9, 2004, https://www.nyt.com.

8. Julie Jargon, "McDonald's All-Day Breakfast Is Luring in Consumers, Study Finds," Wall Street Journal, December 8, 2015, http://www.wsj.com/articles/mcdonalds-all-day-breakfast-isluring-in-customers-study-finds-1449609778?cb=logged0.9060535116359343 (accessed March 3, 2016).

9. Phil LeBeau, "Business Travelers Increasingly Prefer Ride-Hailing Services over Car Rentals, Taxis," CNBC, January 30, 2018, https://www.cnbc.com/2018/01/29/business-travelers-increasingly-prefer-ride-hailing-services-over-car-rentals-taxis.html; Johana Bhuiyan, "Uber Powered Four Billion Rides in 2017. It Wants To Do More—and Cheaper—in 2018," Recode, January 5, 2018, https://www.recode.net/2018/1/5/16854714/uber-four-billion-rides-coo-barney-harford-2018-cut-costs-customer-service (accessed May 29, 2018).

10. Judith Wallenstein and Urvesh Shelat, "What's Next for the Sharing Economy?" Boston Consulting Group, October 4, 2017, https://www.bcg.com/publications/2017/strategy-technology-digitalwhats-next-for-sharing-economy.aspx (accessed May 29, 2018).

11. "JetBlue Celebrates 20th Birthday, 20 Years of Award-Winning Customer Service and Low Fares," JetBlue.com, February 11, 2020, http://mediaroom.jetblue.com/investor-relations/press-releases/2020/02-11-2020-145835585.

12. Paula D. Englis, Basil G. Englis, Michael R. Solomon, and Aard Groen, "Strategic Sustainability and Triple Bottom Line Performance in Textiles: Implications of the Eco-Label for the EU and Beyond," Business as an Agent of World Benefit Conference, United Nations and the Academy of Management, Cleveland, OH, 2006.

13. M. K. Khoo, S. G. Lee, and S. W. Lye, "A Design Methodology for the Strategic Assessment of a Product's Eco-Efficiency," International Journal of Production Research 39 (2001): 245–74; C. Chen, "Design for the Environment: A Quality-Based Model for Green Product Development," Management Science 47, no. 2 (2001): 250–64; Elizabeth Corcoran, "Thinking Green," Scientific American 267, no. 6 (1992): 44–46; Amitai Etzioni, "The Good Society: Goals beyond Money," The Futurist (2001): 68–69; M. H. Olson, "Charting a Course for Sustainability," Environment 38, no. 4 (1996): 10–23. See also U.S. Environmental Protection Agency, "What Is Sustainability," https://www.epa.gov (accessed April 7, 2014).

14. Bombas, "Giving Back," https://bombas.com/pages/givingback (accessed May 29, 2018).

15. G. A. Wyner, "Scorecards and More: The Value Is in How You Use Them," Marketing Research, Summer, 6–7; C. F. Lunbdy and C. Rasinowich, "The Missing Link: Cause and Effect Linkages Make Marketing Scorecards More Valuable," Marketing Research, Winter 2003, 14–19.

16. Marketing Accountability Standards Board, "Finance and Marketing Bond at MillerCoors," March 10, 2016, https://themasb.org/finance-and-marketing-bond-at-millercoors/ (accessed March 27, 2016).

17. Jeff Beer, "25 Predictions for What Marketing Will Look Like in 2020," Fastcocreate, March 4, 2015, http://www.fastcocreate.com/3043109/sector-forecasting/25-predictions-for-what-marketing-will-looklike-in-2020; Daniel Newman, "10 Top Trends Driving the Future of Marketing," Forbes, CMO Network, April 14, 2015, https://www.forbes.com/sites/danielnewman/2015/04/14/10-top-trends-driving-the-future-of-marketing/#81f287c5f97b (accessed March 25, 2016).

18. Prakriti Singhania, Nairita Gangopadhyay, Anya George Tharakan, Rupesh Bhat, and Preetha Devan, "2020 Global Marketing Trends," Deloitte Development LLC, 2019, https://www2.deloitte.com/content/dam/Deloitte/uk/Documents/consultancy/deloitte-uk-consulting-global-marketing-trends.pdf (accessed June 7, 2020).

19. Vinod Janapala, "The Future of E-Commerce: Best Predictions for 2020," Customer Think, March 20, 2020, https://customerthink.com/the-future-of-e-commerce-best-predictions-for-2020/ (accessed June 10, 2020).

20. Adam Tacy, "Embracing Service-Dominant Logic," SolvInnov.com, updated November 23, 2019, http://solvinnov.com/service-dominant-logic-part-1/(accessed June 21, 2020).

21. Christine Crandell, "Customer Co-Creation Is The Secret Sauce To Success," Forbes, June 10, 2016, https://www.forbes.com/sites/

christinecrandell/2016/06/10/customer_cocreation_secret_
sauce/#6bf72d45b6dc (accessed June 18, 2020).

22. Jeep, "Frequently Asked Questions," http://jeepjamboreeusa.
com/faq (accessed May 29, 2018).

23. PR Newswire, "Look No Further, Fall's 'Best Fest' is Back: Samuel
Adams Celebrates 30th Anniversary of OctoberFest,"August 19,
2019, https://www.prnewswire.com/news-releases/look-no-
further-falls-best-fest-is-back-samuel-adams-celebrates-30th-
anniversary-of-octoberfest-300903163.html (accessed June 10, 2020).

24. Roberto A. Ferdman, "How Coca-Cola Has Tricked Everyone into
Drinking So Much of It," *Washington Post*, October 5, 2015, https://
www.washingtonpost.com/news/wonk/wp/2015/10/05/howcoca-
cola-gets-its-way/ (accessed March 20, 2016).

25. Siddharth Cavale, "Coke Revenue Misses Estimates as Soda Sales
Slow," *Reuters*, February 18, 2014, https://www.reuters.com/arti-
cle/2014/02/18/us-cocacola-results-idUSBREA1H0WH20140218
(accessed April 7, 2014); Neil Hughes, "Apple's Domestic Mac
Sales Surge 28.5% as Overall PC Market Shrinks 7.5%," January 9,
2014, https://appleinsider.com/articles/14/01/09/apples-domestic-
mac-sales-surge-285-as-overall-pc-market-shrinks-75 (accessed
April 7, 2014); Annalyn Censky, "Dunkin' Donuts to Double U.S.
Locations," *CNN*, January 4, 2012, http://money.cnn.
com/2012/01/04/news/companies/dunkin_donuts_locations
(accessed April 7, 2014).

26. Michael E. Porter, *Competitive Advantage: Creating and Sustaining
Superior Performance* (New York: Free Press, 1985).

27. Carrie Melissa Jones, "7 Examples of Awesome User-Generated
Content Campaigns," *CMX*, May 2, 2017, https://cmxhub.com/
7-examples-of-awesome-user-generated-content-campaigns/
(accessed May 29, 2018).

28. Carrie Melissa Jones, "7 Examples of Awesome User-Generated
Content Campaigns," *CMX*, May 2, 2017, https://cmxhub.com/
7-examples-of-awesome-user-generated-content-campaigns/
(accessed May 29, 2018).

29. Frito-Lay North America, "PepsiCo's Doritos Brand Reveals the Five
Consumer-Created Commercials Competing for $1 Million Grand
Prize," January 2, 2014, https://www.fritolay.com/news/pepsico-
s-doritos-brand-reveals-the-five-consumer-created-commercials-
competing-for-1-million-grand-prize (accessed April 6, 2014).

30. Kenneth E. Clow and Donald E. Baack, *Integrated Advertising, Promotion, and Marketing Communications*, 7th ed. (Upper Saddle
River, NJ: Pearson, 2016).

31. Some material adapted from a presentation by Matt Leavey, Prentice Hall Business Publishing, July 18, 2007.

32. This section adapted from Michael R. Solomon, *Consumer Behavior: Buying, Having, and Being*, 8th ed. (Upper Saddle River, NJ:
Prentice Hall, 2008).

33. Jeff Surowiecki, *The Wisdom of Crowds* (New York: Anchor, 2005);
Jeff Howe, "The Rise of Crowdsourcing," *Wired*, June 2006,
https://www.wired.com/wired/archive/14.06/crowds.html
(accessed October 3, 2007).

34. Andrew Yoo, "Lego Ideas: Crowdsourcing the Next Big Hit,"
March 20, 2017, https://digital.hbs.edu/platform-digit/submis-
sion/lego-ideas-crowdsourcing-the-next-big-hit/; "Lego Ideas,"
August 3, 2017, https://ideas.lego.com/blogs/a4ae09b6-0d4c-
4307-9da8-3ee9f3d368d6/post/f20a58da-a8fd-4a2c-a0db-
3a094de6fe21 (accessed May 28, 2018).

35. *AdAge*, "FTC calls B.S. on Luminosity's Deceptive 'Brain Training'
Advertising," January 5, 2016, https://adage.com/article/news/
ftc-calls-b-s-lumosity-brain-training-company-pay-2m/302006
(accessed June 17, 2020).

36. E. J. Schultz, "Judge Orders Bud Light to Remove 'No Corn
Syrup' from Packaging Handing MillerCoors a Win," *Advertising
Age*, September 4, 2019, https://adage.com/article/cmo-strategy/
judge-orders-bud-light-remove-no-corn-syrup-packaging-hand-
ing-millercoors-win/2194731 (accessed June 17, 2020).

37. Parts of this section are adapted from Michael R. Solomon, *Consumer Behavior: Buying, Having, and Being*, 7th ed. (Upper Saddle
River, NJ: Prentice Hall, 2007).

38. Thomas C. O'Guinn and Ronald J. Faber, "Compulsive Buying: A
Phenomenological Explanation," *Journal of Consumer Research* 16
(September 1989): 154.

39. Associated Press, "Center Tries to Treat Web Addicts," *New York
Times*, September 5, 2009, https://www.nytimes.com/2009/09/06/
us/06internet.html (accessed June 8, 2010).

40. "Advertisers Face Up to the New Morality: Making the Pitch,"
July 8, 1997.

41. Courtni Casanova, "Disruptive Marketing: What Is It?" Copy-
press, https://www.copypress.com/blog/disruptive-marketing-
what-is-it/ (accessed June 17, 2020).

42. Lindsay Stein and Oliver McAteer, "Campaign US Reveals Top 10
Marketing Disruptors of 2019," CampaignUS, December 19, 2019,
https://www.campaignlive.com/article/campaign-us-reveals-
top-10-marketing-disruptors-2019/1669355 (accessed June 10,
2020); Steve Harvey, "All Shook Up: Disruptive Marketing Techniques for the Non-Conventional Marketer," Fabrikbrands.com,
February 22, 2018, https://fabrikbrands.com/disruptive-marketing-
techniques/ (accessed June 23, 2020); Kelly Springs-Kelley, "These
Disruptive Marketing Examples Will Inspire You," March 17,
2018, https://elevate-staffing.com/these-disruptive-marketing-
examples-will-inspire-you/ (accessed December 6, 2020).

43. Justin Gillis and Nadja Popovich, "The U.S. Is the Biggest Carbon
Polluter in History. It Just Walked Away from the ParisClimate
Deal," *New York Times*, June 1, 2017, https://www.nytimes.com/
interactive/2017/06/01/climate/us-biggest-carbon-polluter-in-
history-will-it-walk-away-from-the-paris-climate-deal.html
(accessed May 22, 2018).

44. https://www.carbonfootprint.com/ (accessed May 22, 2018).

45. Based on Khadeeja Safdar, "StockX, Hub for Sneakerheads, Is Latest
$1 Billion Unicorn," *The Wall Street Journal*, June 26, 2019, https://
www.wsj.com/articles/stockx-hub-for-sneakerheads-is-latest-1-
billion-unicorn-11561571959; Juliette Tafreschi, "'I Am One of the Top
Buyers on StockX'," *SportsWear International*, December 12, 2018,
https://www.sportswear-international.com/news/stories/Online-
marketplace-I-am-one-of-the-top-buyers-on-StockX-15047; Luke
Denne, "Michael Jordan Sneakers Sell for $560,000 at Sotheby's Auc-
tion," *NBC News*, May 18, 2020, https://www.nbcnews.com/news/
sports/michael-jordan-sneakers-sell-560-000-sotheby-s-auction-
n1209086; Sheila Marikar, "The Founder of StockX Turned His
Hobby into a Billion-Dollar Business in 3 Years. Then He Turned
Over the Reins. Now What?" *Inc.*, December 17, 2019, https://www.
inc.com/magazine/202002/sheila-marikar/stockx-josh-luber-
sneaker-resale-marketplace-scott-cutler-detroit-founder-ceo.html;
Dan Hyman, "A Nasdaq for Sneakerheads? StockX Aims to Tame
'Chaos' of Luxury Market," *The New York Times*, July 6, 2018, https://
www.nytimes.com/2018/07/06/business/smallbusiness/stockx-
sneakerheads-luxury-goods.html?auth=login-email&login=email;
Josh Luber, "Why Sneakers Are a Great Investment," *Ted Talks*,
accessed July 27, 2020, https://www.ted.com/talks/josh_luber_
why_sneakers_are_a_great_investment?language=en; Fastco Works,
"One-Stop Xmas Shopping at the Coolest 'Store' on the Internet,"
Fast Company, December 5, 2019, https://www.fastcompany.
com/90438587/one-stop-xmas-shopping-at-the-coolest-store-on-
the-internet; Ashwin Rodrigues, "What Is StockX? Everything You
Need to Know about the Billion-Dollar Sneaker Empire," *Fortune*,
July 21, 2019, https://fortune.com/2019/07/21/what-is-stock-x-
marketplace/; Keagan Pang, "StockX – Trading Exchange for Sneakers," hbs.edu, October 16, 2019, https://digital.hbs.edu/
platform-digit/submission/stockx-trading-exchange-for-sneakers;
Michelle Toh, "This Billion-Dollar Startup Is Turning Sneakers into a
'Stock Market'," *CNN*, September 26, 2019, https://www.cnn.
com/2019/09/25/tech/stockx-detroit-sneaker-startup/index.html;
James Chen, "Unicorn," *Investopedia*, March 31, 2020, https://www.
investopedia.com/terms/u/unicorn.asp; Fastco Works, "The Innovative 'Stock Exchange' That's Changing the Way We Value – and
Buy – Rare Sneakers," *Fast Company*, November 14, 2019, https://
www.fastcompany.com/90429014/the-innovative-stock-exchange-
thats-changing-the-way-we-value-and-buy-rare-sneakers.

2 Global, Ethical, and Sustainable Marketing

Tom Szaky

Meet Tom Szaky

▼ A Decision Maker at TerraCycle

Tom Szaky is CEO of TerraCycle, a global social business based in Trenton, New Jersey. Born in 1982 to two physicians, Tom and his family fled communist Hungary after the Chernobyl disaster, stopping in Germany and Holland before settling in Canada, where he is a citizen. He went to public school and learned about business and entrepreneurship in capitalist North America.

He became fascinated by garbage. Having come from a country with little to a world where everything was available and overconsumption was the norm, he was astounded by the things people threw in the trash; the first television set he ever saw was one being thrown in the garbage. Growing up around this helped him understand that waste is a modern idea. Then, he came to America to study business, and the rest is history.

Tom's Info

What I do when I'm not working: Spend time with friends and family. I travel constantly for the business. When I do have time off, I stay at my home along the Delaware River in New Jersey, where I like to work on do-it-yourself projects in my backyard, building fun things like ziplines and treehouses for my sons!

First job out of school: To be perfectly honest, TerraCycle. I came up with the idea for TerraCycle when I was a 19-year-old freshman at Princeton University and dropped out of the Ivy League to grow the business. Before that, I'd focused on learning everything I could about entrepreneurship, teaching myself how to code at 14 and building a

website. But TerraCycle was my first job, and it's what I've been doing ever since.

What drives me: Waste is a simple concept—something either is, or it isn't—but the economics surrounding it, and how we can eliminate it, is complex. Solving for this by making "the right thing" the more profitable and rewarding thing to do has been a lifelong puzzle of mine, and one that business can get behind with the right framing. Business is the most powerful vehicle to change in the world. Being a part of that change and driving it into the future is what drives me.

My management style:
I consider myself more of a coach than a manager. It's important to me that my staff, many of whom are responsible for very

high-profile projects and interacting with clients, are provided the tools to come to their own conclusions. I can be quite hands-off until I'm needed to step in.

Don't do this when interviewing with me:
Ask me questions with answers that are available on the Internet! I am more than happy to provide insights, but it gets a bit

boring to answer questions about things that are found on our website.

My pet peeve:
Not giving 100% or striving to realize potential. Every person is capable of pushing the limits of an idea, a project, or their own personal growth. I myself tend to work a certain way, so I expect this of my colleagues and peers, as well.

Here's my problem...

Real **People**, Real **Choices**

There is a global epidemic of waste caused by the world's dependence on "single-use" items—consumption of products and packaging designed to be used once or a handful of times and then disposed of. Prior to the 1950s, products were made to be reusable. Today, we make and buy 70 times more stuff, most of it going to landfills or incinerators within 12 months of purchase.

This is a problem that gets worse with every year of population growth. In the past few years, consumers, increasingly concerned with plastic pollution and the waste caused by disposability, are looking to companies to take responsibility and provide solutions.

Tom came up with the idea for TerraCycle in 2001. Originally, the concept (vermicompost, which Tom's friend in Canada proved made fabulous plant fertilizer) was a submission to Princeton University's annual Entrepreneurship Club Business Plan Competition, which caught his attention with a grand prize of $5,000.

As a college student bottling plant fertilizer (produced by feeding Princeton University's food waste to worms) in trash-picked soda bottles, selling an entire product made of garbage eventually got him thinking: *What if we eliminate the very idea of waste?* Soon Tom dropped out of Princeton to focus on the business full-time.

Today, TerraCycle operates in 21 countries (and counting!), working with some of the world's largest brands, retailers, and manufacturers to collect and recycle products and packaging that currently go to landfill or incineration. TerraCycle is the parent company to Loop, a new circular shopping platform that empowers consumers to shop for favorite brands in durable, reusable packaging. Since he started the company, Tom has written four books and been an executive producer of a reality docuseries about TerraCycle.

TerraCycle helps businesses capture the value of their difficult-to-recycle products and packaging, offers national access to first-of-its-kind recycling solutions, and both educates and empowers their customers in regard to recycling. But Tom's team understands that recycling is not the main solution to waste: it is just a way to treat the symptoms. Disposability is the root cause.

Knowing what we know about the economics of waste and why waste exists, Tom found it imperative to apply this to a new model of production and consumption that offers the virtues of convenience, cost, aesthetics, and function demanded by today's consumer, as well as the waste-free wisdom of durable, refillable, community-based models like "the milkman," versions of which deliver consumables like eggs, milk, butter, and oil in durable containers. Mass production, synthetic materials, and disposability took off in the 1950s and never stopped, phasing out durable, reusable, and sharing economy models almost entirely. Recycling and recovery systems cannot handle the complexity or volume of material generated by the world's consumption, which is

now accustomed to the virtues of single-use. In order to get the world to shop differently, Tom's team needed to create a solution that would satisfy all the stakeholders—producers, retailer, and consumers.

At the World Economic Forum Annual Meeting in Davos, Switzerland, in 2017, TerraCycle unveiled the world's first recyclable shampoo bottle made from beach plastic for the world's #1 shampoo brand, Head & Shoulders. Tom's company teamed up with Head & Shoulders' parent company Procter & Gamble and its partner SUEZ in Europe to source beach plastic that volunteers collected by hand. The beach plastic bottle project was a revolutionary initiative at the time, since expanding to additional brands and markets around the world, and one that would go on to win an award from the United Nations.

Behind the scenes, another potentially world-changing concept had been incubating at TerraCycle. Internally called "Phase 2" to the beach bottle project, the idea was a durable packaging model in which companies create durable versions of their own goods previously housed in single-use packaging. The products would be offered in a combination of glass, stainless steel, aluminum, and engineered plastics designed to last at least 100 uses; when they would finally wear out, TerraCycle would be able to recycle them.

By adapting the circular economy principles of durability and use of renewable resources, recovering, reusing, and repurposing whenever possible, this project had the potential to drive a paradigm shift around producer responsibility, consumerism, and what people are really looking for in their products. But, as with all things first-of-their-kind, it would require significant investment of time and money, and, most importantly, boldness.

Those first conversations with the brand partners and retailers would be about proposing a break from the status quo and linear economy, which for so long had been very effective in meeting consumers' needs, creating jobs, and generating growth. Conversations are often about timing, and when everyone gathered at Davos, it seemed like the perfect opportunity.

Tom considered his **options** 1·2·3

1 Option
Introduce Loop at the Davos meeting. With so many stakeholders gathered in one place, TerraCycle could gain access to a big and influential audience in order to get buy-in from organizations around the world. When multiple stakeholders endorse an idea at once, this reduces the risk for each of them. Davos is an event where businesses, governments, brands, and luminaries are in one spot and poised to make deals that will change the world economy. TerraCycle was riding the success of its beach bottle project with P&G, so this could be a good time to propose another radical idea.

On the other hand, this was the announcement of the beach plastic bottle to the world, not necessarily it coming to market at retail. The first 150,000 Head & Shoulders bottles, the world's largest production run of recyclable shampoo bottles made with beach plastic at the time, were slated to hit shelves in Paris, France, that summer. The teams had a significant amount of work to put into the product launch so it would be successful and sell, and it was too soon to speak on the ROI the partnership promised.

A big conversation taking place during a big announcement has a degree of risk. It might've felt like the wrong timing or an overstep to propose something that had never been done before. Plus, a successful conversation had its own risks to the beach bottle project—if time, money, and attention were diverted to Loop development, beach bottle project sales might suffer.

2 Option **Wait to announce the Loop model.** For now, enjoy the incredible response TerraCycle got with the beach plastic bottle project initiative, and then propose the new idea after its success was apparent. The success of the beach plastic bottle and launch in other markets would provide TerraCycle additional credibility and leverage with existing brand partners and potential collaborators. In addition, promoting, marketing, and continuing to source and produce material for the beach plastic bottle required significant management of resources, including energy and time. Waiting a bit to dive into another line of business would allow the company to focus on the beach plastic bottle and be sure it got done right.

On the other hand, TerraCycle's entire business model is built on production and consumption models that haven't existed before. The concepts behind Loop aren't entirely new, calling upon the waste-free wisdom of models like "the milkman," which placed the responsibility and ownership of durable, reusable packaging with the producers of the products they contained and allowed consumers to return their consumables to be refilled, so it was only a matter of time before other platforms came to market. Offering trusted brands in upgraded containers (including what might be the world's most functional, beautiful pint of ice cream), consumers could enjoy products they love while eliminating packaging waste—a "win-win" for profit and sustainability.

Consumers connect with the sustainability angle, but they are interested in the prospect of a better product. One of the many downsides to disposable

packaging is the reduction of consumer delight: the positive, emotional response one has when interacting with a product. For the same reasons we aren't served with disposable eating utensils and paper plates at fancy restaurants, we are delighted by products housed in glass or metal, or beautiful dinnerware.

Durable versions of consumer goods previously housed in single-use packaging may sound exclusive, but the goal is to keep containers useful for much longer, allow people to get what they really want out of the things they buy, and create an upgrade for products the world already uses.

It had always been Tom's method to go with his gut and strike while the iron is hot, and to have waited would have not been his style at all! The world had been ready for a solution to single-use, and waiting would prolong a problem Tom and his team believed was possible to solve.

3 Option **Don't pursue the concept of a durable packaging system at all.** TerraCycle has been long known for "recycling the non-recyclable." Today, people are aware that public recycling is failing, that more of what we try to recycle correctly gets thrown away, and that the tariffs on foreign garbage in the East have destabilized our recycling system even further. But back in 2017, this was only beginning to come to light for the public. Just collecting and recycling the "difficult-to-recycle" is a huge improvement over current conditions, and an entirely new model might be too ambitious. Public recycling was suffering, so TerraCycle was more important than ever. So much of the value the company adds for its customers is education and its status as experts in the waste space. Leaning into its solid identity as a recycling company could allow for increased focus on the issues around recycling. On the other hand, TerraCycle is on a mission to eliminate the idea of waste. To only focus on recycling would be to ignore its root cause: single-use and disposability.

Now, put yourself in Tom's shoes. Which option would you choose, and why?

You Choose

Which **Option** would you choose, and **why**?
☐ Option 1   ☐ Option 2   ☐ Option 3

2.1 Take a Bow: Marketing on the Global Stage

OBJECTIVE

Understand the big picture of international marketing and the decisions firms must make when they consider globalization.

Here's an important question: Do you primarily see yourself only as a resident of Smalltown, USA, or as a member of a global community? The reality is that you and all your classmates are citizens of the world and participants in a global marketplace. It is likely that you eat bananas from Ecuador, drink beer from Mexico, and sip wine from Australia, South Africa, or Chile. When you come home, you may take off your shoes that were made in Thailand, put your feet up on the cocktail table imported from Indonesia, and watch the World Cup football (soccer) match being played in Brazil or Canada on your Smart TV while checking your Facebook page on your smartphone, both made in China. Hopefully, you also have some knowledge and concern for important world events such as the "Brexit" vote in which Britain separated itself from the European Union; the mass killings, systematic rape, and torture of the Rohingya people in Myanmar; the continuing problems in Syria as the once-thought-defeated Islamic State continues to fight Syrian forces;[1] and the growing concern about North Korea's nuclear weapons. And on a more positive note you may even be looking for an exciting career with a firm that does business around the globe.

Firms doing business in this global economy face uncertainty in the future of the global marketplace. For a number of years, consumers and world leaders have argued that the development of free trade and a single global marketplace will benefit us all because it allows people who live in developing countries to enjoy the same economic benefits as citizens of more developed countries.

There are other reasons that many leaders want a single marketplace. One important reason comes from fears that the **Greenhouse Effect** may threaten the future of the planet. What is the Greenhouse Effect? In simple terms, our factories and automobiles continue to pump more and more carbon dioxide (the most important of the greenhouse gases) into our atmosphere while at the same time we cut down the rain forests and reduce the amount of oxygen the trees add to the atmosphere. This increase in greenhouse gases causes the Earth to get warmer, just like a greenhouse provides a warm place for tender plants. The result, many believe, is **climate change**, a warming of the Earth, which will have disastrous effects on the planet.[2] These fears have caused many to demand international agreements that would force industries and governments to develop and adhere to the same environmental standards to protect the future of the planet.

Of course, there is another side to the issue of a single marketplace. The **Arab Spring**, a series of anti-government protests and uprisings in a number of Arab countries, was largely aided by new social media tools available to people in the region. These protests gave hope to many that dictatorships in countries in the Middle East would become democracies and bring a better life to peoples of the countries. Instead, new violent, radical groups such as ISIS took over large portions of these countries. This was accompanied by a growing number of terrorist attacks in other parts of the world, causing citizens and country leaders to propose greater restrictions on immigration and on trade with countries that aid or harbor terrorists. Finally, the COVID-19 pandemic has made clear the tremendous differences between the have and have-not countries, making it essential that more is done to help the poorest nations.[3]

You may be asking, "What do these current events have to do with a marketing course?" Whether we like it or not, we are a global community. Everything that happens in any part of the world has a potential to influence the likelihood of marketers' success and what marketers need to do to be successful at home and around the globe. We'll be talking about these influences in this chapter and throughout the book.

The global marketing game is exciting, the stakes are high, and it's easy to lose your shirt. Competition comes from both local and foreign firms, and differences in national laws, customs, and consumer preferences can make your head spin. In this section, we will first discuss the status of world trade today. Then, we'll look at the decisions firms must make as they consider their global opportunities.

Greenhouse Effect
The turning of our atmosphere into a kind of greenhouse as a result of the addition of carbon dioxide and other greenhouse gases.

climate change
A significant change in the measures of climate, including major changes in temperature, precipitation, or wind patterns, that occurs over several decades or longer.

Arab Spring
A series of anti-government protests and uprisings in a number of Arab countries facilitated by new social media tools available to people in the region.

World Trade

World trade refers to the flow of goods and services among different countries—the total value of all the exports and imports of the world's nations. From 2007 to 2009, the world suffered a global economic crisis that resulted in dramatic decreases in worldwide exports. This was followed by a number of years of increasing economic prosperity and increasing growth in world trade with world exports of merchandise increasing from $12 trillion in 2009 to nearly $19 trillion in 2019. Just how much is $19 trillion? Think about it this way: A recent lottery prize grew to a whopping $1 billion. If a lottery awarded a $1 billion prize every day, it would take more than 43 years to equal $19 trillion. The decline in 2015 was primarily due to declining commodity prices and changing exchange rates rather than to declines in trade volume. Of course, not all countries participate equally in the trade flows among nations. Understanding the "big picture" of who does business with whom is important to marketers when they devise global trade strategies.

world trade
The flow of goods and services among different countries—the value of all the exports and imports of the world's nations.

Figure 2.1 *Process* | Steps in the Decision Process to Enter Global Markets

Entering global markets involves a sequence of decisions.

Step 1: Whether to Go Global

Step 2: Which Market(s) to Enter

Step 3: Level of Commitment

Step 4: How to Adapt Marketing Mix Strategies
- **Localize**
- **Standardize**

countertrade
A type of trade in which goods are paid for with other items instead of with cash.

It's often a good thing to have customers in remote markets, but to serve their needs well requires flexibility and the ability to adapt to local social and economic conditions. For example, you may have to adapt to the needs of foreign trading partners when those firms can't pay cash for the products they want to purchase. Believe it or not, the currencies of as many as 100 countries—from the Chinese Yuan to the Indian Rupee—are *inconvertible,* usually due to government restrictions. This means you can't spend or exchange them outside the country's borders. In some countries, because sufficient cash or credit simply is not available, trading firms work out elaborate **countertrade** deals in which they trade (or *barter*) their products with each other or even supply goods in return for tax breaks from the local government.

Our ever-increasing access to products from around the world does have a dark side: The growth in world trade in recent years has been accompanied by a glut of unsafe products—toys with lead paint, toothpaste containing poisonous diethylene glycol, and more recently, crayons laced with cancer-causing asbestos—many of which came from China.[4] In 2014, the European Commission's early warning system for dangerous products (RAPEX) reported a notable increase in alerts of unsafe products; of the more than 2,000 alert issues the commission received, almost two-thirds of the unsafe products came from China.[5] Although most Chinese manufacturers make quality products, some unscrupulous producers have damaged the reputation of Chinese manufacturers and prompted U.S. and European officials to increase their inspections of Chinese imports.

Should We Go Global?

Figure 2.1 shows that when firms consider going global their decisions include four steps:

- *Step 1.* "Go" or "no go"—is it in our best interest to focus exclusively on our home market or should we cast our net elsewhere as well?

- *Step 2.* If the decision is "go," which global markets are most attractive? Which country or countries offer the greatest opportunity for us?

- *Step 3.* What market-entry strategy, or rather, what level of commitment is best? As we'll see, it's pretty low risk to simply export products to overseas markets. On the other hand, although the commitment and the risk are substantial if the firm decides to build and run manufacturing facilities in other countries, the potentially greater payoff may be worth the extra risk.

- *Step 4.* How do we develop successful marketing mix strategies in these foreign markets—should we standardize what we do across all the countries where we operate or develop a unique localized marketing strategy for each country?

We'll look at the first of these decisions now—whether or not to go global.

Although the prospect of millions—or even billions—of consumers salivating for your goods in other countries is tempting, not all firms can or should go global. When they make these decisions, marketers need to consider a number of factors that may enhance or detract from their success abroad. Let's review two that are critical to the decision: domestic demand and the competitive advantage the firm enjoys at home.

Look at Market Conditions and Opportunities

Many times, a firm decides it's time to go global because the opportunity for growing the business and greater profit within its domestic market has already peaked and may even be declining while foreign markets offer opportunities for large growth. Of course, if there is still room to grow business and profits at home, it may not be a good idea to invest in the larger global market for now.

Starbucks has served coffee to just about every American who drinks it. The company opened its first store in 1971 in Seattle. After conquering its home city, the company spread across the United States. The company's global expansion began in 1996, when it opened its first store outside of North America in Tokyo. Starbucks has opened stores in additional countries every year since. Today, Starbucks operates more than 30,000 stores in 80 markets.[6] That's a lot of lattes.

Consider Your Competitive Advantage

In Chapter 1, we discussed how firms create a competitive advantage over rivals. When firms enter a global marketplace, this challenge is even greater. There are more players involved, and typically local firms have a "home-court advantage." It's like soccer—increasing numbers of Americans play the game, but they are up against an ingrained tradition of soccer fanaticism in Europe and South America, where kids start dribbling a soccer ball when they start to walk.

If a firm wants to go global, it needs to examine the competitive advantage that makes it successful in its home country. Will this leg up "travel" well to other countries? If the answer is yes, then a firm is probably wise to consider globalization more seriously. Starbucks, long known for its product quality, superior customer service, fair treatment of employees, and respect for local cultures, is experiencing great growth overseas as well as strong sales in the United States.[7]

Now that we've discussed this first step in the global decision process, we'll look at important factors that help marketers make decisions about what markets to enter, including global trade controls that governments have in place. We'll also look at the various elements of the external environment that influence marketing decisions both at home and abroad. Finally, we'll examine marketers' decisions on the level of commitment and if and how to adapt marketing strategies used in the domestic market for success in other countries.

2.2 Understand International, Regional, and Country Global Trade Controls

OBJECTIVE
Explain how
international
organizations such as
the World Trade
Organization (WTO),
the World Bank, the
International Monetary
Fund (IMF), economic
communities, and
individual country
regulations facilitate
and limit a firm's
opportunities for
globalization.

Even the most formidable competitive advantage does not guarantee success in foreign markets. Many governments participate in activities that support the idea that the world should be one big open marketplace, where companies from every country are free to compete for business. The actions of others frequently say the reverse. In many countries, the local government may "stack the deck" in favor of domestic competitors. Often, they erect roadblocks (or at least those pesky speed bumps) designed to favor local businesses over outsiders, making it even more difficult to expand into foreign markets. Indeed, in the United States, the issue of whether to regulate trade to give American companies an advantage—or to lessen the advantage that companies based in other countries have from their own governments—remains one of the most divisive issues in political and business circles.

Initiatives in International Cooperation and Regulation

In recent years, a number of international initiatives have diminished barriers to unfettered world trade. Most notably, after World War II, the United Nations established the **General Agreement on Tariffs and Trade (GATT)**, which did much to establish free trade among nations. During a meeting in 1984 known as the Uruguay Round, GATT created the **World Trade Organization (WTO)**. With 164 members and 23 observer states seeking membership, the WTO member nations account for around 98 percent of world trade. The WTO has

General Agreement on Tariffs and Trade (GATT)
International treaty to reduce import tax levels and trade restrictions.

World Trade Organization (WTO)
An organization that replaced GATT; the WTO sets trade rules for its member nations and mediates disputes between nations.

made giant strides to create a single, open world market. It is the only international organization that deals with the global rules of trade between nations. Its main function is "to ensure that trade flows as smoothly, predictably and freely as possible."[8]

The WTO also tackles other issues that stand in the way of an open and fair world market. Perhaps you have spent time in other countries, and noticed the huge numbers of luxury watches, leather bags, and current music CDs that sell for ridiculously low prices. Who can resist a Rolex watch for $20? Of course, there is a catch: They're fake or pirated illegally. Protection of copyright and patent rights is a huge headache for many companies, and it's a priority the WTO tries to tackle. *Pirating* is a serious problem for companies because illegal sales significantly erode their profits. All too often, we see news headlines about police confiscating millions of dollars' worth of goods—from counterfeit luxury handbags to fake Viagra.[9]

Two additional organizations have a strong influence on the advancement of global trade: the **World Bank** and the **International Monetary Fund (IMF)**. The World Bank, founded in 1944 and owned by its 189 member countries, is an international lending institution. The goal of the World Bank is to reduce poverty and better peoples' lives by improving economies and promoting sustainable development. In pursuit of this goal, the World Bank lends about $20 billion a year to development projects. The poorest countries may have up to 50 years to repay the loans without interest.[10]

The primary purpose of the IMF, also founded in 1944, is to ensure the stability of the international monetary exchange by controlling fluctuations in **foreign exchange rates**, also referred to as **forex rates**. Exchange rates are simply the price of one currency in terms of another currency. Stabilizing exchange rates can help to prevent severe **balance of payments** problems and thereby make it possible for countries to trade with each other. A country's balance of payments is a statement of how much trade a country has going out compared to how much it has coming in. If a country is buying more than it is selling, it will have a negative balance of payments (which is not necessarily a bad thing).[11] Conversely, a country, such as China, that sells more than it buys from other countries has a positive balance of payments.

Protected Trade: Quotas, Embargoes, and Tariffs

Whereas the WTO works for free trade, some governments adopt policies of **protectionism** when they enforce rules on foreign firms to give home companies an advantage. Many governments set **import quotas** on foreign goods to protect domestic employment and industries. A second justification for quotas is to protect against unfair foreign trade practices such as dumping (the pricing of imports below production cost). Quotas may also be necessary for national security. By protecting defense-related industries, a country will lessen dependence on foreign imports in the event of a war.[12] Quotas can make goods more expensive to a country's citizens because the absence of cheaper foreign goods reduces pressure on domestic firms to lower their prices. For example, when President Donald Trump placed tariffs on solar panels (30 percent) and washing machines (up to 50 percent) in order to aid U.S. manufacturers, there was concern that consumers would be the ones who would ultimately pay in higher prices for these products.[13]

Of course, these tariffs were only a small part of the longer-term trade war between the U.S. and China, the world's two largest economies and its superpowers. From 2018 to 2020, President Trump introduced tariffs on $550 billion in Chinese goods in order to reduce the U.S. trade deficit, protect American manufacturing, and fight against China's "unfair trade practices," i.e., theft of intellectual property and the forced transfer of American technology to China. The coronavirus outbreak emerged in Wuhan, China, in December 2019, shutting down China's economy for an extended period. Wuhan, as a center for the manufacture of car parts, highlights the likely consequences of continuing problems between the world's two largest economies.[14]

An **embargo** is an extreme quota that prohibits commerce and trade with a specified country altogether. For over 50 years, hardcore cigar smokers in the United States have had to do without as the U.S. government prohibited the import of Cuban cigars as well as rum and other

---

World Bank
An international lending institution that seeks to reduce poverty and better people's lives by improving economies and promoting sustainable development.

International Monetary Fund (IMF)
An international organization that seeks to ensure the stability of the international monetary exchange by controlling fluctuations in exchange rates.

foreign exchange rate (forex rate)
The price of a nation's currency in terms of another currency.

balance of payments
A statement of how much trade a country has going out compared to how much it has coming in. If a country is buying more than it is selling, it will have a negative balance of payments.

protectionism
A policy adopted by a government to give domestic companies an advantage.

import quotas
Limitations set by a government on the amount of a product allowed to enter a country.

embargo
A quota completely prohibiting specified goods from entering or leaving a country.

products because of political differences with its island neighbor. In 2017, President Trump extended the ban under the Trading with the Enemy Act on Cuban products for at least one more year. Still, the U.S. government has moved toward the normalization of relations between the two countries, meaning Americans may again enjoy these uniquely Cuban products.

Governments also use **tariffs**, or taxes on imported and exported goods, to give domestic competitors an advantage in the marketplace by making foreign competitors' goods more expensive than their own products and to raise revenue for the government. New Balance is the largest major sneaker company that produces shoes in the United States. They make or assemble more than four million pairs per year in the United States, a limited portion of their sales. According to the Department of Commerce, the average U.S. tariff for footwear is 10.8 percent, much higher than the average for all industrial products of 1.5 percent.[15] No wonder those Nike Air Jordan III Retro Infrared 23 shoes are so expensive![16]

tariffs
Taxes on imported goods.

Economic Communities

Groups of countries may also band together to promote trade among themselves and make it easier for member nations to compete elsewhere. These **economic communities** coordinate trade policies and ease restrictions on the flow of products and capital across their borders. Economic communities are important to marketers because they set policies in areas such as product content, package labeling, and advertising regulations. The United States, for example, was for many years a member of the *North American Free Trade Agreement (NAFTA)*, which included the United States, Canada, and Mexico. NAFTA was renegotiated and on July 1, 2020, was officially replaced when the three countries approved a new agreement that made major changes in rules for automakers and U.S. dairy product sales to Canada. The new agreement is named the United States-Mexico-Canada Agreement, or USMCA.[17]

economic communities
Groups of countries that band together to promote trade among themselves and to make it easier for member nations to compete elsewhere.

The European Union (EU) represents more than 500 million consumers, more than 300 million of whom use the euro as their currency. In June 2016, U.K. voters approved the United Kingdom's divorce or withdrawal from the European Union, causing alarm and concern around the globe. This action is referred to as **Brexit**, the merging of the words *Britain* and *exit*—a shorthand way of saying Britain's exit from the EU. Brexit was originally scheduled to officially take place on March 29, 2019 but was delayed until January 31, 2020 with the transition to be completed by December 31, 2020.[18] The long-term effects of this move will only be known after the passage of time. Table 2.1 lists the world's major economic communities.

Brexit
Term used to refer to the U.K.'s (**Brit**ain's) **exit** from the European Union.

Table 2.1	Some Major Economic Communities Around the World	
Community	**Member Countries**
Andean Community (www.comunidadandina.org)	Bolivia, Colombia, Ecuador, Peru
Association of Southeast Asian Nations (ASEAN) (www.aseansec.org)	Brunei, Cambodia, Indonesia, Lao PDR, Malaysia, Myanmar, Philippines, Singapore, Thailand, Vietnam
Common Market for Eastern and Southern Africa (COMESA) (www.comesa.int)	Burundi, Comoros, Democratic Republic of the Congo, Djibouti, Egypt, Eritrea, Ethiopia, Kenya, Libya, Madagascar, Malawi, Mauritius, Rwanda, Seychelles, Sudan, Swaziland, Uganda, Zambia, Zimbabwe
European Union (EU) (www.Europa.eu.int)	Austria, Belgium, Bulgaria, Croatia, Cyprus, Czech Republic, Denmark, Estonia, Finland, France, Germany, Greece, Hungary, Ireland, Italy, Latvia, Lithuania, Luxembourg, Malta, Netherlands, Poland, Portugal, Romania, Slovakia, Slovenia, Spain, Sweden
	(In 2016, the United Kingdom voted to withdraw from the EU on March 29, 2019.)
MERCOSUR (www.mercosur.org)	Brazil, Paraguay, Uruguay, Argentina
U.S.-Mexico-Canada Agreement (USMCA) (a renegotiated agreement replacing NAFTA) (https://www.trade.gov/usmca)	Canada, Mexico, United States
South Asian Association for Regional Cooperation (SAARC) (www.saarc-sec.org)	Afghanistan, Bangladesh, Bhutan, India, Maldives, Nepal, Pakistan, Sri Lanka

2.3 Analyze the External Marketing Environment

Whether or not you decide to venture out of your own country (at least for now) to succeed, you can't simply bury your head in the sand and ignore what's going on in the rest of the world. You can be sure your competitors aren't! Marketing planning demands that marketers understand the firm's internal and external environments. We'll talk about the internal environment of a firm in Chapter 3. In this chapter, we'll look at how an understanding of a firm's external environment is even more important if your firm has decided to go global.

The **external environment** consists of elements outside the firm that may affect it either positively or negatively. The key elements of the external environment are the economic environment, competitive environment, technological environment, political and legal environments, and the sociological environment. Because managers can't directly control these external factors, they must be aware and respond to them in marketing planning.

Things can happen very quickly, and new developments can trip up even the most sophisticated marketers. Just ask Tata Motors, which is a major player in the Indian auto industry. In 2016, Tata prepared to launch a new hatchback with the name Zica. Oops—that name was too close to the Zika virus that was spreading around the world—so the company quickly renamed the car Tiago.[19]

And, if you have decided to go global, understanding local conditions in a potential new country or in regional markets helps you to figure out where to go. Figure 2.2 provides a snapshot of these different external environments we'll dive into now.

The Economic Environment

After several rocky years of economic stumbling caused by the Great Recession of 2008–2009, the global economy made giant strides toward a full comeback. The global economy grew steadily through 2019. When the coronavirus pandemic hit the world in 2020,

external environment
The uncontrollable elements outside an organization that may affect its performance either positively or negatively.

Figure 2.2 *Snapshot* │ Elements of the External Environment

It's essential to understand elements of the firm's external environment to succeed in both domestic and global markets.

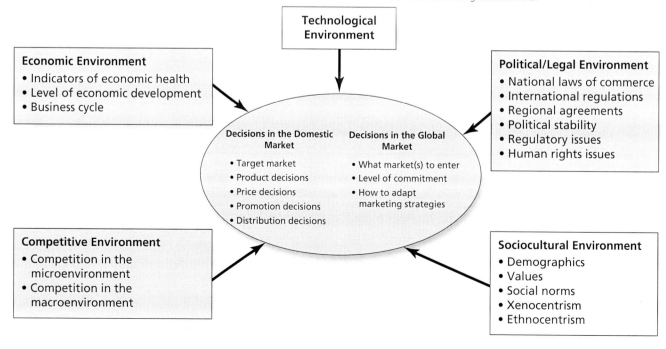

authorities quickly implemented what the International Monetary Fund called the "Great Lockdown," closing borders, schools and businesses and outlawing large gatherings. Many lost their jobs—26 million in the U.S. during a 5-week period. The WTO predicted a decrease in world trade between 12.9 and 30.0 percent. Experts were unable to predict when the world economy would return to a more normal state.[20]

Marketers need to understand the state of the economy from two different perspectives: (1) the overall economic health and level of development of a country and (2) the current stage of its business cycle. Let's take a look at each now.

Indicators of Economic Health

Just as a doctor takes your temperature during a medical checkup, companies need to know about the overall "health" of a country's *economic environment* before they conduct a more detailed exam. You can easily find information about most countries in the *World Factbook* of the Central Intelligence Agency (CIA) (no, you don't need high-level security clearance to access this information online).

The most commonly used measure of economic health is a country's **gross domestic product (GDP)**: the total dollar value of goods and services it produces within its borders in a year. Table 2.2 shows the GDP and other economic and demographic characteristics of a sampling of countries. In addition to total GDP, marketers may also compare countries on the basis of *per capita GDP*: the total GDP divided by the number of people in a country. The *per capita* GDP is the better indicator of economic health because it is adjusted for the population size of each country.

gross domestic product (GDP)
The total dollar value of goods and services produced by a nation within its borders in a year.

Still, these comparisons may not tell the whole story. *Per capita* GDP can be deceiving, because of the income inequality where the wealth of a country may be concentrated in the hands of a few. In these cases, most citizens don't have the means to obtain basic necessities. Furthermore, the costs of the same goods and services are much lower in some global markets. This is why it's important for companies that want to enter a foreign market to consider exchange rates as well.

The foreign exchange (forex) rate that we mentioned earlier is simply the price of a nation's currency in terms of what a bank will exchange it for with another currency. For example, if we want to know how much a U.S. dollar is worth in countries that are members of the European Union, we might find that it is only worth 92.0 cents in Europe ($1 = €0.92). If our neighbors in Europe look at the same exchange rate with the euro as the base currency, they would find that a euro is worth about 9 percent more in the United States (i.e., the forex rate would be (€1 = $1.09). Why does the exchange rate matter? The rate determines the price of a product in a different country and thus a firm's ability to sell outside its borders. If the dollar becomes stronger so that, for example, it takes fewer dollars to equal one euro, a dollar can buy more French wine or escargot, and customers in the United States will buy more of it. If the dollar drops in value compared to the euro, then the dollar will buy less when you hike through Italy, whereas European tourists will flock to the United States for a "cheap" vacation.

Of course, GDP and exchange rates alone do not provide the information marketers need to decide if a country's economic environment makes for an attractive market. They also need to consider whether they can conduct "business as usual" in another country. A country's **economic infrastructure** refers to the availability of the resources that make doing business in a country possible. These resources include transportation, distribution networks, financial institutions, communications networks, and energy resources. For example, countries with less-developed financial institutions may operate as a cash economy in which consumers and business customers must pay for goods and services with cash rather than with credit cards or checks. This may lead to false reporting of incomes of both businesses and individuals, which in turn may create inaccurate GDP figures and lower the tax revenues for the country. The physical infrastructure is equally important. In poorer countries without good road systems, sellers may use donkey carts, hand trucks, or bicycles to deliver goods to the many small retailers who are their customers.

economic infrastructure
The quality of a country's distribution, financial, and communications systems.

| Table 2.2 | Selected Comparisons of Economic and Demographic Characteristics |

	Democratic Republic of the Congo	India	China	Brazil	Russia	United States	Qatar
Ranking*	3	68	118	107	137	180	191
Total GDP	$68.6 billion	$9.474 trillion	$25.36 trillion	$3.248 trillion	$4.016 trillion	$19.49 trillion	$339.5 billion
Per capita GDP	$800	$7,200	$18,200	$15,600	$27,900	$59,800	$124,100
Population below poverty level	63%	21.90%	3.30%	4.20%	13.30%	15.10%	N/A
Inflation rate	41.50%	3.60%	1.60%	3.40%	3.70%	2.10%	0.40%
Unemployment rate	N/A	8.50%	3.90%	12.80%	5.20%	4.40%	8.90%
Population	101.78 million	1,326 million	1,394 million	211.72 million	141.72 million	332.64 million	2.44 million
Birthrate per 1,000 population	41.0	18.2	11.6	13.6	10.0	12.4	9.3
Population growth rate	3.18%	1.10%	0.32%	0.67%	−0.16%	0.72%	1.55%
Population aged 0–14	46.38%	26.31%	17.29%	21.11%	17.24%	18.46%	12.84%
Population aged 15–24	19.42%	17.51%	11.48%	16.06%	9.54%	12.91%	11.78%
Population aged 25–54	28.38%	41.56%	46.81%	43.83%	43.38%	38.92%	70.66%
Population aged 55–64	3.36%	7.91%	12.08%	9.78%	14.31%	12.86%	3.53%
Population aged 65 and older	2.47%	6.72%	12.34%	9.21%	15.53%	16.85%	1.19%
Life expectancy	61 yrs	69.7 yrs	76.1 yrs	74.7 yrs	71.9 yrs	80.3 yrs	79.4 yrs
Literacy rate	77.0%	74.4%	96.8%	93.2%	99.7%	N/A	93.5%
School life expectancy	10 yrs	12 yrs	14 yrs	15 yrs	16 yrs	16 yrs	12 yrs
Cell phones per 100 population	38	91	119	99	161	129	167
Internet users	3.8%	29.5%	53.2%	59.7%	76.4%	76.2%	94.3%

*Based on values expressed in current international dollars, reflecting a single year's (the current year) currency exchange rates and purchasing-power-parity (PPP) adjustments. The ranking goes from the poorest (#1) to the wealthiest (#189).

Source for ranking: Luca Ventura, "The Poorest Countries in the World," *Global Finance Magazine*, April 17, 2019, https://www.gfmag.com/global-data/economic-data/the-poorest-countries-in-the-world (accessed July 21, 2020); data based on Central Intelligence Agency (CIA), The World Factbook, https://www.cia.gov/library/publications/the-world-factbook/docs/profileguide.html (accessed July 21, 2020).

Level of Economic Development

level of economic development
The broader economic picture of a country.

standard of living
An indicator of the average quality and quantity of goods and services consumed in a country.

least developed country (LDC)
A country at the lowest stage of economic development.

When marketers scout the world for opportunities, it helps to consider a country's **level of economic development**. Economists look past simple facts such as growth in GDP to decide this; they also look at what steps the country is taking to reduce poverty, inequality, and unemployment. Analysts also take into account a country's **standard of living**, an indicator of the average quality and quantity of goods and services a country consumes. They describe the following basic levels of development:

1. As we said earlier, a country at the lowest stage of economic development is a **least developed country (LDC).** In most cases, its economic base is agricultural. Analysts consider many nations in Africa and South Asia to be LDCs. In LDCs, the standard of living is low, as are literacy levels. Opportunities to sell many products, especially

luxury items such as diamonds and caviar, are minimal because most people don't have enough spending money. They grow what they need and barter for the rest. These countries are attractive markets for staples such as rice and inexpensive goods such as shoes and fabrics from which people can make clothing. In addition, they present opportunities for new products that these consumers need, such as solar-operated cell phones and computers that will survive without air conditioning.

2. When an economy shifts its emphasis from agriculture to industry, standards of living, education, and the use of technology rise. These countries are **developing countries**. In such locales, there may be a viable middle class, often composed largely of entrepreneurs working hard to run successful small businesses. Because more than 8 out of 10 consumers now live in developing countries, the number of potential customers and the presence of a skilled labor force attract many firms to these areas. Marketers see these developing countries as the future market for consumer goods like skin care products and laundry detergents.

> **developing countries**
> Countries in which the economy is shifting its emphasis from agriculture to industry.

Within these LDCs and developing countries is a group of consumers known as the **bottom of the pyramid (BOP)**, which is the collective name for the group of more than 4 billion consumers throughout the world who live on less than $2 a day.[21] These BOP consumers represent a potentially huge marketing opportunity with purchasing power parity of $5 billion. They also present a big challenge for marketers, as unlike other consumer groups, they generally are unable to afford to purchase "inventory," such as a bottle of shampoo. Procter & Gamble, Unilever, and other companies meet these needs when they offer cleaning products, fabric softeners, and shampoo that can be used in cold water in affordable one-use **sachet** packaging.

> **bottom of the pyramid (BOP)**
> The collective name for the group of consumers throughout the world who live on less than $2 a day.

> **sachet**
> Affordable one-use packages of cleaning products, fabric softeners, shampoo, and other items for sale to consumers in least developed and developing countries.

The largest of the developing or newly industrialized countries—Brazil, Russia, India, China, and South Africa—are referred to as the **BRICS countries**, or simply as the BRICS. Originally known as "BRIC," they became BRICS when South Africa joined in 2010. These five countries are the fastest growing of the developing countries; with more than 3 billion people, they represent over 41 percent of the world's population. Their total GDP of $16.6 trillion is equivalent to about 22 percent of the gross world product (GWP). Marketers are attracted to these countries because of the masses of consumers who are not wealthy but who are beginning their move toward economic prosperity.[22] The BRICS present exciting opportunities to marketers, but we must approach with caution because of the many ups-and-downs that make these economies unstable. As examples, the political crisis in Brazil discourages foreign investment, Russia's "oil rush" has been reduced to a trickle because of the drop in oil prices, and China's exploding economy is starting to sputter.

> **BRICS countries**
> Also referred to as the BRICS, Brazil, Russia, India, China, and South Africa are the fastest growing of the developing countries. With more than 3 billion people, they represent over 41 percent of the world's population and about 22 percent of the gross world product.

3. A **developed country** (also referred to as a *more developed country* or a *more economically developed country*) boasts sophisticated marketing systems, strong private enterprise, and bountiful market potential for many goods and services. Such countries are economically advanced, and they offer a wide range of opportunities for international marketers.

> **developed country**
> A country that boasts sophisticated marketing systems, strong private enterprise, and bountiful market potential for many goods and services.

Before we leave the topic of levels of economic development, we need to explain the country designations used to avoid any confusion if you find different designations being used. The terms used here (*least developed*, *developing*, and *developed*) were developed and used by the UN for many years. The UN has very recently changed their country designations to *developed economies*, *economies in transition*, and *developing economies*. In addition, the World Bank changed to classifications of countries by Gross National Income (GNI)/per capita (*high*, *upper-middle*, *lower-middle*, and *low*). And there are other designations used by some economists that include *industrial developed economies*, *developing economies*, *less developed countries*, *least developed countries*, *emerging markets*, *transition economies*, and *frontier economies*. We are continuing to use the older UN terms as they still remain in use by many.[23]

Group of 7 (G7)
An informal forum of the seven most economically developed countries that meets annually to discuss major economic and political issues facing the international community. Formerly the G8, Russia was excluded from the group as a result of its invasion of Crimea in 2014.

In 1976, the most economically developed countries in the world—France, West Germany, Italy, Japan, the United Kingdom, and the United States—formed what became known as the Group of Six, or G6. Later with the addition of Canada in 1976 and Russia in 1998, the G6 became the Group of Eight (G8). In 2014, Russia's membership was revoked because of its involvement in the Crimean crisis, so we are down to the **Group of Seven (G7)**.[24] The purpose of the G7 is to provide a way for these countries, democracies with highly developed economies, to deal with major economic and political issues that other countries and the international community face. In addition to topics of the world economy and international trade, G7 summits have more recently included discussions of other issues, such as energy, terrorism, unemployment, the information highway, crime and drugs, arms control, and the environment.[25]

The Business Cycle

business cycle
The overall patterns of change in the economy—including periods of prosperity, recession, depression, and recovery—that affect consumer and business purchasing power.

The **business cycle** describes the overall pattern of changes or fluctuations of an economy. All economies go through cycles of *prosperity* (high levels of demand, employment, and income), *recession* (falling demand, employment, and income), and *recovery* (gradual improvement in production, lowering unemployment, and increasing income). A severe recession is a *depression*, a period during which prices fall but there is little demand because few people have money to spend and many are out of work.

Inflation occurs when prices and the cost of living rise while money loses its purchasing power because the cost of goods escalates. During inflationary periods, dollar incomes may increase, but real income—what the dollar will buy—decreases because goods and services cost more.

The business cycle is especially important to marketers because of its effect on customer purchasing behavior. During times of prosperity, consumers buy more goods and services. Marketers try to grow their businesses, maintain inventory levels and develop new products that meet customers' willingness to spend. During periods of recession, such as that experienced by countries all over the globe beginning in 2008, consumers simply buy less. They may also "trade down" as they substitute less expensive or lower-quality brands to stretch a dollar (or euro, or other currency).

The Competitive Environment

A second important element of a firm's external environment is the *competitive environment*. For products ranging from toothpaste to sport utility vehicles, firms must keep abreast of what the competition is doing so they can develop new product features, new pricing schedules, or new advertising to maintain or gain market share. As we will see, marketers need to understand their competitive position among product alternatives in their microenvironment and in the structure of their industries, that is, their macroenvironment.

competitive intelligence (CI)
The process of gathering and analyzing publicly available information about rivals.

Like players in a global chess game, marketing managers size up their competitors according to their strengths and weaknesses, monitor their marketing strategies, and try to predict their next moves. To do this, an increasing number of firms around the globe engage in **competitive intelligence (CI)** activities where they gather and analyze publicly available information about rivals from such sources as the Internet, the news media, and publicly available government documents, such as building permits and patents. Successful CI means that a firm learns about a competitor's new products, its manufacturing processes, or the management styles of its executives. Then the firm uses this information to develop superior marketing strategies (we'll learn more about collecting market intelligence in Chapter 4).

Competition in the Microenvironment

Competition in the *microenvironment* means the product alternatives from which members of a target market may choose. We think of these choices at three different levels:

discretionary income
The portion of income people have left over after paying for necessities such as housing, utilities, food, and clothing.

1. **Discretionary income** or the amount of money people have left after they pay for necessities such as housing, utilities, food, and clothing. Do we plow "leftover" money

into a new computer tablet, donate it to charity, or turn over a new leaf and lose those extra pounds by investing in a healthy lifestyle? These choices vary by country. For Russians, the bulk of monthly income goes to food, alcohol, and tobacco. In the United States, healthcare is the biggest expenditure. In Japan, housing costs take just over a quarter of the average income, while in Saudi Arabia almost 10 percent is spent on furniture.[26]

2. **Product competition**, where other organizations offer different ways to satisfy the same consumers' needs and wants. So, for example, if a couch potato decides to use some discretionary income to get buff (i.e., in shape), he or she may consider whether either joining a health club or buying a used Soloflex machine on eBay to pump iron at home might be a good idea.

3. **Brand competition**, where competitors offer similar goods or services, vying for consumer dollars, euros, or pounds. So, our flabby friend who decides to join a gym still must choose among competitors within this industry, such as Gold's Gym, Soul Cycle, or the YMCA, or he or she may forgo the exercise thing altogether and just buy bigger pants.

Competition in the Macroenvironment

When we talk about examining competition in the *macroenvironment*, we mean that marketers need to understand the big picture—the overall structure of their industry. This structure can range from one firm having total control to numerous firms that compete on an even playing field.

1. No, it's not just a board game: A **monopoly** exists when one seller controls a market. Because the seller is "the only game in town," it feels little pressure to keep prices low or to produce quality goods or services. In most U.S. industries today, the government attempts to ensure consumers' welfare by limiting monopolies through the prosecution of firms that engage in activities that would limit competition and thus violate antitrust regulations.

2. In an **oligopoly**, there are a relatively small number of sellers, each holding substantial market share, in a market with many buyers. Because there are few sellers, the actions of each directly affect the others. Oligopolies most often exist in industries that require substantial investments in equipment or technology to produce a product. The airline industry is an oligopoly.

3. In a state of **monopolistic competition**, many sellers compete for buyers in a market. Each firm, however, offers a slightly different product, and each has only a small share of the market. For example, many athletic shoe manufacturers, including Nike, New Balance, and Under Armour, vigorously compete with one another to offer consumers some unique benefit—even though only Adidas (at least for now) offers you a $250 computerized running shoe that senses how hard the ground is where you are running and adapts to it.

4. Finally, **perfect competition** exists when there are many small sellers, each offering basically the same good or service. In such industries, no single firm has a significant impact on quality, price, or supply. Although true conditions of perfect competition are rare, agricultural markets (in which there are many individual farmers, each producing the same corn or jalapeño peppers) come the closest.

product competition
When firms offering different products compete to satisfy the same consumer needs and wants.

brand competition
When firms offering similar goods or services compete on the basis of their brand's reputation or perceived benefits.

monopoly
A market situation in which one firm, the only supplier of a particular product, is able to control the price, quality, and supply of that product.

oligopoly
A market structure in which a relatively small number of sellers, each holding a substantial share of the market, compete in a market with many buyers.

monopolistic competition
A market structure in which many firms, each having slightly different products, offer unique consumer benefits.

perfect competition
A market structure in which many small sellers, all of whom offer similar products, are unable to have an impact on the quality, price, or supply of a product.

The pandemic disrupted our lives in many ways. One was the instability it created in distribution channels that resulted in many product shortages and stockouts, especially as people engaged in panic buying and hoarding during the early days of the virus.

The Technological Environment

The *technological environment* profoundly affects marketing activities. Of course, the Internet is the biggest technological change in marketing within recent times—even bigger than hoverboards! Online sales offer consumers virtually anything they want (and even some things they don't want) without ever leaving home.

Some people believe the next innovations to be game changers in marketing are already here. Some of these are: In 2013, Amazon CEO Jeff Bezos surprised CBS journalist Charlie Rose with the announcement that Amazon had been secretly working on "Prime Air," a project to use "octocopters" or *drones* or *unmanned aerial vehicles (UAVs)* to deliver packages to homes all over the country within 30 minutes.[27] UPS has introduced a program to deliver for companies such as CVS Pharmacy using drones.

self-driving (autonomous) vehicle
A self-driving or autonomous car (also known as a *driverless car* or *robotic car*) and unmanned ground vehicle is a vehicle that is capable of sensing its environment and navigating without human input.

A second game-changing innovation is **self-driving**, **driverless**, or **autonomous vehicles**, that is, automobiles, delivery vans, and now tractor-trailers without a human at the wheel. These autonomous cars and other vehicles are capable of sensing the environment and navigating (safely, we hope) without traditional controls like steering wheels and pedals or a human driver. Think the driverless 18-wheeler is at least 20 years away? With companies including Uber, Tesla, Volvo, Google, BMW, GM, and Ford working on autonomous vehicles, it's a pretty good bet that we will see them a lot sooner.

Ever want a personal assistant at your beck and call? Amazon has plans for Alexa to be just that. Alexa can already control over 85,000 smart home products from TVs to doorbells and execute over 100,000 skills. By increasing Alexa's mastery of AI fundamentals and language, Amazon will enable Alexa will to recognize what activities go together. Going out for the evening? Ask Alexa to book movie tickets for you and she will ask if you want dinner before and an Uber to get home—and then handle it all.[28]

Successful marketers continuously scan the external business environment in search of ideas and trends to spark their own research efforts. When inventors feel they have come across something exciting, they usually want to protect their exclusive right to produce and sell the invention by applying for a **patent**. This is a legal document that grants inventors exclusive rights to produce and sell a particular invention in that country.

patent
A legal mechanism to prevent competitors from producing or selling an invention, aimed at reducing or eliminating competition in a market for a period of time.

The Political and Legal Environment

The *political and legal environment* refers to the local, state, national, and global laws and regulations that affect businesses. Legal and regulatory controls can be prime motivators for many business decisions. Although firms that choose to remain at home have to worry about local regulations only, global marketers must understand more complex political issues that can affect how they are allowed to do business around the world.

American Laws

U.S. laws governing business generally have one or both of two purposes. Some, such as the Sherman Antitrust Act and the Wheeler-Lea Act, make sure that businesses compete fairly with each other. Others, such as the Food and Drug Act and the Consumer Product Safety Commission Act, make sure that businesses don't take advantage of consumers. Although some businesspeople argue that excessive legislation only limits competition, others say that laws ultimately help firms because they maintain a level playing field for businesses and support troubled industries.

Table 2.3 lists a few of the major federal laws that protect and preserve the rights of U.S. consumers and businesses. Federal and state governments have created a host of regulatory agencies—government bodies that monitor business activities and enforce laws. Table 2.4 lists some of the agencies whose actions affect marketing activities.

Table 2.3	Significant American Legislation Relevant to Marketers	
Law	**Purpose**
Sherman Antitrust Act (1890)	Developed to eliminate monopolies and to guarantee free competition. Prohibits exclusive territories (if they restrict competition), price fixing, and predatory pricing.
Food and Drug Act (1906)	Prohibits harmful practices in the production of food and drugs.
Federal Trade Commission (FTC) Act (1914)	Created the Federal Trade Commission to monitor unfair practices.
Robinson-Patman Act (1936)	Prohibits price discrimination (offering different prices to competing wholesalers or retailers) unless cost is justified.
Wheeler-Lea Amendment to the FTC Act (1938)	Revised the FTC Act. Makes deceptive and misleading advertising illegal.
Lanham Trademark Act (1946)	Protects and regulates brand names and trademarks.
Consumer Credit Protection Act (1968)	Protects consumers by requiring full disclosure of credit and loan terms and rates.
Child Protection and Toy Safety Act (1969)	Sets standards for child-resistant packaging.
National Do Not Call Registry (2003)	Established by the Federal Trade Commission to allow consumers to limit number of telemarketing calls they receive.
Credit Card Accountability, Responsibility, and Disclosure Act of 2009	Bans unfair rate increases, prevents unfair fee traps, requires disclosures be in plain language, and protects students and young people.
The Affordable Care Act of 2013	Mandates healthcare coverage for Americans who do not receive benefits through an employer. Revises insurance regulations by eliminating denial of coverage for preexisting conditions, ending lifetime limits on coverage, and so on.
Digital Accountability and Transparency Act of 2014 (DATA Act)	Gives consumers access to files of personal information a data broker compiles, the ability to correct inaccuracies, and the chance to opt out of the sale of those data to other companies.
USA Freedom Act of 2015	A result of Edward Snowden's revelations about the National Security Agency's (NSA) practices regarding collecting and monitoring of phone conversations. Requires that phone metadata be stored by phone companies, not the U.S. government.
The Tax Cuts and Jobs Act of 2017	A sweeping update to the U.S. tax code designed to lower taxes on businesses and individuals and create higher wages, more jobs, and a larger, dynamic economy. The bill makes large reductions in the corporate tax rate.
Telephone Robocall Abuse Criminal Enforcement and Deterrence Act of 2019 (TRACED Act)	This bill implements a forfeiture penalty for violations of the prohibition on certain robocalls and requires voice service providers to develop call authentication technologies.
Data Privacy Laws	At present there are no federal laws relating to data protection, only laws with specific targets, e.g., financial institutions, telecommunications companies, educational organizations, personal health information, credit report information, telemarketing, and direct marketing. The 50 states, however, have literally hundreds of privacy and data security laws. A number of states are also in various stages of enacting new laws that will address data privacy across sectors.[29]

Political Constraints on Trade

Global firms know that the political actions a government takes can drastically affect their business operations. At the extreme, of course, when two countries go to war, the business environment changes dramatically.

Short of war, a country may impose *economic sanctions* that prohibit trade with another country, as the United States has done with several countries, including Cuba, North Korea, and, more recently, Russia. U.S. sanctions against Russia began after Russia invaded the Crimea region of Ukraine in 2014. This includes financial and economic sanctions with additional sanctions being added later such as trade (embargos) and corporate sanctions. The United States and the European Union have since then placed numerous additional sanctions on the country, companies, and individuals, including government officials, freezing assets and suspending funding.[30]

In some situations, internal pressures may prompt the government to take over the operations of foreign companies that do business within its borders. **Nationalization** occurs when the domestic government seizes private assets, usually declaring the assets the

nationalization
When a government or state seizes a business enterprise, natural resource, or other asset and justifies this action as being in the best interest of the country or state. Reimbursement is typically not required.

Table 2.4	U.S. Regulatory Agencies and Responsibilities
Regulatory Agency	**Responsibilities**
Consumer Financial Protection Bureau (CFPB)	Responsible for consumer protection in the financial sector. The CFPB develops and enforces rules for bank and nonbank financial institutions, including credit unions, securities firms, payday lenders, mortgage-servicing operations, foreclosure relief services, debt collectors, and other financial companies operating in the United States.
Consumer Product Safety Commission (CPSC)	Protects the public from potentially hazardous products. Through regulation and testing programs, the CPSC helps firms make sure their products won't harm customers.
Environmental Protection Agency (EPA)	Develops and enforces regulations aimed at protecting the environment. Such regulations have a major impact on the materials and processes that manufacturers use in their products and thus on the ability of companies to develop products.
Federal Communications Commission (FCC)	Regulates telephone, radio, TV, and more recently the use of the Internet. FCC regulations directly affect the marketing activities of companies in the communications industries, and have indirect effects on all firms that use these media.
Federal Trade Commission (FTC)	Enforces laws, primarily through fines, against deceptive advertising and product labeling regulations.
Food and Drug Administration (FDA)	Enforces laws and regulations on foods, drugs, cosmetics, and veterinary products. FDA approval is required before marketers can introduce many products to the market.

The U.K.'s decision to withdraw from the E.U. (European Union) will reverberate for many years as trade regulations and other laws get revised in the age of "Brexit."

expropriation
When a government or state seizes a foreign-owned asset, normally with some compensation for company owners or individuals (but often not for the full value).

local content rules
A form of protectionism stipulating that a certain proportion of a product must consist of components supplied by industries in the host country or economic community.

property of the state. It happens without any reimbursement and the country typically justifies this action as being in the best interest of the country or state. In contrast, **expropriation** is when a government seizes a foreign company's assets and reimburses the company owners (often not for the full value). One of the more famous examples of nationalization occurred when Egyptian president Gamal Abdel Nasser nationalized the Suez Canal Company and much of the privately owned land, factories, and apartment buildings in 1956. Later, between 2000 and 2010, many families of previous owners of land sued the government and were given some payment for the property. Similarly, following World War II, Germany and other European countries nationalized privately owned businesses. In 1959, following the Cuban Revolution, the Cuban government confiscated all foreign-owned private companies, most of which were owned by U.S. firms or individuals. Now that the United States has normalized relations with Cuba, will these firms seek reimbursement for their lost property?

Regulatory Constraints on Trade

Governments and economic communities regulate what products are allowed in the country, what products should be made of, and what claims marketers can make about them. Other regulations ensure that the host country gets a piece of the action. **Local content rules** are a form of protectionism that stipulates that a certain proportion of a product must consist of components and services supplied by service providers in the host country or economic community. Countries that frequently use local content rules include Argentina, Brazil, China, India, Indonesia, Russia, Saudi Arabia, and the U.S.[31] For example, Brazil has recently tightened its local content rules regarding the manufacture and assembly of wind turbines. Under these rules, a minimum of 70 percent of the steel plates and 100 percent of the cement used to build the towers must be of Brazilian origin. In addition, the tower's nacelles (the assemblies that house the machinery) must be assembled locally.[32] Such rules ensure that Brazil is able to create more domestic manufacturing jobs for its citizens.

Human Rights Issues

Some governments and companies are vigilant about denying business opportunities to countries that mistreat their citizens. They are concerned about conducting trade with local firms that exploit their workers or that keep costs down by employing children or prisoners for slave wages or by subjecting workers to unsafe working conditions, like locked factory doors. Nike, once the poster child for unsafe labor practices, has spent almost two decades admitting to and correcting its formerly abusive practices with increased wages and factory audits, and is now a company others can learn from and look up to.[33]

The biggest human rights problem in our world today is human slavery. The 2018 Global Slavery Index reported that over 40 million men, women, and children in 167 countries were victims of modern slavery. These men, women, and children are bought and sold in public markets and forced to work in factories, on fishing boats, in mines, at construction sites, in stores, on farms, or in homes as maids, often without a salary. Many are subjected to beating. Countries with the highest prevalence of human slavery include North Korea, Eritrea, Burundi, the Central African Republic, Afghanistan, Mauritania, South Sudan, Pakistan, Cambodia, and Iran.[34]

The **U.S. Generalized System of Preferences (GSP)** is a program Congress established to promote economic growth in the developing world. GSP regulations allow developing countries to export goods duty free to the United States. The catch is that each country must constantly demonstrate that it is making progress toward improving the rights of its workers. On the other side of the coin, the low wages that U.S. firms can pay to local workers often entices them to expand or entirely move their operations overseas. Although they provide needed jobs, some companies have been criticized for exploiting workers when they pay wages that fall below local poverty levels, for damaging the environment, or for selling poorly made or unsafe items to consumers.

The mention of human rights issues may elicit images of hungry children in developing countries. In some countries, including the U.S., the COVID-19 pandemic has created conflict between the goals of saving lives and saving the economy—hence creating new human rights issues. This is played out by workers in delivery jobs, meat-packing plants, and other businesses that provide services to those staying home. Some workers are required to work by their employers or face dismissal while others must work for an income for survival.

U.S. Generalized System of Preferences (GSP)
A program to promote economic growth in developing countries by allowing duty-free entry of goods into the United States.

The Sociocultural Environment

The *sociocultural environment* refers to the characteristics of the society, the people who live in that society, and the culture that reflects the values and beliefs of the society. Whether at home or in global markets, marketers need to understand and adapt to the customs, characteristics, and practices of its citizens. Basic beliefs about cultural priorities, such as the role of family or proper relations between the sexes, affect people's responses to products and promotional messages in any market.

To understand some of these values requires knowledge of a culture's history. For example, someone who appreciates that South Korea has long had a significant U.S. military presence might not be surprised to learn that SPAM—that American mystery meat—sells $235 million of the pork shoulder product there every year. During the Korean War, food was scarce and only a select few Koreans could gain access to PX stores on U.S. military bases. As a result, the humble product became a status symbol, and it remains so today though many young Koreans who love to order "military stew" have no idea of its origins.[35]

Demographics

The first step toward understanding the characteristics of a society is to look at its **demographics**. These are statistics that measure observable aspects of a population, such as population size, age, gender, ethnic group, income, education, occupation, and family structure. The information demographic studies reveal is of great value to marketers when they want to predict the size of markets for many products, from home mortgages to brooms and can

demographics
Statistics that measure observable aspects of a population, including size, age, gender, ethnic group, income, education, occupation, and family structure.

AIJEK BERRY/AFP/Getty Images

An "arisan" Tupperware gathering in Indonesia.

openers. We'll talk more about how demographic factors impact marketing strategies in Chapter 7.

Tupperware's explosive growth in overseas markets illustrates the importance of demographics. Faced with a static market in the U.S., the company is prospering by planting its flag in other countries where there are more favorable conditions. One such sweet spot is Indonesia. It turns out there is an Indonesian tradition called an *arisan* ("gathering") where women meet with a group of friends to socialize, share recipes, and even pool their money to buy gifts for one another. Tupperware, which relies on social networks like these, sends sellers to arisans to promote their products and to recruit new agents. For the container company, it's a natural fit.[36]

Values

cultural values
A society's deeply held beliefs about right and wrong ways to live.

Every society has a set of **cultural values**, or deeply held beliefs about right and wrong ways to live, that it imparts to its members.[37] Those beliefs influence virtually every aspect of our lives, even the way we mark the time we live them. For example, for most Americans, *punctuality* is a core value; indeed, business leaders often proclaim that "time is money." For countries in Latin America and other parts of the world, this is not true. If you schedule a business meeting at 10:00 a.m., you can be assured most people are not expected to arrive until around 10:30—or later.

collectivist cultures
Cultures in which people subordinate their personal goals to those of a stable community.

Differences in cultural values often explain why marketing efforts that are a big hit at one time can flop just a few years later. The cultural icon Barbie doll was introduced in 1959, and sported curly bangs and a black-and-white-striped swimsuit. In 1971, Malibu Barbie was introduced. In the 1980s, the McDonald's waitress Barbie and the first black Barbie were added. Then in 2015, the Barbie Fashionistas were brought to market. These ethnically diverse dolls included 3 distinct body types (petite, curvy, and tall), 7 skin tones, 22 eye colors, and 24 hairstyles to reflect the growing cultural value of diversity and to keep Barbie a cultural icon for parents to buy their kids.[38] In 2018, Mattel introduced a new gang of Barbie Fashionistas that included 40 dolls, 7 body types, 11 skin tones, and 28 hairstyles. Next Gen Ken came in three body types: broad, slim, and original, and new looks that included a man bun, cornrows, and freckles.[39]

When the coronavirus caused many families and their children to shelter in place, Mattel introduced #ThankYouHeroes, a new, special edition line of collectible action figures and Little People Community Champions. These new figures honor the many people caring for COVID-19 patients and the everyday heroes who are working to keep communities up and running. In 2020 the Barbie line added Inspiring Women role models, dolls that included Rosa Parks, Ella Fitzgerald, Sally Ride, Florence Nightingale, and Billy Jean King. Barbie is again one of the hottest items on the toy shelf.[40]

One important dimension on which cultures differ is their emphasis on collectivism versus individualism. In **collectivist cultures**, such as those we find in Venezuela,

Kraft Heinz Corporation

The dual values of taking good care of our children and maximizing health and well-being combine for a powerful 1-2 punch as parents seek out organic food for their kids.

Pakistan, Taiwan, Thailand, Turkey, Greece, and Portugal, people tend to subordinate their personal goals to those of a stable community. In contrast, consumers in **individualist cultures**, such as the United States, Australia, Great Britain, Canada, and the Netherlands, tend to attach more importance to personal goals, and people are more likely to change memberships when the demands of the group become too costly.[41]

While individualistic cultures may be more likely to encourage creativity, entrepreneurship, and a prosperous economy, individualist cultures may be far less suited to controlling a contagious pandemic. To prevent spread of a disease, all individuals need to engage in wearing masks, social distancing, and self-quarantining, a collectivist focus. In an individualist culture, people are more likely to defy government orders and engage in mass protests calling for their rights. Controlling pandemics may require that countries move from individualistic values toward collectivist ones, where people feel responsible for others in the community.[42]

You may not do the Downward-Facing Dog, but if, like many consumers, you love to shop at Lululemon, you probably look like you do. The *yoga* craze is sweeping America, but not surprisingly, it's (for now, at least) even bigger in India, where it originates. *Yoga* is closely tied to other long-standing spiritual practices in that country that link to food, medicinal treatments (*Ayurveda*), and even home furnishings. Indian consumers crave modern versions of these products, and a new wave of businesspeople known as the "Baba Cool Movement" are giving them what they want as they market healthy items based upon ancient beliefs. For example, Baba Ramdev is a *swami* (holy man), but he's also an effective marketer who translates traditional values into modern versions. He and other entrepreneurs have been so successful that sales of large multinationals have suffered. They in turn have to adapt or die—that is why Colgate recently introduced toothpastes containing the extract of neem, an Indian tree, and charcoal that Indian villagers use to clean their teeth.[43]

Social Norms

Values are general ideas about good and bad behaviors. From these values flow **social norms**, or specific rules that dictate what is right or wrong, acceptable or unacceptable, within a society. Social norms indicate what ways to dress, how to speak, what to eat (and how to eat), and how to behave. For example, local customs dictate the appropriate hour at which the meal should be served—many Europeans, Middle Easterners, and Latin Americans do not begin dinner until around 9:00 p.m. or later, and they are amused by American visitors, whose stomachs growl by 7:00 p.m. Customs tell us how to eat the meal, including such details as the utensils, the table etiquette, and even the appropriate apparel for dinnertime (no thongs at the dinner table!).

Conflicting customs can be a problem when U.S. marketers try to conduct business in other countries, where executives have different ideas about what is proper or expected. These difficulties even include body language; people in Latin countries tend to stand much closer to each other than do Americans, and they will be insulted if their counterpart tries to stand farther away.

In many countries, even casual friends greet each other with a kiss (or two) on the cheek. In the United States, a kiss on the cheek of a person of the opposite sex is the norm—and one kiss only, please. In Spain and other parts of Europe, kissing includes a kiss on each cheek for both people of the same and the opposite sex, whereas in the Middle East, unless a special friend, it is unacceptable for a man to kiss a woman or a woman to kiss a man. Instead, it is the norm to see two men or two women holding hands or walking down the street with their arms entwined.

individualist cultures
Cultures in which people tend to attach more importance to personal goals than to those of the larger community.

social norms
Specific rules dictating what is right or wrong, acceptable or unacceptable.

Amnesty International campaigns for human rights around the world. This Swiss ad aims to combat domestic abuse.

Courtesy of Amnesty International Chile

While social norms tend to change slowly over time, certain events, such as the Industrial Revolution and the Internet, have quickly created important changes in social norms. These paradigm shifts mean the usual way of thinking about or doing something is replaced by a new and different way. During the COVID-19 pandemic, some new social norms evolved. These included Zoom happy hours, elbow bumps instead of handshakes, and WFH (work from home).

Language

The language barrier is one obvious problem that confronts marketers who wish to break into foreign markets. A notice at a hotel in Acapulco proclaimed, "The manager has personally passed all the water served here." These translation snafus are not just embarrassing. They can affect product labeling and usage instructions, advertising, and personal selling as well. It's vital for marketers to work with local people who understand the subtleties of language to avoid confusion. Tell that to Audi, which may encounter a bit of trouble when it sells its new e-tron line of electric cars in France. In the French language, the word *étron* doesn't conjure up images of speed, sustainability, or sophistication—it means another four-letter word that starts with *s*.[44]

Consumer Xenocentrism

consumer xenocentrism
Consumer belief that products produced in other countries are superior to those produced at home.

The term *xenocentrism* refers to the belief that another country or countries is superior to one's own. **Consumer xenocentrism** refers to the belief that products produced in another country are superior to those produced in one's own. For example, many Americans believe that Europeans or Japanese produce superior automobiles and that French or Spanish wine is better than what is produced in California vineyards.[45]

Consumer Ethnocentrism

consumer ethnocentrism
Consumers' feeling that products from their own country are superior or that it is wrong to buy products produced in another country.

Ethnocentrism refers to the belief that one's own national or ethnic group is superior to others. Similarly, **consumer ethnocentrism** refers to consumers' beliefs about products produced in their country versus those from another. Consumers may feel that products from their own country are superior, or they may feel it is wrong, immoral, or unpatriotic to buy products produced in another country. Consumer ethnocentrism can cause consumers to be unwilling to try products made elsewhere.

Disruption in the Global Marketplace

In Chapter 1, we explained disruptive marketing that turns existing marketing rules upside down and changes how customers think about an industry as a whole. The global marketplace provides an even greater array of disruptive forces that can challenge marketers. Merriam-Webster defines *disruption* as the "act or process of disrupting something: a break or interruption in the normal course or continuation of some activity, process, etc."[46] In other words, disruption comes from some change in the status quo. Some of the major sources of change around the globe include the distribution of wealth, education, the infrastructure necessary for businesses to operate, government, public health, demographics, changes in the natural environment, telecommunications, and technology.

Distribution of wealth refers to how income is distributed across a population. Is the concentration of financial and physical assets distributed fairly evenly among individuals? Is there the opportunity for individuals to move up from their existing circumstances? How large is the gap between the income of the top and bottom levels of the economy?

In countries where the wealth is held by a small percentage of the population and there is limited or no chance for rising above the current status, consumers feel hopeless and oppressed. History shows that this disruption not only limits growth opportunities for businesses but also may create unrest and even revolution.

Access to education over time can be the equalizer in populations, providing opportunities for those who are trapped on the lower rungs of the income ladder to break free. Education is a win-win for consumers who can find jobs that lead to a better quality of life, for governments who not only gain in tax revenues but also in support of the population, and businesses that have increasing markets for products and an educated workforce.

Infrastructure includes the physical, organizational, and digital structure needed for a society to successfully function. In today's world this includes not only roads, bridges, and power grids but also Wi-Fi towers, high-quality Internet services, and closed-circuit security cameras. The digital infrastructure is essential to business success, quality of life, strong financial systems and governments, and, of course, business operations.

Governments at the local, regional, national, and international levels are another potential source of disruption. For example, in countries which have corrupt and/or inept government officials, the opportunities for consumers, for local and foreign investment, and for an advancing society may not be possible. In addition, global news of citizen protests, violence, and general unrest can damage leading industries, such as tourism, thus creating hardships for all. In countries which have governing bodies that have free elections and regular planning cycles and that make good regulatory decisions, businesses and consumers can be successful.

Public health includes not only quality healthcare availability but also health-related consumer behavior, government regulation, conflict, and religious beliefs. The suffering and disruption caused by the global coronavirus pandemic beginning in 2020 was felt in different degrees by countries with good and poor public health systems. Education and government also played a huge part in the difference.

Demographics refers to the characteristics of a population. Earlier in this chapter, we presented statistics about a small but varied group of countries that included data on per capita GDP, percentage population below the poverty level, unemployment rate, life expectancy, literacy rates, and the percentages of populations in various age groups. These data make it easy to understand why demographics are an important factor in disruption in some parts of the world.

Changes in the natural environment, including weather events, climate fluctuations, rising sea levels, drought, and extreme high/low temperatures, are sources of disruption that, in the short run, are difficult or impossible to be controlled or changed. These changes in the natural environment are sources of disruption for agricultural production, infrastructure, supply chains, and populations due to deaths, diseases, and extreme economic loss. The opportunity to prevent negative global disruptions related to the natural environment is possible for the future but not guaranteed.

Media and telecommunications include all of the many different ways in which individuals share information and learn about the world, including social networks, news organizations, digital platforms, video streaming services, and 5G.[47]

2.4 How "Global" Should a Global Marketing Strategy Be?

Going global is not a simple task. Even a company known for its keen marketing prowess can make blunders when it reaches beyond its familiar borders. Disney, for example, learned several lessons from mistakes it made when it opened Hong Kong Disneyland:[48]

- Bigger parks are better. Unlike giant American parks, which Chinese visitors to the United States are accustomed to, Hong Kong Disneyland is Disney's smallest park, easily seen in a single day.

- Cinderella who? Chinese visitors know characters from recent movies like *Toy Story*, but they didn't grow up hearing about Cinderella, so that emotional connection to Disney's traditional characters is lacking, even though they're seen throughout the park.

When Disney opened its first mainland China Disney theme park in June 2016, in Shanghai, it was clear that the company learned its lesson. Unlike the Hong Kong Disneyland, the new park includes the Enchanted Storybook Castle—the largest Disney castle on the planet—and six unique and unforgettable lands that relate to Disney characters that Chinese families are familiar with: Mickey Avenue, Gardens of Imagination, Fantasyland, Adventure Isle, Treasure Cove, and Tomorrowland. There is also a Toy Story hotel.[49]

Company-Level Decisions: The Market Entry Strategy

If a firm decides to expand beyond its home country, it must make important decisions about how to structure its business and whether to adapt its product marketing strategy to accommodate local needs. Just like a romantic relationship, a firm must determine the level of commitment it is willing to make to operate in another country. This commitment ranges from casual involvement to a full-scale "marriage." At one extreme the firm simply exports its products, whereas at the other extreme it directly invests in another country by buying a foreign subsidiary or opening its own stores or manufacturing facility. This decision about the extent of commitment entails a trade-off between *control* and *risk*. Direct involvement gives the firm more control over what happens in the country, but its risk also increases if the operation is not successful.

Let's review four globalization strategies representing increased levels of involvement: exporting, contractual agreements, strategic alliances, and direct investment. Table 2.5 summarizes these options.

Table 2.5 | Market-Entry Strategies

Strategy	Exporting Strategy	Contractual Agreements		Strategic Alliances	Direct Investment
Level of risk	Low	Medium		Medium	High
Level of control	Low	Medium		Medium	High
Options	Sell on its own	Licensing	Franchising	Joint venture, where firm and local partner pool their resources	Complete ownership, often buying a local company
	Rely on export merchants	License a local firm to produce the product	A local firm adopts your entire business model		
Advantages	Low investment, so presents the lowest risk of financial loss	Avoid barriers to entry	Local franchisee avoids barriers to entry	Easy access to new markets	Maximum freedom and control
	Can control quality of product	Limit financial investment and thus risk	Limit financial investment and risk	Preferential treatment by governments and other entities	Avoid import restrictions
	Avoid difficulties of producing some products in other countries				
Disadvantages	May limit growth opportunities	Lose control over how product is produced and marketed, which could tarnish company and brand image	Franchisee may not use the same-quality ingredients or procedures, thus damaging brand image	High level of financial risk	Highest level of commitment and financial risk
	Perceived as a "foreign" product	Potential unauthorized use of formulas, designs, or other intellectual property			Potential for nationalization or expropriation if government is unstable

Exporting

If a firm chooses to export, it must decide whether it will attempt to sell its products on its own or rely on intermediaries to represent it in the target country. These specialists, or **export merchants**, understand the local market and can find buyers and negotiate terms. An exporting strategy allows a firm to sell its products in global markets and cushions it against downturns in its domestic market. Because the firm actually makes the products at home, it is able to maintain control over design and production decisions. The U.S., for example, exports Harley-Davidson motorcycles (HOGS) and Kentucky bourbon.

export merchants
Intermediaries a firm uses to represent it in other countries.

Contractual Agreements

The next level of commitment a firm can make to a foreign market is a contractual agreement with a company in that country. Two of the most common forms of contractual agreements are licensing and franchising:

1. In a **licensing agreement**, a firm (the *licensor*) gives another firm (the *licensee*) the right to produce and market its product in a specific country or region in return for royalties on goods sold. The licensee is able to avoid many of the barriers to entry that the licensor would have but the licensor also loses control over how the product is produced and marketed. There are, however, added risks, not the least of which is that by sharing product designs and technologies, firms may be a target for violations of intellectual property rights, infringement with regard to patents, and copyright or trademark violations. Such misappropriation of trade secrets can violate either civil or criminal laws depending on the type of intellectual property involved.

licensing agreement
An agreement in which one firm gives another firm the right to produce and market its product in a specific country or region in return for royalties.

2. **Franchising** is a form of licensing that gives the franchisee the right to adopt an entire way of doing business in the host country. Firms need to monitor these operations carefully to ensure the partner maintains their brand image. In 2019, the top three global franchises were KFC US LLC, McDonald's, and Pizza Hut LLC.[50]

franchising
A form of licensing involving the right to adapt an entire system of doing business.

Strategic Alliances

Firms that choose to develop an even deeper commitment to a foreign market enter a **strategic alliance** with one or more domestic firms in the form of a **joint venture**, in which two or more firms create a new entity. Strategic alliances also allow companies easy access to new markets and preferential treatment in the partner's home country. U.S. company Uber and South Korean automaker Hyundai Motor announced in 2020 an agreement to develop electric air taxis. This agreement will allow them to compete in the race for flying cars to ease urban congestion.[51]

strategic alliance
Relationship developed between a firm seeking a deeper commitment to a foreign market and a domestic firm in the target country.

joint venture
A strategic alliance in which a new entity owned by two or more firms allows the partners to pool their resources for common goals.

Direct Investment

An even deeper level of commitment occurs when a firm expands internationally through ownership. When a firm buys all or part of a domestic firm, it can take advantage of a domestic company's political savvy and market position in the host country. The United Nations reported that in 2018 the top three nations receiving global foreign direct investment were the United States ($252 billion), China ($139 billion), and Hong Kong ($116 billion).[52]

Marketing Mix Strategies: To "P" or Not to "P?"

In addition to "big-picture" decisions about how a company will operate in other countries, managers must decide on how to market their product in each country. Do they need to modify or create new Four Ps—product, price, promotion, and place—to suit local conditions?

When they go global, marketers ask such questions as these:

1. To what extent will the company need to adapt its marketing communications to the specific styles and tastes of each local market?
2. Will the same product appeal to people there?
3. Will it have to be priced differently?
4. And, of course, how does the company get the product into people's hands?

Marketers must decide which is better—*standardization* or *localization*? Advocates of standardization argue that basic needs and wants are the same everywhere. A focus on the similarities among cultures means a firm doesn't have to make any changes to its marketing strategy to compete in foreign countries and can realize large economies of scale because it can spread the costs of product development and promotional materials over many markets. Widespread, consistent exposure also helps create a global brand like Coca-Cola because it forges a strong, unified image all over the world.

In contrast, those in favor of localization feel that the world is not *that* small; you need to tailor products and promotional messages to local environments. These marketers argue that each culture is unique, with a distinctive set of behavioral and personality characteristics. If you visit the World of Coca-Cola in Atlanta, you can sample the products Coke sells around the globe.

Product Decisions

A firm can choose from three distinct localization/standardization strategies when it develops a product for a global market: to offer the same, a modified, or a new product:

1. A **straight extension strategy** (standardization) retains the same product for domestic and foreign markets. The Apple iPad is a good example of a straight extension strategy. No matter where you go in the world, every iPad is basically the same.

2. A **product adaptation strategy** (modified localization) recognizes that in many cases people in different cultures do have strong and different product preferences. Sometimes these differences can be subtle yet important. In South Korea, for example, the familiar pink-and-orange neon Dunkin' Donuts sign beckons customers inside to sample its gourmet coffee and traditional glazed doughnuts, but also on the menu are items influenced by Korean fare, such as black rice doughnuts, jalapeño sausage pie doughnuts, and rice sticks.[53] KFC, which is the most popular fast food chain in China, serves its chicken along with such local dishes as congee and egg tarts in their Shanghai restaurants.[54]

   A product adaptation strategy also means a company adapts the same basic product to sync with local sensibilities. You may fondly recall Thomas the Tank Engine and his locomotive pals from your youth. Thomas is, in fact, one of the world's largest toy and TV franchises that delivers more than $1 billion per year to Mattel, which bought the company in 2012. Mattel started to catch some heat about the lack of diversity of Thomas's friends, who are primarily male and white. Mattel's answer: The company introduced 14 new friends who represent different countries. You can decide whether these new characters are valuable additions to the team, or if they just reflect cultural stereotypes. Here are some examples of them:[55]

   Raul of Brazil: "feisty" and "strong and agile"
   Yong Bao of China: "driven to achieve and make progress"
   Ashima of India (female): "shows no fear" and "happy to help out"
   Carlos of Mexico: "proud" and "always wearing a smile"

3. A **product invention strategy** (localization) means a company develops a new product as it expands to foreign markets. In some cases, a product invention strategy takes the form of **backward invention**. For example, there are still nearly 1.5 billion people, or more than

---

straight extension strategy
Product strategy in which a firm offers the same product in both domestic and foreign markets.

product adaptation strategy
Product strategy in which a firm offers a similar but modified product in foreign markets.

product invention strategy
Product strategy in which a firm develops a new product for foreign markets.

backward invention
Product strategy in which a firm develops a less advanced product to serve the needs of people living in countries without electricity or other elements of a developed infrastructure.

20 percent of the world's population, who have no access to reliable electricity, primarily in Africa, Asia, and the Middle East. Some clever inventions help those living in the poorest countries. Examples of these include a portable water filtration system, shoes designed to grow when your feet grow, inexpensive glasses that children can adjust until they see clearly, and a lamp that can provide light for up for eight hours and charge battery-operated devices while requiring only two tablespoons of salt in a glass of water.[56]

Promotion Decisions

Marketers must also decide whether it's necessary to modify how they speak to consumers in a foreign market. Some firms endorse the idea that the same message will appeal to everyone around the world, whereas others feel the need to customize it. When Unilever introduced its Dexona deodorant to China with dreams of selling its product to billions of Chinese, sales were far below expectations. Both biology and cultural differences account for this—scientists have found that East Asian consumers simply don't have body odor issues and less than 10 percent of China's population uses deodorant. In order to give female Chinese consumers a reason to buy deodorant, Nivea has introduced deodorants with whitening functions in a market where fair skin is prized.[57]

Price Decisions

Similar to the three product strategies discussed (product extension, product adaptation, and product invention), marketers have three pricing alternatives: extension or **ethnocentric pricing**, adaptation or **polycentric pricing**, and **geocentric pricing**. With ethnocentric pricing strategies, the price of a product is the same around the globe. When a firm uses a polycentric pricing policy, the global subsidiaries or distributors set their own prices based on their understanding of their market environment without concern for the coordination of prices from one country to another. For example, Starbucks uses a polycentric pricing policy to build its affordable luxury brand image. In the United States, the price of Starbucks is higher than other coffee chains—on average a latte costs about $2.75. Even in countries where labor is cheaper, the same latte costs more. For example, a latte is priced higher in three of the BRICS countries: Russia $12.32, India $7.99, and China $7.18. In countries such as these, people see Starbucks as a symbol of having a luxurious life, and they are willing to pay the high price.[58]

A geocentric pricing strategy establishes a global price floor or minimum for a product but also recognizes that unique local market conditions such as costs, income levels, competition, and the rest of the global marketing program must be considered in setting the price in each global market.

It's often more expensive to manufacture a product in a foreign market than at home. This may occur when there are higher costs stemming from transportation, tariffs, differences in currency exchange rates, and the need to source local materials. To ease the financial burden of tariffs on companies that import goods, some countries have established **free trade zones**. These are designated areas where foreign companies can warehouse goods without paying taxes or customs duties until they move the goods into the marketplace.

One danger of pricing too high is that competitors will find ways to offer their product at a lower price, even if they do so illegally. **Gray market goods** are items that are imported without the consent of the trademark holder. Although gray market goods are not counterfeit, they may be different from authorized products in warranty coverage and compliance with local regulatory requirements. Products such as toothpaste and pharmaceuticals may have the same formula but consist of inferior ingredients. The Internet offers exceptional opportunities for marketers of gray market goods ranging from toothpaste to textbooks. But, as the saying goes, "If it seems too good to be true, it probably is."

Another unethical and often illegal practice is **dumping**, through which a company prices its products lower than it offers them at home. This removes excess supply from

ethnocentric pricing
A pricing strategy where the firm sets a single price for a product around the globe.

polycentric pricing
A pricing strategy where the local partners set the prices for the product in each global market.

geocentric pricing
A pricing strategy that establishes a global price floor for a product but recognizes local conditions in setting the price in each market.

free trade zones
Designated areas where foreign companies can warehouse goods without paying taxes or customs duties until they move the goods into the marketplace.

gray market goods
Items manufactured outside a country and then imported without the consent of the trademark holder.

dumping
A company tries to get a toehold in a foreign market by pricing its products lower than it offers them at home.

home markets and keeps prices up there. And dumping isn't restricted to just retail products—agricultural products can be dumped too.

Place/Distribution Decisions

Getting your product to consumers in a remote location can be quite a challenge. It's essential for a firm to establish a reliable distribution system if it's going to succeed in a foreign market. Marketers used to dealing with a handful of large wholesalers or retailers in their domestic market may have to rely instead on thousands of small "mom and pop" stores or distributors, some of whom transport goods to remote rural areas on oxcarts, wheelbarrows, or bicycles. In LDCs, marketers may run into problems when they want to package, refrigerate, or store goods for long periods.

So far, we've talked about marketers' need to understand the external environment and make good marketing mix decisions to be successful both at home and globally. In the next section, we'll discuss an even more important part of long-term marketing success: ethical marketing practices.

2.5 Ethics Is Job One in Marketing Planning

OBJECTIVE

Understand the importance of ethical marketing practices.

It's hard to overemphasize the importance of ethical marketing decisions. Businesses touch many stakeholders, and they need to do what's best for all of them where possible. On a more selfish level, unethical decisions usually come back to bite you later. The consequences of low ethical standards become visible when you consider the number of highly publicized corporate scandals that have made news headlines since the turn of the century. The fallout from unethical practices often means people lose their jobs and even their pensions. Stockholders lose their investments and consumers pay for worthless merchandise or services.

OxyContin is an opioid painkiller introduced to the U.S. by Purdue in 1996 as a 12-hour timed-release dosage of oxycodone. By crushing or dissolving the 12-hour pills, drug abusers could ingest the entire dose at one time, thus causing fatal overdoses.

The Sackler-family-owned Purdue Pharma, maker of OxyContin, used unethical marketing practices. Such practices led Purdue to become the major contributor to the opioid crisis that caused the deaths of 400,000 individuals.

Purdue's aggressive marketing of OxyContin included visiting doctors, paying for their meals and travel, providing gifts, and funding pain treatment groups. Some of the company's marketing messages minimized the potential for OxyContin to lead to addiction, for which it paid over $600 million in fines in 2007. In 2010, Purdue changed the OxyContin formulation to one that could not be turned into a powder and thus not be easily snorted or injected. This caused many abusers to turn to heroin, which led to an increase in heroin overdose deaths.

Purdue announced in September 2019 that it had filed bankruptcy and agreed to pay $10 billion to address the opioid crisis and get money to those who had suffered in the opioid crisis and agencies battling it.[59]

Ethical Philosophies

Of course, what constitutes ethical behavior is often different for different people. We can point to various ethical philosophies and look at how each guides people to make their decisions. Table 2.6 presents a few of these different philosophies and how they reflect on ethical decision making.

Patagonia thrives in part due to the company's ethical business practices. This ad received a lot of praise for actually encouraging customers to buy used Patagonia products instead of new ones.

Table 2.6	Some Common Ethical Philosophies	
Ethical Philosophy	Description of the Ethical Decision	Questions for Decision Making
Utilitarian approach	The decision that provides the most good or the least harm (i.e., the best balance of good and harm).	Which option will produce the most good and do the least harm?
Rights approach	The decision that does the best job of protecting the moral rights of all affected. These include the following: • The right to decide what kind of life to lead • The right to be told the truth • The right not to be injured • The right to privacy	Which option best respects the rights of all who have a stake in the decision?
Fairness or justice approach	The decision that treats all human beings equally—or, if unequally, then fairly based on some standard that is defensible.	Which option treats people equally?
Common good approach	The decision that contributes to the good of all in the community.	Which option best serves the community as a whole, not just some members?
Virtue approach	The decision that is in agreement with certain ideal virtues. Honesty, courage, compassion, generosity, tolerance, love, fidelity, integrity, fairness, self-control, and prudence are all examples of virtues.	Which option leads me to act as the sort of person I want to be?

For example, if one uses the **utilitarian approach** to make a decision on different safety features to include in a new product, the ethical choice is the one that provides the most good and the least harm. The **rights approach** seeks to protect the rights of all. The **fairness** or **justice approach** advocates treating all human beings equally so that decisions about employee compensation would pay everyone the same or would allow one to justify why one salary is higher than another. The good of all in the community is the focus of the **common good approach**, while certain ideal values drive decisions under the **virtue approach**.

Of course, there are other factors that influence behavior. **Ethical relativism** suggests that what is ethical in one culture is not necessarily the same as in another culture. In other words, what is right or wrong is relative to the moral norms within the culture. Business leaders who have experienced a sheltered life in American companies are often shocked to find that they cannot expect the same ethical standards of some others in the global community. Westerners, for example, are often painfully honest. If an American business contact cannot meet a deadline or attend a meeting or provide the needed services, he or she will normally say so. In other cultures, the answer, even if untrue, will always be "yes." Westerners see such dishonest answers as unethical, but in some areas of the world, people believe saying "no" to any request is extremely rude—even if there's no way they intend to honor the request.

Codes of Business Ethics

Ethics are rules of conduct—how most people in a culture judge what is right and what is wrong. **Business ethics** are basic values that guide the behavior of individuals within a business organization. Ethical values govern all sorts of marketing planning decisions that managers make, including what goes into their products, where they source raw materials, how they advertise, and what type of pricing they establish. Developing sound business ethics is a major step toward creating a strong relationship with customers and others in the marketplace.

utilitarian approach
Ethical philosophy that advocates a decision that provides the most good or the least harm.

rights approach
Ethical philosophy that advocates the decision that does the best job of protecting the moral rights of all.

fairness or **justice approach**
Ethical philosophy that advocates the decision that treats all human beings equally.

common good approach
Ethical philosophy that advocates the decision that contributes to the good of all in the community.

virtue approach
Ethical philosophy that advocates the decision that is in agreement with certain ideal values.

ethical relativism
Suggests that what is ethical in one culture is not necessarily the same as in another culture.

business ethics
Basic values that guide a firm's behavior.

code of ethics
Written standards of behavior to which every-one in the organization must subscribe.

To let employees and other stakeholders know definitively what is expected of them, many firms develop their own **code of ethics**—written standards of behavior to which everyone in the organization must subscribe—as part of the planning process. For example, AT&T's *Code of Business Conduct*, a 5-page document available via its website at www.att.com, details its expectations of each director, officer, and employee in areas of honest and ethical conduct, conflicts of interest, disclosure, compliance, reporting and accountability, corporate opportunities, confidentiality, fair dealing, protection, and proper use of company assets.[60]

Of course, even the best code of ethics won't protect customers and the reputation of the organization unless employees are rewarded for ethical behavior. Wells Fargo found this out the hard way when they offered employees incentives to open more accounts by cross-selling other banking products to customers. Employees not only increased their cross-selling but some created fake accounts in the names of existing customers, resulting in Wells Fargo firing 5,300 employees.[61]

To help marketers adhere to ethical behavior in their endeavors, the American Marketing Association (AMA) developed a code of ethics for marketers. We present the highlights of that code in Table 2.7.

Is Marketing Unethical?

Most marketers want to be ethical. Some follow the rights approach philosophy and behave ethically because it's the right thing to do, whereas others are motivated by a desire not to get into trouble with consumers or government regulators. Still, there are examples of questionable or unethical marketing. We'll discuss some of these criticisms here:

Table 2.7	Highlights of the American Marketing Association Statement of Ethics

Ethical Norms and Values for Marketers

PREAMBLE

The American Marketing Association commits itself to promoting the highest standard of professional ethical norms and values for its members (practitioners, academics, and students). Norms are established standards of conduct that are expected and maintained by society and/or professional organizations. Values represent the collective conception of what communities find desirable, important and morally proper. Values also serve as the criteria for evaluating our own personal actions and the actions of others. As marketers, we recognize that we not only serve our organizations but also act as stewards of society in creating, facilitating, and executing the transactions that are part of the greater economy. In this role, marketers are expected to embrace the highest professional ethical norms and the ethical values implied by our responsibility toward multiple stakeholders (e.g., customers, employees, investors, peers, channel members, regulators, and the host community).

ETHICAL NORMS

As marketers, we must:

1. **Do no harm.**
2. **Foster trust in the marketing system.**
3. **Embrace ethical values.**

ETHICAL VALUES

Honesty—to be forthright in dealings with customers and stakeholders.

Responsibility—to accept the consequences of our marketing decisions and strategies.

Respect—to acknowledge the basic human dignity of all stakeholders.

Transparency—to create a spirit of openness in marketing operations.

Citizenship—to fulfill the economic, legal, philanthropic, and societal responsibilities that serve stakeholders.

IMPLEMENTATION

We expect AMA members to be courageous and proactive in leading and/or aiding their organizations in the fulfillment of the explicit and implicit promises made to those stakeholders.

The American Marketing Association helps its members adhere to ethical standards of business through its Code of Ethics.

Source: Copyright © American Marketing Association. Reprinted with permission from the American Marketing Association.

1. *Marketing serves the rich and exploits the poor:* Many marketers are concerned about their bottom line, but they also want to provide a better quality of life for all consumers, that is, the societal marketing concept that we discussed in Chapter 1. But there are exceptions. For example, because of decreasing sales of cigarettes in developed countries, tobacco companies target smokers in LDCs and developing countries and thus contribute to the health problems of those populations.[62]

2. *Products are not safe:* Whether marketers are truly dedicated to providing their customers with the safest products possible or because of the fear of government regulation and liability issues, most firms do make safe products and, if they find a problem, quickly notify customers and recall the defective product.

3. *Poor-quality products:* Many people bemoan the loss of U.S. manufacturing, feeling that imported products such as textiles and furniture are of poor quality. Product quality, however, is determined by what consumers want in a product. Do you want a refrigerator that lasts 50 years? Home appliance manufacturers could design and sell that, but would consumers be willing to pay what it would cost? Until consumers are willing to pay for higher quality, marketers have to provide products at the prices consumers want.

4. *Planned obsolescence:* To remain profitable, marketers must offer new products after an existing product has been on the market a period of time. The iPhone is an example. Have you noticed that about the time your cellular provider contract runs out, there is a newer and better iPhone that you just must have? For many people, this is a good thing because new phones have better features. There are others who still like their old flip phone and will use it until it falls apart in their hands.

5. *Easy consumer credit makes people buy things they don't need and can't afford:* Many are concerned about businesses such as payday loan and car title loan companies that charge interest rates that can exceed 400 percent annually. Their customers often are people with limited financial resources and even less knowledge about how to manage their money. One firm leases tires to consumers who can't afford to buy them. Of course, by the time the tires are paid off, the customer has spent enough to buy several sets of tires.

When Is a Bribe Not a Bribe? Ethical Issues for Global Business

In many LDCs and developing countries, salaries for midlevel people are, sadly, very low; the economy runs on a system we would call *blatant bribery* or *extortion*. Some of these "payments" are only petty corruption, and the "favors" are inconsequential, whereas others may involve high-level government or business officials and can have devastating consequences. If you need to park your car or your delivery truck illegally where there are no parking spaces, you give a little money to a police officer who is willing to accept a bribe. If the shopkeeper wants an officer to watch over his store, he finds an officer who is willing to do so in exchange for a shirt from his stock once in a while. If an importer wants to get her merchandise out of customs before it spoils, she pays off a government worker who can hold up her shipment for weeks. And if someone wants the contract to build a new building or wants an unsafe building to pass inspection—well, you get the idea. We mentioned earlier that a cash economy can lead to inaccurate GDPs and reduced tax revenues. Bribery and extortion are also more likely to occur in cash economies where there is no paper (or digital) trail of income or expenditures.

Bribery occurs when someone voluntarily offers payment to get an illegal advantage. **Extortion** occurs when someone in authority extracts payment under duress. The Foreign Corrupt Practices Act of 1977 (FCPA), however, puts U.S. businesses at a disadvantage because it bars them from paying bribes to sell overseas. The FCPA does, however, allow payments for "routine governmental action . . . such as obtaining permits, licenses, or other official documents; processing governmental papers, such as visas and work orders; [and] providing police protection."[63]

bribery
When someone voluntarily offers payment to get an illegal advantage.

extortion
When someone in authority extracts payment under duress.

2.6 Sustainability: Marketers Do Well by Doing Good

OBJECTIVE

Explain the role of sustainability in marketing planning.

In Chapter 1, we saw that many firms today have adopted a *triple-bottom-line orientation*. These firms don't just look at their financial successes but also focus on how they contribute to their communities (their social bottom line) and create sustainable business practices (the environmental bottom line). Today, many believe that sustainability is no longer an option. It's necessary, it's happening, and it will continue to be a part of strategic planning into the future.

Why are sustainable business practices so important? It's really simple. All of the things we need today or in the future to maintain life as we know it depend on the natural resources of our planet—air, water, and our mineral resources in the earth. Today, our Earth's population continues to grow at staggering rates. Economic growth, especially the growth in developing countries, means we consume our natural resources at higher rates. The massive growth of developing countries like China and India doesn't just provide expanding marketing opportunities; the growing middle classes in these countries look at the lives of consumers in developed countries and want that same life, thus creating even greater levels of unsustainable consumption. And climate control is no longer a debatable issue as people all around the globe are seeing signs of devastation.

green customers
Those consumers who are most likely to actively look for and buy products that are eco-friendly.

Sustainability Is a Sensible Business Decision

To understand sustainable marketing better, we might go back to the societal marketing concept discussed in Chapter 1: marketers must satisfy customers' needs in ways that also benefit society and deliver profit to the firm. Those are also the goals of Tom Szaky whom we met in the beginning of this chapter. Tom is CEO of TerraCycle, a social business focusing on solving problems of overconsumption and waste, two major challenges for sustainability. Sustainability means the firm seeks to sustain itself and, at the same time, the long-term future of society.

Today we see an increasing number of firms moving toward greater sustainability by increasing operational efficiencies, decreasing their use of raw materials, conserving energy, increasing the use of recycled materials, and preventing the discharge of wastes into the natural and social environment.[64]

Developing a Sustainable Marketing Mix

We can examine how some companies already implement sustainable marketing practices to gather some clues about the best ways to do that as we tweak our target marketing and Four Ps to do well by doing good:

- *Target marketing strategies:* Marketers need to understand the attitudes of their customers toward sustainability. They must know which consumers are willing to pay a few cents more for an environmentally friendly product. This allows marketers to successfully target **green customers**—those consumers who are most likely to actively look for and buy products that are eco-friendly.

The Kraft Heinz Company

American consumers' values are changing as many more of us are prioritizing "natural" food products that don't contain extra additives.

- *Product strategies:* Sustainable product strategies include the use of environmentally friendly and recycled materials in products and in packaging. Marketers need to develop and put into production more environmentally friendly products, such as electric automobiles. Some firms also strive to choose **fair trade suppliers**. This term refers to companies that outsource production only to firms that pay workers in developing countries a fair/living wage.

- *Price strategies:* Many consumers would like to buy green products, but they don't because the price is higher than comparable traditional products. Sustainable marketing practices aim to establish prices for green products that are the same or close to the prices of other products. A truly sustainable strategy actually reduces prices in the long term because it encourages more efficiency and less waste.

- *Place/distribution strategies:* Sustainable distribution strategies can include retailers who focus on a reduction in the use of energy to benefit from both monetary savings and the loyalty of green consumers. Both producers and retailers can choose to buy from nearby suppliers to reduce dependence on long-haul trucking, a major source of air pollution. Within the food industry in particular, we witness the growing trend of

fair trade suppliers
Companies that pledge to pay a fair price to producers in developing countries, to ensure that the workers who produce the goods receive a fair wage, and to ensure that these manufacturers rely where possible on environmentally sustainable production practices.

Alta Gracia is a Fair Trade producer that sells collegiate branded apparel made in the Dominican Republic through campus book stores in the U.S. It pays employees a living wage (three times the nation's minimum wage of $150 a month), and they receive health insurance, a pension, vacation days, and maternity leave.

This ad for the African Conservation Foundation encourages consumers to play a role in sustainable behavior.

locavorism
The trend for shoppers to actively look for products that come from farms within 50–100 miles of where they live.

locavorism—the trend in which shoppers actively look for products that come from farms within 50 to 100 miles of where they live.[65]

- *Promotion strategies:* The most obvious sustainable promotion strategies are those that inform customers of the firm's commitment to the planet and future generations through advertising and other messages. But there are other opportunities. The cost of creating a TV commercial is enormous and may take two or three days of shooting to complete. Some firms have begun to "reuse" old commercials while letting customers know that this is their way of practicing sustainability.

Sustainable Customer Behavior

A sustainability approach doesn't end with an improvement in manufacturing processes. Marketers also need to motivate customers to seek out, pay for, and use sustainable options. Many do buy products that minimize the use of natural resources; encourage the use of recycled, reused, and repurposed products; purchase fair trade and organic food; use environmentally friendly cleaning products and toiletries not tested on animals; and share cars, even at the expense of higher prices, less convenience, and lower product performance. Consumers can be an important part of sustainable marketing practices when they become knowledgeable about environmental concerns and environmentally friendly products.

2.7

OBJECTIVE

Recognize which industry and which work environment (both domestic and international) are best for you.

Brand You: Finding the Right Fit

Taylor is excited and eager to begin his journey of developing a personal brand. He recognizes that a personal brand will not only help him land an internship or a first job, but also allow him to control his career options in the future. Taylor understands that marketing is about meeting needs. Employers are looking for people who are able to accomplish tasks and solve problems. A personal brand will allow Taylor to discover and communicate what makes him unique and sets him apart from other job candidates.

If you have had an opportunity to visit different college campuses, you know that each one "feels" different. Some seem cold and impersonal while others are warm and inviting. The inviting ones are places where students like to be and spend time just enjoying each other. This is because different campuses, like different organizations, have different organizational cultures. Just like you found a college that was the "right fit," you need to find an industry that is the best fit for your style. Will you be more comfortable in the conservative culture of a financial institution, or do you crave the freedom of coming to work in jeans and flip-flops at a company like Zappos, where the culture is much more relaxed?

In this section, you will learn how to:

- Recognize the industry that provides the best fit for you
- Discover which work environment is best for you
- Understand options to consider in an international career

Organizational Culture

Just like we define the culture of a group of people as the values, beliefs, and customs of that group, values, beliefs, and customs are important parts of an organizational culture. For an organization, values are deeply held beliefs about the right and wrong way to run a business.

These beliefs may have been influenced by the values of the founder of the business and over time have become so strongly entrenched that they are difficult if not impossible to change. In many organizations, deeply ingrained ways of doing things may include everything from the when and where you eat your lunch to what you can place in your office or cubicle. For example, some companies expect employees to follow company guidelines in their dress and in the treatment of vendors and channel members. In very structured organizations, new ideas often must run up the appropriate chain of command and receive approval before they can be implemented. In less structured organizations, employees have more freedom to try out a new idea and see how it works. At Zappos, the Internet retailer, no one, not even the CEO, has an office; everyone has the same sized cubicle, which they are encouraged to decorate to express themselves. They can do their work in any part of the campus they wish and even take a nap in a room full of hammocks, placed there just for that purpose.

During the coronavirus pandemic, employees at all levels of many organizations began working at home. It remains to be seen if these organizations will adjust their values, beliefs, and customs or return to their previous more formal cultures.

Observe the culture while you are on every job interview. It's the small things that you see (or don't see) that can tell you so much about the organization's culture. Are the people you meet as you walk through the hallways friendly, smiling, and enthusiastic? Do they look like they enjoy working there, or do they seem to be less than excited about their jobs?

It's okay to ask about the organization's culture during the job interview. You can ask such questions as "How would you describe the company culture?" and "What is an average work day here like?" to get a feel for the culture of the organization. In addition, it's always a good idea to ask the same questions of each person with whom you interview to see if you get consistent responses. Some other things that you can observe and that will tell you a lot about the work environment are:

The location of the business. This element refers to the look of the building and the design of its workspaces. Does everyone have a cubicle or office, or are workspaces open and configured around a hub? Do employees work at home some or all of the time?

The personality of key players. Who is more important: scientists, dealmakers, or others?

The management philosophy and style. Do managers micromanage every detail, or do they set goals and then step aside so employees can accomplish them?

Risk-taking. Does the company take risks, or is it financially conservative? What are the consequences if an employee makes a mistake?

Ethics. Does the company have a code of ethics? Do employees follow the code?

Social responsibility. Does the organization contribute to the public good? Is it a good citizen in its community?

You can learn many of these things on a company website and from business or trade publications, such as *Advertising Age* and *Fortune* magazine. The best source may be from someone in your network who works for the organization—and be sure to seek this person's insight before your interview.

Differences among Industries

While much of an organization's culture is influenced by the size, management philosophy, and CEO's personal style, the culture of the company may also be heavily influenced by the culture of the industry.

The following list provides information about the work environment in some key industries.

Agriculture, Mining, and Construction *(agribusiness, petrochemical, forestry, aquaculture, residential/commercial construction)*

Employees are likely to be practical people who take pride in their skills and accomplishments. College grads get jobs in project management, finance, marketing, and sales.

Manufacturing/Research and Development *(automotive, aerospace, clothing, pharmaceuticals, computers)*

Employees face strict timelines, tight budgets, and quality control standards. Detail-oriented, level-headed problem solvers do best with these companies.

Sales/Marketing *(autos, clothing, food, retail stores and Web-based sellers, cosmetics)*

Employees need quantitative and analytical skills to work in this fast-paced, fluid environment. There is little tolerance for failure, and jobs are suited for high achievers with creative ideas and high energy.

Information/Media/Entertainment *(publishing, mass media, software publishing, telecommunications, advertising, public relations, film)*

These industries offer entry-level jobs that require technical skills such as editing, researching, and reporting. Creativity and fresh ideas are important for successful careers.

Finance/Insurance *(banking, commercial real estate, insurance, securities, venture capitalists)*

Employees in this sector must have personal integrity and self-confidence. Jobs require a detailed mind, a full understanding of the financial world, and "looking the part."

Professional and Business Services *(computer systems design, employment services, benefits consultants, management, scientific and technical consulting, public accounting and legal firms, client services organizations)*

Jobs require excellent communication skills, technical skills, a talent for building client relationships, self-discipline, and enjoyment in selling your expertise and knowledge.

Education and Health Services *(edutainment—e.g., video, e-learning; psychological and social services; educational institutions; hospitals; clinics; fitness trainers; nutritionists)*

Employees enjoy work that makes a difference in the lives of others.

Leisure/Hospitality/Culture *(restaurants, hotels, resorts, recreational facilities, parks, entertainment, museums, art galleries)*

Employees like serving other people or helping them enjoy their time off, can stay cool under pressure, and are willing to work for low pay. Employees have flexible hours, making time to pursue other interests.

Government/Not-for-Profits/Nongovernmental Organizations *(federal, state, and local agencies; politicians; city managers; planners; foundations; not-for-profit organizations; charities; service organizations)*

These jobs are good for those who enjoy working to solve complex issues. People work in a collegial work environment.

Transportation and Utilities *(trucking firms, expediters, airlines, electric companies, alternative fuels)*

Jobs require professional skills, sensitivity to customer needs, the ability to implement business plans, and the ability to balance the sometimes conflicting goals of customer service and profitability. Many jobs offer collegial work environments, challenges, and service to others.

Landing a Job Overseas

The world is fast becoming a global marketplace. BMW and Mercedes automobiles may be made by German companies, but many of their cars are made in the U.S. At the same time, U.S. automaker General Motors manufactures vehicles in Canada, Mexico, China,

Germany, Turkey, Brazil, Argentina, Australia, and South Africa, and Toyota makes its cars in 18 countries, including Argentina, Belgium, Indonesia, Poland, South Africa, the U.S., and, oh yes, Japan, just to name a few. After the global economy recovers from the pandemic, you may wish to join the ranks of others who have enjoyed the life-changing experience of working in another country. There are many global firms that provide employment opportunities for short- or longer-term work in another country. In addition to the opportunity to live somewhere else and to travel, these jobs provide invaluable learning experiences. Being able to do business on the international stage and working successfully with other cultures can't be learned in the classroom.

Generally, it is easier to find these jobs from home, beginning by securing a position with a multinational corporation in your own country. Once you have acquired skills and gained some job experience, you'll be ready to apply for a transfer to a branch in a different country. One way you can increase your marketability in the global job market is to study abroad while working on your degree.

Taylor has learned that, just as there are big differences among the cultures (values, beliefs, and norms) of various countries and groups of people, the corporate cultures of companies and industries often vary greatly. He also recognizes that to get a job that is a great "fit" for him, he needs to learn as much as possible about a potential employer's culture by observation and by asking questions during the job interviewing process. He also knows that in today's global marketplace there may be exciting opportunities for working in other countries.

Objective **Summaries** and **Key Terms**

2.1 Objective Summary

Understand the big picture of international marketing and the decisions firms must make when they consider globalization.

The increasing amount of world trade—the flow of goods and services among countries—may take place through cash, credit payments, or countertrade. A decision to go global often comes when further domestic growth opportunities dwindle and the firm perceives likelihood for success in foreign markets as a result of a competitive advantage. After a firm has decided to go global, they must consider which markets are most attractive, what market-entry strategy is best, and how to best develop the marketing mix.

Key Terms

Greenhouse Effect
climate change
Arab Spring
world trade
countertrade

2.2 Objective Summary

Explain how international organizations such as the World Trade Organization (WTO), the World Bank, the International Monetary Fund (IMF), economic communities, and individual country regulations facilitate and limit a firm's opportunities for globalization.

Established by the General Agreement on Tariffs and Trade (GATT) in 1984, the World Trade Organization with its 164 members seeks to create a single open world market where trade flows "smoothly, predictably and freely as possible." Some governments, however, adopt policies of protectionism with rules designed to give home companies an advantage. Such policies may include trade quotas, embargoes, or tariffs that increase the costs of foreign goods. Many countries have banded together to form economic communities to promote free trade.

Key Terms

General Agreement on Tariffs and Trade (GATT)
World Trade Organization (WTO)
World Bank
International Monetary Fund (IMF)
foreign exchange rate (forex rate)
balance of payments
protectionism
import quotas
embargo
tariffs
economic communities
Brexit

2.3 Objective Summary

Understand how factors in a firm's external business environment influence marketing strategies and outcomes in both domestic and global markets.

The economic environment refers to (1) the economic health of a country (normally measured by its GDP or per capita GDP and its economic infrastructure), (2) the level of economic development (that may classify the country as developed, developing, or least developed), and (3) the stage in the business cycle. Marketers use competitive intelligence to examine brand, product, and discretionary income competition in the microenvironment. They also consider the structure of the industry in the macroenvironment, that is, whether the industry is classified as a monopoly, an oligopoly, monopolistic competition, or pure competition. A country's political and legal environment includes laws and regulations that affect business. Marketers must understand any local political constraints, that is, the prospects for nationalization or expropriation of foreign holdings, regulations such as local content rules, and labor and human rights regulations. Because technology can affect every aspect of marketing, marketers must be knowledgeable about technological changes, often monitoring government and private research findings. Marketers also examine a country's sociocultural environment, including demographics, values, social norms and customs, language, and ethnocentricity.

Key Terms

external environment
gross domestic product (GDP)
economic infrastructure
level of economic development
standard of living
least developed country (LDC)
developing countries
bottom of the pyramid (BOP)
sachet
BRICS countries
developed country
Group of 7 (G7)
business cycle
competitive intelligence (CI)
discretionary income
product competition
brand competition
monopoly
oligopoly
monopolistic competition
perfect competition
self-driving (autonomous) vehicle
patent
nationalization
expropriation
local content rules
U.S. Generalized System of Preferences (GSP)
demographics
cultural values
collectivist cultures
individualist cultures
social norms
consumer xenocentrism
consumer ethnocentrism

2.4 Objective Summary

Explain some of the strategies and tactics that a firm can use to enter global markets.

Different foreign-market-entry strategies represent varying levels of commitment for a firm. Exporting of goods entails little commitment but allows little control over how products are sold. Contractual agreements such as licensing or franchising allow greater control. With strategic alliances through joint ventures, commitment increases. Finally, the firm can choose to invest directly by buying an existing company or starting a foreign subsidiary in the host country. Firms that operate in two or more countries can choose to standardize their marketing strategies by using the same approach in all countries or to localize by adopting different strategies for each market. The firm needs to decide whether to sell an existing product, change an existing product, or develop a new product. In many cases, the promotional strategy, the pricing strategy, the place/distribution strategy, and the product itself must be tailored to fit the needs of consumers in another country.

Key Terms

export merchants
licensing agreement
franchising
strategic alliance
joint venture
straight extension strategy
product adaptation strategy
product invention strategy
backward invention
ethnocentric pricing
polycentric pricing
geocentric pricing
free trade zones
gray market goods
dumping

2.5 Objective Summary

Understand the importance of ethical marketing practices.

Ethical business practices are important in order for the firm to do the best for all stakeholders and to avoid the consequences of low ethical standards for the firm and to society. Differing philosophies of ethics provide different results in ethical decision making. Business ethics, values that guide the firm, are often used to develop a business code of ethics. Although most marketers do make ethical decisions, there are examples of actions that justify some of the criticisms of marketing. The ethical environment in some countries can cause problems for marketers if they do not understand the differences in ethical perspectives. In many least developed and developing countries, corruption is a major stumbling block for Western businesses. Bribery and extortion are accepted ways of doing business and present ethical dilemmas for U.S. companies who must abide by the Foreign Corrupt Practices Act of 1977 (FCPA).

Key Terms

utilitarian approach
rights approach
fairness or **justice approach**
common good approach
virtue approach
ethical relativism
business ethics
code of ethics
bribery
extortion

2.6 Objective Summary

Explain the role of sustainability in marketing planning.

With growing world populations and increasing demand for products, sustainable business practices are necessary for life in the future. Many firms practice sustainability when they develop target marketing and product, price, place/

distribution, and promotion strategies designed to protect the environment and the future of our communities.

Key Terms

green customers
fair trade suppliers
locavorism

2.7 Objective Summary

Recognize which industry and which work environment (both domestic and international) are best for you.

Job seekers need to find the industry and the work environment that are best for them. They also need to understand options to consider in an international career. Companies, like different countries and groups of people, have an organizational culture that holds unique beliefs about the right and wrong way to run a business and these beliefs may be strongly entrenched. Job seekers should observe clues to the culture and the work environment, including the location of the business, the personality of key players, the management philosophy and style, the level of risk-taking behavior, and the company's ethics and social responsibility.

As the world becomes a global marketplace, many companies provide employment opportunities for short- or long-term work in another country. Such jobs provide learning that can't be found in a classroom.

Chapter **Questions** and **Activities**

Concepts: Test Your Knowledge

2-1. Describe the market conditions in the home market and those in other countries that influence a firm's decision to enter foreign markets.

2-2. Explain what *world trade* means. What is the role of the WTO and economic communities in encouraging free trade? What is the role of the World Bank and the International Monetary Fund in global trade? Describe and explain the reasons for protectionism, import quotas, embargoes, and tariffs.

2-3. What factors are used to evaluate the economic health of a country? Explain the level of economic development of countries. What is a bottom-of-the-pyramid (BOP) consumer? How do marketers create products specifically targeted for this group?

2-4. What aspects of the political and legal environment influence a firm's decision to enter a foreign market? Why are human rights issues important to firms in their decisions to enter global markets? Describe what is meant by a country's technological and sociocultural environments.

2-5. What is ethnocentrism? What is xenocentrism?

2-6. How is a firm's level of commitment related to its level of control in a foreign market? Describe the four globalization strategies representing different levels of involvement for a firm: exporting, contractual agreements, strategic alliances, and direct investment.

2-7. What are the arguments for standardization of marketing strategies in the global marketplace? What are the arguments for localization? What are some ways a firm can standardize or localize its marketing mix?

2-8. Describe the utilitarianism, rights, fairness or justice, common good, and virtue approaches to ethical decision making. What is ethical relativism?

2-9. Why is sustainability such an important piece of a company's overall marketing strategy? What are some ways that companies can incorporate sustainability into each of the Four Ps of marketing?

Activities: Apply What You've Learned

2-10. *In Class, 10–25 Minutes for Teams* Using the data in Table 2.2, select two countries that are substantially dissimilar from one another. Then, select one of the products below. Use the data for the two countries to develop arguments for why each of the two countries would and/or would not be a good opportunity for expansion of the market for your product.

1. High-end, American-designed home furniture
2. Environmentally sound home air conditioning systems
3. A well-designed but inexpensive kids bicycle
4. A water purification system that makes water potable and does not require electricity

2-11. *Creative Homework/Short Project* With several members of your class, assume you are in the marketing department for a low-end retail store chain; you might think of a chain similar to Dollar General. Your firm has decided to begin an expansion into the global market. Currently you are considering building stores in France, Ecuador, Brazil, and Australia. Gather information about these countries using the CIA Factbook available online and other sources. Using the data you have about each country, develop ideas on the pros and cons of entering each country. Which country do you feel is best? Present your findings to your class.

2-12. *For Further Research (Individual)* Consider the six different ethical philosophies described in the chapter. Apply these six philosophies to one of the following ethical dilemmas. What would be the most ethical decision for each? Explain why you think so. Which would you be most likely to follow?

Decisions:

1. You see a classmate go through the backpack of another student in the restroom, remove some items, and then leave. Should you ignore what you saw, report it, or do something else?

2. You are the president of a school club, which gives you access to the club's money. You need to buy a new tire for your car but you won't have enough money for a week. You are considering borrowing the money from the club and paying it back in a week. What should you do?

3. You have been assigned to a class project team. In a different class, you have been on a team with one of the members of your current team, and you know he or she refuses to do any work but expects others on the team to help him or her out. What are your options, and what should you do?

2-13. *In Class, 10–25 Minutes for Teams* Assume you are the director of marketing for a U.S. firm that produces one of the products listed below. Your firm is considering going after the Indian market and is faced with the decision of the best entry strategy. Should your firm simply export their products, or would a strategic alliance, licensing, a joint venture, or direct investment be a better choice? Develop your ideas for a best entry strategy. Be specific in your recommendations for a strategy, how to implement the strategy, and your reasons for your recommendations.

Products:

1. Tablets (similar to the iPad) targeting the consumer market
2. Expansion of your discount retail store chain
3. Short-term (from an hour up) auto rentals

2-14. *Creative Homework/Short Project* Consumer ethnocentrism is the tendency for individuals to prefer products from one's own culture. Consumer xenocentrism is the tendency for individuals to prefer products from a country not their own. Sometimes people think products made at home are better than imported goods, while others think that imported goods are superior to those produced domestically. Develop a small study to find out what students at your university think about products made at home and abroad. Develop a survey that asks other students to evaluate 10 or more products (not brands) that are imported versus made at home. You might wish to ask if they feel the domestic or imported products are superior in quality and which they would purchase. Prepare a report on your study for your class.

2-15. *In Class, 10–25 Minutes for Teams* Some people argue that our environment is not in jeopardy and that sustainability efforts will only make products more expensive. Plan a debate in your class with two teams, one arguing that climate change is a real threat to our planet and our future and that we must have sustainability efforts and the other arguing against the need for sustainability efforts.

2-16. *For Further Research (Individual)* McDonald's is a company that is all-in globally, having become a staple in over 100 countries around the world. Take a look at the menu items available in four different countries. Why are the offerings so different? Why do you think McDonald's chose to change their menu selections?

2-17. *For Further Research (Groups)* Assume you are part of a small business in the United States that manufactures portable gas barbecue grills and has decided to enter the global marketplace. What type of market entry strategy would be best suited for your company and why? What decisions should the company make around product, price, place, and promotion to ensure success?

Concepts: Apply Marketing Metrics

Many Western firms see their futures in the growing populations of developing countries, where 8 out of 10 consumers now live. Consumers from the BRICS countries—Brazil, Russia, India, China, and South Africa—offer new opportunities for firms because growing numbers are accumulating significant amounts of disposable income. These new consumers are creating big business opportunities for companies that are innovative enough to serve them. Success requires companies to develop a set of key capabilities, including:

- Customer insight: An understanding of local customers and their unique needs is essential.
- People and culture: Culture trumps brand. Companies that don't possess an iconic brand need to adopt a culture of being willing to tailor products to customers' needs rather than attempting to market products from Canada in emerging markets.
- Research and development: Companies must strike a careful balance between local relevance and global scale, paying careful attention to how innovations developed with one set of customers in mind can be reapplied elsewhere.

- Operations and business model: Companies must consider how to tailor their pricing structure or business model when developing products and services aimed at this new emerging "spend" class.[66]

But how do firms measure their success in these developing markets? Firms in developed countries normally use standard marketing metrics, such as customer awareness, customer satisfaction, increases in market share or profits, return on customer investment, or return on marketing investment. But these metrics are based on standard market-entry strategies with full-size products and correspondingly typical pricing and promotional strategies—very different from the approach just described. Hence, these metrics are likely not too useful for the new markets in the developing world, where many millions of people buy streamlined versions of a firm's products at a fraction of their usual price.

2-18. Based on what you learned in the chapter about developing markets, what are some of the idiosyncracies of doing marketing in those markets where one must appeal to consumers with small but growing disposable income?

2-19. How would the success of entry into BRICS markets best be measured by marketers—that is, what metrics would be more useful than the typical metrics used in developed countries? Be creative and develop a list of several possible metrics that firms might use to measure their success in these new developing markets. *Hint:* Keep closely in mind what firms hope to accomplish by increasing their presence and sales in those markets.

Choices: What Do You Think?

2-20. *Critical Thinking and Ethics* Assume you are the CMO for an athletic shoe company. Over 75 percent of your sales comes from the United States and Europe. You have outsourced your shoe production to Firm ABC in Guatemala for 30+ years, but recent reports in the world news have suggested that your supplier is using child labor to produce its goods. The reports show the children are forced to work 70 or more hour weeks in unclean conditions without adequate air conditioning and with few breaks. You are considering switching to Firm XYZ in Honduras that produces an identical product in a sustainable manner and provides both green marketing and fair labor certifications. The only downside is that Firm XYZ's product is 43 percent more expensive than what you are currently purchasing from Firm ABC. The switch would require you to increase the price of your shoes, which would likely impact your sales. Were your sales to decrease, there is the possibility of layoffs and plant closings. You are also aware of the importance of ethics and sustainability to today's consumers. Answer the following questions:

   a. What are the potential positive and negative outcomes (in addition to those already discussed) of continuing to purchase product from Firm ABC?

   b. What are the potential positive and negative outcomes (other than those already discussed) of changing suppliers and purchasing product from Firm XYZ?

   c. Which firm would you choose using the utilitarian approach to decision making? Why?

   d. Which firm would you choose using the rights approach to decision making? Why?

   e. Which firm would you personally choose? Why?

2-21. *Critical Thinking* Do you think companies that operate in the U.S. should be able to use bribes to compete in countries where bribery is an accepted (and legal) form of doing business? Why or why not?

2-22. *Critical Thinking* Some countries have been critical of the export of American culture via movies, television, music, and many American consumer goods by U.S. businesses. What about American culture might be objectionable? Can you think of some products that U.S. marketers export that can be objectionable to some foreign markets? What is the solution to the problem?

2-23. *Critical Thinking* Some of the U.S. population supports free trade, whereas others are unhapppy, even angry, that the government has reduced regulations on imports of such products as textiles and furniture, causing factories to shut down and employees to lose their jobs. They feel that the U.S. government should legislate greater regulation of imported goods to give American companies an advantage or at least to lessen the advantage that companies in other countries receive from their government. What do you think? How do you justify your answer?

2-24. *Critical Thinking* In 1999, several single European nations banded together to form the European Union and converted their individual monetary systems over to the euro. In June 2016, the U.K. (the only EU country that did not adopt the euro) voted to leave the EU (a plan named *Brexit*) with the actual separation coming in December 2020. Many are concerned that this will be the beginning of the end for the European Union. What do you think about Brexit and the future of the EU? What effect do you think this will have on other economic communities? What about the possibility of a single world currency?

2-25. *Critical Thinking* Think about a company that you are familiar with that has a "cause marketing" program. Why do you think that company chose that specific cause to support? Do you think the firm's customers are more loyal to the company because of this program? Why or why not?

Miniproject: Learn by Doing

The purpose of this miniproject is to gain experience in understanding what it takes to move a product that is successful in its home market into a global market in which it will continue to be successful. Assume that you are the director of marketing for a firm that produces its own high-end brands of makeup, skin care, and hair care products for both men and women that are sold only in its own retail outlets. The products have been endorsed by a number of male and female musicians who are highly popular with young people around the world.

2-26. Describe your local competitive advantage and why you believe this competitive advantage will serve you globally.

2-27. Determine which global market(s) is or are most attractive for your products. Will you target a single country or an economic community? Describe your reasoning.

2-28. Decide which market-entry strategy you will pursue. Again, explain your reasoning.

2-29. Describe your marketing mix strategy:
- How might you need to adapt your products?
- What other product decisions do you need to make?
- How will you promote your products?
- How will you price your products?
- What place/distribution decisions must you consider?

Prepare a short presentation to share with your class.

Marketing in Action **Case**   Real Choices at Walmart

When businesses consider expanding into a new region of the world, the number of potential customers in the area is a major consideration. Perhaps that's why India, with its 1.38 billion people, is so attractive to Walmart, the brick-and-mortar king of retailing and a major force in online shopping. In 2018, the Indian retail market generated $800 billion a year in sales and was headed toward $1 trillion in the next two years, according to research firm Forrester. Online sales represented only about $20 billion of that amount. Betting on the growth of online retail in India, Walmart made a $16 billion investment in locally owned online retailer Flipkart.

Most retail sales in India are through small individual "mom-and-pop" stores. Over the previous decade, Walmart had tried to break into the market, but those small store owners were able to influence government regulators to create limitations on foreign direct investment (FDI) by international retailers. At that point, Walmart's presence there had been limited to 21 Best Price wholesale member-only stores (with plans to add 50 more). The investment in Flipkart provided a way for Walmart to reach the massive Indian market.

Flipkart was founded in 2007 by two college friends and former Amazon employees and began as an online bookseller. Understanding that many Indians saw paying online with credit cards as risky, Flipkart allowed buyers to pay cash when their order was delivered. The company was also known for its many delivery drivers on motorcycles with huge backpacks filled with merchandise. In its 2017 fiscal year, Flipkart had net sales of $4.6 billion, a fraction of Walmart's $485 billion, but an impressive 40 percent of online sales in the country. Flipkart had more than 10 million customers and 100,000 sellers, and it made more than 500,000 deliveries every day.

But Walmart wasn't the only U.S. online retailer looking to capture the Indian online market. Walmart's investment in Flipkart was, at least in part, to fend off rival Amazon that already had strong online sales in India. At the time, Amazon claimed they had the most downloaded shopping app in India and founder Jeff Bezos said the company planned to invest more in the Indian market. Early in 2020, Bezos said the company would invest $1 billion in digitizing small- and medium-sized businesses to facilitate their online operations.

Walmart's investment provided financial stability for Flipkart and a stronger presence for Walmart in India. The investment positioned Walmart to move into brick-and-mortar outlets if regulatory limitations changed. The investment was also good news for Indian consumers, who would benefit from an expanded Flipkart and the merchandising expertise Walmart would bring.

But not everyone was happy with the move. The Confederation of All India Traders, which represented 60 million businesses in India, objected that the investment was "a clear attempt to control and dominate the retail trade of India by Walmart." Their fear was that the deal would create an uneven playing field and encourage predatory pricing, a pricing strategy in which a company sets a very low price for the purpose of driving competitors out of business. Others warned that the Walmart and Flipkart cultures might clash. Flipkart is "very aggressive and numbers driven," according to Flipkart seller Devita Saraf, with a "flexible, entrepreneurial energy. They are constantly working on acquiring new customers." Walmart "may know retail but may not know India. India is a complicated market. You have to have the right partners to understand the customer."

Walmart's investment seems to have paid off. Flipkart's share of the Indian market grew from 40 percent in 2017 to 60 percent in 2019, eclipsing rival Amazon's share, believed to be about 30 percent. The company got an added bonus by acquiring a digital payments subsidiary as part of the Flipkart deal. Its PhonePe unit facilitates payment via smartphone, a business that has received a valuation from outside investors as high as $10 billion. This market alone has huge potential and is projected to grow to $1 trillion by 2023. But the way forward will not be easy for Walmart as the Indian government is carefully controlling the company's expansion. In 2020, the government rejected Flipkart's plan to move into food retail because it claimed that Flipkart's plan did not comply with regulatory guidelines.

Walmart's indirect play in India illustrates the creative approaches that marketers must take to reach new global markets. With this investment, Walmart became the dominant online player in the massive Indian market and is positioned well for further growth. Whether its $16 billion bet continues to pay off will depend on its strategic actions and those of its competitors, but most of all on how India's massive consumer base reacts to this "invasion."[67]

Questions for Discussion

2-30. What other options for global expansion (besides Flipkart) were available to Walmart for expansion in India?

2-31. What external factors should Walmart have taken into consideration as it considered expansion in India?

2-32. Many citizens of India fit into the group of consumers known as the *bottom of the pyramid (BOP)*. What additional strategies could Walmart execute through Flipkart to serve consumers in this group?

Chapter **Notes**

1. Fawaz Gerges, "The Islamic State Has Not Been Defeated," *New York Times*, March 23, 2019, https://www.nytimes.com/2019/03/23/opinion/isis-defeated.html?searchResultPosition=1 (accessed May 3, 2020).

2. Henry Fountain, "Climate Change Is Accelerating, Bringing the World 'Dangerously Close' to Irreversible Change," December 4, 2019, https://www.nytimes.com/2019/12/04/climate/climate-change-acceleration.html (accessed May 3, 2020).

3. Alpaslan Ozerdem, "Coronavirus and the Least Developed Countries," March 23, 2020, Thomson Reuters Foundation News, https://news.trust.org/item/20200323155755-uo6f3/ (accessed May 3, 2020).

4. Myron Levin and Stuart Silverstein, "Asbestos Found in Imported Crayons and Toy Fingerprint Kits," *FairWarning*, July 8, 2015, http://www.fairwarning.org/2015/07/asbestos-in-toys/ (accessed April 3, 2016); Emily Stewart, "China Has a History of Selling Dangerous Products to U.S. Consumers," *The Street*, March 3, 2015, http://www.thestreet.com/story/13063992/1/china-has-a-history-of-selling-dangerous-products-to-us-consumers.html (accessed April 4, 2016).

5. European Commission, "Clothing and Toys Top List of Dangerous Consumer Items in EU," March 26, 2014, http://www.europa-nu.nl/id/vjif6kwwgdyi/nieuws/clothing_and_toys_top_list_of_dangerous (accessed April 15, 2014).

6. http://www.starbucks.com/business/international-stores.

7. http://www.starbucks.com/business/international-stores.

8. World Trade Organization, "Annual Report 2014," https://www.wto.org/english/res_e/booksp_e/anrep_e/anrep15_e.pdf (accessed April 1, 2016).

9. Katie Thomas, "Facing Black Market, Pfizer Is Looking Online to Sell Viagra," *New York Times*, May 6, 2013, https://www.nytimes.com/2013/05/07/business/pfizer-begins-selling-viagra-online.html (accessed April 14, 2014).

10. The World Bank Group, "Who We Are," https://www.worldbank.org/en/who-we-are (accessed July 21 2020).

11. Todaro and Smith, "Economic Development Glossary," *Economic Development*, 8th ed. (New York: Addison Wesley, 2003); http://www.compilerpress.ca/ElementalEconomics/270%20Developmental/Todano%20&%20Smith%20Glossary%208th%20Ed.htm (accessed July 21, 2020); Food and Agricultural Organization of the United Nations, "Document 10: Glossary of Economic and Institutional Terminology," http://www.fao.org/docrep/006/y5137e/y5137e0f.htm (accessed April 4, 2016).

12. Lumen, "Barriers to Trade," https://courses.lumenlearning.com/boundless-economics/chapter/barriers-to-trade/ (accessed May 3, 2020).

13. Paul Davidson, "Trump Tariffs on Solar Panels, Washing Machines Could Raise Prices," *USA Today*, January 24, 2018, https://www.usatoday.com/story/money/2018/01/24/trump-tariffs-solarpanels-washing-machines-could-raise-prices/1059542001/ (accessed February 15, 2018).

14. Lucy Colback, "How to Navigate the US-China Trade War," *Financial Times*, February 28, 2000, https://www.ft.com/content/6124beb8-5724-11ea-abe5-8e03987b7b20 (accessed May 12, 2020).

15. Marc Bain, "(Not) Made in the USA, Your Sneakers Are a Case Study in Why Trump's America-First Trade Policy is Nonsense," *Quartz Media US*, December 20, 2016, https://qz.com/859628/your-nikesneakers-are-a-case-study-in-why-trumps-protectionist-americafirst-trade-policy-is-nonsense/ (accessed February 5, 2018).

16. Investopedia, "Which Products and Companies Rely on Protective Tariffs to Survive?" http://www.investopedia.com/ask/answers/051315/what-are-examples-products-and-companies-rely-protective-tariffs-survive.asp (accessed April 5, 2016).

17. Mark Landler and Alan Rappeport, "Trump Hails Revised Nafta Trade Deal, and Sets Up a Showdown With China," *New York Times*, October 1, 2018, https://www.nytimes.com/2018/10/01/politics/nafta-deal-trump-canada-mexico.html (accessed October 2, 2018); Jim Tankersley, "Trump Just Ripped Up Nafta. Here's What's in the New Deal," *New York Times*, October 1, 2018, https://www.nytimes.com/2018/10/01/business/trump-nafta-usmca-differences.html (accessed October 2, 2018) ; U.S. Customs and Border Protection, U.S.-Mexico-Canada Agreement (USMCA), https://www.cbp.gov/trade/priority-issues/trade-agreements/free-trade-agreements/USMCA (accessed December 5, 2020).

18. BBC News, "Brexit: All You Need to Know about the UK Leaving the EU," 17 February 2020, https://www.bbc.com/news/uk-politics-32810887 (accessed May 5, 2020).

19. Saritha Rai, "Deadly Zika Virus Claims First Corporate Victim: Tata's Zica Car In India," *Forbes*, February 3, 2016, https://www.forbes.com/sites/saritharai/2016/02/03/deadly-zika-virus-claims-first-corporate-victim-tatas-zica-car-in-india/#5f04b797422e (accessed July 21, 2020).

20. Yen Nee Lee, "7 Charts Show How the Coronavirus Pandemic Has Hit the Global Economy," *CNBC*, April 24, 2020, https://www.cnbc.com/2020/04/24/coronavirus-pandemics-impact-on-the-global-economy-in-7-charts.html (accessed May 2, 2020).

21. C. K. Prahalad, *The Fortune at the Bottom of the Pyramid* (Upper Saddle River, NJ: Wharton School Publishing, 2010), xiv.

22. Mark Koba, "BRICS: CNBC Explains," *CNBC*, August 11, 2011, http://www.cnbc.com/id/44006382 (accessed April 4, 2016); Ian Talley, "'BRICS' New World Order Is Now on Hold," *The Wall Street Journal*, January 19, 2016, http://www.wsj.com/articles/brics-new-world-order-is-now-on-hold-1453240108 (accessed April 4, 2016).

23. United Nations, "Country Classification: Data Sources, Country Classifications and Aggregation Methodology," https://www.un.org/en/development/desa/policy/wesp/wesp_current/2014wesp_country_classification.pdf (accessed May 15, 2020); World Bank Data Team, "New Country Classifications by Income Level: 2019–2020," July 1, 2019, https://blogs.worldbank.org/opendata/new-country-classifications-income-level-2019-2020 (accessed May 15, 2020).

24. Alison Smale and Michael D. Shear, "Russia Is Ousted from Group of 8 by U.S. and Allies," *New York Times*, March 24, 2014, http://www.nytimes.com/2014/03/25/world/europe/obama-russia-crimea.html (accessed April 15, 2014).

25. G7 Information Center, "What Are the G7 and G8?" http://www.g7.utoronto.ca/what_is_g8.html (accessed February 12, 2010).

26. Arwen Armbrecht, "What Do Different Nationalities Spend Their Money On?" *World Economic Forum* (January 2016), https://www.weforum.org/agenda/2016/01/what-do-different-nationalities-spend-their-money-on/ (accessed April 6, 2016).

27. CBS News, "Amazon Unveils Futuristic Plan: Delivery by Drone," December 1, 2013, https://www.cbsnews.com/news/amazon-unveils-futuristic-plan-delivery-by-drone/ (accessed April 4, 2016).

28. Karen Hao, "Inside Amazon's Plan for Alexa to Run Your Entire Life," *MIT Technology Review*, November 5, 2019, https://www.technologyreview.com/2019/11/05/65069/amazon-alexa-will-run-your-life-data-privacy/ (accessed May 2, 2020).

29. DLA Piper, "Data Protection Laws of the World—United States," last modified January 27, 2020, https://www.dlapiperdataprotection.com/index.html?t=law&c=US (accessed May 11, 2020).

30. Dianne E. Rennack and Cory Welt, "U.S. Sanctions on Russia: An Overview," Congressional Research Service, updated March 23, 2020, https://fas.org/sgp/crs/row/IF10779.pdf (accessed May 2, 2020).

31. Hanna Deringer, Fredrik Erixon, Philipp Lamprecht, and Erik van der Marel, "The Economic Impact of Local Content Requirements: A Case Study of Heavy Vehicles," January 2018, European Centre for International Political Economy (ECIPE), https://ecipe.org/publications/the-economic-impact-of-local-content-requirements/ (accessed May 5, 2020).

32. Stephan Nielsen, "Brazil Local Content Rules Hurting Major Wind Suppliers," Renewable Energy World, October 7, 2013, https://www.renewableenergyworld.com/2013/10/07/brazil-local-content-rules-hurting-major-wind-manufacturers/#gref (accessed April 16, 2014).

33. Max Nisen, "How Nike Solved Its Sweatshop Problem," May 9, 2013, https://www.businessinsider.com/how-nike-solved-its-sweatshop-problem-2013-5 (accessed April 16, 2014).

34. Arantxa Underwood, "Which Countries Have the Highest Rates of Modern Slavery and Most Victims?" Thomson Reuters Foundation, July 31, 2018, https://reliefweb.int/report/world/which-countries-have-highest-rates-modern-slavery-and-most-victims (accessed March 24, 2020); Walk Free Foundation, "The Global Slavery Index 2018," July 20, 2018, https://reliefweb.int/report/world/global-slavery-index-2018 (accessed March 21, 2020).

35. Choe Sang-Hun, "In South Korea, Spam Is The Stuff Gifts Are Made Of," New York Times, January 26, 2014, http://www.nytimes.com/2014/01/27/world/asia/in-south-korea-spam-is-the-stuff-gifts-are-made.html (accessed April 6, 2016).

36. Joe Cochran, "Tupperware's Sweet Spot Shifts to Indonesia," New York Times, February 28, 2015, https://www.nytimes.com/2015/03/01/world/asia/tupperwares-sweet-spot-shifts-to-indonesia.html (accessed April 6, 2016).

37. Richard W. Pollay, "Measuring the Cultural Values Manifest in Advertising," Current Issues and Research in Advertising 6 (1983): 71–92.

38. Shan Li, "Barbie Breaks the Mold with Ethnically Diverse Dolls," Los Angeles Times, January 28, 2016, http://www.latimes.com/business/la-fi-mattel-barbie-20160128-story.html (accessed February 5, 2018).

39. Mattel, Barbie Fashionistas, The New Crew, https://barbie.mattel.com/en-us/about/fashionistas.html (accessed February 12, 2018).

40. Mattel Newsroom, "Mattel Unveils Special Edition #ThankYouHeroes Collection from Fisher-Price to Honor Today's Heroes," https://news.mattel.com/news/mattel-unveils-special-edition-thankyouheroes-collection-from-fisher-price-xae-to-honor-today-s-heroes (accessed March 25, 2020).

41. Daniel Goleman, "The Group and the Self: New Focus on a Cultural Rift," New York Times, December 25, 1990, http://www.nytimes.com/1990/12/25/science/the-group-and-the-self-new-focus-on-a-cultural-rift.html (accessed December 4, 2014); Harry C. Triandis, "The Self and Social Behavior in Differing Cultural Contexts," Psychological Review 96 (July 1989): 506; Harry C. Triandis et al., "Individualism and Collectivism: Cross-Cultural Perspectives on Self-Ingroup Relationships," Journal of Personality and Social Psychology 54 (February 1988): 323.

42. Meghan O'Rourke, "The Shift Americans Must Make to Fight the Coronavirus," The Atlantic, March 12, 2020, https://www.theatlantic.com/ideas/archive/2020/03/we-need-isolate-ourselves-during-coronavirus-outbreak/607840/ (accessed May 11, 2020).

43. Getta Anand, "A Yoga Master, the King of 'Baba Cool,' Stretches Out an Empire," New York Times, April 1, 2016, http://www.nytimes.com/2016/04/02/world/asia/a-yoga-master-the-king-of-baba-cool-stretches-out-an-empire.html?smprod=nytcoreiphone&smid=nytcore-iphone-share&_r=0 (accessed April 6, 2016).

44. "Oh, Crap: Audi Mucks Up E-Tron Name in French," AutoBlog, September 13, 2010, http://www.autoblog.com/2010/09/13/oh-crap-audi-mucks-up-e-tron-name-in-french/ (accessed April 6, 2016).

45. Your Dictionary, "Examples of Ethnocentrism," https://examples.yourdictionary.com/examples-of-ethnocentrism.html (accessed May 5, 2020).

46. https://www.merriam-webster.com/dictionary/disruption.

47. Amy Webb, "The 11 Sources of Disruption Every Company Must Monitor," Disruption 2020, MIT Sloan Management Review, pp. 43–48, https://sloanreview.mit.edu/article/the-11-sources-of-disruption-every-company-must-monitor/ (accessed May 28, 2020).

48. Shaun Rein, "Shanghai Disney Must Deliver 'Big' Experience," CNBC, April 11, 2011, http://www.cnbc.com/id/42528017 (accessed April 21, 2014).

49. https://www.shanghaidisneyresort.com/en/destinations/theme-park/.

50. "2020 Top Global Franchise Rankings," Entrepreneur.com, https://www.entrepreneur.com/franchises/topglobal (accessed May 5, 2020).

51. Hyunjoo Jin and Joyce Lee, "Uber, Hyundai Motor Team Up to Develop Electric Air Taxi," Reuters, January 6, 2020, https://www.reuters.com/article/uber-hyundai-motor/uber-hyundai-motor-team-up-to-develop-electric-air-taxi-idUSL4N29B25H (accessed May 4, 2020).

52. United Nations Conference on Trade and Development, "Global Foreign Direct Investment Slides for Third Consecutive Year," June 12, 2019, https://unctad.org/en/pages/newsdetails.aspx?OriginalVersionID=2118 (accessed May 5, 2020).

53. Matt Viser, "Dunkin' Donuts Jumps on Asia's Coffee Craze," Boston Globe, March 30, 2014, https://kimsaebom.wordpress.com/2014/04/24/dunkin-donuts-jumps-on-asias-coffee-craze/#:~:text=SEOUL%20%E2%80%94%20It%20is%20a%20Saturday,as%20if%20at%20a%20nightclub (accessed April 14, 2014).

54. Stefon Walters, "Adaptations in International Marketing," AZCentral, updated August 23, 2019, https://yourbusiness.azcentral.com/adaptations-international-marketing-1558.html (accessed May 5, 2020).

55. Brooks Barnes, "Thomas the Tank Engine's Expanding World," New York Times, March 25, 2016, https://www.nytimes.com/2016/03/26/business/media/thomas-the-tank-engines-expanding-world.html (accessed April 6, 2016).

56. Cameron Dwyer, "10 Brilliant Inventions That Can Change Poor People's Lives," When on Earth.net, https://whenonearth.net/10-brilliant-inventions-that-can-change-poor-peoples-lives/ (accessed May 3, 2020).

57. Owen Guo, "Aiming at China's Armpits: When Foreign Brands Misfire," New York Times, February 2, 2018, https://www.nytimes.com/2018/02/02/business/china-consumers-deodorant.html (accessed March 18, 2018).

58. Paul Reynolds, "Countries Where Buying Starbucks Is the Most and Least Extravagant," Value Penguin, updated August 9, 2019, https://www.valuepenguin.com/countries-where-buying-starbucks-most-and-least-extravagant (accessed May 5, 2020).

59. Walter Pavlo, "State AGs Called to Settle with Purdue Pharma," Forbes, March 19, 2020, https://www.forbes.com/sites/walterpavlo/2020/03/19/state-ags-called-to-settle-with-purdue-pharma/#2fddff5a2faa (accessed May 19, 2020).

60. AT&T.com, "AT&T Inc. Code of Ethics," https://investors.att.com/~/media/Files/A/ATT-IR/governance-documents/att-code-of-ethics-2012.pdf (accessed May 5, 2020).

61. Mark Pastin, "The Surprise Ethics Lesson of Wells Fargo," Huffington Post, January 20, 2017, updated January 21, 2018, https://www.huffingtonpost.com/mark-pastin/the-supriseethics-lesson_b_14041918.html (accessed February 15, 2018).

62. Duff Wilson, "Cigarette Giants in Global Fight on Tighter Rules," New York Times, November 13, 2010, http://www.nytimes.com/2010/11/14/business/global/14smoke.html?_r=1 (accessed April 16, 2014).

63. "Foreign Corrupt Practices Act of 1977 (as Amended)," http://www.usdoj.gov/usao/eousa/foia_reading_room/usam/title9/47mcrm.htm (accessed May 15, 2008).

64. Joan Voight, "Green Is the New Black: Nike among Marketers Pushing Sustainability," Adweek, October 23, 2013, http://www.adweek.com/news/advertising-branding/green-new-blacklevis-nike-among-marketers-pushing-sustainability-153318 (accessed March 10, 2014).

65. Common Dreams, "'Locavorism on the Rise Everywhere': US Consumers Turn to Smaller, Local Farms," May 8, 2012, http://www.commondreams.org/headline/2012/05/08 (accessed April 23, 2014).

66. Kevin McKenzie, "How Do I Sell My Products to BRIC Countries," *Business Vancouver*, May 27, 2013, https://biv.com/article/2013/05/ask-the-experts-how-do-i-sell-my-products-to-bric- (accessed May 22, 2018).

67. Based on "India Population (2020) – Worldometer," Worldometers. Info, accessed July 25, 2020, https://www.worldometers.info/world-population/india-population/; Corinne Abrams, Sarah Nassauer, and Douglas MacMillan, "Walmart Takes on Amazon with $15 Billion Bid for Stake in India's Flipkart," *Wall Street Journal (Eastern Ed.)*, May 4, 2018, https://www.wsj.com/articles/walmart-seeking-to-buy-stake-in-indian-e-commerce-giant-flipkart-1525437107; Michelle Chapman and Anne D'Innocenzio, "Walmart Makes a $16 Billion Bet on India's Booming Economy," 2018, *Associated Press*, May 9, 2018, https://apnews.com/e182e1ccad4e4c19a6f50c472e02c5a3/Walmart-makes-a-$16-billion-bet-on-India's-booming-economy; Sharanya Haridas, "What India Loves and Hates about Walmart Acquiring Flipkart," *Forbes*, May 9, 2018, https://www.forbes.com/sites/sharanyaharidas/2018/05/09/walmart-acquiring-flipkart-16b-india-loves-hates-amazon/#7adbbb45d72d; Isobel Asher Hamilton, "Amazon Plans to Invest $1 Billion in India, and CEO Jeff Bezos Said a US-India Alliance Will Be Most Important This Century," *Business Insider*, January 15, 2020, https://www.businessinsider.com/jeff-bezos-said-amazon-is-investing-1-billion-in-india-2020-1; Nishant Arora, "Amazon, Flipkart May Face Tough Challenge in 2020 as Reliance Firms Up Plans," *Live Mint*, December 29, 2019, https://www.livemint.com/industry/retail/amazon-flipkart-may-face-tough-challenge-in-2020-as-reliance-firms-up-plans-11577594279227.html; Saritha Rai, "Walmart Got a $10 Billion Surprise after Buying Flipkart," *Bloomberg*, July 9, 2019, https://www.bloomberg.com/news/articles/2019-07-09/walmart-payment-unit-is-raising-funds-at-up-to-10-billion-value; Manish Singh, "India Rejects Walmart-Owned Flipkart's Proposed Foray into Food Retail Business," *TechCrunch*, May 31, 2020, https://techcrunch.com/2020/05/31/india-rejects-walmart-owned-flipkarts-proposed-foray-into-food-retail-business/.

3 Strategic Market Planning

Robert Roncska

Meet Robert "Navy Bob" Roncska
▼ A Decision Maker at AdventHealth

Robert "Navy Bob" Roncska, a former U.S. Navy commodore, joined the healthcare industry in 2018 as Executive Director for patient safety for AdventHealth based in Orlando, Florida. After 15 months, he was promoted to the newly created position of Executive Director of high reliability and unit culture, helping oversee more than 48 hospitals and 8,500 licensed beds across seven states. During his career, he was a Commodore of Submarine Squadron Seven in Pearl Harbor, Hawaii, responsible for the safe operation, maintenance, and mission-execution of 10 *Los Angeles*-class nuclear-powered submarines, totaling 1,700 sailors and $25 billion in assets. He retired with the rank of Captain in mid-2018.

Prior to being Commodore, Captain Roncska served as commanding officer of the USS *Texas*, a *Virginia*-class nuclear-powered submarine that was the first-ever submarine of its type certified for arctic operations. Bob led the USS *Texas* under the ice sheet of the North Pole and Arctic Circle, earning it the Best Performing Ship award in the squadron and the highest retention rate in the Pacific Fleet for two consecutive years.

Prior to that, Bob carried the "Nuclear Football," which contained the nuclear launch codes; served as Naval Aide; and was responsible for the safety of the Office of the President under President George W. Bush, who warmly dubbed him "Navy Bob."

Currently, Bob serves on the Florida Safety Council Chamber Board of Directors, alongside executive safety professionals from Walt Disney World, Coca-Cola, Florida Blue, and the University of Central Florida. The Florida Chamber Safety Council was launched by the Florida Chamber of Commerce to serve Florida as an incubator for education, research, and leadership with the goal of making Florida the country's safest state. Captain Roncska was instrumental in the pairing of AdventHealth and the Safety Council to launch a campaign that brings awareness to mental health issues as a result of the COVID-19 pandemic and resources for help.

Bob also serves on IMPower's board of directors. IMPower is a leading Florida-based, not-for-profit organization focusing on mental health, substance misuse, and child well-being. IMPower offers personal attention, counseling, assistance, and inspiration to those in need and serves the community by providing outpatient mental health services, substance misuse treatment, telepsychiatry, foster care and adoption service, prevention programs, and residential youth support. During his tenure on IMPower's board, he has helped them organize their capital campaign and facilitated a substantial grant from AdventHealth to increase IMPower's ability to provide mental health programs for its young and vulnerable clients.

Bob's personal belief that "you either get better or get worse, you never stay the same," has propelled him to continue his personal growth journey. He is now pursuing an Executive Doctorate of Business Administration at Crummer Graduate School of Business at Rollins College. He has been married to his wife, Stephanie, for more than 28 years and has two children, Sophia and Zachary. They live in Winter Park, Florida.

What do I do when I'm not working:

I enjoy physical activities and strongly believe in the health benefits I get from being active. In my early years, I played football, wrestled, participated in track and field, and rowed crew. As an adult, I began running marathons and eventually started to do triathlons and have successfully completed two Ironman triathlons. Although not currently competing in triathlons, I still bike and run almost every day.

First job out of school:

I joined the Nuclear Navy as an Ensign on my college graduation day. I was assigned as the nuclear chemistry and radiological division officer on the USS *West Virginia* (SSBN 736) Gold crew, a ballistic missile nuclear submarine stationed in Kings Bay, Georgia.

Career high:

My career high was commanding my own submarine, the USS *Texas* (SSN-775). I took a low-performing submarine to the number one ranked ship in our squadron, with the highest retention rate in the Pacific Fleet. I particularly enjoyed our time performing Arctic operations in which we certified the first *Virginia*-class submarine for such operations and conducting numerous missions vital to National Security. Although I was a top-ranked commanding officer, the true high was bonding with my crew as if they were my own family and watching the sailors grow and succeed.

My motto to live by:

"Good ideas are not adopted automatically. They must be driven into practice with courageous impatience."
– Hyman Rickover

What drives me:

A genuine and intrinsic desire to help people and to pay it forward.

My management style:

I believe strongly in the Leader Membership Exchange Theory. Building relationships and creating a family with my teams is the most effective and fulfilling way to lead. Instead of focusing on myself, I focus on the individual and team relationships.

Don't do this when interviewing with me:

Speak disrespectfully of others.

My pet peeve:

Blaming others for failures and not taking personal responsibility.

Here's my problem...

Real **People**, Real **Choices**

American businesses and governments—along with their long-term strategic goals—suddenly ground to a halt as COVID-19 cases sharply rose in the U.S. during the first months of 2020.

AdventHealth, a healthcare system of 48 hospitals, 80,000 employees, serving over 5 million patients per year, had planned to unveil its 2025 and 2030 vision for the company at an executive conference in Orlando, Florida. But with the pandemic rapidly spreading, it was forced to cancel the conference and put many of its long-term strategic goals on hold.

AdventHealth had been on a continuous journey to make its hospitals as safe as possible, driven both by its mission "to extend the healing ministry of Christ" as a Seventh-day Adventist–sponsored organization and its strategic goals as a modern healthcare system. The majority of its hospitals receive "A" grades for patient safety by the Leapfrog Group, a third-party hospital grading system. But AdventHealth didn't want to just make the grade. In combination with its mission and strategy, AdventHealth wanted a clinical DNA and culture that prized safety.

Part of this strategic desire stemmed from the 1999 landmark report, "To Err Is Human: Building a Safer Health Care System," which revealed that an estimated 44,000 to 98,000 people die each year from preventable medical errors. The report forced the entire industry to take a hard look at its managerial practices and culture.

Amy C. Edmondson, a leadership and management professor at Harvard Business School, researched the issue and discovered that healthcare teams with a culture of "psychological safety" welcomed open discussion of their medical errors. The discussion led to collaboration, addressing the underlying issues, and successfully preventing future harm. Whereas one nurse might hide a medical error for fear of getting in trouble, for example, another nurse might report a medical error immediately because "you're never afraid to tell the nurse manager." In other words, the second nurse had psychological safety.

As Edmondson said in a *Harvard Business Review* podcast in 2019: "Psychological safety is about candor, being direct . . . being able to say, 'I made a mistake,' and being willing to ask for help when you're in over your head." In psychologically safe workplaces, results and performances improved, and not just in healthcare.

The nuclear Navy embraced these and other safety principles through its "Five Principles of High Reliability," which were first instituted in the 1950s by Admiral Hyman Rickover. Since that time, the Navy has operated more than 200 mobile nuclear reactors underwater for a combined 6,500 years of operation without a single Reactor Accident, making the nuclear Navy the industry gold standard for high reliability. In 2018, AdventHealth hired U.S. Navy nuclear submarine Captain Bob Roncska after he retired from the military to bring the safety secrets of the Navy and promote a culture of highly reliable and safe hospital units to AdventHealth as part of its strategic goals.

After 15 months with the company, Bob was promoted to support hospital unit culture for the entire system, overseeing a team of safety officers as well as a new project that pioneered an innovative communication technology that included a digital touchscreen. These screens and their additional educational component on safe cultures were being rolled out to 108 AdventHealth hospital units the year COVID-19 hit. It was hefty strategic work for the company that suddenly floundered as all AdventHealth executive teams pivoted to deal with COVID-19 crisis.

AdventHealth's strategic goals for improving unit culture were put on hold. Bob and his team knew they had to redirect their focus. How could he and his team make the best use of their time to advance strategy as the company managed the crisis? If they continued with the unit culture work, how could they ensure they didn't get in the way and distract from the crisis management work? Did Bob and his team need to drop what they were doing to see whether they could help too?

As the new Executive Director of high reliability and unit culture for all AdventHealth, Bob was responsible for successfully carrying out his and AdventHealth's strategic duties at a time when his fellow leaders were preoccupied with an unprecedented dilemma.

Bob considered his **options** 1·2·3

1 Option
Do nothing. Relatively new to the company and certainly not expected to continue his work, which involved meetings with hospital leaders throughout the organization, Bob could tell his teams to rest during the pandemic and focus on the projects already launched. Indeed, in many cases, leadership requested he pause his work to allow hospital units and clinical leaders to prepare for a potential surge of patients, which was when demand for COVID-19 services would overwhelm the hospital's capacity and supplies on hand. However, by waiting, Bob might lose precious time and momentum advancing the unit culture project, a project that was still, if not more, vital to the safety of the hospital. If and when AdventHealth deemed it safe to begin resuming normal operations, it could be difficult to restart his work.

2 Option
Bob could get partially involved with the crisis. With his leadership experience operating nuclear reactors underwater with a submarine crew in the Navy, he was well-qualified to speak on safety—an important issue during the COVID-19 pandemic. Bob could leverage his existing team and knowledge of clinical operations to the company's benefit as it dealt with COVID-19. Hospital leaders who might need an extra hand could also tap Bob and his team for their heavy workloads. One potential drawback was that his strategic work, which the company hired him to do, would continue to flounder. While taking solace in helping others handle an unprecedented emergency, Bob's main team and the company's strategic vision would continue to get sidelined and get confused with crisis

management. AdventHealth's important work, and the safe and quality care of its millions of annual patients, could be affected.

3 Option
Bob could go all in. He could use the communication tools and education intended to develop psychological safety in the hospital unit to support teams dealing with the COVID-19 crisis instead. This way, he would further the work the team was already doing with the communication technology that AdventHealth was implementing and advance unit culture, while also helping the hospital system with COVID-19 in an innovative fashion. When AdventHealth pivoted back to normal operations, hospital leaders throughout the system would be familiar with AdventHealth and Bob's strategic work and mission. Their familiarity would make their engagement and buy-in easier as he continued his work. But Bob still risked getting in the way as leadership teams worked around the clock to plan and react to the pandemic. If his project wasn't helpful, it could hinder both the company's handling of the crisis and the strategic work AdventHealth wanted to achieve.

Now, put yourself in Bob's shoes. Which option would you choose, and why?

You Choose

Which **Option** would you choose, and **why**?
☐ **Option 1**   ☐ **Option 2**   ☐ **Option 3**

3.1 Business Planning: Compose the Big Picture

OBJECTIVE
Explain business planning and its three levels.

As you read in the chapter's opening vignette, AdventHealth promoted Bob Roncska to develop and execute an important new plan for organizational cultural enhancement for its entire chain of hospitals. But no sooner had he started the position than—zap—the COVID-19 crisis hit. And what industry was more disrupted by COVID-19 than healthcare? Probably none. So what happens when unexpected roadblocks impact great plans? Well, that's why firms need well-trained *business* students like you—plans are not static, changes that impact a plan happen with great regularity (usually not as dramatically as COVID-19, though), and as former U.S. President and five-star General Dwight Eisenhower famously said: "Plans are nothing; planning is everything."

The wisdom of Eisenhower's simple statement for marketers (and everybody who does planning) is that a *plan* is merely a static narrative captured on paper or in bytes. *Planning*, on the other hand, is an organic, changeable, and ever-evolving *process* that must be managed with great skill. This is a book about marketing; hence, much of our discussion of planning in this chapter centers on *market* planning. But note that the chapter title is "Strategic Market Planning" and that extra word *strategic* (a derivative of the word *strategy*) is actually really important. **Strategy** is the execution of the elements of a plan based on goals and objectives to bring about a desired future. It is often said that strategy is both an art and a science, and as you read about the process of planning in this chapter, you will pick up on how important it is to be both creative and analytical in planning.

Careful planning enables a firm to speak in a clear voice in the marketplace so that customers understand what the firm is and what it has to offer that competitors don't—especially

strategy
The execution of the elements of a plan based on goals and objectives to bring about a desired future.

as it decides how to create value for customers, clients, partners, and society at large. In this chapter, you will experience the power of effective business planning—and especially market planning—and lay the groundwork for your own capability to do successful planning.

We think this process is really important. That's why we're starting with a discussion about what planners do and the questions they need to ask to be sure they keep their companies and products on course. In many ways, developing great business planning is like taking an awesome digital photo with your smartphone (maybe a selfie?)—hence the title of this section. The metaphor works because success in photography is built on capturing the right information in the lens of your camera, positioning the image correctly, and snapping the picture you'll need to set things in motion. A business plan is a lot like that.

The knowledge you gain from going through a formal planning process is worth its weight in gold. Without market planning as an ongoing activity in a business, there's no real way to know where you want the firm to go, how it will get there, or even if it is on the right or wrong track right now. There's nothing like a clear road map when you're lost in the wilderness. And speaking of road maps, we even include a handy guide as a supplement at the end of this chapter that shows you step-by-step how to build a marketing plan and where to find the information throughout the book to be able to do it. This road map will be highly useful as you make your way through the book, keeping the big-picture viewpoint of marketing in mind no matter which chapter you're reading.

What exactly is **business planning**? Put simply, it's an ongoing process of decision making that guides the firm in both the short term and the long term. Planning identifies and builds on a firm's strengths, and it helps managers at all levels make informed decisions in a changing business environment. *Planning* means that an organization develops objectives before it takes action. In large firms like IBM, Ford, PepsiCo, or Amazon that operate in many markets, planning is a complex process involving many people from different areas of the company's operations. At a small business like Mac's Diner in your hometown, however, planning is quite different in scope. Yet regardless of firm size or industry, great planning can only increase the chances of success.

In the sections that follow, we'll look at the different steps in an organization's planning. First, we'll see how managers develop a **business plan** to specify the decisions that guide the entire organization or its business units. Then we'll examine the entire strategic planning process and the stages in that process that lead to the development and implementation of a **marketing plan**—a process and resulting document that describes the marketing environment, outlines the marketing objectives and strategies, and identifies how the company will implement and control the strategies embedded in the plan. To keep the journey through the process smooth, we'll take it a step at a time through three distinct levels of planning.

The Three Levels of Business Planning

We all know in general what planning is—we plan a vacation or a great Saturday night party. Some of us even plan how we're going to study and get our assignments completed without stressing out at the last minute. When businesses plan, the process is more complex. As Figure 3.1 shows, planning occurs at three levels: strategic, functional, and operational. The top level is big-picture stuff, like a picture of a sweeping landscape. In contrast, the bottom level specifies the "nuts-and-bolts" actions the firm will need to take to get there, more like a close-up photo.

First-Level Planning

Strategic planning is the managerial decision process that matches the firm's resources (such as its financial assets and workforce) and capabilities (the things it is able to do well because of its expertise and experience) to its market opportunities for long-term growth. In a strategic plan, top management—usually the chief executive officer (CEO), president, and other top executives—define the firm's purpose and specify what the firm hopes to achieve over

business planning
An ongoing process of making decisions that guides the firm both in the short term and in the long term.

business plan
A plan that includes the decisions that guide the entire organization.

marketing plan
A document that describes the marketing environment, outlines the marketing objectives and strategy, and identifies how the company will implement and control the strategies embedded in the plan.

strategic planning
A managerial decision process that matches an organization's resources and capabilities to its market opportunities for long-term growth.

Figure 3.1 *Snapshot* | Levels of Business Planning

During planning, an organization determines its objectives and then develops courses of action to accomplish them. In larger firms, planning takes place at the strategic, functional, and operational levels.

Strategic Planning	**Functional (Market)** Planning	**Operational** Planning
Planning done by corporate and/or SBU-level management 1. Define the mission 2. Evaluate the internal and external environment 3. Set organizational or SBU objectives 4. Establish the business portfolio (if applicable) 5. Develop growth strategies	Planning done by top functional-level management, such as the firm's chief marketing officer (CMO) 1. Perform a situation analysis 2. Set marketing objectives 3. Develop marketing strategies 4. Implement and control the marketing plan	Planning done by supervisory managers 1. Develop action plans to implement the marketing plan 2. Use marketing metrics to monitor how the plan is working

the next five years or so. For example, AdventHealth's strategic plan may set an objective to decrease medical errors by 10 percent each year over the next five years. In recent years, partly due to more aggressive entry into online retailing by firms such as Walmart and Target, Amazon publicly has had a goal to achieve more physical touchpoints with customers (partly for product pickup and partly for convenient product returns) and also to increase their grocery business. Voilà! Suddenly they acquired Whole Foods and also established a return goods relationship with Kohl's, which kills the proverbial two birds with one stone.[1]

It is important to note that for larger firms, like Procter & Gamble (P&G), Samsung, General Electric, and many others, strategic planning takes place both at the corporate level and also at the level of individual and unique organizational areas of focus. These are called **strategic business units (SBUs)**, which are individual units within the firm that operate like separate businesses, with each having its own mission, business objectives, resources, managers, and competitors. For example, P&G has amazingly diverse product groups, including separate businesses in disposable baby diapers, laundry products, paper products, feminine care, razors and blades, cleaning products, oral care, and others. While planning is certainly done at the overall P&G corporate level, much of the real street planning is done by the SBUs because the markets and competitors are so different between them.[2]

strategic business units (SBUs)
Individual units within the firm that operate like separate businesses, with each having its own mission, business objectives, resources, managers, and competitors.

Second-Level Planning

The next level of planning is **functional planning**. This level gets its name because it involves the various functional areas of the firm, such as marketing, finance, and human resources. Vice presidents or functional directors of these areas usually manage the process of functional planning. We refer to the functional planning that marketers do as **market planning**. The person in charge of such planning may have the title of director of marketing, vice president of marketing, chief marketing officer, or something similar. Such marketers might set an objective to gain 40 percent of a particular market by successfully introducing three new products during the coming year. This objective is part of a marketing plan. Market planning typically includes both a broad three- to five-year marketing plan to support the firm's strategic plan and a detailed annual plan for the coming year. Each of P&G's SBUs have a marketing plan for the overall product category (razors and blades, for example) but also separate marketing plans for products within the category that are targeted to very different markets (for example, men's and women's shaving products). The planning process is led by each SBU's head of marketing and supported by the SBU's marketing team. These SBU marketing plans must make sense within the context of P&G's overall marketing

functional planning
A decision process that concentrates on developing detailed plans for strategies and tactics for the short term, supporting an organization's long-term strategic plan.

market planning
The functional planning marketers do. Market planning typically includes both a broad three- to five-year marketing plan to support the firm's strategic plan and a detailed annual plan for the coming year.

plan—that is, an SBU's marketing plan must not create conflict or inconsistencies with the overall marketing plan for the SBU.

Third-Level Planning

Still farther down the planning ladder are the managers who are responsible for planning at a third level called **operational planning**. In marketing, these include people such as sales managers, marketing communication managers, brand managers, and market research managers. This level of planning focuses on the day-to-day execution of the functional plans and includes detailed annual, semiannual, or quarterly plans. Operational plans might show exactly how many units of a product a salesperson needs to sell per month or how many TV commercials the firm will place on certain networks during a season. At the operational planning level, a P&G manager may develop plans for a social media marketing campaign to promote a new product pre-release via Instagram.

> **operational planning**
> A decision process that focuses on developing detailed plans for day-to-day activities that carry out an organization's functional plans.

Of course, marketing managers don't just sit in their offices dreaming up plans without any concern for the rest of the organization. Put more directly—market planning doesn't take place in a vacuum! Even though we've described each layer separately, *all business planning is an integrated activity.* This means that at a complex organization like AdventHealth that has 48 hospitals and 80,000 employees and serves over 5 million patients per year, strategic, functional, and operational plans must work together for the benefit of the whole, always within the context of the organization's mission and objectives. So planners at all levels must consider good principles of accounting, the financial well-being of the organization, and the requirements for staffing and human resource management—that is, they must keep the big picture in mind even as they plan for their little corner of the organization's world.

In the next sections, we'll further explore planning at each of the three levels that we've just introduced.

3.2 Strategic Planning: Frame the Picture

OBJECTIVE
Describe the steps in strategic planning.

Many large firms realize it's risky to put all their eggs in one basket and rely on only one product, so they have become multiproduct companies with self-contained divisions organized around product lines or brands.

In firms with multiple SBUs (as illustrated previously by P&G), the first step in strategic planning is for top management to establish a mission for the entire corporation. Top managers then evaluate the internal and external environments of the business and set corporate-level objectives that guide decision making within each individual SBU. In firms that are not large enough to have separate SBUs, strategic planning simply takes place at the overall firm level. Whether or not a firm has SBUs, the process of strategic planning is basically the same. Let's look at the planning steps in a bit more detail, guided by Figure 3.2.

Step 1: Define the Mission, Vision, and Values

Ideally, top management's first step in the strategic planning stage is to answer questions such as the following:

- What business are we in?
- What do we believe in as an organization?
- What customers should we serve?
- How should we develop the firm's capabilities and focus its efforts?

Figure 3.2 *Process* | Steps in Strategic Planning

The strategic planning process includes a series of steps that results in the development of growth strategies.

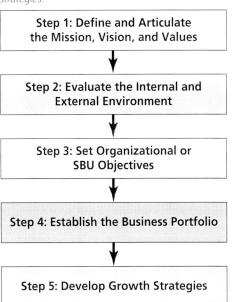

Step 1: Define and Articulate the Mission, Vision, and Values
Step 2: Evaluate the Internal and External Environment
Step 3: Set Organizational or SBU Objectives
Step 4: Establish the Business Portfolio
Step 5: Develop Growth Strategies

mission (or **purpose**)
A firm's core reason for being.

mission statement
A formal statement in an organization's strategic plan that describes the overall purpose of the organization and what it intends to achieve in terms of its customers, products, and resources.

vision
What a firm aspires to do or be in the future.

vision statement
A firm's articulation of its vision.

organizational values
The core attributes valued by the firm that most closely reflect the firm's culture.

situation analysis
An assessment of a firm's internal and external environments.

internal environment
The controllable elements inside an organization, including its people, its facilities, and how it does things that influence the operations of the organization.

In many firms, the answers to questions such as these become the lead items in the organization's strategic plan. A firm's **mission** is basically its purpose—its core reason for being. It follows logically that a **mission statement** is a formal document that describes the organization's overall purpose and what it intends to achieve in terms of its customers, products, and resources. For example, P&G's mission statement (which they call a "purpose statement"), reads: "We will provide branded products and services of superior quality and value that improve the lives of the world's consumers, now and for generations to come. As a result, consumers will reward us with leadership sales, profit and value creation, allowing our people, our shareholders and the communities in which we live and work to prosper."[3] The ideal mission statement is not too broad, too narrow, or too shortsighted. A mission that is too broad will not provide adequate focus for the organization. It doesn't do much good to claim, "We are in the business of making high-quality products" or "Our business is keeping customers happy," because it is hard to find a firm that doesn't make these claims. It's also important to remember that the need for a clear mission statement applies to virtually any type of organization.

You may be interested to know that for most firms, the mission statement is anything but a secret from the marketplace. That is, smart firms make their mission statements very visible to customers and other stakeholders as a way to trumpet the good work they do. Southwest has had a good run positioning itself as a "fun" airline. Their purpose (mission) is to "Connect people to what's important in their lives through friendly, reliable, and low-cost air travel." It's hard to argue that this isn't what Southwest does. Mission statements reflect what firms do now, but a **vision** is what a firm aspires to do or be in the future. This is articulated in a **vision statement**, and for Southwest it is "To be the world's most loved, most efficient, and most profitable airline." Pretty audacious, yes. But a vision is meant to be aspirational, and given Southwest's long success record, don't count them out for achieving that vision. Finally, **organizational values** reflect core attributes valued by the firm that most closely reflect its culture. P&G, for example, articulates its core values as integrity, leadership, ownership, passion for winning, and trust. These elements play a guiding role in how P&G does business including how they approach strategic planning.[4]

In Chapter 9, you will learn quite a lot about branding—for now, suffice it to say that brands, in order to be perceived by customers as authentic, must embody their organization's mission, vision, and values.

Southwest Airlines has always been very focused on hiring and developing employees who reflect the "Southwest Spirit" to customers. Anyone who has flown on Southwest can attest to the fact that the atmosphere is lively and fun, and flight attendants are likely to do most any crazy stunt—bowling in the aisle or serenading the captain and first officer (and passengers) with a favorite tune. One of our favorites is a guy who does galloping horse hooves and neighing sounds during takeoff and landing. For Southwest, a real strength—one that's hard for the competition to crack—lies in this employee spirit.

Step 2: Evaluate the Internal and External Environment

The second step in strategic planning is to assess the firm's internal and external environments. We refer to this process as a **situation analysis**, but it's also sometimes called *environmental analysis*, or a *business review*. The analysis includes a discussion of the firm's internal environment, which can identify a firm's strengths and weaknesses, as well as the external environment in which the firm does business so the firm can identify opportunities and threats.

By **internal environment** we mean all the controllable elements inside a firm that influence how well the firm operates. Internal strengths may lie in the firm's technologies. What is the firm able to do well that other firms would find difficult to duplicate? What patents does it hold? A firm's physical facilities can be an important strength or weakness, as can its level of financial stability, its relationships with suppliers, its corporate reputation, its ability to produce consistently high-quality products, and its ownership of strong brands in the marketplace. Internal elements include a firm's structure, organizational culture, and all sorts of assets—financial and otherwise.

Internal strengths and weaknesses often reside in the firm's employees—the firm's *human and intellectual capital*. What skills do the employees have? What kind of training have they had? Are they loyal to the firm? Do they feel a sense of ownership? Has the firm been able to attract top researchers and good decision makers?

Recall from Chapter 2 that the *external environment* consists of elements outside the firm that may affect it either positively or negatively. For AdventHealth and almost all organizations really, the external environment for today's businesses is global, so marketers engaged in planning must consider elements such as the economy, competition, technology, law, ethics, and sociocultural trends. Unlike elements of the internal environment that management can control to a large degree, the firm can't directly control these external factors, so management must respond to them through its planning process.

The pandemic injected a host of uncontrollable elements into the strategic planning process.

In Chapter 2, you read about the various elements of the external environment in which marketing takes place, within the context of today's global enterprise. In particular, you got a strong sense of how the COVID-19 global crisis has impacted marketing generally. You gained an appreciation of why it is important for you to be aware that opportunities and threats can come from any part of the external environment. On the one hand, trends or currently unserved customer needs may provide opportunities for growth. On the other hand, if changing customer needs or buying patterns mean customers are turning away from a firm's products, it's a signal of possible danger or threats down the road. Even successful firms have to change to keep up with external environmental pressures. Prior to the global pandemic, the U.S. healthcare sector was quoted as representing around $3.5 trillion in spending, accounting for about 18 percent of U.S. GDP. Obviously environmental elements have a major impact on this sector, and as one of the largest providers in the sector, AdventHealth must be highly skilled at monitoring potential trends in the external environment, assessing the impact of those trends, and developing and executing plans to maximize their organizational effectiveness within the dynamic environment.

What is the outcome of an analysis of a firm's internal and external environments? Marketers often synthesize their findings from a situation analysis into a format called a **SWOT analysis**. This document summarizes the ideas from the situation analysis. It provides a clear focus on the meaningful strengths (S) and weaknesses (W) in the firm's internal environment and on the opportunities (O) and threats (T) coming from outside the firm (the external environment). A SWOT analysis enables a firm to develop strategies that make use of what the firm does best in seizing opportunities for growth while at the same time avoiding external threats that might hurt the firm's sales and profits.

SWOT analysis
An analysis of an organization's strengths and weaknesses and the opportunities and threats in its external environment.

Step 3: Set Organizational or SBU Objectives

After they construct a mission statement, top management translates it into *organizational* or *SBU objectives*. These goals are a direct outgrowth of the mission statement and broadly identify what the firm hopes to accomplish within the general time frame of the firm's long-range business plan. If the firm is big enough to have separate SBUs, each unit will have its own objectives relevant to its operations.

To be effective, objectives need to be *specific, measurable* (so firms can tell whether they've met them), *attainable*, and *sustainable over time*. Attainability is especially important—firms that establish "pie-in-the-sky" objectives they can't realistically obtain can create frustration for their employees (who work hard but get no satisfaction of

The pandemic pushed some technologies, like Zoom and other videoconferencing platforms, to the forefront of the new normal.

accomplishment) and other stakeholders in the firm, such as vendors and shareholders who are affected when the firm doesn't meet its objectives. That a firm's objectives are sustainable over time is also critical—usually there's little advantage to investing in attaining an objective for only a very short term. This often happens when a firm underestimates the likelihood that a competitor will come to market with a better offering. Without some assurance that an objective is sustainable over time, the financial return on an investment likely will not be positive.

Objectives may relate to revenue and sales, profitability, the firm's standing in the market, return on investment, productivity, product development, customer satisfaction, social responsibility, and many other attributes. To ensure measurability, marketers increasingly try to state objectives in numerical terms. For example, a firm might have as an objective a 10 percent increase in profitability over the next fiscal year. It could reach this objective by increasing productivity, by reducing costs, or by selling off an unprofitable division. Or it might meet this 10 percent objective by developing new products, investing in new technologies, or entering a new market.

The entire videoconferencing industry was put in a position of having to ramp up capabilities and bandwidth very quickly when business travel shut down during the initial months of the COVID-19 crisis in 2020. Zoom, WebEx, Microsoft Teams, and other providers had plans in place for 2020 that included objectives that were developed in early 2019 without any inkling of what was to come. In such cases, there are two characteristics that separate winners from losers in market planning. The first is the ability to be a **nimble organization**, which in business means that a firm has the culture, leadership, and operational capability to change very rapidly as external conditions demand. Closely related to the strategic concept of *nimble* is the ability for a firm to pivot successfully once things change. A **strategic pivot** is the operationalization of a rapid demand to change the business model, business direction, product line, or market focus, including the ability to rapidly increase output, to satisfy unexpected new and/or different demand. In early 2020, literally within a few weeks, the videoconferencing providers had to rapidly adapt not only to increased volume but also to widely varying new uses of their technologies, which required a nimble approach and a number of strategic pivots to ensure demand for the now-critical virtual communication channels was fulfilled.[5]

Step 4: Establish the Business Portfolio

For companies with several different SBUs, strategic planning includes making decisions about how to best allocate resources across these businesses to ensure growth for the total organization. Each SBU has its own focus within the firm's overall strategic plan, and each has its own target market and strategies to reach its objectives. Just like an independent business, each SBU is a separate *profit center* within the larger corporation—that is, each SBU within the firm is responsible for its own costs, revenues, and profits. These items can be accounted for separately for each SBU.

Just as we call the collection of different stocks an investor owns a *portfolio*, the range of different businesses that a large firm operates is its **business portfolio**. These different businesses usually represent different product lines, each of which operates with its own budget and management. Having a diversified business portfolio reduces the firm's dependence on one product line or one group of customers. For example, the travel restrictions and soured economy in 2020 meant that consumers didn't travel as much, making a bad year for Disney theme park attendance and cruises, but Disney is very diversified and their leaders found that some of the losses were made up by stay-at-homers who watch Disney's TV networks or stream Disney shows and who purchase Mickey Mouse collectibles from the Disney website.

nimble organization
A firm with the culture, leadership, and operational capability to change very rapidly as external conditions demand.

strategic pivot
The operationalization of a rapid demand to change a firm's business model, business direction, product line, or market focus, including the ability to rapidly increase output, to satisfy unexpected new and/or different demand.

business portfolio
The group of different products or brands owned by an organization and characterized by different income-generating and growth capabilities.

Historically, Disney Cruise Line has been an important element in The Walt Disney Company's business portfolio.

Portfolio analysis is a tool management uses to assess the potential of a firm's business portfolio. It helps management decide which of its current SBUs should receive more—or less—of the firm's resources and which of its SBUs are most consistent with the firm's overall mission. There are a host of portfolio models available. To illustrate how one works, let's examine the especially popular model the Boston Consulting Group (BCG) developed: the **BCG growth–market share matrix**.

The BCG model focuses on determining the potential of a firm's existing SBUs to generate cash that the firm can then use to invest in other businesses. Note that when we say SBU, in many cases this represents broad product groups. So as in the P&G example earlier, one might analyze razors and blades (like their Gillette line) in one BCG category and cleaning products (like Swiffer) in another. The BCG matrix in Figure 3.3 shows that the vertical axis represents the attractiveness of the market: the *market growth rate*. Even though the figure shows "high" and "low" as measurements, marketers might ask whether the total market for the SBU's products is growing at a rate of 10, 50, 100, or 200 percent annually.

The horizontal axis in Figure 3.3 shows the SBU's current strength in the market through its relative market share. Here, marketers would look at the ratio of an SBU's share to that of the rival in the third-ranked market position. Combining the two axes creates four quadrants representing four different types of SBUs. Each quadrant of the BCG grid uses a symbol to describe business units that fall within a certain range for market growth rate and market share. Let's take a closer look at each cell in the grid:

- **Stars** are SBUs with products that have dominant market shares in high-growth markets. Because the SBU has a dominant share of the market, stars generate large revenues, but they also require large amounts of funding to keep up with production and promotion demands. Hence, stars need investment capital from other parts of the business because they don't generate it themselves. Of course, any profits generated directly by stars presumably would be reinvested right back in the star. For example, in recent years, Disney has viewed its studios as a star and has been able to generate significant revenues from its acquisition of Lucasfilm nearly a decade ago and the intellectual property within the *Star Wars* universe. *Star Wars Episode IX: The Rise of Skywalker* took in about $1.1 billion worldwide on a near-record budget of about $275 million![6]—not a bad return on investment for "the Mouse"! The key question for Disney is, will this "really" be the last of the *Star Wars* saga as was publicly announced? We'll let you decide if you believe it is or isn't!

- **Cash cows** have dominant market shares in low-growth-potential markets. Because there's not much opportunity for new companies, competitors don't often enter the market. At the same time, the SBU is well established and enjoys a high market share that the firm can sustain with minimal funding. Firms usually milk cash cows of their profits to fund the growth of other SBUs. Of course, if the firm's objective is to increase revenues, having too many cash cows with little or no growth potential can become a liability. For Disney, its theme parks unit fits into the cash cow category in that global sales have been basically steady for an extended period of time. This cash cow status could spring over to star status now that the Star Wars: Galaxy's Edge theme parks are operational at both their Orlando and Anaheim facilities. However, for Disney these in-person experiential elements of their

portfolio analysis
A management tool for evaluating a firm's business mix and assessing the potential of an organization's strategic business units.

BCG growth–market share matrix
A portfolio analysis model developed by the Boston Consulting Group that assesses the potential of successful products to generate cash that a firm can then use to invest in new products.

stars
SBUs with products that have dominant market shares in high-growth markets.

cash cows
SBUs with dominant market shares in low-growth-potential markets.

Figure 3.3 *Snapshot* | BCG Matrix

The Boston Consulting Group's (BCG) growth–share matrix is one way a firm can examine its portfolio of different SBUs and their related products. By categorizing SBUs as stars, cash cows, question marks, or dogs, the matrix helps managers make good decisions about how the firm should grow.

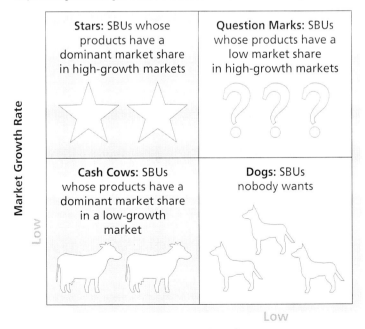

Source: Product Portfolio Matrix, © 1970, The Boston Consulting Group.

When The Walt Disney Company acquired Marvel Comics, the idea was to add another star to its BCG product portfolio.

question marks
SBUs with low market shares in fast-growth markets.

dogs
SBUs with small shares of slow-growth markets. They are businesses that offer specialized products in limited markets that are not likely to grow quickly.

business are totally dependent on an individual's willingness and ability to travel to them, which of course was disrupted phenomenally by the COVID-19 crisis of 2020.

- **Question marks**—sometimes called *problem children*—are SBUs with low market shares in fast-growth markets. When a business unit is a question mark, the key issue is whether through investment and new strategy it can be transformed into a star. For example, the firm could pump more money into marketing the product and hope that relative market share will improve. But the problem with question marks is that—despite investment—many times they make a beeline straight into the annals of market failures. Hence, the firm must carefully evaluate the likelihood that investment in a question mark will pay off—otherwise, it may find itself "throwing good money after bad" if it gains nothing but a negative cash flow and disappointment. For Disney, as with many retailers, its brick-and-mortar operation falls into the question-mark category because its performance has softened over recent years. Like most retail operators today, the online version of the Disney Store provides a better growth trajectory than the four-walls version.

- **Dogs** command small shares of slow-growth markets. They are businesses that offer specialized products in limited markets that are not likely to grow quickly. When possible, large firms may sell off their dogs to smaller firms that may be able to nurture them—or they may take the SBU's products off the market. Disney, being a savvy strategic planner, over a decade ago apparently identified its Miramax film studio as a long-term dog (to Pluto and Goofy: no pun intended) because they sold it off after a 17-year involvement with that studio.[7] Interestingly, more recently ESPN has shown signs of significant underperformance on profits due to pressures throughout the cable television industry. So far, Disney is hanging onto ESPN, but many have speculated in recent years about a potential divestment.[8]

Like Disney, AdventHealth could use the BCG matrix to evaluate its various offerings to make important decisions about where to invest for future growth. It would look across its product lines and the markets in which it operates to assess the market growth rate and relative market share, determine the degree to which each has greater or lesser potential to serve, and decide which to invest further in as well as what other products and markets could be developed. More on product and market development in the next section! One area of Disney's product portfolio that has gone from a star to a potential dog in rapid order is the Disney Cruise line business. Post-global pandemic, whether people will be generally willing to venture out on big boats for long periods of time at the same level as in the past remains to be seen.

Step 5: Develop Growth Strategies

Although the BCG matrix can help managers decide which SBUs they should invest in for growth, it doesn't tell them much about *how* to make that growth happen. Should the growth of an SBU come from finding new customers, from developing new variations of the product, or from some other growth strategy? Part of strategic planning at the SBU level entails evaluating growth strategies.

Marketers use the product–market growth matrix, shown in Figure 3.4, to analyze different growth strategies. The vertical axis in

Figure 3.4 *Snapshot* | Product–Market Growth Matrix

Marketers use the product–market growth matrix to analyze different growth strategies.

Product Emphasis

	Existing **Products**	**Products**
Existing Markets	**Market penetration strategy** • Seek to increase sales of existing products to existing markets	**Product development strategy** • Create growth by selling new products in existing markets
Markets	**Market development strategy** • Introduce existing products to new markets	**Diversification strategy** • Emphasize both new products and new markets to achieve growth

Market Emphasis

the matrix represents opportunities for growth either in existing markets or in new markets. The horizontal axis considers whether the firm would be better off putting its resources into existing products or whether it should acquire new products. The matrix provides four fundamental marketing strategies: market penetration, market development, product development, and diversification:

McDonald's has reenergized its marketing strategy, partly by doubling down on automation.

- **Market penetration strategies** seek to increase sales of existing products to existing markets, such as current users, nonusers, and users of competing brands within a market. Venerable McDonald's, while certainly quite financially successful, has been losing market share to other options for most of the last decade. Everyone in the QSR (quick-service restaurant) industry, from Taco Bell to Popeyes, has taken a proverbial bite out of McDonald's business. But recently, new top management at the golden arches has energized substantial growth by executing what it calls its "Velocity Growth Plan." You've probably noticed the changes, as this business plan has been progressing steadily toward the three key components of its strategy: technology, delivery, and experience of the future (EOTF) restaurants. The tech component includes focus on its global mobile app, self-order kiosks, and digital menu boards. These elements, coupled with the fact that basically every U.S. store has been or will be remodeled or totally razed and rebuilt, has sparked a major re-penetration of "Micky D's" in the very challenging QSR marketplace.[9]

market penetration strategies
Growth strategies designed to increase sales of existing products to current customers, nonusers, and users of competitive brands in served markets.

- **Market development strategies** introduce existing products to new markets. This strategy can mean expanding into a new geographic area, or it may mean reaching new customer segments within an existing geographic market. Cuba is a major potential market for all sorts of U.S. products and services, and it sits just 90 miles from Miami. While growth into the market has been hampered recently by general cutbacks in the airline industry, U.S. airlines are running regular service into Havana from several key Florida cities for the first time in nearly 60 years. These routes have high potential for growth if tensions ease and commerce becomes more normalized over the next several years.[10]

market development strategies
Growth strategies that introduce existing products to new markets.

- **Product development strategies** create growth by selling new products in existing markets. *Product development* may mean extending the firm's product line by developing new variations of the item, or it may mean altering or improving the product to provide enhanced performance. With continued declines in its core soft drink business as more consumers avoid sugar, Coca-Cola is engaged in a highly publicized product development strategy with new entries across the beverage spectrum. For example, Diet Coke has launched several sexy new flavors—namely Ginger Lime, Feisty Cherry, Zesty Blood Orange, and Twisted Mango—that come in sleek 12-ounce cans and are sold as on-the-go singles and eight-packs. By the way, it looks like Feisty Cherry is the top taste winner among the four with one rater stating, "We thought it had more of that authentic soda shop cherry flavor (as compared to that juice from the maraschino jar taste)."[11] Coke knows that there's likely no turning back from market tastes toward real sugar, so its approach to developing products across other beverage categories is a smart one.[12]

product development strategies
Growth strategies that focus on selling new products in existing markets.

diversification strategies
Growth strategies that emphasize both new products and new markets.

Cuba represents a promising market development growth strategy for American companies, so long as the U.S. government moves forward with easing access to the island. Firms of all kinds are waiting in the wings to "invade" the island once they get the green light.

- **Diversification strategies** emphasize both new products and new markets to achieve growth. Earlier you read about Amazon's first foray into supermarket brick-and-mortar

Jazzy new flavors are part of Diet Coke's product development strategy.

with its acquisition of Whole Foods in 2017. This move was a calculated diversification strategy for the distribution giant, and as a result, the company now can offer new products in new markets. Although at the time some pundits pooh-poohed the move as Amazon just flexing their financial strength—and it is true that on the surface a pairing of a broad-based distributor with a high-end specialty food retailer seemed a bit odd—experts have come around to understand that the move was brilliant if for no other reason than it gives Amazon a greater physical presence to hawk its Prime offering.[13]

To review what we've learned so far, strategic planning includes developing the mission statement, assessing the internal and external environment (resulting in a SWOT analysis), setting objectives, establishing the business portfolio, and developing growth strategies. In the next section, we'll look at marketers' functional plans as we examine the process of market planning.

3.3 Market Planning: Develop and Execute Marketing Strategy

Until now, we have focused on fairly broad strategic plans. This big-picture perspective, however, does not provide details about how to reach the objectives we set. Strategic plans "talk the talk" but put the pressure on lower-level functional-area managers, such as the marketing manager, production manager, and finance manager, to "walk the walk" by developing the functional plans—the nuts and bolts—to achieve organizational and SBU objectives. Because you're taking a marketing course and this is a marketing text (but you knew that!), our focus at the functional planning level is naturally on developing marketing plans, which is the next step in planning as we showed back in Figure 3.1.

The Four Ps of the marketing mix we discussed in Chapter 1 remind us that successful firms must have viable *products* at *prices* consumers are willing to pay, a way to *promote* the products to the right consumers, and the ability to get the products to the *place* where consumers want to buy them.

Making this happen requires a tremendous amount of planning by the marketer. The steps in this market planning process are quite similar to the steps at the strategic planning level. An important distinction between strategic planning and market planning, however, is that marketing professionals focus much of their planning efforts on issues related to the *marketing mix*—the firm's product, its price, promotional approach, and distribution (place) methods. In the end, as you learned in Chapter 1, marketing focuses on creating, communicating, delivering, and exchanging offerings that have value, and market planning plays a central role in making these critical components of marketing successful. Let's use Figure 3.5 as a guide to look at the steps involved in the market planning process in a bit more detail.

Figure 3.5 *Process* | Steps in Market Planning

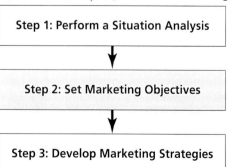

Step 1: Perform a Situation Analysis

The first step to develop a marketing plan is to conduct an analysis of the *marketing environment*. In Chapter 2, you learned about four key external elements that impact marketers: the economic, technological, political and legal, and sociocultural environments. To analyze the environment, managers build on the company's SWOT analysis and search out information about the environment that specifically affects the marketing plan. For example, for AdventHealth to develop an effective marketing communication program for any one of its service offerings, it's not enough to have just a general understanding of the target market. AdventHealth needs to know *specifically* what media potential patients like to connect with, what messages about the hospital's services are most likely to make them choose AdventHealth, and how they prefer to communicate with the organization about new services and customer care issues. And make no mistake about it—hospitals have competitors too! AdventHealth is one of the largest hospital groups in the U.S. and it has a wide variety of competitors for services across its wide market base. As such, AdventHealth must know how those disparate competitors market to potential patients so that they can customize their own market planning from locale to locale across the country.

Step 2: Set Marketing Objectives

Once marketing managers have a thorough understanding of the marketing environment, the next step is to develop specific marketing objectives. How do marketing objectives differ from corporate objectives? Generally, marketing objectives are more specific to the firm's marketing mix–related elements. Think of the connection between business objectives and marketing objectives this way: Business objectives guide the entire firm's operations, whereas marketing objectives state what the marketing function must accomplish if the firm is ultimately to achieve these overall business objectives. So for AdventHealth, setting marketing objectives means deciding what the firm wants to accomplish in terms of a product line's marketing mix–related elements: product development, pricing strategies, or specific marketing communication approaches.

Step 3: Develop Marketing Strategies: Target Markets and the Marketing Mix

In the next stage of the market planning process, marketing managers develop their actual marketing strategies—that is, they make decisions about what activities they must accomplish to achieve the marketing objectives. Usually this means they decide which markets to target and actually develop the marketing mix strategies—product, price, promotion, and place (supply chain)—to support how they want to position the product in the market. At this stage, marketers must figure out how they want consumers to think of their product compared with competing products.

As we mentioned in Chapter 1, the target market is the market segment(s) a firm selects because it believes its offerings are most likely to win those customers. The firm assesses the potential demand—the number of consumers it believes are willing and able to pay for its products—and decides if it is able to create a sustainable competitive advantage in the marketplace among target consumers.

Marketing mix decisions identify how marketing will accomplish its objectives in the firm's target markets by using product, price, promotion, and place. To make the point, we'll stick with airlines to provide examples of each of these marketing mix strategy components:

- Because the product is the most fundamental part of the marketing mix—firms simply can't make a profit without something to sell—carefully developed *product strategies* are essential to achieve marketing objectives. Product strategies include decisions such as product design, packaging, branding, support services (e.g., maintenance); if there will be variations of the product; and what product features will provide the unique benefits targeted customers want. In the U.S., Alaska Airlines is consistently rated #1 in overall customer satisfaction. A few years ago, Alaska became the first carrier to fly a version of the Boeing 737 aircraft that offers a type of overhead bin that can hold 48 percent more luggage than a standard pivot bin.[14] If you've ever packed a carry-on bag with the express purpose of not having to deal with the cost and hassle of checking a bag, only to find when you get to the gate that the bins are full and you have to check the bag anyway, you might be tempted by Alaska's bigger bins and book them over other carriers.[15]

- A *pricing strategy* determines how much a firm charges for a product. Of course, that price has to be one that customers are willing to pay. If not, all the other marketing efforts are futile. In addition to setting prices for the final consumer, pricing strategies usually establish prices the company will charge to wholesalers and retailers. A firm may base its pricing strategies on costs, demand, or the prices of competing products. In recent years, most airlines have been charging extra fees (checked baggage, anyone?) for services and perks they used to include in the ticket price, a practice known as *debundling*, in an effort to increase their revenues. While most U.S. airlines "nickel and dime" passengers to distraction, Southwest Airlines—who we featured earlier and who also gets high marks in customer satisfaction—has a very simple system that doesn't charge for checked luggage or carry-ons; nor do they charge for the standard snack fare of peanuts and pretzels. Southwest's pricing strategy has helped it be a consistent leader both in profitability and in customer satisfaction.[16]

- A *promotional strategy* is how marketers communicate a product's value proposition to the target market. Marketers use promotion strategies to develop the product's message and the mix of advertising, sales promotion, public relations and publicity, direct marketing, and personal selling that will deliver the message. Many firms use all these elements to communicate their message to consumers. At the luxury end of the airline spectrum, it's hard to top Singapore Airlines, which for the second straight year was rated the best first-class cabin experience. The new Singapore offering has been promoted widely as "Ultra-Lux Suites" in which each pampered passenger gets his or her own suite, complete with a Poltrona Frau leather armchair that is 21 inches wide and reclines up to 135 degrees. Except for takeoff and landing, it will be able to swivel and adjust into various seated and lounging positions. What's more, if you've got the cash, your suite will have entirely separate, stowable beds that will measure up at 27 inches wide by 76 inches long and will be dressed with a cotton Lalique duvet and two pillows. Competition at the super high end of international air travel is fierce because the profit potential is very high, so carriers pull out all stops to target messaging and imagery about their offering to this discerning segment of customers.[17]

- *Distribution strategies* outline how, when, and where the firm will make the product available to targeted customers (the *place* component). When they develop a distribution strategy, marketers must decide whether to sell the product directly to the final customer or to sell through retailers and wholesalers. And the choice of which retailers should be involved depends on the product, pricing, and promotion decisions. Back in the "old days," airlines used to sell tickets in person at city ticket offices, by phone directly to customers, or through independent travel agents. Obviously, customers now largely purchase tickets online, often through third-party travel websites. And there are benefits to this strategy, especially for consumers. For example, travelers can see at a glance the best airline fares and flight schedules; get bundle discounts for booking multiple travel services, such as flights, hotels, and car rentals; and get access to promotional specials through website features like Expedia's "Today's Amazing Flight Deals." This page is especially attractive for leisure travelers with flexibility on date of travel, as it typically lists a wide array of bargains spanning the U.S. and beyond, all anchored on the flyer's home departure city.[18]

Step 4: Implement and Control the Marketing Plan

Once the marketing plan is developed, it's time to get to work and make it succeed. In practice, marketers spend much of their time managing the various elements involved in implementing the marketing plan. Once AdventHealth understands the marketing environment, determines the most appropriate objectives and strategies, and gets its ideas organized and on paper in the formal plan, the rubber really hits the road. Like all organizations, how AdventHealth actually implements its plan is what will make or break it in the marketplace.

During the implementation phase, marketers must have some means to determine to what degree they actually meet their stated marketing objectives. Often called **control**, this formal process of monitoring progress entails three steps:

1. Measure actual performance.
2. Compare this performance to the established marketing objectives or strategies.
3. Make adjustments to the objectives or strategies on the basis of this analysis. This issue of making adjustments brings up one of the most important aspects of successful market planning: Marketing plans aren't written in stone, and marketers must be flexible enough to make such changes when changes are warranted.

control
A process that entails measuring actual performance, comparing this performance to the established marketing objectives, and then making adjustments to the strategies or objectives on the basis of this analysis.

For effective control, AdventHealth has to establish appropriate *metrics* related to each of its marketing objectives and then track those metrics to know how successful the marketing strategy is and determine whether it needs to change the strategy along the way. For example, what happens if AdventHealth sets an objective for the of a year to increase its patient usage for a particular service by 20 percent, but after the first quarter, sales are only up 5 percent? The *control process* means that market planners would have to look carefully at *why* the company isn't meeting its objectives. Is it due to internal factors, external factors, or a combination of both? Depending on the cause, AdventHealth would then have to adjust the marketing plan's strategies (such as to implement alterations in the components of the service, modify the price, change the way the product is delivered, or increase or alter promotion). Alternatively, AdventHealth could decide to adjust the marketing objective so that it is more realistic and attainable. This scenario illustrates the important point we made earlier in our discussion of strategic planning: Objectives must be specific and measurable but also *attainable* (and *sustainable over time*) in the sense that if an objective is not realistic, it can become demotivating for everyone involved in the marketing plan.

For AdventHealth and all firms, effective control requires appropriate **marketing metrics**, which are specific measures that help marketers watch the performance of their marketing campaigns, initiatives, and channels, and when appropriate, serve as a control mechanism. Two common ways that metrics can be categorized include: (1) **activity metrics**, which are focused on measuring and tracking specific activities taken within a firm that are part of different marketing processes; and (2) **outcome metrics**, which are focused on measuring and tracking specific events identified as key business outcomes that result from marketing processes. An example of an activity metric is the number of calls that a salesperson makes to customers over a month, whereas a related outcome metric is the number of orders gained from sales calls made during that month.

marketing metrics
Specific measures that help marketers watch the performance of their marketing campaigns, initiatives, and channels, and when appropriate, serve as a control mechanism.

activity metrics
Metrics focused on measuring and tracking specific activities taken within a firm that are part of different marketing processes.

outcome metrics
Metrics focused on measuring and tracking specific events identified as key business outcomes that result from marketing processes.

Metrics are very important in marketing today and it is particularly important to understand that marketers must balance attention to marketing control and the measurement of marketing performance against sustainability and corporate social responsibility (CSR) objectives, which you read about in Chapter 2. Recall that sustainability has to do with firms doing well by doing good—that is, paying attention to important issues such as ethics, the environment, and social responsibility as well as the bottom line. In market planning, we certainly don't want to drive firms toward strategies that compromise sustainability by focusing only on controlling relatively short-term aspects of performance.

Today's CEOs are keen to quantify just how an investment in marketing has an impact on the firm's success, financially and otherwise, over the long haul. You've heard of the financial term *return on investment (ROI)*—in a marketing context we refer to **return on marketing investment (ROMI)**. *In fact, it's critical to consider marketing as an investment rather than an expense*; this distinction drives firms to use marketing more strategically to enhance the business. For many firms today, ROMI is the metric du jour to analyze how the marketing function contributes to the bottom line.

return on marketing investment (ROMI)
Quantifying just how an investment in marketing has an impact on the firm's success, financially and otherwise.

So, what exactly is ROMI? It is the revenue or profit margin (both are widely used) generated by investment in a specific marketing campaign or program divided by the cost of that program (expenditure) at a given risk level (the risk level is determined by management's analysis of the particular program). Again, the key word is *investment*—that is, in the planning process, thinking of marketing as an investment rather than an expense keeps managers focused on using marketing dollars to achieve specific objectives.[19]

Here's a quick and simple example of the ROMI concept. Let's say that a relatively routine marketing campaign costs $30,000 and generates $150,000 in new revenue. Thus, the ROMI for the program is 5.0 (the ROI is five times the investment). If the firm has a total marketing budget of $250,000 and an objective for new revenue of $1,000,000, then the ROMI hurdle rate could be considered 4.0 ($1,000,000/$250,000), meaning that each program should strive to meet or exceed that ROMI benchmark of $4.00 in revenue for every $1.00 in marketing expenditure. Because the marketing campaign exceeds the ROMI hurdle rate, it would be deemed acceptable to proceed with that investment.[20]

For an organization to use ROMI properly it must (1) identify the most appropriate and consistent measure to apply, (2) combine review of ROMI with other critical marketing metrics (one example is marketing payback—how quickly marketing costs are recovered), and (3) fully consider the potential long-term impact of the actions ROMI drives (i.e., is the impact sustainable for the organization over the long term?).[21] Fortunately for the marketer, there are many other potential marketing metrics beyond ROMI that measure specific aspects of marketing performance.

Action Plans

How does the implementation and control step actually get operationalized within a marketing plan? One convenient way is through the inclusion of a series of **action plans** that support the various marketing objectives and strategies within the plan. The best way to use action plans (which also are sometimes called *marketing programs*) is to include a separate action plan for each important element involved in implementing the marketing plan. Table 3.1 provides a template for an action plan.

action plans
Individual support plans included in a marketing plan that provide guidance for implementation and control of the various marketing strategies within the plan. Action plans are sometimes referred to as *marketing programs*.

For example, let's consider the use of action plans in the context of supporting the objective we came up with for AdventHealth earlier to increase patient usage of a particular service by 20 percent in the first quarter of the year. To accomplish this, the marketing plan would likely include a variety of strategies related to how AdventHealth would use the marketing mix elements to reach this objective. Important questions would include the following:

- What are the important needs and wants of this target market of patients?
- How will the service be positioned in relation to this market?
- What will be the branding strategies?
- What will be the pricing strategy for this market?
- How will the service be promoted to them?
- What is the best approach to distribute the service to the market?

Any one of these important strategic issues may require several action plans to implement.

Action plans also help managers when they need to assign responsibilities, timelines, budgets, and measurement and control processes for market planning. In Table 3.1, notice that these four elements are the final items that an action plan documents. Sometimes when we view a marketing plan in total, it can seem daunting and nearly impossible to actually implement. Like most big projects, implementation of a marketing plan is best done one step at a time, paying attention to maximizing the quality of executing that step. In practice, what happens is that marketers combine the input from these last four elements of each action plan to form the overall implementation and control portion of the marketing plan. Let's examine each element a bit further.

Assign Responsibility

A marketing plan can't be implemented without people. And not everybody who will be involved in implementing a marketing plan is a marketer. The truth is, marketing plans

Table 3.1	Action Plan Template
Title of the action plan	Give the action plan a relevant name.
Purpose of the action plan	What do you hope to accomplish by the action plan—that is, what specific marketing objective and strategy within the marketing plan does it support?
Description of the action plan	Be succinct—but still thorough—when you explain the action plan. What are the steps involved? This is the core of the action plan. It describes what must be done in order to accomplish the intended purpose of the action plan.
Responsibility for the action plan	What person(s) or organizational unit(s) are responsible for carrying out the action plan? What external parties are needed to make it happen? Most importantly, who specifically has final "ownership" of the action plan—that is, who within the organization is accountable for it?
Timeline for the action plan	Provide a specific timetable of events leading to the completion of the plan. If different people are responsible for different elements of the timeline, provide that information.
Budget for the action plan	How much will implementation of the action plan cost? This may be direct costs only or may also include indirect costs, depending on the situation. The sum of all the individual action plan budget items will ultimately be aggregated by category to create the overall budget for the marketing plan.
Measurement and control of the action plan	Indicate the appropriate metrics, how and when they will be measured, and who will measure them.

touch most areas of an organization. Upper management and the human resources department will need to deploy the necessary employees to accomplish the plan's objectives. You learned in Chapter 1 that marketing isn't the responsibility only of a marketing department. Nowhere is that idea more apparent than in marketing plan implementation. Sales, production, quality control, shipping, customer service, finance, information technology—the list goes on—all will likely have a part in making the plan successful.

Create a Timeline

Notice that each action plan requires a timeline to accomplish its various tasks. A timeline is essential to include in the overall marketing plan. Most marketing plans portray the timing of tasks in flowchart form so that it is easy to visualize when the pieces of the plan will come together. Marketers often use *Gantt charts* or *PERT charts*, popular in operations management, to portray a plan's timeline. These are the same types of tools that a general contractor might use to map out the different elements of building a house from the ground up. Ultimately, managers develop budgets and the financial management of the marketing plan around the timeline so they know when cash outlays are required.

Set a Budget

Each element of the action plan links to a *budget item*, assuming there are costs involved in carrying out the plan. Forecasting the needed expenditures related to a marketing plan is difficult, but one way to improve accuracy in the budgeting process overall is to ensure estimates for expenditures for the individual action plans that are as accurate as possible. At the overall marketing plan level, managers create a master budget and track it throughout the market planning process. They report variances from the budget to the parties responsible for each budget item. For example, a firm's vice president of sales might receive a weekly or monthly report that shows each sales area's performance against its budget allocation. The vice president would note patterns of budget overage and contact affected sales managers to determine what, if any, action they need to take to get the budget back on track. The same approach would be

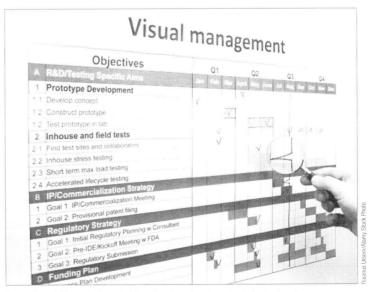

Gantt charts help marketers stick to a timeline when they do strategic planning.

repeated across all the different functional areas of the firm on which the budget has an impact. In such a manner, the budget itself becomes a critical element of control.

Decide on Measurements and Controls

Previously, we described the concept of control as a formal process of monitoring progress to measure actual performance, compare the performance to the established marketing objectives or strategies, and make adjustments to the objectives or strategies on the basis of this analysis. The metric(s) a marketer uses to monitor and control individual action plans ultimately forms the overall control process for the marketing plan. Metrics can serve as **leading indicators** or **lagging indicators** of marketing outcomes. Leading indicators provide insight into the performance of *current efforts* in a way that allows a marketer to adjust relevant marketing activities, (hopefully) resulting in performance improvements against the current action plan. Lagging indicators reflect the performance of an action plan based on outcomes realized. Lagging indicators provide a basis for review and analysis of the action plan with implications for improvement that are focused beyond the scope of the current action plan itself. That is, they provide post hoc insights for next actions.

It is an unfortunate fact that many marketers do not consistently do a good job of measurement and control, which, of course, compromises their market planning. And remember that selection of good metrics needs to take into account short-term objectives balanced against the firm's focus on long-term sustainability.

Operational Planning: Day-to-Day Execution of Marketing Plans

Recall that planning happens at three levels: strategic, functional (such as market planning), and operational. In the previous section, we discussed market planning—the process by which marketers perform a situation analysis, set marketing objectives, and develop, implement, and control marketing strategies. But talk is cheap: The best plan ever written is useless if it's not properly carried out. That's what **operational plans** are for. They put the pedal to the metal by focusing on the day-to-day execution of the marketing plan.

The task of operational planning usually falls to first-line managers, such as sales managers, marketing communication managers, digital marketing managers, brand managers, and market research managers. Operational plans generally cover a shorter period of time than either strategic plans or marketing plans—perhaps only one or two months—and they include detailed directions for the specific activities to be carried out, who will be responsible for them, and timelines for accomplishing the tasks. In reality, the action plan template we provide in Table 3.1 is most likely applied at the operational level.

Significantly, many of the important marketing metrics managers use to gauge the success of plans actually get used at the operational planning level. For example, sales managers in many firms are charged with the responsibility of tracking a wide range of metrics related to the firm–customer relationship, such as number of new customers, sales calls per month, customer turnover, and customer loyalty. The data are collected at the operational level and then sent to upper management for use in planning at the functional level and above. In Chapter 5, you will learn how a customer relationship management (CRM) system helps to facilitate this process.

Agile Marketing and the Strategic Market Planning Process

So far in this chapter, you've had a thorough indoctrination to planning at three levels—strategic, functional, and operational. Sometimes, though, reading about planning—especially market planning—can make it seem like the process is neat, orderly, and predictable. We assure you, in today's fast-paced competitive marketplace, for many products, market planning is far from neat, orderly, and predictable! In fact, in markets such as high tech, in startups, and in hypercompetitive environments, taking the slow boat to developing a marketing plan may mean that the market opportunity passes you by before the ink dries on the paper.

---

leading indicators
Performance indicators that provide insight into the performance of *current efforts* in a way that allows a marketer to adjust relevant marketing activities, (hopefully) resulting in performance improvements against the current action plan.

lagging indicators
Performance indicators that provide insight into the performance of an action plan based on outcomes realized.

operational plans
Plans that focus on the day-to-day execution of the marketing plan. Operational plans include detailed directions for the specific activities to be carried out, who will be responsible for them, and timelines to accomplish the tasks.

Earlier in the chapter, you were introduced to the concepts of nimble organization and strategic pivot. Now it's time to build on these elements and create a framework for applying them within the planning process. In business environments where speed of planning and execution is especially sensitive for competitive success, *agility* becomes a watchword for marketers. **Agility** is about being nimble, being able to move quickly and easily in response to rapid changes and new challenges. This new strategic perspective is called **agile marketing**, which refers to using data and analytics to continuously source promising opportunities or solutions to problems in real time, deploying tests quickly, evaluating the results, and rapidly iterating (doing it over and over). At scale, a high-functioning agile marketing organization can run hundreds of marketing campaigns simultaneously and generate multiple new ideas every week.[22]

The notion of agile marketing is adopted largely from a software development context. In that field, agility is usually based on a methodology called **Scrum**, which had the original goal to embrace the uncertainty and creativity that already governed software development. Perhaps oversimplifying a bit, in a software development context, Scrum advocates that whenever you start a project, you should regularly check in, see whether what you're doing is heading in the right direction, and verify that it's actually what people want.[23] Scrum provides a framework that aims to create a culture of transparency, inspection, and adaptation while making it easier for team members to produce consistently great products. This approach lays out steps to achieve these objectives:

1. Sprint planning
2. Daily Scrum (also known as *daily standup*)
3. Sprint review
4. Sprint retrospective

Note that in agile marketing, the word *sprint* is used in place of *plan* or *planning* to overtly call out the need for speed in planning and execution of marketing strategies.

How can marketers apply this approach? Basically an organization creates an elite team, kind of like a special forces operation in the military. They are removed from their daily assignments, and instead they meet in a "war room" to plot their quick strike. These groups should be small enough that everyone can communicate with one another easily. Jeff Bezos of Amazon specified they should be "two-pizza teams"—that is, teams no bigger than can be fed by two pizzas. A "Scrum master" leads the team, setting priorities and managing "sprints" (one- to two-week cycles of work). The group's mission (should they choose to accept it!) is to execute a series of quick-turnaround experiments designed to create real bottom-line impact. For example, a retailer might want to test a lot of different approaches to optimizing conversion on its website (such as the percentage of people who visit the site and actually buy something).[24]

At this point, going much further into explanations of the Scrum process will take us down a scary black hole to techie land. For your purposes as a marketing student, we bring up the concept of agile marketing just to be sure that you understand that market planning isn't always quite as methodical as the process may seem when you read about it. And in hypercompetitive markets in which success depends on speed of marketing strategy development and execution, you may well find yourself in the middle of Scrum as your business aims to stay nimble.

Digital Disruption and Strategic Market Planning

We have to admit, sometimes when you read about planning in a book like ours, it sounds very stepwise—very neat and tidy. Something like a recipe, and if you follow the steps, the dish is good. Unfortunately, in reality that's a false sense of security. Organizations that go through planning processes like an exercise in checking boxes and filling in blanks will most likely underperform in the dynamic marketplace of the 2020s. And the attitude in some firms that we do planning because "it's January and in January we always do our planning"—planning for planning's sake—misunderstands the spirit of what you've read so far in this chapter. Planning is an organic, ever-changing process, and once a plan is

agility
The ability to be nimble, or to move quickly and easily.

agile marketing
Using data and analytics to continuously source promising opportunities or solutions to problems in real time, deploying tests quickly, evaluating the results, and rapidly iterating (doing it over and over).

Scrum
A popular methodology for executing agile marketing.

digital disruption
The effect of digital technologies and digital business models on an organization's value proposition and its resulting position in the markets in which it competes.

digital vortex
The inexorable movement of industries toward a "digital center" in which business models, offerings, and value chains are all digitized to the maximum extent possible.

contingency planning
Planning that assesses the risk of a variety of possible, mostly external, environmental factors and their potential level of impact on the firm's ability to add value and serve its market through its offerings.

scenarios
The multiple strategic paths a firm develops in contingency planning.

"done," conditions surrounding it immediately begin to change and constant adaptation becomes necessary. Hence: Be nimble, execute strategic pivot, and practice agile marketing!

In any contemporary chapter on strategic market planning that's worth its salt, two concepts deserve mention that taken together should be key drivers to more effective planning. First is the concept of **digital disruption**, which is the effect of digital technologies and digital business models on an organization's value proposition and its resulting position in the markets in which it competes. Second is the concept of the **digital vortex**, which is the inexorable movement of industries toward a "digital center" in which business models, offerings, and value chains are all digitized to the maximum extent possible. You learned what a value proposition and a value chain are in Chapter 1. The net of these phenomena of digital disruption and the digital vortex is that traditional (i.e., traditional stepwise) processes to strategic market planning are pretty well suited to more stable, non-disrupted products and markets (remember the product-market growth matrix earlier in this chapter). Such stable environments can better allow for year-long goals and annual repetitive planning processes. But in more and more sectors today—and AdventHealth's sector is a prime example—that level of stability no longer exists as digital disruption and the digital vortex are rapidly redefining what customers want and expect.

Bottom line: All of us as students of strategic market planning today need to expect and actually embrace constant change as a fundamental truth. This calls for building in **contingency planning** that better takes into account the market uncertainties and constancy of change in business today. Put succinctly, contingency planning assesses the risk of a variety of possible, mostly external, environmental factors and their potential level of impact on the firm's ability to add value and serve its market through its offerings. That is, what is the likelihood of certain possible future events or circumstances to impact the efficacy of a plan? Based on this assessment, enlightened firms develop and prepare for multiple strategic paths that are often referred to as **scenarios**. Because these firms have thought through and documented these different scenarios in advance within the context of their plan, if and when one or more of these potentialities occur, they're in a much better place to strategically pivot and nimbly redirect resources to successfully execute a scenario's strategies. In this high-stakes game, the ability to do this well heavily defines winners and losers.

A great example of the need for contingency planning was the way many universities approached the prospects of reopening for the fall 2020 semester. During the summer beforehand, school leaders mapped out multiple scenarios, including opening with all students attending in person, opening with all students engaged through online learning, and a hybrid approach in which students made use of both learning modalities. Regardless of industry, could anyone have fully understood in advance the likelihood, scope, and potential impact of the global pandemic that began in early 2020 on their businesses and prepared in advance accordingly? That's a question for the ages in strategic market planning. But going forward, there's no doubt that one of the many organizational lessons learned from the crisis will be the importance of finding a balance between planning as a process and executing broad organizational agility.

Make Your Life Easier! Use the Market Planning Template

Ultimately, the planning process we've described in this section is documented in a formal, written marketing plan. You'll find a template for building a marketing plan in the Supplement at the end of this chapter. The template will come in handy as you make your way through the book, as each chapter will give you information you can use to "fill in the blanks" of a marketing plan. You will note that the template is cross-referenced with the questions you must answer in each section of the plan. It also provides you with a general road map of the topics covered in each chapter that need to flow into building the marketing plan. By the time you're done, we hope that all these pieces will come together and you'll understand how real marketers make real choices.

As we noted previously, a marketing plan should provide the best possible guide for the firm to successfully market its products. In large firms, top management often requires such a written plan because putting the ideas on paper encourages marketing managers to formulate concrete objectives and strategies. In small entrepreneurial firms, a well-thought-out marketing plan is often the key to attracting investors who will help turn the firm's dreams into reality.

3.4 Brand You:
Planning Your Career

OBJECTIVE
Understand how to develop a strategic plan for a successful career.

Taylor feels he is making progress in developing his personal brand. He is able to identify the characteristics of different organizational cultures and recognize the uniqueness of different industries. Now it's time to develop his strategic Brand You plan.

Now that we've learned how organizations plan at three different levels, we need to examine how you, the prospective employee of these organizations, can effectively plan your career.

Great brands like Google, Apple, Coke, and Amazon.com don't just happen overnight. In fact, it takes time, research, and consideration to create a compelling brand. This is true for products, places, and people like you. In this section, you'll first learn the importance of career planning. Then we'll talk about how to create a personal mission statement, identify your strengths and weaknesses, and see career opportunities in trends and changes in the business environment.

In the early part of 2020, the global COVID-19 pandemic meant people in most countries in the world engaged in self-quarantining. As non-essential businesses closed and millions lost their jobs, the economy took a major hit. Students graduating from colleges were unsure if they could find a job.

The good news is that there are always some companies needing new employees. Even better news, your personal brand that defines you and makes you unique and compelling can put you ahead of other less-prepared job candidates.

Whether you are the type of person who normally plans or one who leaves things to the last minute, career planning is essential. As CEO of your own personal brand, you want to speak in a clear voice so that employers (your customers) understand who you are and what you have to offer.

To increase your chances of success when you are looking for an internship or full-time job, start planning *NOW*. Leaving career decisions until your senior year is risky. Without a clear sense of direction, you'll miss important opportunities to find internships with companies that might hire you or contacts that could lead to job offers.

Creating a career plan involves a series of decisions, starting with your personal mission statement and ending with implementation and control of your career strategies. To achieve your goals, you'll need to drill down from the big picture of your career plan to the details—the actions you'll need to take to make your plan a reality.

Your Personal Strategic Plan

We often hear people ask, "What do I want to be when I grow up?" If they're changing careers, the question is modified slightly to "What do I want to be *this time* when I grow up?" Career planning isn't about *being* anything—you're already a real live human being. It's about *doing*. Rephrase the question to "What do I want to do with my skills and knowledge now?" With this question in mind, you'll be able to create a flexible plan that allows you to adapt to changes in the workplace—and there will be many!

Businesses deliberately set a time frame of five years for their strategic plans. In today's rapidly changing world, longer views usually prove to be meaningless. The probability of accurately forecasting developments in technology, business practices, and customer expectations beyond five years is very low. A relatively short time frame gives businesses the flexibility to adapt to changes as they occur. A five-year plan for your career is about the right length of time too. Your plan should be flexible enough to adapt to changes in the workplace.

Beyond five years, it's hard to predict what may happen in your job, your company, your profession, or your industry. In addition, your own personal interests and needs are likely to change several times over your lifetime.

Although businesses look at five-year time frames for their strategic plans, they actually review and revise them every year. Likewise, you should review your career plan every year. That way you'll be able to make incremental changes and not discover too late that your skills are obsolete and you have to start in an entirely new career direction.

Define Your Mission

Organizations start their strategic plans with a mission statement. The mission defines the organization's overall purpose and what it hopes to achieve in terms of its customers, products, and resources. Like an organization's mission statement, **your mission statement defines your overall purpose and what you hope to achieve in the future**. It should be narrow enough to give you a sense of focus but broad enough to adapt to future opportunities. A well-thought-out mission statement will help guide your search for a career choice now and in the future.

To develop your mission, think about:

- What's important to you
- Who you are
- What you stand for
- What you like to do
- Why you want to do it

Because your mission statement will guide your actions and let others know about you, your top values will give you some clues about a mission that describes your purpose for working. For example, if your top value is community, you might try a mission statement similar to this: "To support activities that sustain our environment." With more and more consumers who are passionate about protecting the global environment, many companies are responding to that passion. Your mission statement would therefore give you many career options, such as working for the Environmental Protection Agency (EPA), starting a community garden in a low-income neighborhood, promoting a new technology to reduce pollution, or implementing new forest management practices. As varied as these options are, each is aligned with the mission.

Here are some points that will help you write a great mission statement.

- Make it memorable.
- Focus on a single theme; don't try to be all things to all people.
- Make it clear and concise (it should fit on the back of your business card).
- It should energize you and rally you to action.
- It should serve to guide you as you make career decisions.

Organizations and businesses don't hide their mission statement. You'll often see it displayed on a wall, in brochures, on websites, and even on coffee cups. Find a way to display your mission statement. It will help you stay focused on your career goals and guide your decisions. Here are some ideas to consider: Print it on the back of your business card, post it on your website, or hang it on the wall where you'll see it every day.

Your Internal Analysis

As we learned earlier in this chapter, the next step in strategic planning is to conduct a situation analysis that examines your internal and external environments. From your internal analysis, you will be able to identify your skills and talents, characteristics that provide insights into your strengths and weaknesses. Your inventory of skills will help you identify a career direction. Careers that require these skills will rise to the top of your choices while jobs that do not can be dropped from consideration.

Taylor's Mission Statement—Step 1

Taylor started writing his personal mission statement by identifying the things that he really enjoyed or thought he would enjoy.

- Solving challenging strategic problems
- Working with data to make fact-based decisions
- Interacting with people
- Helping people
- Persuading people to see a different or new point of view
- Working on major marketing projects and delivering results
- Working for an industry-leading corporation that cares about its employees and society
- Giving back to the community

Taylor's Mission Statement—Step 2

After creating and fine-tuning this list, Taylor crafted the key points into a few sentences that would become the foundation of his mission statement.

> I enjoy working with people and using data to solve complex marketing challenges. I think it would be good to start my career at a large corporation so I can be exposed to and learn as much as I can about marketing and bringing new products to market. I would ultimately like to be in a leadership role in marketing. It's important to me that the company I choose to work for is community-minded and gives back to society in some way.

Taylor's Mission Statement—Step 3

After thinking about it for a week or so, Taylor reviewed his mission statement again. He felt it captured who he is and what he wants to do, but it seemed a bit long and wasn't memorable. He eventually evolved his mission statement into the one below.

> To connect consumers with brands that provide positive value or utility and give back to the community.

This concise statement summarizes Taylor's passion for marketing and his focus on community service. Based on this mission statement, he could pursue a career in a variety of industries. It also gives him flexibility to work for an established company or even start his own firm. Most important, it gives a clear framework by which to make career choices.

Your inventory of skills will help you in several ways. If you are looking for a career direction, knowing your skills will help you identify good career choices. In addition, you will be able to clearly describe your skills to potential employers when asked what you have to offer.

Your External Analysis

One reason businesses scan the external environment is to look for new opportunities. Changes in the economy, regulations, consumers, competitors, and popular culture can have a profound impact on a firm's fortunes. Business leaders know it's imperative to identify these shifts and adapt to them.

In the same way, frequently scanning the external environments brings to light the opportunities and threats that you face in your career planning. Your career success will also depend on frequently scanning the external environment. On the negative side are such facts as the growth in technology that has allowed employers to replace people with robotics or the popularity of outsourcing manufacturing to the least developed countries. At the same time, it's important to remember that the world is full of new opportunities. Ever since scientists broke the genetic code, biotechnology has been growing exponentially. The advent of global terrorism has fueled the growth of security products and services. The retirement of baby boomers, the largest generation in history, will create many jobs related to leisure activities and antiaging products. Scanning the external environment also means you can stay up to date with trends in your industry and profession, giving you a head start on potential new opportunities for your career.

Your Career SWOT

Now that you've identified your mission and your strengths (skills), and you've discovered some trends that may impact your career, you're ready to try out your personal SWOT analysis. SWOT stands for *strengths* (S) and *weaknesses* (W) that are within your control and *opportunities* (O) and *threats* (T) that are outside your control but can influence your career. Your SWOT analysis will help guide your career direction and help you craft your personal brand message in the form of your cover letter and résumé and even in your approach to job interviews.

Career Objectives

After you have your SWOT analysis, it's time to write your career objectives. Objectives are specific goals that you want to achieve by a given time. For example, one of your career objectives might be:

> *Obtain a marketing internship at a major corporation for summer of this year.*

Worded this way, the objective is SMART—*specific (S), measurable (M), attainable (A), realistic (R),* and *timebound (T).* SMART objectives give you the capability of measuring whether you have achieved them. Note that the following objective is not SMART and is not measurable:

Obtain a position in sales.

Rather the objective should be stated as:

Obtain a sales position at a food marketing company by June of this year.

From Strategic Planning to Success

Does a personal strategic plan guarantee success in your job? In a career, it's not just doing your job—it's caring about the job, the company, the people you work with, and the results you achieve. Success requires a large dose of self-discovery to find what you really care about.

Students often start their career planning by asking the question, *"What do I want to be when I grow up?"* A question that fits our changing times better is, *"What do I want to do now?"* This keeps you open to exciting possibilities that will develop.

The most important part of career planning is to identify what you like to do . . . and what you don't like to do. You will be more successful in a career using the skills you enjoy.

Taylor knows that he cannot wait until his senior year to plan for a career—he must do that NOW. As a first step, Taylor examined the values that he used as the foundation of his mission statement. In addition, he has identified his own strengths and weaknesses and the opportunities and threats he faces in the external career environment. After summarizing all of this in his SWOT analysis, Taylor has created well-thought-out career objectives. Taylor is pleased with the progress he has made on his personal brand and feels he is on the right track for his career.

Objective **Summaries** and **Key Terms**

3.1 Objective Summary

Explain business planning and its three levels.

Business planning is the ongoing process of decision making that guides the firm in both the short term and the long term. A business plan, which includes the decisions that guide the entire organization or its business units, is different from a marketing plan, which is a process and resulting document that describes the marketing environment, outlines the marketing objectives and strategies, and identifies how the company will implement and control the strategies embedded in the plan.

Planning takes place at three key levels. Strategic planning is the managerial decision process that matches the firm's resources and capabilities to its market opportunities for long-term growth. Large firms may have a number of self-contained divisions called *strategic business units (SBUs).* In such cases, strategic planning takes place at both the overall corporate level and within the SBU. Functional planning gets its name because the various functional areas of the firm, such as marketing, finance, and human resources, get involved. And operational planning focuses on the day-to-day execution of the functional plans and includes detailed annual, semiannual, or quarterly plans.

Key Terms

strategy
business planning

business plan
marketing plan
strategic planning
strategic business units (SBUs)
functional planning
market planning
operational planning

3.2 Objective Summary

Describe the steps in strategic planning.

For large firms that have a number of self-contained business units, the first step in strategic planning is for top management to establish a mission for the entire corporation. Top managers then evaluate the internal and external environment of the business and set corporate-level objectives that guide decision making within each individual SBU. In small firms that are not large enough to have separate SBUs, strategic planning simply takes place at the overall firm level.

The first step in strategic planning is defining the mission—a formal document that describes the organization's overall purpose and what it hopes to achieve in terms of its customers, products, and resources. Step 2 is to evaluate the internal and external environment through a process known as *situational analysis,* which is later formatted as a SWOT analysis that identifies the organization's strengths, weaknesses, opportunities, and threats. Step 3 is to set organizational or SBU objectives that are specific, measurable, attainable, and sustainable. Step 4 is to establish the business portfolio, which is the range of different businesses that a large firm operates. To determine how best to allocate resources to the various businesses, or units, managers use the Boston Consulting Group (BCG) growth–market share matrix to classify SBUs as stars, cash cows, question marks, or dogs. The final step, Step 5, in strategic planning is to develop growth strategies. Marketers use the product–market growth matrix to analyze four fundamental marketing strategies: market penetration, market development, product development, and diversification.

Key Terms

mission (or **purpose**)

mission statement

vision

vision statement

organizational values

situation analysis

internal environment

SWOT analysis

nimble organization

strategic pivot

business portfolio

portfolio analysis

BCG growth–market share matrix

stars

cash cows

question marks

dogs

market penetration strategies

market development strategies

product development strategies

diversification strategies

3.3 Objective Summary

Describe the steps in market planning.

Once big-picture issues are considered, it's up to the lower-level functional-area managers, such as the marketing manager, production manager, and finance manager, to develop the functional marketing plans—the nuts and bolts—to achieve organizational and SBU objectives. The steps in this market planning process are quite similar to the steps at the strategic planning level. An important distinction between strategic planning and market planning, however, is that marketing professionals focus much of their planning efforts on issues related to the Four Ps of the marketing mix. Managers start off by performing a situational analysis of the marketing environment. Next, they develop marketing objectives specific to the firm's brand, sizes, and product features. Then, marketing managers select the target market(s) for the organization and decide what marketing mix strategies they will use. Product strategies include decisions about products and product characteristics that will appeal to the target market. Pricing strategies state the specific prices to be charged to channel members and final consumers. Promotion strategies include plans for advertising, sales promotion, public relations, publicity, personal selling, and direct marketing used

to reach the target market. Distribution (place) strategies outline how the product will be made available to targeted customers when and where they want it. Once the marketing strategies are developed, they must be implemented, which is the last step in developing the marketing plan. Control is the measurement of actual performance and comparison with planned performance. Maintaining control implies the need for concrete measures of marketing performance called *marketing metrics*.

Operational planning is done by first-line managers, such as sales managers, marketing communication managers, and market research managers, and focuses on the day-to-day execution of the marketing plan. Operational plans generally cover a shorter period of time and include detailed directions for the specific activities to be carried out, who will be responsible for them, and timelines for accomplishing the tasks. To ensure effective implementation, a marketing plan must include individual action plans, or programs, that support the plan at the operational level. Each action plan necessitates providing a budget estimate, schedule, or timeline for its implementation and appropriate metrics so that the marketer can monitor progress and control for discrepancies or variation from the plan. Sometimes, variance from a plan requires shifting or increasing resources to make the plan work; other times, it requires changing the objectives of the plan to recognize changing conditions.

Agile marketing has become an important competitive necessity in many markets in which fast-paced change makes standard market planning processes too slow. Agile marketing relies on a methodology called *Scrum* that comes out of the software development space to provide a step-wise approach to increasing speed of product development.

Key Terms

control

marketing metrics

activity metrics

outcome metrics

return on marketing investment (ROMI)

action plans

leading indicators

lagging indicators

operational plans

agility

agile marketing

Scrum

digital disruption

digital vortex

contingency planning

scenarios

3.4 Objective Summary

Understand how to develop a strategic plan for a successful career.

It's not enough just to get a job; career planning is essential. You want to let employers (your customers) understand who you are and what you have to offer. A clear sense of direction will keep you from missing important opportunities. Creating a flexible career plan that allows you to adapt to changes in the workplace involves a series of decisions. Your career plan, like the strategic plans of businesses, should be for about five years because it's difficult to predict changes in the industry, company, job, and your interests and needs for longer periods. While a career plan can be for five years, you should review annually just as businesses review their strategic plans every year, thus avoiding your skills becoming obsolete.

A carefully devised personal career plan mission statement defines your overall purpose and what you hope to achieve in the future. Like a business, let people know your mission state-

ment. After developing a mission statement, you should conduct a situation analysis that examines your internal and external environments to identify your skills and your weaknesses and the opportunities and threats in your external environment. Following up with a SWOT analysis will help guide your career and help you craft your personal brand message in a cover letter and résumé and in job interviews. Your personal SWOT can be followed by developing career objectives.

Chapter **Questions** and **Activities**

Concepts: Test Your Knowledge

3-1. What is a marketing plan? How does it differ from a business plan?

3-2. Describe the three levels of business planning: strategic, functional, and operational planning. Think about Disney and how they would plan at the three levels. Describe each level. Who do you think does the planning for each level? What do you imagine is covered in each of the three plans?

3-3. What is a mission statement? What role does it play in the planning process?

3-4. Describe the five steps in the strategic planning process.

3-5. Describe three elements of an organization's internal environment. Explain the SWOT analysis and its relationship to the firm's internal and external environments.

3-6. What is a business portfolio analysis such as the BCG growth–market share matrix? If a product is classified as a cash cow in a firm's BCG matrix, what does this mean? What are the implications for strategic planning for a cash cow?

3-7. List and explain the four characteristics that make an objective effective?

3-8. Describe the four business growth strategies: market penetration, product development, market development, and diversification.

3-9. Explain the four steps in the market planning process.

3-10. What is return on marketing investment (ROMI)? How does considering marketing as an investment instead of an expense affect a firm?

3-11. What is an action plan? Why are action plans such an important part of market planning? Why is it so important for marketers to break the implementation of a marketing plan down into individual elements through action plans?

3-12. Give an example of operational planning that supports a marketing plan. Describe what that plan might include.

Activities: Apply What You've Learned

3-13. *Creative Homework/Short Project* As a marketing student you know that large firms often organize their operations into a number of strategic business units (SBUs). In these large corporations, strategic planning is done at both the corporate and SBU levels. Medium

and small businesses also engage in strategic planning by developing a single plan for their entire organization. Select one SBU that is part of a large corporation. Select one successful medium-sized business. How do you think strategic planning is alike for these two organizations? In what ways is strategic planning for the two different? Would you rather work for an SBU of a large corporation or a medium-sized business?

3-14. *Creative Homework/Short Project* Assume that you are the marketing director for Mattel Toys. Your boss, the company vice president for marketing, has decided that it's time to develop some new objectives for some of their product lines as the company begins market planning. Your VP has asked you to help out by writing several initial objectives. Select any product line at Mattel and develop several objectives that fulfill the criteria for objectives discussed in the chapter.

3-15. *In Class, 10–25 Minutes for Teams* Select one of the following products that you all use.
- Shampoo
- Toothpaste
- Deodorant
- Flavored water
- Athletic or running shoes

Discuss the product among the members of your team. Make a list of the different product attributes each person uses in selecting their favorite brand or brands. Was it the fragrance, the shiny hair you have when you use it, or something else? Now, assume you are a marketing consultant. Based on this information, develop a recommendation to the firm for a new product that you believe would be successful. Develop a complete description of the product and why you are recommending it.

3-16. *In Class, 10–25 Minutes for Teams* As an employee of a business consulting firm that specializes in helping people who want to start a small business, you have been assigned a client who is interested in developing a new concept in pet care. The new business will offer a variety of services for customers: grooming, bathing, daycare, longer-term boarding, obedience training, and having healthy organic pet foods for sale. There will also be a veterinarian on staff to handle regular check-ups and immunizations as well as pet illnesses, accidents, and other emergencies. As you begin thinking about the potential success of this new business concept, you realize that it is essential that the client has a strong marketing plan from the start. Take a role-playing approach to present your argument to the client as to why they need to spend the money on your services to create a formal marketing plan.

3-17. *For Further Research (Individual)* Identify a small business in your community that has enjoyed a successful operation for at least 10 years. Make an appointment for your team to talk with the owners and/or managers when it is convenient for them. With your team, develop a list of questions to ask. These might include why and when they started the business, the greatest challenges for them in the beginning, the greatest challenges for them now, if they had a marketing plan and whether they think a marketing plan is helpful to a new small business. Make a written report and give a presentation to your class on your findings.

3-18. *Individual written assignment.* An important part of planning is a SWOT analysis, understanding an organization's strengths, weaknesses, opportunities, and threats. Select one of the businesses listed below. Prepare a SWOT analysis that includes three or four items in each of the four SWOT categories.

Panera Bread
Applebee's
Dunkin' Donuts
Domino's Pizza
Olive Garden

Concepts: Apply Marketing Metrics

You learned in the chapter that most marketers today feel pressure to measure (quantify) their level of success in market planning. They do this by setting and then measuring marketing objectives. One popular metric is market share, which in essence represents the percentage of total product category sales your products represent versus category competitors. For example, recent statistics indicate that Lenovo holds the number-one market share in global PC sales with about 21 percent, topping HP with about 19 percent. Ranked third through fifth are Dell, Apple, and Acer, respectively.[25] But, despite its common appearance in marketing objectives, market share has been heavily criticized as a metric. Often it can become more of a "bragging right" for a firm than a profit enhancer. This is because—especially in situations like the global PC market that is seeing heavy annual declines in sales as tablets and other devices replace PCs—investing in being number one in market share may deflect focus away from more lucrative new and growing product lines.

3-19. Under what conditions do you believe market share as a metric is important to a firm? What are the potential pitfalls of relying too much on market share as a key metric? What self-defeating behaviors might this over-reliance lead a firm to undertake?

3-20. Come up with some other product categories besides PCs that are declining and identify the firms within those categories that have the highest market share. What does their profit picture look like?

Choices: What Do You Think?

3-21. Defining the mission is identified as the first major step in the strategic planning process. Many companies display their mission statement on their website, making it readily accessible to the public. Do you think a company should make it available for everyone to see? Why or why not? Are there any specific situations or factors to consider that would lead you to recommend not doing so?

3-22. Strategic planning is an intensive process that takes a good bit of time and company resources. Is this process useful to small businesses? What are the pros of developing a strategic plan for small businesses? Are there any cons, and if so, what are they? What are five mistakes that small businesses can make because they do not have a business plan? How can a business plan make them more successful?

3-23. Within the BCG matrix, products that earn the dog label have limited market potential for the firm and also only hold a small relative market share. Products identified as dogs within this framework are typically obvious candidates for divestment, but are there any cases where doing so would not be wise for an organization? That is, why would a firm want to hold onto a dog?

3-24. Most planning involves strategies for growth. But is growth always the right direction to pursue? Can you think of situations where a contraction strategy would be better than a growth strategy? Do you know of any organizations that have actually planned to get smaller to increase their success? (Hint: Use the Internet for information.)

3-25. To be effective in strategic planning, a firm must be transparent—sharing the big picture with employees is critical to achieving success at the lowest levels of planning. What issues do you think might arise if a company decides not to fully share its strategic plan details with employees? How might this impact functional planning? How about operational planning? Why do you think it is important that all three areas of planning are aligned?

3-26. Many companies operate on the mentality that "marketing is an expense." Do you agree that marketing is an expense, or should marketing be treated as an investment? Should there be a business standard as to whether marketing is treated as an expense/investment, or should individual organizations be given the freedom to choose which line item to assign it to? Explain your reasoning.

Miniproject: Learn by Doing

The purpose of this miniproject is to gain an understanding of market planning through actual experience.

3-27. a. Select one of the following for your market planning project:
- Yourself (in your search for a career)
- Your university
- A specific department in your university
- A new health club
- A new spa
- A new brand of toothpaste

b. Next, develop the following elements of the market planning process:
- A mission statement
- A SWOT analysis
- Objectives

- A description of the target market(s)
- A positioning strategy
- A brief outline of the marketing mix strategies—the product, pricing, distribution, and promotion

strategies—that satisfy the objectives and address the target market

c. Prepare a brief outline of a marketing plan using the basic template provided in this chapter as a guide.

Marketing in Action **Case**   Real Choices at P&G

Do you love doing laundry? If so, you are the exception! The American Cleaning Institute says that cleaning our clothes is our fifth-most-loathed household chore, right behind cleaning the kitchen, dusting, mopping, and cleaning the bathroom. A Labor Department study found that Americans spend up to 375 hours per year keeping our clothes looking great (or at least presentable). For many of us, doing that task means grabbing a box or bottle of P&G's product, Tide detergent. In an effort to continue to dominate the garment-care segment, P&G is trying a new initiative as part of its growth strategy—Tide Cleaners.

Launched in 1946 as "The Washday Miracle," Tide has been the number one laundry detergent in the U.S. since 1949. About 40 million Americans use it each year. Regular innovations have helped the brand to stay on top, including Liquid Tide, Tide Pods, and Tide to Go stain releaser pens. While clearly the leader among its industry rivals, P&G also has to stay on top of changing demographic and consumer behavior trends that influence how Americans do laundry—or avoid doing it. The company identified a growing desire among consumers to "outsource" this unpleasant chore, so it realized it's not enough just to sell a popular detergent if customers start to pay others to wash their clothes instead.

P&G began to explore a service-oriented approach to meeting consumers' garment-care needs. The company initially launched a dry-cleaning chain as a venture to sell more detergent and to learn about consumers' laundry preferences—kind of a "real life" laboratory to observe what people do with dirty clothes. Sure enough, P&G started to pick up on changes, especially among millennials and Gen Z consumers. Compared to their parents, they tend to wear their clothing many more times before they wash them. And they appear to be less loyal to leading laundry brands than their parents.

P&G also observed that these younger customers are willing to pay for on-demand services like DoorDash, UberEats, and GrubHub. In general, they're just more used to using apps and hiring others to do routine tasks for them, such as food delivery and rides around town.

That spells opportunity for expanded laundry services. For some younger people, it's a practical matter—their urban apartments don't have washer-dryer hookups, or the shared laundry room or neighborhood laundromat may be far away. Consumers are also trying to recover time in their jam-packed schedules, particularly those in the millennial and Gen Z generations who place a high value on their free time. "It's critical we go for this because it's a natural extension of the brand," according to Sundar Raman, vice president of P&G North American Fabric Care. "The time people spend on chores is decreasing, and there's less and less consumption happening at home. The market for out-of-home laundry is just as big as for in-home and growing faster."

From its start with dry-cleaning outlets, Tide Cleaners has expanded to include wash-and-fold laundry and lockers in city buildings where you can drop off and pick up your laundry. Its Tide University won't earn you college credits, but it will free up some time for you to study if you attend one of the 20 schools

where the service is currently available. There's no need to drive to an off-campus shop or to find a locker somewhere for a drop-off. Just load up your bag with dirty clothes and give it to the friendly attendant who drives a truck right onto your campus. Tide Cleaners uses a personalized mobile app to communicate with customers, a must for the digitally savvy market it wants to attract. The app can also track your laundry as it moves through the cleaning process, using bar-coded laundry bags and chips attached to dry-clean–only garments.

P&G's marketing for Tide Cleaners is focused primarily on direct mail, email, digital, and posters. It also produced a video ad with the tagline "Life, Not Laundry." But its biggest marketing effort is the expansion of its physical locations. The company now plans to increase to 2,000 outlets by the end of 2020, most of which will be operated by franchisees. If doing laundry every day all day sounds good to you, save up your money: franchisees are required to have $1.1 million in liquid capital and a net worth of $2 million. Each of these locations prominently displays the familiar Tide logo, which not only identifies it as a drop-off point for laundry but reinforces the brand imagery for purchasers of Tide products for home use. The impact on product sales could be one of the biggest wins out of the initiative for P&G, as it connects directly to consumers and collects valuable behavioral information about its customers.

Not everyone agrees with the wisdom of P&G's move into laundry services. "We've watched Tide over the years, and they haven't had a long-term strategy yet," according to Wayne Wudyka, owner of competitor Huntington Company, the largest dry-clean franchiser in the U.S. "When I look at the economics of what they are doing, it's counterintuitive." The dry-cleaning industry has been declining in recent years, and while Tide Cleaners is not yet profitable, P&G believes its expanded set of services is a ground floor opportunity as more people choose to outsource their fifth-least-favorite chore. Competitors know it's dangerous to underestimate the power of a 70-year-old brand, owned by a company known for its heavy investment in marketing. Digital marketing consultant Judge Graham sees Tide Cleaners as a win for P&G: "Tide understands that they have a legacy, old brand, and if it's not them, others will come up with this idea," he said. "They get to own this market, and I suspect they'll see a spike in their traditional retail sales as people perceive Tide as this 'Uberesque' sort of innovative brand."[26]

Questions for Discussion

3-28. What factors in an evaluation of the external environment might have led P&G to pursue the Tide Cleaners initiative? What other factors should it consider as it further develops and promotes Tide Cleaners?

3-29. Review the Product-Market Growth Matrix in Figure 3.4. Which of the four approaches is P&G using with its Tide Cleaners initiative? What other growth strategies could it use to stimulate further growth?

3-30. With the Tide Cleaners venture, P&G is responding to consumers' choice to spend their money on a service to realize the benefit they seek rather than through the purchase of a product. What other industries are—or should be—taking a similar approach?

Chapter **Notes**

1. Nick Turner, Selina Wang, and Spencer Soper, "Amazon to Acquire Whole Foods for $13.7 Billion," Bloomberg Technology, June 16, 2017, https://www.bloomberg.com/news/articles/2017-06-16/amazon-to-acquire-whole-foods-in-13-7-billion-bet-on-groceries (accessed March 8, 2018); Kelly Tyco, "Have an Amazon Return to Send Back? Kohl's Stores are Now Accepting Amazon Returns," *USA Today*, July 8, 2019, https://www.usatoday.com/story/money/2019/07/08/kohls-stores-now-accepting-amazon-returns-no-box-required/1629966001/ (accessed May 5, 2020).

2. https://us.pg.com/brands/ (accessed March 6, 2020).

3. https://us.pg.com/policies-and-practices/purpose-values-and-principles/ (accessed March 6, 2020).

4. http://investors.southwest.com/our-company/purpose-vision-and-the-southwest-way/ (accessed May 5, 2020); https://us.pg.com/policies-and-practices/purpose-values-and-principles/ (accessed May 5, 2020).

5. "Impact of COVID-19 on the Video Conferencing Market, 2020," https://www.businesswire.com/news/home/20200416005739/en/Impact-COVID-19-Video-Conferencing-Market-2020 (accessed May 9, 2020).

6. Chaim Gartenberg, "The Rise of Skywalker Is Proof That Star Wars Needs to Reinvent Itself," *The Verge*, January 15, 2020, https://www.theverge.com/2020/1/15/21067480/star-wars-rise-of-skywalker-box-office-performance-results-disney-future (accessed May 9, 2020).

7. Michael Cieply and Brooks Barnes, "Disney Sells Miramax for $660 Million," *The New York Times*, July 30, 2010, http://www.nytimes.com/2010/07/31/business/media/31miramax.html?_r=0 (accessed April 22, 2014).

8. James Freeman, "More Problems at ESPN," *The Wall Street Journal*, May 9, 2017, https://www.wsj.com/articles/more-problems-atespn-1494369199 (accessed March 7, 2018).

9. Rebekah Schouten, "McDonald's Sees Success from its 'Most Ambitious Plan in History'," *Food Business News*, May 1, 2019, https://www.foodbusinessnews.net/articles/13711-mcdonalds-sees-success-from-its-most-ambitious-plan-in-history (accessed May 8, 2020).

10. http://www.skyscanner.com/flights-to/cu/airlines-that-flytocuba.html (accessed March 14, 2018).

11. Lisa Kimanski, "We Tried the New Diet Coke Flavors and Here's What We Thought," *Taste of Home*, https://www.tasteofhome.com/article/we-tried-new-diet-coke-flavors/ (accessed May 6, 2020).

12. Rachel Arthur, "What's Hitting the Shelves? New Diet Coke Flavors, Premium Juice, and Survival Beer," *Beverage Daily*, January 28, 2018, https://www.beveragedaily.com/Article/2018/01/23/What-s-hitting-the-shelves-New-beverage-launches-January-2018# (accessed March 8, 2018).

13. Dennis Green, "How Whole Foods Went From a Hippie Natural Food Store to Amazon's $13.7 Billion Grocery Weapon," *Business Insider*, May 2, 2019, https://www.businessinsider.com/whole-foods-timeline-from-start-to-amazon-2017-9 (accessed May 7, 2020).

14. "Alaska Airlines Increases Overhead Storage Nearly 50 Percent with First 737 Featuring New Boeing Space Bins," *PR Newswire*, October 9, 2015, http://www.prnewswire.com/news-releases/alaska-airlines-increases-overhead-storage-nearly-50-percent-with-first-737-featuring-new-boeing-space-bins-300157186.html (accessed March 22, 2016).

15. Ibid.

16. "Despite Inflammatory Incidents, Airline Customer Satisfaction Keeps Improving, JD Powers Finds," May 10, 2017, http://www.jdpower.com/press-releases/jd-power-2017-north-america-airline-satisfaction-study (accessed March 7, 2018).

17. Mark Matsousek, "The 20 Airlines With the Best First-Class Experience," *Business Insider*, June 21, 2019, https://www.businessinsider.com/airlines-best-first-class-experience-skytrax-2019-6 (accessed May 9, 2020); Eric Rosen, "First Look at Singapore Airlines' Amazing New First Class Suites," *Forbes*, November 27, 2017, https://www.forbes.com/sites/ericrosen/2017/11/02/first-look-at-singapore-airlines-amazing-new-first-class-suites/#7b7ed0b011b0 (accessed March 10, 2018).

18. http://www.expedia.com/flight-deals (accessed December 7, 2020).

19. Gordon A. Wyner, "Beyond ROI: Make Sure the Analytics Address Strategic Issues," *Marketing Management* 15 (May/June 2006): 8–9.

20. Guy R. Powell, *Return on Marketing Investment* (Albuquerque, NM: RPI Press, 2002), 4–6.

21. Ibid.

22. Andrea Fryrear, "Using Scrum for Marketing: An In-Depth Introduction," January 12, 2017, http://www.agilesherpas.com/scrummarketing-intro/ (accessed March 16, 2018); http://www.scrum.org/resources/what-is-scrum (accessed March 16, 2018).

23. David Edelman, Jason Heller, and Steven Spittaels, "Agile Marketing: A Step-by-Step Guide," McKinsey & Co., November 2016, https://www.mckinsey.com/business-functions/marketingand-sales/our-insights/agile-marketing-a-step-by-step-guide (accessed March 19, 2018).

24. Tim Ambler, "Don't Cave In to Cave Dwellers," *Marketing Management*, September/October 2006, 25–29.

25. International Data Corporation, "PC Market Finishes 2015 as Expected, Hopefully Setting the Stage for a More Stable Future, According to IDC," January 12, 2016, http://www.idc.com/getdoc.jsp?containerId=prUS40909316 (accessed March 19, 2016).

26. Based on P. J. Bednarski, "Tide Now Making It Easier to Do Wash 'On Demand'," *MediaPost*, February 20, 2019, https://www.mediapost.com/publications/article/332241/tide-now-making-it-easier-to-do-wash-on-demand.html; Erica Sweeney, "Tide Plots Nationwide Ambitions for Mobile On-Demand Laundry Service," *MarketingDive*, February 20, 2019, https://www.marketingdive.com/news/tide-plots-nationwide-ambitions-for-mobile-on-demand-laundry-service/548722/; "About Us," Tide.Com, Tide corporate website, accessed July 27, 2020, https://tide.com/en-us/about-tide/about-us; Janelle Nanos, "Tide Wants to Do Your Laundry for You – So I Let Them Do Mine," *The Boston Globe*, July 19, 2019, https://www.bostonglobe.com/business/2019/07/19/tide-cleaners-wants-your-laundry-for-you-let-them-mine/qkqxJXwDUDdknYQEbcvLJP/story.html; Sharon Terlep, "P&G Takes Tide to the Cleaners," *The Wall Street Journal*, September 3, 2019, https://www.wsj.com/articles/p-g-takes-tide-to-the-cleaners-11567503001; Jack Neff, "Procter & Gamble Goes Nationwide with Its Tide Laundry Service," *AdAge*, February 19, 2019, https://adage.com/article/cmo-strategy/tide-cleaners-launches-national-rollout-plan-2-000-locations/316677; Imogen Watson, "P&G launches 'Tide Cleaner App' – A Laundry Solution for Time-Constrained Consumers," *The Drum*, February 20, 2019, https://www.thedrum.com/news/2019/02/20/pg-launches-tide-cleaner-app-laundry-solution-time-constrained-consumers; "Choose Your School," UniversityLaundry.Com, Tide corporate website, accessed July 27, 2020, https://www.universitylaundry.com/register?returnUrl=%2Fhome%2Fmap; Nathaniel Meyersohn, "Who Knew, Tide Does Dry Cleaning. Now It's Expanding Business," *CNN*, February 20, 2019, https://www.cnn.com/2019/02/20/business/tide-cleaners-laundry-service/index.html; Suman Bhattacharyya, "P&G Is Testing a Tide-Branded Laundry Service," *Digiday*, February 20, 2019, https://digiday.com/retail/pg-testing-tide-branded-laundry-service/.

OUTLINE
C. DEVELOP MARKETING STRATEGIES
3. Pricing Strategies

QUESTION
● How will we price our product to the consumer and through the channel?

CHAPTER
Chapter 10: Price: What Is the Value Proposition Worth?

build a
Marketing Plan

HOW TO USE This Template

Here's a handy template that serves as a road map both to develop a marketing plan and to guide you through the course.

1. The first column provides the basic marketing plan **OUTLINE**.

2. The second column gives you **QUESTIONS** you must answer in each of the sections of the marketing plan.

3. The third column shows you where to go to find the answers as you work your way through the **CHAPTERS** of the book.

By the time you're done, all these pieces will come together and you'll understand how real marketers make real choices.

The Marketing Plan OUTLINE

A. PERFORM A SITUATION ANALYSIS
1. Internal Environment

2. External Environment

3. SWOT Analysis

B. SET MARKETING OBJECTIVES

C. DEVELOP MARKETING STRATEGIES
1. Select Target Markets and Positioning

2. Product Strategies

3. Pricing Strategies

4. Distribution Strategies

5. Promotional Strategies

D. IMPLEMENT AND CONTROL THE MARKETING PLAN
1. Action Plans (for all marketing mix elements)
2. Responsibility

3. Timeline

4. Budget

5. Measurement and Control

QUESTIONS the Plan Addresses	CHAPTERS Where You'll Find These Questions
• How does marketing support my company's mission, objectives, and growth strategies? • What is the corporate culture and how does it influence marketing activities? • What has my company done in the past with its: Target markets? Products? Pricing? Promotion? Supply chain? • What resources, including management expertise, does my company have that make us unique? How has the company added value through its offerings in the past?	**Chapter 1:** Welcome to the World of Marketing: Create and Deliver Value **Chapter 2:** Global, Ethical, and Sustainable Marketing **Chapter 3:** Strategic Market Planning **Chapter 4:** Market Research **Chapter 5:** Marketing Analytics: Welcome to the Era of Data-Driven Insights!
• What data does the company need in order to develop the plan and make evidence-based marketing decisions? • What is the nature of the overall domestic and global market for our product? How big is the market? Who buys our product? • What are the key trends in the economic environment? The competitive environment? The technological environment? The political and legal environment? The sociocultural environment?	
• Based on this analysis of the internal and external environments, what are the key Strengths, Weaknesses, Opportunities, and Threats (SWOT)?	
• What does marketing need to accomplish to support the objectives of my firm?	**Chapter 2:** Global, Ethical, and Sustainable Marketing **Chapter 3:** Strategic Market Planning
• How do consumers and organizations go about buying, using, and disposing of our products? • Which segments should we select to target? If a consumer market: What are the relevant demographic, psychographic, and behavioral segmentation approaches and the media habits of the targeted segments? If a business market: What are the relevant demographics of the purchasing firm? • How will we position our product for our market(s)?	**Chapter 4:** Market Research **Chapter 5:** Marketing Analytics: Welcome to the Era of Data-Driven Insights! **Chapter 6:** Understand Consumer and Business Markets **Chapter 7:** Segmentation, Target Marketing, and Positioning
• What is our core product? The actual product? The augmented product? • What product line / product mix strategies should we use? • How should we package, brand, and label our product?	**Chapter 8:** Product I: Innovation and New Product Development **Chapter 9:** Product II: Product Strategy, Branding, and Product Management
• How will we price our product to customers (either end-user consumers, business customers, or both)? How much must we sell to break even at this price? What pricing tactics should we use?	**Chapter 10:** Price: What Is the Value Proposition Worth?
• How do we get our product to customers in the best and most efficient manner? • How do we integrate supply chain elements to maximize the value we offer to our customers and other stakeholders? • What do we need to do to ensure customers have a great experience with us? • How can attention to service quality enhance our success?	**Chapter 11:** Deliver the Goods: Determine the Distribution Strategy **Chapter 12:** Deliver the Customer Experience
• How do we develop a consistent message about our product? • What approaches to each of the promotional options should we use? • What (if any) role should a sales force play in the promotion plan?	**Chapter 13:** Promotion I: Planning and Advertising **Chapter 14:** Promotion II: Social Media Platforms and Other Promotion Elements
• What is the title, purpose, and description of each action plan? • Who is responsible for accomplishing each action plan? • What is the timing for the elements of each action plan? • What budget do we need to successfully execute each action plan? • How and when will progress on each action plan be measured, by what metrics, and by whom?	**Chapter 3:** Strategic Market Planning **Chapter 4:** Market Research **Chapter 5:** Marketing Analytics: Welcome to the Era of Data-Driven Insights!

4 Market Research

Meet Cindy Bean

▼ A Decision Maker at Campbell Soup Company

Cindy Bean is manager of Consumer Insights at Campbell Soup Company. Since joining Campbell in 2010, Cindy has spent most of her time leading Consumer Insights on one of two New Ventures teams responsible for shaping and driving an enterprise-wide innovation pipeline against identified areas of consumer need. Cindy's team is made up of cross-functional leaders who iteratively identify areas of exploration, and rapidly prototype and validate ideas that result in solutions or new product opportunities. Cindy has been a part of launching the successful Dinner Sauce line of products that includes Skillet Sauces, Slow Cooker Sauces, Oven Sauces, and most recently Grill Sauces.

Prior to Campbell, Cindy worked in a variety of industries, managing a variety of businesses. Cindy worked as a Qualitative Research Consultant, achieving her moderating certification. She synthesized and interpreted sales and market share data, competitive intelligence, syndicated research, current industry conditions, and other relevant information to deliver the monthly state of the vision care business to Johnson & Johnson's Vistakon executives (J&J's Vision Care Division). She improved marketing effectiveness for Wyeth Pharmaceutical's (now Pfizer) Women's Health Care products by planning, designing, and managing a portfolio-wide consumer segmentation study, and she led the insights for the antidepressant drug Pristiq. She led research activities for McNeil Consumer Healthcare's Tylenol pediatrics, upper respiratory products, and the Sleep franchise (Tylenol PM and Simply Sleep). And she managed research functions within The Vanguard Group's Institutional business, including company 401(k) and 403(b) plans.

Cindy holds a bachelor's degree from Drexel University and an MBA from Pennsylvania State University.

Cindy's Info

What I do when I'm not working: When I'm not spending time with my husband and two kids, I'm practicing yoga, reading a book, or trying out a new recipe.

First job out of school: Financial Analyst at The Vanguard Group

A job-related mistake I wish I hadn't made: Taking too long to launch a new product. Perfection does not exist, but it's easier to get closer to what the

consumer wants by seeing them interact with it in real time and tweaking as we go.

Business book I'm reading now: *Thinking, Fast and Slow* by Daniel Kahneman

My motto to live by: Worry only about what you can control.

What drives me: Besides being a positive role model for my kids, I have a constant need to

understand people to the point of knowing how to make their lives better.

My management style: Highly collaborative and action-oriented

Don't do this when interviewing with me: Tell vague stories about your past when I'm looking for clear examples of your actions

My pet peeve: People not being accountable for their actions

Here's my problem...

Real **People**, Real **Choices**

A few years ago, Campbell set out on a mission to grow an otherwise stagnant soup business. Canned soup still is popular among baby boomers. However, younger consumers just aren't as interested. They turn to alternatives, like microwaveable and mini meals (such as pizza and tacos). Campbell realized its core business would be at risk if the company couldn't come up with products to entice the emerging group of millennial consumers who are between the ages of 18 and 34. These customers are 25 percent of the U.S. population, or approximately 80 million people. They spend a lot of money on food, but very little of it on soup.

To understand what makes millennials tick, Campbell went through a deep immersion. They scrutinized millennials' culture and habits to learn what kind of soups appeal to them. Cindy led a cross-functional innovation team that conducted dozens of extensive face-to-face, in-depth interactions with young consumers, both one-on-one and in groups. The team ate meals with young people in their homes, checked out their pantries, and tagged along with them on shopping trips to the supermarket.

After that immersion, the team listed all the pain points millennials associated with canned soup. For example, they told the team millennials think that these products are too "processed" and that they taste bland, homogeneous, and unexciting. Another common complaint was the lack of healthy ingredients these consumers look for, such as quinoa and on-trend veggies, like kale. The team found this group includes "flexitarians"—that is, consumers who eat vegetarian for a few days and then eat meat on the weekends, for special occasions, to satisfy a craving, etc. They tend to care about sustainability, local sourcing, and company practices.

As a result of these insights, Cindy's team then created concepts and prototypes to test their potential solutions for the pain points they identified. The team continued to put these ideas in front of a series of focus groups as they fine-tuned their solutions based on the feedback they got from actual millennials.

This process gave Cindy's team some great insights about what they could do to boost Campbell's appeal to millennials. One no-brainer was to change the packaging from a can to a pouch; the respondents told the team that a pouch communicates a "fresher ingredients" message. And the team knew the flavor profile of the soup had to be bolder than the varieties that baby boomers are used to. They ultimately aligned on the following as the guardrails to create this new product platform:

- Young adults are looking for satisfying, easy meals for one.
- Products should satisfy demanding tastes for a more flavorful life.
- Products should always deliver of-the-moment flavors and show packaging from a trusted brand.

However, given Campbell's current portfolio of soups, Cindy's team needed to position this millennial-focused platform differently from existing products they already sold under the Campbell's name. Specifically, most of the ideas they tested overlapped with Campbell's Slow Kettle brand. The Slow Kettle brand was created to bring Campbell into the packaged premium soup category. Because consumers were becoming more interested in the rich, complex flavors they enjoy from restaurant soups, the team saw an opportunity to bring that experience home. Campbell's culinary team created Slow Kettle to create a "prepared with care" feeling even though it still comes from the supermarket soup aisle. The flavors are familiar, the soups are hearty and filling, the quality is better than that of other canned soups, and the package is meant to convey a homemade feeling (Slow Kettle comes in a tub, like Tupperware). The brand skews toward higher-income millennials. Because the price point is at a premium for the category, $3.25, it represents a small but interesting opportunity for Campbell.

Clearly Cindy's team needs to do more work to figure out the best way to create a new offering that grabs millennials' attention and makes it clear that this is "not your father's soup," while at the same time avoiding confusion with the Slow Kettle brand.

Courtesy of Cindy Bean/Campbell Soup Company

Courtesy of Cindy Bean/Campbell Soup Company

Cindy considered her **options** 1·2·3

1 **Option**

Carve out a new space within the soup portfolio for this millennial-driven soup offering. They would have to demonstrate that the new offering serves a unique need for prepared soup that is not already available in Campbell's other brands. This strategy would give them an opportunity to build a new brand from scratch entirely based on millennials' needs. The brand could include soups but also possibly other food products, such as mini-meals and hearty on-the-go snacks, positioned to meet the needs of the millennial. This new product line would be so distinct that they wouldn't have to worry about cannibalizing sales from other parts of their portfolio, especially Slow Kettle. However, it's expensive and risky to build a brand. They would have to commit to at least a three-year investment to build awareness and encourage trial. Because Campbell does offer somewhat similar products, like Slow Kettle, if they fail to create a really tight message to set apart the new brand, they might shoot themselves in the foot by injecting some confusion into the marketplace.

2
Option

Reposition an existing brand to be the face of the millennial portfolio. Campbell's Slow Kettle Brand already has many elements that could meet the needs of these young consumers. With a few tweaks, they could probably transform it into the kind of product that would resonate with this target market. This approach would involve less investment than building an entirely new brand, and they already have the internal manufacturing capability to turn out these soups. On the other hand, they could commit the cardinal sin when marketing to millennials: offer a product they perceive as inauthentic. Because the Slow Kettle brand has already been on the market, these savvy young consumers might decide that a few tweaks to an existing offering doesn't really speak to them. Millennials run from products they view as "fake" faster than soup boils on a hot stove.

3
Option

Don't take the risk, and stick with their existing solutions. Investing in a unique millennial product might be just too costly and time-consuming, and it's possible that a new solution wouldn't deliver enough return on investment to justify their efforts. This conservative solution would allow Campbell to focus their resources on maintaining their solid (though stagnant) base business. They could ramp up their advertising to appeal to the nostalgia of the familiar Campbell brand, because millennials sometimes do respond well to this

kind of appeal. On the other hand, if this stay-the-course strategy backfires, they risk becoming irrelevant to an entire generation of new consumers. In that event, they would continue to experience a decline in their bottom line as an aging group of loyal consumers eventually dies off. And, if competitors eventually enter the millennial space, Campbell might be forced to sit on the sidelines as they capture this valuable target. The team knows that most consumer-packaged-goods (CPG) companies are taking similar steps to satisfy this new generation. Many traditional brands are transitioning to natural colors, removing artificial sweeteners and high fructose corn syrup, and in some cases, moving toward a non-GMO label to address consumers' concerns about genetically modified food. There's no doubt that changes are coming.

Now, put yourself in Cindy's shoes. Which option would you choose, and why?

You Choose

Which **Option** would you choose, and **why**?
☐ **Option 1**   ☐ **Option 2**   ☐ **Option 3**

4.1 Knowledge Is Power

OBJECTIVE
Explain the role of a marketing information system and a marketing decision support system in marketing decision making.

In Chapter 3 you learned about market planning. We considered how the COVID-19 crisis forced marketers to rapidly, and hopefully nimbly, adjust their marketing plans to account for changes in the external and internal environments that created the need for change in marketing strategy. An important question is: Just how are those decisions about changing plans and strategies made? That is, what are the informational inputs to marketers that allow them to make the best decisions? The answer is research, and in particular **market research**. Market research refers to the process of collecting, analyzing, and interpreting data about customers, competitors, and the business environment to improve marketing effectiveness. (Note that in practice, the term *marketing research* is often used interchangeably with market research, but to be precise, marketing research is broader in scope and often refers to the type of research that academics in marketing conduct about the field, whereas market research refers to the type of research that marketing practitioners conduct about markets and consumers.) In 2020, once it became clear that the global crisis was going to significantly impact the way consumers acquire products, services, and information, marketing managers very rapidly began conducting research to gain insights that allowed for exceptionally quick changes in how their firms were going to market and how they were communicating with their customers.

At Campbell Soup, Cindy Bean's issue centers on how to better appeal to millennials with what is basically a very traditional product—soup. When people of all generations found themselves "locked down" during March and April of 2020, Campbell found themselves in the totally unexpected position of having to substantially ramp up production to keep up with steeply increased consumption of "comfort foods." It seems that soup in general has that unique combination of convenience, comfort, nutrition, and family connotation that really "hit the spot" during that period when most people were holed up together at home (you probably experienced this!). In addition, to the great fortune of Campbell, other massively consumed products during those days included pastas (which of course

market research
The process of collecting, analyzing, and interpreting data about customers, competitors, and the business environment in order to improve marketing effectiveness.

require sauces) and snacks. Campbell was all too happy to serve those product needs in the form of Prego and Goldfish! From a market research standpoint, the rapid turn of events prompted Campbell to ramp up data collection—from both consumers and its retailers—to shift and increase production and distribution as rapidly as possible toward the areas experiencing the most consumer demand. Without that information, shelves no doubt would have been even more empty of the most popular items than they were otherwise.[1]

Without a doubt, successful market planning means that managers make informed decisions to guide the organization. But how do marketers actually arrive at those decisions? Specifically, how do they find out what they need to know to develop marketing objectives, select a target market, position (or reposition) their product, and develop product, price, promotion, and place strategies?

The answer is (drumroll . . .): information. Information is the fuel that runs the marketing engine. There's a famous acronym in the marketing information systems field: **GIGO**, which stands for *garbage in, garbage out*. To make good decisions, marketers must have information that is not "garbage"—rather, it must be accurate, up to date, and relevant. To understand these needs, marketers first must engage in various forms of research and data collection to identify them.

In this chapter, which kicks off Part Two of the book, we will discuss a variety of tools that marketers use to get that information. Then in Chapter 5, we'll drill down further on applying market research for decision making via marketing analytics. In the chapters that follow, we will look closely at how and why both consumers and organizations buy, and we will explore how marketers sharpen their focus via target marketing.

Disruption and Market Research

Before we jump into the topic of market research, here's a question for you: A marketer who conducts research to learn more about his customers shouldn't encounter any ethical challenges, right? Well, maybe in a perfect world. In reality though, several aspects of market research are fraught with the *potential* for ethics breaches. **Market research ethics** refers to taking an ethical and aboveboard approach to conducting market research that does no harm to the participant in the process of conducting the research.

Central to the issue of market research ethics in the current digital era, much of the information collected about consumers nowadays comes from various online means. And when an organization collects data—whether via digital or other means—important issues of privacy and confidentiality come into play. **Data privacy** (or information privacy) refers to the ability an organization or individual has to determine what data collected can be shared with third parties. Marketers must be clear when they work with research respondents about how they will use the data and give respondents full disclosure on their options for confidentiality and anonymity. **Confidentiality** refers to a condition in which the researcher knows the identity of a research subject, but takes steps to protect that identity from being discovered by others. **Anonymity** is a condition in which the identity of individual subjects is not known to researchers. As a result of the heightened public attention to these issues, marketers have found themselves in the position of having to develop deep professional partnerships with both the information technology and legal departments in their firms. Ultimately, the field of **risk management** in marketing has grown exponentially in recent years, mostly related to issues of **data security** and market research. In a nutshell, risk management refers to the practice of identifying potential risks in advance, analyzing them, and taking precautionary steps to reduce/curb the risk. Along those lines, for market researchers any data collection and storage process must be subjected to rigorous risk management analysis. Nobody wants their brand to join the Top 15 worst data breaches list! And this discussion brings us back to marketing ethics. For example, it is unethical to collect data under the guise of market research when your real intent is to develop a **database** of potential customers for direct marketing. A database is an organized collection (often electronic) of data that can be searched and queried to provide information about contacts, products, customers, inventory, and more. Firms that abuse the trust of respondents run a serious risk of damaging their reputation when word gets out that they are engaged in unethical research practices. This makes it difficult to attract participants in future research projects—and it "poisons the well" for other companies when consumers believe that they can't trust them.

A key takeaway for you as a student of marketing is that market research—when executed ethically, professionally, and with high consumer confidence in the security of the data—is highly beneficial not only to marketers for developing plans and strategies but for consumers who benefit from products and services more attuned to their needs. The success of products you buy from Amazon, the ads you click (or try to make go away) while enjoying YouTube, the price you pay at Chick-fil-A for that Grilled Chicken Club and Waffle Fries, and nearly every other imaginable product and service that is marketed to the public is heavily influenced by market research and the interpretation of the data. Hence, the content of this chapter is very important for anyone who wants to do marketing well. Back to GIGO again, if the data is bad and the interpretation of it is worse, some rotten marketing decisions are bound to happen!

Market research is a huge topic and is the subject of one or multiple courses in any marketing degree program. To help you sort out many of the most important ideas, this chapter gives you a succinct guided tour of the most important concepts in market research, starting with the big picture concept of a marketing information system and then systematically walking you through each step in the market research process. And don't be afraid that this chapter's message is too technical, overly statistical, or only relevant for advanced marketers! Our job here is to give you a nice overview of how and why market research adds huge value to marketers' knowledge for planning and decision making. It's an indispensable marketing tool.

Notice that the title of this section is Knowledge Is Power. That about says it all—without the knowledge that only well-interpreted data can provide, marketers are at a huge competitive disadvantage in their ability to compete through the marketing strategy and planning elements you learned about in Chapter 3. Put another way, when marketers throw perfectly good money against marketing strategies that are based on poorly conducted and interpreted market research, the likelihood of success with consumers is very low.

The Marketing Information System

marketing information system (MIS)
A process that first determines what information marketing managers need and then gathers, sorts, analyzes, stores, and distributes relevant and timely marketing information to system users.

Many firms use a **marketing information system (MIS)** to collect information. The MIS is a process that first determines what information marketing managers need. Then, it gathers, sorts, analyzes, stores, and distributes relevant and timely marketing information to users. As shown in Figure 4.1, the MIS system includes three important components:

1. Four types of data (internal company data, market intelligence, market research, and acquired databases)
2. Computer hardware and software to analyze the data and to create reports
3. Output for marketing decision makers

Various sources "feed" the MIS with data, and then the system's software "digests" it. MIS analysts use the output to generate a series of regular reports for various decision makers.

Let's take a closer look at each of the four different data sources for the MIS.

Internal Company Data

The *internal company data system* uses information from within the organization to produce reports on the results of sales and marketing activities. Internal company data include a firm's sales records—information such as which customers buy which products in what quantities and at what intervals, which items are in stock and which are back-ordered because they are out of stock, when items were shipped to the customer, and which items have been returned because they are defective.

Often, an MIS allows both marketers and also salespeople and sales managers in the field to access relevant information through a company **intranet**. This is an internal corporate communications network that uses Internet technology to link company departments, employees, and databases. Intranets are secured so that only authorized employees have access. Nowadays, savvy marketing organizations make sure that access and usability of this valuable internal information is maximized by creating an appealing interface for employees called a **marketing dashboard**. A marketing dashboard is a comprehensive display and access system providing company personnel with up-to-the-minute information necessary to make decisions. Marketing dashboards often include such elements as data on actual sales versus forecasts, progress on marketing plan objectives, distribution channel effectiveness, current price competition, and whatever other metrics and information are uniquely relevant to the particular employee's role in the firm.[2] *Dashboard* is a good label because, similar to the dashboard of your car, the idea of a marketing dashboard is to make information contained within the company intranet convenient, attractively displayed, and available in real time.

Marketers often rely on salespeople and sales managers in the field to influence customers to purchase. A great marketing dashboard allows these folks to easily access the company intranet and find information available on the MIS system. This type of sales support by marketing means that the sales force can better serve their customers because they have immediate and well-organized access to information on pricing, inventory levels, production schedules, shipping dates, and purchasing history for all of their customers. Marketing managers at company headquarters also can see daily or weekly sales data by brand or product line from the internal company data system. They can view monthly sales reports to measure progress toward sales goals and market share objectives. For example, buyers and managers at Walmart's headquarters in Arkansas use up-to-the-minute sales information they obtain from store cash registers around the country so they can quickly detect problems with products, promotions, price competitiveness, and even the firm's distribution system. Related to company intranets and marketing dashboards is the concept of *customer relationship management (CRM)*, which we'll develop more fully in Chapter 5.

Market Intelligence

As we saw in Chapter 2, to make good decisions, marketers need to have information about the marketing environment. Thus, a second important element of the MIS is the **market intelligence system**, a method by which marketers get information about what's going on in the world that is relevant to their business. Although the name *intelligence* may suggest cloak-and-dagger spy activities, in reality nearly all the information that companies need about their environment—including the competitive environment—is available by monitoring everyday sources: company websites, industry trade publications, and direct field observations of the competitive marketplace.

And because salespeople are the ones "in the trenches" every day, talking with customers, distributors, and prospective customers, they are a key to sourcing this valuable information. Retailers and other service providers often employ **mystery shoppers** to experience the way actual customers are handled by providers. And this goes for both online and in-person customer experiences. (Imagine being paid to take flights to cool locations!) Other information may come from speaking with organizational buyers about competing

Figure 4.1 *Process* | The Marketing Information System

A firm's marketing information system (MIS) stores and analyzes data from a variety of sources and turns the data into information for useful marketing decision making.

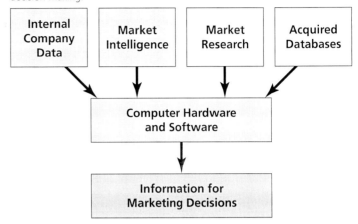

intranet
An internal corporate communication network that uses Internet technology to link company departments, employees, and databases.

marketing dashboard
A comprehensive display and access system providing company personnel with up-to-the-minute information necessary to make decisions.

market intelligence system
A method by which marketers get information about what's going on in the world that is relevant to their business.

mystery shoppers
Individuals employed by retailers and other service providers to experience and report back on the way actual customers are handled.

reverse engineering
The process of physically deconstructing a competitor's product to determine how it's put together.

products, attending trade shows, or simply purchasing, using, and even **reverse engineering** competitors' products, which means physically deconstructing the product to determine how it's put together.

Marketing managers may use market intelligence data to predict fluctuations in sales as a result of a variety of external environmental factors you read about in Chapter 2, including economic conditions, political issues, and events that heighten consumer awareness. They may also use the data to forecast the future so that they will be on top of developing trends. Television networks have observed how consumers increasingly binge-watch shows through platforms such as Netflix, Amazon Prime Video, Disney+, and others, and as a result, they have begun to offer their shows in ways that appeal to the changing preferences and expectations of consumers. And during the COVID-19 lockdown period, consumers gorged on content from streaming services not only in terms of hours on end spent binge-watching but also in branching out and subscribing to a number of different streaming services! This resulted in a huge leap in product trial and acceptance, and no doubt dealt a blow to the networks and cable.[3]

Market Research

As mentioned earlier, market research refers to the process of collecting, analyzing, and interpreting data about customers, competitors, and the business environment to improve marketing effectiveness. Although companies collect market intelligence data continuously to keep managers abreast of happenings in the marketplace, market research also is called for when managers need unique information to help them make specific decisions. Whether their business is selling cool fashion accessories to teens or industrial coolant to factories, firms succeed when they know what customers want, when they want it, where they want it—and what competing firms are doing about it. In other words, the better a firm is at obtaining valid market information, the more successful it will be. Therefore, virtually all companies rely on some form of market research, though the amount and type of research they conduct varies dramatically. In general, market research data available in an MIS come in two flavors: syndicated research reports and custom research reports.

syndicated research
Research by firms that collect data on a regular basis and sell the reports to multiple firms.

Syndicated research is general information that specialized firms collect on a regular basis and subsequently sell to other firms. Nielsen's Scarborough, for instance, surveys local consumers across the United States in over 100 media markets to understand media trends, shopping habits, consumer attitudes, healthcare behaviors, and more. These insights assist clients in media planning, brand strategy, and market development.[4] And the Q Score scoring system, owned by Marketing Evaluations Inc., is a quotient (or percentage) that indicates the proportion of people who have heard of a given celebrity who also consider them as one of their favorites. This is sometimes referred to as a "positive Q Score." A "negative Q Score" can be calculated too, being the proportion of people who have heard of a given celebrity who also consider them "poor" or "fair."

Twice a year, a representative sample of men and women are presented with a list of 1,800 celebrities and asked to rate them on a six-point scale from "Never heard of" to "One of my favorites." And who do you think was right at the top in a recent calculation? Ta-da . . . none other than country music legend Dolly Parton! Dolly is called out in a divided America as a "great unifier," scoring in the top 10 most loved celebrities globally (and also one of the least hated!)[5]

custom research
Research conducted for a single firm to provide specific information its managers need.

As valuable as it may be, syndicated research doesn't provide all the answers to marketing questions because the information it collects typically is broad but shallow. For example, it gives good insights about general trends, such as who is watching what TV shows or what brand of perfume is hot this year. In contrast, a firm conducts **custom research** to provide answers to specific questions. This kind of research is especially helpful for firms when they need to know more about *why* certain trends have surfaced. In contrast to syndicated research, custom research can provide a tailored approach for researching more niche topics. What if candy giant Hershey is considering entering the growing snack bar segment and wants to obtain information about current snack bars in the marketplace, particularly Clif and KIND. This calls for examination beyond Hershey's traditional brands and markets. And they would likely also want to look at different product formulations and enhancements to see if it is possible to find a viable competitive slot within the overall category. This type of information need would call for a custom research project.[6]

Some firms maintain an in-house research department that conducts studies on its behalf. Many firms, however, hire outside research companies that specialize in designing and conducting projects based on the needs of the client. Hint: This is a great career path if you love solving puzzles and getting into the weeds about what makes consumers tick! These custom research reports are another kind of information an MIS includes. Marketers may use market research to identify opportunities for new products, promote existing ones, or provide data about the quality of their products, who uses them, and how.

Acquired Databases

A large amount of information that can be useful in marketing decision making is available in the form of external databases. Firms acquire these databases from any number of sources. For example, some companies are willing to sell their customer database to noncompeting firms. Government databases—including the massive amounts of economic and demographic information the U.S. Census Bureau, Bureau of Labor Statistics, and other agencies collect—are available at little or no cost. State and local governments may make some information, such as automobile license data, available for a fee.

Sophisticated companies like Harrah's closely track what people do in venues like Las Vegas so they can send promotional materials tailored to specific entertainment preferences (like Lance Burton here).

Earlier we discussed databases and data security in general. Nowadays, the use of databases for marketing purposes has come under increased government scrutiny because some consumer advocates are quite concerned about the potential invasion of privacy such use may cause. Using the data to analyze overall consumer trends is one thing—using it for outbound direct mailings and unsolicited phone calls and emails has evoked a backlash in a tidal wave of "do-not-call" lists and antispam laws. Maybe you have noticed that when you sign up for most anything online that requires your contact information, you receive an invitation to "opt out" of receiving promotional mailings from the company or from others who may acquire your contact information from the organization later. By law, if you decide to opt out, companies cannot use your information for marketing purposes.

We'll further explore the overall issue of database usage by marketers in the context of the popular phrase "Big Data" in Chapter 5. For now, just know that it's a good bet that every website or mobile link you search—and maybe even every tweet or Facebook message you post today—will wind up in a marketer's database.

Marketing Decision Support System

As we have seen, a firm's MIS generates regular accessible information for decision makers on what is going on in the internal and external environment. But sometimes this information alone (no matter how well organized with a slick marketing dashboard) is still inadequate for decision making. Different managers may want different information, and in some cases, the problem they must address is too vague or unusual for the MIS process to easily answer. As a result, many firms beef up their MIS with a **marketing decision support system (MDSS)**. An MDSS includes analysis and interactive software that allows marketing managers, even those who are not computer experts, to access MIS data and conduct their own analyses, often within the context of the company intranet.

marketing decision support system (MDSS)
The data, analysis software, and interactive software that allow managers to conduct analyses and find the information they need.

Table 4.1	Comparison of Questions an MIS versus an MDSS Might Answer

Questions an MIS Answers	Questions an MDSS Answers
What were our company sales of each product during the past month and the past year?	Has our decline in sales simply reflected changes in overall industry sales, or is there some portion of the decline that industry changes cannot explain?
What changes are happening in sales in our industry, and what are the demographic characteristics of consumers whose purchase patterns are changing the most?	Do we see the same trends in our different product categories? Are the changes in consumer trends similar among all our products? What are the demographic characteristics of consumers who seem to be the most and the least loyal?
What are the best media to reach a large proportion of heavy, medium, or light users of our product?	If we change our media schedule by adding or deleting certain media buys, will we reach fewer users of our product?

At its essence, an MDSS includes sophisticated statistical and modeling software tools. Statistical software allows managers to examine complex relationships among factors in the marketplace. For example, a marketer who wants to know how consumers perceive his or her company's brand in relation to the competition's brand might use a sophisticated statistical technique called *multidimensional scaling* to create a "perceptual map," or a graphic presentation of the various brands in relationship to each other. You'll see an example of a perceptual map in Chapter 7.

MDSS is very sophisticated and its modeling software allows decision makers to examine possible or preconceived ideas about relationships in the data—to ask "what-if" questions. As examples, media modeling software might enable marketers to see what would happen if they made certain decisions about where to place their advertising and sales data, and an analytical model might allow brand managers to see how many consumers would stay with the brand versus switching under different conditions over time. Table 4.1 gives a few other examples of the different marketing questions an MIS and an MDSS might answer, providing a vivid contrast of the capabilities of each to add value to marketing decision making.

4.2 Evidence-Based Decision Making in Marketing

OBJECTIVE

Understand the concept of evidence-based decision making toward gaining customer insights.

As a consumer, you inherently know that it's getting easier all the time for organizations to collect huge amounts of data. **Data** are raw, unorganized facts that need to be processed. Analysts then process, organize, structure, and present the data so that it is useful for decision making. This transformation creates **information**, which is interpreted data. But there is a downside to knowing too much! All of these data can be overwhelming—and not very useful—if no one has any idea what they all mean. The old saying about the ocean—"water, water everywhere and not a drop to drink!"—can be repurposed as "data, data everywhere and nothing insightful to find!"

You are studying marketing at a time in which the buzzwords for marketers are **evidence-based decision making**, which quite simply refers to a marketer's capability to utilize all of the relevant information available (the "evidence") in order to make the best possible marketing decisions. Sounds logical and pretty easy, right? Well, not so fast on that. Many decisions in marketing end up getting made through more of a READY➔FIRE➔AIM approach, unfortunately meaning that little or no market research went into the decision-making process. Note: Agile marketing, which we discussed in Chapter 3, is *not* READY➔FIRE➔AIM decision making! Rather, in agile marketing, the idea is to both acquire and analyze the evidence quickly, gaining speedy insights for good decisions.

data
Raw, unorganized facts that need to be processed.

information
Interpreted data.

evidence-based decision making
A marketer's capability to utilize all of the relevant information available in order to make the best possible marketing decisions.

Of course, sometimes more information is available than other times, and in some cases, time pressures can lead to simply making a decision with the information you've got at the moment. But everything else being equal, successful marketers of today and the future are going to have to buy into the mantra of evidence-based decision making and then gear up their firm's data collection and analysis capabilities accordingly—because the alternative is being left in the dust by competitors who do have a strong capability in this area. This is such an important strategic issue for marketers and for firms that a whole new subfield of marketing called *data analytics* has emerged. **Data analytics** in marketing is the process of examining raw data to discover trends, answer questions, and gain insights in order to make evidence-based decisions. Chapter 5 provides a rich introduction to the whole area of data analytics in marketing.

Closely related to evidence-based decision making is the concept of **customer insights**, which at its core refers to the collection, deployment, and interpretation of information that allows a business to acquire, develop, and retain its customers. That is, the *insights* are the evidence that allows for better decisions! Like Cindy Bean at Campbell, most companies today maintain a dedicated team of experts whose jobs are to sift through all the information available to support market planning decisions. This group does its best to understand how customers interact with the organization (including the nasty encounters they may have) and to guide planners when they think about future initiatives.

The job of executing a companywide evidence-based approach to decision making is more complicated than it sounds. Traditionally, most companies have operated in "silos," so that, for example, the people in new product development would have zero contact with anyone in customer service who actually had to deal with complaints about the items they designed. The insights manager is like an artist who has to work with a lot of different colors on a palette—the job is to integrate feedback from syndicated studies, marketing research, customer service, loyalty programs, and other sources to paint a more complete picture the organization can use. As such, this function in the organization usually plays a supporting role across the firm's strategic business units (SBUs).

For example, to gain greater insight into the preferences and characteristics of those consumers who made purchases within a specific product line of soups, a product line manager at Campbell could reach out to Cindy Bean's consumer insights team for help. The team would then gather a wide array of data about the specific types of consumers who enjoy soup from that product line as well as other data, such as frequency of purchases by consumer segment and what key factors influence consumption of specific types of soup by consumer segment. Cindy's team no doubt would deliver this information in an easy-to-understand format to highlight the most actionable insights. This analysis would enable the manager of the product line to determine how to better allocate resources to drive market performance of the products. Like Campbell, many organizations are "catching the wave" by adding customer (consumer) insights departments. This growing trend in turn offers new and promising job opportunities for graduates who know how to fish for usable knowledge in the huge information ocean.

data analytics
The process of examining raw data to discover trends, answer questions, and gain insights in order to make evidence-based decisions.

customer insights
The collection, deployment, and interpretation of information that allows a business to acquire, develop, and retain its customers.

4.3 Steps in the Market Research Process

OBJECTIVE
List and explain the steps and key elements of the market research process.

The collection and interpretation of information is hardly a one-shot deal that managers engage in "just out of curiosity." Ideally, market research is an ongoing process—a series of steps marketers take repeatedly to learn about the marketplace. Whether a company conducts the research itself or hires another firm to do it, the goal is the same: to help managers make informed marketing decisions. Figure 4.2 provides a great road map of the steps in the research process. You can use it to track our discussion of each step.

Figure 4.2 *Process* | Steps in the Market Research Process

The market research process includes a series of steps that begins with defining the problem or the information needed and ends with the finished research report for managers.

Define the Research Problem

- Specify the research objectives
- Identify the consumer population of interest
- Place the problem in an environmental context

↓

Determine the Research Design

- Determine whether secondary data are available
- Determine whether primary data are required
  —Exploratory research
  —Descriptive research
  —Causal research

↓

Choose the Method to Collect Primary Data

- Determine which survey methods are most appropriate
  —Mail questionnaires
  —Telephone interviews
  —Face-to-face interviews
  —Online questionnaires
- Determine which observational methods are most appropriate
  —Personal observation
  —Unobtrusive measures
  —Mechanical observation

↓

Design the Sample

- Choose between probability sampling and nonprobability sampling

↓

Collect the Data

- Translate questionnaires and responses if necessary
- Combine data from multiple sources (if available)

↓

Analyze and Interpret the Data

- Tabulate and cross-tabulate the data
- Interpret or draw conclusions from the results

↓

Prepare the Research Report

- In general, the research report includes the following:
  —An executive summary
  —A description of the research methods
  —A discussion of the results of the study
  —Limitations of the study
  —Conclusions and recommendations

Step 1: Define the Research Problem

The first step in the market research process is to clearly understand what information managers need. This step is called *defining the research problem*. You should note that the word *problem* here does not necessarily refer to "something that is wrong" but instead refers to the overall questions for which the firm needs answers. Defining the problem has three components:

1. *Specify the research objectives:* What questions will the research attempt to answer?

2. *Identify the consumer population of interest:* What are the characteristics of the consumer group(s) of interest?

3. *Place the problem in an environmental context:* What factors in the firm's internal and external business environment might influence the situation?

It's not as simple as it may seem to provide the right kind of information for each of these pieces of the problem. Suppose a luxury car manufacturer wants to find out why its sales are not keeping pace with other luxury competitors. The research objective could center on any number of possible questions: Is the firm's advertising failing to reach the right consumers? Is the right message being sent? Do the firm's cars have a particular feature and related benefit (or lack of one) that turns customers away? Does a competitor offer some features and benefits that have better captured customer imaginations? Is there a problem with the firm's reputation for providing quality service? Do consumers believe the price is right for the value they get? The particular objective researchers choose depends on a variety of factors, such as the feedback the firm gets from its customers, the information it receives from the marketplace, and sometimes even the intuition of the people who design the research.

Often the focus of a research question comes from marketplace feedback that identifies a possible problem. Volvo, long known for the safety records of its cars, continues to have a tough time competing with luxury brands like Mercedes-Benz, BMW, Lexus, and Audi. Resulting research question: How might Volvo improve its market share among luxury car buyers?

The *research objective* determines the consumer population the company will study. In the case of Volvo, the research might focus on current owners to find out what they especially like about the car. Or it could be directed at non-owners to understand their lifestyles, what they look for in a luxury automobile, or their beliefs about the Volvo brand that discourage them from buying the cars. Actually, the Volvo scenario is a real one, and in contemplating the best move, the company chose to focus on *why consumers didn't buy the competing brands*. Volvo marketers figured it would be a good idea to identify the "pain points" shoppers experienced when they looked at rivals so that they could try to address these objections with their own marketing activities (a pretty smart approach!).

So what did Volvo find out? Its research showed that many car shoppers were too intimidated by the "ostentatious" image of Mercedes and BMW to consider actually buying one. Others felt that too many of their neighbors were driving a Lexus, and they wanted to make more of an individual statement. Volvo's vice president of marketing explained that Volvo owners' "interpretation of luxury is different but very real. They're more into life's experiences, and more into a Scandinavian simple design [of vehicles] versus a lot of clutter. They are very much luxury customers and love luxury products, but they don't feel a need to impress others." Based on the research findings, Volvo developed a new ad campaign, showing consumers that it was OK—and even desirable—to be different. The company even pokes fun at rival luxury brands. In one TV commercial, a sophisticated woman sits at a stoplight in her Mercedes-Benz SUV and checks out her makeup in the rearview mirror. Another woman pulls up next to her in a Volvo XC60—but she's more down to earth. The Volvo driver looks into her own rearview mirror. The difference is she makes a funny face to make her kids in the backseat crack up. The voice-over says, "Volvos aren't for everyone, and we kinda like it that way."[7]

This Volvo example illustrates the evidence-based decision making approach very well as it has ramped up its research and development (R&D). The insights the company identified led Volvo to double down on its own uniqueness. This clear positioning and compelling messaging within the luxury car market has contributed mightily to a turnaround in sales and profit performance for the firm. Their lesson learned is that great marketing *works*—and the odds of doing great marketing go way up when evidence-based decision making yields just the right insights to spark an appropriate strategy change.[8]

Step 2: Determine the Research Design

Once we isolate specific problems, the second step of the research process is to decide on a plan of attack. This plan is the **research design**, which specifies exactly what information marketers will collect and what type of study they will do. Research designs fall into two broad categories based on whether the analysts will use primary or secondary data (see Figure 4.3). All marketing problems do not call for the same research techniques, and marketers solve many problems most effectively with a combination of approaches.

research design
A plan that specifies what information marketers will collect and what type of study they will do.

Research with Secondary Data

The first question marketers must ask when they determine their research design is whether the information they require to make a decision already exists. For example, a coffee producer that needs to know the differences in coffee consumption among different demographic and geographic segments of the market may find that the information it needs is available from one or more studies already conducted by the National Coffee Association, the leading trade association of U.S. coffee companies and a major generator of industry research. Information that has been collected for some purpose other than the problem at hand is **secondary data**.

secondary data
Data that have been collected for some purpose other than the problem at hand.

Figure 4.3 *Process* | Market Research Designs

For some research problems, secondary data may provide the information needed. At other times, one of the primary data collection methods may be needed.

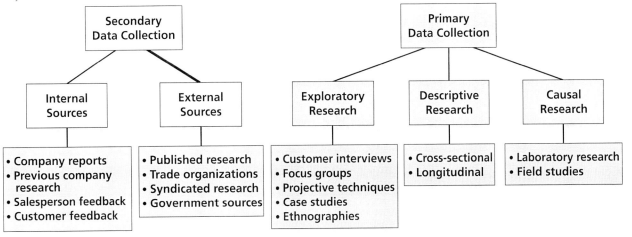

Many marketers thrive on going out and collecting new, "fresh" data from consumers. In fact, getting new data seems to be part of the marketing DNA. However, if secondary data are available, it saves the firm time and money because it has already incurred the expense to design a study and collect the data. Sometimes the information that marketers need may be "hiding" right under the organization's nose in the form of company reports; previous company research studies; feedback received from customers, salespeople, or stores; or even in the memories of longtime employees (it's amazing how many times a manager commissions a study without knowing that someone else who was working on a different problem already submitted a similar report!).

More typically, though, researchers need to look elsewhere for secondary data. They may obtain reports published in popular and business press, studies that private research organizations or government agencies conduct, and published research on the state of the industry from trade organizations. For example, many companies subscribe to reports such as the *National Consumer Study*, a survey conducted by syndicated research firm MRI-Simmons. The company publishes results that it then sells to marketers, advertising agencies, and publishers. Access to its data is even available in some college libraries. This database contains more than 60,000 data variables with usage behavior on all major media, over 500 product categories, and over 8,000 brands. Data from MRI-Simmons can give a brand manager a profile of who uses a product, identify heavy users, or even provide data on what information sources a target market is likely to consult prior to purchase.[9] As examples, popular online sources of useful data for marketers include Opinion Research Corporation (ORC), the U.S. Census Bureau and Bureau of Labor Statistics, the American Marketing Association, and LexisNexus.

Research with Primary Data

Of course, secondary data are not always the answer. When a company needs to make a specific decision, marketers often collect **primary data**: information they gather directly from respondents to specifically address the question at hand. Primary data include demographic and psychological information about customers and prospective customers, customers' attitudes and opinions about products and competing products, as well as their awareness or knowledge about a product and their beliefs about the people who use those products. In the next few sections, we'll talk briefly about the various design options for collecting primary data.

Exploratory Research

Marketers use **exploratory research** to come up with ideas for new strategies and opportunities or perhaps just to get a better handle on a problem they are currently experiencing with a product. Because the studies are usually small scale and less costly than other techniques, marketers may do this to test their hunches about what's going on without too much risk or expense. We refer to most exploratory research as **qualitative research**, which means the results of the research project tend to be nonnumeric and instead might be detailed verbal or visual information about consumers' attitudes, feelings, and buying behaviors. In contrast, **quantitative research** produces numeric results that can be analyzed using a variety of statistical programs. Four primary examples of exploratory research are *in-depth interviews* (sometimes called just depth interviews), *focus groups* (which can be in person or virtual), *case studies*, and *ethnography*. Let's take a closer look at each of these approaches.

primary data
Data from research conducted to help make a specific decision.

exploratory research
A technique that marketers use to generate insights for future, more rigorous studies.

qualitative research
Research with results that provide detailed verbal or visual information about consumers' attitudes, feelings, and buying behaviors rather than offering numeric data.

quantitative research
Research that produces numeric results that can be analyzed using a variety of statistical programs.

The Finish brand did extensive marketing research to better understand how consumers use the product.

Exploratory studies often involve in-depth probing of a few consumers who fit the profile of the "typical" individual of interest in a study. An **in-depth interview** is a relatively unstructured personal interview with a single respondent, conducted by a highly skilled interviewer. The purpose of in-depth interviews is to understand the underlying motivations, beliefs, attitudes, and feelings of respondents on a particular subject. Researchers may interview consumers, salespeople, or other employees about products, services, ads, or stores. They may simply "hang out" and watch what people do when they choose among competing brands in a store aisle, and then approach them with some questions. Firms often locate places where the consumers of interest tend to be and ask questions in these settings. For example, some researchers find that younger

Focus groups are a very popular technique to do exploratory research.

people often are too suspicious or skeptical in traditional research settings, so they may interview them while they wait in line to buy concert tickets or in clubs.

A **focus group** is the technique that market researchers employ most often for exploratory research. Focus groups typically consist of five to nine consumers who have been recruited because they share certain characteristics (they all play golf at least twice a month, are women in their 20s, etc.). These people sit together to discuss a product, ad, or some other marketing topic a discussion leader introduces. Typically, the leader records (by videotape or audiotape) these group discussions, which may be held at special interviewing facilities that allow for observation by the client who watches from behind a one-way mirror. As a result of insights it gathered from focus groups, MillerCoors decided to revise the packaging design for one of its brands to brighten it up and better appeal to consumers. The company heard from millennials in focus group sessions that the packaging on its Blue Moon Belgian White Ale was perceived as "dark," "lonely," and "mystical," which prompted the change in packaging to a more "perky" motif.[10]

Today it's common to find focus groups in cyberspace as well as in person. Firms such as IKEA and Volvo use online focus group sites that resemble other social networking sites. IKEA used consumer consulting boards, also known as a **market research online community (MROC)**, in five different countries to solicit feedback for an update of its catalog.[11] An MROC is a privately assembled group of people, usually by a market research firm or department, used to gain insight into customer sentiments and tendencies. MROCs are useful for many market research questions, including those about product ideas, branding strategies, and packaging decisions.[12] In a different approach from IKEA's, Volvo launched a focus group via TweetChat, Twitter's chat platform, to gather feedback about advertisements that the firm had developed. Volvo marketers said that the instant feedback they got from consumers helped strike the right balance in the ads. The rapid back-and-forth between the company and the online community allows for real-time data collection.[13]

The **case study** is a comprehensive examination of a particular firm or organization. In business-to-business market research in which the customers are other firms, for example, researchers may try to learn how one particular company makes its purchases. The goal is to identify the key decision makers, to learn what criteria they emphasize when they choose among suppliers, and perhaps to learn something about any conflicts and rivalries among these decision makers that may influence their choices.

Another qualitative approach is **ethnography**, which uses a technique that marketers borrow from anthropologists who immerse themselves with a specific cultural group for months or even years. Some market researchers visit people's homes or participate in real-life

in-depth interview
A relatively unstructured personal interview with a single respondent, conducted by a highly skilled interviewer.

focus group
A product-oriented discussion among a small group of consumers led by a trained moderator.

market research online community (MROC)
A privately assembled group of people, usually by a market research firm or department, utilized to gain insight into customer sentiments and tendencies.

case study
A comprehensive examination of a particular firm or organization.

ethnography
An approach to research based on observations of people in their own homes or communities.

consumer activities to get a handle on how they really use products. Imagine having a researcher follow you around while you shop and while you use the products you bought to see what kind of consumer you are. This is basically marketing's version of a reality show—though, we hope, the people they study are a bit more "realistic" than the ones on TV!

Descriptive Research

We've seen that marketers have many exploratory research tools in their arsenal, including in-depth interviews, focus groups, case studies, and ethnography to help them better define a problem or opportunity. These are usually modest studies of a small number of people—enough to get some indication of what is going on but not enough for the marketer to feel confident about generalizing what she observes to the rest of the population.

descriptive research
A tool that probes more systematically into the problem and bases its conclusions on large numbers of observations.

The next step in market research, then, often is to conduct **descriptive research**. This kind of research probes systematically into the marketing problem and bases its conclusions on a large sample of participants. Descriptive research is most often quantitative research, in which results typically are expressed in quantitative terms—averages, percentages, or other statistics that result from a large set of measurements. In such quantitative approaches to research, the project can be as simple as counting the number of Listerine bottles sold in a month in different regions of the country or as complex as statistical analyses of responses to a survey mailed to thousands of consumers about their flavor preferences in mouthwash. In each case, marketers conduct the descriptive research to answer a specific question, in contrast to the "fishing expedition" they may undertake in exploratory research. However, don't downplay the usefulness of qualitative approaches—initial qualitative market research serves to greatly inform and shape subsequent quantitative approaches.

cross-sectional design
A type of descriptive technique that involves the systematic collection of quantitative information.

questionnaire
A survey research instrument (either on paper or electronic) consisting of a series of questions for the purpose of gathering information from respondents.

longitudinal design
A technique that tracks the responses of the same sample of respondents over time.

Market researchers who employ descriptive techniques most often use a **cross-sectional design**. This approach usually involves the systematic collection of responses to a **questionnaire**, which is a survey research instrument (either on paper or electronic) consisting of a series of questions for the purpose of gathering information from respondents. They may collect the data on more than one occasion but usually not from the same pool of respondents.

In contrast to these one-shot studies, a **longitudinal design** tracks the responses of the same sample of respondents over time. Market researchers sometimes create consumer panels to get information; in this case, a sample of respondents who are representative of a larger market agrees to provide information about purchases on a weekly or monthly basis. Southwest Airlines, who has always benefited from cult-like loyalty of its customers, has a longstanding Customer Advisory Council that is billed as a "panel of trusted advisors made up of customers like yourself." In this firm's culture, it's like a community—a place to interact with other Southwest customers, and share opinions, thoughts, and ideas with the goal of helping to shape the future of the airline. Such an approach is very smart, as it takes full advantage of both solidifying loyalty from members and also provides a solid platform for gaining customer insights for Southwest's decision making.[14]

Causal Research

It's a fact that purchases of both diapers and beer peak between 5 p.m. and 7 p.m. Can we say that purchasing one of these products caused shoppers to purchase the other as well—and, if so, which caused which? Does taking care of a baby drive a parents to drink? Or is the answer simply that this happens to be the time when young parents stop at the store on their way home from work to pick up a bottle of wine and a box of Pampers?[15]

And what about hemlines? Since the 1920s, George Taylor's "hemline index" has posited that the length of women's hemlines reflects overall economic health. The theory originated at a time when women wore silk stockings—when the economy was strong, they shortened their hemlines to show off the stockings; when the economy took a dive, so did the hemlines to cover up the fact that women couldn't afford the fancy stockings. Don't believe it? The same was true in 2009 when runway designs were "shockingly short" and the stock market rallied 15 percent for the year.[16] And how about more recently? Well, true to form, through 2017 into January 2018, the market rose 33 percent, only to begin experiencing some waffling through the spring. And guess what? The market was very bullish and skirts were getting shorter. Then, as fall 2018 ready-to-wear collections began to roll out, a look at their longer hemlines suggested the economy and Wall Street might be headed for some tough times. But investors might not want to panic just yet. There's also the "Super Bowl Indicator" to consider, which suggests that a win by a team in the National Football Conference means it will be a good year for stocks. A win by an American Football Conference team suggests a bear market. These and other "superstitions" aren't necessarily accurate, but they illustrate the faith many of us place in correlated events. Place your bets (both on your stocks and on your team)![17]

The descriptive techniques we've mentioned do a good job of providing valuable information about what is happening in the marketplace, but by its nature, descriptive research can only *describe* a marketplace phenomenon—it cannot tell us *why* it occurs. Sometimes marketers need to know if something they've done has brought about some change in behavior. For example, does placing one product next to another in a store mean that people will buy more of each? We can't answer this question through simple observation or description.

There's an old question about whether the sun comes up because the rooster crows. Questions like that relate to "causality"—that is, what causes what? To get this answer, market researchers turn to **causal research**, which attempts to identify cause-and-effect relationships between two or more things (like the sun rising and the rooster crowing!). Which one causes the other?

causal research
A technique that attempts to understand cause-and-effect relationships.

Marketers use causal research techniques when they want to know if a change in something (e.g., placing cases of beer next to a diaper display) is responsible for a change in something else (e.g., a big increase in diaper sales). They call the factors that might cause such a change *independent variables* and the outcomes *dependent variables*. The independent variable(s) cause some change in the dependent variable(s). In our example, then, the beer display is an independent variable, and sales data for the diapers are a dependent variable—that is, the study would investigate whether an increase in diaper sales *depends* on the proximity of beer. Researchers can gather data and test the causal relationship statistically.

This form of causal research often involves using experimental designs. **Experiments** attempt to establish causality by ruling out alternative explanations, and to maintain a high level of control, experiments may entail bringing subjects (participants) into a lab so that researchers can control precisely what they experience. For the diaper example, a group of parents might be paid to come into a testing facility and enter a "virtual store" on a computer screen. Researchers would then ask them to fill a grocery cart as they click through the virtual aisles. The experiment might vary the placement of the diapers—next to shelves of beer in one scenario and near paper goods in another scenario. The objective of the experiment would be to find out which placement gets more of the parents to put diapers into their carts.

experiments
A technique that tests predicted relationships among variables in a controlled environment.

Step 3: Choose the Method to Collect Primary Data

When the researcher decides to work with primary data, the next step in the market research process is to figure out just how to collect it. We broadly describe primary data collection methods as either *survey* or *observation*. There are many ways to collect data, and marketers try new ones all the time. In fact, today, more and more marketers are turning to sophisticated brain scans to directly measure a consumer's brain for reactions to various advertisements or products. This **neuromarketing** approach uses technologies such as functional magnetic resonance imaging (fMRI) to measure brain activity in order to better understand why consumers make the decisions they do. Some firms have even invested in their own labs and in-house scientists to establish an ongoing neuromarketing research program.

neuromarketing
A type of brain research that uses technologies such as functional magnetic resonance imaging (fMRI) to measure brain activity in order to better understand why consumers make the decisions they do.

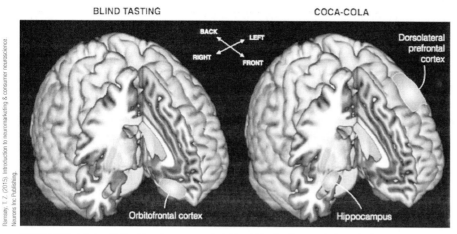

BLIND TASTING

COCA-COLA

Neuromarketing is a useful tool to gain consumer insights and feedback on products and ads.

Neuromarketing has gained increasing popularity among companies such as Facebook, Twitter, and Time Warner as a tool to understand consumer reactions to elements of various forms of marketing communication. For instance, Samsung and the firm NeuroInsight worked together to analyze the brain activity of iPhone and Samsung users to develop television commercials that appealed specifically to Apple enthusiasts. Their biometric research found that Apple users responded best to ads that identified problems with iPhones and solutions offered by Samsung products. Industry heavyweight Nielsen has invested in neuromarketing in a major way, purchasing Neuro-Focus and Innerscope to facilitate studying eye tracking, facial coding, and other biometric measures.[18] Because most of us don't have access to fMRI machines to conduct market research, we'll focus more in this section on explaining other methods to collect primary data.

In contrast to neuromarketing for primary data collection, surveys provide a more traditional approach. Survey methods involve some kind of interview or other direct contact with respondents who answer questions. Questionnaires can be administered on the phone, in person, through the mail, or over the Internet. Table 4.2 summarizes the advantages and disadvantages of different survey methods for collecting data.

Questionnaires

survey research

The collection of information from respondents via their answers to questions.

Survey research is simply the collection of information from respondents via their answers to questions. This approach frequently involves the use of a questionnaire, which was introduced to you a bit earlier in the chapter. Some folks get a bit confused between "survey" and "questionnaire"—but it's easy to keep the two concepts straight—not all survey research involves a questionnaire in the traditional sense. But questionnaires are very frequently used (you've no doubt responded to many of them), and in this section let's take a closer look at questionnaires as a research tool.

Questionnaires differ in their degree of structure. With a totally *unstructured questionnaire*, the researcher loosely determines the items in advance. Questions may evolve from the respondent's answers to previous questions. At the other extreme, the researcher uses a *completely structured questionnaire*, asking every respondent the exact same questions, and each participant responds to the same set of fixed choices. You have probably experienced this kind of questionnaire, where you might have had to respond to a statement by saying if you "strongly agree," "somewhat agree," and so on. *Moderately structured questionnaires* ask each respondent the same questions, but the respondent is allowed to answer the questions in his or her own words.

Mail questionnaires are easy to administer and offer a high degree of anonymity to respondents. On the downside, because the questionnaire is printed and mailed, researchers have little flexibility in the types of questions they can ask and little control over the circumstances under which the respondent answers them. Mail questionnaires also take a long time to get back to the company and are likely to have a much lower response rate than other types of data collection methods because people tend to ignore them.

Telephone interviews usually consist of a brief phone conversation in which an interviewer reads a short list of questions to the respondent. There are several problems with using telephone interviews as a data collection method. The respondent may not feel comfortable speaking directly to an interviewer, especially if the survey is about a sensitive

Table 4.2 | Advantages and Disadvantages of Survey Data Collection Methods

Data Collection Method	Advantages	Disadvantages
Mail questionnaire	• Respondents feel anonymous • Low cost • Good for ongoing research	• May take a long time for questionnaires to be returned • Low rate of response; many consumers may not return questionnaires • Inflexible questionnaire format • Length of questionnaire is limited by respondents' interest in the topic • Unclear whether respondents understand the questions • Unclear who is responding • No assurance that respondents are being honest
Telephone interviews	• Fast • High flexibility in questioning • Low cost • Limited interviewer follow-up • Limited questionnaire length	• Decreasing levels of respondent cooperation • High likelihood of respondent misunderstanding • Respondents cannot view materials • Cannot survey households without phones • Consumers screen calls with answering machines and caller ID • Do-not-call lists allow many research subjects to opt out of participation
Face-to-face interviews	• Flexibility of questioning • Can use long questionnaires • Can determine whether respondents have trouble understanding questions • Take a lot of time • Can use visuals or other materials	• High cost • Interviewer bias a problem
Online questionnaire	• Instantaneous data collection and analysis • Questioning very flexible • Low cost • No interviewer bias • No geographic restrictions • Can use visuals or other materials	• Unclear who is responding • No assurance that respondents are being honest • Limited questionnaire length • Unable to determine whether respondent understands the question • Self-selected samples

subject. Another problem with this method is that the growth of **telemarketing**, in which businesses sell directly to consumers over the phone, has eroded consumers' willingness to participate in phone surveys. In addition to aggravating people by barraging them with telephone sales messages (usually during dinnertime!), some unscrupulous telemarketers disguise their pitches as research. They contact consumers under the pretense of doing a study when, in fact, their real intent is to sell the respondent something or to solicit funds for some cause. This in turn prompts increasing numbers of people to use voicemail and caller ID to screen calls, further reducing the response rate. And, as we noted previously, state and federal *do-not-call lists* allow many would-be research subjects to opt out of participation in both legitimate market research and unscrupulous telemarketing.[19]

The rise of robocalls in recent years prompted the U.S. Congress to pass the "TRACED Act," which was signed by the President in December 2019 (TRACED stands for Telephone Robocall Abuse Criminal Enforcement and Deterrence). A **robocall** is an unsolicited phone call—most often from an unscrupulous source—that uses a computerized autodialer to deliver a pre-recorded message, as if from a robot. The same principle works with "robo-texts," with an equal degree of annoyance to consumers. Robocalls often rely on the use of **spoofed numbers**, which are numbers used that look familiar to the intended receiver but

telemarketing
The use of the telephone to sell directly to consumers and business customers.

robocall
An unsolicited phone call—most often from an unscrupulous source—that uses a computerized autodialer to deliver a pre-recorded message, as if from a robot.

spoofed numbers
Numbers used that look familiar to the intended receiver but are actually fake.

Some unscrupulous companies poison the well for legitimate marketing researchers by using robocall techniques that most of us aren't fond of at all.

intercept research
A study in which researchers recruit shoppers in malls or other public areas.

are actually fake. The intent is to make it easier for consumers to identify robocalls so that they can avoid answering them as well as to provide stiff new penalties for offenders who flout the law. The legislation requires telecom carriers to implement, at no extra charge, a number-authentication system to help consumers identify who's calling. The magnitude of this problem for legitimate marketers is profound, as U.S. consumers received around 60 billion robocalls in 2019.[20]

Using *face-to-face interviews*, a live interviewer asks questions of one respondent at a time. Although in "the old days" researchers often went door-to-door to ask questions, that's much less common today because of fears about security and because the large numbers of two-income families make it less likely to find people at home during the day. Typically, today's face-to-face interviews occur as part of **intercept research**, an approach in which researchers recruit consumers in public areas, such as stores or highly trafficked walkways. You've probably experienced this scenario—you're in a public area minding your own business when before you know it, a smiling person holding a clipboard stops you to see if you are willing to answer a few questions. A classic example occurs during a leisurely vacation with the family at a resort hotel when, as you're walking down the corridor to have a leisurely lunch, you encounter a representative of the hotel's timeshare division who starts out with a questionnaire and—if you fit the profile—ends with an invitation to a "free" session on the benefits of vacation ownership.

Intercept research offers good opportunities to get feedback about new package designs, styles, or even reactions to new foods or fragrances. However, because only certain groups of the population probably frequent the locale of the intercept, an intercept study may not provide the researcher with a representative sample of the population (unless the population of interest is highly correlated with the characteristics of the respondents). In addition to being more expensive than mail or phone surveys, intercept research has the disadvantage that respondents may be reluctant to answer questions of a personal nature in a face-to-face context.

Online questionnaires are extremely popular, but the use of such questionnaires is not without concerns. Many researchers question the quality of responses they will receive—particularly because (as with mail and phone interviews) no one can be really sure who is typing in the responses on the computer. In addition, it's uncertain to what degree savvy online consumers are truly representative of the general population that is purported to be of interest to the researcher.[21]

Observational Methods

A second major primary data collection method is *observation*. This term refers to situations where the researcher simply records the consumer's behaviors.

When researchers use *personal observation*, they simply watch consumers in action to understand how they react to marketing activities. Although a laboratory allows researchers to exert control over what test subjects see and do, marketers don't always have the luxury of conducting this kind of "pure" research. But it is possible to conduct field studies in the real world, as long as the researchers still can control the independent

Automakers sometimes enlist the help of car show models to conduct market research such as probing attendees for the reasons why they like or don't like a vehicle on display.

variables. For example, a diaper company might choose two grocery stores that have similar customer bases in terms of age, income, and so on. With the cooperation of the grocery store's management, the company might place its diaper display next to the beer in one store and next to the paper goods in the other and then record diaper purchases parents make over a two-week period. If a lot more parents buy diapers in the first store than in the second (and the company was sure that nothing else was different between the two stores, such as a dollar-off coupon for diapers being distributed in one store and not the other), the diaper manufacturer might conclude that the presence of beer in the background does indeed result in increased diaper sales.

The Nielsen Company uses "People Meters" to record patterns of TV watching.

When they suspect that subjects will probably alter their behavior if they know someone is watching them, researchers may use **unobtrusive measures** to record traces of physical evidence that remain after people have consumed something. For example, instead of asking a person to report on the alcohol products currently in their home, the researcher might go to the house and perform a "pantry check" by actually counting the bottles in their liquor cabinet. Another option is to sift through garbage to search for clues about each family's consumption habits. The "garbologists" can tell, for example, which soft drink is accompanied by what kind of food. Because people in these studies don't know that researchers are looking through products they've discarded, the information is totally objective—although a bit smelly!

unobtrusive measures
Measuring traces of physical evidence that remain after some action has been taken.

Mechanical observation is a method of primary data collection that relies on nonhuman devices to record behavior. For example, one of the classic applications of mechanical observation is the Nielsen Company's famous use of People Meters—boxes the company attaches to the TV sets of select viewers to record patterns of TV watching. The data that Nielsen obtains from these devices indicate who is watching which shows. These "television ratings" help network clients determine how much to charge advertisers for commercials and which shows to cancel or renew. Nielsen also measures user activity on digital media. The research company has more than 250,000 Internet users across 30,000 sites and 25 countries covering all the potential devices that a consumer would use to access digital media.[22] This allows Nielsen to give clients a more updated understanding of how viewers interact with their favorite TV shows. For example, it tracks the number of TV-related tweets people post and provides demographic information including age and gender of individuals who post TV-related tweets.[23]

mechanical observation
A method of primary data collection that relies on machines to capture human behavior in a form that allows for future analysis and interpretation.

Similarly, Nielsen Audio (formerly Arbitron) deploys thousands of Portable People Meters (PPMs).[24] PPMs resemble pagers and automatically record the wearer's exposure to any media that has inserted an inaudible code into its promotion, such as TV ads or shelf displays. Thus, when the consumer is exposed to a broadcast commercial, cinema ad, or other form of commercial, the PPM registers, records, and time-stamps the signal. Portability ensures that all exposures register; this eliminates obtrusive people meters and written diaries that participants often forget to fill out.[25]

Another form of mechanical observation that some firms use is **eye tracking technology**. This method relies on portable or stationary equipment to track the movement of a participant's eyes, and it can provide greater insight into what people look at and for how long they look at it. For marketers, this provides the opportunity to better understand how consumers engage with various forms of marketing of a visual nature. Examples of its use include tracking the viewing of print, television, and mobile ads, and product placement in televised sporting events. Improvements in the portable or wearable version of eye tracking technology offer greater opportunities for data to be gathered outside of lab settings—in the "real world"—thus offering potential for more applicable insights for marketers.[26]

eye tracking technology
A type of mechanical observation technology that uses sensors and sophisticated software to track the position and movement of an individual's eyes in order to gain context-specific insights into how individuals interact with and respond to different visual elements and stimuli.

Some retailers use sophisticated technology to observe where shoppers travel in their stores so they can identify places that attract a lot of traffic and those that are dead spots. In some cases, these "heat maps" use the signals from shoppers' mobile phones to record their movements through the aisles.

Online Research

The COVID-19 crisis obviously had a profound impact on marketers' ability to collect data face-to-face. But fortunately, most firms realized a good while ago that an online approach is a superior way to collect data—it's fast, it's relatively cheap, and it lends itself well to forms of research from simple questionnaires to online focus groups. In fact, some large companies like P&G now collect the vast portion of their consumer intelligence online. Developments in online research are happening quickly, so let's take a look at where things are headed.

There are two major types of information from online research. One type is information that organizations gather when they track consumers surfing the Web. The second type is information they gather more selectively through questionnaires on websites, including, of course, social media sites, through email, or from focus groups that virtual moderators conduct in chat rooms. Most social media platforms, such as Twitter and Facebook, offer numerous ways to analyze trends and conduct market research. By simply searching the latest posts and popular terms—or, as marketers refer to it, "scraping the Web"—you can gain insight into emerging trends and see what customers are talking about in real time. One example of this approach is conducting hashtag searches on Twitter. By setting up a few searches with hashtags related to your brand, industry, or product, you can receive instant notifications when customers, clients, or competitors use key terms.[27]

A very popular approach to online research applies the concept of ethnography defined earlier to understand what consumers discuss about brands online (hint: a lot!). **Netnography** (cleverly labeled such because it combines the net and ethnography) is a form of qualitative research that tracks the consumption patterns and conversations of online consumers. It focuses on the social groups that customers create to inform one another about products, services, and brands. Companies like Campbell use this approach to identify the "genuine voices" of consumers and how they talk about brands—for example, gaining buyers' suggestions about how they use products to generate new recipes or applications.[28]

Back in Chapter 1, you learned that crowdsourcing is a practice where firms outsource marketing activities (such as selecting an ad) to a community of users. This approach provides a place where market researchers can post requests to gain community insights. Using crowdsourcing platforms, such as Amazon Mechanical Turk (MTurk) and CrowdFlower, for collecting market research data can potentially be quicker and less costly than other methods marketers use to gather a large amount of responses because of the large audience of workers available to the firm and the relatively lower prices for them to perform required tasks.[29] For market research that requires the inclusion of a specific group of respondents, such a platform may not be well suited, and instead seeking out focused panel data may be more appropriate.

You may like to share selfies with friends, but did you know that it's possible companies are diving into TikTok, Instagram, and Pinterest to take a close look at your latest gems as well? Some firms use special software to scan photos to identify logos, facial expressions, and contexts so that they can learn more about how consumers use a client's brands in daily life. There are huge numbers of photos and videos to look at. Over 40 billion photos and videos have been shared on the Instagram platform since its inception and 95 million more are shared every day! The practice is so new that privacy concerns are just starting to bubble up.[30] For now, think twice about what you post—the potential for unexpected issues is growing, including a growing trend of catfishing. A **catfish** is someone who pretends to be someone else online. This person completely assumes a fake identity and goes the extra mile to make their victim believe that they are exactly who they say they are. Given marketing's increasing reliance on data from these types of platforms, catfishing could impact the integrity of the research that marketers think they're conducting!

netnography
A form of qualitative research that tracks the consumption patterns and conversations of online consumers.

catfish
Someone who pretends to be someone else online.

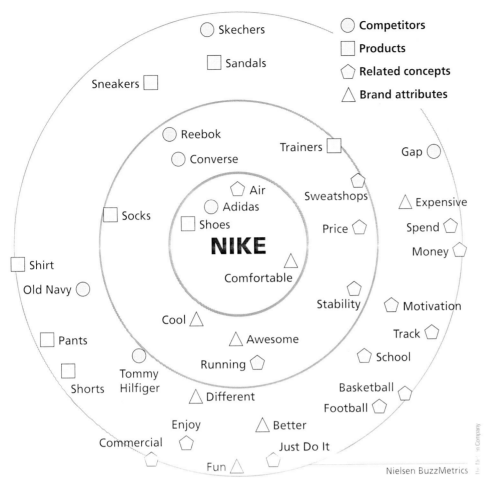

Some research firms use sophisticated software to search the web for thousands of product postings that when taken together give the client a heads-up on what consumers are saying about their brand.

Across all of its platforms and forms, the Internet offers unprecedented ability to track consumers as they search for information on Google and other search engines. We've become so accustomed to just looking up stuff online that *google* long ago became a verb (as has *friend* in Facebook's case). As consumers enter search terms like "lowest prices on J Brand jeans" or "home theaters," these queries become small drops in the ocean of data available to marketers that engage in online behavioral tracking. How do they know what we're looking at online? Beware the Cookie Monster! **Cookies** are text files that a website sponsor inserts into a user's hard drive when the user connects with the site. Cookies remember details of a visit to a website and track which pages the user visits. Some sites request or require that visitors "register" on the site by answering questions about themselves and their likes and dislikes. In such cases, cookies also allow the site to access these details about the customer.

The technology associated with cookies allows websites to customize services, such as when Amazon recommends new books to users on the basis of what books they have ordered in the past. Consider this one: It is late evening, and you should be studying, but you just can't make yourself do it. So you grab your tablet and sign in to Netflix. And like every other time you sign in, Netflix offers up a bunch of movies and TV shows to tempt you away from the textbooks. But how does Netflix know what you want to see—sometimes they seem to anticipate your tastes better than your friends can!

No, there isn't someone sitting at their office whose only job is to follow you around online to guess what you'll want to see next. These surprising connections are the results of

cookies

Text files inserted by a website sponsor into a web surfer's hard drive that allow the site to track the surfer's moves.

predictive technology
Analysis techniques that use shopping patterns of large numbers of people to determine which products are likely to be purchased if others are.

predictive technology, which uses shopping patterns of large numbers of people to determine which products are likely to be purchased if others are—except in this case what you're "shopping" for is movies to watch. To figure out what movies or TV shows you are likely to enjoy, Netflix trained teams of people to watch thousands of movies and tag them according to attributes such as "goriness" or "plot conclusiveness." Netflix then combines those attributes with the viewing habits of millions of users.[31] And voilà—Netflix knows just what to serve up to satisfy your viewing fix.

You can block cookies or curb them by changing settings on your computer, although this makes life difficult if you are trying to log on to many sites, such as online newspapers or travel agencies that require this information to admit you. The information generated from tracking consumers' online journeys has become big business, and in massive quantities, it has become popularly known as *Big Data*, a topic we will discuss in more detail in Chapter 5. To date, the Federal Trade Commission has relied primarily on firms and industries to develop and maintain their own standards instead of developing its own extensive privacy regulations, but many would like to see that situation changed, and much discussion is afoot at all levels of government regarding online privacy rights. Proponents advocate the following guiding principles:

- Information about a consumer belongs to the consumer.
- Consumers should be made aware of information collection.
- Consumers should know how information about them will be used.
- Consumers should be able to refuse to allow information collection.
- Information about a consumer should never be sold or given to another party without the permission of the consumer.

No data collection method is perfect, and online research is no exception—though many of the criticisms of online techniques also apply to offline techniques. One potential problem is the representativeness of the respondents. Many segments of the consumer population, mainly the economically disadvantaged and elderly, do not have the same level of access to the Internet as other groups.

In addition, in many studies (just as with mail surveys or mall intercepts), there is a *self-selection bias* in the sample. That is, because respondents have accepted invitations to take part in online studies, by definition they tend to be the people who like to participate in surveys. As with other kinds of research, such as live focus groups or panel members, it's not unusual to encounter "professional respondents"—people who just enjoy taking part in studies (and getting paid for it). Quality online research specialists, such as Harris Interactive, Survey Sampling International (SSI), and Toluna, address this problem by monitoring their participants and regulating how often they are allowed to participate in different studies over a period of time. However, unfortunately, with the proliferation of online data collection, many new and unproven data providers continue to come into the industry. Therefore, in terms of online research, the venerable phrase *caveat emptor* (let the buyer beware) rules.

There are other disadvantages of online research. Hackers can actually try to influence research results. Competitors can learn about a firm's marketing plans, products, advertising, and other proprietary elements when they intercept information from these studies (though this can occur in offline studies just as easily). Because cheating has become so rampant, some

cross-browser digital fingerprinting
An approach to identifying fake responses to online questionnaires by correlating specific computers used with multiple browsers.

companies today use a new technology called **cross-browser digital fingerprinting** to identify a specific computer even when that machine is using a different browser to access the same website. This approach allows companies to identify respondents who fake responses or professionals who game the industry by doing as many surveys as possible.[32]

Data Quality: Revisiting GIGO—Garbage In, Garbage Out

We've seen that a firm can collect data in many ways, including focus groups, ethnographic approaches, observational studies, online surveys, and controlled experiments, among others. But how much faith should marketers place in what they find out from the research? This question gets at the center of the efficacy of evidence-based decision making. That is, one can derive consumer insights based on evidence, but without knowledge of the quality of the data that was translated into information and eventually the insights, it's impossible for marketers to gauge the potential of their decisions to actually be the optimal ones!

Think of it this way: All too often, marketers who commission a study assume that because the researchers give them a massive report full of impressive-looking numbers and tables, they must be looking at the "truth." Unfortunately, there are times when this "truth" is really just one person's interpretation of the facts. At other times, the data researchers use to generate recommendations are flawed. Early in this chapter we brought up GIGO: "garbage in, garbage out."[33] That is, your conclusions can be only as good as the *quality* of the information you use to make them. Typically, three factors influence the quality of research results—validity, reliability, and representativeness.

Validity is the extent to which the research actually measures what it was intended to measure. Validity can be further broken down into internal validity and external validity. **Internal validity** refers to the extent that the research design was set up in such a manner that what was intended to be measured was accurately measured and not obscured (for instance, by the accidental inclusion of any factors not intended to be included in the study). This is typically accomplished in a highly controlled setting (such as a laboratory) where it is easier to avoid the introduction of extraneous factors that could muddy the results obtained. **External validity** refers to the extent that research results are practically applicable to the relevant target market (and not just the specific study participants who were intended to represent that target market). Another way of thinking about this is whether the research findings would hold up when leveraged out in the real world.

Validity was part of the problem underlying one of the most famous debacles in marketing history—the New Coke fiasco in the 1980s. At that time, Coca-Cola (one of the world's more prolific brands) underestimated people's loyalty to its flagship soft drink after it replaced "Old Coke" with a new, sweeter formula in an attempt to attract more Pepsi drinkers. This blunder was so huge that we still talk about it today even though it happened before your humble authors were even born (well, not quite . . .)! But seriously, every student of marketing should know about this one. In a blind taste test, the company assumed testers' preferences for one anonymous cola over another was a valid measure of consumers' preferences for a cola brand. Arguably, we can also say that the use of a sip test is flawed (and lacking degrees of external validity) in that it is set up so that consumers try the colas in small quantities, as opposed to the larger quantities more typically experienced by consumers when enjoying a can, a bottle, or a glass of cola in a more leisurely setting.[34] Coca-Cola found out the hard way that measuring taste only is not the same as measuring people's deep allegiances to their favorite soft drinks. After all, Coke is a brand that elicits strong consumer loyalty and is nothing short of a cultural icon. Tampering with the flavors was like attacking motherhood and apple pie. Sales eventually recovered after the company brought back the old version as "Coca-Cola Classic."[35]

Reliability is the extent to which the research measurement techniques are free of errors. Sometimes, for example, the way in which a researcher asks a question creates error by biasing people's responses. Imagine that a hipster male interviewer who works for El Dorado rum stops female college students on spring break in South Padre Island campus and asks them if they like rum products and would they like a free taste. Do you think their answers might change if they were asked the same questions on an anonymous survey they received in the mail? Most likely, their answers would be different because people are reluctant to disclose what they actually do when their responses are not anonymous. Researchers try to maximize reliability by thinking of several different ways to ask the same questions, by asking these questions on several occasions, or by using several analysts to interpret the responses. Thus, they can compare responses and look for consistency and stability.

validity
The extent to which research actually measures what it was intended to measure.

internal validity
The extent to which the results of a research study accurately measure what the study intended to measure by ensuring proper research design, including efforts to ensure that any potentially confounding factors were not included or introduced at any point during the execution of the research study.

external validity
The extent to which the results of a research study can be generalized to the population its sample was intended to represent, providing a higher level of confidence that the findings can be applied outside of the setting where the research was conducted.

reliability
The extent to which research measurement techniques are free of errors.

Figure 4.4 *Snapshot* | Completion Test

It can be especially difficult to get accurate information from children. Researchers often use visuals, such as this Japanese completion test, to encourage children to express their feelings. The test asked boys to write in the empty balloon what they think the boy in the drawing will answer when the girl asks, "What program do you want to watch next?"

representativeness
The extent to which consumers in a study are similar to a larger group in which the organization has an interest.

sampling
The process of selecting respondents for a study.

probability sample
A sample in which each member of the population has some known chance of being included.

Reliability is a problem when the researchers can't be sure that the consumer population they're studying even understands the questions. For example, kids are difficult subjects for market researchers because they tend to be undependable reporters of their own behavior, they have poor recall, and they often do not understand abstract questions. In many cases, children cannot explain why they prefer one item over another (or they're not willing to share these secrets with grown-ups).[36] For these reasons, researchers have to be especially creative when they design studies involving younger consumers. Figure 4.4 shows part of a completion test that a set of researchers used to measure children's preferences for TV programming in Japan.

Representativeness is the extent to which consumers in the study are similar to a larger group in which the organization has an interest. This criterion underscores the importance of **sampling**: the process of selecting respondents for a study. The issue then becomes how large the sample should be and how to choose these people. We'll talk more about sampling in the next section.

Step 4: Design the Sample

Once the researcher defines the problem, decides on a research design, and determines how to collect the data, the next step is to decide from whom to obtain the needed information. Of course, he or she *could* collect data from every single customer or prospective customer, but this would be extremely expensive and time consuming if possible at all (this is what the U.S. Census spends millions of dollars to do every 10 years). Not everyone has the resources of the U.S. government to poll *everyone* in their market. So they typically collect most of their data from a small proportion, or *sample*, of the population of interest. Based on the answers from this sample, researchers generalize to the larger population. Whether such inferences are accurate or inaccurate depends on the type and quality of the study sample. There are two main types of samples: probability and nonprobability samples.

Probability Sampling

In a **probability sample**, each member of the population has some known chance of being included. Using a probability sample ensures that the sample represents the population and that inferences we make about the population from what members of the sample say or do are justified. For example, if a larger percentage of younger consumers versus older consumers in a probability sample say they prefer action movies to musicals, one can infer with confidence that a larger percentage of younger consumers would also rather see a character get sliced and diced than singing a love song.

The most basic type of probability sample is a *simple random sample*, in which every member of a population has a known and equal chance of being included in the study. For example, if we simply take the names of all 40 students in a class, put them in a hat, and draw one out, each member of the class has a 1 in 40 chance of being included in the sample. In most studies, the population from which the sample will be drawn is too large for a hat, so marketers use a computer program to generate a random sample from a list of members.

Sometimes researchers use a *systematic sampling procedure* to select members of a population; they select the *n*th member of a population after a random start. For example, if we want a sample of 10 members of your class, we might begin with the second person on the roll and select every fourth name after that—the second, sixth, tenth, fourteenth, and so on. Researchers know that studies that use systematic samples are just as accurate as those that use simple random samples. But unless a list of members of the population of interest is already in a computer data file, it's a lot simpler just to create a simple random sample.

Yet another type of probability sample is a *stratified sample,* in which a researcher divides the population into segments that relate to the study's topic. For example, imagine you want to study what movies most theatergoers like. You have learned from previous studies that younger and older consumers in the population differ in their attitudes toward different types of movies—younger consumers like action movies, and older consumers like musicals. To create a stratified sample, you would first divide the population into younger and older segments. Then, you would randomly select respondents from each of the two segments in proportion to their percentage of the population. In this way, you have created a sample that is proportionate to the population on a characteristic that you know will make a difference in the study results.

Nonprobability Sampling

Sometimes researchers do not believe that the time and effort required to develop a probability sample is justified, perhaps because they need an answer quickly or just want to get a general sense of how people feel about a topic. They may choose a **nonprobability sample**, which entails the use of personal judgment to select respondents—in some cases, they just ask anyone they can find. With a nonprobability sample, some members of the population have no chance at all of being included. Thus, there is no way to ensure that the sample is representative of the population. Results from nonprobability studies can be generally suggestive of what is going on in the real world but are not necessarily definitive.

A **convenience sample** is a nonprobability sample composed of individuals who just happen to be available when and where the data are being collected. For example, if you were to simply stand in front of the student union and ask students who walk by to complete your questionnaire, the "guinea pigs" you get to agree to do it would be a convenience sample.

Finally, researchers may also use a *quota sample*, which includes the same proportion of individuals with certain characteristics as in the population. For example, if you are studying attitudes of students in your university, you might just go on campus to find freshmen, sophomores, juniors, and seniors in proportion to the number of members of each class in the university. The quota sample is much like the stratified sample except that, with a quota sample, the researcher uses his or her individual judgment to select respondents.

nonprobability sample
A sample in which personal judgment is used to select respondents.

convenience sample
A nonprobability sample composed of individuals who just happen to be available when and where the data are being collected.

Step 5: Collect the Data

At this point, the researcher has determined the nature of the problem to address. She chose a research design that will specify how to investigate the problem and what kinds of information (data) she will need. The researcher has also selected the data collection and sampling methods. Once she's made these decisions, the next task is to collect the data.

We noted previously that the quality of your conclusions is only as good as the data you use. The same logic applies to the people who collect the data: *The quality of research results is only as good as the poorest interviewer in the study.* Careless interviewers may not read questions exactly as written, or they may not record respondent answers correctly. So marketers must train and supervise interviewers to make sure they follow the research procedures exactly as outlined. In the next section, we'll talk about some of the problems in gathering data and some solutions.

Challenges to Gathering Data in Foreign Countries

Conducting market research around the world is big business for U.S. firms—for the top 50 companies (as measured by revenue), 52 percent of their income comes from work done *outside* the United States—that totals nearly \$15 billion.[37] However, as we saw in Chapter 2, market conditions and consumer preferences vary worldwide, and there are major differences in the sophistication of market research operations and the amount of data available to global marketers. In Mexico, for instance, because there are still large areas where native tribes speak languages other than Spanish, researchers may end up bypassing these groups in surveys. In Egypt, where the government must sign off on any survey, the approval process can take months or years. And in many developing countries, infrastructure is an impediment to executing phone or mail surveys, and lack of online connectivity blocks web-based research.

Connecting with consumers in developing countries that lack up-to-date technological infrastructure can be challenging.

back-translation
The process of translating material to a foreign language and then back to the original language.

For these and other reasons, choosing an appropriate data collection method is difficult. In some countries, many people may not have phones, or low literacy rates may interfere with mail surveys. Understanding *local customs* can be a challenge, and *cultural differences* also affect responses to survey items. Both Danish and British consumers, for example, agree that it is important to eat breakfast. However, the Danish sample may be thinking of fruit and yogurt, whereas the British sample has toast and tea in mind. Sometimes marketers can overcome these problems by involving local researchers in decisions about the research design.

Another problem with conducting market research in global markets is *language*. Sometimes translations just don't come out right. In some cases, entire subcultures within a country might be excluded from the research sample. In fact, this issue is becoming more and more prevalent inside the U.S. as non-English speakers increase as a percentage of the population.

To overcome language difficulties, researchers use a process of **back-translation**, which requires two steps. First, a native speaker translates the questionnaire into the language of the targeted respondents. Then, someone fluent in the second language translates this new version back into the original language to ensure that the correct meanings survive the process. Even with precautions such as these, researchers must interpret the data they obtain from other cultures with care.

Step 6: Analyze and Interpret the Data

Once market researchers collect the data, what's next? It's like a spin on the old "if a tree falls in the woods" question: "If results exist, but there's no one to interpret them, do they have a meaning?" Let's leave the philosophers out of it and just say that marketers would answer "no." Data need interpretation if the results are going to be useful.

To understand the important role of data analysis, let's take a look at a hypothetical research example. Say a global company that markets frozen foods wishes to better understand two key groups of consumers' preferences for varying levels of fat content in their diets. They conducted a descriptive research study where they collected primary data via online questionnaires. Because they know that dietary preferences relate to country of residence of consumers (among other aspects), they used a stratified sample that includes 175 consumers in Western Europe and 175 consumers in the United States.

Typically, marketers first tabulate the data, as Table 4.3 shows—that is, they arrange the data in a table or other summary form so they can get a broad picture of the overall responses. The data in Table 4.3 indicate that 43 percent of the sample prefers a low-fat meal. In addition, there may be a desire to cross-classify or cross-tabulate the answers to questions by other variables. *Cross-tabulation* means that we examine the data that we break down into *subgroups*—in this case, Western Europeans and Americans separately—to see how results vary between categories. The cross-tabulation in Table 4.3 reveals that 59 percent of Western Europeans versus only 27 percent of Americans prefer a meal with low-fat content. Researchers may wish to apply additional statistical tests that you may learn about in subsequent courses (now, there's something to look forward to!).

Based on the tabulation and cross-tabulations, the researcher interprets the results and makes recommendations. For example, the study results in Table 4.3 may lead to the

| Table 4.3 | Examples of Data Tabulation and Cross-Tabulation Tables |

Fat Content Preference (number and percentages of responses)

Do you prefer a meal with high-fat content, medium-fat content, or low-fat content?

Questionnaire Response	Number of Responses	Percentage of Responses
High fat	21	6
Medium fat	179	51
Low fat	150	43
Total	350	100

Fat Content Preference by Western European versus American Consumers (number and percentages of responses)

Do you prefer a meal with high-fat content, medium-fat content, or low-fat content?

Questionnaire Response	Number of Western Europeans	Percentage of Western Europeans	Number of Americans	Percentage of Americans	Total Number	Total Percentage
High fat	4	2	17	10	21	6
Medium fat	68	39	111	64	179	51
Low fat	103	59	47	27	150	43
Total	175	100	175	100	350	100

conclusion that Western Europeans are more likely than Americans to be concerned with a low-fat diet. Based on these data, the researcher might then recommend that the firm target primarily Western Europeans when it introduces a new line of low-fat foods.

Step 7: Prepare the Research Report

The final step in the market research process is to prepare a report of the research results. In general, a research report must clearly and concisely tell the readers—top management, clients, creative departments, and many others—what they need to know in a way that they can easily understand and that won't bore you to tears (just like a good textbook should keep you engaged). A typical research report includes the following sections:

- An executive summary of the report that covers the high points of the total report
- An understandable description of the research methods
- A complete discussion of the results of the study, including the tabulations, cross-tabulations, and additional statistical analyses
- Limitations of the study (no study is perfect)
- Conclusions drawn from the results and the recommendations for managerial action based on the results

4.4 Brand You: Career and Internship Information and Research

Taylor recognizes the importance of a good "fit" with the company and industry where he will work and spend his career. He also knows that he must investigate the culture of companies where he is interviewing. Understanding this, he is set to research different companies and industries in planning his personal brand.

How many times has someone asked you, "What do you want to do when you finish college?" While you may not know the answer to the question now, this is an excellent time to begin finding out more about your options. Yes, you need to find where there are some cool jobs, but at the same time, you also need to explore careers.

Just as a brand manager or a professional salesperson or an online retailer continuously gathers and analyzes information about his/her customers and other important factors relative to the product's success, your success in marketing yourself for a great internship or your dream job requires that you have information. And the more information you have, the better decisions about your marketing strategy you can make. This section can help you to:

- Know how to gather relevant information
- Understand how trends will potentially affect your career
- Identify resources you can use to find companies

Good Research Strategies

Knowing how to research career options is a valuable skill not only for your immediate future but also for your entire career. Very few people stay in the same job with the same company for the entirety of their work life. The research skills you learn now will be just as useful to you in the future. These skills include focusing on the big picture, evaluating your assumptions, and asking the right questions.

Focus on the Big Picture

Begin your research by examining industries and professions rather than specific job titles. Industries and professions are stable—many have survived for centuries. If you are interested in logistics and transportation, you not only need to know what is new and exciting now; you also need to know what is in the planning stages. What jobs will there be and what skills will be needed to fill those jobs if driverless "18-wheelers" begin moving goods across the country?

Investigate Your Assumptions

What exactly do brand managers, professional salespeople, or marketing researchers do in their jobs? You probably have ideas about what these jobs are like. While you may think you know a lot about a field or a particular job, some of your ideas may be based on assumptions. Your research should provide you with facts that can either support or challenge these assumptions. It's not enough just to know what the salary for a particular job is or what skills are needed. You also need to know what a person in that job does day after day. Many students who have interned with a firm in a job they thought they wanted have found they hate the job—an incredibly important benefit from an internship.

Ask the Right Questions

Some questions you might include in your research that will be helpful are:

- What kind of people do well in this field?
- What are the typical projects people in this job do?
- What is the work environment like?
- How is technology changing this field?
- What changes are anticipated in the way work is performed?
- What factors influence advancement in this job?

How to Begin and End Your Search

Many students see their career search as a giant undertaking and have no idea how to begin. A good research strategy is to search from the general to the specific. *Begin searching industries, then companies, and finally specific jobs.* You should also gather information from different sources to get different opinions from different perspectives.

You might also consider talking with your professors. While not all professors are tuned into the latest in a particular industry, many have experience working in an industry or have consulted with companies. If they can't answer your questions, it is likely they can refer you to people who can.

Gathering Information Online and Offline

Yes, we all use the Internet to get information. In fact, many of us spend entirely too much time surfing the Web. You may be less familiar with sites that will be helpful in providing career-related information. A few useful online sites that will be useful for beginning your research are listed below.

Online Sources of Information

Websites	Type of Information
www.hoovers.com www.bls.gov/oco www.online.onetcenter.org	Information on industries
www.career-advice.monster.com www.rileyguide.com www.salary.com	Career planning
www.associationjobboards.com	Professional associations
www.bizjournals.com	Local business journals
www.businessweek.com www.wsj.com CNNmoney.com/fortune	Lists of businesses
www.linkedin.com	Professional social network
Your campus career center website	Career planning
Online industry trade magazines	Provide email newsletters and websites with industry news
www.glassdoor.com	Anonymous reviews of companies and their management by employees and former employees

There are also offline sources of information that you should access in your research. A few of these are:

- Your campus career center
- Your campus library or a public library
- Your campus alumni association
- Networking events
- Professional organizations

Taylor has learned that he needs to develop research skills now to keep up with trends that will affect his career. This will include first looking at the big picture of industries rather than jobs, investigating his assumptions, and asking the right questions of both online and offline sources.

Objective **Summaries** and **Key Terms**

4.1 Objective Summary

Explain the role of a marketing information system and a marketing decision support system in marketing decision making.

To successfully compete in today's marketplace, marketers must ensure that the information they need for decision making is well organized and easily accessible. A marketing information system (MIS) is composed of internal data, market intelligence, market research data, acquired databases, and computer hardware and software. Firms use an MIS to gather, sort, analyze, store, and distribute information needed by managers for marketing decision making. Then, firms often deploy an intranet, which is an internal corporate communication network that uses Internet technology to link company departments, employees, and databases. Nowadays, savvy marketing organizations make sure that access and usability of this valuable internal information is maximized by creating an appealing interface for employees called a *marketing dashboard*, which is a comprehensive display and access system providing company personnel with up-to-the-minute information necessary to make decisions. Finally, the marketing decision support system (MDSS) allows managers to use analysis software and interactive software to access MIS data and to conduct analyses and find the information they need about their products and services.

Key Terms

market research
GIGO
market research ethics
data privacy
confidentiality
anonymity
risk management
data security
database
marketing information system (MIS)
intranet
marketing dashboard
market intelligence system
mystery shoppers
reverse engineering
syndicated research
custom research
marketing decision support system (MDSS)

4.2 Objective Summary

Understand the concept of evidence-based decision making toward gaining customer insights.

You are studying marketing in an era of evidence-based decision making. For marketers to be successful in creating and executing marketing strategies, they must be able to effectively convert data to information that allows them to derive useful and dependable customer insights. Organizations today are collecting massive amounts of data, but they need customer insight specialists to sift through that data in order to make it useful. The concept of customer insights refers to the collection, deployment, and interpretation of information that allows a business to acquire, develop, and retain its customers. This information supports market planning decisions and guides planners in future business initiatives.

Key Terms

data
information
evidence-based decision making
data analytics
customer insights

4.3 Objective Summary

List and explain the steps and key elements of the market research process.

The research process begins by defining the problem and determining the research design or type of study. Next, researchers choose the data collection method—that is, whether there are secondary data available or whether primary research with a communication study or through observation is necessary. Then, researchers determine what type of sample is to be used for the study and collect the data. The final steps in the research are to analyze and interpret the data and prepare a research report.

Exploratory research typically uses qualitative data collected by individual interviews, focus groups, or observational methods, such as ethnography. Descriptive research includes cross-sectional and longitudinal studies. Causal research goes a step further by designing controlled experiments to understand cause-and-effect relationships between independent marketing variables, such as price changes, and dependent variables, such as sales.

Researchers may choose to collect data via survey methods and observation approaches. Survey approaches include mail questionnaires, telephone interviews, face-to-face interviews, and online questionnaires. A study may use a probability sample, such as a simple random or stratified sample, in which inferences can be made to a population on the basis of sample results. Nonprobability sampling methods include a convenience sample and a quota sample. The researcher tries to ensure that the data are valid, reliable, and representative.

Internet-based research, including the use of various social media platforms, accounts for a rapidly growing proportion of all market research. Online tracking uses cookies to record where consumers go on a website. Consumers have become increasingly concerned about privacy and how this information is used and made available to others. Online approaches also provide an attractive alternative to traditional communication data collection methods because of its speed and low cost. Many firms use the Internet to conduct online focus groups.

Key Terms

research design
secondary data
primary data
exploratory research
qualitative research
quantitative research
in-depth interview
focus group
market research online community (MROC)
case study
ethnography
descriptive research
cross-sectional design
questionnaire
longitudinal design
causal research
experiments
neuromarketing
survey research
telemarketing
robocall
spoofed numbers
intercept research
unobtrusive measures
mechanical observation
eye tracking technology
netnography
catfish
cookies

predictive technology
cross-browser digital fingerprinting
validity
internal validity
external validity
reliability
representativeness
sampling
probability sample
nonprobability sample
convenience sample
back-translation

4.4 Objective Summary

Understand how to research both online and offline resources to search for a job or internship.

Your success in marketing yourself for an internship or a job requires information. Knowing how to research career options is a valuable skill for your immediate future and for your entire career. These research skills include focusing on the big picture, that is, an industry rather than a single job, evaluating your assumptions by learning what a person in that job does day after day, and asking the right questions about the people in the field—typical projects, the work environment, expected changes, and factors influencing advancement.

A good research strategy is to begin searching industries, then companies, and finally specific jobs. It is also good to gather information from different sources to get different opinions from different perspectives. You should be sure to include Internet sites that provide career-related information.

Chapter **Questions** and **Activities**

Concepts: Test Your Knowledge

4-1. What is a marketing information system (MIS)? What types of information does it include? What is the marketing decision support system (MDSS)? What additional benefit is provided by an MDSS over an MIS?

4-2. What is a marketing dashboard? What is marketing intelligence? Explain how each of these help in marketing decision making.

4-3. Why is defining the problem to be researched critical to ultimate success with the research project?

4-4. Explain the difference between primary data and secondary data. What are some ways market researchers use exploratory research data?

4-5. What techniques can marketers use to gather data using exploratory research? How is this type of data collection useful?

4-6. What is syndicated research? What is custom research? What are the benefits of each?

4-7. Describe the purpose of causal research. How does it differ from descriptive research?

4-8. What are the main methods used to collect primary data?

4-9. GIGO—garbage in, garbage out—is mentioned in the chapter. What is the significance of this concept to market research?

4-10. What are the seven steps in the market research process? Provide a short description of each.

4-11. What unique issues must researchers consider when they plan to collect data online?

4-12. When we consider data quality, what are the differences among validity, reliability, and representativeness? How can you know the data have high levels of these characteristics?

4-13. What are some ethical problems associated with marketing research?

4-14. What is a cross tabulation? How are cross tabulations useful to analyze and interpret data?

Activities: Apply What You've Learned

4-15. *In Class, 10–25 Minutes for Teams* Your firm is planning to begin marketing a consumer product in several global markets. You have been given the responsibility of developing plans for market research to be conducted in Mexico, France, and China. In a role-playing situation, present the difficulties you expect to encounter, if any, in conducting research in each of these areas.

4-16. *Creative Homework/Short Project* Your company recently launched a new "dry" shampoo. Although initial sales were strong, they have steadily declined over the last year and a half. You have decided to conduct further market research, but first you have to define the research problem. What are your research objectives? What is the population of interest? How does the problem fit within the environmental context? Prepare a short report that clearly and fully defines the research problem for your product.

4-17. *Creative Homework/Short Project* As an account executive with a market research firm, you are responsible for deciding on the type of research to be used in various studies conducted for your clients. For each of the following client questions, list your choices of research approaches.

   a. Will TV or online advertising be more effective for a local bank to use in its marketing communication plan?
   b. Should a California winemaker operating on a national scale switch from bottling its mid-tier wine ($9 to $15 per bottle) with corks to bottling it with screwcaps?
   c. Are consumers more likely to buy brands from firms that support strong sustainability initiatives?
   d. What existing features of an e-commerce site selling clothing to women are most important for making a purchase decision?

4-18. *Creative Homework/Short Project* The increasing use of telemarketing combined with the shrinking number of home (landline) phones has made it difficult for marketing researchers to conduct phone surveys. How can marketers overcome this challenge? What other methods might they use to obtain similar data?

4-19. *In Class, 10–25 Minutes for Teams* Your market research firm is planning to conduct surveys to gather information for a number of clients. Your boss has asked you and a few other new employees to do some preliminary work. She has asked each of you to choose three of the topics (from among the following six listed) that will be included in the project and to prepare an analysis of the advantages and disadvantages of each of these communication methods of collecting primary data: mail questionnaires, telephone interviews, face-to-face interviews, and online questionnaires.

   a. The amount of sports nutrition drinks consumed in a city
   b. Why a local bank has been losing customers
   c. How heavily the company should invest in manufacturing and marketing home fax machines
   d. The amount of money being spent "over the state line" for lottery tickets
   e. What local doctors would like to see changed in the city's hospitals
   f. Consumers' attitudes toward several music celebrities

4-20. *For Further Research (Individual)* Some companies use neuromarketing to gain an edge over their competitors. Research at least two companies that employ this technique. Explain how they use neuromarketing to gain a competitive advantage and assess whether the value of the information these marketers gained was worth the investment. (Hint: Just start by googling the term *neuromarketing*.)

4-21. *For Further Research (Individual)* Many different types of syndicated research are important to marketers. Use online company resources to learn about the methodology for three of the following syndicated research studies. After you have become familiar with the methodologies, write a report with your thoughts about the pros and cons of the data.

   a. Arbitron ratings
   b. Neilsen ratings
   c. Claritas PRIZM
   d. Q Scores or Q-ratings
   e. Simmons National Survey

Concepts: Apply Marketing Metrics

Marketers historically have tended to rely too much on click-through rates as a metric for success of web advertising. *Click-through rate (CTR)* is a metric that indicates the percentage of website users who have decided to click on an advertisement to visit the website or Web page associated with it. Technically, click-through rate is the number of times a click is made on the advertisement divided by the total impressions (the times an advertisement was served up to the consumer during the visit to the website):

$$\text{Click-through rate (\%)} = \frac{\text{Number of click-throughs}}{\text{Number of impressions}}$$

Although providing useful information, click-through rates merely measure quantity, not quality, of consumer response. Consider what you learned in this chapter about various approaches to market research.

4-22. What other two or three data collection approaches to measuring the success of a web advertising campaign might be fruitful in providing more meaningful data than just clicks? (Hint: Just because the metric relates to the Web doesn't mean non-web-based research approaches are inappropriate.[38])

Choices: What Do You Think?

4-23. *Critical Thinking* This chapter introduces Q Scores (also known as Q-ratings), which are used to track the way that the public perceives different celebrities. A positive (and ideally high) Q Score indicates a positive perception, whereas a negative Q Score indicates a negative perception of a celebrity. Is it possible for a celebrity to have a particular type of image or reputation for which a negative Q Score might be beneficial from a commercial standpoint? Explain your answer and provide examples.

4-24. *Ethics* Some telemarketers attempt to disguise themselves as market researchers who want to ask you questions when their real intent is to sell something to the consumer. What is the impact of this practice on legitimate researchers? What do you think might be done about this practice?

4-25. *Critical Thinking* Do you believe that there could be a relationship between the amount of compensation received for actively participating in a research study and the level of effort put forth by a participant in that study? Are there forms of research that are more or less susceptible to such a relationship?

4-26. *Critical Thinking* The use of loyalty programs in the marketplace allow companies to collect more and more data on customers. Some consumers do not realize this information is being compiled and used to market to them. Do you think there are any privacy or ethical concerns with this practice? Why or why not?

4-27. *Critical Thinking* More and more companies are starting to employ customer insight specialists to make sense of the data collected about their customers. Do you think this position is really needed within companies, or is it just a fad? Explain your reasoning.

4-28. *Ethics* Sometimes firms use data to determine a segment of customers that is unprofitable and work to prune out these customers. Do you think this is an acceptable practice? Why or why not?

4-29. *Critical Thinking* Market researchers use focus groups to discuss a product or a   concept with consumers. List three types of products that you think would benefit the most from a focus group study. Select one of these. Develop a set of 10 discussion questions to provide the information the marketer will need.

4-30. *Ethics* One of the potential opportunities offered by neuromarketing is the capability to look at patterns in brain activity and identify (a) how the presence of different product attributes and variations of those attributes can help to predict what choices a consumer considers prior to their actually making those choices

and (b) how those attributes can be manipulated to influence other choices without the consumer realizing the impact that those changes are having on their choices. Do you believe that marketers should be able to use this type of knowledge to their advantage? Would you have any personal qualms with doing so?

Miniproject: Learn by Doing

The purpose of this miniproject is to familiarize you with market research techniques and to help you apply these techniques to managerial decision making.

4-31. With a group of three other students in your class, select a small retail business or quick-service restaurant to use as a "client" for your project. (Be sure to get the manager's permission before you conduct your research.) Then, choose one topic from among the following possibilities to develop a study problem:

- Employee–customer interactions
- The busiest periods of customer activity
- Customer perceptions of service
- Customer likes and dislikes about the menu
- Customer likes and dislikes about the environment in the place of business
- The benefits customers perceive to be important
- The age groups that frequent the place of business
- The buying habits of a particular age group
- How customer complaints are handled

1. Develop a plan for the research.
   a. Define the research question as you will study it.
   b. Choose the type of research approach you will use.
   c. Select the techniques you will use to gather data.
   d. Develop the mode and format for data collection.
2. Conduct the research.
3. Write a report (or develop a class presentation) that includes the five parts shown in step 7 of the market research process covered in the chapter.

Marketing in Action **Case**   Real Choices at LEGO

Understanding market preferences can be as challenging as assembling LEGO's 7,541-piece Millennium Falcon—which can be yours for only $799. The Danish toymaker known for its building sets made of colorful plastic "bricks" found that it needed a variety of research methodologies to determine what their young customers really want. They have also learned that even the best research does not guarantee long-term financial success.

Founded by Ole Kirk Kristiansen in 1932, the LEGO Group has grown to become the world's largest toy manufacturer by sales. However, in 2004, the company was on the brink of bankruptcy. What happened? LEGO aggressively leveraged its popular brand by moving into action figures and video games, believing that kids no longer wanted to spend time playing

with old-fashioned plastic bricks. When CEO Jørgen Vig Knudstorp took over that year, the company was losing $1 million per day. In pursuit of a turnaround, Knudstorp focused not on adding new product lines but on understanding LEGO's customers and what "play" actually meant to them.

To gain this insight, LEGO did not pursue normal market research techniques, like surveys and focus groups. Instead, it turned to advanced techniques like using MRI scans of kids' brains, noting which parts light up as they play with different toys. They also ventured into the science of *anthropology*, the study of humans and human behavior and societies. Their goal was to get to the roots of customer behaviors, a process that LEGO's consultants ReD Associates call *sensemaking*. LEGO's researchers actually lived with families in the U.S. and Germany (presumably with their permission!), and they spent months interviewing parents and children, shopping with them, creating video diaries, and studying toy shops.

Through this deeper market research, LEGO learned that children were not too busy to spend time building LEGOs. In fact, they like to play as an escape from their overly orchestrated lives. They not only have the time, but they have the desire to "achieve mastery" by honing a skill like building their creations made of LEGO bricks. This insight on why children play provided LEGO with a new focus that returned them to their roots and propelled the company to revenue growth that nearly quintupled between 2007 and 2016 to $6 billion.

This growth trajectory came to a screeching halt in 2017 when LEGO saw revenue drop for the first time in 13 years, creating the need to shed about 1,400 jobs. Analysts pointed to competition from programmable robotic kits that appeal to kids in an increasingly digital world. Internal challenges plagued the toymaker as well. Expecting continued growth, LEGO had created an organizational structure with many layers that made reacting to changing trends slow and marketing strategy implementation tedious. More fundamentally, inaccurate forecasting led them to manufacture more product than needed, leading to a sell off at lower profit margins.

A new CEO was installed in 2017, and he moved the company back on a positive path with a focus on expanding LEGO's company-owned retail stores in order to fill a void left by the bankruptcy of Toys "R" Us. Many of these stores were in China, where LEGO's research found that kids played in very similar ways as kids of other nationalities. The company also introduced new products in the digital arena, including an augmented-reality app that uses a mobile device or tablet to animate LEGO bricks. The company is also spending $150 million to create LEGO bricks made from plants, not plastic, in order to meet growing demands for more sustainable products.

LEGO's recent history shows both the promise of creative market research and its limitations. Effective research is a foundation for the evidence-based approach to decision making you learned about in Chapter 3. But their recent challenges show that research alone—even using the most innovative methods—does not guarantee business success. Consistent success comes from asking the right questions, making the right interpretations, and ultimately implementing the right strategies.[39]

Questions for Discussion

4-32. What are some of the sources of information LEGO used to form their strategy? Which are secondary sources? Which are primary sources?

4-33. How could information contained in a marketing information system or a marketing decision support system help LEGO make future strategic decisions?

4-34. What additional research could help LEGO in their ongoing strategic planning?

Chapter **Notes**

1. Kennedy Rose, "Campbell Soup Sees Unprecedented Demand for Products as Prego and Goldfish Sales Soar," *Philadelphia Business Journal*, March 25, 2020, https://www.bizjournals.com/philadelphia/news/2020/03/25/campbell-soup-sees-unprecedented-demand-for.html (accessed May 16, 2020).

2. Patrick LaPointe, *Marketing by the Dashboard Light: How to Get More Insight, Foresight, and Accountability from Your Marketing Investments* (New York: ANA, 2005).

3. "Coronavirus Viewing: More People are Sampling Multiple Streaming Services," Wendy Lee, *Los Angeles Times*, April 14, 2020, https://www.latimes.com/entertainment-arts/business/story/2020-04-14/coronavirus-more-people-sampling-streaming (accessed May 15, 2020).

4. Nielsen, "Solutions: Nielsen Scarborough," http://www.nielsen.com/us/en/solutions/capabilities/scarborough-local.html (accessed March 13, 2018).

5. Louise Grimmer and Martin Grimmer, "Dolly Parton is a 'great unifier' in a divided America. Here's why," *The Conversation*, November 24, 2019, https://www.abc.net.au/news/2019-11-25/how-marketers-measure-dolly-partons-magic/11733972 (accessed May 26, 2020).

6. Ariella Gintzler, "Clif Bar and Kind are Fighting: Here's Why," *Outside*, June 12, 2019, https://www.outsideonline.com/2398140/clif-bar-kind-fight (accessed May 18, 2020).

7. Quoted in Dale Buss, "Unapologetically, Volvo Aims Its New Campaign at True Believers," *Forbes*, April 15, 2013, https://www.forbes.com/sites/dalebuss/2013/04/15/unapologetically-volvo-aims-its-new-ads-at-true-believers/#213932c86e76 (accessed April 4, 2015).

8. Nick Gibbs, "How Volvo Defied the Odds," *Automotive News*, April 17, 2017, http://www.autonews.com/article/20170417/RETAIL01/304179963/volvo-sales-united-states-up (accessed March 28, 2018).

9. MRI-Simmons, "National Consumer Study," https://www.mrisimmons.com/solutions/national-studies/national-consumer-study/ (accessed May 20, 2020).

10. Greg Trotter, "MillerCoors Works to Keep Leinenkugel, Blue Moon Rising," *Chicago Tribune*, March 22, 2016, http://www.chicagotribune.com/business/ct-blue-moon-leinenkugel-craftbeer-0323-biz-20160322-story.html (accessed May 10, 2018).

11. Tom De Ruyck, "Inspirational Online Dialogues," October 14, 2013, http://rwconnect.esomar.org/inspirational-online-dialogues (accessed August 12, 2016).

12. Decision Analyst, "Online Communities," http://www.decisionanalyst.com/services/onlinecommunities.dai (accessed April 9, 2016).

13. Karl Greenberg, "Volvo Uses Twitter Chat for Digital Focus Group," *MediaPost*, May 29, 2013, https://www.mediapost.com/publications/article/201309/volvo-uses-twitter-chat-for-digitalfocus-group.html?edition=60600 (accessed August 12, 2016).

14. https://www.southwestadvisorycouncil.com/Portal/default.aspx (accessed May 19, 2020).

15. Matt Richtel, "The Parable of the Beer and Diapers," *The Register*, August 15, 2006, http://www.theregister.co.uk/2006/08/15/beer_diapers (accessed April 8, 2016).

16. John Carney, "Hemlines Are Plunging, Is Economy Next?," *CNBC*, February 16, 2012, https://www.cnbc.com/id/46414411 (accessed April 4, 2016).

17. Arthur Zaczkiewicz, "Bear Market Ahead? If Hemline Theory Holds, Then Maybe," *WWD*, February 7, 2018, http://wwd.com/business-news/business-features/hemline-theory-1202539760/ (accessed March 28, 2018).

18. Jack Neff, "Neuromarketing Exits 'Hype Cycle,' Begins to Shape TV Commercials," *AdAge*, April 19, 2016, http://adage.com/article/cmo-strategy/neuromarketing-exits-hype-cycle-begins-shape-tv-ads/303582/ (accessed March 14, 2018).

19. Direct Marketing Association, "Where Marketers Can Obtain State Do-Not-Call Lists," http://www.the-dma.org/government/donotcalllists.shtml (accessed April 2, 2016).

20. Octavia Blanco, "How the New Robocall Law would Protect Consumers," *Consumer Reports*, December 19, 2019, https://www.consumerreports.org/robocalls/how-traced-act-robocall-law-will-protect-consumers/ (accessed May 21, 2020).

21. The Praxis Group, Inc., "Research Overview: Telephone versus Online Research—Advantages and Pitfalls," Fall 2007, http://www.praxisgroup.net/TPG%20Phone%20Versus%20Online%20WP.pdf (accessed April 1, 2016).

22. Nielsen, "Solutions: How We Measure," http://www.nielsen.com/us/en/solutions/measurement.html (accessed March 14, 2018).

23. Nielsen Social, "Social Content Ratings," http://www.nielsensocial.com/product/nielsen-twitter-tv-ratings/ (accessed March 26, 2016).

24. Nielsen, "Solutions: Nielsen Audio," http://www.nielsen.com/us/en/solutions/capabilities/audio.html (accessed March 26, 2016).

25. Corey Deitz, "What Is the Portable People Meter and How Does It Work?" *Lifewire*, http://radio.about.com/od/forprofessionals/a/What-Is-Arbitrons-Portable-People-Meter-And-How-Does-It-Work.htm (accessed March 26, 2016).

26. Tobii Pro, "Advertising," http://www.tobiipro.com/fields-of-use/marketing-consumer-research/advertising/ (accessed March 26, 2016).

27. Ray Nelson, "How to Use Social Media for Marketing Research," *Social Media Today*, March 19, 2013, https://www.socialmediatoday.com/content/how-use-social-media-market-research (accessed April 5, 2016).

28. Robert V. Kozinets, "Netnography: The Marketer's Secret Ingredient," MIT Technology Review, October 14, 2010, https://www.technologyreview.com/2010/10/14/199923/netnography-the-marketers-secret-ingredient/ (accessed March 30, 2018).

29. Pritam Nagrale, "Top 12 Crowdsourcing Sites Like MTurk to Find Micro Jobs," *Money Connexion*, February 10, 2018, http://money-connexion.com/top-10-crowdsourcing-sites-like-mturk.htm (accessed March 14, 2018).

30. Mary Lister, "33 Mind-Boggling Instagram Stats and Facts for 2018," *WordStream*, January 18, 2018, https://www.wordstream.com/blog/ws/2017/04/20/instagram-statistics (accessed March 14, 2018).

31. Alexis Madrigal, "How Netflix Reverse Engineered Hollywood," *The Atlantic*, January 2, 2014, http://www.theatlantic.com/technology/archive/2014/01/how-netflix-reverse-engineered-hollywood/282679 (accessed April 5, 2016).

32. Dan Goodin, "Now Sites Can Fingerprint You Online Even When You Use Multiple Browsers," *ARS Technica*, February 13, 2017, https://arstechnica.com/information-technology/2017/02/now-sites-can-fingerprint-you-online-even-when-you-use-multiple-browsers/ (accessed March 14, 2018).

33. Bruce L. Stern and Ray Ashmun, "Methodological Disclosure: The Foundation for Effective Use of Survey Research," *Journal of Applied Business Research* 7 (1991): 77–82.

34. Malcolm Gladwell, *Blink* (New York: Hachette Book Group, 2007), 159.

35. Michael E. Ross, "It Seemed Like a Good Idea at the Time," *MSNBC*, April 22, 2005, http://www.nbcnews.com/id/7209828#.WuBdvlMvw-4 (accessed April 7, 2016).

36. Gary Levin, "New Adventures in Children's Research," *Advertising Age*, August 9, 1993, 17.

37. *2019 Market Leaders Green Book Report*, December 10, 2019, https://www.mrweb.com/drno/news29031.htm (accessed May 19, 2020).

38. Neil T. Bendle, Paul W. Farris, Phillip E. Pheifer, and David J. Reibstein, *Marketing Metrics: The Manager's Guide to Measuring Marketing Performance* (Upper Saddle River, NJ: Wharton School Publishing, 2015).

39. Based on The LEGO Group, "Millennium Falcon," accessed July 24, 2020, https://www.lego.com/en-us/product/millennium-falcon-75192; The LEGO Group, "About Us," accessed July 24, 2020, https://www.lego.com/en-us/aboutus/lego-group/the_lego_history; Saabira Chaudhuri, "Lego Commits to China Expansion as Revenue Climbs," *Wall Street Journal (Eastern Ed.)*, March 4, 2020, https://www.wsj.com/articles/lego-commits-to-china-expansion-as-revenue-climbs-11583310205; Richard Feloni, "How Lego Came Back from the Brink of Bankruptcy," *Business Insider*, February 10, 2014, http://www.businessinsider.com/how-lego-made-a-huge-turnaround-2014-2; Christian Madsbjerg and Mikkel B. Rasmussen, "An Anthropologist Walks into a Bar," *Harvard Business Review*, March 2014, https://hbr.org/2014/03/an-anthropologist-walks-into-a-bar; Wadavi, "LEGO – Market Research as the Building Block to Success," *Wordpress.Com*, April 18, 2016, https://mpk732t12016clusterb.wordpress.com/2016/04/18/lego-market-research-as-the-building-block-to-success/; Mikkel B. Rasmussen, "Why Your Legos Are as Addictive as Your iPhone," *Fortune*, January 29, 2017, http://fortune.com/2017/01/29/why-your-legos-are-as-addictive-as-your-iphone/; Wikipedia contributors, "Anthropology," *Wikipedia, The Free Encyclopedia*, July 13, 2020; "How Lego Can Rebuild Its Business - Knowledge@Wharton," Upenn.Edu, accessed July 25, 2020, http://knowledge.wharton.upenn.edu/article/lego-can-recover-slump/; Sabira Chaudhuri, "Lego Hits Brick Wall with Sales, Sheds 8% of Global Workforce," *The Wall Street Journal*, September 5, 2017, https://www.wsj.com/articles/lego-to-slash-1-400-jobs-posts-first-sales-drop-in-13-years-1504599603; Bel Booker, "Lego's Growth Strategy: How the Toy Brand Innovated to Expand," *Attest Blog*, September 12, 2019, https://www.askattest.com/blog/brand/legos-growth-strategy-how-the-toy-brand-innovated-to-expand; Saabira Chaudhuri, "Lego Returns to Growth as It Builds on U.S. Momentum," *The Wall Street Journal*, February 27, 2019; https://www.wsj.com/articles/lego-returns-to-growth-as-it-builds-on-china-expansion-11551259001; Anne Michaud, "Lego's Quest to Make Plant-Based Toy Bricks Is Met with Skepticism," *The Wall Street Journal*, June 21, 2019, https://www.wsj.com/articles/legos-quest-to-make-plant-based-toy-bricks-is-met-with-skepticism-11561125040.

5 Marketing Analytics: Welcome to the Era of Data-Driven Insights!

Josh Barbieri

Meet Josh Barbieri

▼ A Decision Maker at the Philadelphia Phillies

Josh Barbieri is in his 19th season with the Philadelphia Phillies, where he serves as Director, Business Analytics. In his current role with the club, Josh leads a data-driven team that works daily with all departments on the business side of the organization helping to improve and automate various business processes involving data. Josh and his team are responsible for data infrastructure, business application development, business intelligence, and predictive analytics.

Josh has a background in enterprise business intelligence software and in-memory data warehousing methodologies, and he possesses knowledge in several programming languages. Born in Philadelphia, Josh earned a B.S. degree from Philadelphia University, with a double major in Accounting and Management Information Systems.

Josh's Info

What I do when I'm not working:
Spend time with my wife, Lauren, and twins, Josh and Vivian

Career high:
Working for the Phillies; riding down Broad Street on a float celebrating the 2008 World Champion Philadelphia Phillies

My hero:
My parents for instilling a strong work ethic and providing me the opportunity and encouragement to pursue my career goals

My motto to live by:
Be a lifelong learner. Work hard and empower others, and you will accomplish more than you ever thought possible.

What drives me:
I love to build stuff!

My management style:
Hire talented people and get out of the way.

Don't do this when interviewing with me:
Use your mobile phone.

Here's my problem...

Real **People**, Real **Choices**

The baseball legend Yogi Berra once said, "Baseball is 90% mental. The other half is physical." Although his math skills were a little off, today the mental aspects of the sport are even more important than they were in Berra's day. Although baseball has always thrived on stats, now sophisticated data analytics go light-years beyond the simple practice of recording "Ks" on a piece of paper. The book and movie *Moneyball* helped to fuel the Big Data revolution; author Michael Lewis told the story of how the 2002 Oakland A's used data about players' performances to help the team sign undiscovered talents and decide on matchups and plays that would be more likely to propel them past big-spending teams like the New York Yankees.[1]

Fast forward to today: Virtually every professional team in baseball and other big-time sports now relies heavily on data-driven approaches to decision making. Managers rely on their analysts to guide them as they figure out how to spot stars, how to predict their performance, and what to pay them. Each team's marketers dip into data as well; they trust their data analysts to guide them in decisions such as pricing, sales offers, and operational efficiencies. In the end, however, executives in these areas balance industry experience with data to make the most informed decisions.

Josh's Business Analytics team assists the Phillies in transforming both structured and unstructured data into meaningful information that the team— and its marketing team—can easily access and analyze. They are tasked with examining and developing strategies that promote data-driven decision making with the overall vision of centralizing, organizing, and visualizing all business information while enabling real-time access to analytics.

Josh's team works collaboratively with all departments on the business side. For example, it produces predictive models the team uses to forecast how many fans will renew their season tickets. Using five years of historical data (key variables include tenure, games attended, and secondary market activity, among other things), the team delivers real-time visualizations that compare everything from ticket sales and revenue to how many hot dogs the concessions sell during a game.

In 2015, the team faced the growing challenge of optimizing how it stores big data and how to efficiently organize and disseminate information in an actionable way. At the time, it had sufficient business intelligence tools; however, as Josh's team continued to acquire more data sources, this became increasingly challenging to manage at scale. Josh was getting a lot of requests that involved blending multiple systems together. For example, stakeholders wanted data that blended online sales and attendance (in-park), and these were housed on two different platforms. He needed a better way to combine and analyze vast amounts of data in order to deliver accurate predictions to the marketing team and others within the Phillies organization.

The analysts needed to modernize their development approach, shift to a self-service business intelligence (BI) model that allowed them to directly query their databases without going through a third party, and upgrade the team's data infrastructure to support the expanding head count of the Analytics department and the growing list of business units that it services.

The question was, how could the Phillies modernize how it used Big Data in a way that would be the most efficient and allow the team to make the best use of all the information it collected on fans, concessions, retail, and other data sources? There was a need for a new approach that had to be designed to outlast the changes of underlying source systems and consolidate information from disparate data sources in real time. Josh wanted to be in control so his team could deliver releases on time and tailored to the needs of the Phillies' business users, such as integrating with Major League Baseball's (MLB) "Wheelhouse" data platform. MLB has a team of data engineers that publishes new feeds to each team on a frequent basis. For example, MLB developed a metric it calls Fan Avidity that measures how passionate different customer segments are about the teams they follow. This kind of information

is invaluable, and Josh's team is always looking for ways to incorporate these insights with the team's marketers.

Josh had a vision for a new system that would truly harness the power of Big Data to benefit different team stakeholders. For example, he wanted to provide real-time sales information through a mobile app to sales and ticket office personnel. He also hoped to deliver advanced predictive models to concessions managers to forecast how many fans will attend games at Citizens Bank Park. The concessionaire is very data driven because tracking exactly what sells under different conditions creates efficiency and reduces waste. This collaboration affords a variety of managers the information they need to staff accordingly and to acquire the right amount of hot dogs, T-shirts, and other merchandise for each game. Josh also hoped to encourage data users to get "more bang for the buck" by delivering vast amounts of information in visual formats (sometimes called *dashboards*) so that they could see more quickly just what insights they could derive by looking at a lot of complex yet powerful relationships among various data sources.

Josh and his team considered their options 1·2·3

1 Option **Build an enterprise data warehouse internally.** Although a team always has to work with vendors, it's risky to rely on them to safeguard one of the team's most important assets—data. If Josh's team took on the task of building the data warehouse themselves, they would be in full control of what it was able to do. But of course, this is a huge undertaking and the team would have to allocate personnel to support the platform after it gets deployed. If something went wrong, there wouldn't be a vendor to call in a panic—it would be on the team to fix the problem.

2 Option **Outsource the data enterprise platform.** If Josh brought in a vendor to overhaul the team's data platform, this would free up members of his team to do the other things required of them, such as engaging new departments with its capabilities. He could spend more time educating other areas of the business on how his team can help with data organization, analysis, and visualizations. On the other hand, this solution would mean giving up a lot of control over how the platform would work and also the extent to which Josh's team could modify it in the future. In addition, Josh estimated that outsourcing this work would cost the team more than one million dollars—and that amount doesn't include hosting and maintenance fees and additional enhancements charged by the hour.

3 Option **Wait for a vendor to deliver this as a packaged service.** There were several vendors with whom Josh's team worked closely that touted a turnkey solution. They told Josh that he would not need to invest in additional staff because they would operate the system. On the other hand, the Phillies' specific needs wouldn't be a priority, because these vendors offered data systems that were designed to work for every team that subscribed to their services. As a result, Josh would have to trade personalization for efficiency because the output wouldn't be customized to the Phillies' specific data needs.

Now, put yourself in Josh's shoes. Which option would you choose, and why?

You Choose

Which **Option** would you choose, and **why**?

☐ **Option 1**   ☐ **Option 2**   ☐ **Option 3**

5.1

OBJECTIVE

Explain how
marketers increase
long-term success
and profits by
practicing customer
relationship
management (CRM).

Customer Relationship Management (CRM): A Key Decision Tool for Marketers

customer relationship management (CRM)

A systematic tracking of consumers' preferences and behaviors over time to tailor the value proposition as closely as possible to each individual's unique wants and needs.

A good place to kick off our discussion of how marketers use large quantities of data and advanced analytic tools is by introducing the concept of **customer relationship management (CRM)**. The big data revolution was fueled in part by the success of sports teams using data analytics to enhance their on-field performance. However, Josh Barbieri and the Phillies quickly recognized the potential to leverage customer data using CRM as a means to enhance the overall customer experience. CRM systems serve as a central hub of customer data for most successful firms, integrating various data sources that can be used to develop powerful analytical capabilities oriented toward enhancing an organization's relationship with its customers. For example, Josh and his marketing team use this type of data to predict ticket renewals and in-game attendance, which allows them to anticipate potential demand for concessions and merchandise and to maximize points of contact with fans. Vast amounts of data have enabled marketers to understand and interact with customers in ways that would never have been possible in the past. Did you know that chief marketing officers (CMOs) now spend more on technology than do chief information officers (CIOs)? There are over 5,000 vendors that sell technology specifically for *marketing analytics* (we'll formally define this term later in the chapter), and this number grows tremendously each year! This explosion has created a new category of technology called **MarTech**, which is a blending of marketing and technology, especially digital technologies.[2]

MarTech

Short for "marketing technology," this term is commonly used to denote the fusion of marketing and technology. A particular focus is placed on the application of marketing through digital technologies.

This blending of functionality, enabled by advanced technology not available to marketers until recently, has begun to impact how firms organize themselves and do business even at their highest levels. It's even affecting titles and roles in the company **C-suite**, the top executive teams of firms so-named because they are composed of all the "chief" officer roles, like CEO (chief executive officer), COO (chief operating officer), CFO (chief financial officer), CIO (chief information officer), CMO (chief marketing officer), and sometimes others. An organization-wide focus on CRM, enabled by MarTech, has sparked a trend toward adding a new C-suite role called **chief customer officer (CCO)**. The CCO is a firm's leading voice of all things customer related. In some C-suites, it replaces the traditional CMO role, and in others, it augments that role. This trend is a very visible example of a deep commitment to a *customer orientation,* which, as you learned in Chapter 1, is a business approach that prioritizes the satisfaction of customers' needs and wants in order to enhance the customer experience.[3]

C-suite

A popular term for a firm's top executive team, so-called because of the "chief" titles of each officer, such as chief executive officer (CEO).

chief customer officer (CCO)

An increasingly popular C-suite role, the CCO is positioned as a firm's leading force of all things customer related.

Why Is CRM So Effective?

Now it's time to drill down a bit more on how firms actually accomplish this prioritization. Toward this end, most highly successful firms embrace CRM programs that involve systematically tracking consumers' preferences and behaviors over time to tailor the value proposition as closely as possible to each individual's unique wants and needs. CRM allows firms to talk to individual customers and to adjust elements of their marketing programs in light of how each customer reacts.[4] The CRM trend facilitates **one-to-one marketing**, which includes several steps:[5]

one-to-one marketing

Facilitated by CRM, one-to-one marketing allows the organization to customize some aspect of the goods or services it offers to each customer.

1. Identify customers and get to know them in as much detail as possible.
2. Differentiate among these customers in terms of both their needs and their value to the company.

3. Interact with customers and find ways to improve cost efficiency and the effectiveness of the interaction.

4. Customize some aspect of the goods or services that you offer to each customer. This means treating each customer differently based on what the organization has learned about him or her through prior interactions.[6]

Remember, successful one-to-one marketing depends on CRM, which allows a company to identify its best customers, stay on top of their needs, and increase their satisfaction.[7]

At its core, CRM is about communicating with customers and about customers being able to communicate with a company "up close and personal." CRM systems are applications that use computers, specialized computer software, databases, and often the Internet to capture information at each **touchpoint**, which is any point of direct interface between customers and a company (online, by phone, or in person).

These systems include everything from websites that let you check on the status of a bill or package to call centers that solicit your business. When you log on to the FedEx website to track a lost package, that's part of a CRM system. When you get a phone message from the dentist reminding you about your appointment tomorrow to get a root canal, that's CRM (sorry about that). And when you get a call from the car dealer asking how you like your new vehicle, that's also CRM. Remember how we said in Chapter 4 that information is the fuel that runs the marketing engine? It is through CRM that companies act on and manage the information they gather from their customers.

Marketing Automation

It quickly can become overwhelming to think about how to both maintain and utilize all of the data that can be collected from customers through all potential touchpoints. To help reduce the cognitive load (and clerical effort) required to fully take advantage of all this data, firms deploy **marketing automation**. This term refers to a set of systems and technologies that the organization can use to put in place a set of rules for handling different processes without human intervention. These rules can relate to the collection and processing of data, as well as the execution of different customer-oriented actions.

Consider, for example, a potential customer who has subscribed to receive an email notification whenever someone posts on your company's blog. A few weeks later, he or she reads and comments on a blog post that discusses the value that a client obtained from one of your company's products. Then, in a few more days, he or she downloads a document from your website that outlines the technical features of that same product.

At this point, if you're on your toes, it should be increasingly clear that the potential customer has a fair amount of interest in one of your company's products. But with everything else that's going on, it is often easy for managers to miss these activity patterns. In this example, an organization could use a marketing automation system from the onset to watch for sequenced events like this, and based on an understanding of their contextual significance and relationship with each other, it could instruct the system to send out an email to the potential customer inviting her to speak to a sales representative, attend a webinar, or pursue other follow-up options. The system can also direct the customer to a personalized landing page on the company website that is updated in real time based on the previous viewing behaviors associated with their unique IP address. Such customized responses greatly increase the likelihood of customer follow-through.

The firm Synduit is a vivid example of marketing automation at work. Synduit provides affordable, professional, creative, and comprehensive marketing solutions for small businesses in the service sector. Think of them as a virtual marketing department for businesses that otherwise could not afford these types of services. One of the secrets of success for Synduit is the highly personalized customer exchanges with a very special salesperson

touchpoint
Any point of direct interface between customers and a company (online, by phone, or in person).

marketing automation
A group of systems and technologies that can be used to establish a set of rules for handling different marketing-related processes without human intervention.

named Barry. Although most of Barry's customers send emails back and forth with him for months as they move through the sales process, they have no idea that he actually is 100 percent automated!

Synduit's sales process has four stages, each consisting of a sequence of automated emails from Barry intended to move potential customers (or leads) to the next stage of the sales process. A **lead** is an individual or firm with a potential interest in buying something you sell. Leads are converted into paying customers through the **sales funnel**, which is the process through which a company finds, qualifies, and sells its products to buyers. The metaphor of a funnel is used to describe the process because a large number of potential customers may begin at the top-end of the sales process, but only the most qualified prospects advance through the process and only a fraction of these people actually end up making a purchase. (You'll learn more about sales later in Chapter 14.) The sales funnel for Synduit looks something like this:

lead
An individual or firm with a potential interest in buying something you sell.

sales funnel
The process through which a company finds, qualifies, and sells its products to buyers.

- Step 1: New leads are added to a seven-week email sequence, each receiving a total of 14 emails from Barry.

- Step 2: If a lead fills out a "let's chat" form, Barry initiates a six-email sequence to schedule a call.

- Step 3: The lead is added to one of two email sequences—sequence one if Barry will be converting the sale or sequence two if Barry will need to nurture the lead. **Lead nurturing** is the automated process of sending personalized and relevant content to the prospect to build their trust, making it more likely that they will eventually make a purchase.

lead nurturing
The automated process of sending personalized and relevant content to the prospect to build their trust, making it more likely that they will eventually make a purchase.

- Step 4: Barry sends a series of post-conversion anniversary emails at 6 months, 12 months, and 24 months. By automating 90 percent of the sales process and personalizing each email and landing page over time to reflect the lead's current stage in the sales process, Synduit has successfully created an efficient and effective sales process that avoids the inconsistencies of human error.[8]

Connecting with Customers

As we noted previously, CRM doesn't just drive automated methods; it also plays a key role in enabling employees to maximize high-touch and personal relationships with customers. For example, consider the experience of USAA, which began as an insurance company catering to the military market and today is a leading global financial services powerhouse. In 1922, when 25 army officers met in San Antonio and decided to insure each other's vehicles, they could not have imagined that their tiny organization would one day serve 6 million members and become the only fully integrated financial services company in America. Unlike State Farm, Allstate, and other traditional insurance providers, USAA does not provide field agents with an office where you can go to sit down and shoot the breeze about your latest fishing trip. In fact, USAA's employees conduct business almost entirely over the phone. But just ask any USAA member how they feel about the service, and you'll get a glowing report.

The secret sauce in USAA's success is largely its state-of-the-art CRM system. No matter where on the globe you are, no matter what time of day or night, a USAA representative will pull up your profile, and you'll feel that he or she knows you. Of course, it takes a good dose of employee training to enable those folks to use the system to its potential. But USAA does a great job of building and maintaining long-term customer relationships and, more importantly, getting customers to move many or all of their business over to USAA, including banking, credit cards, money management, investments, and financial planning. To further build loyalty, USAA even runs an online company store that sells all sorts of popular product lines and brands at discounted prices for members.[9]

USAA's success helps illustrate and explain why CRM has become a driving philosophy in many successful firms. Gartner, a leading information technology (IT) research firm, notes that the CRM market reached $48.2 billion in 2018 and global CRM revenues are expected to reach over $80 billion in 2025.[10]

Clearly, CRM has increasingly become an important part of how businesses operate, with no signs of that trend slowing down. CRM trends predict a continued movement toward mobile devices and better integration with voice, text, and video as cloud-based systems are becoming more popular than on-premise applications. The ability to access CRM software from multiple devices and locations has led to remarkable gains for businesses in terms of customer satisfaction, sales, and business process efficiency.[11] Here are some great examples of CRM at work:

- Amazon.com is the world champion master of the happy customer approach to CRM. For loyal users, Amazon tracks visits so that it can customize product recommendations on the website as well as enable the delivery of relevant product recommendations and promotions via email.[12] Given that Amazon has become a true one-stop shop for everything from streaming entertainment to designer clothing to organic groceries, the Amazon homepage has become more of a lifestyle guide than an online retail site. On Amazon's homepage, a user can find product recommendations organized into sections that relate to such factors as past browsing and shopping behavior, including movie and music preferences, and observed relationships between a product that the user recently purchased and one or more products that the user has not yet purchased. This focus on personalizing the customer experience helps keep customers engaged during each of their visits and helps ensure that they continue to come back for more.

- Adidas delivers one-to-one marketing through its application of top CRM provider Salesforce.com (often referred to as simply "Salesforce"). Its Salesforce application enables Adidas to collect a wide array of data around customers to better understand each one as an individual. Whereas in the past, athletic apparel consumers traditionally began their purchase journey in a physical store, the website is now the dominant entry channel. Tracking every touchpoint with the customer—each customer service interaction, each product view, and each purchase—allows Adidas to adapt the messaging it presents, as well as when and how the consumer sees it. The data it gathers also allows Adidas to create new products based on customer wants. Its Salesforce CRM system empowers over 1,100 Adidas customer care agents to deliver faster and smarter service in whatever format each customer prefers—phone, email, web, or social media.[13]

- Disney launched MyMagic+, a system that allows Disney World visitors to more efficiently plan out their vacation experience and reduce the need to carry around tickets and other items previously necessary to tour the park. Visitors can book events in advance, reserve times on rides, and review the park activities that they have experienced in the past, to name a few of the main features. MyMagic+ is designed to be partnered with either a wearable computer called the Disney Magic Band or the My Disney Experience app on a smartphone, both of which enable users to verify all of the actions they have taken through the MyMagic+ system without carrying around receipts or other forms of proof. In addition, they can use the wearable Magic Band or My Disney Experience app to make transactions while in the park. (Note that Disney will stop providing Magic Bands for free in 2021 because the same benefits will be available from the My Disney Experience app.) The benefits and convenience for visitors are obvious, but for Disney, another big advantage is the amount of data it can collect on visitors' behavior and actions. These data better enable the firm to understand how to communicate with each customer and manage each relationship more effectively.[14] Yep—one-to-one marketing even within a massive theme park!

Measuring Marketing Success

Back in Chapter 3 we talked about the importance of setting goals and objectives as part of good marketing planning. In addition to having a different mindset, companies that successfully practice CRM have different goals, use different measures of success, and look at customers in some different ways compared to firms that do not deploy CRM. As you learned in Chapter 1, *metrics* are measurements or "scorecards" that marketers use to identify the effectiveness of different strategies or tactics. Put another way, metrics are numbers that tell you whether or not something is working the way it should and how much progress you are making toward achieving your marketing goals. Given the vast amount of data potentially available, CRM facilitates the capability for users to look at a plethora of potential *marketing metrics*. Recall from Chapter 3 that these are measures that help marketers watch the performance of their marketing campaigns, initiatives, and channels, and, when appropriate, serve as a control mechanism. So how do you choose the right metrics? A good CRM strategy based on SMART goals is the key to successfully identifying which metrics are most appropriate. Let's have a look at how to set and measure these goals.

SMART Goals

Here's a fundamental question for marketers: Why invest in CRM? Well, the primary focus of any CRM initiative should be to *help a company achieve its goals and objectives!* Are goals and objectives the same thing? Technically no, but the words are often used interchangeably. They both describe desired outcomes and results that an organization wants to achieve. What distinguishes goals from objectives is mainly the timeframe (goals tend to be longer term), the level of concreteness (objectives tend to be more micro-level), and the impact they have on an organization (goals have a more lasting impact). For our purposes here, we're going to speak in terms of goals rather than objectives, but the following concepts can be applied to objectives as well.

SMART goals

Goals that meet the criteria of being specific, measurable, achievable, relevant, and timely.

Back to CRM—a critical first step in implementing a successful CRM strategy is to identify the goals it seeks to support. **SMART goals** are goals that meet the criteria of being specific, measurable, achievable, relevant, and timely. They provide a sense of direction to increase the likelihood of goal achievement. Figure 5.1 explains the five criteria that make up a SMART goal.[15]

Here's an example to help clarify the difference between a SMART goal and one that is not-so-SMART! A common goal of CRM is to "strengthen customer relationships," but what exactly does that mean? To begin, this statement is not *specific*. It does not identify which customers should or should not be included as part of the goal, what customer relationship elements are relevant, or what the intended action plan might be. Next, as stated it is not *measurable* as it does not describe how the strength of customer relationships actually will be assessed. This is particularly important given that there are several criteria that could indicate strengthened customer relationships. For example, both a decrease in customer churn and an increase in customer conversion rates could be indicative of strengthened customer relationships (you will learn what those two metrics mean later in the chapter). Because the goal essentially is not measurable, it is nearly impossible to determine either if it is *achievable* or how *relevant* it is to the broader objectives of the company. Finally, it is not *timely* because there is no timeline associated with this goal and, therefore, no sense of urgency and motivation to achieve the goal—that is, *when do we want to achieve it?*

An alternative goal statement that meets the SMART criteria might be: "To increase customer conversion rates for new referral customers by 15 percent by the end of Quarter 4, as tracked and measured by our CRM software. To achieve this, we will use our CRM software to enhance personalized communications between our sales teams and newly referred customers." This goal statement includes a specific action (increase customer conversion rates for new referral customers), a quantifiable goal and how it will be measured (by 15 percent as measured by CRM software), specified tools for achieving the goal (CRM

Figure 5.1 | SMART Goals

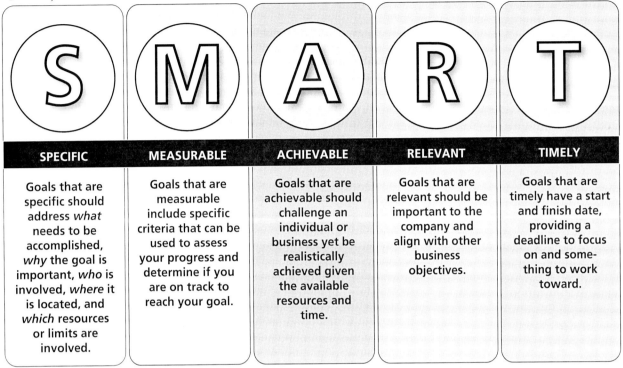

SPECIFIC	MEASURABLE	ACHIEVABLE	RELEVANT	TIMELY
Goals that are specific should address *what* needs to be accomplished, *why* the goal is important, *who* is involved, *where* it is located, and *which* resources or limits are involved.	Goals that are measurable include specific criteria that can be used to assess your progress and determine if you are on track to reach your goal.	Goals that are achievable should challenge an individual or business yet be realistically achieved given the available resources and time.	Goals that are relevant should be important to the company and align with other business objectives.	Goals that are timely have a start and finish date, providing a deadline to focus on and something to work toward.

software to enhance personalized communications), and it ties directly to broader business objectives (strengthen customer relationships) and sets a deadline (by the end of Quarter 4). Setting goals that are well defined, attainable, and meaningful and then developing the motivation, action plan, and needed support to achieve them greatly increase the chances of successfully meeting those goals. And that is just SMART business!

CRM Metrics and Key Performance Indicators (KPIs)

Now that you have a better understanding of how to set SMART goals, it is time to decide how you should measure and track those goals. There are three main categories of CRM metrics that businesses should be particularly focused on: user adoption metrics, customer perception metrics, and business performance metrics.[16]

1. **User adoption metrics** are focused on the extent to which employees are using the CRM system as intended, including various IT metrics, such as number of logins and data completeness.

2. **Customer perception metrics**, such as satisfaction, are concerned with the extent to which customer experiences are enhanced as a result of CRM.

3. **Business performance metrics** typically receive the most attention because they directly assess outcomes related to the profitability of a company.

The number of potential business performance metrics available to choose from can be overwhelming (see Table 5.1 for numerous examples), but firms identify their **key performance indicators (KPIs)** that they consider to be especially important to their success. Remember reading about Josh Barbieri and the Phillies at the beginning of this chapter? Josh and his marketing team use a variety of commonly used real-time KPIs, as well as industry-specific metrics such as Fan Avidity, which was created by MLB. You'll find more information about several of the metrics that firms use as KPIs in the Chapter 5 supplement at the end of this chapter. Table 5.1 identifies these as the boldfaced metrics.

user adoption metrics
Metrics focused on the extent to which employees are using the CRM system as intended, including various IT metrics, such as number of logins and data completeness.

customer perception metrics
Metrics, such as satisfaction, that are concerned with the extent to which customer experiences are enhanced as a result of CRM.

business performance metrics
Metrics that directly assess outcomes related to the profitability of a company.

key performance indicators (KPIs)
The critical indicators of progress toward an intended result.

Table 5.1	Examples of CRM Business Performance Metrics*

Marketing Metrics	Sales Metrics	Service Metrics
• **Customer acquisition cost**	• **Conversion rate**	• **Customer churn rate**
• **Customer lifetime value (CLV)**	• **Length of sales cycle**	• **Net promoter score**
• **Percentage of marketing-originated customers**	• **Share of customer wallet**	• **Return on experience**
• Number of campaigns	• Number of prospects	• Customer effort score
• Number of campaign responses	• Number of new customers	• Number of cases handled
• Number of campaign purchases	• Number of retained customers	• Number of cases closed the same day
• Revenue generated by campaign	• Close rate	• Average number of service calls per day
• Number of customer referrals	• Average size of sale	• Complaint time to resolution
• Number of web page views	• Renewal rate	• Number of customer call backs
• User goal completion rate on the web	• Number of sales calls made	• Average service cost per service interaction
• Time per website visit	• Number of sales calls per opportunity	• Service level agreement (SLA) compliance rate
• Cross-sell ratio	• Amount of new revenue	• Calls lost before being answered
• Up-sell ratio	• Number of open opportunities	• Average call handling time
• Email list growth rate	• Sales stage duration	
	• Number of proposals given	

*For more detailed information on the **boldfaced metrics** above that firms use as KPIs, please refer to to the Chapter 5 supplement at the end of this chapter.

5.2

Big Data A popular term to describe the exponential growth of data—both structured and unstructured—in massive amounts that are hard or impossible to process using traditional database techniques.

Big Data: Zettabytes Rule

CRM systems provide a great internal organizational data repository. But as more consumer experiences shift into the digital space and new means of connecting and interacting with both individuals and corporations become possible and widely accepted, it is no surprise that *Big Data* is becoming an increasingly important concept. You were briefly introduced to **Big Data** in Chapter 1, where you learned that it is the popular term to describe the exponential growth of data—both structured and unstructured—in massive amounts that are hard or impossible to process using traditional database techniques.

According to SAS, a leading provider of data analytics software, "Big Data refers to the ever-increasing volume, velocity, variety, variability and complexity of information."[17] Think about the amount of time that you spend online looking up information through search engines such as Google, connecting with friends on social media sites such as Facebook and Twitter, listening to music on sites such as Spotify and YouTube, or myriad other activities on the Web or through a mobile app that all of us engage in, and you'll begin to comprehend the sheer volume of data that we (perhaps unwittingly) create each and every day.

Each action you take online leaves a digital footprint, and all of your footprints—especially when analysts combine them with the footprints of thousands or even millions of others—have the potential to yield valuable insights for a wide range of stakeholders within society. Table 5.2 provides some examples of common user actions that create these valuable footprints for marketers to follow. As you review this table, you'll get a strong sense for why marketers are compelled to play close attention to the ethical use of data. The ethical downsides of abuse are potentially significant, especially as they pertain to privacy threats, confidentiality, transparency, and identity protection.

The hugely successful Netflix show *House of Cards* became one of Netflix's first original programs thanks in part to the use of Big Data. Following the success of that show, Netflix has continued to build an impressive showcase of original programming. This is because the movie platform is able to use a treasure trove of consumer data it pulls from its site to

Table 5.2	Examples of Data Created on Digital Platforms	
	Examples of User Actions	Potential Use of the Related Data for a Marketer
Facebook	"Like" an Internet celebrity's Facebook page	Data representing each "like" are recorded and associated with the individual user who committed the action. For example, if a marketer believes that the related Internet celebrity is well suited to endorse a product for female millennials, the Internet celebrity could show the marketer the related "like" data that would show that the majority of her followers fall within the correct age range and gender for which the marketer's product is designed to appeal.
YouTube	Watch a video	Data are recorded representing the view of the video and based on the characteristics of the video (e.g., its topic); related videos will be recommended to the user in the future that have the potential to increase the user's engagement on the platform (e.g., views of videos and time spent). A marketer could see that a large enough group of users view videos within the given topic and choose to use YouTube to distribute a video ad to users within this group (based on the assumption that the related video topic attracts a group of consumers with interests relevant to the product being advertised).
	Skip an ad displayed before a video	Data are recorded representing the action of pressing the "Skip Ad" button for the user. If the marketer saw that a particular video ad was being skipped often enough through a review of this data in aggregate (across all users who were exposed to the ad), this could provide a good basis to dig deeper and determine if there are specific issues with the content of the video ad or the audience(s) to which it is delivered.

help inform content acquisitions, including consumer viewing habits (e.g., when, where, and with what devices consumers watch) and content preferences. Recall Chapter 4's coverage of *predictive technology*; we talked about how Netflix trained teams of people to watch thousands of movies and tag them according to attributes such as "goriness" or "plot conclusiveness" to figure out what movies or TV shows you are likely to enjoy—and thus improve the site's ability to make better recommendations.

All of this data helps Netflix to more accurately predict whether it would be a sound decision to buy the rights to a show like *House of Cards* or to re-launch entirely new seasons of shows like *Arrested Development* that were cancelled for low ratings while amassing a cult-like following among loyal fans. Netflix makes these decisions based on a high degree of confidence that the company can find a suitable group of current (and perhaps potential) customers who would enjoy the shows and promptly start binge-watching them. Netflix also uses all of this data to create personalized marketing that will help attract viewers to programming they may not otherwise watch. For instance, they feature multiple versions of previews for their shows based on the viewing habits of users. Someone who just finished the final season of *Arrested Development* will see a picture of Jason Bateman (a star of the series) as the main preview icon for the movie *Hancock* starring Will Smith, even though Jason Bateman plays a supporting role in the movie and never appeared on any of the movie posters for the film. In a similar way, the Netflix home screen now lists the "Top 10 in the U.S. Today" to recommend the ten shows that have received the most views over the previous week. Netflix leverages large quantities of data to drive a wide array of choices of what shows and movies to license, which ones to buy the rights to and produce, and which ones to suggest to each customer.[18]

For marketers, Big Data has potential to provide competitive advantages in three main areas:

1. Identifying new opportunities through analytics that yield greater return on investment (ROI) on marketing efforts

2. Turning insights gained into goods and services that are better aligned with the desires of consumers

3. Delivering communications on goods and services to the marketplace more efficiently and effectively

Tesla uses advanced technology to communicate with drivers.

Internet of Things (IoT)
Describes a system in which everyday objects are connected to the Internet and in turn are able to communicate information throughout an interconnected system.

web scraping
The process of using computer software to extract large amounts of data from websites.

sentiment analysis
The process of identifying a follower's attitude (e.g., positive, negative, or neutral) toward a product or brand by assessing the context or emotion of his or her comments.

The amount of data that all of us produce does not appear to be slowing down either, as new technologies continue to enhance the ways we connect to people, machines, and organizations. The **Internet of Things (IoT)** is a term that increasingly appears in articles and stories on technology trends. It describes a system in which everyday objects are connected to the Internet and in turn are able to communicate information throughout an interconnected system.[19]

Areas that would become part of this network include medical devices, cars, toys, video games, and even a six-pack of beer in your refrigerator—the list goes on and on. Within the context of Big Data, this means that an even larger amount of data will be accessible, offering insight into the extent and ways in which consumers use everyday objects. Like the marketing automation technologies we mentioned previously, this knowledge will allow companies to automate processes that were previously done manually. We're already seeing these changes in multiple ways—just ask anyone who tasks Alexa with turning on smart lights, warming up the house, brewing coffee automatically (thanks to an Alexa smart plug), and announcing the weather, news, traffic, and calendar updates for the day over an Echo speaker.

The term *IoT* is typically reserved for devices that wouldn't usually be generally expected to have an Internet connection, such as light bulbs, doorbells, and electrical outlets. For marketers, this interconnection of objects and collection of data means gaining insights into how we use products via data captured through sensors embedded in products that track a user's interaction with the product. This information is then transmitted via an Internet connection at or near real time. Not only does this enable us to gain greater knowledge about how people use products, but it can be done on a scale that traditional market research can achieve only through astronomical financial investments—essentially tracking the actions of each and every product user!

So it's easy to begin to see how much data we would produce in a world where the Internet of Things has fully taken hold. Tesla has made significant changes in how it communicates with customers based on IoT information. The automaker actually uses the car itself as a relationship manager—it's able to monitor for necessary repairs, record user habits and preferences, and upgrade performance with constant software downloads. The approach is creating a new normal for the automotive industry—that is, a "persistently connected product." And all the data collected based on this capability makes Tesla much smarter when it comes to selling aftermarket features. The company also can predict when the time is right to begin messaging the Tesla user about new models in advance of his or her next purchase.[20]

Big Data Creation, Sources, and Usage

The millions of pieces of information that make up Big Data originate from a number of different sources. Figure 5.2 provides the most important sources of Big Data for marketers.

1. *Social media sources:* With an increasing array of social media sites that boast a large number of consumers interacting with each other, with brands, and with other entities, a wealth of information is being produced about how individuals feel about products and just about everything else in their lives. It is not uncommon today for consumers to either praise or condemn a product online. That information can be very valuable to marketers not only in terms of what they're saying but also in terms of factors that triggered them to say it. Today, several companies engage in **web scraping** (using computer software to extract large amounts of data from websites), **sentiment analysis** (a process of identifying a follower's attitude [e.g.,

positive, negative, or neutral] toward a product or brand by assessing the context or emotion of comments they post), and other advanced techniques that involve analyzing and mapping millions of posts on Facebook, Twitter, and other social media platforms to track what people say about their experiences with goods and services. They depict the themes in these posts visually so that managers can easily see the kinds of words customers use in their posts. (Hint: If your brand's name appears a lot of the time with terms like "awful" or "sucks," you probably have a problem.)

2. *Corporate IT sources:* These are the sources of data within the organization that might include CRM databases, web analytic databases (e.g., Google Analytics), enterprise resource planning (ERP) databases (you'll learn about ERP in Chapter 11), and even accounting-related databases. Each of these sources can contain a treasure trove of information on an organization's customers, but unfortunately these databases often exist in "silos" such that one group in the company may not share this information with others in the firm. Thus, each group gets only an incomplete picture of its customers. Fortunately, marketing is in a great position to cut across these groups to mine these databases and connect the dots!

3. *Government and nongovernmental organization sources:* The government provides many types of data, from extracted U.S. Census results (quickly check out www.census.gov to begin to be overwhelmed with census data) to data on the economic conditions in developing countries that allow marketers to better understand the demographics of consumers at home and the opportunities for global expansion. Ever-increasing types and amounts of accessible and machine-readable government-generated data will continue to provide new opportunities for enterprising marketers who can figure out how to navigate the numerous datasets that are available free of charge.[21]

4. *Commercial entity sources:* Many companies today collect data in large quantities to sell to organizations that can derive value from them. For some provider firms, this activity is their primary source of revenue; for others, it is a nice additional source of revenue over and above their principal business activities. For example (and this may or may not come as a surprise to you), many credit card companies, such as American Express and MasterCard, sell your purchase data to advertisers so that they can better target their ads. And supermarkets like Safeway for years have sold **scanner data**—data derived from all those items you scan at the cash register when you check out with your customer rewards number (which just happens to have your demographic profile information in its record!). Supermarkets sell the data in aggregated form so that it's not possible to identify the actions of a specific customer, but scanner data still provide extremely useful information to both manufacturers and retailers about how much shoppers buy in different categories and which brands they choose.[22]

Figure 5.2 *Snapshot* | Sources of Big Data for Marketers

Big Data can come from many sources. These sources can be both within and outside of the organization and created and compiled from different groups.

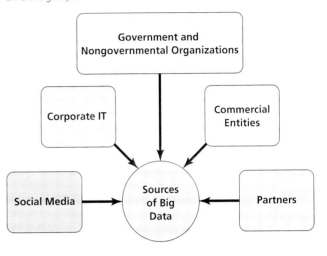

scanner data
Data derived from items that are scanned at the cash register when you check out with your loyalty card.

The rewards number you use at the supermarket or local coffee shop provides valuable data about your purchase history.

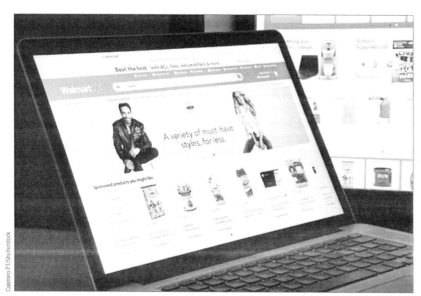

Casimiro PT/Shutterstock

Walmart's Retail Link connects the store chain with suppliers.

5. *Partner database sources:* In Chapter 11, you will read about different members of a channel of distribution. Many firms today have adopted a **channel partner model** in which there is a two-way exchange of information between purchasing organizations and their vendors through shared or integrated IT systems. If you're the producer of a product that is sold by a large retailer such as Walmart, think about the information and insights you could gain from access to the consumer information that Walmart gathers from its interactions with shoppers in its stores, on its website, and within the Walmart app.

Indeed, Walmart in particular is already well known for employing this approach through its vendor management system known as *Retail Link*, which provides real-time purchase data to suppliers, making it possible for them to track purchase data for their products in real time. Vendors are able to manage the process of replenishment so that they can ensure that their products are available for consumers exactly when and where they need them. In addition, for marketers, this provides a valuable source of purchase data in real time that they can use to analyze purchase patterns within different Walmart locations. It also saves Walmart the costs of having to manage this process themselves.[23]

For organizations, being able to leverage large amounts of data to yield new insights and provide a clearer understanding of both consumers and internal business operations is an attractive proposition and a potential source of competitive advantage. As we noted in the previous section, increased integration within supply chains allows organizations to more efficiently track the movement of goods at every point. This helps them to create a more efficient balance between supply and demand and can create greater confidence among supply chain members when it comes to supplying either raw materials or products at exactly the point when they are needed (more on this when we discuss distribution and, in particular, *just-in-time (JIT)* delivery and inventory techniques in Chapter 11). Ultimately, this means cost savings that retailers can pass down to the consumer in the form of lower prices.

Data Mining

Who says you can't have too much of a good thing? For organizations today, the challenge with data is not about having enough of it. To the contrary, many have far more information than they can handle! Remember that in the opening vignette this is the specific problem that Josh Barbieri and the Phillies were facing! Big Data can easily exacerbate the problem of **information overload**, in which the marketer is buried in so much data that it becomes nearly paralyzing to decide which of it provides useful information and which does not.

Most *marketing information systems* include internal customer transaction databases, and many include acquired databases. Often, these databases are extremely large. To take advantage of the massive amount of data now available, a sophisticated analysis technique called **data mining** is now a priority for many firms. This refers to a process in which analysts sift through Big Data (often measured in zettabytes—much larger than gigabytes or even terabytes) to identify unique patterns of behavior among different customer groups. To give you a sense of the scale, 1 zettabyte is equal to 1,024 terabytes or 3.4 years of 24/7 full HD video recording!

channel partner model
A relationship between channel partners in which a two-way exchange of information between purchasing organizations and their respective vendors is facilitated through shared or integrated IT systems.

information overload
A state in which the marketer is buried in so much data that it becomes nearly paralyzing to decide which of the data provide useful information and which do not.

data mining
A process in which analysts sift through Big Data (often measured in zettabytes—much larger than gigabytes or even terabytes) to identify unique patterns of behavior among different customer groups.

To get a flavor of how data mining aids in marketing decision making, let's consider a couple of examples:

- Upscale restaurant Oriole in Chicago relies on data mining to identify its frequent customers and enhance their service experience. When a first reservation is made, a customer profile is created. At the end of the customer's first experience, the profile is updated to provide enough information to enable Oriole staffers to delight customers the next time by better personalizing their dining experience with things like wine and food suggestions, conversational prompts, and even server assignment based on matching interests (sports, music, etc.) between servers and patrons. The savvy restauranteurs also use the data they collect to categorize their menu items into four quadrants: greatest hits, underperformers, one-hit wonders that are popular with first-time guests but not with repeat visitors, and hidden gems that regulars like and first-timers don't typically notice.[24]

- The trendy "cheap-chic" retailer Target discovered by mining its data that it could predict if a customer was pregnant well before they start buying baby items. Using a Guest ID number that is tied to a customer's credit card, name, or email address and tracks every purchase they make, Target was able to identify some useful shopping patterns among women who signed up for their baby registries to create a "pregnancy prediction" score. However, the company quickly became the center of a widespread social media frenzy when a man learned of his daughter's pregnancy because Target sent her coupons for baby items. While Target never actually violated any privacy policies, the general public felt the targeted marketing was too invasive and just plain creepy! This is one of the most notorious examples of data ethics and the potential for misuse.[25]

In a marketing context, data mining uses computers that run sophisticated programs so that analysts can combine different databases to understand relationships between buying decisions, exposure to marketing messages, and in-store promotions. These operations are so complex that often companies need to build a **data warehouse** (which can cost more than $10 million) simply to store and process the data.[26] As you've no doubt read in the news because it can be controversial, marketers at powerful consumer data generators Google, Netflix, Amazon, Facebook, and Twitter are into data mining big time. For example, Facebook has access to vast sums of data created as a result of the various posts, comments, and reactions by the two billion plus users that use the social media platform on a daily basis.[27]

As the IoT continues to grow and household products become increasingly interconnected, the need for **edge computing** is evolving. Edge computing allows data to be processed and stored faster, which means real-time applications, such as Tesla's self-driving capability, become more efficient. If Tesla's Autopilot feature were to rely on remote servers hundreds of miles away, a small data delay could result in a tragic accident.[28]

Primary Data Types for Data Mining

As data mining techniques improve and software becomes more adept at understanding and analyzing information in its various formats, the ability to gain deeper insights about consumers from data is increasing. Data in electronic format can be considered either structured or unstructured. **Structured data** are what you might find in an Excel spreadsheet or in a statistics table on a sports website, such as ESPN.com. These datasets typically are either numeric or categorical; they usually are organized and formatted in a way that is easy for computers to read, organize, and understand; they can be inserted into a database in a seamless fashion; and, typically, they can be easily placed within rows and columns.

data warehouse
A system to store and process the data that result from data mining.

edge computing
The practice of processing data near the edge of the network where the data is being generated, instead of in a centralized data processing warehouse.

structured data
Data that (1) are typically numeric or categorical; (2) can be organized and formatted in a way that is easy for computers to read, organize, and understand; and (3) can be inserted into a database in a seamless fashion.

Digital assistants like Alexa are our new guardian angels. They help us to live more efficiently, but in the process they also provide a lot of valuable (and hopefully anonymous) data to marketers about what people are buying and asking for.

Massive data warehouses—also sometimes called "server farms"—store the huge amounts of information that marketers need for data mining and examining purchasing patterns in order to yield insights about customer preferences.

unstructured data
Nonnumeric information that is typically formatted in a way that is meant for human eyes and not easily understood by computers.

emotion analysis
A sophisticated process for identifying and categorizing the emotions a follower possesses in relation to a product or brand by assessing the content of that communication.

Figure 5.3 *Process* | Structured and Unstructured Data Examples

Far more unstructured data than structured data are created on a daily basis through different business processes, but both have the potential to offer marketers greater insights into their customers and markets.

Structured Data	Unstructured Data
• Date	• Body of Emails
• Time	• Tweets
• Census Data	• Facebook Status Update Messages
• Facebook "Likes"	• Video Transcripts

In contrast, **unstructured data** contain nonnumeric information that is typically formatted in a way that is meant for human eyes and not easily understood by computers.[29] A good example of unstructured data is the body of an email message. The email carries a lot of meaning to a human but poses a greater challenge for a machine to understand or organize. Figure 5.3 lists other examples of different types of structured and unstructured data.

In the past, data mining and data analysis were focused on structured data because computers could easily analyze a large number of data points at one time. For instance, a baseball statistician can put into a computer all of the "at bats" that a player has had throughout the course of a season along with the associated outcomes and easily tell the computer to predict the player's batting average for the year (as well as a number of other useful measures). This output yields a better understanding of each player's performance on the field.

It becomes more challenging—but also potentially more interesting—to derive meaning from large quantities of *unstructured* data. For instance, imagine that you are the social media manager for a company that sells candy bars and you spend a lot of time engaging with customers through Facebook and Twitter. You are lucky to have a lot of likes and followers and a high level of interaction as well, but you're not satisfied with these data and believe that this is only the tip of the iceberg. In addition, you know that all of these comments from your customers could be a source of a lot of great information—the only problem is that there are thousands of them flooding in, and you're only one person. How could you possibly find the time to effectively analyze their contents and discern valuable patterns from all of this information? Even a huge team would have significant challenges trying to cull through the vast amount of unstructured data customers create every day when they talk about different companies online.

Technology to the rescue! Significant advances in data-analytic technologies make the process of unstructured data analysis easier through the development of computer logic that can search through and extract patterns from large amounts of textual data. It also makes it more cost-effective through the use of automated processes as opposed to manual intervention (imagine having to sift through every message by hand to pull out and record the information that you believed was meaningful).[30] The other advantage is that these types of technologies give unstructured data a "structure," enabling it to be shared and leveraged when combining it with data sources held elsewhere in an organization.

Previously in the chapter, we introduced *sentiment analysis*, which is commonly used with social media data to determine the attitudes held by consumers in relation to a brand. As technology becomes even more advanced, marketers are moving beyond sentiment (which might simply be recorded as either positive, negative, or neutral) into a wide range of more complex feelings and emotions. This method, known as **emotion analysis**, can analyze the content of social media communications within the context of a specific brand or product and determine what emotional category or categories the communication fits within. The media conglomerate Viacom (which includes MTV, Nickelodeon, and BET to name a few) recently chose to use a technology startup called Canvs for emotion analysis to offer its advertising partners greater insight into how viewers are reacting to the advertisements they place through Viacom's programming and other content offerings. Canvs is able to categorize comments into 56 categories (in other words, provide and translate *unstructured data* into *structured data*) that include such categories as "trippy," "awkward," "guilty pleasure," and "mindblown." The company is able to do this by allowing its algorithm to look at social media comments within the context of the company's own database of more than 4 million words and phrases, which include shorthand expressions popular on social media as well as generation-specific vernacular (e.g., "bae" and "on fleek").[31] Being able to leverage both structured and unstructured data in data mining efforts offers marketers the opportunity to gain a deeper understanding of their customers.

Data mining helps marketers to build bonds with repeat customers—like "sneakerheads" who love to drop a lot of cash on vintage models.

Data Mining: Applications for Marketers

A key theme of this chapter and the previous chapter is that better understanding of both current and potential customers should be a central goal for all marketers. Every interaction the firm has with a consumer—every touchpoint, regardless of which department might facilitate the interaction—can provide valuable information for marketers to leverage. Data mining techniques that enhance the value of Big Data provide opportunities for marketers to increase organizational performance. To help identify the data needed for these efforts and bring them together, organizations often assemble teams of individuals from different functions, such as marketing, sales, in-store operations, and IT, to help identify and gather the needed data sources for analysis.[32]

As illustrated in Figure 5.4, data mining has four important applications for marketers:[33]

1. *Customer acquisition:* Many firms include demographic and other information about customers in their database. For example, a number of supermarkets offer weekly special price discounts for store "members." These stores' membership application forms require that customers indicate their age, family size, address, and so on. With this information, the supermarket determines which of its current customers respond best to specific offers and then sends the same offers to noncustomers who share the same demographic characteristics.

Figure 5.4 *Snapshot* | Uses of Data Mining

Data mining has four primary applications for marketers.

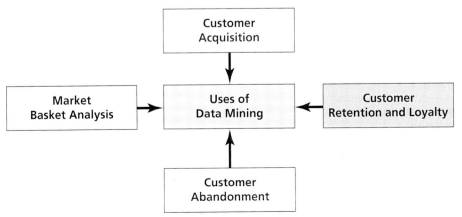

2. *Customer retention and loyalty:* The firm identifies big-spending customers, who may or may not be at risk of defecting, and then targets them with special offers and inducements other customers won't receive to reward them for their loyalty and increase their likelihood of retention.[34] Keeping the most profitable customers coming back is a great way to build business success because—here we go again!—keeping good customers is less expensive than constantly finding new ones.

3. *Customer abandonment:* Strange as it may sound, sometimes a firm wants customers to take their business elsewhere because servicing them actually costs the firm too much. Today, this is popularly called "firing a customer." Here are six warning signs for customers who bring more trouble than they're worth: they make unreasonable demands, they want everything for nothing, they're always slow to pay, they don't listen to you, they don't respond to you, or they show a lack of basic respect.[35] For example, Amazon recently ignited some controversy when the company started to revoke Prime memberships from customers who returned too many items.[36] The idea isn't to immediately cut the cord with a customer on first evidence of these issues, but rather to be on the lookout for patterns of such problems with customers and to first try to work out any issues. But ultimately, even if you're like Post Malone and "not good at goodbyes," sometimes that's exactly what you need to say to customers who are not working out.

4. *Market basket analysis:* This type of analysis develops focused promotional strategies based on the records of which customers have bought certain products. Hewlett-Packard, for example, carefully analyzes which of its customers recently bought new printers and targets them to receive emails about specials on ink cartridges and tips to get the most out of their machines. Another example is when a user purchases one item on Amazon and then is recommended a set of items that other users who purchased the first item also purchased (such as recommending an Amazon Fire TV stick after a customer purchases an Amazon Echo Dot).

Data Scientists: Transforming Big Data into Winning Information

In Chapter 4, we talked about the important role of customer insights for marketing decision making. Being able to transform data into insights and leveraging data to enhance the way that organizations interact with consumers is a really challenging proposition. It is one that analysts execute with the help of powerful databases and complex software. These analysts (also known as *business intelligence developers*) are employed by the biggest names in technology. A **data scientist** uses skills in mathematics, computer science, and trend analysis to explore multiple, disparate data sources to discover hidden insights that will provide a competitive advantage.[37] These individuals frequently have Ph.D.s, often command six-figure starting salaries (according to Glassdoor.com, the median salary as of 2020 was $113,309[38]), and are becoming an increasingly important source of competitive advantage for organizations that want to leverage Big Data. Traditional data analysts often looked at one data source, whereas data scientists typically look at multiple sources of data across the organization.

If you have ever used LinkedIn, you'll be interested to learn that one of the most frequently used features on the site was developed through experimentation by one of the organization's data scientists, Jonathan Goldman. Specifically, Goldman developed the "People You May Know" feature on the site, where LinkedIn users whom you may know in real life are shown two profiles at a time. Goldman accomplished this by developing a way to assess and score users based on common elements, such as shared tenures at educational institutions, and then sorting the profiles displayed through the feature from the highest to the lowest scores (to a limit). The idea was originally implemented as an advertisement on the site to generate interest in the message. Sure enough, the site's managers discovered that this feature had a click rate that was 30 percent higher than average. Soon after that,

data scientist
An individual who uses skills in mathematics, computer science, and trend analysis to explore multiple, disparate data sources to discover hidden insights that will provide a competitive advantage.

top management within the organization signed off on adding "People You May Know" as a standard feature.[39]

These and many other insights exemplify what data scientists are able to generate and the value they can yield for organizations. As more data become available from multiple sources, organizations will most likely continue to need people with the skill and curiosity to transform data into information (any interest on your part in being a data scientist?).

Augmented Intelligence: Enhancing Consumer Experiences with Big Data

In 2014, Amazon first introduced to the market the Echo, touted as a product fueled by "far-field technology" that combines voice recognition with additional data analysis to become a virtual assistant to the user. The Echo relies on artificial intelligence and machine learning (two terms that are often used in tandem) to work its magic, allowing it to get more and more accurate results the more data it gets.

Specifically, **artificial intelligence (AI)** refers to the broader concept of machines being able to carry out tasks in a way that humans would consider "smart," while **machine learning** is the application of AI based on the idea that machines can and should have access to data and engage in learning for themselves.[40]

The Echo even analyzes characteristics of the user's speech, such as frequency and pitch, to try to determine the emotion in a person's voice. The Echo can remember what a person has said previously and then apply that knowledge to subsequent interactions! At first blush, all of this AI-enabled friendliness from a device might still be a little unsettling, and scattered incidents where Amazon's Alexa weirdly laughed at users or even recorded their conversations and emailed them to others remind us there are still a few kinks companies need to work on.[41] If they're able to resolve these important privacy issues, imagine how convenient it is to have a digital friend that knows (and even anticipates) your every whim![42]

Thanks to AI, what used to be science fiction is now a reality that already impacts you on a daily basis. If you happen to own a smartphone that uses a facial recognition system . . . that's AI! Although some industries and businesses are more advanced than others, AI is still at a very early stage of development overall. Yet almost all aspects of how we work and live have become increasingly digitized over the last 10 years. Analysts estimate that AI will drive nearly $2.9 trillion worth of business value worldwide in 2021,[43] and that number could grow to $15.7 trillion by 2030.[44] When used effectively, the primary value that AI delivers for a business is helping to deliver better customer experiences. This is where the concept of **augmented intelligence** comes into play. Whereas the ultimate goal of AI is to create systems that operate without humans, augmented intelligence seeks to create systems that make humans better, smarter, and happier by being more efficient with automatization. Figure 5.5 illustrates the four main types of desired results for AI applications.

Reality Check for Marketers: Ethical Considerations in Using Big Data

Today, as consumers, most of us are pretty well conditioned to the reality that data about us is being used by the organizations that we patronize. But let's not get too complacent about this brave new world of Big Data! While the tone in the discussion of the preceding topic is positive in the sense that marketers greatly benefit from consumer-supplied data as this data allow for more customized and customer-satisfying service experiences, marketers must be diligent that a very high level of **cybersecurity** is maintained at all times. Cybersecurity implies a strong commitment by firms to protect digital data, such as those in an electronic database, from destructive forces and from the unwanted actions of unauthorized users. This could occur via a **cyberattack**, which is an attempt to gain illegal

artificial intelligence (AI)
The broad concept of machines being able to carry out tasks in a way that humans would consider "smart."

machine learning
The application of AI based on the idea that machines can and should have access to data and engage in learning for themselves.

augmented intelligence
The application of AI to help people make better decisions.

cybersecurity
A strong commitment by firms to protect digital data, such as those in an electronic database, from destructive forces and from the unwanted actions of unauthorized users.

cyberattack
An attempt to gain illegal access to a computer or computer system for the purpose of causing damage or harm.

Figure 5.5 *Snapshot* | Key Types of Desired Results of AI Applications

	Human in the Loop	No Human in the Loop
Hardwired/Specific Systems	**Assisted Intelligence** AI systems that assist humans in making decisions or taking actions. Hard-wired systems that do not learn from their interactions. **Example:** Machines in an assembly line	**Automation** Automation of manual and cognitive tasks that are either routine or nonroutine. This does not involve new ways of doing things—it automates existing tasks. **Example:** A thermostat that automatically adjusts temperature settings based on pre-determined criteria
Adaptive Systems	**Augmented Intelligence** AI systems that augment human decision making and continuously learn from their interactions with humans and the environment. **Example:** Software that informs a bank loan officer about a high credit risk for an individual with a previous bankruptcy	**Autonomous Intelligence** AI systems that can adapt to different situations and can act autonomously without assistance. **Example:** Self-driving cars

Source: Adapted from PricewaterhouseCoopers, "Sizing the prize: What's the real value of AI for your business and how can you capitalise?" https://www.pwc.com/gx/en/issues/analytics/assets/pwc-ai-analysis-sizing-the-prize-report.pdf

hacker
A person who illegally gains access and sometimes tampers with information in a computer system.

data breach
The intentional or unintentional release of secure or private/confidential information to an untrusted environment.

access to a computer or computer system for the purpose of causing damage or harm. Cyberattacks are most often perpetrated by a **hacker**, which is a person who illegally gains access and sometimes tampers with information in a computer system. Another possibility is some other type of **data breach**, which is the intentional or unintentional release of secure or private/confidential information to an untrusted environment. Ultimately, marketers and their organizations have an obligation to protect customer data from unauthorized users, but customers must also be wary of how organizations use all of this data and the potential that exists to intentionally mislead customers.

Data Security

In Chapter 2, you read that ethics is "job one" for marketers and learned about the importance of firms having codes of business ethics. Toward that end, ethicists make a strong case that marketers and their organizations have a high ethical and moral obligation to exhibit full transparency with customers about how, when, and why data are being collected from them as well as the intended uses of those data. Failure to do so can result in a massive loss of trust by customers. Data aspects are a critical part of any modern code of business ethics. Famous and game-changing examples of wholesale trust breaches based on data include the cyberattack on Target in late 2013 that hacked into 41 million of the retail giant's customer payment card accounts and Facebook's admission in early 2018 that in 2017 the data of 2.2 billion users had been compromised. As a result of these circumstances, both of these venerable firms severely damaged—some would say irreparably—customer confidence and trust in their integrity and perhaps permanently sullied their brand images.[45]

Unfortunately, some organizations seem to never learn. In 2018, Facebook was again exposed for its poor data security when it was revealed that 87 million of its users had been shared with third-party firm Cambridge Analytica, the UK firm that worked with Donald Trump's election team to build a software program to attempt to predict and influence voters. They got the data via surreptitious means when hundreds of thousands of users were paid a fee to take a personality test and in doing so consented to have their data collected. The associated app also harvested information about the participants' friends. Facebook discovered the information had been harvested in late 2015 but failed to alert users until their hand was forced in April 2018. It appears that data privacy continues to be a vault that Facebook can't seem to keep closed, with another data breach in 2019 that exposed user IDs, phone numbers and names of nearly 267 million Facebook users. How many more failures of cybersecurity can Facebook endure and continue to maintain their constituency? Only time will tell, but the solution lies squarely in Facebook's culture and organizational will to make the security of its patrons' data its utmost priority.[46]

Deep Learning and Misinformation

Since the early 2000s, popular late-night talk show host Conan O'Brien has frequently entertained millions of his viewers with segments that show him interviewing famous celebrities and world leaders using still photos and superimposed talking mouth videos. These segments became fan favorites because they hilariously characterize famous individuals making funny and sometimes controversial remarks that they would likely never make in real life, but there is never any doubt among viewers that these interviews are not real. But what if viewers were to watch these same interviews with the same funny and controversial remarks, except instead of a still photo and superimposed mouth it was the actual celebrity or world leader delivering those remarks? Or at least, it looks and sounds like the actual celebrity or world leader! Although this may sound like something only possible in a *Mission: Impossible* movie, recent advancements in AI and **deep learning** make **deepfake** videos a very real and potentially dangerous phenomenon based on coding that's freely available online.

A number of deepfake videos started showing up online in 2019, but it was an ad for State Farm in 2020 that introduced millions of consumers, perhaps unknowingly, to its potential. The commercial created immediate buzz among consumers as it appeared to show footage from a 1998 ESPN segment in which an analyst made surprisingly accurate predictions about the future, including ESPN's 2020 hit documentary *The Last Dance*. The YouTube channel *Ctrl Shift Face* features a variety of iconic movie scenes starring all new actors, demonstrating how convincing this technology can be. Despite how believable these videos may appear, subtle cues such as face discolorations, incorrect lighting, audio and video that are slightly out of sync, and blurriness where the face meets the neck and hair (among other elements) can help identify that a video is a deepfake, at least for now. However, as technology improves at an exponential rate, critics anticipate that deepfakes will be indistinguishable from real images in the very near future as the capability to generate deepfake images accelerates much faster than the ability to detect them.

Synthesia, a software company that uses AI to create synthetic media generated by computers, used deepfake technology to create a global campaign video for the Malaria Must Die initiative that generated more than 800 million impressions! The video featured soccer star David Beckham who appeared to speak 9 different languages, providing an altered message depending on the intended audience.[47] This same technology could allow marketers to create personalized marketing messages that feature celebrities identifying consumers by name. Of course, part of the reason Synthesia's campaign was so successful was complete transparency about the technology used to create it. Although this type of video editing may seem amusing and harmless when it's done for entertainment and viewers know they are being fooled by AI technology, the concern becomes much more

deep learning
A subset of machine learning that allows machines to solve complex problems even when using a dataset that is very diverse, unstructured, and interconnected.

deepfake
A realistic-looking photo or video of people doing or saying things they did not actually do or say.

troubling when it is used to share misinformation. Consider the implications of deepfake videos featuring supposed experts promoting inferior or dangerous products and brands, corporate spokespeople misrepresenting the values of organizations or their target audiences, or well-known politicians engaging in illegal activities. The old adage "seeing is believing" may no longer apply in a world of AI and Big Data.

Blockchain and Big Data Challenges

With all of this talk about data security, data breaches, and using AI-driven technologies to share misinformation, it may seem that the risks associated with Big Data are insurmountable. As the name suggests, Big Data deals with huge volumes of data that continue to evolve and grow exponentially. The task of storing so much data in a secure manner, cleaning the data, and detecting fraud in the data has become extremely difficult and labor-inducive.

Thankfully, there is a possible solution for most of these biggest challenges relating to Big Data and protecting consumers in a digital world. **Blockchain** is a type of database that exists on multiple computers simultaneously, containing "blocks" of data that are linked together as "chains" of immutable data. Blockchain offers a level of unmatched data security because no single entity owns the data, which is cryptographically stored, making it almost impossible to tamper with the data even if it gets stolen. On top of all that security, the blockchain is transparent so the data can be traced back to its origin point by anyone who wants to see it. What all of this means is that blockchain offers the potential to help data scientists ensure data integrity, prevent malicious activities, make predictions, analyze data in real time, and manage data sharing.

Examples of Internet privacy violations seem limitless while highlighting a fundamental lack of choice for consumers to share or not share their data. We've already mentioned Facebook's data breaches, but they have also been criticized in the past for deliberately sharing user's names (and the names of their friends) with advertisers. Even Disney was sued for allegedly spying on children who frequently used one of its 42 gaming apps and sharing the data with advertisers without parental consent.[48]

Blockchain could help consumers protect their own data and privacy by allowing them to choose which data to share with businesses and advertisers in exchange for discounts or loyalty rewards. With so many apparent benefits, why isn't blockchain more widely utilized? In short, blockchain is still relatively immature and its lack of scalability—the ability to handle a lot of transactions all at once—is a major issue, which also means that it is more expensive than traditional data storage. One additional limitation of blockchain is that a very large network is vital to its success because data that only exists on a few computers is vulnerable to attack. It may not be the holy grail of data security, but blockchain has the potential to greatly impact the data security world.

blockchain
A time-stamped series of immutable records of data that is managed by a cluster of computers not owned by any single entity.

5.3 A Primer on Analytics

OBJECTIVE
Describe what marketing analytics include and how organizations can leverage both marketing analytics and predictive analytics to improve marketing performance.

Marketing analytics have become a critically important part of a marketer's toolbox as technological advances enable consumers to engage in an increasing number of activities online that were previously possible only within the physical space. In a general sense, we can think of analytics as the identification, interpretation, and articulation of patterns within data that one or more groups view as meaningful.[49]

At its core, **marketing analytics** comprises a group of technologies and processes that enable marketers to collect, measure, analyze, and assess the effectiveness of marketing efforts. Marketing analytics solutions provide marketers with a holistic means to look at the

marketing analytics
A group of technologies and processes that enable marketers to collect, measure, analyze, and assess the effectiveness of marketing efforts.

performance of different marketing initiatives.[50] They are capable of providing a level of analysis and a degree of accuracy and speed that is crucial in our data-driven world. Put simply, then, marketing analytics takes the Big Data and makes sense of it for use in marketing decision making! That is, the breadth and depth of information that today's marketers have at their disposal requires the ability to leverage technology that can move through massive and often disparate datasets to provide useful information that can power decisions and help marketers better understand the value of their investments.

The need to be able to tie specific actions in advertising to measurable results (such as sales) has been a long-standing challenge for marketers. Especially for those who have spent money on TV advertising, billboards, and other forms of traditional advertising, there is a real challenge to quantify the value of these efforts. You may have seen a TV advertisement for McDonald's featuring a Big Mac and chosen the next day to purchase one because of the advertisement, but how would anyone else know that it was that commercial that pushed you over the fast-food edge, as opposed to any of the other marketing investments that McDonald's has made? Digital marketing offers an attractive solution due to the easy application of marketing analytics it brings. It enables marketers to get a better sense of the specific ROI they receive when they use a specific channel as opposed to the guesswork of earlier days.

Connect Digital Marketing Channels to Marketing Analytics

One of the perennial challenges marketers face is being able to determine the effectiveness of different marketing campaigns and channels. This is because it is not always clear where a lead came from, or what led to a purchase by a consumer, without being able to track it from its origin. For instance, did a consumer learn about and ultimately purchase a product because of the commercial he or she saw on TV, because of the ad he or she viewed in a magazine, or perhaps both? For traditional media, such as TV and magazines, it is still not always clear what actions yield the greatest impact for the marketer.

However, with the proliferation of digital media and digital marketing channels, it has become more straightforward to understand what actions on the part of marketers drive consumers to ultimately make a decision that aligns with the interests of the organization. **Digital marketing channels** are those specific means of distribution through which digital marketing communications can be delivered to current and potential customers. The distribution of communications through digital marketing channels often requires the use of one or more technology platforms that serve as intermediaries.

Let's consider as an example a fictional clothing company that has decided to send out a promotional email to let you know about its new fall collection (and hopefully induce a purchase). The email includes images of a few models who wear some of the clothing items, a link to a specific part of the website that displays the fall collection, and a special promotional code to input at checkout (e.g., FALL20) that will take 20 percent off of any fall collection items that the recipient chooses to purchase.

Now, let's see how marketing analytics kick in to help this retailer. Hint: In the next paragraph, we are going to note some of the key parts of the process by which the company can record data (watch for the phrase *data recorded*) based on your hypothetical actions in the scenario. Figure 5.6 illustrates this process in terms of the relationship between some of your actions in this scenario, the specific data created as a result of those actions, and the data's potential analytics-related applications.

OK, here goes. You receive the email in your inbox, read the subject line, and decide to open the email (*data recorded*). After reviewing the email's contents, you decide that you are interested in checking out the new fall collection, so you click the link to that part of the website (*data recorded*). You take a look at a few of the specific details related to the items by clicking links corresponding to their individual product pages (*data recorded*) and ultimately

digital marketing channels
The paths of distribution through which a company's digital marketing communications can be delivered to reach their respective audiences.

choose to add a sweater to your shopping cart (*data recorded*). You go to the checkout page (*data recorded*), input the promotional code, select a button to process it (*data recorded*), and then pay for the item (*data recorded*).

All of the data the preceding paragraph identified as "recorded" now can be transformed using marketing analytics to gain a greater understanding of whether the related email campaign is achieving a satisfactory ROI for this retailer. Presumably, you were not the only one who received the promotional email, and it is likely that other variations of it were distributed (perhaps with higher and lower discounts, as well as different images of models in different clothing items). Each of these variations would be identifiable within the data, and the marketer could analyze at a more detailed level how each variation

Figure 5.6 *Process* | Digital Marketing Channel Example

This figure illustrates examples of several aspects of a digital marketing channel initiative for a fictional clothing company.

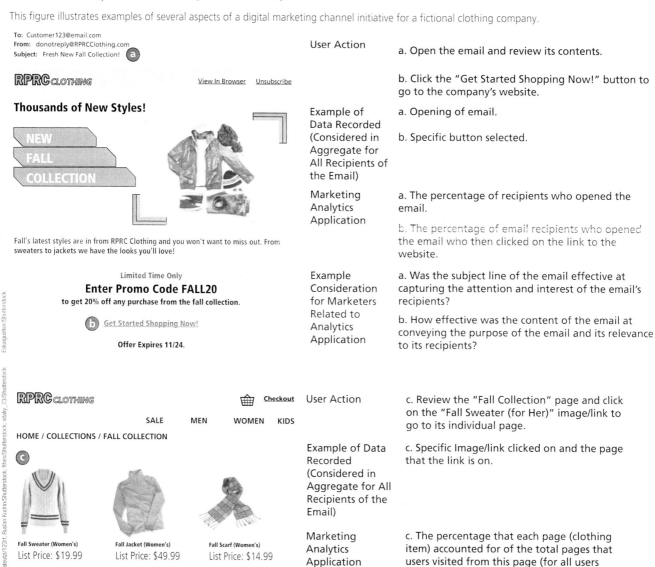

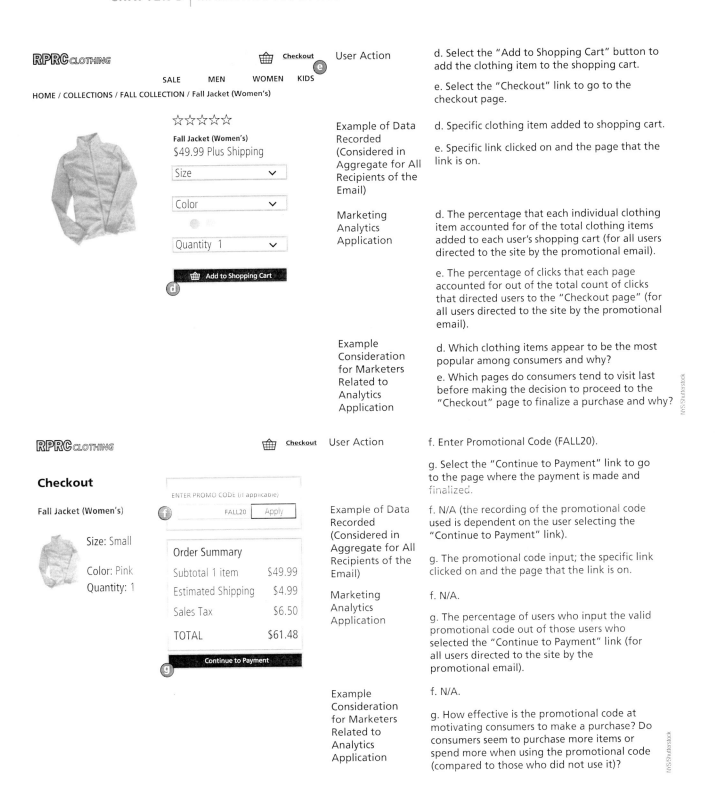

User Action	d. Select the "Add to Shopping Cart" button to add the clothing item to the shopping cart.	
	e. Select the "Checkout" link to go to the checkout page.	
Example of Data Recorded (Considered in Aggregate for All Recipients of the Email)	d. Specific clothing item added to shopping cart.	
	e. Specific link clicked on and the page that the link is on.	
Marketing Analytics Application	d. The percentage that each individual clothing item accounted for of the total clothing items added to each user's shopping cart (for all users directed to the site by the promotional email).	
	e. The percentage of clicks that each page accounted for out of the total count of clicks that directed users to the "Checkout page" (for all users directed to the site by the promotional email).	
Example Consideration for Marketers Related to Analytics Application	d. Which clothing items appear to be the most popular among consumers and why?	
	e. Which pages do consumers tend to visit last before making the decision to proceed to the "Checkout" page to finalize a purchase and why?	
User Action	f. Enter Promotional Code (FALL20).	
	g. Select the "Continue to Payment" link to go to the page where the payment is made and finalized.	
Example of Data Recorded (Considered in Aggregate for All Recipients of the Email)	f. N/A (the recording of the promotional code used is dependent on the user selecting the "Continue to Payment" link).	
	g. The promotional code input; the specific link clicked on and the page that the link is on.	
Marketing Analytics Application	f. N/A.	
	g. The percentage of users who input the valid promotional code out of those users who selected the "Continue to Payment" link (for all users directed to the site by the promotional email).	
Example Consideration for Marketers Related to Analytics Application	f. N/A.	
	g. How effective is the promotional code at motivating consumers to make a purchase? Do consumers seem to purchase more items or spend more when using the promotional code (compared to those who did not use it)?	

performed in terms of the ultimate goal of driving sales as well as along each step in the process leading to a sale.

Perhaps best of all, the marketer can now measure the investment associated with each variation of the email promotion (and the effort as a whole) relative to its cost and identify how the company might make further improvements. In its simplest form, the retailer might conduct an **A/B test**, which is a method to test the effectiveness of altering one characteristic of a marketing asset (e.g., a web page, a banner advertisement, or an email). Essentially, this involves sending out two variations of the same message to determine if one version "pulls

A/B test

A method to test the effectiveness of altering one characteristic of a marketing asset (e.g., a web page, a banner advertisement, or an email).

click-through rate (CTR)
A metric that indicates the percentage of website users who have decided to click on an advertisement to visit the website or Web page associated with it.

higher" than the other. The test is conducted by randomly exposing some users to the original version and other users to an altered version. The behavior of users within each group is recorded, and the results are used to determine if the altered version performs better on some measure of interest such as **click-through rate (CTR)**. CTR is a metric that indicates the percentage of website users who have decided to click on an advertisement to visit the website or Web page associated with it. When you compare the power of this test to the old-fashioned approach of "Let's run an ad in the Sunday paper and see what store traffic looks like on Monday!", you can easily appreciate the benefit of the A/B test approach.

Connect with Consumers across Digital Marketing Channels

To help understand the increasing value that marketing analytics offers to organizations, it is important to recognize how much the way that we ingest information has changed over time. As we'll see in later chapters, today's consumer has evolved into an omnichannel media user. This means that most of us get our information about the world from multiple sources, including computers, tablets, and phones, and we freely move from one to another in the course of a day. With more individuals having access to and spending time on the Internet, digital marketing has become an increasingly important element of the marketer's toolbox. According to the Pew Research Center, in 2020, 90 percent of Americans used the Internet (up from 50 percent in 2000), and 73 percent used social networking sites (up from only 5 percent in 2005!).[51]

Across the globe, more people use the Internet for an increasingly wider array of purposes. Who knows how many more functions will be made faster, easier, or more intuitive as developers continually introduce new apps? As the ways in which consumers engage with media shift, digital marketers must reinvent their strategies to keep up. Globally, some markets average more than 45 percent of their media budget devoted to digital marketing.[52] It's not that people are spending less time consuming media—consumption has actually risen in recent years. Rather, the critical change is that consumers now seek information from more diverse channels. In particular, they have become much more digitally savvy (and increasingly impatient!) with traditional promotional techniques and intolerant of intrusive or irrelevant messages common with old-style, "one-size-fits-all" promotion approaches.[53] As marketers continue to feel pressure to demonstrate the ROI or ROX of their efforts, the emphasis on digital marketing and specifically digital commerce will most likely continue into the future.

The options for investment in digital marketing channels are diverse; consumers spend large amounts across a variety of options. Figure 5.7 illustrates six major groupings of different digital marketing channels: video marketing, personalized email, content marketing, social media, search engines, and digital ad networks. Artificial intelligence plays an important role in many of these channels as chatbots are expected to account for 85 percent of customer service and voice search to account for more than 50 percent of searches in 2020. Note that in Chapter 14 we will discuss digital promotional options that are available to marketers in detail. For example, for all of these entities a lot of money can be made by selling advertising space to organizations. Facebook, which more than a billion people use, offers users the ability to create a profile for free, but its business model relies heavily on being able to generate revenue by selling

Figure 5.7 *Snapshot* | Major Digital Marketing Channels

Digital marketing channels are typically broken up into six main categories. Within these, there are multiple types of marketing efforts and campaigns that marketers can develop and track.

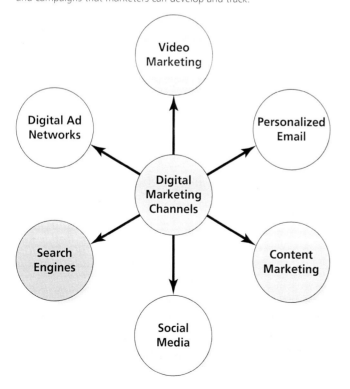

advertisements on the site. Increasingly (and prompted by the widespread criticisms about the way Facebook targets users that even led to a #DeleteFacebook movement), social networking sites are looking for creative ways to provide advertisements on their sites in a way that does not put people off.[54] The objective is to create a source of value for organizations that does not compromise the website's user experience and relevance.

In addition, most, if not all, social networking sites invest a lot of effort to offer their advertisers access to analytic tools and capabilities that will help them to assess and further optimize the performance of their marketing efforts. For instance, the popular Internet meme generator and image-sharing platform Imgur added advanced analytic capabilities to help its users and advertisers better understand how their images were spreading. The added capabilities allowed users to go beyond just knowing how many views an image has to understanding things such as how many of those views are being captured in a given day and in a given hour, which websites are linking back to the original version of the image, and where within those websites the image is shared. Bottom line, advertisers can use Imgur's analytics to track the performance of their images in order to better understand the specific stages on the path to going viral (or not viral) and to see where the image was best received.[55]

Business Models for Digital Marketing

For marketers, investments in digital marketing are especially attractive because their cost is often directly tied to specific actions users take. For instance, Google's paid search ads can be purchased or bid upon on a **cost-per-click** basis. This means the cost of the advertisement is charged only each time an individual clicks the advertisement and is directed to the web page that the marketer placed within the advertisement. This method of charging for advertisements is common for online vendors of advertisement space. Other methods of purchasing advertisements digitally include **cost-per-impression**, in which the cost of the advertisement is charged each time the advertisement shows up on a page that the user views.

Companies that sell online advertising space commonly use both of these methods to charge for advertisements. Cost-per-click purchases of advertisements are typically more expensive, as they demand a higher level of interaction from the user (i.e., the users have actually visited the page on which the ad appears and hence are one step closer to becoming a customer). In contrast, cost-per-impression purchases of advertisements can provide a good value, but they typically require a greater leap of faith because it's not so easy to measure the value of an impression (or view of an advertisement). For instance, if a marketer knew (or had a good idea) that a certain number of impressions from an advertisement translated into a specific number of clicks, then he or she would be able to more accurately estimate the cost of the ad in terms of clicks even while using a cost-per-impression structure to price advertisements. In this way, the marketer would be able to obtain a better value through cost-per-impression pricing as opposed to cost-per-click pricing.

One advantage of digital marketing is that data come in at the speed at which data travel, which is almost instantaneous. This means that marketers can track the performance of digital marketing initiatives and determine their performance both in the very short term and over the long term. Marketing analytics enable them to capture these data across all of the channels in which they have invested and present the data in a way that provides valuable insights into the performance of each channel.

cost-per-click
An online ad purchase in which the cost of the advertisement is charged only each time an individual clicks the advertisement and is directed to the web page that the marketer placed within the advertisement.

cost-per-impression
An online ad purchase in which the cost of the advertisement is charged each time the advertisement shows up on a page that the user views.

Imgur is a popular image-sharing platform that hosts more than 650 million images and attracts up to 1.5 million uploads daily. The vast amount of data it tracks helps provide powerful analytics to marketers wanting to understand how images are shared and where they travel online, to better understand what drives the popularity of digital marketing content that goes viral.[56]

Marketing Accountability within Digital Marketing Channels: A Specialty Headphones Example

Imagine you have an e-commerce website to sell specialty headphones and you have begun to invest in attracting new customers to your website. You've purchased some online banner advertisements that are being strategically shown to individuals who visit different music websites, and you've also purchased some ads on Facebook that are showing up as sponsored posts in people's feeds who frequently "like" different indie rock bands' pages. You've even looked into **search engine optimization (SEO)**, which is a systematic process to ensure that your firm comes up at or near the top of lists of typical search phrases related to your business. As a result, you've hired an SEO specialist to help ensure that your website ranks highly on search engines such as Google and Bing when people type in search phrases such as "high-quality head-phones" and "best way to listen to music."

Now that you have invested in your different marketing channels, you start to see that sales are increasing. It seems as though your investment in all of these different digital marketing channels is paying off, but what if some are paying off more than others because they are engaging more effectively with your target audience and in turn helping to create more sales? How would you determine which channels to invest in even more and which to drop like a hot potato?

Answer: Marketing analytics would enable you to analyze the performance of all of these channels to help you make the best investment of your marketing dollars moving forward. To understand what's really working on your e-commerce site, you might look to see whether more sales come from your customers who arrive at your site because they typed a search term into Google or whether those who come to the site via a Facebook ad spend more. Or you might find that the banner advertisements bring in relatively few customers and that the transactions they make are relatively small.

If you compare the average cost per customer transaction from each of these channels against the average value of the customer transaction from each channel, it would become clear which channel provides your e-commerce site with the most value. You might even discover that one of these channels costs more than it wins in sales! Table 5.3 provides sample data for the preceding specialty headphones example as an illustration of how you could perform the relevant calculations for each digital marketing channel. In the example, you will see that SEO provides the highest sales, but Facebook ads actually provide the greatest amount of value per customer transaction (or profitability per transaction). This insight might encourage our specialty headphone company to invest more heavily in Facebook advertising in the future.

Without marketing analytics and the data digital marketing initiatives produce, this result would have been more challenging to determine, and as a result, there would have been more waste within your e-commerce site's marketing mix. These are the types of challenging questions that companies such as Zappos.com, Wayfair.com, and Overstock.com deal with every day as they look to ensure that their marketing investments provide a healthy ROI. Marketing analytics help them to better understand how their different marketing channels perform.

It is worth noting that some caution can be beneficial when you rely on marketing analytics data to attribute a specific effort to a related outcome. For example, suppose an individual sees a TV advertisement for a product and decides to go online to learn more about it. At that point, he or she comes across a banner advertisement online that includes a coupon for the product. Then, he or she clicks the banner advertisement to redeem the coupon and buy the product. On the surface, to a marketer it might look as though all of the credit for the sale should go to the banner advertisement because the marketer has no awareness of the influence that the TV advertisement has had on the consumer. As we can see, however, that conclusion is not entirely accurate. The risk we

Table 5.3	Marketing Performance Calculation and Comparison: Specialty Headphones Example		
Digital Marketing Channel	Average Customer Transaction (Total Sales Attributed to Channel/Total Number of Customers Acquired through Channel)	Average Cost per Customer Transaction (Total Spend Attributed to Channel/Total Number of Customers Acquired through Channel)	Average Value of Digital Marketing Channel Investment (Average Customer Transaction—Average Cost per Customer)
Banner Ads	$450,000 (Sales)/10,000 (Customer Transactions) = **$45 (Average Customer Transaction)**	$100,000 (Spent)/10,000 (Customer Transactions) = **$10 (Average Cost per Customer Transaction)**	$45 (Avg. Customer Transaction) −$10 (Avg. Cost per Customer Transaction) = **$35 (Average Value of Digital Marketing Channel Investment)**
Facebook Ads	$1,200,000 (Sales)/15,000 (Customer Transactions) = **$80 (Average Customer Transaction)**	$240,000 (Spent)/15,000 (Customer Transactions) = **$16 (Average Cost per Customer Transaction)**	$80 (Avg. Customer Transaction) − $16 (Avg. Cost per Customer Transaction) = **$64 (Average Value of Digital Marketing Channel Investment)**
Search Engine Optimization	$2,100,000 (Sales)/40,000 (Customer Transactions) = **$55 (Average Customer Transaction)**	$200,000 (Spent)/40,000 (Customer Transactions) = **$5 (Average Cost per Customer Transaction)**	$55 (Avg. Customer Transaction) − $5 (Avg. Cost per Customer Transaction) = **$50 (Average Value of Digital Marketing Channel Investment)**
Total across Channels (Sum of Total Values in Each Channel Input into the Formulas)	$3,575,000 (Sales)/65,000 (Customer Transactions) = **$55 (Average Customer Transaction)**	$440,000 (Spent)/65,000 (Customer Transactions) = **$6.77 (Average Cost per Customer Transaction)**	$57.69 (Avg. Customer Transaction) − $6.77 (Avg. Cost per Customer Transaction) = **$50.92 (Average Value of Digital Marketing Channel Investment)**

illustrate here is the misappropriation of the value that one particular effort has had in delivering a specific result.

Being able to determine the effectiveness of digital marketing depends on having clear goals we can track and measure. In the case of an e-commerce site, one defined goal would most likely be the completion of a transaction with a consumer. However, for a business consulting company's website, the goal might be to get a prospective client to submit a request for information about what the consulting company can do to help with their particular problem. And being able to tie these data into a CRM system that tracks the individual from the point of filling out a request for information to when he or she ultimately becomes a customer enables the company to look back at the specific digital marketing initiative (or initiatives) that motivated that customer to come to the website in the first place. This provides greater insight into what particular channels and factors help to create new business.

This specialty headphones example serves to illustrate how marketers can bring together different pieces of Big Data. Remember that comprehensive information about a customer resides in different parts of the organization—in this case, in the CRM system along with what is currently captured in the marketing analytics system for web-based interactions. By applying marketing analytics, the organization can transform these data into a more complete picture of each customer as well as each marketing channel to better understand where to make future investments or how to adjust current marketing campaigns. Understanding each customer's full story enables marketers to better understand how to weave their own actions and communications into the fabric of that story in a way that is meaningful and compelling.

Marketing Accountability within Nondigital Marketing Channels

Although we have paid a lot of attention to marketing analytics within the context of digital marketing channels and efforts, we would be remiss not to take a little time to discuss how we can also use marketing analytics to generate insights related to nondigital marketing channels. In particular, direct mail, which we will discuss as a promotion tool in Chapter 13, is one type of nondigital marketing channel that can be set up so that we can more effectively measure its value using marketing analytics. You might be asking yourself at this stage, how can you know that a direct mail marketing campaign led to a sale (or some other desired action)? The key is to put in place a mechanism to identify those current or potential customers who were targeted by a specific direct mail campaign and tie them to the specific desired goal (e.g., making a purchase).

To see how this works, let's revisit the hypothetical clothing company we discussed earlier that sent out a promotional email to alert consumers of its new fall collection. As you may recall, one of its components was a promotional code that a customer could enter to redeem a discount. A direct mail campaign intended to generate sales of a product or service can use similar tactics by creating a unique promotional code to measure the effectiveness of the campaign. When a customer enters that code (either in an online store or a physical store), the company can confidently attribute that transaction to the related direct mail campaign. Knowing how many direct mail items were sent out with the related promotional code (and the cost of doing so) along with how many times the code was used (and the total dollar amount of the related transactions) gives the company strong evidence of how effective the campaign was.

Another tactic is to use a specific URL within a direct mail campaign that we don't display elsewhere. The URL could link to a **landing page**, which is a single page on a website that is built for a particular direct marketing opportunity. Landing pages are usually designed to include specific information that is logically connected to the content of the marketing communication that led the user to the page. It typically features one or more interactive elements that let the user engage in one or more actions the marketer desires (e.g., responding to an invitation to attend an online webinar). Marketing analytics then associate each visitor to the landing page with the related direct mail campaign. Then, the company can determine how effective the specific campaign was at encouraging people to (a) RSVP for the event and (b) actually show up for the event.

We can apply similar tactics to other types of nondigital marketing channels to get a better picture of how effective they are at reaching the marketer's particular goals for a campaign. Essential to such an approach is being able to isolate the relationship between a specific marketing effort and its desired outcome. Hence, using campaign-specific identifiers, such as unique promotional codes, URLs, QR codes, or phone numbers for customer follow-up, allows the direct marketer to tie a specific effort to a specific response. This link provides maximum opportunity to apply marketing analytics capabilities to understand the performance of the campaign.[57] No more wondering what worked and what didn't!

Predictive Analytics

Can we predict the future? Up to this point, we've looked at how organizations can leverage marketing analytics to better understand how *current* marketing channels and initiatives perform—in other words, to understand how to validate the value of decisions we have already made and potentially to create fact-based triggers that will enable us to better determine how to make future investments. Another intriguing area for any marketer is the ability to actually *predict* the future and thus better understand the value of their marketing campaigns even *before* they implement them. This method is called **predictive analytics**.

One interesting application of predictive analytics is what Amazon calls **anticipatory shipping**. This is a data-driven system of delivering products to customers before they

landing page
A single page on a website that is built for a particular direct marketing opportunity.

predictive analytics
Uses large quantities of data within variables that have identified relationships to more accurately predict specific future outcomes.

anticipatory shipping
A system of delivering products to customers before they place an order, utilizing predictive analytics to determine what customers want and then shipping the products automatically.

place an order, utilizing predictive analytics to determine what customers want, and then shipping the products automatically. Fascinating, right? It sounds almost like science fiction, but it's based on solid data analytic assumptions about what customers in a specific area are likely to buy based upon their past behavior. Amazon then ships those products to a more local shipment hub; this heads-up allows the customer to receive the product (that they didn't realize they want yet!) in record time, as it will be located much closer to the customer when the order actually occurs. You'll read more about this and other logistics and supply chain topics in Chapter 11. The big win for firms like Amazon is that getting the right goods moving like this cuts overall delivery time and thus may dissuade customers from visiting brick-and-mortar retailers instead of shopping online.[58]

This crystal-ball scenario is where predictive analytics can increasingly provide significant value to marketers. These techniques use large quantities of data and variables that the analysts know relate to one another to more accurately predict specific *future* outcomes (the key with "predictive" analytics is this focus on the future, not just the present).[59] Certainly, organizations have used these techniques for decades to help forecast sales and other important measures of business performance and outcomes, but don't fool yourself into thinking there's nothing new or exciting within this area. Thanks to Big Data and the new-age data mining capabilities we've discussed, the types of future outcomes that we can predict and the level of accuracy possible with those predictions now enable marketers to obtain more accuracy than ever before when they forecast successful future marketing investments. As we discussed previously, Target's "pregnancy prediction score" is one example of how predictive analytics can be applied to anticipate consumer needs.

Clearly, finding that sweet spot of providing valuable services and support to customers when those particular customers need them is mission critical in today's global competitive marketplace. Toward that end, predictive analytics and marketing analytics in general enable great execution of marketing strategies.

5.4

OBJECTIVE

Understand how to create and use a personal database to manage your career.

Brand You: Creating, Organizing, and Mining Your Personal Career Big Data—For the Lifetime of Your Career

Previously, we saw how Taylor searched for information on industries and professions. Now he needs to take the next step of developing, nurturing, and maintaining relationships with prospective employers and others in a personal career database.

It's not enough to just make contacts with the hiring managers that have job offers. As we've said before, you need to begin planning for your career now. Just as marketers use databases to maximize sales of their products now and in the future, you need to develop a personal database of people, companies, and job opportunities for the life of your career. While you may not want or get a job in a certain firm now, you never know when you will have a different opportunity with the same company and even the same hiring manager whether he/she's at that company or has moved on to a new job him/herself.

This is the same customer relationship management (CRM) that you learned about earlier in this chapter. CRM allows firms to talk with individual customers and adjust elements of their marketing program to meet the unique needs of each customer—a concept called *one-to-one marketing* that is discussed earlier in this chapter. It's a smart plan for marketing Brand You throughout your career. The basis for all CRM programs is a good database.

Think about it this way. If you know of a great job with XYZ company in Georgia or in Germany, and you remember you interviewed with someone with that company 15 years ago but can't remember much about the person or the interview process, wouldn't it be great to have that information at your fingertips?

Today, smartphone apps are available to develop lists of contacts. In some, you can take a snapshot of a business card and the app will add it to the database in the proper order. There is also inexpensive software for your laptop that may meet your needs better. No matter what software you use, it's best to have the flexibility to add some new information as you move through your career.

Some of the information you may want to have in your database about contacts may include:

- Name
- Nickname or other name
- Address (include city, state, and country as separate fields—later you may wish to search your database for individuals who are in Kentucky or Arizona, etc.)
- Email address
- Phone numbers (office and cell if possible)
- Position
- Company
- Date your entry was made (You may add additional information as the contact moves to new positions over the years, and having the date of entry will be helpful.)
- Nature of your contact with this person
- If the contact is from a job interview, include the type of job, whether you received an offer, and whether you accepted or declined the offer
- Any other relevant information about the person, his/her position, the company, etc.
- Many people also scan business cards into their database
- If you attend meetings, speeches, or other events, be sure to make notes on the people speaking and their presentations, and add these to your database. Again, devise a way that this information is accessible
- Be sure to include your professors, classmates, and others in your professional and personal network

The key to creating the most useful database is to include all the relevant information that you believe might be useful to you now and/or in the future when you will mine your database for managing your career. And as you learned earlier in this chapter, data mining is useful to marketers for (among other things) customer acquisition and increasing customer retention and loyalty. You will no doubt find your personal database is useful to you for these purposes, as illustrated below.

Customer Acquisition

In your job search, customer acquisition is getting a new job. You may also think of it as acquiring a new job contact. New contacts are always important because you never know who might be of help to you in your career. For example, contacts can provide you with information about their company or about a competitor in their industry, giving you a step up compared to other job candidates.

Customer Retention

When we talk about brands, such as a pair of shoes or a smartphone, we say we want our brand to have top-of-mind awareness. This means that when a customer thinks of shoes, your brand is the first that comes to mind. In the same way, you want a potential employer or any other contact to keep you on the top of his or her mind awareness, especially when a firm plans on making a hire. Many people will tell you they have never applied for a job. Rather, they were hired because of all the great jobs they have had and because someone recommended them to a potential employer. It's always a good thing when others remember you as someone who would be a good person to work with.

One thing you might do to keep your brand on top of mind and to maintain a relationship with a prospective employer or other contact is to send them something of value, such as:

- A news article or website that mentions (in a complimentary way) their firm
- An article/website that mentions (in a complimentary way) the individual's winning an award, being promoted, getting a new job, etc.
- An article/website that provides information on something about new directions or new technology in their industry
- If they are local to you, an article with good news about a member of their family
- If you change jobs, a quick email about your move, letting them know that a job with their firm is still one of your top career goals

Most important: Begin your database now. What can happen if you wait, you ask? At worst, you will never begin. At best, you may never include some of the great contacts you have already made.

Taylor now understands the usefulness and importance of enhancing the management of his career with a personal database. He is excited about beginning the process right now instead of waiting and hopes that his marketing class will give him a better understanding of what information will be useful in the database.

Objective **Summaries** and **Key Terms**

5.1 Objective Summary

Explain how marketers increase long-term success and profits by practicing customer relationship management (CRM).

Companies using CRM programs establish relationships and differentiate their behavior toward individual customers on a one-to-one basis through dialogue and feedback. The ability to effectively manage all of the available data has been greatly aided by marketing automation capabilities, which facilitate the capability of sales and marketing professionals to gain critical insights from customer data. Companies that successfully practice CRM have the capability for users to look at a wide range of marketing metrics based on the data collected within the CRM system. A critical first step in implementing a successful CRM strategy is to identify the goals it seeks to support. A good CRM strategy based on SMART goals is the key to successfully identifying which metrics are most appropriate, SMART being an acronym for **s**pecific, **m**easurable, **a**chievable, **r**elevant, and **t**imely. Three key categories of metrics are marketing metrics, sales metrics, and service metrics. Key performance indicators (KPIs) are the most critical indicators of progress toward key intended results (goals). Some of the popular KPIs marketers track are customer acquisition cost (CAC), customer lifetime value (CLV), conversion rate, length of sales cycle, share of wallet, customer churn rate, net promoter score (NPS), and return on experience (ROX).

Key Terms

customer relationship management (CRM)

MarTech

C-suite

chief customer officer (CCO)

one-to-one marketing

touchpoint

marketing automation

lead

sales funnel

lead nurturing

SMART goals

user adoption metrics

customer perception metrics

business performance metrics

key performance indicators (KPIs)

5.2 Objective Summary

Understand Big Data and data mining, and how marketers can put these techniques to good use.

Big Data refers to data that are growing in terms of both volume and velocity. It comes from a wider range of sources within different functions within organizations as well as society at large. Big Data offers marketers the ability to gain a deeper understanding of their customers when properly leveraged through methods such as data mining. When marketers use data mining, they methodically sift through large datasets using computers that run sophisticated programs to understand relationships among things like consumer buying decisions, exposure to marketing messages, and in-store promotions. Data mining leads to the ability to make important decisions about which customers to invest in further, which to abandon, and where the greatest opportunities for new investments lie.

Key Terms

Big Data
Internet of Things (IoT)
web scraping
sentiment analysis
scanner data
channel partner model
information overload
data mining
data warehouse
edge computing
structured data
unstructured data
emotion analysis
data scientist
artificial intelligence (AI)
machine learning
augmented intelligence
cybersecurity
cyberattack
hacker
data breach
deep learning
deepfake
blockchain

5.3 Objective Summary

Describe what marketing analytics include and how organizations can leverage both marketing analytics and predictive analytics to improve marketing performance.

Marketing analytics offer marketers the means to better understand and analyze the wealth of data that are now at their disposal. With the proliferation of digital marketing and the speed at which data can be captured and analyzed, marketers are able to gain insights at or near real time in regard to the performance of their marketing investments. This capability to analyze across channels (both physical and digital) the performance of their different marketing initiatives provides a means through which to more precisely identify *where value is being created*. Predictive analytics have the potential to help marketers identify outcomes before they occur and, in turn, make smarter decisions as they plan marketing campaigns and investments.

Key Terms

marketing analytics
digital marketing channels
A/B test
click-through rate (CTR)
cost-per-click
cost-per-impression
search engine optimization (SEO)
landing page
predictive analytics
anticipatory shipping

5.4 Objective Summary

Understand how to create and use a personal database to manage your career.

For management of the life of your career, you need to develop a personal database of people, companies, and job opportunities. The personal database will allow you to use CRM for marketing Brand You.

Be sure to include all the relevant information that you believe might be useful to you now and/or in the future in your database, including the individual's name, company, contact information, and information about previous contacts with the individual.

Your database will be important throughout your career for getting a new job (customer acquisition) and for maintaining relationships with prospective employers and their key employees (customer retention and loyalty). Such relationships are enhanced when you can send contacts something of value, such as a news story that mentions the firm.

Chapter **Questions** and **Activities**

Concepts: Test Your Knowledge

5-1. What is CRM? Why is CRM effective? What is one-to-one marketing? What are touchpoints?

5-2. What is marketing automation and how is it used in marketing?

5-3. Explain the term *SMART goals*. What are key performance indicators?

5-4. Describe the various sources of Big Data for marketers.

5-5. Explain customer acquisition cost (CAC). Explain customer lifetime value (CLV). What are marketing-originated customers? Explain share of wallet.

5-6. Explain the churn rate. Explain net promoter score (NPS). What is marketing ROI? What is marketing ROX? Why is ROX a better measure than ROI? How do marketers measure ROX?

5-7. Explain the three ways that Big Data helps firms create a competitive advantage.

5-8. Explain the Internet of Things (IoT). Give two examples of the IoT.

5-9. What is structured data? What is unstructured data? Explain the four applications for data mining.

5-10. What is the role of the data scientists? What is artificial intelligence? What is machine learning?

5-11. Explain the meaning of *blockchain*. What does blockchain have to do with cybersecurity?

5-12. Explain marketing analytics. What are digital marketing channels? Explain how digital marketing channels and marketing analytics help marketers in decision making. How might an A/B test be incorporated with the use of digital marketing channels and marketing analytics?

5-13. What is predictive analytics? What are some examples of how a firm might use predictive analytics to improve its efficiency?

Activities: Apply What You've Learned

5-14. *For Further Research (Individual)* For this assignment, you are going to act as a manual version of a software program that conducts sentiment analysis. First, you must locate a Facebook page for a popular brand you use or know of. You must make sure that the site includes comments from consumers. Select a sample of comments (between five and seven that do not contain any explicit words or expressions) created by users in response to a specific brand's post on their Facebook page. Copy the comments down and categorize the sentiment within each comment as "positive," "negative," or "neutral." Include what specific elements of each comment most clearly support your categorization of it (e.g., use of punctuation, context, inclusion of specific words, use of slang, etc.). What insights should a marketing manager responsible for the related brand take away from these comments? Develop a short presentation for your class.

5-15. *Creative Homework/Short Project* Assume that you are the digital marketing manager for a local law firm that specializes in divorce and auto accident cases. You have decided to implement a search engine optimization campaign to ensure your firm is one of the top listings. Make a list of at least 10 words and phrases you think are likely to be the most searched by potential customers. Consider both your geography and your legal areas of specialty. Rank them in order with the most important at the top of the list.

5-16. *Creative Homework/Short Project* You have been asked by your boss to weigh in on whether Instagram advertising or search engine advertising through Google

would be a better use of company funds. Your boss has provided her opinion on the matter: "Pictures on Instagram are just more compelling than little blocks of text in a search engine's results." You need to gather data and assess the potential solutions on your own.
  a. What data and metrics would you need to evaluate Google search engine advertising effectiveness?
  b. What data and metrics would you need to evaluate Instagram advertising effectiveness?
  c. Take the time to research the two options and gather some real data. What would you recommend to your boss? Why?

5-17. *In Class, 10–25 Minutes for Teams* As an admissions manager for a college or university, you are interested in exploring the use of predictive analytics within the admissions process to bring in students with a higher likelihood of graduating from the school and achieving greater levels of success both during and after their studies. With another student who is acting as your boss, the admissions director, discuss the specific reasons that predictive analytics might be of value to making admissions decisions on students. Be sure to discuss any areas where you might need to proceed with caution.

5-18. *Creative Homework/Short Project* Assume you are working in the market research unit of a firm that practices DTC (Direct-to-Consumer) marketing to sell its mattresses. Your assignment is to plan an A/B test of the main visual on your company's landing page. Develop a detailed plan for the A/B test and submit it to your instructor.

5-19. What is cost-per-click? What is cost-per-impression? Develop a detailed scenario of how an imaginary company might use marketing analytics and digital marketing channels to gain insight into the cost of each channel in relation to how much the firm gains in sales. What are some ways marketers might use analytics to measure the value of nondigital marketing channels?

Concepts: Apply Marketing Metrics

For this exercise, please refer to the Chapter 5 Supplement on CRM Metrics and Key Performance Indicators (KPIs). In particular, review the discussion of *customer lifetime value (CLV)* and *share of wallet*. Often a firm's loyalty (or rewards) program serves as a key enabler of CRM capabilities based on the customer data such programs generate.

Back in 2017, Macy's revamped its popular Star Rewards loyalty program as one measure to combat sliding brick-and-mortar sales and also promote more online shopping at Macy's, which resulted in sales gains.[60] Go to their website (www.macys.com) and review the current information about their Star Rewards program.

5-20. In what ways could Macy's expect to measure customer lifetime value (CLV) and share of wallet based on data collected within the context of a reward program such as this?

5-21. How would data be collected for each element, and how might management at Macy's use that data to provide loyal customers with a very strong relationship with the firm?

Choices: What Do You Think?

5-22. *Ethics* CRM relies on data collected from customers to create customized or one-to-one experiences for those customers. Data are collected at various touchpoints—places in which the customer interfaces with the firm to provide information, such as at a checkout lane, on the phone, on the website, and so on. Do firms have an obligation to explain to customers that they are collecting information from them to populate and drive their CRM initiative, or is it inherently obvious in today's world that such practices are routine? In general, what is your personal viewpoint of database-driven positioning strategies? What are the potential pros and cons to the company and to the customer?

5-23. *Critical Thinking* Are there any potential challenges that would arise from companies using predictive analysis as a key marketing strategy? What are some examples? What are the potential benefits to companies that invest in this form of marketing and do it well?

5-24. *Critical thinking* The *Internet of Things* refers to the increased proliferation of devices that are connected to the Internet and that in turn can be connected to each other. Although there are a number of benefits to this level of connectivity for both society and businesses, there are also a number of risks and ethical issues. Thinking about the Internet of Things, what kinds of devices (physical objects) providing data and what kinds of data could create what kinds of risks for consumers? Do the benefits outweigh the downsides?

5-25. *Ethics* Many apps that you use are able to remain free to users through the sale of advertising and by monetizing the data of the individuals using the technology. This includes apps for social media, gaming, and news. Do you feel there is a limit to what information these companies are able to share with third parties? What types of information should not be shared? Would you be willing to pay for usage of the app to eliminate this type of data sharing?

5-26. *Critical Thinking* Spending on digital marketing has trended upward in recent years, and with so many individuals using the Internet for extended periods of time, it is easy to understand why. Some organizations spend more than half of their budget on digital marketing. How do you think they justify committing such substantial amounts of money to digital efforts? Do you believe that more companies should invest primarily in digital marketing? What groups or factors would indicate to you that digital marketing does not make sense as an investment? Many of these companies have not decreased their budgets for other media advertising in order to increase digital marketing; they have simply increased their total marketing budgets. Does this make sense to you? Why or why not?

5-27. *Critical Thinking* A study conducted by Adobe found that 77 percent of marketers surveyed believe that data on customer purchase histories can improve marketing performance, yet only 21 percent actually use it. Similarly, 88 percent believe that behavioral data can have a similar impact, but only 20 percent use it.[61] These statistics highlight a contradiction between the perception of marketing analytics' value and the actual frequency of execution of marketing analytics. Why do you think this is? If you were in charge of implementing marketing analytics in an organization, what hurdles would you expect to encounter and from whom, and how would you overcome them?

5-28. *Ethics* Do you believe it is right for companies to target a higher (or lower) cost service to a consumer based on a data-driven observation that the consumer possesses characteristics typically associated with a willingness to spend more (or less) money on the related service? Does this constitute a form of discrimination that would make you uncomfortable as a marketer who is exploring the possibility of employing this strategy? What about if you were the consumer on the receiving end of it?

Miniproject: Learn by Doing

Different types of businesses use different approaches to engaging with both current and potential consumers online. A company's website is usually a key source of information for potential and current customers. The purpose of this project is to gain a deeper understanding of how marketing analytics can be implemented in order to gain greater insights into and enable more effective control of marketing efforts.

    a. Select three company websites. These should include one e-commerce site (e.g., Amazon), one consulting company (e.g., IBM Global Services), and one consumer-packaged-goods company or brand (e.g., Procter & Gamble's Tide).

    b. For each company's website, list what you believe the objectives of the organization are as communicated through the website, and identify specific conversion actions on the website that would most closely align with these goals. For example, customer acquisition might be supported and ultimately achieved by getting users to sign up for an email newsletter, which would be defined as a conversion action.

5-29. Rank the conversion actions in order of importance and include an explanation of why you have ordered them as such. Identify whether they are short-term oriented as they relate to the organization's objectives or long-term oriented (or, in some cases, both) and why.

5-30. If you could choose only two marketing metrics (remember metrics, not conversions) to track for each of these websites, identify which two you would select for each website and explain why.

5-31. Some of the websites visited should have a request-for-information form on them. Often, this is one of the ways that marketers begin to collect information on a customer to place within their CRM system. Locate this form and identify what information it is asking for. Write down the different potential uses of this information for the organization and in what ways it might be used by marketers to further engage with the customer. What are some creative ways that you would recommend leveraging these data for each website analyzed in terms of future communications? Develop a presentation about your project and the results for your class.

Marketing in Action **Case**   Real Choices at Spotify

Whether it's firing us up for a workout or helping to mend a broken heart, music can play a meaningful role in our lives. Streaming music market leader Spotify understands this. The company uses data analytics to connect us to music it thinks we'll love, and also to connect the artists who create that music to their fans.

Founded in Sweden in 2006, Spotify began as an alternative to other music download services—both legal and illegal. The company shook up the music industry by offering customers music from Spotify's vast library we pay for in one of two ways: with our time or with our money. Subscribers can listen for free but be interrupted by ads, or they can pay a subscription fee for ad-free listening. The fee-based service adds other nice features like the ability to choose tracks, unlimited track skipping, listening offline, and higher-quality audio.

Music lovers have embraced Spotify's model, catapulting the firm to rise to a dominant position in music streaming (2019 stats show a 35 percent market share compared to 19 percent for Apple Music and 15 percent for Amazon Music). But music creators—the artists—generally have not been so enthusiastic. This is largely because Spotify makes deals with record labels; by the time the money trickles down to artists the royalties can be pretty small. This famously caused Taylor Swift to pull her music catalog from Spotify in 2014 (although she later reversed herself).

Spotify's active user count tops 286 million, with 130 million of those on its paid Premium service. And with all that downloading, track choosing, and skipping, the company collects a *lot of data*, which it uses to understand and support customer preferences. A popular service is the company's Discover Weekly feature, which provides a personalized playlist each week. It serves up songs you haven't heard before, composed of tunes that Spotify's algorithms believe you'll like—think of it as sort of a personalized mixtape (if you are too young to know what a mixtape is, then you'll have to google it!). You can also create and name your own playlists, like one for romantic evenings at home and another for that weekend barbecue bash in the backyard. Overall, one of the best value-adding elements of Spotify is the sheer scope of the music available—all genres, virtually any artists, and millions of songs, right on your desktop, tablet, or mobile device.

Spotify is also using its vast data and analytical prowess to both win back skeptical artists who've left and also to attract new artists who are so important to the firm's future success. The company launched its Spotify for Artists app that gives artists access to data about their fans, including which playlists create new fans for the artist and how many streams the artist's music is getting. The app also gives artists some control over their presence on the service, with the ability to update bios, post playlists, and specify which track is the "artist's pick." And Spotify's Fans First program helps to identify the artist's most passionate fans, allowing the musicians to target them with special offers. In 2019, the company acquired the music-production service SoundBetter, which allows record labels to promote new music to specific Spotify listeners. Spotify expects this "two-sided marketplace" focused on tools and services supporting artists and their representatives to grow by 50 percent in 2020.

The usefulness of Spotify's vast data stretches well beyond listeners and fans. It also contains a treasure trove of marketing-relevant information that can help advertisers choose which users it most wants to reach. Spotify for Brands is a program that allows marketers of all sorts of goods and services to laser-focus their ads, using insights gleaned from the data that, according to its website, "reflect the real people behind the devices." Music is driven by consumers' real or desired self-identities, a factor that many companies use in advertising. The data also help to determine optimal ad placement timing. Selling Gatorade? Playing an ad at the end of a workout sounds good.

Today, Spotify differentiates itself from its competitors by the deeper way that it views customer data. But in its early days of using data analytics, the firm focused mostly on standard fare, such as keeping track of online customers after they left its website (known as retargeting). Now Spotify has reimagined customers as not simply clicks or transactions, but rather as unique human beings with changing needs, wants, and preferences that influence their choices in music and in products. As such, Spotify's goal is to build lasting connections with its users and other stakeholders, understanding how people consume the music they select and then applying those insights to better serve its customers and support its advertising clients' goals.

What roles will data analytics play in the next chapter of Spotify's growth? While chipping away at competitors' market share in the core business of music streaming is fine, the big prize likely will come by pursuing other ventures. Imagine almost anything connected to music and its stakeholders, from smart speakers to selling exclusive lines of makeup that its artists use. Do you like to listen to podcasts? In 2019, Spotify acquired two big producers of podcasts, Anchor and Gimlet Media, signaling a big focus on this other hot audio product in the future. Spotify is in the midst of a remarkable transformation in which artists are moving from foes to fans of its offerings and business model. Whatever direction it takes, it's fairly certain that Big Data and smart use of analytics will drive those strategies, resulting in deep understanding of Spotify's stakeholders and providing them with a great experience with the firm's offerings.[62]

Questions for Discussion

5-32. Review the four steps in one-to-one marketing. How is Spotify following each of these to support their marketing efforts?

5-33. What are some examples of unstructured data that Spotify is probably using in their analysis?

5-34. Could Spotify use the Internet of Things with their service? Share a couple of innovations they could add that would fit into this category.

Chapter **Notes**

1. Michael Lewis, *Moneyball: The Art of Winning an Unfair Game*, New York: W.W. Norton & Company, 2004.

2. Gaetano DiNardi, "9 Essential B2B Marketing Trends That Will Pick Up Steam in 2018," December 18, 2017, https://www.insidesales.com/insider/technology/b2b-marketing-trends-2018 (accessed May 21, 2018).

3. Nathan Isaacs, "The CMO+Chief Customer Officer: The Beyonce & Jay-Z of the C-Suite," *act-on*, January 8, 2018, www.act-on.com/blog/chief-customer-officer-cmo/ (accessed May 26, 2018).

4. "A Crash Course in Customer Relationship Management," *Harvard Management Update*, March 2000 (Harvard Business School reprint U003B); Nahshon Wingard, "CRM Definition—Customer-Centered Philosophy," October 26, 2009, http://ezinearticles.com/?CRM-Definition—Customer-Centered-Philosophy&id=933109 (accessed May 21, 2018).

5. Don Peppers and Martha Rogers, *The One-to-One Future* (New York: Doubleday, 1996).

6. Don Peppers, Martha Rogers, and Bob Dorf, "Is Your Company Ready for One-to-One Marketing?" *Harvard Business Review*, January–February 1999, 151–60.

7. Quoted in Cara B. DiPasquale, "Navigate the Maze," Special Report on 1:1 Marketing, *Advertising Age*, October 29, 2001, S1: 2.

8. "5 Creative Ways Small Businesses Are Using Marketing Automation," VentureHarbour, https://www.ventureharbour.com/5-creative-ways-small-businesses-using-marketing-automation/.

9. Leonard L. Berry, *On Great Service: A Framework for Action* (New York: Free Press, 1995); Paul T. Ringenbach, *USAA: A Tradition of Service* (San Antonio, TX: Donning, 1997).

10. Denis Pombriant, "Your CRM Tech TL:DR Thoughts for 2018," *Diginomica*, January 3, 2018, https://diginomica.com/2018/01/03/your-crm-tech-tldr-for-2018/ (accessed March 27, 2018); "Gartner Says Worldwide Customer Experience and Relationship Management Software Market Grew 15.6% in 2018," June 17, 2019, https://www.gartner.com/en/newsroom/press-releases/2019-06-17-gartner-says-worldwide-customer-experience-and-relati; Milja Milenkovic, "31 Sizzling CRM Statistics to Help Your Business Soar," September 19, 2019, https://www.smallbizgenius.net/by-the-numbers/crm-statistics/#gref.

11. Manohar Chapalamadugu, "6 Trends to Watch in 2018," *Destination CRM*, January 13, 2018, http://www.destinationcrm.com/Articles/Web-Exclusives/Viewpoints/6-CRM-Trends-to-Watch-in-2018-122717.aspx (accessed March 27, 2018); "54 Key CRM Software Statistics: 2020 Market Share Analysis & Data," FinancesOnline, https://financesonline.com/crm-statistics-analysis-of-trends-data-and-market-share/#link12.

12. JP Mangalindan, "Amazon's Recommendation Secret," July 30, 2012, http://fortune.com/2012/07/30/amazons-recommendation-secret/ (accessed May 21, 2018).

13. Salesforce, "Adidas," https://www.salesforce.com/customer-success-stories/adidas (accessed May 21, 2018).

14. "My Magic Plus FAQ," http://www.disneytouristblog.com/mymagic-plus-faq (accessed May 21, 2018).

15. Rachel Burns, "CRM Goals: 4 Objectives for Your CRM Strategy," May 17, 2019, https://www.activecampaign.com/blog/crm-goals.

16. Neil Davey, "CRM Metrics: What Should You Monitor and Measure?," March 14, 2018, https://www.mycustomer.com/selling/crm/crm-metrics-what-should-you-monitor-and-measure.

17. SAS, "Big Data, Bigger Marketing," www.sas.com/en_us/insights/big-data/big-data-marketing.html (accessed May 21, 2018).

18. David Carr, "Giving Viewers What They Want," February 24, 2013, http://www.nytimes.com/2013/02/25/business/media/for-house-of-cards-using-big-data-to-guarantee-its-popularity.html?_r=0 (accessed May 21, 2018); Michael Dixon, "How Netflix Used Big Data and Analytics to Generate Billions," April 5, 2019, https://seleritysas.com/blog/2019/04/05/how-netflix-used-big-data-and-analytics-to-generate-billions/.

19. Friedemann Mattern and Christian Floerkemeier, "From the Internet of Computers to the Internet of Things," *Informatik-Spektrum* 33 (2010): 107–21; Steve Ranger, "What Is the IoT? Everything You Need to Know about the Internet of Things Right Now," February 3, 2020, https://www.zdnet.com/article/what-is-the-internet-of-things-everything-you-need-to-know-about-the-iot-right-now/.

20. Vinay Iyengar and Jeffrey Rayport, "'When Consumer Packaged Goods Start Acting Like Software," *Venture Beat*, March 25, 2018, https://venturebeat.com/2018/03/25/when-consumer-packaged-goods-start-acting-like-software/ (accessed March 27, 2018).

21. Hudson Hollister, "Data Companies' Plan to Transform Government in 2018: Introducing Our Policy Agenda," January 16, 2018, https://www.datacoalition.org/data-companies-plan-to-transform-government-in-2018-introducing-our-policy-agenda/ (accessed May 21, 2018).

22. Jim Edwards, "Yes, Your Credit Card Company Is Selling Your Purchase Data to Online Advertisers," April 16, 2013, www.businessinsider.com/credit-cards-sell-purchase-data-to-advertisers-2013-4 (accessed May 21, 2018).

23. Todd Traub, "Wal-Mart Used Technology to Become Supply Chain Leader," July 2, 2012, www.arkansasbusiness.com/article/85508/wal-mart-used-technology-to-become-supply-chain-leader?page=all (accessed May 21, 2018).

24. Karen Stabiner, "To Survive in Tough Times, Restaurants Turn to Data-Mining," *New York Times*, August 25, 2017, www.nytimes.com/2017/08/25/dining/restaurant-software-analytics-data-mining.html (accessed May 21, 2018).

25. Kashmir Hill, "How Target Figured Out a Teen Girl Was Pregnant before Her Father Did," *Forbes*, February 16, 2012, https://www.forbes.com/sites/kashmirhill/2012/02/16/how-target-figured-out-a-teen-girl-was-pregnant-before-her-father-did/#76a5743d6668.

26. Pan-Ning Tan, Michael Steinbach, and Vipin Kumar, *Introduction to Data Mining* (New York: Addison-Wesley, 2005).

27. "Number of monthly active Facebook users worldwide as of 4th quarter 2017," *Statista*, Q4 2017, https://www.statista.com/statistics/264810/number-of-monthly-active-facebook-users-worldwide/ (accessed March 29, 2018).

28. Andrew Herbert, "Data Analytics & Artificial Intelligence Trends in 2019," April 22, 2019, https://medium.com/datadriveninvestor/data-analytics-artificial-intelligence-trends-in-2019-1032c44d9ce8.

29. Joe F. Hair Jr., "Knowledge Creation in Marketing: The Role of Predictive Analytics," *European Business Review* 19 (2007): 303–15.

30. Goutam Chakraborty and Murali Krishna Pagolu, "Analysis of Unstructured Data: Applications of Text Analytics and Sentiment Mining," *SAS Paper* 1288 (2014): 1–14.

31. Todd Spangler, "Viacom to Track Emotional Responses to Social Ads, Content," January 25, 2016, http://variety.com/2016/digital/news/viacom-canvs-emotional-social-media-ads-1201687790/ (accessed May 21, 2018).

32. Thor Olavsrud, "What Is Data Ops?," November 21, 2017, https://www.cio.com/article/3237694/analytics/what-is-dataops-data-operations-analytics.html (accessed May 16, 2018).

33. Pang-Ning Tan et al., *Introduction to Data Mining*, 2nd ed. (New York: Pearson, 2018).

34. Werner Reinartz and V. Kumar, "The Mismanagement of Customer Loyalty," *Harvard Business Review* 80 (7): 86–97.

35. Nellie Akalp, "6 Reasons to Fire a Client," May 6, 2014, www.forbes.com/sites/allbusiness/2014/05/06/6-reasons-to-fire-a-client/#31d0d2e5c512 (accessed May 16, 2018).

36. Felix Salmon, "Amazon Should Be Very Careful about Banning Customers for Making Too Many Returns," May 25, 2018, https://slate.com/business/2018/05/amazon-is-banning-customers-for-making-too-many-returns.html (accessed May 29, 2018).

37. SAS, "What Is a Data Scientist?" https://www.sas.com/en_us/insights/analytics/what-is-a-data-scientist.html (accessed May 21, 2018).

38. Glassdoor, https://www.glassdoor.com/Salaries/data-scientist-salary-SRCH_KO0,14.htm (accessed May 16, 2018).

39. Thomas H. Davenport and D. J. Patil, "Data Scientist: The Sexiest Job of the 21st Century," *Harvard Business Review*, October 2012, http://hbr.org/2012/10/data-scientist-the-sexiest-job-of-the-21st-century/ar/1 (accessed May 13, 2016).

40. Bernard Marr, "What Is the Difference between Artificial Intelligence and Machine Learning?," *Forbes*, December 6, 2016, www.forbes.com/sites/bernardmarr/2016/12/06/what-is-the-difference-between-artificial-intelligence-and-machine-learning/#192ecfd52742 (accessed May 26, 2018).

41. Niraj Chokshi, "Is Alexa Listening? Amazon Echo Sent Out Recording of Couple's Conversation," *New York Times*, May 25, 2018, https://www.nytimes.com/2018/05/25/business/amazon-alexa-conversation-shared-echo.html (accessed May 29, 2018).

42. James Ovenden, "How Amazon Alexa Works," *Innovation Enterprise*, https://channels.theinnovationenterprise.com/articles/how-amazon-alexa-works (accessed May 16, 2018).

43. "Gartner Says AI Augmentation Will Create $2.9 Trillion of Business Value in 2021," August 5, 2019, https://www.gartner.com/en/newsroom/press-releases/2019-08-05-gartner-says-ai-augmentation-will-create-2point9-trillion-of-business-value-in-2021 (accessed May 26, 2020).

44. "Sizing the Prize: PwC's Global Artificial Intelligence Study: Exploiting the AI Revolution," https://www.pwc.com/gx/en/issues/data-and-analytics/publications/artificial-intelligence-study.html (accessed May 26, 2020).

45. Kevin McCoy, "Target to Pay $18.5M for 2013 Data Breach That Affected 41 Million Consumers," *USA Today*, May 23, 2017, https://www.usatoday.com/story/money/2017/05/23/target-pay-185m-2013-data-breach-affected-consumers/102063932/ (accessed May 26, 2018); Mohit Kumar, "Facebook Admits Public Data of its 2.2 Billion Users Has Been Compromised," *The Hacker News*, April 4, 2018, https://thehackernews.com/2018/04/facebook-data-privacy.html (accessed May 26, 2018).

46. Nadeem Badshah, "Facebook to Contact 87 Million Users Impacted by Data Breach," *The Guardian*, April 8, 2018, www.theguardian.com/technology/2018/apr/08/facebook-to-contact-the-87-million-users-affected-by-data-breach (accessed May 26, 2018).

47. Garett Sloane, "What Marketers Need to Know about Deepfake," October 16, 2019, https://adage.com/article/digital/what-marketers-need-know-about-deepfakes/2206586 (accessed June 1, 2020); https://www.synthesia.io/post/david-beckham (accessed August 6, 2020).

48. Sam Mire, "Blockchain in Marketing: 7 Possible Use Cases," November 26, 2018, Disruptor Daily, https://www.disruptordaily.com/blockchain-use-cases-marketing/ (accessed June 1, 2020).

49. Wikipedia, "Analytics," https://en.wikipedia.org/wiki/Analytics (accessed May 21, 2018).

50. http://www.pewresearch.org/fact-tank/2018/03/05/some-americans-dont-use-the-internet-who-are-they/ (accessed May 27, 2018); SAS, "Marketing Analytics: What It Is and Why It Matters," www.sas.com/en_us/insights/marketing/marketing-analytics.html (accessed May 21, 2018).

51. Monica Anderson, Andrew Perrin, and Jingjing Jiang, "11% of Americans Don't Use the Internet. Who Are They?" Pew Research Center, March 5, 2018, http://www.pewinternet.org/fact-sheet/social-media/ (accessed May 27, 2018); Pew Research Center, "Internet/Broadband Fact Sheet," February 5, 2018, http://www.pewinternet.org/fact-sheet/internet-broadband/ (accessed May 21, 2018); Pew Research Center, "Social Media Fact Sheet," February 5, 2018, http://www.pewinternet.org/fact-sheet/social-media (accessed May 21, 2018); Shannon Schumacher and Nicholas Kent, "8 Charts on Internet Use around the World as Countries Grapple with COVID-19," Pew Research Center, April 2, 2020, https://www.pewresearch.org/fact-tank/2020/04/02/8-charts-on-internet-use-around-the-world-as-countries-grapple-with-covid-19/ (accessed May 27, 2020).

52. Chris Leone, "How Much Should You Budget for Marketing in 2020?," https://www.webstrategiesinc.com/blog/how-much-budget-for-online-marketing-in-2014.

53. BCG, "The Digital Marketing Revolution Has Only Begun," May 10, 2017, www.bcg.com/en-ca/publications/2017/sales-consumer-insights-digital-marketing-revolution-has-only-just-begun.aspx (accessed May 21, 2018).

54. Henry Timms and Jeremy Heimans, "Commentary: #DeleteFacebook Is Just the Beginning. Here's the Movement We Could See Next," *Fortune*, April 16, 2018, http://fortune.com/2018/04/16/delete-facebook-data-privacy-movement/ (accessed May 21, 2018).

55. Nathan Ingrahan, "Imgur's New Analytics Tools Let Users and Advertisers See How Their Images Go Viral," *The Verge*, January 28, 2014, http://www.theverge.com/2014/1/28/5351618/imgurs-new-analytics-tool-lets-users-and-advertisers-see-how-images-go-viral (accessed May 21, 2018).

56. https://www.globenewswire.com/news-release/2014/01/28/1248406/0/en/Imgur-Analytics-Platform-Reveals-Data-Around-the-Lifecycle-of-Images-Online.html (accessed October 16, 2020).

57. Mail Shark, "How To Track and Measure Direct Mail," https://www.themailshark.com/resources/guides/how-to-track-measure-direct-mail/ (accessed May 21, 2018).

58. Megan Ray Nichols, "Amazon Wants to Use Predictive Analytics to Offer Anticipatory Shipping," January 16, 2018, SmartData Collective, www.smartdatacollective.com/amazon-wants-predictive-analytics-offer-anticipatory-shipping (accessed May 21, 2018).

59. Hair, "Knowledge Creation in Marketing."

60. Phil Wahba, "Macy's Is Overhauling Its Rewards Program to Bring Back Straying Shoppers?," *Fortune*, September 17, 2017, http://fortune.com/2017/09/27/macys-loyalty-shoppers/ (accessed May 22, 2018).

61. Wes Nichols, "Secrets of Successful Analytics Adoption," *Forbes*, July 22, 2013, www.forbes.com/sites/forbesinsights/2013/07/22/secrets-of-successful-marketing-analytics-adoption (accessed May 16, 2016).

62. Based on "How Many Users Do Spotify, Apple Music and Streaming Services Have?" Musically.Com, accessed July 25, 2020, https://musically.com/2020/02/19/spotify-apple-how-many-users-big-music-streaming-services/; Jeff Parsons, "History of Spotify: How the Swedish Streaming Company Changed the Music Industry," Mirror.Co.Uk, April 3, 2018, https://www.mirror.co.uk/tech/history-spotify-how-swedish-streaming-12291542; Bernard Marr, "The Amazing Ways Spotify Uses Big Data, AI and Machine Learning to Drive Business Success," *Forbes*, October 30, 2017, https://www.forbes.com/sites/bernardmarr/2017/10/30/the-amazing-ways-spotify-uses-big-data-ai-and-machine-learning-to-drive-business-success/#4df4b114bd2f; "Music for Everyone," Spotify.com, accessed July 25, 2020, https://www.spotify.com/us/; Hilary Weaver, "Taylor Swift Gives In, a Little, to Spotify," *Vanity Fair*, November 7, 2017, https://www.vanityfair.com/style/2017/11/taylor-swift-gives-in-to-streaming-services; Amy Watson, "Spotify's Monthly Active Users," *Statista*, May 11, 2020, https://www.statista.com/statistics/367739/spotify-global-mau/; Anne Steele, "Spotify Agrees to Buy Ringer and Reports Growth in Users," *The Wall Street Journal*, February 5, 3030, https://www.wsj.com/articles/spotify-adds-subscribers-swings-to-loss-as-it-invests-in-podcasts-11580900543; Alexandra Bruell, "Spotify Has Big Ambitions for Ad Business," *The Wall Street Journal*, August 17, 2017, https://www.wsj.com/articles/spotify-has-big-ambitions-for-ad-business-1502964001; Dawn Papandrea, "Spotify's CMO on Using Data to Create Content Marketing Hits," *Insights*, June 7, 2017, https://insights.newscred.com/spotify-cmo-data-content-marketing/; Tom Turula, "Spotify Will Now Sell Listeners Makeup Products Inspired by Popular Music Artists," *Business Insider*, November 13, 2017, http://www.businessinsider.com/spotify-to-sell-makeup-products-2017-11?r=UK&IR=T.

63. Satish Kota, "68% of Customers Leave You If You Don't Care for Them," http://www.reputationxl.com/charts-infographics/68-of-customers-leave-you-if-you-dont-care-for-them/.

CRM Metrics and Key Performance Indicators (KPIs)

While all metrics track and provide data about general business processes, KPIs are the critical measures that demonstrate how effectively a company is achieving key business goals. This supplement provides some of the most commonly used KPIs for assessing CRM success. In addition, this supplement includes an explanation for how to calculate these metrics using simple generalized formulas, with the understanding that some of these metrics can also be calculated using complex formulas that are industry or firm specific.

Customer Acquisition Cost (CAC)

customer acquisition cost (CAC)
The cost of convincing a potential customer to buy a product or service.

Every dollar that goes into the marketing process has the ultimate objective to acquire customers. Therefore, it should be no surprise that an important KPI to consider is **customer acquisition cost (CAC)**, which is the cost of convincing a potential customer to buy your particular product or service. In addition to telling you the price per lead (potential customer), this metric helps you estimate the total amount you should spend for your lead generation efforts. You can calculate the CAC simply by dividing the overall marketing and sales expenditures for a given time period by the number of customers you acquire during that same time period. For example, if FunCo Inc. spent $100,000 in sales and marketing over a one-year period and acquired 1,000 customers during that period, the CAC is $100.

As Figure 5.1-S illustrates, CAC is a metric that every business wants to reduce. If a company can obtain revenues from customers by spending less money to do so, the company's profit margin improves, and it makes a larger profit—even though it still receives the same amount from its customers! Companies with annual or monthly contracts may also be interested in the time to recoup customer acquisition cost, as this will allow them to determine how soon a customer becomes profitable for them.

customer lifetime value (CLV)
Represents how much profit a firm expects to make from a particular customer, including each and every purchase he or she will make from them now and in the future.

Customer Lifetime Value (CLV)

Customer lifetime value (CLV) represents how much profit a firm expects to make from a particular customer, including each and every purchase he or she will make from them now and in the future.

Thus, this metric describes the potential profit that a single customer's purchase of a firm's products generates over the customer's lifetime. You just learned that FunCo Inc. has a CAC of $100. But how do you know if this is a number that FunCo's marketers will be delighted about, or if it is so high the survival of the company is in jeopardy?

Figure 5.1-S | Calculate Customer Acquisition Cost

$$\frac{\text{Sales \& Marketing Costs}}{\text{\# of New Customers}} = \text{Customer Acquisition Cost}$$

If the average order customers place is $250 and FunCo has a markup of 100 percent on all products, the company makes $125 on every sale and it generates $25 ($125 – CAC of $100) from each customer to pay salaries, advertising, and other general expenses. But that's for a one-time purchase—what happens if the customer makes more than one purchase over a lifetime? To calculate CLV, you need four pieces of information:

1. *Average purchase value*, which is the average purchase amount each time a customer buys from you
2. *Average purchase frequency rate*, which is how many times per year the average customer buys from you
3. *Average customer value*, which is how much money the average customer spends with you per year
4. *Average customer lifespan*, which is how long the average customer continues to buy from you

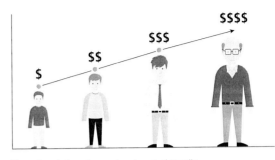

The value of all customers is not created equally.

Once you have all this information, it's very straightforward to calculate your company's CLV. Just multiply the average customer value by the average customer lifespan.

Now, let's see how this impacts FunCo. You already know the average purchase value for FunCo is $250—this is the average size of an order mentioned above. If the average purchase frequency rate is six purchases per year and the average customer lifespan is five years, the CLV of each customer is $7,500.

That means that Company A is able to turn a $100 investment into $7,500 of revenue! It just makes sense that a firm's profitability and long-term success will be far greater if it develops long-term relationships with its customers, so that those customers buy from it again and again. Costs will be far higher and profits lower if each customer's purchase is a first-time sale. That's why we keep repeating this mantra: *It's much more profitable to retain an existing customer than to acquire a new one.* Figure 5.2-S illustrates the CLV calculation.

Figure 5.2-S | Calculate Customer Lifetime Value (CLV)

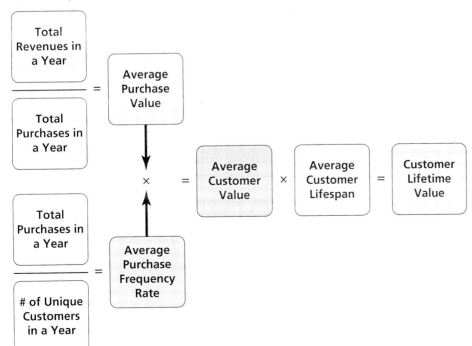

Figure 5.3-S | Calculate Marketing-Originated Customer Percentage

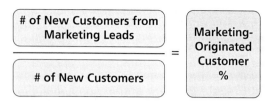

Percentage of Marketing-Originated Customers

This metric helps you to understand the impact of your marketing campaign efforts by showing what portion of your total customer acquisitions directly originated from marketing efforts. To compute, take all of your new customers in a given time period and look at what percentage of them started with a marketing-generated lead. A **marketing-generated lead** is a warm, inbound lead in which a potential customer comes to your company with an interest in your goods or services, resulting from your marketing efforts. This percentage may be as high as 80 percent for companies with primarily marketing-generated leads or as low as 10 percent for companies with primarily sales-generated leads, which are cold, outbound leads generated by people in the sales department.

marketing-generated lead
An inbound sales lead in which a potential customer contacts a company with an interest in their goods or services, resulting from their marketing efforts.

Conversion Rate

conversion rate
The number of sales leads converted into customers from various channels such as search marketing, personal selling, email marketing, and mobile marketing.

One of the primary goals of any CRM system is to make it easier for the sales team to convert marketing leads into paying customers. This is called a **conversion rate**, and as Figure 5.4-S illustrates, it represents the number of leads we turn into customers from various channels such as search marketing, personal selling, email marketing, and mobile marketing.

For example, if you had 100 new leads during the past year and 20 of those leads were converted to paying customers, the sales-to-lead conversion rate would be 20 percent.

Figure 5.4-S | Calculate Conversion Rate

There are a number of approaches available to help increase conversion rates, including lead nurturing (discussed earlier); setting up killer landing pages that attract, inform, and engage consumers; and connecting your CRM and marketing automation platform. Recall our prior discussion of Synduit—these are all approaches that have already been integrated into Synduit's automated sales process. No wonder Barry the automated salesperson is so effective!

Length of Sales Cycle

sales cycle
The series of events that takes place from the moment a salesperson first engages with a prospect up until the moment when the sale is made.

A **sales cycle** refers to the series of events that takes place from the moment a salesperson first engages with a prospect up until the moment when the sale is made. These elements are illustrated in Figure 5.5-S. If a prospect first talks with a firm's sales team in early June and then finally makes a purchase in early December, the sales cycle is approximately seven months.

Many sales processes can be very long, typically ranging from three to nine months, so finding ways to shorten them can be extremely valuable. In general, the more expensive the product or service and the more people involved in the decision process, the longer the sales cycle will be (Boeing's sales cycle for orders for new jets is multiple years!).

Although it's true a salesperson can't always control factors such as these, CRM software can help identify

Figure 5.5-S | The Sales Cycle

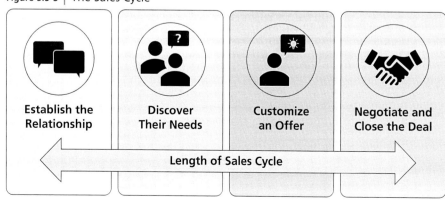

bottlenecks in the sales process and identify areas for improvement, leading to greater efficiency in a firm's sales process, which is advantageous since it means you sell more in less time!

Share of Wallet

As we emphasized earlier, an axiom in business is that it's always easier and less expensive to keep an existing customer than to get a new one. A share of customer wallet, or more frequently just **share of wallet**, is the percentage of that individual customer's purchase of a product over time that is the same brand. In Chapter 6 you'll learn about *customer loyalty*—share of wallet is closely related to customer loyalty. That is, loyalty should result in a higher share of wallet to a particular brand.

Referring to Figure 5.6-S, let's say that a consumer buys six pairs of shoes a year—two pairs from each of three different manufacturers. Assume that one shoemaker has a CRM system that allows it to send letters to its current customers inviting them to receive a special price discount or a gift if they buy more of the firm's shoes during the year. If the firm can get the consumer to buy three or four or perhaps all six pairs from it, it has increased its share of wallet. And that may not be too difficult because the customer already likes the firm's shoes. Without the CRM system, the shoe company would probably use traditional advertising to increase sales, which would be far costlier than the customer-only direct mail campaign. So the company can increase sales and profits at a much lower cost than it would spend to get one, two, or three new customers.

Great CRM systems develop loyal customers who are willing to forget about your competitors when it's time to part with their hard-earned cash (or rack up more credit card debt!).

Figure 5.6-S | Share of Wallet

$$\frac{\text{Amount Spent on Your Products}}{\text{Total Amount Spent on Category}} = \text{Share of Wallet}$$

share of wallet
The percentage of an individual customer's purchase of a product that is a single brand.

Customer Churn Rate

Despite best intentions and great marketing, sometimes it's just not in the cards to retain every customer! Hence, marketers track **customer churn rate**. Sometimes referred to as *customer churn* or the *rate of attrition*, the customer churn rate is the rate at which customers stop doing business with a company.

The customer churn rate KPI is crucial: Nearly 70 percent of customers who stop doing business with a company do so because they believe the company doesn't care about them! Thankfully, CRM and marketing automated systems are designed specifically to support a firm's capability to make customers feel wanted.

A super simple calculation of customer churn rate is the number of customers you lose in a time period divided by the number of customers you started with at the beginning of that period. This basic approach is a great starting point because it is easily understandable and easily comparable, and if needed, a deeper dive into customer churn might consider much more information, such as how customers are counted, the moment of churn, sample size, timeframe chosen, customer segments, seasonality, and other business-specific factors. Figure 5.7-S illustrates how to calculate basic customer churn rate.[63]

customer churn rate
The percentage of a company's customers (for a given span of time) who by the end of that time span can no longer be considered customers of the company (e.g., because they have cancelled their contract for a service or they have stopped shopping at the related retail location).

Figure 5.7-S | Customer Churn Rate

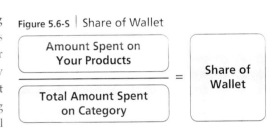

$$\frac{\text{\# of Customers Lost in Time Period}}{\text{\# of Customers at the Beginning of Time Period}} = \text{Customer Churn Rate}$$

Net Promoter Score

Customer satisfaction is one of the most important customer success metrics because it is associated with increasing sales. The **net promoter score (NPS)** is a quick and effective way to assess customer satisfaction—you've probably seen it in quick surveys you've taken after you buy something.

NPS simply asks customers, "How likely is it that you will recommend our products to your colleague or friend?" on a scale from 0 (not at all likely) to 10 (very likely). Referring to Figure 5.8-S, we then group respondents into one of three categories based on their answers. Customers who respond with a 9 or 10 are *promoters*—they are really pumped about what your business has done for them (and want to tell all their friends!). The customers who give an answer in the range of 7 or 8 are *passives*—they are satisfied with your business, but they aren't very excited about it (and warning: they're vulnerable to competitive offerings). Finally, those customers who score 6 or below are *detractors*—they are unhappy customers who can damage a brand with negative word-of-mouth (and they are likely to switch to competitors).

The NPS could be particularly useful in helping to identify specific customers who are to some degree displeased, so marketers can work hard to address these customer frustrations and hopefully ward off future bad reviews before they happen again. It's also a great tool to identify brand ambassadors who will communicate with and sell to other customers.

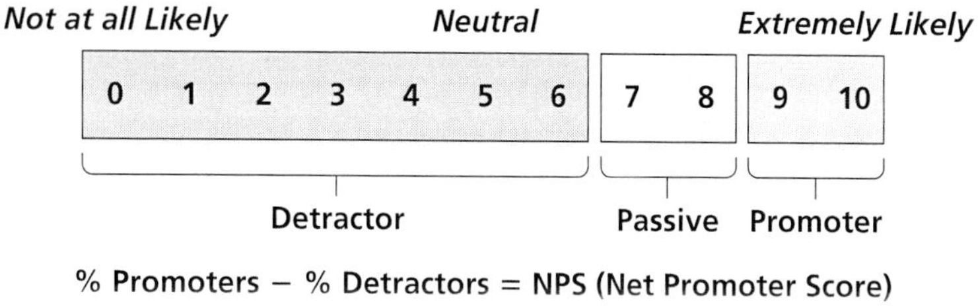

Let us share a word of caution about relying *exclusively* on NPS as a marker of success in customer relationships. Even though marketers frequently consider NPS among the most powerful metrics to develop strategies that increase sales and hopefully gain repeat purchase, it is important to keep in mind that NPS only tells you how customers feel about your business *at a specific moment*. That means this metric is not by its nature a dependable indicator of customer retention or customer churn because these involve repeated interactions with the company over time. And, importantly, in and of itself, it doesn't tell you *why* customers feel the way they do or what needs to change in order to grow your business. Thus, NPS is best used along with other relevant customer-related metrics.

Figure 5.8-S | New Promoter Score (NPS)

Not at all Likely   *Neutral*   *Extremely Likely*

| 0 | 1 | 2 | 3 | 4 | 5 | 6 | 7 | 8 | 9 | 10 |

Detractor   Passive   Promoter

% Promoters − % Detractors = NPS (Net Promoter Score)

Return on Experience

An overwhelming number of marketers have started to concentrate on how to enhance the experience of customers by more meaningfully engaging them and creating an omnichannel digital marketing approach (we will discuss this more in the next section of the chapter). Such an approach sparks the need for metrics related to **return on experience (ROX)** of the customer. An ROX approach helps companies measure the *real value of personalized customer experiences*.

ROX begins with mapping a customer's **purchase journey**, which is the process or roadmap a customer follows to become aware of, consider and evaluate, and decide to purchase a product or service. The key is to identify touchpoints and discover factors that impact customers the most. Then, focus turns to improving those experiences for a more positive business outcome. Unlike most of the metrics we have already discussed, ROX is not a single, universally applicable metric because the calculation of ROX will be unique for each company based on KPIs that are specific to that company, its product lines, and its unique customer relationship goals and strategies.

This means that calculating this metric can be a bit tricky, but it's definitely worth the effort. A fairly simple example should help illustrate how ROX could be calculated. Let's imagine you run a small, but successful app-based mobile delivery service to pick up and deliver food to students who live on campus, and you recently decided you want to improve the customer experience. Here's a step-by-step look at getting to the important ROX amount:

- The first step in calculating ROX is to determine the key elements of the customer's journey with you. Don't you imagine that delivery time is an important element here? So in order to reduce delivery times for your service, you decide to hire five additional delivery drivers to each work three days per week, which reduces the average delivery time by 20 percent. The shorter delivery time allows for an additional 20 orders per day to be delivered and reduces your cost per delivery from $3.00 to $2.25. Pretty nice so far, right?

- Guess what—customers really appreciated the shorter delivery time, which translates into an increase in the average purchase value from $7.25 to $9.50! Now we're talking some real money. Let's see if we can calculate the net value of benefits from your efforts to enhance this customer experience. Prior to hiring additional delivery drivers, the average number of orders delivered per day was 60. Thanks to the shorter delivery times, that number increased to 80.

- Based on the average cost of $3.00 per delivery, it would have cost you $240 to deliver 80 orders prior to hiring additional delivery drivers. However, with your newly reduced cost per delivery, it now only costs you $180 to deliver the same number of orders. That's a savings of $60 per day, which translates into $1,800 for the month ($60 per day × 30 days).

- And we're not done calculating the net value of benefits yet! Remember the average purchase value increased by $2.25. That translates into $180 in additional revenue per day ($2.25 × 80 deliveries) and an additional $5,400 per month ($180 × 30 days). If you add the amount you saved for the month ($1,800) to the amount of additional revenue you generated during the month, you determine that your net value of benefits is $7,200 for the first month.

- And how much was spent to accomplish those savings? Each new driver worked 18 hours per week for four weeks and received $10 per hour, making your one-month total investment $3,600. Now that we have calculated your benefits and costs, we can figure out your return on experience: $7,200/$3,600 × 100 = 200 percent ROX. Way to go—it looks like hiring additional drivers was worth the investment!

Figure 5.9-S illustrates the basic concept of ROX.

Figure 5.9-S | Return on Experience

$$\frac{\text{Net Value of Benefits}}{\text{Cost of Investment}} \times 100 = \text{Return on Experience}$$

Key Terms

customer acquisition cost (CAC)
customer lifetime value (CLV)
marketing-generated lead
conversion rate
sales cycle
share of wallet
customer churn rate
net promoter score (NPS)
return on experience (ROX)
purchase journey

6 Understand Consumer and Business Markets

Dondeena Bradley

Meet Dondeena Bradley
▼ A Decision Maker at WW International, Inc.

Dondeena Bradley is an innovation strategist, health and well-being expert, and a visionary in the area of health innovation. At the time of this case study, Dondeena led global innovation at WW International. Prior to WW, she was at PepsiCo, serving as Vice President, Nutrition Ventures, and Vice President, Nutrition R&D. Her previous food and nutrition experience includes Johnson & Johnson, Campbell's Soup, and Mars, International. Her education includes a Doctor of Philosophy, Food Science, from Ohio State University, a Master of Science from Purdue University, and a Bachelor of Science from Anderson University.

Dondeena's Info

What I do when I'm not working:
Reading, sketching, and live music

First job out of school:
Research Scientist, Mars, International

Business book I'm reading now:
SuperBetter by Jane McGonigal

My management style:
Collaborative, co-creative, and emergent

My pet peeve:
People talking over each other

Here's my problem...

Real **People**, Real **Choices**

In the early 1960s, WW founder Jean Nidetch began inviting friends into her Queens, New York, living room once a week to talk about their lives and how to stay on their diets. Today, that group of friends has grown to millions of women and men around the world who have joined WW to lose weight and lead healthier lives.

More than 50 years after WW was founded, the need for this kind of support has never been greater. Two out of three American adults are overweight, and one-third are obese. We spend more than $60 billion per year on weight-loss solutions, ranging from diet drinks and gym memberships to programs like WW and competitors like Jenny Craig and Nutrisystem.[1] Healthcare providers and employers are grappling with the best way to address this costly epidemic. And losing weight continues to be a top priority for many consumers.

Yet there has been a shift in how people think about weight loss. Today's consumers don't want dieting, deprivation, and restriction; they want a more holistic and personalized solution that integrates healthier eating, fitness, and emotional well-being. They are also looking for success to be measured by more than just the number on the scale.

In an age of infinite options and choices, it is getting harder to get people to "join" or commit to a single program. Many people opt for a "do-it-yourself" approach using smartphones, apps, and trackers as well as customized diets and exercise regimens that fit their preferences and needs. Many consumers say they don't want a one-size-fits-all approach like WW International, and that they aren't all that interested in carving out time for weekly meetings that don't seem current.

In January 2016, in response to this changing landscape, WW launched a new "Beyond the Scale" program that takes a more personalized approach based on each member's unique lifestyle, goals, and challenges. After an initial assessment, each member receives a custom program that includes daily and weekly SmartPoints targets (to encourage them to eat better), a personalized activity goal (to nudge them to move more), and education and inspiration tailored to their unique situation.

Members can choose to participate in the program online, in person, or both. A typical member's experience consists of attending weekly meetings, each lasting about 45 minutes, at a WW location where an inspiring leader who has been successful using the program supports the member group in achieving their stated weight-loss goals.

Whether a member engages online or in person, the challenge for WW is to find relevant ways to help them stay motivated, inspired, and positive week after week—because the weight-loss journey is typically a long haul, and clinical evidence shows that happier people tend to make healthier choices.

As leader of the global innovation team, Dondeena's job was to focus on transforming the WW face-to-face business. Her challenge was to modernize the experience for today's busy, "always on" consumer and to appeal to more people than the segment of age 50+ women that make up WW's core customer base.

Dondeena's team also was asked to address the seasonal/cyclical nature of a business that starts strong at the beginning of the year and typically goes downhill from there. The fact is, after a big marketing and membership "burst" in January when new year / new me resolutions are at a peak, engagement and attendance at WW begins to decline significantly throughout the year—as people lose motivation, their commitment wanes, and it gets harder to stay on track.

There's no doubt that people still want the benefits that WW delivers, but Dondeena had to think hard about new ways for the company to show up and deliver its services given the realities of consumer behavior today.

Dondeena considered her **options** 1·2·3

Option 1

Make the weekly meetings more productive and entertaining. Mix them up with lectures by lifestyle experts, and offer classes in yoga, Pilates, and other forms of exercise to provide a "one-stop shopping" experience for attendees. These offerings would be attractive to busy people who want to maximize their "bang for the buck" when they allocate time to weight loss. They would also sync nicely with the broader consumer trend of a heightened interest in wellness that continues to spread through the mainstream U.S. population. On the other hand, these activities would dilute the core WW experience, which is unique because it emphasizes group support and provides a forum for people to share their anxieties and frustrations when they try to lose weight. In addition, WW had no expertise in these areas, so becoming a broader lifestyle-oriented company would be a departure from the company's strategic mission. Plus, it would require a massive amount of training for the company's field of 10,000+ meeting leaders and service providers.

Option 2

Design an immersive well-being event that would debunk and shift current assumptions about WW International (dated, diet-focused, boring) and give participants a contemporary, compelling, life-changing experience. This event would be unique and unexpected enough to energize current members, re-engage those who have left, and entice individuals who have never considered WW before. It would capitalize on trends of people increasingly paying for "experiences" that range from 45-minute group cycling classes at Soul Cycle to four-day Wanderlust retreats at a Hawaiian resort, featuring yoga, meditation, chefs, and performers. The event would generate a lot of word of mouth (a critical driver to the WW business), and Dondeena's team could use feedback on the first one to modify subsequent events and determine whether this plan is feasible. On the other hand, a large dramatic event would be a far stretch from the traditional WW model. It might alienate core members who expect WW to be focused on food, not holistic practices and approaches. It would also require a lot of resources to plan and execute a novel experience like this from scratch.

Option 3

Organize a transformative event, but partner with an existing organization like Wanderlust to leverage their experience and infrastructure. Instead of trying to reinvent the wheel, WW could move quickly to market with a proven business model and a competent cosponsor that knows how to stage a complicated event for hundreds or thousands of people. On the other hand, a partner wouldn't be as familiar with the needs of the weight-loss community, so the experience might not be as authentic for WW's customers. In addition, even if the event were successful, WW International would not "own" it, so the value to the company's ongoing program might be hard to assess.

Now, put yourself in Dondeena's shoes. Which option would you choose, and why?

You Choose

Which **Option** would you choose, and **why**?

☐ Option 1   ☐ Option 2   ☐ Option 3

6.1 The Consumer Decision-Making Process

OBJECTIVE

Define *consumer behavior*, and explain the purchase decision-making process.

Compelling new products, clever packaging, and creative advertising surround us, clamoring for our attention—and our money. And that's not all—the Internet allows us to shop on our mobile phones and tablets 24/7 from any location, it provides information on a gazillion different products from just about as many sellers, and it gives us product and seller reviews by other consumers.

But consumers don't all respond in the same way. Each of us is unique, with our own reasons to choose one product over another. Remember: The focus of the marketing concept is to satisfy consumers' wants and needs. To accomplish that crucial goal, we first need to appreciate what those wants and needs are. What causes one consumer to step into an International House of Pancakes for an order of IHOP Rooty Tooty Fresh 'N Fruity® Pancakes, whereas another opts for a quick Starbucks latte and Danish, and a third will only eat a healthy serving of "natural" Kashi cereal and fruit? And what, other than income, will cause one consumer to buy that box of Kashi cereal only when it's "on deal" while her neighbor never even looks at the price?

consumer behavior
The process involved when individuals or groups select, purchase, use, and dispose of goods, services, ideas, or experiences to satisfy their needs and desires.

Consumer behavior is the process individuals or groups go through to select, purchase, use, and dispose of goods, services, ideas, or experiences to satisfy their needs and desires. Marketers recognize that consumer decision making is an ongoing process; it's much more than what happens the moment a consumer forks over the cash and in turn receives a good or service.

Let's go back to the shoppers who want to buy a box of dry cereal. Although this may seem like a simple purchase, in reality, there are quite a few steps in the process that cereal marketers need to understand. The first decision in the purchasing process is where to buy your cereal. If you eat a lot of it, you may choose to make a special trip to a warehouse-type retailer that sells super-duper-sized boxes rather than just picking up a box while you're at the local supermarket. If you want to choose from healthier organic alternatives, you may browse for cereal at Whole Foods or a local food co-op. If you are one of those people who hates to waste money, you may go to a *limited assortment supermarket*, also referred to as an *extreme value food retailer*, such as Aldi or Lidl. Of course, if you get a craving for cereal in the middle of the night, you may dash to the local convenience store. Then, what type of cereal do you buy? Do you eat only low-fat, high-fiber bran cereals, or do you go for the sugar-coated varieties with marshmallows? Of course, you may also like to have a variety of cereals available so you can mix and match.

Marketers also need to know how and when you consume their products. Do you eat cereal only for breakfast, or do you snack on it while you sit in front of the TV at night? Do you eat certain kinds of cereal only at certain times (like sugary kids' cereals that serve as comfort food when you pull an all-nighter)? What about storing the product (if it lasts that long)? Do you have a kitchen pantry where you can store the supersized box, or is space an issue?

And there's more. Marketers also need to understand the many factors that influence each of these steps in the consumer behavior process—internal factors unique to each of us, situational factors at the time of purchase, and the social influences of people around us. In this chapter, we'll talk about how all these factors influence how and why consumers do what they do. But first we'll look at the types of decisions consumers make and the steps in the decision-making process.

Not All Decisions Are the Same

Old-school researchers assumed that consumers carefully collect information about competing products, determine which products possess the characteristics or product attributes important to their needs, weigh the pluses and minuses of each alternative, and arrive at a

Figure 6.1 *Snapshot* │ The Consumer Decision-Making Continuum

Decisions characterized as extensive problem solving versus habitual decision making differ in a number of ways.

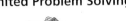

Habitual Decision Making	Limited Problem Solving	Extensive Problem Solving

Level of Involvement
Low	Moderate	High

Risk
Low	Low to Moderate	High

Information Search
Respond to environmental cues	Moderate search	Extensive search and careful processing

Marketing Actions
Provide environmental cues at point-of-purchase, such as product displays		Provide information via advertising salespeople, websites, social media, etc. Educate consumers on product benefits, risks of wrong decisions, etc.

satisfactory decision. But how accurate is this picture of the decision-making process? Is this the way *you* buy cereal?

Although it does seem that people take these steps when they make an important purchase, such as a new car, is it realistic to assume that they do this for *everything* they buy, like that box of cereal? Today, we realize that decision makers actually employ a set of approaches that range from painstaking analysis to pure whim, depending on the importance of what they are buying and how much effort they choose to put into the decision.[2] As we see in Figure 6.1, researchers think in terms of an "effort" continuum that is anchored on one end by *habitual decision making*, such as deciding to purchase a box of cereal, and at the other end by *extensive problem solving*, such as deciding to purchase a new car.

When consumers engage in extensive problem solving, they do indeed carefully go through the steps Figure 6.2 outlines: problem recognition, information search, evaluation of alternatives, product choice, and postpurchase evaluation.

When we make habitual decisions, however, we make little or no conscious effort. Rather, the search for information and the comparison of alternatives may occur almost instantaneously, as we recall what we have done in the past and the satisfaction we received. You may, for example, simply throw the same brand of cereal in your shopping cart week after week without thinking about it too much. Many decisions fall somewhere in the middle and are characterized by *limited problem solving*, which means that we do *some* work to make decisions but not a great deal. This is probably how you decide on a new pair of running shoes or a cool new case for your smartphone. Just how much effort do we put into our buying decisions? The answer depends on our level of **involvement**—how important we perceive the consequences of the purchase to be.

Figure 6.1 shows the decision-process continuum and some of the differences between extensive problem solving, limited problem solving, and habitual decision making. Of course, habitual decision making, limited problem solving, and extensive problem solving are not discrete categories. Rather, we think of our product purchases as being on a continuum on which each purchase we make is at a slightly different point.

As a rule, we are more involved in the decision-making process for products when we think the decision may be risky in some way. **Perceived risk** may be present if the product is expensive or complex and hard to understand, such as a new computer or a sports car.

involvement
The relative importance of perceived consequences of the purchase to a consumer.

perceived risk
The belief that choice of a product has potentially negative consequences, whether financial, physical, or social.

Figure 6.2 *Process* | The Consumer Decision-Making Process

The consumer decision-making process involves a series of five steps.

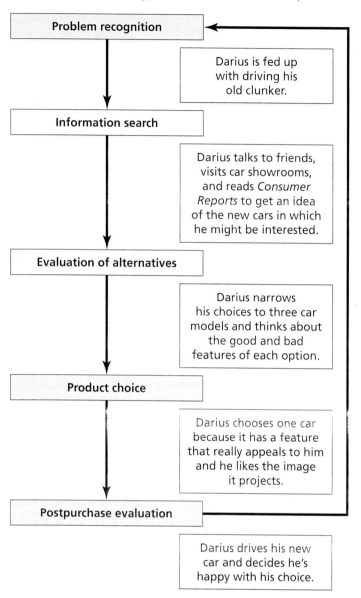

Perceived risk also can play a role when we think that making a bad choice will result in embarrassment or social rejection. For example, a young woman might decide against purchasing a nice-looking and functional Nine West purse from Kohl's for fear that she might be teased or ridiculed by her sorority sisters who all sport trendy Coach handbags. Perceived risk may also be higher if the consumer has little or no knowledge or experience in the product category and/or when there is little information available to help in the decision-making process.

When perceived risk is low—such as when we buy a box of cereal—we experience a low amount of involvement in the decision-making process. In these cases, we're not overly concerned about which option we choose because it is not especially important or risky. The worst-case scenario is that you don't like the taste and pawn off the box on your unsuspecting roommate! In *low-involvement* situations, the consumer's decision is often a response to environmental cues, such as when you decide to try a new type of cereal because the grocery store prominently displays it at the end of the aisle, known as an *end cap*. Under these circumstances, managers must concentrate on how a store displays products at the time of purchase to influence the decision maker.

For *high-involvement* purchases, such as when we buy a house or a car, we are more likely to carefully process all the available information and to have thought about the decision well before we buy the item. The consequences of the purchase are important and risky, especially because a bad decision may result in significant financial losses, aggravation, or social embarrassment. Most of us would not just saunter into an auto dealer's office at lunchtime and casually plunk down a deposit on a new Tesla Roadster. For high-involvement products, managers must start to reduce perceived risk by educating the consumer about why their product is the best choice well in advance of the time that the person is ready to make a decision.

To understand each of the steps in the decision-making process, we'll follow the fortunes of a consumer named Darius, who, as Figure 6.2 shows, is in the market for a new ride—a highly involved purchase decision, to say the least.

Step 1: Problem Recognition

problem recognition
The process that occurs whenever the consumer sees a significant difference between his or her current state of affairs and some desired or ideal state; this recognition initiates the decision-making process.

Problem recognition occurs whenever a consumer sees a significant difference between his or her current state of affairs and some desired or ideal state. This can occur in either of two ways: when the current state changes or when the desired state changes. A woman whose 10-year-old Hyundai has recently spent lots of time at the mechanic's shop recognizes that she has a problem; her car no longer meets her ideal state of providing her with reliable transportation. A man who sees his buddies getting admiring stares in their "cool" cars while he gets laughs for his old clunker also recognizes he has a problem; his current state has not changed but his ideal state necessitates the purchase of a new car. Problem recognition is also why clothing and home décor designers create new styles in new colors every few years. They hope consumers will suddenly realize that they must have new clothes and totally redecorate their apartment or risk social disapproval. The pandemic, for example, made many consumers realize that they suddenly needed all sorts of hygienic products, like sanitary wipes—or even a closetful of toilet paper. In the case of buying a car, this is an even bigger challenge now that the pandemic has caused many more people to buy online or by appointment, rather than just dropping into dealerships as they used to do. To counter such concerns, online auto dealers offer free no-touch delivery and a week to decide to return the vehicle if they are not satisfied.[3]

Do marketing decisions have a role in consumers' problem recognition? Although most problem recognition occurs spontaneously or when a true need arises, marketers often develop creative advertising messages that stimulate consumers to recognize that their current state (that old car) just doesn't equal their desired state (a shiny new convertible). Figure 6.3 provides examples of marketers' responses to consumers' problem recognition and the other steps in the consumer decision-making process.

Step 2: Information Search

Once Darius recognizes his problem—he wants a newer car—he needs adequate information to resolve it. **Information search** is the step of the decision-making process in which the consumer checks their memory and surveys the environment to identify what options might solve their problem. Advertisements on TV, information we "google" on the Internet, and videos on YouTube, for example, often provide valuable guidance during this step. Darius might rely on recommendations from his friends, Facebook groups for drivers, information he finds at www.caranddriver.com, brochures from car dealerships, or the manufacturers' websites. We'll talk more about opportunities for consumers to gather information in the digital world in Chapter 14.

> **information search**
> The process whereby a consumer searches for appropriate information to make a reasonable decision.

The information search step includes discovering what alternatives are available and which meet our personal needs. We call the alternatives a consumer knows about the **evoked set** and the ones he or she seriously considers the **consideration set**. If a brand isn't in the consumer's evoked set, there's pretty much zero chance of purchase. That's why marketers know it's important for consumers to be exposed to messages about their brand frequently, thus ensuring a place in the consumers' evoked set.

> **evoked set**
> All of the alternative brands a consumer is aware of when making a decision.

> **consideration set**
> The alternative brands a consumer seriously considers when making a decision.

Increasingly, consumers use the Internet to search for information about products. Search engines, such as Google (www.google.com) and Bing (www.bing.com), help consumers locate useful information as they search millions of web pages for key words and return a list of millions of sites that contain those key words. We'll talk more about marketing and search engines in Chapter 13.

Comparison-shopping agents (shopbots), such as Bizrate.com or Pricegrabber.com, are web applications that can help online shoppers find what they are looking for at the lowest price. In addition to listing where a product is available and the price, these sites often provide customer reviews and ratings of the product and the sellers. They enable consumers to view both positive and negative feedback about the product and the online retailer from other consumers. It is estimated that more than 10 million consumers check shopbots before placing an order online. Other very popular shopbots include Google Shopping, Yahoo Shopping, CamelCamelCamel, and Pronto.[4]

> **comparison-shopping agents (shopbots)**
> Web applications that help online shoppers find what they are looking for at the lowest price and provide customer reviews and ratings of products and sellers.

Increasingly, consumers also search out other consumers' opinions and experiences through networking websites such as YouTube and Facebook. We'll talk more about these sites and others similar to them later in the chapter. Shopbots are so popular with consumers that new services have sprung up all over the world. Pricena, launched in the United Arab Emirates, is now helping shoppers find deals in Egypt, Saudi Arabia, and Kuwait.[5] In the U.S., there are several site-specific shopbots that search the vast array of products on sites like eBay and Craigslist. Shopbots also provide a great way for marketers to compare their prices to those of their competitors and to adjust their prices to be more competitive.

Figure 6.3 *Process* | Responses to Decision Process Stages

Understanding the consumer decision process means marketers can develop strategies to help move the consumer from recognizing a need to being a satisfied customer.

Stage in the Decision Process	Marketing Strategy	Example
Problem recognition	Encourage consumers to see that existing state does not equal desired state	• Create TV commercials showing the excitement of owning a new car
Information search	Provide information when and where consumers are likely to search	• Target marketing communications with traditional and digital media to media vehicles and Internet sites with high target-market viewership • Provide sales training that ensures knowledgeable salespeople • Make new-car brochures available in dealer showrooms • Design exciting, easy-to-navigate, and informative websites • Provide information on blogs and social networks to encourage word-of-mouth strategies • Use search marketing to ensure that your website has preferential search engine positioning • Participate in consumer review/advisory websites such as tripadvisor.com
Evaluation of alternatives	Understand the criteria consumers use in comparing brands and communicate own brand superiority	• Conduct research to identify most important evaluative criteria • Create advertising and other marketing communications that include reliable data on superiority of a brand (e.g., miles per gallon, safety, comfort)
Product choice	Understand choice heuristics used by consumers and provide communication that encourages brand decision	• Advertise "Made in America" (country of origin) • Stress long history of the brand (brand loyalty)
Postpurchase evaluation	Encourage accurate consumer expectations	• Provide honest messages in all marketing communications and sales presentations

Step 3: Evaluation of Alternatives

Once Darius identifies his options, it's time to decide on a few true contenders. There are two components to this stage of the decision-making process. First, a consumer armed with information identifies a small number of products in which he or she is interested. Then, he or she focuses on **determinant attributes**, the features most important to differentiate and compare among the product choices. In reality, consumers' search for information and evaluation of alternatives occur simultaneously. As consumers gather information about different brands in a product category, it would be impossible not to do some evaluation of the brands, leaving some in their consideration set while not including others. Darius has always wanted a red Ferrari. But after he allows himself to daydream for a few minutes, he returns to reality and reluctantly admits that an Italian sports car is probably not in the cards for him right now. He decides that the cars he likes—and can actually afford—are the Nissan Versa, the Mazda3 hatchback, the Chevrolet Sonic, and the Honda Fit. He narrows down his options as he considers only affordable cars that come to mind or that his Facebook friends suggest.

Now it's decision time. Darius has to look more systematically at each of the four possibilities and identify the important product characteristics, what marketers refer to as **evaluative criteria**, he will use to decide among them. The characteristics may be power, comfort, price, the style of the car, and, yes, even safety. Keep in mind that marketers often play a role in educating consumers about which product characteristics they should use as evaluative criteria—usually they will "conveniently" emphasize the dimensions on which their product excels.

Atkins Nutritionals, Inc., was founded by Dr. Robert Atkins, author of the best seller about low-carb dieting, *Dr. Atkins' Diet Revolution*. For decades, the medical profession argued that low-fat diets were healthy and Atkins diets were not. It was not until about 15 years ago that research—demonstrating that the low-fat, low-carb Atkins diet was superior for everyone, not just for dieters—changed the minds of the medical community. Today, consumers, even those who are not trying to lose weight, strive for a healthy lifestyle, which means a low-carb, low-fat, high-protein diet. To address the changing health values for those consumers, Atkins promotes its products as part of a healthy lifestyle for everyone, whether you want to lose weight or not.[6]

To make sure customers like Darius come to the "right" conclusions in their evaluation of the alternatives, marketers must understand which criteria consumers use and which they believe are more and less important. With this information, sales and advertising professionals can point out a brand's superiority on the most important criteria as *they* have defined them.

Step 4: Product Choice

When Darius examines his alternatives and takes a few test drives, it's time to "put the pedal to the metal." Deciding on one product and acting on this choice is the next step in the decision-making process. After agonizing over his choice for a few weeks, Darius decides that even though the Nissan Versa and the Honda Fit both have attractive qualities, the Fit offers the affordability he needs, and its carefree image reflects how he wants to be perceived by others. All this thinking about cars is *driving* him crazy, and he's relieved to make a decision to buy the Fit and get on with his life.

So just how do consumers like Darius choose among the alternatives they consider? These decisions often are complicated because it's hard to juggle all the product characteristics in your head. One car may offer better gas mileage, another is $2,000 cheaper, whereas another boasts a better safety record. How do we make sense of all these qualities and arrive at a decision?

For extended problem-solving decisions, we often consider all of the characteristics and the relative importance to us of each one. This type of decision uses **compensatory decision rules** that allow information about attributes of competing products to be

determinant attributes
The features most important to differentiate and compare among the product choices.

evaluative criteria
The dimensions consumers use to compare competing product alternatives.

compensatory decision rules
The methods for making decisions that allow information about attributes of competing products to be averaged in some way.

averaged in some way. The poor standing of one attribute can potentially be offset by the good standing of another. For example, Darius may find one car has a better fuel efficiency record, while a second has better styling. Darius might choose the better looking one because the coolness factor compensates for the lower fuel efficiency.

Realistically, there are only so many times we exert this much "cognitive sweat" when we make decisions—life is too short! Many times, we rely upon simple rules of thumb, or heuristics, instead of painstakingly learning all the ins and outs of every product alternative. These **heuristics** provide consumers with shortcuts that simplify the decision-making process. One such heuristic is price = quality; many people willingly buy the more expensive brand because they assume that if it costs more, it must be better (even though this isn't always true). Does this mean that consumers who use this heuristic are not good decision makers? Not at all. Most consumers have bought a very low-priced box of cereal, a new pair of running shoes, or a bottle of shampoo, only to be disappointed with the product's performance. In other words, many times it's actually a smart move to use a heuristic that is based on our prior experience.

Perhaps the most common heuristic is **brand loyalty**; this occurs when we consciously choose to buy the same brand over and over. As you might guess, brand loyalty is the Holy Grail for marketers. People form preferences for a favorite brand and then may never change their minds in the course of a lifetime, making it extremely difficult for rivals to persuade them to switch.

Still another heuristic is based on *country of origin*. We assume that a product has certain characteristics if it comes from a certain country. In the car category, many people associate German cars with fine engineering and Swedish cars with safety. Darius assumed that the Japanese Honda Fit would be more dependable than the Kia or the Chevrolet, so he factored that into his decision.

Step 5: Postpurchase Evaluation

In the last step of the decision-making process, the consumer evaluates just how good a choice he or she made. Everyone has experienced regret after making a purchase ("What was I *thinking*?"), and (hopefully!) we have all been pleased with something we've bought. The evaluation of the product results in a level of **consumer satisfaction/dissatisfaction**. This refers to the overall feelings, or attitude, a person has about a product after he or she purchases it.

Just how do we decide if we're satisfied with what we bought? When we buy a product, we have some *expectations* of product quality. How well a product or service meets or exceeds these expectations determines customer satisfaction. In other words, we tend to assess product quality by comparing what we have bought to a preexisting performance standard.

Think about the customer who finds his new car gets 25 mpg. If his expectation is the same 25 mpg, he will be satisfied; if his expectation is 20 mpg, he will be extremely satisfied; but if, based on the information he received before he purchased the vehicle, he expects to get 30 mpg, he will be dissatisfied.

We form our product expectations via a mixture of information from marketing communications, informal information sources such as friends and family, and our own prior experience with the product category. That's why it's important that marketers *manage expectations* of their product through advertising and other communications. One moral: To prevent or diminish consumers experiencing buyer's remorse, don't overpromise! No product is perfect, so don't claim that yours is. Holiday Inn motels found that out the hard way: At one point the chain's slogan was, "No surprises." Inevitably, some guests were surprised (and not in a good way), so the line had to be scrapped.

Even when a product performs up to expectations, consumers may experience regret, or **buyer's remorse**, after they make a purchase. When we reject product alternatives with attractive features, we may second-guess our decision. Darius, for example, might begin to think, "Maybe I should have chosen the Mazda3—Mazda makes great cars and the hatchback would be so cool for hauling all my things around." To generate satisfied customers

heuristics
A mental rule of thumb that leads to a speedy decision by simplifying the process.

brand loyalty
A pattern of repeat product purchases, accompanied by an underlying positive attitude toward the brand, based on the belief that the brand makes products superior to those of its competition.

consumer satisfaction/dissatisfaction
The overall feelings or attitude a person has about a product after purchasing it.

buyer's remorse
The anxiety or regret a consumer may feel after choosing from among several similar attractive choices.

and (hopefully) avoid buyer's remorse, marketers often seek to reinforce purchases through follow-up communications with the customer after the sale.

The Hive Mind: Consumer Decision Making in the Digital Age

What we have just described is the traditional model of consumer decision making. Google refers to the moment when the consumer decides to make a purchase as **ZMOT**, short for *zero moment of truth*. Today, ZMOT occurs on mobile phones, laptops, and any other type of wired device. ZMOT is just as, if not more, likely to occur at home, in the car, at work, or in the gym as it is in a store.

Consumers have also changed *how* they make decisions. Today, consumers are far more likely to spend hours seeking information, even for small purchases. The "always on" consumers make decisions collectively by seeking advice from their social networks. And, of course, the traditional steps in the consumer decision-making process are changing as well. Here are some ways they are changing:

- Problem recognition is likely to occur collectively as consumers continuously search Google and ask, "How can I know what I want until I read what other people say?"
- Information search is big business as companies spend almost $40 billion per year on search engine advertising. Still, the consumer looking for the perfect pair of jeans is more likely to check out teenage fashion blogs, such as *Style Rookie* and *Tolly Dolly Posh*. Want ideas for a new cool bedroom makeover or an over-the-top pair of sunglasses? Image banks such as Pinterest offer hundreds, if not thousands, of visuals.
- Evaluation of alternatives presents another challenge: We have too many choices, which is referred to by researchers as **hyperchoice**. Studies show that consumers actually make poorer decisions and feel more frustrated when they have a lot of choices than when they have only a few.
- When it comes to product choice, many consumers make purchases online and on their phone without ever entering a brick-and-mortar store. Brick-and-mortar retailers bemoan the fact that some consumers visit retail stores to see, touch, feel, and even get advice on a product before making the actual purchase online for a cheaper price.
- During much of the first half of 2020, the COVID-19 pandemic caused consumers worldwide to quarantine themselves at home. Brick-and-mortar consumer sales plummeted while online sales grew. A number of large retailers were forced to file for bankruptcy, including JCPenney, Neiman Marcus, and JCrew.[7]
- In April 2020, U.S. retail sales fell 16.4 percent while manufacturing output fell 13.7 percent, both records. In contrast, the sales of online retailers, such as Amazon.com, grew 8.4 percent. Overall retail spending declined 20 percent in April 2020 compared to April 2019. Clothing store sales declined 90 percent while sales at department stores, bars, restaurants, and sporting goods stores were cut in half. Many questioned what the impact of this would be on brick-and-mortar retailing in the future.[8]
- In the traditional decision-making process, postpurchase evaluation involved consumers getting confirmation of their good purchase decision via compliments from others. Today, social media provides constant feedback as consumers post everything from selfies at concerts to photos of what's on their plate, popularly called **food porn**.

Changes in Consumer Decision Making: Welcome to AI

As we discussed in Chapter 5, *artificial intelligence (AI)* is rapidly moving forward in its influence on both consumer and B2B behavior. AI in the simplest terms is intelligence demonstrated by machines rather than the natural intelligence of humans. AI enables computer systems to perform such tasks as visual perception, speech recognition, decision making, and language translation.

ZMOT
Google's term for the *zero moment of truth* when the consumer decides to make a purchase, often on a smartphone, tablet, or laptop.

hyperchoice
A term used to describe the condition in which consumers have too many choices, leading them to make poorer decisions and experience greater frustration.

food porn
Social media posts featuring consumers' photos of their meals.

AI has the possibility to change the behavior of consumers and marketers.[9]

- For consumers, AI is already in many parts of our lives. iPhone's Siri and Amazon's Alexa, for example, follow our requests because of AI.

- Ride sharing services Lyft and Uber are only possible because of AI and machine learning. AI figures out the price of the fare, the estimated arrival time, and the route the ride will take. Lyft and Uber anticipate their fares will drop when they move to using driverless or autonomous cars. This will be possible because of the same AI and machine learning.[10]

- For marketers, AI can generate advertising messages that are customized to individual customers based on their preferences.

- **Chatbots** are computer programs that use either voice or text to allow consumers to talk with a computer through the use of AI. Chatbots use natural language processing and artificial intelligence to understand what a customer or client needs. AI chatbots learn as they go and become smarter with more interactions. Rated as one of the best chatbots, the World Health Organization's Health Alert bot helps people protect themselves from infections, provides consumers with travel advice, and, during the coronavirus pandemic, worked to dispel the false information that spread around the globe.[11] While marketers are hoping that they will soon sound like real people, there is no evidence that consumers care so long as they get accurate information.

- Email marketing (the sort that is approved by consumers) is one of the most effective forms of marketing today. AI can create personalized emails to individual customers based on their previous purchases, what brands they have searched or purchased, and what pages they spend the most time on. Sixty-one percent of consumers enjoy their weekly or daily promo emails, which probably explains why email marketing results in more sales than social media and search combined.

In a study, business students wrote complaint letters to companies. The companies responded with a free sample, a letter of apology, or no response at all. When the company sent a free sample, attitudes toward the company improved significantly; when the company sent a letter of apology, there was no change in attitude; and when the company did not respond, the attitude was more negative than before.[12]

In addition to understanding the mechanics of the consumer decision-making process, marketers need to understand what influences in consumers' lives affect this process. As we see in Figure 6.4, there are three main influences in the decision-making process: internal, situational, and social influences. All of these factors work together to affect the ultimate choice each person makes.

chatbots
A computer program that uses either voice or text to allow consumers to talk with the computer's AI capability.

Figure 6.4 *Process* | Influences on Consumer Decision Making

A number of different factors in consumers' lives influence the consumer decision-making process. Marketers need to understand these internal and external influences and which ones are important in the purchase process.

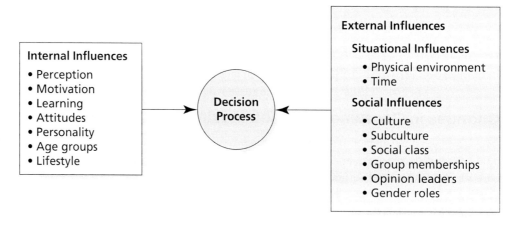

6.2 Internal Influences on Consumers' Decisions

OBJECTIVE

Explain how internal factors influence consumers' decision-making processes.

What is your dream car? It may be a sporty Ferrari. However, your roommate dreams of a tricked-out Mustang, and your dad is set on owning a cool new Tesla Roadster. As the saying goes, "That's why they make chocolate and vanilla." We can attribute much of these differences to internal influences on consumer behavior—those things that cause each of us to interpret information about the outside world, including which car is the best, differently from one another.

Perception

Perception is the process by which people select, organize, and interpret information from the outside world. We receive information in the form of sensations. As you can see in Figure 6.5, our sensory receptors—eyes, ears, nose, mouth, and skin—have immediate responses to sights, sounds, smells, tastes, and textures. We try to make sense of the sensations we receive as we interpret them in light of our past experiences.

We are bombarded with information about products—thousands of ads both on- and off-line, in-store displays, special offers, our friends' opinions posted on Facebook, and on and on. The perception process has important implications for marketers: As we absorb and make sense of the vast quantities of information that compete for our attention, the odds are good that any single message will get lost in the clutter. And, if we do notice the message, there's no guarantee that the meaning we give it will be the same one the marketer intended. To improve the likelihood that a consumer will notice and make sense of a message correctly, marketers need to understand the three steps that occur during this process: *exposure*, *attention*, and *interpretation*.

perception
The process by which people select, organize, and interpret information from the outside world.

Exposure

The stimulus must be within range of people's sensory receptors to be noticed; in other words, people must be physically able to see, hear, taste, smell, or feel the stimulus. For example, the lettering on a highway billboard must be big enough for a passing motorist to read easily, or the message will be lost. **Exposure** is the extent to which a person's sensory receptors are capable of registering a stimulus.

Marketers work hard to achieve exposure for their products, but sometimes it's just a matter of making sure that cool people use your product—and that others observe them doing so.

Many people believe that even messages they *can't* see will persuade them to buy advertised products. Claims of **subliminal advertising** messages being hidden in ice cubes or baked into the tops of crackers have been surfacing since the 1950s. A survey of American consumers found that almost two-thirds believe in the existence of subliminal advertising, and more than one-half are convinced that this technique can get them to buy things they don't really want.[13]

exposure
The extent to which a person's sensory receptors are capable of registering a stimulus.

subliminal advertising
Supposedly hidden messages in marketers' communications.

Figure 6.5 *Process* | An Overview of the Perceptual Process Sensory Stimuli

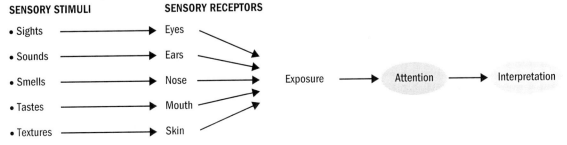

There is not much evidence to support the argument that this technique actually has any effect at all on our perceptions of products, and even less that marketers are or ever have used subliminal advertising methods. But still, concerns persist. ABC once rejected a commercial for KFC that invites viewers to slowly replay the ad to find a secret message, citing the network's long-standing policy against subliminal advertising. The ad (which other networks aired) is a seemingly ordinary pitch for KFC's $0.99 Buffalo Snacker chicken sandwich. But if you replay it slowly on a digital video recorder, it tells you that viewers can visit KFC's website to receive a coupon for a free sandwich. Ironically, this technique is really the *opposite* of subliminal advertising because instead of secretly placing words or images in the ad, KFC blatantly publicized its campaign by informing viewers that it contains a message and how to find it.[14] The short story: Hidden messages are intriguing and fun to think about (if a little scary), but they don't really work. Sorry for the letdown—and don't bother trying to read this paragraph backward.

Attention

attention
The extent to which a person devotes mental processing to a particular stimulus.

As you drive down the highway, you pass hundreds, maybe thousands, of other cars. But to how many do you pay attention? Probably only one or two—the bright pink and purple VW Bug and the Honda with the broken taillight that cut you off at the exit ramp. **Attention** is the extent to which we devote mental-processing activity to a particular stimulus.

Because attention is critical to advertising effectiveness, marketers continue to look for ways to ensure that consumers will attend to their messages. Some factors that influence consumers' likelihood of devoting processing activity to a stimulus include the following:

- *Personal needs and goals:* Consumers are more likely to pay attention to messages that speak to their current needs. A car that almost causes you to be in an accident will speak to your current need to get where you are going safely. That's the same reason you're far more likely to notice an ad for a fast-food restaurant when you're hungry.

- *Size:* A larger magazine or newspaper ad or a longer TV commercial is more likely to command attention.

- *Novelty:* Stimuli that present something unexpected tend to grab our attention. That includes the red-and-white polka-dot VW bug driving in front of us, ads that are in black and white in an all-color world, or ads in unconventional places, such as painted on a sidewalk, on the backs of shopping carts, or on bathroom walls. Novelty can also make product packaging stand out. When Pepsi came out with Pepsi One and Coke introduced Coca-Cola Zero in black cans, these new versions stood out on store shelves.

multitasking
Moving back and forth between various activities, such as checking emails, watching TV shows, sending instant messages, and so on.

Another problem marketers face when it comes to attention is **multitasking**, which occurs when we flit back and forth between emails, TV channels, text messages, and so on. For college students, more serious multitasking involves getting those three term papers that are due the same day completed on time—while still catching the latest episode of *The Bachelor*. Today, multitasking is so prevalent that it is considered the norm. Most jobs require multitasking skills of some sort. Prospective employers list the ability to multitask successfully in their job descriptions. Career counselors may advise you to have examples ready of how you have handled multiple tasks or projects in the past.[15] But as we'll see later in the book, this process creates headaches for marketers who want you to pay full attention to what they're saying!

rich media
A digital advertising term for an ad that includes advanced features, like video and audio elements, that encourage viewers to interact and engage with the content.

Online advertisers keep innovating to get visitors to watch their messages. Some have turned to **rich media**, a digital advertising term for an ad that includes advanced features, like video and audio elements, that encourage viewers to interact and engage with the content. The web page for the 2020 Corvette Stingray RWD Convertible allows potential buyers to see the car with different colors and trims and even allows you to see what your Stingray would look like with the full-length dual–racing-stripe package and the wing-style spoiler—for just a little over $86,000.[16] Online rich media for the

Metropolitan Museum of Art allows web visitors to view a moving panorama of an exhibit or to examine details of a painting by clicking the image.

Interpretation

Interpretation is the process of assigning meaning to a stimulus based upon prior associations we have with it and assumptions we make about it. Two people can see or hear the same event, but their interpretation of it can be as different as night and day, depending on what they had expected the stimulus to be. In one study, kids ages 3 to 5 who ate McDonald's French fries served in a McDonald's bag overwhelmingly thought they tasted better than those who ate the same fries out of a plain white bag. Even carrots tasted better when they came out of a McDonald's bag—more than half the kids preferred them to the same carrots served in a plain package! Ronald would be proud.[17]

interpretation
The process of assigning meaning to a stimulus based on prior associations a person has with it and assumptions he or she makes about it.

Motivation

Motivation is an internal state that drives us to satisfy needs. Once we activate a need, a state of tension exists that drives the consumer toward some goal that will reduce this tension by eliminating the need. Have you ever been on an interstate highway and seen a billboard with a giant picture of a hamburger available at the next exit, realized how good a big fat juicy hamburger would taste at that moment, and decided to pull off the road for it? That's motivation at work.

motivation
An internal state that drives us to satisfy needs by activating goal-oriented behavior.

Psychologist Abraham Maslow developed an influential approach to motivation.[18] He formulated a **hierarchy of needs** that categorizes motives according to five levels of importance, the more basic physical needs being on the bottom of the hierarchy and the higher spiritual and psychological needs at the top. The hierarchy suggests that before a person can meet needs at a given level, he or she must first meet the lower level's needs—somehow those hot new 7 For All Mankind jeans don't seem as enticing when you don't have enough money to buy food. Later Maslow amended the model by adding a sixth level to the hierarchy, *self-transcendence*. Consumers seeking to achieve this level focus on some higher goal outside themselves through altruistic endeavors or spiritual awakening. Relevant products for this level might be organizations that provide assistance to others and religious organizations. Have you done your downward-facing dog in yoga class today?[19]

hierarchy of needs
An approach that categorizes motives according to five levels of importance, the more basic needs being on the bottom of the hierarchy and the higher needs at the top.

As you can see from Figure 6.6, people start at the lowest level with basic physiological needs for food and sleep. Then, they progress to higher levels to satisfy more complex needs, such as the need to be accepted by others or to feel a sense of accomplishment. Ultimately, they can reach the highest-level needs, where they will be motivated to attain such goals as self-fulfillment. As the figure shows, if marketers understand the level of needs relevant to consumers in their target market, they can tailor their products and messages to them. For example, when an insurance company reassures you that "you're in good hands with Allstate," it's addressing your need for safety.

gamification
A strategy in which marketers apply game design techniques, like awarding points, badges, or levels, to nongame experiences in order to engage consumers.

Marketers use their understanding of consumer needs for prestige, status, and accomplishment when they use **gamification**. This term refers to a hot new strategy in which marketers apply game design techniques to non-gaming contexts, like shopping. They often do this by awarding points or badges to motivate consumers. Nike+, for example, allows consumers to earn points and set goals to push themselves to exercise more. Stride gum introduced "Gumulon," the world's first chewing-based mobile game. Players position the camera on their mobile

Consumers purchase many products, such as bathtubs, for both functional and aesthetic reasons.

Figure 6.6 *Snapshot* | Maslow's Hierarchy of Needs and Related Products

Abraham Maslow proposed a hierarchy of needs that categorizes motives. Savvy marketers know they need to understand the level of needs that motivates a consumer to buy a particular product or brand.

HIGHER-LEVEL NEEDS

Relevant Products		Example
Hobbies, travel, education	**SELF-ACTUALIZATION** Self-Fulfillment, Enriching Experiences	U.S. Army–"Be all you can be."
Cars, furniture, credit cards, stores, country clubs, liquors	**EGO NEEDS** Prestige, Status, Accomplishment	Royal Salute Scotch–"What the rich give the wealthy."
Clothing, grooming products, clubs, drinks	**BELONGINGNESS** Love, Friendship, Acceptance by Others	Pepsi–"You're in the Pepsi generation."
Insurance, alarm systems, retirement, investments	**SAFETY** Security, Shelter, Protection	Allstate Insurance–"You're in good hands with Allstate."
Medicines, staple items, generics	**PHYSIOLOGICAL** Water, Sleep, Food	Quaker Oat Bran–"It's the right thing to do."

LOWER-LEVEL NEEDS

Source: Adapted from Maslow, Abraham H.; Frager, Robert D.; Fadiman, James, *Motivation and Personality*, 3rd Ed., ©1987. Reprinted and electronically reproduced by permission of Pearson Education, Inc., Upper Saddle River, New Jersey.

devices to use their mouths to control the intergalactic game. A simple chewing motion causes the main character, Ace, to jump and advance through levels of the game, which takes place in a cavernous outer space mine (on the planet "Gumulon"). Although it's too soon to tell if this strategy is just a fad, at least for today, gamification is a multibillion-dollar industry.[20] Would you study more if you could collect badges for your efforts?

Learning

learning
A relatively permanent change in behavior caused by acquired information or experience.

Learning is a change in behavior caused by information or experience. Psychologists who study learning have advanced several theories to explain the learning process, and these perspectives are important because a major goal for marketers is to "teach" consumers to prefer their products. We refer to the two major perspectives on how people learn as *behavioral* and *cognitive learning*.

Behavioral Learning

behavioral learning theories
Theories of learning that focus on how consumer behavior is changed by external events or stimuli.

Behavioral learning theories assume that learning occurs as the result of experience and the connections we form between events. In one type of behavioral learning, **classical conditioning**, a person perceives two stimuli at about the same time. After a while, the person transfers his or her response from one stimulus to the other. For example, an ad shows a product and a breathtakingly beautiful scene so that (the marketer hopes) you will transfer the positive feelings you get when you look at the scene to the advertised product. During the recent pandemic, auto makers and other advertisers developed commercials that thanked people for helping those who were suffering from the pandemic and reminded viewers that "we will" get through this.

classical conditioning
The learning that occurs when a stimulus eliciting a response is paired with another stimulus that initially does not elicit a response on its own but will cause a similar response over time because of its association with the first stimulus.

Another common form of behavioral learning is **operant conditioning**, which occurs when people learn that their actions result in rewards or punishments. This feedback

operant conditioning
Learning that occurs as the result of rewards or punishments.

Figure 6.7 *Snapshot* | Consumers Learn in Many Ways

Behavioral Learning: <u>Consumers Learn through Experience and Connections between Events</u>

Theories	Occurs When	Marketing Application
Classical conditioning	Product paired with positive stimulus	Ads showing product with beautiful scenery/music
Operant conditioning	Consumers receive a reward for action	Consumers receive a gift with purchase of a product

Cognitive Learning

Theories	Occurs When	Marketing Application
Information acquisition	Consumers make connection between ideas	Rational/informational ads
Observational learning	Consumers observe what happens to others	Ads showing good or bad effects of using/not using a product

influences how they will respond in similar situations in the future. Just as a rat in a maze learns the route to a piece of cheese, consumers who receive a "reward," like the toy that you used to get in your Happy Meal at McDonald's, will be more likely to buy that brand again. We don't like to think that marketers can train us like lab mice, but like it or not, that kind of feedback does reward us for the behavior and makes it more likely that we'll repeat it in the future.

Cognitive Learning

In contrast to behavioral theories of learning that emphasize simple stimulus-response connections, **cognitive learning theory** views people as problem solvers who learn as they proactively absorb new information. Supporters of this viewpoint stress the role of creativity and insight during the learning process. *Cognitive learning* occurs when consumers make a connection between ideas or by observing things in their environment.

Observational learning occurs when people watch the actions of others and note what happens to them as a result. They store these observations in memory and at some later point use the information to guide their own behavior. Marketers often use this process to create advertising and other messages that allow consumers to observe the benefits of using their products. Health clubs and manufacturers of exercise equipment feature ripped men and women pounding away on treadmills, whereas mouthwash makers imply that fresh breath is the key to romance.

Now we've discussed how the three internal processes of perception, motivation, and learning influence consumer behavior. But the results of these processes—the interpretation

cognitive learning theory
Theory of learning that stresses the importance of internal mental processes and that views people as problem solvers who actively use information from the world around them to master their environment.

observational learning
Learning that occurs when people watch the actions of others and note what happens to them as a result.

the consumer gives to a marketing message or action—differ depending on unique consumer characteristics. Let's talk next about some of these characteristics: existing consumer attitudes, the personality of the consumer, and consumer age groups.

Attitudes

attitude
A learned predisposition to respond favorably or unfavorably to stimuli on the basis of relatively enduring evaluations of people, objects, and issues.

An **attitude** is a lasting evaluation of a person, object, or issue.[21] Consumers have attitudes toward brands, such as whether McDonald's or Wendy's has the best hamburgers. They also evaluate more general consumption-related behaviors, such as whether high-fat foods, including hamburgers, are a no-no in a healthy diet. Marketers often measure consumer attitudes because they believe attitudes predict behavior—people like Darius who think Honda Fit is a "cool" car are more likely to buy one than consumers who cherish the plush comfort of a big Lexus or Audi. To make attitude measurement meaningful, marketers understand that a person's attitude has three components: affect, cognition, and behavior. This is easy to remember—just think of it as the **ABC Theory of Attitudes**.

ABC Theory of Attitudes
A term for referring to attitudes that brings to mind the three components of attitudes.

Affect is the *feeling* component of attitudes. This term refers to the overall emotional response a person has to a product. Affect is usually dominant for expressive products, such as perfume, where we choose a fragrance if it makes us feel happy.

affect
The feeling component of attitudes; refers to the overall emotional response a person has to a product.

In other cases, advertisers try to arouse more negative emotions to get our attention and create a bond with their products. This new trend even has a name, **sadvertising**. Ads that provoke a good cry are all around us; think about all the adorable puppies and ponies you see in modern Super Bowl spots.[22] These emotional reactions actually cause physiological changes, such as an increase in pulse and sweating when a well-done commercial really gets to us. Some advertising researchers measure heart rate and skin conductivity and track the eye gaze of consumers while they view ads over the Internet, mobile devices, and TVs.[23] This technique is so common that Taco Bell spoofed it to advertise its new Quesarito, a combination of a quesadilla and a burrito. The chain developed overly dramatic tearjerker ads—including one where two friends have an emotional "reunion" after being apart for only six days—to convey the message that some things are better together.[24]

sadvertising
Advertising designed to arouse negative emotions in order to get our attention and create a bond with the brand's products.

cognition
The knowing component of attitudes; refers to the beliefs or knowledge a person has about a product and its important characteristics.

Cognition, the *knowing* component, refers to the beliefs or knowledge a person has about a product and its important characteristics. Cognition is important for complex products, such as computers, for which we may develop beliefs on the basis of technical information.

This ad for sparkling water containing CBD suggests that the product influences our feelings and emotions—the affect component of our attitudes.

Behavior, the *doing* component, involves a consumer's intention to do something, such as the intention to purchase or use a certain product. For products such as cereal, consumers act (purchase and try the product) on the basis of limited information and then form an evaluation of the product simply on the basis of how the product tastes or performs.

Personality and the Self: Are You What You Buy?

Personality is the set of unique psychological characteristics that consistently influences the way a person responds to situations in the environment. One adventure-seeking consumer may always be on the lookout for new experiences and cutting-edge products, whereas another is happiest in familiar surroundings where he or she can use the same brands over and over. Today, popular online matchmaking services like Match.com, Matchmaker.com, and eHarmony.com offer to create your "personality profile" and then hook you up with other members whose profiles are a good match.

A person's **self-concept** is his or her attitude toward himself or herself. The self-concept is composed of a mixture of beliefs about one's abilities and observations of one's own behavior and feelings (both positive and negative) about one's personal attributes, such as body type or facial features. The extent to which a person's self-concept is positive or negative can influence what products he or she buys and even the extent to which he or she fantasizes about changing his or her life.

Self-esteem refers to how positive a person's self-concept is. Our society is obsessed with the self. Consumers track their health and diet on apps like Fitbit, they post their relationship updates on Facebook, and they spend billions on apparel and beauty products to "edit" the person that others see.

The "selfie" epidemic is another symptom of this infatuation, as people go to great lengths to record their presence at parties, museums, and many other locations. According to one study, 39.4 percent of people take one to five selfies a day, and 14.4 percent admit to taking 30 or more a day. Ninety-three million selfies are posted on Internet sites per day, and 10 are posted on Instagram every 10 seconds.[25] About half of the respondents were OK with the idea of snapping selfies during childbirth, and one in five think it's OK to take them during a funeral![26]

As Dondeena at WW International knows, the appeal of many products relates directly to their promise to improve self-image. A lot of these appeals focus on body parts and how people feel about their physical appearance. Of course, in our society "thin is in," and women are constantly bombarded with images of anorexic-looking models. That focus may be starting to change as the movement toward more realistic body ideals gains steam. Alpine Butterfly sells vibrant, fashionable swimwear in sizes large to 5XL, while Swimsuits For All launched its first "fatkini" collection. Sports Illustrated, Eloquii, Forever21, and Fashion Nova all released plus-size swim collections in 2017. These new brands are starting to take a bigger share of the $20 billion swimwear industry.[27]

Age

A person's age is another internal influence on purchasing behavior. Many of us feel we have more in common with those of our own age because we share a common set of experiences and memories about cultural events, whether these involve Woodstock, Woodstock II, or even Woodstock III. Goods and services often appeal to a specific age group. Although there are exceptions, it is safe to assume that most fans who download Rihanna's cuts are younger than those who buy Barbra Streisand songs.

Age is important, but regardless of how old we are, what we buy often depends more on our current position in the **family life cycle**—the stages through which family members pass as they grow older. Singles (of any age) are more likely to spend money on expensive cars, entertainment, and recreation. Couples with small children purchase baby furniture, insurance, and a larger house, whereas older couples whose children have "left the nest" are more likely to buy a retirement home in Florida.

behavior
The doing component of attitudes; involves a consumer's intention to do something, such as the intention to purchase or use a certain product.

personality
The set of unique psychological characteristics that consistently influences the way a person responds to situations in the environment.

self-concept
An individual's self-image that is composed of a mixture of beliefs, observations, and feelings about personal attributes.

family life cycle
A means of characterizing consumers within a family structure on the basis of different stages through which people pass as they grow older.

We transition to different positions in the family life cycle—and some changes merit a celebration.

lifestyle
The pattern of living that determines how people choose to spend their time, money, and energy and that reflects their values, tastes, and preferences.

activities, interests, and opinions (AIOs)
Measures of consumer activities, interests, and opinions used to place consumers into dimensions.

Marketers know that the family life cycle is often a better predictor of purchasing behavior than simple demographics alone. Take, for example, a 40-year-old single man. He graduated from a top engineering school and has a great job with an annual salary of around $175,000. What is he spending his money on? Luxury vacations? Expensive electronics? Dinners at top restaurants? Expensive cars? Now take a man of the same age and income who is married, and with his husband has a 10-year-old daughter, a 17-year-old son entering college in the fall, and a 19-year-old who is a student at an Ivy League school. What do you think he spends his money on (whatever he has left)? Get the picture?

Lifestyle

Demographic characteristics, such as age, income, and family life cycle, tell marketers *what* products people buy, but they don't reveal *why*. Two consumers can share the same demographic characteristics yet be totally different people—all 20-year-old male college students are hardly identical to one another. That's why marketers often further profile consumers in terms of their lifestyles. A **lifestyle** is a pattern of living that determines how people choose to spend their time, money, and energy and that reflects their values, tastes, and preferences. Dondeena and WW Intenational understand that members have unique lifestyles, goals, and challenges. That understanding is behind the more personalized "Beyond the Scale" program that provides a custom plan for each member.

Savvy marketers often try to identify how consumers' lifestyle preferences create opportunities for products and services that relate to their values. Consider, for example, the growing cannabis revolution. Almost overnight, legal pot has become big business, with revenues in the United States of close to $3 billion per year already. As more states decide to legalize marijuana, businesses large and small are rushing in to satisfy customers' needs for not only weed but also related items (Oreos, anyone?). The magazine *High Times*, founded by a former drug smuggler way back in 1974, is a trade paper for this lifestyle. Today, it's at the forefront of the revolution. It hosts the High Times Cannabis Cups, weekend festivals that feature more than 500 vendors, seminars, and appearances by celebrities such as Ice Cube and David Arquette. Now it's moving into other ventures, including nightclubs that offer cannabis menus and merchandise, such as socks emblazoned with pot leaves.[28]

To identify consumers' lifestyles, marketers turn to *psychographics*, which groups consumers according to psychological and behavioral similarities. One way to do this is to describe people in terms of their **activities, interests, and opinions (AIOs)**. These dimensions are based on preferences for vacation destinations, club memberships, hobbies, specific political and social viewpoints, food, and fashion, and so on. Using data from large samples, marketers create profiles of customers who resemble one another in terms of their activities and patterns of product use.[29] A related and very popular technique today is to tell a detailed story about the life of a "typical" brand user. This persona becomes the rallying point for the company as he or she helps the marketing team to visualize how real people actually integrate the brand into their daily lives. We'll talk more about psychographics in Chapter 7.

Yoga has quickly become a central part of many people's lifestyles.

6.3

OBJECTIVE

Show how situational factors and consumers' relationships with other people influence consumer behavior.

Situational and Social Influences on Consumers' Decisions

We've seen that internal factors, such as how people perceive marketing messages, their motivation to acquire products, and their unique personalities, age groups, family life cycle, and lifestyle, influence the decisions people make. In addition, situational and social influences—factors external to the consumer—have a big impact on the choices consumers make and how they make them.

Situational Influences

When, where, and how we shop—what we call *situational influences*—shape our purchase choices. Some important situational cues are our physical surroundings and time pressures.

Marketers know that dimensions of the physical environment, including factors such as decor, smells, lighting, music, and even temperature, can significantly influence consumption. When casino operators replaced old school "one-armed bandits" with electronic slot machines that no longer made the familiar whirring noises when players pulled the handle, earnings fell by 24 percent.[30] And the Hard Rock Hotel in Orlando, Florida, boosted ice cream sales by 50 percent simply by spraying a waffle cone scent into the air outside its shop.[31]

Sensory marketing appeals to consumers' five senses: taste, sight, touch, smell, and hearing. Sensory marketing is becoming big business. Specialized companies sell scents to hotels, car manufacturers, and even banks (like customers don't know what money smells like). Some offer individual scents, like vanilla, whereas others sell combinations of popular scents. Brands such as Cinnabon make sure the aroma of fresh baked cinnamon rolls floats down the mall to attract consumers. Does this tactic work? The scent is so successful that some locations heat brown sugar and cinnamon just to keep hungry consumers pouring in.[32]

But for some retailers, it's not enough to have just any scent; these retailers use scents that not only appeal to their customers but also enhance their brand. For example, at the Benetton store in Chicago, customers enjoy a bright spring fragrance similar to Benetton's Verde cologne. Abercrombie & Fitch use their signature cologne, Fierce, to create a musky scent in their stores.[33] And, coming soon: Books, movies, and even clothing that will deliver specific scents via pellets that you insert into your iPhone![34] Marketers term this strategy **sensory branding**.[35] Let's see how some other situational factors influence the consumer decision-making process.

sensory marketing
Marketing techniques that link distinct sensory experiences, such as a unique fragrance, with a product or service.

sensory branding
The use of distinct sensory experiences not only to appeal to customers but also to enhance a brand.

The Physical Environment

It's no secret that physical surroundings strongly influence people's moods and behaviors. Despite all their efforts to presell consumers through advertising, marketers know that the store environment influences many purchases. For example, one study of purchasing habits showed that consumers decide on about three out of every four of their supermarket product purchases in the aisles (so always eat before you go to the supermarket). The study also showed that in-store marketing and branding had a strong influence on shoppers' purchasing decisions.[36]

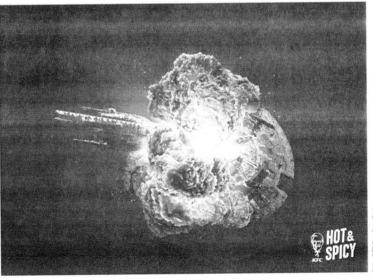

KFC boasts about the impact of its new menu item on our sensory receptors.

Bass Pro Shops provide fun experiences that allow customers to try out their products under realistic conditions.

The Purchase Setting

Two dimensions, *arousal* and *pleasure*, determine whether a shopper will react positively or negatively to a store environment. In other words, the person's surroundings can be either dull or exciting (arousing) and either pleasant or unpleasant. Just because the environment is arousing doesn't necessarily mean it will be pleasant—we've all been in crowded, loud, hot stores that are anything but. The importance of these surroundings explains why many retailers focus on packing as much entertainment as possible into their stores. For example, Bass Pro Shops, a chain of outdoor sports equipment stores built in the style of an enormous hunting lodge, features giant aquariums, waterfalls, trout ponds, archery and rifle ranges, putting greens, and fish and wildlife mounts at every turn. It also offers free classes (for adults and kids) in everything from ice fishing to conservation to meat processing. Every Easter, Bass Pro Shops offers free family events at their stores where families can pose with the Easter Bunny and take home a free 4-by-6 color photo, enjoy kid's craft activities, and participate in an old-fashioned Easter egg hunt.[37] And if all that sensory overload leaves you famished, many of the more than 60 Bass Pro Shops locations have on-site restaurants.

Time

Every country has a set of core values and beliefs, even if they vary slightly from one region to another. The core values of a country set it apart from other cultures. When people list the core American values, they are likely to include "time" as one.

Time is also one of consumers' most limited resources. We talk about "making time" or "spending time," and we remind one another that "time is money." Marketers know that the time of day, the season of the year, and how much time a person has to make a purchase affect decision making.

time poverty
Consumers' belief that they are more pressed for time than ever before.

Indeed, many consumers, especially college students, believe that they are more pressed for time than ever before. This sense of **time poverty** makes consumers responsive to marketing innovations that allow them to save time, including services such as drive-through lanes at pharmacies, to-your-door grocery delivery, and mobile pet grooming. Time poverty is a major factor in the increasing demand for online college courses by students who need to fit getting their degree in between family commitments, jobs, and an occasional trip to the gym.

Then, of course, there is the "always open" convenience of "stores" on the Web, ready to serve you whenever, wherever, and however you want. In fact, online shopping is growing at about seven times the rate of overall retail spending in the United States. Consumers browse products on mobile devices while in brick-and-mortar stores (known as **showrooming**) and 71 percent say they are searching for the lowest product prices online from any smart device (known as **webrooming**).[38]

showrooming
Consumers browsing products on their mobile devices while in a brick-and-mortar store.

webrooming
Consumers comparing prices of products online.

But this doesn't mean your favorite brick-and-mortar store is going away anytime soon. The Internet gives marketers the opportunity to drive traffic to their stores with coupons, mobile apps, email, etc. Stores can then adapt their in-store services to meet customer needs, offering data-driven personalization of the shopping experience. Rent the Runway is an e-commerce brand that opened showrooms in major U.S. cities only after developing an online presence. Customers sign in when they enter the store, making it easy for store "stylists" to recommend dresses and accessories based on previous purchases. Rent the Runway makes the process easy for customers by providing a pre-paid, pre-addressed package to return the purchase.[39]

Disruption in Consumer Behavior: The COVID-19 Pandemic

Beginning in early 2020, the lives of consumers around the globe were dramatically changed. The "norm" disappeared overnight and was replaced by new behaviors, including self-quarantining, social distancing, wearing medical masks, and the closing of stores and service providers except those considered "essential." Is this not *the* definition of disruption? The most important question that marketers need answered is, "What is the new normal going to be?" Below are some of the speculated possibilities.[40]

1. **Mobile will dominate the new norm.** During the COVID-19 pandemic, consumers of all ages became more comfortable with digital and mobile devices, including smartphones, tablets, watches, wearable gadgets, such as Microsoft's new **HoloLens** and others. Microsoft's HoloLens 2 was used during the pandemic to help doctors treat people with COVID-19. With simple hand gestures, doctors can look at x-rays, scans, and test results while communicating with colleagues in a virus-free room.[41]

2. **Transparency will be part of all successful business–customer relationships.** During the COVID-19 pandemic, consumers began to value family and relationships more. What customers will continue to want most from corporations is communication and engagement. The old model of communications with traditional broadcast media will no longer work. Furthermore, customers will demand even greater transparency. "Authentic" companies, including those that admit their mistakes (a trend called "**flawsome**"), and companies that have a solid commitment to social responsibility will form connections with their customers, gain customer support and loyalty, and be heavily rewarded.[42]

3. **User-generated content will be the most disruptive in terms of marketing activities.** During the pandemic, consumers, even those who hadn't used social media before, spent more and more time on social media. Corporations will need to give control of their marketing communications to consumers who will gladly provide user-generated content. Traditional branded content will be ignored, while greater influence will come from online reviews, social media posts, and blogs. In the future, corporations must work to earn positive content by their products and by their corporate values and actions. Content co-creation between brands and consumers will become an important trend in marketing communications.[44]

4. **Social networks will grow to rival the original Internet.** Social networks have become an important source of information for consumers, especially in the time of crisis. Research has shown that much of the success of the Arab Spring uprisings would not have happened without the abundant use of social networks. Today, the future of social networks may mean becoming not another channel but *the* channel or another Internet itself. **Social graphs** map the relationships of everybody in studies to better understand the importance of social media. Social graphs are not only becoming more popular but are indispensable. The growth of these graphs has been possible due to mobile, broadband, and high-quality content on social media sites such as Facebook, Instagram, Twitter, Tumblr, LinkedIn, Pinterest, and Snapchat.[45]

5. **Personalized, data-driven disruptive marketing will take precedence.** The difference between data-driven marketing and **data-driven disruptive marketing** is that data-driven disruptive marketing is relationship oriented, where the content of a marketing action acts to build trust. Data-driven marketing is old fashioned "push" messaging facilitated by Big Data. Thus, marketers who successfully use data-driven disruptive marketing to focus on building relationships around good products will be rewarded, while followers with shabby products and poor service will fail.[46]

HoloLens
Microsoft's mixed reality headset that is a combination of hardware, mixed reality, and artificial intelligence (AI).

flawsome
Flawsome is a new term that combines two words *flaws* and *awesome*. Flawsome describes a person who accepts themselves despite their flaws and knows that they are awesome regardless. It would not be wrong to say that it is the word which best describes a person and every minutiae associated with them.[43]

social graph
A graph that represents social relations between people or other entities. A social graph is a representation of a social network. The social graph has been referred to as "the global mapping of everybody and how they are related."

data-driven disruptive marketing
Relationship-oriented marketing where the use of data and the content of marketing is used to build trust.

6. **Consumers will change brand loyalty.** Early in the COVID-19 pandemic, popular goods, including toilet tissue and bread, disappeared from store shelves. When consumers found store shelves empty, they turned to substitute brands and products. This was particularly seen in certain food product categories, including dairy, pasta, canned goods, frozen foods, bread, baked goods, and paper products. As a result, more consumers tried private label brands, not only because they were still on the shelves but also because they normally sell for a lower price. This made good sense to consumers because of uncertainty about incomes. In several studies, consumers indicated they would stay with the new private label brand even after the pandemic was past and the new normal was arriving.

7. **Consumers will transition to digital shopping.** A significant change during the pandemic was the movement of consumers away from in-store buying to online buying. This was particularly apparent in grocery shopping, where digital had not been heavily used prior to the pandemic. Many consumers used online grocery buying for the first time during the pandemic, and many say they will continue as long as the pandemic is around. What they will do after that is not clear. Many consumers will likely return to brick-and-mortar grocery shopping because of the social benefits they receive from the in-store experience of shopping.[47]

8. **In-homing will become part of the new normal.** During the pandemic, consumers adopted a new somewhat-normal—**in-homing**. They still worked, but at home. They still ate, but not at restaurants; instead, they learned to cook and ate only at home. They added subscriptions to TV streaming services, but they gave up discretionary spending at movie theaters. They stopped driving because they so seldom left home, meaning a tank of gas could last a month or more. So, will the new normal include **in-homing**? Consumers who learned to cook while quarantined at home may continue to do so. What about consumers who set up a gym in their basement—will they return to a gym membership? And it's a pretty good bet that consumers will keep their streaming services. A large portion of the workforce may decide (or be told by their employers) to continue working from home. And all of these changes will change the demand for various goods and services.[48]

in-homing

A pattern of living in which almost all activities are done in the home.

Social Influences on Consumers' Decisions

Although we are all individuals, we are also members of many groups that influence our buying decisions. Families, friends, and classmates often sway us, as do larger groups with which we identify, such as ethnic groups and political parties. Now let's consider how social influences, such as values, culture, social class, trends within the larger society, and influential friends and acquaintances affect the consumer decision-making process. And, of course, today this includes Facebook and other online friends.

Values (Again)

As we saw in Chapter 2, cultural values are deeply held beliefs about right and wrong ways to live.[49] Marketers who understand a culture's values can tailor their product offerings accordingly. But over time, cultural values change. Consider, for example, that the values for collectivist countries differ greatly from those of individualistic cultures, where immediate gratification of one's own needs comes before all other loyalties. In collectivist cultures, loyalty to a family or a tribe overrides personal goals. Today, we see the economic growth of some collectivist countries, such as India, Japan, and China, making many consumers more affluent—and more individualistic. For marketers, this means growth opportunities in the travel business, luxury goods, sports activities like tennis and golf, and entertainment.

Trends

Personal values of consumers are shared by many members of the culture and they change over time. Because consumer trends evolve from consumer values, consumer trends change also, making it critical that marketers remain knowledgeable about which trends exist and which are predicted for the future. These trends dictate marketing activities. Here are some of the major trends we can predict:

- **The sharing economy:** We already see the blurring of the boundaries between producer and consumer. In the sharing economy, everyday people become hoteliers and taxi drivers. An increasing number of consumers are sharing automobiles and renting their power and gardening tools by leasing them when needed.
- **Authenticity and personalization:** Driven by a dislike for big corporations and mass-market products, many consumers demand individualized experiences and artisanal products.
- **Blurring of gender roles:** Individuals, corporations, and governments are moving away from a two-gender standard. More people are refusing to identify themselves as male or female.
- **Diversity and multiculturalism:** Racial and ethnic differences will continue to disappear as people are exposed to a diverse group of others in the workplace, in the media, and online. Following a racial profiling scandal, Starbucks closed each of its 8,000 stores for diversity training, showing consumers that Starbucks prizes equity in communities.
- **Healthy and ethical living:** Consumers will continue to focus on wellness, physical fitness, and environmental sustainability. Economic inequality will dictate which consumers will follow this trend as less affluent consumers will not be able to afford healthy and sustainable products. Unilever demonstrates its commitment to sustainability in its mission and its products. The 28 brands in Unilever's Sustainable Living division have grown 69 percent faster than the rest of the company's business due to the support of environmentally conscious consumers.
- **Interconnection and the Internet of Things:** As AI (artificial intelligence) continues to grow, so will the Internet of Things. Consumers in larger numbers will invest in wearable computers that monitor physical activity and smart homes.

Culture

We can think of **culture** as a society's personality. It is the values, beliefs, customs, and tastes a group of people produces or practices. Although we often assume that what people in one culture (especially our own) think is desirable or appropriate will be appreciated in other cultures as well, that's far from the truth. For example, simply translating American marketing messages or brand names into French (café chain Au Bon Pain) or German (Yoplait Greek Yogurt) or any other language doesn't mean those messages will be accepted by French- or German-speaking consumers—especially those living in the United States who have a strong desire to maintain their ethnic identity. Instead, marketers must "recognize that all consumers buy brands that empower their cultural relevancy."[50] That means developing relationships with customers and considering their family and religious values.

culture
The values, beliefs, customs, and tastes a group of people produces or practices.

Subcultures

A **subculture** is a group that coexists with other groups in a larger culture but whose members share a distinctive set of beliefs or characteristics, such as members of a religious organization or an ethnic group. **Microcultures** are groups of consumers who identify with a specific activity or art form. These groups form around TV shows, like *Tiger King*; movies, like *Star Wars*; online games, like Candy Crush Saga; and leisure activities, like e-sports. Of course, one of the best known microcultures for many years has been the Deadheads, fans

subculture
A group within a society whose members share a distinctive set of beliefs, characteristics, or common experiences.

microcultures
Groups of consumers who identify with a specific activity or art form.

of the popular American rock band the Grateful Dead, who performed from 1965 to 1995. Ask your grandparents to tell you about the Grateful Dead, or better still, buy them some Grateful Dead t-shirts for Christmas on the group's website. Social media have been a real boon to subcultures and microcultures; they provide an opportunity for like-minded consumers to share their thoughts, photos, videos, and so on. More on these important new sharing platforms later in the book.

For marketers, some of the most important subcultures are demographic (such as age), racial, and ethnic groups because many consumers identify strongly with their heritage, and products that appeal to this aspect of their identities appeal to them. We will talk more about these subculture groups in Chapter 7. To grow its business, Clorox got down and dirty with its Latino/a consumers. After studying how Latino/a individuals traditionally clean their homes, Clorox introduced its Clorox Fraganzia line of cleaning products to meet all of their cleaning needs—a thorough process of cleaning, disinfecting, and aromatizing. Even the Fraganzia line's toilet-bowl cleaners, in the shape of little baskets, or *canastillas*, look like those people use in Latin America.[51]

Conscientious Consumerism: An Emerging Lifestyle Trend

Powerful new social movements within a society also contribute to how consumers make decisions about what they want and what they don't. One such influence is **consumerism**, the social movement directed toward protecting consumers from harmful business practices. Much of the current focus of consumerism is about business activities that harm the environment and the potential damage to our planet. Worries about climate change, entire species going extinct, widespread exposure to carcinogens and harmful bacteria, and many other issues are front and center.

As consumers and the media place more and more emphasis on this, many of us are much more mindful of environmental issues when we shop and when we make decisions about the foods we eat, the clothes we wear, the buildings in which we live and work, and the cars we drive. And marketers are following the consumerism call to action. Patagonia is a company widely known for its focus on the environment. Patagonia's re\\\collection line uses recycled down, wood, polyester, labels, zippers, and buttons.[52] In January 2019, Patagonia announced that it was changing its focus from "doing no harm" to a more proactive stance. Patagonia's goal is to make its supply chain carbon neutral by 2025.[53] Some analysts call this new value **conscientious consumerism**.[54] We see evidence of its impact everywhere, in the form of vegan restaurants, electric cars, recycling activities, solar heating panels on homes, and more.

Social Class

Social class is the overall rank of people in a society. People who are within the same class tend to exhibit similarities in occupation, education, and income level, and they often have similar tastes in clothing, decorating styles, and leisure activities. Class members also share many political and religious beliefs as well as preferences for AIOs.

Many marketers design their products and stores to appeal to people in a specific social class. Working-class consumers tend to evaluate products in more utilitarian terms, such as sturdiness or comfort instead of trendiness or aesthetics. They are less likely to experiment with new products or styles, such as modern furniture or colored appliances, because they tend to prefer predictability to novelty.[55] Marketers need to understand these differences and develop products and communication strategies that appeal to different social classes.

Luxury goods often serve as **status symbols**, visible markers that provide a way for people to flaunt their membership in higher social classes (or at least to make others believe they are members). The bumper sticker "He who dies with the most toys wins" illustrates the desire to accumulate these badges of achievement. However, it's important to note that over time, the importance of different status symbols rises and falls. For example, when

James Dean starred in the 1956 movie *Giant*, the Cadillac convertible was the ultimate status symbol car in the United States. Today, wealthy consumers who want to let the world know of their success are far more likely to choose a Mercedes, a Tesla, or even a humbler Prius.

In addition, traditional status symbols today are available to a much wider range of consumers around the world with rising incomes. This change fuels demand for mass-consumed products that still offer some degree of *panache*, or style. Think about the success of companies like Nokia, H&M, Zara, ING, Dell Computers, Gap, Nike, EasyJet, or L'Oréal. They cater to a consumer segment that analysts label **mass class**. This term refers to the hundreds of millions of global consumers who now enjoy a level of purchasing power that's sufficient to let them afford high-quality products offered by well-known multinational companies.

Pricey Christian Louboutin shoes provide women with an expensive and highly visible status symbol.

Group Membership

Anyone who's ever "gone along with the crowd" knows that people act differently in groups than they do on their own. When there are more people in a group, it becomes less likely that any one member will be singled out for attention, and normal restraints on behavior may evaporate (think about the last wild party you attended). In many cases, group members show a greater willingness to consider riskier alternatives than they would if each member made the decision alone.[56]

A **reference group** is a set of people that a consumer wants to please or imitate. Consumers *refer* to these groups when they decide what to wear, where they hang out, and what brands they buy. This influence can take the form of family and friends; a sorority or fraternity; a respected statesman, like Martin Luther King Jr.; celebrities, like Angelina Jolie; or even (dare we say it) your professors. Marketers often try to cultivate a loyal community of fans who will spread the word about their clothing, cars, music, sports teams, and movies. Nobody does this better than Lucasfilm for its *Star Wars* franchise. The studio even employs a full-time head of fan relations.[57]

mass class
The hundreds of millions of global consumers who now enjoy a level of purchasing power that's sufficient to let them afford high-quality products.

reference group
An actual or imaginary individual or group that has a significant effect on an individual's evaluations, aspirations, or behavior.

opinion leader
A person who is frequently able to influence others' attitudes or behaviors by virtue of his or her active interest and expertise in one or more product categories.

Opinion Leaders

If, like Darius, you are in the market for a new car, is there a certain person to whom you'd turn for advice? An **opinion leader** is a person who influences others' attitudes or behaviors because they believe that he or she possesses expertise about the product.[58] Opinion leaders usually exhibit high levels of interest in the product category. They continuously update their knowledge as they read blogs, talk to salespeople, or subscribe to podcasts about the topic. Because of this involvement, opinion leaders are valuable information sources.

Unlike commercial endorsers, who are paid to represent the interests of just one company, opinion leaders have no ax to grind and can

Beginning with *Star Wars: Episode I* in 1999, Lucasfilm Ltd. has hosted a huge gathering every other year called *Star Wars Celebration* that attracts almost 50,000 Jedis, Wookiees, and Stormtroopers.

impart both positive and negative information about the product (unless they're being compensated to blog on behalf of a brand, which is actually quite common these days!). In addition, these knowledgeable consumers often are among the first to buy new products, so they absorb much of the risk and reduce uncertainty for others who are not as courageous.

Gender Roles

gender roles
Society's expectations regarding the appropriate attitudes, behaviors, and appearance for men and women.

Some of the strongest pressure to conform comes from our **gender roles**, or society's expectations regarding the appropriate attitudes, behaviors, and appearances of men and women.[59] Of course, marketers play a part in teaching us how society expects us to act as men and women. Marketing communications and products often portray people according to the dominant gender role expectations in the culture.

Traditional gender stereotypes focused on women as caretakers and men as breadwinners. The rise in women's labor force participation since the 1960s and the increasing number of dual-income households have changed society's expectations. Every day, we encounter societal influences that indicate what "proper" gender roles should be and that teach us as consumers which products are appropriate for each gender.

In every society, however, there are people who don't adhere to the male/female dichotomy. The LGBTQ+ (lesbian, gay, bisexual, transgender, and questioning) population in the U.S. is about 3/4 the size each of the Latino/a population and the Black population. The buying power of this community is estimated at almost $1 trillion. Still, many of those who identify as LGBTQ+ keep their sexual orientation or gender identity hidden from most others. Recent cultural movements such as the Pride movement and the #MeToo movement, which looks critically at how men view women, will hopefully lead to greater acceptance of and openness toward individuals who deviate from or challenge dominant gender roles.[60]

Gender roles have a big impact on sales of many products. For example, it was not that many years ago that men in most cultures would not consider using a skincare product, as all skincare products were deemed only for women. Today, men's use of skincare products is accepted in many cultures. A growing number of well-known skincare brands now offer products for men—from moderately priced Olay, L'Oréal, and Neutrogena to the more expensive luxury brands Clinique, Dior, and Chanel. Men's grooming products are projected to grow from around $60 billion in 2018 to $81 billion in 2024.[61]

The good news is that gender roles do vary across cultures and are changing. While the old custom of wives in a household doing all the cooking, cleaning, and child care, and only husbands working outside the home still exists in some cultures, that is being replaced with a greater sharing of responsibilities. In more and more households, both partners, irrelevant of gender, participate in all activities.

Furthermore, the view of the main breadwinner is changing. In one study, almost 40 percent of married working women bring in *more* than their partner.[62]

Still, some gender-typed products that reflect exaggerated consumer expectations of gender rather than reality persist. For years, many consumers and feminists have claimed that the Barbie doll reinforces unrealistic ideas about what women's bodies should look like. In response, Mattel recently reintroduced its traditional blonde Barbie in a variety of skin tones, hairstyles, and outfits to attract a more diverse market. In 2018, the company even released new versions based upon role models like Amelia Earhart.[63]

Today, many brands are using their advertising and other marketing activities to (hopefully) limit the influence of outdated gender roles that encourage discrimination. Whether by their choice of programming content, by where their ads appear, or by the content of the ads themselves, we find a greater number of brands giving support to the acceptance of all LBGTQ+ people.

Ignacio Ferrándiz/Alamy Stock Photo

As consumers experience more and more gender-neutral ad campaigns for makeup, a growing trend is for men to wear cosmetic products like manscara.

6.4 Business Markets: Buying and Selling When the Customer Is Another Organization

OBJECTIVE

Understand the characteristics of business-to-business markets and how marketers classify business-to-business customers.

You might think most marketers spend their days dreaming up the best way to promote cutting-edge products for consumers—like new apps for your iPhone, a new power drink to keep you fit, or some funky shoes to add to your collection.

But this is not the whole picture. Many marketers know that the "real action" also lies in products that companies sell to businesses and organizations rather than to end-user consumers like you—software applications to make a business more efficient, safety goggles for industrial plants, the carts shoppers push in super-markets, or the sensors that keep track of your luggage at the airport. In fact, some of the most interesting and lucrative jobs for young marketers are in businesses you've never heard of because these companies don't deal directly with consumers.

Like an end consumer, a business buyer makes decisions—but with an important difference: The purchase may be worth millions of dollars, and both the buyer and the seller have a lot at stake (maybe even their jobs). A consumer may decide to buy two or three T-shirts at one time, each emblazoned with a different design. *Fortune* 500 companies, such as ExxonMobil, PepsiCo Inc., and FedEx, buy thousands of employee uniforms embroidered with their corporate logos in a single order.

Consider these transactions: P&G contracts with several advertising agencies to promote its brands at home and around the globe. The Metropolitan Opera buys costumes, sets, and programs. Mac's Diner buys a case of canned peas from BJ's Wholesale Club. The U.S. government places an order for 3,000 new HP laser printers. Emirates Airlines signs a $16 billion order for up to 36 of the superjumbo 500-passenger Airbus A380s.[64]

All these exchanges have one thing in common: They're part of *business-to-business (B2B) marketing*. As we saw in Chapter 1, this is the marketing of goods and services that businesses and other organizations buy for purposes other than personal consumption. Some firms resell these goods and services, so they are part of a *channel of distribution*, a concept we'll revisit in Chapter 11 and Chapter 12. Other firms use the goods and services they buy to produce still other goods and services that meet the needs of their customers or to support their own operations. These **business-to-business (B2B) markets**, also called **organizational markets**, include manufacturers and other product producers, wholesalers, retailers, and a variety of other organizations, such as hospitals, universities, and governmental agencies.

To put the size and complexity of business markets into perspective, let's consider a single product—a pair of jeans. A consumer may browse through several racks of jeans and ultimately purchase a single pair, but the buyer who works for the store at which the consumer shops had to purchase many pairs of jeans in different sizes, styles, and brands from different manufacturers. Each of these manufacturers purchases fabrics, zippers, buttons, and thread from other manufacturers, which in turn purchase the raw materials to make these components. In addition, all the firms in this chain need to purchase equipment (maybe a machine to make all those holes in just the right places), electricity, labor, computer systems, legal and accounting services, insurance, office supplies, packing materials, and countless other goods and services. So, even a single purchase of a pair of 7 For All Mankind jeans is the culmination of a series of buying and selling activities among many organizations; many people have been keeping busy while you're out shopping! In this section, we'll first talk about the different types of business customers that buy goods and services, the different types of B2B purchases, and the steps in the B2B decision process. Finally, we'll look at B2B e-commerce and digital marketing.

business-to-business (B2B) markets
The group of customers that includes manufacturers, wholesalers, retailers, and other organizations.

organizational markets
Another name for business-to-business markets.

Types of Business-to-Business Customers

As we noted before, many firms buy products in business markets so they can produce other goods. Other B2B customers resell, rent, or lease goods and services. Still other customers, including governments and not-for-profit institutions, such as the Red Cross or a local church, serve the public in some way. In this section, we'll look at the three major classes of B2B customers shown in Figure 6.8 (producers, resellers, and organizations). Then, we'll look at how marketers classify specific industries.

Producers

producers
The individuals or organizations that purchase products for use in the production of other goods and services.

Producers purchase products for the production of other goods and services that they, in turn, sell to make a profit. For this reason, they are customers for a vast number of products from raw materials to goods that still other producers manufacture. For example, Dell buys microprocessor chips from Intel and AMD that go into its line of computers, and Marriott hotels buys linens, furniture, and food to produce the accommodations and meals their guests expect. In addition to manufacturers of goods, the fishing, agricultural, and lumber industries are considered producers.

Resellers

resellers
The individuals or organizations that buy finished goods for the purpose of reselling, renting, or leasing to others to make a profit and to maintain their business operations.

Resellers, including both brick-and-mortar stores and online sellers, buy finished goods for the purpose of reselling, renting, or leasing to consumers and other businesses. Although resellers do not actually produce goods, they do provide their customers with the time, place, and possession utility we talked about in Chapter 1 because they make the goods available to consumers when and where they want them. For example, Walmart buys toothpaste, peanuts, kids' shoes, and about a gazillion other products to sell in its more than 11,500 stores worldwide.[65]

Increasingly, large retail businesses such as Walmart, Walgreen's, and Kroger Supermarkets and wholesale clubs such as Costco and Sam's have taken over the functions that were previously the job of wholesalers and distributors. This means that there are fewer of these resellers today. More on this in Chapter 12.

Figure 6.8 *Snapshot* │ The Business Marketplace

The business marketplace consists of three major categories of customers: producers, resellers, and organizations. B2B marketers must understand the different needs of these customers if they want to build successful relationships with them.

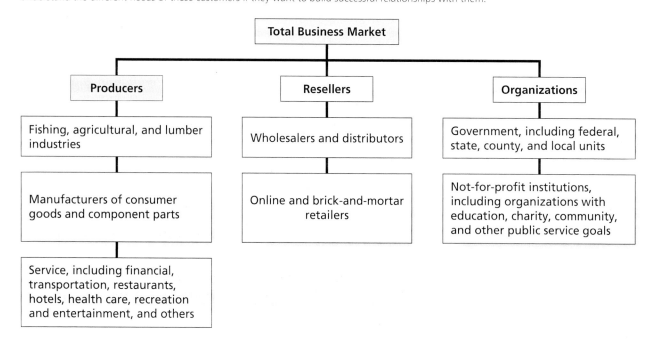

Government and Not-for-Profit Organizations

Governments and not-for-profit institutions are two other types of organizations in the business marketplace. **Government markets** make up the largest single business and organizational market in the United States. The U.S. government market includes more than 3,000 county governments, 35,000 municipalities and townships, 37,000 special district governments, 50 states and the District of Columbia, plus the federal government. The Bureau of Economic Analysis (BEA) reported that in 2016, spending by governments was $3,267 billion—actually more than the "mere" $3,057 billion that businesses spent.[66]

And of course, there are thousands more government customers around the globe, and many of those governments are just about the only customers for certain products, such as jet bombers and nuclear power plants. But many government expenditures are for more familiar items. Pens, pencils, and paper for offices; cots, bedding, and toiletries for jails and prisons; and cleaning supplies for routine facilities maintenance are just a few examples of items that consumers buy one at a time but that governments purchase in bulk.

As we said in Chapter 1, not-for-profit or nongovernmental organizations (NGOs) are organizations with educational, community, and other public service goals, such as hospitals, churches, universities, museums, and charitable and cause-related organizations, like the Salvation Army and the Red Cross. These institutions tend to operate on low budgets. Because nonprofessional part-time buyers who have other duties often make purchases, these customers may rely on marketers to provide more advice and assistance before and after the sale.

government markets
The federal, state, county, and local governments that buy goods and services to carry out public objectives and to support their operations.

The North American Industry Classification System

In addition to looking at B2B markets within these three general categories, marketers rely on the **North American Industry Classification System (NAICS)** to identify their customers. This is a numerical coding of industries the United States, Canada, and Mexico developed. Table 6.1 illustrates how the NAICS coding system works. NAICS replaced the U.S. Standard Industrial Classification system in 1997 so that the North American Free Trade Agreement (NAFTA) countries could compare economic and financial statistics.[67] The NAICS reports the number of firms, the total dollar amount of sales, the number of employees, and the growth rate for industries, all broken down by geographic region. Many firms use the NAICS to assess potential markets and to determine how well they are doing compared to others in their industry group.

Firms may also use the NAICS to find new customers. A marketer might first determine the NAICS industry classifications of his or her current customers and then evaluate the sales potential of other firms occupying these categories.

North American Industry Classification System (NAICS)
The numerical coding system that the United States, Canada, and Mexico use to classify firms into detailed categories according to their business activities.

Table 6.1 The North American Industry Classification System: A Sample

		Frozen Fruit Example		Wireless Telecommunications Example
Sector (two digits)	31–33	Manufacturing	51	Information
Subsector (three digits)	311	Food manufacturing	517	Telecommunications
Industry group (four digits)	3114	Fruit and vegetable preserving and specialty food manufacturing	5173	Wired and wireless telecommunications carriers
Industry (five digits)	31141	Frozen food manufacturing	51731	Wired and wireless telecommunications carriers
U.S. industry (six digits)	311411	Frozen fruits, fruit juice, and vegetables, manufacturing	517312	Wireless telecommunications carriers (except satellite)

Source: United States Census Bureau, "North American Industry Classification System," https://www.census.gov/cgi-bin/sssd/naics/naicsrch?code=311411&search=2017%20NAICS%20Search (accessed March 10, 2018).

Factors That Make a Difference in Business Markets

In theory, the same basic marketing principles should hold true in both consumer and business markets—firms identify customer needs and develop a marketing mix to satisfy those needs. For example, take the company that makes the desks and chairs for a university classroom. Just like a firm that markets consumer goods, the classroom furniture company first must create an important competitive advantage for its target market of universities. Next, the firm develops a marketing mix strategy that begins with a product—classroom furniture that will withstand years of use by thousands of students, while it provides a level of comfort that a good learning environment requires (and you thought those hardback chairs were intended just to keep you awake during class). The firm must offer the furniture at prices that universities will pay and that will allow the firm to make a reasonable profit. Then, the firm must develop a sales force or other marketing communication strategy to make sure the university (and hundreds of others) considers—and hopefully chooses—its products when it furnishes classrooms.

Although marketing to business customers does have a lot in common with consumer marketing, there are differences that make this basic process more complex.[68] Figure 6.9 summarizes the key areas of difference, and Table 6.2 provides a more extensive set of comparisons between the two types of markets.

Multiple Buyers

In business markets, products often must do more than satisfy an individual's needs. They must meet the requirements of everyone involved in the company's purchase decision. If you decide to buy a new chair for your room or apartment, you're the only one you must satisfy. For your classroom, the furniture must satisfy not only students but also faculty, administrators, campus planners, and the people at your school who actually do the purchasing. If your school is a state or other governmental institution, the furniture may also have to meet certain government-mandated engineering standards. If you have a formal green initiative, the purchase must satisfy environment-friendly criteria.

Number of Customers

Organizational customers are few and far between compared to end-user consumers. In the United States, there were 128.6 million consumer households but only 32.5 million businesses and other organizations in 2019.[69]

Size and Cost of Purchases

B2B products dwarf consumer purchases both in the quantity of items ordered and in how much a single item may cost. A company that rents uniforms to other businesses, for

Figure 6.9 *Snapshot* | Key Differences in Business versus Consumer Markets

There are a number of differences between business and consumer markets. To be successful, marketers must understand these differences and develop strategies specific to organizational customers.

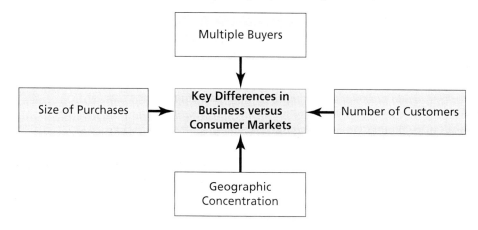

| Table 6.2 | Differences between Organizational and Consumer Markets |

Organizational Markets	Consumer Markets
• Purchases made for some purpose other than personal consumption	• Purchases for individual or household consumption
• Purchases made by someone other than the user of the product	• The ultimate user often makes the purchase
• Several people frequently make the decisions	• Individuals or small groups like couples and families usually decide
• Purchases made according to precise technical specifications based on product expertise	• Purchases often based on brand reputation or personal recommendations with little or no product expertise
• Purchases made after careful weighing of alternatives	• Purchases frequently made on impulse
• Purchases based on rational criteria	• Purchases based on emotional responses to products or promotions
• Purchasers often engage in lengthy decision processes	• Individual purchasers often make quick decisions
• Interdependencies between buyers and sellers; long-term relationships	• Buyers engage in limited-term or one-time-only relationships with many different sellers
• Purchases may involve competitive bidding, price negotiations, and complex financial arrangements	• Most purchases made at "list price" with cash or credit cards
• Products frequently purchased directly from producer	• Products usually purchased from someone other than producer of the product
• Purchases frequently involve high risk and high cost	• Most purchases are relatively low risk and low cost
• Limited number of large buyers	• Many individual or household customers
• Buyers often geographically concentrated in certain areas	• Buyers generally dispersed throughout total population
• Products often complex; classified based on how organizational customers use them	• Products: consumer goods and services for individual use
• Demand derived from demand for other goods and services, generally inelastic in the short run, subject to fluctuations, and may be joined to their demand for other goods and services	• Demand based on consumer needs and preferences, is generally price elastic, steady over time, and independent of demand for other products
• Promotion emphasizes personal selling	• Promotion emphasizes advertising including online and social media

example, buys hundreds of large drums of laundry detergent each year to launder its uniforms. In contrast, even a hard-core soccer family who deals with piles of dirty socks and shorts goes through a box of detergent only every few weeks.

Organizations purchase many products, such as a highly sophisticated piece of manufacturing equipment, computer-based marketing information systems that can cost a million dollars or more, and a dozen or so new jetliners costing billions. Recognizing such differences in the size of purchases allows marketers to develop effective marketing strategies.

Geographic Concentration

Another difference between business markets and consumer markets is *geographic concentration*, meaning that many business customers may locate in a single region of the country. Whether they live in the heart of New York City or in a small fishing village in Oregon, consumers buy and use toothpaste and TVs. For years, Silicon Valley, a 50-mile-long corridor close to the California coast, has been home to thousands of electronics and software companies because of its high concentration of skilled engineers and scientists. For B2B marketers who wish to sell to these markets, this means that they can concentrate their sales efforts and perhaps even locate distribution centers in a single geographic area.

B2B Demand

Demand in business markets differs from consumer demand. Most demand for B2B products is derived, inelastic, fluctuating, and joint. Understanding how these factors influence B2B demand is important for marketers when they forecast sales and plan effective marketing strategies. Of course, these are not always the biggest factors in successful marketing. During the COVID-19 pandemic in 2020, both consumer and business demand experienced large declines causing both small mom-and-pop businesses and large corporations to declare bankruptcy or just close. Let's look at each of these concepts in a bit more detail.

Derived Demand

derived demand
Demand for business or organizational products caused by demand for consumer goods or services.

Consumer demand is based on a direct connection between a need and the satisfaction of that need. But business customers don't purchase goods and services to satisfy their own needs. Businesses instead operate on **derived demand** because a business's demand for goods and services comes either directly or indirectly from consumers' demand for what it produces.

To better understand derived demand, take a look at Figure 6.10 (beginning at the bottom). Demand for forestry products comes from the demand for pulp, which in turn is derived from the demand for paper that publishers buy to make the textbooks you may use in your classes. The demand for textbooks comes from the demand for education (yes, education is the "product" you're buying—with the occasional party or football game thrown in as a bonus). As a result of derived demand, the success of one company may depend on another company in a different industry. The derived nature of business demand means that marketers must constantly be alert to changes in consumer trends that ultimately will have an effect on B2B sales. So, if fewer students attend college and those who do increasingly choose to purchase digital textbooks, the forestry industry has to find other sources of demand for its products.

Figure 6.10 *Process* | Derived Demand

B2B demand is derived demand. That is, the demand is derived directly or indirectly from consumer demand for another good or service. Some of the demand for forestry products is derived indirectly from the demand for corrugated boxes to ship all those online purchases we make.

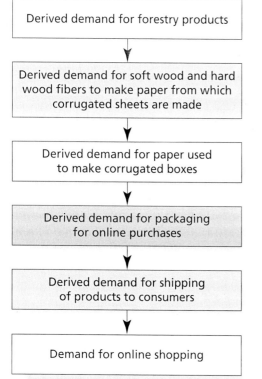

Inelastic Demand

Inelastic demand means that it usually doesn't matter if the price of a B2B product goes up or down—business customers still buy the same quantity. Demand in B2B markets is mostly inelastic because what an individual firm sells often is just one of the many parts or materials that go into producing the consumer product. It is not unusual for a large increase in a business product's price to have little effect on the final consumer product's price.

For example, you can buy a BMW M4 Coupe "loaded" with options for just over $80,000.[70] To produce the car, BMW purchases thousands of different parts. If the price of tires, batteries, or stereos goes up or down, BMW will still buy enough to meet consumer demand for its cars. As you might imagine, increasing the price by $30 or $40 or even $100 won't change consumer demand for the M4—so demand for parts remains the same. (If you have to ask how much it costs, you can't afford it!). We'll discuss inelastic demand more in Chapter 10.

Fluctuating Demand

Business demand also is subject to greater fluctuations than is consumer demand. There are two reasons for this. First, even modest changes in consumer demand can create large increases or decreases in business demand. Take, for example, air travel. A reluctance to fly due to fears about becoming infected with COVID-19 is one of many disturbances that can cause airlines to postpone or cancel orders for new equipment. This change in turn creates a dramatic decrease in demand for planes from manufacturers such as Boeing and Airbus.

A product's life expectancy is another reason for fluctuating demand. Business customers tend to purchase certain products infrequently. They may need to replace some types of large machinery only every 10 or 20 years. Thus, demand for such products fluctuates—it may be high one year when a lot of customers' machinery wears out but low the following year because everyone's old machinery works fine. Marketers can also generate fluctuating demand. When Boeing or Airbus develops jetliners that are more fuel efficient, airlines may decide they can increase profits by buying a whole new fleet and selling their old planes to a global market for used aircraft.

Joint Demand

Joint demand occurs when two or more goods are necessary to create a product. For example, BMW needs tires, batteries, and spark plugs to make that M4 that piqued your interest earlier. If the supply of one of these parts decreases, BMW will be unable to manufacture as many automobiles, so it will not buy as many of the other items either.

joint demand
Demand for two or more goods that are used together to create a product.

6.5 Business Purchase Situations and the Business Buying Decision Process

OBJECTIVE
Identify and describe the different business purchase situations and the business buying decision process, including the use of e-commerce and social media.

So far we've talked about how B2B markets are different from consumer markets and about the different types of customers that make up business markets. In this section, we'll discuss some of the important characteristics of business buying situations. This is important because just like companies that sell to end-user consumers, a successful B2B marketer needs to understand how his or her customers make decisions. Armed with this knowledge, the company is able to participate in the buyer's decision process from the start.

The Buyclass Framework

Like end-user consumers, business buyers spend more time and effort on some purchases than on others. This usually depends on the complexity of the product and how often they need to make the decision. A **buyclass** framework, as Figure 6.11 illustrates, identifies the degree of effort required of the firm's personnel to collect information and make a purchase decision. These classes, which apply to three different buying situations, are straight rebuys, modified rebuys, and new-task buys. Of course, in reality, the complexity and frequency of the decision may place the purchase anywhere on a continuum ranging from the simplest rebuy to a highly complicated new-task buy.

buyclass
One of three classifications of business buying situations that characterizes the degree of time and effort required to make a decision.

straight rebuy
A buying situation in which business buyers make routine purchases that require minimal decision making.

Straight Rebuy

A **straight rebuy** refers to the routine purchase of items that a B2B customer regularly needs. The buyer has purchased the same items many times before and routinely reorders them when supplies are low, often from the same suppliers. Reordering the items takes little time. Buyers typically maintain a list of approved vendors that have demonstrated their ability to meet the firm's criteria for pricing, quality, service, and delivery. GE Healthcare's customers routinely purchase its line of basic surgical scrubs (the clothing and caps doctors and nurses wear in the operating room) without much evaluation on each occasion.

Because straight rebuys often contribute the "bread-and-butter" revenue a firm needs to maintain a steady stream of income, many business marketers go to great lengths to cultivate and maintain relationships with customers who submit reorders on a regular basis.

Figure 6.11 *Snapshot* | Elements of the Buyclass Framework

The classes of the buyclass framework relate to three different organizational buying situations: straight rebuy, modified rebuy, and new-task buy.

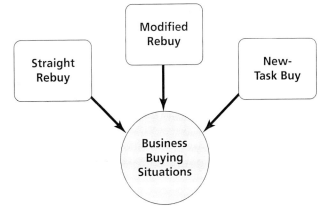

Salespeople may regularly call on these customers to personally handle orders and to see if there are additional products the customer needs—and to take the purchasing agent to lunch. The goal is to be sure that the customer doesn't even think twice about just buying the same product every time he or she runs low. Rebuys keep a supplier's sales volume up and help cover selling costs.

Modified Rebuy

Life is sweet for companies whose customers automatically do straight rebuys. Unfortunately, these situations don't last forever. A **modified rebuy** occurs when a firm decides to shop around for suppliers with better prices, quality, or delivery times. This situation also can occur when the organization confronts new needs for products it already buys. A buyer who purchased many Dell laptops for its salesforce, for example, may choose to reevaluate several other options when it is time for the firm to replace these older machines.

Modified rebuys require more time and effort than straight rebuys. The buyer generally knows the purchase requirements and has a few potential suppliers in mind. Marketers know that modified rebuys can mean that some vendors get added to a buyer's approved supplier list, whereas others may be dropped. So even if in the past a company purchased its laptops from Dell, this doesn't necessarily mean it will do so in the future as Apple, HP, and other companies introduce faster, smaller, lighter, and more powerful computers.

New-Task Buy

A first-time purchase is a **new-task buy**. Uncertainty and risk characterize buying decisions in this classification, and these decisions require the most effort because the buyer has no previous experience on which to base them.

Your university, for example, may decide (if it hasn't done so already) to put more money into online education that requires the purchase of state-of-the-art software to digitally proctor exams. This is a complex new-task buy for a school. In new-task buying situations, not only do buyers lack experience with the product, but they also are often unfamiliar with firms that supply the product. Supplier choice is critical, and buyers gather much information about quality, pricing, delivery, and service from several potential suppliers.

Marketers know that to get the order in a new-buy situation, they must develop a close working relationship with the business buyer. There are many situations in which marketers focus on selling their product by wooing people who recommend their products—over and above the end consumers who actually buy them. To use an example close to home, think about all of the goods and services that make up the higher-education industry. For instance, even though you are the one who shelled out the money for this extremely awesome text, your professor was the one who made the exceptionally wise decision to assign it. He or she made this choice (did we mention it was a really wise choice?) only after carefully considering numerous texts and talking to several publishers' sales representatives.

Professional Buyers and Buying Centers

Just as it is important for marketers of consumer goods and services to understand their customers, it's essential that B2B marketers understand who handles the buying for their business customers. Large retailers, for example, will often have a large number of trained professional buyers, each assigned to a single product category, who perform a buying function in B2B markets. These people have titles such as *purchasing agents, procurement officers*, or *directors of materials management*.

Although some consumers like to shop 'til they drop almost every day, most of us spend far less time roaming the aisles. However, professional purchasers do it all day, every day—it's their job and their business to buy. These individuals focus on economic factors beyond the initial price of the product, including transportation and delivery charges, accessory products or supplies, maintenance, and other ongoing costs. They are

---

modified rebuy

A buying situation classification used by business buyers to categorize a previously made purchase that involves some change and that requires limited decision making.

new-task buy

A new business-to-business purchase that is complex or risky and that requires extensive decision making.

Table 6.3	Roles in the Buying Center	
Role	Potential Player	Responsibility
• Initiator	• Production employees, sales managers, almost anyone	• Recognizes that a purchase needs to be made
• User	• Production employees, secretaries, almost anyone	• Individual(s) who will ultimately use the product
• Gatekeeper	• Buyers, purchasing agents	• Controls flow of information to others in the organization
• Influencer	• Engineers, quality control experts, technical specialists, outside consultants	• Affects decision by giving advice and sharing expertise
• Decider	• Purchasing agents, managers, CEOs	• Makes the final purchase decision
• Buyer	• Purchasing agents	• Executes the purchase decision

responsible for selecting quality products and ensuring their timely delivery. And, in our retailer example, they are responsible for the final impact on the company's bottom line for their purchases. They shop as if their jobs depend on it—because they do.

Many times in business buying situations, several people—ranging from a production worker to the CFO—work together to reach a decision. The **buying center** is a cross-functional team of people in the organization who participate in the decision-making process. Although this term may conjure up an image of "command central" buzzing with purchasing activity, a buying center is not a place at all. Generally, the members of a buying center have some expertise or interest in the particular decision, and as a group they are able to make the best decision.

Depending on the complexity of the purchase and the size of the buying center, a participant may assume one, several, or all of the six roles that Table 6.3 shows. Let's review them now.

- The *initiator* begins the buying process by first recognizing that the firm needs to make a purchase. A production employee, for example, may notice that a piece of equipment is not working properly and notify a supervisor that it is slowing up the production line. Depending on the initiator's position in the organization and the type of purchase, the initiator may or may not influence the actual purchase decision. For marketers, it's important to make sure that individuals who might initiate a purchase are aware of improved products they offer.

- The *user* is the member of the buying center who actually needs the product. The user's role in the buying center varies. For example, a firm's administrative assistants may be asked to give their input on the features a new copier should have because they will be chained to the machines for several hours a day. Marketers need to inform users of their products' benefits, especially if the benefits outweigh those that competitors offer.

- The *gatekeeper* is the person who controls the flow of information to other members. Typically, the gatekeeper is the purchasing agent, who gathers information and materials from salespeople, schedules sales presentations, and controls suppliers' access to other participants in the buying process. For salespeople, developing and maintaining strong personal relationships with gatekeepers is critical to being able to offer their products to the buying center.

- An *influencer* affects the buying decision when he or she dispenses advice or shares expertise. Highly trained employees, like engineers, quality control specialists, and other technical experts in the firm, generally have a great deal of influence in purchasing equipment, materials, and component parts the company uses in production. The influencers may or may not wind up using the product. Marketers need to identify key influencers in the buying center and persuade them of their product's superiority.

buying center
The group of people in an organization who participate in a purchasing decision.

- The *decider* is the member of the buying center who makes the final decision. This person usually has the greatest power within the buying center; he or she often has power within the organization to authorize spending the company's money. For a routine purchase, the decider may be the purchasing agent. If the purchase is complex, a manager or even the CEO may be the decider. The decider is critical to a marketer's success and deserves a lot of attention in the selling process.
- The *buyer* is the person who has responsibility to execute the purchase. The buyer obtains competing bids, negotiates contracts, and arranges delivery dates and payment plans. Once a firm makes the purchase decision, marketers turn their attention to negotiating the details of the purchase with the buyer. Successful marketers are well aware that providing exemplary service in this stage of the purchase can be a critical factor in achieving future sales from this client.

The Business Purchase Decision Process

We've seen that there are a number of players in the business buying process, beginning with an initiator and ending with a buyer. To make matters even more challenging to marketers, members of the buying team go through several stages in the decision-making process before the marketer gets an order. The *business buying decision process*, as Figure 6.12 shows, is a series of steps similar to those in the consumer decision process we discussed previously in this chapter. To help understand these steps, let's say you've just started working at the Way Radical Skateboard Company and your boss just assigned you to the buying center for the purchase of new software for web page design—a new-task buy for your firm.

Step 1: Recognize the Problem

As in consumer buying, the first step in the business buying decision process occurs when someone sees that a purchase can solve a problem. For straight rebuy purchases, this may occur because the firm has run out of paper, pens, or garbage bags. In these cases, the buyer places the order, and the decision-making process ends. Recognition of the need for modified rebuy purchases often comes when the organization wants to replace outdated equipment, when technology changes, or when an ad, brochure, or some other marketing communication offers the customer a better product or one at a lower price.

Two events may occur in the problem-recognition step. First, a member of the firm makes a request or requisition, usually in writing. Today, as firms are moving the purchasing process into their larger data management system, the request is likely to be in online form. Then, depending on the complexity of the purchase, the firm may form a buying center. The need for new-task purchases often occurs because the firm wants to enhance its operations in some way or a smart salesperson tells the business customer about a new product that will increase the efficiency of the firm's operations or improve the firm's end products.

Step 2: Search for Information

In the second step of the decision process (for purchases other than straight rebuys), the buying center searches for information about products and suppliers. Members of the buying center may individually or collectively refer to reports in trade magazines and journals, seek advice from outside consultants, and pay close attention to marketing communications from different manufacturers and suppliers. Of course, just like individual consumers, business buyers will certainly access online sources of information. As in consumer marketing, it's the job of marketers to make sure that information is available when and where business customers want it—by placing ads in trade magazines, by mailing brochures and other printed material to prospects, by using search engine marketing and/or

Figure 6.12 *Process* | Steps in the Business Buying Decision Process

The steps in the business buying decision process are the same as those in the consumer decision process. But for business purchases, each step may be far more complex and require more attention from marketers.

Step 1: Recognize the problem
• Make purchase requisition or request
• Form buying center, if needed

↓

Step 2: Search for Information
• Develop product specifications
• Identify potential suppliers
• Obtain proposals and quotations

↓

Step 3: Evaluate the Alternatives
• Evaluate proposals
• Obtain and evaluate samples

↓

Step 4: Select the Product and Supplier
• Issue purchase order

↓

Step 5: Evaluate Postpurchase
• Survey users
• Document performance

optimization as well as other means of communication via the Internet, and by having a well-trained sales force regularly calling on customers to build long-term relationships. We'll talk more about how B2B firms can use the Internet and social media to increase their sales later in this chapter.

There are thousands of specialized publications out there that cater to just about any industry you can think of. Usually sponsored by leading industry trade associations, each is bursting with information from competing companies that cater to a specific niche. Who needs that fluffy romance novel at the beach? Try leafing through the latest issue of *Chemical Processing* or *Meat and Poultry Magazine* instead. And, of course, these publications are also or only available online.

Sometimes, B2B marketers try to get the information about their product into the hands of buyers via less specialized media. For example, in recent years Aflac—the American Family Life Assurance Company of Columbus (the firm behind the famous duck)—has heavily advertised on TV even though most of its customers are in the B2B space. In fact, many end-user consumers don't have the foggiest notion what Aflac sells—but they sure love to "quack up" over the duck's antics. The truth is, Aflac's primary business is working with businesses (more than 400,000 of them, in fact) to enhance their employee benefits packages with various types of insurance and other benefits in order to improve recruiting and retention of the firms' people. But their strategy of advertising directly on mass media was brilliant; now when an organizational buyer or human resources manager searches for these services, Aflac's name will surely be at the top of the list. Now there's a duck that's not out of water![71]

Business buyers often develop **product specifications**, that is, a written description of the quality, size, weight, color, features, quantity, training, warranty, service terms, and delivery requirements for the purchase. When the product needs are complex or technical, engineers and other experts are the key players who identify specific product characteristics they require and determine whether the organizations can get by with standardized, off-the-shelf items or if they need to acquire customized, made-to-order goods and services. Once the product specifications are in hand, the next step is to identify potential suppliers and obtain written or verbal proposals, or *bids*, from one or more of them. For standardized or branded products in which there are few if any differences in the products of different suppliers, this may be as simple as an informal request for pricing information, including discounts, shipping charges, and confirmation of delivery dates. At other times, the potential suppliers receive a formal online *request for proposal* or *request for quotation* that requires detailed information from vendors.

product specifications
A written description of the quality, size, weight, and other details required of a product purchase.

Step 3: Evaluate the Alternatives

In this stage of the business buying decision process, the buying center assesses the proposals it receives. Total spending for goods and services can have a major impact on the firm's profitability, so, all other things being equal, price can be a primary consideration. Pricing evaluations must take into account discount policies for certain quantities, returned-goods policies, the cost of repair and maintenance services, terms of payment, and the cost of financing large purchases. For capital equipment, cost criteria also include the life expectancy of the purchase, the expected resale value, and disposal costs for the old equipment. In some cases, the buying center may negotiate with the preferred supplier to match the lowest bidder.

Although a firm often selects a bidder because it offers the lowest price, there are times when it bases the buying decision on other factors. For example, in its lucrative B2B market, American Express wins bids for its travel agency business because it offers extra services. A company that produces and sells high-tech medical equipment to hospitals may offer a free loaner if an item needs servicing or repairs while other vendors do not.

The more complex and costly the purchase, the more time buyers spend searching for the best supplier—and the more marketers must do to win the order. In some cases, a

customer reference program
A formalized process by which customers formally share success stories and actively recommend products to other potential clients, usually facilitated through an online community.

company may even ask one or more of its current customers to participate in a **customer reference program**. In these situations, customers formally share success stories and actively recommend products to other potential clients, often as part of an online community composed of people with similar needs.

Marketers often make formal presentations and product demonstrations to the buying center group. In the case of installations and large equipment, they may arrange for buyers to speak with or even visit other customers to examine how the product performs. For less complex products, the buying firm may ask potential suppliers for samples of the products so that its people can evaluate them personally. The buying center may ask salespeople from various companies to demonstrate their software for your Way Radical group so that you can all compare the capabilities of different products.

Step 4: Select the Product and Supplier

Once buyers have assessed all proposals, it's time for the rubber to hit the road. The next step in the buying process is the purchase decision when the group selects the best product and supplier to meet the organization's needs. Reliability and durability rank especially high for equipment and systems that keep the firm's operations running smoothly without interruption. For some purchases, warranties, repair service, and regular maintenance after the sale are important.

single sourcing
The business practice of buying a particular product from only one supplier.

One of the most important decisions a buyer makes is how many suppliers can best serve the firm's needs. Sometimes having one supplier is more beneficial to the organization than having multiple suppliers. **Single sourcing**, in which a buyer and seller work quite closely, is particularly important when a firm needs frequent deliveries or specialized products. Single sourcing also helps assure consistency of quality of materials input into the production process. But reliance on a single source means that the firm is at the mercy of the chosen supplier to deliver the needed goods or services without interruption. If the single source doesn't come through, the firm's relationship with its own end users will likely be affected.

However, using one or a few suppliers rather than many has its advantages. A firm that buys from a single supplier becomes a large customer with a lot of clout when it comes to negotiating prices and contract terms. Having one or a few suppliers also lowers the firm's administrative costs because it has fewer invoices to pay, fewer contracts to negotiate, and fewer salespeople to see than if it uses many sources.

multiple sourcing
The business practice of buying a particular product from several different suppliers.

In contrast, **multiple sourcing** means buying a product from several different suppliers. Under this system, suppliers are more likely to remain price competitive. And if one supplier has problems with delivery, the firm has others to fall back on. The automotive industry practices this philosophy: A vehicle manufacturer often won't buy a new product from a supplier unless the vendor's rivals also are capable of making the same item. This policy tends to stifle innovation, but it does ensure a steady supply of parts to feed to the assembly line.

reciprocity
A trading partnership in which two firms agree to buy from one another.

Sometimes supplier selection is based on **reciprocity**, which means that a buyer and seller agree to be each other's customers by saying, essentially, "I'll buy from you, and you buy from me." For example, a firm that supplies parts to a company that manufactures trucks would agree to buy trucks from only that firm.

The U.S. government frowns on reciprocal agreements and often determines that such agreements between large firms are illegal because they limit free competition; new suppliers simply don't have a chance against the preferred suppliers. Reciprocity between smaller firms, that is, firms that are not so large as to control a significant proportion of the business in their industry, is legal in the United States if both parties voluntarily agree to it. In other countries, reciprocity is a practice that is common and even expected in B2B marketing.

outsourcing
The business buying process of obtaining outside vendors to provide goods or services that otherwise might be supplied in house.

Outsourcing occurs when firms obtain outside vendors to provide goods or services that might otherwise be supplied in-house. For example, Sodexo is the world's largest outsourcer for quality-of-life services, including food and facilities management services in 80 countries. Sodexo serves 15 million consumers at 13,000 client sites in North America alone.[72] Colleges and universities are a major category of clientele for Sodexo (are they your school's vendor?) because these educational institutions want to focus on educating students rather than preparing and serving food. (Fortunately, your professors don't have to cook as well as teach!)

Outsourcing is an increasingly popular strategy, but in some cases, it can be controversial. Many critics object when U.S. companies contract with companies or individuals in remote places like China or India to perform work they used to do at home, a process known as **offshoring**. These tasks range from complicated jobs like writing computer code to fairly simple ones like manning reservations desks, staffing call centers for telephone sales, and even taking drive-through orders at U.S. fast-food restaurants. (Yes, in some cases, it's actually more efficient for an operator in India to relay an order from a customer for a #3 Burger Combo to the restaurant's cooks than for an on-site person to take the order.)

Yet another type of buyer–seller partnership is **reverse marketing**. Instead of sellers trying to identify potential customers and then "pitching" their products, buyers try to find suppliers that can produce specifically needed products and then attempt to "sell" the idea to the suppliers. Often large poultry producers practice reverse marketing. Perdue supplies baby chickens, chicken food, financing for chicken houses, medications, and everything else necessary for farmers to lay "golden eggs" for the company. This assures the farmer that he or she will have a buyer while at the same time Perdue knows it can rely on a steady supply of chickens.

offshoring
A process by which U.S. companies contract with companies or individuals in remote places like China or India to perform work they used to do at home.

reverse marketing
A business practice in which a buyer firm attempts to identify suppliers who will produce products according to the buyer firm's specifications.

Step 5: Evaluate Postpurchase

Just as consumers evaluate purchases, an organizational buyer assesses whether the performance of the product and the supplier lives up to expectations. The buyer surveys the users to determine their satisfaction with the product as well as with the installation, delivery, and service that the supplier provides. For producers of goods, this may relate to the level of satisfaction of the final consumer of the buying firm's product. Has demand for the producer's product increased, decreased, or stayed the same? By documenting and reviewing supplier performance, a firm decides whether to keep or drop the supplier.

An important element in postpurchase evaluation is measurement. When you think about measuring elements of a customer's experience with a company and its products and brands, we'll bet you automatically think about end-user consumers—like travelers' views of their Marriott hotel stay or the taste of that new Starbucks coffee flavor. Similarly, in the B2B world, managers pay a lot of attention to the feedback they get from their customers about the purchases they've made.

B2B E-Commerce and Social Media

We know that the Internet transformed marketing—from the creation of new products to providing more effective and efficient marketing communications to the actual distribution of some products. This is certainly true in business markets as well. **Business-to-business (B2B) e-commerce** refers to Internet exchanges of information, goods, services, and payments between two or more businesses or organizations. It's not as glitzy as consumer e-commerce, but it sure has changed the way businesses operate. Using the Internet for e-commerce allows business marketers to link directly to suppliers, factories, distributors, and their customers, radically reducing the time necessary for order and delivery of goods, tracking sales, and getting feedback from customers.

In the simplest form of B2B e-commerce, the Internet provides an online catalog of goods and services that businesses need. Companies find that their Internet site is important for delivering online technical support, product information, order status information, and customer service to corporate customers. Many companies, for example, save millions of dollars a year when they replace hard-copy manuals with electronic downloads. And, of course, B2B e-commerce creates some exciting opportunities for a variety of B2B service industries.

business-to-business (B2B) e-commerce
Online exchanges between two or more businesses or organizations.

Intranets and Extranets

Although the Internet is the primary means of B2B e-commerce, many companies maintain an *intranet*, which provides a more secure means of conducting business. As we said in Chapter 4, this term refers to an internal corporate computer network that uses Internet technology to link a company's departments, employees, and databases. Intranets give access only to authorized employees. They allow companies to process internal transactions with greater control and consistency because of stricter security measures than those they can use on the entire web. Businesses also use intranets to videoconference, distribute internal documents, communicate with geographically dispersed branches, and train employees.

extranet

A private, corporate computer network that links company departments, employees, and databases to suppliers, customers, and others outside the organization.

In contrast to an intranet, an **extranet** allows certain suppliers, customers, and others outside the organization to access a company's internal system. A business customer that a company authorizes to use its extranet can place orders online. Extranets can be especially useful for companies that need to have secure communications between the company and its dealers, distributors, or franchisees. As you can imagine, intranets and extranets are cost efficient and save money for organizations.

In addition to saving companies money, extranets allow business partners to collaborate on projects (such as product design) and build relationships. GE's extranet, the Trading Process Network, began as a set of online purchasing procedures and has morphed into an extensive online extranet community that connects GE with large buyers, such as Con Edison.

The Dark Side of B2B E-Commerce

Doing business the web-enabled way sounds great—perhaps too great. There are indeed security risks because so much information gets passed around in cyberspace. You've no doubt heard stories about hackers obtaining vast lists of consumers' credit card numbers from a number of retailers, including Target and Macy's. In 2018, two global organizations, Facebook and the Winter Olympics, were both hacked.[73] But companies have even greater worries. When hackers break into company sites, they can destroy company records and steal trade secrets. Both B2C and B2B e-commerce companies worry about *authentication* and ensuring that transactions are secure. This means making sure that only authorized individuals are allowed to access a site and place an order. Your university may have already instituted an authentication system whereby the system must make an individual contact with you once a week or so in order to access your grades, your Blackboard account, or how much you owe in parking fines. Maintaining security also requires firms to keep the information transferred as part of a transaction, such as a credit card number, from criminals' hard drives.

Well-meaning employees can also create security problems. They can give out unauthorized access to company computer systems by being careless about keeping their passwords into the system a secret. For example, hackers can guess at obvious passwords—nicknames, birth dates, hobbies, or a spouse's name.

malware

Software designed specifically to damage or disrupt computer systems.

Some employees (and even nonemployees) are not so well-meaning; they deliberately create security breaches by leaking confidential documents or hacking into an organization's computer system for sensitive information. Edward Snowden became famous (or, rather, infamous) for his role in leaking thousands of classified documents to the media while working as a consultant for the National Security Agency. And Target's computer system was breached when hackers installed **malware** (software designed specifically to damage or disrupt computer systems) that captured more than 40 million credit card numbers and other customer data despite safeguards the retailer had in place.[74]

spyware

Software that covertly gathers information from an individual's or an organization's computer.

Another security risk comes from **spyware**, software that covertly gathers information from an individual's or an organization's intranet without them giving consent or even knowing it. Much of spyware is for the purpose of tracking and storing movements on the Web in order to send those pop-up ads that we all enjoy so much. Of course, there is also more malicious spyware that seeks not just to track users but also to steal user logins and credit card and bank information. All this has made it necessary for organizations to maintain antimalware and antispyware protection in addition to antivirus software.

To increase security of their Internet sites and transactions, most companies now have safeguards in place—firewalls and encryption devices, to name the two most common methods, though, as we saw with Target, even these safeguards aren't always 100 percent hacker-proof. A **firewall** is a combination of hardware and software that ensures that only authorized individuals gain entry into a computer system. The firewall monitors and controls all traffic between the Internet and the intranet to restrict access. Companies may even place additional firewalls within their intranet when they wish only designated employees to have access to certain parts of the system. Although firewalls can be fairly effective (even though none is totally foolproof), they require costly, constant monitoring.

firewall
A combination of hardware and software that ensures that only authorized individuals gain entry into a computer system.

Encryption means scrambling a message so that only another individual (or computer) with the right "key" can unscramble it. Otherwise, it looks like gobbledygook. The message is inaccessible without the appropriate encryption software—kind of like a decoder ring your favorite superhero might wear. Without encryption, it would be easy for unethical people to get a credit card number by creating a "sniffer" program that intercepts and reads messages. A sniffer finds messages with four blocks of four numbers, copies the data, and voilà!—someone else has your credit card number.

encryption
The process of scrambling a message so that only another individual (or computer) with the right "key" can unscramble it.

Despite firewalls, encryption, and other security measures, web security for B2B marketers remains a serious problem. The threat to intranet and extranet usage goes beyond competitive espionage. The increasing sophistication of hackers and Internet criminals who create viruses, worms, and other approaches to disrupting individual computers and entire company systems means that all organizations—and consumers—are vulnerable to attacks and must remain vigilant.

B2B and Social Media

Although most of us associate business use of social media such as Facebook, LinkedIn, and Twitter with consumer marketing, B2B organizations are increasing their use of and their budgets for social media:[75]

- A recent study found three social media sites that B2B marketers are most likely to use: LinkedIn (89 percent), Twitter (77 percent), and Facebook (76 percent). Importance ratings for the three sites were lower: LinkedIn (71 percent), Twitter (55 percent), and Facebook (38 percent).
- Eighty-three percent used social media content to deliver their content marketing tactics.[76]

As with consumer marketing, a number of strategies can be successful in using social media marketing for B2B firms.[77] First, social media sites are good sources of information to identify target audiences. It's helpful to know which potential customers your competitors interact with on social media. And, one of the most important uses of social media for both consumer marketers and business marketers is to monitor what your customers and others say about your product, your firm, and your competitors. A number of tools, such as Google Analytics, Radian6, and Social Mention, have been developed for this purpose. Social media provide platforms for marketers or consumers to join in conversations, get answers to their questions, and share experiences. Marketers who understand social media contribute to conversations on Twitter, Facebook, and blogs. They give good answers to questions and establish their credibility and a leadership position in the industry.

6.6 Brand You: Why Employers Buy

Taylor has made great progress in developing a strategic plan for his personal brand. He has created a personal mission statement and identified his personal strengths and weaknesses as well as his skills and talents. Looking at the external environment, Taylor has determined where the best opportunities for him are. In addition, he has looked at trends in the field that will impact his career long term. Based on this, he has completed a SWOT analysis for his career opportunities. He has made a list of industries and companies that would likely be in the market for an employee with his knowledge and skills and where he believes he would like to work. Now it is time to examine his potential customers and how he can satisfy their needs for a new employee or intern, thus convincing them to "buy" him.

In Chapter 1 of this book, we discussed how a product can be a good, a service, a person, or a place. Just like any other product, to successfully market a person—in this case, you—requires an understanding of why employers buy. In your job search, employers are your customers.

Step 1: Understand the Employer's Decision Process

We hate to tell you, but getting a job is not about you. It's about the company's needs. Just as marketing a pair of shoes or a smartphone or a hamburger isn't about the seller; it's about satisfying consumer needs. That means you must learn to tell your story about how your experiences, skills, expertise, and personal characteristics will bring value to the company or client.

You might think about this in the same way we've discussed how understanding the steps consumers go through in the decision process can help marketers keep the customer moving toward purchase and eventual brand loyalty.

1. *Problem recognition:* Seeing a difference between the current state and some desired state. Such is the case when someone retires or the company's growth creates needs for more employees. The hiring manager has an open position, and his organization is not complete until someone new is hired.

2. *Information search:* The hiring manager normally posts the position when a new hire is needed.

3. *Evaluation of alternatives:* The hiring manager reviews the résumés, interviews some candidates, and conducts background checks.

4. *Product choice:* The hiring manager makes the decision to extend an offer to one of the qualified candidates.

5. *Postpurchase evaluation:* Most organizations have a probationary time frame, normally three to six months, after which they will evaluate the employee, provide feedback, and make a decision whether to keep the new employee.

Step 2: Understand the Process of Creating Brand You

Branding is a process of determining who you are. How can you differentiate yourself from the hundreds or thousands of other college grads who are also looking for a job? This means focusing on your benefits—the value you add to an organization. Creating Brand You is not an attempt to "fake it." It's all about understanding the ways in which you can add value to an organization and be able to verbalize them.

Think about it this way. If you were the boss and you were hiring someone, what kind of person would you want? What skills and knowledge would they need to do the job and to meet the future needs of the organization? Would you want someone who is dependable? A creative thinker? A multitasker? Outgoing? A team player? A great problem solver?

Now is the time to review your mission statement and your SWOT analysis. From this, you decide what you have to offer as your core competency. What is the thing you do best that will add value to the organization?

Taylor now understands the steps in the decision process of the manager who will be hiring a new employee or intern. He has focused on what the employer is likely to be looking for in job applicants and has reviewed his mission statement and SWOT analysis in order to clearly articulate what core competencies he has to offer an organization.

With these insights into his job search, he is ready to move forward with development of his Brand You strategies.

Objective **Summaries** and **Key Terms**

6.1 Objective Summary

Define *consumer behavior*, and explain the purchase decision-making process.

Consumer behavior is the process individuals or groups go through to select, purchase, use, and dispose of goods, services, ideas, or experiences to satisfy their needs and desires. Consumer decisions differ greatly, ranging from habitual, repeat (low-involvement) purchases to complex, extended problem-solving activities for important, risky (high-involvement) purchases. When consumers make important purchases, they go through a series of five steps. First, they recognize there is a problem to be solved. Then, they search for information to make the best decision. Next, they evaluate a set of alternatives and judge them on the basis of various evaluative criteria. At this point, they are ready to make their purchasing decision. Following the purchase, consumers decide whether the product matched their expectations and may develop anxiety, regret, or buyer's remorse.

Key Terms

consumer behavior
involvement
perceived risk
problem recognition
information search
evoked set
consideration set
comparison-shopping agents (shopbots)
determinant attributes
evaluative criteria
compensatory decision rules
heuristics
brand loyalty
consumer satisfaction/dissatisfaction
buyer's remorse
ZMOT
hyperchoice
food porn
chatbots

6.2 Objective Summary

Explain how internal factors influence consumers' decision-making processes.

Several internal factors influence consumer decisions. Perception is how consumers select, organize, and interpret stimuli. Motivation is an internal state that drives consumers to satisfy needs. Learning is a change in behavior that results from information or experience. Behavioral learning results from external events, whereas cognitive learning refers to internal mental activity. An attitude is a lasting evaluation of a person, object, or issue and includes three components: affect, cognition, and behavior. Personality influences how consumers respond to situations in the environment. Marketers seek to understand a consumer's self-concept to develop product attributes that match some aspect of the consumer's self-concept.

Consumers' age, family life cycle, and lifestyle are also strongly related to consumption preferences. Marketers may use psychographics to group people according to activities, interests, and opinions that may explain reasons for purchasing products.

Key Terms

perception
exposure
subliminal advertising
attention
multitasking
rich media
interpretation
motivation
hierarchy of needs
gamification
learning
behavioral learning theories

classical conditioning
operant conditioning
cognitive learning theory
observational learning
attitude
ABC Theory of Attitudes
affect
sadvertising
cognition
behavior
personality
self-concept
family life cycle
lifestyle
activities, interests, and opinions (AIOs)

6.3 Objective Summary

Show how situational factors and consumers' relationships with other people influence consumer behavior.

Situational influences include our physical surroundings and time pressures. Dimensions of the physical environment create arousal and pleasure and can determine how consumers react to the environment. The time of day, the season of the year, and how much time one has to make a purchase also affect decision making. Consumers' overall preferences for products are determined by their membership in cultures and subcultures and by cultural values, such as collectivism and individualism. Consumerism is a social movement directed toward protecting consumers from harmful business practices. Social class, group memberships, and opinion leaders are other types of social influences that affect consumer choices. A reference group is a set of people a consumer wants to please or imitate, and this affects the consumer's purchasing decisions. Purchases also result from conformity to real or imagined group pressures.

Another way social influence is felt is in gender roles, the expectations of society regarding the proper roles for men and women and what products are appropriate for each gender. Today, as cultures and gender roles are changing, many marketing programs include ads and other strategies that give support to the acceptance of all LGBTQ+ people and thus discourage discrimination.

Key Terms

sensory marketing
sensory branding
time poverty
showrooming
webrooming
HoloLens
flawsome
social graph
data-driven disruptive marketing
in-homing
culture
subculture
microcultures

consumerism
conscientious consumerism
social class
status symbols
mass class
reference group
opinion leader
gender roles

6.4 Objective Summary

Understand the characteristics of business-to-business markets and how marketers classify business-to-business customers.

B2B markets include business or organizational customers that buy goods and services for purposes other than personal consumption. Business customers include producers, resellers, governments, and not-for-profit organizations. Producers purchase materials, parts, and various goods and services needed to produce other goods and services to be sold at a profit. Resellers purchase finished goods to resell at a profit as well as other goods and services to maintain their operations. Governments and other not-for-profit organizations purchase the goods and services necessary to fulfill their objectives. The NAICS, a numerical coding system developed by NAFTA countries, is a widely used classification system for business and organizational markets.

There are a number of major and minor differences between organizational and consumer markets. To be successful, marketers must understand these differences and develop strategies that can be effective with organizational customers. For example, business customers are usually few in number, they may be geographically concentrated, and they often purchase higher-priced products in larger quantities. Business demand derives from the demand for another good or service, is generally not affected by price increases or decreases, is subject to great fluctuations, and may be tied to the demand and availability of some other good.

Key Terms

business-to-business (B2B) markets
organizational markets
producers
resellers
government markets
North American Industry Classification System (NAICS)
derived demand
joint demand

6.5 Objective Summary

Identify and describe the different business purchase situations and the business buying decision process, including the use of e-commerce and social media.

The buyclass framework identifies the degree and effort required to make a business purchase decision. Purchase situations can be straight rebuy, modified rebuy, and new-task buying. A buying center is a group of people who work together to make a buying decision. The roles in the buying center are (1) the initiator, who recognizes the need for a purchase; (2) the user, who will ultimately use the product; (3) the gatekeeper, who controls the flow of information to others; (4) the influencer, who shares advice and expertise; (5) the decider, who makes the final decision; and (6) the buyer, who executes the purchase. The steps in the business buying process are similar to those in the consumer decision process but are often somewhat more complex. For example, in the search for information, B2B firms often develop written product specifications, identify potential suppliers, and obtain proposals and quotations.

B2B e-commerce refers to Internet exchanges of information, goods and services, and payments between two or more businesses or organizations. B2B firms often maintain intranets that give access only to employees or extranets that allow access to certain suppliers and other outsiders. Firms often install firewalls and use encryption to prevent problems from hackers and other threats to the security of the firm's intranets and extranets. B2B firms are increasingly using social media to gather information on target audiences, increase brand exposure and web traffic, monitor what customers and others are saying, and provide a platform for conversations with customers.

Key Terms

buyclass
straight rebuy
modified rebuy
new-task buy
buying center
product specifications
customer reference program
single sourcing
multiple sourcing
reciprocity
outsourcing
offshoring
reverse marketing
business-to-business (B2B) e-commerce
extranet
malware
spyware
firewall
encryption

6.6 Objective Summary

Understand what prospective employers are looking for in an employee and how you can meet their needs, thus increasing your chances that the employer will "buy" or hire you.

Getting a job is about the company's needs, meaning you must learn to tell how your experiences, skills, expertise, and personal characteristics will bring value to the company. Employers follow the same process in deciding on a new employee as consumers do in their purchase decisions (problem recognition, information search, evaluation of alternatives, product choice, and postpurchase evaluation).

To differentiate yourself from other job applicants, you should focus on your benefits—that is, understanding the ways you can add value to an organization and being able to verbalize them. Analyzing your mission statement and SWOT analysis will help you identify what you have as your core competency.

Chapter **Questions** and **Activities**

Concepts: Test Your Knowledge

6-1. What is consumer behavior and why is it important for marketers to understand consumer behavior?

6-2. Explain habitual decision making, limited problem solving, and extended problem solving. What is the role of perceived risk in the decision process?

6-3. Explain the steps in the consumer decision-making process.

6-4. What is perception? What is Maslow's hierarchy? What is gamification?

6-5. What is behavioral learning? What is cognitive learning? What are attitudes and personality? What is the family life cycle?

6-6. What are the three components of attitudes?

6-7. In what ways did the COVID-19 pandemic change consumer behavior?

6-8. What are values, trends, cultures, subcultures, and microcultures, and how do they shape consumer behavior.

6-9. What is the significance of social class to marketers?

6-10. What are reference groups, and how do they influence consumers? What are opinion leaders?

6-11. What are gender roles? How does marketing influence gender roles? What changes in gender roles have come about in recent years and how have marketing activities influenced this change?

6-12. How do B2B markets differ from consumer markets?

6-13. Explain what we mean by derived demand, inelastic demand, fluctuating demand, and joint demand.

6-14. Describe the buyclass framework. What are new-task buys, modified rebuys, and straight rebuys?

6-15. What is a buying center? What are the roles of the members in a buying center?

6-16. How do the steps in the consumer decision process differ from the steps in the business buying process?

6-17. What is single sourcing? Multiple sourcing? Outsourcing?

6-18. Explain the role of intranets and extranets in B2B e-commerce. Describe the security issues firms face in B2B e-commerce and some safeguards firms use to reduce their security risks.

Activities: Apply What You've Learned

6-19. *Creative Homework/Short Project* This chapter indicated that consumers go through a series of steps (from problem recognition to postpurchase evaluation) as they make purchases. Write a detailed report describing what you as a consumer would do in each of these steps when deciding to purchase one of the following products:

a. A new suit for a job interview
b. A new smartphone
c. Tickets for a movie for you and a date
d. A bottle of shampoo
e. A new lamp for your desk where you study

Then, make suggestions for what marketers might do to make sure that consumers like you who are going through each step in the consumer decision process move toward the purchase of their brand. (*Hint:* Think about product, place, price, and promotion strategies.)

6-20. *In Class, 10–25 Minutes for Teams* During the last week of class, your professor explains how she wants to employ a gamification strategy next semester to further motivate and engage students, and she is asking for your help. Develop a simple gamification strategy that she can use in the classroom. Describe what the goals should be, how progress will be measured, and what the reward system will be.

6-21. *Creative Homework/Short Project* You probably had more than one school in mind before you ultimately decided on the college or university you are now attending. To better understand how consumers make decisions, prepare an outline that shows how internal influences like perception, motivation, and so on had an impact on the decision you made about which school to attend. Include specific examples for each type of internal influence in your outline.

6-22. *For Further Research (Individual)* You work for a firm that produces and sells high-end digital cameras. You are concerned about the effects of current consumer trends, including improved quality of in-phone cameras and the decrease in photo printing. Others in your firm do not share your concerns—they think "business as usual" will be adequate. Develop a memo for upper management that outlines your concerns, the impact you think the trends could have on the business, and what the company could do to help decrease the chance of negative results.

6-23. *For Further Research (Groups)* We learned in this chapter that when considering a product need, consumers have an evoked set of brands and a consideration set of brands. With some of your classmates, conduct a simple research study and explain your results using the following steps:

a. Select a product that students in college might purchase.
b. Develop a questionnaire that you will ask student participants to complete. The questionnaire should ask students to list all of the brands of the product

you have selected that they are aware of. Give them at least five minutes to complete this question.
c. Then, ask them to tell you which ones they would seriously consider buying if they were going to make a purchase today.
d. Develop a report using the results of the survey. What conclusions can you draw from the research?

6-24. *Creative Homework/Short Project* Assume you are employed in the marketing department of a firm that makes transmissions for BMW automobiles. You are part of a buying center that is addressing several needed purchases. One is a new-task buy, one is a modified rebuy, and one is a straight rebuy. First, list a product that you imagine would fall into each of the three categories for the firm. Then, describe the steps you would think the buying center would go through in each of the three buys. Write a brief report on your ideas.

6-25. *In Class, 10–25 Minutes for Teams* With your team members, make a list of the ways in which the values of your age subculture, the values of your parents' age subculture, and the values of your grandparents' age subculture differ and are alike. You might want to think of this in terms of categories, e.g., values regarding money or values regarding different purchases. Next, develop your assumptions as to why these differences exist. Make a brief presentation to your class.

Concepts: Apply Marketing Metrics

B2B customers (clients) are busy professionals and thus are notoriously reluctant to take time to provide data to marketers. To measure important issues described in the chapter, such as overall client satisfaction, service quality by the vendor firm, level of customer engagement, repurchase intentions, and speed and effectiveness of problem resolution, marketers must employ the most user-friendly and efficient data collection methods available when dealing with these professional business clients. Otherwise, it is highly unlikely that they will take time to provide any useful data for market planning and decision making.

6-26. Take a few minutes to go back and briefly review what you learned in Chapter 4 about the different approaches to collecting data. Propose an approach to collecting the types of information from a busy B2B customer in a way that is most likely to result in his or her cooperation. Be as specific as you can in describing your chosen approach and explain why you selected it. Then, explain your recommendation and justification for it.

Choices: What Do You Think?

6-27. *Critical Thinking* Changing demographics and cultural values are important to marketers. List at least three current trends that may affect the successful marketing of the following products:

a. Toys
b. Electronics

c. Education
d. Clothing
e. Travel and tourism
f. Automobiles

6-28. *Critical Thinking* Consumers often buy products because they feel pressure from reference groups to conform. Does conformity exert a positive or a negative influence on consumers? With what types of products is conformity more likely to occur?

6-29. *Ethics* Marketers have been shelling out the bucks on sensory marketing techniques for years to appeal to your subconscious mind. And studies show that it works. But is sensory marketing fair? Some say it's a way to enhance the purchasing process, while others say marketers are unethically manipulating consumers. What are some of the pros and cons associated with sensory marketing? What is your position?

6-30. *Critical Thinking* Mobile commerce (m-commerce) takes place via a smartphone or tablet instead of a desktop or laptop computer. How has m-commerce changed the way consumers shop? What do marketers need to do now and in the future to better support their m-commerce customers? What do you think the future of m-commerce will be?

6-31. *Critical Thinking* The practice of buying business products based on sealed competitive bids is popular among all types of business buyers. What are the advantages and disadvantages of this practice to buyers? What are the advantages and disadvantages to sellers? Should companies always give the business to the lowest bidder? Why or why not?

6-32. *Critical Thinking* What are some potential benefits and what are some potential negative outcomes of a culture's gender roles? We said that gender roles are changing today. Describe the changes you have seen in gender roles in the past two years.

6-33. *Ethics* Many firms in developed countries such as the U.S. contract with companies in least developed countries to perform work that they used to do at home, a process called *offshoring*. This practice has received much criticism for a number of different reasons. What do you think about offshoring? Is it unethical, and if so, in what ways? Who is benefitting from this practice and how? Who is being hurt by this practice and how?

6-34. *Critical Thinking* Do you think that subliminal advertising is illegal? Do you think it should be illegal if it is not? Do you believe it exists and is being used by marketers today? Do you think most people agree with you? Why do you think it is discussed so much?

Miniproject: Learn by Doing

The purpose of this miniproject is to increase your understanding of the process that consumers go through when making a purchase decision. First, select one of the following products (or some other product of your choice) that now, or in the future, you might be in the market for:

- New or used car
- Spring break vacation
- Apartment
- Computer or smartphone

6-35. *Problem Recognition* Describe the situation or event that might lead you to purchase this product.

6-36. *Information Search* Use the Internet to gather some initial information about the product you chose. Visit at least two stores or locations where the product may be purchased to gather further information.

6-37. *Evaluation of Alternatives* Identify at least five alternative product options that you are interested in. Narrow down your selection to two or three choices. Which are the most feasible? What are the pros and cons of each?

6-38. *Product Choice* Make a final decision about which product you will purchase. Describe the heuristics that aided in your decision making.

6-39. *Postpurchase Evaluation* If this is a product you have actually purchased, explain the reasoning behind your current satisfaction or dissatisfaction with the product. If not, develop several reasons you might be satisfied or dissatisfied with the product.

6-40. Prepare a report that explains in detail the decision-making process for the product in your purchase scenario.

Marketing in Action **Case**   Real Choices at Anheuser-Busch InBev

Can beer drinkers distinguish between the taste of one brand of beer and another? Research studies say they can't. This is one reason that beer marketing has traditionally focused more on establishing an identity for the brand and less on differentiating it from competitors. In recent years, however, beer consumers have shown that they actually want something different in the products they choose, driving them not just to new brands, but to whole new categories of alcoholic beverages. The popularity of so-called "hard" seltzers is the latest example of this shift in behavior. Market leader Anheuser-Busch InBev hopes to capitalize on this trend with its line of spiked seltzer drinks.

Anheuser-Busch InBev (commonly called AB InBev) is the parent company of the brand Budweiser, the undisputed "King of Beers." The company has a massive portfolio of brands—some 500—including well-known names Corona, Stella Artois, Michelob Ultra and the best-selling beer in the U.S., Bud Light. Until recently, the most seismic shift in beer consumer preferences was toward less filling, lower calorie brews. Anheuser-Busch did not pioneer this category (Miller Lite was first in 1975), but it later took over leadership with Bud Light. While traditional beer is still the largest category of alcohol in the U.S., a 2019 study showed the category is shrinking, falling from 22.3 percent of in-store sales to 17.7 percent. Some consumers reduced their alcohol consumption, while others moved to the more distinctive "craft" brews. In the last two years, many of these traditional beer drinkers moved to flavored malt beverages, of which hard seltzers are the most popular.

A focus on health and wellness helped drive the popularity of light beer, and it's driving much of the interest in the new seltzer products. A 2020 survey found that 59 percent of beer drinkers had reduced beer drinking for health reasons. Sixty-two percent said they were most concerned about weight gain, and 29 percent reported that they count calories most or all of the time when they drink. A Nielsen study found that those who choose craft beers were looking for more variety, as well as better quality and more flavor options. Much of this trend is driven by younger drinkers—millennials and Gen Zers—who think of traditional beer as stale and unhealthy. These more "mindful" drinkers are also more adventurous. They look for something different in their beverages (along with a buzz), and hard seltzer producers like AB InBev are happy to oblige.

AB InBev is attacking the seltzer market with several brands that focus on different demographics. Its Bon & Viv is a premium product targeted toward non-beer drinkers, particularly millennial women. Natural Light Seltzer targets a market familiar to you: college age drinkers of its popular Natural Light beer. This offering is priced for the lower budgets of its target market; it costs about 20 percent less than mainstream alternatives. But the company's biggest play is the leveraging of its top brand with the introduction of Bud Light Seltzer. Priced between its other two seltzer offerings, AB InBev hopes this new product in its portfolio will attract the average "backyard beer drinker" who is looking for a crisp alternative from a familiar brand. The numbers are right for the health-conscious imbiber: 100 calories, 1 gram of sugar, 2 grams of carbs, and 5 percent alcohol. For variety (or adventure), you get a choice of Black Cherry, Lemon Lime, Strawberry, or Mango.

The company is serious about seltzers, with plans to invest an additional $100 million into the category. It launched the brand with an ad that takes place in the real town of Seltzer, Pennsylvania, where a fictitious mayor sums up the company's ambitions for the product, saying "If you love Bud Light, you'll love Bud Light Seltzer. If you don't love Bud Light, you'll love Bud Light Seltzer." As further proof of its commitment, Bud Light Seltzer was promoted with a 60-second Super Bowl ad in 2020 that the new product shared with its namesake, Bud

Light. To create extra buzz, the company let social media users select which of two ads actually made it to the Super Bowl.

The future looks pretty sparkling for seltzers. While growing by over 212 percent in 2019, the subcategory still represented only 2.6 percent of the overall beer market. AB InBev hopes it can capture 20 percent of the market with its three seltzer brands. Compared to craft beers that have many small producers, hard seltzer is largely driven by national brands, which of course plays to the strengths of a company like AB InBev with its huge distribution network. The hard seltzer category, worth $1.75 billion in 2019, is expected to grow to $4.7 billion by 2022. Fifty percent of alcohol drinkers haven't even tried seltzer yet, a factor that AB InBev thinks plays to its advantage due to the high awareness of its existing beer brands. But AB InBev is playing catchup in the market. Early 2020 numbers claimed only nine percent market share for Bud Light Seltzer, and 2019 share numbers for Bon & Viv and Natural Light Seltzer landed at 5 percent and 2 percent, respectively. This combined 16 percent share is still far behind market leader White Claw, whose share in 2019 was 59 percent.

AB InBev's chief marketing officer, Pedro Earp, understands how beer consumers have changed. He observes, " . . . years ago, you could create an average product or a product that didn't have a lot of functional difference and you could really use mass advertising to drive emotional differentiation. The world has completely changed. Consumers are much more savvy about what's a great product or not. So true product differentiation became a much more important factor than emotional differentiation." He added, " . . . you need to understand your consumers much better, their passion points and needs." The company's challenge ahead is to understand and respond to those changing consumer tastes with beverage tastes that beer drinkers will continue to buy.[78]

Questions for Discussion

6-41. What factors do you believe drive beer drinkers' buying behavior? How can beer marketers best respond to those preferences with adjustments to the marketing mix?

6-42. What are the unique characteristics of GenZ beer consumers that the AB InBev marketing team should consider? How do these influence each of the four parts of the marketing mix?

6-43. In 2016, bottled water eclipsed carbonated soft drinks in sales. What could AB InBev learn from that industry's experience and the strategy executed by market leaders Coca-Cola and Pepsi?

Chapter **Notes**

1. Geoff Williams, "The Heavy Price of Losing Weight," *U.S. News & World Report,* January 2, 2013, http://money.usnews.com/money/personal-finance/articles/2013/01/02/the-heavy-price-of-losing-weight (accessed December 24, 2015).
2. James R. Bettman, "The Decision Maker Who Came in from the Cold," Presidential Address, in *Advances in Consumer Research*, vol. 20, ed. Leigh McAllister and Michael Rothschild (Provo, UT: Association for Consumer Research, 1990); John W. Payne, James R. Bettman, and Eric J. Johnson, "Behavioral Decision Research: A Constructive Processing Perspective," *Annual Review of Psychology 4*

(1992): 87–131; for an overview of recent developments in individual choice models, see Robert J. Meyer and Barbara E. Kahn, "Probabilistic Models of Consumer Choice Behavior," in *Handbook of Consumer Behavior*, ed. Thomas S. Robertson and Harold H. Kassarjian (Englewood Cliffs, NJ: Prentice Hall, 1991), 85–123.
3. Benjamin Preston, "Coronavirus Is Pushing Car Dealerships into Online Sales and Home Delivery," *Consumer Reports*, April 8, 2020, https://www.consumerreports.org/buying-a-car/corona-virus-pushing-car-dealerships-into-online-sales-and-home-delivery/

4. Reza Merchant, "21+ Best Price Comparison Websites for Your Online Products in 2020," *Cloudways*, April 20, 2020, https://www.cloudways.com/blog/price-comparison-websites/ (accessed May 16, 2020).

5. Yousra Zaki, "5 Apps That Help You Save Money in the UAE," *Gulf News*, March 5, 2018, http://gulfnews.com/guides/life/5-appsthat-help-you-save-money-in-the-uae-1.2118978 (accessed March 10, 2018); https://ae.pricena.com (accessed February 28, 2018).

6. Jessica Wohl, "Atkins Hires Rob Lowe to Promote Its 'Lifestyle' (It's Not Just a Diet)," *Advertising Age*, January 3, 2018, http://adage.com/article/cmo-strategy/atkins-hires-rob-lowe-promote-lifestyle-a-diet/311791/ (accessed February 15, 2018); Atkins, "How It Works," https://www.atkins.com/how-it-works (accessed May 16, 2020).

7. Suzanne Kapner and Andrew Scurria, "J.C. Penney, Pinched by Coronavirus, Files for Bankruptcy," *The Wall Street Journal*, May 15, 2020, https://www.wsj.com/articles/j-c-penney-pinched-by-coronavirus-files-for-bankruptcy-11589582224?mod=djemalertNEWS (accessed May 15, 2020).

8. Harriet Torry, "Coronavirus Lockdowns Trigger Rapid Drop in Retail Sales Factory Output," *The Wall Street Journal*, May 15, 2020, https://www.wsj.com/articles/coronavirus-lockdowns-trigger-record-spending-drops-on-shopping-eating-out-11589535000?mod=djemalertNEWS (accessed May 15, 2020).

9. Joshua Nite, "This Changes Everything: How AI Is Transforming Digital Marketing," Toprankblog.com, February 19, 2018, http://www.toprankblog.com/2018/02/artificial-intelligence-transforming-marketing/ (accessed March 25, 2018).

10. James Maguire, "12 Examples of Artificial Intelligence: AI Powers Business," Datamation.com, September 13, 2019, https://www.datamation.com/artificial-intelligence/examples-of-artificial-intelligence.html (accessed May 25, 2020).

11. Michael Keenan, "The 15 Best Chatbot Examples in 2020," Manychat, March 16, 2020, https://manychat.com/blog/chatbot-examples/#WHO-health-alert (accessed May 16, 2020).

12. Gary L. Clark, Peter F. Kaminski, and David R. Rink, "Consumer Complaints: Advice on How Companies Should Respond Based on an Empirical Study," *Journal of Services Marketing* 6 (Winter 1992): 41–50.

13. Michael Lev, "No Hidden Meaning Here: Survey Sees Subliminal Ads," *New York Times*, May 3, 1991, D7.

14. "ABC Rejects KFC Commercial, Citing Subliminal Advertising," Wall Street Journal Interactive Edition, March 2, 2006.

15. Alison Doyle, "Multitasking Definition, Skills, and Examples," *The Balance*, February 15, 2018, https://www.thebalance.com/multitasking-skills-with-examples-2059692 (accessed March 10, 2018).

16. https://www.chevrolet.com/performance/corvette/build-and-price/config (accessed December 15, 2020).

17. Nicholas Bakalar, "If It Says McDonald's, Then It Must Be Good," *New York Times*, August 14, 2007, https://www.nytimes.com/2007/08/14/health/nutrition/14nugg.html (accessed August 14, 2007).

18. Abraham H. Maslow, *Motivation and Personality*, 2nd ed. (New York: Harper & Row, 1970).

19. Mark E. Koltko-Rivera, "Rediscovering the Later Version of Maslow's Hierarchy of Needs: Self-Transcendence and Opportunities for Theory, Research, and Unification," *Review of General Psychology* 10(4): 302–317 (December 2006); https://www.researchgate.net/publication/232510315_Rediscovering_the_later_version_of_Maslow's_hierarchy_of_needs_Self-transcendence_and_opportunities_for_theory_research_and_unification (accessed Mar 27 2018); John G. Messerly, "Summary of Maslow on Self-Transcendence," *Reason and Meaning*, Institute for Ethics and Emerging Technologies, February 4, 2017, https://ieet.org/index.php/IEET2/more/Messerly20170204 (accessed March 10, 2018).

20. An Coppens, "Gamification Trends for 2018," Gamification Nation, January 3, 2018, https://gamificationnation.com/gamification-trends-2018/ (accessed March 10, 2018).

21. Robert A. Baron and Donn Byrne, *Social Psychology: Understanding Human Interaction*, 5th ed. (Boston: Allyn & Bacon, 1987).

22. Rae Ann Fera, "The Rise of Sadvertising: Why Brands Are Determined to Make You Cry," *Fast Company*, May 4, 2014, http://www.fastcocreate.com/3029767/the-rise-of-sadvertising-whybrands-are-determined-to-make-you-cry (accessed April 13, 2016).

23. Ryan Nakashima, "Disney to Create Lab to Test Ads for ABC, ESPN," *Sydney Morning Herald*, May 13, 2008, https://www.smh.com.au/technology/disney-to-create-lab-to-test-ads-for-abc-espn-20080513-2djh.html (accessed September 2, 2020).

24. Tim Nudd, "Taco Bell Makes Fun of 'Sadvertising' with a Not-So-Poignant Story of Not-So-Long-Lost Friends," *Adweek*, July 17, 2017, http://www.adweek.com/creativity/taco-bell-makes-fun-of-sadvertising-with-a-not-so-poignant-story-of-not-so-long-lost-friends/ (accessed March 10, 2018).

25. Paige Meyer, "The Selfie Generation," *HQ Press*, December 9, 2018, https://www.hqpress.org/blog-2/2018/11/20/the-selfie-generation (accessed May 15, 2020).

26. David Moye, "Millennials Are Surprisingly Chill with Funeral Selfies," *The Huffington Post*, September 28, 2015, http://www.huffingtonpost.com/entry/selfie-survey-20-percent-funerals_us_5605bddee4b0af3706dc592c (accessed April 13, 2016).

27. "Alpine Butterfly Swimwear Empowers Plus-Size Women," *Canvas8*, August 24, 2017, https://www.canvas8.com/signals/2017/08/24/plus-swimwear.html (accessed January 24, 2018).

28. Alex Williams, "High Times Wants to Be the Playboy of Pot," *The New York Times*, April 2, 2016, https://www.nytimes.com/2016/04/03/style/high-times-wants-to-be-the-playboy-of-pot.html (accessed April 13, 2016).

29. Alfred S. Boote, "Psychographics: Mind over Matter," *American Demographics*, April 1980, 26–29; William D. Wells, "Psychographics: A Critical Review," *Journal of Marketing Research* 12 (May 1975): 196–213.

30. Shiv, "Sensory Marketing: Using the Senses for Brand Building," March 3, 2014, http://marketingfaq.net/branding/sensory-marketing-and-branding (accessed April 29, 2014).

31. Aroma Marketing, "Research/Case Studies," https://www.sensorymax.com/aroma-marketing/research-case-studies-aroma.html (accessed April 29, 2014).

32. Helena Horton, "Sensory Marketing—How to Appeal to Your Customers through All 5 Senses," January 30, 2017, Pro Motion, Inc., https://promotion1.com/2017/01/30/sensory-marketing-appeal-customers-5-senses/ (accessed September 2, 2020).

33. Air-Scent, "A Retailer's Guide to Scenting Department Stores & Boutiques," July 16, 2019, https://www.airscent.com/guide-to-scenting-retail-environments/ (accessed May 14, 2019).

34. Roxie Hammill and Mike Hendricks, "Scent Received, With a Tap of a Smartphone," *The New York Times*, July 8, 2015, http://www.nytimes.com/2015/07/09/technology/personaltech/scent-received-with-a-tap-of-a-smartphone.html?ref=business&_r=1- (accessed April 13, 2016).

35. Ibid.

36. Jack Grant, "Shoppers Make More Purchase Decisions In-Store," June 2012, http://www.cpgmatters.com/In-StoreMarketing0612.html (accessed April 27, 2014).

37. Bass Pro Shops, "Free Easter Family Fun Offered at Bass Pro Shops and Cabela's," March 21, 2018, http://press.basspro.com/free-easter-family-fun-offered-at-bass-pro-shops-and-cabelas/ (accessed March 25, 2018).

38. Morgan Kelleher, "The Future of Brick-And-Mortar: Enhancing the Customer Experience," *Forbes*, Community Voice, January 23, 2018, https://www.forbes.com/sites/forbescommunicationscouncil/2018/01/23/the-future-of-brick-and-mortar-enhancing-the-customer-experience/#3e2ae0f53ce3 (accessed March 25, 2018).

39. Ibid.

40. Courtni Casanova, "Disruptive Marketing: What Is it?," *Copy-press*, https://www.copypress.com/blog/disruptive-marketing-what-is-it/ (accessed May 31, 2020).

41. Insight.com, "Next Level Exploration," https://www.insight.com/en_US/shop/partner/microsoft/hardware/hololens.html (accessed May 22, 2020).

42. Courtni Casanova, "Disruptive Marketing: What Is it?," *Copy-press*, https://www.copypress.com/blog/disruptive-marketing-what-is-it/ (accessed May 31, 2020).

43. Womensweb, "Why Be Only Awesome When You Can Be 'Simply Flawsome'?," December 14, 2017, https://www.womensweb.in/2017/12/why-awesome-can-be-flawsome-dec17wk3/ (accessed May 31, 2020).

44. Courtni Casanova, "Disruptive Marketing: What Is it?," *Copy-press*, https://www.copypress.com/blog/disruptive-marketing-what-is-it/ (accessed May 31, 2020).

45. Ibid.

46. Ibid.

47. Jason Goldberg, "The Impact Of COVID-19 on U.S. Brands and Retailers," *Forbes*, March 29, 2020, https://www.forbes.com/sites/jasongoldberg/2020/03/29/the-impact-of-covid-19-on-us-brands-and-retailers/#4a0aae661452 (accessed May 24, 2020).

48. Ibid.

49. Richard W. Pollay, "Measuring the Cultural Values Manifest in Advertising," *Current Issues and Research in Advertising* 6(1) (1983): 71–92.

50. Glenn Llopis, "Don't Sell to Me! Hispanics Buy Brands That Empower Their Cultural Relevancy," *Forbes*, May 14, 2012, https://www.forbes.com/sites/glennllopis/2012/05/14/dont-sell-to-me-hispanics-buy-brands-that-empower-their-cultural-relevancy/#2cbf003c661c (accessed April 29, 2014).

51. Michelle Saettler, "General Mills, Clorox Target Hispanic Mobile Shoppers via Bilingual Promotions App," https://www.marketingdive.com/ex/mobilemarketer/cms/news/strategy/17575.html (accessed December 15, 2020).

52. Philip Kotler and Christian Sarkar, "Finally, Brand Activism!," *The Marketing Journal*, January 9, 2017, http://www.marketingjournal.org/finally-brand-activism-philip-kotler-and-christian-sarkar/ (accessed March 25, 2018).

53. Cara Salpini, "Patagonia Doubles Down on Sustainability," *Retail Drive*, January 16, 2019, https://www.retaildive.com/news/patagonia-doubles-down-on-sustainability/546144/ (accessed May 18, 2020).

54. Emily Burg, "Whole Foods Is Consumers' Favorite Green Brand," *Marketing Daily*, May 10, 2007, https://www.mediapost.com/publications/article/60116/whole-foods-is-consumers-favorite-green-brand.html%3Fedition (accessed May 10, 2007).

55. Stuart U. Rich and Subhash C. Jain, "Social Class and Life Cycle as Predictors of Behavior," *Journal of Marketing Research* 5 (February 1968): 41–49.

56. Nathan Kogan and Michael A. Wallach, "Risky Shift Phenomenon in Small Decision-Making Groups: A Test of the Information Exchange Hypothesis," *Journal of Experimental Social Psychology* 3 (January 1967): 75–84; Arch G. Woodside and M. Wayne DeLozier, "Effects of Word-of-Mouth Advertising on Consumer Risk Taking," *Journal of Advertising* (Fall 1976): 12–19.

57. Brooks Barnes, "For Lucasfilm, the Way of Its Force Lies in Its 'Star Wars' Fans," *The New York Times*, April 17, 2015, http://www.nytimes.com/2015/04/18/business/media/for-lucasfilm-the-way-of-its-force-lies-in-its-star-wars-fans.html (accessed April 13, 2016).

58. Everett M. Rogers, *Diffusion of Innovations*, 3rd ed. (New York: Free Press, 1983).

59. Kathleen Debevec and Easwar Iyer, "Sex Roles and Consumer Perceptions of Promotions, Products, and Self: What Do We Know and Where Should We Be Headed?," in *Advances in Consumer Research*, vol. 13, ed. Richard J. Lutz (Provo, UT: Association for Consumer Research, 1986), 210–14; Lynn J. Jaffe and Paul D. Berger, "Impact on Purchase Intent of Sex-Role Identity and Product Positioning," *Psychology and Marketing* (Fall 1988): 259–71.

60. "Comprehensive* List of LGBTQ+ Vocabulary Definitions," https://www.itspronouncedmetrosexual.com/2013/01/a-comprehensive-list-of-lgbtq-term-definitions/ (accessed November 19, 2020); Colin Poitras, "The 'Global Closet' is Huge—Vast Majority of World's Lesbian, Gay, Bisexual Population Hide Orientation, YSPH Study Finds," Yale School of Medicine, June 13, 2019, https://medicine.yale.edu/news-article/20510/ (accessed November 19, 2020).

61. Katie Powers, "Shattering Gendered Marketing," American Marketing Association, September 3, 2019, https://www.ama.org/marketing-news/shattering-gendered-marketing/ (accessed Novermber 19, 2020); Statista, "Size of the Global Men's Grooming Products Market from 2018 to 2024 (in billion U.S. dollars)," https://www.statista.com/statistics/287643/global-male-grooming-market-size/ (accessed November 19, 2020).

62. Natalie Angier, "The Changing American Family," *New York Times*, November 25, 2013, http://www.nytimes.com/2013/11/26/health/families.html?_r=0, (accessed November 19, 2020).

63. Lisa Gutierrez, "Kansas Aviator Amelia Earhart Is Now an 'Inspiring' Barbie Doll," *The Kansas City Star*, March 7, 2018, http://www.kansascity.com/latest-news/article203870239.html (accessed March 10, 2018).

64. Christopher Jasper and Benjamin D Katz, "Airbus Handed A380 Lifeline with $16 Billion Emirates Order," *Bloomberg*, January 18, 2018, https://www.bloomberg.com/news/articles/2018-01-18/emirates-orders-20-a380s-worth-9-billion-in-vital-program-boost (accessed February 28, 2018).

65. Walmart, "Location Facts," https://corporate.walmart.com/our-story/our-locations (accessed May 15, 2020).

66. "Government Purchases," *Investopedia*, https://www.investopedia.com/terms/g/governmentpurchases.asp (accessed March 10, 2018).

67. U.S. Census Bureau, "North America Industry Classification System (NAICS)," https://www.census.gov/cgi-bin/sssd/naics/naicsrch?code=311411&search=2017%20NAICS%20Search (accessed March 7, 2018).

68. F. Robert Dwyer and John F. Tanner, *Business Marketing: Connecting Strategy, Relationships, and Learning* (Boston: McGraw-Hill, 2008); Edward F. Fern and James R. Brown, "The Industrial/Consumer Marketing Dichotomy: A Case of Insufficient Justification," *Journal of Marketing* (Spring 1984): 68–77.

69. Erin Duffin, "Number of Households in the U.S. from 1960 to 2019," *Statista*, November 28, 2019, https://www.statista.com/statistics/183635/number-of-households-in-the-us/ (accessed May 16, 2020).

70. "2018 BMW M4 Pricing," *Edmunds*, https://www.edmunds.com/bmw/m4/2018/?utm_medium=sem&utm_source=bing&utm_account=edmunds_2011&utm_campaign=bmw_m4_tier_1&utm_adgroup=bmw-m4-years&utm_term=bmw_m4_2017&utm_content=utm_migration&utm_device=c&utm_matchtype=bb&msclkid=f71e0f88a43d12cd73315516a1b04630 (accessed March 2, 2018).

71. Aflac, "Aflac for Business," https://www.aflac.com/business/default.aspx (accessed February 23, 2010).

72. Sodexo Quality of Life Services, "About Us," https://www.sodexousa.com/home/about-us.html (accessed March 25, 2018).

73. Ellen Nakashima, "Russian Spies Hacked the Olympics and Tried to Make It Look Like North Korea Did It, U.S. Officials Say," *The Washington Post*, February 24, 2018, https://www.washingtonpost.com/world/national-security/russian-spies-hacked-the-olympics-and-tried-to-make-it-look-like-north-korea-did-it-us-officials-say/2018/02/24/44b5468e-18f2-11e8-92c9-376b4fe57ff7_story.html (accessed March 25, 2018).

74. Michael Riley, Ben Elgin, Dune Lawrence, and Carol Matlack, "Missed Alarms and 40 Million Stolen Credit Card Numbers: How Target Blew It," *Bloomberg Businessweek*, March 13, 2014, https://

www.bloomberg.com/news/articles/2014-03-13/target-missed-warnings-in-epic-hack-of-credit-card-data (accessed April 26, 2014).

75. Tom Pick, "83 Exceptional Social Media and Marketing Statistics for 2014," April 20, 2014, https://www.business2community.com/social-media/83-exceptional-social-media-marketing-statistics-2014-0846364#!FfTg2 (accessed March 19, 2014).

76. Content Marketing Institute, B2B Content Marketing, https://contentmarketinginstitute.com/wp-content/uploads/2016/09/2017_B2B_Research_FINAL.pdf (accessed March 26, 2018).

77. Ryan Nakashima, "Disney to Create Lab to Test Ads for ABC, ESPN," *USA Today*, May 12, 2008, https://www.usatoday.com/tech/products/2008-05-12-1465558386_x.htm (accessed February 24, 2010); Sylvia Jensen, "How Do B2B Companies Use Social Media?" https://www.scu.edu/ethics/practicing/decision (accessed March 21, 2014); J. J. McCorvey, "How to Use Social Media for B2B Marketing," *Inc.*, July 29, 2010, https://www.inc.com/guides/2010/07/how-to-use-social-media-for-b2b-marketing.html (accessed March 15, 2014); Allen Narcisse, "Planning Your B2B Marketing Approach to Social Media: 3 Key Angles," January 22, 2014, https://www.business2community.com/b2b-marketing/planning-b2b-marketing-approach-social-media-3-key-angles-0744273 (accessed September 2, 2020).

78. Based on: BizCommunity, "Drinkers Cannot Discern between Major Beer Brands," *BizCommunity*, August 18, 2014, https://www.bizcommunity.com/Article/196/597/117649.html; "Market Study Beer Rebranding," *Stealingshare.com*, n.d., https://www.stealingshare.com/pages/beer-rebranding/ (accessed July 26, 2020); "Market Share of Leading Beer Suppliers in the United States from 2014 to 2019," https://www-statista-com.go.asbury.edu/statistics/972647/leading-beer-suppliers-market-share-us/ (accessed July 26, 2020); Bob Woods, "Anheuser-Busch Invests $100 Million in Hard Seltzer, the New Drink Craze," *CBNC*, January 13, 2020, https://www.cnbc.com/2019/11/16/anheuser-busch-invests-100-million-in-hard-seltzer-the-drink-craze.html; Ab-Inbev.com, "Our Brands," https://www.ab-inbev.com/our-brands/our-beers.html (accessed July 26, 2020); Colman Andrews, "Most Popular Beer Brands in America Dominated by Anheuser-Busch, Molson Coors," *USA Today*, March 18, 2020, https://www.usatoday.com/story/money/2020/03/18/the-most-popular-beer-brands-in-america/111416118/; Millerlite.com, "Our Beer," https://www.millerlite.com/our-beer (accessed July 26, 2020); Nat Ives, "Whatssup? Anheuser-Busch InBev Looks for New Markets," *The Wall Street Journal*, October 27, 2019, https://www.wsj.com/articles/whassup-anheuser-busch-inbev-looks-for-new-markets-11572228300; Nat Ives, "Bud Light Will Share a Super Bowl Ad with Its New Hard Seltzer Extension," *The Wall Street Journal*, January 8, 2020, https://www.wsj.com/articles/bud-light-will-share-a-super-bowl-ad-with-its-new-hard-seltzer-extension-11578514593; Will Cowling, "Are Consumer Beer Drinking Habits Changing?" *New Good*, February 8, 2020,
https://www.newfoodmagazine.com/article/105390/are-consumer-beer-drinking-habits-changing/; Justin Kendall, "Power Hour: Nielsen Shares 2019 Craft Beer Consumer," *Brewbound*, July 23, 2019, https://www.brewbound.com/news/power-hour-nielsen-shares-2019-craft-beer-consumer-insights; Commetric, "Beer in the Media: A Tale of Shifting Consumer Tastes – Commetric," *Commetric.com*, December 29, 2019, https://commetric.com/2019/12/29/beer-in-the-media-a-tale-of-shifting-consumer-tastes/; Jeanette Settembre, "Anheuser-Busch Banks on Hard Seltzer as Beer Drinking Declines," *FOX Business*, January 9, https://www.foxbusiness.com/markets/budweiser-anheuser-busch-bud-light-seltzer-white-claw; Cathy Siegner, "AB InBev Takes Another Shot at the Hard Seltzer Category," *FOODDIVE*, August 12, 2019, https://www.fooddive.com/news/ab-inbev-takes-another-shot-at-the-hard-seltzer-category/560671/; Jennifer Maloney, "Natty Light, the King of Cheap Beers, Goes After Hard Seltzer," *The Wall Street Journal*, August 9, 2010, https://www.wsj.com/articles/natty-light-the-king-of-cheap-beers-goes-after-hard-seltzer-11565391254; Jessi Devenyns, "Bud Light Seltzer Hits Shelves Next Year as AB InBev Invests $100M in the Segment," *FOODDIVE*, November 20, 2019, https://www.fooddive.com/news/bud-light-seltzer-hits-shelves-next-year-as-ab-inbev-invests-100m-in-the-s/567714/; Ethan Jakob Craft, "Bud Light Retires Its 'Dilly Dilly' World Ahead of New Seltzer Campaign," *AdAge*, January 10, 2020, https://adage.com/article/special-report-super-bowl/bud-light-retires-its-dilly-dilly-world-ahead-new-seltzer-campaign/2226401; E. J. Schultz, "Bud Light Will Ask Social Media to Pick Which Post Malone Spot to Air during the Super Bowl," *AdAge*, January 29, 2920, https://adage.com/article/special-report-super-bowl/bud-light-seltzer-will-ask-social-media-pick-which-post-malone-spot-air-during-super-bowl/2231486; Charles Passy, "Bud Light Makes a Move into Hard Seltzer Just in Time for Super Bowl 2020," *Market Watch*, February 1, 2020, https://www.marketwatch.com/story/bud-light-says-its-new-strawberry-hard-seltzer-goes-great-withcheesecake-2020-01-31; Saabira Chaudhuri, "Budweiser Brewer Shares Dive as It Loses More U.S. Market Share," *The Wall Street Journal*, February 27, 2020, https://www.wsj.com/articles/budweiser-brewer-takes-profit-hit-loses-more-u-s-market-share-11582793027; Michael O'Connor, "Big Beer Pops Top on New Hard Seltzer Brands in 2020," *S&P Global Market Intelligence*, February 5, 2020, https://www.spglobal.com/marketintelligence/en/news-insights/latest-news-headlines/big-brewers-pop-top-on-new-hard-seltzer-brands-in-2020-56743493; Lauren Eads, "10 of the Biggest Hard Seltzer Brands," *Thedrinksbusiness.com*, https://www.thedrinksbusiness.com/2020/04/10-of-the-biggest-hard-seltzer-brands/11/ (accessed July 26, 2020); Jennifer Maloney, "PepsiCo Gives Its 'Premium' Water a Super Bowl Push," *The Wall Street Journal*, January 24, 2017, http://www.wsj.com/articles/pepsico-gives-its-premium-water-a-super-bowl-push-1485253982.

7 Segmentation, Target Marketing, and Positioning

Meet Jen Sey
▼ A Decision Maker at Levi Strauss

Jen Sey has been with Levi Strauss & Co. for 21 years, holding a variety of leadership positions within the Marketing, Strategy and Ecommerce teams. In 2013, Jen became the Global Chief Marketing Officer for the Levi's® brand and in 2018 was appointed Senior Vice President & Chief Marketing Officer, Levi Strauss & Co., overseeing marketing for the company's portfolio of brands. She is also a member of the company's global leadership team, which guides the strategic direction for LS&Co.

Jen has received numerous awards, including the distinction of being named one of *AdAge*'s Top 40 Marketers Under 40 in 2006, one of *Brand Innovators*' Top 50 Women in Marketing in 2015, one of *Billboard Magazine*'s Top 25 Most Powerful People in Music and Fashion, and being a recipient of the 2018 CMO Social Responsibility Award. She was also featured on *Forbes*' CMO Next List for 2018: 50 Chief Marketers Who Are Redefining the CMO Role. In 2018, under Sey's direction, the Levi's brand was awarded a Silver Cannes Lions award for the "Circles" advertising campaign, and most recently, in 2019, she was named one of *Forbes*' Most Influential CMOs.

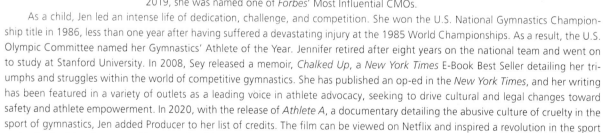

As a child, Jen led an intense life of dedication, challenge, and competition. She won the U.S. National Gymnastics Championship title in 1986, less than one year after having suffered a devastating injury at the 1985 World Championships. As a result, the U.S. Olympic Committee named her Gymnastics' Athlete of the Year. Jennifer retired after eight years on the national team and went on to study at Stanford University. In 2008, Sey released a memoir, *Chalked Up*, a *New York Times* E-Book Best Seller detailing her triumphs and struggles within the world of competitive gymnastics. She has published an op-ed in the *New York Times*, and her writing has been featured in a variety of outlets as a leading voice in athlete advocacy, seeking to drive cultural and legal changes toward safety and athlete empowerment. In 2020, with the release of *Athlete A*, a documentary detailing the abusive culture of cruelty in the sport of gymnastics, Jen added Producer to her list of credits. The film can be viewed on Netflix and inspired a revolution in the sport under the hashtag #gymnastalliance, with athletes around the world coming forward to share their stories of abuse in the sport and to call for change.

Jen is on the Board of Directors for the Red Tab Foundation, an organization within Levi Strauss & Co. committed to the mission of employees helping employees and retirees in times of need. She also serves on the 49ers Foundation Board, an organization that seeks to empower Bay Area Youth through a collective of innovative and community-focused education strategies.

Jen lives in San Francisco, California, with her husband, Daniel, and her four children, Virgil, Wyatt, Oscar, and Ruth.

Here's my problem...

Real **People**, Real **Choices**

The Levi's brand was losing relevance and market share. Although technically they were the leader in denim in terms of market share, it didn't necessarily feel like they were leading; their market share was being eaten up by premium brands and then, most recently, fast fashion. Levi's needed to reposition for success—in terms of both financial and equity performance and the overall future health of the brand. They needed to create a clear brand value proposition that was relevant and differentiated, broadly appealing and globally viable. Jen's job was to lead this process and create a long-standing marketing campaign off of this positioning, while inspiring the organization more broadly with this brand direction.

cultural icon James Dean. The actor's appearance in the 1950s movie *Rebel Without a Cause* wearing a white shirt, leather jacket, and a pair of Levi's 501s is one of the most legendary images in pop culture. On the other hand, this link with originality no longer made the statement it used to. Many jeans and apparel brands were making this claim (justified or not). Jen couldn't be sure that this position would differentiate Levi's in the market and give people a reason to choose Levi's versus another brand. However, there was no question that Levi's had a legitimate claim to this space if they chose to remind consumers of their long heritage.

Jen considered her options 1·2·3

1 **First and foremost, Jen looked at the obvious: Levi's is *the* original blue jean.** The founder, Levi Strauss, and tailor, Jacob Davis, obtained a U.S. patent on the process of putting rivets in men's work pants in 1873, and the company had a rich history that spanned almost 150 years. This positioning asserted the brand's innovator status; it was the oldest and also the first. No other company could make this claim. No one else created the blue jean—or the product category. Although this was a powerful statement, it wasn't that relevant to modern consumers. It didn't give them a reason to choose the brand *today*. Levi's knew that millennials value authenticity, but they needed to either promote this attribute more forcefully or give them additional reasons to choose their brand.

2 **Jen also looked at a different definition of *originality*.** Her idea was that "originality" meant not only "first." This concept also referred to the quality of being new, fresh, creative, and independent. Jen looked at creating an association between the brand and the wearer with a position built on the idea that *Levi's is as original as you are*. This statement was relevant and aspirational. Everyone wants to see themselves as original, unique, and individualistic. And it was certainly believable for Levi's to be associated with this position. The brand had long told a story about individuality, most notably through its strong association with the

3 **As Jen embarked on research with consumers around the world, she heard a lot of people talk about all the amazing life experiences they have had in their Levi's.** They related stories about road trips, first loves, concerts, and all-night dance parties. They talked about the bond they have with their Levi's because of these experiences. And they said that they did not have this kind of relationship with their other jeans or clothing items. The relationship with their Levi's jeans was special. This inspired the idea: You wear other jeans but you live your life in Levi's. This claim was highly differentiated, and more importantly, it made an emotional connection with customers. The downside was that blue jeans were now more of a fashion-oriented product than they used to be. Levi's needed to drive a style message in addition to an emotional message. And this connection wasn't as strong in all of the brand's global markets. For example, in China, where people hadn't been wearing Levi's for very long, people hadn't had time to forge these connections yet.

Now, put yourself in Jen's shoes. Which option would you choose, and why?

You Choose

Which **Option** would you choose, and **why**?

☐ Option 1   ☐ Option 2   ☐ Option 3

243

7.1 Target Marketing: Select and Enter a Market

OBJECTIVE

Identify the steps in the target marketing process.

Way back in Chapter 1, we defined a market as all the customers and potential customers who share a common need that can be satisfied by a specific product, who have the resources to exchange for it, who are willing to make the exchange, and who have the authority to make the exchange. At this point in your study of marketing, you know that key goals of the marketer are to create value, build customer relationships, and satisfy needs. But in our modern, complex society, it's naive to assume that everyone's needs are the same—even for a pair of blue jeans.

market fragmentation

The creation of many consumer groups due to a diversity of distinct needs and wants in modern society.

Today, it's a complex task to understand people's differing needs because technological and cultural advances create a condition of **market fragmentation**. This means that people's diverse interests and backgrounds naturally divide them into numerous groups with distinct needs and wants. Because of this diversity, the same good or service will not appeal to everyone.

One need look no further than higher education—a market you as a student likely know quite a lot about—for a great example of market fragmentation! The COVID-19 crisis hit higher ed really hard. Many colleges and universities had to change their instructional delivery from in-person to online almost literally overnight. The rapidity of the shifts caused major disruption for faculty and students, especially at schools that had little experience with distance learning platforms. Like all markets, there were winners and there were losers. Schools that were already deeply experienced with online delivery—Arizona State University and Western Governors University are two standouts—were incredibly well-positioned to shine during the changeover semester as well as to attract new students for Fall 2020 who elected to hold off attending traditional in-person classes for a while. Other players that benefited from the rapid shift in consumer preferences for classes closer to home were local community colleges and major urban universities, such as the University of South Florida in Tampa and the University of Texas at Arlington. With all the uncertainty, many students (and their parents) liked the idea of erring on the side of caution and staying close to home for classes. Higher ed in the U.S. is highly fragmented, with lots of choices ranging from large to small, public to private, and in-person to online to blended. A key question for schools going forward is how will the experiences of the COVID-19 crisis impact the longer-term nature of the field? How will consumers of higher ed prefer to pursue their degrees in the future (if they pursue degrees at all!)?[1]

In Chapter 1, you learned the term *mass market*, meaning all possible customers in a market regardless of the differences in their specific needs and wants. Marketers must balance the efficiency of mass marketing, where they can offer the same items to everyone, with the effectiveness that comes when they offer each individual exactly what he or she wants. Mass marketing certainly costs much less—when we offer one product to everyone, we eliminate the need for separate advertising campaigns and distinctive packages for each item. However, consumers see things differently. From their perspective, the best strategy would be to offer the perfect product just for them. Unfortunately, that's often not realistic.

In the QSR, or quick serve restaurant, space, Chick-fil-A's drive-through is legendary among consumers looking for a great experience. In 2019, the National Restaurant Association reported that 39 percent of consumers used a drive-through more than the year before. And we all know about the massive spike in drive-through in 2020 due to the COVID-19 closures and then reduction in inside dining seats. While Chick-fil-A's drive-through falls behind others in pure speed, what analysts find is that friendliness of service and accuracy of order trump speed and just about everything else when it comes to consumer satisfaction. Essentially, Chick-fil-A carves out a difference from competitors on those two critical components, and the small difference in average wait time doesn't bother their customers one bit![2]

Figure 7.1 *Process* | Steps in the Target Marketing Process

Target marketing strategy consists of three separate steps. Marketers first divide the market into segments based on customer characteristics, then select one or more segments, and finally develop products to meet the needs of those specific segments.

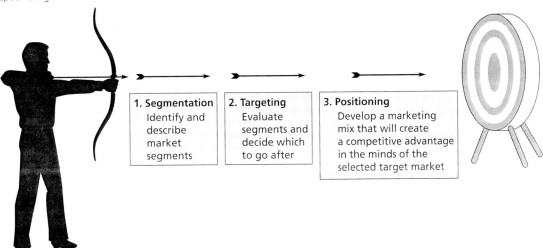

1. Segmentation
Identify and describe market segments

2. Targeting
Evaluate segments and decide which to go after

3. Positioning
Develop a marketing mix that will create a competitive advantage in the minds of the selected target market

Like Chick-fil-A in the QSR market, all marketers must understand that creating key differences in their products and services in order to meet different consumer needs, wants, and preferences is a core concept—and it is the central theme of this chapter. That is, instead of trying to sell the same thing to everyone, marketers select a **target marketing strategy** in which they divide the total market into different segments based on customer characteristics, select one or more segments, and develop products to meet the needs of those specific segments. Figure 7.1 illustrates the three-step process of segmentation, targeting, and positioning, and it's what we're going to check out in this chapter. Let's start with the first step—segmentation.

target marketing strategy
Dividing the total market into different segments on the basis of customer characteristics, selecting one or more segments, and developing products to meet the needs of those specific segments.

7.2   Step 1: Segmentation

OBJECTIVE
Understand the need for market segmentation and the approaches available to do it.

Segmentation is the process of dividing a larger market into smaller pieces based on one or more meaningful, shared characteristics. This process is a way of life for almost all marketers in both consumer and business-to-business markets. The truth is that you can't please all the people all the time, so you need to take your best shot. Marriott, for example, segments its market as it offers 30 separate brands that range from the value-oriented Courtyard to the deluxe Ritz-Carlton. In fact, with the acquisition of Sheraton and its stable of brands, some might say that Marriott risks a fine line between clarity in the minds of consumers about what each of those brands represents and offering an appropriate number of choices for different lodging needs.

This sort of situation has resulted in a marketing malady called **oversegmentation**, when consumers may become confused if an organization offers too many choices. In Marriott's case, can you recite the key differences between a Fairfield Inn and a 4 Points by Sheraton, or between a Weston and a Renaissance?[3]

Just how do marketers segment a population? How do they divide the whole pie into smaller slices they can "digest"? The marketer must decide on one or more useful **segmentation variables**—that is, dimensions that divide the total market into fairly homogeneous groups, each with different needs and preferences. In this section, we'll take a look at this process, beginning with the types of segmentation variables that marketers use to divide up end-user consumers. Then, we'll move on to business-to-business segmentation.

segmentation
The process of dividing a larger market into smaller pieces based on one or more meaningfully shared characteristics.

oversegmentation
A marketing malady that occurs when consumers may become confused if an organization offers too many choices.

segmentation variables
Dimensions that divide the total market into fairly homogeneous groups, each with different needs and preferences.

Segment Consumer Markets

At one time, it was sufficient to divide the sports shoe market into athletes and non-athletes. But take a walk through any sporting goods store today and you'll quickly see that the athlete market has fragmented in many directions. Shoes designed for jogging, basketball, tennis, cycling, cross-training, and even skateboarding beckon us from the aisles. We need several segmentation variables if we want to slice up the market for all the shoe variations available today. First, not everyone is willing or able to drop several hundred bucks on the latest sneakers, so marketers consider income. (Note: A pair of Chanel x Pharrell Williams x adidas Originals will set you back almost $11,000!).[4] Second, men may be more interested in basketball shoes for shooting hoops with the guys, whereas women snap up the latest Pilates styles, so marketers also consider gender. Because not all age groups are equally interested in buying specialized athletic shoes, we slice the larger consumer "pie" into smaller pieces in a number of ways, including demographic, psychographic, and behavioral differences. In the case of demographic segmentation, there are several key subcategories of demographics: age (including generational differences), gender, family life cycle, income and social class, ethnicity, and place of residence, sometimes referred to separately as *geographic segmentation*. Figure 7.2 summarizes the dominant approaches to segmenting consumer markets.

In the sections that follow, we'll consider each of these segmentation approaches in turn, but first a note of caution. When it comes to marketing to some groups—in particular, lower-income individuals, the poorly educated, nonnative-language speakers, and children—it is incumbent on marketers to exercise the utmost care not to take undue advantage of their circumstances. In Chapter 2, we introduced a global segment called the bottom of the pyramid (BOP), which is the collective name for the group of more than 4 billion consumers throughout the world who live on less than $2 a day. Ethical marketers must be sensitive to the different conditions in which people find themselves and proactively work to uphold a high level of honesty and trust with all segments of the public. Doing so is nothing short of marketing's social responsibility.

One other caveat is needed before we jump into our discussion of different market segments. Identifying segments is not, repeat *not*, intended by marketers as a form of stereotyping. The idea of segmenting markets is to identify groups of consumers with similar needs so that marketing to them can be done more efficiently and effectively versus a mass-market approach. That doesn't necessarily mean that we want to pigeonhole a group of people because they happen to share an important characteristic, such as gender or race.

Figure 7.2 *Snapshot* | Segmenting Consumer Markets

Consumer markets can be segmented by demographic, geographic, psychographic, and behavioral criteria.

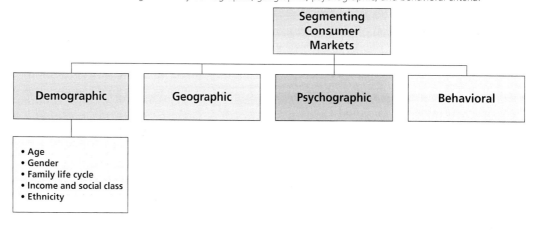

Demographic Segmentation: By Age

As you learned in Chapter 2, *demographics* are statistics that measure observable aspects of a population, including size, age, gender, ethnic group, income, education, occupation, and family structure. These descriptors are vital to identify the best potential customers for a good or service. Because they represent objective characteristics, they usually are easy to identify, and then it's just a matter of tailoring messages and products to relevant age groups. Consumers of different age groups have different needs and wants. Members of a generation tend to share the same outlook, values, and priorities. When these characteristics are combined for purposes of market segmentation and targeting, such an approach is called **generational marketing**. Let's take a close look at several of these generational groups in the sections below.

Children

For example, *children* are an attractive age segment for many marketers. Although kids obviously have a lot to say about purchases of toys and games, they influence other family purchases as well (just watch them at work in the grocery store!). According to a recent YouGov Omnibus survey, 42 percent of parents said that they gave in to a child's request to buy a product when the child put substantial effort into arguing for the purchase.

Savvy children are famous for negotiation tactics such as promising to do more chores or to work harder in school to get better grades.[5] It's not hard to see how these persuasive little guys could quickly wear down a parent's resistance—buying the item is easier than fighting the fight. For Netflix, developing content to win over children to the platform has become a key strategy. The streaming giant recently announced it will be investing around $1 billion a year on dozens of high profile animation projects for the kiddies (and lots of their parents, no doubt). Netflix recognizes the importance of this segment in cementing its position as the main source of entertainment for families and as a key source of growth in delivering long-term customer value.[6]

Generation Z

Generation Z (iGen) describes individuals who were born after 1994 (the iGen label of course refers to them as iPhone junkies). This is the first generation of the 21st century, and it's the most diverse we've ever experienced: 55 percent are White, 24 percent are Latino/a, 14 percent are Black, and 4 percent are Asian. They are accustomed to blurred gender roles, where household responsibilities don't split along traditional lines. And, of course, they are **digital natives** who spend a big chunk of their time online, so they expect brands to engage them in two-way digital conversations.

Move over millennials! Marketers are gearing up to focus on the promise of the next wave of young consumers. Having grown up during the Great Recession, kids today are not as likely to believe in an idealized, carefree world. They research brands via their devices before they shop, and then they seek out retailers that offer new technologies in-store, such as smartphone self-checkout, interactive shopping screens, and virtual try-on for clothing.[7] They learn about new styles from around the globe via social media, so they are equally at home watching *Ozark* or listening to Korean K-pop. Their idols are "self-made" Internet stars like the Swedish video producer PewDiePie, who has the world's most-subscribed-to YouTube channel (with 104 million subscribers and over 4,100 videos) and the teenage video sensation Evan, who has 25 million followers.[8] And on TikTok, which is growing in popularity, Charli D'Amelio has over 55 million followers!

Korean K-pop is a global music phenomenon that young people in many countries love.

Imaginechina Limited/Alamy Stock Photo

Generation Z wields up to $143 billion in spending power, without accounting for their influence on other household purchases. Their peers inspire many of these purchases, so online and social media reviews are more important than ever to retailers.[9] Much of this money goes toward "feel-good" products: music, video games, cosmetics, and fast food—with the occasional tattoo or hookah pen thrown in as well. Because this generation is so interested in many different products and have the resources to obtain them, many marketers avidly court the youth market.[10] Snapchat has designed a platform that contains cool features that appeal heavily to a younger crowd, including teenagers (for example, a feature that allows you to manipulate selfies by incorporating features of a unicorn into your face). The platform is designed to make it hard for one user (say, for instance, a parent) to eavesdrop on the activity of another user (say, for instance, the child of that parent) without knowing their username. Reliable tracking reports that 41 percent of U.S. teens claim Snapchat as their most important social app, but with Instagram closely behind at 35 percent.[11]

Millennials (Generation Y)

Generation Y (millennials)
The group of consumers born between 1979 and 1994.

Generation Y, often called **millennials** or "echo boomers," consists of people born between the years 1979 and 1994. This age segment is the first generation to grow up online. Generation Y is an attractive market for a host of consumer products because of its size (approximately 25 percent of the population) and free-spending nature—as a group, it spends about $1.3 trillion annually.[12] By the way, don't get the idea that Gen Z is just an extension of the millennials. That could not be farther from the truth! Among other famously proposed differences: Gen Z tends to be more pragmatic, while millennials tend more toward idealism; Gen Z is more focused on saving money than on the customer experience, while millennials tend toward the opposite; and Gen Z sets a higher bar for expecting innovation from companies than do millennials.[13]

But Generation Y consumers can be hard to reach through traditional media because they resist reading and increasingly turn off the TV to opt instead for streaming video and digital video recordings. As a result, many marketers have had to develop other ways to reach this generation "where they live," which is in large measure through their smartphones and tablets, using social media and related technology. We'll talk more about the shift to new-age marketing communications techniques later in this book.

We already know that Gen Yers are tech savvy, but what else defines them as a generation compared to past generations? A Pew Research study shows that compared to past generations (when they were in the same age range), Gen Yers are more racially diverse and more highly educated. In addition, a greater proportion of them have never been married when compared to other generations (68 percent compared to 56 percent for Generation X, which is the next closest generation).[14]

Generation X

Generation X
The group of consumers born between 1965 and 1978.

The group of consumers born between 1965 and 1978 consists of 46 million Americans known as **Generation X**, who unfortunately and undeservedly came to be called *slackers* or *busters* (for the "baby bust" that followed the "baby boom"). Many of these people have a cynical attitude toward marketing—a chapter in a famous book called *Generation X* is titled "I Am Not a Target Market!"[15]

Despite this tough reputation, members of Generation X, the oldest of whom are now in their early 50s, have mellowed with age. In retrospect, they also have developed an identity for being an entrepreneurial group. One study revealed that Gen Xers led much of the modern technology revolution, and now firms seek them out for their entrepreneurial talents. Many people in this segment were determined to have stable families after being brought up as latchkey children themselves as both their parents put in long days at work. Gen Xers tend to view the home as an expression of individuality rather than material success. More than half are involved in home improvement and repair projects.[16] So much for Gen Xers as slackers!

Baby Boomers

Baby boomers—often called simply "boomers"—are consumers born between 1946 and 1964 who are now in their 50s to 70s and are an important segment to many marketers—if for no other reason than that there are so many of them who have a lot of money. The baby boom occurred when soldiers came flooding home after World War II and there was a rush to get married and start families. Back in the 1950s and 1960s, couples started having children younger and had more of them than the previous generation. The resulting glut of kids really changed the infrastructure of the country: more single-family houses, more schools, migration to the suburbs, and freeways to commute from home to work.

More recently, some research has suggested that it may be beneficial for marketers to treat this generational segment as two different groups for the purpose of considering their discretionary and nondiscretionary spending capabilities. A survey by Gallup indicates that there are significant differences between baby boomer spending for those born in the first half of the generation's age range ("leading-edge boomers") compared with those born in the second half of the generation's age range ("trailing-edge boomers"). In general, the trailing-edge boomers find themselves spending significantly more on nondiscretionary items (e.g., house maintenance, groceries, etc.) than their leading-edge boomer counterparts.

One explanation for this difference in spending capabilities between these two groups may relate to differences in financial obligations. The older group of baby boomers (over age 70) most likely has reached a point where they are no longer paying off mortgages or higher education debts. Maybe you've seen those bumper stickers on retirees' cars and RVs: "We're spending our children's inheritance." Annoying to their kids, perhaps, but a wake-up call to marketers.[17]

Currently, the U.S. Census Bureau estimates that there are slightly more than 49 million Americans aged 65 or older and they account for just over 15 percent of the population, an increase from prior years.[18] To better accommodate the senior market, companies are changing their stores and their products. In one of the more dramatic shifts, CVS in recent years has remade its image around broad-based health care with the older half of the baby boomers squarely in their sights. The firm's Minute Clinics already serve an important need for fast, efficient, and convenient care, and over the next few years, CVS will be opening 1500 HealthHubs that will be more staff-intensive to offer customers a more personalized experience and medical advice specific to their needs. All this momentum at CVS was triggered by their recent merger with Aetna, and the firm is well suited to serve a broad spectrum of baby boomers' needs.[19]

Demographic Segmentation: By Gender

Many products, from fragrances to fashion apparel and accessories, specifically appeal to men or women. Traditional segmenting by gender often starts at an early age—even diapers come in pink for girls and blue for boys. While society's perspective on gender has changed in recent years and there's been a shift toward less rigid and binary definitions of gender, most marketing continues to categorize products for men or for women. In some cases, manufacturers develop parallel products to appeal to each sex. For example, male grooming products have traditionally been Gillette's priority since the company's founder, King Gillette (yes, his first name was actually King), introduced the safety razor in 1903. But today, the Venus line by Gillette is a top-selling razor for women of all ages.

A growing number of people are taking a more fluid attitude toward gender—that is, beyond the traditional male/female dichotomy. **Gender identity** is the personal sense of one's own gender. Gender identity can correlate with a person's assigned sex at birth or can differ from it. Gender expression typically reflects a person's gender identity, but this is not always the case. **Androgyny** refers to the possession of both masculine and feminine traits. Nowadays, marketers are more frequently making a distinction between *sex-typed* people—who are stereotypically masculine or feminine—and *androgynous* people. Androgyny can create

baby boomers
The group of consumers born between 1946 and 1964.

gender identity
The personal sense of one's own gender that may or may not correlate with a person's assigned sex at birth.

androgyny
The possession of both masculine and feminine traits.

The fashion world is witnessing an explosion of androgynous brands that both men and women wear, like MeUndies.

gender-bending products
Traditionally sex-typed items adapted to the opposite gender.

Me Too movement
A movement against sexual harassment and sexual abuse of women that went viral on social media with the hashtag #MeToo.

new target markets for savvy marketers who create products for that growing segment. One way to do this is for a firm to take a current product sold to one gender and test the waters with it or an adaptation of it for the opposite gender. When this approach is successful, the result is **gender-bending products**, which are traditionally sex-typed items adapted to the opposite gender. The fashion apparel industry is often an initial conduit for such expansion, often sparked by a superstar's wardrobe statement. For example, Beyoncé's January drop in January 2020 of her Ivy Park collection included a subtle shift: It was positioned as gender neutral. Whether you want to call it androgyny, gender neutrality, or unisex, gender expression is being reworked, especially by younger-generation consumers who are heavily abandoning the notion of binary definitions of male and female. Savvy marketers should be quick to serve this emerging market with new and smart offerings.[20]

Recently, the **Me Too movement** against sexual harassment and sexual abuse of women has gained substantial momentum. Multiple high-profile examples of such abuse have played out before the global media. The movement has spread rapidly and virally as a hashtag (#MeToo) on social media. The attention has served as a very positive force for marketers to step back and ensure that gender biases do not unwittingly creep into their messaging. During the holiday season in 2019, high-end exercise equipment marketer Peloton ran an ad in which a man gave a woman a Peloton bike as a gift that was quickly spoofed by comedians as it became meme fodder for social media. Peloton's stock price fell 9 percent when the online outrage was at its peak. And though the company assured consumers that the ad was created to "celebrate (a) fitness and wellness journey," reaction to the ad on social media was overwhelmingly negative, with many users comparing it to an episode of "Black Mirror," the tech-centric dystopian Netflix satire that fictionalizes the dangers of the digital age. An important lesson for marketers is that while segmentation is obviously an exceptionally beneficial activity, care must be taken to ensure that messaging to various segments is not up for misinterpretation.[21]

Demographic Segmentation: By Family Life Cycle

Because family needs and expenditures change over time, one way to segment consumers is to consider the stage of the family life cycle they occupy. (You learned about the family life cycle in Chapter 6.) Not surprisingly, consumers in different life cycle segments are unlikely to need the same products, or at least they may not need these things in the same quantities. Single-person households have grown over the years, influenced by such factors as changing views toward marriage and other shifting lifestyle choices. This trend is expected to continue to grow over time and is projected to have an impact on marketing in many industries, including housing and health care.[22] A report from the research firm the NPD Group noted that recent growth in snack food consumption could be attributed largely to the growth in single-person households.[23]

But not all attempts at marketing to the family life cycle succeed. Gerber once tried to market single-serving food jars to single seniors—a quick meal for one person who lives alone. The manufacturer called these containers "Singles." However, Gerber's strong identification with baby food worked against it: The product flopped because their target market was embarrassed to be seen buying baby food.[24]

As families age and move into new life stages, different product categories ascend and descend in importance. At different stages in families, individual family members of varying demographic differences may well be more or less likely to exercise, go to bars and movies, and consume alcohol. Older couples and single adults are more likely to use maintenance services. Seniors are a prime market for resort condominiums and golf products. Marketers need to identify the family life cycle segment of their target consumers by examining purchase data by family life cycle group.

In 2016, the first baby boomer turned 70. Within that group, there are millions of single women who have the time, desire, and financial means to do some active, world-trotting travel. The website *Sixty and Me* is very bullish on providing great travel options to this market segment to push their experiences out to the limit. One truly tempting example is a do-it-yourself learning vacation at Oxford University, England. Topics vary from year to year but typically include creative writing, Shakespeare, philosophy, and British literature and poetry.[25]

Demographic Segmentation: By Income and Social Class

The distribution of wealth is of great interest to marketers because it determines which groups have the greatest **buying power**. Buying power can help marketers to determine how to better match different products and versions of products to different consumer groups based on an understanding of what discretionary and nondiscretionary allocations of funds they are able to make. After a more than 50-year run during which the truly wealthy just kept getting richer, the Great Recession that began in 2007 took some of the wind out of their sails because of heavy investment losses. Then in early 2020, the COVID-19 crisis hit and it whacked the global economy mightily. By May of that year, over 40 million Americans had filed for unemployment and the real jobless rate was quoted at about 24 percent. Obviously, at this writing the punch line to this story has not yet played out. But presuming the economy slowly cranks back up, this hard hit to the economy will have long-lasting effects on many consumers' (and businesses') incomes and spending power. A resulting trickle-down effect is that marketers must rapidly pivot their marketing plans and strategies to account for shifts in spending capabilities and priorities of customers both in the consumer and business markets.[26]

In the past, it was popular for marketers to consider *social class segments*, such as upper class, middle class, and lower class. However, many consumers buy not according to where they actually fall in that framework but rather according to the image they wish to portray. In recent years, luxury car manufacturers such as Mercedes, BMW, and Audi have developed versions of cars that are priced at less than half the price they charge for one of their traditional models. Seeking to attract consumers who view the brands as aspirational purchases, the approach has been so successful at increasing sales and market share that *avant-garde* electric luxury car manufacturer Tesla offers a "low-end" Model III for about half the price of its most expensive model to compete for these consumers, and the company has struggled since the launch to keep up with orders.[27]

Demographic Segmentation: By Race and Ethnicity

A consumer's national origin is often a strong indicator of his or her preferences for specific magazines or TV shows, foods, apparel, and leisure activities. Marketers need to be aware of these differences and sensitivities—especially when they invoke outmoded stereotypes—to appeal to consumers of diverse races and ethnic groups. A new U.S. census was taken in 2020, and those results won't be posted for a couple of years, but let's take a look at ethnic populations based on the figures that are available.

Black, Asian, and Latino/a individuals are the largest racial and ethnic groups in the U.S. The Census Bureau projects that by the year 2050, White individuals will make up just less than 50 percent of the population (compared to 74 percent in 1995) as these other groups grow. Let's take a closer look at each of these important segments.

Black individuals comprise more than 13 percent of the U.S. population.[28] Many marketers recognize the huge impact of this segment and work hard to identify products and services that will appeal to these consumers. The movie industry is no exception—the 2018

buying power
A concept in segmentation that can help marketers to determine how to better match different products and versions of products to different consumer groups based on an understanding of what discretionary and nondiscretionary allocations of funds they are able to make.

The hit movie *Crazy Rich Asians* appealed to many Asian-Americans, and it also crossed over into the mainstream market.

blockbuster film *Black Panther*, starring a full Black cast, quickly earned over $1 billion worldwide within less than two months of its U.S. release, at the time challenging the total revenues of both *Star Wars: The Last Jedi* and *The Avengers*. The *Black Panther* sensation was game-changing for marketers who recognize the huge purchasing power of many different racial and ethnic groups. Importantly, the fact that the film showcased a Black superhero in the starring role who was widely embraced by people of all colors gave strong impetus for marketers to better develop marketing approaches based on how ethnicities are blending rather than proliferate old approaches solely focused on race and ethnicity.[29]

Although their numbers are still small relative to several other ethnicities, Asian Americans are the fastest-growing minority group in the U.S. Between 2000 and 2015, the Asian American population grew by 72 percent to reach over 20 million individuals. By 2055, Asian Americans are projected to make up a whopping 38 percent of all U.S. immigrants, making them the nation's largest immigrant group.[30] Of course projections of this nature depend heavily on the direction in which U.S. immigration laws go over the next several years.

For marketers, the Asian American segment is especially attractive given its substantial buying power, which is estimated to be $1 trillion. The average family income of Asian American households is $20 thousand higher than the U.S. average![31] The sensational hit film *Crazy Rich Asians* brought the Asian success culture to millions of Americans who otherwise knew very little of this robust ethnic segment. BuzzFeed makes an effort to court Asian Americans by publishing content on topics and experiences highly relatable to this group, such as posts tailored to specific Asian subsegments, like "22 Signs You Grew Up with Immigrant Chinese Parents" and "21 Annoying Comments Filipinos Are Tired of Hearing." This approach to delivering fresh and specifically relatable content to different segments enables BuzzFeed to connect with distinct cultural groups of Asian Americans as well as other types of consumer segments.[32] It also makes BuzzFeed attractive to marketers who want to develop **content marketing** that will resonate with specific customer groups. This term refers to the strategy of establishing thought leadership in the form of bylines, blogs, commenting opportunities, videos, sharable social images, and infographics. A key departure is that these messages look like the kind of content that "ordinary" people post rather than the traditional advertising messages consumers are used to seeing.

The Latino/a population is a real emerging superstar segment for this decade, a segment that mainstream marketers today actively cultivate. Latino/a individuals have overtaken Black individuals as the nation's largest minority group, although the growth rate has leveled off.[33] In the United States, Latino/a buying power has reached $1.4 trillion—nearly three times where the segment's buying power was in 2010. Latino/a individuals now represent nearly 10 percent of total U.S. buying power![34]

As with any ethnic group, appeals to Latino/a consumers need to take into account cultural differences. For example, Latino/a individuals didn't appreciate the famously successful mainstream "Got Milk?" campaign because biting, sarcastic humor is not part of their culture. In addition, the notion of milk deprivation is not funny to a Latina mother—if she runs out of milk, this means she has failed her family. To make matters worse, "Got Milk?" translates as "Are you lactating?" in Spanish. Thus, new Spanish-language versions were changed to "And you, have you given them enough milk today?" with tender scenes centered on cooking *flan* (a popular pudding) in the family kitchen. And Taco Bell's "Yo quiero Taco Bell" uttering Chihuahua dog was put out to pasture years ago. (You can check out classic ads from both these campaigns on YouTube.)

content marketing
The strategy of establishing thought leadership in the form of bylines, blogs, commenting opportunities, videos, sharable social images, and infographics.

It is not an overstatement to say that Latino/a youth are changing mainstream culture. Many of these consumers are "young biculturals" who bounce back and forth between hip-hop and rock en Español, blend Mexican rice with spaghetti sauce, and spread peanut butter and jelly on tortillas. In fact, we find many bicultural Latino/a individuals in both younger and older age groups—one study reported that fully 44 percent of the Latino/a population identifies as bicultural. Within that group there are those who place a greater emphasis on preserving their heritage and those who are more open to experimenting with it in the context of new cultural influences.[35]

One caution about the Latino/a, or *Hispanic*, market is that the term *Hispanic* itself actually is a misnomer. For example, Cuban Americans, Mexican Americans, and Puerto Ricans may share a common language, but their history, politics, and culture have many differences. Marketing to them as though they are a homogeneous segment can be a big mistake. However, the term is still widely used as a demographic descriptive. As one unique example, in recent years in part due to the devastating effects of 2017's Hurricane Maria on their home island, hundreds of thousands of Puerto Ricans have relocated to the mainland U.S. The largest recipient of these new consumers was the Central Florida area (Metro Orlando), and marketers have actively been cultivating their business in that major metropolitan area over the past few years.[36] Early predictions for the 2020 Census are that the number of Hispanic teens will grow by 62 percent, compared with 10 percent growth in teens overall. They seek spirituality, strong family ties, and color in their lives—three hallmarks of Latino/a culture. Music crossovers from the Latin charts to mainstream lead the trend, including pop idols Enrique Iglesias, Marc Anthony, and Reggaeton sensation Daddy Yankee. And in perhaps one of the most high-profile statements ever of the popularity of Latino/a entertainers, the 2020 SuperBowl LIV in Miami featured an all-Latino/a–themed halftime extravaganza that included Shakira, Jennifer Lopez, Bad Bunny, and J Balvin. In the U.S., for marketers the Latino/a community of consumers is clearly a segment of tremendous potential.

An important outcome of the increase in multiethnicity is the opportunity for increased cultural diversity in the workplace and elsewhere. **Cultural diversity**—a management practice that actively seeks to include people of different sexes, races, ethnic groups, and religions in an organization's employees, customers, suppliers, and distribution channel partners—is now business as usual rather than an exception. Marketing organizations benefit from employing people of all kinds because they bring different backgrounds, experiences, and points of view that help the firm develop strategies for its brands that will appeal to diverse customer groups.

Geographic Segmentation

Recognizing that people's preferences often vary depending on where they live, many marketers tailor their offerings to specific geographic areas, an approach called **geographic segmentation**. Google Earth and other similar applications of a **geographic information system (GIS)** have ramped up geographic approaches to segmentation. A GIS system can elegantly combine a geographic map with digitally stored data about the consumers in a geographic area. Thus, market information by geographic location is much more convenient for use in market planning and decision making than ever before.

When marketers want to segment regional markets even more precisely, they sometimes combine geography with demographics using the technique of **geodemography**. A basic assumption of geodemography is that "birds of a feather flock together"—people who live near one another share similar characteristics. Sophisticated statistical techniques identify geographic areas that share the same preferences for household items, magazines, and other products. This lets marketers construct segments of households with a common pattern of preferences. This way, they can hone in on those customers most likely to be interested in its specific offerings, in some cases so precisely that families living on one block will belong to a segment, whereas those on the next block will not.

cultural diversity
A management practice that actively seeks to include people of different sexes, races, ethnic groups, and religions in an organization's employees, customers, suppliers, and distribution channel partners.

geographic segmentation
An approach in which marketers tailor their offerings to specific geographic areas because people's preferences often vary depending on where they live.

geographic information system (GIS)
A system that combines a geographic map with digitally stored data about the consumers in a particular geographic area.

geodemography
A segmentation technique that combines geography with demographics.

One widely used geodemographic system is PRIZM, which is a large database developed by Nielsen Claritas. This system classifies the U.S. population into 68 segments based on various socioeconomic data, such as income, age, race, occupation, education, and household composition as well as lifestyle attributes that are critical to marketing strategies; shopping patterns such as where they vacation, what they drive, and their favorite brands; and media preferences. The 68 segments range from the highly affluent "Young Digerati" and "Country Squires" to the lower-income "Family Thrifts" and "Park Bench Seniors" neighborhoods. To give you a flavor of what the profiles are like, here's one for Group 34, "Young & Influential," who are profiled as "midscale younger mostly without kids."

- *Young & Influential* is a segment of younger, lower middle-class households that might not have high incomes but are nonetheless influential in their communities and social networks and are very tech savvy. The segment is a common address for middle-class singles and couples who are more preoccupied with balancing work and leisure pursuits and who live in apartment complexes surrounded by ball fields, health clubs, and casual-dining restaurants. Sound like anyone you know?

geotargeting
Marketing to a set of specific users based on their current real-time location.

One interesting specific approach to location-based targeting is **geotargeting**, which is marketing to a set of specific users based on their current real-time location.[37] When you sign up for Domino's offers, you are asked to provide your address in the opt-in process. This is a geotargeting company's dream. Once the customer is done ordering, Domino's can begin to geotarget in several different ways, including ZIP code, time zone, store location, and state. It's a rich vein of advertising possibilities. For example, a Domino's location in a college town may send out special offers the night of a game. A store in a location currently experiencing a thunderstorm might advertise that ordering in is better than braving the elements. The opportunities for targeted advertising are endless once you grab the address of your customers, and Domino's does so with the lure of cheesy goodness at discount prices.[38]

micromarketing
The ability to identify and target very small geographic segments that sometimes amount to individuals.

Ultimately, highly precise geodemographic segmentation enables marketers to practice **micromarketing**, which is the ability to identify and target small geographic segments that sometimes amount to just one or a few individuals—a concept closely related to that of *one-to-one marketing*, which you read about in Chapter 5. These elements are both enabled by CRM (customer relationship management), another topic in that chapter.

Segment by Psychographics

Demographic and geographic information is useful, but it does not always provide enough information to divide consumers into meaningful segments. Although we can use demographic variables to discover, for example, that on family visits to Walt Disney World in Orlando younger kids prefer the Magic Kingdom while mom and dad might rather spend the day country-hopping at EPCOT, savvy marketers (which Disney surely is!) know that preferences are more complex than just the demographic variable of customer age. In fact, really successful firms often combine approaches to segmentation, and one of the most useful and more sophisticated methods is to segment customers by psychographics.

psychographics
The use of psychological, sociological, and anthropological factors to construct market segments.

As we said in Chapter 6, **psychographics** segment consumers in terms of psychological and behavioral similarities, such as shared *activities, interests, and opinions, or AIOs*.[39] Marketers often develop profiles of the typical customers for whom they desire to paint a more vivid picture. Although some marketers and their creative agencies develop their own psychographic techniques to classify customers, others subscribe to services that divide the entire U.S. population into segments and then provide this information to clients for use in proprietary marketing project applications, such as strategy planning. The best known of these systems is **VALS™**, which is a product of Strategic Business Insights (SBI). VALS™ divides U.S. adults into eight groups according to what drives them psychologically as well as by their economic resources.

VALS™
A psychographic segmentation system that divides U.S. adults into eight groups according to what drives them psychologically as well as by their economic resources.

One segment that combines a psychographic/lifestyle component with a heavy dose of generational marketing is the **gamer segment**, sometimes referred to as the *gamer generation*—"gamer" as in "video games," of course. This group grew up playing video games as second nature for primary recreation, and as they have entered college and the workforce, they continue to carry many gaming sensibilities with them. Video gaming is clearly a lifestyle, and much as the company Google turned into the generic verb *to google* in the 2000s, in this decade, the buzz term du jour is *gamification*, which, as we saw in Chapter 6, is a strategy in which marketers apply game design techniques, often by awarding points or badges to nongame experiences, to drive consumer behavior (e.g., the gamification of practice exams where you might earn badges for getting right answers and then move to the next level of difficulty in your homework). And, by the way, just in case you didn't know, a **badge** is some type of milestone or reward a player earns when he or she progresses through a gamified application. And . . . you're a participant in a gamification strategy if you're a Starbucks Rewards member. In that case you accumulate "stars" with each latte you buy that you can redeem for prizes, like free refills.

E-sports is a booming market, as millions of members of the gamer generation watch their favorite players and teams compete.

dpa picture alliance/Alamy Stock Photo

Marketers would be wise to think about what sorts of badges might appeal to the gamer segment as this segment becomes more and more engaged as consumers who are highly likely to do much of their shopping online.

Segment by Behavior

People may use the same product for different reasons, on different occasions, and in different amounts. So, in addition to demographics and psychographics, it is useful to study what consumers actually do with a product. **Behavioral segmentation** slices consumer segments on the basis of how they act toward, feel about, or use a product.

One way to segment on the basis of behavior is to divide the market into users and nonusers of a product. Then, marketers may attempt to reward current users or try to win over new ones. In addition to distinguishing between users and nonusers, marketers can describe current customers as heavy, moderate, and light users. They often do this according to a rule of thumb we call the **80/20 rule**: 20 percent of purchasers account for 80 percent of the product's sales (the ratio is an approximation, not gospel). This rule means that it often makes more sense to focus on the smaller number of people who are really into a product rather than on the larger number who are just casual users.

The 80/20 rule brings the concept of **customer loyalty** to the forefront. In many product categories, we see fierce competition among rival firms to keep their critical 20 percent loyalists highly engaged and connected with the brand and thus much less likely to switch to a competitor's offering. The competitive intensity to attract and keep loyal customers is very high, and Starbucks remains one of the trend setters. The Starbucks Rewards program we just mentioned blends loyalty, convenience, and services by offering rewards for customer behaviors the firm wants to see reinforced. Members earn stars for the frequency and amount of purchase, and receive benefits such as customized beverages, free upgrades, members-only happy hours, and "jumping the line" perks. Starbucks Rewards ensures that customers are fully integrated with the Starbucks app for mobile payment. The goal is to make these top customers as "sticky" to Starbucks as possible. In fact, **customer stickiness** has actually become part of the common lexicon in marketing, and it means just what you'd expect: that you have a strong bond to a particular brand. In the end, Starbucks Rewards members spend an incredible three times more with the company than the average customer![40]

gamer segment
A consumer segment that combines a psychographic/lifestyle component with a heavy dose of generational marketing.

badge
A milestone or reward earned for progressing through a video game.

behavioral segmentation
A technique that divides consumers into segments on the basis of how they act toward, feel about, or use a good or service.

80/20 rule
A marketing rule of thumb that 20 percent of purchasers account for 80 percent of a product's sales.

customer loyalty
A customer's low likelihood of switching to a competitor's offering, especially because of being highly engaged and connected with their current brand.

customer stickiness
Highly cultivated customers who are likely to follow through on an intended purchase, buy the product repeatedly, and recommend it to others.

Stephen Saks Photography/Alamy Stock Photo

The Biltmore Estate in Asheville, North Carolina, increased attendance during its annual Christmas celebration as part of a strategy to segment by usage occasion. The estate's marketers developed four separate strategies to target different types of visitors, including heavy users who have made a Christmas pilgrimage an annual family tradition.

experiential loyalty
Customer loyalty that results not just in increased purchases but also in an enhanced broader experience for the customer.

usage rate
A measurement that reflects the quantity purchased or frequency of use among consumers of a particular product or service.

long tail
A new approach to segmentation based on the idea that companies can make money by selling small amounts of items that only a few people want, provided they sell enough different items.

usage occasions
An indicator used in behavioral market segmentation based on when consumers use a product most.

Such deep attention through their loyalty programs to not just increased purchase but also to enhancing the broader customer experience has sparked the new buzzword **experiential loyalty**. Marketers crave this because customers who have a very close relationship-driven experience with a brand and offering tend to yield the highest customer lifetime value (CLV), which was discussed in Chapter 5. The concept of CLV may sound similar to that of ROMI (return on marketing investment), which you learned about in Chapter 3, but there's actually a big difference. ROMI is about the success of marketing investments on a large scale at the overall firm level. In contrast, CLV tracks data at the individual customer level. This is accomplished when firms can link engagement level and purchases to specific customers, and a key way firms do this is through customer data from their loyalty programs.

A related concept to the 80/20 rule and customer loyalty and stickiness in behavioral segmentation is **usage rate**, which reflects the quantity purchased or frequency of use among consumers of a particular product or service. The highest-use segments are often incredibly profitable over the long run and may contribute the majority of profits to a particular offering's bottom line.

Although the 80/20 rule and its related concepts still hold true in the majority of situations, the Internet's ability to offer an unlimited choice of goods to billions of people has changed how marketers think about segmentation. An approach called the **long tail** turns traditional thinking about the virtues of selling in high volume on its head. The basic idea is that we need no longer rely solely on big hits (like blockbuster movies or best-selling books) to find profits. Companies can also make money when they sell small amounts of items that only a few people want—if they sell enough different items.

For many companies, the selling of digital products that can be transferred to purchasers through an Internet connection helps to support a long-tail approach because it reduces the cost of storage of products and allows for the fulfillment of consumer demand on an as-needed basis. Amazon, the Apple iTunes Store, and the Google Play Store are prime examples of sites that are set up to be able to benefit from the large and small sales of a wider array of goods, which should also benefit both the big and small sellers that offer products through their platforms.

Another way to segment a market on the basis of behavior is to look at **usage occasions**, or when consumers use the product most. We associate many products with specific occasions, whether time of day, holidays, business functions, or casual get-togethers. Businesses often divide up their markets according to when and how their offerings are in demand. Ruth's Chris Steakhouse is by far the market leader in the high-end steak restaurant category, featuring USDA prime beef as its signature dish. Ruth's is well aware that it is a special-occasion location—graduations, birthdays, promotions, you name it—and folks want to celebrate at Ruth's. And they are all too happy to accommodate, often surprising guests with special table decorations for the occasion and a nice dessert treat, compliments of the chef.

And in the online space, Google enables its advertising clients to target certain ads to certain segments of search engine users based on data such as Google domain, query entered, IP address, and language preference. This way, companies can have Google automatically sort and send the intended ad to certain market segments. Thus, it is possible for advertisers on Google to tailor their automatically targeted ads based on seasonality—you will see more TurboTax ads on Google pages during tax season, even if people aren't querying about tax software.[41]

Segment B2B Markets

We've reviewed the segmentation variables marketers use to divide up the consumer pie, but how about all those B2B marketers out there? Adding to what you learned about business markets in Chapter 6, it's important to know that segmentation also helps them better understand their customers. Although the specific variables may differ, the underlying logic of classifying the larger market into manageable pieces that share relevant characteristics is the same whether the product you sell is pesto or pesticides.

Organizational demographics are organization-specific dimensions that marketers use to describe, classify, and organize different organizations for the purpose of segmenting business-to-business markets. Organizational demographics also help a B2B marketer understand the needs and characteristics of its potential customers. These classification dimensions include the size of the firms (either in total sales or in number of employees), the number of facilities, whether they are a domestic or a multinational company, their purchasing policies, and the type of business they are in. B2B markets may also be segmented on the basis of the production technology they use and whether the customer is a user or a nonuser of the product.

Many industries use the North American Industry Classification System (NAICS) we discussed in Chapter 6 to obtain information about the size and number of companies operating in a particular industry. B2B marketers often consult general informational business and industry databases on the web, such as D&B Hoovers, for insight and up-to-date information on private and public companies worldwide.

organizational demographics
Organization-specific dimensions that can be used to describe, classify, and organize different organizations for the purpose of segmenting business-to-business markets.

Disruption in Segmentation: When Everybody's a Segment of One

In Chapter 5, you read all about how the great strides in CRM, marketing analytics, and related advancements in the science side of the marketing field are transforming the way marketing is done. Perhaps nowhere within the marketing toolkit is the impact of these elements more profound than in market segmentation. Consider predictive analytics, for example. Boiled down to its essence and in layman's terms, predictive analytics—driven by artificial intelligence (AI) capabilities—strives to help marketers know what a customer is likely to need and want even before the customer takes the very first step toward purchase. And further, anticipatory shipping also relies on AI to actually go ahead and take the leap to supply you with that offering. So long as this works well, customers actually really like the ease and convenience of just letting it flow.

The above approach facilitates the advent of the concept of a **segment of one**, which refers to tracking the activity and preferences of a single potential customer and then tailoring products or ads for that individual according to their behaviors. Once that customer is on board and fully vetted and represented in the provider's CRM system, it's really just a matter of tracking and applying the AI-driven analyses to put much of that customer's relationship and experience with the provider onto a sort of autopilot mode. Obviously not all customers will partake in the opportunity to be served in what may appear to be a bit of a sterile manner such as this. But back to our discussion about generational marketing—approaches to need fulfillment that include convenience, digitally-driven solutions, and high dependability of process all score really high marks with the younger generations. And the capabilities to execute against a segment of one are getting stronger and stronger all the time.

segment of one
Tracking the activity and preferences of a single potential customer and then tailoring products or ads for that individual according to their behaviors.

So in the end, the disruption to market segmentation of this trend is that much of the traditional "groupings" of customers with different needs for marketing purposes is likely to eventually become moot. You will learn in Chapter 14 how the marketing communication mix is also skewing toward more and more digital/social approaches, which means that segments of one can also be well communicated with by the provided one-to-one, and vice-versa. Does this negate all the concepts you've just read in this section on market segmentation? We don't think so—the various approaches to segmentation you've learned about here are certainly still valid and heavily utilized today. But in the future—we'll see.

7.3 Step 2: Targeting

OBJECTIVE

Explain how marketers evaluate segments and choose a targeting strategy.

targeting
A strategy in which marketers evaluate the attractiveness of each potential segment and decide in which of these groups they will invest resources to try to turn them into customers.

target market
The market segments on which an organization focuses its marketing plan and toward which it directs its marketing efforts.

Way back in Figure 7.1, we saw that target marketing strategy consists of three steps: segmentation, targeting, and positioning. And in the last section we've seen that the first step in a target marketing strategy is segmentation, in which the firm divides the market into smaller groups that share certain characteristics. The next step is **targeting**, in which marketers evaluate the attractiveness of each potential segment and decide in which of these groups they will invest resources to try to turn them into customers. The customer group or groups they select are the firm's **target market**, which, as you learned in Chapter 1, is the segment(s) on which an organization focuses its marketing plan and toward which it directs its marketing efforts.

In this section, we'll review the three phases of targeting: evaluate market segments, develop segment profiles, and choose a targeting strategy. Figure 7.3 illustrates these three phases.

Phases of Targeting

Phase 1: Evaluate Market Segments

Just because a marketer identifies a segment does not necessarily mean that it's a useful target. A viable target segment should satisfy the following requirements:

- *Are members of the segment similar to each other in their product needs and wants and, at the same time, different from consumers in other segments?* Without real differences in consumer needs, firms might as well use a mass-marketing strategy. It's a waste of time to develop two separate lines of skin care products for working women and nonworking women if both segments have the same complaints about dry skin.

- *Can marketers measure the segment?* Marketers must know something about the size and purchasing power of a potential *segment* before they decide if it's worth their efforts.

- *Is the segment large enough to be profitable now and in the future?* For example, a graphic designer who hopes to design web pages for Barbie doll collectors must decide whether there are enough hard-core aficionados to make this business worthwhile and whether the trend will continue.

- *Can marketing communications reach the segment?* It is easy for marketers to identify TV programs or magazines that will efficiently reach older consumers, consumers with certain levels of education, or residents of major cities because the media *they* prefer are easy to identify. However, it is unlikely that marketing communications can reach only left-handed blondes with multiple piercings who listen to Taylor Swift overdubbed in Mandarin Chinese.

Figure 7.3 *Process* | Phases of Targeting

Targeting involves three distinct phases of activities.

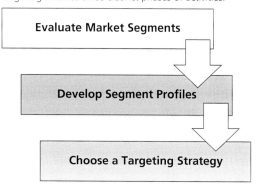

- Evaluate Market Segments
- Develop Segment Profiles
- Choose a Targeting Strategy

- *Can the marketer adequately serve the needs of the segment?* Does the firm have the expertise and resources to satisfy the segment better than the competition? Some years ago venerable consumer-packaged-goods manufacturer P&G decided there was money to be made in salty snacks, so with great fanfare, it entered the market with Pringles. Pringles came with the unique twist of being sold in vacuum-packed cans instead of

It's often useful to develop a buyer persona that describes a typical customer so that the entire marketing team has the same profile in mind.

in bags like most potato chips. But Frito-Lay has dominated the salty snack space for decades, and while P&G had some degree of success with the novel Pringles, there was just no way to beat Frito-Lay's distribution and marketing expertise. A few years ago, Pringles was acquired by snack food giant Kellogg's, which, as the second-largest snack company in the world, is in a much better position to compete with Frito-Lay.

Phase 2: Develop Segment Profiles

segment profile
A description of the "typical" customer in a segment.

Once a marketer identifies a set of usable segments, it is helpful to generate a profile of each to really understand segment members' needs and to look for business opportunities. This segment profile is a description of the "typical" customer in that segment. A **segment profile** might, for example, include customer demographics, location, lifestyle information, and a description of how frequently the customer buys the product. When the marketers of General Mills' product Hamburger Helper decided to target cash-strapped millennials, they had to adjust the image they presented on social media. On one April Fools' Day, the packaged food company announced through social media the release of a mixtape titled "Watch the Stove" containing five light-hearted Hamburger Helper–themed rap songs created by a group of college students at McNally Smith's College of Music. The mixtape was well received and was played more than 270,000 times on SoundCloud by 5 p.m. on the day of release. One of the company's marketing communications planners describes the target segment of consumers as "a young, urban, millennial guy making Hamburger Helper in his dorm room."[42]

personas
Fictional characters created by marketers that represent different key potential user types for an offering.

A very useful tool in profiling market segments is the use of **personas**. Personas are fictional characters created by marketers that represent different key potential user types for an offering. They represent different needs, experiences, behaviors, and goals of different individuals. Marketers use personas to step outside of their own personal viewpoint and biases about who their customers are and to recognize that different people have uniquely different needs and expectations. For example, a travel firm might use the following set of personas to identify the marketing approaches most likely to appeal to each: the Experience Seeker, the Chill Out, the Family Bonder, and the All-Business. Each of these categories of the travel consumer would be fully fleshed out to represent the core needs they hope to fulfill from the travel experience. From the labels of these personas, can you imagine the differences in imagery, narrative, and persuasive appeals the travel firm's marketers might deploy to attract each type of traveler? For example, the Family Bonder persona most likely represents a couple with children and maybe an extended family who enjoy taking vacations together and focus both on fun activities as well as family renewal time. Marketers typically have fairly sophisticated templates for articulating the descriptions of personas they believe represent their most fruitful market segments.[43]

Phase 3: Choose a Targeting Strategy

A basic targeting decision centers on how finely tuned the target should be: Should the company go after one large segment or focus on meeting the needs of one or more smaller segments? Let's look at four targeting strategies: undifferentiated, differentiated, concentrated, and customized.

undifferentiated targeting strategy
Appealing to a broad spectrum of people.

A company like Walmart that selects an **undifferentiated targeting strategy** appeals to a broad spectrum of people. If successful, this type of operation can be efficient because production, research, and promotion costs benefit from *economies of scale*—it's cheaper to develop one product or one advertising campaign than to choose several targets and create separate products or messages for each. But the company must be willing to bet that people have similar needs so that the same product and message will appeal to many customers. Walmart is the quintessential undifferentiated retailer because it aims to appeal to pretty much anybody who wants to buy something.

A company that chooses a **differentiated targeting strategy** develops one or more products for each of several customer groups with different product needs. A differentiated strategy is called for when consumers choose among well-known brands that have distinctive images and the company can identify one or more segments that have distinct needs for different types of products.

As a PR stunt, Domino's created customized billboards specifically targeting "holdouts" who hadn't yet tried its new pizza versions.

When you think of auto manufacturers, Volvo and Suburu come to mind as brands with a differentiated targeting strategy. Both get you from point A to point B like any other car. But each has its own unique place in the consumer market. Volvo historically has built a reputation as an exceptionally safe vehicle, as has Suburu. But Volvo comes across as appealing to a bit older and more traditional crowd, while Suburu works hard to have a more edgy—even a bit quirky—appeal.

Differentiated marketing can also involve connecting one product with multiple segments by communicating differently to appeal to those segments. Again, using the venerable "Got milk?" campaign as an example, one of the campaign's most classic ads featured Aerosmith's Steven Tyler to appeal to both aging boomers who got into the band in the 1970s and Gen Xers who discovered the band in the 1990s as a result of Run-DMC's remake of "Walk This Way." Then, amazingly, millennials discovered Tyler during his run as a judge on *American Idol*. Talk about multigenerational appeal!

When a firm offers one or more products to a single segment, it uses a **concentrated targeting strategy**. Smaller firms that do not have the resources or the desire to be all things to all people often do this. Consider the cell phone brand Jitterbug—a great example of concentrated targeting. The company GreatCall Wireless developed it back in the mid-2000s as a simple, straightforward product. It immediately ran counter to the trend toward increasingly technologically sophisticated cell phones (and smartphones) by offering a flip cell phone with fewer and larger buttons, as well as a focused range of capabilities. The original Jitterbug was primarily targeted toward seniors with a desire for a simpler communication device. But over the years, it has evolved to offer options including a model that "resembles" a smartphone in appearance (important for today's seniors to "look hip") but with a streamlined range of choices on its touchscreen interface and features such as an urgent care button that are of particular value to this older segment.[44]

Ideally, marketers should be able to define segments so precisely that they can offer products that exactly meet the unique needs of each individual or firm. This level of concentration does occur (we hope) in the case of personal or professional services we get from doctors, lawyers, and hairstylists. A **customized marketing strategy** also is common in industrial contexts where a manufacturer often works with one or a few large clients and develops products that only these clients will use.

differentiated targeting strategy
Developing one or more products for each of several distinct customer groups and making sure these offerings are kept separate in the marketplace.

concentrated targeting strategy
Focusing a firm's efforts on offering one or more products to a single segment.

customized marketing strategy
An approach that tailors specific products and the messages about them to individual customers.

Blacksocks practices a highly concentrated targeting strategy.

Of course, in most cases, this level of segmentation is neither practical nor possible when mass-produced products such as computers or cars enter the picture. However, advances in computer technology, coupled with the new emphasis on building solid relationships with customers, have focused managers' attention on devising new ways to tailor specific products and the messages about them to individual customers. This targeting approach is referred to as **mass customization**, where a manufacturer modifies a basic good or service to meet an individual's specific needs.[45]

mass customization
An approach that modifies a basic good or service to meet the needs of an individual.

7.4 Step 3: Positioning

OBJECTIVE
Recognize how marketers develop and implement a positioning strategy.

The final stage of developing a target marketing strategy is to provide consumers who belong to a targeted market segment with a good or service that meets their unique needs and expectations. **Positioning** means developing a marketing strategy to influence how a particular market segment perceives a good or service in comparison to the competition. A key word in this definition is *perceives*—that is, positioning is in the eye of the beholder.

positioning
Developing a marketing strategy to influence how a particular market segment perceives a good or service in comparison to the competition.

A firm may truly believe that its customers think about its offering in a certain way, but unless market research bears this out, what the marketer "thinks" doesn't matter, as it is trumped by what the consumer perceives. To position a brand, marketers must clearly understand the criteria target consumers use to evaluate competing products and then convince them that their product, service, or organization will meet those needs. In addition, the organization has to come up with a plan to communicate this position to its target market.

Steps in Positioning

Figure 7.4 shows the steps marketers go through to decide just how to position their product or service: analyze competitors' positions, offer a good or service with a competitive advantage, finalize the marketing mix, and evaluate responses and modify as needed. Let's take a closer look at each of these positioning steps.

Step 1: Analyze Competitors' Positions

direct competitors
Competitors whose offerings are very similar to yours.

indirect competitors
Competitors whose offerings are different from yours but potentially could provide the same benefits and satisfy the same customer needs as your offerings do.

The first stage is to analyze competitors' positions in the marketplace. To develop an effective positioning strategy, marketers must understand the current lay of the land. What competitors are out there, and how does the target market perceive them? And it's important to realize that competitors come in two flavors: **direct competitors**, whose offerings are very similar to yours, and **indirect competitors**, whose offerings are different from yours but potentially could provide the same benefits and satisfy the same customer needs as your offerings do.

Sometimes the indirect competition can be more important than the direct, especially if it represents an emerging consumer trend. For years, McDonald's developed positioning strategies based only on its direct competition, which it defined as other large fast-food hamburger chains (translation: Burger King and Wendy's). McDonald's failed to realize that, in fact, many indirect competitors fulfilled consumers' needs for a quick, tasty, convenient meal—from supermarket delis to frozen microwavable single-serving meals to call-ahead takeout from full-service restaurants like Applebee's, Olive Garden, Outback,

Figure 7.4 *Process* | Steps in Positioning

Four key steps comprise the decision-making process in positioning.

and Chili's—all of whom have convenient curbside service instead of backed-up drive-through lines. Ultimately, McDonald's began to understand that it must react to this indirect competition by serving up a wider variety of adult-friendly food and shoring up lagging service. These days, the company also offers its McCafé concept, with coffee products aimed squarely at taking business away from morning mainstays Starbucks and Dunkin', along with a tasty breakfast menu all day long.

Step 2: Define Your Competitive Advantage

The second stage is to offer a good or service with a competitive advantage to provide a reason why consumers will perceive the product as better than that of the competition. Toward this end, a **positioning statement** can help the company frame internally how a product is positioned so that any associated marketing communication remains focused on articulating to consumers the specific *value* offered by a product. Positioning statements typically include the segment(s) to which the product is targeted, the most important claim (differentiator) to be attributed to the product for the targeted segment(s), and the most important piece of evidence that supports the claim made about the product. If the company offers only a "me-too product," it can induce people to buy for a lower price. Other forms of competitive advantage include offering a superior image (Giorgio Armani), a unique product feature (Levi's 501 button-fly jeans), better service (Cadillac's roadside assistance program), or even better-qualified people (the legendary salespeople at Nordstrom department stores).

positioning statement
An expression of a product's positioning that is internally developed and maintained in order to support the development of marketing communication that articulates the specific *value* offered by a product.

Step 3: Finalize the Marketing Mix

Once they settle on a positioning strategy, the third stage for marketers is to finalize the marketing mix as they put all the pieces into place. The elements of the marketing mix must match the selected segment. This means that the good or service must deliver benefits that the segment values, such as convenience or status. Put another way, it must add value and satisfy consumer needs (sound familiar?). Furthermore, marketers must price this offering at a level these consumers will pay, make the offering available at places they are likely to go, and correctly communicate the offering's benefits in locations where these targets are likely to take notice. In other words, the positioning strategy translates into the organization's marketing mix that we discussed in Chapter 1.

Beginning with Chapter 8, all the remaining chapters in the book provide you with the details of developing strategies for each element of the marketing mix: product, price, physical distribution, and promotion. The sum of these individual marketing mix strategies results in the overall positioning strategy for your offering.

Step 4: Evaluate Responses and Modify as Needed

In the fourth and final stage, marketers evaluate the target market's responses so they can modify strategies if necessary. Over time, the firm may find that it needs to change which segments it targets or even alter a product's position to respond to marketplace changes. A change in positioning strategy is **repositioning**, and it's fairly common to see a company try to modify its brand image to keep up with changing times. Take as an example Charles Schwab, which used to be pegged primarily as a self-service stock brokerage. Competition in the budget broker business, especially from online brokers, prompted Schwab's repositioning to a full-line, full-service financial services firm that still pays attention to frugal prices for its services. Think of it this way: There's not much value Schwab can add as one of a dozen or more online providers of stock trades. In that environment, customers simply view the firm as a commodity (i.e., just a way to buy stocks) with no real differentiation. Schwab still has its no-frills products, but the real growth in sales and profits comes from its expanded product

repositioning
Redoing a product's position to respond to marketplace changes.

The SoBe Beverage Company started in Miami's South Beach (hence the name "So-Be") in 1996 when the founders saw a lizard on the art deco façade of the Abbey Hotel, and the rest is history. SoBe has masterfully executed the process of segmentation, target marketing, and positioning and today boasts such flavors as Morning Patrol, Tsunami, Offshore Breeze, and South Beach Sunset.

retro brands
A once-popular brand that has been revived to experience a popularity comeback, often by riding a wave of nostalgia.

perceptual map
A technique to visually describe where brands are "located" in consumers' minds relative to competing brands.

neglected segment
An unserved or underserved market segment for which opportunity may exist for a new product entry.

lines and provision of more information—both online and through personal selling—that warrant higher fees and build deeper customer relationships. Today, Charles Schwab aptly uses the tagline "A modern approach to investing and retirement"—offering a wide range of services to customers in whatever way they want to engage with the firm.

Repositioning also occurs when a marketer revises a brand thought to be inextricably past its prime. Sometimes these products rise like a phoenix from the ashes to ride a wave of nostalgia and return to the marketplace as **retro brands**—venerable brands like Oxydol laundry detergent, Breck Shampoo, Ovaltine cereal, Frontier airlines, and Tab cola all are examples of brands that at one point were nearly forgotten but then got a new lease on life.[46] If you want to check out an interesting set of retro brands, take a look at RetroBrands USA's website. Their mission is to revive "abandoned" consumer iconic brands they've acquired and to bring them back to the marketplace by partnering with interested investors. Some of the brands they have acquired in a "fire sale" are Chipwich (ice cream sandwich with chocolate chips), Mr. Microphone (transmit your voice to the nearest radio), Puss 'N Boots (cat food), and Aspergum (that's right— aspirin in gum).[47]

Perceptual Maps

An important aspect of product positioning is to develop an identity for the product that the target market will prefer over competing brands. How do marketers determine where their product actually stands in the minds of consumers? One solution is to ask consumers what characteristics are important and how competing alternatives would rate on these attributes, too. Marketers use this information to construct a **perceptual map**—a vivid way to construct a picture of where products or brands are "located" in consumers' minds.

To illustrate, let's consider the positioning of steak restaurants in the U.S. Figure 7.5 provides a perceptual map of several popular brands portrayed on two key dimensions of the customer experience—formal versus casual atmosphere and high versus low variety menu. Marketers obtain this information directly from market research in which consumers provide their perceptions of each brand on these two dimensions. This knowledge can be very useful for any of the players on the map because it gives them a starting point for potentially repositioning their brand if, for example, trends indicate more opportunity in one quadrant or another. So if Ruth's Chris decides the market is trending toward higher menu variety and wants to add a few new items, that would position it more in line with Fleming's and Del Frisco's than at present, which has implications for its marketing strategy.

Perceptual maps can aid marketers by revealing an unserved or underserved area. This might represent a **neglected segment**, which is an unserved or underserved market segment for which opportunity may exist for a new product entry. If so, you will want to move quickly to capture the segment and define the standards of comparison for the category. In our perceptual map on steak restaurants, there is an obvious void in the quadrant of casual atmosphere and low menu variety. To the clever marketer, this might spark the possibility of a smaller, Chipotle-sized steak place that serves a very limited menu and caters to the fast-casual crowd. Good food, limited menu, and an easy and pleasant dining stop.

Figure 7.5 *Snapshot* | Perceptual Map

Perceptual mapping allows marketers to identify consumers' perceptions of their brand in relation to the competition.

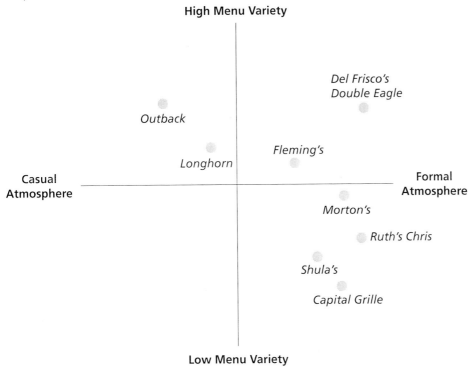

7.5 Brand You: Sharpening Your Focus with Target Marketing

OBJECTIVE

Understand the importance of target marketing and the three steps— segmentation, targeting, and positioning—for managing a successful career.

Taylor now understands the decision process a manager is likely to use in hiring a new employee or intern. He has focused on what the employer is likely to be looking for in job applicants and has reviewed his mission statement and SWOT analysis. Now it's time to develop effective Brand You marketing strategies.

Many young job seekers make the mistake of using an unfocused approach. Lacking direction makes it hard if not impossible to know what industries and what firms to contact or what to say. In fact, you won't know how to develop a clear message about the value you have to offer and what to emphasize about your skills, talents, and experiences. This, in turn, makes it difficult to write a résumé or develop dynamic answers to interview questions. Just like individual consumers, businesses and other organizations seeking to buy/hire a new employee are not all alike. You'll find that using a target marketing strategy will make your job search less difficult and you'll find a job more quickly. Think about it this way—if you just tossed a coin each semester to decide what courses you would take, you might end up with electives in pre-med, theater, and accounting. Just like you carefully choose the courses you take each semester, your Brand You job search should be carefully planned and targeted.

Target Marketing

Just as the consumer market includes people with vastly different interests and backgrounds, hiring organizations are highly diverse. When looking for a job, it makes sense to target one or a few specific types of organizations. As we discussed earlier in this chapter, the target marketing process includes three steps: segmentation, targeting, and positioning. These same steps can be applied to targeting when the market includes companies who are seeking employees.

1. **Segmentation** is the process of dividing the market (in this case, companies or organizations) into groups. Think about the hospitality industry. Businesses in the industry include restaurants, hotels, resorts, and casinos. Identifying and gathering information about the different groups or segments allows you to decide which segments or business sectors you want to pursue.

2. **Targeting** is the process of evaluating the attractiveness of each segment and deciding which are worth spending resources on to turn into potential customers. The group becomes the **target market**. In your search for work, your resources are time and energy. Targeting means you can focus all of those resources where you are likely to get the greatest return. If you choose to have more than one target market, you'll need to adapt your message (your résumé, cover letter, and interview responses) for each market.

3. **Positioning** is placing your brand in the minds of consumers in relation to other brands. In this case, the customer is a prospective employer, and the competition is made up of other job candidates. Positioning helps you recognize what makes you unique and has value to prospective customers. The more you can position yourself as a person who can provide the skills and competencies that meet an employer's unique needs, the better your chances for being hired.

Once you've developed your marketing materials (your résumé and cover letters), examine the response you're getting from employers. The purpose of a résumé is to get requests for an interview. If it isn't doing that, you may need a different strategy for contacting employers or a more effective cover letter and résumé.

Choosing a Targeting Strategy

At this point, you may be asking if you should go after a single segment or several. That depends on how sure you are about a single sector and how large it is. If the single sector has limited potential employers, you may be better off targeting more than one segment.

Bringing Your Personal Brand to Life

Brands come to life and gain appeal when they have an identifiable personality (think Aflac duck versus the GEICO gecko). To bring your brand to life, build on your own personality. A helpful way to do this is to create a list of personality traits and adjectives you want to incorporate into the brand identity for the product (you). Your brand identity includes your personality characteristics, skills, and behaviors that demonstrate what you can accomplish. These things, taken together, are what make you unique; they are the things you'll want to emphasize as you communicate your own personal brand to others.

In a job interview, it's important for you to be you. Let your personality come through; don't try to create a new one. The right attitude to have during a job interview is, "Here I am. Here is what I stand for. Here is what I care about. If you want someone like me, I'm ready!"

Taylor understands the importance of target marketing and is already planning how he will segment his potential job market. He is also working on a list of his own personality characteristics that he will build on to become the best job candidate he can possibly be.

Objective **Summaries** and **Key Terms**

7.1 Objective Summary

Identify the steps in the target marketing process.

Marketers must balance the efficiency of mass marketing, serving the same items to everyone, with the effectiveness of offering each individual exactly what he or she wants. To accomplish this, instead of trying to sell something to everyone, marketers follow these steps: (1) select a target marketing strategy, in which they divide the total market into different segments based on customer characteristics; (2) select one or more segments; and (3) develop products to meet the needs of those specific segments.

Key Terms

market fragmentation
target marketing strategy

7.2 Objective Summary

Understand the need for market segmentation and the approaches available to do it.

Market segmentation is often necessary in today's marketplace because of market fragmentation—that is, the splintering of a mass society into diverse groups due to technological and cultural differences. Most marketers can't realistically do a good job of meeting the needs of everyone, so it is more efficient to divide the larger pie into slices in which members of a segment share some important characteristics and tend to exhibit the same needs and preferences. Marketers frequently find it useful to segment consumer markets on the basis of demographic characteristics, including age, gender, family life cycle, social class, race or ethnic identity, and place of residence. A second dimension, psychographics, uses measures of psychological and social characteristics to identify people with shared preferences or traits. Consumer markets may also be segmented on the basis of how consumers behave toward the product, for example, their brand loyalty, usage rates (heavy, moderate, or light), and usage occasions. B2B markets are often segmented on the basis of industrial demographics, type of business based on the North American Industry Classification codes, and geographic location.

Key Terms

segmentation
oversegmentation
segmentation variables
generational marketing
Generation Z (iGen)
digital natives
Generation Y (millennials)
Generation X
baby boomers

gender identity
androgyny
gender-bending products
Me Too movement
buying power
content marketing
cultural diversity
geographic segmentation
geographic information system (GIS)
geodemography
geotargeting
micromarketing
psychographics
VALS™
gamer segment
badge
behavioral segmentation
80/20 rule
customer loyalty
customer stickiness
experiential loyalty
usage rate
long tail
usage occasions
organizational demographics
segment of one

7.3 Objective Summary

Explain how marketers evaluate segments and choose a targeting strategy.

To choose one or more segments to target, marketers examine each segment and evaluate its potential for success as a target market. Meaningful segments have wants that are different from those in other segments, can be identified, can be reached with a unique marketing mix, will respond to unique marketing communications, are large enough to be profitable, have future growth potential, and possess needs that the organization can satisfy better than the competition.

After marketers identify the different segments, they estimate the market potential of each. The relative attractiveness of segments also influences the firm's selection of an overall marketing strategy. The firm may choose an undifferentiated, differentiated, concentrated, or custom strategy based on the company's characteristics and the nature of the market.

Key Terms

targeting
target market
segment profile
personas
undifferentiated targeting strategy
differentiated targeting strategy

concentrated targeting strategy
customized marketing strategy
mass customization

retro brands
perceptual map
neglected segment

7.4 Objective Summary

Recognize how marketers develop and implement a positioning strategy.

After marketers select the target market(s) and the overall strategy, they must determine how they wish customers to perceive the brand relative to the competition—that is, should the brand be positioned like, against, or away from the competition? Marketers can compare brand positions by using such research techniques as perceptual mapping. In developing and implementing the positioning strategy, firms analyze the competitors' positions, determine the competitive advantage offered by their product, tailor the marketing mix in accordance with the positioning strategy, and evaluate responses to the marketing mix selected. Marketers must continually monitor changes in the market that might indicate a need to reposition the product.

Key Terms

positioning
positioning statement
direct competitors
indirect competitors
repositioning

7.5 Objective Summary

Understand the importance of target marketing and the three steps—segmentation, targeting, and positioning—for managing a successful career.

Using a target marketing strategy can make the job search easier, faster, and more successful. A target market strategy helps you develop a clear message about your value and what skills and experiences to emphasize in order to write a résumé that will target one or a few types of businesses.

Target marketing includes three steps: segmentation, targeting, and positioning. Segmentation is the process of dividing the market (companies or organizations) into groups. Targeting is evaluating the attractiveness of each segment and deciding which one is worth resources to turn into a customer, that is, your target market. Positioning yourself among other job candidates with prospective employers helps you recognize what makes you unique and has value to prospective customers.

Other decisions you face in target marketing include identifying whether a single segment or several is best and what type of brand personality should be part of your Brand You. In your job interview, be sure that your personality comes through rather than one you have created.

Chapter **Questions** and **Activities**

Concepts: Test Your Knowledge

7-1. What is market segmentation, and why is it an important strategy in today's marketplace? What is market fragmentation, and what are its consequences for marketers?

7-2. What is a target marketing strategy?

7-3. Describe the three major racial and ethnic groups in the United States (the Black, Asian, and Latino/a populations). How do they provide unique segments for many products? Describe the steps in target marketing.

7-4. List and explain the major demographic characteristics frequently used in segmenting consumer markets.

7-5. Explain generational marketing. What is Generation Z? Generation Y? Generation X? Baby boomers?

7-6. What is behavioral segmentation?

7-7. What are some of the ways marketers segment B2B markets?

7-8. List and explain the criteria marketers use to determine whether a segment may be a good candidate for targeting.

7-9. Explain the differences between undifferentiated, differentiated, concentrated, and customized marketing strategies. What is mass customization?

7-10. What is product positioning? What do marketers mean by creating a brand personality? What examples can you come up with of uses of brand anthropomorphism?

7-11. How do marketers use perceptual maps to help them develop effective positioning strategies?

7-12. Explain content marketing and geodemography. What is customer loyalty and customer stickiness?

Activities: Apply What You've Learned

7-13. *Creative Homework/Short Project* You are an entrepreneur who is designing a new line of boutique hotels located along California's coastline. Each of the 100 guest rooms in each hotel will offer upscale decor, Wi-Fi, a mini bar stocked with high-end snacks, premium beers, and top-label liquors for a nightly rate of $315. The hotels will have a spa, an onsite restaurant, and a separate full-service bar that features local musicians. Describe in detail the demographics—age, gender, family life cycle, income and social class, ethnicity, and place of residence—of your target customer.

7-14. *Creative Homework/Short Project.* Assume that a small regional microbrewery has hired you to help them with their target marketing. They are pretty unsophisticated about marketing—you will need to explain some things to them and provide ideas for their future. In the past, the microbrewery has simply produced and sold a single beer brand to the entire market—a mass-marketing strategy. As you begin your work, you come to believe that the firm could be more successful if it developed a target marketing strategy. Write a memo to the owner outlining the following:

a. The basic reasons for doing target marketing in the first place
b. The specific advantages of a target marketing strategy for the microbrewery
c. An initial "short list" of possible target segment profiles

7-15. *In Class, 10–25 Minutes for Teams* Assume you are the owner of a local dance studio that offers tap, jazz, ballet, hip-hop, and tumbling classes to children and teens (ages 2–18). To better market your classes to potential students and families in your town, you are developing a segment profile of a typical dancer at your studio. Write a descriptive segment profile, or "persona," of the target consumer. Share your description with the class.

7-16. *In Class, 10–25 Minutes for Teams* As an account executive for a marketing consulting firm, your newest client is a university—your university. You have been asked to develop a positioning strategy for the university. With your team, develop an outline of your ideas, including the following:

a. Who are your competitors?
b. What are the competitors' positions?
c. What target markets are most attractive to the university?
d. How will you position the university for those segments relative to the competition?

7-17. *Creative Homework/Short Project* Imagine you are the marketing director for a new potato chip brand called CRUNCH and that you have been charged with determining what kind of brand personality the product should have in order for it to have broad appeal with members of Generation Z. Describe the desired brand personality and identify specific elements of the marketing mix (product, place, price, promotion) that should be implemented to assist in establishing the desired brand personality.

7-18. *Creative Homework* Choose a food category that you know well and that has several brands that compete in the marketplace. Develop a perceptual map for that category. First, you will need to create two dimensions on which you will compare the brands (see Figure 7.5 to see how it was done for the steakhouse industry). Once you have your dimensions, place the brands in the quadrants based on how closely they fit those descriptions. Be prepared to share your results with the class.

Concepts: Apply Marketing Metrics

When it comes to metrics, good data about the characteristics of the various consumer segments that you may wish to ultimately target is critical because target marketing is ultimately a strategic investment of resources in the segments that appear

to have the best return on investment. In this chapter, we mentioned that VALS™ is a well-known approach to psychographic segmentation.

7-19. To make the power of the psychographic technique and resulting information for decision making come alive, let's find out your own VALS™ category.

a. Go to the VALS™ website (either google it or go directly to www.strategicbusinessinsights.com and click the VALS™ tab on the homepage).
b. Click "Take the VALS™ Survey." Complete all the questions, and click SUBMIT to view your results.
c. What is your VALS™ type? Review the information on the website that describes it (found under the tabs About VALS™/VALS™ Types) along with the other VALS™ types.
d. What is your reaction to learning your own VALS™ type? Are you surprised with the result, or was it consistent with what you would have expected? Why or why not?
e. What insights does the knowledge of your VALS™ type provide relative to your own consumer behavior?

Choices: What Do You Think?

7-20. *Ethics* Some critics of marketing have suggested that market segmentation and target marketing lead to an unnecessary proliferation of product choices that wastes valuable resources. These critics suggest that if marketers didn't create so many different product choices, there would be more resources to feed the hungry and house the homeless and provide for the needs of people around the globe. Are the results of segmentation and target marketing harmful or beneficial to society as a whole? Should firms be concerned about these criticisms? Why or why not?

7-21. *Ethics* Some businesses market unwholesome products to the elderly, disabled veterans, and similar segments. Should these groups warrant special concern or protection? Should marketers be required to use different criteria to market to these groups? How involved should the government be in overseeing and protecting marketing messages to these at-risk groups?

7-22. *Critical Thinking* Companies sometimes find themselves in a situation where they need to reposition to keep up with changing times. Recently automaker Cadillac has developed new vehicle models that they felt would appeal to a younger demographic than the traditional Cadillac buyer. What suggestions would you make to Cadillac on how to reposition to reach this new audience? Do you think a brand with a long history and reputation in one category can successfully change how the public views them? Why or why not?

7-23. *Ethics* Gamification was discussed in Chapter 6. For specific segments of a market, a gamification approach might help elicit a desired behavior from consumers, and of course in many cases the desired behavior is an increase in consumption of the related product. When a product is generally associated with potential health problems if consumed in large quantities (e.g., alcohol, sugar), should a marketer be allowed to engage the consumer in gamification activities or similar "fun" approaches that encourage or induce excessive consumption of the product?

7-24. *Critical Thinking* Marketers commonly ask celebrities to endorse products, but tying a brand to a celebrity can come with risks. What if that celebrity falls out of favor with the public as the result of something they do or say that is perceived negatively? How would you determine if the signing of a celebrity to an endorsement deal is worth the risk? What would you want to know to make that determination and reduce the risk potential? Think of an example of a celebrity endorsement in recent history that has gone bad—what happened, how did it impact the brand, and did they recover?

Miniproject: Learn by Doing

This miniproject will help you to develop a better understanding of how firms make target marketing decisions. The project focuses on the market for men's athletic shoes.

a. Gather ideas about different dimensions useful for segmenting the men's athletic shoes market. You may use your own ideas, but you probably will also want to examine advertising and other marketing communications developed by different athletic shoe brands.
b. Based on the dimensions for market segmentation that you have identified, develop a questionnaire and conduct a survey of consumers. You will have to decide which questions should be asked and which consumers should be surveyed.
c. Analyze the data from your research and identify the different potential segments.
d. Develop segment profiles that describe each potential segment.
e. Generate several ideas for how the marketing strategy might be different for each segment based on the profiles.
f. Define your competitive advantage that you believe will be important to the segments you have identified.

7-25. Develop a presentation (or write a report) outlining your ideas, your research, your findings, and your marketing strategy recommendations.

Marketing in Action **Case**   Real Choices at ThirdLove

Market fragmentation is an apt target marketing term because market segments often form by breaking off (like a fragment) from a larger market. This idea is at the core of the origin story of the online lingerie company ThirdLove, which focused on attracting women who felt excluded by the products and promotional tactics of market leader Victoria's Secret. As the company's sales have skyrocketed, its marketing strategies—and its target market definition—have evolved to respond to changing market priorities.

In 2011, ThirdLove cofounder Heidi Zak, a Silicon Valley tech professional, was engaged in the shopping experience that many women find unpleasant and confusing—shopping for a bra at Victoria's Secret. While she was fine with shopping at Victoria's Secret as a younger woman, she was now so embarrassed to leave the store with the retailer's pink bag that she hid it in her backpack.

Shortly after this bad experience, she and her husband, David Spector, started ThirdLove to provide a way to get a quality, properly fitted bra without going into a store. Its target was a group of women who had moved on from Victoria's Secret, either due to their age or a different outlook. "They [are] going after a customer that Victoria's Secret wasn't," according to Lori Greeley, former CEO of Victoria's Secret and now a ThirdLove board member. "As Victoria's Secret continued to put so much of its focus on the teenage college student, you could see that there were women who were looking for somewhere to graduate to."

Given Zak's and Spector's prior work experience at Google, it's no surprise that ThirdLove's initial focus was on the use of a smartphone app to properly size its product for customers. Customers would take two photos in form-fitting clothing and

send them to ThirdLove for analysis. Computer vision technology (similar to technology that NASA's Mars Rover used) and patented algorithms allowed the company to determine the right size for the customer. Privacy concerns and problems with the app eventually led to its replacement with a 60-second "Fit Finder" questionnaire. The same patented algorithms used with the app were now applied to the questionnaire answers to provide an optimal fit. Once a size was determined, another ThirdLove innovation made sure it could properly fit the customer: half sizes. While a standard practice with shoemakers, ThirdLove was the first bra company to offer its line with these options.

Over its relatively short life, ThirdLove has fine-tuned its brand messaging and with it, the implicit definition of its target market. In its early years, lead designer Ra'el Cohen was not enthusiastic about offering larger sizes, saying "we will never be a plus-size company." More recently, the company has fully embraced body positivity. Now it offers over 80 sizes and prominently features plus-size models in its advertising. Launched in 2018, these larger sizes generated $1 million in the first five days, and they sold out in three weeks.

The company has expanded this new focus to include a general emphasis on inclusivity that has become a hallmark of ThirdLove. CEO Heidi Zak says, "We believe the future is building a brand for every woman, regardless of her shape, size, age, ethnicity, gender identity, or sexual orientation. This shouldn't be seen as groundbreaking; it should be the norm." In Zak's view, a focus on inclusivity means that the company does not have to have different marketing strategies for different generations but can welcome all ages through offering a variety of products and sizes.

ThirdLove is not the only company that offers online lingerie. Competitors include Adore Me, American Eagle's Aerie, and True&Co. One major competitor has become less of a threat to ThirdLove's growth—the retailer that effectively started it all for founders Zak and Spector, Victoria's Secret. In 2020, after years of slumping sales (in part due to competitors like ThirdLove), an agreement was made to sell the pioneer in retail lingerie to a private equity firm at a price well below some analysts' estimates of its value. While the deal eventually fell through, CEO Zak was quick to respond to the news, seeing it as an indication of Victoria Secret's incorrect focus: "This is a positive step for our industry, which was historically dominated by unrealistic ideals and images of what femininity and sexy should be."

Lingerie is a $13 billion market in the U.S. and $100 billion globally. As of fall 2019, ThirdLove was expecting sales of $125 million for the year and had a reported valuation of $750 million. But the company aspires to capture even more of the lingerie market and is also thinking about how to apply its precision fitting skills to swimsuits and athletic wear.

The company that started by using technology to ensure a great fit continues to use data to recommend products, drive repeat purchases and better understand who its customers are. As ThirdLove continues to grow, an understanding of its target market's changing needs and priorities will help ensure there is a good fit, not only with its fashion products but with the marketing strategies the company employs to meet its customers' needs and to communicate its value proposition. Cofounder David Spector is optimistic about the future of ThirdLove. He states, "We're really proud of our team and what we've accomplished to date. But we're just getting started."[48]

Questions for Discussion

7-26. ThirdLove offers a product that females from teen years through senior citizens can use, but it believes that defining its market based on "inclusivity" eliminates the need to utilize generation-specific marketing strategies. What are the benefits and risks of this approach?

7-27. Create a brief profile that describes the original customer ThirdLove targeted when the company began.

7-28. What is ThirdLove's competitive advantage? Use this information to form a basic positioning statement for the company.

Chapter **Notes**

1. "How Will the Pandemic Change Higher Education?," *The Chronicle of Higher Education* 66, no. 27 (April 2020): 12, https://link-gale-com.ezproxy.rollins.edu/apps/doc/A623696221/PROF?u=wint4 7629&sid=PROF&xid=c33d9a99 (accessed May 31, 2020).

2. Alicia Kelso, "Chick-fil-A Has the Slowest Drive-Thru in Fast Food; Here's Why Customers Keep Coming Back," *Food and Drink*, October 9, 2019, https://www.forbes.com/sites/aliciakelso/2019/10/09/chick-fil-a-has-the-slowest-drive-thru-in-fast-food-heres-why-it-doesnt-matter/#4cfdb1005ec3 (accessed May 29, 2020).

3. Deanna Ting and Greg Oates, "Every One of Marriott's 30 Hotel Brands, Explained," *Skift*, September 21, 2016, https://skift.com/2016/09/21/every-one-of-marriotts-30-hotel-brands-explained/ (accessed March 17, 2018); Brooks Barnes, "But It Doesn't Look Like a Marriott: Marriott International Aims to Draw a Younger Crowd," *The New York Times*, January 4, 2014, http://www.nytimes.com/2014/01/05/business/marriott-international-aims-to-draw-a-younger-crowd.html?ref=business (accessed April 18, 2016).

4. Chris Danforth, "Top 10 Most Valuable Sneakers," *High Snobiety*, February 1, 2018, https://www.highsnobiety.com/p/top-10-valuable-sneakers-2017-q1/ (accessed May 27, 2020).

5. Anne Gammon and Kristen Harmeling, "Children Have Refined Pester Power and Make Savvy Shoppers," June 11, 2015, https://today.yougov.com/news/2015/06/11/children-make-savvy-shoppers-have-refined-pester-p/ (accessed April 1, 2016).

6. Drew Harwell, "Netflix Is Coming for Your Kids," *Washington Post*, March 28, 2016, https://www.washingtonpost.com/news/the-switch/wp/2016/03/28/netflix-is-coming-for-your-kids/ (accessed April 1, 2016).

7. Andrew Mettle, "4 Things You Need to Know About Gen Z's Shopping Habits," *Inc.*, November 27, 2017, https://www.inc.com/andrew-medal/how-to-give-gen-z-ers-shopping-experience-they-want.html (accessed March 15, 2018).

8. Adapted from Michael R. Solomon, *Consumer Behavior; Buying, Having, and Being*, 12th ed. (Hoboken, NJ: Pearson Education, 2016); John Lynch, "These Are the 19 Most Popular YouTube Stars in the World—And Some Are Making Millions," *Business Insider*, February 2, 2018, http://www.businessinsider.com/most-popular-youtubers-with-most-subscribers-2018-2 (accessed April 9, 2018).

9. Jeff Fromm, "How Much Financial Influence Does Gen Z Have?," *Forbes*, January 10, 2018, https://www.forbes.com/sites/jefffromm/2018/01/10/what-you-need-to-know-about-the-financial-impact-of-gen-z-influence/#5d956dc056fc (accessed March 23, 2018).

10. Amy Barrett, "To Reach the Unreachable Teen," *BusinessWeek*, September 18, 2000, 78–80.

11. "Most Popular Social Networks of Teenagers in the United States from Fall 2012 to Fall 2019," *Statista*, https://www.statista.com/statistics/250172/social-network-usage-of-us-teens-and-young-adults/ (accessed May 30, 2020).

12. Zofia Antonow, "41 Revealing Statistics about Millennials Every Marketer Should Know," *Ascend*, June 6, 2017, www.agencyascend.com/blog/41-revealing-statistics-about-millennials-every-marketer-should-know (accessed May 19, 2018).

13. Heike Young, "Millennials vs. Gen Z: How Are They Different," *Salesforce Blog*, April 8, 2019, https://www.salesforce.com/blog/2017/10/how-millennials-and-gen-z-are-different.html#:~:text=Gen%20Z%20is%20pragmatic%3B%20millennials, and%20adults%20in%20their%20lives.&text=Meanwhile%2C%20those%20in%20Gen%20Z,grew%20up%20during%20the%20recession (accessed June 11, 2020).

14. Eileen Patten and Richard Fry, "How Millennials Today Compare with Their Grandparents 50 Years Ago," March 19, 2015, https://www.pewresearch.org/fact-tank/2015/03/19/how-millennials-compare-with-their-grandparents/#!1 (accessed April 1, 2016).

15. Douglas Coupland, *Generation X: Tales for an Accelerated Culture* (New York: St. Martin's Press, 1991).

16. Marshall Lager, "The Slackers' X-cellent Adventure," *CRM*, November 1, 2008, https://www.destinationcrm.com/Articles/Editorial/Magazine-Features/The-Slackerse28099-X-cellent-Adventure-51406.aspx (accessed April 10, 2016).

17. John H. Fleming, "Baby Boomers Are Opening Their Wallets," January 30, 2015, https://www.gallup.com/businessjournal/181367/baby-boomers-opening-wallets.aspx (accessed April 1, 2016).

18. "The Nation's Older Population Is Still Growing," U.S. Census Bureau, June 22, 2017, https://www.census.gov/newsroom/press-releases/2017/cb17-100.html#table1 (accessed March 17, 2018).

19. Tara Bannow, "CVS to Aggressively Expand Health Care Services in Stores," *Modern Healthcare*, June 4, 2019, https://www.modern-healthcare.com/patient-care/cvs-aggressively-expand-health-care-services-stores (accessed May 25, 2020).

20. Katie Smith, "Gender-Bending: Say Goodbye to Old Stereotypes," *Inside Retail Australia*, February 5, 2020, https://insideretail.com.au/news/gender-bending-say-goodbye-to-old-stereotypes-202002 (accessed June 10, 2020).

21. Aimee Ortiz, "Peloton Ad Is Criticized as Sexist and Dystopian," *The New York Times*, December 3, 2019, https://www.nytimes.com/2019/12/03/business/peloton-bike-ad-stock.html (accessed May 30, 2020).

22. Daniel Bachman and Akrur Barua, "Single-Person Households: Another Look at the Changing American Family," November 12, 2015, https://www2.deloitte.com/us/en/insights/economy/behind-the-numbers/single-person-households-and-changing-american-family.html (accessed April 1, 2016).

23. NPD Group, "Growing Single-Person Households Have Increasing Influence on Snacking Behavior," August 11, 2015, https://www.npd.com/wps/portal/npd/us/news/press-releases/2015/growing-single-person-households-have-increasing-influence-on-snacking-behavior/ (accessed April 1, 2015); John Stanton, "A Closer Look at the Single Household," July 18, 2013, https://www.foodprocessing.com/articles/2013/market-view-single-household/ (accessed April 10, 2016).

24. "Glass Baby Bottles in Demand," June 1, 2008, www.brandpackaging.com/CDA/Articles/Trends_Next_Now/BNP_GUID_9-5-2006_A_1000000000000352222 (accessed April 10, 2016).

25. "Six Amazing Vacations for Single Women Over 60," *Sixty and Me*, https://sixtyandme.com/senior-travel-6-amazing-vacations-for-single-women-over-60/ (accessed May 26, 2020).

26. Lance Lambert, "Over 40 million Americans Have Filed for Unemployment during the Pandemic—Real Jobless Rate over 23.9%," *Fortune*, May 28, 2020, https://fortune.com/2020/05/28/us-unemployment-rate-numbers-claims-this-week-total-job-losses-may-28-2020-benefits-claims-job-losses/ (accessed May 30, 2020).

27. Christopher Rauwald and Mark Clothier, "Luxury Car Makers Bet on Lower-Priced Rides," *Bloomberg*, January 16, 2014, https://www.bloomberg.com/news/articles/2014-01-16/luxury-car-makers-bet-on-lower-priced-rides (accessed April 10, 2016); Tom Randall, "How Tesla's Model 3 Could Conquer Low-End Luxury," *Bloomberg*, March 22, 2016, https://www.bloomberg.com/news/features/2016-03-22/how-tesla-model-3-can-complete-its-take-over-of-the-u-s-luxury-market (accessed April 18, 2016); Ben Thompson, "Can Elon Musk Meet Demand for the Tesla Model 3?" *The Christian Science Monitor*, April 4, 2016, https://www.csmonitor.com/Business/2016/0404/Can-Elon-Musk-meet-demand-for-the-Tesla-Model-3-video (accessed April 18, 2016).

28. U.S. Census Bureau, "Quick Facts," July 2017, https://www.census.gov/quickfacts/fact/table/US/PST045216 (accessed March 26, 2018).

29. Scott Mendelson, "Box Office: 'Black Panther' Pacing to Top 'Last Jedi' and 'Avengers,'" *Forbes*, March 15, 2018, www.forbes.com/sites/scottmendelson/2018/03/15/box-office-black-panther-pacing-to-top-star-wars-the-last-jedi-and-avengers/#628f7a59e79f (accessed March 28, 2018).

30. Gustavo López, Neil G. Ruiz, and Eileen Patten, "Key Facts about Asian Americans, a Diverse and Growing Population," *Pew Research Center*, September 8, 2017, https://www.pewresearch.org/fact-tank/2017/09/08/key-facts-about-asian-americans/ (accessed March 19, 2018).

31. Vic Marcus, "The Spending Power of Asian Americans," *NWI Global*, September 18, 2017, https://www.nwiglobal.com/blog/the-buying-power-of-asian-americans/ (accessed March 20, 2018).

32. Yuriy Boykiv, "How BuzzFeed Is Winning with Asian-Americans," *AdAge*, August 5, 2015, https://adage.com/article/digitalnext/buzzfeed-winning-asian-americans/299823/ (accessed April 1, 2015).

33. Jens Manuel Krogstad, "U.S. Hispanic Population Growth Has Leveled Off," *Pew Research Center*, August 3, 2017, https://www.pewresearch.org/fact-tank/2017/08/03/u-s-hispanic-population-growth-has-leveled-off/ (accessed March 21, 2018); U.S. Census Bureau, "United States Census 2000," https://www.census.gov/main/www/cen2000.html (accessed March 22, 2006); "Latinas Are a Driving Force behind Hispanic Purchasing Power in the U.S.," *Nielsen*, August 1, 2013, https://www.nielsen.com/us/en/insights/article/2013/latinas-are-a-driving-force-behind-hispanic-purchasing-power-in-/ (accessed May 28, 2014); Elinor Kinnier, "Five Trends Emerging among U.S. Hispanics: The New General Market," April 2008, www.amg-inc.com/AMG/news/4-08-5trends-hispanicmkt.html (accessed February 25, 2010).

34. Mark Melzer, "UGA: Hispanic Buying Power in U.S. Soars to $1.4 Trillion," *Atlanta Business Chronicle*, March 2, 2017, www.bizjournals.com/atlanta/news/2017/03/02/uga-hispanicbuying-power-in-u-s-soars-to-1-4.html (accessed March 26, 2018).

35. Nielsen, "Measuring the Bicultural Hispanic Consumer beyond Just Language and Demographic Data," September 3, 2015, https://www.nielsen.com/us/en/news-center/2015/measuring-the-bicultural-hispanic-consumer-beyond-just-language-and-demographic-data/ (accessed April 2, 2016).

36. Kyle Arnold, "Demand Grows in Orlando for Puerto Rican Food, Beer," *Orlando Sentinel Blog*, http://eleven11communications.com/demand-grows-in-orlando-for-puerto-rican-food-beer/ (accessed June 9, 2020); Stefen Rayer, "Estimating the Migration of Puerto Ricans to Florida Using Flight Passenger Data," *Bureau of Economic and Business Research*, University of Florida, October 3, 2018, https://www.bebr.ufl.edu/sites/default/files/Research%20Reports/puerto_rican_migration.pdf (accessed May 29, 2020).

37. Andrew Tate, "Are Geotargeting Facebook Ads Right for Your Business?", *AdEspresso*, October 11, 2017, https://adespresso.com/blog/geo-targeting-facebook-ads/ (accessed April 7, 2018).

38. "Dominos Uses Text Messages for Hyperlocal Advertising," *4 Great Examples of Geotargeting*, December 12, 2018, https://www.nativ3.io/blog/4-great-examples-of-geotargeting/ (accessed May 25, 2020).

39. Lewis Alpert and Ronald Gatty, "Product Positioning by Behavioral Life Styles," *Journal of Marketing* 33 (April 1969): 65–69; Emanuel H. Demby, "Psychographics Revisited: The Birth of a Technique," *Marketing News*, January 2, 1989, 21; William D. Wells, "Backward Segmentation," in *Insights into Consumer Behavior*, ed. Johan Arndt (Boston: Allyn & Bacon, 1968), 85–100.

40. Patrick Spenner and Karen Freeman, "To Keep Your Customers, Keep It Simple," *Harvard Business Review*, May 2012, https://hbr.org/2012/05/to-keep-your-customers-keep-it-simple (accessed April 7, 2018); Katherine Parsons and Darren (Daz) McCall, "A New Approach to Brand Loyalty—How to Stand Out in the Experience Age," *Retail Touch Points*, March 9, 2018, https://retailtouchpoints.com/features/executive-viewpoints/a-new-approach-to-brand-loyalty-how-to-stand-out-in-the-experience-age (accessed March 20, 2018).

41. "Choose Where and When Ads Appear," https://support.google.com/adwords/topic/3119119?hl=en&ref_topic=3119071 (accessed April 10, 2016).

42. Polly Mosendz, "Why Hamburger Helper's Rap-Mixtape Marketing Stunt Worked," *Bloomberg*, April 1, 2016, http://www.bloomberg.com/news/articles/2016-04-01/why-hamburger-helper-s-rap-mixtape-marketing-stunt-worked (accessed April 2, 2016).

43. Rikke Dam and Teo Siang, "Personas – A Simple Introduction," *Interaction Design Foundation*, March 29, 2019, https://www.interaction-design.org/literature/article/personas-why-and-how-you-should-use-them (accessed May 29, 2020).

44. GreatCall, https://www.greatcall.com/phones-devices (accessed April 2, 2016); Dyna, https://dynallc.com/jitterbug-honored-as-best-small-company-by-the-american-society-on-aging-2008/ (accessed April 2, 2016).

45. Chip Bayers, "The Promise of One to One (a Love Story)," *Wired*, May 1998, 130.

46. Arundhati Parmar, "Where Are They Now? Revived, Repositioned Products Gain New Life," *Marketing News*, April 14, 2003, 1(3).

47. https://retrobrands.net (accessed April 5, 2018).

48. Based on: Natalie Robehmed, "Next Billion – Dollar Startup: Entrepreneurs Create $750M Bra Business by Exposing Victoria's Weakness," *Forbes*, October 18, 2018, https://www.forbes.com/sites/natalierobehmed/2018/10/18/next-billion-dollar-startup-entrepreneurs-create-750m-bra-business-by-exposing-victorias-weakness/#48b16e724d03; Tom Ryan, "To Get Online Bra-Fitting Right, ThirdLove Is Going Physical," *Forbes*, August 1, 2019, https://www.forbes.com/sites/retailwire/2019/08/01/to-get-online-bra-fitting-right-thirdlove-is-going-physical/#2553ec092661; Clare O'Connor, "Want A Bra That Fits Perfectly? This Billionaire-Backed App Helps With Just Your iPhone," *Forbes*, February 10, 2014, https://www.forbes.com/sites/clareoconnor/2014/02/10/want-a-bra-that-fits-perfectly-this-billionaire-backed-app-helps-with-just-your-iphone/#28b7aad36b0b; Carey Dunne, "Ex-Googler Invents A Better Way to By Bras," *Fast Company*, March 28, 2014, https://www.fastcompany.com/3028267/ex-googler-invents-a-better-way-to-buy-bras?partner=newsletter; WBR Insights, "ThirdLove Boosts Retention and Referrals with New VIP Tiers Loyalty Program," *eTail*, https://etailwest.wbresearch.com/thirdlove-vip-tiers-loyalty-program-strategy-retention-referrals-boost-ty-u (accessed August 24, 2020); Richard Collings, "ThirdLove to Open Stores in Select Markets and Add Creative Agencies," *Adweek*, February 20, 2020, https://www.adweek.com/retail/thirdlove-to-open-stores-in-select-markets-and-add-creative-agencies/; Admin, "A Pivot From Tech to Empowerment at Bra Startup ThirdLove," *Public News Update*, November 19, 2019, https://publicnewsupdate.com/a-pivot-from-tech-to-empowerment-at-bra-startup-thirdlove/; Kellie Ell, "Victoria's Secret Hires First Plus-size Model, But Some Say It's Too Late," *Wbresearch.Com*, October 9, 2019, https://wwd.com/fashion-news/intimates/plus-size-models-lingerie-industry-1203339476/; Pamela Bump, "7 Brands That Got Inclusive Marketing Right," *Hubspot.Com*, https://blog.hubspot.com/marketing/inclusive-marketing-campaigns (accessed August 24, 2020); Heidi Zak, "How to Market the Same Products to Different Generations, From Baby Boomers to Millennials," *Inc.*, July 2, 2019, https://www.inc.com/heidi-zak/how-to-market-same-products-to-different-generations-from-baby-boomers-to-millennials.html; Jim Weiker, "L Brands to Sell Victoria's Secret to Private Equity Firm," *The Daily Item*, February 23, 2020, https://www.dailyitem.com/business/l-brands-to-sell-victorias-secret-to-private-equity-firm/article_63d6cf6f-f885-54bd-8ba7-1690c80ca689.html; "Unfiltered," *Unfiltered.tv*, https://unfiltered.tv/interview/1a0d277efbc44ffab26cecd4f5b7f4e5 (accessed August 24, 2020); Katie Roof, "ThirdLove Takes on Victoria's Secret, But Faces Challenges," *The Wall Street Journal*, January 7, 2020, https://www.wsj.com/articles/thirdlove-takes-on-victorias-secret-but-faces-challenges-11579293194; Ingrid Lunden, "ThirdLove, the Direct-To-Consumer Lingerie Startup, Gets a $55M Boost," *TechCrunch*, February 26, 2019, https://techcrunch.com/2019/02/26/thirdlove-the-direct-to-consumer-lingerie-startup-gets-a-55m-boost/; L. Rittenhouse, "Five Lessons on Navigating the Direct-To-Consumer Landscape," *AdAge*, September 12, 2019, https://adage.com/article/digital/five-lessons-navigating-direct-consumer-landscape/2196476; Gabriela Barkho, "'The Next Few Years Will Be a Telling Time For DTC': ThirdLove's Heidi Zak Says It's Time For Thoughtful Investing," *ModernRetail*, February 27, 2020, https://www.modernretail.co/retailers/the-next-few-years-will-be-a-telling-time-for-dtc-thirdloves-heidi-zak-says-its-time-for-thoughtful-investing/; Shoshy Ciment, "Cofounder Of Victoria's Secret Rival ThirdLove Says His Goal Was to Put the Lingerie Giant Our of Business," *Business Insider*, February 27, 2020, https://www.businessinsider.com/thirdlove-cofounder-wanted-to-put-victorias-secret-out-of-business-2020-2.

8 Product I: Innovation and New Product Development

Sheryl Adkins-Green

Meet Sheryl Adkins-Green

▼ A Decision Maker at Mary Kay

Sheryl Adkins-Green, Mary Kay's Chief Marketing Officer, supports the success of millions of Independent Beauty Consultants by leading the global brand marketing strategy, new product development, advertising, digital marketing, social media, and customer insights that keep the Mary Kay brand and business opportunity relevant and competitive. Staying true to its direct-selling model, Mary Kay is currently enriching the lives of women in nearly 40 countries.

Sheryl brings a wealth of global sales and marketing knowledge to the Chief Marketing Officer role. She thrives on pursuing opportunities in key areas such as new business development, digital innovation, and strategic alliances.

Sheryl received a BS in retailing, *cum laude*, from the University of Wisconsin, and she holds an MBA from Harvard Business School. She is a @Forbes Top 50 CMO influencer who was named one of the Most Powerful Women in Corporate America by *Black Enterprise* magazine in 2019. Sheryl was named one of the 2018 Dallas Power 50 Awardees by the Texas Diversity Council, and in 2017, she was named one of the Most Influential Women in Direct Selling. In 2016, Sheryl was included in the "Top Women in Marketing Technology" list by Brand Innovators. In 2012, she was honored to be the first recipient of the Global Marketer Award from the Academy of Marketing Sciences.

Closely aligning with Mary Kay's focus on improving women's economic independence, Sheryl is actively involved in the community through the Mary Kay Foundation's mission of finding cures for cancers affecting women and stopping the incidence of violence against women. In addition to serving on the Texas Christian University Board of Trustees, she serves on the board of the Dallas Museum of Art and AT&T Performing Arts Center. She currently resides in Dallas with her husband and their two sons.

Sheryl's Info

First job out of business school:
Assistant Product Manager, Gaines Dog Food, Kraft Foods

Business book I'm reading now:
Leadershift: The 11 Essential Changes Every Leader Must Embrace by John C. Maxwell

My hero:
My father

My motto to live by:
"Picture an invisible sign around each person's neck that says, 'Make me feel important.'" — Mary Kay Ash

What drives me:
Connecting people and ideas to create value

My management style:
Situational—it depends on the business need and the skill sets of the team members involved. Typically, my preference is to delegate and empower my team. My priority as a leader is to develop more leaders. When an urgent situation demands decisiveness, or when a challenge is significantly greater than my team can handle successfully, I will get more involved, and when necessary, take charge.

My pet peeve:
People who interrupt others, especially when they start giving an answer before they've heard the entire question!

Here's my problem...

Mary Kay Ash, a true business trailblazer, founded her beauty company more than 55 years ago with three goals: Develop rewarding opportunities for women, offer irresistible products, and make the world a better place. That dream has blossomed into a multibillion-dollar company with millions of independent sales force members in nearly 40 countries. Mary Kay is dedicated to investing in the science behind beauty and manufacturing cutting-edge skin care, color cosmetics, nutritional supplements, and fragrances.

Mary Kay entered the China market in 1995, and by 2018, Mary Kay China had grown to become one of the largest Mary Kay markets. Historically, the China beauty market was driven primarily by the skin care category, and Mary Kay's patented age-fighting skin care products enjoyed tremendous success. For many years, the market for color cosmetics in China was underdeveloped compared to Europe, Latin America, and North America. Women in China had a preference for a more subtle, "natural" look. Although Mary Kay China did offer color makeup as part of the product portfolio, sales from the color category represented less than 10 percent of the total Mary Kay China wholesale revenue, in contrast to many other Mary Kay markets where the color category represented 40 percent or more of the total Mary Kay wholesale revenue.

In more recent years, as the popularity of Korean beauty, also known as *K-beauty*, products grew rapidly, so did interest in and demand for color makeup. Fueled by celebrities and key opinion leaders (KOLs) in China, the color makeup category began growing at a double-digit rate. Competition in the color category also grew dramatically as global, Korean, and Chinese brands accelerated new product activity to meet rapidly growing demand.

In the Chinese language the word *crisis* is composed of two characters, one representing danger and the other, opportunity. The rapid growth of the color category certainly represented a revenue opportunity for Mary Kay China. There was "threat," however, that if Mary Kay did not move quickly, the company would miss the opportunity to help its independent sales force attract new customers, particularly Gen Z consumers who were looking for new and exciting makeup products. Beauty consumers in China were becoming younger, and the purchasing power of the 18–24 group was rising.

In 2018, Sheryl received an urgent request to provide Mary Kay China with a fresh color product portfolio as quickly as possible to capture the sales opportunity and, more importantly, to help the independent sales force attract new customers.

trend experts, the Mary Kay color product portfolio was updated every quarter to keep pace with the latest trends.

This option was attractive, because Mary Kay could quickly get these existing products that it already sold successfully around the world into the Chinese market. By utilizing the global Mary Kay color line to increase market share in the color category, Mary Kay China would be able to tap into and increase awareness of the Mary Kay brand in China using global marketing assets, tutorials, etc. On the other hand, while the Mary Kay brand was well-known and respected, it could be viewed by the younger target audience as "mature" rather than "young and trendy." And while the Mary Kay color portfolio was "on-trend," it did not specifically capture the latest makeup trends being promoted by China's KOLs and the influential K-pop stars.

2 Option

Create a new line of color cosmetics specifically developed for the China market. This would allow the company to customize a range of products specifically for the target audience. By addressing the preferences of the China beauty consumer, Mary Kay could compete more effectively with the growing number of local cosmetic brands that were gaining in popularity. But this course would require significant time and product development resources. Since these products would be brand new, it would also be difficult to forecast product demand, and introducing them would require more marketing investment compared to being able to leverage the already well-known Mary Kay brand.

3 Option

Adapt a successful regional color line, Mary Kay @Play, for the China market. Mary Kay @Play is a trendy line of color products sold primarily in Mary Kay's Latin America markets. This was offered in addition to the "classic" Mary Kay color product line and appealed to a younger demographic. This option could quickly leverage existing Mary Kay @Play color products as well as those already in development. And the Mary Kay @Play products would help to build awareness of the Mary Kay brand while conveying a more modern, youthful image. However, although existing products could be quickly adapted, these products were developed to complement the bold, colorful fashion trends of Latin American countries such as Brazil and Colombia.

Now, put yourself in Sheryl's shoes. Which option would you choose, and why?

You Choose

Which **Option** would you choose, and **why**?
☐ Option 1   ☐ Option 2   ☐ Option 3

Sheryl considered her **options** 1·2·3

1 Option

Leverage the broad range of color makeup products sold globally under the Mary Kay Brand. At the time of the request, Mary Kay offered a full range of makeup products around the world, everything from brushes to blushes to more than 100 shades of lip color. Under the guidance of global celebrity makeup artists and fashion

---

8.1 Build a Better Mousetrap— and Add Value

OBJECTIVE

Explain how value is derived through different product layers.

"Build a better mousetrap, and the world will beat a path to your door." Although we've all heard that adage, the truth is that just because a product is better, there is no guarantee it will succeed. For decades, the Woodstream Corp. built Victor-brand wooden mousetraps. Then, the company decided to build a better one. Woodstream's product-development people researched the eating, crawling, and nesting habits of mice (hey, it's a living). They built prototypes of different mousetraps to come up with the best possible design and tested them in homes. Then, the company unveiled the sleek-looking "Little Champ," a black plastic miniature inverted bathtub with a hole. When the mouse went in and ate the bait, a spring snapped upward—and the mouse was history.

Sounds like a great new product (unless you're a mouse), but the Little Champ failed. Woodstream studied mouse habits, *not* consumer preferences. The company later discovered that husbands set the trap at night, but in the morning, it was the wives who disposed of the "present" they found waiting for them. Unfortunately, many of them thought the Little Champ looked too expensive to throw away, so they felt they should empty the trap for reuse. This was a task most women weren't willing to do; they wanted a trap they could happily toss into the garbage.[1]

Woodstream's failure in the "rat race" underscores the importance of creating products that provide the benefits people want rather than just new gizmos that sound like a good idea. It also tells us that any number of products, from low-tech cheese to high-tech traps, potentially deliver these benefits. Despite Victor's claim to be the "World's Leader in Rodent Control Solutions," in this case, cheese and a shoebox could snuff out a mouse as well as a high-tech trap.

We need to take a close look at how products successfully trap consumers' dollars when they provide value. In Chapter 1, we saw that the *value proposition* is the consumer's perception of the benefits he or she will receive if he or she buys a good or service. So the marketer's task is twofold: first, to create a better value than what's out there already and, second, to convince customers that this is true.

This chapter and the next one focus on the decisions marketers need to make in order to create and maintain successful products. As we defined it in Chapter 1, a *product* is a tangible good, service, idea, or some combination of these that satisfies consumer or business customer needs through the exchange process; it is a value-adding bundle of **attributes**, including features, functions, benefits, and uses as well as its brand and packaging. Because of the broad range of possibilities for bundles of attributes, instead of saying *product*, it has become common for marketers to substitute the more generic term **offering** to denote the broadest possible range of sources of value for the product. But to keep things simpler, in this chapter, we will use the more basic term *product*.

Products can be physical goods, services, ideas, people, or places. A **good** is a *tangible* product, something that we can see, touch, smell, hear, taste, or possess. It may take the form of a pack of yummy cookies, a shiny new iPad, a house, a part used in production of that Tesla Model 3 you might like to buy, or a chic but pricey Christian Louboutin bag for women or men. (Ever price one of these babies—it can set you back a couple thousand dollars!) In contrast, *intangible* products—services, ideas, people, and places—are products that we can't always see, touch, taste, smell, or possess. We'll talk more about intangible products in Chapter 12.

Welcome to Part 3 of this book, Develop the Value Proposition for the Customer. The key word here is *develop*, and a large part of the marketer's role in developing the value proposition is to create and market products innovatively. In this chapter, we'll first examine what a product is and see how marketers classify consumer and business-to-business (B2B) products. Then, we'll go on to look at new products, how marketers develop new products, and how markets accept them (or not).

More broadly speaking, Parts 3 and 4 of the book take you systematically through all of the elements of the marketing mix's four Ps: product and price in Part 3 and distribution ("place") and promotion in Part 4. As you learned in Chapter 7, developing and executing a great marketing mix is the heart and soul of positioning strategy. And the place to start is with your product—as an old saying in marketing goes, "If the product ain't right, the rest don't matter."

attributes
Include features, functions, and uses of a product. Marketers view products as a bundle of attributes that includes the packaging, brand name, benefits, and supporting features in addition to a physical good.

offering
A generic term often used by marketers to denote the broad range of possibilities of product attributes and sources of product value.

good
A tangible product that we can see, touch, smell, hear, or taste.

Layers of the Product Concept

No doubt you've heard someone say, "It's the thought, not the gift that counts." Sometimes that's just an excuse for a lame present, but more broadly it means that the gift is a sign or symbol that the gift giver has remembered you. When we evaluate a gift, we may consider the following: Was it presented with a flourish? Was it wrapped in special paper? Was it obviously a "regift"—something the gift giver had received as a gift but wanted to pass on to you (like last year's fruitcake or that funky vase that clashes with everything else in the house)? These dimensions are a part of the total gift you receive in addition to the actual goodie in the box.

Like a gift, a product is everything that a customer receives in an exchange. As Figure 8.1 shows, we distinguish among three distinct layers of the product—the core product, the actual product, and the augmented product. When they develop product strategies, marketers need to consider how to satisfy customers' wants and needs at each of these three layers—that is, how they can create value. Let's consider each layer in turn.

The Core Product

The **core product** consists of all the benefits the product will provide for consumers or business customers. As we noted in Chapter 1, a *benefit* is an outcome that the customer receives from owning or using a product. Wise old marketers (and some wise young marketers, too) will tell you, "A marketer may make and sell a half-inch drill bit, but a customer buys a half-inch hole." This tried-and-true saying reminds us that people buy the core product—in this case, the ability to make a hole. If a new product, such as a laser, comes along that provides that outcome in a better way or more cheaply, the drill-bit maker has a problem. The moral of this story? *Marketing is mostly about supplying benefits*, not just creating features and

core product
All the benefits the product will provide for consumers or business customers.

Figure 8.1 Snapshot | Layers of the Product

A product is everything a customer receives—the basic benefits, the physical product and its packaging, and the "extras" that come with the product.

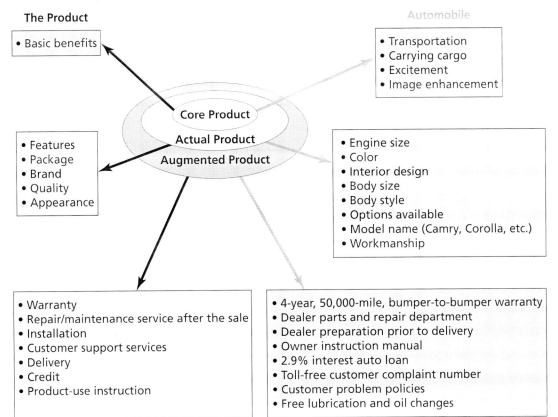

functionality. And benefits are the foundation of any value proposition, which we defined in Chapter 1 as a marketplace offering that fairly and accurately sums up the value the buyer will receive if the good or service is purchased.

Many products actually provide multiple benefits. For example, the primary benefit of a car is transportation—all cars (in good repair) offer the ability to travel from point A to point B. But products also provide customized benefits—benefits customers receive because manufacturers add "bells and whistles" to win them over. Some drivers simply want that Toyota Corolla for basic, dependable, and economical transportation; others appreciate that Prius Prime hybrid with its plug-in capabilities for the ultimate environmentally friendly experience, and still others crave a top-of-the-line Toyota Land Cruiser for the ultimate in off-road luxury and performance. The point is that all three of these options get you from point A to point B in roughly the same time, but different consumers seek wildly different benefits from a vehicle purchase and some are willing to pay a lot more (about $60K more in the case of the Land Cruiser versus the Corolla) for the product that can best satisfy their needs and wants. Therein lies the power of product marketing—and why a basic mousetrap is not the universal answer!

The Actual Product

actual product
The physical good or the delivered service that supplies the desired benefit.

augmented product
The actual product plus other supporting features, such as a warranty, credit, delivery, installation, and repair service after the sale.

The second layer—the **actual product**—is the physical good or the delivered service that supplies the desired benefit. For example, when you buy a washing machine, the core product is the ability to get clothes clean, but the actual product is a large, square metal apparatus. When you get a medical exam, the core service is maintaining your health, but the actual one is a lot of annoying poking and prodding. The actual product also includes the unique features of the product, such as its appearance or styling, the package, and the brand name. Samsung makes a wide range of flat-screen TVs in dozens of sizes from low-end, low-price to other models that might cause you to mortgage your house. But in the end, all offer the same core benefit of enabling you to maximize your viewing experience the next time you sit down for some binge streaming from Netflix.

The Augmented Product

Finally, marketers offer customers an **augmented product**—the actual product plus other supporting features, such as a warranty, credit, delivery, installation, and repair service after the sale. Marketers know that adding these supporting features to a product is an effective way for a company to stand out from the crowd.

Way back in 2003, Apple forever changed the music industry when it created its iTunes Store, which augmented the basic product of music by allowing consumers to download favorites directly to their digital music and video libraries and conveniently saving them the trouble of correctly inserting, labeling, and sorting the new music. This innovation no doubt dealt a blow to firms that manufactured stands designed to hold hundreds of CDs. Apple's augmented product (convenience, extensive selection, and ease of use) continues to pay off handsomely for the company in sales and profits, and customers adore the fact that you can do it all on your device of choice. As streaming services for music like Spotify rose in popularity, Apple adapted to the change in consumer preferences by creating Apple Music. Apple Music offers users the ability to access an extensive collection of songs (to the tune of 60 million compared to a mere 50 million at Spotify!) for a monthly fee as opposed to purchasing songs or albums individually.[2] And of course, with the rise of smart TVs now, Apple has fiercely expanded into that growing space with the Apple TV App (tagline: All your TV, all in one app).[3]

This diet dessert offers a value proposition of good taste without the extra calories.

8.2 How Marketers Classify Products

OBJECTIVE

Describe how
marketers classify
products.

So far, we've learned that a product may be a tangible good or an intangible service or idea and that there are different layers to the product through which a consumer can derive value. Now we'll build on these ideas as we look at how products differ from one another. Marketers classify products into categories because they represent differences in how consumers and business customers feel about products and how they purchase different products. Such an understanding helps marketers develop new products and a marketing mix that satisfies customer needs.

Let's first consider differences in consumer products based on how long the product will last and on how the consumer shops for the product. Then, we will discuss the general types of B2B products.

How Long Do Products Last?

Marketers classify consumer goods as durable or nondurable depending on how long the product lasts. You expect a refrigerator to last many years, but a gallon of milk will last only a week or so until it turns into a science project. **Durable goods** are consumer products that provide benefits over a period of months, years, or even decades, such as cars, furniture, and appliances. In contrast, we consume **nondurable goods**, such as *People* magazine and fresh sushi, in the short term.

We are more likely to purchase durable goods under conditions of *high involvement* (as we saw in Chapter 6), whereas nondurable goods are more likely to be *low-involvement* decisions. When consumers buy a new car or a house, most will spend a lot of time and energy on the decision process. When marketers offer high-involvement products, they need to understand consumers' desires for different product benefits and the importance of warranties, service, and customer support. So they must be sure that consumers can find the information they need. One way is to provide a frequently asked questions (FAQ) section on a company website. Another is to host a Facebook page or Twitter feed, start a YouTube channel, build a message board, or create a blog to build a community around the product. When a company itself sponsors such forums, the firm can keep track of what people say about its products and provide a place for users to share information with each other as well as ask questions of the company related to specific products. For high-tech products, this is especially valuable to support the consumer's experience and ensure they are able to gain maximum value from what they buy. Our friends at Apple maintain a popular online forum called Apple Support Communities, where loyalists can find answers, ask questions, and connect with the whole community of Apple users from around the world.[4]

In contrast to the higher-involvement mode for durable goods, consumers usually don't "sweat the details" so much when they choose among nondurable goods. There is little if any search for information or deliberation. Sometimes this means that consumers buy whatever brand is available and is reasonably priced. In other instances, they base their decisions largely on past experience. Because a certain brand has performed satisfactorily before, customers often see no reason to consider other brands, and they choose the same one out of habit.

How Do Consumers Buy Products?

Marketers also classify products based on where and how consumers buy the product. Figure 8.2 portrays product classifications in the consumer and business marketplaces. We'll consider the consumer market first in which we think of both goods and services as

durable goods
Consumer products that provide benefits over a long period of time, such as cars, furniture, and appliances.

nondurable goods
Consumer products that provide benefits for a short time because they are consumed, such as food, or are no longer useful, such as newspapers.

Figure 8.2 *Snapshot* | Classification of Products

Products are classified differently depending on whether they are in the consumer or business market.

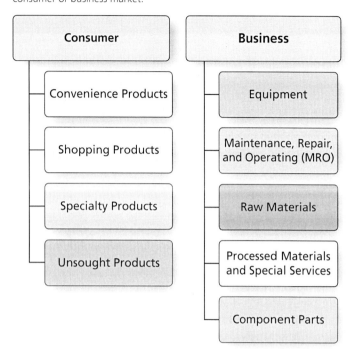

convenience product

A consumer good or service that is usually low priced, widely available, and purchased frequently with a minimum of comparison and effort.

staple products

Basic or necessary items that are available almost everywhere.

consumer packaged good (CPG), or **fast-moving consumer good (FMCG)**

A low-cost good that is consumed quickly and replaced frequently.

impulse products

A product people often buy on the spur of the moment.

convenience products, shopping products, specialty products, or unsought products. Recall that in Chapter 6 we talked about how consumer decisions differ in terms of effort consumers put into habitual decision making versus limited problem solving versus extended problem solving—a useful idea on which to base our understanding of why it's important to classify products.

A **convenience product** typically is a nondurable good or service that consumers purchase frequently with a minimum of comparison and effort. As the name implies, consumers expect these products to be handy, and they will buy whatever brands are easy to obtain. In general, convenience products are low priced and widely available. You can buy a gallon of milk or a loaf of bread at most any grocery store, drugstore, or convenience store. Consumers generally already know all they need or want to know about a convenience product, devote little effort to purchases, and willingly accept alternative brands if their preferred brand is not available in a convenient location.

What's the most important thing for marketers of convenience products? You guessed it—make sure the product is easily obtainable in all the places where consumers are likely to look for it. It's a good guess that shoppers don't put a lot of thought into buying convenience products, so a company that sells products like white bread might focus its strategy on promoting awareness of a brand name (ever try Bunny Bread? It's white bread at its finest!) as opposed to providing a detailed "spec sheet" we might expect to find for a smartphone or other durable product.

There are several types of convenience products:

- **Staple products**, such as milk, bread, and gasoline, are basic or necessary items that are available almost everywhere. Most consumers don't perceive big differences among brands. A particular category of staple products is called *consumer packaged goods*. A **consumer packaged good (CPG)**, or **fast-moving consumer good (FMCG)**, is a low-cost good that we consume quickly and replace frequently.

  Like staple products in general, CPGs (or FMCGs) are also frequently purchased but are less basic, with more variations than general staples. Importantly, they are also more brand-centric, and consumers tend to perceive more differences in product quality, features, and benefits, so the brands are heavily advertised. And in terms of distribution, giant retailers use CPGs and FMCGs to bring shoppers into the store, thus building foot traffic and increasing the chances that other types of products will also end up in shopping baskets (see the discussion on impulse and shopping products that follows). As the early days of the COVID-19 crisis began to settle in on the U.S., shopping carts certainly filled up with bleach, hand sanitizer, and other obligatory coronavirus prep items. But along with those necessities, purchases often included multiple large-sized boxes of Hostess Twinkies and Ding Dongs. This business bump of these venerable FMCGs led to an unforecasted spike in the company's first quarter revenues—and no doubt ultimately also to the obligatory "COVID 15" (as in pounds) experienced by so many folks during the lockdown! It's great to be a staple product![5]

- While a staple is something we usually decide to buy in advance (or at least before the fuel needle sits on "E" for too long), we buy **impulse products** on the spur of the moment. Ever been in line at the supermarket and at the very last moment been lured by a *People* magazine cover at the checkout stand into forking over the rack price of $5.99?

Whether the hijinks of the British Royals or a screaming headline about Kelly Clarkson "Inside her shocking divorce," when you've succumbed to the purchase, you're acting on impulse. When they want to promote impulse products, marketers have two challenges: (1) to create a product or package design that "reaches out and grabs the customer" and (2) to make sure their product is highly visible, for example, by securing prime end-aisle or checkout-lane space. That's why you'll often find brightly colored packages of yellow creme Oreos on end caps in the spring or cheery packages of gum, nuts, and candy in checkout lines. Package design and placement is becoming ever more important as customers come through the lines with "mobile blinders" on—that is, customers with mobile phones in hand are more likely to send texts or check Instagram while they stand in line, so they don't even notice the impulse products beckoning for their attention.

In the past, firms often pushed coupons and promotions to shoppers in-store through their smartphones. While this is clearly still done, today the more integrated practice of **geofencing marketing** has become prevalent. Geofencing is the use of GPS or RFID technology to create a virtual geographic boundary, enabling software to trigger a response when a mobile device enters or leaves a particular area. So if you're Walgreens and have stores chock full of lovely and tempting impulse product treats, wouldn't you want to ping a shopper on entry about the 3 for $2.00 special on single candy bars you're running in order to generate some incremental sales?[6] Note that another related concept, called *proximity marketing* (or *beacon marketing*), will be introduced and discussed later in Chapter 12.

- As the name suggests, we purchase **emergency products** when we're in dire need; examples include bandages, umbrellas, and something to unclog the nasty bathroom sink. Because we need the product badly and immediately, price and sometimes product quality may be irrelevant to our decision to purchase.

In contrast to convenience products, **shopping products** are goods or services for which consumers will spend time and effort to gather information on price, product attributes, and product quality. For these products, consumers are likely to compare alternatives before they buy.

Tablet computers are a good example of a shopping product. They offer an ever-expanding array of features and functions, and new versions constantly enter the market. The shopper has many trade-offs and decisions to make about a variety of features that can be bundled, including speed, screen size, functionality, weight, and battery life. And tablet manufacturers understand your decision dilemma: They take great pains to communicate comparisons to you in their advertising—and, as you might expect, they usually find a way to make their version seem superior.

Specialty products have unique characteristics that are important to buyers at almost any price. When gas prices are down, hybrid vehicles are less cost-effective versus standard cars, yet many consumers still opt to shell out the premium prices to purchase them because of the importance they place on being environmentally friendly. Specialty products often have luxury connotations for which consumers are willing to pay a higher price to achieve a desired image—Blue Buffalo and Orijen gourmet dog foods versus mere Purina or Pedigree, for example. The pricey brands court dog owners who won't compromise what they feed their pets any more than they would compromise what they feed the human members of the family. Lucky Dog Cuisine boasts "Cooked, all natural, fresh food for your dog shipped directly from our kitchen to yours—right to your door!" The hit to the wallet of some of these high-end hound brands can easily run into multiple thousands of dollars annually![7]

Consumers usually know a good deal about specialty products, and they tend to be loyal to specific brands. Generally, a specialty product is an extended problem-solving purchase that requires a lot of effort to choose, meaning that firms that sell these kinds of

geofencing marketing
The use of GPS or RFID technology to create a virtual geographic boundary, enabling software to trigger a response when a mobile device enters or leaves a particular area.

emergency products
Products we purchase when we're in dire need.

shopping products
Goods or services for which consumers spend considerable time and effort gathering information and comparing alternatives before making a purchase.

specialty products
Goods or services that have unique characteristics and are important to the buyer and for which he or she will devote significant effort to acquire.

products need to create marketing strategies that make their products stand apart from the rest.

Unsought products are goods or services (other than convenience products) for which a consumer has little awareness or interest until a need arises. When a college graduate lands his or her first "real" job, typically retirement plans and disability insurance are unsought products. It requires a good deal of advertising or personal selling to interest young people in these kinds of products—just ask any life insurance salesperson. One solution may be to make pricing more attractive; for example, reluctant consumers may be more willing to buy an unsought product for "only pennies a day" than if they have to think about their yearly or lifetime cash outlay.

How Do Businesses Buy Products?

While consumers purchase products for their own use, as we saw in Chapter 6, organizational customers purchase items to enable them to produce still other goods or services. Marketers classify B2B products based on how organizational customers *use* them. As with consumer products, when marketers know how their business customers use a product, they are better able to design products and craft an appropriate marketing mix. Let's briefly review the five different types of B2B products that Figure 8.2 depicts.

- **Equipment** refers to the products an organization uses in its daily operations. *Heavy equipment*, sometimes called *installations* or *capital equipment*, includes items such as the sophisticated robotics Ford uses to assemble automobiles. Installations are big-ticket items and last for a number of years. Desktop computers, desks, and chairs are examples of *light* or *accessory equipment*; they are portable, cost less, and have a shorter life span than capital equipment.

- **Maintenance, repair, and operating (MRO) products** are goods that a business customer consumes in a relatively short time. *Maintenance products* include light bulbs, mops, cleaning supplies, and the like. Repair products are items such as nuts, bolts, washers, and small tools. *Operating supplies* include computer paper and oil to keep machinery running smoothly. Although some firms use a sales force to promote MRO products, most rely on online sales or telemarketing approaches in order to keep prices as low as possible.

- **Raw materials** are products of the fishing, lumber, agricultural, and mining industries that organizational customers purchase to use in their finished products. For example, a food company transforms soybeans into tofu, and a steel manufacturer changes iron ore into large sheets of steel that other firms use to build automobiles, washing machines, and lawn mowers.

- Firms produce **processed materials** when they transform raw materials from their original state. A builder uses treated lumber to add a deck onto a house. A company that creates aluminum cans for Monster, Red Bull, and Rockstar buys aluminum ingots to make them.

- In addition to tangible processed materials, some business customers purchase **specialized services** from outside suppliers. These may be equipment based, such as repairing a copy machine or fixing an assembly line malfunction, or non-equipment-based, such as market research and legal services. These services are essential to the operation of an organization but are not part of the production of a product.

- **Component parts** are manufactured goods or subassemblies of finished items that organizations need to complete their own products. For example, a computer manufacturer needs silicon chips to make a computer, and an automobile manufacturer needs batteries, tires, and fuel injectors.

unsought products
Goods or services for which a consumer has little awareness or interest until the product or a need for the product is brought to his or her attention.

equipment
Expensive goods that an organization uses in its daily operations that last for a long time.

maintenance, repair, and operating (MRO) products
Goods that a business customer consumes in a relatively short time.

raw materials
Products of the fishing, lumber, agricultural, and mining industries that organizational customers purchase to use in their finished products.

processed materials
Products created when firms transform raw materials from their original state.

specialized services
Services that are essential to the operation of an organization but are not part of the production of a product.

component parts
Manufactured goods or subassemblies of finished items that organizations need to complete their own products.

8.3

Disruption in Marketing:
Innovation and Design Thinking Now Drive Product Success

"New and improved!" What exactly do we mean when we use the term *new product*? The Federal Trade Commission says that (1) a product must be entirely new or changed significantly to be called *new* and that (2) a product may be called new for only six months.

That definition is fine from a legal perspective. From a marketing standpoint, though, a new product, or an **innovation**, is *anything* that customers perceive as new and different. Innovation has its roots in an even more elemental concept that is a hot topic in boardrooms of most organizations today: creativity. **Creativity** describes a phenomenon in which something new and somehow valuable is created. That is, the outcome is original and worthwhile and can be most anything tangible or intangible—an idea, a joke, an artistic or literary work, a painting or musical composition, a novel solution to a problem, an invention, and of course, a new product. Scientific research into creativity provides strong evidence of the importance of creative processes in the production of novel, useful products.[8]

Recently, organizations desiring to accelerate the pace of innovation have been incorporating **design thinking** into their processes to gain an edge over competitors. Design thinking, which is also called *human-centered design*, draws upon logic, imagination, intuition, and systemic reasoning to explore possibilities of what could be—and to create desired outcomes that benefit the end user (the customer).[9] Design thinking requires an organizational culture that values **ideation**, which means idea generation through a process characterized by the alternation of divergent and convergent thinking, typical of the design-thinking process. **Divergent thinking** means coming up with as many new ideas as possible and exploring new "out-of-the-box" alternatives. To achieve divergent thinking, it is important to have a diverse group of people involved in the process. In contrast, **convergent thinking** moves toward a more analytical focus on the different ideas in order to come to a decision on the best choice, a process that ensures the design-thinking process will achieve the desired outcome and not just be an exercise in throwing ideas on the wall.

Figure 8.3 lays out the process steps in design thinking. First, marketers need to empathize to gain a deep understanding of the problem space and users, including their issues and goals. With sufficient understanding of those elements, the marketer is then in a position to clearly articulate the problem(s) to be addressed through the design thinking process and move to the ideation phase. Next comes the creation of a prototype solution followed by testing of the efficacy of that solution with real users. Design teams use design thinking to tackle ill-defined/unknown problems (aka, "wicked problems") because the mindset for design thinking centers on reframing these in human-centric ways to focus on what's most important for users.[10]

Sometimes an innovation may be relatively minor, such as the thousands of new versions of current products that come onto the market regularly—for example Lay's Chesapeake Bay Crab Spice potato chips and Cheerios Oat Crunch Oats 'N Honey cereal.

innovation
A product that consumers perceive to be new and different from existing products.

creativity
A phenomenon in which something new and somehow valuable is created.

design thinking
A process that draws upon logic, imagination, intuition, and systemic reasoning to explore possibilities of what could be—and to create desired outcomes that benefit the end user (the consumer). Design thinking is also referred to as *human-centered design*.

ideation
Idea generation through a process characterized by the alternation of divergent and convergent thinking, typical of the design-thinking process.

divergent thinking
Coming up with as many new ideas as possible and exploring new "out-of-the-box" alternatives.

convergent thinking
After successful divergent thinking, convergent thinking moves toward analyzing the different ideas in order to come to a decision on the best choice.

Figure 8.3 *Snapshot* | Process Steps in Design Thinking

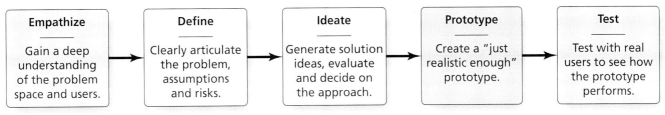

Empathize	Define	Ideate	Prototype	Test
Gain a deep understanding of the problem space and users.	Clearly articulate the problem, assumptions and risks.	Generate solution ideas, evaluate and decide on the approach.	Create a "just realistic enough" prototype.	Test with real users to see how the prototype performs.

HP-22S

Ever heard of a slide rule (on top above)? HP's scientific calculators made slide rules obsolete, and your smartphone's functions now make most stand-alone calculators obsolete.

But other times innovation can bring game-changing products, such as the iPhone triple camera technology that has three 12MP cameras behind one telephoto, one wide-angle, and one ultra-wide angle lens, coupled with their new "Deep Fusion" computational photography tech that drives those cameras! Innovation might result in a new way to game on the go, which is enabled by the Nintendo Switch that comes with its touchscreen sandwiched between a pair of removable controllers and also has its own battery and storage, or in a simple way to amuse children and adults, such as the fidget spinner. Historically, the highest-impact innovations have been completely new products that provide benefits never available before. A great example is the original HP scientific calculator that nearly overnight made the slide rule obsolete (if the term *slide rule* is foreign to you, we suggest googling it—a slide rule is how engineers used to make complex calculations before HP's innovation). In this section and the next, we focus heavily on the concept and process of product innovation. When done well, innovation contributes mightily to organizational success!

Types of Innovations

Innovations differ in their *degree* of newness, and this helps determine how quickly the target market will adopt them. Because innovations that are more novel require us to exert greater effort to figure out how to use them, they are slower to spread throughout a population than new products that are similar to what is already available.

As Figure 8.4 shows, marketers classify innovations into three categories based on their degree of newness: continuous innovations, dynamically continuous innovations, and discontinuous innovations. However, it is better to think of these three types as ranges along a continuum that goes from a very small change in an existing product to a totally new product. We can then describe the three types of innovations in terms of the amount of change they bring to people's lives. For example, the first automobiles caused tremendous changes in the lives of people who were used to getting places by "horse power." Then airplanes came along and opened the entire world to us. And now, with innovations like the TripLingo app, you can communicate easily while traveling abroad. TripLingo comes with a real-time translator—just speak into your phone, and it speaks back to you, at whatever speed you choose. Extras include a culture guide (for quirky dress code and etiquette help), a currency converter, and a slang section for times when you want to be a little less formal.[11]

On the idea side, Airbnb changed how travelers book a place to stay at their destinations (by allowing virtually anyone to rent out space in their own homes), and of course Uber's app provides an easy way to get to a destination (and also cuts down on confusion between you and your driver when there is a language barrier). While you're visiting those new places, you can also use the SitOrSquat App to find the nearest restroom and to even see a rating in advance on its cleanliness. It's worth noting that this service is brought to you by P&G's Charmin brand of toilet paper (apropos, right?). Plus, you'll naturally also want to know if it is free to use or if the restroom's establishment expects you to buy a cup of coffee from them to be able to "use the facilities"![12]

Figure 8.4 *Snapshot* | Types of Innovations

Three types of innovations are continuous, dynamically continuous, and discontinuous, based on their degree of newness.

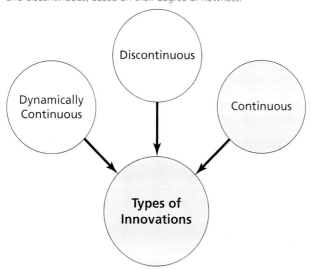

Continuous Innovations

A **continuous innovation** is a modification to an existing product, such as when Samsung and others reinvigorated the TV market by offering thinner sets that featured high-definition viewing. This type of modification can set one brand apart from its competitors. For example, people associate Volvo cars with safety—in fact, their taglines include "Safety first, always" and "You're not just driving a car, you're driving a promise." Those are strong words, and Volvo backs them up with a steady stream of safety-related innovations.

The consumer doesn't have to learn anything new to use a continuous innovation. From a marketing perspective, this means that it's usually relatively easy to convince consumers to adopt this kind of new product. For example, the current generation of smart TVs didn't require television buyers to change their behaviors very much. We all know what a television is and how it works, and we all still want a large screen. The technology's continuous innovation simply gives users the added benefits of accessing online features like Netflix, Hulu, Amazon Prime, and Disney+ without needing another product to facilitate the connection.

A **knockoff** is a new product that copies, with slight modification, the design of an original product. Firms deliberately create knockoffs of clothing and jewelry, often with the intent to sell to a larger or different market. For example, companies may copy the *haute couture* clothing styles of top designers and sell them at lower prices to the mass market. It's likely that a cheaper version of the gown Charlize Theron wears to the Academy Awards ceremony will be available at numerous websites within a few days after the event. It is difficult to legally protect a design (as opposed to a technological invention) because an imitator can argue that even a slight change—different buttons or a slightly wider collar on a dress or shirt—means the knockoff is not an exact copy.

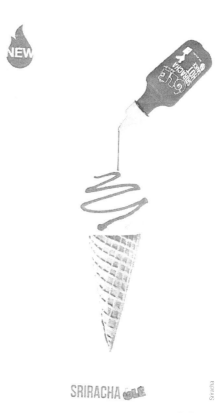

SRIRACHA

Some continuous innovations simply involve finding new ways to use existing products.

Dynamically Continuous Innovations

A **dynamically continuous innovation** is a pronounced modification to an existing product that requires a modest amount of learning or change in behavior to use it. Here's a great example: The history of audio equipment is a series of dynamically continuous innovations (no, the industry didn't start out with streaming and downloads). For many years, consumers enjoyed listening to their favorite Frank Sinatra songs on record players (actually, when first introduced, they were called *gramophones*). In the 1960s, teeny boppers screamed and swooned as they listened to the Beatles on a continuous-play eight-track tape (requiring the purchase of an eight-track tape player, of course). Then came cassette tapes to listen to the Eagles (oops, now a cassette player is needed). In the 1980s, consumers could hear Metallica songs digitally mastered on compact discs (that, of course, required the purchase of a new CD player).

But of course, in the 1990s, recording technology moved one big step forward with MP3 technology. MP3 allowed Madonna fans to download music from the Internet or to exchange electronic copies of the music with others, and when mobile MP3 players hit the scene in 1998, fans could download the tunes directly into a portable player. Then, in 2001, Apple Computer introduced its first iPod and two years later came the Apple iTunes Store. With the original iPod, music fans could take 1,000 songs with them wherever they went. By 2010, iPods could hold 40,000 songs, 25,000 photos, and 200 hours of video.[13] Today, of course, we take for granted that most music fans go to the Apple iTunes Store or Spotify to download songs and to get suggestions for new music they might enjoy, since you can obviously now do all of this on your smartphone! With improving data plans and coverage as well as Wi-Fi being available almost everywhere outside the home, it's easier than ever to stream music on your smartphone or tablet as opposed to downloading it on a device. But if you do want something more retro, yes—you can still purchase an iPod! In fact, in 2020 the iPod Touch 8th Generation was launched complete with an Apple-designed A11 bionic chip and a beautiful liquid retina display. Flip phone anyone?[14]

continuous innovation
A modification of an existing product that sets one brand apart from its competitors.

knockoff
A new product that copies, with slight modification, the design of an original product.

dynamically continuous innovation
A change in an existing product that requires a moderate amount of learning or behavior change.

discontinuous innovation
A totally new product that creates major changes in the way we live.

convergence
The coming together of two or more technologies to create a new system with greater benefits than its separate parts.

disruptive innovation
An innovation that creates a new market and value chain and eventually disrupts an existing market and value chain, displacing established market-leading firms, products, and alliances.

first-mover advantage
Being the first firm to enter a market with a new product, perhaps as a disruptive innovator.

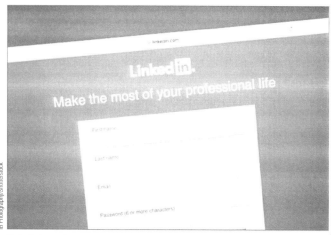
LinkedIn has a first-mover advantage with its extensive network of business executives.

research and development (R&D)
A well-defined and systematic approach to how innovation is done within the firm.

Discontinuous Innovations

To qualify as a **discontinuous innovation**, the product must create *major changes* in the way we live. Consumers have to learn a great deal to be able to effectively use a discontinuous innovation because no similar product has ever been on the market. Major inventions, such as the airplane, the car, and the TV, are the sort of innovations that radically changed modern lifestyles. Another discontinuous innovation, the personal computer—developed in fairly close parallel to the rise of the Internet—changed the way we shop and allowed more people to work from home or anywhere else. Since the advent of PCs, the move toward processing the same information on tablets and on handheld devices became a follow-up journey in dynamically continuous innovation. One particular type of discontinuous innovation is **convergence**, which means the coming together of two or more technologies to create new systems that provide greater benefit than the original technologies alone. A classic example of convergence technology is smartphones, which combine the functionality of a telephone, a camera, a music player, and a digital personal assistant (among other things) into one device.

What's the next discontinuous innovation? Is there a product out there already that will gain that distinction? Usually, marketers know for sure only through 20/20 hindsight; in other words, it's tough to plan for the next really big one (what the computer industry calls the "killer app"). Speculating now, but perhaps the Elon Musk/SpaceX approach will be seen as one of the major discontinuous innovations of the decade. It is touted as the first private industry–led program in the history of U.S. space travel, and with every launch, hopes grow higher and plans more confident that we'll look back on the technology as our entrée into the next phase of what ultimately may become viable commercial space travel. Check back with us on this in about 20 years, please!

At the organizational strategy level, the concept of discontinuous innovation gets translated to **disruptive innovation**, which refers to an innovation that creates a new market and value chain and eventually disrupts an existing market and value chain, displacing established market-leading firms, products, and alliances. As you learned in Chapter 2 and Chapter 3, prior to engaging in market planning, an important part of the process is scanning the external environment—including the competitive environment—to seek out trends that may impact the business. Part of the art and science of marketing strategy is working to predict and ultimately get ahead of anticipated future disruptive innovations and hopefully gain a **first-mover advantage** in the market by being the firm that leads the disruption! A great example was the success of LinkedIn as a new default mechanism for professional job searches in many industries. As a social media platform at its roots, LinkedIn has grown to usurp online employment websites like Monster and CareerBuilders as a go-to place for much job-hunting as well as for recruiting. But even disruptive innovators cannot sit back on their laurels! In recent years, the rise of Indeed as a simpler, more straighforward, and considerably more focused website for professional job seekers has posed a significant threat to the more cluttered feel of LinkedIn.[15]

8.4 New Product Development

OBJECTIVE
Show how firms develop new products.

Building on our knowledge of the concept of creativity and the different types of innovations, we'll now turn our attention to how firms actually develop new products. This process is based on expenditures in **research and development (R&D)**, which in most organizations is a well-defined and systematic approach to how it innovates. Investors and financial markets closely scrutinize R&D investments because these expenditures tend to predict how robust the firm's oncoming new product stream will be. In fact, R&D investment in and of itself is often a central metric for organizational commitment to innovation. Higher levels of R&D activity are inherently more competitively important in some industries versus others (high tech and pharmaceuticals are examples on the high side), but in any firm new product development is fueled by investment in R&D.

There are seven phases in the process of **new product development (NPD)**, as Figure 8.5 shows: idea generation, product concept development and screening, marketing strategy development, business analysis, technical development, market test, and commercialization. Let's take a quick look at what goes on during each of these phases.

Phase 1: Ideation (or Idea Generation)

As we discussed earlier, in the ideation (or idea generation) phase of product development, marketers use a variety of sources to come up with great new product ideas that provide customer benefits and that are compatible with the company mission. Sometimes ideas come from customers. Ideas also come from salespeople, service providers, and others who have direct customer contact. **Value co-creation** refers to the process by which an organization creates worth through collaborative participation by customers and other stakeholders in the new product development process.

The name "Lego" is an abbreviation of the two Danish words "leg godt," meaning "play well." The 90-year-old product exhibited strong sales and financial performance during the COVID-19 crisis, and the firm donated $50 million to help support families during the crisis. In a marketing and innovation coup, Lego developed an online platform called *Lego Ideas* where users can suggest new Lego sets and seek to have them turned into physical products by the company. Lego Ideas enables users to provide a description, create a visual representation (either physically or digitally using Legos), and specify the characteristics of their proposed Lego set. Then, any new ideas that attract more than 10,000 supporters in a two-year period on the platform move into a review phase, at which point Lego determines whether or not it's feasible to turn the idea into a mass-produced Lego set. As part of the vetting process, folks who throw their support behind a particular proposed product answer a series of questions to determine market potential (questions related to perceived price, segments of the market the set would appeal to, complexity of building the set, etc.). This approach to value co-creation has yielded creative new ideas, including sets targeted to older Lego *aficionados*, such as Luke's Diner from *The Gilmore Girls* and *The Big Bang Theory* set.[16] It's important to note that such a value co-creation approach is in stark contrast to "traditional" approaches in which firms develop products behind a curtain and send them to market, hoping that customers connect with the intended value proposition of the new offering.

Often firms use market research activities, such as the focus groups we discussed in Chapter 4, in their search for new product ideas. For example, a company like ESPN that wants to develop new channels or change the focus of its existing channels might hold focus group discussions across different groups of sports-minded viewers to get ideas for new types of programs.

Phase 2: Product Concept Development and Screening

The second phase in developing new products is **product concept development and screening**. Although ideas for products initially come from a variety of sources and, it is hoped, through co-creation with customers and others, ultimately the responsibility usually falls to marketers to manage the process and expand these ideas into more complete product concepts. Product concepts describe what features the product should have and the benefits those features will provide for consumers. Of course, just because an idea is unique doesn't

Figure 8.5 *Process* | Phases in New Product Development

New product development generally occurs in seven phases.

Phase 1: Idea Generation

Phase 2: Product Concept Development and Screening

Phase 3: Marketing Strategy Development

Phase 4: Business Analysis

Phase 5: Technical Development

Phase 6: Test Marketing

Phase 7: Commercialization

new product development (NPD)
The phases by which firms develop new products, including idea generation, product concept development and screening, marketing strategy development, business analysis, technical development, test marketing, and commercialization.

value co-creation
The process by which benefits-based value is created through collaborative participation by customers and other stakeholders in the new product development process.

product concept development and screening
The second step of product development in which marketers test product ideas for technical and commercial success.

mean it will sell. How about the Japanese company (Satis) that invented an app to allow your smartphone to control your toilet? It lets you flush and lift the seat without touching the commode. But wait, there's more: You can play music through the toilet's speakers and store your "usage history" in a "toilet diary" to track your progress. Now this idea is flush with possibilities![17]

In new product development, failures often come as frequently (or more so) than successes, and it is critical to screen ideas for *both* their technical and commercial value. When screening, marketers examine the chances that a new product concept might be successful while they weed out concepts that have little chance to make it in the market. They estimate **technical success** when they decide whether the new product is technologically feasible—is it possible to actually build this product? Then, they estimate **commercial success** when they decide whether anyone is likely to buy the product. Lego uses its Lego Ideas process to estimate the potential commercial success of a new product in terms of the number of supporters the idea attracts. Its potential technical success comes into play only if the product gains enough support to make it to Lego's internal review. If the product concept reaches this benchmark, the company will then conduct an analysis of whether it can actually produce it.

Phase 3: Marketing Strategy Development

The third phase in new product development is to develop a marketing strategy to introduce the product to the marketplace, a process we began to talk about back in Chapter 3. This means that marketers must identify the target market, estimate its size, and determine how they can effectively position the product to address the target market's needs. And, of course, marketing strategy development includes planning for pricing, distribution, and promotion expenditures both for the introduction of the new product and for the long run.

Phase 4: Business Analysis

Once a product concept passes the screening stage, the next phase is a **business analysis**. Even though marketers have evidence that there is a market for the product, they still must find out if the product can make a profitable contribution to the organization's product mix. How much potential demand is there for the product? Does the firm have the resources it will need to successfully develop and introduce the product?

The business analysis for a new product begins with assessing how the new product will fit into the firm's total product mix. Will the new product increase sales, or will it simply take away sales of existing products (a concept called *cannibalization* that we'll discuss further in Chapter 9)? Are there possible synergies between the new product and the company's existing offerings that may improve visibility and the image of both? And what are the marketing costs likely to be?

Phase 5: Technical Development

If a new product concept survives the scrutiny of a business analysis, it then undergoes **technical development**, in which a firm's engineers work with marketers to refine the design and production process. A classic example of the technical development phase involves goTenna, which launched a product to enable people to be able to communicate with each other using their smartphones while in an area without cell phone coverage. The product ingeniously uses radio signals to create a network between multiple goTenna devices that, along with the company's smartphone app, provides a means of communication between multiple users of the product within a given area. One valuable application of goTenna is during wilderness excursions, where potentially intense weather

technical success
Indicates that a product concept is feasible purely from the standpoint of whether or not it is possible to physically develop it, regardless of whether it is perceived to be commercially viable.

commercial success
Indicates that a product concept is feasible from the standpoint of whether the firm developing the product believes there is or will be sufficient consumer demand to warrant its development and entry into the market.

business analysis
The step in the product development process in which marketers assess a product's commercial viability.

technical development
The step in the product development process in which company engineers refine and perfect a new product.

New flavors need to undergo rigorous technical development so companies can be sure they will satisfy consumers' expectations.

conditions make it even more difficult to receive cell phone signals. The goTenna's design is lightweight, it's easy to attach to the outside of a backpack or one of the belt loops on a pair of pants, and it's water-resistant. Although many of these characteristics were most likely identified to some degree during an earlier stage of the product development process, the company's marketers needed to work with the engineering team during the technical development phase to more fully flesh them out into a tangible form that fits with both consumer needs and the internal capabilities of the company.[18]

The better a firm understands how customers will react to a new product, the better its chances of commercial success. For this reason, typically a company allocates resources to develop one or more physical versions or **prototypes** of the product. Prospective customers may evaluate these mock-ups in focus groups or in field trials at home.

A relatively new aspect of the technical development phase of new product development is enabled by the increasing popularization of 3D printing. Marketers in firms as diverse as Coca-Cola, Volkswagen, Nokia, and BelVita are engaging customers directly in product development processes through this technology. For example, as part of Nokia's 3D Printing Community Project, the mobile phone manufacturer made available a 3D printing kit for its customers enabling them to print out customized covers for one of its smartphones. And Volkswagen encouraged patrons to become their own car designers though The Polo Principle campaign in which people were allowed to take control of the 3D printer used to create the original VW Polo car model via a website. Then, the consumers could create their very own versions, from which 40 ideas were finally 3D-printed and displayed in Copenhagen. Afterward, the consumers/designers had the chance to take the mini-car version of their design home—one of the ideas was even turned into a full-sized VW Polo![19] And marketers at Trek bicycles are using 3D printing to both speed up and increase accuracy in developing product prototypes, thus accelerating overall product design cycles. Trek now produces four times as many prototypes as before, while also improving overall speed to market.[20]

Prototypes also are useful for people within the firm. Those involved in the technical development process must determine which parts of a finished good the company will make and which ones it will buy from other suppliers. In the case of manufacturing goods, the company may have to buy new production equipment or modify existing machinery. Someone has to develop work instructions for employees and train them to make the product. When it's a matter of a new service process, technical development includes decisions such as which activities will occur within sight of customers versus in the "backroom" and whether the company can automate parts of the service to make delivery more efficient.

Technical development sometimes requires the company to apply for a *patent*. As you learned in Chapter 2, because patents legally prevent competitors from producing or selling the invention, this legal mechanism may reduce or eliminate competition in a market for many years so that a firm gains some time to recoup its investments in technical development.

prototypes
Test versions of a proposed product.

Phase 6: Market Test

The next phase of new product development is running a **market test**, or **test market**. This usually means the firm tries out the complete marketing plan—the distribution, advertising, and sales promotion—in a small slice of the market that is similar to the larger market it ultimately hopes to enter with full force.

There are both pluses and minuses to market tests. On the negative side, market tests are extremely expensive. It can cost more than a million dollars to conduct a market test even in a single city. A market test also gives the competition a free look at the new product, its introductory price, and the intended promotional strategy—and an opportunity to get to the market first with a competing product. On the positive side, when they offer a new product in a limited area, marketers can evaluate and improve the marketing program.

market test, or **test market**
Testing the complete marketing plan in a small geographic area that is similar to the larger market the firm hopes to enter.

Sometimes, market tests uncover a need to improve the product itself. At other times, market tests indicate product failure, providing an advanced warning that allows the firm to save millions of dollars by "pulling the plug."

For years, the manufacturer of venerable Listerine wanted to introduce a mint-flavored version of its classic gold formulation to compete more directly with P&G's pleasant-tasting Scope (it originally introduced this alternative under the brand Listermint). Unfortunately, every time they tried to run a market test, P&G found out, and the rival poured substantial extra advertising and coupons for its Scope brand into the test market cities. This counterattack reduced the usefulness of the test market results for Listerine when its market planners tried to decide whether to introduce Listermint nationwide. Because P&G's aggressive response to Listermint's market tests actually *increased* Scope's market share in the test cities, there was no way to determine how well Listermint would actually do under normal competitive conditions. The company went ahead and introduced Listermint nationally anyway, but the new brand achieved only marginal success, and the company ultimately pulled it from the market. Today, thanks to better product development, the Listerine brand itself is available in mint flavor as well as several other choices and is hands down the top-selling U.S. mouthwash brand, with sales of over $354 million annually.[21]

Because of the potential problems and expense of market tests, marketers instead may use special computer software to conduct a **simulated market test** that imitates the introduction of a product into the marketplace. These simulations allow the company to see the likely impact of price cuts and new packaging—or even to determine where in the store it should try to place the product. The process entails gathering basic research data on consumers' perceptions of the product concept, the physical product, the advertising, and other promotional activity. The test market simulation model uses that information to predict the product's success much less expensively (and more discreetly) than a traditional test market. As this technology improves, traditional test markets may become a thing of the past.

simulated market test
Application of special computer software to imitate the introduction of a product into the marketplace, allowing the company to see the likely impact of price cuts and new packaging—or even to determine where in the store it should try to place the product.

Phase 7: Commercialization

The last phase in new product development is **commercialization**. This means the launching of a new product, and it requires full-scale production, distribution, advertising, sales promotion—the works. For this reason, commercialization of a new product cannot happen overnight. A launch requires planning and careful preparation.

Commercialization is expensive, but the Internet makes it much easier for start-ups to obtain the funding they need to get their new products into the market. Today, we witness the explosive growth of **crowdfunding**, where innovative websites such as Kickstarter.com, Indiegogo.com, and Crowdfunder.com continue to grow in popularity as fundraising mechanisms for entrepreneurs and small companies. On these sites, individuals can choose to either donate money (often in exchange for a product sample) or actually invest in the company. Even during the height of the early onset of the COVID-19 crisis, crowdfunding proved highly viable. Indiegogo, for example, reported a number of highly successful fundraising initiatives at the time, including $1.6 million for Babymaker (a lightweight e-bike similar to traditional entry-level bicycles), $1.5 million for Midia (a revolutionary air conditioning unit that stays nearly silent while running and consumes 35 percent less energy than conventional AC units), and $3.5 million for Niche Zero (hailed as a game-changer in coffee grinding, aiming at making barista-quality coffee available within any home kitchen).[22] Under this commercialization model, even small contributions add up when hundreds or thousands of people like an idea and pitch in.

As launch time nears, preparations gain a sense of urgency. First, the social media campaigns are likely to crank up, and hopefully insiders will then start to buzz about the new product on Twitter and in the blogosphere. Then, sales managers will have to explain special incentive programs to salespeople, who in turn will educate all of their customers in the channel of distribution. Soon the media announce to prospective customers why they

commercialization
The final step in the product development process in which a new product is launched into the market.

crowdfunding
Online platforms that allow thousands of individuals to each contribute small amounts of money to fund a new product from a start-up company.

should buy and where they can find the new product. And all of this has to be orchestrated with the precision of a symphony, with every player on top of his or her part, else the introduction into the market can easily disappoint customers when they first try to buy.

The late Apple innovation genius Steve Jobs was never one to squelch precommercialization hype about his new product introductions. It has been estimated that Apple achieved prelaunch publicity worth more than $500 million on the original iPhone before it spent a single penny on any actual paid advertising. And the introduction of the original iPad back in 2010 was no exception to the Apple hype-creation machine. Jobs claimed that the iPad would offer an experience superior to that of netbooks (a popular term at the time for notebook computers). He argued that the 751 million people who at that time owned iPhones and iPod Touches already knew how to use the iPad because it uses the same operating system and touch-screen interface. Well, as they say, the rest is history. Since 2010, the iPad and its bevy of competitors have had a major impact on how we work and entertain ourselves.[23] The iPad introduction is a perfect segue to the next section on adoption and diffusion of innovation.

8.5 Adoption and Diffusion of New Products

OBJECTIVE
Explain the process of product adoption and the diffusion of innovations.

In the previous section, we talked about the steps marketers take to develop new products from generating ideas to launch. Now we'll look at what happens *after* that new product hits the market—how an innovation spreads throughout a population.

A painting is not a work of art until someone views it. A song is not music until someone sings it. In the same way, new products do not satisfy customer wants and needs until the customer actually uses (consumes) them—hence the word *consumer*. **Product adoption** is the process by which a consumer or business customer begins to buy and use a new good, service, or idea.

The term **diffusion** describes how the use of a product spreads throughout a population. One way to understand how this process works is to think about a new product as if it were a computer virus that spreads from a few computers to infect many machines. A brand might just slog around—sometimes for years and years. At first, only a small number of people buy it, but change happens in a hurry when the process reaches the moment of critical mass. This moment of truth is called the **tipping point**.[24] After they spend months or even years to develop a new product, the real challenge for firms is to get consumers to buy and use the product and to do so quickly and in sufficient quantities so they can recover the costs of product development and launch. To accomplish this, marketers must understand the product adoption process.

Next, we'll discuss the stages in this process. We'll also see how consumers and businesses differ in their eagerness to adopt new products and how the characteristics of a product affect its adoption (or "infection") rate.

Stages in Consumers' Adoption of a New Product

Whether the innovation is the next breakthrough in smartphones or a better mousetrap, individuals and organizations pass through six stages in the adoption process. Figure 8.6 shows the **adoption pyramid**, which reflects how a person goes from being unaware of an innovation through stages from the bottom up of awareness, interest, evaluation, trial, adoption, and confirmation. At every stage in building the pyramid, people drop out of the process, so the proportion of consumers who wind up actually using the innovation on a consistent basis is a mere fraction of those who are exposed to it.

product adoption
The process by which a consumer or business customer begins to buy and use a new good, service, or idea.

diffusion
The process by which the use of a product spreads throughout a population.

tipping point
In the context of product diffusion, the point when a product's sales spike from a slow climb to an unprecedented new level.

adoption pyramid
Reflects how a person goes from being unaware of an innovation through stages from the bottom up of awareness, interest, evaluation, trial, adoption, and confirmation.

A new product is more likely to experience diffusion if it is visible to others, which may help explain why fanny packs are making a bit of a fashion comeback.

Figure 8.6 *Process* | Adoption Pyramid

Consumers pass through six stages in the adoption of a new product—from being unaware of an innovation to becoming loyal adopters. The right marketing strategies at each stage help ensure a successful adoption.

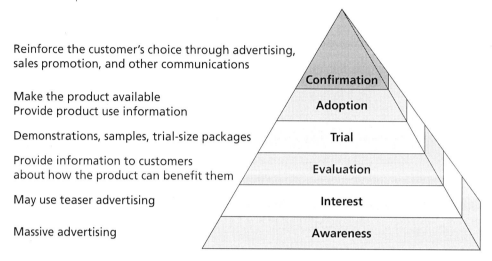

Reinforce the customer's choice through advertising, sales promotion, and other communications

Make the product available
Provide product use information

Demonstrations, samples, trial-size packages

Provide information to customers about how the product can benefit them

May use teaser advertising

Massive advertising

Confirmation
Adoption
Trial
Evaluation
Interest
Awareness

Awareness

Awareness that the innovation exists at all is the first step in the adoption process. To educate consumers about a new product, marketers may conduct a massive advertising campaign: a **media blitz**. For example, Tropicana identified a "problem" that it shares with many other venerable brands: How to keep the image of a long-standing market leader fresh and relevant without alienating its loyal base? Toward this goal, PepsiCo launched a new campaign for Tropicana that is a case study in how to wrap old, familiar virtues in cutting-edge trends. The Tropicana brand story rests on a solid foundation because it's firmly entrenched in a consumer ritual—a series of actions we repeat on a regular basis because they help to articulate important meanings and continuity in our lives. Like orange juice every morning for breakfast! Hence, Tropicana's Sip Your Sunshine campaign strives to update the justification for including the juice in the family breakfast ritual. PepsiCo explained the campaign's objective as highlighting "authentic moments of brightness that bind us. Our goal is to inspire consumers to stop, enjoy and even celebrate the instances that bring little moments of happiness into their lives, and that sometimes we take for granted—like watching the sunrise or starting off the day with a delicious glass of orange juice."[25]

media blitz
A massive advertising campaign that occurs over a relatively short time frame.

Interest

For some of the people who become aware of a new product, a second stage in the adoption process is *interest*. In this stage, a prospective adopter begins to see how a new product might satisfy an existing or newly realized need. Interest also means that consumers look for and are open to additional information about the innovation. We know there are many Apple fans reading this book, and as mentioned earlier, the Apple iPad was originally launched way back in 2010, but recently the company released a new 9.7-inch iPad with the Apple Pencil. Consumers' interest quickly peaked as they learned about its innovative new features, such as the Retina Display that has a higher pixel density than traditional Apple displays, all-day battery life, the ability to sketch on-screen, and a faster processor. Ads featuring the sleek new products filled the airwaves on TV, and pop-ups seemed to burst on to every website. Apple's efforts to produce a lower-priced product with superior features quickly paid off by generating substantial interest as the company tried to regain some of the users it lost to Samsung in recent years.[26]

On the adoption pyramid, Apple wants to encourage interest by sponsoring a Facebook page.

However, this approach doesn't work with all products, so marketers often design teaser advertisements that give prospective customers just enough information about the new product to make them curious and to stimulate their interest. Despite marketers' best efforts, however, some more consumers drop out of the process at this point.

Evaluation

In the *evaluation* stage, we weigh the costs and benefits of the new product. On the one hand, for complex, risky, or expensive products, people think about the innovation a great deal before they will try it. For example, a firm will carefully evaluate spending hundreds of thousands of dollars on manufacturing robotics prior to purchase. Marketers for such products help prospective customers see how such products can benefit them.

In a very unique and innovative approach, Callaway (the golf club manufacturer) partnered with Boeing to deploy some of the aerodynamic know-how and design elements that Boeing has developed for use in airplanes into the development of a new set of drivers. Although some consumers might be initially skeptical of the end product of this partnership, Callaway has worked hard to educate consumers on why this odd coupling of two companies has resulted in better performing golf clubs. To drive home the point (pun intended), Callaway convinced several of its sponsored pro golf players to use the new clubs in the Masters tournament. If this product is good enough for arguably the most prestigious tournament in golf, it stands to reason that it would make a great addition to most casual golfers' arsenals.[27]

As you read earlier in the chapter, in the case of impulse products a person may do very little planning or search effort before deciding to purchase. This phenomenon is called an **impulse purchase**, like the Screaming Goat novelty item that sits on a tree stump and screams whenever you touch it (seriously—that's the product). Why does it do this, you might ask? Because "sometimes world events just seem so overwhelming and you need an outlet for your feelings." And yes, this product peaked on the impulse purchase charts in the first half of 2020 (makes sense, right?).[28]

Some potential adopters will evaluate an innovation positively enough to move on to the next stage. Those who do not think the new product will provide adequate benefits drop out at this point.

impulse purchase
A purchase made without any planning or search effort.

Trial

Trial is the stage in the adoption process when potential buyers will actually experience or use the product for the first time. Often marketers stimulate trial when they provide opportunities for consumers to sample the product.

Diet Coke, as part of a full brand relaunch in North America, recently rolled out a new campaign to showcase the brand's four bold new flavors, new packaging, and new design. The "Because I Can" campaign centered on doing things that make you happy in life, no matter what others may think. In addition to a creative new TV and outdoor campaign, Diet Coke executed a major nationwide sampling push at events and festivals to encourage people to try (or retry) the brand. Product trial can result in high rates of adoption by the target market, provided its members enjoy the product.[29] Those who do not are unlikely to adopt the new product and fall out at this point.

Adoption

In the *adoption* stage, a prospect actually buys the product (hooray, a sale!). Does this mean that all individuals or organizations that first choose an innovation are permanent customers? No, and that's a mistake many firms make. Marketers need to provide follow-up contacts and communications with adopters to ensure they are satisfied and remain loyal to the new product over time.

Confirmation

After he or she adopts an innovation, a customer weighs expected versus actual benefits and costs. Favorable experiences make it more likely that the customer will become a loyal adopter as initially positive opinions result in *confirmation*. Of course, nothing lasts forever; even a loyal customer may decide that a new product no longer meets his or her expectations and reject it. Hence, marketers understand that reselling the customer in the confirmation stage is often quite important. They provide advertisements, sales presentations, and other communications to reinforce a customer's choice.

Adopter Categories

As we saw previously, *diffusion* describes how the use of a product spreads throughout a population. Of course, marketers prefer their entire target market to immediately adopt a new product, but this is not the case. Both consumers and business customers differ in their willingness to try something new, lengthening the diffusion process by months or even years. Based on adopters' roles in the diffusion process, experts classify them into five categories, as shown in Figure 8.7: innovators, early adopters, early majority, late majority, and laggards.[30]

Some people like to try new products. Others are so reluctant that you'd think they're afraid of anything new (know anyone like that?). Many innovative technology products are released as a **beta test** to allow usage and feedback from a small number of users who are willing to test the product under normal, everyday conditions of use. The types of innovative technologies commonly beta tested are often called a **bleeding-edge technology**—one that is not yet ready for release to the market as a whole, potentially because of issues

beta test
Limited release of a product, especially an innovative technology, to allow usage and feedback from a small number of customers who are willing to test the product under normal, everyday conditions of use.

bleeding-edge technology
An innovative technology that is not yet ready for release to the market as a whole, potentially because of issues related to reliability and stability, but is in a suitable state to be offered for beta testing to evaluate consumer perceptions of its performance and identify any potential issues in its usage.

Figure 8.7 *Snapshot* | Categories of Adopters

Because consumers differ in how willing they are to buy and try a new product, it often takes months or years for most of the population to adopt an innovation.

Innovators 2.5% | Early Adopters 13.5% | Early Majority 34% | Late Majority 34% | Laggards 16%

related to reliability and stability, but is in a suitable state for beta testing and user feedback.[31] To understand how the adopter categories differ, we'll focus below on a threaded example of the adoption of one specific technology—a blast from the past that has had a big impact on all of us today—Wi-Fi (did you know that *Wi-Fi* is short for *wireless fidelity*?). What would we do without it? You'll enjoy getting a little history of how it began and how it got to what we take for granted today!

Innovators

Innovators make up roughly the first 2.5 percent of adopters. This segment is extremely adventurous and willing to take risks with new products. Innovators are typically well educated, younger, better off financially than others in the population, and worldly. Innovators who were into new technology knew all about Wi-Fi well before other people had even heard of it. Because innovators pride themselves on trying new products, they purchased laptops with Wi-Fi cards way back in ancient history (1999) when Apple first introduced them in its Mac laptops.

innovators
The first segment (roughly 2.5 percent) of a population to adopt a new product.

Early Adopters

Early adopters, approximately 13.5 percent of adopters, buy product innovations early in the diffusion process but not as early as innovators. Unlike innovators, early adopters are concerned about social acceptance, so they tend to gravitate toward products they believe will make others think they are cutting-edge or fashionable. Typically, they are heavy media users and often are heavy users of the product category. Others in the population often look to early adopters for their opinions on various topics, making early adopters critical to a new product's success. For this reason, marketers often heavily target them in their advertising and other communications efforts. Remember that the innovators pretty much already have the new product in hand before most early adopters purchase.

early adopters
Those who adopt an innovation early in the diffusion process but after the innovators.

Columnists who write about personal technology for most popular magazines and tech websites were testing Wi-Fi in the mid-2000s. They experienced some problems (like PCs crashing when they set up a wireless network at home), but still they touted the benefits of wireless connectivity. Road warriors adopted the technology as Wi-Fi access spread into airports, hotels, city parks, and other public spaces. Intel, maker of the Centrino mobile platform, launched a major campaign with field-leading Condé Nast's *Traveler* magazine and offered a location guide to T-Mobile hot spots nationwide.

Early Majority

The **early majority**, roughly 34 percent of adopters, avoid being either first or last to try an innovation. They are typically middle-class consumers and are deliberate and cautious. Early majority consumers have slightly above-average education and income levels. When the early majority adopts a product, we no longer consider it new or different—that is, when it gets into their hands, it is, in essence, "established." By 2002, Wi-Fi access was available in more than 500 Starbucks cafés, and monthly subscription prices were dropping rapidly (from $30 to $9.95 per month).

early majority
Those whose adoption of a new product signals a general acceptance of the innovation.

Late Majority

Late majority adopters, about 34 percent of the population, are older, are even more conservative, and typically have lower-than-average levels of education and income. The late majority adopters avoid trying a new product until it is no longer risky. By that time, the product has become an economic necessity for them, or there is pressure from peer groups to adopt. By 2004, Wi-Fi capability was being bundled into almost all laptops, and you could connect in mainstream venues, like McDonald's restaurants and sports stadiums. Cities across the country began considering blanket Wi-Fi coverage throughout the entire town through WiMAX (Worldwide Interoperability for Microwave Access) technology, a wireless communication standard.

late majority
The adopters who are willing to try new products when there is little or no risk associated with the purchase, when the purchase becomes an economic necessity, or when there is social pressure to purchase.

laggards
The last consumers to adopt an innovation.

Laggards

Laggards, about 16 percent of adopters, are the last in a population to adopt a new product. Laggards are typically lower in income level and education than other adopter categories and are bound by tradition. By the time laggards adopt a product, it may already be superseded by other innovations. By 2006, it would have seemed strange if Wi-Fi or a similar capability was not part of the standard package in even the lowest-priced laptop computer, and people began to become annoyed if Wi-Fi access wasn't available just about everywhere they might go.[32]

So now you know a bit about the diffusion of innovation of Wi-Fi. And understanding these adopter categories allows marketers to develop strategies that will speed the diffusion or widespread use of their products. For example, early in the diffusion process, marketers may put greater emphasis on gaining buzz through targeted social media and advertising in special-interest magazines and websites to attract innovators and early adopters. Later, they may lower the product's price or come out with lower-priced models with fewer "bells and whistles" to attract the late majority. We will talk more about strategies for new and existing products in the next chapter.

Product Factors That Affect the Rate of Adoption

Not all products are successful, to say the least. Let's see if you've ever heard of these classic boo-boos in new product introduction:

- *Clairol Look of Buttermilk shampoo:* Consumers pondered what exactly *was* the "look of buttermilk" and why would they want it?

- *Betamax video player:* Sony refused to allow anyone else to make the players, and the rest of the industry went to VHS format.

- *Cheetos Lip Balm:* Eating Cheetos may be a guilty pleasure, but why would anyone want that flavor stuck on their lips all day?[33]

- *Heinz multicolored ketchup:* What's better than red ketchup? Blue, green, or purple, of course! Consumers, however, didn't equate the look with the flavor.

- *Wow! Chips:* Frito-Lay thought fat-free chips would be a smash hit among the health conscious. Too bad the main ingredient, Olestra, caused stomach cramping and other abdominal issues.[34]

- *Coors Rocky Mountain Sparkling Water:* Despite Coors' efforts to equate their beer's quality with the pureness of the Rocky Mountain water used to produce it, the Coors brand and its famous water source did not translate into successful sales of a sparkling water line. Perhaps this was because consumers were confused as to why a company known for brew was selling sparkling water with a label similar to the one on its more familiar beer cans and bottles.[35] And along the same vein—how about Bud Light Seltzer, which debuted in four flavors in early 2020? It will be interesting to track this one over the longer run to see if Anheuser-Busch has better luck than Coors in sticking a beer brand onto a non-beer product.

The reason for most product failures is really pretty simple: Consumers simply did not perceive that the product satisfied a need better than competitive products already on the market. If you *could* predict which new products will succeed and which will fail, you'd quickly be in high demand as a marketing guru by companies worldwide. That's because companies make large investments in new products, but failures are all too frequent. Experts suggest that between one-third and one-half of all new products fail. As you might expect, a lot of people try to develop research techniques that enable them to predict whether a new product will be hot or not.

Researchers identify five characteristics of innovations that affect the rate of adoption: relative advantage, compatibility, complexity, trialability, and observability.[36] The degree to which a new product has each of these characteristics affects the speed of diffusion. It may take years for a market to widely adopt a new product. As an example to better understand why each of these characteristics is important, let's take a closer look at the humble microwave oven—a product that was highly innovative in its early days but now is generally a low-priced staple of every kitchen (and every college apartment and dorm):

- **Relative advantage** describes the degree to which a consumer perceives that a new product provides superior benefits. In the case of the microwave oven, consumers in the 1960s did not believe that the product provided important benefits that would improve their lives (realize that until at least the 1970s, "traditional" male and female family and household roles were highly predominant). But by the late 1970s, that perception had changed because more women had entered the workforce. So in the 1960s, quite a few more women had all day to prepare the evening meal, so they didn't really need the microwave (yes, at that time there were very few males in the "househusband" role—that's really changed today!). In the 1970s, however, when many women left home for work at 8 a.m. and returned home at 6 p.m., an appliance that would "magically" defrost a frozen chicken and cook it in 30 minutes provided a genuine advantage.

- **Compatibility** is the extent to which a new product is consistent with existing cultural values, customs, and practices. Did consumers see the microwave oven as being compatible with existing ways of doing things? Hardly. Cooking on paper plates? If you put a paper plate in a conventional oven, you'll likely get a visit from the fire department. By anticipating compatibility issues early in the new-product-development stage, marketing strategies can address such problems in planning communications and consumer education programs, or there may be opportunities to alter product designs to overcome some consumer objections.

- **Complexity** is the degree to which consumers find a new product or its use difficult to understand. Many microwave users today haven't a clue about how a microwave oven cooks food. When appliance manufacturers introduced the first microwaves, they explained that this new technology causes molecules to move and rub together, which creates friction that produces heat. Voilà! Cooked pot roast.

- **Trialability** is the ease of sampling a new product and its benefits. Marketers took an important step in the 1970s to speed up adoption of the microwave oven product trial. Just about every store that sold microwaves invited shoppers to visit the store and sample an entire meal a microwave cooked. Finally, consumers began to understand what the product even was and what it could do!

- **Observability** refers to how visible a new product and its benefits are to others who might adopt it. The ideal innovation is easy to see. For example, for a generation of kids, scooters like the Razor became the hippest way to get around as soon as one preteen saw his or her friends flying by. That same generation observed its friends trading Pokémon cards and wanted to join in (were you part of this craze when you were younger?). In the case of the microwave, it wasn't quite so readily observable for its potential adopters—only close friends and acquaintances who visited someone's home would likely see an early adopter using it. But the fruits of the microwave's labors—tasty food dishes—created lots of buzz at office watercoolers and social events, and its use spread quickly. Too bad they didn't have social media back then—if they had, it's a sure bet that the rate of adoption of microwaves would have been a whole lot faster.

relative advantage
The degree to which a consumer perceives that a new product provides superior benefits.

compatibility
The extent to which a new product is consistent with existing cultural values, customs, and practices.

complexity
The degree to which consumers find a new product or its use difficult to understand.

trialability
The ease of sampling a new product and its benefits.

observability
How visible a new product and its benefits are to others who might adopt it.

Since its introduction, the venerable microwave oven has gone from being an expensive cutting-edge innovation to a low-priced staple product.

8.6 Brand You: Creating Your Value Proposition

OBJECTIVE

Be prepared to develop your personal value proposition.

Taylor now knows it is essential to be focused in his approach to looking for a job and a career. This can be accomplished by completing the three steps of target marketing: segmentation, targeting, and positioning. Taylor knows that the next step is to develop the "product" he will offer prospective employers. It's time to move forward with developing his value proposition.

Previously in this chapter, we discussed the value proposition that was introduced in Chapter 1. The value proposition is the consumer's perception of the benefits he or she will receive when purchasing a good or service. The marketer has two tasks: (1) create a better value (product) than what is available from other sellers and (2) convince customers that this is true.

Creating your Brand You value proposition is about answering these questions: What do you have to offer a prospective employer? How do you stand out among all the other students and graduates competing for an internship or full-time job? You also must clearly answer these questions before you write your résumé and cover letter.

As we discussed, a product is a bundle of features, functions, benefits, and uses, as well as its brand and packaging. Products have three distinct and important layers: the core product, the actual product, and the augmented product. This same concept of product layers applies to your personal brand. You are not simply a student who has taken marketing classes; you are a highly motivated student with interests and experiences in the area of marketing (*actual product*) who can help your target market (company) increase sales and provide a higher level of customer service (*core product*), and you are willing to work flexible hours, put your social networking skills to work to connect with customers, and relocate to other parts of the country (or globe) for the right job (*augmented product*).

You are the most important product you will ever market, whether you are a marketing major or a math major. Take the time to focus on and develop your features (actual product), benefits (core product), and extras (augmented product). When you implement the concept of product layers, you can easily see what you have to offer a prospective employer.

Add to Your Product Layers

To position yourself far ahead of your competitors (other students seeking the same job), you need to add to your product layers. Some ways to do that include:

- Volunteer to work with a not-for-profit organization. If you know how to use social media as a marketing tool, offer to help the organization gain support in the community and showcase the work they do.

- Establish a blog business. You can contract with local small businesses to develop blogs on their company websites, thus creating buzz for their products and their brand. Alternatively, you might try setting up your own blog for local not-for-profit organizations, perhaps even acquiring sponsorship income.

- "Blog for a job." Develop a social network for job-hunting students at your campus. Provide leadership and space for people to share networking ideas, discuss job-search strategies, and vent frustrations. Your blog will generate lots of ideas and one just might lead to the perfect job for you!

Of course, if you think these ideas sound great but you don't know how to set up a blog or use social media for marketing, now is a great time to learn. There are plenty of folks on your campus or in various businesses who would be happy to help an ambitious student. Plus, you will have another skill to add to your actual product.

The Core Product—Your Benefits

The core product consists of all the benefits you can provide for your customer. Defining benefits is a little more difficult than identifying features (your skills and knowledge). Benefits are the outcomes or results that occur because of your efforts. Examples of benefits are higher sales, increased customer satisfaction, improved brand recognition, lower costs, and higher profits. Benefits will become critical elements of your value proposition. Knowing these benefits and being able to discuss them is the secret to communicating effectively, whether you are interviewing for a job or writing a dynamic résumé.

You can also add to your product layers in other ways. Involvement in (not just joining) a campus organization or a charity or professional organization enhances the layers of your brand.

You'll have the opportunity to work with many different kinds of people and even gain leadership experience.

The Actual Product—Your Features

Most of us take our strengths, talents, and skills for granted. However, once you know your strengths—that is, the skills you like using, the things you are good at—it will be much easier to know the profession or industry in which you fit best. In addition to your skills, potential employers will evaluate your attitudes and your presentation.

Employers seek a person who is committed to his or her career and to quality job performance. Before you go on a job interview, ask yourself, if you were recruiting someone for this position, what attitudes do you think would be important? After you've identified attitudes that are important to the employers, think of things you've done that demonstrate those attitudes. There's a place for these actions on your résumé and in the job interview.

Another important part of your package is how you present yourself when job hunting and meeting people. Your first real impression will likely be made in the first few seconds—right about the time you say, "My name is . . . ." Looking professional takes planning and effort. Some suggestions are:

- Dress in business attire for interviews. When in doubt, choose a conservative look.
- The eyes have it—make eye contact with everyone with whom you interview.
- Leave cell phones and all other electronic devices turned off and out of sight.
- The perfect accessory is a smile—for everyone you encounter, not just the interviewer.

The Augmented Product—Your Extras

If you've purchased a car, it may have been the extras, such as the warranty or the interest rate, that clinched the deal for you. What are the "extras" you can offer an employer?

- Are you willing to travel? To work overtime?
- Consider offering to take classes or attend training to pick up a skill that would be useful to the employer.
- You might offer to work on contract, as a temp through an employment agency, or as an intern. Working arrangements like these involve less risk on the part of the employer and give both of you an opportunity to test the match between you and the position.

Taylor has come a long way in developing the all-important value proposition that he is hoping employers will buy. He has identified his best features that will provide benefits for an employer plus the extras he feels will be valuable to firms in his chosen industry— the core, actual, and augmented layers of his personal brand. But Taylor knows that he isn't finished yet. He still needs to develop a plan to communicate the value proposition to prospective customers.

Objective **Summaries** and **Key Terms**

8.1 Objective Summary

Explain how value is derived through different product layers.

Products can be physical goods, services, ideas, people, or places. A good is a *tangible* product, something that we can see, touch, smell, hear, taste, or possess. In contrast, *intangible* products—services, ideas, people, and places—are products that we can't always see, touch, taste, smell, or possess. Marketers think of the product as more than just a thing that comes in a package. They view it as a bundle of attributes that includes the packaging, brand name, benefits, and supporting features in addition to a physical good. The key issue is the marketer's role in creating the value proposition to develop and market products appropriately.

The core product is the basic product category benefits and customized benefit(s) the product provides. The actual product is the physical good or delivered service, including the packaging and brand name. The augmented product includes both the actual product and any supplementary services, such as warranty, credit, delivery, installation, and so on.

Key Terms

attributes
offering
good
core product
actual product
augmented product

8.2 Objective Summary

Describe how marketers classify products.

Marketers generally classify goods and services as either consumer or B2B products. They further classify consumer products according to how long they last and by how they are purchased. Durable goods provide benefits for months or years, whereas nondurable goods are used up quickly or are useful for only a short time. Consumers purchase convenience products frequently with little effort. Customers carefully gather information and compare different brands on their attributes and prices before buying shopping products. Specialty products have unique characteristics that are important to the buyer. Customers have little interest in unsought products until a need arises. Business products are for commercial uses by organizations. Marketers classify business products according to how they are used. For example, equipment might be classified among the following: maintenance, repair, and operating (MRO) products; raw materials; processed materials; specialized services; and component parts.

Key Terms

durable goods
nondurable goods
convenience product
staple products

consumer packaged good (CPG), or fast-moving consumer good (FMCG)
impulse products
geofencing marketing
emergency products
shopping products
specialty products
unsought products
equipment
maintenance, repair, and operating (MRO) products
raw materials
processed materials
specialized services
component parts

8.3 Objective Summary

Understand the importance and types of product innovations.

Innovations are anything consumers perceive to be new. Understanding new products is important to companies because of the fast pace of technological advancement, the high cost to companies of developing new products, and the contributions to society that new products can make. Marketers classify innovations by their degree of newness. A continuous innovation is a modification of an existing product, a dynamically continuous innovation provides a greater change in a product, and a discontinuous innovation is a new product that creates major changes in people's lives.

Key Terms

innovation
creativity
design thinking
ideation
divergent thinking
convergent thinking
continuous innovation
knockoff
dynamically continuous innovation
discontinuous innovation
convergence
disruptive innovation
first-mover advantage

8.4 Objective Summary

Show how firms develop new products.

In new product development, marketers generate product ideas from which product concepts are first developed and then screened. Next, they develop a marketing strategy and conduct a business analysis to estimate the profitability of the new product. Technical development includes planning how the product will be manufactured and may mean obtaining a patent. Next, an actual or a simulated test market may be conducted to assess the effectiveness of the new product in the market. Finally, in the commercialization phase, the product is launched, and the entire marketing plan is implemented.

Key Terms

research and development (R&D)
new product development (NPD)
value co-creation
product concept development and screening
technical success
commercial success
business analysis
technical development
prototypes
market test, or test market
simulated market test
commercialization
crowdfunding

8.5 Objective Summary

Explain the process of product adoption and the diffusion of innovations.

Product adoption is the process by which an individual begins to buy and use a new product, whereas the diffusion of innovations is how a new product spreads throughout a population. The stages in the adoption process are awareness, interest, trial, adoption, and confirmation. To better understand the diffusion process, marketers classify consumers—according to their readiness to adopt new products—as innovators, early adopters, early majority, late majority, and laggards.

Five product characteristics that have an important effect on how quickly (or if) a new product will be adopted by consumers are relative advantage, compatibility, product complexity, trialability, and observability. Similar to individual consumers, organizations differ in their readiness to adopt new products based on characteristics of the organization, of its management, and of the innovation.

Key Terms

product adoption
diffusion
tipping point
adoption pyramid
media blitz
impulse purchase
beta test
bleeding-edge technology
innovators
early adopters
early majority
late majority
laggards
relative advantage
compatibility
complexity
trialability
observability

8.6 Objective Summary

Be prepared to develop your personal value proposition.

Creating your value proposition is about identifying what you have to offer a prospective employer and how you can stand out among all the others competing for an internship or full-time job.

You, like other products, have three layers: you are a highly motivated student with education, interests, and experiences in the area of marketing (*actual product*) who can help your target market (company) increase sales (*core product*), and you can work flexible hours, connect with customers, and relocate for the right job (*augmented product*).

You can add to your product layers through such activities as volunteer work, involvement with campus activities, and establishing a blog. You should talk about your skills, not just list experiences. To enhance your actual product, be sure to make a good first impression and dress in business attire.

Chapter **Questions** and **Activities**

Concepts: Test Your Knowledge

8-1. What is a good? What are the differences between tangible and intangible products?

8-2. Explain what marketers mean by the core product, the actual product, and the augmented product.

8-3. What are the two ways marketers classify products? What is the difference between a durable good and a nondurable good? What are the main differences among convenience, shopping, and specialty products?

8-4. What types of products are bought and sold in B2B markets?

8-5. What is a new product? Why is understanding new products so important to marketers? Innovations are classified according to their degree of newness. What are the different levels of newness used by marketers? Why is it so important for marketers to understand in which category an innovation belongs?

8-6. Explain ideation, divergent thinking, and convergent thinking.

8-7. What is R&D, and what is its importance to marketers and the product development process?

8-8. List and explain the steps marketers undergo to develop new products.

8-9. What is crowdfunding? How does it help products get to market?

8-10. Explain the stages a consumer goes through in the adoption of a new product.

8-11. List and explain the categories of adopters.

8-12. What product factors affect the rate of adoption of innovations?

Activities: Apply What You've Learned

8-13. *Creative Homework/Short Project* Assume that you are a member of the marketing department for a firm that is producing a smart kitchen that will allow all your large and small appliances to communicate with each other, meaning less work for you. In developing this product, you realize that it is important to provide a core product, an actual product, and an augmented product that meets the needs of customers. Develop an outline of how your firm might provide these three product layers in the smart kitchen.

8-14. *In Class, 10–25 Minutes for Teams* Firms go to great lengths to develop new product ideas. Many firms are now using the ideation process, which includes divergent thinking first, followed by convergent thinking. With a group of other students, participate in ideation by first coming up with new product ideas for one of the following (or some other product of your choice):

- A set of golf clubs using the newest technology
- A new flavor potato chip
- A new type of university

   Then, with your class, use convergent thinking to screen the ideas for possible further product development.

8-15. *Creative Homework/Short Project* You are a member of a new product team with your company that has developed a computer that carries a perpetual charge—no plug-in required! You are considering conducting a test market for this new product. Outline the pros and cons for test marketing this product. What are your recommendations?

8-16. *For Further Research (Individual)* Choose an innovative product that has been recently introduced into the marketplace. Research how the product was introduced. Using the adopter categories in the chapter, identify the characteristics of the consumers who you expect would be the innovators for this product. Provide evidence of specific behaviors and characteristics that support the placement of these consumers within that adopter category.

8-17. *For Further Research (Individual)* Take a look at the fast-changing in-home media marketplace. In the past year or so, there have been a number of new alternatives in the market for consumers, including new free streaming services, new subscription streaming services, additional cable channels, and more. These have been added to older options like the Roku and Firestick. First, conduct research to create a list of new services. Using the five characteristics that affect rate of adoption (relative advantage, compatibility, complexity, trialability, and observability), rate each of the new services on these characteristics. Based on this evaluation, which services do you think will be most quickly adopted? Which ones do you think will take the longest to catch on? Which of the innovator services do you feel will fail? Which of our current services will also disappear? Support your answers.

8-18. *For Further Research (Individual)* Sometimes products are massively successful because consumers find a use for them separate from what the developing company initially envisioned. Find two products online that fit this description and identify their initial intended use(s), then what other use(s) consumers found for them, and finally whether companies adjusted their marketing efforts around the products after becoming aware of how consumers were actually using the products.

Concepts: Apply Marketing Metrics

In the chapter, we define creativity and discuss how it relates to innovation. Innovation can be measured in terms of number of successful new products as well as a variety of secondary measures related to those products (e.g., new product launches per year or per employee and success rate versus failure rate—cast on the basis of how the firm defines product success and failure). Innovation is fueled by R&D expenditures, as the chapter notes.

   But what about measuring creativity itself? Some experts have argued that an over focus on metrics can negatively impact creativity.[37] They might argue that the phrase "creativity metric" is an oxymoron. There's always been a right-brain/left-brain argument that to be optimally successful, marketing has to nurture both the creative and the analytical. Has the proliferation of marketing metrics over the past decade squelched essential creativity emanating from the right brain?

8-19. What is your viewpoint about measuring creativity? Do you believe it is more constructive or damaging to organizational innovation? Support your opinions.

8-20. Point out a few well-known organizations that you believe are quite creative. How do you know that they are creative—that is, what specific evidence can you cite that indicates that a high level of creativity is practiced?

Choices: What Do You Think?

8-21. *Critical Thinking* Technology has changed the speed at which new products enter—and leave—the marketplace. What are three products you think technology will impact in the future? How do you see technology changing them? Will this impact how consumers use the product in the future?

8-22. *Critical Thinking* Discontinuous innovations are totally new products—something seldom seen in the marketplace. These innovations are often referred to as *disruptive innovations*. What are some examples of discontinuous innovations introduced in the past 50 years? Why are there so few discontinuous innovations? What products have companies recently introduced that you believe will end up being regarded as discontinuous innovations?

8-23. *Ethics* For several decades, consumer products—everything from vaccines to cosmetics—have been tested on animals. Do you think product testing on animals should be legal or illegal? Does your position change depending on what kind of animal the product is tested on (e.g., a mouse versus a dog)? What are some instances of when it would be acceptable or unacceptable to test products on animals (e.g., medical necessity versus enhancing one's looks)?

8-24. *Ethics* Some companies opt to increase the price of certain types of products when there is an increased need for them—think rain ponchos on a rainy day in a theme park. Because consumers need the product immediately, price and quality are typically irrelevant. Explain the potential positive and negative implications of this practice. Is this practice illegal? Should it be illegal or not?

8-25. *Critical Thinking* Consider the differences in marketing to consumer markets versus business markets. Which aspects of the processes of product adoption and diffusion apply to both markets? Which aspects are unique to one or the other? Provide evidence of your findings.

8-26. *Ethics* In this chapter, we explained that knockoffs are slightly modified copies of original product designs. Should knockoffs be illegal? Who is hurt by knockoffs? Is the marketing of knockoffs good or bad for consumers in the short run? In the long run?

8-27. *Critical Thinking* It is not necessarily true that all new products benefit consumers or society. What are some new products that have made our lives better? What are some new products that have actually been harmful to consumers or to society? Is there a way to monitor or "police" new products that are introduced to the marketplace? What would you recommend?

8-28. *Critical Thinking* The augmented product represents the add-ons—the extras manufacturers add to stand out from the crowd. Think about purchasing a car. As a consumer, what types of supporting features would you require before making your purchase? Do you think these extras could ever make up for a sub-par product?

Miniproject: Learn by Doing

What product characteristics do consumers think are important in a new product? What types of service components do they demand? Most important, how do marketers know how to develop successful new products? This miniproject is designed to let you make some of these decisions as you walk through several steps of the new product development process.

8-29. Develop a presentation that summarizes your efforts for each of the following phases of new product development:

a. Phase 1: Idea generation: Create (in your mind) a new product item that might be of interest to college students such as yourself. Develop a written description and possibly a drawing of this new product. Describe the three layers of the product.

b. Phase 2: Product concept development and screening: Describe what features the product should have and the benefits those features will provide for consumers. Estimate both the technical success and the commercial success of the product.

c. Phase 3: Marketing strategy development: Develop a simple marketing plan that identifies the target market and how you can position the product to meet that market's needs.

Assume now that you have undergone a thorough business analysis (phase 4) and have built a prototype of the product (phase 5).

d. Phase 6: Market test: Describe your product to five other college students, as if you had an actual prototype of the product. What is their overall opinion of the new product? Would they try the product? How could you influence them to buy the product?

e. Phase 7: Commercialization: Based on the information you have collected, determine whether you are ready to launch the product. If not, describe the reasons why.

Marketing in Action **Case**   Real Choices at Nature On Tap

Sometimes innovation is less about invention and more about just noticing what's around you. That's what organic water company Nature On Tap learned when it created its company's flagship product. Product developers there discovered something that consumers considered new and different, even though it had been around for more than a thousand years—tapped birch water.

If you're a frequent purchaser of brands like Dasani or Aquafina, it's probably no surprise to you that bottled water is big business. U.S. per capita consumption of bottled water is now over 44 gallons per year, 7 gallons higher than the amount of carbonated soft drinks we consume. Selling over $34 billion of a ubiquitous product (water) that is readily available almost for free is an impressive marketing feat. Of course, bottled water consumers are not just buying a commodity. They are willing to pay a premium for what they regard as the health benefits they'll get from how the water is filtered and/or sourced.

Enter Nature On Tap with an innovation. For centuries people have tapped the waterlike sap of the birch tree for refreshment and health. According to the University of Maryland Medical Center, the slightly sweet beverage contains a high level of manganese—a quite efficacious mineral that, according to experts, can help to regulate blood sugar, fight "free radicals," and support bone structure through calcium absorption. To add to the value proposition, birch water also contains trace amounts of xylitol, a natural sugar alcohol that the California Dental association says can help prevent tooth decay.

Birch water fits into a product category known as "alternative water," with the category's most famous formula being the very popular coconut water. Sales of that beverage were projected to reach over $4 billion worldwide by 2020. Nature On Tap realized that consumers were looking for that next "superdrink," and the company concluded that birch water was "it," especially given the lower sugar content (and calories) versus coconut water. In addition to the benefit claims noted earlier, birch water also contains *saponin*, which may have anti-inflammatory benefits and can lower cholesterol.

Nature On Tap has taken full advantage of the storytelling opportunities that the nature of its product affords. It readily offers up imagery of the beautiful birch forests of Finland, where farmers tap the trees for a truly unique beverage that is "pure, hydrating, cleansing and straight from the tree." The package is also unique—a cylinder made of 75 percent wood-based paperboard that looks like a portion of a birch tree.

But while Nature On Tap is riding a birch high, the truth is that birch is not the only plant in the forest. Other companies are busily pursuing their own versions of wonder water. Maple, bamboo, olive, artichoke, and even cactus are all vying for a place on water connoisseurs' palates. And closer to home, it has competitors right in the birch water segment, such as Sibberi, Sapp, BelSeva, TreeVitalise, and Treo.

Beyond the growing competitive challenges, Nature On Tap has a unique production and supply chain quirk due to the short two-week window its product can be harvested! This circumstance highlights the criticality of very accurate sales forecasting and precise distribution targets. And like all the products in the category, birch water marketers must deal with often confusing and contradictory claims and counterclaims regarding product benefits. For example, one dietician notes that a cup of oats has about the same amount of manganese as a bottle of birch water and costs about $0.21—far less than the over $3 you're likely to pay for a bottle of Tapped Birch Water.

Nevertheless, as a small player in a niche market, Nature On Tap has a great product story, gets generally positive press, and has built a distribution network that includes leading retailers such as Sainsbury's in the U.K., Whole Foods, and Amazon. Its ability to excel over competitors and continue to grow will depend on how well it keeps up the product innovation and creative marketing that is the hallmark of its story so far.[38]

Questions for Discussion

8-30. What kind of innovation is Tapped Birch Water—continuous, dynamically continuous, or discontinuous? Why?

8-31. What other innovations should the company pursue to continue growing?

8-32. Perhaps you, like many consumers, may have just become aware of tapped birch water. What could the company do to move consumers higher in the adoption pyramid?

Chapter **Notes**

1. Woodstream Corp., www.victorpest.com (accessed April 11, 2016).

2. Lexy Savvides and Vanessa Hand Orellana, "Apple Music vs. Spotify: The Best Music Streaming Service for You," August 3, 2020, *CNET*, https://www.cnet.com/news/spotify-vs-apple-music-choosing-the-best-music-streaming-service-in-2020/ (accessed June 30, 2020).

3. https://www.apple.com/tv

4. https://discussions.apple.com/welcome

5. Brian Sozzi, "Coronavirus Outbreak May Have Unleashed Panic Buying of Hostess Twinkies and Ding Dongs," *Yahoo! Finance*, March 5, 2020, https://finance.yahoo.com/news/coronavirus-outbreak-may-have-unleashed-panic-buying-of-hostess-twinkies-and-ding-dongs-210034011.html (accessed June 29, 2020).

6. Barry Berman, "Planning and Implementing Effective Mobile Marketing Programs," *Business Horizons* 59, no. 4 (2016): 431–39. https://doi:10.1016/j.bushor.2016.03.006.

7. https://luckydogcuisine.com/

8. Michael D. Mumford, "Where Have We Been, Where Are We Going? Taking Stock in Creativity Research," *Creativity Research Journal* 15 (2003): 107–20; Robert J. Sternberg, "Creativity," in *Cognitive Psychology* (6 ed.) (Cengage Learning, 2011), 479.

9. Linda Naiman, "Design Thinking as a Strategy for Innovation," *Creativity at Work*, https://www.creativityatwork.com/design-thinking-strategy-for-innovation/ (accessed April 12, 2018).

10. "Design Thinking: Solve Complex Problems Using an Iterative, Experimental, Human-Centered Approach that Rapidly Delivers Value," *ecity interactive*, https://design.ecityinteractive.com/ (accessed July 7, 2020).

11. Dominic Preston, "The Best Language Learning Apps," *TechAdvisor*, February 19, 2018, https://www.techadvisor.co.uk/feature/software/bestlanguage-learning-apps-3655778/ (accessed April 2, 2018).

12. Emily Price, "15 Best Travel Apps for Your Next Trip," *CNN*, November 20, 2017, https://www.cnn.com/travel/article/best-travel-apps/index.html (accessed April 2, 2018); https://www.charmin.com/en-us/about-us/sitorsquat

13. Apple Inc., "iPod + iTunes Timeline," https://www.apple.com/pr/products/ipodhistory (accessed April 11, 2016); "iPod Q&A," http://www.everymac.com/systems/apple/ipod/ipod-faq/how-many-songs-does-ipod-hold-capacity.html (accessed April 11, 2016).

14. https://www.apple.com/ipod-touch/

15. https://www.indeed.com/

16. "6 Projects Qualify for the Second 2017 LEGO Ideas Review," LEGO Ideas, September 4, 2017, https://ideas.lego.com/blogs/a4ae09b6-0d4c-4307-9da8-3ee9f3d368d6/post/0d0f90c2-71d4-421e-8765-e7ea5f141f7f (accessed April 10, 2018); "15 LEGO Sets That Started as LEGO Ideas," Den of Geek, http://www.denofgeek.com/us/imported-articles/lego/265552/15-lego-sets-that-started-as-lego-ideas (accessed April 10, 2018); Afdel Azis, "Lego Donates $50 Million to Support Families during COVID-19," *Forbes*, April 15, 2020, https://www.forbes.com/sites/afdhelaziz/2020/04/15/lego-donates-50-million-to-support-families-during-covid19/#18b644925794 (accessed July 1, 2020).

17. Anita Li, "Smartphone-Controlled Toilet Features Remote Lid, Speakers, App," *Mashable*, December 15, 2012, https://mashable.com/2012/12/15/smartphone-controlled-toilet/?utm_source=feedburner&utm_medium=email&utm_campaign=Feed%3A+Mashable+%28Mashable%29#hhvMklnHAZqp (accessed April 29, 2016).

18. goTenna, "How It Works," http://www.gotenna.com/pages/how-it-works (accessed April 9, 2016); "goTenna Releases goTenna Pro X, an Open Platform, Interoperable, Tactical Mesh Networking Device," *CISION PR Newswire*, March 28, 2019, https://www.prnewswire.com/news-releases/gotenna-releases-gotenna-pro-x-an-open-platform-interoperable-tactical-mesh-networking-device-300819940.html (accessed July 2, 2020).

19. "5 Ways How 3D Printing Takes Marketing to a New Level," *Drupa*, September 29, 2017, https://blog.drupa.com/en/5-ways-how-3dprinting-takes-marketing-to-a-new-level-2/ (accessed April 16, 2018).

20. "3D Printing Makes Great Products Better," *Javelin*, www.javelin-tech.com/3d-printer/industry/consumer-goods/ (accessed April 16, 2018).

21. M. Shahbandeh, "Sales of Leading Mouthwash/Dental Rinse Brands in the United States in 2018," *Statista*, February 21, 2020, https://www.statista.com/statistics/195543/sales-of-leading-us-mouthwash-brands-in-2012-and-2013/ (accessed July 7, 2020).

22. Matt Fleck, "Crowdfunding in the Time of COVID-19," *Indiegogo Blog*, April 2, 2020, https://go.indiegogo.com/blog/2020/04/crowdfunding-time-of-covid19.html (accessed July 3, 2020).

23. Brad Stone, "Analysts Ask if the iPad Can Live Up to Its Hype," *The New York Times*, March 28, 2010, https://www.nytimes.com/2010/03/29/technology/29apple.html (accessed April 11, 2016).

24. Malcolm Gladwell, *The Tipping Point* (Newport Beach, CA: Back Bay Books, 2002).

25. Michael R. Solomon, "Mindfulness: Tropicana Shows Us It's Not Just for Breakfast Any More," *Forbes*, January 17, 2020, https://www.forbes.com/sites/michaelrsolomon/2020/01/17/mindfulness-tropicana-shows-us-its-not-just-for-breakfast-anymore/#4547449275dd (accessed July 8, 2020).

26. "Apple Introduces New 9.7-inch iPad with Apple Pencil Support," Apple Newsroom, March 27, 2018, https://www.apple.com/newsroom/2018/03/apple-introduces-new-9-7-inch-ipad-with-apple-pencil-support/ (accessed April 10, 2018).

27. Taylor Bloom, "Multiple Players at the Masters Are Using Clubs Designed by Boeing," *SportTechie*, April 9, 2016, http://www.sporttechie.com/2016/04/09/multiple-players-at-the-masters-are-using-clubs-designed-by-boeing (accessed April 9, 2016).

28. Melanie Aman, "26 Impulse Buys That Were Totally Worth It According to Reviewers," *BuzzFeed*, June 1, 2020, https://www.buzzfeed.com/melanie_aman/impulse-buys-that-were-totally-worth-it-according-to (accessed July 7, 2020).

29. "Because I Can: Diet Coke Launches Campaign to Support Rebrand in North America," January 26, 2018, http://www.coca-colacompany.com/stories/diet-coke-because-i-can- (accessed April 8, 2018).

30. Everett Rogers, *Diffusion of Innovations* (New York: Free Press, 1983), 247–51.

31. Techopedia, "Bleeding Edge," https://www.techopedia.com/definition/23222/bleeding-edge (accessed April 11, 2016).

32. "Wi-Fi's Big Brother," *Economist*, March 13, 2004, 65; William J. Gurley, "Why Wi-Fi Is the Next Big Thing," *Fortune*, March 5, 2001, 184; Joshua Quittner, "Cordless Capers," *Time*, May 1, 2000, 85; Scott Van Camp, "Intel Switches Centrino's Gears," *Brandweek*, April 26, 2004, 16; Benny Evangelista, "SBC Park a Hot Spot for Fans Lugging Laptops," *San Francisco Chronicle*, April 26, 2004, A1; Todd Wallack, "Santa Clara Ready for Wireless," *San Francisco Chronicle*, April 19, 2004, D1; Glenn Fleishman, "Three Essays on Muni-Fi You Should Read," https://wifinetnews.com/archives/2008/05/three_essays_on_muni-fi_you_should_read.html (accessed December 21, 2020).

33. Geoffrey James, "The 21 Worst Product Flops of All Time," *Inc.*, April 7, 2016, https://www.inc.com/geoffrey-james/the-21-worst-product-flops-of-all-time.html (accessed April 3, 2018).

34. "Top 10 Failed Products," www.smashinglists.com/top-10-failed-products/2 (accessed April 11, 2016).

35. Market Watch, "12 Worst American Product Flops," April 10, 2015, http://www.marketwatch.com/story/12-worst-american-product-flops-2015-04-10 (accessed April 9, 2016); Jenny N. Zhang, "Believe It or Not, Bud Light's New Bubbly Water Isn't Just Bud Light," *EATER*, November 7, 2019, https://www.eater.com/2019/11/7/20953335/bud-light-seltzer-hard-spiked-seltzer-anheuser-busch (accessed July 9, 2020).

36. Rogers, *Diffusion of Innovations*, chap. 6.

37. Patrick Sarkissian, "Why Metrics Are Killing Creativity in Advertising," March 10, 2010, https://adage.com/article/guest-columnists/viewpoint-metrics-killing-creativity-advertising/142600 (accessed April 11, 2016).

38. Based on: Seánan Forbes, "This Energizing Drink Has Half the Calories of Coconut Water and More B Vitamins Than Green Juice," *Prevention*, February 23, 2017, https://www.prevention.com/food-nutrition/g20508414/energizing-drink/; International Bottled Water Association, "Bottled Water's Retail Dollar Sales Increased 5.2 Percent from 2018 to 2019, Beverage Marketing Corporation Data Indicates," Vending Marketwatch, May 26, 2020, https://www.vendingmarketwatch.com/coffee-service/water-equipment-coolers-filters-accessories-etc/news/21139681/bottled-waters-retail-dollar-sales-increased-52-percent-from-2018-to-2019-beverage-marketing-corporation-data-indicates; Kay Taylor, "People Are Drinking Less Pepsi and Coke Than Ever – And It Reveals the Power of the 'Biggest Marketing Track of the Century,'" *Business Insider*, May 7, 2018, http://www.businessinsider.com/pepsi-coke-decline-while-bottled-water-grows-2018-5; Jeremy Mikula, "Should You Be Drinking Birch Water?," *Chicago Tribune*, April 6, 2017, http://www.chicagotribune.com/lifestyles/health/sc-birch-water-health-0503-20170406-story.html; Caroline McGuire, "Forget Coconut Water – BIRCH Water Is the Craze Everyone Will Be Obsessed with in 2015: The Detoxing Super-Liquid Is Even Supposed to Even Reduce Cellulite!," *Daily Mail*, November 10, 2014, http://www.dailymail.co.uk/femail/article-2828686/Forget-coconut-water-BIRCH-water-craze-obsessed-2015-detoxing-super-liquid-reduce-cellulite.html; Rebecca Seal, "Birch Water: Big Business?" *Financial Times*, June 10, 2016, https://www.ft.com/content/8590acdc-2dc8-11e6-a18d-a96ab29e3c95; Paul Lederer, "TAPPED - How to Tap Birch Tree Vimeo 03 05 17," YouTube, May 19, 2017, https://www.youtube.com/watch?v=3Sjud7tgSDw; Richard Baird, "New Packaging for Tapped Birch Water by Horse, United Kingdom" BP&O, October 27, 2015, http://bpando.org/2015/10/27/package-design-tapped-birch-water/; Kiran Pulidindi and Hemant Pandey, "Plant Based Waters Market Size Will Exceed $10bn by 2024," *Global Market Insights*, June 5, 2017, https://www.gminsights.com/pressrelease/plant-based-waters-market; Christopher Rich, "Impact of COVID-19 on Global Birch Water Market Share, Size, Revenue (2020-2019)," *Best News Monitoring*, July 17, 2020, https://bestnewsmonitoring.com/global-birch-water-market-report/; "100% Pure Organic Birch Water (12x250ml) — TAPPED," http://www.tappedtrees.com/shop/12-x-organic-birch-water (accessed July 27, 2020); Laura Hill, "Birch Water Brand Tapped Looks to Asia to Expand Global Presence," *Welltodo Global Wellness News*, January 8, 2018, https://www.welltodoglobal.com/birch-water-brand-tapped-looks-asia-expand-global-presence/; TÅPPED Organic Birch Water (12 x 250ml). Amazon.com, https://www.amazon.co.uk/Birch-Water-case-of-12/dp/B01MTC3EPD (accessed July 27, 2020).

9 Product II: Product Strategy, Branding, and Product Management

Meet Aaron Keller

▼ A Decision Maker at Capsule

Aaron Keller is the cofounder of Capsule, a brand consultancy built on a design-thinking platform. This means the agency starts with deep empathy for the people who will use the products and then finds ways to optimize the intersections between brand and individual. His background includes working with clients to solve complex design challenges, identifying new revenue opportunities, and rebuilding lagging brands. Aaron spent his undergraduate years at the University of St. Thomas, obtained a graduate degree at the Carlson School of Management, and developed a specialty in retail while at the University of Manchester, England. Capsule's clients include Patagonia, Herman Miller, Target, Panda Express, Craftsman, SmartWool, Medtronic, Red Wing Shoes, 3M, General Mills, Jack Daniels, Fisher-Price, Mattel, and Leatherman Tools. Aaron is the author of three books, two in a series called *Design Matters*, and he recently co-authored *The Physics of Brand*.

Aaron's Info

What I do when I'm not working:
Most of my time outside of work I spend with my family, hiking, biking, and going on trips around the world. We also spend a substantial amount of time on a nonprofit my daughter founded called Read Indeed (readindeed.org), sorting books, planning, and putting on fundraising events. When I'm not with my immediate family, I'm with my biking family, road biking across Iowa or biking from Colorado to Utah on a ride with friends from SmartWool.

First job out of school:
I went from an internship in marketing at my father's engineering firm to a full-time job at Yamamoto Moss. They're a Minneapolis-based brand strategy and design firm where I cut my teeth and learned the real-world business of a design consulting firm.

Career high:
There are three, tied for first in my career. Working with Patagonia twice on substantial projects is one. Writing and publishing our third book, *The Physics of Brand*, is the second. And surviving the near destruction of our firm due to the departure of a partner in the first year of business.

A job-related mistake I wish I hadn't made:
There are so many, it is hard to count. We founded our firm with three partners, but only two remain. The third partner was a mistake in some ways, but this also taught us some valuable lessons. We are the firm we are today because of this third partner.

Here's my problem...

Real **People**, Real **Choices**

Patagonia as a brand is iconic, but like any other business, they need to be sustainable in revenue and in their relationship with the planet. Their sales of base layer (long underwear) items were facing a challenging competitive environment. In these situations, every element of a brand has to pull its weight in order to convince shoppers to give it a chance. True to its mission, Patagonia's packaging was regarded as the most sustainable—it consisted of two rubber bands wrapped around a sushi-rolled product and a large hang tag. Despite the package design's small environmental footprint, Aaron felt that the design might be a candidate for revamping in order to make more of an impact at the point-of-purchase.

about others touching their undergarments. This choice would also mean minimal investment and likely a small improvement to sales because it would be easier to ship the products to stores as they would come in standard sizes. And the poly bags Patagonia used to ship its current packages all over the world would be removed from the cycle, and that alone would be an environmental win. On the other hand, Patagonia takes a leadership position in much of the corporate culture, so this would be in contrast to that natural behavior.

Aaron considered his options 1·2·3

1 Option

Ignore the problem. Keep using the minimal packaging that was designed by Patagonia's founder Yvon Chouinard and had been widely acknowledged in a variety of media as a standard for environmentally responsible packaging. The client could continue to stay true to its mission of sustainability, while it saved the money required to change out its packaging. However, sales of the products within the packages would probably continue to decline over time.

2 Option

Redesign the packaging to be like everyone else. Create a box with a drawer because this format is standard across much of the base layer category. In fact, Patagonia had already sold these products in boxes in Germany because shoppers there were finicky

3 Option

Conduct a complete redesign of the structure, packaging graphics, and display of the product line. This would be the riskiest option because it would force the client to revamp its distribution system in order to ship the new packages efficiently. It also wasn't clear if the company's founder and the client's internal teams would approve such a radical change. However, this option would also offer the greatest potential upside for the brand because it would remain environmentally friendly but create a greater impact on store shelves.

Now, put yourself in Aaron's shoes. Which option would you choose, and why?

You Choose

Which **Option** would you choose, and **why**?
☐ Option 1   ☐ Option 2   ☐ Option 3

9.1 Product Planning: Develop Product Objectives and Product Strategy

OBJECTIVE
Discuss the product objectives and strategies a firm may choose.

What makes one product fail and another succeed? It's worth reemphasizing what you learned in Chapter 3: *Firms that plan well succeed.* Product planning plays a big role in the firm's *market planning.* And among the famous four Ps of the marketing mix, each P is not created equal—that is, the best pricing, promotion, and physical distribution strategies cannot overcome fundamental problems with the product over the long run! Hence, product planning takes on special significance in marketing.

Figure 9.1 *Process* | Steps to Manage Products

Effective product strategies come from a series of orderly steps.

```
┌─────────────────────────────────────┐
│      Develop Product Objectives     │
│  • For individual products          │
│  • For product lines and mixes      │
└─────────────────────────────────────┘
                  │
                  ▼
┌─────────────────────────────────────┐
│      Design Product Strategies      │
└─────────────────────────────────────┘
                  │
                  ▼
┌─────────────────────────────────────┐
│   Make Tactical Product Decisions   │
│  • Product branding                 │
│  • Packaging and labeling design    │
└─────────────────────────────────────┘
                  │
                  ▼
┌─────────────────────────────────────┐
│   Organize for Product Management   │
└─────────────────────────────────────┘
```

product management
The systematic and usually team-based approach to coordinating all aspects of a product's strategy development and execution.

product objectives
The direction and focus that marketers establish for their products, which ultimately support the broader marketing objectives of the business unit and are consistent with the firm's overall mission.

Strategies outlined within the product specify how the firm expects to develop a value proposition that will meet marketing objectives. Product planning is guided by the continual process of **product management**, which is the systematic and usually team-based approach to coordinating all aspects of a product's strategy development and execution. In some companies, product management is sometimes also called *brand management*, and the terms refer to essentially the same thing. The organization members who coordinate these processes are called *product managers* or *brand managers*. The essential difference between the two is that brand managers focus on creating a company brand around a product, while product managers aim to develop and market new goods and services. Both are interested in the opinions of buyers, but the focus of the opinion is different for each. We discuss the role of these individuals in more detail later in the chapter.

As more and more competitors enter the global marketplace and as technology moves forward at an ever-increasing pace, firms create products that grow, mature, and then decline at faster and faster speeds. Our discussion in Chapter 3 of agility and agile marketing underscores that smart and agile product management strategies are more critical than ever. Marketers just don't have the luxury of trying one thing, finding out it doesn't work, and then trying the next thing; they have to multitask when it comes to product management, and product managers should be an integral part of the Scrum process you saw in Chapter 3!

In Chapter 8, we talked about how marketers think about products—both core and augmented—and about how companies develop and introduce new products. In this chapter, we finish the product part of the story as we see how companies manage products, and then we examine the steps in product planning, shown in Figure 9.1. These steps include developing product objectives and the related strategies required to successfully market products as they evolve from "newbies" to tried-and-true favorites—and in some cases, finding new markets for these favorites. Next, we discuss branding and packaging, two of the more important tactical decisions product planners make. Finally, we examine how firms organize for effective product management. Let's start with an overview of how firms develop product-related objectives.

Getting Product Objectives Right

When marketers develop product strategies, they make decisions about product benefits, features, styling, branding, labeling, and packaging. But what do they want to accomplish? Clearly stated **product objectives** provide focus and direction. They should support the broader marketing objectives of the business unit in addition to being consistent with the firm's overall mission. For example, the objectives of the firm may focus on return on investment (ROI). Marketing objectives then may concentrate on building market share or the unit or dollar sales volume necessary to attain that ROI. Product objectives need to specify how product decisions will contribute to reaching a desired market share or level of sales.

Remember back in Chapter 5 when we talked about SMART goals—that is, goals that are specific, measurable, attainable, realistic, and timely. What distinguishes goals from objectives is mainly the timeframe (goals tend to be longer term), the level of concreteness (objectives tend to be more micro-level), and the impact they have on an organization (goals have a more lasting impact). To be effective, product objectives must meet the SMART criteria! Consider, for example, how Amy's, a popular organic and health-conscious frozen ethnic entrée manufacturer, might state its product objectives:

- "In the upcoming fiscal year, reduce the fat and calorie content of our products by 15 percent to satisfy consumers' health concerns."
- "Introduce three new products this quarter to the product line to take advantage of increased consumer interest in Mexican foods."

- "During the coming fiscal year, improve the pasta entrées to the extent that consumers will rate them better tasting than the competition."

Embedded within these bullets, the marketer has ensured that each element of SMART is addressed.

Planners must keep in touch with their customers so that their objectives accurately respond to their needs. In Chapter 2, we introduced you to the idea of *competitive intelligence*, and an up-to-date knowledge of competitive product innovations is important to develop product objectives. Above all, these objectives should consider the *long-term implications* of product decisions. Planners who sacrifice the long-term health of the firm to reach short-term sales or financial goals choose a risky course. Product planners may focus on one or more individual products at a time, or they may look at a group of product offerings as a whole. Next, we briefly examine both of these approaches. We also look at one important product objective: product quality.

Objectives and Strategies for Individual Products

Everybody loves the MINI Cooper (anything small is cute, right?). But it wasn't just luck or happenstance that turned this product into a global sensation. Just how do you launch a new car that's only 151–158 inches long (depending on the model) and makes people smile when they see it? Its parent company, BMW, succeeded by deliberately but gently poking fun at the MINI Cooper's small size from the beginning of the brand. The original launch of the MINI Cooper included bolting the MINI onto the top of a Ford Excursion with a sign reading, "What are you doing for fun this weekend?" BMW also mocked up full-size MINIs to look like coin-operated kiddie rides you find outside grocery stores with a sign proclaiming, "Rides $16,850. Quarters only." The advertising generated buzz in the 20- to 34-year-old target market, and today the MINI is no joke.

As a smaller brand, the MINI never had a huge advertising budget—in fact, it was the first new car in modern times in which the initial launch didn't include TV advertising. Instead, the MINI launched with print, outdoor billboards, and online ads. And of course, it has an active and ongoing social media presence. This is because the objective wasn't a traditional heavy-handed car launch that beats prospects over the head with massive TV ads; rather, BMW envisioned a "discovery process" by which target consumers would find out about the brand on their own and fall in love with it. They used *brand storytelling* to its fullest potential (watch for a discussion of this concept a little later in this chapter). Ads promoted "motoring" instead of driving, and magazine inserts included MINI-shaped air fresheners and

MINI Cooper makes a virtue of its small size.

pullout games. *Wired* magazine even ran a cardboard foldout of the MINI suggesting that readers assemble and drive it around their desks making "putt-putt" noises. *Playboy* came up with the idea of a six-page MINI "centerfold" complete with the car's vital statistics and hobbies. By the end of its first year on the market, the MINI was rated the second-most memorable new product of the year!

As with the MINI, product strategies often focus on a single new product. (As an interesting sidebar, the original MINI was 142 inches long, but enough customers complained about the cramped quarters in the MINI's backseat—it is, after all, a "mini"—that BMW acquiesced and introduced a "larger MINI." Now that's an oxymoron—something like a "jumbo shrimp"!)[1] Strategies for individual products may be quite different, depending on the situation: new products, regional products, mature products, or other differences. For new products, not surprisingly, the objectives relate heavily to producing a very successful introduction.

Figure 9.2 *Process* | Objectives for Single and Multiple Products

Product objectives provide focus and direction for product strategies. Objectives can focus on a single product or a group of products.

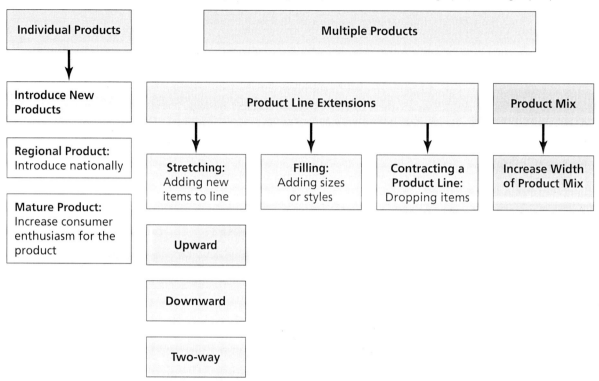

After a firm experiences success with a product in a local or regional market, it may decide to introduce it nationally. Chick-fil-A opened its doors in Atlanta in 1967 and slowly became a regional player in the quick-service restaurant industry across the Southeast. Fast-forward to today, the company is ranked #3 in sales among all U.S. restaurant chains with over 2,400 restaurants in 47 of the 50 states and Washington, D.C., and it is consistently rated #1 in customer satisfaction scores in quick service.[2]

For mature products, like Oreo (dating back to 1912), product objectives may be focused on how to leverage the brand to develop new varieties of the product that appeal to changing consumer tastes. Oreo regularly introduces limited edition flavors, like Chocolate Marshmallow and Caramel Coconut.[3] And after months of speculation and a $50,000 contest to guess the flavor, Oreo finally revealed its new mystery flavor: ta-da . . . .Churro Oreos![4]

Objectives and Strategies for Multiple Products

Although a small firm might get away with a focus on one product, larger firms often sell a set of related products. This means that strategic decisions affect two or more products simultaneously. In this situation, the firm must think in terms of its entire portfolio of products. As Figure 9.2 shows, product planning means developing *product line* and *product mix* strategies to encompass multiple offerings.

product line
A firm's total product offering designed to satisfy a single need or desire of target customers.

A **product line** is a firm's total product offering to satisfy a group of target customers. For example, as we saw in Chapter 4, Campbell's Soup offers several different brands to satisfy different consumer tastes and needs. One is Campbell's Slow Kettle soup, which is positioned as a more luxurious experience for more discerning consumers. Slow Kettle is preservative-free, features creative combinations of ingredients, and employs a slow simmer method of cooking to draw out each soup's unique flavor. On the other hand, Campbell's Soup on the Go is positioned as a quick snack for those with limited time to eat. Soup on the Go features simple soups packaged in a cup that is microwavable for heating, easy to grip with one hand, and consumed by tilting the container in the same way one would do with a can of soda.

The **product line length** is determined by the number of separate items within the same category—in Campbell's case, a total of nine brands each with multiple **stock-keeping units (SKUs)**. A SKU is a unique identifier for each distinct product. Hence, for Campbell's Soup on the Go, each SKU would represent a unique item within the brand, which, in this case, would be each of the different soup recipes sold under that brand.[5]

In terms of product line strategies, two primary approaches are used. A **full-line product strategy** targets many customer segments to boost sales potential. In contrast, a **limited-line product strategy**, with fewer product variations, can improve the firm's image if consumers perceive it as a specialist with a clear, specific position in the market. A great example is Rolls-Royce Motor Cars, which BMW also owns (how about that—from MINI Coopers to Rolls—quite a stable of brands!). Rolls-Royce makes expensive, handcrafted cars built to each customer's exact specifications and for decades maintained a unique position in the automobile industry. Every Rolls Phantom that rolls out the factory door is truly a unique work of art.[6]

In a **product line extension**, organizations create a strategy to expand a particular product line by adding more brands or models. Procter & Gamble acquired Merck's KGaA consumer health products unit to add vitamin and food supplements to P&G's existing portfolio of over-the-counter pharmacy items and thus take advantage of the growth of nonprescription home remedy sales. The product line extension was touted in the business press as a coup for P&G that gave them control of new brands in a lucrative market.[7]

When a firm decides to extend its product line, it must decide on the best direction to go—which usually means either stretching the line upward or downward in price. If a firm's current product line includes middle- and lower-end items, an **upward product line stretch** adds new items—higher-priced entrants that claim better quality or offer more bells and whistles.

Over the last decade, Kia has been working to stretch its low-priced product line upward with new brand-building activities and a new luxury car in part because of rival Hyundai's success with its Genesis model. Toward that objective, Kia launched its luxury K900, positioning it between the BMW 5-Series (at about $50,000) and the BMW 7-Series (at ... ... ucts in the mid-to-low priced category to offering a high-end product, and the K900 experienced this firsthand in the few years since it was launched. Lower-than-expected sales motivated Kia to cut the manufacturer's suggested retail price (MSRP) of the Premium trim version of the car (one tier below the Luxury trim version initially launched) down to $50,900 by 2018.[9] To date, Kia has not experienced anything close to the success at the high end as has Hyundai's Genesis, which is now branded as simply Genesis similarly to the way Toyota brands Lexus separately from Toyota in order to better target luxury car buyers (since the core brands of Hyundai and Toyota are not associated with the luxury market).

Conversely, a **downward product line stretch** augments a line when it adds new items at the lower-priced end. Here, the firm must take care not to blur the images of its higher-priced, upper-end offerings. Rolex, for example, most likely will not want to run the risk of cheapening its image with a new watch line to compete with Timex or Swatch. In some cases, a firm may come to the realization that its current target market is too small. In this case, the product strategy may call for a **two-way product line stretch** that adds products at both the upper- and lower-priced ends, a potentially very tricky strategy to execute successfully.

A **filling-out product strategy** adds sizes or styles not previously available in a product category. Mars Candy did this when it introduced Reese's Minis as a knockoff of its already crazy-popular full-sized product. In other cases, the best strategy may actually be to reduce the size of a product line, particularly when some of the items are not profitable and the complexity of managing them becomes detrimental to the company. Nestlé

---

product line length
Determined by the number of separate items within the same category.

stock-keeping unit (SKU)
A unique identifier for each distinct product.

full-line product strategy
A product line strategy that targets many customer segments to boost sales potential.

limited-line product strategy
A product line strategy that has fewer product variations in order to send a signal of exclusivity or specialization to the market.

product line extension
A strategy to expand an existing product line by adding more brands or models.

upward product line stretch
A product line extension strategy that adds new items toward the higher-priced end of the market.

downward product line stretch
A product line extension strategy that adds new items toward the lower-priced end of the market.

two-way product line stretch
A product line extension strategy that simultaneously expands new items both toward the higher and lower ends of the market.

filling-out product strategy
A strategy to add sizes or styles not previously available in a product category.

agreed to sell its candy business to Ferrero, maker of Nutella, for $2.8 billion. Included in the deal were chocolate favorites such as Baby Ruth, Butterfinger, and Raisinets. Nestlé's goal in divesting its candy business was to reorient the company toward healthier—and more profitable—food options in markets with greater projected growth than candy.[10]

We've seen that there are many ways a firm can modify its product line to meet the competition or take advantage of new opportunities. To further explore these product strategy decisions, let's stick with the P&G theme and return to the "glamorous" world of dish detergents. By the way, P&G basically invented the product management system that is widely used in firms around the world, so it's certainly fitting to focus on this giant consumer products company. What does P&G do if the objective is to increase market share? One possibility would be to expand its line of liquid dish detergents—as the company did with its move to expand Gain's popularity from laundry soap to dishwashing liquid. If the line extension meets a perceived consumer need the company doesn't currently address, this would be a good strategic objective. Gain brought a bevy of laundry loyalists into its new category in dishes, making for a great base of business on which to build.

But whenever a manufacturer extends a product line or a product family, there is risk of **cannibalization**. This occurs when the new item eats up sales of an existing brand as the firm's current customers simply switch to the new product. That may explain why P&G's Gain dishwashing positioning is all about the unique Gain scent. For Gain Flings (basically the Gain equivalent of Tide Pods), the message to consumers is "get 50 percent more of that original Gain scent you love—it's music to your nose!"

Product Mix Strategies

A firm's **product mix** describes its entire range of products. When they develop a product mix strategy, marketers usually consider the product mix width, which is the number of different product lines the firm produces. If it develops several different product lines, a firm reduces the risk of putting all its eggs in one basket. Normally, firms develop a mix of product lines that have some things in common.

Beer is a great product to consider when we think about product mix strategies. It's a fragmented industry in the U.S., and several major players account for huge market share. A smaller craft brewer might control almost 5 percent of U.S. sales. But even with that massive volume, A-B InBev is always on the lookout for new beverage products to add to its mix. And given the rise in popularity of craft beers, in a controversial move Craft Brew Alliance (maker of the Kona brand) actively courted acquisition by A-B InBev. Citing distribution and marketing capabilities as prime drivers, the two firms see the product mix pairing as a happy marriage that benefits both consumers and enhances A-B InBev's product appeal to the growing segment of craft beer drinkers. But craft brew purists always wince a bit when a big global brewery acquires a small brand![11]

Quality as a Product Objective: TQM and Beyond

Product objectives often focus on **product quality**, which is the overall ability of the product to satisfy customer expectations. Quality is tied to how customers *think* a product will perform, not necessarily to some technological level of perfection. That is, for all intents and purposes, perception is reality. Product quality objectives coincide with marketing objectives for higher sales and market share and with the firm's objectives for increased profits.

In 1980, just when the economies of Germany and Japan were finally rebuilt from World War II and were threatening American markets with a flood of new products, an NBC documentary on quality titled *If Japan Can Do It, Why Can't We?* fired a first salvo to the American public—and to American CEOs—to warn that American product quality was

cannibalization
The loss of sales of an existing brand when a new item in a product line or product family is introduced.

product mix
The total set of all products a firm offers for sale.

product mix width
The number of different product lines the firm produces.

product quality
The overall ability of the product to satisfy customer expectations.

becoming inferior to that of other global players.[12] So began the *total quality management (TQM)* revolution in American industry. You learned in Chapter 1 that TQM is a business philosophy that calls for company-wide dedication to the development, maintenance, and continuous improvement of all aspects of the company's operations. Indeed, some of the world's most admired, successful companies—top-of-industry firms such as Nordstrom, 3M, Boeing, and Coca-Cola, to name a few—endorse a total quality focus.

Product quality is one way that marketing adds value to customers. However, TQM as an approach to doing business is far more sophisticated and impactful than simply paying attention to products that roll off the assembly line. TQM firms promote a culture among employees that *everybody* working there serves its customers—even employees who never interact with people outside the firm. In such cases, coworkers are **internal customers**— other employees with whom they interact, and these employees harbor an attitude and belief that providing a high quality of service internally will ultimately have an impact on external customers' experiences with the firm and its offerings. This **internal customer mindset** comprises the following four beliefs: (1) employees who receive my work are my customers, (2) meeting the needs of employees who receive my work is critical to doing a good job, (3) it is important to receive feedback from employees who receive my work, and (4) I focus on the requirements of the person who receives my work.

The bottom line is that TQM maximizes external customer satisfaction by involving all employees, regardless of their function, in efforts to continually improve quality. This results in products that perform better and more fully meet customer needs. For example, TQM firms encourage all employees, even the lowest-paid factory workers, to suggest ways to improve products—and then reward them when they come up with good ideas.

TQM fired the first shot on product quality, and since then many companies around the world look to the uniform standards of the International Organization for Standardization (ISO) for quality guidelines. This Geneva-based organization developed a set of criteria to improve and standardize product quality in Europe. The **ISO 9000** is a broad set of guidelines that establish voluntary standards for quality management. These guidelines ensure that an organization's products conform to the customer's requirements.

ISO subsequently has developed a variety of other standards, including ISO 14000 which concentrates on environmental management, and ISO 22000 on food safety management. Because many countries in the European Union and other European countries prefer suppliers with ISO 9000 and ISO 14000 certification, U.S. companies must comply with these standards to be competitive there.[13]

One way that companies can improve quality is to use the **Six Sigma** method. The term *Six Sigma* comes from the statistical term *sigma*, which is a standard deviation from the mean. Six Sigma refers to six standard deviations from a normal distribution curve. In practical terms, that translates to no more than 3.4 defects per million—getting it right 99.9997 percent of the time. As you can imagine, achieving that level of quality requires a rigorous approach (try it on your term papers—even when you use spell-check!), and that's what Six Sigma offers. The method involves a five-step process called *DMAIC* (define, measure, analyze, improve, and control). The company trains its employees in the method, and as in karate, they progress toward "black belt" status when they successfully complete all the levels of training. Employees can use Six Sigma processes to remove defects from services, not just products. In these cases, a "defect" means failing to meet customer expectations. For example, hospitals use Six Sigma processes to reduce medical errors, and airlines use the system to improve flight scheduling.

It's fine to talk about product quality, but what exactly is it? Figure 9.3 summarizes the many aspects of product quality. In some cases, product quality means durability. For example, athletic shoes shouldn't develop holes after their owner shoots hoops for a few weeks. Reliability also is an important aspect of product quality—-customers want to know that a McDonald's hamburger is going to taste the same at any location. For many

internal customers
Coworkers who interact and harbor the attitude and belief that all activities ultimately impact external customers.

internal customer mindset
An organizational culture in which all organization members treat each other as valued customers.

ISO 9000
Criteria developed by the International Organization for Standardization to regulate product quality in Europe.

Six Sigma
A process whereby firms work to limit product defects to 3.4 per million or fewer.

Figure 9.3 *Snapshot* | Product Quality

Some product objectives focus on quality, which is the ability of a product to satisfy customer expectations—no matter what those expectations are.

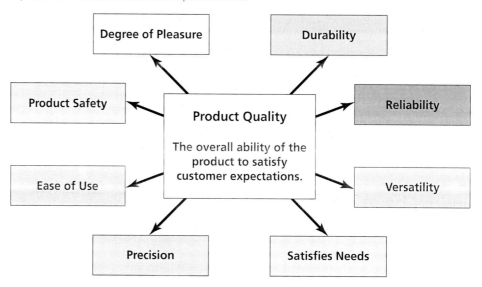

customers, a product's versatility and its ability to satisfy their needs are central to product quality.

For other products, quality means a high degree of precision. For example, purists compare HDTVs in terms of the number of pixels and their refresh rate. Quality, especially in business-to-business (B2B) products, also relates to ease of use, maintenance, and repair. Yet another crucial dimension of quality is product safety. Finally, the quality of products, such as a painting, a movie, or even a wedding gown, relates to the degree of aesthetic pleasure they provide. Of course, evaluations of aesthetic quality differ dramatically among people. To one person, the quality of a mobile device may mean simplicity, ease of use, and a focus on reliability in voice signal, whereas to another, it's the cornucopia of apps and

The 3-D printer has opened the door to a lot of creative product innovation, such as these pint-sized versions of Fiat automobiles.

9.2 Marketing throughout the Product Life Cycle

OBJECTIVE

Understand how firms manage products throughout the product life cycle.

Many products have long lives. Others are "here today, gone tomorrow." The **product life cycle (PLC)** is a useful way to explain how the market's response to a product and marketing activities change over the life of a product. In Chapter 8, we talked about how marketers introduce new products, but the launch is only the beginning. Product marketing strategies must evolve and change as they continue through the product life cycle.

Alas, some brands don't have long to live. We'll bet neither your parents nor grandparents can remember the Rambler car or Evening in Paris perfume (you should look these products up online sometime!). In contrast, other brands seem almost immortal. For example, Coca-Cola has been the number-one cola brand for more than 120 years, General Electric has been the number-one light bulb brand for over a century, and Kleenex has been the number-one tissue brand for more than 80 years.[14] Let's take a look at the stages of the PLC, which Figure 9.4 shows. In addition, Figure 9.5 provides insights on marketing mix strategies throughout each phase of the PLC.

product life cycle (PLC)
A concept that explains how products go through four distinct stages from birth to death: introduction, growth, maturity, and decline.

introduction stage
The first stage of the product life cycle, in which slow growth follows the introduction of a new product in the marketplace.

Introduction Stage

Like people, products are born, they "grow up," and eventually they die. We divide the life of a product into four stages. The first stage we see in Figure 9.4 is the **introduction stage**. Here, customers get the first chance to purchase the good or service. During this early stage, a single company usually produces the product. If it clicks and is profitable, competitors usually follow with their own versions.

During the introduction stage, the goal is to get first-time buyers to try the product. Sales (hopefully) increase at a steady but slow pace. As is also evident in Figure 9.4, the

Some new products struggle to get market acceptance. Google had to withdraw its controversial Glass product due in part to concerns about privacy. The technology is now being adapted to manufacturing contexts, but don't be surprised if it reappears in some form for consumers around the late 2020s.

Figure 9.4 Snapshot | The Product Life Cycle (PLC)

The PLC helps marketers understand how a product changes over its lifetime and suggests how to modify their strategies accordingly.

$ Sales and Profits	Introduction Stage	Growth Stage	Maturity Stage	Decline Stage
	No profits because the company is recovering R&D costs	Profits increase and peak	Sales peak	Market shrinks: Sales fall
				Sales
			Profit margins narrow	Profits fall
				Profits
0				

Time

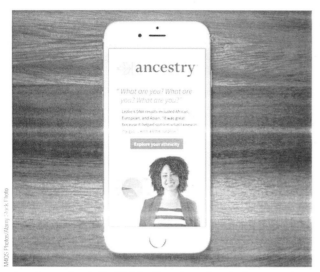

Ancestry.com, founded in 1996, is still growing as they develop new markets and new uses for the app.

company usually does not make a profit during this stage. Why? Research-and-development (R&D) costs and heavy spending for advertising and promotional efforts cut into revenue.

As Figure 9.5 illustrates, during the introduction stage, pricing may be high to recover the R&D costs (demand permitting) or low to attract a large number of consumers. For example, when the popular AncestryDNA direct-to-consumer genealogical test was first launched, the pricing strategy was stable at $99 for several years. Then, as more competitors entered and the newness of the concept began to wear off, occasional promotions brought the price down $10 or so for short periods. Fast-forward to 2020 and beyond. Check out the Zouton aggregator website for Ancestry deals and coupons. Now, every sort of double-digit discount imaginable is available for the consumer. Probably nobody pays "full price" (whatever full price means).[15]

How long does the introduction stage last? As we saw in the microwave oven example in Chapter 8, it can be quite long. A number of factors come into play, including marketplace acceptance and the producer's willingness to support its product during start-up. Sales for hybrid cars started out pretty slowly except for the Prius, but now with broader consumer acceptance of the value of hybrid vehicles and greater levels of sales, hybrids can be considered well past the introduction stage. As of mid-2020, Tesla Model 3 usurped everything else at the top of the introduction quadrant. However, consumer demand was much higher than Tesla's problem-plagued production process could deliver against, raising the specter of a red-hot product introduction fizzling

Figure 9.5 *Snapshot* | Marketing Mix Strategies and Other Characteristics through the Product Life Cycle

Marketing mix strategies (the four Ps) and other characteristics change as a product moves through the life cycle.

Characteristic	Introduction	Growth	Maturity	Decline
Product	Single company produces single product	New competitors enter the market creating new variations of the product	New features added; sales are mostly replacement products	Number of variations reduced
Goals	Get first-time buyers to try the new product	Encourage brand loyalty	Attract new users	Remain profitable; decide whether to keep or phase out product
Sales	Increase at a steady but slow pace	Rapid increase	Peak, then level off, often decline	Continue to decline
Profits	Negative	Increase and peak	Profit margins narrow	Declining
Pricing	High: recover R&D costs Low: attract large numbers of customers	May need to reduce because of increased competition	Price to maintain market share	May reduce if product can remain profitable
Marketing Communication	Informing customers	Heavy advertising to counter new competition	Reminder advertising	Decreased to maintain profitability

before achieving a growth stage unless the production issues could be fully and permanently rectified.[16]

It is important to note that many products *never* make it past the introduction stage. Infamous examples include New Coke (1985—a product that tasted more like Pepsi), RJ Reynolds Smokeless Cigarettes (1989—introductory marketing investment of $325 million), Coors Rocky Mountain Spring Water (1990—a really bad idea for a product line extension), and Orbitz Soda (1999—the bottles, consistency, and flecks suspended in the liquid looked like a Lava Lamp from the '70s).[17] For a new product to succeed, consumers must first know about it. Then, they must believe that it is something they want or need. Marketing during this stage often focuses on informing consumers about the product, how to use it, and its promised benefits.

However, this isn't nearly as easy as it sounds: Would you believe that the most recent data indicate that as many as 95 percent of new products introduced each year fail? Shocking as that number is, it's true. Adding to the litany of previously mentioned product flops, have you ever heard of Apple's Newton PDA? How about Colgate Lasagna or Jack Daniels mustard? Probably not! These product blunders—which must have seemed good to some product manager at the time but sound crazy now—certainly didn't last on shelves very long. Ever heard of Google Glass, a headset that you wear like a pair of glasses? They included a small screen tucked into the upper corner of the frame that kept users constantly plugged in to email, calls, and other notifications. The sky-high price, issues around privacy, and cultural backlash helped the product enter and exit the market quickly. It was likely a product a little ahead of its time—so don't count it out as a **product relaunch** for the future.

Firms occasionally relaunch old or former products using principles of segmentation, target marketing, and positioning to reposition an existing product for reintroduction into the product life cycle. The approach typically involves a change to the product itself or to the way it is marketed in order to make it available as a new product to increase sales. It's noteworthy that the product failure examples above (as are many) were backed by big companies and attached to already well-known brands. Just think of the product introduction risks for start-ups and unknown brands![18]

Growth Stage

In the **growth stage**, sales increase rapidly while profits increase and peak. Marketing's goal here is to encourage brand loyalty by convincing the market that this brand is superior to others. In this stage, marketing strategies may include the introduction of product variations to attract market segments and increase market share. Tablets and smartphones are examples of products that are still in the growth stage, as worldwide sales continue to increase. Continual new product innovations fuel what seems for now to be an endless growth opportunity, and in the U.S., Apple and Samsung command the majority of smartphone revenues. When you look at a pattern of market share from year to year, it looks like a see-saw effect—Apple is up when they introduce a next-gen phone; then Samsung is up when theirs comes out. But between those two, prices have remained quite high and demand very solid. And the way these products are marketed in the U.S. contributes to keeping prices high since sales of data plans are mostly on multi-year contracts.[19]

When competitors appear on the scene, marketers must heavily rely on advertising and other forms of promotion. Price competition may develop, driving profits down. Some firms may seek to capture a particular segment of the market by positioning their product to appeal to a certain group. And, if it initially set the price high, the firm may now reduce it to meet increasing competition. We've seen some of this in the U.S. in recent years in the smartphone space, with several innovative new players entering and also with a few cellular providers bringing more flexibility into their data plans. When will the growth phase for cellular phones be over? Hard to project—but as of now, it looks like solid growth on the horizon.

U.S. Photos/Alamy Stock Photo

Orbitz soda had a swift demise.

product relaunch
Using principles of segmentation, target marketing, and positioning to reposition an existing product for reintroduction into the product life cycle.

growth stage
The second stage in the product life cycle, during which consumers accept the product and sales rapidly increase.

Maturity Stage

The **maturity stage** of the PLC is usually the longest. Sales peak and then begin to level off and even decline while profit margins narrow. Competition gets intense when remaining competitors fight for their share of a shrinking pie. Firms may resort to price reductions and reminder advertising ("Did you brush your teeth today?") to maintain market share.

Because most customers have already accepted the product, they tend to buy to replace a worn-out item or to take advantage of product improvements. For example, almost everyone in the U.S. owns a TV (there are still more homes without indoor toilets than without a TV set), meaning that most people who buy a new set replace an older one—especially when TV stations nationwide stopped using analog signals and began to broadcast exclusively in a digital format. TV manufacturers hope that a lot of the replacements will be sets with the latest-and-greatest new technology—Samsung would love to sell you a smart TV to replace that worn-out basic model. During the maturity stage, firms try to sell their product through as many outlets as possible because availability is crucial in a competitive market. Consumers will not go far to find one particular brand if satisfactory alternatives are close at hand.

To remain competitive and maintain market share during the maturity stage, firms may tinker with the marketing mix to extend this profitable phase for their product. Food manufacturers constantly monitor consumer trends, which of late have been heavily skewed toward healthier eating. This has resulted in all sorts of products that trumpet their low-carb, organic, or no-trans-fat credentials.

Decline Stage

The **decline stage** of the PLC is characterized by a decrease in overall product category sales. The reason may be obsolescence forced by new technology—where (other than in a museum) do you see a typewriter today? See many people using flip phones recently? Although a single firm may still be profitable, the market as a whole begins to shrink, profits decline, there are fewer variations of the product, and suppliers pull out. In this stage, there are usually many competitors, but none has a distinct advantage.

A firm's major product decision in the decline stage is whether to keep the product at all. An unprofitable product drains resources that the firm could use to develop newer products. If the firm decides to keep the product, it may decrease advertising and other marketing communication to cut costs and reduce prices if the product can still remain profitable. If the firm decides to drop the product, it can eliminate it in two ways: (1) phase it out by cutting production in stages and letting existing stocks run out or (2) simply dump the product immediately. If the established market leader anticipates that there will be some residual demand for the product for a long time, it may make sense to keep the product on the market. The idea is to sell a limited quantity of the product with little or no support from sales, merchandising, advertising, and distribution and just let it "wither on the vine."

Here's a question for you: Can a product that has begun the journey downward to decline ever regain momentum and achieve new growth on the PLC? The answer is yes, but it is usually very difficult and requires application of several of the key principles of segmentation, target marketing, and positioning, which you learned about in Chapter 7. There, you read that *repositioning* is a change in positioning strategy in which a company tries to modify its brand image to keep up with changing times. Venerable Listerine (far and away the #1 selling oral hygiene rinse) has gone through multiple repositioning strategies during its lengthy run as a successful product. Named after Joseph Lister, a pioneer of antiseptic surgery, Listerine was developed in 1879 by Joseph Lawrence, a chemist in St. Louis, Missouri. Over its 140-year history it has been marketed first as primarily an all-purpose antiseptic, then a mouth freshener, and then through extensions of the brand to a variety of new products it has expanded its reach to address indications such as gingivitis, cavities, whitening, and sensitivity. While it may be rare to find products that have had as many successful journeys through the PLC as Listerine, this brand's experiences clearly illustrate that with savvy marketing it's definitely possible to get a "new lease on your product life cycle!"[20]

9.3 Branding and Packaging:
Create Product Identity

OBJECTIVE

and packaging strategies contribute to product identity.

Successful marketers keep close tabs on their products' life cycle status, and they plan accordingly. Equally important, though, is to give that product an *identity* and a *personality*. For example, the mere word *Disney* evokes positive emotions around fun, playfulness, family, and casting day-to-day cares out the window. Folks pay a whole lot of money at Disney's theme parks in Florida and California (as well as in France, China, and Japan) to act on those emotions. Disney achieved its strong identity through decades of great branding. Branding along with packaging are extremely important (and expensive) elements of product strategies.

What's in a Name (or a Symbol)?

How do you identify your favorite brand? By its name? By the logo (how the name appears)? By the package? By some graphic image or symbol, such as Nike's swoosh? A **brand** is a name, term, symbol, or any other unique element of a product that identifies one firm's product(s) and sets it apart from the competition. Consumers easily recognize the Coca-Cola logo, the Jolly Green Giant (a *trade character*), and the triangular red Nabisco logo (a *brand mark*) in the corner of the box. Branding provides the recognition factor products need to succeed in regional, national, and international markets.

A brand name is probably the most used and most recognized form of branding. Smart marketers use brand names to maintain relationships with consumers "from the cradle to

Meal and then convert them over time to its more adult Pico Guacamole with Artisan Grilled Chicken (accompanied, they hope, by a Side Salad, Fruit 'N Yogurt Parfait for dessert, and a Turtle Macchiato to drink).

A good brand name may position a product because it conveys a certain image (Ford Mustang, which is now well over 50 years old) or describes how it works (Drano, for your worst-clogged pipes). Brand names such as Caress and Shield help position these different brands of bath soap by saying different things about the benefits they promise. Irish Spring soap provides an unerring image of freshness (can't you just smell it now?). Apple's use of "i-everything" is a brilliant branding strategy because it conveys individuality and personalization—characteristics that millennial buyers prize. And Mr. Clean—well, that about says it all, doesn't it?

How does a firm select a good brand name? Expert brand designers say there are four "easy" tests: *easy to say, easy to spell, easy to read*, and *easy to remember*—like P&G's Swiffer, Tide, Pampers, Bold, Gain, Downy, Bounty, and Crest (P&G is the undisputed branding king of all time). And the name should also pass the "fit test" on four dimensions:

1. Fit the target market
2. Fit the product's benefits
3. Fit the customer's culture
4. Fit legal requirements

brand
A name, term, symbol, or any other unique element of a product that identifies one firm's product(s) and sets it apart from the competition.

When it comes to graphics for a brand symbol, name, or logo, the rule is that it must be recognizable and memorable. No matter how small or large, the triangular Nabisco logo in the corner of the box is a familiar sight. And it should have visual impact. That means that from across a store or when you quickly flip the pages in a magazine, the brand will catch your attention. Apple's apple with the one bite missing never fails to attract.

trademark
The legal term for a brand name, brand mark, or trade character; trademarks legally registered by a government obtain protection for exclusive use in that country.

A **trademark** is the legal term for a brand name, brand mark, or trade character. The symbol for legal registration in the U.S. is a capital "R" in a circle: ®. Marketers register trademarks to make their use by competitors illegal. Because trademark protection applies only in individual countries where the owner registers the brand, unauthorized use of marks on counterfeit products is a huge headache for many companies.

A firm can claim protection for a brand even if it has not legally registered it. In the U.S., *common-law protection* exists if the firm has used the name and established it over a period of time (sort of like a common-law marriage). Although a registered trademark prevents others from using it on a similar product, it may not bar its use for a product in a completely different type of business. Consider the range of unrelated "Quaker" brands: Quaker Oats (cereals), Quaker Funds (mutual funds), Quaker State (motor oil), Quaker Bonnet (gift food baskets), and Quaker Safety Products Corporation (firemen's clothing). A court applied this principle when Apple Corp., the Beatles' music company, sued Apple Inc. in 2006 over its use of the Apple logo. The plaintiff wanted to win an injunction to prevent the technology company from using the Apple logo in connection with its iPod and iTunes products; it argued that the application to music-related products came too close to the Beatles' musical products. The judge didn't agree; instead he ruled that Apple Inc. clearly used the logo to refer to the download service, not to the music itself.[21]

Why Brands Matter

Why do brands matter, you ask? Perhaps the most simple way to put it is this: If brands don't matter, then why not sell everything with simple generic labels? Brands matter because a brand is a lot *more* than just the product it represents—the best brands build an emotional connection with their customers. Think about the most popular diapers—they're branded Pampers and Luvs, not some functionally descriptive name like Absorbency Master or Dry Bottom. The point is that Pampers and Luvs *as brands* evoke the joys of parenting, not the utility of the diaper.

Marketers spend huge amounts of money on new product development, advertising, and promotion to develop strong brands. When they succeed, this investment creates **brand equity**. This term describes a brand's value over and above the value of the generic version of the product. For example, how much extra will you pay for a shirt with the American Eagle Outfitters logo on it than for the same shirt with no logo or, worse, the logo of an "inferior" brand? The difference reflects the eagle's brand equity in your mind.

brand equity
The value of a brand to an organization.

Brand equity means that a brand enjoys customer loyalty because people believe it is superior to the competition. For a firm, brand equity provides a competitive advantage because it gives the brand the power to capture and hold onto a larger share of the market and to sell at prices with higher profit margins. For example, among pianos, the Steinway name has such powerful brand equity that its market share among concert pianists is 95 percent.[22]

Marketers identify different levels of loyalty (or lack thereof) by observing how customers feel about the product. At the lowest level, customers really have no loyalty to a brand, and they will change brands for any reason—often they will jump ship if they find something else at a lower price. At the other extreme, some brands command fierce devotion, and loyal users will go without rather than buy a competing brand.

Escalating levels of attachment to a brand begin when consumers become aware of a brand's existence. Then, they might look at the brand in terms of what it literally does for them or how it performs relative to competitors. Next, they may think more deeply about the product and form beliefs and emotional reactions to it. The truly successful brands, however, are those that truly "bond" with their customers so that people feel they have a real relationship with the product. Here are some of the types of relationships a person might have with a product, each of which is enhanced by the particular branding:

- *Self-concept attachment:* The product helps establish the user's identity. (For example, do you feel better in Ralph Lauren or Cherokee clothing, which is a Walmart staple?)
- *Nostalgic attachment:* The product serves as a link to a past self. Doritos' new Flamin' Hot Nacho flavor scored a major nostalgia coup in 2019's Super Bowl LIII when Chance the Rapper appeared in a commercial with the Backstreet Boys. The connection? "I want it that way" of course. The new flavor created its own campaign called #NowItsHot.[23]
- *Interdependence:* The product is a part of the user's daily routine. (Could you get through the day without a Starbucks coffee?)
- *Love:* The product elicits emotional bonds of warmth, passion, or other strong emotion. (Hershey's Kiss, anyone?)[24]

Ultimately, the way to build strong brands is to forge strong bonds with customers—bonds based on **brand meaning**. This concept encompasses the beliefs and associations that a consumer has about the brand. In many ways, the practice of brand management revolves around the management of meanings. Brand managers, advertising agencies, package designers, name consultants, logo developers, and public relations firms are just some of the collaborators in a global industry devoted to the task of *meaning management*.

Closely related to brand meaning is the idea of **brand personality**. In a way, brands are like people: We often describe them in terms of personality traits. We may use adjectives such as *cheap, elegant, sexy,* or *cool* when we talk about a store, a perfume, or a car. A product positioning strategy often aims to create a brand personality for a good or service—a distinctive image that captures its character and benefits. For example, an advertisement for *Elle France* for women* or *cool* as amazing, this fashion magazine for women proclaimed, "She is not a reply card. She is not a category. She is not shrink-wrapped. *Elle* is not a magazine. She is a woman."

One of the more effective ways to give a brand a personality in the minds of consumers is to engage in deliberate marketing actions that make the brand seem more human. The phenomenon of attributing to a brand human characteristics is known as **brand anthropomorphism**, and we can see it in action when, for instance, a brand's Twitter account makes a quirky comment in reply to someone's tweet (that is, "humanizing the brand through a response") or through the interactions of a brand's mascot in a commercial. M&M'S were first introduced commercially in 1941 by Forrest Mars, Sr., son of the founder of candy giant Mars, Inc. He got the idea for the candy after observing soldiers eating chocolate pellets with a hard shell during the Spanish Civil War. The candy was made with a hard shell so that soldiers could carry the chocolate during warm weather. There's no doubt those delicious "melts in your mouth, not in your hand" goodies are an amazing product, but in recent years credit for the brand's success goes mostly to that comedic ensemble of characters named Red, Green, Yellow, Blue, Orange, and Ms. Brown that have done the heavy lifting for the brand's popularity.[25]

Products as people? It seems funny to say, yet marketing researchers find that most consumers have no trouble describing what a product would be like "if it came to life." People often give clear, detailed descriptions, including what color hair the product would have, the type of house it would live in, and even whether it would be thin, overweight, or somewhere in between.[26] If you don't believe us, try doing this yourself.

brand meaning
The beliefs and associations that a consumer has about the brand.

brand personality
A distinctive image that captures the character and benefits of a good or service.

brand anthropomorphism
The assignment of human characteristics and qualities to a brand.

Today, for many consumers brand meaning builds virally as people spread its story online. "Tell to sell," once a mantra of top Madison Avenue ad agencies, has made a comeback as marketers seek to engage consumers with compelling stories rather than peddle products in hit-and-run fashion with interruptive advertising, like 30-second TV commercials—which millennials largely block out anyway. The method of **brand storytelling** captures the notion that powerful ideas do self-propagate when the audience is connected by digital technology. It conveys the constant reinvention inherent in interactivity in that whether via blogging, content creation through YouTube, or photo sharing on Instagram, there will always be new and evolving perceptions and dialogues about a brand in real time.

Airbnb is a great example of a company that has used brand storytelling to connect with consumers and further establish its identity as the premier online marketplace and hospitality service for people to lease or rent short-term lodging. The company underwent a rebranding effort that included the changing of its brand logo to what the company calls the *Bélo*: the universal symbol of belonging. The symbol looks partially like an upside-down heart, partially like an uppercase "A," and it includes an element that resembles the location pin symbol. For Airbnb, the rebrand and accompanying branding campaign provided an opportunity to tell a story that fits with the brand's identity, one that is centered on the experience of being able to feel a sense of belonging wherever a person uses the services Airbnb provides.[27] If we could name the key elements that make a brand successful, what would they be? Here is a highly respected list of 10 characteristics of the world's top brands:[28]

1. The brand excels at delivering the benefits customers truly desire.
2. The brand stays relevant.
3. The pricing strategy is based on consumers' perceptions of value.
4. The brand is properly positioned.
5. The brand is consistent.
6. The brand portfolio and hierarchy make sense.
7. The brand makes use of and coordinates a full repertoire of marketing activities to build equity.
8. The brand's managers understand what the brand means to consumers.
9. The brand is given proper support, and that support is sustained over the long run.
10. The company monitors sources of brand equity.

Products with strong brand equity provide exciting opportunities for marketers. A firm may leverage a brand's equity via **brand extensions**—new products it sells with the same brand name. Because of the existing brand equity, a firm is able to sell its brand extension at a higher price than if it had given it a new brand, and the brand extension will attract new customers immediately. Of course, if the brand extension does not live up to the quality or attractiveness of its namesake, there is a risk of **brand dilution**, in which the contrast between the brand extension's less positive characteristics and the more positive characteristics of the brand can lead to a shift in how consumers perceive the brand. Ultimately, this result can impact brand equity as well as brand loyalty and sales. In the pursuit of greater sales and market share, many luxury automakers, such as Audi and BMW, have been using their brand names to sell lower-end models with prices more accessible to a less affluent segment of consumers. Some marketers have voiced concerns over the impact this may have on the value of these brands, which in the past have been heavily associated with luxury and exclusivity.[29]

One other related approach is **sub-branding**, or creating a secondary brand within a main brand that can help differentiate a product line to a desired target group. Marriott hotels are a leader in sub-branding, having launched a multitude of sub-brands over the history of the company. From Residence Inn by Marriott to Courtyard by Marriott,

brand storytelling
Compelling stories told by marketers about brands to engage consumers.

brand extensions
A new product sold with the same brand name as a strong existing brand.

brand dilution
A reduction in the value of a brand typically driven by the introduction of a brand extension that possesses attributes that adversely contrast with the current attributes consumers associate with the brand.

sub-branding
Creating a secondary brand within a main brand that can help differentiate a product line to a desired target group.

Springhill Suites by Marriott, AC Hotels by Marriott, and on and on—the company understands the power of using an established principal brand to launch alternate products. The addition of the Starwood stable of sub-brands brings Marriott's total number of sub-brands to over 30! The question is: With that many sub-brands, can each of them possibly maintain and convey a unique brand meaning and personality?[30]

Branding Strategies

Because brands contribute to a marketing program's success, a major part of product planning is to develop and execute branding strategies. Marketers have to determine which branding strategy approach(es) to use. Figure 9.6 illustrates the options: individual or family brands, national or store brands, generic brands, licensing, and cobranding. This decision is critical, but it is not always an easy or obvious choice.

Individual Brands versus Family Brands

Part of developing a branding strategy is to decide whether to use a separate, unique brand for each product item—an *individual brand strategy*—or to market multiple items under the same brand name—a **family brand**, or *umbrella brand*, strategy. Individual brands may do a better job of communicating clearly and concisely what the consumer can expect from the product, whereas a well-known company, like Hyatt Hotels, may find that its high brand equity and reputation in one category (e.g., Hyatt Regency and Grand Hyatt at the high end) can sometimes "rub off on" or "trickle down to" brands in newer, lower-priced categories (e.g., Hyatt Place and Hyatt House).

The decision whether to family brand often depends on characteristics of the product and whether the company's overall product strategy calls for introduction of a single, unique product or for the development of a group of similar products. For example, Microsoft serves as a strong umbrella brand for a host of diverse, individually branded products, like Windows 10, Office 2019, Xbox One X, and Bing. In contrast, Unilever and P&G prefer to brand each of their beauty care and household products separately (for most of the products, you'd never know who the manufacturer is unless you look at the small print on the back label).

But there's a potential dark side to having too many brands, particularly when they become undifferentiated or even confusing in the eyes of the consumer as a result of poor positioning or, alternatively, when those brands begin to stray too far from a related parent brand, which results in a loss of synergy. A few years back, the iconic firm Coca-Cola Company announced a "One Brand" global strategy to attempt to address growing complexity among its various sub-brands that are primarily labeled Coca-Cola (Coca-Cola, Coca-Cola Zero, Diet Coke, etc.). It's unclear that this original strategy had the desired impact on consumer markets, and more recently the company has shifted to a philosophical branding approach labeled "Coke's Way Forward." Under this approach, "Coca-Cola is evolving its business strategy to become a total beverage company by giving people more of the drinks they want—including low and no-sugar options across a wide array of categories—in more packages sold in more locations."[31] The challenge for a company with as many brands and sub-brands as Coca-Cola is finding the best balance between individual branding approaches and parlaying the family brand. For instance, is it a positive, negative, or neutral attribute for consumers that Tropicana orange juice is a Coke product?

Figure 9.6 *Snapshot* | Branding Strategies

Marketers have several branding strategy options from which to choose.

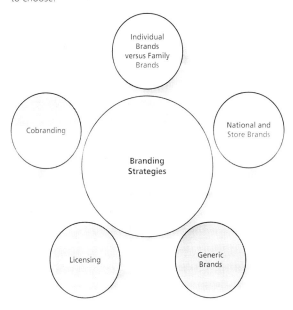

family brand
A brand that a group of individual products or individual brands share.

Campbell's uses a family branding strategy to identify its Chunky line of soups.

National and Store Brands

national or **manufacturer brands**
Brands that the product manufacturer owns.

private-label brands
Brands that a certain retailer or distributor owns and sells.

Retailers today often are in the driver's seat when it comes to deciding what brands to stock and push. In addition to choosing from producers' brands, called **national** or **manufacturer brands**, retailers decide whether to offer their own versions. **Private-label brands**, also called *store brands*, are the retail store or chain's exclusive trade name. Target boasts many private labels, including Goodfellow & Co, Market Pantry, Simply Balanced, and Hearth & Hand, covering most every category of goods they offer. Their trendy kid's clothing line, Cat & Jack, raked in over $2 billion in its first year![32]

Interestingly, if a retailer stocks a unique brand that consumers can't find in other stores, it's much harder for shoppers to compare "apples to apples" across stores and simply buy the brand where they find it sold for the lowest price. As such, private labels represent a major roadblock to price transparency online because consumers can't easily use the Internet to compare private label prices to national brand prices before purchase. Grocery giant Aldi markets 90 percent of its products under private label brands. Aldi's product strategy is to introduce new products in line with market trends at high quality but for lower prices than national brand names. And as consumers become more concerned with healthier eating, Aldi has made sure that its private label brands are free of synthetic colors, trans fats, and MSG. Competitors that sell mostly national brands can cut prices on those brands, but that hurts their overall profitability. Aldi can reduce prices on national brands but still make a ton of money on its more profitable private-label products.[33]

Generic Brands

generic branding
A strategy in which products are not branded and are sold at the lowest price possible.

An alternative to either national or store branding is **generic branding**, which is basically no branding at all. Generic branded products are typically packaged in white with black lettering that names only the product itself (e.g., "Green Beans"). Generic branding is one strategy to meet customers' demand for the lowest prices on standard products, such as dog food or paper towels. Generic brands first became popular during the inflationary period of the 1980s when consumers became especially price conscious. More recently, Walmart has aggressively disrupted the pharmacy business by offering some types of generic prescriptions, such as basic antibiotics. Their website hawks "$4 prescriptions—save big on generic medications," "Walmart customers have saved over $3 billion over the years with our $4 prescriptions," and "you can save no —no insurance needed."

Licensing

licensing
An agreement in which one firm sells another firm the right to use a brand name for a specific purpose and for a specific period of time.

Some firms choose to use a **licensing** strategy to brand their products. This means that one firm sells another firm the right to use a legally protected brand name and other associated elements for a specific purpose and for a specific period of time. Why should an organization sell its name? Licensing can provide instant recognition and consumer interest in a new product, and this strategy can quickly position a product for a certain target market as it trades on the high recognition of the licensed brand among consumers in that segment. For example, the popular toy brand Shopkins entered into a licensing agreement with Build-A-Bear so that customers creating their own furry friends at Build-A-Bear stores across the nation can choose to make a Shopkins bear. An exclusive collectible Shopkins figurine is included with every purchase—a must-have for Shopkins fans trying to complete their collection![35]

A familiar form of licensing occurs when movie producers license their properties to manufacturers of a seemingly infinite number of products. So each time a blockbuster Harry Potter movie hit the screens, a plethora of Potter products packed the stores. In addition to toys and games, there was Harry Potter candy, clothing, all manner of back-to-school items, home items, and even wands and cauldrons. At its heyday back in 2010, with considerable fanfare, Harry and the gang showed up in the form of a major attraction at Universal Orlando called *The Wizarding World of Harry Potter*. The next addition, called "Diagon

Alley," opened for business in the summer of 2014. Since then, other Wizarding Worlds have opened in Los Angeles and Osaka, Japan.[36]

Cobranding

Cobranding is an agreement between two brands to market a new product. A great example of a wildly successful cobranding strategy is GoPro and Red Bull. GoPro doesn't just sell portable cameras, and Red Bull doesn't just sell energy drinks. Instead, both have established themselves as **lifestyle brands**, which are brands that seek to inspire, guide, and motivate people with the goal of contributing to the consumer's way of life. For both GoPro and Red Bull in particular, the representative lifestyle is one that's action-packed, adventurous, fearless, and usually pretty extreme. Hence they're very compatible brands, and these shared values made them a perfect pairing for cobranding, especially those surrounding action sports. So GoPro equips athletes and adventurers from around the world with the tools and funding to capture things like races, stunts, and action sport events on video, and Red Bull uses its experience and reputation to run and sponsor these events. They've collaborated a lot, but probably their biggest collaboration stunt was "Stratos," in which Felix Baumgartner jumped from a space pod more than 24 miles above Earth's surface with a GoPro strapped to his person. Not only did he set three world records that day, but he also embodied the value of reimagining human potential that defines both the GoPro and Red Bull brands.[37]

A new and fast-growing variation on cobranding is **ingredient branding**, in which branded materials become "component parts" of other branded products.[38] This is the strategy behind brands that are willing to pay more for their raw materials so they can have the tag of a supplier on the product. One great example is Patagonia—they promote the fact that many of their products are lined with Polartec, a special performance lining that keeps its wearer warmer, cooler, or dryer depending on the need. This showcases that even highly regarded and well-known brands like Patagonia understand the benefit of showcasing what's inside the product that makes it special.[39]

The practice of ingredient branding has two main benefits. First, it attracts customers to the host brand because the ingredient brand is familiar and has a strong brand reputation for quality. Second, the ingredient brand's firm can sell more of its product, not to men-

cobranding
An agreement between two brands to work together to market a product.

lifestyle brands
Brands that seek to inspire, guide, and motivate people with the goal of contributing to the consumer's way of life.

ingredient branding
A type of branding in which branded materials become "component parts" of other branded products.

Disruption in Branding: Toward Social Justice and Marketing's Responses

In the summer of 2020, in the midst of the COVID-19 crisis, a significant movement toward greater social justice related to racial equality was rekindled by several tragic events that resulted in harm and death to individuals of color. A pattern of these types of events stretching over time, coupled with a plethora of other well-documented racially motivated injustices, caused many people to begin to reexamine themselves in earnest—their own attitudes, beliefs, and behaviors related to people of color—and ultimately to question their own actions and those of their institutions. Because marketing is squarely in the center of organizations' communication, branding, and imagery about itself, its values, and its products, very rapidly brand and marketing leaders began to audit their stable of brands and marketing strategies to ensure that they were not contributing to the pain and hurt represented by the historical inequities of race.

As a result, several highly visible consumer brands began to be a focus for reexamination, including the Washington Redskins football team (owned by Dan Snyder), Aunt Jemima (owned by Quaker Oats, a subsidiary of Pepsico, Inc.), Eskimo Pie (owned by Dreyers Grand Ice Cream), Mrs. Butterworth's (owned by Conagra Foods), and Uncle Ben's (owned by Mars, Inc.). Subsequently, all committed to rebranding and re-imaging their products via retiring or substantially reimagining these legacy brands and creating new

rebranding
Taking an established brand and intentionally and strategically creating a new name, concept, symbol, design, imagery, and messaging in order to develop a new, differentiated identity in the minds of consumers and other stakeholders.

brands, new imagery, and new messaging void of any hint of racism. While the brands mentioned are very visible examples, no doubt numerous other brands—large and small, famous and obscure—embarked at the time on a similar road to **rebranding**, which means taking an established brand and intentionally and strategically creating a new name, concept, symbol, design, imagery, and messaging in order to develop a new, differentiated identity in the minds of consumers and other stakeholders.

As one example, Aunt Jemima, the 130-year-old brand of pancake mix and related products, historically has featured a Black woman on the package who was originally dressed as a minstrel character. "We recognize Aunt Jemima's origins are based on a racial stereotype," Kristin Kroepfl, vice president and chief marketing officer of Quaker Foods North America, said in a news release at the time. "As we work to make progress toward racial equality through several initiatives, we also must take a hard look at our portfolio of brands and ensure they reflect our values and meet our consumers' expectations." Kroepfl said that over the years the company had worked to incrementally "update" the brand to be more "appropriate and respectful," but that the events culminating in summer 2020 made it clear that it was time to realize that incremental changes are insufficient.

Among the examples above, Mrs. Butterworth's rebrand may be the most complex. In its case, the actual syrup bottle itself is fashioned as a matronly woman. And while the race of Mrs. Butterworth, which has been on shelves for nearly 60 years, has not been confirmed, many have suspected her to be Black. Conagra Brands announced a full brand and packaging review, issuing the following statement: "The Mrs. Butterworth's brand, including its syrup packaging, is intended to evoke the images of a loving grandmother. We stand in solidarity with our Black and Brown communities and we can see that our packaging may be interpreted in a way that is wholly inconsistent with our values." In a world where the company said it's "heartbreaking and unacceptable that racism and racial injustices exist," Conagra Brands vowed to be "part of the solution" and work to "progress toward change."

A key takeaway from these events is that you, as a student of marketing, have the opportunity to make significant contributions to the future of the field by ensuring that your branding strategies do not create undue offense to any group. Vigilance is required because branding is one of the most powerful and highest impact elements in all of marketing. It's up to the marketer not to misuse or abuse the power of branding—especially in ways that might hurt and offend others.

Packages and Labels: Branding's Little Helpers

How do you know if the soda you are drinking is "regular" or "caffeine free"? How do you keep your low-fat grated cheese fresh after you have used some of it? Why do you like that little blue box from Tiffany's so much? The answer to all these questions is effective packaging and labeling. So far, we've talked about how marketers create product identity with branding. In this section, we'll learn that packaging and labeling decisions also help to create product identity. We'll also talk about the strategic functions of packaging and some of the legal issues that relate to package labeling.

package
The covering or container for a product that provides product protection, facilitates product use and storage, and supplies important marketing communication.

A **package** is the covering or container for a product, but it's also a way to create a competitive advantage. The important functional value of a package is that it protects the product. For example, packaging for computers, TV sets, and stereos protects the units from damage during shipping and warehousing. Cereal, potato chips, or packs of grated cheese wouldn't be edible for long if packaging didn't provide protection from moisture, dust, odors, and insects. The multilayered, soft box for the chicken broth you see in Figure 9.7 prevents the ingredients inside from spoiling. In addition to protecting the product, effective packaging makes it easy for consumers to handle and store the product. Review the different elements pointed out in Figure 9.7—collectively, they illustrate how packaging serves a number of different functions.

Over and above these utilitarian functions, however, a package communicates brand personality. Effective product packaging uses colors, words, shapes, designs, and pictures

Figure 9.7 *Snapshot* | Functions of Packaging

Great packaging provides a covering for a product, and it also creates a competitive advantage for the brand.

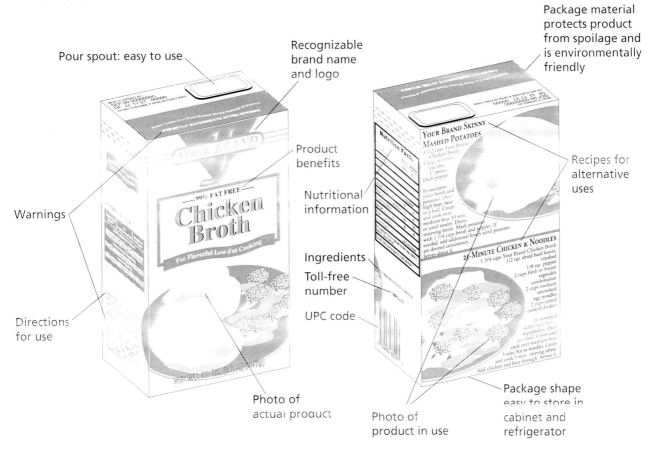

Pour spout: easy to use

Recognizable brand name and logo

Package material protects product from spoilage and is environmentally friendly

Product benefits

Warnings

Nutritional information

Recipes for alternative uses

Ingredients

Toll-free number

UPC code

Directions for use

Photo of actual product

Photo of product in use

Package shape easy to store in cabinet and refrigerator

to provide brand and name identification for the product. In addition, packaging provides product facts, including flavor, fragrance, directions for use, suggestions for alternative uses, recipes, safety warnings, and ingredients. Packaging may also include warranty information and a toll-free telephone number for customer service.

A final communication element is the **Universal Product Code (UPC)**, which is the set of black bars or lines printed on the side or bottom of most items sold in grocery stores and other mass-merchandising outlets. The UPC is a national system of product identification. It assigns each product a unique 10-digit number. These numbers supply specific information about the type of item (grocery item, meat, produce, drugs, or discount coupon), the manufacturer (a five-digit code), and the specific product (another five-digit code). At checkout counters, electronic scanners read the UPC bars and automatically transmit data to a computer in the cash register so that retailers can easily track sales and control inventory.

Design Effective Packaging

Should the package have a resealable zipper, feature an easy-to-pour spout, be compact for easy storage, be short and fat so it won't fall over, or be tall and skinny so it won't take up much shelf space? Effective package design involves a multitude of decisions.

Planners must consider the packaging of other brands in the same product category. For example, when Pringles potato chips were introduced, they were deliberately packaged in a cylindrical can instead of in bags like Lay's and others. This was largely out of necessity because Pringles' manufacturer (which back then was P&G) didn't have all the local trucks to deliver to stores that Frito-Lay did and the cans

Universal Product Code (UPC)

A set of black bars or lines printed on the side or bottom of most items sold in grocery stores correspond to a unique 10-digit number.

Sr.

Jr.

1/2 the fat, 1/3 the calories of regular ice cream. Now in *New* cups.

Introducing multiple package sizes is one way to accomplish product line expansion.

kept the chips fresher much longer. However, quickly after product introduction, Pringles discovered that not all customers would accept a radical change in packaging and retailers may be reluctant to adjust their shelf space to accommodate such packages. To partly answer the concern, Pringles (today marketed by Kellogg's) now comes in a diverse array of products and package types and sizes, including Screamin' Dill Pickle, Baconator, Memphis BBQ, and yes—even Rotisserie Chicken![42]

Packaging can speak to some of the intangible characteristics of a product's brand, such as its personality, heritage, and premium image. After years and years of resistance to major change in look, back in 2016 venerable Jim Beam underwent a global packaging redesign to reflect a more premium and unified image for the products within its portfolio. Specific changes meant to help unify the products under the brand included the prominent display of the Jim Beam signature "rosette" logo. In addition, to keep the heritage of the brand in the minds of consumers, the portraits on the side of the Jim Beam White bottle, which feature seven generations of Beam family distillers, were refreshed to improve the quality of the images. Specific Jim Beam products also had elements of the bottle updated to further communicate the premium nature of the different product offerings within the brand. This was the first-ever global packaging redesign in the 220-plus-year history of the brand! More recently, Jim Beam has continued its brand freshen-up by launching the first campaign for an iconic American bourbon featuring a woman. The company partnered with actress Mila Kunis, a genuine bourbon drinker. Consumer research showed that young guys see Mila as someone who is real, approachable, and fun, while women see her as strong, confident, and inspirational. For the millennial set, it was a home run and has given the brand a new trajectory with this next-gen target market.[43]

Firms that wish to act in a socially responsible manner must also consider the environmental, social, and economic impact of packaging. For instance, shiny gold or silver packaging transmits an image of quality and opulence, but certain metallic inks are not biodegradable. Some firms are developing innovative **sustainable packaging** that involves one or more of the following: elements that can be produced from previously used materials, elements that use materials in their development that can be repurposed after use, materials that require fewer resources to cultivate, and materials and processes that are generally less harmful to the environment. Of course, there is no guarantee that consumers will accept such packaging. They didn't take to plastic pouch refills for certain spray-bottle products even though the pouches may take up less space in landfills than the bottles do. They didn't like pouring the refill into their old spray bottles. Still, customers have accepted smaller packages of concentrated products, such as laundry detergent, dishwashing liquid, and fabric softener.

What about the shape: Square? Round? Triangular? Hourglass? Toiletry manufacturer Mennen once had an aftershave and cologne line called Millionaire that it packaged in a gold pyramid-shaped box. How about an old-fashioned apothecary jar that consumers can reuse as an attractive storage container? What color should it be? White to communicate purity? Yellow because it reminds people of lemon freshness? Brown because the flavor is chocolate? Sometimes, we can trace these decisions back to personal preferences. The familiar Campbell's Soup label—immortalized as art by Andy Warhol—is red and white because a company executive many years ago liked the football uniforms at Cornell University!

Finally, there are many specific decisions brand managers must make to ensure that a product's packaging reflects well on its brand and appeals to the intended target market. What graphic information should the package show? Someone once quipped, "Never show the dog eating the dog food." Translation: Should there be a picture of the product on the package? Must green bean cans always show a picture of green beans? Should there be a picture that demonstrates the results of using the product, such as

sustainable packaging
Packaging that involves one or more of the following: elements that can be produced from previously used materials, elements that use materials in their development that can be repurposed after use, materials that require fewer resources to cultivate, and materials and processes that are generally less harmful to the environment.

Newton's athletic shoes come in sustainable packaging.

beautiful hair? Should there be a picture of the product in use, perhaps a box of crackers that shows them with delicious-looking toppings arranged on a silver tray? Should there be a recipe or coupon on the back? Of course, all these decisions rely on a marketer's understanding of consumers, ingenuity, and perhaps a little creative luck.

Store brands have unique packaging opportunities. Some store brands opt for **copycat packaging**, mimicking the look of the national branded product they want to knock off. Walgreens is a master of such copycat packaging—look on any shelf in its medicinal categories, and you will see a Walgreens brand proudly merchandised on the shelf (at a very attractive price!) right next to the leading national brand in that category, with the package design and colors so similar that you have to look carefully to discern what you are actually buying.[44]

Walgreens does a great job of copycat packaging—that is, creating a similar look to national brands.

Labeling Regulations

The Federal Fair Packaging and Labeling Act of 1966 controls package communication and labeling in the U.S. This law aims to make labels more helpful to consumers by providing useful information. More recently, the requirements of the *Nutrition Labeling and Education Act of 1990* forced food marketers to make sweeping changes in how they label products. Since August 18, 1994, the U.S. Food and Drug Administration (FDA) requires most foods sold in the U.S. to have labels telling, among other things, how much fat, saturated fat, cholesterol, calories, carbohydrates, protein, and vitamins are in each serving of the product. These regulations force marketers to be more accurate when they describe the contents of their products. Juice makers, for example, must state how much of their product is real juice rather than sugar and water.

As of January 1, 2006, the FDA also requires that all food labels list the amount of trans fat in the food directly under the line for saturated fat content. The new labeling reflects scientific evidence showing that consumption of trans fat, saturated fat, and dietary cholesterol raises "bad" cholesterol levels, which increases the risk of coronary heart disease. The trans fat line was the first significant change on the Nutrition Facts panel since it was established.[45] Recently, additional changes have been mandated that must be implemented by 2020, including increasing font sizes for calories, number of servings, and serving sizes, and displaying additional details on added sugars and actual amounts of vitamin D, calcium, iron, and potassium.[46]

copycat packaging
Packaging designed to mimic the look of a similar or functionally identical national branded product often meant to lead the consumer to perceive the two products as comparable.

9.4 Organize for Effective Product Management

OBJECTIVE
Describe how marketers structure organizations for new and existing product management.

Of course, firms don't create great products, brands, and packaging—people do. Like all elements of the marketing mix, product strategies are only as effective as their managers make them and carry them out. In this section, we'll talk about how firms organize both to manage existing products and to develop new products.

Manage Existing Products

In small firms, a single marketing manager usually handles the marketing function. This individual is responsible for new product planning, advertising, working with the company's few sales representatives, marketing research, and just about everything else. But in

Figure 9.8 *Snapshot* | Types of Product Management

Product management can take several forms: brand managers, product category managers, and market managers, depending on the firm's needs and the market situation.

Three Types of Product Management

brand manager
An individual who is responsible for developing and implementing the marketing plan for a single brand.

product category manager
An individual who is responsible for developing and implementing the marketing plan for all the brands and products within a product category.

market manager
An individual who is responsible for developing and implementing the marketing plans for products sold to a particular customer group.

larger firms, there are a number of managers who are responsible for different brands, product categories, or markets. As illustrated in Figure 9.8, depending on the organization's needs and the market situation, product management may include brand managers, product category managers, and market managers. Let's take a look at how each operates.

Brand Managers

Sometimes, a firm sells several or even many different brands within a single product category. Take the laundry section in the supermarket, for example. In the detergent category, P&G brands are Bold, Gain, and Tide. In such cases, each brand may have its own **brand manager** who coordinates all marketing activities for a brand; these duties include positioning, identifying target markets, research, distribution, sales promotion, packaging, and evaluating the success of these decisions.

Although this job title and assignment (or something similar) is still common throughout industry, some big firms are changing the way they allocate responsibilities. For example, today P&G's brand managers function more like internal consultants to cross-functional teams located in the field that have responsibility for managing the complete business of key retail clients across all product lines. Brand managers still are responsible for positioning of brands and developing and nurturing brand equity, but they also work heavily with folks from sales, finance, logistics, and others to serve the needs of the major retailers that make up the majority of P&G's business.

By its very nature, the brand management system is not without potential problems. If they act independently and sometimes competitively against each other, brand managers may fight for increases in short-term sales for their own brand, potentially to the detriment of the overall product category for the firm. They may push too hard with coupons, cents-off packages, or other price incentives to a point at which customers will refuse to buy the product when it's not "on deal." Such behavior can hurt long-term profitability and damage brand equity.

Product Category Managers

dination. Take IBM, for example. Originally known as a computer manufacturer, IBM now generates much of its revenue from a wide range of consulting and related client services across the spectrum of IT applications (the company hasn't sold personal computers in over a decade, having spun off its ThinkPad business to the Chinese firm Lenovo in 2005). In cases such as IBM, P&G, and similar multi–product line firms, organizing for product management may include a **product category manager**, who coordinates the mix of product lines within the more general product category and who considers the addition of new product lines based on client needs.

Market Managers

Some firms have developed a **market manager** structure in which different people focus on specific customer groups rather than on the products the company makes. This type of organization can be especially useful when firms offer a variety of products that serve the needs of a wide range of customers. For example, GE serves the following customer markets: aviation, healthcare, power, renewable energy, digital industry, additive manufacturing, venture capital and finance, and lighting. Such firms serve their customers best when they focus separately on each of these very different markets. And in case you're wondering why home appliances aren't on the list, yes, the GE brand is still on ranges, washers, dryers, microwaves, and refrigerators, but it's just a brand now—they're not actually made by GE anymore!

Organize for New Product Development

You read in Chapter 8 about the steps in new product development and learned earlier in this chapter about the importance of the introduction phase of the PLC. Because launching new products is so important, the management of this process is a serious matter. In some instances, one person handles new product development, but within larger organizations, new product development almost always requires many people. Often especially creative people with entrepreneurial skills get this assignment.

The challenge in large companies is to enlist specialists in different areas to work together in **venture teams**, which focus exclusively on the new product development effort. Sometimes the venture team is located away from traditional company offices in a remote location called a "skunk works." This colorful term originated with the Skunk Works, an illicit distillery in the comic strip *Li'l Abner*. Because illicit distilleries were bootleg operations, typically located in an isolated area with minimal formal oversight, organizations adopted the colorful description "skunk works" to refer to a small and often isolated department or facility that functions with minimal supervision (not because of its odor).[47]

venture teams
Groups of people within an organization who work together to focus exclusively on the development of a new product.

9.5 Brand You: Managing the Product—You

OBJECTIVE
Understand how to manage your career so as to adapt and flourish in a changing work environment.

Taylor made great progress in developing his value proposition, that is, what value a prospective employer will receive in hiring him. He has spent time recognizing, evaluating, and adding to his product layers. He knows that a product is a bundle of features, functions, benefits, and uses plus its brand and packaging.

If you normally watch the Super Bowl every year, it's a good bet that you pay attention to the commercials. Whether they're funny, use sex appeal, or tell a story that touches your heart, the commercials that you think are great are able to deliver a clear value proposition in about 30 seconds.

You might be wondering what a 30-second Super Bowl commercial has to do with launching and managing your career. When someone asks you about your career interests, even in a job interview, that's all the time you have to tell what you want to do. Think of it as a Super Bowl commercial for your personal brand, a commercial in which you must deliver your compelling value proposition. What makes you different? What do you have to offer? Why would a company manager want to hire you instead of someone else? Your value proposition should answer all of these questions.

If you think that commercials are only for marketing majors, think again. If you are interviewing for a position as a law clerk, special education teacher, research assistant, nurse, videographer, or website developer, you need to have your value proposition fine-tuned and ready to deliver in virtually any situation, including networking and job interviews.

No one is going to do it for you. You have to do it for yourself.

Your Value Proposition—The Key to Success

You may have already been on an interview or two where the interviewer starts by saying, "So, tell me about yourself." In these cases, your 30-second value proposition is the perfect reply. From there, you can tell your brand story based on what you say in your value proposition statement.

Your value proposition is a short, simple statement that includes four key pieces of information:

- Who you are
- What you have accomplished
- What makes you unique and how you bring value to an organization
- What you want to do

Your value proposition is a summary of the information you created about your product layers put together in a few simple sentences that you can say in any situation. In fact, your value proposition is also referred to as your **elevator pitch** because you should be able to share it with someone in the 30 seconds it takes for the average elevator ride.

Your value proposition that needs to be clearly communicated in your elevator pitch should outline your features, benefits, and extras, such as the one below.

"Hi. My name is Gabriela Land. I'm a marketing major with marketing research experience and creative writing skills, and I'm really excited about combining these interests. While in school, I completed an internship that gave me the chance to work on developing a social media marketing plan for the City of Spartanburg. As a result of my plan, attendance at several city events, including the Spring Fling, increased significantly."

And remember, you need to practice, practice, practice, and constantly improve your elevator pitch.

elevator pitch
A statement that details your value proposition in about 30 seconds, the average time it takes for an elevator ride.

Launch Your Career with Marketable Skills

A college degree isn't the only ticket you're likely to need to launch your career. Many recruiters say they don't interview students who haven't shown the effort to get real-world experience through internships, service learning, or cooperative learning programs.

Internships

Most recruiters and hiring managers will tell you that the best way to get a job is to have at least one internship or co-op on your résumé. Internships provide opportunities to gain valuable work-related experience. They also provide an opportunity to explore the real work world and decide if this truly is the career for you. With an internship, you are enhancing your academic education with practical career-related experience. The result? You'll gain marketable skills and build your résumé.

Your first step is to decide what you hope to gain from an internship. You might want an internship to help you evaluate your career goal, learn new skills to beef up your résumé, gain networking connections, or all of these. Knowing what you want to accomplish will help you evaluate internship offers and, inevitably, you'll be asked about your goals when you interview.

Through an internship, you gain firsthand experience that you can't learn in a class or a textbook. And an internship can also be valuable to help you learn what you *don't* want to do.

Volunteering

While internships are an excellent way to gain practical experience, you can learn about the real world in other ways. Volunteering for a not-for-profit, professional, or campus organization can help you gain valuable experience while you are making a difference. No matter what profession you want to pursue, volunteering can help you make your mark.

Manage Your Career by Remaining Employable

Think about how people and companies have changed in your short lifetime. Ten years ago, there were even some marketing professors who were totally convinced that social media was a fad that would go away and had no business in a marketing class. Employee skills are now outdated in three to five years, and new jobs will emerge (each year) that involve tasks that don't even exist today.

Develop a Flexible Career Plan

Although you can't know exactly what the future holds, you can be proactive and create a flexible career plan that allows for uncertainty. Plan your career to keep up with continuous changes in the world of work. As you add new skills to your portfolio, you'll be ready for challenges you couldn't imagine when you launched your career. Many successful people are surprised by their achievements—they didn't necessarily aspire to their current roles. Their success occurred because they kept on learning and were willing to take risks when opportunity came knocking.

Expand Self-Awareness

By following the steps to develop your career plan, you've seen that the cornerstone of good planning is awareness of your strengths and preferences. Most working adults know that in the future they will have five to seven careers. Periodically take an inventory of your updated skills and preferences and map out new territory for your personal brand.

Communicate Your Value

Marketing *you* is a never-ending process. Keep an eye on the next big work project, company shift, or product innovation, and position yourself to participate in completing the task(s). That means being able to sell yourself. Once inside a company, learn what the organization values. Ask to see the strategic plan. Look for ways to align your work with your employer's strategic goals. Anticipate the skills that will be relevant in the future and map out a strategy to develop them.

Going Up!

Your elevator pitch should give someone a summary of your value proposition. It should be no longer than the time it takes for an average elevator ride and should tell someone who you are, what you've done that makes you unique, and what you want to do.

impor how has a plan to manage his career introduction his resume there is a crucial but very important practical career-related experience through an internship for a semester before he graduates. He knows that he must be able to communicate his value proposition to others in an elevator pitch that takes only around 30 seconds.

Objective **Summaries** and **Key Terms**

9.1 Objective Summary

Discuss the product objectives and strategies a firm may choose.

Product planning is guided by the continual process of product management. Objectives for individual products may be related to introducing a new product, expanding the market of a regional product, or rejuvenating a mature product. For multiple products, firms may decide on a full- or a limited-line strategy. Often, companies decide to extend their product line with an upward, downward, or two-way stretch; with a filling-out strategy; or by contracting a product line. Firms that have multiple product lines may choose a wide product mix with many different lines or a narrow one with few. Product quality objectives refer to the durability, reliability, degree of precision, ease of use and repair, or degree of aesthetic pleasure. One way that companies can improve quality is to use the Six Sigma method.

Key Terms

product management
product objectives
product line
product line length
stock-keeping unit (SKU)

full-line product strategy
limited-line product strategy
product line extension
upward product line stretch
downward product line stretch
two-way product line stretch
filling-out product strategy
cannibalization
product mix
product mix width
product quality
internal customers
internal customer mindset
ISO 9000
Six Sigma

9.2 Objective Summary

Understand how firms manage products throughout the product life cycle.

The product life cycle explains how products go through four stages from birth to death. During the introduction stage, marketers seek to get buyers to try the product and may use high prices to recover R&D costs. During the growth stage, characterized by rapidly increasing sales, marketers may introduce new product variations. In the maturity stage, sales peak and level off. Marketers respond by adding desirable new product features or market-development strategies. During the decline stage, firms must decide whether to phase a product out slowly, drop it immediately, or, if there is residual demand, keep the product.

Key Terms

product life cycle (PLC)
introduction stage
product relaunch
growth stage
maturity stage
decline stage

9.3 Objective Summary

Explain how branding and packaging strategies contribute to product identity.

A brand is a name, term, symbol, or other unique element of a product used to identify a firm's product. A brand should be selected that has a positive connotation and that is recognizable and memorable. Brand names need to be easy to say, spell, read, and remember and should fit the target market, the product's benefits, the customer's culture, and legal requirements. To protect a brand legally, marketers obtain trademark protection. Brands are important because they help maintain customer loyalty and because brand equity or value means a firm is able to attract new customers. Firms may develop individual brand strategies or market multiple items with a family or umbrella brand strategy. National or manufacturer brands are owned and sold by producers, whereas private-label

or store brands carry the retail or chain store's trade name. Licensing means a firm sells another firm the right to use its brand name. In a cobranding strategy, two brands form a partnership to market a new product.

Packaging is the covering or container for a product and serves to protect a product and to allow for easy use and storage of the product. The colors, words, shapes, designs, pictures, and materials used in package design communicate a product's identity, benefits, and other important product information. Package designers must consider cost, product protection, and communication in creating a package that is functional, aesthetically pleasing, and not harmful to the environment. Product labeling in the U.S. is controlled by a number of federal laws aimed at making package labels more helpful to consumers.

Key Terms

brand
trademark
brand equity
brand meaning
brand personality
brand anthropomorphism
brand storytelling
brand extensions
brand dilution
sub-branding
family brand
national or manufacturer brands
private-label brands
generic branding
licensing
cobranding
lifestyle brands
ingredient branding
rebranding
package
Universal Product Code (UPC)
sustainable packaging
copycat packaging

9.4 Objective Summary

Describe how marketers structure organizations for new and existing product management.

To successfully manage existing products, the marketing organization may include brand managers, product category managers, and market managers. Large firms, however, often give new product responsibilities to new product managers or to venture teams, groups of specialists from different areas who work together for a single new product.

Key Terms

brand manager
product category manager
market manager
venture teams

9.5 Objective Summary

Understand how to manage your career so that you will be able to adapt and flourish in a changing work environment.

Like a Super Bowl commercial, you will need to deliver a compelling value proposition that tells what you offer that would make an employer hire you rather than someone else in 30 seconds. The value proposition is a summary of the product layers in a few simple sentences, often referred to as your *elevator pitch*.

Having one or more internships that give real-world experience allows you to launch your career with marketable skills.

You can also learn about the real world through volunteering for a not-for-profit, professional, or campus organization.

Employee skills are now outdated in three to five years, and new jobs will emerge (each year) that involve tasks that don't even exist today. To continue success in a career, you should create a flexible career plan that allows for uncertainty. Plan your career to keep up with continuous changes in the world of work by continuing to learn and add new skills to your portfolio.

Key Terms

elevator pitch

Chapter **Questions** and **Activities**

Concepts: Test Your Knowledge

9-1. What is a company's product line? List and explain the different product line extensions that marketers may use. What is a company's product mix? What product mix strategy do marketers usually consider?

9-2. What are two reasons a firm might determine it should expand a product line? What are two reasons for contracting a product line? What do we mean by a product mix strategy?

9-3. How do marketers define product quality? What are the dimensions of product quality? How has e-commerce affected the need for quality product objectives?

9-4. Explain the product life cycle concept. List and describe the stages of the product life cycle.

9-5. What are some ways products are managed during the different stages of the product life cycle?

9-6. What is a brand? What are the characteristics of a good brand name? How do firms provide legal protection for their brands?

9-7. In discussing branding, marketers may talk about brand equity, brand meaning, brand personality, and brand anthropomorphism. Explain each of these terms.

9-8. What are individual and family brands? A national brand? A store brand?

9-9. What does it mean to license a brand? What is cobranding?

9-10. What are the functions of packaging? What are some important elements of effective package design?

9-11. What should marketers know about package labeling?

9-12. Describe some of the ways firms organize the marketing function to manage existing products. What are the ways firms organize for the development of new products?

Activities: Apply What You've Learned

9-13. *In Class, 10–25 Minutes for Teams* Think of products you are familiar with in the marketplace. Brainstorm with your group and identify at least three products (not specific brands) that fall into each of the product life cycle categories—introduction, growth, maturity, and decline. Are any of the products you identified in a transition stage? Discuss what marketing strategies you would suggest for each brand. Present your results to your class.

9-14. *Creative Homework/Short Project* Assume you are in the marketing area for an automobile firm such as BMW. You have been tasked with identifying cobranding opportunities. Determine four companies/brands that would work well in being paired with BMW. Describe each of the cobranding opportunities, and outline the advantages that would result from each.

9-15. *In Class, 10–25 Minutes for Teams* Assume that you are working in the marketing department of a major manufacturer of athletic shoes. Your firm is introducing a new product, a line of disposable sports clothing. That's right—wear it once and toss it! You wonder if it would be better to market the line of clothing with a new brand name or use one family brand name that has already gained popularity with your existing products. Make a list of the advantages and disadvantages of each strategy. Develop your recommendation.

9-16. *In Class, 10–25 Minutes for Teams* As an entrepreneur, you know you want to open a new unique and innovative food store that sells only healthy organic food items. You are trying to decide on the kind of products you should carry. Discuss the importance of national brands, store brands, and generic brands. Which brand or brands will your new store carry? Briefly explain your decision.

9-17. *Creative Homework/Short Project* Assume that you have been recently hired by Kellogg's, the cereal company. You have been asked to work on a plan for redesigning the packaging for Kellogg's Frosted Flakes, Kellogg's top-selling cereal. In a role-playing situation, present the following report to your marketing superior:

Discussion of the problems or complaints customers have with current packaging

Discussion of the pros of the current packaging design and appearance

Several different package alternatives

Your recommendations for changing packaging or for keeping the packaging the same

9-18. *For Further Research (Individual)* You are interested in the role that Six Sigma plays with regard to product quality. Using the Internet, research the concept of Six Sigma and find at least two case studies on companies that employ Six Sigma in their day-to-day activities. Summarize your findings in a short report.

Concepts: Apply Marketing Metrics

The chapter introduced you to the concept of brand equity, an important measurement of the value vested in a product's brand in and of itself. Different formulas for calculating brand equity exist. One well-publicized approach is that of Interbrand, which annually publishes a variety of Best Brands lists, including its Best 100 Global Brands. Type "Interbrand Best Global Brands" into any search engine and click the current year's Best Global Brands Rankings (the list is a grid with brand icons for each of the cells and data indicating the recent year's estimated increase or decrease in brand equity). Select any two to three brands in which you have keen interest. For each, observe whether brand equity has been trending up or down over the past few years.

9-19. What is it about each of your selected brands that attracts your interest?

9-20. What is your opinion about why your selected brand's equity is what it is and whether it is trending upward or downward?

Choices: What Do You Think?

9-21. *Critical Thinking* Brand equity means that a brand enjoys customer loyalty, perceived quality, and brand-name awareness. To what brands are you personally loyal? What is it about the product that creates brand loyalty and, thus, brand equity?

9-22. *Critical Thinking* Are there specific products that you purchase where branding does not matter and has never mattered to you? What characteristics of the related products and your own individual preferences can help explain why this might be the case?

9-23. *Critical Thinking* Quality is an important product/service objective, but quality can mean different things for different goods and services, such as durability, precision, aesthetic appeal, and so on. What does quality mean for the following goods/services?

   a. Laptop computer
   b. Haircut
   c. Athletic wear
   d. A gym or fitness center
   e. New automobile
   f. College education

9-24. *Ethics* How do you think a company's behavior toward its customers and its community impact purchase? Have you ever purchased (or not purchased) a brand because of what you knew about their environmental initiatives? How about their stand and actions on controversial issues such as race or gender discrimination, political loyalty, or treatment of employees? What type of issues do you think could cause a decline in sales for a company?

9-25. *Critical Thinking* There are many products in the marketplace that keep the same packaging year after year, even when there may be a newer best practice. Take a look at the list of products below and think about the brand that you use. Write down any issues you have with the packaging of your preferred brand. Now think about a competitive brand in each category—do they have any benefits your package doesn't have? What ways could your preferred brand's packaging be improved? What benefits could the marketer hope to achieve if they took your suggestions?

   a. A dozen donuts
   b. Powder laundry detergent
   c. Deodorant
   d. Gallon of milk
   e. Potato chips
   f. Candy bar

9-26. *Ethics* If a company knows that a snack or beverage is typically consumed in a single sitting (such as a bottle of soda or a bag of chips), is it ethical for that company to include on the product's nutrition label values based on the identification of multiple servings within the product (that is, the nutrition values displayed would represent a single serving of the product that is less than the whole product, making it necessary to multiply those values by the number of servings to identify the total nutritional value of the package)?

9-27. *Ethics* You learned in this chapter that it's hard to *legally* protect brand names across product categories—Quaker and Apple, for example, and also Delta, which is an airline and a faucet. But what about the *ethics* of borrowing a name and applying it to some unrelated products? Think of some new business you might like to start up. Now consider some possible names for your product or service. Include a few brands in other, unrelated categories. Do you think it would be ethical to borrow one of those names? Why or why not?

Miniproject: Learn by Doing

In any supermarket in any town, you will surely find thousands of examples of product packaging. This miniproject is designed to give you a better understanding of how branding, cobranding, and packaging all work together to compete for your purchasing dollars.

   a. Go to a typical supermarket in your community.
   b. Select two product categories of interest to you: ice cream, cereal, laundry detergent, soup, frozen meals, and so on.
   c. For each product category, visit that area of the store. Write down a list of the three items that attract your attention first. Identify what it was about the product that attracted your attention (the brand, cobrand, or package design).
   d. For each of the three products, identify which you are most likely to buy based on the first look alone. Explain why you chose this product.

9-28. Pick up each of three products and study their package design and any information you can find about the product. Now which product are you most likely to buy? Explain why you chose this product.

9-29. Present a summary to your class on what you learned about the brands and packaging in your two product categories.

Marketing in Action **Case**   Real Choices at Helen of Troy

Did you drink your eight glasses of water today? Medical experts say that specific advice is outdated, but the need for water drives many of us to grab a Dasani, Aquafina, or other brand of bottled water out of a vending machine. Many consumers now get their water out of the tap or water fountain and keep it cool in a stylish reusable water bottle. One brand of water bottle has managed to become the top choice for water consumers—the Hydro Flask that the Helen of Troy corporation manufactures. Its rise to number one was driven in large part by establishing and maintaining a strong brand that some customers say they not only prefer but *love*.

The Hydro Flask was created in 2009 by a couple who were tired of drinking lukewarm water. Travis Rosbach and his girlfriend Cindy Weber improved upon the double-wall vacuum insulation bottles that the Thermos Brand invented back in 1904 by making its new bottles stylish and colorful and remarkably effective at keeping cold drinks cold. They first sold their innovation at the county fair and later at farmers' markets in Bend, Oregon, an area full of hikers and campers. As proof of their product's thermal capability, the founders put ice in the bottles the day before and then showed prospective customers how the ice cubes were still floating inside—even after having been in the hot sun for a day. That demonstration converted many prospects to customers and led them not only to buy the product but to bring their friends to see this new bottle.

The original inventors sold their ownership stake to an investor to keep up with the company's growth, and that investor was later acquired and would become part of the company.

The new corporate owner brought both money and distribution relationships that helped propel Hydro Flask's growth even further. External factors also played a role. A greater interest in more nutritious eating and exercise contributed to an awareness of the role of water in good health. This contributed to bottled water's growth in popularity, surpassing the sales of carbonated drinks in 2016. But some consumers were concerned about the environmental impact of all those plastic bottles. The 2008 recession may have also impacted reusable water bottle sales as consumers tightened their budgets.

Hydro Flask's marketing efforts, most notably its focus on design and variety in its product offerings, have also helped. In addition to perfecting its fundamental cooling functionality, the company focused on the aesthetics of its product. The bottle's exterior is powder-coated, a painting technique that looks great and is durable with a slight texture to it for an easier grip. A variety of bright colors and a whimsical logo make the product noticeable—particularly since it is too large to hide away in a backpack. The company also employed an approach similar to the technique used in the company's early farmers' market days to win over distributors. Hydro Flask sales reps would leave bottles of ice water at dealer offices and then ask them to call when the ice melted.

These marketing efforts, with some help from the external factors, led to significant sales growth; in 2019, purchases of Hydro Flask increased 239 percent. But the more impressive part of the Hydro Flask story is the depth of affection that its customers have for the brand and its products. Founder Rosbach recalls that his first customer at that county fair almost started crying when he saw the unmelted ice in the bottle. Whitney Todosiev, a Palos Verdes High School junior, says about her Hydro Flask, "Now that I have one, I realize that I love mine." She has even given her bottle a name: Barry. According to Scott Allan, the brand's former global general manager, "Customers came up to us and didn't just say, 'We love your product' or 'We love your company,'" says Allan. "They were saying, 'We love your brand.'"

What's behind all this brand love? Customers clearly appreciate the functional value the product delivers (that ice just won't melt). But they also seem to like what the product and brand say about them as users. Carrying a water bottle communicates that health is important and that exercise or outdoor activities are part of one's life. It could also signal concern for the environment. These priorities are hallmarks of a particular type of consumer known as "VSCO girls," so named for their prolific use of the photo sharing app VSCO. These teens are known for their "beachy, California style" and their concern for the environment. They are also concerned with having all the right accessories, including the Hydro Flask, that appear in many of their social media posts. Hydro Flask's focus on personalization allows VSCO girls and other customers not only to choose their bottle style and color but to cover it with stickers and other marks of their personal style.

The attraction to reusable bottles is not limited to teens; 74 percent of millennials reported owning one. "With millennials, fitness and health are themselves signals," says Tülin Erdem, a marketing professor at NYU. "They drink more water and carry it with them, so it's an item that becomes part of them and their self-expression." One researcher suggested that the water bottle has become a "comforting, adulty 'binky,'" with users having one they take when they exercise, one for the car, and one they use at the office.

The tendency to own more than one Hydro Flask is one key to the brand's continued growth. Hydro Flask offers limited-edition series and opportunities to mix and match different colors and accessories, which supports a marketing strategy called "just one more." The company also has the opportunity to expand internationally and to move into new categories like insulated grocery totes and hydration packs. The success of these growth plans will largely depend on whether the Hydro Flask continues to be the reusable bottle among VSCO girls and the other consumers who love to use it and love to talk about their love for the brand. Among those is a fan of the brand who said, "I will be buried with all of my different sizes of Hydro Flask. Maybe by then Hydro Flask will come out with a coffin, so I can be buried in that, too." How's that for lifetime value?[48]

Questions for Discussion

9-30. What brand (in a different product category than reusable water bottles) do you love or at least have a strong affection for? Translate the reasons that you love your brand into generic attributes to which other brands could aspire (for example, "high quality" or "rugged").

9-31. For the brand you identified above, which attributes that you listed do not directly relate to the performance of the product (for example, "sophisticated")? What marketing tactics may have influenced your inclusion of those brand attributes in your list?

9-32. Helen of Troy has a history of growth and expansion of its product offerings. Its goal for the future is to continue growing its products, including the Hydro Flask. Describe three possible growth strategies Helen of Troy might consider for Hydro Flask. What are the pros and cons of each? Which one would you recommend and why?

Chapter **Notes**

1. David Kiley, "The Mini Bulks Up," *NBC News*, January 27, 2006, https://www.nbcnews.com/id/10992248/ns/business-us_business/t/mini-bulks/ (accessed April 15, 2016).

2. Michael F. Haverluck, "Chick-fil-A Now #3 Restaurant Chain in U.S.," *NE News Now*, June 21, 2019, https://onenewsnow.com/business/2019/06/21/chick-fil-a-now-3-restaurant-chain-in-us (accessed July 13, 2020); Tim Pierce, "Chick-fil-A Tops the List for Customer Satisfaction, Again," *Washington Examiner*, June 25, 2019, https://www.washingtonexaminer.com/news/chick-fil-a-tops-the-list-for-customer-satisfaction-again (accessed July 13, 2020).

3. Laurie Dixon, "Oreo is Dropping TWO New Flavors in 2020, and We Can't Wait!," *Taste of Home*, November 8, 2019, https://www.tasteofhome.com/article/oreo-is-dropping-new-flavors-in-2020/ (accessed July 13, 2020).

4. Morgan Raum, "Oreo Unveils New Churro Cookie as Its New Mystery Flavor," *People.com*, December 2, 2019, https://people.com/food/oreo-unveils-new-churro-cookie-as-its-latest-mystery-flavor/ (accessed July 13, 2020.)

5. Campbell's Soup, https://www.campbells.com/campbell-soup/ (accessed July 15, 2016).

6. Rolls-Royce Motor Cars, https://www.rolls-roycemotorcars.com (accessed April 15, 2016).

7. Natasha Bach, "Why Procter & Gamble Is Buying Merck KGaA's Consumer Health Unit in a Whopper of a Deal," *Fortune*, April 19, 2018, https://fortune.com/2018/04/19/procter-and-gamble-merck-kgaa-deal/ (accessed April 19, 2018).

8. [...] K900 Car," *Chicago Tribune*, May 16, 2014, http://-articles.chicagotribune.com/2014-05-16/marketplace/sns-rt-us-kiamotors-k900-20140515_1_luxury-brand-bernie-woodall-k900 (accessed April 15, 2016).

9. Jay Ramey, "2015 Kia K900 Luxury Sedan Gets $5,000 Price Cut," *Autoweek*, January 28, 2015, https://autoweek.com/article/car-news/2015-kia-k900-luxury-sedan-gets-5000-price-cut (accessed April 15, 2016).

10. Caitlin Dewey, "Why Nestle Sold Its U.S. Candy Business—and Bought a Vitamin Company," *The Washington Post*, January 17, 2018, https://www.washingtonpost.com/news/wonk/wp/2018/01/17/why-nestle-sold-its-u-s-candy-business-and-bought-a-vitamin-company/?utm_term=.a1d32f6fee9e (accessed April 20, 2018).

11. Rich Duprey, "The Anheuser-Busch Acquisition of Craft Beer Alliance Faces Growing Anti-Trust Scrutiny," *The Motley Fool*, February 13, 2020, https://www.fool.com/investing/2020/02/13/the-anheuser-busch-acquisition-of-craft-brew-allia.aspx (accessed July 10, 2020); Chris Furnari, "Anheuser-Busch InBev Completes Acquisition Of Craft Brew Alliance," *Forbes*, September 30, 2020, https://www.forbes.com/sites/chrisfurnari/2020/09/30/anheuser-busch-inbev-completes-acquisition-of-craft-brew-alliance/?sh=537e5f382a8a (accessed December 22, 2020).

12. Geoffrey Colvin, "The Ultimate Manager," *Fortune*, November 22, 1999, 185–87.

13. International Organization for Standardization, https://www.iso.org/iso/home/standards.htm (accessed April 15, 2016).

14. Al Ries and Laura Ries, *The Origin of Brands* (New York: Collins, 2005).

15. Arvind Chatterjee, "Ancestry Membership Discounts: Save 26% on All Major Categories," *Zouton.com*, April 20, 2020, https://zouton.com/news/ancestry-membership-discounts (accessed July 11, 2020).

16. Tom Randall, "Tesla's Model 3 Is Now America's Best-Selling Electric Car," *Bloomberg*, April 3, 2018, https://www.bloombergquint.com/technology/tesla-s-model-3-is-the-best-selling-electric-car-in-the-u-s (accessed May 7, 2018); Faiz Siddiqui, "TESLA Lost $700 Million in the First Quarter with Model 3 Problems," *The Washington Post*, April 24, 2019, https://www.washingtonpost.com/technology/2019/04/24/tesla-lost-million-first-quarter-model-problems/ (accessed July 11, 2020).

17. Ben Gilbert, "25 of the Biggest Failed Products from the World's Biggest Companies," *Business Insider*, May 4, 2018, https://www.businessinsider.com/biggest-product-flops-in-history-2016-12 (accessed May 7, 2018).

18. "When Corporate Innovation Goes Bad—The 110 Biggest Product Failures of All Time," *CB Insights*, April 13, 2017, https://www.cbinsights.com/research/corporate-innovation-product-fails/ (accessed April 20, 2018).

19. "Global Smartphone Shipments Market Share by Vendor from the 2nd Quarter 2014 to the 1st Quarter 2020," *Statista*, https://www.statista.com/statistics/671213/worldwide-market-share-of-leading-smartphone-manufacturers/ (accessed July 14, 2020).

20. Listerine, https://www.listerine.com, accessed May 5, 2018; "History of Listerine: From Surgery Antiseptic to Modern Mouthwash," https://www.listerine.com/about (accessed July 10, [...]

21. Eric Pfanner, "Apple Wins Trademark Case with Beatles," *The New York Times*, May 8, 2006, https://www.nytimes.com/2006/05/08/business/07cnd-apple.html#:~:text=LONDON%2C%20May%208%20%E2%80%94%20Apple%20Computer,of%20the%20bitten%2Dapple%20symbol (accessed September 14, 2020).

22. "The Most Famous Name in Music," *Music Trades* 118, no. 12 (September 2003).

23. Beatriz da Costa, "Chance the Rapper Remixes Backstreet Boys 'I Want It That Way' for Doritos' Super Bowl Commercial," *Vibe*, January 29, 2019, https://www.vibe.com/2019/01/chance-the-rapper-backstreet-boys-super-bowl-commercial (accessed July 10, 2020).

24. Susan Fournier, "Consumers and Their Brands: Developing Relationship Theory in Consumer Research," *Journal of Consumer Research* 24 (March 1998): 343–73.

25. Laura O'Reilly, "How 6 Colorful Characters Propelled M&M's to Become America's Favorite Candy," *Business Insider*, March 26, 2016, https://www.businessinsider.com/the-story-of-the-mms-characters-2016-3 (accessed July 13, 2020).

26. For an example of how consumers associate food brands with a range of female body shapes, see Martin R. Lautman, "End-Benefit Segmentation and Prototypical Bonding," *Journal of Advertising Research*, June/July 1991, 9–18.

27. Austin Carr, "Airbnb Unveils a Major Rebranding Effort That Paves the Way for Sharing More Than Homes," *Fast Company*, July 16, 2014, https://www.fastcompany.com/3033130/most-innovative-companies/airbnb-unveils-a-major-rebranding-effort-that-paves-the-way-for-sh (accessed April 16, 2016).

28. Kevin Lane Keller, "The Brand Report Card," *Harvard Business Review*, January–February 2000 (Harvard Business School reprint R00104).

29. Jeremy Sinek, "As Luxury Makers Offer Cheaper Cars, Does It Help or Devalue the Brand?" *The Globe and Mail*, April 12, 2016, https://www.theglobeandmail.com/globe-drive/news/industry-news/as-luxury-makers-offer-cheaper-cars-does-it-help-or-devalue-the-brand/article29539479/ (accessed April 16, 2016).

30. Meghan Hunter, "Do You Know the Difference between Marriott Hotel Brands?," *Million Mile Secrets*, May 19, 2020, https://million-milesecrets.com/guides/marriott-hotel-brands/#:~:text=Here%20are%20the%2032%20current,Autograph%20Collection%20Hotels (accessed May 11, 2020).

31. https://www.coca-colacompany.com/brands/coca-cola (accessed December 22, 2020).

32. Elaine Lowe, "How Private Labels Could Be Amazon's, Target's Next Cash Cow," October 27, 2017, https://www.investors.com/news/target-amazon-private-label-exclusive-brands/ (accessed April 24, 2018).

33. Pamela DeLoatch, "Aldi Racks Up More Than 200 Private Label Awards," January 3, 2018, https://www.fooddive.com/news/grocery-aldi-racks-up-more-than-200-private-labelawards/513813/ (accessed April 24, 2018).

34. Walmart, "$4 Prescriptions," https://www.walmart.com/cp/$4-prescriptions/1078664 (accessed May 4, 2018).

35. "Shopkins License Agreement with Build-a-Bear Workshop," October 13, 2017, https://shopkinsworld.com/shopkins-licenseagreement-build-bear-workshop (accessed April 24, 2018).

36. Tony Lisanti, "Warner Bros. and the Magic World of Harry Potter," June 1, 2009, http://www.licensemag.com/license-global/warnerbros-and-magic-world-harry-potter (accessed April 16, 2016); Morgan Korn, "Universal Makes Big Bet on Harry Potter Again," June 23, 2014, https://finance.yahoo.com/blogs/daily-ticker/universal-s-diagon-alley-opens-july-8-151552286.html (accessed April 16, 2016); Leo Sun, "Theme Park Sales Again," April 1, 2016, http://www.fool.com/investing/general/2016/04/01/harrypotter-may-boost-comcast-corps-theme-park-sa.aspx (accessed April 16, 2016).

37. "7 Examples of Successful Cobranding Partnerships and Why They're So Great," *MyBlog*, June 20, 2019, http://hypbrands.com/marketing/7-examples-of-successful-co-branding-partnerships-and-why-theyre-so-great/ (accessed July 14, 2020); Stefania Saviolo and Antonio Marazza, *Lifestyle Brands: A Guide to Aspirational Marketing* (London: Palgrave Macmillan, 2013).

38. D. C. Denison, "The Boston Globe Business Intelligence Column," *Boston Globe*, May 26, 2002.

39. Richard Kestenbaum, "What 'Ingredient Brands' Are and Why They're Important," *Forbes*, February 4, 2018, https://www.forbes.com/sites/richardkestenbaum/2018/02/04/what-ingredient-brands-are-and-why-theyre-important/#1ae981417c36 (accessed April 24, 2018).

40. Stephanie Thompson, "Brand Buddies," *Brandweek*, February 23, 1998, 26–30; Jean Halliday, "L.L. Bean, Subaru Pair for Co-Branding," *Advertising Age*, February 21, 2000, 21.

41. Ben Kesslen, "Aunt Jemima Brand to Change Name, Remove Image that Quaker Says Is 'Based on a Racial Stereotype'," *NBC News*, June 7, 2020, https://www.nbcnews.com/news/us-news/aunt-jemima-brand-will-change-name-remove-image-quaker-says-n1231260 (accessed July 14, 2020); Aris Folly, "Company Behind Mrs. Butterworth's Now Doing 'Complete Brand and Packaging Review,'" June 18, 2020, https://thehill.com/blogs/blog-briefing-room/news/503368-company-behind-mrs-butter-worths-now-doing-complete-brand-and (accessed July 14, 2020).

42. Pringles, "Favorites," https://www.pringles.com/us/products/favorites.html?gclid=EAIaIQobChMI27GIyN7N6gIVgq_ICh0uVg3GEAAYASABEgJZhPD_BwE (accessed July 13, 2020).

43. "Jim Beam Family DNA Informs Bourbon Bottle Redesign," *Packaging World*, April 16, 2016, https://www.packworld.com/design/materials-containers/article/13370140/jim-beam-family-dna-informs-bourbon-bottle-redesign (accessed April 16, 2016); "The Revival of Jim Beam: How the Equality Movement by StrawberryFrog Saved an American Icon," *The Drum Network*, September 20, 2019, https://www.thedrum.com/news/2018/09/20/the-revival-jim-beam-how-the-equality-marketing-movement-strawberryfrog-saved (accessed July 11, 2020).

44. Aaron Baar, "Accidental Purchases: Blame Package Design," *Marketing Daily/MediaPost News*, October 29, 2010, https://www.mediapost.com/publications/article/116283/accidental-purchases-blame-package-design.html (accessed April 16, 2016).

45. "Labels to Include Trans Fat," *San Fernando Valley Business Journal*, January 19, 2004, 15.

46. U.S. Food & Drug Administration, "Changes to the Nutrition Facts Label," https://www.fda.gov/Food/GuidanceRegulation/GuidanceDocumentsRegulatoryInformation/LabelingNutrition/ucm385663.htm (accessed April 24, 2018).

47. Professor Jakki Mohr, University of Montana, personal communication (April 2004).

48. Based on: Hrefna Palsdottir, "Drink 8 Glasses of Water a Day: Fact or Fiction?" *Healthline*, November 8, 2016, https://www.healthline.com/nutrition/8-glasses-of-water-per-day#section2; Priscella Vega, "Hydro Flask Started Out at Farmers Markets. Here's How It Got So Huge," *Los Angeles Times*, February 23, 2020, https://www.latimes.com/business/story/2020-02-23/hydro-flask-water-bottle-why-is-it-special; Kai Burkhardt, "The Hydro Flask Is a Gen Z Trend We Can Get Behind," *CNN*, October 24, 2019, https://www.cnn.com/2019/10/24/cnn-underscored/hydro-flask-review/index.html#:~:text=The%20Hydro%20Flask%20craze%20is,plastic%20bottle%20in%20your%20hand; Harris Newman, "The Birth of a Brand," *Oregon Business*, March 29, 2019, https://www.oregonbusiness.com/article/sponsored/item/18713-the-birth-of-a-brand; Ann Binlot, "Hydro Flask Celebrates a Decade of Keeping Warm Drinks Hot and Chilled Beverages Cold," *Forbes*, December 29, 2019, https://www.forbes.com/sites/abinlot/2019/12/29/hydro-flask-celebrates-a-decade-of-keeping-warm-drinks-hot-and-chilled-beverages-cold/#48ff8d187c43; Jacob Gallagher, "The Latest Eco-Friendly Status Symbol? Water Bottles," *The Wall Street Journal*, October 7, 2019, https://www.wsj.com/articles/the-latest-eco-friendly-status-symbol-water-bottles-11570458600; International Bottled Water Association, "Bottled Water's Retail Dollar Sales Increased 5.2 Percent from 2018 to 2019, Beverage Marketing Corporation Data Indicates," *Vending Market Watch*, May 26, 2020, https://www.vendingmarketwatch.com/coffee-service/water-equipment-coolers-filters-accessories-etc/news/21139681/bottled-waters-retail-dollar-sales-increased-52-percent-from-2018-to-2019-beverage-marketing-corporation-data-indicates; Thomas J. Ryan, "Conversation with Hydro Flask's Retiring General Manager Scott Allan," *SGB Media*, January 29, 2020, https://sgbonline.com/conversation-with-hydro-flasks-general-manager-scott-allan/; Caroline Kelm, "Hydro Flask Introduces New Refreshingly Bold Logo," *Snews*, May 12, 2017, https://www.snewsnet.com/press-release/hydro-flask-introduces-new-refreshingly-bold-logo; Tim Newcomb, "Why Are Hydro Flask Bottles Suddenly Everywhere?," *Popular Mechanics*, February 23, 2019, https://www.popularme-chanics.com/adventure/outdoor-gear/a25657823/hydro-flask/; inventRightTV, "How Travis Invented Hydro Flask, The Most Used Water Bottle in the World!," *YouTube*, February 12, 2020, https://www.youtube.com/watch?v=szdbseI5P60 (August 4, 2020); Becky Pemberton, "The VSCO Girl Is the Latest Gen-Z Craze to Go Viral – And Everyone Loves to Hate It," *The Sun*, September 25, 2019, https://www.thesun.co.uk/fabulous/10001715/vsco-girl-gen-z-craze-viral/; Becky Hughes, "What Does VSCO Think About the 'VSCO Girls'?," *The New York Times*, August 20, 2019, https://www.nytimes.com/2019/08/30/style/vsco-girls.html; Amanda Mull, "How Fancy Water Bottles Became a 21st-Century Status Symbol," *The Atlantic*, February 12, 2019, https://www.theatlantic.com/health/archive/2019/02/luxury-water-bottles/582595/; Thomas J. Ryan, "Hydro Flask Delivers 'Fantastic' Year," *SGB Media*, April 29, 2020, https://sgbonline.com/hydro-flask-delivers-fantastic-year/.

10 Price: What Is the Value Proposition Worth?

Auto Europe

Meet Imad Khalidi
▼ A Decision Maker at Auto Europe

Imad Khalidi is President and CEO of Auto Europe, a major international car rental provider. He was born in Jerusalem and graduated from Jean-Baptiste de La Salle College and Birzeit College, affiliated with American University of Beirut. He attended two full-time management courses at the INSEAD in Fontainebleau, France. Imad speaks five languages.

In 1990, he joined Auto Europe as Executive Vice President, rising to the position of President in 1991. Imad brought with him an extensive knowledge of the industry, including prior background as a District Manager with the Hertz Corporation. He has guided Auto Europe from being a "car rental broker" to a leader in European car rental services. In 1994, he expanded the company's services to include scheduled air service and European hotel accommodations. In 1997, he led the company to an IPO with the company traded publicly on NASDAQ. Imad has won numerous travel industry awards, including being named the ASTA [...] member of the Year.

Auto Europe is a major provider of rental vehicles in cities throughout Europe. Most of its end customers are American tourists who are visiting Europe and want to be sure they have a safe and reliable vehicle at their disposal when they tour in various countries. Unlike the typical car rental in the U.S. that lasts about three days, the rentals that Auto Europe provides are more likely to be for at least 10 days. The company has 600 employees and rents about 2.1 million cars per year. The employees own stock in the company, and Imad is constantly challenged to maintain a healthy cash flow so that he can meet his payroll and make money for these stakeholders.

Auto Europe is a wholesale organization. It doesn't compete with other car rental companies, like Hertz and Avis. Instead it works *with* them to procure vehicles for customers. These agencies like to work with Auto Europe because the company helps them to fill gaps during slow periods—for example, when business travel decreases in the summer months and tourists flock to European cities. Unlike retail rental companies, Auto Europe does not actually have any cars in inventory. When a customer arranges for a vehicle, the company finds one that retail firms like Hertz and Avis have available in a European city. A lot of its business comes from travel agents who earn a commission when they arrange for a rental on behalf of a client.

Imad's Info

What I do when I'm not working:
Read

First job out of school:
Bellboy

Career high:
CEO

My hero:
Gandhi

My motto to live by:
Give people a chance.

What drives me:
Challenge

My management style:
Teamwork

My pet peeve:
Wasting resources

Here's my problem...

Real **People**, Real **Choices**

Auto Europe for the most part does not compete on price, but rather on quality service. While college students and other young people look to platforms like Priceline to find the lowest possible rental fees, Auto Europe's customers tend to be more affluent. Because they work through travel agents who add about 15–20 percent to travel packages when they take a commission, clients for the most part are willing to pay a premium in order to ensure that they will get a car that doesn't break down at midnight in a deserted European village.

Auto Europe tries to be flexible to some degree on fees, but there is a limit to how much Imad and his team are willing to cut prices. They prefer to emphasize that customers will receive a very high level of service. For example, if a car does break down in that deserted village, Auto Europe provides free 24-hour assistance to fix or replace it.

Still, these relatively wealthy customers didn't get that way by just giving away their hard-earned money! Many of them do try to get a lower price for the vehicles they book. Imad frequently gets requests to cut prices when a customer finds a similar car that's available elsewhere for a lower price. For example, a typical request might be an upscale Mercedes E 240 rental that Imad rents for $1,000 per week. Because the Mercedes is more in demand and costs more, Imad has to pay a higher price to obtain it for a customer compared to some other models that are available. Many Americans who travel throughout Europe prefer to drive a European car with a tony (upscale) image, like a Mercedes. Still, the customer may find another dealer who offers a General Motors car for $900 and then ask Imad to match that price for the Mercedes.

Imad considered his **options** 1·2·3

Option 1
Match the price and provide the Mercedes for $900 instead of $1,000. Imad loses money on this deal, so obviously it's not a very attractive option. On the other hand, this discount makes the customer happy. If he or she turns into a repeat client as a result, the short-term loss can turn into a long-term profit.

Option 2
Offer to provide the same GM car at $890 to keep things apples-to-apples. This makes the customer happy and Imad still turns a profit. However, Imad makes substantially less than if he rents the Mercedes for $1,000. If the client insists he or she still wants the Mercedes for $900, Imad may lose him or her as a customer. In that case, Imad may try to offer a compromise price for the Mercedes, such as $950, in order to keep the customer.

Option 3
Continue to offer the Mercedes for $1,000 and explain that this vehicle is more valuable than the GM car, so it's worth it to pay a premium. The customer may choose to shop further, and he or she may possibly find the Mercedes elsewhere for less than $1,000 (but more than $900). In this case, Imad loses the business completely. However, when the customer does the homework on the pricing environment, he does Imad a favor because he alerts him that he needs to adjust his pricing to be more competitive.

Now put yourself in Imad's shoes. Which option would you choose and why?

You Choose

Which **Option** would you choose, and **why**?

☐ Option 1 ☐ Option 2 ☐ Option 3

10.1 "Yes, but What Does It Cost?"

OBJECTIVE
Explain the importance of pricing and how marketers set objectives for their pricing strategies.

"If you have to ask how much it is, you can't afford it!" We've all heard that, but how often do you buy something without asking the price? If price weren't an issue, we'd all drive dream cars, take trips to exotic places, and live like royalty. In the real world, though, most of us need to at least consider a product's price before we buy it.

In the past two chapters, we've talked about creating and managing products. But to create value for customers, marketers must do more than just create a fantastic new (or existing) widget with all the bells and whistles consumers want. Equally (if not more) important is pricing the new offering so that consumers are willing to fork over their hard-earned cash to own the product. The question of what to charge for a product is a central part of the marketing plan.

In this chapter, we'll tackle the basic question—what is price? We'll look at pricing objectives and the roles that demand, costs, revenues, and

Digital currency systems such as Bitcoin may disrupt the way we think about money.

Maurice Savage/Alamy Stock Photo

341

the environment play in the pricing decision process. Then, we'll explore specific pricing strategies and tactics. Finally, we'll look at the dynamic world of pricing on the Internet and at some psychological, legal, and ethical aspects of pricing.

What Is Price?

As we said in Chapter 1, *price* is the assignment of value, or the amount the consumer must exchange to receive the offering or product. Price, of course, has many names. We pay college *tuition*, *rent* for our apartment, *interest* on our credit card balance, a lawyer's or a doctor's professional *fee*, an insurance *premium*, a *toll* to use a road or a bridge, and a taxi, airplane, or bus *fare*.

Payment may also be in the form of goods, services, favors, votes, or anything else that has *value* to the other party. Long before societies minted coins or printed paper money, people exchanged one good or service for another. This practice, called *bartering*, still occurs today. For example, someone who owns a home at a mountain ski resort may exchange a weekend stay for car repair or dental work. No money changes hands, but there still is an exchange of value (just ask the Internal Revenue Service).

Other nonmonetary costs often are important to marketers. What is the cost of wearing seat belts? What is it worth to people to camp out in a clean national park? What does it cost to have cleaner air? To recycle? It is also important to consider an *opportunity cost*, or the value of something we give up to obtain something else. For example, the cost to obtain a college degree includes more than tuition; it also includes the income that the student could have earned by working instead of going to classes (no, we're not trying to make you feel guilty). And what about a public service campaign designed to reduce alcohol-related accidents? The cost to the individual is either agreeing to abstain and be a designated driver or shelling out for taxi or Uber fare. The value is reducing the risk of having a serious or possibly fatal accident. Unfortunately, too many people feel the chance of having an accident is so slim that the cost of abstaining from drinking is too high.

As Figure 10.1 shows, the elements of price planning include six steps: developing pricing objectives, estimating demand, determining costs, evaluating the pricing environment, choosing a pricing strategy, and developing pricing tactics. In this chapter, we talk about how marketers go through these steps for successful price planning.

Step 1: Develop Pricing Objectives

The first crucial step in price planning is to develop pricing objectives. These must support the broader objectives of the firm, such as maximizing shareholder value, as well as its overall marketing objectives, such as increasing market share. Figure 10.2 provides examples of different types of pricing objectives. Let's take a closer look at these.

Profit Objectives

As we discussed in Chapter 2, often a firm's overall objectives relate to a certain level of profit it hopes to realize. When pricing strategies are determined by profit objectives, the focus most often is on a target level of profit growth or a desired net profit margin. A profit objective is important to firms that believe profit is what motivates shareholders and bankers to invest in a company.

Because firms usually produce an entire product line or a product mix, profit objectives may focus on pricing for the firm's entire portfolio of products. In such cases, marketers develop pricing strategies that maximize the profits of the entire portfolio rather than focusing on the costs or profitability of each individual product.

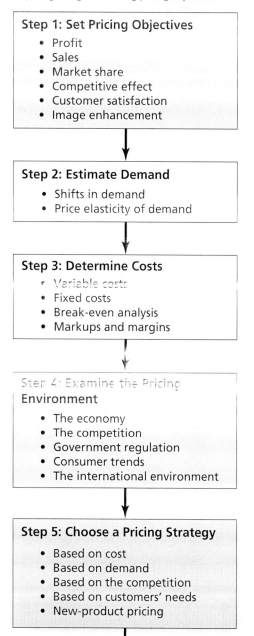

Figure 10.1 *Process* | Elements of Price Planning

Successful price planning includes a series of six orderly steps beginning with setting pricing objectives.

Step 1: Set Pricing Objectives
- Profit
- Sales
- Market share
- Competitive effect
- Customer satisfaction
- Image enhancement

Step 2: Estimate Demand
- Shifts in demand
- Price elasticity of demand

Step 3: Determine Costs
- Variable costs
- Fixed costs
- Break-even analysis
- Markups and margins

Step 4: Examine the Pricing Environment
- The economy
- The competition
- Government regulation
- Consumer trends
- The international environment

Step 5: Choose a Pricing Strategy
- Based on cost
- Based on demand
- Based on the competition
- Based on customers' needs
- New-product pricing

Step 6: Develop Pricing Tactics
- For individual products
- For multiple products
- Distribution-based tactics
- Discounting for channel members

Figure 10.2 *Process* | Pricing Objectives

The first step in price planning is to develop pricing objectives that support the broader objectives of the firm.

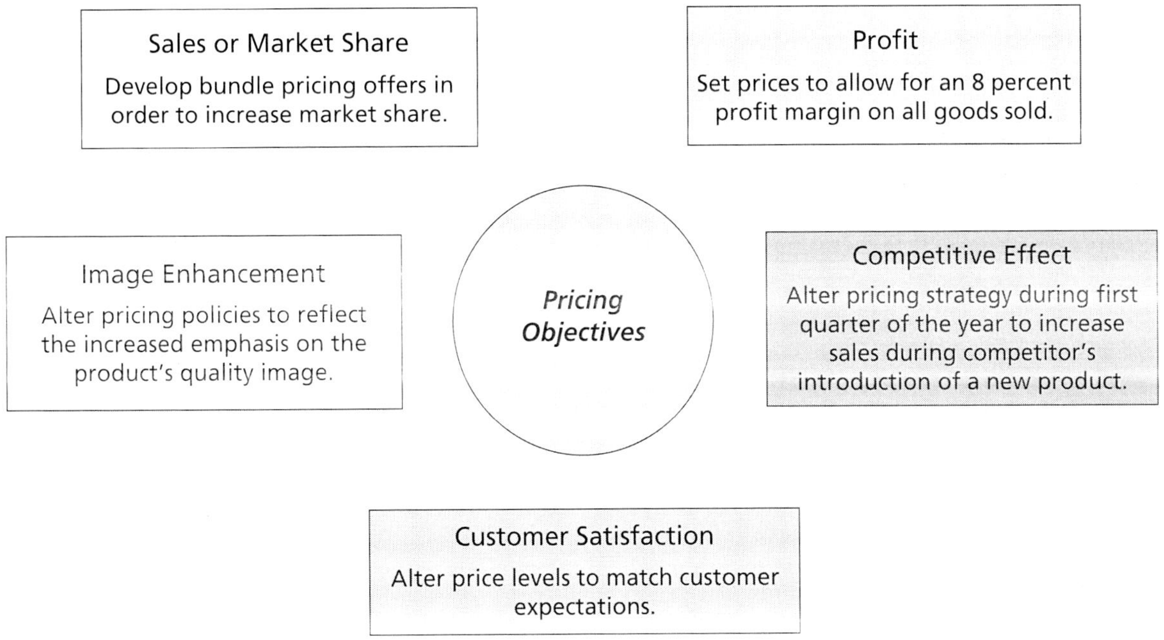

Sales or Market Share	Profit
Develop bundle pricing offers in order to increase market share.	Set prices to allow for an 8 percent profit margin on all goods sold.

Pricing Objectives

Image Enhancement	Competitive Effect
Alter pricing policies to reflect the increased emphasis on the product's quality image.	Alter pricing strategy during first quarter of the year to increase sales during competitor's introduction of a new product.

Customer Satisfaction

Alter price levels to match customer expectations.

For example, it may be better to price one product especially high and lose sales on it if that decision causes customers to instead purchase a product that has a higher profit margin. That's why many retail chains are happy if you buy their own store brand. While the store brand is a lower cost to you, the retailer may sell the product for 35 or 40 percent more than they pay for it, while with the national brand, the price has only a 30 percent markup on their cost. We'll talk more about markups a little later in this chapter.

Although profits are an important consideration in the pricing of all goods and services, ... popular fads in the 1950s, mopeds and Pet Rocks in the 1970s, and Beanie Babies, the Furby, and rollerblades in the 1990s. Today's fads include the *Tiger King* TV show, CBD oil, goat yoga, glamorous sneakers, AI-inspired artwork, Peloton workouts, cryotherapy (where you spend three minutes in a chamber where the temperature is between minus 230 and minus 300 degrees), and eating Tide pods (yes, really!). Because fads such as these have a very short market life (and your life will be pretty short if you eat those Tide pods), the profit objective is essential to allow the firm to recover its investment in a short time. In such cases, the firm must harvest profits before customers lose interest and move on to the next cool idea.

Sales or Market Share Objectives

Often the objective of a pricing strategy is to maximize sales (either in dollars or in units) or to increase market share, the percentage of a market in terms of sales units or revenue accounted for by a specific firm, product line, or brand. Does setting a price intended to increase unit sales or **market share** simply mean pricing the product lower than the competition? Sometimes, yes. Providers of cable and satellite TV services, such as Spectrum, Xfinity, DIRECTV, and AT&T U-verse, relentlessly offer consumers better deals that include more TV, wireless Internet, and telephone service. But lowering prices is not always necessary to increase market share. If a company's product has a competitive advantage, keeping the price at the same level as other firms may satisfy sales and/or market share objectives. Lowering prices can lead to a "price war" when consumers switch from one producer to another simply because the price changes.

market share
The percentage of a market (defined in terms of either sales units or revenue) accounted for by a specific firm, product line(s), or brand(s).

Competitive Effect Objectives

Sometimes strategists design the pricing plan to dilute the competition's marketing efforts. In these cases, a firm may deliberately try to preempt or reduce the impact of a rival's pricing changes. This is referred to as **competitive-effect pricing**, or **market-based pricing**. Generally, all airlines offer the exact or almost the same prices for the routes they fly. That is, until low-cost carriers such as Spirit or Frontier Airlines move in. That's what happened when these two airlines moved into Philadelphia and the cost of the one-way fare between Detroit and Philadelphia went from over $300 to $183 on all carriers, including Delta Air Lines and American Airlines.[1] When the COVID-19 pandemic forced consumers all over the globe to self-quarantine, airline travel dropped so low that airlines were grounding significant portions of their fleets. For those who chose to fly, competitive-effect pricing continued and all airlines slashed prices similarly. Some one-way flights were priced as low as $14.[2]

Customer Satisfaction Objectives

Many quality-focused firms believe that profits result from making customer satisfaction their primary objective. These firms believe that if they focus solely on short-term profits, they will lose sight of their objective to retain customers for the long term that we discussed in Chapter 1. In 2014, retail giant Walmart, long known as the "everyday low price" leader, introduced Savings Catcher, a tool within its mobile app that customers could use to ensure they were getting the lowest price on more than 80,000 food and household products when compared to the advertised prices of those of the competitors in the same geographic area. Customers could scan the receipt with the Walmart phone app and the Savings Catcher tool would automatically compare the prices on the receipt with the advertised prices at other local stores. Savings were returned to the customer in the form of an e-gift card that could be used for future Walmart purchases.[3] In 2019, Walmart announced it was ending the Savings Catcher program, earning the anger of customers who wanted to stage a boycott.[4]

Image Enhancement Objectives

Consumers often use price to make inferences about the quality of a product. In fact, marketers know that price is often an important means of communicating not only quality but also image to prospective customers. The image-enhancement function of pricing is particularly important with **prestige products** (or luxury products) that have a high price and appeal to status-conscious consumers. Most of us would agree that the high price tag on a Rolex watch, a Louis Vuitton handbag, or a Rolls-Royce car, although representing the higher costs of producing the product, is vital to shaping an image of an extraordinary product that only the wealthy can afford (not counting the "real" Rolex you buy for $10 from that shady guy on the street).

From the iPhone's introduction, Apple used prestige pricing to ensure an image of a premium brand that is a more refined and polished alternative compared to cheaper smartphones. The company also applied this strategy when it introduced the iPhone X with its infrared facial recognition and wireless charging in 2017 at a price of around $1,000. By 2020, Apple sales had fallen as many consumers decided to keep their current iPhone rather than invest $1,000 or more in a newer one. In April 2020, Apple added a lower-priced phone to their line. The iPhone SE (2020) was priced at $399 for the 64GB model and $449 for 128GB.[5]

A Rolex watch is a prestige product that tends to gain value over time.

10.2 Costs, Demand, Revenue, and the Pricing Environment

OBJECTIVE

Describe how marketers use costs, demand, revenue, and the pricing environment to make pricing decisions.

Once a marketer decides on its pricing objectives, it is time to begin the actual process of price setting. To set the right price, marketers must understand a variety of quantitative and qualitative factors that can mean success or failure for the pricing strategy. As Figure 10.3 shows, these include an estimate of demand, knowledge of costs and revenue, and an understanding of the pricing environment.

Figure 10.3 *Process* | Factors in Price Setting

To set the right price, marketers must understand a variety of quantitative and qualitative factors.

Costs	Demand
Revenue	Pricing Environment

Step 2: Estimate Demand

The second step in price planning is to estimate demand. *Demand* refers to the quantity of a good or service that consumers and business customers are willing and able to buy at a given price in a given time period. Because demand normally changes with changes in price, marketers must know how much consumers are willing to buy at different prices. Obviously, marketers should know the answer to this question before they set prices. Therefore, one of the earliest steps marketers take in price planning is to estimate demand for their products.

Demand Curves

Economists use a graph of a *demand curve* to illustrate the effect of price on the quantity demanded of a product. The demand curve, which can be a curved or straight line, shows the quantity of a product that customers will buy in a market during a period of time at various prices if all other factors remain the same.

Figure 10.4 shows demand curves for normal and prestige products. The vertical axis for the demand curve represents the different prices that a firm might charge for a product (*P*). The horizontal axis shows the number of units or quantity (*Q*) of the product demanded. The demand curve for most goods (that we show on the left side of Figure 10.4) slopes downward and to the right. As the price of the product goes up (P_1 to P_2), the number of units that customers are willing to buy goes down (Q_1 to Q_2). If prices decrease, customers

Figure 10.4 *Snapshot* | Demand Curves for Normal and Prestige Products

There is an inverse relationship between price and demand for normal products. For prestige products, demand will increase—to a point—as price increases or will decrease as price decreases.

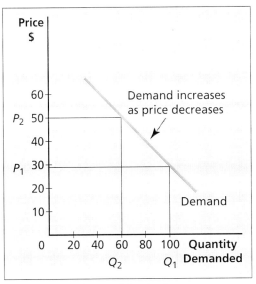

Normal Products

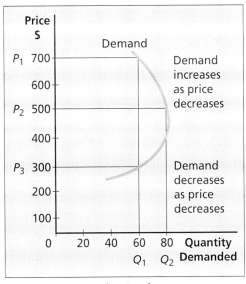

Prestige Products

will buy more. This is the *law of demand*. For example, if the price of bananas goes up, customers will probably buy fewer of them. And if the price gets really high, customers will eat their cereal without bananas.

There are, however, exceptions to this typical price–demand relationship. In fact, there are situations in which (otherwise sane) people desire a product more as it *increases* in price. For prestige products such as luxury cars or jewelry, a price hike may actually result in an *increase* in the quantity consumers demand because they see the product as more valuable. In such cases, the demand curve slopes upward. The right-hand side of Figure 10.4 shows the "backward-bending" demand curve we associate with prestige products. If the price increases, consumers perceive the product to be more desirable and demand is likely to increase. You can see that if the price increases from P_3 to P_2, the quantity demanded increases from Q_1 to Q_2. On the other hand, if the price decreases, consumers think the product is less desirable. This is what happens if the price begins at P_2 and then goes up to P_3; quantity decreases from Q_2 to Q_1. Still, the higher-price/higher-demand relationship has its limits. If the firm increases the price too much (say, from P_2 to P_1), making the product unaffordable for all but a few buyers, demand will begin to decrease. The direction the backward-bending curve takes shows this.

Shifts in Demand

The demand curves we've shown assume that all factors other than price stay the same. But what if they don't? What if the company improves the product? What happens when there is a glitzy new advertising campaign that turns a product into a "must-have" for a lot of people? What if stealthy *paparazzi* catch Brad Pitt using the product at home and the photo gets thousands of "likes" on Facebook? Any of these things could cause an *upward shift* of the demand curve. An upward shift in the demand curve means that at any given price, demand is greater than before the shift occurs.

Figure 10.5 shows the upward shift of the demand curve as it moves from D_1 to D_2. At D_1, before the shift occurs, customers will be willing to purchase the quantity Q_1 (or 80 units in Figure 10.5) at the given price, P (or $60 in Figure 10.5). For example, customers at a particular store may buy 80 barbecue grills at $60 a grill. But then the store runs a huge advertising campaign featuring Rihanna on her patio using the barbecue grill. The

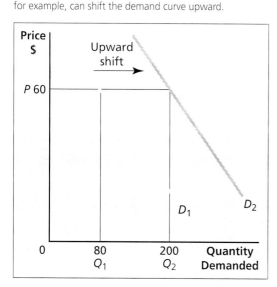

Figure 10.5 *Snapshot* | Shift in the Demand Curve

Changes in the environment or in company efforts can cause a shift in the demand curve. A great advertising campaign, for example, can shift the demand curve upward.

the quantity demanded has changed to Q_2. In our example, the store is now selling 200 barbecue grills at $60 per grill. From a marketing standpoint, this shift is the best of all worlds. Without lowering prices, the company can sell more of its product. As a result, total revenues go up, and so do profits, unless, of course, the new promotion costs as much as those potential additional profits.

Demand curves may also shift downward. For example, if a rumor spreads at warp speed on Twitter that the gas grill was faulty and could cause dangerous fires, even with the price remaining at $60, the curve would shift downward, and the quantity demanded would drop so that the store could sell only 30 or 40 grills.

Estimate Demand

It's extremely important for marketers to understand and accurately estimate demand. Plans for production of the product as well as marketing activities and budgets must all be based on reasonably accurate estimates of potential sales.

So how do marketers reasonably estimate potential sales? Marketers predict total demand first by identifying the number of buyers or potential buyers for their product, i.e., their target market, and then multiplying

Table 10.1	Estimating Demand for Pizza	
Number of families in market	180,000
Average number of pizzas per family per year	6
Total annual market demand	1,080,000
Company's predicted share of the total market	3 percent
Estimated annual company demand	32,400 pizzas
Estimated monthly company demand	2,700 pizzas
Estimated weekly company demand	675 pizzas

that estimate times the average amount each member of the target market is likely to purchase. Table 10.1 shows how a small business, such as a start-up pizza restaurant, estimates demand in markets it expects to reach. For example, the pizza entrepreneur may use U.S. Census data to determine that there are 180,000 consumer households in his geographic market who normally buy pizza from various retail pizza outlets in the area. While some households buy a pizza or more every week and some never buy pizza at all, we could estimate that each household would purchase an average of six pizzas a year. The total annual demand is 1,080,000 pizzas (hold the anchovies on at least one of those, please).

Once the marketer estimates total demand, the next step is to predict what the company's market share is likely to be. The company's estimated demand is then its share of the whole (estimated) pie. In our pizza example, the entrepreneur may feel that he can gain 3 percent of this market, or about 2,700 pizzas per month—not bad for a new start-up business. Of course, such projections need to take into consideration other factors that might affect demand, such as new competitors entering the market, changing consumer tastes—like a sudden demand for low-carb takeout food, or the Surgeon General proclaiming that pizza is the most perfect food for a healthy diet—but we knew that already!

Price Elasticity of Demand

Marketers also need to know how their customers are likely to react to a price change. In particular, it is critical to understand whether a change in price will have a large or small impact on demand. How much can a firm increase or decrease its price until it sees a marked change in sales? If the price of a pizza increases by $1, will people switch to subs and burgers? What would happen if the pizza went up $2? Or even $5?

Price elasticity of demand is a measure of the sensitivity of customers to changes in price: If the price changes by 10 percent, what will be the percentage change in demand for the product? The word *elasticity* indicates that changes in price usually cause demand to stretch or retract like a rubber band. We calculate price elasticity of demand as follows:

price elasticity of demand
The percentage change in unit sales that results from a percentage change in price.

$$\text{Price elasticity of demand} = \frac{\text{Percentage change in quantity demanded}}{\text{Percentage change in price}}$$

Sometimes customers are sensitive to changes in prices, and a change in price results in a substantial change in the quantity they demand. In such instances, we have a case of **elastic demand**. In other situations, a change in price has little or no effect on the quantity consumers are willing to buy. We describe this as **inelastic demand**. Let's use the formula in this example: Suppose the pizza maker finds (from experience or from marketing research) that lowering the price of his pizza 10 percent (from $10 per pizza to $9) will cause a 15 percent increase in demand. He would calculate the price elasticity of demand as 15 divided by 10. The price elasticity of demand would be 1.5. If the price elasticity of demand is greater than one, demand is elastic; that is, consumers respond to the price decrease by demanding more. Or, if the price increases, consumers will demand less. Figure 10.6 shows these calculations.

elastic demand
Demand in which changes in price have large effects on the amount demanded.

inelastic demand
Demand in which changes in price have little or no effect on the amount demanded.

Figure 10.6 *Snapshot* | Price Elasticity of Demand

Marketers know that price elasticity of demand is an important pricing metric.

Elastic demand

Price changes from $10 to $9.

$10 – 9 = $1

1/10 = 10% change in price

Demand changes from 2,700 per month to 3,100 per month

$$3,100$$
$$- 2,700$$

Increase

$$400 \text{ pizzas}$$

Percentage increase   400/2,700 = .148 ~ 15% change in demand

Price elasticity of demand = $\dfrac{\text{percentage change in quantity demanded}}{\text{percentage change in price}}$

Price elasticity of demand = $\dfrac{15\%}{10\%}$ = 1.5

Inelastic demand

Price changes from $10 to $9.

$10 – 9 = $1

1/10 = 10% change in price

Demand changes from 2,700 per month to 2,835 per month

$$2,835$$
$$- 2,700$$

Increase

$$135 \text{ pizzas}$$

Percentage increase   135/2,700 = 0.05 ~ 5% change in demand

Price elasticity of demand = $\dfrac{\text{percentage change in quantity demanded}}{\text{percentage change in price}}$

Price elasticity of demand = $\dfrac{5\%}{10\%}$ = 0.5

Our pizza restaurant entrepreneur doesn't really care about elasticity—he only cares about his bottom line. As Figure 10.7 illustrates, when demand is elastic, changes in price and in total revenues (total sales) work in opposite directions. If the price is increased, total sales/revenues decrease. If the price is decreased, total sales/revenues increase. With elastic demand, the demand curve shown in Figure 10.7 is more horizontal. With an elasticity of demand of 1.5, a decrease in price will increase the pizza maker's total revenue.

If demand is price inelastic, can marketers keep raising prices so that revenues and profits will grow larger and larger? And what if demand is elastic? Does it mean that marketers can never raise prices? The answer to these questions is "no" (surprise!). Elasticity of demand for a product often differs for different price levels and with different percentages of change. If we calculate the difference in demand with a price increase from $8 to $10, it will be quite different from the same $2 increase from $17 to $19 and so on.

Other factors can affect price elasticity and sales. Consider the availability of *substitute* goods or services. If a product has a close substitute, its demand will be elastic; that is, a change in price will result in a change in demand as consumers move to buy the substitute product. For example, all but the most die-hard cola fans might consider Coke and Pepsi close substitutes. If the price of Pepsi goes up, many people will buy Coke instead. Marketers of products with close substitutes are less likely to compete on price because they recognize that doing so could result in less profit as consumers switch from one brand to another.

Figure 10.7 *Snapshot* | Price-Elastic and Price-Inelastic Demand

Price elasticity of demand represents how demand responds to changes in prices. If a price increase results in little change in demand, then demand is said to be price inelastic. If a price increase results in a large change in demand, demand is price elastic.

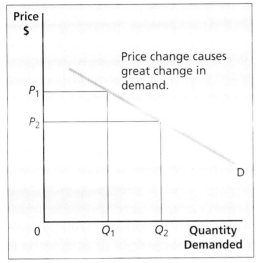

Elastic Demand

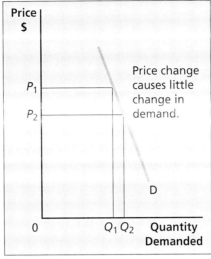

Inelastic Demand

Changes in prices of other products also affect the demand for an item, a phenomenon we label **cross-elasticity of demand**. When products are substitutes for each other, an increase in the price of one will increase the demand for the other. For example, if the price of bananas goes up, consumers may instead buy more strawberries, blueberries, or apples. However, when products are *complements*—that is, when one product is essential to the use of a second—an increase in the price of one decreases the demand for the second. So if the price of gasoline goes up, consumers may drive less, carpool, or take public transportation, and thus demand for tires (as well as gasoline) will decrease. That's the reason the U.S. government rationed gasoline during WWII. There was no shortage of gasoline, but there was a shortage of tires. So, knowing this by rationing gasoline, consumers were restricted how much they could drive each week. This resulted in tires lasting longer so that people didn't lose their means of transportation.

cross-elasticity of demand
When changes in the price of one product affect the demand for another item.

Step 3: Determine Costs

Estimating demand helps marketers to determine possible prices to charge for a product. It tells them how much of the product they think they'll be able to sell at different prices. Knowing this brings them to the third step in determining a product's price: making sure the price will cover costs. Before marketers can determine price, they must understand the relationship of cost, demand, and revenue for their product. In this section, we'll talk about different types of costs that marketers must consider in pricing. Then, we'll show how marketers use that information to make pricing decisions.

Variable and Fixed Costs

It's obvious that the cost of producing a product plays a big role when firms decide what to charge for it. If an item's selling price is lower than the cost to produce it, it doesn't take a rocket scientist to figure out that the firm will lose money. Before we look at how cost influences pricing decisions, we need to understand the different types of costs that firms incur.

First, a firm incurs **variable costs**—the per-unit costs of production that will fluctuate depending on how many units or individual products a firm produces. For example, if it takes 25 cents worth of nails—a variable cost—to build one bookcase, it will take 50 cents

variable costs
The costs of production (raw and processed materials, parts, and labor) that are tied to and vary by the number of units produced.

Figure 10.8 *Snapshot* | Variable Costs for Bookcases at Different Levels of Production

Variable Costs to Produce 100 Bookcases		*Variable Costs to Produce 200 Bookcases*		*Variable Costs to Produce 500 Bookcases*	
Wood	$13.25	Wood	$13.25	Wood	$9.40
Nails	0.25	Nails	0.25	Nails	0.20
Paint	0.50	Paint	0.50	Paint	0.40
Labor (3 hours × $12.00 per hr)	$36.00	Labor (3 hours × $12.00 per hr)	$36.00	Labor (2½ hours × $12.00 per hr)	$30.00
Cost per unit	$50.00	Cost per unit	$50.00	Cost per unit	$40.00
Multiply by number of units	100	Multiply by number of units	200	Multiply by number of units	500
Cost for 100 units	$5,000	Cost for 200 units	$10,000	Cost for 500 units	$20,000

One bookcase = one unit.

worth for two, 75 cents worth for three, and so on. Make cents? For the production of bookcases, variable costs would also include the cost of lumber and paint as well as the wages the firm would pay factory workers.

Figure 10.8 shows some examples of the average variable cost (the variable cost per unit) and the total variable costs at different levels of production (for producing 100, 200, and 500 bookcases). If the firm produces 100 bookcases, the average variable cost per unit is $50, and the total variable cost is $5,000 ($50 × 100). If it doubles production to 200 units, the total variable cost now is $10,000 ($50 × 200).

In reality, it's usually more complex to calculate variable costs than what we've shown here. As the number of bookcases the factory produces increases or decreases, average variable costs may change. For example, if the company buys just enough lumber for one bookcase, the lumberyard will charge top dollar. If it buys enough for 100 bookcases, the guys at the lumberyard will probably offer a better deal. And if it buys enough for thousands of bookcases, the company may cut variable costs even more. Even the cost of labor goes down with increased production because manufacturers are likely to invest in labor-saving equipment (a fixed cost) that allows workers to produce bookcases faster. Figure 10.8 shows this is the case. By purchasing wood, nails, and paint at a lower price (because of a volume discount) and by providing a means for workers to build bookcases more quickly, the company reduces the cost per unit to produce 500 bookcases to $40 each.

Variable costs don't always go down with higher levels of production. Using the bookcase example, at some point the demand for the labor, lumber, or nails required to produce the bookcases may exceed the supply: The bookcase manufacturer may have to pay employees higher overtime wages to keep up with production. The manufacturer may have to buy additional lumber from a distant supplier that will charge more to cover the costs of shipping. The cost per bookcase rises. You get the picture.

fixed costs

Costs of production that do not change with the number of units produced.

Fixed costs are costs that *do not* vary with the number of units produced—the costs that remain the same whether the firm produces 1,000 bookcases this month or only 10. Fixed costs include rent or the cost of owning and maintaining the factory; utilities to heat or cool the factory; equipment, such as saws, hammers, and other hand tools; a sophisticated assembly line; robotics; and paint sprayers used in the production of the product. Although the wages of factory workers to build the bookcases are part of a firm's variable costs, the salaries of a firm's executives, accountants, human resources specialists, marketing managers, and other personnel not involved in the production of the product are fixed costs. So too are other costs, such as advertising and other marketing activities, at least in the short term. All these costs are constant no matter how many units of the product the factory manufactures.

Average fixed cost is the fixed cost per unit—the total fixed costs divided by the number of units (bookcases) produced and sold. Although total fixed costs remain the same no matter how many units are produced, the average fixed cost will decrease as the number of units produced increases. Say, for example, that a firm's total fixed costs of production are $300,000. If the firm produces one unit, it applies the total of $300,000 to the one unit. If it produces two units, it applies $150,000, or half of the fixed costs, to each unit. If it produces 10,000 units, the average fixed cost per unit is $30 and so on. As we produce more and more units, average fixed costs go down, and so does the price we must charge to cover fixed costs.

Of course, like variable costs, in the long term, total fixed costs may change. The firm may find that it can sell more of a product than it has manufacturing capacity to produce, so it builds a new factory, its executives' salaries go up, and more money goes to purchase manufacturing equipment.

Combining variable costs and fixed costs yields **total costs** for a given level of production. As a company produces more and more of a product, both average fixed costs and average variable costs may decrease. Then, output may continue to increase, requiring the organization to pay its workers overtime or higher salaries, and/or to pay more for materials such as the lumber used in our bookcase example. In this case, the average variable costs may start to increase. If these variable costs ultimately rise faster than average fixed costs decline, this will result in an increase to average total costs. Similarly, increasing production may mean increased fixed costs. As total costs fluctuate with differing levels of production, the price that producers have to charge to cover those costs changes accordingly. Therefore, marketers need to calculate the minimum price necessary to cover all costs—the *break-even price*.

Break-Even Analysis

Break-even analysis is a metric marketers use to examine the relationship between costs and price. This method lets them determine what sales volume the company must reach at a given price before it will completely cover its total costs and past which it will begin to turn a profit. Simply put, the **break-even point** is the point at which the company doesn't lose any money and doesn't make any profit. All costs are covered, but there isn't a penny

many units of a product they will have to sell at a given price to exceed the break-even point and be profitable.

Figure 10.9 uses our bookcase example to demonstrate break-even analysis assuming the manufacturer charges $100 per unit. The vertical axis represents the amount of costs and revenue in dollars, and the horizontal axis shows the quantity of goods the manufacturer produces and sells. The break-even model assumes that there is a given total fixed cost and that variable costs per unit do not change with the quantity produced.

In this example, let's say that the total fixed costs (the costs for the factory, equipment, marketing, and electricity) are $200,000 and that the average variable costs (for materials and labor) are constant. The figure shows the total costs (variable costs plus fixed costs) and total revenues if varying quantities are produced and sold. The point at which the total revenue and total costs lines intersect is the break-even point. If sales are above the break-even point, the company makes a profit. Below that point, the firm will suffer losses.

To determine the break-even point, the firm first needs to calculate the **contribution per unit**, or the difference between the price the firm charges for a product (the revenue per unit) and the

average fixed cost
The fixed cost per unit produced.

total costs
The total of the fixed costs and the variable costs for a set number of units produced.

break-even analysis
A method for determining the number of units that a firm must produce and sell at a given price to cover all its costs.

break-even point
The point at which the total revenue and total costs are equal and above which the company makes a profit; below that point, the firm will suffer a loss.

contribution per unit
The difference between the price the firm charges for a product and the variable costs.

Figure 10.9 Snapshot | Break-Even Analysis Assuming a Price of $100

Using break-even analysis, marketers can determine what sales volume must be reached before the company makes a profit. This company needs to sell 4,000 bookcases at $100 each to break even.

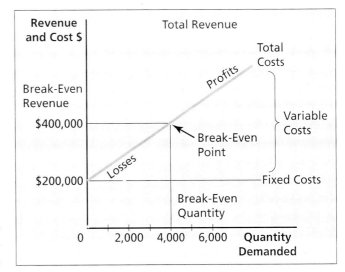

variable costs. This figure is the amount the firm has after it pays for the wood, nails, paint, and labor to *contribute* to meeting the fixed costs of production and any profit. For our example, we will assume that the firm sells its bookcases for $100 each. Using the variable costs of $50 per unit that we had before, contribution per unit is the selling price (SP) minus the variable costs (VC)—in this case, $100 − $50 = $50. Using the fixed cost for the bookcase manufacturing of $200,000, we can now calculate the firm's break-even point in units of the product:

$$\text{Break-even point (in units)} = \frac{\text{Total fixed costs}}{\text{Contribution per unit to fixed costs}}$$

$$\text{Break-even point (in units)} = \frac{\text{Total fixed costs}}{(\text{SP} - \text{VC})}$$

$$\text{Break-even point (in units)} = \frac{\$200,000}{\$50} = 4,000 \text{ units}$$

We see that the firm must sell 4,000 bookcases at $100 each to meet its fixed costs and to break even. We can also calculate the break-even point in dollars. This shows us that to break even, the company must sell $400,000 worth of bookcases:

$$\text{Break-even point (in dollars)} = \frac{\text{Total fixed costs}}{1 - \dfrac{\text{Variable cost per unit}}{\text{Selling price}}}$$

$$\text{Break-even point (in dollars)} = \frac{200,000}{1 - \dfrac{\$50}{\$100}} = \frac{\$200,000}{1 - 0.5} = \frac{\$200,000}{0.5} = \$400,000$$

After the firm's sales have met and passed the break-even point, it begins to make a profit. How much profit? If the firm sells 4,001 bookcases, it will make a profit of $50. If it sells 5,000 bookcases, we calculate the profit as follows:

$$\begin{aligned} \text{Profit} &= \text{Quantity above break-even point} \times \text{Contribution per unit} \\ &= 1,000 \times \$50 \\ &= \$50,000 \end{aligned}$$

Often a firm will set a *profit goal*, the dollar profit figure it wants to earn. Its managers may calculate the break-even point with a certain dollar profit goal in mind. In this case, it is not really a "break-even" point we are calculating because we're seeking profits. It's more of a "target amount." If our bookcase manufacturer thinks it is necessary to realize a profit of $50,000, his calculations look like this:

$$\text{Break-even point (in units) with target profit included} = \frac{\text{Total fixed costs} + \text{Target profit}}{\text{Contribution per unit to fixed costs}}$$

$$\text{Break-even point (in units) with target profit included} = \frac{\$200,000 + 50,000}{\$50} = 5,000 \text{ units}$$

Knowing the break-even point is equally important to small or large businesses. The owner of a restaurant that is already meeting its fixed costs and making a profit knows that if he can increase his sales, the contribution margin portion of all new sales will be profit. If an automaker can cut its costs by obtaining component parts for a lower price, the contribution margin and profits will increase with no increase in sales. This is the reason many U.S. firms have moved overseas where labor costs are lower or where governments have lower corporate tax rates. Because of significant changes made by **The Tax Cuts and Jobs Act of 2017 (TCJA of 2017)** to the way that domestic businesses are taxed on overseas earnings, the hope/expectation is that these changes will result in companies returning jobs/investment to the U.S.

Break-even analysis does not provide an easy answer for pricing decisions. Yes, it provides answers about how many units the firm must sell to break even and to make a profit,

The Tax Cuts and Jobs Act of 2017 (TCJA of 2017)
A major overhaul of personal and corporate taxes enacted by Congress in 2017.

but without knowing whether demand will equal that quantity at that price, companies can make big mistakes.

Markups and Margins: Pricing through the Channel

So far, we've talked about costs simply from the perspective of a manufacturer selling directly to a consumer. But in reality, most products are not sold directly to consumers or business buyers. Instead, a manufacturer may sell a consumer good to a wholesaler, distributor, or jobber who in turn sells to a retailer who finally sells the product to the ultimate consumer. In organizational markets, the manufacturer may sell his or her product to a distributor who will then sell to the business customer. Each of these members of the channel of distribution buys a product for a certain amount and adds a **markup** amount to create the price at which they will sell a product. This markup amount is the **gross margin**, also referred to as the **retailer margin** or the **wholesaler margin** when discussing pricing through the channel of distribution. The margin must be great enough to cover the fixed costs of the retailer or wholesaler and leave an amount for a profit. When a manufacturer sets a price, he or she must consider these margins. To understand pricing through the channel better, Figure 10.10 shows a simple example of channel pricing.

Of course, we all know that the traditional channel of distribution has changed dramatically in the past few years due to the growth of large retailers such as Walmart, Target, and online retailer-wholesaler Amazon combined with the equally incredible growth of e-commerce. Increasingly, manufacturers are selling directly to retailer chains, e-commerce sellers, or to final consumers. In this chapter, we assume the more complex traditional model with manufacturers selling to wholesalers or distributors who then sell to retailers who make the product available to the consumer. We will talk more about this in Chapters 11 and 12.

markup
An amount added to the cost of a product to create the price at which a channel member will sell the product.

gross margin
The markup amount added to the cost of a product to cover the fixed costs of the retailer or wholesaler and leave an amount for a profit.

retailer margin
The margin added to the cost of a product by a retailer.

wholesaler margin
The amount added to the cost of a product by a wholesaler.

Figure 10.10 *Snapshot* | Markups through the Channel

Producers of products need to remember that organizations at each level of the channel must set the price of the product to cover their fixed costs and make a profit.

Retailer	
Manufacturer's suggested retail price (MSRP) or list price	$20.00
Retailer's required margin to cover fixed costs and make a profit	− 30% = $ 6.00
	$14.00
Price to the retailer must be $14.00 or less	

Wholesaler	
Price the retailer pays for the product	$14.00
Wholesaler's required margin to cover fixed costs and make a profit	− 20% = $ 2.80
	$11.20
Price the manufacturer charges the wholesaler must be $11.20 or less.	

Manufacturer	
Manufacturer's revenue from sale of item to the wholesaler	$11.20
Manufacturer's variable costs per unit	− $7.85
Manufacturer's contribution	$3.35

list price, or **manufacturer's suggested retail price (MSRP)**
The price that the manufacturer sets as the appropriate price for the end consumer to pay.

Many times, a manufacturer builds its pricing structure around list prices. A **list price**, which we also refer to as a **manufacturer's suggested retail price (MSRP)**, is the price that the manufacturer sets as the appropriate price for the end consumer to pay. In Figure 10.10 we have a consumer good with an MSRP of $20, the price that the retailers will charge a consumer. But, as we said, retailers need money to cover their fixed costs and their profits. Thus, the retailer may determine that he must have a certain percentage gross or retailer margin—in this case, 30 percent. This means that the retailer must be able to buy the product for $14 or less. If the channel of distribution also includes a wholesaler or distributor, the wholesaler/distributor must be able to mark up the product to pay their fixed costs and profits. This means that the wholesaler must also have a certain percentage gross or wholesaler margin—in our example, 20 percent.

This means that the wholesaler must be able to buy the product for $11.20 or less to cover his fixed costs and profits. Thus, the manufacturer will sell the product not for $20 but for $11.20. Of course, the manufacturer may sell the product to the wholesaler for less than that, but he cannot sell it for more and meet the margin requirements of the retailer and the wholesaler. If the manufacturer's variable costs for producing the product are $7.85, then his contribution to fixed costs is $11.20 − $7.85, or $3.35. This is the manufacturer's contribution and the amount that would be used to calculate the break-even point.

Step 4: Examine the Pricing Environment

In addition to demand and costs, marketers look at factors in the firm's external environment when they set prices. The fourth step in developing pricing strategies is to examine and evaluate the external pricing environment. In this section, we will discuss some important external influences on pricing strategies—the economic environment, competition, and consumer trends.

The Economy

Broad economic trends, like those we discussed in Chapter 2, tend to influence pricing strategies. The business cycle, inflation, economic growth, and consumer confidence in the economy all help to determine whether a firm should keep prices stable, reduce them, or even raise them. Of course, the upswings and downturns in a national economy do not affect all product categories or all regions equally. Marketers need to understand how economic trends will affect their particular businesses.

In general, during *recessions*, like the Great Recession that began in late 2007 and the even greater economic problems created by the COVID-19 pandemic in 2020, consumers grow more price sensitive. They switch brands to get a better price and patronize discount stores and warehouse outlets. They are less likely to take luxury vacations; instead, they're happy with a "staycation" where they entertain the family at home. Many consumers lose their jobs, and others are fearful of losing theirs. Even wealthy households, relatively unaffected by the recession, tend to cut back on their consumption. As a result, to keep businesses in operation during periods of recession, some firms find it necessary to cut prices to levels at which they cover their costs but don't make a profit.

During the Great Recession, Starbucks' strategy to cope with the downturn was to keep a premium image while the chain retained price-sensitive customers who threatened to defect to lower-priced competitors, such as McDonald's. To do this, Starbucks raised the prices of its sugary coffees with several ingredients, such as Frappuccinos and caramel macchiatos, by 10, 15, or even 30 cents. At the same time, the company reduced prices of more popular beverages, such as lattes and brewed coffee, from 5 to 15 cents.

While the kneejerk reaction to a recession is to lower prices in order to hold onto business, sometimes that strategy can be disastrous. Domino's Pizza instead worked on its core product—pizza. A consumer survey revealed negative customer perceptions of Domino's "cardboard crust" and "ketchup sauce." In response, Domino's did what many would believe is unthinkable: The company admitted its product stinks. Domino's overhauled its recipe for an improved pizza, and then it aggressively promoted this change. This brought customers in the door and doubled profits.[7]

There are also some economic trends that influence what consumers see as an acceptable or unacceptable price range for a product and thus allow firms to change prices. *Inflation* may give marketers causes to either increase or decrease prices. First, inflation gets customers accustomed to price increases, even when inflation goes away. This allows marketers to make real price increases, not just those that adjust for the inflation. Of course, during periods of inflation, consumers may cut back on purchases because they grow fearful of the future and worry about whether they will have enough money to meet basic needs. Then, as in periods of recession, inflation may cause marketers to lower prices and temporarily sacrifice profits to maintain sales levels.

P&G responded to a difficult economic environment by lowering prices on products—from Duracell batteries to Pampers diapers.

The Competition

Marketers try to anticipate how the competition will respond to their pricing actions. It's not always a good idea to fight the competition with lower and lower prices. Pricing wars can change consumers' perceptions of what is a "fair" price, leaving them unwilling to buy at previous price levels.

As we discussed in Chapter 2, most industries belong to one of three industry structures—an oligopoly, monopolistic competition, or pure competition. The industry structure a firm belongs to will influence price decisions. In general, firms like Delta Airlines that do business in an oligopoly, in which the market has few sellers and many buyers, are more likely to adopt status quo pricing objectives in which the pricing of all competitors is similar. Such objectives are attractive to oligopolistic firms because avoiding price competition allows all players in the industry to remain profitable. Of course, this doesn't mean that firms in an oligopoly can just ignore pricing by the competition. When one airline raises or lowers the price for its flights, the other airlines follow.

In a business like the restaurant industry, which is characterized as monopolistic competition in which there are many sellers, each offering a slightly different product, it is possible for firms to differentiate products and to focus on nonprice competition. Then each firm prices its product on the basis of its cost without much concern for matching the exact price of competitors' products.

Organizations like wheat farmers who function in a market characterized as pure competition have little opportunity to raise or lower prices. Rather, supply and demand directly influence the price of products like wheat, soybeans, corn, and fresh peaches.

Government Regulation

Another important factor in the environment that influences how marketers develop pricing strategies is government regulation. Governments in the U.S. and some other countries develop two different types of regulations that affect pricing. First, regulations for employee health care, environmental protection, occupational safety, and highway safety, just to mention a few, cause the costs to produce many products to increase. Other regulations on specific industries, such as those imposed by the Food and Drug Administration on the production of food and pharmaceuticals, increase the costs of developing and producing those products.

Credit Card Responsibility and Disclosure Act
Limits credit card rates and other fees.

Affordable Care Act
Provides access to health care for all Americans.

sharing economy
A consumer activity where consumers share goods and services that is facilitated by an online platform.

Uber
A peer-to-peer sharing service offering shared rides, food delivery, and transportation worldwide via websites and mobile apps.

Airbnb
A sharing service for consumers to lease or rent short-term lodging, including holiday cottages, apartments, homestays, hostel beds, and hotel rooms.

shopping for control
Consumers, facing a world with terrorism and political unrest, value products and services that provide some degree of control, such as smart home technology or gated communities.

In addition, some regulations directly address prices. Recently, Congress enacted the **Credit Card Responsibility and Disclosure Act**, which limits credit card rates and other fees.[8] In March 2010, a massive healthcare overhaul bill known as the **Affordable Care Act** was enacted. The legislation, which took effect in 2013–2014, offers all Americans access to health care, including those with preexisting conditions who in the past have often been denied coverage.[9]

Government regulations create some problems in the international environment. In countries including Egypt, the Philippines, Thailand, Bangladesh, and Zimbabwe, to name a few, the government dictates prices for a range of products from bread to pharmaceuticals. Pricing regulations are enacted to maintain affordability of staple foods and goods, to prevent price gouging during shortages, and to slow inflation. When this kind of government control makes it impossible to produce their products and make a profit, a firm's only options are to use cheaper ingredients or not make their products available in that market.

Consumer Trends

Consumer trends also can strongly influence prices. Culture and demographics determine how consumers think and behave, so these factors have a large impact on all marketing decisions. One current consumer trend is referred to as the **sharing economy** in which consumers share goods and services with each other. **Uber** and **Airbnb** are examples of how consumers are sharing their assets while making some extra money from the service. We'll talk more about the sharing economy in Chapter 12. Another current consumer trend is saving time by *buying time*. More and more consumers choose to buy ready-made food, shop locally or online, enjoy "daycation" deals where hotels and spas offer access to a room or hotel amenities such as a pool for the day, and use digital timesaving devices such as robot vacuum cleaners. **Shopping for control** is a response to the almost daily reports of terrorism and political unrest that have made the world a scary place for many consumers. This has led consumers to value products and services that provide some degree of predictability and control in an uncertain world. For example, consumers may install smart home technology or move to gated communities.[10] Need a new refrigerator? The Samsung Family Hub 2.0 allows you to see inside your refrigerator, stream music from Pandora or Spotify, hear and speak to someone who rings your Ring doorbell, create memos and a digital photo album, manage events in your life with a calendar, watch the same TV program playing on another TV in the house, find great recipes, order dinner from GrubHub, or order groceries and have them delivered in one hour.[11]

We would be remiss if we did not mention again that the worldwide pandemic in 2020 caused a major upheaval in the lives of millions of people. While we do not yet know what changes in consumers' lives, their attitudes, and their purchase trends will occur, the past tells us that there will be changes. In pricing as in every element of marketing strategy, marketers will have to find the best alternatives.

The International Environment

As we discussed in Chapter 2, the marketing environment often varies widely from country to country. This can have important consequences in developing pricing strategies. Can a company standardize prices for all global markets, or must it adjust to local conditions?

For some products, such as jet airplanes, companies like Boeing and Airbus standardize their prices. This is possible, first, because about the only customers for the wide-bodies and other popular jets are major airlines and governments of countries that buy for their military or for use by government officials. Second, companies that build planes have little or no leeway to cut their costs without sacrificing safety.

For other products, including most consumer goods, unique environmental factors in different countries mean that marketers must adapt their pricing strategies. As we noted in Chapter 2, the economic conditions in developing countries often mean that consumers simply cannot afford $3 or $4 or more for a bottle of shampoo or laundry detergent. As a result, marketers offer their brands at lower prices, even selling some in one-use packages called *sachets*, which we discussed in Chapter 2. In other cases, companies must save on costs by using less expensive ingredients in their brands to provide toothpaste or soap that is affordable.

Finally, channels of distribution often vary both in the types and sizes of available intermediaries and in the availability of an infrastructure to facilitate product distribution. Often these differences can mean that trade margins will be higher, as will the cost of getting the products to consumers.

10.3 Identify Strategies and Tactics to Price the Product

OBJECTIVE

Understand key pricing strategies and tactics.

An old Russian proverb says, "There are two kinds of fools in any market. One doesn't charge enough. The other charges too much."[12]

In modern business, there seldom is any one-and-only, now-and-forever, best pricing strategy. Like playing a game of chess, making pricing moves and countermoves requires thinking two and three moves ahead. Figure 10.11 provides a summary of different pricing strategies and tactics. Price planning is influenced by psychological issues and strategies and by legal and ethical issues.

Step 5: Choose a Pricing Strategy

The next step in price planning is to choose a pricing strategy. Some strategies work for certain products, with certain customer groups, in certain competitive markets, whereas others do not. When is it best for the firm to undercut the competition and when is it best to just meet the competition's prices? When is the best pricing strategy one that considers costs only, and when is it best to use one based on demand?

Pricing Strategies Based on Cost

Marketing planners often choose cost-based strategies because they are simple to calculate and are relatively risk free. They promise that the price will at least cover the costs the company incurs to produce and market the product.

Figure 10.11 *Snapshot* | Pricing Strategies and Tactics

Marketers develop successful pricing programs by choosing from a variety of pricing strategies and tactics.

Pricing Strategies	Pricing Tactics

• Based on cost
  Cost plus
• Based on demand
  Target costing
  Yield management
• Based on the competition
  Price leadership
• Based on customers' needs
  Value (EDLP) pricing
• New product pricing
  Skimming pricing
  Penetration pricing
  Trial pricing
	• Pricing for individual products
	  Two-part pricing
	  Payment pricing
	  Subscription pricing
	• Pricing for multiple products
	  Price bundling
	  Captive pricing
	• Distribution-based pricing
	• Discounting for channel members

Cost-based pricing methods have drawbacks, however. They do not consider factors such as the changing prices of inputs, the nature of the target market, demand, competition, the product life cycle, and the product's image. Moreover, although the calculations for setting the price may be simple and straightforward, estimating costs accurately may prove difficult.

Think about firms like 3M, General Electric, and Nabisco, all of which produce many different products. How does a cost analysis allocate the costs for the plant, research and development, equipment, design engineers, maintenance, and marketing personnel among the different products so that the pricing plan accurately reflects the cost to produce any one product? For example, how do you allocate the salary of a marketing executive who oversees several different products? Should the cost be divided equally among all products? Should costs be based on the actual number of hours spent working on each product? Or should costs be assigned based on the revenues generated by each product? There is no one right answer. Even with these limitations, though, cost-based pricing strategies often are a marketer's best choice.

The most common cost-based approach to pricing a product is **cost-plus pricing**, in which the marketer totals all the costs for the product and then adds an amount (or marks up the cost of the item) to arrive at the selling price. Many marketers, especially retailers and wholesalers who often must set the price for tens of thousands of products, use cost-plus pricing because of its simplicity; users need only know or estimate the unit cost and add the markup.

You may wonder how a retailer or a wholesaler determines the markup percentage. In many cases, the markup percentage is a matter of tradition or rules of thumb. Many retailers mark up clothing, gifts, and other items by keystone pricing, or **keystoning**, a pricing strategy in which the retailer simply doubles the cost of the item (100 percent markup) to determine the price.[13] Restaurants typically triple the costs (200 percent markup) of the food that goes into a menu item and quadruple (300 percent markup) the cost of alcoholic beverages.[14]

To calculate cost-plus pricing, marketers usually calculate either a markup on cost or a markup on selling price. With both methods, you calculate the price by adding a predetermined percentage to the cost, but as the names of the methods imply, for one the calculation uses a percentage of the costs, and for the other, a percentage of the selling price. Which of the two methods is used seems often to be little more than a matter of "the way our company has always done it." You'll find more information about cost-plus pricing and how to calculate markup on cost and markup on selling price in the Chapter 10 Supplement at the end of this chapter.

Pricing Strategies Based on Demand

In 1960, Lee Iacocca, then the Ford Division general manager, noted forecasts that the baby boomer generation was coming of age, which meant that Ford would face an increasing number of young car buyers. There were also indications that these young car buyers would like a stylish sports car but couldn't afford the $4,000 to $7,000 price tag on the Ford Thunderbird or the GM Corvette. Under Iacocca's direction, Ford began developing a car that had the style and features young drivers desired but at a cost they could afford. This car, of course, was the iconic Ford Mustang. Priced at an amazingly low $2,500, Ford sold more than 400,000 Mustangs in the first year and in two years made over $1 billion in profits from the car.[15]

Demand-based pricing means that the firm bases the selling price on an estimate of volume or quantity that it can sell in different markets at different prices. To use any of the pricing strategies based on demand, firms must determine how much product they can sell in each market and at what price. In some cases, organizations such as local governments can actually regulate behavior by manipulating the prices people pay for services. For example, several major cities, including London and Shanghai, use a

cost-plus pricing
A method of setting prices in which the seller totals all the costs for the product and then adds an amount to arrive at the selling price.

keystoning
A retail pricing strategy in which the retailer doubles the cost of the item (100 percent markup) to determine the price.

demand-based pricing
A price-setting method based on estimates of demand at different prices.

congestion pricing strategy to reduce their horrendous traffic jams. They have succeeded by creating "congestion zones" where drivers must pay a high fee for the privilege of operating their cars during peak times.[16] You may have encountered express lanes on local highways that charge a higher toll to access less-crowded roads—you get what you pay for.

As we noted previously, marketers often use customer surveys, in which consumers indicate whether they would buy a certain product and how much of it they would buy at various prices. They may obtain more accurate estimates by conducting an experiment like the ones we described in Chapter 4. Two specific demand-based pricing strategies are target costing and yield management pricing. Let's take a quick look at each approach.

Today, firms find that a new product can be more successful if they match price with demand using a **target costing** process.[17] With target costing, firms first use marketing research to identify the quality and functionality needed to satisfy attractive market segments and what price they are willing to pay *before* they design the product. As Figure 10.12 shows, the next step is to determine what margins retailers and dealers require as well as the profit margin the producer firm requires. On the basis of this information, managers can calculate the target cost—the maximum it can cost the firm to manufacture the product. If the firm can meet customer quality and functionality requirements and control costs to meet the required price, it will manufacture the product. If not, it abandons the product.

Yield management pricing is another type of demand-based pricing strategy that hospitality businesses, like airlines, hotels, and cruise lines, use. These businesses charge different prices to different customers to manage capacity while they maximize revenues. Many service firms practice yield management pricing because they recognize that different customers have different sensitivities to price; some customers will pay top dollar for an airline ticket, whereas others will travel only if there is a discount fare. The goal of yield management pricing is to accurately predict the proportion of customers who fall into each category and allocate the percentages of the airline's or hotel's capacity accordingly so that no product goes unsold.

congestion pricing
Pricing strategy of charging a high fee for operating cars during peak traffic times to reduce congestion.

target costing
A process in which firms identify the quality and functionality needed to satisfy customers and what price they are willing to pay before the product is designed; the product is manufactured only if the firm can control costs to meet the required price.

yield management pricing
A practice of charging different prices to different customers to manage capacity while maximizing revenues.

Figure 10.12 *Snapshot* | Target Costing Using a Jeans Example

With target costing, a firm first determines the price at which customers would be willing to buy the product and then works backward to design the product in such a way that it can produce and sell the product at a profit.

Step 1: Determine the price customers are willing to pay for the jeans
  $79.99

Step 2: Determine the markup required by the retailer
  40% (.40)

Step 3: Calculate the maximum price the retailer will pay, the price customers are willing to pay minus the markup amount

  Formula: Price to the retailer = Selling price × (1.00 – markup percentage)
       Price to the retailer = $79.99   × (1.00 – .40)
             = $79.99   × 0.60 =   **$47.99**

Step 4: Determine the profit required by the firm
  15% (.15)

Step 5: Calculate the target cost, the maximum cost of producing the jeans
  Formula: Target cost = Price to the retailer × (1.00 – profit percentage)
       Target cost = $47.99 × 0.85 =   **$40.79**

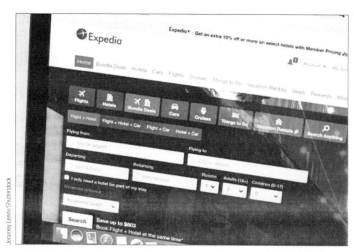

Travel platforms provide greater price transparency when passengers want to compare airfares across companies.

An airline, for example, may charge two prices for the same seat—say, a full fare of $899 and a discount fare of $299. (In reality, of course, the airlines charge a much greater number of different fares.) The airline uses information about past flights to predict how many seats it can fill at full fare and how many it can sell only at the discounted fare. The airline begins months ahead of the date of the flight with a basic allocation of seats—perhaps it will place 25 percent of the seats in the full-fare "bucket" and 75 percent in the discount-fare "bucket." As flight time gets closer, the airline might make a series of adjustments to the allocation of seats in the hope of selling every seat on the plane at the highest price possible. If the New York Mets need to book the flight, chances are the airline will be able to sell some of the discount seats at full fare, which in turn decreases the number available at the discounted price. If, as the flight date nears, the number of full-fare ticket sales falls below the forecast, the airline will move some of those seats over to the discount bucket. Then the suspense builds! The pricing game continues until the day of the flight as the airline attempts to fill every seat by the time the plane takes off. This is why you may find one price for a ticket on Travelocity.com or Expedia.com a month before the flight, a much higher price two weeks later, and a very low price the last few days before the flight. This also tells you why you often see the ticket agents at the gate frantically looking for "volunteers" who are willing to give up their seats because the airline sold more seats than actually fit in the plane.

Pricing Strategies Based on the Competition

Sometimes a firm's pricing strategy involves pricing its wares near, at, above, or below the competition's prices. In the "good old days," when U.S. automakers had the American market to themselves, pricing decisions were straightforward: Industry giant General Motors would announce its new car prices, and Ford, Chrysler, Packard, Studebaker, Hudson, and the others got in line or dropped out. A **price leadership** strategy, which usually is the rule in an oligopolistic industry that a few firms dominate, may be in the best interest of all players because it minimizes price competition. Price leadership strategies are popular because they provide an acceptable and legal way for firms to agree on prices without ever coordinating these rates with each other.

Pricing Strategies Based on Customers' Needs

Retailers typically practice one of two pricing strategies based on customers' needs: EDLP and high/low pricing. Firms that practice **value pricing**, or **everyday low pricing (EDLP)** develop a pricing strategy that promises good quality and durable products at reasonable prices every day. Many successful retail chains around the world—including Walmart, Home Depot, Office Depot, and Target—all adopt a deliberate policy of EDLP. Because of their size, these firms are able to demand billions of dollars in cost efficiencies from their suppliers and pass the savings on to customers.

The **high/low pricing**, or **promo pricing**, strategy means retailers have prices that are higher than EDLP chains, normally the MSRP or list price, but they run frequent, often weekly, promotions that heavily discount some products. So what happens if retailers seek to switch from one strategy to the other? Sears, for example, has switched from high/low to EDLP and then back to high/low. JCPenney also tried to switch from a high/low strategy to EDLP and failed.

Both Sears and JCPenney suffered great financial losses during the 2007 recession and again during the COVID-19 pandemic as did many retailers. By 2020, Sears had only 182 of its previous 3,500 stores remaining and survival seemed unlikely. JCPenney initiated a

price leadership
A pricing strategy in which one firm first sets its price and other firms in the industry follow with the same or similar prices.

value pricing, or **everyday low pricing (EDLP)**
A pricing strategy in which a firm sets prices that provide ultimate value to customers.

high/low pricing, or **promo pricing**
A retail pricing strategy in which the retailer prices merchandise at list price but runs frequent, often weekly, promotions that heavily discount some products.

highly successful curbside pickup program and other customer-pleasing changes following the recession and appeared to be successfully reinventing itself until the COVID-19 pandemic led Penney to file for bankruptcy.[18]

New Product Pricing

New products are vital to the growth and profits of a firm, but they also present unique pricing challenges. When a product is new to the market or when there is no established industry price norm, marketers may use a skimming pricing strategy, a penetration pricing strategy, or trial pricing.

A **skimming price** means that the firm charges a high, premium price for its new product with the intention of reducing it in the future in response to market pressures. If a product is highly desirable and offers unique benefits, demand is price inelastic during the introductory stage of the product life cycle, allowing a company to recover research and development (R&D) and promotion costs. When rival products enter the market, the firm lowers the price to remain competitive. Firms that focus on profit objectives when they develop their pricing strategies often set skimming prices for new products. The Sony PlayStation 3 was originally sold at $599 in the U.S. market, but it was gradually reduced to less than $200.[19] For skimming pricing to be successful, there should be little chance that competitors can get into the market quickly. With highly complex, technical products, it will take time for competitors to put a rival product into production.

Penetration pricing is the opposite of skimming pricing. In this situation, the company prices a new product very low to sell more in a short time and gain market share early. Another reason marketers use penetration pricing is to discourage competitors from entering the market. The firm that first introduces a new product has an important advantage. Experience shows that a pioneering brand often is able to maintain dominant market share for long periods. Campbell's soup, with the iconic red label, is a brand that was first to market in 1895 and still dominates the industry today.[20]

Trial pricing means that a new product carries a low price for a limited time to generate a high level of customer interest. Unlike penetration pricing, in which the company maintains the low price, the company increases the trial price after the introductory period. The idea is to win customer acceptance first and make profits later, as when a new health club offers an introductory membership to start pulling people in or a cable TV company offers a great low price for six months if you sign up for their TV, Internet, and phone bundle, after which you will pay much more.

Price Segmentation

Most markets are made up of consumers who have widely different characteristics. As we discussed in Chapter 7, we refer to these as *market segments*. Just as the same product may not be best for all segments, the best price for a product differs among market segments. **Price segmentation** is the practice of charging different prices to different market segments for the same product. For example, Captain George's Seafood Restaurant in Myrtle Beach, South Carolina, segments buffet pricing by age. They offer an adult buffet for $35.99, but access to the same buffet for children ages 5–12 is $19.99.[21] Segmenting on quantity occurs when the price of one large pizza is $9 but you can get two for $15. Of course marketers must be careful when using customer characteristics as criteria for price differences to avoid discriminating against some customers. The use of characteristics such as gender, race, religion, or ethnic group typically is illegal and should generally be avoided.

When the demand for a product differs during predictable periods, sellers often develop a pricing plan that sets prices higher during periods with higher demand. In the same way, a seller may segment based on the time when the purchase is made. This **peak load pricing** received its name because it was originally used for pricing by electric utility companies. Movie theaters offer lower daytime ticket prices, restaurants offer "early bird"

skimming price
A very high, premium price that a firm charges for its new, highly desirable product.

penetration pricing
A pricing strategy in which a firm introduces a new product at a very low price to encourage more customers to purchase it.

trial pricing
Pricing a new product low for a limited period of time to lower the risk for a customer.

price segmentation
The practice of charging different prices to different market segments for the same product.

peak load pricing
A pricing plan that sets prices higher during periods with higher demand.

Ride-sharing platforms like Uber use a surge pricing strategy that calibrates fares to demand.

discounts, and the cost of resort hotel rooms is much higher during the summer for beach resorts and winter for resorts on the slopes.

As we discussed earlier, Uber is a global online transportation company. Consumers can use the Uber app on their smartphones to request a trip, which is then routed to Uber drivers who use their own cars. Uber uses a **surge pricing** strategy; it raises the price of its product as demand goes up (as on a rainy Saturday night) and lowers it as demand declines. Think twice before hailing an Uber on New Year's Eve—you may be better off renting a limo!

Bottom-of-the-Pyramid Pricing

Marketers face a different challenge when they wish to get a foothold in countries with huge populations of people with the lowest incomes, the bottom-of-the-pyramid countries. These marketers need to develop **bottom-of-the-pyramid pricing**, prices that are low enough to appeal to the large numbers of these consumers. One approach (discussed in Chapter 2) is to sell nondurable products in smaller packages for just a few cents. A second option is for people, perhaps an entire village, to share a product such as a cell phone, a computer, or a refrigerator.

Step 6: Develop Pricing Tactics

Once marketers have developed pricing strategies, the last step in price planning is to implement them. The methods companies use to set their strategies in motion are their *pricing tactics*.

Pricing for Individual Products

Pricing tactics, the way marketers present a product's price, can make a big difference in the success of the product:

- **Two-part pricing** requires two separate types of payments to purchase the product. For example, golf and tennis clubs charge yearly or monthly fees plus fees for each round of golf or tennis.

- **Payment pricing** makes the consumer think the price is "do-able" by breaking up the total price into smaller amounts payable over time. For example, Home Shopping Network (HSN) and some infomercials offer payment pricing for many of their products. You might buy a UHD Smart TV for a single price of over $1,000 or 6 FlexPay of less than $200. The payment price sounds much better than forking over a thousand dollars at one time!

- **Subscription pricing** is a strategy where a seller offers or even requires that customers pay a periodic fee for access to a product. Magazine and newspaper subscriptions have been popular for decades. Today, subscription pricing is more likely to be used for services such as access to Microsoft and Adobe computer programs and streaming television networks, such as Netflix, Disney+, and Hulu. Some goods are also sold with subscription pricing. Amazon offers many nondurable goods, such as shampoo, toothpaste, or even Red Bull Energy drinks, at a 15% discounted price for customers who opt for regular deliveries.

- **Decoy pricing** is a strategy where a seller offers at least three similar products. Two of them have comparable but more expensive prices than the third, and one of these two

surge pricing
A pricing plan that raises prices of a product as demand goes up and lowers it as demand slides.

bottom-of-the-pyramid pricing
Innovative pricing strategy in which brands that wish to get a foothold in bottom-of-the-pyramid countries appeal to consumers with the lowest incomes.

two-part pricing
Pricing that requires two separate types of payments to purchase the product.

payment pricing
A pricing tactic that breaks up the total price into smaller amounts payable over time.

subscription pricing
Pricing tactic where customers pay on a periodic basis, normally monthly or yearly, for access to a product.

decoy pricing
A pricing strategy where a seller offers at least three similar products; two have comparable but more expensive prices and one of these two is less attractive to buyers, thus causing more buyers to buy the higher-priced, more attractive item.

is less attractive to buyers than the other. The result is that people will more often choose the more attractive of the two higher-priced items. As an example, think about an electronics retailer who would like for his customers to buy a specific, higher-priced laptop with a higher margin that will mean more profits for him. With decoy pricing, he will offer three different laptops—we'll call them models A, B, and C. Model A is a stripped-down, no-name brand laptop, much lower priced than either model B or model C, and unlikely to attract many sales. One of the two higher-priced items, say model B, has a larger hard drive, superior screen resolution and more RAM than model C. In this case, model C is the decoy. When consumers compare it to model B, they will naturally buy model B, just as the retailer wanted them to do.

A retailer or wholesaler may hold a **clearance sale** to reduce inventory of seasonal and outdated items to make room for new merchandise.

Pricing for Multiple Products

A firm may sell several products that consumers typically buy at one time. As fast-food restaurants like Burger King know, a customer who buys a burger for lunch usually springs for a soft drink and fries as well. The purchase of a single-serve coffee brewer means you also need to purchase lots of K-cup coffee pods. The two most common tactics for pricing multiple products are price bundling and captive pricing.

Price bundling means selling two or more goods or services as a single package for one price—a price that is often less than the total price of the items if bought individually. Traditional cable TV providers, like AT&T U-verse, Comcast Xfinity, and Spectrum, have gotten into the price bundling act as they entice their customers to sign on for a package of cable TV, high-speed Internet, and local or, in some cases, wireless phone service.

From a marketing standpoint, price bundling makes sense. If we price products separately, it's more likely that customers will buy some but not all the items. They might choose to put off some purchases until later, or they might buy from a competitor. Whatever revenue a seller loses from the reduced prices for the total package, it often makes up for in increased total purchases.

Captive pricing is a pricing tactic a firm uses when it has two products that work only when used together. The firm sells one item at a very low price and then makes its profit on the second high-margin item. This tactic has been used for many years to sell shaving products where the razor is relatively cheap but the blades are not. Similarly, companies such as HP and Canon offer consumers a desktop printer that also serves as a fax, copier, and scanner for under $100 to keep selling the very high-priced ink cartridges.

Distribution-Based Pricing

Distribution-based pricing is a pricing tactic that establishes how firms handle the cost of shipping products to customers near, far, and wide. Characteristics of the product, the customers, and the competition figure in the decision to charge all customers the same price or to vary according to shipping cost.

F.O.B. pricing is a tactic business-to-business (B2B) marketers use. F.O.B. stands for *free on board*, which refers to who pays for the shipping. Also—and this is important—*title passes to the buyer* at the F.O.B. location. **F.O.B. factory pricing**, or **F.O.B. origin pricing**, means that the cost of transporting the product from the factory to the customer's location is the responsibility of the customer. **F.O.B. delivered pricing** means that the seller pays both the cost of loading and the cost of transporting to the customer, amounts it added into the selling price.

clearance sale
A closeout or clearance sale is a discount sale of inventory either by retailer or wholesaler. Clearances are meant to help sell unwanted inventory that may be seasonal or outdated in order to make room for new merchandise and minimize the financial impact of products that were not popular.

price bundling
Selling two or more goods or services as a single package for one price.

captive pricing
A pricing tactic for two items that must be used together; one item is priced very low, and the firm makes its profit on another, high-margin item essential to the operation of the first item.

F.O.B. factory pricing, or **F.O.B. origin pricing**
A pricing tactic in which the cost of transporting the product from the factory to the customer's location is the responsibility of the customer.

F.O.B. delivered pricing
A pricing tactic in which the cost of loading and transporting the product to the customer is included in the selling price and is paid by the manufacturer.

Delivery terms for pricing of products sold in international markets are similar:[22]

- *CIF* (cost, insurance, freight) is the term used for ocean shipments and means the seller quotes a price for the goods (including insurance), all transportation, and miscellaneous charges to the point of debarkation from the vessel.
- *CFR* (cost and freight) means the quoted price covers the goods and the cost of transportation to the named point of debarkation, but the buyer must pay the cost of insurance. The *CFR* term is also used for ocean shipments.
- *CIP* (carriage and insurance paid to) and *CPT* (carriage paid to) include the same provisions as CIF and CFR but are used for shipment by modes other than water.

When a firm uses **uniform delivered pricing**, it adds a preset shipping cost to the price, no matter what the distance from the manufacturer's plant—within reason. Uniform delivered pricing is most likely to be used when shipping charges are very low. For example, when you order the latest Harry Potter book, you may pay the cost of the book plus $3.99 for shipping and handling, no matter what the actual cost of the shipping to your particular location. Internet sales, catalog sales, home TV shopping, and other types of nonstore retail sales usually use uniform delivered pricing.

Freight absorption pricing means the seller takes on part or all of the cost of shipping. This policy works well for high-ticket items, for which the cost of shipping is a negligible part of the sales price and the profit margin. Marketers are most likely to use freight absorption pricing in highly competitive markets or when such pricing allows them to enter new markets. Online marketers such as Amazon.com have found that offering free shipping makes a big difference to consumers and to their sales volume. Even traditional big-box retailers are getting in on the trend—Target recently announced free two-day shipping on any size order for its RedCard holders.[23]

Discounting for Channel Members

So far, we've talked about pricing tactics used to sell to end customers. Now we'll talk about tactics firms use to price to members of their *distribution channels*:

- *Trade or functional discounts:* We discussed previously how manufacturers often set a list or suggested retail price for their product and then sell the product to members of the channel for less, allowing the channel members to cover their costs and make a profit. Thus, the manufacturer's pricing structure will normally include **trade discounts** to channel intermediaries. These discounts are usually set percentage discounts off the suggested retail or list price for each channel level. In today's marketing environment dominated by large retail chains such as Walmart, Costco, and Target, the retailers dictate the amount of the trade discount, and the larger their size, the more power they have in the channel. We'll talk more about channel power in Chapter 11.
- *Quantity discounts:* To encourage larger purchases from distribution channel partners or from large organizational customers, marketers may offer **quantity discounts**, or reduced prices for purchases of larger quantities. *Cumulative quantity discounts* are based on a total quantity bought within a specified time period, often a year, and encourage a buyer to stick with a single seller instead of moving from one supplier to another. Cumulative quantity discounts often take the form of *rebates*, in which case the firm sends the buyer a rebate check at the end of the discount period or, alternatively, gives the buyer credit against future orders. *Noncumulative quantity discounts* are based only on the quantity purchased with each individual order and encourage larger single orders but do little to tie the buyer and the seller together.
- *Cash discounts:* Many firms try to entice their customers to pay their bills quickly by offering **cash discounts**. For example, a firm selling to a retailer may state that the terms of the sale are "2 percent 10 (days), net 30 (days)," meaning that if the retailer or organizational customer pays the producer for the goods within 10 days, the amount

---

uniform delivered pricing
A pricing tactic in which a firm adds a standard shipping charge to the price for all customers regardless of location.

freight absorption pricing
A pricing tactic in which the seller absorbs the total cost of transportation.

trade discounts
Discounts off list price of products to members of the channel of distribution who perform various marketing functions.

quantity discounts
A pricing tactic of charging reduced prices for purchases of larger quantities of a product.

cash discounts
A discount offered to a customer to entice them to pay their bill quickly.

due is cut by 2 percent. The total amount is due within 30 days, and after 30 days, the payment is late.

- *Seasonal discounts:* **Seasonal discounts** are price reductions offered only during certain times of the year. For seasonal products such as snow blowers, lawn mowers, and water-skiing equipment, marketers use seasonal discounts to entice retailers and wholesalers to buy off-season and either store the product at their locations until the right time of the year or pass the discount along to consumers with off-season sales programs. Alternatively, they may offer discounts when products are in season to create a competitive advantage during periods of high demand.

seasonal discounts
Price reductions offered only during certain times of the year.

10.4 Pricing and Innovations in Payment for E-Commerce

OBJECTIVE
Understand the opportunities for Internet pricing strategies and innovations in payment.

As we have seen, price planning is a complex process in any firm. But if you are operating in the "wired world," get ready for even more pricing options!

Because sellers are connected to buyers around the globe as never before through the Internet, corporate networks, and wireless setups, marketers can offer deals they tailor to a single person at a single moment. On the other hand, they're also a lot more vulnerable to smart consumers, who can easily check out competing prices with the click of a mouse.

Many experts suggest that technology is creating a consumer revolution that might change pricing forever—and perhaps create the most efficient market ever. The music industry provides the most obvious example: Music lovers from around the globe purchase and download tens of billions of songs from numerous Internet sites and apps, including iTunes, Google Play, Amazon Music, and Bandcamp.[24] Sixty-eight percent of smartphone users who live in the U.S. stream music on their device every day.[25] And as you know, some of those people pay little to nothing for their tunes.

Pricing Advantages for Online Shoppers

The Internet also allows consumers to gain more control over the buying process while it creates unique pricing challenges for marketers. Both consumers and marketers have access to sophisticated "shopbots" that provide them with the best price on all kinds of products. As one illustration, a comparison study found that the price of an Otter Box Defender Series iPhone case ranged from a high of $59.90 at OtterBox.com to a low of $44.20 at Amazon.com. Shopbots and search engines mean that consumers are no longer at the mercy of firms that dictate a price they must accept.

dynamic pricing
A pricing strategy in which the price can easily be adjusted to meet changes in the marketplace.

Detailed information about what products actually cost manufacturers, available from sites such as Consumerreports.org, can give consumers more negotiating power when shopping for new cars and other big-ticket items. Finally, e-commerce potentially can lower consumers' costs because of the gasoline, time, and aggravation they save when they avoid a trip to the mall.

Dynamic Pricing Strategies

One of the most important opportunities the Internet offers marketers is **dynamic pricing**, in which the seller can quickly and easily adjust prices to meet changes in the marketplace. If a

Online music streaming means some customers pay little or nothing for their tunes, transforming price planning in the music industry.

sipscreens/Alamy Stock Photo

brick-and-mortar retail store wants to change prices, employees/workers must place new price tags on items, create and display new store signage and media advertising, and input new prices into the store's computer system. For B2B marketers, employees/workers must print catalogs and price lists and distribute to salespeople and customers. These activities can be very costly to a firm, so they simply don't change their prices often.[26] The Internet also enables firms that sell to other businesses (B2B firms) to change their prices rapidly as they adapt to changing costs.

Online Auctions

online auctions
E-commerce that allows shoppers to purchase products through online bidding.

For consumers who have lots of stuff in their attics that they need to put in someone else's attic, the Internet means an opportunity for sellers to find ready buyers through consumer-to-consumer (C2C) sites. While most consumers are familiar with eBay and Etsy, many have never heard of other auction sites such as eCrater, Bonanzle, eBid, and CQout. These too are some of the many **online auctions** that allow shoppers to bid on everything from bobbleheads to health-and-fitness equipment to a Sammy Sosa home-run ball. Auctions are a powerful Internet pricing strategy. Perhaps the most popular auctions are the C2C auctions such as those on eBay. The eBay auction is an *open auction*, meaning that all the buyers know the highest price bid at any point in time. On many Internet auction sites, the seller can set a *reserve price*, which is a price below which the item will not be sold.

A *reverse auction* is a tool firms use to manage their costs in B2B buying. Although in a typical auction, buyers compete to purchase a product, in reverse auctions sellers compete for the right to provide a product at, the buyers hope, a low price.

A popular and profitable online auction site is StockX. StockX specializes in offering retro athletic shoes and other clothing and promotes itself as the first stock market for things. Like those on Wall Street and other stock markets around the globe, buyers place bids and sellers place asks. When the two meet, a transaction automatically happens. One seller who sells on both StockX and the similar site, Stadium Goods, sold a pair of Air Jordans for $20,000.

Freemium Pricing Strategies

freemium pricing
A business strategy in which a product in its most basic version is provided free of charge but the company charges money (the premium) for upgraded versions of the product with more features, greater functionality, or greater capacity.

Perhaps the most exciting new pricing strategy is **freemium pricing** (a mix of *free* and *premium*). Freemium is a business strategy in which a company provides its most basic version of a product free of charge but then charges (the premium) for upgraded versions of the product with more features, greater functionality, or greater capacity.[27] The freemium pricing strategy has been most popular in digital offerings such as software media, games, or web services where the cost of one additional copy of the product is negligible. Companies that have followed the new pricing strategy include Dropbox, Inc., SurveyMonkey, Spotify, and Skype.

The very popular video game Candy Crush Saga is a freemium video game with a revenue of $230 million a year. So how do they make so much money? The idea is that if you give your product away, you will build a customer base of consumers willing to pay for added benefits. While you can download and play Candy Crush for free, if you really want to win at the 5000 levels, you can choose to pay for special features to help when the game gets more difficult.[28]

While there are many advantages for consumers in e-commerce, there are some companies and individuals who stalk the Web to engage in unethical or illegal practices. We'll talk about one of these, Internet price discrimination, next.

Internet Price Discrimination

Of course, the Internet allows firms to do more than just adjust prices as a result of external factors such as changing costs or competitive activity. The promise of the Internet is that it allows consumers to quickly comparison shop for the lowest price, all the while sitting in their pajamas at home. Many firms, it seems, use the same technology to practice **Internet price discrimination**.

Internet price discrimination is an Internet pricing strategy that charges different prices to different buyers for the same product based on order size or geographic location.[29] A *Wall Street Journal* investigation found that a Swingline stapler on Staples.com was priced at $15.79 for one customer and $14.29 for another who lived just a few miles away based on their location and their distance from either an OfficeMax or an Office Depot store.[30]

Marketers know that they will maximize profits if they charge each customer the most that person is willing to pay. Although this is not practical, placing customers into groups based on where they live, how close they are to the retailer or a competitor, the cost of doing business in the area, or their Internet browsing history can greatly increase profits. Some sites even offer customers a discount if they use a mobile device. A shopper who uses a smartphone to find a hotel room on sites like Orbitz.com or CheapTickets.com may find rooms for as much as 50 percent less than they would otherwise pay.

Is Internet price discrimination illegal? As we said in our discussion of price segmentation, as long as companies don't charge different prices based on a demographic characteristic such as gender or race, it is not. Sometimes, however, it's difficult to tell how the company makes these decisions. For example, a recent report found that *The Princeton Review*, which charges different prices for its SAT prep service to consumers who live in different zip codes, is almost twice as likely to offer a higher price to Asians who ask for an online quote compared to non-Asians. This doesn't necessarily mean the company is intentionally discriminating against Asians, but rather that these consumers are more likely to live in zip codes assigned to the higher rates. As the company responded, "The areas that experience higher prices will also have a disproportionately higher population of members of the financial services industry, people who tend to vote Democratic, journalists, and any other group that is more heavily concentrated in areas like New York City."[31]

Innovations in Payment Systems

The digital revolution has created a new world of ways consumers conduct transactions with both business and other consumers. The very successful of these provide value, security, and convenience for both buyer and seller. Some you are familiar with are online auctions and digital/mobile wallets. Others that are increasingly popular are cryptocurrency, digital installment plans, buy-now-pay-later (BNPL) opportunities, collaborative savings and consumption, rent-to-own programs, and peer-to-peer (P2P) lending.

Cryptocurrency

The most recent addition to the value exchange is digital currency. A **cryptocurrency** is one type of digital currency that uses cryptography for security. While there are over two thousand different cryptocurrencies, the five most important and most frequently traded are Bitcoin, Ethereum, Ripple, Litecoin, and Tether.[32]

These cryptocurrencies are digital tokens with no physical backup. Note: Don't plan on walking around with a shiny new Bitcoin in your pocket; they don't really exist in the sense that you can touch or see one![33]

You can buy **Bitcoin** on several *Bitcoin exchanges*, or individuals can purchase them from each other using mobile apps that store their Bitcoins in a "virtual wallet." Today, most Bitcoin transactions are by people who speculate on the future prices of Bitcoin and hope to earn enormous returns in the future.

A feature that makes Bitcoin and other digital currencies attractive to many around the globe is that it is *organic*. This means that it is not issued by any central authority. The entire records of the Bitcoin network are stored on every one of the thousands of computers that help maintain the network. That is the feature that prevents cryptocurrency such as Bitcoin

Internet price discrimination
An Internet pricing strategy that charges different prices to different buyers for the same product based on order size or geographic location.

cryptocurrency
A digital currency that uses cryptography for security.

Bitcoin
The most popular and fastest-growing cryptocurrency.

from being controlled by any government or organization. This network of computers that maintains the database of all Bitcoin transactions is called the *blockchain*.

There are distinct advantages to cryptocurrency. For consumers, it eliminates the risk of credit card fraud that entices criminals to steal personal customer information and credit card numbers. To pay for your purchase, you use your smartphone to take a picture of the QR code displayed by the cash register. You click Confirm, and your app pays for your purchase.[34]

There is also a societal benefit from the use of cryptocurrencies. Many lower-income consumers do not have bank accounts. Instead, they must often pay fees of 10 percent or higher each time they need to send a money order to a payee. With cryptocurrencies, such payments would cost only a fraction of that amount. Many believe that digital currencies will contribute to increased quality of life for those who live in the world's poorest countries.

Cryptocurrencies can be sent electronically anywhere in the world in a few minutes. That's good news for folks who need to make large international money transfers that would take weeks with traditional transfers going through banks—not to mention that you get the money back that you loaned a friend right away!

There are no "middlemen" (like banks) involved in the process that collect transaction fees (which is why many businesses like this option). However, it also means that transactions occur only from person to person, so there is no record of them, and this opens the potential for Bitcoins to show up in illegal transactions (such as funding terrorism or laundering drug money).

While cryptocurrency remains controversial, many believe that our future will be financed this way—in the long term, the world's banking system will be based on digital currency. Some people believe that within 10 years, Bitcoin or another cryptocurrency will be the only money in the world. But don't get rid of those dollars just yet!

Digital and Mobile Wallets

While there are some consumers who still like to pull out a checkbook and write checks as they stand in the grocery line, many consumers, especially the younger ones, are using digital wallets. A **digital wallet** is a financial account that consumers can use to store funds, make transactions, and track payments by computer. The digital wallet software may be in a bank's mobile app or may be a payment platform such as PayPal and Alipay. Digital wallets are also the main means of moving cryptocurrencies such as Bitcoin from one owner to another. A **mobile wallet** is an app on a smartphone that may store credit card, debit card, and rewards card information as well as coupons. Mobile wallets are a convenient way to make purchases and payments.

digital wallet
A financial account used to store funds, make transactions, and track payments.

mobile wallet
A smartphone app that stores credit card and other information in order to make purchases/payments.

In developing nations, digital wallets allow consumers to participate more fully in the global financial system. Digital wallets mean individuals can accept and make payments and even receive funds from individuals in other nations. Digital wallets do not require a bank account with a physical firm or branch, often allowing those in more rural areas to connect. In Africa, where 80 percent of the population have mobile phones, the M-Pesa mobile payment system has over 200 million consumer subscribers. Digital and mobile wallets mean consumers in developing countries can move away from cash economies to safer, more secure financial systems and participate in the world's growing economy.

The leading digital wallets are Google Pay, Apple Pay, Samsung Pay, Android Pay, and PayPal. Of these leading brands, only PayPal works across all major devices. Other popular digital wallets include the Starbucks mobile app,

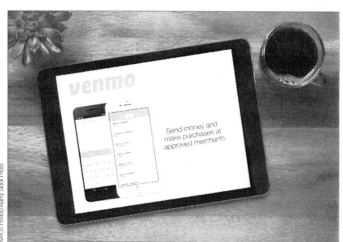

Venmo is one of several popular digital wallets that facilitate person-to-person transactions that are much safer than cash.

M4OS Photos/Alamy Stock Photo

which gives users points toward free coffee, and Venmo (now owned by PayPal), which is a social commerce app that facilitates easy payments among friends. Venmo can be used to transfer funds to friends or for your group of friends to share the cost of lunch. Square is another type of app that allows both individual and small business sellers to buy, sell, and send money using both Apple and Android devices.

Buy-Now-Pay-Later (BNPL)

A controversial innovation in payments is the **buy-now-pay-later (BNPL)** or "afterpay" payment option. Services like Afterpay, Affirm, and Openpay give shoppers the opportunity to get the product up front while financing the payment over three or four months. The BNPL options have been criticized because young consumers can quickly get into debt and damage their credit scores.

BNLP is, in many ways, just a new twist on the older retail layaway plans offered by retailers that began during the Great Depression. These programs allowed consumers without adequate financial resources to pay for goods interest-free over time. With layaway programs, the clothing or Christmas toys remained with the retailer until they were paid for.

buy-now-pay-later (BNPL)
Services that allow consumers to get a product now and pay for it over three or four months.

Save-Now-Buy-Later (SNBL)

Similar to BNPL programs, another installment payment process is the **save-now-buy-later (SNBL)** offering. Apps such as U.S.-based Reel and the U.K.'s Cashmere offer luxury items for sale. Potential buyers can save up for higher-priced items instead of paying by credit. The customer is given suggestions for payment plans (e.g., $50 per week for six months). Once the savings plan is agreed upon, the amount is automatically removed from the customer's bank account. When the amount is saved, the customer can order the item.

save-now-buy-later (SNBL)
A payment process whereby payments are automatically drafted from a customer's bank account; when the agreed-upon amount is saved, the customer can order the item.

Collaborative Savings and Consumption

Collaborative savings and consumption programs also allow consumers to make payments over a period of time. With so many wonderful things to buy, many of us have problems saving. To help consumers save for a down payment on a house or an exotic vacation, Stepladder offers consumers a collaborative saving and consumption program. All Stepladder members are placed into small groups. Each individual in the group contributes a set amount to a central pot. Every 30 days, a member is randomly selected to withdraw the entire monthly contribution. The group remains intact until every member has drawn out the monthly sum. Cashmere has begun a similar program.

collaborative savings and consumption
A savings plan where members are placed into small groups and make monthly payments. One member is selected randomly every 30 days to withdraw the entire monthly contributions.

P2P Lending

Also new to the sharing economy is the concept of **peer-to-peer (P2P) lending**, or **social lending**, which allows individuals to borrow money from other individuals. P2P lending companies provide both borrower and lender with assistance as eBay assists its buyers and sellers. P2P increases the rate of return for investors and decreases the cost of borrowing for the borrower. For many consumers who seek greater control of their work and leisure, are suspicious of large institutions, or just hate banks, P2P lending is very attractive. Of course, to borrow from a P2P lender, a borrower must have good credit and lenders' funds are not insured. Despite the problems, P2P lending seems to be growing in popularity.

peer-to-peer (P2P) lending, or **social lending**
Allows individuals to borrow money from other individuals giving the lender higher rates and the borrower lower rates than banks.

Rent-to-Own

The "sharing economy" we talked about earlier has changed consumers' attitudes towards renting and swapping clothes. And, renting a high-quality item such as a prom dress or even a wedding gown might be a way to try before you buy—the prom dress, that is. **Rent-to-own** is not new. Retailers that offer furniture for homes and for offices have for many years offered consumers and businesses the ability to rent furniture and at the end of a set rental period, the buyer owns the merchandise. The biggest downside to rent-to-own programs is that the total price is usually substantially higher than the price of the product if bought outright.

rent-to-own
A buyer rents an item and at a set end of the rental period, the buyer owns the merchandise.

Disruption on the Consumer Side of the Exchange

How many times have you heard these sayings?

"Money doesn't grow on trees."

"When I was young, I thought money was the most important thing in the world; now that I'm older, I know it is."

"I know money doesn't bring you happiness, but neither does being broke."

Well, if you think about money as paper dollars or Euros or Japanese yen, you may be in for a big surprise. Many experts say we will soon have a **cashless society**. With the use of digital currency and smartphone apps, more and more consumers are using cash less often if at all.

During the coronavirus pandemic, many were concerned about getting the virus from everything from cardboard boxes to doorknobs to, yes, paper money. The medical experts said there was no way to wash paper money. Washing hands was the only way to deal with virus-contaminated cash.

Sweden is the country closest to being cashless. In Sweden only about one percent of the country's GDP circulates in cash compared to 11 percent in the eurozone and eight percent in the U.S. In February of 2020, Sweden's central bank began an experiment with its own digital currency, the e-krona.

For many, it's a win-win game. Businesses like it because it increases security and digital currency is also less expensive to handle. Consumers like it because it's convenient. Retailers say that without cash, they're able to speed up transactions while reducing the risk of theft and the costs of securing and toting large amounts of cash to the bank. For governments, cashless payments are preferable because there is a record of each transaction, making it less likely that someone can avoid taxes.

Swish is a very popular payment smartphone app backed by the major Swedish banks that can be used for transferring money. For those who are concerned about the security of smartphones, one firm, Biohax, has developed a microchip that can be inserted under the skin of a consumer's hand. The chip allows Biohax clients to pay for everything from expensive travel to snacks from a vending machine with a wave.

Of course, not everyone in Sweden thinks cashless is a good thing. Older consumers are concerned they will forget their access number to use digital money. Charity groups are concerned that individuals subject to domestic abuse won't be able to hide money away if their abuser has taken control of their bank account.

Will other countries, including the U.S., become cashless in the 2020s decade? Experts suggest not so, but the number of places where you can opt not to use cash will grow while there may also be an increase in the number of places you are not allowed to use cash. We also know that the number of Americans still using cash for even small purchases has declined from 46 percent of purchases in 2015 to 37 percent in 2020.[35]

cashless society
An economic state where financial transactions are executed through the transfer of digital information—usually in the form of a credit card, debit card, mobile wallet, or digital currency such as Bitcoin—rather than with banknotes.

10.5 Psychological, Legal, and Ethical Aspects of Pricing

OBJECTIVE
Describe the psychological, legal, and ethical aspects of pricing.

So far, we've discussed how marketers use demand, costs, and an understanding of the pricing environment to plan effective pricing strategies and tactics. There are, however, other aspects of pricing that marketers must understand and deal with to maximize the effectiveness of their pricing plans. In this section, we discuss a number of psychological, legal, and ethical factors related to pricing that are important for marketers. Figure 10.13 provides a quick look at these aspects of pricing.

Figure 10.13 *Snapshot* | Psychological, Legal, and Ethical Aspects of Pricing

Price planning is influenced by psychological issues and strategies and by legal and ethical issues.

Psychological Issues in Pricing	Psychological Pricing Strategies
• Buyers' Expectations • Internal Reference Prices • Price-Quality Inferences	• Odd-Even Pricing • Price Lining • Prestige Pricing
Legal and Ethical Issues in B2C and C2C Pricing	Legal and Ethical Issues in B2B Pricing
• Bait-and-Switch • Loss-Leader Pricing • Misleading Merchandising • Price Gouging	• Price Discrimination • Price-Fixing • Predatory Pricing

Psychological Issues in Setting Prices

Much of what we've said about pricing depends on economists' notion of a customer who evaluates price in a logical, rational manner. For example, we express the concept of demand by a smooth curve, which assumes that if a firm lowers a product's price from $10 to $9.50 and then from $9.50 to $9 and so on, then customers will simply buy more and more. In the real world, though, it doesn't always work that way; consumers aren't nearly as rational as that! Let's look at some psychological factors that keep economists up at night.

Buyers' Pricing Expectations

Often consumers base their perceptions of price on what they perceive to be the customary or *fair price*. For example, for many years a candy bar or a pack of gum was priced at five cents (yes, five). Consumers would have perceived any other price as too high or low. It was a nickel candy bar—period. So when inflation kicked in and costs went up, some candy-makers tried to shrink the size of the bar instead of changing the price. Eventually, inflation prevailed, consumers' salaries rose, and that candy bar goes for as much as 30 times one nickel today—a price that consumers would have found unacceptable a few decades ago.

When the price of a product is above or even sometimes when it's below what consumers expect, they are less willing to purchase the product. If the price is above their expectations, they may think it is a rip-off. If it is below expectations, consumers may think quality is below par. By understanding the pricing expectations of their customers, marketers are better able to develop viable pricing strategies. These expectations can differ across cultures and countries. For example, in one study researchers in southern California found that Chinese supermarkets charge significantly lower prices (only half as much for meat and seafood) than mainstream American supermarkets in the same areas.[36]

Internal Reference Prices

Sometimes consumers' perceptions of the price of a product depend on their **internal reference price**. That is, based on past experience, consumers have a set price or a price range in mind that they refer to when they evaluate a product's cost. The reference price may be the last price paid, or it may be the average of all the prices they know of for similar products. No matter what the brand, the normal price for a loaf of sandwich bread is about $2.00. In some stores it may be $1.89, and in others it is $2.89, but the average is $2.00. If

internal reference price
A set price or a price range in consumers' minds that they refer to in evaluating a product's price.

consumers find a comparable loaf of bread priced much higher than this—say, $3.99—they will feel it is overpriced and grab a competing brand. If they find bread priced significantly lower—say, at $0.89 or $0.99 a loaf—they may shy away from the purchase as they wonder "what's wrong" with the bread (no, we don't think that's why they call it *Wonder Bread*).

In some cases, marketers try to influence consumers' expectations of what a product should cost when they use reference pricing strategies. For example, manufacturers may compare their price to competitors' prices when they advertise. Similarly, a retailer may display a product next to a higher-priced version of the same or a different brand. The consumer must choose between the two products with different prices.

Two results are likely: On the one hand, if the prices (and other characteristics) of the two products are fairly close, the consumer will probably feel the product quality is similar. This is an *assimilation effect*. The customer might think, "The price is about the same, so they must be alike. I'll be smart and save a few dollars." And so the customer chooses the lower-priced item because the low price makes it look attractive next to the higher-priced alternative. This is why store brands of deodorant, vitamins, pain relievers, and shampoo sit beside national brands, often accompanied by a shelf talker pointing out how much shoppers can save if they purchase the store brands. On the other hand, if the prices of the two products are too far apart, a *contrast effect* in which the customer equates the gap with a big difference in quality may result. The consumer may think, "Gee, this lower-priced one is probably not as good as the higher-priced one. I'll splurge on the more expensive one." Using this strategy, an appliance store may place an advertised $300 refrigerator next to a $699 model to convince a customer that the bottom-of-the-line model just won't do.

Price–Quality Inferences

Imagine that you go to a shoe store to check out running shoes. You notice one pair that costs $89.99. On another table, you see a second pair that looks almost identical to the first pair—but its price is only $24.95. Which pair do you want? Which pair do you think is the better quality? Many of us will pay the higher price because we believe the bargain-basement shoes aren't worth the risk at any price.

Consumers make *price–quality inferences* about a product when they use price as a cue or an indicator of quality. (An *inference* means we believe something to be true without any direct evidence.) If consumers are unable to judge the quality of a product through examination or prior experience, they usually assume that the higher-priced product is the higher-quality product.

In fact, new research on how the brain works even suggests that the price we pay can subtly influence how much pleasure we get from the product. Brain scans show that—contrary to conventional wisdom—consumers who buy something at a discount experience *less* satisfaction than people who pay full price for the very same thing. For example, in one recent study, volunteers who drank wine that they were told cost $90 a bottle actually registered more brain activity in pleasure centers than did those who drank the very same wine but who were told it only cost $10 a bottle. Researchers call this the *price-placebo effect*. This is similar to the placebo effect in medicine where people who think they are getting the real thing but who are actually taking sugar pills still experience the effects of the real drug.[37]

Psychological Pricing Strategies

Setting a price is part science, part art. Marketers must understand psychological responses to prices when they decide what to charge for their goods or services.

Odd–Even Pricing

In the U.S. market, we usually see prices in dollars and cents—$1.99, $5.98, $23.67, or even $599.95. We see prices in even dollar amounts—$2, $10, or $600—far less often. The reason? Marketers assume that there is a psychological response to odd prices that differs from the response to even prices. Habit might also play a role here. Whatever the reason, research shows that prices ending in 99 rather than 00 can increase sales by 21–34 percent, depending on other factors. That's a huge amount of sales, so it's no surprise that 60 percent of U.S. prices end in a 9.[38]

But there are some instances in which even prices are the norm or perhaps a necessity. Theater and concert tickets, admission to sporting events, and lottery tickets tend to be priced in even amounts. Professionals normally quote their fees in even dollars. Would you want to visit a doctor or dentist who charged $39.99 for a visit, or would you be concerned that the quality of medical care was less than satisfactory? Many luxury items, such as jewelry, golf course fees, and resort accommodations, use even dollar prices to set them apart.

Prices ending not in whole dollars but in .98 or .99 or some other odd number, can dramatically increase sales.

Restaurants (and the menu engineers who work with them) have discovered that how prices for menu items are presented has a major influence on what customers order—and how much they pay. When prices are given with dollar signs or even the word dollar, customers spend less. Thus, a simple 9 is better on a menu than $9. For high-end restaurants, the formats that end in 9, such as $9.99, indicate value but not quality.[39]

Price Lining

Marketers often apply their understanding of the psychological aspects of pricing in a practice they call **price lining**, whereby items in a product line sell at different prices, or *price points*. If you want to buy a new digital camera, you will find that most of the leading manufacturers have one "stripped-down" model for $100 or less. A better-quality but still moderately priced model likely will be around $200, whereas a professional-quality camera with multiple lenses might set you back $1,000 or more. Another great example can be found at your local car wash! Typically, customers are able to select from one of several package options—the lower-priced choices offering a basic wash, while the higher-end packages include extras like a hot wax or wheel detail. Price lining provides the different ranges necessary to satisfy each segment of the market.

Why is price lining a smart idea? From the marketer's standpoint, it's a way to maximize profits. In theory, a firm would charge each individual customer the highest price that customer is willing to pay. If the maximum one particular person is willing to pay for a digital camera is $150, then that will be the price. If another person is willing to pay $300, that will be his price. But charging each consumer a different price is really not possible. Having a limited number of prices that generally fall at the top of the different price ranges that customers find acceptable is a more workable alternative.

price lining
The practice of setting a limited number of different specific prices, called *price points*, for items in a product line.

Prestige or Premium Pricing

Finally, although a "rational" consumer should be more likely to buy a product or service as the price goes down, in the real world, this assumption sometimes gets turned on its head. Remember that previously in the chapter we talked about situations where we want to meet an image-enhancement objective to appeal to status-conscious consumers. For this reason, sometimes luxury goods marketers use **prestige pricing**, or **premium pricing**, in which they keep the price of the product artificially high to maintain a favorable image of the product based on price only. Prestige pricing relies on the price–quality inference that we talked about before. Tumi, a luxury luggage maker, began cutting promotional activity to protect the premium nature of the brand. Their high-end price point is targeted specifically at the upscale business traveler.[40] Contrary to the "rational" assumption that we are more likely to purchase a product or service as the price goes down, in these cases, believe it or not, people tend to buy more as the price goes up!

prestige pricing, or **premium pricing**
A pricing strategy used by luxury goods marketers in which they keep the price artificially high to maintain a favorable image of the product.

Legal and Ethical Considerations in B2C and C2C Pricing

The free enterprise system is founded on the idea that the marketplace will regulate itself. Prices will rise or fall according to demand. Firms and individuals will supply goods and services at fair prices if there is an adequate profit incentive. Unfortunately, the business world includes the greedy and the unscrupulous.

Deceptive Pricing Practices: Bait-and-Switch

bait-and-switch
An illegal marketing practice in which an advertised price special is used as bait to get customers into the store with the intention of switching them to a higher-priced item.

Unscrupulous businesses may advertise or promote prices in a deceptive way. The Federal Trade Commission (FTC), state lawmakers, and private bodies such as the Better Business Bureau have developed pricing rules and guidelines to meet the challenge. They say retailers (or other suppliers) must not claim that their prices are lower than a competitor's unless that claim is true. A going-out-of-business sale should be the last sale before going out of business. A fire sale should be held only when there really was a fire.

Another deceptive pricing practice is the **bait-and-switch** tactic, whereby a retailer will advertise an item at a very low price—the *bait*—to lure customers into the store. An example might be a budget model TV that has been stripped of all but the most basic features. But it is almost impossible to buy the advertised item—salespeople like to say (privately) that the item is "nailed to the floor." The salespeople do everything possible to get the unsuspecting customers to buy a different, more expensive item—the *switch*. They might tell the customer "confidentially" that "the advertised item is really poor quality, lacking important features, and full of problems." It's complicated to enforce laws against bait-and-switch tactics because these practices are similar to the legal sales technique of "trading up." Simply encouraging consumers to purchase a higher-priced item is acceptable, but it is illegal to advertise a lower-priced item when it's not a legitimate, bona-fide offer that is available if the customer demands it. Another example of a bait-and switch tactic is hotels that lure consumers in with extremely low room rates and then at booking slap on many additional fees and surcharges that sometimes double the advertised price of the room.[41] The FTC may determine if an ad is a bait-and-switch scheme or a legitimate offer by checking to see if a firm refuses to show, demonstrate, or sell the advertised product; disparages it; or penalizes salespeople who do sell it.

Loss-Leader Pricing and Unfair Sales Acts

loss-leader pricing
The pricing policy of setting prices very low or even below cost to attract customers into a store.

Not every advertised bargain is a bait-and-switch. Some retailers advertise items at very low prices or even below cost and are glad to sell them at that price because they know that once in the store, customers may buy other items at regular prices. Marketers call this **loss-leader pricing**; they do it to build store traffic and sales volume. For example, grocery stores know that a sale on chicken is sure to pack the aisles, and they are banking on the fact that while you are in the store, you will fill your cart with many other items you need, at regular price.[42] These retailers use loss-leader pricing—boneless, skinless chicken breasts for $2.98/lb.—to get you to choose their store for your weekly shopping. In the same way, you can buy markers, glue, and other school supplies in July and August for less than half of what they are at other times of the year.

unfair sales acts
State laws that prohibit suppliers from selling products below cost to protect small businesses from larger competitors.

Some states frown on loss-leader practices, so they have passed legislation called **unfair sales acts** (also called *unfair trade practices acts*). These laws or regulations prohibit wholesalers and retailers from selling products below cost. These laws aim to protect small wholesalers and retailers from larger competitors because the "big fish" have the financial resources that allow them to offer loss leaders or products at very low prices—they know that the smaller firms can't match these bargain prices. Meijer, a Michigan-based grocer, was accused of violating a Depression-era law in Wisconsin. Several complaints were filed, citing 37 products that were being sold at less than cost, including ice cream, tomatoes, and bananas.[43]

Misleading Merchandising

Sometimes, the merchandising activities in the retail store are deceptive or at least suspicious. Consumers assume that items in an end-aisle display are being sold at a discounted price. When retailers display regularly priced merchandise in these displays, they may be accused of taking advantage of consumers.

Consumers also assume that the larger bottle or box of something is a better deal. Not always true! Although government regulations now require that grocers and other retailers of food post the price per ounce, pound, and such, on store shelves, few consumers seem to look at these labels.

Price Gouging

"He Has 17,700 Bottles of Hand Sanitizer and No Place to Sell Them" is a headline from a major metropolitan newspaper. The article referred to brothers from Tennessee who set out the day after the first death from COVID-19 in the U.S. in search of hand sanitizer. They cleaned the shelves of hand sanitizer and antibacterial wipes wherever they drove through Tennessee and Kentucky. They also ordered pallets more of sanitizer and wipes. The products were then listed for sale online and sold for between $8 and $70 each. The next day the Internet site pulled items and those on thousands of other listings for sanitizer, wipes, and face masks. Online auction sites followed with even stricter measures.

Price gouging occurs when a seller, either a business organization or an individual consumer, seeks to take advantage of extreme needs to charge exorbitant prices for items. While price gouging is illegal, the relevant laws are different in different states. In California, increasing prices "more than 10 percent after an emergency is declared" is considered price gouging, while New York's law refers to sellers who charge an "unconscionably excessive price" during emergencies. The Tennessee law defines price gouging as "unreasonable prices for essential goods and services . . . in direct response to a disaster." The Tennessee attorney general's office began investigating the case a few days after the headline.

The price gouging laws are civil laws rather than criminal laws, meaning that the offender can only be fined. In the first few weeks of the pandemic, some states collected hundreds of thousands of dollars in fines.

Most of us question the morality of hoarding potentially life-saving products in order to make a profit. Those using e-commerce in price gouging may attempt to justify it as "fixing the inefficiencies in the marketplace."[44]

price gouging
An illegal act in which a seller seeks to take advantage of an emergency or extreme need to charge exorbitant prices for items.

Legal Issues in B2B Pricing

Of course, illegal pricing practices are not limited to B2C pricing situations. Some of the more significant illegal B2B pricing activities include price discrimination, price fixing, and predatory pricing.

Illegal B2B Price Discrimination

The *Robinson–Patman Act* includes regulations against price discrimination in interstate commerce. Price discrimination regulations prevent firms from selling the same product to different retailers and wholesalers at different prices if such practices lessen competition. In addition to regulating the price companies charge, the Robinson–Patman Act specifically prohibits offering such "extras" as discounts, rebates, premiums, coupons, guarantees, and free delivery to some but not all customers.

There are exceptions, however:

- The Robinson–Patman Act does not apply to products sold to consumers—only those sold to resellers.
- A discount to a large channel customer is legal if it is based on the quantity of the order and the resulting efficiencies, such as transportation savings.
- The act allows price differences if there are physical differences in the product, such as different features. A name-brand appliance may be available through a large national retail chain at a lower price than an almost identical item a higher-priced retailer sells because only the chain sells that specific model.

Price-Fixing

Price-fixing occurs when two or more companies conspire to keep prices at a certain level. *Horizontal price-fixing* occurs when competitors making the same product jointly determine what price they each will charge. Of course, parallel pricing among firms in industries in which there are few sellers is not in and of itself considered price-fixing. There must be an exchange of pricing information between sellers to indicate illegal price-fixing actions. The Sherman Antitrust Act of 1890 specifically makes this practice, referred to as *collusion*, illegal. In 2017, the Canadian Competition Bureau found grocery giant Loblaw guilty of participating in a scheme to increase the prices of packaged bread products in a 16-year-long conspiracy. Loblaw's parent company, George Weston, came forward to report the collusion on the promise of immunity from prosecution. According to George Weston, officials from their company and officials at Canada Bread Company communicated directly at least 15 times about raising the price of baked goods to the end consumer. Loblaw claims that other grocery chains were involved, including Walmart, Sobeys, and Giant Tiger.[45]

Vertical price fixing occurs when manufacturers or wholesalers attempt to force retailers to charge a certain price for their product. When vertical price-fixing occurs, the retailer that wants to carry the product must charge the "suggested" retail price. The *Consumer Goods Pricing Act* of 1976 limited this practice, leaving retail stores free to set whatever price they choose without interference by the manufacturer or wholesaler. Today, retailers don't need to adhere to "suggested" prices.

Predatory Pricing

Predatory pricing means that a company sets a very low price for the purpose of driving competitors out of business. Later, when they have a monopoly, they turn around and increase prices. The Sherman Act and the Robinson–Patman Act prohibit predatory pricing. For example, online retailer Amazon was accused of predatory pricing centered on its book sales in 2014. Due to its sheer size, Amazon is able to sell books at a discounted rate to customers looking for a deal. The concern is that, over time, this discount option will capture the vast majority of the market share, making it virtually impossible for other retailers to succeed. The claim was that Amazon's aggressive pricing model could trickle down to authors and push the amount they were paid for their work down to nearly nothing.[46]

10.6 Brand You: How Much Are You Worth?

Taylor has made great progress in developing his job search strategy. He has identified his personal strengths and weaknesses, analyzed the job environment to identify where the best opportunities for him are, made a list of industries and companies that would likely be in the market for an employee with his knowledge and skills, and identified where he believes he would like to work. He also knows that he must address the difficult but very important topic of price—how much he can expect in terms of compensation from a prospective employer.

While you, like almost all of us, want to make as much money as possible in your new job, you will be successful in your job search only if you have some important information. Specifically, you need to know what price (the job offer) is competitive in your job market and then set realistic expectations. You also need to know how much you actually need to meet your financial obligations.

Step 1: Realistic Expectations

To understand salary, you need to understand value. For example, would you pay $10.00 to download a song on iTunes when the going price is $0.99 to $1.29 per song? Unlikely because that would not be a good value. The same concept holds true for employers. An employer is not going to offer you a $75,000 annual salary for a job as a human resources assistant when most other companies are paying around $40,000 for a comparable job. Just as you know the going price for a song download, you should know the standard compensation for the job you want to pursue. Employers, just like all consumers, have expectations about what a product (you) is worth. Various factors, including competition, demand, economic conditions, and other elements in the environment, impact the salary you can expect. Marketers of shoes or hamburgers or smartphones know that to sell their products, they must try to come as close to "reasonable" as possible when deciding on price. In the same way, your chances of obtaining work increase when you set reasonable salary expectations.

Think of yourself as a product. In the job market, your price is your salary, or more specifically, your total compensation, the total you are paid for performing a job, including all additional elements such as commissions, bonus, benefits, and other perks or extras that an employer is willing to give in exchange for your valuable skills. Here is a quick glossary of words you should know to maximize your earnings.

- **Base salary**: Annual salary on which commissions and bonuses are calculated. (For example, a 5 percent bonus on a $30,000 base salary is $1,500, whereas a 5 percent bonus on a $35,000 base salary is $1,750.)
- **Commission**: Additional compensation that is paid based on the amount of goods or services sold (usually applies to sales positions).
- **Bonus**: Additional compensation that is paid based on performance or achievement of a prespecified goal.
- **Stock options**: Additional compensation in the form of ownership of the company. Usually stock options are shares of stock that may be purchased by the employee.
- **Benefits**: Compensation elements that may include insurance (usually medical, dental, optical), vacation and sick days, day care, tuition reimbursement, 401(k), and others; benefits vary by company, so it's best to ask to see the benefits package.
- **Other perks**: Some companies include subsidized cafeterias, office services such as a concierge, game tables, free coffee and snacks, flex hours, low-cost day care, drop-in medical clinics, and other "extras" that help offset your living expenses or make it more attractive to work at the company. In addition, some positions may include a car allowance or other transportation allowance as part of compensation.

Step 2: Know What You're Worth

To have an accurate idea of what you're worth, you need to do some research, preferably early in your personal branding process. Some suggestions for this are:

- Talk with people you know in the industry, including friends and recent graduates, about what you can expect given the economy, competition, and your background for the position you are seeking.
- Search the Internet for sites that provide details on compensation for various jobs. Salary.com and Payscale.com are two sites that provide information on total compensation for thousands of different positions.
- The U.S. government's Bureau of Labor Statistics website provides information on over 800 jobs at https://www.bls.gov/bls/blswage.htm.

Just as marketers know that shoes or smartphones with more features are more valuable to consumers, thus meriting a higher price, you can add to your value while still in school. Some ways to increase your value are listed below:

Have one or more internships while in school. Internships give relevant experience to communicate on your résumé and in interviews. Plus, they provide networking contacts that can be of use to you for many years to come.

Gain work experience while in college—any type will be good, but if it's related to your future career, even better.

Give a good impression from your first letter or phone call to your last interview and be professional.

Keep in touch with internship, job, and other contacts in case a full-time position becomes available in the future.

Send a thank-you note, handwritten, in the mail, within 24 hours of your interview visit—and show off your writing skills at the same time.

Step 3: Know How Much You Need

In addition to knowing about salaries for different jobs in different places, you also need to understand how much it will cost you to live in different places since the cost of everything from food to apartments to gasoline varies from city to city. Websites such as bestplaces.net provide information on the cost of living in various cities. You can use that information to help in determining what the minimum salary must be for you to live in an area.

Of course, to get closer to a realistic estimate of what it will cost *you* to live in an area, you have to develop a personal estimate of monthly expenses, or a budget. Your budget should include all your possible expenses:

- Housing (both rent or mortgage payments and furnishings)
- Utilities
- Food (both groceries and eating out)
- Clothing purchases and cleaning
- Transportation
- Home or renters, auto, and any other insurance
- Childcare if applicable
- Education loan payments
- Other recurring bills and debts, such as payments on an auto loan if not included with transportation
- Savings
- Discretionary spending (movies, reading, other entertainment)
- Amount that will be taken out of your pay for health insurance, social security, your 401(k) contributions, state and federal withholding taxes, and any other deductions

Armed with this information, you should be able to develop a salary range that is realistic for the prospective employer and one with which you can enjoy your job and your life.

Salary Question Dos and Don'ts

Don't ask about salary in the interview.

Do wait until the employer brings up the topic.

Do have a salary range in mind that you are seeking.

Do, when asked, "What are your salary expectations?" say, "I'm sure you have a very competitive compensation package."

Do, if the employer persists, give your predetermined salary range by saying something like, "I'm looking for a base salary between $30,000 and $35,000 with competitive benefits."

Do be sure to put your salary range higher than you want. If you want $28,000, ask for a minimum range of $30,000.

Taylor has done his pricing work. He knows that the average salary for the entry-level job he is applying for in his area of the country is $37,500, or a little over $3,000 a month. He also knows that his expenses will be around $2,500 each month.

It's time for Taylor's job interview and the discussion of salary goes something like this:

Interviewer: What are your salary expectations?

Taylor: I'm sure you have a very competitive compensation package.

Interviewer: Yes, but how much will it take for you to accept the position?

Taylor: I'm looking for a base salary between $35,000 and $40,000 with competitive benefits.

Taylor has successfully made it through the uncomfortable topic of salary.

Objective **Summaries** and **Key Terms**

10.1 Objective Summary

Explain the importance of pricing and how marketers set objectives for their pricing strategies.

Pricing is important to firms because it creates profits and influences customers to purchase or not. Prices may be monetary or nonmonetary, as when consumers or businesses exchange one product for another. Effective pricing objectives are designed to support corporate and marketing objectives and are flexible. Pricing objectives often focus on a desired level of profit growth or profit margin, on sales (to maximize sales or to increase market share), on competing effectively, on increasing customer satisfaction, or on communicating a certain image.

Key Terms

market share
competitive-effect pricing, or market-based pricing
prestige products

10.2 Objective Summary

Describe how marketers use costs, demand, revenue, and the pricing environment to make pricing decisions.

In developing prices, marketers must estimate demand and determine costs. Marketers often use break-even analysis to

help in deciding on the price for a product. Break-even analysis uses fixed and variable costs to identify how many units must be sold at a certain price to begin making a profit. Marketers must also consider the requirements for adequate trade margins for retailers, wholesalers, and other members of the channel of distribution. Like other elements of the marketing mix, pricing is influenced by a variety of external environmental factors. This includes economic trends, such as inflation and recession, and the firm's competitive environment—that is, whether the firm does business in an oligopoly, a monopoly, or a more competitive environment. Government regulations can also affect prices by increasing the cost of production or through actual regulations of a firm's pricing strategies. Consumer trends that influence how consumers think and behave may also influence pricing. Although marketers of some products may develop standardized pricing strategies for global markets, unique environmental factors in different countries mean marketers must localize pricing strategies.

Key Terms

price elasticity of demand
elastic demand
inelastic demand
cross-elasticity of demand
variable costs
fixed costs
average fixed cost
total costs
break-even analysis

break-even point
contribution per unit
The Tax Cuts and Jobs Act of 2017 (TCJA of 2017)
markup
gross margin
retailer margin
wholesaler margin
list price, or manufacturer's suggested retail price (MSRP)
Credit Card Responsibility and Disclosure Act
Affordable Care Act
sharing economy
Uber
Airbnb
shopping for control

10.3 Objective Summary

Understand key pricing strategies and tactics.

Although easy to calculate and "safe," frequently used cost-based strategies do not consider demand, the competition, the stage in the product life cycle, plant capacity, or product image. The most common cost-based strategy is cost-plus pricing.

Pricing strategies based on demand, such as target costing and yield management pricing, can require that marketers estimate demand at different prices in order to be certain they can sell what they produce. Strategies based on the competition may represent industry wisdom but can be tricky to apply. A price leadership strategy is often used in an oligopoly.

Firms that focus on customer needs may consider everyday low price or value pricing strategies. An alternative consumer pleasing strategy is a high/low pricing strategy. New products may be priced using a high skimming price to recover research, development, and promotional costs or a penetration price to encourage more customers and discourage competitors from entering the market. Trial pricing means setting a low price for a limited time.

Other pricing strategies include pricing segmentation, peak load pricing, surge pricing, bottom-of-the-pyramid pricing, and decoy pricing.

To implement pricing strategies with individual products, marketers may use two-part pricing or payment pricing tactics. For multiple products, marketers may use price bundling, wherein two or more products are sold and priced as a single package. Captive pricing is often chosen when two items must be used together; one item is sold at a very low price, and the other at a high, profitable price.

Distribution-based pricing tactics, including F.O.B. pricing (for domestic shipments), uniform delivered pricing, and freight absorption pricing, address differences in how far products must be shipped. Similar pricing tactics are used for products sold internationally.

Pricing for members of the channel may include trade or functional discounts, cumulative or noncumulative quantity discounts to encourage larger purchases, cash discounts to encourage fast payment, and seasonal discounts to spread purchases throughout the year or to increase off-season or in-season sales.

Key Terms

cost-plus pricing
keystoning
demand-based pricing
congestion pricing
target costing
yield management pricing
clearance sale
price leadership
value pricing, or everyday low pricing (EDLP)
high/low pricing, or promo pricing
skimming price
penetration pricing
trial pricing
price segmentation
peak load pricing
surge pricing
bottom-of-the-pyramid pricing
two-part pricing
payment pricing
subscription pricing
decoy pricing
price bundling
captive pricing
F.O.B. factory pricing, or F.O.B. origin pricing
F.O.B. delivered pricing
uniform delivered pricing
freight absorption pricing
trade discounts
quantity discounts
cash discounts
seasonal discounts

10.4 Objective Summary

Understand the opportunities for Internet pricing strategies and innovations in payment.

E-commerce may offer firms an opportunity to initiate dynamic pricing—meaning prices can be changed frequently with little or no cost. Auctions offer opportunities for customers to bid on items in C2C, B2C, and B2B e-commerce. The Internet also allows firms to practice freemium pricing, in which basic versions of digital products are given to customers for no charge. The Internet allows buyers to compare products and prices, gives consumers more control over the price they pay for items, and has made customers more price sensitive.

Key Terms

dynamic pricing
online auctions
freemium pricing
Internet price discrimination
cryptocurrency
Bitcoin

digital wallet
mobile wallet
buy-now-pay-later (BNPL)
save-now-buy-later (SNBL)
collaborative savings and consumption
peer-to-peer (P2P) lending, or social lending
rent-to-own
cashless society

10.5 Objective Summary

Describe the psychological, legal, and ethical aspects of pricing.

Consumers may express emotional or psychological responses to prices. Customers may use an idea of a customary or fair price as an internal reference price in evaluating products. Sometimes marketers use reference pricing strategies by displaying products with different prices next to each other. A price–quality inference means that consumers use price as a cue for quality. Customers respond to odd prices differently than to even-dollar prices. Marketers may practice price lining strategies in which they set a limited number of different price ranges for a product line. With luxury products, marketers may use a prestige or premium pricing strategy, assuming that people will buy more if the price is higher.

Most marketers try to avoid unethical or illegal pricing practices. One deceptive pricing practice is the illegal bait-and-switch tactic. Many states have unfair sales acts, which are laws against loss-leader pricing that make it illegal to sell products below cost. Federal regulations prohibit predatory pricing, price discrimination, and horizontal or vertical price-fixing.

Key Terms

internal reference price
price lining
prestige pricing, or premium pricing
bait-and-switch
loss-leader pricing
unfair sales acts
price gouging
price-fixing
predatory pricing

10.6 Objective Summary

Understand the important considerations in job compensation, how to set realistic expectations, and improve your chances of getting a great first job.

Students and others seeking a job need to know what price (the job offer) is competitive when seeking a job. Realistic expectations come from an understanding of potential value offered to a prospective employee—i.e., how much the employee (product) is worth. Compensation for various jobs may include base salary, commission, bonus, stock options, benefits, and other perks.

Students can add to their value to a prospective employer through internships or work experience combined with professional job search protocol. The price or compensation expectations also depend on the necessary amount needed to cover living expenses, savings, and debt. These expenses include such basics as housing, utilities, food, clothing, and recurring bills, such as student and auto loans. Amounts withheld by the employer for various taxes, health insurance, and retirement savings must also be considered.

Chapter **Questions** and **Activities**

Concepts: Test Your Knowledge

10-1. What is price, and why is it important to a firm? Describe and give examples of the following types of pricing objectives: profit, market share, competitive effect, customer satisfaction, and image enhancement.

10-2. Explain how the demand curves for normal products and for prestige products differ. What are demand shifts and what are some ways that marketers can cause them to occur? How do firms go about estimating demand? How can marketers estimate the elasticity of demand?

10-3. Explain variable costs, fixed costs, average variable costs, average fixed costs, and average total costs. What is break-even analysis?

10-4. List and explain the five areas of the environment that influence pricing.

10-5. Explain and give an example of target costing, yield management pricing, leader pricing, and EDLP.

10-6. For new products, explain skimming pricing, penetration pricing, and trial pricing. Give examples of situations in which each would be the best choice.

10-7. How do marketers customize pricing with price segmentation, peak load pricing, and surge pricing? What are some ways marketers can price to meet the needs of bottom-of-the-pyramid consumers?

10-8. Explain decoy pricing. Is decoy pricing ethical?

10-9. Explain and give examples of two-part pricing, payment pricing, price bundling, captive pricing, and distribution-based pricing tactics.

10-10. What is dynamic pricing? What is Internet price discrimination? What is the difference between the two?

10-11. Explain these psychological aspects of pricing: price–quality inferences, odd–even pricing, internal reference price, price lining, and prestige pricing.

10-12. Explain these ethical and legal problems in B2B pricing: B2B price discrimination, price-fixing, price gouging, and predatory pricing.

Activities: Apply What You've Learned

10-13. *Creative Homework/Short Project* Assume that you are an entrepreneur who runs a bakery that sells gluten-free breads and cakes. You believe that the current economic conditions merit an increase in the price of your baked goods. You are concerned, however, that increasing the price might not be profitable because you are unsure of the price elasticity of demand for your products. Develop a plan for the measurement of price elasticity of demand for your products. What findings would lead you to increase the price? What findings would cause you to rethink the decision to increase prices? Develop a presentation for your class outlining (1) the concept of elasticity of demand, (2) why raising prices without understanding the elasticity would be a bad move, (3) your recommendations for measurement, and (4) the potential impact on profits for elastic and inelastic demand.

10-14. *In Class, 10–25 Minutes for Teams* For each of the following products, determine at least three different prices that might be charged. Then, survey each of the individuals within your group to find out how much of each product they would buy at each price point for each of the products. For each product, calculate the price elasticity of demand to determine whether the demand is elastic or inelastic.

a. Cups of coffee per month
b. Movie tickets per month
c. Concert tickets per year

10-15. *For Further Research (Groups)* In this chapter, we talked about different forms of digital money and about the possibility of a cashless society. Plan and execute a simple research project with students at your university. You need to find out:

a. What type(s) of digital cash they currently use if any.
b. What they see as benefits and disadvantages of using that digital cash.
c. What they see as benefits and disadvantages of a cashless society
d. How they would react if their government moved to a cashless society.

Prepare a report for your class.

10-16. *Creative Homework/Short Project* Your textbook has talked about a number of different available and popular cryptocurrencies. Using the Internet, find as many different types of cryptocurrencies that are currently exchanged as you can. Pick five of these and gather enough information on them to be able to compare them. Take notes on your findings. Pick three that you think are the best and two that are the least promising. Rank the five and write a description of each, including your comments about their benefits and weaknesses. Present a report to your class.

10-17. *For Further Research (Individual)* In this chapter, we talked about how airlines use yield management pricing to ensure that every seat is filled on every flight, thus maximizing profits. Go to the websites of at least two different airlines. Check the prices of a flight for each airline approximately three weeks from "now." Then, check the prices for the same flights in less than a week, in one week, and in two weeks. Write a report on your findings and what they tell you about airline pricing.

10-18. *For Further Research (Groups)* Select one of the product categories below. Identify two different firms that offer consumers a line of product offerings in the category. For example, Dell, HP, and Apple each market a line of laptop computers, whereas Hoover, Dyson, and Bissell offer lines of vacuum cleaners. Using the Internet or by visiting a retailer who sells your selected product, research the product lines and pricing of the two firms. Based on your research, develop a presentation on the price lining strategies of the two firms. Your presentation should discuss (1) the specific price points of the product offerings of each firm and how the price lining strategy maximizes revenue, (2) your ideas for why the specific price points were selected, (3) how the price lining strategies of the two firms are alike and how they are different, and (4) possible reasons for differences in the strategies.

a. Laptop computers
b. Vacuum cleaners
c. Smart TVs
d. Smartphones

Concepts: Apply Marketing Metrics

Contribution per unit and break-even analysis are two popular and very useful metrics for marketing decision making. These analyses are essential to determine if a firm's marketing opportunity will mean a financial profit or loss. As explained in the chapter, *contribution per unit* is the difference between the price the firm charges for a product and the variable costs. Break-even analysis that includes contribution tells marketers how much must be sold to break even or to earn a desired amount of profit.

Let's assume that Touch of Beirut Brands is a Los Angeles–based producer of Lebanese specialty foods and ingredients. In the past, the firm has marketed primarily through restaurant distributors to small mom-and-pop Lebanese cuisine restaurants around the U.S. But recently they've developed a marketing plan to sell a combination hummus and pita slices packaged product that is ready to eat—sort of like the famous boxed Oscar Mayer Lunchables. They've branded the new product "Hummus-to-Go," and outlets will be Whole Foods and other supermarkets that stock healthier fare.

The company plans to use social media to gain buzz around the new product but will also be spending money on advertising and sales promotion through coupons to consumers and price incentives to distributors and retailers. Whole Foods would like to be able to sell the boxes at retail for $5. Because the retailer typically requires a 30 percent markup, Touch of Beirut's price to the supermarkets will be $3.50 per box. The unit variable costs for the product, including packaging, will be $1.25.

Touch of Beirut estimates its advertising and promotion expenses for the first year will be $2,500,000.

10-19. What is the contribution per unit for Hummus-to-Go?

10-20. What is the break-even volume for the first year that will cover the planned advertising and promotion (1) in units and (2) in dollars?

10-21. How many units of Hummus-to-Go must Touch of Beirut sell to earn a total profit of $1,000,000?

10-22. Based on the above, does this seem like a good business venture to you? Why or why not?

Choices: What Do You Think?

10-23. *Ethics* Several online stores now sell products to consumers at different prices based on the user's information, such as geographic location—which determines your proximity to competitors and your area's average income. Although this practice, known as *Internet price discrimination*, is not illegal, some would say it is unethical. Do you believe this practice is unethical? Should this practice be illegal? If you think the practice should be legal, should retailers be required to put a disclaimer on their site? Explain your reasoning.

10-24. *Critical Thinking* Two-part pricing and payment pricing are tactics that are designed to make things more affordable for customers and better meet their needs. List two products where you feel consumers would benefit if a two-part pricing tactic were used. What are two products where you feel consumers would benefit if a payment pricing tactic were used? Explain your reasoning for these decisions.

10-25. *Ethics* Many successful retailers use a loss leader pricing strategy, in which they advertise an item at a price below their cost and sell the item at that price to get customers into their store. They feel that these customers will continue to shop with their company and that they will make a profit in the long run. Do you consider this an unethical practice? Who benefits and who is hurt by such practices? Do you think the practice should be made illegal, as some states have done? How is this different from bait-and-switch pricing?

10-26. *Ethics* In this chapter, we talked about price gouging during the COVID-19 epidemic. Many people sell things they own on one of the online auctions, such as eBay, at prices above the regular or list price. Think about each of the following products and decide if you think the pricing is unethical. Should it be illegal to sell at this price?

a. An antique Chinese vase priced at $1,000.00
b. The doll every little girl seems to want for Christmas at 15 percent above MSRP
c. The doll every little girl seems to want for Christmas at 75 percent above MSRP
d. A brand of deodorant that is no longer being produced priced at double the MSRP
e. A pair of collectible limited-edition NBA basketball shoes priced at $20,000

10-27. *Critical Thinking* You work as a marketer for a large chain of upscale skin care boutiques that offer all-natural skin and beauty products. The price of your ingredients has been rising steadily for over two years, cutting into your profits. To continue making the products, you must either increase your prices or use less expensive ingredients. Your research tells you that the market won't tolerate a price increase, so you have decided to use the less expensive ingredients from new suppliers. What, if anything, do you tell your customers? What are some of the possible ramifications of this decision for your business, your customers, and your suppliers?

10-28. *Critical Thinking* Some retailers sell their own store brands that compete with well-known national brands. Typically, the store brands are sold right beside the name-brand product on the shelf with a much lower price. The hope is to convince the consumer to purchase the store brand because it is offered at a lower price point with the same ingredients (and sometimes even eerily similar packaging). Is this practice fair to the national brands? If you were the brand manager for Advil, how would you market your product and set your pricing to combat the competition?

Miniproject: Learn by Doing

The purpose of this miniproject is to help you become familiar with how consumers respond to different prices by conducting a series of pricing experiments. For this project, you should first select a product category that students such as yourself normally purchase. It should be a moderately expensive purchase, such as athletic shoes, a smartphone, or a piece of luggage. You should next obtain two photographs of items in this product category or, if possible, two actual items. The two items should not appear to be substantially different in quality or in price.

Note: You will need to recruit separate research participants for each of the activities listed in the next section.

10-29. *Experiment 1: Reference Pricing*

a. Place the two products together. Place a sign on one with a low price. Place a sign on the other with a high price (about 50 percent higher will do). Ask your research participants to evaluate the quality of each of the items and to tell which one they would probably purchase.
b. Reverse the signs and ask other research participants to evaluate the quality of each of the items and to tell which one they would probably purchase.

c. Place the two products together again. This time place a sign on one with a moderate price. Place a sign on the other with a price that is only a little higher (less than 10 percent higher). Again, ask research participants to evaluate the quality of each of the items and to tell which one they would probably purchase.

d. Reverse the signs and ask other research participants to evaluate the quality of each of the items and to tell which one they would probably purchase.

10-30. *Experiment 2: Odd–Even Pricing* For this experiment, you will only need one of the items from experiment 1.

a. Place a sign on the item that ends in 99 cents (e.g., $62.99). Ask research participants to tell you if they think the price for the item is very low, slightly low, moderate, slightly high, or very high. Also ask them to evaluate the quality of the item and to tell you, on a scale of 1 to 10, with 10 being very likely, how likely they would be to purchase the item.

b. This time place a sign on the item that is slightly lower but that ends in 0 cents (e.g., $60). Ask different research participants to tell you if they think the price for the item is very low, slightly low, moderate, slightly high, or very high. Also ask them to evaluate the quality of the item and to tell you how likely they would be to purchase the item.

Develop a presentation for your class in which you discuss the results of your experiments and what they tell you about odd–even pricing and about assimilation and contrast effects in price perceptions.

Marketing in Action **Case**   Real Choices at United Airlines

Correctly setting prices in any industry is challenging, but air travel can be an especially complex proposition. On the same plane, you'll have one customer who is primarily schedule focused and willing to pay a higher rate to get to a business meeting on time sitting next to a leisure traveler who planned a trip months in advance and just wants to get the lowest fare possible. And then there is the perishability issue—when the wheels go up, any empty seats can no longer produce revenue at any price. This is the environment that United Airlines and other carriers face every day.

United Airlines is one of the leaders in an industry that has seen many companies come and go since the beginning of commercial air travel in 1914. Along with American Airlines and Delta, United is considered one of the "big three" in air travel. Formerly a part of airplane manufacturer Boeing, the company was formed in 1931 and today claims to have the world's "most comprehensive global route network." In 2019, United offered 4,989 daily departures taking 162 million passengers per year to 362 destinations in 61 countries.

In recent years, United has found itself in competition with a new class of airline known as ULCCs: *ultra-low-cost carriers*. You may have flown on one of these economical (or "cut rate") carriers, such as Spirit, Frontier, and Allegiant. Southwest Airlines also offers low fares, but (along with JetBlue) is instead considered to be in the *low-cost carrier* category, as these companies offer some standard services not available with the ULCCs. What distinguishes this no-frills class of airline is what they do *not* include as part of the fare: reserved seats, snacks, drinks, ability to carry on a bag, in-flight entertainment, seats that recline, leg room, and, often, on-time arrivals. These flights are not about service but instead are all about getting you from point A to B at the lowest price possible.

To compete with low-cost carriers, United first took a run at creating an LCC of its own. Called *Ted*, the airline had its own separate planes. Skeptics joked that the name stood for "the end of United." While United survived, Ted was discontinued after five years.

United then tried to compete with low-cost carriers by creating an additional fare class: Basic Economy. The prices are low like those of the ULCCs; and so are the services: no seat selection, no seat assigned until day of departure when middle seats may be the only seats available, no ticket changes, no refunds, and—one of the biggest restrictions—no full-sized carry-ons. The fare savings are not huge—typically between $20 and $30 each way—but enough to attract customers who are very price sensitive, including many in the millennial generation. "Big three" compatriots American and Delta have followed suit with versions of the fare class.

So far, Basic Economy seems to be a huge success for United and other airlines. In addition to keeping some customers away from the ULCCs, United is able to sell a small portion of its unused inventory to attract travelers to its airline, hoping they will continue to be a United customer. United is also able to "upsell" some customers to a better (and more profitable) class of service. In 2019, the company was able to upsell 60 to 70 percent of bookings from Basic Economy to a standard fare. It also makes significant revenues on fees when travelers decide they need that overhead bin after all, often paying more in total than they would have by purchasing a standard economy ticket. When United introduced Basic Economy fares in 2016, it projected that between fees and upgrades, the program would earn an additional one billion dollars by 2020.

While United tries to be very transparent about the differences between standard and economy fares, an unintended consequence of the pricing has been the creation of a sort of class system in the coach compartment of its planes. Standard economy passengers, including some with "elite" status based on miles flown, resent Basic Economy passengers taking precious overhead bin space. On another airline, one passenger spent the night in jail after a battle for the bin with a fellow traveler, and in another case, the conflict turned into a fist fight. So much for "Flying the Friendly Skies!"

The pandemic of 2020 caused a massive upheaval in the global transportation industry, with air traffic down by 95 percent in April of that year. This downturn led to major decreases in fares; by one estimate, the median price of a domestic U.S. flight dropped by over 47 percent. Major external events like the pandemic along with new technology, additional competitors, and changes in consumer preferences will require the airline industry to continue to evolve. To continue to survive, United Airlines will have to carefully manage its pricing process to meet the needs of all the classes of passengers that it serves.[47]

Questions for Discussion

10-31. Consider the issue of price elasticity for the two broad classes of United's customer base: leisure travelers and business travelers. Is the demand for air travel from each of these customer groups generally elastic or inelastic?

10-32. As seen above, competition is a big factor in United's pricing decisions. What other factors in the external environment should marketers consider in their flight scheduling and ticket pricing?

10-33. Consumers can be fickle. Assume competitors change their pricing strategies and consumers abandon United's Basic Economy class. What are three suggestions for ways United might adjust its offerings and pricing in order to gain long-term customer loyalty?

Chapter **Notes**

1. Micah Maidenberg, "How Low-Cost Airlines Alter the Economics of Flying," *New York Times*, https://www.nytimes.com/2017/09/01/business/budget-airlines-ticket-prices.html (accessed March 25, 2018).

2. Dan Burns, "How COVID-19 Affected U.S. Consumer Prices in March," *Reuters*, April 10, 2020, https://www.reuters.com/article/us-health-coronavirus-usa-prices/how-covid-19-affected-us-consumer-prices-in-march-idUSKCN21S20H (accessed May 1, 2020).

3. Jayme Kinsey, "WALMART SAVINGS CATCHER APP—REVIEW WITH PROS AND CONS," *So Not Niche Blog*, January 5, 2016, http://www.sonotniche.com/so-not-niche-blog/walmart-savings-catcher-app-review-with-pros-and-cons (accessed September 23, 2020).

4. "Walmart Ending Savings Catcher Program," *Progressive Grocer*, March 20, 2019, https://progressivegrocer.com/walmart-ending-savings-catcher-program (accessed (March 26, 2020).

5. Vindu Goel, "At $1,000, Apple's iPhone X Crosses a Pricing Threshold," *New York Times*, September 10, 2017, https://www.nytimes.com/2017/09/10/technology/apple-iphone-price.html (accessed March 26. 2018); Antonio Villas-Boas, Malarie Gokey and Monica Chin, "Apple Sells Several Different iPhone Models — Here's How Much They All Cost," *Business Insider*, April 15, 2020, https://www.businessinsider.com/iphone-price (accessed March 26, 2020); Tripp Mickle, "Apple Unveils Low-Priced iPhone in Bid to Capture Emerging Markets," *Wall Street Journal*, April 15, 2020, https://www.wsj.com/articles/apple-unveils-low-priced-iphone-in-bid-to-capture-emerging-markets-11586965159 (accessed March 26, 2020).

6. "This Day in History," https://www.history.com/this-day-in-history/seventeen-states-put-gasoline-rationing-into-effect (accessed May 23, 2014).

7. Claire Bradley, "6 Companies Thriving in the Recession," *Investopedia*, August 23, 2010, https://www.investopedia.com/financial-edge/0810/6-companies-thriving-in-the-recession.aspx (accessed March 265, 2018).

8. Jennifer Waters, "It's a New Day for Credit Cards," *Wall Street Journal*, February 21, 2010, https://online.wsj.com/article/SB126670472534749217.html?KEYWORDS5credit1card1rate1regulations (accessed March 3, 2010).

9. "Key Features of the Affordable Care Act by Year," https://www.hhs.gov/healthcare/facts/timeline/timeline-text.html (accessed May 10, 2014); Rick Ungar, "The Real Numbers on 'The Obamacare Effect' Are In—Now Let the Crow Eating Begin," *Forbes*, March 10, 2014, https://www.forbes.com/sites/rickungar/2014/03/10/the-real-numbers-on-the-obamacare-effect-are-in-now-let-the-crow-eating-begin (accessed May 20, 2014).

10. Daphne Kasriel-Alexander, "Top 10 Global Consumer Trends for 2016," *Euromonitor International*, December 18, 2016, https://blog.euromonitor.com/update-on-our-top-10-global-consumer-trends-for-2016-agnostic-shoppers/ (accessed December 22, 2020).

11. Samsung, "Apps Available on Your Family HubTM Refrigerator," https://www.samsung.com/us/explore/family-hub-refrigerator/apps/ (accessed March 26, 2020).

12. Steward Washburn, "Pricing Basics: Establishing Strategy and Determining Costs in the Pricing Decision," *Business Marketing*, July 1985, reprinted in Valerie Kijewski, Bob Donath, and David T. Wilson, eds., *The Best Readings from Business Marketing Magazine* (Boston: PWS-Kent, 1993), 257–69.

13. Robert L. Steiner, "The Inverse Association Between the Margins of Manufacturers and Retailers," *Review of Industrial Organization* 8 (1993): 717–40, As cited in Robert M. Schindler, *Pricing Strategies: A Marketing Approach* (Thousand Oaks, CA: SAGE Publications, Inc., 2012), 23.

14. Charles L. Ilvento, *Profit Planning and Decision Making in the Hospitality Industry* (Dubuque, IA: Kendall/Hunt Publishing Company, 1996), 154. As cited in Robert M. Schindler, *Pricing Strategies: A Marketing Approach* (Thousand Oaks, CA: SAGE Publications, Inc., 2012), 23.

15. David Adodaher, *Iacocca* (New York: Macmillan Publishing Co., 1982), 126, as cited in Robert M. Schindler, *Pricing Strategies: A Marketing Approach* (Thousand Oaks, CA: SAGE Publications, Inc., 2012), 37.

16. "II. What Is Congestion Pricing?," U.S. Department of Transportation (February 1, 2017), https://ops.fhwa.dot.gov/publications/congestionpricing/sec2.htm (accessed April 6, 2018).

17. Robin Cooper and W. Bruce Chew, "Control Tomorrow's Costs through Today's Design," *Harvard Business Review*, January–February 1996, 88–97.

18. Erin McDowell, "The Rise and Fall of Sears, Once the Largest and Most Powerful Retailer in the World," *Business Insider*, https://www.businessinsider.com/rise-and-fall-of-sears-bankruptcy-store-closings (accessed March 26, 2020).

19. Jim Riley, "Q&A – Explain Price Skimming," Tutor2u, December 21, 2009, https://www.tutor2u.net/business/blog/qa-explain-price-skimming (accessed May 12, 2014).

20. Campbell's, "About Us," https://www.campbellsoupcompany.com/about-campbell/ (accessed May 8, 2014).

21. Captain George's, https://captaingeorges.com/pricing-location/myrtle-beach-sc (accessed March 23, 2018).

22. Universal Cargo, "Incoterms Definitions Part 2: CFR, CIF, CPT, CIP," February 14, 2013, https://www.universalcargo.com/incoterms-definitions-part-2-cfr-cif-cpt-cip/ (accessed September 23, 2020).

23. "RedCard," Target, https://www.target.com/c/redcard/-/N-4tfyn#?lnk=snav_rd_solr_redcard (accessed October 12, 2018).

24. Megan Gibson, "Happy 10th Birthday, iTunes!," *Time*, April 28, 2013, https://entertainment.time.com/2013/04/28/happy-10th-birthday-itunes (accessed May 8, 2014).

25. "Music Goes Mobile as More Smartphone Users Stream Songs," *eMarketer*, August 13, 2013, https://www.emarketer.com/Article/Music-Goes-Mobile-More-Smartphone-Users-Stream-Songs/1010126 (accessed May 10, 2014).

26. Adam Tanner, "Different Customers, Different Prices, Thanks to Big Data," *Forbes*, March 26, 2014, https://www.forbes.com/sites/adamtanner/2014/03/26/different-customers-different-prices-thanks-to-big-data (accessed May 23, 2014).

27. Kyle Poyar, "Everything You Need to Know About Freemium Pricing," *Open View*, August 27, 2020, https://openviewpartners.com/blog/freemium-pricing-guide/#.X2wCAGhKhGk (accessed September 23, 2020).

28. Rebecca April May, "Candy Crush Saga Prepares 5,000th Level and Plans for 10 More Years of Puzzles," *Game Central*, July 2, 2019, https://metro.co.uk/2019/07/02/candy-crush-saga-prepares-5000th-level-and-plans-for-10-more-years-of-puzzles-10104154/ (accessed March 26, 2020).

29. Alexandra Twin, "Price Discrimination," *Investopedia*, https://www.investopedia.com/terms/p/price_discrimination.asp (accessed May 23, 2014).

30. Jennifer Valentino-DeVries, Jeremy Singer-Vine, and Ashkan Soltani, "Websites Vary Prices, Deals Based on Users' Information," *Wall Street Journal*, December 24, 2012, https://online.wsj.com/news/articles/SB10001424127887323777204578189391881534 (accessed May 1, 2014).

31. Quoted in Julia Angwin, Surya Mattu, and Jeff Larson, "The Tiger Mom Tax: Asians Are Nearly Twice as Likely to Get a Higher Price from Princeton Review," *Pro Publica*, September 1, 2015, https://www.propublica.org/article/asians-nearly-twice-as-likely-to-get-higher-price-from-princeton-review (accessed April 20, 2016).

32. Nathan Reiff, "The 10 Most Important Cryptocurrencies Other Than Bitcoin," *Investopedia*, January 8, 2020, https://www.investopedia.com/tech/most-important-cryptocurrencies-other-than-bitcoin/ (accessed March 26, 2020); Paul Vigna and Eun-Young Ieona, "Cryptocurrency Scams Took in More Than $4 Billion in 2019," *Wall Street Journal*, February 8, 2020 (accessed March 22, 2020.)

33. Nathaniel Popper, "What Is Bitcoin and How Does It Work?" *New York Times*, October 1, 2017, https://www.nytimes.com/2017/10/01/technology/what-is-bitcoin-price.html (accessed March 22, 2018).

34. Ibid.

35. Ethan Wolff-Mann, "Coronavirus Crisis: How to Deal with Potentially Contaminated Money," *Yahoo Finance*, March 26, 2020, https://finance.yahoo.com/news/coronavirus-crisis-how-to-deal-with-potentially-contaminated-money-182126373.html (accessed May 19, 2020); Giovanni Immordino and Francesco Flaviano Russo, "Cashless Payments and Tax Evasion," *European Journal of Political Economy*, https://www.sciencedirect.com/science/article/abs/pii/S0176268017302239 (accessed May 19, 2020); Morgan Meaker, "Sweden's Cashless Society Dream Isn't All It's Cracked Up to Be," *Wired*, April 6, 2020, https://www.wired.co.uk/article/sweden-cashless-society (accessed May 19, 2020).

36. David Ackerman and Gerald Tellis, "Can Culture Affect Prices? A Cross-Cultural Study of Shopping and Retail Prices," *Journal of Retailing* 77 (2001): 57–82.

37. Shankar Vedantam, "Eliot Spitzer and the Price-Placebo Effect," *Washington Post*, March 17, 2008, https://www.washingtonpost.com/wp-dyn/content/article/2008/03/16/AR2008031602168.html (accessed May 27, 2008).

38. William J. Boyes, Allen K. Lynch, and William Stewart, "Why Odd Pricing?" *Journal of Applied Social Psychology* 37, no. 5 (May 2007): 1130–40; Robert M. Schindler and Thomas M. Kibarian, "Increased Consumer Sales Response through Use of 99-Ending Prices," *Journal of Retailing* 72 (1996): 187–99.

39. Sarah Kershaw, "Using Menu Psychology to Entice Diners," *New York Times*, December 22, 2009, https://www.nytimes.com/2009/12/23/dining/23menus.html?scp51&sq5Using%20Menu%20Psychologyu%20to%20Entice%20Diners&st5cse (accessed March 3, 2010).

40. Shelly Banjo and Brooke Sutherland, "Don't Buy the Kate Spade Deal Hype," *Bloomberg*, March 28, 2017, https://www.bloomberg.com/gadfly/articles/2017-03-28/kate-spade-takeover-premium-hype-overblown (accessed March 23, 2018).

41. Victoria Rosenthal, "US Hotel Fees and Surcharges Expected to Reach Record Levels in 2017," *Hotel Management*, September 28, 2017, https://www.hotelmanagement.net/operate/u-s-hotelfees-surcharges-expected-to-reach-record-levels-2017 (accessed March 23, 2018).

42. Stephanie Rosenbloom, "Back-to-School Discounts Are Deeper, More Creative," *New York Times*, August 14, 2008, https://www.nytimes.com/2008/08/15/business/15retail.html (accessed March 4, 2010).

43. Shandra Martinez, "Meijer Investigated in Wisconsin for Pricing Too Low," *Michigan Live*, August 19, 2015, http://www.mlive.com/business/west-michigan/index.ssf/2015/08/meijer_investigated_in_wiscons.html (accessed March 23, 2018).

44. Jack Nicas, "He Has 17,700 Bottles of Hand Sanitizer and Nowhere to Sell Them," *New York Times*, March 14, 2020, https://www.nytimes.com/2020/03/14/technology/coronavirus-purell-wipes-amazon-sellers.html.

45. Mario Anzuoni, "Loblaws losing consumer trust after bread price fixing story, Dalhousie study finds," *CBC News*, March 20, 2018, https://www.cbc.ca/news/business/grocery-bread-price-fixing-grocery-trust-dalhousie-1.4584400 (accessed September 23, 2020).

46. Drew Sandholm, "Amazon's Predatory Pricing Questioned," *CNBC*, June 30, 2014, https://www.cnbc.com/2014/06/30/amazons-predatory-pricing-questioned.html (accessed March 23, 2018).

47. Based on: Tim Sharp, "World's First Commercial Airline/The Greatest Moments in Flight," *Space.com*, May 22, 2018, https://www.space.com/16657-worlds-first-commercial-airline-the-greatest-moments-in-flight.html; Edward Russell, "American and Delta Were the World's Largest Airlines in 2019," *The Points Guy*, January 23, 2020, https://thepointsguy.com/news/worlds-largest-airlines-2019-american-delta-united/; United Airlines, "Corporate Fact Sheet," https://newsroom.united.com/corporate-fact-sheet (accessed May 24, 2018); "The End of The Low Cost Carrier (LCC)," *Your Mileage May Vary*, January 19, 2020, https://yourmileagemayvary.net/2020/01/19/the-end-of-the-low-cost-carrier-lcc/ (accessed August 4, 2020); Asheville Regional Airport, "Legacy to Low Cost: How Different Types of Airlines Work," *Asheville Regional Airport*, January 27, 2016, https://flyavl.com/article/legacy-low-cost-how-different-types-airlines-work (accessed August 4, 2020); Justin Bachman, "What Do You Want, Cheap Airfare or an On-Time Flight?," *Bloomberg*, July 31, 2017, https://www.bloomberg.com/news/articles/2017-07-31/what-do-you-want-cheap-airfare-or-an-on-time-flight; Micheline Maynard, "The Media Business: Advertising; United Airlines Unveils Ted, Its Low-Fare Airline and Hope for the Future," *New York Times*, November 21, 2003, https://www.nytimes.com/2003/11/21/business/media-business-advertising-united-airlines-unveils-ted-its-low-fare-airline-hope.html; Benjamin Zhang, "Major Airlines Are Finally Taking on the Biggest Threat to Their Business," *Business Insider*, December 11, 2017, http://www.businessinsider.com/how-airlines-combat-low-cost-competition-2017-12?utm_source=hearst&utm_medium=referral&utm_content=allverticals#comments; Michael Goldstein, "Made for Millennials: Basic Economy Fare Shakes Up Passengers, Airlines," *Forbes*, September 7, 2017, https://www.forbes.com/sites/michaelgoldstein/2017/09/07/made-for-millennials-basic-economy-fare-shakes-up-passengers-airlines/#683d041a34cd; James Eagleman, "United Basic Economy vs Economy: What's the Difference?" *Traveling Light*, May 28, 2020, https://travelinglight.com/united-basic-

economy-vs-economy/; Emily Price, "The Future of Air Travel Smells Like Inequality," *Fortune*, August 9, 2017, http://fortune. com/2017/08/09/airlines-united-inequality/; Michael Goldstein, "Looking Back on 2017: The Resistible Rise of Basic Economy," *Forbes*, December 29, 2017, https://www.forbes.com/sites/ michaelgoldstein/2017/12/29/looking-back-on-2017-the-resistible-rise-of-basic-economy/#7bbe5b964857; Courtney Miller, "The Evolution of Basic Economy – an Update," *Visual Approach*, September 10, 2019, https://visualapproach.io/the-evolution-of-basic-economy/; Kathryn Creedy, "There's A Better Way to Handle This Basic Economy Problem," *Flyertalk*, August 6, 2019, https://www.flyertalk.com/articles/a-better-way-to-resell-basic-economy-fares.html; A. W., "'Basic Economy' Class Is Winning Over Flyers," *The Economist*, June 19, 2017, https:// www.economist.com/gulliver/2017/06/19/basic-economy-class-is-winning-over-flyers; Chuck Schumer, "Schumer: In Just a Few Weeks, United Airlines Will Charge Extra Fee To Store Luggage in 'Overhead Bin'; Once Again, An Airline Trying to Charge Expensive & Annoying Fees, Squeezing the Pockets of Countless New Yorkers?," December 4, 2016, https://www. schumer.senate.gov/newsroom/press-releases/schumer-in-just-a-few-weeks-united-airlines-will-charge-extra-fee-to-store-luggage-in-overhead-bin-once-again-an-airline-trying-to-charge-expensive-and-annoying-fees-squeezing-the-pockets-of-countless-new-yorkers (accessed August 4, 2020); Michael Goldstein, "Battle Over Bin Space: Class Conflict Coming to Economy Cabin," *Forbes*, December 12, 2017, https://www. forbes.com/sites/michaelgoldstein/2017/12/12/battle-over-bin-space-class-conflict-coming-to-economy-cabin/#320f4edd3c49; Mark Ellwood, "Coronavirus Air Travel: These Numbers Show the Massive Impact of the Pandemic," *Conde Nast Traveler*, April 13, 2020, https://www.cntraveler.com/story/coronavirus-air-travel-these-numbers-show-the-massive-impact-of-the-pandemic.

Marketing Math

To develop marketing strategies to meet the goals of an organization effectively and efficiently, it is essential that marketers understand and use a variety of financial analyses. This supplement provides some of these basic financial analyses, including a review of the income statement, balance sheet, and some basic performance ratios. In addition, this supplement includes an explanation of some of the specific calculations that marketers use routinely to set prices for their goods and services.

Income Statement and Balance Sheet

The two most important documents used to analyze the financial situation of a company are the income statement and the balance sheet. The *income statement* (which is sometimes referred to as the *profit and loss statement,* or the *P&L*) provides a summary of the revenues and expenses of a firm—that is, the amount of income a company received from sales or other sources, the amount of money it spent, and the resulting income or loss that the company experienced.

The major elements of the income statement are as follows:

- **Gross sales** are the total of all income the firm receives from the sales of goods and services.
- **Net sales revenue** is the gross sales minus the amount for returns and promotional or other allowances given to customers.
- **Cost of goods sold** (sometimes called the *cost of sales*) is the cost of inventory or goods that the firm has sold.
- **Gross margin** (also called *gross profit*) is the amount of sales revenue that is in excess of the cost of goods sold.
- **Operating expenses** are expenses other than the cost of goods sold that are necessary for conducting business. These may include salaries, rent, depreciation on buildings and equipment, insurance, utilities, supplies, and property taxes.
- **Operating income** (sometimes called *income from operations*) is the gross margin minus the operating expenses. Sometimes accountants prepare an *operating statement*, which is similar to the income statement except that the final calculation is the operating income—that is, other revenues or expenses—and taxes are not included.
- **Other revenue and expenses** are income or expenses other than those required for conducting the business. These may include items such as interest income and expenses and any gain or loss experienced from the sale of property or plant assets.
- **Taxes** are the amount of income tax the firm owes calculated as a percentage of income.
- **Net income** (sometimes called *net earnings* or *net profit*) is the excess of total revenue over total expenses.

Table 10S.1 shows the income statement for an imaginary company, DLL Incorporated. DLL is a typical merchandising firm. Note that the income statement is for a specific year and includes income and expenses inclusively from January 1 through December 31.

Table 10S.1	DLL Inc. Income Statement for the Year Ended December 31, 2019		
Gross sales		$253,950	
Less: Sales returns and allowances	$ 3,000		
Sales discounts	2,100	5,100	
Net sales revenue			$248,850
Cost of goods sold			
Inventory, January 1, 2019		60,750	
Purchases	135,550		
Less: Purchase returns and allowances	1,500		
Purchase discounts	750		
Net purchases	133,300		
Plus: Freight-in	2,450	135,750	
Goods available for sale		196,500	
Less: Inventory, December 31, 2019		60,300	
Cost of goods sold			136,200
Gross margin			112,650
Operating expenses			
Salaries and commissions		15,300	
Rent		12,600	
Insurance		1,500	
Depreciation		900	
Supplies		825	
Total operating expenses			31,125
Operating income			81,525
Other revenue and (expenses)			
Interest revenue		1,500	
Interest expense		(2,250)	(750)
Income before tax			80,775
Taxes (40%)			32,310
Net income			$ 48,465

The following comments explain the meaning of some of the important entries included in this statement.

- DLL Inc. has total or gross sales during the year of $253,950. This figure was adjusted, however, by deducting the $3,000 worth of goods returned and special allowances given to customers and by $2,100 in special discounts. Thus, the actual or net sales generated by sales is $248,850.
- The cost of goods sold is calculated by adding the inventory of goods on January 1 to the amount purchased during the year and then subtracting the inventory of goods on December 31. In this case, DLL had $60,750 worth of inventory on hand on January 1. During the year, the firm made purchases in the amount of $135,550. This amount, however, was reduced by purchase returns and allowances of $1,500 and by purchase discounts of $750, so the net purchases are only $133,300.

There is also an amount on the statement labeled "freight-in." This is the amount spent by the firm in shipping charges to get goods to its facility from suppliers. Any expenses for freight from DLL to its customers (freight-out) would be an operating expense. In this case, the freight-in expense of $2,450 is added to net purchase costs. Then, these costs of current purchases are added to the beginning inventory to show that during the year the firm had a total of $196,500 in goods available for sale. Finally, the inventory of goods held on December 31 is subtracted from the goods available for sale to reveal the total cost of goods sold of $136,200.

We mentioned that DLL Inc. is a merchandising firm—a retailer of some type. If DLL were instead a manufacturer, calculation of the cost of goods sold would be a bit more complicated and would probably include separate figures for items, such as inventory of finished goods, the "work-in-process" inventory, the raw materials inventory, and the cost of goods delivered to customers during the year. Continuing down the previous income statement we have the following:

- The cost of goods sold is subtracted from the net sales revenue to get a gross margin of $112,650.
- Operating expenses for DLL include the salaries and commissions paid to its employees, rent on facilities or equipment, insurance, depreciation of capital items, and the cost of operating supplies. DLL has a total of $31,125 in operating expenses, which is deducted from the gross margin. Thus, DLL has an operating income of $81,525.
- DLL had both other income and expenses in the form of interest revenues of $1,500 and interest expenses of $2,250, making a total other expense of $750, which was subtracted from the operating income, leaving an income before taxes of $80,775.
- Finally, the income before taxes is reduced by 40 percent ($32,310) for taxes, leaving a net income of $48,465. The 40 percent is an average amount for federal and state corporate income taxes incurred by most firms.

The *balance sheet* lists the assets, liabilities, and stockholders' equity of the firm. Whereas the income statement represents what happened during an entire year, the balance sheet is like a snapshot; it shows the firm's financial situation at one point in time. For this reason, the balance sheet is sometimes called the *statement of financial position*.

Table 10S.2 shows DLL Inc.'s balance sheet for December 31. Assets include any economic resource that is expected to benefit the firm in the short or long term. *Current assets* are items that are normally expected to be turned into cash or used up during the next 12 months or during the firm's normal operating cycle. Current assets for DLL include cash, securities, accounts receivable (money owed to the firm and not yet paid), inventory on hand, prepaid insurance, and supplies: a total of $84,525. *Long-term assets* include all assets that are not current assets. For DLL, these are furniture and fixtures (less an amount for depreciation) and land, or $45,300. The *total assets* for DLL are $129,825.

A firm's *liabilities* are its economic obligations, or debts that are payable to individuals or organizations outside the firm. *Current liabilities* are debts due to be paid in the coming year or during the firm's normal operating cycle. For DLL, the current liabilities—the accounts payable, unearned sales revenue, wages payable, and interest payable—total $72,450. *Long-term liabilities* (in the case of DLL, a note in the amount of $18,900) are all liabilities that are not due to be paid during the coming cycle. *Stockholders' equity* is the value of the stock and the corporation's capital or retained earnings. DLL has $15,000 in common stock and $23,475 in retained earnings for a total stockholders' equity of $38,475. Total liabilities always equal total assets—in this case, $129,825.

Table 10S.2	DLL Inc. Balance Sheet: December 31, 2019		

Assets

Current assets			
Cash		$ 4,275	
Marketable securities		12,000	
Accounts receivable		6,900	
Inventory		60,300	
Prepaid insurance		300	
Supplies		150	
Total current assets			84,525
Long-term assets—property, plant, and equipment			
Furniture and fixtures	$42,300		
Less: Accumulated depreciation	4,500	37,800	
Land		7,500	
Total long-term assets			45,300
Total assets			$129,825

Liabilities

Current liabilities			
Accounts payable	$70,500		
Unearned sales revenue	1,050		
Wages payable	600		
Interest payable	300		
Total current liabilities		72,450	
Long-term liabilities			
Note payable		18,900	
Total liabilities			91,350
Stockholders' equity			
Common stock		15,000	
Retained earnings		23,475	
Total stockholders' equity			38,475
Total liabilities and stockholders' equity			$129,825

Important Financial Performance Ratios

How do managers and financial analysts compare the performance of a firm from one year to the next? How do investors compare the performance of one firm with that of another? As the book notes, managers often rely on various metrics to measure performance.

Often, a number of different financial ratios provide important information for such comparisons. Such *ratios* are percentage figures comparing various income statement items to net sales. Ratios provide a better way to compare performance than simple dollar sales or cost figures for two reasons. They enable analysts to compare the performance of large and small firms, and they provide a fair way to compare performance over time

Table 10S.3	Hypothetical Operating Ratios for DLL Inc.		
Gross margin ratio	$= \dfrac{\text{Gross margin}}{\text{Net sales}}$	$= \dfrac{\$112{,}650}{\$248{,}850}$	$= 45.3\%$
Net income ratio	$= \dfrac{\text{Net income}}{\text{Net sales}}$	$= \dfrac{\$48{,}465}{248{,}850}$	$= 19.5\%$
Operating expense ratio	$= \dfrac{\text{Total operating expenses}}{\text{Net sales}}$	$= \dfrac{\$31{,}125}{248{,}850}$	$= 12.5\%$
Returns and allowances ratio	$= \dfrac{\text{Return and allowances}}{\text{Net sales}}$	$= \dfrac{\$3{,}000}{248{,}850}$	$= 1.2\%$

without having to take inflation and other changes into account. In this section, we will explain the basic operating ratios. Other measures of performance that marketers frequently use and that are also explained here are the inventory turnover rate and return on investment (ROI).

Operating Ratios

Measures of performance calculated directly from the information in a firm's income statement (sometimes called an *operating statement*) are called the *operating ratios*. Each ratio compares some income statement item to net sales. The most useful of these are the *gross margin ratio*, the *net income ratio*, the *operating expense ratio*, and the *returns and allowances ratio*. These ratios vary widely by industry but tend to be important indicators of how a firm is doing within its industry. The ratios for DLL Inc. are shown in Table 10S.3.

- **Gross margin ratio** shows what percentage of sales revenues is available for operating and other expenses and for profit. With DLL, this means that 45 percent, or nearly half, of every sales dollar is available for operating costs and for profits.
- **Net income ratio** (sometimes called the *net profit ratio*) shows what percentage of sales revenues is income or profit. For DLL, the net income ratio is 19.5 percent. This means that the firm's profit before taxes is about 20 cents of every dollar.
- **Operating expense ratio** is the percentage of sales needed for operating expenses. DLL has an operating expense ratio of 12.5 percent. Tracking operating expense ratios from one year to the next or comparing them with an industry average gives a firm important information about the efficiency of its operations.
- **Returns and allowances ratio** shows what percentage of all sales is being returned, probably by unhappy customers. DLL's returns and allowances ratio shows that only a little over 1 percent of sales is being returned.

Inventory Turnover Rate

The *inventory turnover rate*, also referred to as the *stockturn rate*, is the number of times inventory or stock is turned over (sold and replaced) during a specified time period, usually a year. Inventory turnover rates are usually calculated on the basis of inventory costs, sometimes on the basis of inventory selling prices, and sometimes by number of units.

In our example, for DLL Inc., we know that for the year the cost of goods sold was $136,200. Information on the balance sheet enables us to find the average inventory. By adding the value of the beginning inventory to the ending inventory and dividing by 2, we can compute an average inventory. In the case of DLL, this would be as follows:

$$= \frac{\$60,750 + \$60,300}{2} = \$60,525$$

Thus,

$$\text{Inventory turnover rate} \atop \text{(in cost of goods sold)} = \frac{\text{Costs of goods sold}}{\text{Average inventory at cost}} = \frac{\$136,200}{\$60,525} = 2.25 \text{ times}$$

Return on Investment

Firms often develop business objectives in terms of *return on investment (ROI)*, and ROI is often used to determine how effective (and efficient) the firm's management has been. First, however, we need to define exactly what a firm means by *investment*. In most cases, firms define investment as the total assets of the firm. To calculate the ROI, we need the net income found in the income statement and the total assets (or investment) found in the firm's balance sheet.

Return on investment is calculated as follows:

$$\text{ROI} = \frac{\text{Net income}}{\text{Total investment}}$$

For DLL Inc., if the total assets are $129,825, then the ROI is as follows:

$$\frac{\$48,465}{\$129,825} = 37.3\%$$

Sometimes, return on investment is calculated by using an expanded formula:

$$\text{ROI} = \frac{\text{Net profit}}{\text{Sales}} \times \frac{\text{Sales}}{\text{Investment}}$$
$$= \frac{\$48,465}{\$248,850} \times \frac{\$248,850}{\$129,825} = 37.3\%$$

This formula makes it easy to show how ROI can be increased and what might reduce ROI. For example, there are different ways to increase ROI. First, if the management focuses on cutting costs and increasing efficiency, profits may be increased while sales remain the same:

$$\text{ROI} = \frac{\text{Net profit}}{\text{Sales}} \times \frac{\text{Sales}}{\text{Investment}}$$
$$= \frac{\$53,277}{\$248,850} \times \frac{\$248,850}{\$129,825} = 41.0\%$$

But ROI can be increased just as much without improving performance simply by reducing the investment—by maintaining less inventory:

$$\text{ROI} = \frac{\text{Net profit}}{\text{Sales}} \times \frac{\text{Sales}}{\text{Investment}}$$
$$= \frac{\$48,465}{\$248,850} \times \frac{\$248,850}{\$114,825} = 42.2\%$$

Sometimes, however, differences among the total assets of firms may be related to the age of the firm or the type of industry, which makes ROI a poor indicator of performance. For this reason, some firms have replaced the traditional ROI measures with *return on assets managed* (ROAM), *return on net assets* (RONA), or *return on stockholders' equity* (ROE).

Price Elasticity

Price elasticity, discussed in Chapter 10, is a measure of the sensitivity of customers to changes in price. Price elasticity is calculated by comparing the percentage change in quantity to the percentage change in price:

$$\text{Price elasticity of demand} = \frac{\text{Percentage change in quantity}}{\text{Percentage change in price}}$$

$$= \frac{(Q_2 - Q_1)/Q_1}{(P_2 - P_1)/P_1}$$

where Q = quantity and P = price.

For example, suppose a manufacturer of jeans increased its price for a pair of jeans from \$30 to \$35. But instead of 40,000 pairs being sold, sales declined to only 38,000 pairs. The price elasticity would be calculated as follows:

$$E = \frac{(38,000 - 40,000)/40,000}{(\$35.00 - 30.00)/\$30.00} = \frac{-0.05}{0.167} = 0.30$$

Note that elasticity is usually expressed as a positive number even though the calculations create a negative value.

In this case, a relatively small change in demand (5 percent) resulted from a fairly large change in price (16.7 percent), indicating that demand is inelastic. At 0.30, the elasticity is less than 1.

On the other hand, what if the same change in price resulted in a reduction in demand to 30,000 pairs of jeans? Then, the elasticity would be as follows:

$$E = \frac{(30,000 - 40,000)/40,000}{(\$35.00 - 30.00)/\$30.00} = \frac{-0.25}{0.167} = 1.50$$

In this case, because the 16.7 percent change in price resulted in an even larger change in demand (25 percent), demand is elastic. The elasticity of 1.50 is greater than 1.

Note: Elasticity may also be calculated by dividing the change in quantity by the average of Q_1 and Q_2 and dividing the change in price by the average of the two prices. However, we have chosen to include the formula that uses the initial quantity and price rather than the average.

Cost-Plus Pricing

As noted in Chapter 10, the most common cost-based approach to pricing a product is *cost-plus pricing*, in which a marketer figures all costs for the product and then adds an amount to cover profit and, in some cases, any costs of doing business that are not assigned to specific products. The most frequently used type of cost-plus pricing is *straight markup pricing*. The price is calculated by adding a predetermined percentage to the cost. Most retailers and wholesalers use markup pricing exclusively because of its simplicity; users need only obtain the unit cost and add the designated markup.

The first step requires that the unit cost be easy to estimate accurately and that production rates are fairly consistent. As Table 10S.4 shows, we will assume that a jeans manufacturer has fixed costs (the cost of the factory, advertising, managers' salaries, etc.) of $2,000,000. The variable cost, per pair of jeans (the cost of fabric, zipper, thread, and labor) is $20. With the current plant, the firm can produce a total of 400,000 pairs of jeans, so the fixed cost per pair is $5. Combining the fixed and variable costs per pair means that the jeans are produced at a total cost of $25 per pair and the total cost of producing 400,000 pairs of jeans is $10,000,000.

The second step is to calculate the markup. There are two methods for calculating the markup percentage: markup on cost and markup on selling price. Examples of both are shown in Table 10S.4. For *markup on cost pricing,* just as the name implies, a percentage of

Table 10S.4 | Markup Pricing Using Jeans as an Example

Step 1: Determine Costs

1.a: Determine total fixed costs

Management and other nonproduction-related salaries	$ 750,000	
Rental of factory	600,000	
Insurance	50,000	
Depreciation on equipment	100,000	
Advertising	500,000	
Total fixed costs	**$2,000,000**	

1.b: Determine fixed costs per unit

Number of units produced = 400,000

Fixed cost per unit ($2,000,000/400,000)		**$5.00**

1.c: Determine variable costs per unit

Cost of materials (fabric, zipper, thread, etc.)	$ 7.00	
Cost of production labor	10.00	
Cost of utilities and supplies used in production process	3.00	
Variable cost per unit		**$20.00**

1.d: Determine total cost per unit

$20.00 + $5.00 = $25.00

Total cost per unit		**$25.00**

Total cost for producing 400,000 units = $10,000,000

Step 2: Determine markup and price

Manufacturer's markup on cost (assuming 20% markup)

Formula: Price = Total cost + (Total cost × Markup percentage)

Manufacturer's price to the retailer		**$30.00**
= $25.00 + ($25.00 × 0.20) = $25.00 + 5.00 =		

Retailer's markup on selling price (assuming 40% markup)

Formula: $\text{Price} = \dfrac{\text{Total cost}}{(1.00 - \text{Markup percentage})}$

Retailer's price to the consumer $= \dfrac{\$30.00}{(1.00 \times 40)} = \dfrac{\$30.00}{0.60} =$		**$50.00**

Retailer's alternative markup on cost (assuming 40% markup)

Formula: Price = Total cost + (Total cost × Markup percentage)

Retailer's price to the consumer

$30.00 + ($30.00 × 0.40) = $30.00 + $12.00 =		**$42.00**

the cost is added to the cost to determine the firm's selling price. As you can see, we have included both methods in our example shown in Table 10S.4.

Markup on Cost

For markup on cost, the calculation is as follows:

$$\text{Price} = \text{Total cost} + (\text{Total cost} \times \text{Markup percentage})$$

But how does the manufacturer or reseller know which markup percentage to use? One way is to base the markup on the total income needed for profits, for shareholder dividends, and for investment in the business. In our jeans example, the total cost of producing the 400,000 pairs of jeans is $10,000,000. If the manufacturer wants a profit of $2,000,000, what markup percentage would it use? The $2,000,000 is 20 percent of the $10 million total cost, so 20 percent. To find the price, the calculations would be as follows:

$$\text{Price} = \$25.00 + (\$25.00 \times 0.20) = \$25.0 + \$5.00 = \$30.00$$

Note that in the calculations, the markup percentage is expressed as a decimal; that is, $20\% = 0.20, 25\% = 0.25, 30\% = 0.30$, and so on.

Markup on Selling Price

Some resellers—that is, retailers and wholesalers/distributors—set their prices using a markup on selling price. The markup percentage here is the seller's gross margin, the difference between the cost to the wholesaler or retailer and the price needed to cover overhead items, such as salaries, rent, utility bills, advertising, and profit. For example, if the wholesaler or retailer knows that it needs a margin of 40 percent to cover its overhead and reach its target profits, that margin becomes the markup on the manufacturer's selling price. Markup on selling price is particularly useful when firms negotiate prices with different buyers because it allows them to set prices with their required margins in mind.

Now let's say a retailer buys the jeans from the supplier (wholesaler or manufacturer) for $30 per pair. If the retailer requires a margin of 40 percent, it would calculate the price as a 40 percent markup on selling price. The calculation would be as follows:

$$\text{Price} = \frac{\text{Total cost}}{1.00 - \text{Markup percentage}}$$

$$\text{Price} = \frac{\$30.00}{(1.00 - 0.40)} = \frac{\$30.00}{0.60} = \$50.00$$

Therefore, the price of the jeans with the markup on selling price is $50.00.

Just to compare the difference in the final prices of the two markup methods, Table 10S.4 also shows what would happen if the retailer uses a markup on cost method. Using the same product cost and price with a 40 percent markup on cost would yield $42, a much lower price. The markup on selling price gives you the percentage of the selling price that the markup is. The markup on cost gives you the percentage of the cost that the markup is. In the markup on selling price, the markup amount is $20, which is 40 percent of the selling price of $50. In the markup on cost, the markup is $12, which is 40 percent of the cost of $30.

Supplement **Problems** Test Your Marketing Math

10S-1. Assume that you are in charge of pricing for a firm that produces pickles. You have fixed costs of $4,200,200. Variable costs are $0.65 per jar of pickles. You are selling your product to retailers for $0.98. You sell the pickles in cases of 24 jars per case. (*Hint:* Note that the pickle producer cannot sell pickles except in full jars and in full cases. Therefore, you need to be careful and round up when calculations result in a partial jar or a partial case.)

   a. How many jars of pickles must you sell to break even?

   b. How much must you sell in dollars to break even?

   c. How many jars of pickles must you sell to break even plus make a profit of $1,000,000?

   d. Assume a retailer buys your product for $0.98. His business requires that he price products with a 30 percent markup on cost. Calculate his selling price.

   e. Assume you have an MSRP of $1.69 for the pickles. If a retailer has a required 40 percent retailer margin on all products he sells, what is the most he is willing to pay the producer for the pickles?

   f. A clothing retailer knows that to break even and make a profit, he needs to have a minimum retailer margin (also referred to as a *contribution margin* or *gross margin*) of at least 60 percent. If he is to sell a pair of shorts for the manufacturer's suggested retail price of $59.99, what is the most he can pay the manufacturer for the shorts and maintain his margin?

   g. A salesperson is developing a quote for a landscaping company that wants to buy six commercial riding mowers. His cost for each mower is $2,750. His firm requires that he have a 35 percent margin on all equipment sold, so he is using a markup on selling price to calculate his quote to the buyer. What will his quote be per mower if he uses a 35 percent markup on selling price?

10S-2. Executives of Studio Recordings Inc. produced the latest compact disc by the Starshine Sisters Band, titled *Sunshine/Moonshine*. The following cost information pertains to the CD.

   a. CD package $0.65/CD

   b. Songwriters' royalties $0.55/CD

   c. Recording artists' royalties $0.90/CD

   d. Advertising and promotion $2,400,000

   e. Studio Recording Inc.'s overhead $350,000

   f. Selling price to the CD distributor $9.50

Calculate the following:

   1. Contribution per CD unit

   2. Break-even volume in CD units and dollars

   3. Net profit if 1 million CDs are sold

   4. Necessary CD unit volume to achieve a $500,000 profit

10S-3. A distributor of equipment and supplies for physician's offices and other similar healthcare customers requires that their salespeople negotiate with customers to get the best price possible. At the same time, the distributor management knows that to cover overhead costs such as salary, rent, and utility bills plus provide a satisfactory level of profit, they need a margin of 45 percent. Therefore, the salespeople use a markup on selling price to calculate their quotes. If the company buys cases of disposable examination gowns for $288, what is the lowest price the salesperson can quote the customer?

10S-4. "Green Stuff" is a regional chain of small restaurants. The Green Stuff menu includes only salads, all priced at $8.95, and beverages. Each restaurant serves an average of 800 salads a week at that price. The company wants to raise the price of their salads to $10.95 but is concerned that the price increase will lower sales volume and could actually lower total revenue for the stores. To determine whether they should raise salad prices, the company has tested the higher price of $10.95 in some of their stores. The results of their study showed that when the price of the salads was increased, average store sales declined from 800 salads per week to 650.

Calculate the price elasticity of demand for Green Stuff's price increase experiment. What conclusions can be drawn from the price increase experiment? What would you recommend that Green Stuff do?

10S-5. Assume a firm has the following year end results on their income statement:

Net sales	$1,450,000
Gross margin	$789,000
Net income	$432,000
Operating expenses	$158,999
Returns and allowances	$14,300

Based on this, calculate their gross margin ratio, net income ratio, operating expense ratio, and returns and allowances ratio. How do you interpret each of these ratios?

11 Deliver the Goods: Determine the Distribution Strategy

Used with permission from Michael Ford.

Meet Michael Ford

▼ A **Decision Maker** at BDP International

Michael Ford is a career professional in international transportation, specializing in import/export documentation and regulatory compliance. He is responsible for BDP International's Regulatory Compliance unit. Michael's activities include developing and administering the company's consulting arm in value-added product offerings, such as regulatory compliance, supply chain security, duty drawback, customer education, and logistics process analysis/management, and all topical governmental issues connected with the handling and administration of export and import cargo. Michael's leadership in communication and system logic on governmental rules and regulations is central to BDP's ability to understand and resolve complex regulatory issues quickly, decisively, and with minimal impact on customers.

Michael has been associated with BDP for more than 36 years. Before his current role, he headed the company's regional ocean export service division as vice president. For the past 20 years, he has worked with and served as an advocate for some of the world's leading companies, interacting with the U.S. Customs Service and the Department of Commerce/Census Bureau, in the development, piloting, and automation of import and export programs. Among his other affiliations, Ford is the co-chair for trade on the Export Committee in the development of the new Customs ACE system, and he has served with Customs as a member of the Commercial Operations Advisory Council (COAC) and as chair of the Mid-Atlantic District Export Council. Currently, he also chairs the Partner sector with the American Chemistry Council, Responsible Care Committee, and teaches an MBA international logistics course at Saint Joseph's University in Philadelphia. He received a B.A. in Business Administration from Temple University in 1979.

Michael's Info

What I do when I'm not working:
Spend time with family and play basketball

Business book I'm reading now:
Leading Change by John Kotter

My motto to live by:
Work hard and keep things simple.

What drives me:
The opportunity to learn and then share my new knowledge

My management style:
Trust the people who work for you and allow them to make their decisions.

Don't do this when interviewing with me:
Ask me questions about me.

Here's my problem...

Real **People**, Real **Choices**

BDP International, Inc., is the world's premiere international logistics company, specializing in customized logistics solutions powered by exceptional people, industry-leading execution processes, and proprietary technology. BDP is non-asset based; this means it does not own the planes, vessels, and trucks it uses to move clients' goods around the world. This structure gives BDP a lot of flexibility because it can pick and choose the right transportation company to meet the needs of a specific client.

BDP was founded in 1966 in a one-room office of the Philadelphia Customs House with the goal to redefine the business of freight forwarding. The company's founder, Richard Bolte Sr., identified the opportunity to reinvent the complex documentation process of international sales and purchase orders to yield long-term and meaningful savings for his customers.

Since its inception, BDP has focused on finding solutions to complex logistics problems and creating significant value for customers rather than simply moving freight. BDP remains family owned. The continuity of family ownership during BDP's transformation from start-up into a global enterprise has fostered and institutionalized a unique service culture that has remained a hallmark of BDP's unparalleled industry reputation. BDP is one of the only U.S.-headquartered, privately owned freight forwarders with global scale.

PepsiCo is one of BDP's many large corporate clients; BDP works with their organization to move their products around the world. PepsiCo is the parent company of 22 brands that range from Pepsi beverages to Quaker Oats and Frito-Lay. In January 2015, the World Economic Forum (WEF) was holding an important meeting in Davos, Switzerland. Economic decision makers from around the world would be attending, and many of them were involved in leading discussions about many of the current world issues that impact large companies like PepsiCo as well as consumers and the environment. This prominent world stage was the perfect setting for the company's Quaker Foods brand to host a "café" at the conference and use the opportunity to provide attendees with samples of its new "breakfast bars." Quaker's PR/marketing team was eager to showcase this new product line because the company was introducing the bars to the consumer market and this event would provide a global stage for their debut. Two weeks before the start of the conference, Quaker asked BDP to help them get a total of 102 boxes full of these bars to the venue in Davos.

This request wasn't as easy as it sounds. The problem was that the breakfast bars were made in the U.S., and the manufacturing site was not approved by the European Union (EU). The EU imposes very strict controls on the ingredients it allows for import. Switzerland is a member country of the EU, so it follows EU regulations. BDP had a short window to move the goods from the U.S. and persuade Swiss Customs to clear the shipment in time for the conference. If the Quaker products didn't show up in time, the bare shelves at the café would make the client look bad—and this failure, in turn, would be a major black eye for BDP.

BDP had to scramble to understand all of the possible regulatory issues that might gum up the works. The biggest sticking point was that the EU requires all food products to carry a label that lists all of their ingredients, and this label has to be printed in Italian, German, or French; Swiss Customs would not grant a special exemption for English for the conference. If BDP had to unpack each box and relabel more than 4,000 Quaker bars in one of the permitted languages, the additional resources required would make it unrealistic to move the order.

Michael considered his **options** 1·2·3

1
Option

Convince Swiss Customs to allow BDP to put a new label on the outside of each of the 102 boxes rather than on each of the 4,020 individual bars in the shipment. This compromise would allow the products to enter the country. However, the cost to label each box as well as the time required to do so raised the possibility that BDP wouldn't be able to move the goods in time to make the start of the conference. If BDP had to add another label in a different language, this solution would also cover up the normal package and hide other product information.

2
Option

Identify a different Quaker Foods product that is manufactured in Europe, and convince the client to substitute this for the breakfast bars. The client would be able to provide a local product for the conference attendees. On the other hand, Quaker wanted to impress the participants who would come from around the world with its innovativeness, and its new breakfast bars would do that.

3
Option

Provide the list of required ingredients in the requested language as BDP's contact at Swiss Customs proposed. This option would eliminate the cost of labeling every bar or box as well as the additional labor costs and time required to move the boxes on schedule. However, the suggested solution was verbal only; as a result of the bureaucratic process involved, BDP would have to approach Customs when the physical products actually arrived to be cleared and remind the person working at the time about this suggestion. The odds were this would not be the same person who made the suggestion, so BDP would have to take its chances. Inspectors who are confronted with more than 100 boxes to clear sometimes rely on their own judgment about how to handle the shipment. And, BDP would still have to move the boxes from the manufacturing site in the midwestern U.S. to Switzerland in less than a week. The client would have to pay for all the associated costs, and they might not be too happy about that.

Now put yourself in Michael's shoes. Which option would you choose, and why?

You Choose

Which **Option** would you choose, and **why**?
☐ **Option 1**   ☐ **Option 2**   ☐ **Option 3**

11.1 Types of Distribution Channels and Wholesale Intermediaries

physical distribution
The activities that move finished goods from manufacturers to final customers, including order processing, warehousing, materials handling, transportation, and inventory control.

So you've done all the work to understand your target market. You've created your product, and you've priced it too. Your Facebook page is attracting legions of brand fans. But sorry, you're still not done with the marketing mix—now you need to get what you make out into the marketplace (i.e., distribute it). The delivery of goods to customers involves **physical distribution**, which refers to the activities that move finished goods from manufacturers to final customers. As introduced in Chapter 1, a *channel of distribution* is the series of firms or individuals that facilitates the movement of a product from the producer to the final customer. In many cases, these channels include an organized network of producers (or manufacturers), wholesalers, and retailers that develop relationships and work together to make products conveniently available to eager buyers. And, as Michael Ford's decision at BDP International illustrates, the delivery of goods across national borders requires an in-depth understanding of laws and regulations specific to a particular nation or international governing body.

Distribution channels come in different shapes and sizes. The bakery around the corner where you buy your cinnamon rolls is a member of a channel, as are the baked-goods section at the local supermarket, the Starbucks that sells biscotti to go with your double-mocha cappuccino, and the bakery outlet store that sells day-old rolls at a discount.

direct channel
A channel of distribution in which a manufacturer of a product or creator of a service distributes directly to the end customer.

A channel of distribution consists of, at a minimum, a producer—the individual or firm that manufactures or produces a good or service—and a customer. This is a **direct channel**, and when you buy a loaf of bread at a mom-and-pop bakery, you're buying through a direct channel. Firms that sell their own products directly to customers through websites, catalogs, toll-free numbers, or factory outlet stores also use direct channels.

indirect channel
A channel of distribution in which firms sell their products through third parties.

channel intermediaries
Firms or individuals, such as wholesalers, agents, brokers, or retailers, who help move a product from the producer to the consumer or business user. An older term for intermediaries is *middlemen*.

Another approach to distribution is through an **indirect channel**, in which firms sell their products through third parties. These outside entities often include one or more **channel intermediaries**—firms or individuals, such as wholesalers, agents, brokers, and retailers, who in some way help move the product to the consumer or business user. For example, a bakery may choose to sell its cinnamon buns to a wholesaler that will in turn sell boxes of buns to supermarkets and restaurants that in turn sell them to consumers. Another older term for intermediaries that you may still hear on occasion is *middlemen*.

Functions of Distribution Channels

Channels that include one or more organizations or intermediaries often can accomplish certain distribution functions more effectively and efficiently than can a single organization. As we saw in Chapter 2, this is especially true in international distribution channels, where differences among countries' customs, beliefs, and infrastructures can make global marketing a nightmare. Even small companies can succeed in complex global markets when they rely on distributors such as BDP that know local customs and laws.

Overall, channels provide the place, time, and possession utility we described in Chapter 1. They make desired products available when, where, and in the sizes and quantities that customers desire. Suppose, for example, you want to buy that perfect bouquet of flowers for a special someone. You *could* grow them yourself or even "liberate" them from a cemetery if you were *really* desperate (very classy!). Fortunately, you can probably accomplish this task with just a simple phone call or a few mouse clicks, and "like magic" a local florist delivers a bouquet to your honey's door.

Distribution channels provide a number of logistics or physical distribution functions that increase the efficiency of the flow of goods from producer to customer (more on this later in the chapter). How would we buy groceries without our modern system of super-markets that provide convenient in-store shopping or home delivery? We'd have to get our milk from a dairy, our bread from a bakery, our tomatoes and corn from a local farmer, and our flour from a flour mill. And forget about specialty items, such as Monster Energy Drink or KIND Dark Chocolate Nuts and Sea Salt bars. The companies that make these items would have to handle literally millions of transactions to sell to every individual who craves a midday food fix.

Distribution channels create *efficiencies* because they reduce the number of transactions necessary for goods to flow from many different manufacturers to large numbers of custom-ers. This occurs in two ways. The first is **breaking bulk**. Wholesalers and retailers purchase large quantities (usually cases) of goods from manufacturers but sell only one or a few at a time to many different customers. Second, channel intermediaries reduce the number of transactions when they **create assortments**; they provide a variety of products in one loca-tion so that customers can conveniently buy many different items from one seller at one time.

Figure 11.1 provides a simple example of how distribution channels work. This simpli-fied illustration includes five producers and five customers. If each producer sold its prod-uct to each individual customer, 25 different transactions would have to occur—not exactly an efficient way to distribute products. But with a single intermediary who buys from all 5 manufacturers and sells to all 5 customers, we quickly cut the number of transactions to 10. If there were 10 manufacturers and 10 customers, an intermediary would reduce the number of transactions from 100 to just 20. Do the math: Channels are efficient.

The **transportation and storage** of goods is another type of physical distribution func-tion. That is, retailers and other channel members move the goods from the production point to other locations where they can hold them until consumers want them. Channel intermediaries also perform a number of **facilitating functions** that make the purchase pro-cess easier for customers and manufacturers. For example, intermediaries often provide customer services, such as offering credit to buyers.

Many of us like to shop at brick-and-mortar department stores because if we are not happy with the product, we can take it back to the store, where cheerful customer service personnel are happy to give us a refund (at least in theory). But the same facilitating

breaking bulk
Dividing larger quantities of goods into smaller lots in order to meet the needs of buyers.

create assortments
To provide a variety of products in one location to meet the needs of buyers.

transportation and storage
Occurs when retailers and other channel members move the goods from the production point to other locations where they can hold them until consumers want them.

facilitating functions
Functions of channel intermediaries that make the purchase process easier for customers and manufacturers.

Figure 11.1 *Process* | Reduce Transactions via Intermediaries

One of the functions of distribution channels is to provide an assortment of products. Because the customers can buy a number of different products at the same location, this reduces the total costs of obtaining a product.

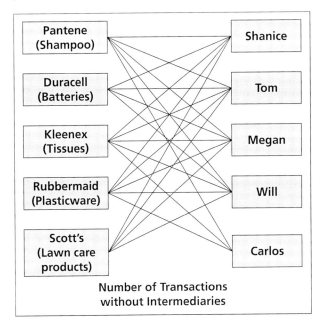

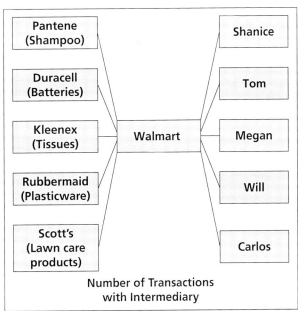

risk-taking functions
The chance retailers take when they buy a product from a manufacturer, as the product might just sit on the shelf if no customers want it.

communication and transaction functions
Happens when channel members develop and execute both promotional and other types of communication among members of the channel.

disintermediation
The elimination of some layers of the channel of distribution to cut costs and improve the efficiency of the channel.

knowledge management
A comprehensive approach to collecting, organizing, storing, and retrieving a firm's information assets.

function happens online with Zappos, Lands' End, and a host of other customer-friendly retailers. These same customer services are even more important in business-to-business (B2B) markets where customers purchase larger quantities of higher-priced products. And channel members perform **risk-taking functions**. For example, if a retailer buys a product from a manufacturer and it just sits on the shelf because no customers want it, he or she is stuck with the item and must take a loss. But hey, that's what outlet malls are for, right? Perishable items present an even greater risk of spoilage and loss, and as such they're potentially a high risk. Blueberries in the U.S. are in season for only a very short period of time. Retailers want to stock up to meet the annual high demand; on the other hand, a carton of semisoft blueberries on the shelf a few weeks past prime is beyond unappealing.

Finally, intermediaries perform **communication and transaction functions** by which channel members develop and execute both promotional and other types of communication among members of the channel. Wholesalers buy products to make them available for retailers, and they sell products to other channel members. Retailers handle transactions with final consumers. Channel members can provide two-way communication for manufacturers. They may supply the sales force, advertising, and other types of marketing communication necessary to inform consumers and persuade them that a product will meet their needs. And the channel members can be invaluable sources of information on consumer complaints, changing tastes, and new competitors in the market.

The Evolution of Distribution Functions

In the future, channel intermediaries that physically handle the product may become obsolete. Already companies are eliminating many traditional intermediaries because they find that they don't add enough value in the distribution channel—a process we call **disintermediation** (of the channel of distribution). Literally, disintermediation means removal of intermediaries! For marketers, disintermediation reduces costs in many ways: fewer employees, no need to buy or lease expensive retail property in high-traffic locations, and no need to furnish a store with fancy fixtures and decor. You can also see this process at work when you pump your own gas, withdraw cash from an ATM, or book a roundtrip flight and a hotel stay with a website such as Expedia.

As with many other aspects of marketing, the Internet is radically changing how companies coordinate among members of a supply chain to make it more effective in ways that end consumers never see. These firms develop better ways to implement **knowledge management**, which refers to a comprehensive approach that collects, organizes, stores, and retrieves a firm's information assets. Those assets include databases and company documents as well as the practical knowledge of employees whose past experience may be relevant to solve a new problem. In the world of B2B, this process probably occurs via an *intranet*, which, as you read in Chapter 4, is an internal corporate communication network that uses Internet technology to link company departments, employees, and databases. But it can also facilitate sharing of knowledge among channel partners because it is a secure and password-protected platform. This more strategic management of information results in a win-win situation for all the partners.

But as with most things cyber, the Internet as a distribution channel brings pain with pleasure. One of the more vexing problems with Internet distribution is

Some wholesalers and retailers assist the manufacturer when they provide setup, repair, and maintenance service for products they handle. Best Buy's Geek Squad is a good example.

the potential for **online distribution piracy**, which is the theft and unauthorized repurposing of intellectual property via the Internet. At the core, such piracy amounts to **copyright infringement**, which is the use of works protected by copyright law without the permission of the copyright holder. Unfortunately, it's just too easy. And this malady comes home to roost in many university situations, including theft or unauthorized use of intellectual property, failure to properly credit sources, and outright plagiarism (we know you'd never engage in these things!).

Let's look at a similar distribution issue in a product category that's probably familiar to you. Unauthorized downloads of music continue to pose a major challenge to the "recording" industry—to the point where the whole nature of the industry has turned topsy-turvy in search of a new business model that works. Many in the music business are rethinking exactly what—and where—is the value-added for what they do. To most (but not yet all) of today's music consumers, the value of a physical CD has plummeted—to the point where many listeners are unwilling to pay anything at all for the artist's work. And more and more musical artists, like Nick Jonas and Demi Lovato, have defected from traditional record labels to introduce their tunes online, where they can control at least some of the channel of distribution.[1] On the other hand, other stars from many eras and genres from Dr. Dre to Neil Young decline to make their albums available on Spotify so that fans can stream them.[2] We're still a long way from a perfect transition to this channel!

In addition to music, TV shows and movies also tend to be obvious targets for piracy online. For a company such as Netflix that legally partners with content providers to make their content available online for a fee, distribution piracy is a serious issue for both parties. Popular messaging apps like Telegram, WhatsApp, and Facebook Messenger have become a forum for people sharing stolen login credentials for services like Netflix and Spotify.[3] Interestingly, Netflix actually adjusts its prices lower in markets outside the U.S. that have higher rates of piracy to attract a larger number of consumers to the legitimate offerings through the company website. In addition, Netflix believes that making legal access to content an easier and more convenient experience can lead to decreases in piracy.

So far, we've learned what a distribution channel is and talked about some of the functions it performs. Now let's find out about specific types of channel intermediaries and channel structures.

Artists like Chance the Rapper have defected from traditional distribution channels to get their recorded music to their fans.

online distribution piracy
The theft and unauthorized repurposing of intellectual property via the Internet.

copyright infringement
The use of works protected by copyright law without the permission of the copyright holder.

wholesaling intermediaries
Firms that handle the flow of products from the manufacturer to the retailer or business user.

Figure 11.2 *Snapshot* | Key Types of Intermediaries

Intermediaries can be independent or manufacturer owned.

```
                    ┌─────────────────────────┐
                    │     Intermediaries      │
                    └─────────────────────────┘
                         ↓                 ↓
      ┌─────────────────────┐   ┌─────────────────────────┐
      │     Independent     │   │   Manufacturer-Owned    │
      │    Intermediaries   │   │     Intermediaries      │
      ├─────────────────────┤   └─────────────────────────┘
      │ • Merchant          │
      │   Wholesalers       │
      │ • Merchandise       │
      │   Agents or         │
      │   Brokers           │
      └─────────────────────┘
```

Wholesaling Intermediaries

How can you get your hands on a new Billie Eilish T-shirt or hoodie? You could pick one up at your local music store, at a trendy clothing store like Hot Topic, or maybe at its online store. You might join hordes of others and buy an "official Billie Eilish concert T-shirt" from vendors during a show. Alternatively, you might get a "deal" on a bootlegged, unauthorized version of the same shirt that a shady guy who stands *outside* the concert venue sells from a battered suitcase. Perhaps you shop online at www.billieeilish.com. Each of these distribution alternatives traces a different path from producer to consumer. Let's look at the different types of wholesaling intermediaries and at different channel structures. Figure 11.2 portrays key intermediary types, and Table 11.1 summarizes the important characteristics of each.

Wholesaling intermediaries are firms that handle the flow of products from the manufacturer to the retailer or business user. There are

Table 11.1 | Types of Intermediaries

Intermediary Type	Description	Advantages
Independent intermediaries	Do business with many different manufacturers and many different customers	Used by most small- to medium-size firms
• **Merchant wholesalers**	Buy (take title to) goods from producers and sell to organizational customers; either full or limited function	Allow small manufacturers to serve customers throughout the world with competitive costs
• Cash-and-carry wholesalers	Provide products for small-business customers who purchase at wholesaler's location	Distribute low-cost merchandise for small retailers and other business customers
• Truck jobbers	Deliver perishable food and tobacco items to retailers	Ensure that perishable items are delivered and sold efficiently
• Drop shippers	Take orders from and bill retailers for products drop-shipped from manufacturer	Facilitate transactions for bulky products
• Mail-order wholesalers	Sell through catalogs, telephone, or mail order	Provide reasonably priced sales options to small organizational customers
• Rack jobbers	Provide retailers with display units, check inventories, and replace merchandise for retailers	Provide merchandising services to retailers
• **Merchandise agents and brokers**	Provide services in exchange for commissions	Maintain legal ownership of product by the seller
• Manufacturers' agents	Use independent salespeople; carry several lines of noncompeting products	Supply sales function for small and new firms
• Selling agents, including export/import agents	Handle entire output of one or more products	Handle all marketing functions for small manufacturers
• Commission merchants	Receive commission on sales price of product	Provide efficiency primarily in agricultural products market
• Merchandise brokers, including export/import brokers	Identify likely buyers and bring buyers and sellers together	Enhance efficiency in markets where there are many small buyers and sellers
Manufacturer-owned intermediaries	Limit operations to one manufacturer	Create efficiencies for large firms
• Sales branches	Maintain some inventory in different geographic areas (similar to wholesalers)	Provide service to customers in different geographic areas
• Sales offices	Carry no inventory; availability in different geographic areas	Reduce selling costs and provide better customer service
• Manufacturers' showrooms	Display products attractively for customers to visit	Facilitate examination of merchandise by customers at a central location

many different types of consumer and B2B wholesaling intermediaries. Some of these are independent, but manufacturers and retailers can own them too.

independent intermediaries
Channel intermediaries that are not controlled by any manufacturer but instead do business with many different manufacturers and many different customers.

Independent Intermediaries

Independent intermediaries do business with many different manufacturers and many different customers. Because no manufacturer owns or controls them, they make it possible for many manufacturers to serve customers throughout the world while they keep prices low.

merchant wholesalers
Intermediaries that buy goods from manufacturers (take title to them) and sell to retailers and other B2B customers.

Merchant wholesalers are independent intermediaries that buy goods from manufacturers and sell to retailers and other B2B customers. Because merchant wholesalers **take title** to the goods (i.e., they legally own them), they assume certain risks and can suffer losses if products are damaged, become outdated or obsolete, are stolen, or just don't sell. On the other hand, because they own the products, they are free to develop their own marketing strategies, including setting the prices they charge their customers. Wait, it gets better: There are several different kinds of merchant wholesalers:

take title
To accept legal ownership of a product and assume the accompanying rights and responsibilities of ownership.

- **Full-service merchant wholesalers** provide a wide range of services for their customers, including delivery, credit, product-use assistance, repairs, advertising, and other promotional support—even market research. Full-service merchant wholesalers often have their own sales force to call on businesses and organizational customers. Some general merchandise wholesalers carry a large variety of different items, whereas specialty wholesalers carry an extensive assortment of a single product line. For example, a candy wholesaler carries only candy and gum products but stocks enough different varieties to give your dentist nightmares for a year.

- In contrast, **limited-service merchant wholesalers** provide fewer services for their customers. Like full-service wholesalers, limited-service wholesalers *take title* to merchandise but are less likely to provide services such as delivery, credit, or marketing assistance to retailers. Specific types of limited-service wholesalers include the following:

  - *Cash-and-carry wholesalers* provide low-cost merchandise for retailers and industrial customers that are too small for other wholesalers' sales representatives to call on. Customers pay cash for products and provide their own delivery. Some popular cash-and-carry product categories include groceries, office supplies, and building materials.

  - *Truck jobbers* carry their products to small business customer locations for their inspection and selection. Truck jobbers often supply perishable items, such as fruit and vegetables, to small grocery stores. For example, a bakery truck jobber calls on supermarkets, checks the stock of bread on the shelves, removes outdated items, and suggests how much bread the store needs to reorder.

  - *Drop shippers* are limited-function wholesalers that take title to the merchandise but never actually take possession of it. Drop shippers take orders from and bill retailers and industrial buyers, but the merchandise is shipped directly from the manufacturer. Because they take title to the merchandise, they assume the same risks as other merchant wholesalers. Drop shippers are important to both the producers and the customers of bulky products, such as coal, oil, or lumber.

  - *Mail-order wholesalers* sell products to small retailers and other industrial customers, often located in remote areas, through catalogs rather than a sales force. They usually carry products in inventory and require payment in cash or by credit card before shipment. Mail-order wholesalers supply products such as cosmetics, hardware, and sporting goods.

  - *Rack jobbers* supply retailers with specialty items, such as health and beauty products and magazines. Rack jobbers get their name because they own and maintain the product display racks in grocery stores, drugstores, and variety stores. These wholesalers visit retail customers on a regular basis to maintain levels of stock and refill their racks with merchandise. Think about how quickly magazines turn over on the rack; without an expert who pulls old titles and inserts new ones, retailers would have great difficulty ensuring that you can buy the current issue of *People* magazine on the first day it hits the streets.

Merchandise agents and brokers are a second major type of independent intermediary. Agents and brokers provide services in exchange for commissions. They may or may not take possession of the product, but they *never* take title; that is, they do not accept legal ownership of the product. Agents normally represent buyers or sellers on an ongoing basis, whereas clients employ brokers for a short period of time:

- *Manufacturers' agents*, or *manufacturers' reps*, are independent salespeople who carry several lines of noncompeting products. They have contractual arrangements with manufacturers that outline territories, selling prices, and other specific aspects of the relationship but provide little if any supervision. Manufacturers normally compensate agents with commissions based on a percentage of what they sell. Manufacturers'

full-service merchant wholesalers
Wholesalers that provide a wide range of services for their customers, including delivery, credit, product-use assistance, repairs, advertising, and other promotional support.

limited-service merchant wholesalers
Wholesalers that provide fewer services for their customers.

merchandise agents and brokers
Channel intermediaries that provide services in exchange for commissions but never take title to the product.

agents often develop strong customer relationships and provide an important sales function for small and new companies.

- *Selling agents*, including *export/import agents*, market a whole product line or one manufacturer's total output. They often work like an independent marketing department because they perform the same functions as full-service merchant wholesalers but do not take title to products. Unlike manufacturers' agents, selling agents have unlimited territories and control the pricing, promotion, and distribution of their products. We find selling agents in industries such as furniture, clothing, and textiles.

- *Commission merchants* are sales agents who receive goods, primarily agricultural products, such as grain or livestock, on *consignment*—that is, they take possession of products without taking title. Although sellers may state a minimum price they are willing to take for their products, commission merchants are free to sell the product for the highest price they can get. Commission merchants receive a commission on the sales price of the product.

- *Merchandise brokers*, including export/import brokers, are intermediaries that facilitate transactions in markets such as real estate, food, and used equipment, in which there are lots of small buyers and sellers. Brokers identify likely buyers and sellers and bring the two together in return for a fee they receive when the transaction is completed.

Manufacturer-Owned Intermediaries

Sometimes manufacturers set up their own channel intermediaries. In this way, they can operate separate business units that perform all the functions of independent intermediaries while still maintaining complete control over the channel:

- *Sales branches* are manufacturer-owned facilities that, like independent wholesalers, carry inventory and provide sales and service to customers in a specific geographic area. We find sales branches in industries such as petroleum products, industrial machinery and equipment, and motor vehicles.

- *Sales offices* are manufacturer-owned facilities that, like agents, do not carry inventory but provide selling functions for the manufacturer in a specific geographic area. Because they allow members of the sales force to locate close to customers, they reduce selling costs and provide better customer service.

- *Manufacturers' showrooms* are manufacturer-owned or -leased facilities in which products are permanently displayed for customers to visit. *Merchandise marts* are often multiple buildings in which one or more industries hold trade shows and many manufacturers have permanent showrooms. Retailers can visit either during a show or all year long to see the manufacturer's merchandise and make B2B purchases.

Types of Distribution Channels

Firms face many choices when they structure distribution channels. Should they sell directly to consumers and business users? Would they benefit if they included wholesalers, retailers, or both in the channel? Would it make sense to sell directly to some customers but use retailers to sell to others? Of course, there is no single best channel for all products. The marketing manager must select a channel structure that creates a competitive advantage for the firm and its products based on the size and needs of the target market. Let's consider some of the factors these managers need to think about.

When they develop distribution (place) strategies, marketers first consider different **channel levels**. This refers to the number of distinct categories of intermediaries that make up a channel of distribution. Many factors have an impact on this decision. What channel members are available? How large is the market? How frequently do consumers purchase the product? What services do consumers require? Figure 11.3 summarizes the different structures a distribution channel can take. The producer and the customer are always members, so the shortest channel possible has two levels. Using a retailer adds a third level, a

channel levels
The number of distinct categories of intermediaries that make up a channel of distribution.

wholesaler adds a fourth level, and so on. Different channel structures exist for both consumer and B2B markets.

And what about services? You will learn in Chapter 12 that services are intangible, so there is no need to worry about storage, transportation, and the other functions of physical distribution. In most cases, the service travels directly from the producer to the customer. However, an intermediary we call an *agent* can enhance the distribution of some services when he helps the parties complete the transaction. Examples of these agents include insurance agents, stockbrokers, and travel agents (no, not everyone books their travel online).

Consumer Channels

As we noted previously, the simplest channel is a direct channel. Why do some producers sell directly to customers? One reason is that a direct channel may allow the producer to serve its customers better and at a lower price than is possible if it included a retailer. A baker who uses a direct channel makes sure that customers enjoy fresher bread than if the tasty loaves are sold through a local supermarket. Furthermore, if the baker sells the bread through a supermarket, the price will be higher because of the supermarket's costs of doing business and its need to make its own profit on the bread. In fact, sometimes this is the *only* way to sell the product because using channel intermediaries may boost the price above what consumers are willing to pay.

Another reason to use a direct channel is *control*. When the producer handles distribution, it maintains control of pricing, service, and delivery—all elements of the transaction. Because distributors and dealers carry many products, it can be difficult to get their sales forces to focus on selling one product. In a direct channel, a producer works directly with customers, so it gains insights into trends, customer needs and complaints, and the effectiveness of its marketing strategies.

Nike is a few years into its sweeping new plan for growth called the Triple Double Strategy (2X). Through it, the company has promised to double its "cadence and impact of innovation," double its speed to market and—most relevant to the consumer channels issue—double its "direct connections with consumers." The cornerstone of the 2X Strategy is the Nike Consumer Experience (NCX), which includes Nike's own direct-to-consumer network, as well as a vastly streamlined slate of wholesale distribution partners. At a time when most big international companies are probably doubling down on the channel strategies that made them successful in order to defend their turf, Nike is bucking the trend by taking more control of their own direct channel to consumers.[4]

Why do producers choose to use indirect channels to reach consumers? A reason in many cases is that customers are familiar with certain retailers or other intermediaries; it's where they always go to look for what they need. Getting customers to change their normal buying behavior—for example, convincing consumers to buy their laundry detergent or frozen pizza from a catalog or over the Internet instead of from the corner supermarket—can be difficult.

In addition, intermediaries help producers in all the ways we described previously. By creating utility and transaction efficiencies, channel members make producers' lives easier and enhance their ability to reach customers. The *producer–retailer–consumer channel* in Figure 11.3 is the shortest indirect channel. Samsung uses this channel when it sells TVs through large retailers such as Best Buy (either their brick-and-mortar stores or their online store). Because the retailers buy in large volume, they can obtain inventory at a low price and then pass these savings on to shoppers (this is what gives them a competitive advantage over smaller, more specialized stores that don't order so many items). The size of these retail giants also means they can provide the physical distribution functions that wholesalers handle for smaller retail outlets, such as transportation and storage.

One fast-growing channel is consumer-to-consumer (C2C). eBay and other similar online platforms facilitate the means for a direct channel of distribution from one consumer to another, including mechanisms for payment, shipping, returns, and providing reviews of the service experience. Some eBay sellers really are businesses, in essence–and there's good income to be made selling on eBay if you rack up a history of excellent reviews from buyers.

Figure 11.3 *Snapshot* | Different Types of Channels of Distribution

Channels differ in the number of channel members that participate.

Major Types of Channels of Distribution

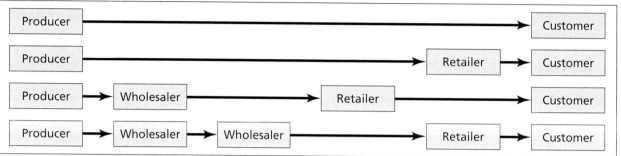

Typical Consumer Channels

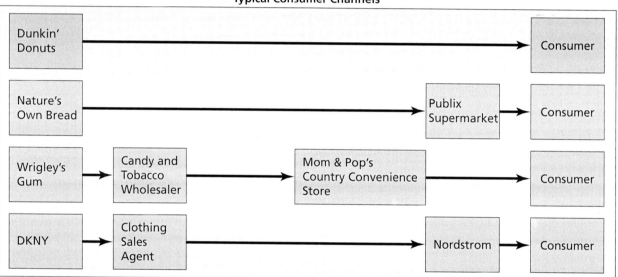

Typical B2B Channels

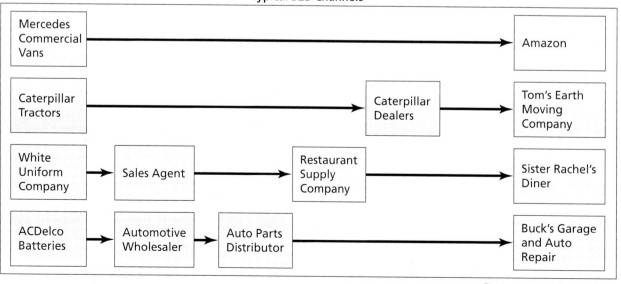

The *producer–wholesaler–retailer–consumer channel* is a common distribution channel in consumer marketing. An example would be a single ice cream factory that supplies, say, four or five regional wholesalers. These wholesalers then sell to 400 or more retailers, such as grocery stores. The retailers, in turn, each sell the ice cream to thousands of customers. In this channel, the regional wholesalers combine many manufacturers' products to supply grocery stores. Because the grocery stores do business with many wholesalers, this arrangement results in a broad selection of products.

You'll read more about retailers in Chapter 12, but given the preceding discussion, this is a good spot to bring up the current and growing craze for instant customer gratification via same-day delivery for virtually anything! If you've never done so, do a quick check online at DoorDash, Instacart, or any of the other similar delivery services that have grown exponentially since the COVID-19 crisis. There you can get fast delivery on everyday essentials from stores like Walmart, Costco, Target, and Walgreens. In the service sector, TaskRabbit's homepage hawks its ability to get you a same-day handyman or mover.[5] And the most exciting thing about all of these new-age channel opportunities is that they're fueled by the gig economy—folks happy to work several independent roles rather than one traditional job, giving them the freedom to work when and at what they want to.

B2B Channels

B2B distribution channels, as the name suggests, facilitate the flow of goods from a producer to an organizational or business customer. Generally, B2B channels parallel consumer channels in that they may be direct or indirect. For example, the simplest indirect channel in industrial markets occurs when the single intermediary—a merchant wholesaler we refer to as an *industrial distributor* rather than a retailer—buys products from a manufacturer and sells them to business customers.

Direct channels are more common in B2B markets versus consumer markets. As we saw in Chapter 6, this is because B2B marketing often means that a firm sells high-dollar, high-profit items (a single piece of industrial equipment may cost hundreds of thousands of dollars) to a market made up of only a few customers. In such markets, it makes sense financially for a company to develop its own sales force and sell directly to customers—in this case, the investment in an in-house sales force pays off.

Dual (or Multiple) and Hybrid Distribution Systems

Figure 11.3 illustrates how simple distribution channels work. Producers, dealers, wholesalers, retailers, and customers alike may actually participate in more than one type of channel, as illustrated earlier by Nike adding its NCX direct-to-consumer network. Similarly, bedding manufacturer Boll & Branch opened its first physical location in a luxury mall in New Jersey despite the fact that its bedding doesn't carry a luxury price tag. The company had a desire to prove that its less expensive bedding was actually better than some of the options with much higher prices—the only way to show the skeptics was to give them an opportunity to feel the difference.[6] And even ubiquitous online distribution channel Amazon took the plunge into brick-and-mortar in the grocery space when it acquired Whole Foods, with the intent to use the stores for product (which has since morphed into a far more lucrative win for the firm). We call these approaches **dual** or **multiple distribution systems**.

The pharmaceutical industry provides another good example of multiple-channel usage. Pharmaceutical companies distribute their products in at least three types of channels:

1. They sell to hospitals, clinics, and other organizational customers directly. These customers buy in quantity, and they purchase a wide variety of products. Because hospitals and clinics dispense pills one at a time rather than in bottles of 50, these outlets require different product packaging than when the manufacturer sells medications to other types of customers.

dual or multiple distribution systems
A system where producers, dealers, wholesalers, retailers, and customers participate in more than one type of channel.

Amazon acquired Whole Foods Market in 2017, creating a now highly successful example of dual distribution system.

2. They rely on an indirect consumer channel when they sell to large drugstore chains, like Walgreens, that distribute the medicines to their stores across the country. Alternatively, some of us would rather purchase our prescriptions in a more personal manner from the local independent drugstore where we can still get an ice cream soda while we wait. In this version of the indirect consumer channel, the manufacturer sells to drug wholesalers that, in turn, supply these independents.

3. Finally, the companies sell directly to third-party payers such as HMOs, PPOs, and insurance companies. But make no mistake—pharmaceutical firms in the U.S. are mindful that the future of healthcare distribution channels is far from clear, despite the failure to repeal the Affordable Care Act.

hybrid marketing system

A marketing system that uses a number of different channels and communication methods to serve a target market.

Instead of serving a target market with a single channel, some companies combine channels—direct sales, distributors, retail sales, and direct mail—to create a **hybrid marketing system**.[7] Believe it or not, the whole world of business actually has not gone paperless (amazing, isn't it)! Hence, companies actually do still buy copying machines (sounds so 1999)—and in large quantities. At one time, you could buy a Xerox copier only directly through a Xerox salesperson. Today, unless you are a very large business customer, you likely will purchase a Xerox machine from a local Xerox authorized dealer or possibly through the Shop Xerox website.[8] Xerox turned to an enhanced dealer network for distribution because such hybrid marketing systems offer companies certain competitive advantages, including increased coverage of the market, lower marketing costs, and a greater potential for customization of service for local markets.

Distribution Channels and the Marketing Mix

Recall that the elements of the marketing mix include product, promotion, place (meaning *channel of distribution*), and price. So how do decisions regarding place relate to the other *three Ps*? For one, place decisions affect pricing. Marketers that distribute products through lower-priced retailers such as Walmart, T.J. Maxx, and Marshalls will have different pricing objectives and strategies than will those that sell to specialty stores like Tiffany or high-end department stores like Nordstrom. And, of course, the nature of the product itself influences the retailers and intermediaries that are used for distribution. Manufacturers select mass merchandisers to sell mid–price-range products while they distribute top-of-the-line products, such as expensive jewelry, through high-end department and specialty stores.

Distribution decisions can sometimes give a product a distinct position in its market. For example, Ultradent Products, Inc., started out selling its teeth-whitening product Opalescence® exclusively through licensed dental professionals. Many other companies' teeth-whitening products are typically sold through traditional retail channels, making them much more easily available. However, Ultradent's approach initially allowed the company to position Opalescence® as a higher-end product endorsed by professional experts. They rely on the dentist and staff to pitch the benefits of the product in a way that carries far more credibility with a patient than an ad by a retailer or manufacturer. So when Ultradent recently launched a take-home version of the product, consumers immediately assumed it would be higher quality and more efficacious than the pedestrian competitors that started out on the grocery shelves.[9]

In addition, the distribution channel *itself*—a cool new way you get the product—may help to position a product in a unique way vis-à-vis the competition. That is, the way you obtain a product can be one of the attributes that makes it appealing. A great example is the hot trend of **subscription boxes**, a business model that is still growing by leaps and bounds every year. Many people love to get surprises in the mail (as long as they're not bills or a jury summons). Today, numerous upstart companies supply these surprises by sending out a box each month filled with items you never knew you wanted but you just have to have. Fun examples include FabFitFun (style, fashion, fitness), CauseBox (sustainable products), Rocksbox (jewelry), Ipsy (makeup), Sips by (tea), HelloFresh (meal kits), Winc (wine), BarkBox (dog supplies), and BOTM (books). The market is split roughly 60–40 women to men, with the latest estimate of global subscription e-commerce market at about $15 billion![10]

The subscription model is booming in popularity. This is a fairly new business model that relies upon regularly scheduled shipments direct from the manufacturer to the consumer.

Ethics in the Distribution Channel

Companies' decisions about how to make their products available to consumers through distribution channels can create ethical dilemmas. For example, because their size gives them great bargaining power when they negotiate with manufacturers, many large retail chains force manufacturers to pay a **slotting allowance**—a fee in exchange for agreeing to place a manufacturer's products on a retailer's valuable shelf space. Although the retailers claim that such fees pay the cost of adding products to their inventory, many manufacturers feel that slotting fees are more akin to highway robbery. Certainly, the practice prevents many smaller manufacturers that cannot afford the slotting allowances from getting their products into the hands of consumers.

It may seem odd to you that in some cases products end up being sold through one or more channels that the manufacturer did not authorize. This practice is known as **product diversion**, and it can be a big problem for manufacturers due to loss of control that results once the product is in the hands of unauthorized distributors and retailers. An additional concern for many manufacturers is that their products, once diverted, will end up being sold at a price or in a form that damages both the brand and the firm's relationship with its authorized distributors. Such practices are common for beauty products that are sold exclusively through salons and other hair care professionals. Salon-quality brands like Tigi, Redken, Pureology, Kérastase, and others actively message to consumers about potential risks associated with buying their products outside of the established professional salon distribution channel, including product counterfeits, old or out-of-date merchandise, diluted formulas, and other safety concerns with their use, such as contamination.[11]

So who perpetrates product diversion? Most often, a **diverter** turns out to be one or more of the manufacturer's own regular customers that purposefully overbuys product when it is offered at special promotional prices, holds it in inventory until the promotion is over, and then sells the product within the channel. Also, retailers or distributors may be tempted to simply divert incidental excess inventory of a product that they do not expect to be able to sell through legitimate means.

Another ethical issue involves the sheer size of a particular channel intermediary—be it manufacturer, wholesaler, retailer, or other intermediary. Walmart, the poster child for giant retailers, has been vilified for years as contributing to the demise of scores of independent competitors (i.e., mom-and-pop stores). In more recent years, the company has begun a very visible program to help its smaller rivals. The program offers financial grants to hardware stores, dress shops, and bakeries near its new urban stores; training on how to

subscription boxes
A new business model for distribution that supplies surprises by sending out a box each month filled with items you never knew you wanted but you just have to have.

slotting allowance
A fee paid in exchange for agreeing to place a manufacturer's products on a retailer's valuable shelf space.

product diversion
The distribution of a product through one or more channels not authorized for use by the manufacturer of the product.

diverter
An entity that facilitates the distribution of a product through one or more channels not authorized for use by the manufacturer of the product.

survive with a Walmart in town; and even free advertising in Walmart stores. Although certainly beneficial to the small fry, Walmart also hopes to benefit from the program in urban settings like Los Angeles and New York, where its plan to build new stores in inner-city neighborhoods has met with mixed reactions from local communities.[12]

Overall, it is important for all channel intermediaries to behave and treat each other in a professional, ethical manner—and to do no harm to consumers (financially or otherwise) through their channel activities. Every intermediary in the channel wants to make money, but behavior by one to maximize its financial success at the expense of others' success is a doomed approach, as ultimately cooperation in the channel will break down. Instead, it behooves intermediaries to work cooperatively in the channel to distribute products to consumers in an efficient manner—making the channel a success for everybody participating in it (including consumers)! Win-win!

11.2 Develop a Channel Strategy

OBJECTIVE

List and explain the steps to plan a distribution channel strategy.

Do customers want products in large or small quantities? Do they insist on buying them locally, or will they purchase from a distant supplier? How long are they willing to wait to get the product? Inquiring marketers want to know!

Channel of distribution planning works best when marketers follow the steps in Figure 11.4. In this section, we first look at how firms decide on distribution objectives, then we examine what influences distribution decisions, and finally we talk about how firms select different distribution strategies and tactics.

Firms that operate within a channel of distribution—manufacturers, wholesalers, and retailers—do **distribution planning**, which is a process of developing distribution objectives, evaluating internal and external environmental influences on distribution, and choosing a distribution strategy.

distribution planning
The process of developing distribution objectives, evaluating internal and external environmental influences on distribution, and choosing a distribution strategy.

Step 1: Develop Distribution Objectives

The first step in a distribution plan is to develop objectives that support the organization's overall marketing goals. How can distribution work with the other elements of the marketing mix to increase profits? To increase market share? To increase sales volume? In general, the overall objective of any distribution plan is to make a firm's product available when, where, and in the quantities customers want at the minimum cost. More specific distribution objectives, however, depend on the characteristics of the product and the market.

For example, if the product is bulky, a primary distribution objective may be to minimize shipping costs. If the product is fragile, a goal may be to develop a channel that minimizes handling. In introducing a new product to a mass market, a channel objective may be to provide maximum product exposure (like BDP's work with its client Quaker) or to make the product available close to where customers live and work. Sometimes marketers make their product available where similar products are sold so that consumers can compare prices.

Step 2: Evaluate Internal and External Environmental Influences

After they set their distribution objectives, marketers must consider their internal and external environments to develop the best channel structure. Should the channel be long or short? Is intensive, selective, or exclusive distribution best? Short, often direct channels may be better suited for B2B marketers for whom customers are geographically concentrated and require high levels of technical know-how and service. Companies frequently sell expensive or complex products directly to final customers. Short channels with selective distribution also make more sense with perishable products because getting the product to the final user quickly is a priority. However, longer channels with more intensive distribution are generally best for inexpensive, standardized consumer goods that need to be distributed broadly and that require little technical expertise.

The organization must also examine issues such as its own ability to handle distribution functions, what channel intermediaries are available, the ability of customers to access these intermediaries, and how the competition distributes its products. Should a firm use the same retailers as its competitors? It depends. Sometimes, to ensure customers' undivided attention, a firm sells its products in outlets that don't carry the competitors' products. In other cases, a firm uses the same intermediaries as its competitors because customers expect to find the product there. For example, you will find Harley-Davidson bikes only in selected Harley "boutiques" and Piaggio's Vespa scooters only at Vespa dealers (no original sales through Amazon for those two!), but you can expect to find Coca-Cola, Colgate toothpaste, and a Snickers bar in every possible outlet that sells these types of items (remember our discussion in Chapter 8 about the nature of convenience products).

Finally, when they study competitors' distribution strategies, marketers learn from their successes and failures. If the biggest complaint of competitors' customers is delivery speed, developing a system that allows same-day delivery can make the competition pale in comparison.

Step 3: Choose a Distribution Strategy

Planning a distribution strategy means making several decisions. First, of course, distribution planning includes decisions about the number of levels in the distribution channel. We already discussed these options in the previous section on consumer and B2B channels, illustrated by Figure 11.3. Beyond the number of levels, distribution strategies also involve two additional decisions about channel relationships: (1) whether a conventional system or a highly integrated system will work best and (2) the proper **distribution intensity**, meaning the number of intermediaries at each level of the channel. The next sections provide insight into making these two distribution strategy decisions.

Decision 1: Conventional, Vertical, or Horizontal Marketing System?

Participants in any distribution channel form an interrelated system. In general, these marketing systems take one of three forms: conventional, vertical, or horizontal.

1. A **conventional marketing system** is a multilevel distribution channel in which members work independently of one another. Their relationships are limited to simply buying and selling from one another. Each firm seeks to benefit, with little concern for other channel members. Even though channel members work independently, most conventional channels are highly successful. For one thing, all members of the channel work toward the same goals—to build demand, reduce costs, and improve customer satisfaction. And each channel member knows that it's in everyone's best interest to treat other channel members fairly.

2. A **vertical marketing system (VMS)** is a channel in which there is formal cooperation among channel members at two or more different levels: manufacturing, wholesaling, and retailing. Firms develop VMSs as a way to meet customer needs better by reducing costs incurred in channel activities. Often, a VMS can provide a level of cooperation and efficiency not possible with a conventional channel, maximizing the effectiveness of the channel while also maximizing efficiency and keeping costs low.

Figure 11.4 *Process* | Steps in Distribution Planning

Distribution planning begins with setting channel objectives and evaluating the environment and results in developing channel strategies and tactics.

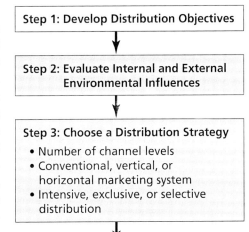

Step 1: Develop Distribution Objectives

Step 2: Evaluate Internal and External Environmental Influences

Step 3: Choose a Distribution Strategy
- Number of channel levels
- Conventional, vertical, or horizontal marketing system
- Intensive, exclusive, or selective distribution

Step 4: Develop Distribution Tactics
- Select channel partners
- Manage the channel
- Develop logistics strategies
  - Order processing
  - Warehousing
  - Materials handling
  - Transportation
  - Inventory control

distribution intensity
The number of intermediaries at each level of the channel.

conventional marketing system
A multiple-level distribution channel in which channel members work independently of one another.

vertical marketing system (VMS)
A channel of distribution in which there is formal cooperation among members at the manufacturing, wholesaling, and retailing levels.

Members share information and provide services to other members; they recognize that such coordination makes everyone more successful when they want to reach a desired target market. There are three types of vertical marketing systems: administered, corporate, and contractual:

administered VMS
A vertical marketing system in which channel members remain independent but voluntarily work together because of the power of a single channel member.

corporate VMS
A vertical marketing system in which a single firm owns manufacturing, wholesaling, and retailing operations.

contractual VMS
A vertical marketing system in which cooperation is enforced by contracts (legal agreements) that spell out each member's rights and responsibilities and how they will cooperate.

a. In an **administered VMS**, channel members remain independent but voluntarily work together because of the power of a single channel member. Strong brands are able to manage an administered VMS because resellers are eager to work with the manufacturer so they will be allowed to carry the product.

b. In a **corporate VMS**, a single firm owns manufacturing, wholesaling, and retailing operations. Thus, the firm has complete control over all channel operations. Retail giant Macy's, for example, owns a nationwide network of distribution centers and retail stores.

c. In a **contractual VMS**, cooperation is enforced by contracts (legal agreements) that spell out each member's rights and responsibilities and how they will cooperate. This arrangement means that the channel members can have more impact as a group than they could alone. In a wholesaler-sponsored VMS, wholesalers get retailers to work together under their leadership in a voluntary chain. Retail members of the chain use a common name, cooperate in advertising and other promotions, and even develop their own private-label products. Examples of wholesaler-sponsored chains are Independent Grocers' Alliance (IGA) food stores and Ace Hardware stores.

retailer cooperative
A group of retailers that establishes a wholesaling operation to help them compete more effectively with the large chains.

In other cases, retailers themselves organize a cooperative marketing channel system. A **retailer cooperative** is a group of retailers that establishes a wholesaling operation to help them compete more effectively with the large chains. Each retailer owns shares in the wholesaler operation and is obligated to purchase a certain percentage of its inventory from the cooperative operation. Associated Grocers and True Value hardware stores are examples of retailer cooperatives.

franchise organizations
A contractual vertical marketing system that includes a *franchiser* (a manufacturer or a service provider) who allows an entrepreneur (the *franchisee*) to use the franchise name and marketing plan for a fee.

Franchise organizations are a third type of contractual VMS. Franchise organizations include a *franchiser* (a manufacturer or a service provider) who allows an entrepreneur (the *franchisee*) to use the franchise name and marketing plan for a fee. In these organizations, contractual arrangements explicitly define and strictly enforce channel cooperation. In most franchise agreements, the franchiser provides a variety of services for the franchisee, such as helping to train employees, giving access to lower prices for needed materials, and selecting a good location. In return, the franchiser receives a percentage of revenue from the franchisee. Usually, the franchisees are obligated to follow the franchiser's business format very closely to maintain the franchise.

From the manufacturer's perspective, franchising a business is a way to develop widespread product distribution with minimal financial risk while at the same time maintaining control over product quality. From the entrepreneur's perspective, franchises are a helpful way to get a start in business.

horizontal marketing system
An arrangement within a channel of distribution in which two or more firms at the same channel level work together for a common purpose.

3. In a **horizontal marketing system**, two or more firms at the same channel level agree to work together to get their product to the customer. Sometimes, unrelated businesses forge these agreements. Most airlines today are members of a horizontal alliance that allows them to cooperate when they provide passenger air service. For example, American Airlines is a member of the **one**world alliance, which also includes British Airways, Cathay Pacific, Finnair, Iberia, Japan Airlines, LATAM, Malaysia Airlines, Qantas, Qatar Airways, Royal Jordanian, S7 Airlines, and SriLankan Airlines. These alliances increase passenger volume for all airlines because travel agents who book passengers on one of the airline's flights will be more likely to book a connecting flight on the other airline. To increase customer benefits, they also share frequent-flyer programs and airport clubs.[13]

Decision 2: Intensive, Exclusive, or Selective Distribution?

How many wholesalers and retailers should carry the product within a given market? This may seem like an easy decision: Distribute the product through as many intermediaries as possible. But guess again. If the product goes to too many outlets, there may be inefficiency and duplication of efforts. For example, if there are too many Honda dealerships in town, there will be a lot of unsold Hondas sitting on dealer lots, and no single dealer will be successful. But if there are not enough wholesalers or retailers to carry a product, the manufacturer will fail to maximize total sales of its products (and its profits). If customers have to drive hundreds of miles to find a Honda dealer, they may instead opt for a Toyota just because of convenience. Thus, a distribution objective may be to either increase or decrease the level of distribution in the market.

Harley-Davidson keeps customers focused only on its brand of motorcycles by using an exclusive distribution strategy, selling products in exclusive boutiques. No Hondas or Yamahas in here.

The three basic choices are intensive, exclusive, and selective distribution. Table 11.2 summarizes five decision factors—company, customers, channels, constraints, and competition—and how they help marketers determine the best fit between distribution system and marketing goals. Read on, and you will find that these categories connect with the concept of convenience products, specialty products, and shopping products you learned about in Chapter 8.

Intensive distribution aims to maximize market coverage by selling a product through all wholesalers or retailers that will stock and sell the product. Marketers use intensive distribution for *convenience products*, such as chewing gum, soft drinks, milk, and bread that consumers quickly consume and must replace frequently. Intensive distribution is necessary for these products because availability is more important than any other consideration in customers' purchase decisions.

In contrast to intensive distribution, **exclusive distribution** means to limit distribution to a single outlet in a particular region. Marketers often sell pianos, cars, executive training programs, TV programs, and many other *specialty products* with high price tags through exclusive distribution arrangements. They typically use these strategies with products that are high priced and have considerable service requirements and when a limited number of buyers exist in any single geographic area. Exclusive distribution enables wholesalers and retailers to better recoup the costs associated with long selling processes for each customer and, in some cases, extensive after-sale service.

intensive distribution
Selling a product through all suitable wholesalers or retailers that are willing to stock and sell the product.

exclusive distribution
Selling a product only through a single outlet in a particular region.

Table 11.2	Characteristics That Favor Intensive versus Exclusive Distribution	
Decision Factor	**Intensive Distribution**	**Exclusive Distribution**
Company	Oriented toward mass markets	Oriented toward specialized markets
Customers	High customer density	Low customer density
	Price and convenience are priorities	Service and cooperation are priorities
Channels	Overlapping market coverage	Nonoverlapping market coverage
Constraints	Cost of serving individual customers is low	Cost of serving individual customers is high
Competition	Based on a strong market presence, often through advertising and promotion	Based on individualized attention to customers, often through relationship marketing

For luxury products, employing an exclusive distribution strategy can support the associations the marketer wants consumers to have with the product (such as exclusivity, quality, or mystique) and ensure that the product is offered by retailers who are well-suited and matched to the task. For example, the ultra-high-end watchmaker Patek Philippe only sells its products through a small group of authorized retailers, and in many cases, each retailer only receives one unit of a new model each year. Authorized dealers are heavily vetted and ultimately are selected based on their fit and ability to sell and service the watches, which can range from 10,000 euros to more than 1 million euros in price. The company does not sell its watches online and does not expect its retailers to do so either.[14]

That said, if you search for a Patek Philippe watch online, you will undoubtedly find some e-commerce sites selling the company's products they were able to acquire through the **gray market**. Gray markets often emerge around high-end luxury goods sold through exclusive distribution. Related to the concept of product diversion introduced previously in the chapter, the gray market represents those channels of distribution that are not formally defined and authorized by the manufacturer for sale of the product. Exchanges that occur in the gray market are not technically illegal (unlike the concept of an illegal "black market"); hence, the use of the intermediate color gray makes sense. But the original manufacturer of the product does not view gray markets as appropriate or beneficial.

Of course, not every situation neatly fits a category in Table 11.2. (You didn't *really* think it would be that simple, did you?) For example, consider professional sports. Customers might not shop for games in the same way they shop for pianos. They might go to a game on impulse, and they don't require much individualized service. Nevertheless, professional sports use exclusive distribution. A team's cost of serving customers is high because of those million-dollar player salaries and multi-million-dollar stadiums.

The alert reader (and/or sports fan) may note that there are some exceptions to the exclusive distribution of sports teams. New York has two football teams and two baseball teams, Chicago fields two baseball teams, and so on. We call market coverage that is less than intensive distribution but more than exclusive distribution **selective distribution** (yes, this type falls between the two). This model fits when demand is so large that exclusive distribution is inadequate but selling costs, service requirements, or other factors make intensive distribution a poor fit. Although a White Sox baseball fan may not believe that the Cubs franchise is necessary (and vice versa), Major League Baseball and even some baseball fans think the Chicago market is large enough to support both teams.

Selective distribution strategies are suitable for most *shopping products*, such as household appliances and electronic equipment, for which consumers are willing to spend time visiting different retail outlets to compare alternatives. For producers, selective distribution means freedom to choose only those wholesalers and retailers that have a good credit rating, provide good market coverage, serve customers well, and cooperate effectively. Wholesalers and retailers like selective distribution because it results in higher profits than are possible with intensive distribution, in which sellers often have to compete on price.

gray market
A distribution channel in which a product's sale to a customer may be technically legal but is at a minimum considered inappropriate by the manufacturer of the related product. Gray markets often emerge around high-end luxury goods sold through exclusive distribution.

selective distribution
Distribution using fewer outlets than intensive distribution but more than exclusive distribution.

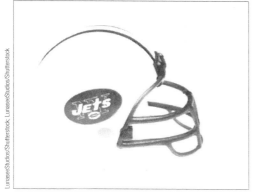

Two professional football teams for one city? Selective distribution.

Step 4: Develop Distribution Tactics

As with planning for the other marketing Ps, the final step in distribution planning is to develop the tactics for distribution necessary to implement the distribution strategy. These decisions are usually about the type of distribution system to use, such as a direct or an indirect channel or a conventional or an integrated channel. Distribution tactics relate to two aspects of the implementation of these strategies: (1) how to select individual channel members and (2) how to manage the channel. We provide insights into making each of these two decisions.

First, it is essential to understand that these two decisions are important because they often have a *direct impact on customer satisfaction*; nobody wants to have to wait for something they've bought! For many small businesses, partnering with Amazon to take advantage of its great distribution prowess is highly attractive. For a competitive fee, fulfillment by Amazon offers third parties the ability to outsource the storage and shipping of products to them. A company such as Instant Pot, which has upended the home-cooking industry and doubled sales every year since 2011, relies on Amazon as a channel member to distribute its products efficiently and at a competitive price. In a recent Prime Day, over 300,000 of these handy multicookers were sold.[15] Consumers who are signed up for Amazon Prime and thus get access to free two-day shipping provide an added bonus for companies that sell their products through Amazon. From its earliest days, Instant Pot took advantage of Amazon's Fulfillment by Amazon program—Amazon warehouses, ships, and handles paperwork for retailers in exchange for a fee. Because of Amazon's size, companies such as Instant Pot can feel more confident that as they scale out their business, Amazon will be able to stay ahead of their need for increased distribution. In times of peak demand, a real advantage of outsourcing distribution versus an internal approach is that Amazon can easily flex to handle the spikes in demand. This flexibility saves a firm like Instant Pot a lot of stress.[16]

Decision 1: Select Channel Partners

When firms agree to work together in a channel relationship, they become partners in what is normally a long-term commitment. Like a marriage, it is important to both manufacturers and intermediaries to select channel partners wisely, or they'll regret the match-up later (and a divorce can be really expensive!). In evaluating intermediaries, manufacturers try to answer questions such as the following: Will the channel member contribute substantially to our profitability? Does the channel member have the ability to provide the services customers want? What impact will a potential intermediary have on channel control?

For example, what small-to-midsize firm wouldn't jump at the chance to have retail giant Walmart distribute its products? With Walmart as a channel partner, a small firm could double, triple, or quadruple its business. But believe it or not, some firms that recognize that size means power in the channel actually decide against selling to Walmart because they are not willing to relinquish control of their marketing decision making. There is also a downside to choosing one retailer and selling only through that one retailer. If that retailer stops carrying the product, for example, the company will lose its one and only customer (perhaps after relinquishing other smaller customers), and it will be back to square one.

Another consideration in selecting channel members is competitors' channel partners. Because people spend time comparing different brands when purchasing a shopping product, firms need to make sure they display their products near similar competitors' products. If most competitors distribute their electric drills through mass merchandisers, a manufacturer has to make sure its brand is there also.

In marketing channels, a firm's dedication to promoting opportunities for a high level of diversity of all types within the channel is a responsibility that should be taken seriously. Hence, many highly socially responsible enterprises run extensive programs to seek out and recruit channel partners from among firms owned and operated by diverse leadership. For example, Coca-Cola Company offers a supplier training program aimed at helping female-owned businesses successfully break into its supply chain. The concept behind this supplier diversity program is the belief that when women succeed, economies and communities greatly benefit.[17]

Decision 2: Manage the Channel

channel leader, or channel captain
The dominant firm that controls the channel.

channel power
The ability of one channel member to influence, control, and lead the entire channel based on one or more sources of power.

Once a manufacturer develops a channel strategy and aligns channel members, the day-to-day job of managing the channel begins. The **channel leader**, or **channel captain**, is the dominant firm that controls the channel. A firm becomes the channel captain because it has more **channel power** relative to other channel members. Channel power is the ability of one channel member to influence, control, and lead the entire channel based on one or more sources of power. This power comes from different potential sources, among which are the following:

- A firm has *economic power* if it has the ability to control resources.
- A firm such as a franchiser has *legitimate power* if it has legal authority to call the shots.
- A producer firm has *reward* or *coercive power* if it engages in exclusive distribution and has the ability to give profitable products and to take them away from the channel intermediaries.

Historically, producers have held the role of channel captain. P&G, for example, developed customer-oriented marketing programs, tracked market trends, and advised retailers on the mix of products most likely to build sales. But as large retail outlets have evolved, giants like Amazon, Home Depot, Target, Walmart, and Walgreens began to assume a channel leadership role because of the sheer size of their operations. Today, it is much more common for the big retailers to dictate their needs to producers instead of producers controlling what products they offer to retailers.

In a classic example, Amazon tried to use its formidable channel power to "persuade" publisher Hachette to meet Amazon's terms regarding e-book pricing by subjecting its books to artificial purchase delays and by limiting the visibility of some Hachette titles in search results. During the time of the dispute, some popular Hachette titles no longer were available for preorder. Ultimately, Amazon and Hachette reached a settlement in which the publisher was still able to set its own prices, but evidence suggests the publisher made some concessions as well behind closed doors.[18]

channel cooperation
Occurs when producers, wholesalers, and retailers depend on one another for success.

Because producers, wholesalers, and retailers depend on one another for success, **channel cooperation** helps everyone. Channel cooperation is stimulated when the channel leader takes actions that make its partners more successful. Examples of this, such as high intermediary profit margins, training programs, cooperative advertising, and expert marketing advice, are invisible to end customers but are motivating factors in the eyes of wholesalers and retailers.

channel conflict
Incompatible goals, poor communication, and disagreement over roles, responsibilities, and functions among firms at different levels of the same distribution channel that may threaten a manufacturer's distribution strategy.

Of course, relations among members in a channel are not always full of sweetness and light. Because each firm has its own objectives, **channel conflict** may threaten a manufacturer's distribution strategy. Such conflict most often occurs between firms at different levels of the same distribution channel. Incompatible goals, poor communication, and disagreement over roles, responsibilities, and functions cause conflict. For example, a producer is likely to feel the firm would enjoy greater success and profitability if intermediaries carry only its brands, but many intermediaries believe they will do better if they carry a variety of brands.

In this section, we've been concerned with the distribution channels firms use to get their products to customers. In the next section, we'll look at the area of logistics—physically moving products through the supply chain—and end by introducing the concept of the supply chain.

11.3 Logistics and the Supply Chain

OBJECTIVE
Discuss the concepts of logistics and supply chain.

Some marketing textbooks tend to depict the practice of marketing as 90 percent planning and 10 percent implementation. Not so! In the "real world" (and in our book), many managers argue that this ratio should be reversed. Marketing success is very much the art of getting the timing right and delivering on promises—*implementation*.

That's why marketers place so much emphasis on efficient **logistics**: the process of designing, managing, and improving the movement of products through the supply chain. Logistics includes purchasing, manufacturing, storage, and transport. From a company's viewpoint, logistics takes place both *inbound* to the firm (raw materials, parts, components, and supplies) and *outbound* from the firm (work in process and finished goods).

Logistics is also a relevant consideration regarding product returns, recycling and material reuse, and waste disposal—**reverse logistics**.[19] As we saw in previous chapters, this is becoming even more important as firms start to more seriously consider *sustainability* as a competitive advantage and put more effort into maximizing the efficiency of recycling to save money and the environment at the same time. So you can see that logistics is an important issue across all elements of the supply chain. Let's examine this process more closely.

The Lowdown on Logistics

Have you ever heard the saying, "An army travels on its stomach"? *Logistics* was originally a term the military used to describe everything necessary to deliver troops and equipment to the right place, at the right time, and in the right condition. In business, logistics is similar in that its objective is to deliver exactly what the customer wants—at the right time, in the right place, and at the right price. As Figure 11.5 shows, logistics activities include order processing, warehousing, materials handling, transportation, and inventory control. This process impacts how marketers physically get products where they need to be, when they need to be there, and at the lowest possible cost.

When a firm does logistics planning, however, the focus also should be on the customer. In the old days when managers thought of logistics as physical distribution only, the objective was to deliver the product at the lowest cost. Today, forward-thinking firms consider the needs of the customer first. The customer's goals become the logistics provider's priorities. And this means that when they make most logistics decisions, firms must decide on the best trade-off between low costs and high customer service. The appropriate goal is not just to deliver what the market needs at the lowest cost but rather to provide the product at the lowest cost possible *as long as the firm meets delivery requirements*. Although it would be nice to transport all goods quickly by air (even by drone), that is certainly not practical. But sometimes air transport is necessary to meet the needs of the customer, no matter the cost.

When they develop logistics strategies, marketers must make decisions related to each of the five functions of logistics depicted in Figure 11.5. For each decision, managers need to consider how to minimize costs while maintaining the service customers want. Let's look closely at each of the five logistics functions.

Order Processing

Order processing includes the series of activities that occurs between the time an order comes into the organization and the time a product goes out the door. After a firm receives an order, it typically sends it electronically to an office for record keeping and then on to the warehouse to fill it. When the order reaches

logistics
The process of designing, managing, and improving the movement of products through the supply chain. Logistics includes purchasing, manufacturing, storage, and transport.

reverse logistics
Includes product returns, recycling and material reuse, and waste disposal.

order processing
The series of activities that occurs between the time an order comes into the organization and the time a product goes out the door.

Figure 11.5 *Process* | The Five Functions of Logistics

When developing logistics strategies, marketers must make decisions related to order processing, warehousing, materials handling, transportation, and inventory control.

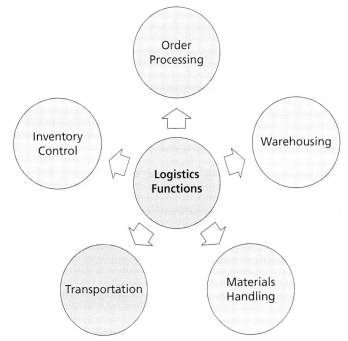

enterprise resource planning (ERP) systems
A software system that integrates information from across the entire company, including finance, order fulfillment, manufacturing, and transportation, and then facilitates sharing of the data throughout the firm.

the warehouse, personnel there check to see if the item is in stock. If it is not, they put the order on back-order status. That information goes to the office and then to the customer. If the item is available, the company locates it in the warehouse, packages it for shipment, and schedules it for pickup by either in-house or external shippers.

Fortunately, many firms automate this process with **enterprise resource planning (ERP) systems**. An ERP system is a software solution that integrates information from across the entire company, including finance, order fulfillment, manufacturing, and transportation. Data need to be entered into the system only once, and then the organization automatically shares this information and links it to other related data. For example, an ERP system ties information on product inventories to sales information so that a sales representative can immediately tell a customer whether the product is in stock.

Warehousing

warehousing
Storing goods in anticipation of sale or transfer to another member of the channel of distribution.

Whether we deal with fresh-cut flowers, canned goods, or computer chips, at some point goods (unlike services) must be stored. Storing goods allows marketers to match supply with demand. For example, gardening supplies are especially big sellers during spring and summer, but the factories that manufacture them operate 12 months of the year. **Warehousing**—storing goods in anticipation of sale or transfer to another member of the channel of distribution—enables marketers to provide *time utility* to consumers by holding onto products until consumers need them.

Part of developing effective logistics means making decisions about how many warehouses are needed and where and what type of warehouse each should be. A firm determines the location of its warehouse(s) by the location of customers and access to major highways, airports, or rail transportation. The number of warehouses often depends on the level of service that customers require. If customers generally demand fast delivery (today or tomorrow at the latest), then it may be necessary to store products in a number of different locations from which the company can quickly ship the goods to the customer. Amazon continues to invest heavily in its fulfillment centers in the U.S. and abroad to keep up with customer demand and ensure that products get to consumers as quickly as possible (increasingly, the same day as ordered).[20]

distribution center
A warehouse that stores goods for short periods of time and that provides other functions, such as breaking bulk.

Firms use private and public warehouses to store goods. Those that use private warehouses have a high initial investment, but they also lose less of their inventory as a result of damage. Public warehouses are an alternative that allows firms to pay for a portion of warehouse space rather than having to own an entire storage facility. Most countries offer public warehouses in all large cities and many smaller cities to support domestic and international trade. A **distribution center** is a warehouse that stores goods for short periods of time and that provides other functions, such as breaking bulk. Most large retailers have their own distribution centers so that their stores do not need to keep a lot of inventory in the back room.

Materials Handling

materials handling
The moving of products into, within, and out of warehouses.

Materials handling is the moving of products into, within, and out of warehouses. When goods come into the warehouse, they must be physically identified, checked for damage, sorted, and labeled. Next, they are taken to a location for storage. Finally, they are recovered from the storage area for packaging and shipment. All in all, the goods may be handled over a dozen separate times. Procedures that limit the number of times a product must be handled decrease the likelihood of damage and reduce the cost of materials handling.

Transportation

transportation
The mode by which products move among channel members.

Logistics decisions take into consideration options for **transportation**, the mode by which products move among channel members. Again, making transportation decisions entails a compromise between minimizing cost and providing the service customers want. As Table 11.3 shows, modes of transportation, including railroads, water transportation, trucks, airways, pipelines, and the Internet, differ in the following ways:

- *Dependability:* The ability of the carrier to deliver goods safely and on time
- *Cost:* The total transportation costs to move a product from one location to another, including any charges for loading, unloading, and in-transit storage
- *Speed of delivery:* The total time to move a product from one location to another, including loading and unloading

Amazon is experimenting with an Amazon Prime Air drone delivery service that has the potential to add a whole new dimension to transportation options for logistics companies.

- *Accessibility:* The number of different locations the carrier serves
- *Capability:* The ability of the carrier to handle a variety of different products, such as large or small, fragile, or bulky
- *Traceability:* The ability of the carrier to locate goods in shipment

Each mode of transportation has strengths and weaknesses that make it a good choice for different transportation needs. Table 11.3 summarizes the pros and cons of each mode:

- *Railroads:* Railroads are best to carry heavy or bulky items, such as coal and other mining products, over long distances. Railroads are about average in their cost and provide moderate speed of delivery. Although rail transportation provides dependable, low-cost service to many locations, trains cannot carry goods to every community.
- *Water:* Ships and barges carry large, bulky goods and are very important in international trade. Water transportation is relatively low in cost but can be slow.

Table 11.3 | A Comparison of Transportation Modes

Transportation Mode	Dependability	Cost	Speed of Delivery	Accessibility	Capability	Traceability	Most Suitable Products
Railroads	Average	Average	Moderate	High	High	Low	Heavy or bulky goods, such as automobiles, grain, and steel
Water	Low	Low	Slow	Low	Moderate	Low	Bulky, nonperishable goods, such as automobiles
Trucks	High	High for long distances; low for short distances	Fast	High	High	High	A wide variety of products, including those that need refrigeration
Air	High	High	Very fast	Low	Moderate	High	High-value items, such as electronic goods and fresh flowers
Pipeline	High	Low	Slow	Low	Low	Moderate	Petroleum products and other chemicals
Internet	High	Low	Very fast	Potentially very high	Low	High	Services such as banking, information, and entertainment

- *Trucks:* Trucks or motor carriers are the most important transportation mode for consumer goods, especially for shorter hauls. Motor carrier transport allows flexibility because trucks can travel to locations missed by boats, trains, and planes. Trucks also carry a wide variety of products, including perishable items. Although costs are fairly high for longer-distance shipping, trucks are economical for shorter deliveries. Because trucks provide door-to-door service, product handling is minimal, and this reduces the chance of product damage.

- *Air:* Air transportation is the fastest and also the most expensive transportation mode. It is ideal to move high-value items such as important mail, fresh-cut flowers, and live lobsters. Passenger airlines, air-freight carriers, and express delivery firms, such as FedEx, provide air transportation. Ships remain the major mover of international cargo, but air transportation networks are becoming more important as international markets continue to develop. And of course, then there are drones—definitely a Next Gen approach to air transportation that's mostly a novelty today but holds great promise for the future. Mostly, firms have their sites on drones to deliver to the "last mile" of a shipment's journey. The precision needed to get the product to its final few blocks can be very expensive, and among the firms ramping up for more drone usage are Amazon, Domino's, Walmart, UPS, and Alphabet (Google's parent).[21]

- *Pipeline:* Pipelines carry petroleum products, such as oil and natural gas and a few other chemicals. Pipelines flow primarily from oil or gas fields to refineries. They are very low in cost, require little energy, and are not subject to disruption by weather.

- *The Internet:* As we discussed previously in this chapter, marketers of services such as banking, news, and entertainment take advantage of distribution opportunities the Internet provides.

Inventory Control

inventory control
Activities to ensure that goods are always available to meet customers' demands.

Another component of logistics is **inventory control**, which means developing and implementing a process to ensure that the firm always has sufficient quantities of goods available to meet customers' demands—no more and no less. This explains why firms work so hard to track merchandise in order to know where their products are and where they are needed in case a low-inventory situation appears imminent.

inventory turnover, or inventory turns
The number of times a firm's inventory completely cycles through during a defined time frame.

One of the most used measures of inventory control is **inventory turnover**, or **inventory turns**, which is the number of times a firm's inventory completely cycles through during a defined time frame (usually in one year). Marketers can measure inventory turnover by using the value of the inventory at cost or at retail, or this metric can even be expressed in units. Just make sure that you're using the same unit of measurement in both the numerator and the denominator! One of the most common formulas is the following:

$$\text{Inventory turnover} \times \text{Annual cost of sales} \div \frac{\text{Average inventory}}{\text{level for the period}}$$

However, the formula requires waiting until the end of the year (or the end of the business's fiscal year). An alternative is using the following "snapshot" number, which takes a rolling approach so that turns can be calculated at any time by looking at cost of sales for the immediately prior 12 months and the current inventory at the end of that period:

$$\text{Inventory turnover} \times \text{Rolling 12-month cost of sales} \div \text{Current inventory}$$

Benchmarks for inventory turnover vary greatly by industry and product line. High-volume/low-margin settings, like supermarkets, may have 12 or more inventory turns per year overall, but some staple goods, like milk and bread, that are bought on every trip may have significantly higher turnover rates. All else equal, a firm can increase its profitability substantially by targeting increases in inventory turnover—selling through Product A 15 times a year instead of 12 naturally improves the bottom line (so long as Product A is profitable). However, if price reductions or promotional expense increases are needed to increase the turns, management will have to carefully calculate whether the increased volume really adds to profits (this is where marketers can get into trouble with the old saying, "We're losing money, but we'll make it up in volume!").

Some companies are even phasing in a sophisticated technology (similar to the EZ Pass system many drivers use to speed through tollbooths) known as **radio frequency identification (RFID)**. RFID lets firms tag clothes, pharmaceuticals, or virtually any kind of product with tiny chips that contain information about the item's content, origin, and destination. This technology has the potential to revolutionize inventory control and help marketers ensure that their products are on the shelves when people want to buy them. Great for manufacturers and retailers, right? But some consumer groups are creating a backlash against RFID, which they refer to as "spy chips." Through blogs, boycotts, and other anti-company initiatives, these groups proclaim that RFID is a personification of the privacy violations George Orwell predicted in his classic book *1984*.[22]

Firms store goods (i.e., they create an *inventory*) for many reasons. For manufacturers, sometimes the pace of production may not match seasonal demand, and as a result, a firm might engage in a practice known as **level loading**. This is a manufacturing approach intended to balance the inventory holding capabilities and production capacity constraints of a manufacturer for a particular product through the implementation of a consistent production schedule, employed both during and beyond periods of peak demand. For example, it may be more economical to produce snow skis year-round and pay to store them for the colder months than to produce them only during the winter season. This is a result of capacity issues related to the number of snow skis that a manufacturer can produce in a given span of time on existing production lines and with its available work force.

Similarly, for channel members that purchase goods from manufacturers or other channel intermediaries, it may be economical to order a product in quantities that don't exactly parallel demand. For example, delivery costs make it prohibitive for a retail gas station to place daily orders for just the amount of gas that people will use that day. Instead, stations usually order truckloads of gasoline, holding their inventory in underground tanks. **Stock-outs**, which are zero-inventory situations resulting in lost sales and customer dissatisfaction, may be very negative. Ever go to the store based on an ad in the newspaper, only to find the store doesn't have the product on hand? In the early days of the COVID-19 crisis, when people initially went into lockdown mode, the Nintendo Switch sold out immediately almost everywhere. Besides all the extra time people suddenly had on their hands, "Animal Crossing: New Horizons" was released right around the same time, creating a double whammy on consumer demand for the Nintendo Switch!

Inventory control has a major impact on the overall costs of a firm's logistics initiatives. If supplies of products are too low to meet fluctuations in customer demand, a firm may have to make expensive emergency deliveries or else lose customers to competitors. If inventories are above demand, unnecessary storage expenses and the possibility of damage or deterioration occur. To balance these two opposing needs, manufacturers turn to **just-in-time (JIT)** inventory techniques with their suppliers. JIT sets up delivery of goods just as they are needed on the production floor. This minimizes the cost of holding inventory while ensuring the inventory will be there when customers need it.

A supplier's ability to make on-time deliveries is the critical factor in the selection process for firms that adopt this kind of system. JIT systems reduce stock to very low levels (or even zero) and time deliveries very carefully to maintain just the right amount of inventory. The advantage of JIT systems is the reduced cost of warehousing. For both manufacturers and resellers that use JIT systems, the choice of supplier may come down to one whose location is nearest. To win a large customer, a supplier may even have to be willing to set up production facilities close to the customer to guarantee JIT delivery.[23]

radio frequency identification (RFID)
Product tags with tiny chips containing information about the item's content, origin, and destination.

level loading
A manufacturing approach intended to balance the inventory holding capabilities and production capacity constraints of a manufacturer for a particular product through the implementation of a consistent production schedule, employed both during and beyond periods of peak demand.

stock-outs
Zero-inventory situations resulting in lost sales and customer dissatisfaction.

just-in-time (JIT)
Inventory management and purchasing processes that manufacturers and resellers use to reduce inventory to very low levels and ensure that deliveries from suppliers arrive only when needed.

A penultimate outcome of great logistics that we can all easily relate to is the trend toward online ordering and in-store pickup, which again was exacerbated by the early lockdown days during the COVID-19 crisis. Best Buy is a great example, as the firm has turned a former lemon into lemonade through its outstanding execution of this capability. In the past, Best Buy suffered mightily from customers "just browsing" in their stores who would then go home after experiencing a product and purchase it for a lower price somewhere else online. But now Best Buy has turned the tables on competitors by creating several quick and convenient options under its Fast Store Pickup program. Today's customers "want it now," and logistics is a key tool to successfully fulfill that want and gain competitive advantage.[24]

Place: Pulling It All Together through the Supply Chain

supply chain
All the activities necessary to turn raw materials into a good or service and put it in the hands of the consumer or business customer.

A **supply chain** includes all the activities necessary to turn raw materials into a good or service and put it into the hands of the consumer or business customer. Sam's Club and its sister company, Walmart, are iconic when it comes to global supply chain effectiveness. To both reduce overall excess inventory and more effectively meet the needs of consumers who increasingly shop both in the company's physical locations and on its website, Walmart has put a strategy in place that enables greater agility within the company's supply chain. Specifically, the retail giant has reduced its total inventory, increased the variety of products sold, and shifted more of its inventory from its physical stores to its distribution centers. They have even implemented **cross-docking** with many of their suppliers where products are transferred off the supplier's truck directly onto a Walmart truck bound for a store with no warehousing at all. With an increasing number of consumers shopping online, these significant operational changes allow Walmart to serve those customers more nimbly. The company can avoid the big increase in overall inventory costs it would incur if it had to maintain separate approaches to inventory management for online versus in-store shoppers.

cross-docking
A supply chain efficiency technique in which products are transferred off a supplier's truck directly onto a buyer's truck bound for the next distribution point, such as a retail store.

In addition, distribution centers are much more efficient at getting products to stores when an expected increase in demand is observed at one location versus implementing an inventory transfer between stores—incredibly, every Walmart store is within 130 miles of a distribution facility. Yet another added benefit of this change is that it frees up in-store employees to focus more on other value-added activities (such as assisting customers) because less time is required to manage inventory in the stock room. All of that said, a reduction of inventory in each store potentially means that some customers will not be able to get a specific product exactly when they wanted it due to increased stock-outs.[25]

Amazon and Walmart clearly understand the potential for supply chain practices to enhance organizational performance and profits, and scores of other firms across most every industry with physical products benchmark against them for best practices. The truth is that distribution may be the "final frontier" for marketing success. To understand why, consider these facts about the other three Ps of marketing. After years of hype, many consumers no longer believe that "new and improved" products really *are* new and improved. Nearly everyone, even upscale manufacturers and retailers, tries to gain market share through aggressive pricing strategies. Advertising and many other forms of promotion are so commonplace today that they have lost some of their impact. Even hot new social media strategies can't sell overpriced or poorly made products, at least not for long. Marketers have come to understand that *place* (the "distribution P") may be the only one of the four Ps to offer an opportunity for really long-term competitive advantage—especially because many consumers now expect "instant gratification" by getting just what they want instantaneously when the urge strikes.

Fast-fashion retailers rely upon very efficient distribution channels to constantly replenish their inventories at a rate that is much faster than traditional stores can match.

That's why savvy marketers are always on the lookout for novel ways to distribute their products. A large part of the marketer's ability to deliver a value proposition rests on the ability to understand and develop effective supply chain strategies. Often, of course, firms may decide to bring in outside companies to accomplish these activities—this is *outsourcing*, which as we learned about in Chapter 6 occurs when firms obtain outside vendors to provide goods or services that might otherwise be supplied in-house. In the case of supply chain functions, outsource firms are most likely organizations with whom the company has developed some form of partnership or cooperative business arrangement.

Supply chain management is the coordination of flows among the firms in a supply chain to maximize total profitability. These "flows" include not only the physical movement of goods but also the sharing of information about the goods—that is, supply chain partners must synchronize their activities with one another. For example, they need to communicate information about which goods they want to purchase (the procurement function), about which marketing campaigns they plan to execute (so that the supply chain partners can ensure there will be enough product to supply the increased demand that results from the promotion), and about logistics (such as sending advance shipping notices to alert their partners that products are on their way). Through these information flows, a company can effectively manage all the links in its supply chain, from sourcing to retailing.

supply chain management
The management of flows among firms in the supply chain to maximize total profitability.

In his classic book *The World Is Flat: A Brief History of the Twenty-First Century*, author Thomas Friedman addresses a number of high-impact trends in global supply chain management.[26] One such development is the trend whereby companies we traditionally know for other things remake themselves as specialists who take over the coordination of clients' supply chains for them. UPS is a great example of this trend. UPS, which used to be "just" a package delivery service, today is much more because it also specializes in **insourcing**. This process occurs when companies contract with a specialist who services their supply chains. Unlike the *outsourcing process* where a company delegates nonessential tasks to subcontractors, insourcing means that the client company brings in an external company to run its essential operations. Although we tend to associate UPS with those little brown trucks that zip around town delivering boxes, the company actually positions itself in the B2B space as a broad-based supply chain consultancy!

insourcing
A practice in which a company contracts with a specialist firm to handle all or part of its supply chain operations.

Finally, in case you're wondering about the difference between a supply chain and a channel of distribution, the major distinguishing feature is the number of members and their functions. A supply chain is broader, consisting of those firms that supply the raw materials, component parts, and supplies necessary for a firm to produce a good or service *plus* the firms that facilitate the movement of that product to the ultimate users of the product. This last part—the firms that get the product to the ultimate users—is the channel of distribution.

Disruption in Logistics and Supply Chain

As a marketing student today, you are poised to experience the impact of several major trends, some disruptive to markets, that will change the face of the field. In fact, in marketing planning and strategy, staying cutting-edge in these areas often yields very high potential for competitive advantages as many firms fail to invest in state-of-the-art logistics and supply chain capabilities.

Technology will drive its share of these opportunities. For example, while the full potential of integrating drones into the distribution mix hasn't yet been realized, it won't be long before it is commonplace to get a pizza air-dropped to your front porch—and this is just the tip of the iceberg. *Artificial intelligence (AI)*, introduced in Chapter 1 and discussed further in Chapter 5, is a key enabling capability behind autonomous, or "driverless," vehicles. Think of how much of the transportation of products in the future can be shifted to autonomous means and what a cost savings this will be for both firms and consumers. Imagine, for example, a whole fleet of Walmart trucks without drivers![27]

Amazon continues to lead the charge toward many of the disruptive changes in logistics and supply chain. In Chapter 5 we defined *anticipatory shipping* as a system of delivering products to customers before they place an order, utilizing predictive analytics to determine what customers want and then shipping the products automatically. For Amazon, their anticipatory shipping algorithm for orders literally gives them the capability to make highly accurate supply and shipping decisions even before a customer's next purchase decisions are fully finalized. At the core, the concept is intended to reduce the time from order to receipt of goods, which creates a win-win outcome for supplier and customer (assuming a high level of accuracy in the algorithm's estimates, of course). This system is so valuable to Amazon's future that they applied for and received a patent on the process, which is officially described by the patent office as "a method for shipping a package of one or more items to the destination geographical area without completely specifying the delivery address at the time of shipment, with the final destination defined en route." Wow—talk about getting ahead of the game! And just because Amazon's approach is patented doesn't mean that other retailers aren't working on perfecting their own versions of the same concept.[28]

In Chapter 1, you were introduced to the concept of the sharing economy in which non-ownership forms of consumption have grown increasingly popular as more consumers continue to turn toward the renting, sharing, lending, and bartering of products and services. This trend has several obvious implications for the future of not only logistics and supply chain but also, more broadly, channels and physical distribution in general. For example, TaskRabbit and other similar crowdsourcing websites enable direct peer-to-peer collaborations for time and skill sharing and contribute to a decreased demand for access to products and services from the traditional corporate marketplace—both business-to-business (B2B) and business-to-consumer (B2C) markets. The key question becomes, how should the elements of supply chain and related aspects be optimally set up and executed in a customer-to-customer (C2C) marketplace instead of those familiar B2C or B2B market scenarios? That is, the trend toward a sharing economy clearly impacts consumer behavior and marketing communication, but don't underestimate its potential impact on market planning and strategy development on how goods and services are distributed as well.

In the end, these examples reinforce the fact that you are very fortunate to be studying marketing at a time of exciting possibilities as well as disruptive changes, both of which create many opportunities for savvy marketers. We believe that logistics and supply chain innovation and optimization represents a huge opportunity for firms to improve their performance with customers, reduce costs, and thus improve their overall competitiveness in the marketplace.

11.4 Brand You: Delivering Your Value Proposition

OBJECTIVE

Understand how to prepare for an interview to maximize your chances of getting the job.

Taylor has done a great job of planning his personal brand. He has used his strengths and weaknesses to develop his core product and understands his potential value in terms of salary and other compensation to potential employers.

Now it is time to think about how he will deliver his value proposition—he needs to begin getting prepared for interviews and his evaluation of job offers.

When we talk about delivering your value proposition, we are talking about making every job interview successful. To do this you will need to:

- Research a company prior to the interview
- Plan for questions you may need to ask and to answer
- Learn how to dress for the interview

Think of the interview like a sales call—an opportunity to sell yourself and build long-term relationships. A salesperson finds out as much as possible about a client and prepares her presentation, focusing on the product benefits that will appeal to each customer. In other words, the salesperson has all the information needed before calling on the client to maximize her chances of making the sale. In the same way, you need to gather as much information about the company and the specific position to maximize your chances of getting the offer.

Step 1: Study the Company

Employers *expect* candidates to research the company and be prepared during an interview. In fact, if you have not researched the company, it will likely be a major strike against you and may immediately take you off the list of possible job candidates.

First, be sure you have a complete job description. Often job postings give only the highlights of positions. It's okay to contact the company's human resources (HR) department and ask for more information before your interview.

Today it's easy to get information about a company online. Study (yes, we mean read and make notes just as you do for exams in your classes) company websites. Be sure you look at all the website pages, especially the "About Us" sections. Look for information about the company, its products, its customers, its various locations, and its top management. Try to find clues about the type of people who work there and the company culture.

You may be able to access additional resources, such as Dun and Bradstreet's Hoovers (www.hoovers.com), through your campus library. Hoovers provides information on more than 85 million companies, including number of employees, locations, how long the company has been in business, any recent mergers or acquisitions, new products and services, global expansion, and lots more.

As your mother may have told you, "Don't put all your eggs in one basket." In the job search, that translates to "Don't look at just one job at a time." Instead, plan a campaign where you will be looking at multiple potential employers all at the same time. Even when you are preparing to interview for one possible job, send out résumés to other companies while at the same time maintaining contact with your network.

Step 2: Prepare Good Questions and Good Answers

In an interview, it is inevitable that you will be asked if you have any questions. Be prepared to ask "good" questions. **Do not** ask about salary and benefits. Instead, show your interest in the job by preparing great questions about the company and the position.

A word of caution: Never take a phone interview on the fly. If you agree to the interview, you may sabotage your chances of getting the job. If you are called, it is acceptable to say you are busy.

Some questions to ask might be:

- What is one word or a few words you would use to describe the company culture?
- What do you think the company will look like in three years?
- What would the ideal person for this position be like?
- What is the single most important skill the person in this position must possess?
- What are some challenges facing the department in the next 90 days? What role will the person in this position play in tackling those challenges?
- What are the next steps in the hiring process?

After the interviewer responds to your questions, you might want to follow up by restating your strengths. For example, suppose the interviewer tells you the ideal person would be committed to achieving goals and learning new skills. Follow up by telling about a specific time when you achieved a goal or discuss how much you've enjoyed learning as a college student.

In the same way, prepare answers for possible questions. Some questions you should be prepared to answer:

- Tell me about yourself.
- What are your biggest weaknesses/strengths?
- Why should we hire you?
- How do you think other people would describe you?
- What do you know about the company?
- Why do you want this job?
- What was your favorite class in college?
- Tell me about a time when you worked on a team.

You may even be asked an unexpected question, just to see how you respond to surprises:

- If you were an animal, which one would you want to be?

And remember, the three most important things in preparing for an interview are **practice**, **practice**, **practice**. At many schools, the career services department offers workshops where students can practice interviewing skills.

Step 3: Close the Interview

Just like a salesperson must ask for the order to get it, you need to ask for the job to get the offer. You can let the interviewer know you want the job by saying something like: "After the research I did before coming in, I was interested in working for your company. Now that I have a better understanding of the job and the advantages of working for your company, I'm even more excited about it. I would really like the opportunity to contribute to your success."

Step 4: Follow Up

This is an absolute must: Write a handwritten thank-you note (preferably not an email) within 24 hours. An alternative is to send an email and then follow up with a handwritten note, thus keeping you on top in the memory of your interviewers. This may sound "old school" but it can be *very* effective to differentiate yourself from your competitors!

In the email and note, you should:

- Thank the interviewer for his or her time and information
- Refer to something specific in the interview—a mutual contact, some connection with the interviewer, or a topic you discussed
- Briefly describe the key reasons you feel you are a good match for the position
- Reiterate your interest in the job
- Be sincere

Call in a week if you haven't heard from the employer to inquire about the status of his or her decision. This signals again your interest in the position. It's OK to check once a week or so.

How to Dress and What to Bring

Your decision on how to dress should be easy: simply *dress professionally*—no matter what the profession. It is always OK to dress professionally and conservatively, even if you are told to dress business casual. First impressions are incredibly important to the success of job hunting!

A portfolio showcases your skills with samples of your work. Bring samples of class projects, internship or volunteer projects, or other activities that demonstrate your skills. If the projects are team projects, attach a description of your personal team participation and what portions of the project you personally prepared. Even if not required, a portfolio can be a powerful tool that places you ahead of other job candidates.

Bring extra copies of your résumé printed on résumé paper in a folder or portfolio. This is important as the interviewer might not be able to locate your résumé at the exact time you are meeting or you may be asked to meet with additional interviewers who do not have a copy.

Taylor has worked hard to prepare the delivery of his value proposition in a job interview. He has made a list of questions to ask and to answer and practiced interviewing with his school's career services counsellors. He has put together a portfolio that will show employers the quality of work from his courses. And his parents have invested in a great new suit.

Objective **Summaries** and **Key Terms**

11.1 Objective Summary

Explain what a distribution channel is, identify types of wholesaling intermediaries, and describe the different types of distribution channels.

A channel of distribution is a series of firms or individuals that facilitates the movement of a product from the producer to the final customer. Channels provide place, time, and possession utility for customers and reduce the number of transactions necessary for goods to flow from many manufacturers to large numbers of customers by breaking bulk and creating assortments. Channel members make the purchasing process easier by providing important customer services.

Wholesaling intermediaries are firms that handle the flow of products from the manufacturer to the retailer or business user. Merchant wholesalers are independent intermediaries that take title to a product and include both full-service merchant wholesalers and limited-service merchant wholesalers. Merchandise agents and brokers are independent intermediaries that do not take title to products. Manufacturer-owned channel members include sales branches, sales offices, and manufacturers' showrooms.

Distribution channels vary in length from the simplest two-level channel to longer channels with three or more channel levels. Distribution channels include direct distribution, in which the producer sells directly to consumers, and to indirect channels, which may include a retailer, wholesaler, or other intermediary. B2B distribution channels facilitate the flow of goods from a producer to an organizational or business customer. Producers, dealers, wholesalers, retailers, and customers may participate in more than one type of channel, called a *dual* or *multiple distribution system*. Finally, some companies combine channels—direct sales, distributors, retail sales, and direct mail—to create a hybrid marketing system.

Key Terms

physical distribution
direct channel

indirect channel
channel intermediaries
breaking bulk
create assortments
transportation and storage
facilitating functions
risk-taking functions
communication and transaction functions
disintermediation
knowledge management
online distribution piracy
copyright infringement
wholesaling intermediaries
independent intermediaries
merchant wholesalers
take title
full-service merchant wholesalers
limited-service merchant wholesalers
merchandise agents and brokers
channel levels
dual or multiple distribution systems
hybrid marketing system
subscription boxes
slotting allowance
product diversion
diverter

11.2 Objective Summary

List and explain the steps to plan a distribution channel strategy.

Firms that operate within a channel of distribution—manufacturers, wholesalers, and retailers—do distribution planning, which is a process of developing distribution objectives, evaluating internal and external environmental influences on distribution, and choosing a distribution strategy. Marketers begin channel planning by developing distribution channel objectives and considering important internal and external environmental factors. The next step is to decide on a distribution strategy, which involves determining the type of distribution channel that is best. Finally, distribution tactics include the selection of individual channel members and management of the channel.

Key Terms

distribution planning
distribution intensity
conventional marketing system
vertical marketing system (VMS)
administered VMS
corporate VMS
contractual VMS
retailer cooperative
franchise organizations
horizontal marketing system
intensive distribution
exclusive distribution
gray market
selective distribution
channel leader, or channel captain
channel power
channel cooperation
channel conflict

11.3 Objective Summary

Discuss the concepts of logistics and supply chain.

Logistics is the process of designing, managing, and improving supply chains, including all the activities that are required to move products through the supply chain. Logistics contributes to the overall supply chain through activities including order processing, warehousing, materials handling, transportation, and inventory control.

A supply chain includes all the activities necessary to turn raw materials into a good or service and put it into the hands of the consumer or business customer. Supply chain management is the coordination of flows among the firms in a supply chain to maximize total profitability.

Key Terms

logistics
reverse logistics

order processing
enterprise resource planning (ERP) systems
warehousing
distribution center
materials handling
transportation
inventory control
inventory turnover, or inventory turns
radio frequency identification (RFID)
level loading
stock-outs
just-in-time (JIT)
supply chain
cross-docking
supply chain management
insourcing

11.4 Objective Summary

Understand how to prepare for an interview to maximize your chances of getting the job.

In the Brand You context, delivering your value proposition is about making every job interview successful. To do this, you will need to:

1. Research a company prior to the interview. Be sure you have a complete job description and use the company's website and other sources to gather more information about the firm and its culture.

2. Plan for questions you may need to ask and to answer. Be prepared to ask good questions about the company and the position but not about salary. Questions that you should be prepared to answer are likely to be about you, your strengths and weaknesses, why you want the job, and why the company should hire you. Always practice your questions and answers. You will want to close the interview by letting the interviewer know you want the job and following up with both an email and a handwritten note.

3. Learn how to dress for the interview. Dress professionally and conservatively. Women should wear a dress or suit and closed-toe, low-heel shoes, and men should wear a coordinated suit, shirt, and tie with clean and polished oxford shoes. You may wish to bring a portfolio of your work and extra copies of your résumé printed on résumé paper.

Chapter **Questions** and **Activities**

Concepts: Test Your Knowledge

11-1. What is a channel of distribution? What are channel intermediaries? What are direct and indirect channel intermediaries?

11-2. Explain the functions of distribution channels.

11-3. Explain the disintermediation of channels of distribution. What is online distribution piracy?

11-4. List and explain the types of independent and manufacturer-owned wholesaling intermediaries.

11-5. What factors are important in determining whether a manufacturer should choose a direct or indirect channel? Why do some firms use hybrid marketing systems?

11-6. What are conventional, vertical, and horizontal marketing systems?

11-7. Explain intensive, exclusive, and selective forms of distribution.

11-8. Explain the four steps in distribution planning. What are the decisions that must be made in developing distribution tactics? What is a channel leader, or channel captain? Explain channel power and channel conflict.

11-9. What is logistics? Explain the five functions of logistics. What is reverse logistics?

11-10. How do warehousing decisions impact delivery time to consumers? What is a distribution center and what functions does it serve? What does Amazon call its distribution centers?

11-11. What is inventory control, and why is it important? How is RFID technology revolutionizing inventory management?

11-12. What is a supply chain, and how is it different from a channel of distribution?

Activities: Apply What You've Learned

11-13. *For Further Research (Individual)* Find an example of disintermediation that has been employed by a particular firm. Research the specific impact of the disintermediation on the organization's operations and its customers' experience with the firm. Evaluate both the pros and the cons of the related example of disintermediation.

11-14. *In Class, 10–25 Minutes for Teams* As the one-person marketing department for a candy manufacturer (your firm makes high-quality, hand-dipped chocolates using only natural ingredients), you are considering making changes in your distribution strategy. Your products have previously been sold through a network of food brokers who call on specialty food and gift stores. But you think that perhaps it would be good for your firm to develop a corporate vertical marketing system (i.e., vertical integration). In such a plan, a number of company-owned retail outlets would be opened across the country. The president of your company has asked that you present your ideas to the company executives. In a role-playing situation with one of your classmates, present your ideas to your boss, including the advantages and disadvantages of the new plan compared with the current distribution method.

11-15. *For Further Research (Individual)* Do a little research and find an example of a company that started out selling its product exclusively online direct to consumers but has now expanded to B2B channels as well.

  a. Why did the business opt to move into the B2B distribution model in addition to online?

  b. Has the move been successful for them? Why or why not?

  Are there opportunities for the firm to expand distribution even further in the future? Provide some ideas.

11-16. *For Further Research (Individual)* Visit the website for FedEx (www.fedex.com). FedEx has positioned itself as a full-service provider of logistics solutions. After reviewing its website, answer the following questions:

  a. What logistics services does FedEx offer its customers?

  b. Who are FedEx's major competitors? What services do they offer?

  c. What does FedEx say to convince prospective customers that its services are better than those of the competition?

11-17. *In Class, 10–25 Minutes for Teams* You are the VP of marketing for a new company that has created a robot lawn mower. Similar to the iRobot Roomba Robot Vacuum, it can mow the lawn using automation and sensors to make it easy to take care of the yardwork without breaking a sweat. Your management team is working to determine a distribution strategy. You have been asked to write up a summary of the benefits and drawbacks for each of the three options for distribution: intensive, exclusive, and selective. Work with your team to comprehensively review each option.

11-18. *Creative Homework/Short Project* Your friend is studying for an upcoming marketing test but doesn't quite understand logistics. Write up a summary of the various logistics functions and devise a short multiple-choice quiz that will help him test his comprehension of the subject.

Concepts: Apply Marketing Metrics

Companies track a wide range of metrics within the supply chain area. Some of the most common ones are the following:
- On-time delivery
- Accuracy of forecasted inventory needs
- Returns processing cost as a percentage of product revenue
- Customer order actual cycle time
- Perfect order measurement

Let's take a look at the last measure in more detail. The perfect order measurement calculates the error-free rate of each stage of fulfilling a purchase order.[29] This measure helps managers track the multiple steps involved in getting a product from a manufacturer to a customer so that opportunities for process improvement can be pinpointed. For example, a company can calculate its error-free rate at each stage and then combine these rates to create an overall metric of order quality. Suppose the company identifies the following error rates:
- Order entry accuracy: 99.95 percent correct (interpret this as 0.5 errors per 1,000 order lines)
- Warehouse pick accuracy: 99.2 percent (8 errors per 1,000 items picked by warehouse staff)
- Delivered on time: 96 percent (40 errors per 1,000 deliveries)
- Shipped without damage: 99 percent (10 damaged items per 1,000 deliveries)
- Invoiced correctly: 99.8 percent (2 errors per 1,000 invoices)

To calculate the perfect order measurement, all the company has to do is combine these individual rates into an overall metric by multiplying them together.

11-19. Calculate the perfect order measurement for the above purchase order process. Interpret your result.

11-20. Do you think the firm should be satisfied with this level of performance? Why or why not? What particular areas need attention, in priority order? How do you suggest motivating employees toward reducing these errors?

11-21. Is a zero error rate realistic? How close should a firm be expected to come to zero errors?

11-22. Given this particular example, what are some things the manufacturer might work on to bring the overall perfect order measurement higher? What would be the key advantages to the firm in making an investment in this improvement?

Choices: What Do You Think?

11-23. *Critical Thinking* Many entrepreneurs choose to start a franchise business rather than "go it alone." Do some research on franchise opportunities. Find an example in both the restaurant and the service industry to review. Do you think these franchise opportunities offer good opportunities to make money? What are the positive and negative aspects of purchasing each of the franchises you have researched? Assuming you were an entrepreneur, would you elect to invest in one, both, or neither of them? Why do you feel this way?

11-24. *Critical Thinking* Would you purchase a durable product (such as a watch) online at a significantly lower price than the MSRP (manufacturer's suggested retail price) if you knew that the retailer was not officially authorized by the product's manufacturer to sell it? Putting ethical concerns aside for a moment, what risks would most concern you about making such a purchase and what steps could the related retailer take to lessen those risks?

11-25. *Critical Thinking* Can a company's reverse logistics system have a significant influence on how a consumer views the organization and its brand? Are there specific types of products for which a company's reverse logistics system could play a more important role in contributing to a customer's view of the organization? For those companies, what characteristics would you expect their reverse logistics systems to have in order to create high added value for a customer?

11-26. *Critical Thinking* Many companies are using technology to cut out the middleman and sell more directly to the consumer—think about music or video downloads, e-books, software, etc. How do you think technology will continue to revolutionize the distribution channel in the future? What are some ways technology is revolutionizing logistics? What other industries might benefit from a more direct-to-consumer model using technology?

11-27. *Critical Thinking* The supply chain concept looks at both the inputs of a firm and the firms that facilitate the movement of the product from the manufacturer to the consumer. Do you think *marketers* should have input into their firm's total supply chain decisions? Why or why not?

11-28. *Ethics* Many large retail chains ask manufacturers to pay a slotting allowance in order for new products to be stocked in their stores. Do you think this process is ethical? Why or why not? How do you believe it might impact smaller manufacturers? What role should government have in regulating such practices?

Miniproject: Learn by Doing

In the U.S., the distribution of most products is fairly easy. There are many independent intermediaries (wholesalers, dealers, distributors, and retailers) that are willing to cooperate to get the product to the final customer. Our elaborate interstate highway system combines with rail, air, and water transportation to provide excellent means for moving goods from one part of the country to another. In many other countries, the means for distribution of products are far less efficient and effective.

For this miniproject, you should first select a consumer product, probably one you normally purchase. Then, use the Internet and other people (e.g., retailers, manufacturers, dealers, and classmates), to gather information to do the following:

a. Describe the path the product takes to get from the producer to you. Draw a model to show each of the steps the product takes. Include as much as you can about transportation, warehousing, materials handling, order processing, inventory control, and so on.

b. Select another country, preferably one that is substantially different from your own country, in which the same or a similar product is sold. Describe the path the product takes to get from the producer to the customer in that country.

c. Determine if the differences between the two countries cause differences in price, availability, or quality of the product.

11-29. Prepare and present a summary of your findings.

Marketing in Action **Case**   Real Choices at Rent the Runway

The big event is only four days away and you just found out that the dress you ordered two months ago will not be arriving until *after* the party. Not so happy? Neither were the hundreds of customers of Rent the Runway when they discovered the garment they were expecting would be arriving late. This was the supply chain fiasco the leader in fashion clothing rental experienced in October of 2019.

Jenn Hyman got the idea for Rent the Runway (RTR) when she was home for a Thanksgiving holiday from her MBA studies at Harvard Business School. Her sister was struggling with a decision about buying an expensive dress for an upcoming event, complaining about the lack of outfits she had available, even though she had a closet full of clothes. Jenn realized that women like her sister were more concerned with the experience of wearing an amazing dress than with owning it. She thought that a rent-by-mail model was a potential solution, and, with classmate Jennifer Fleiss, she began to purchase designer pieces and then rented them to Harvard undergraduate students. After that test marketing effort—and after getting input from more than 50 of their Harvard professors—the two formed Rent the Runway in 2009.

Two big trends helped to propel Rent the Runway's success. The sharing economy (discussed in this chapter) is affecting the way consumers get access to many categories of products, allowing them to use or *experience* the product without having to purchase it. This is especially popular with millennials, either due to financial limitations or a lifestyle goal of "living in the present." The other trend is the "casualization of the workplace" that has caused some women to feel the need to differentiate the outfits they wear to work from day to day. That may seem counterintuitive, as casual clothes would seem to be less expensive than more formal business fashions. But with casualization, women are "layering," purchasing more blouses, pants, jackets and accessories to build out their wardrobes. Since the early 2000s when this more relaxed dress code began to appear, women have been spending on average four percent more of their paychecks on clothing for work.

Rent the Runway meets these needs through a novel approach to stocking your closet. The company started with (and still offers) one-time rentals for special events, but now it earns over 70 percent of its revenue through a monthly subscription service. Customers can select from over 15,000 styles offered by 600 brands. For a monthly fee of $89, $135, or $159, members can rent four items at a time and swap them out over the course of the month either once, twice or an unlimited number of times (for the higher monthly rate). When you are ready to swap, simply send the item back via FedEx or leave it at a convenient drop-off box—no dry cleaning required. It's a fashionista's dream come true.

Managing all these shipments for so many customers—at last count, over six million—is a complex process. Large online retailers like Amazon have a similar challenge, but unlike Amazon, virtually 100 percent of the shipments Rent the Runway sends to customers are also returned, which requires proficiency in *reverse logistics*, the set of processes concerned with product returns, recycling and material reuse, and waste disposal. Add to that the need to clean and, in some cases, repair the products. The final challenge is high customer sensitivity to on-time delivery. With all these challenges, this dream arrangement for fashion customers can easily become a supply chain nightmare.

That nightmare scenario occurred in October 2019 when Rent the Runway's systems were not able to keep up with customer orders. The company's back-end technology systems crashed, leaving order fulfillment workers idle. A new inventory management software system designed to better sort and rack clothes malfunctioned at the company's New Jersey distribution center, affecting six percent of Rent the Runway's special event customers and 14 percent of customers in its subscription programs. Services were put on hold for 11 days

(a lifetime in e-commerce) with orders frozen and those requesting new memberships put on a waiting list. Customers who were counting on receiving a dress in time for an event were understandably angry. They expressed their ire on the phone with the company's customer service team (when the line was finally answered) and more publicly with hundreds of complaints on social media.

To make amends, Rent the Runway provided impacted customers a full refund plus $200 in cash. Founder and CEO Hyman also communicated frequently with customers through heartfelt email messages of apology and a commitment to do better. "You rely on us for meaningful events in your life and to get dressed everyday," the email read. "We realize we have let some of you down, and we need to fix it." She explained the reasons for the delays and attempted to paint a picture of better days to come. While the software that ran the warehouse was the cause of the shutdown, Hyman said that it would ultimately be the key to reducing turnaround times.

Rent the Runway appears to have survived its supply chain failure; during the 11-day shutdown, 1,000 new subscription customers asked to be added to the waitlist. The company has since been valued at 1 billion dollars. Hyman noted, "Interestingly, this warehouse delay that we had I think fostered even greater loyalty in most of our customers, at least that's what we've seen in the last few months." The company is continuing to expand, adding athleisure and ski apparel. RTR has also expanded into children's clothing and items like pillows and throws. It is also supporting travelers through a partnership with W Hotels that allows wardrobe selections to be waiting in a guest's room when she arrives at the hotel.

In a business largely based on trust and word-of-mouth promotion, customer confidence in the quality of the clothing and timely delivery is critical. At this point in its history, it appears that most of Rent the Runway's customers are willing to give the company another chance so that they as customers can continue to enjoy all the benefits its innovative service offers. According to one customer who experienced customer service problems, "I thought about canceling, but oh, it's so addictive."[30]

Questions for Discussion

11-30. Rent the Runway has built its business primarily on the needs of female fashion consumers. Should the company expand its business to include men's clothing? How might delivery/return expectations of male customers differ from those of female customers? What logistics strategies could Rent the Runway use to respond to those differences?

11-31. The sharing economy includes services in many categories that previously required the purchase of physical products. What non-consumable product have you purchased that could be a candidate for a rental approach like that used by Rent the Runway?

11-32. Review the five logistics functions illustrated in Figure 11.5. How should Rent the Runway prioritize these functions for further operational improvement and investment? Explain your assignment of the relative importance of these logistics capabilities.

Chapter **Notes**

1. Tom Barnes, "These Are 9 Artists the Music Industry Will Never Own," *Mic*, May 20, 2015, https://mic.com/articles/118796/these-are-9-artists-that-the-music-industry-will-never-own#.LlG3BpKcz (accessed May 16, 2018).

2. Andrew Unterberger, "8 Artists You Still Can't Find on Any Major Streaming Service," *Billboard*, January 19, 2018, https://www.billboard.com/articles/news/7549739/artists-streaming-services-holdout-not-available (accessed May 16, 2018).

3. Zoe Bernard, "People Are Using the Messaging App Telegram to Share Pirated Movies and Stolen Netflix and Spotify Accounts," *Business Insider*, April 13, 2018, http://www.businessinsider.com/telegram-app-has-become-haven-for-pirated-movies-stolen-netflix-spotify-accounts-report-2018-4 (accessed May 9, 2018).

4. Pamela N. Danziger, "Nike's New Consumer Experience Distribution Strategy Hits the Ground Running," *Forbes*, December 1, 2018, https://www.forbes.com/sites/pamdanziger/2018/12/01/nikes-new-consumer-experience-distribution-strategy-hits-the-ground-running/#2f31adb4f1d0 (accessed July 16, 2020).

5. TaskRabbit, https://www.taskrabbit.com/ (accessed May 16, 2018).

6. "These 11 Online Retailers Opening Brick and Mortar Stores Prove Shopping Trips Aren't Dead," March 2018, http://www.chipchick.com/2018/03/ctk-online-retailers-opening-brick-and-mortar.html/8 (accessed May 9, 2018).

7. Rowland T. Moriarty and Ursula Moran, "Managing Hybrid Marketing Systems," *Harvard Business Review*, November–December 1990, 2–11.

8. Shop Xerox, https://www.shop.xerox.com/ (accessed May 10, 2018).

9. Ultradent Products Inc., "The Opalescence® Story," https://www.ultradent.com/en-us/Dental-Products-Supplies/Tooth-Whitening/Pages/Opalescence-Story.aspx?s_cid=2279 (accessed May 9, 2018).

10. Tony Chen, Ken Fenyo, Sylvia Yang, and Jessica Zhang, "Thinking Inside the Subscription Box: New Research on E-Commerce Consumers," *McKinsey & Company*, February 9, 2018, https://www.mckinsey.com/industries/technology-media-and-telecommunications/our-insights/thinking-inside-the-subscription-box-new-research-on-ecommerce-consumers (accessed July 17, 2020).

11. Geri Beth, "Product Diversions: Why You Should Think Twice," *Get Dolled Up*, March 2, 2016, www.getdolledupmke.com/productdiversion-why-you-should-think-twice/ (accessed May 16, 2018).

12. Jonathan O'Connell, "Wal-Mart Invites Local Businesses to Join it on Georgia Avenue," April 30, 2013, https://www.washingtonpost.com/blogs/capital-business/post/wal-mart-invites-local-business-tojoin-it-on-georgia-avenue/2013/04/30/bc9a60fe-b1ae-11e2-9a98-4be1688d7d84_blog.html (accessed April 25, 2016).

13. Oneworld, "Member Airlines," https://www.oneworld.com/members (accessed April 25, 2016).

14. Sophie Doran, "In Conversation with Thierry Stern, President, Patek Philippe," April 22, 2014, https://luxurysociety.com/articles/2014/04/in-conversation-with-thierry-stern-president-patek-philippe (accessed April 25, 2016); PatekPhilippe, "Authorized Retailers," http://www.patek.com/en/retail-network/authorizedretailers (accessed April 25, 2016).

15. Mara Leighton, "Amazon Sold a Mind-Blowing 300,000 Instant Pots during Prime Day – Here's Why We're Not Surprised," *Business Insider*, July 18, 2018, https://www.businessinsider.com/instant-pot-amazon-prime-day-sales-numbers-2018-7 (accessed July 17, 2020).

16. Gene Marks, "Small Businesses Should Be Thankful for Amazon.com," *Entrepreneur*, December 21, 2017, https://www.entrepreneur.com/article/306378 (accessed May 10, 2018).

17. Coca-Cola, "Stepping Up With STEP: Coke's Supplier Training & Empowerment Program Helps Women-Owned Suppliers Compete and Grow," June 23, 2017, https://www.coca-colacompany.com/stories/stepping-up-with-step (accessed May 10, 2018).

18. David Streitfeld, "Amazon and Hachette Resolve Dispute," *New York Times*, November 13, 2014, https://www.nytimes.com/2014/11/14/technology/amazon-hachette-ebook-dispute.html (accessed April 25, 2016).

19. Toby B. Gooley, "The Who, What, and Where of Reverse Logistics," *Logistics Management* 42 (February 2003): 38–44; James R. Stock, *Development and Implementation of Reverse Logistics Programs* (Oak Brook, IL: Council of Logistics Management, 1998), 20.

20. Aditya Raghunath, "Amazon Set to Open 100,000 Roles in Its Fulfillment and Delivery Network," *The Motley Fool*, March 17, 2020, https://www.fool.com/investing/2020/03/17/amazon-set-to-open-100000-new-roles-in-its-fulfilm.aspx (accessed July 17, 2020).

21. "Why Amazon, UPS, and Even Domino's Is Investing in Drone Delivery Services," *Business Insider Intelligence*, February 12, 2020, https://www.businessinsider.com/drone-delivery-services (accessed July 17, 2020).

22. "Spychipped Levi's Brand Jeans Hit the U.S.," April 27, 2006, www.spychips.com/press-releases/levis-secret-testing.html (accessed April 25, 2016); Katherine Albrecht and Liz McIntyre, *Spychips: How Major Corporations and Government Plan to Track Your Every Purchase and Watch Your Every Move* (New York: Plume, 2006).

23. Faye W. Gilbert, Joyce A. Young, and Charles R. O'Neal, "Buyer-Seller Relationships in Just-in-Time Purchasing Environments," *Journal of Organizational Research* 29 (February 1994): 111–20.

24. Best Buy Fast Store Pickup, https://www.bestbuy.com/site/customerservice/fast-store-pickup/pcmcat218900050012.c?id=pcmcat218900050012 (accessed May 16, 2018).

25. "Walmart: Leading the Way with a Successful Supply Chain," *Skubana*, February 14, 2018, https://www.skubana.com/walmart-leading-way/ (accessed May 10, 2018).

26. Thomas L. Friedman, *The World Is Flat 3.0: A Brief History of the Twenty-First Century* (New York: Picador, 2007).

27. "Artificial Intelligence in the Supply Chain: What Is It and How Is It Used," *Triskele Logistics – The Logistics Blog*, http://triskelogi.com/artificial-intelligence-in-the-supply-chain-what-is-it-and-how-is-it-used/ (accessed May 16, 2018).

28. Lance Ulanoff, "Amazon Knows What You Want Before You Buy It," *Predictive Analytics Times*, June 27, 2014 (originally published in *Mashable*), https://www.predictiveanalyticsworld.com/patimes/amazonknows-what-you-want-before-you-buy-it/3185/ (accessed May 16, 2018).

29. www.supplychainmetric.com/perfect-order-measure.html (accessed May 22, 2018).

30. Based on: Jason Del Rey, "Rent the Runway Customers Are Reporting Horror Stories of Cancelled Dress Deliveries and Customer Service Breakdowns," *VOX*, September 24, 2019, https://www.vox.com/recode/2019/9/24/20881206/rent-the-runway-delivery-delays-customer-service-wait-times-reserve-unlimited; Stacey Widlitz, "Rent the Runway's Recent Troubles Don't Spell Doom for the Company – Or the Rental Economy," *Forbes*, September 29, 2019, https://www.forbes.com/sites/staceywidlitz/2019/09/29/rent-the-runway-a-wobbly-stiletto-by-no-means-a-fall/#1f84496d6733; Matthew, "Rent the Runway Business Model – How Does Rent the Runway Work & Make Money?," *Productmint*, https://productmint.com/rent-the-runway-business-model-how-does-rent-the-runway-make-money/ (accessed August 4, 2020); Philip Levinson, "Rent the Runway's HBS Founders & VCs Create a Cinderella Story," *The Harbus*, February 12, 2012, https://harbus.org/2012/rent-the-runway/;

Samuel Hum, "How Rent the Runway Created a Multi-Million Dollar Legacy," *Referral Candy Blog*, https://www.referralcandy.com/blog/rent-the-runway-marketing-strategy/ (accessed August 4, 2020); Sapna Maheshwari, "They See It. They Like It. They Want It. They Rent It.," *New York Times*, June 8, 2019, https://www.nytimes.com/2019/06/08/style/rent-subscription-clothing-furniture.html; Elisabeth Anne Boniface, "The Changing Consumer Behind Rent the Runway's Success," *Commerce Next*, September 10, 2019, https://commercenext.com/the-changing-consumer-behind-rent-the-runways-success/; David Moin, "Rent the Runway Extends Its Subscription Program," *WWD*, May 24, 2016, https://wwd.com/business-news/retail/rent-the-runway-extends-its-subscription-program-10435514/; Jason Del Rey, "Rent the Runway Stops Accepting New Customers as Operations Melt Down," *VOX*, September 27, 2019, https://www.vox.com/recode/2019/9/27/20887017/rent-the-runway-new-customer-freeze-subscribers-delivery-delays-warehouse-issues; Nora Walsh, "Hotels Aim to Help Guests Travel Lighter," *New York Times*, February 25, 2020, https://www.nytimes.com/2020/02/25/travel/hotels-aim-to-help-guests-travel-lighter.html; Rent the Runway, https://www.renttherunway.com/ (accessed August 4, 2020); Morgan Forde, "Rent the Runway: Fulfilment Software Upgrade Behind Shipment Delays," *Supply Chain Dive*, October 9, 2019, https://www.supplychain-dive.com/news/warehouse-fulfillment-rent-the-runway-delays/563979/; Lauren Thomas, "Rent the Runway Partners with W Hotels So You Can Pack Lighter," *CNBC*, December 5, 2019, https://www.cnbc.com/2019/12/04/rent-the-runway-partners-with-w-hotels-so-you-can-pack-lighter.html; Sarah Nassauer, "Rent the Runway Is Growing Fast, and Struggling to Keep Up," *Wall Street Journal*, July 23, 2019, https://www.wsj.com/articles/rent-the-runway-is-growing-fast-and-struggling-to-keep-up-11563890548?mod=article_inline; "Rent the Runway Says It's Open Again After Supply-Chain Crisis," *Crain's New York Business*, October 8, 2019, https://www.crainsnewyork.com/retail-apparel/rent-runway-says-its-open-again-after-supply-chain-crisis; Phil Wahba, "Rent the Runway Will Stop Taking New Customers Temporarily Amid Operations Chaos," *Fortune*, September 27, 2019, https://fortune.com/2019/09/27/rent-the-runway-stops-taking-new-customers-amid-operations-chaos/; Katie Richards, "Rent the Runway Ends Shutdown Early, Likely with Limited Brand Damage," *Glossy*, October 9, 2019, https://www.glossy.co/fashion/rent-the-runway-ends-shutdown-early-likely-with-limited-brand-damage; Diana Pearl, "Rent the Runway CEO Says Transparency about Logistics Problems Boosted Brand Loyalty," *Adweek*, January 12, 2020, https://www.adweek.com/retail/rent-the-runway-ceo-says-transparency-about-logistics-problems-boosted-brand-loyalty/; Margaux Lushing, "Rent the Runway Launches Athleisure and Ski Apparel Just In Time For Ski Season," *Forbes*, December 4, 2019, https://www.forbes.com/sites/margauxlushing/2019/12/04/rent-the-runway-launches-athleisure-and-ski-apparel-just-in-time-for-ski-season/#7756178e42ef; Richard Kestenbaum, "Rent the Runway Is Expanding into Your Hotel Room. Other Retailers Will Follow," *Forbes*, December 5, 2019, https://www.forbes.com/sites/richardkestenbaum/2019/12/05/rent-the-runway-is-expanding-into-your-hotel-room-other-retailers-will-follow/#5b14fbef60c5.

12 Deliver the Customer Experience

Paula Hopkins

Meet Paula Hopkins
▼ A Decision Maker at PepsiCo

Dr. Paula Hopkins is General Manager / Sr. Market Director – South Florida for the Pepsi Beverages Company. She is responsible for the people, business, and community at the PepsiCo North Beverages Company in South Florida. Since she joined PepsiCo in 1992, Paula has held a variety of roles in finance, operations, and sales in both the field and headquarters. In her most previous role, she served as the Sr. Sales Director for the Walmart East Team, where she led the execution and strategic development of PepsiCo's direct store delivery (DSD) and Gatorade beverage businesses.

Paula completed her doctorate at Rollins Crummer graduate school. Her dissertation examined the role of mentorship on job advancement among executive women. She holds a Master's of Business Administration with a concentration in Marketing from the Crummer Graduate School at Rollins College and a Bachelor of Arts degree from Rollins College. Additionally, during her tenure, Paula has been instrumental in leading many diversity and inclusion efforts across PepsiCo. Her efforts have helped create a more inclusive culture, assisting a generation of professionals to excel in their careers at PepsiCo.

Paula's Info

What I do when I'm not working:
Spend time with family, read, and exercise

First job out of school:
Retail buyer's assistant

A job-related mistake I wish I hadn't made:
Not asking for more resources

Business book I'm reading now:
The Infinite Game by Simon Sinek

My hero:
My mom, Vidonia "Vi" Scott. She died in 2018, and I miss her more today than I did yesterday.

My motto to live by:
I strive to make people feel included. I love Maya Angelou: "People will forget what you said, people will forget what you did, but people will never forget how you made them feel."

What drives me:
The desire to be the BEST version of ME. I strive to be the best version of myself. . .leaving a legacy my family will be proud of.

My management style:
This is hard because I believe that situations require different styles. The ones I use the most are visionary, democratic, transformational, and coaching.

Here's my problem...

Real **People**, Real **Choices**

PepsiCo is a primary sponsor of the National Football League's biggest game of the year, the Super Bowl. Its efforts to engage the audience during Super Bowl 53 in Atlanta went really well, and as January 2020 loomed, it was Paula and her team's turn to do the same—or better—for Super Bowl 54 in Miami. Her job was to be sure that the all-important customer experience for football fans and everyone else in the area included a hefty dose of PepsiCo love. Paula knew it was crucial to deliver the best "game" of her career.

There were a number of stakeholders, including PepsiCo personnel, the Miami community, and the NFL, whom Paula and the marketing team had to convince would get a return on their financial investments and efforts. Marketing programs for the Super Bowl often involve creating commemorative products or special packaging for the event, so, for example, if Paula's team created a new commemorative can or other spinoff, then the people in manufacturing had to be sure they would have enough lead time to set up the machinery to do this to ensure ROI for all stakeholders. Also, PepsiCo's local employees wanted to feel included in the campaign so they could show their pride in the company and the Miami community.

And, ideally, the program would reflect Miami's unique demographics and culture, so Paula and her team wanted to identify ways that the activation (marketing, products, and promotions) could reinforce local pride in the area. That would mean somehow relating to the city's proud Latino/a identity and the region's tropical feel. PepsiCo knew that a huge proportion of its customers in the area identified as Latino/a, so it was imperative to link to Hispanic culture in some way.

Paula's overall objective was to leave fans both at the game and those watching at home with a positive feeling about PepsiCo and to grow the company's brand share by ensuring that every location in Miami had the commemorative product and that the execution and activation in stores and on the street was front and center.

In prior Super Bowls, PepsiCo found success by issuing a special commemorative can that generated excitement in the local market where the game took place. However, in the past, this basically involved adding only the Super Bowl logo to the traditional can. (As with all marketing of beloved brands, people tend to be very cautious when it comes to altering a well-known can design.) But Paula's team wanted to create a unique collector's item for this year's game that would live on well past the event. How far could Paula and the team go to change the game and deliver a culturally relevant Super Bowl 54 while also keeping the focus on the Pepsi brand?

Paula considered her **options** 1·2·3

1 Option **Convert all messaging to Spanish or Spanglish, deliver the first-ever pink-top Pepsi can, and add a big pink *Miami* to the Pepsi 12-packs to play upon a color that many people associate with the city.** This vibrant color change would make the cans stand out (and it didn't hurt that pink is Paula's favorite color!). If Pepsi introduced a new can to commemorate the 2020 Super Bowl, this would itself be a newsworthy story, and it could generate a lot of excitement. However, there was a chance that many consumers wouldn't get the connection, and they might even avoid buying the cans if they didn't think they were the "real" Pepsi they were used to. Pepsi is the company's flagship brand and the #1 seller in the Miami market, so it was important not to risk its premiere standing.

2 Option **Just sync with Pepsi's national promotional activities, and show only the Super 54 logo and NFL shield on the commemorative can.** This option wouldn't otherwise differ in shape or coloration from the traditional Pepsi can. It would minimize confusion because the basic can would be the one that consumers were used to buying. On the other hand, there wouldn't be anything unique or exciting about this promotion, and nothing would tie it to the local culture.

3 Option **The activation program for last year's Super Bowl in Atlanta worked really well.** Why tinker with success? Just repeat the elements again. This would be quite easy to pull off because all of the special marketing and packaging elements from last year were already approved. Paula's team could just turn the key and restart the engine, and she wouldn't have to spend a lot of effort to convince shareholders that this program would be effective. On the other hand, there wasn't anything new and exciting about a promotion that people had already seen. And consumers wouldn't see any connection to the Miami market.

Now put yourself in Paula's shoes. Which option would you choose, and why?

You Choose

Which **Option** would you choose, and **why**?
☐ Option 1   ☐ Option 2   ☐ Option 3

The Customer Experience Is Everything!

OBJECTIVE

Understand marketing's focus on excellent customer experiences in traditional and online retailing and in omnichannel marketing.

Wow! If you need a box of crackers or a pair of shoes or a ticket for a vacation to Cancun, where do you shop? At a supermarket, a large mall, a travel agency? Or do you shop from your living room, wearing your PJs and those cute fuzzy slippers your mother gave you for Christmas, using your laptop or your smartphone? **Retailing**, whether in a brick-and-mortar store or online, remains the final stop on the distribution path—the process by which organizations deliver

retailing
The final stop in the distribution channel in which organizations sell goods and services to consumers for their personal use.

goods and services to consumers for their personal use. But that's about all that you can count on staying the same about retailing. Changes of note include the following:

- To survive, both brick-and-mortar and online retail stores must be able to provide an exceptional *customer experience (CX or CEX)* that we first discussed in Chapter 1.

- Gaining the loyalty of consumers no longer depends on the neat stacks of jeans in a display or the sale prices or the designer labels. Traditional and non-traditional retail stores, online-only and omnichannel merchants, and direct marketing enterprises can all offer these. What matters is the quality of the encounter between the customer and the seller, rather than the type of encounter it is.

- The COVID-19 pandemic has demanded the movement to online formats for just about everything consumers do. From education and employment to grocery, pharmacy, and apparel shopping, online activities dominate the lives of everyone, no matter the age.

- Traditional "the-larger-the-better" shopping malls may soon be extinct, and those who enjoyed them as teens will remember and say, "All day at the mall every Saturday—those were the good times."

Paula Hopkins at PepsiCo knew that plenty of people like to drink Pepsi products. But when they participate in a big event like the Super Bowl, they want more than just a tasty soft drink. They want an exciting experience that will live on in their memories for years to come—and maybe some awesome souvenirs, like a commemorative Pepsi can with a pink top to show off to friends when they return home.

In this section of the chapter, we'll talk about the very important customer experience, referred to as CX or CEX, and how marketers work to provide customers with an excellent experience. Then we'll look at the broader world of retailing, how it has changed, and how it continues to change.

As we said in Chapter 1, it's no longer enough to offer a great product at a reasonable price to create a satisfied customer. The fact is that a lot of companies can do that. While these elements are still important, they're just the ticket to the dance. If you want to win the dance contest, you have to provide a lot more on top of these elements of the marketing mix.

Today, it's all about the experience or the series of experiences that the customer has before, during, or after he or she purchases the good or service. That means it's up to marketers to understand—in detail—every single aspect of the process. Does it take too long to navigate the company's website? Does the product arrive with a thick book of directions that not even a rocket scientist will understand? Does shopping in a store feel like you're fighting unruly crowds at rush hour?

Any bad experience can derail the whole team's efforts, so marketers need to understand every detail to be sure the experience is as painless—and hopefully as enjoyable—as possible. We talked about each of these elements, or *touchpoints*, in Chapter 5, when we discussed the idea of mapping the customer's journey. That attention to detail is exactly what drives the unrelenting focus on the customer experience that successful marketers maintain in today's competitive environment. In this chapter, we'll dig into the online and offline channels that marketers use to deliver a great experience.

Customer experience describes customers' overall assessments of their interactions with a good, service, or retail location. CX is the total of every interaction a customer has with a business, from navigating the company website to talking to customer service to the packaging the product arrives in. *Everything* you do impacts customers' perceptions and their decision to keep coming back or not.

In the old days before e-commerce was a "thing," smart retailers focused on designing brick-and-mortar stores that made shoppers want to visit; maybe they piped in current songs or even encouraged customers to create their own products, as the Build-A-Bear chain does.

That's still a smart approach, but today the situation is a lot more complicated because customers often interact with an organization online as well—and in some cases, they never physically enter a storefront. That means the CX equation has to include both offline and online touchpoints to ensure that today's digital natives (those who were born into an Internet world) have positive interactions regardless of whether they're browsing online in their pajamas, navigating a post-pandemic store with plexiglass barriers and sanitizers everywhere, or perhaps following up on an order with a call center.

Customer Journey Mapping

As we saw in Chapter 5, one of the best ways to understand CX is to use a technique marketers call **customer journey mapping**. Creating a journey map is not for the faint of heart; it requires tremendous attention to even the smallest details that can derail a great experience.

Before you can fix a problem, you have to identify it. That's why making a customer journey map starts with specifying every touchpoint. Communication touchpoints include the company's website, chatbots, email and postal mail correspondence, traditional and digital advertising, and social media postings by the company and by others. Human touchpoints are the customer's interactions with company representatives, including salespeople and customer service agents. Physical touchpoints include the company's physical location if the customer engages the company there, the trucks that carry the products, the uniforms employees wear, as well as the product itself and its packaging. Finally, sensory touchpoints include sounds; sights, such as flashing machines and dim lighting in a casino; and scents, such as fragrance in a cosmetics boutique.

The customer journey is the path (start to finish) the customer traverses to complete a transaction with a business. Think of it like the yellow brick road in *The Wizard of Oz*. The customer travels this path because he or she hopes to get a good outcome at the end. Although we hope there are no evil flying monkeys along the way, there may well be "pain points" that prevent our customer from reaching a happy ending to the story.

A mapping project involves a very precise tracking of the experiences that customers have when they interact with a product, store, or service. One important goal is to identify the "pain points" they encounter along the way to reduce the amount of friction people experience. The customer journey mapping process involves several basic steps:

1. Identify the buyer's persona, as we discussed in Chapter 7.
2. Identify the customer's goals—that is, the objectives they want to accomplish when they interact with the organization. These goals can include easily finding the correct product; one-click ordering; picking up an order that contains the correct merchandise; getting help, such as a refund, if problems occur; or having the same consistent experience each time they repeat this process.
3. Identify the places that buyer touchpoints might occur. These include word of mouth exchanges; websites; brick-and-mortar stores; traditional media; order confirmation texts or emails; a website app; a delivery service; phone, email or chat contact; and even the social media platforms, like Twitter, that the organization uses to communicate with customers.
4. Identify the specific pain points that customers encounter—for example, "there aren't enough registers open."
5. Prioritize and remove these roadblocks.
6. Take the customer journey yourself! Don't just "imagine" what the problems might be. Experience the process from the customer's point of view, not just yours.
7. Update and improve.

Then, take a deep breath and start over. Your ultimate goal is not just to satisfy the customer. If possible, you want to delight him or her also! If you don't, there's a good chance a competitor will.[1]

customer journey mapping
The process of identifying customer touchpoints and tracking the experiences customers have when they interact with a brand or a store as they become aware of, consider and evaluate, and decide to purchase a product in order to improve the customer experience.

12.2 Retailing, 21st-Century Style

Retailing: A Mixed (Shopping) Bag

OBJECTIVE

Define retailing and understand how retailing evolves.

Retailing is big business. In 2019, U.S. retail sales totaled about $21 trillion while e-commerce sales accounted for nearly $3.8 trilllion of that.[2]

More than 1 million retail businesses employ nearly 16 million workers—about 1 of every 10 U.S. workers.[3] Although we tend to associate huge stores, such as Walmart and Sears, with retailing activity, in reality, most retailers are small businesses. Certain retailers, such as Home Depot and Costco, are both wholesalers and retailers because they provide goods and services to both businesses and end consumers.

Retailing has different faces in different parts of the world. In some European countries, don't even think about squeezing a tomato to see if it's too soft or picking up a cantaloupe to see if it smells ripe. Such mistakes will quickly gain you a reprimand from the store clerk, who will choose your oranges and bananas for you. In developing countries like those in Asia, Africa, and South America, retailing often includes many small butcher shops where you won't find hygienically sealed packages of steaks and lamb chops. Instead, sides of beef and lamb proudly hang in store windows so everyone will be assured that the meat comes from healthy animals. Don't feel like cooking tonight? There's no drive-through window for pickup, but even better—there's delivery from McDonald's, Hardee's, or KFC via motor scooters that dangerously dash in and out of traffic just a few minutes away. You can even order your Big Mac or a spicy vegetable dragon roll for delivery online through sites such as Egypt's Otlob.com or Mumbai's Foodkamood.com.

wheel-of-retailing hypothesis
A theory that explains how retail firms change, becoming more upscale as they go through their life cycle.

direct-to-consumer (D2C) retail
E-commerce companies that manufacture, sell, and ship their products without middlemen.

The Sears department store chain started as a mail ordering catalog company in 1892. Its very large catalog, 532 pages by 1895, was well known throughout the country, especially in rural areas where it met the needs of consumers who didn't have a lot of physical stores. The first Sears retail locations were not opened until 1925.[4]

The Evolution of Retailing

Retailing has taken many forms over time, including the peddler who hawked his wares from a horse-drawn cart, a majestic urban department store, an intimate boutique, and a huge "hyperstore" that sells everything from potato chips to snow tires. But now the cart you see inside at your giant local mall that sells new-age jewelry or monogrammed golf balls to passersby has replaced the horse-drawn cart, and you've traded the local hypermarket for your computer, tablet, or smartphone. As the economic, social, and cultural pictures change, different types of retailers emerge, and they often squeeze out older, outmoded types. How can marketers know what the dominant types of retailing will be tomorrow or 10 years from now?

One of the oldest and simplest explanations for these changes is the **wheel-of-retailing hypothesis**. Figure 12.1 shows that new types of retailers begin at the entry phase with low-end strategies as they offer goods at lower prices than their competitors.[5] After they gain a foothold, they gradually trade up as they improve facilities and upgrade merchandise before they move up even more with a high-end strategy. This makes it them vulnerable to still newer entrants that can afford to charge lower prices. And so the wheel turns. The latest turn of the wheel came when cheaper online outlets and **direct-to-consumer (D2C) retail** businesses entered the system post-COVID-19.

The 2020 COVID-19 pandemic turned the wheel of retailing again, as merchants scrambled to meet the needs of consumers for sanitized shopping.

Figure 12.1 *Snapshot* | The Wheel of Retailing

The wheel of retailing explains how retailers change over time.

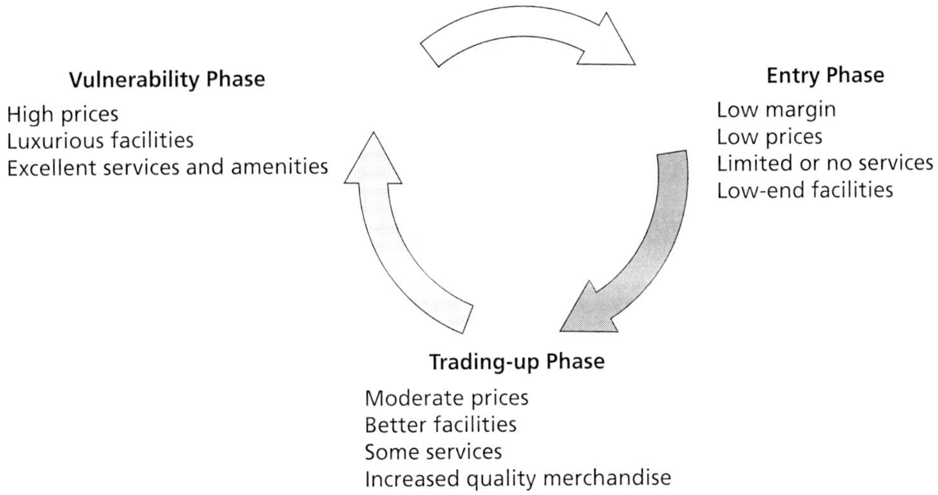

Vulnerability Phase

High prices
Luxurious facilities
Excellent services and amenities

Entry Phase

Low margin
Low prices
Limited or no services
Low-end facilities

Trading-up Phase

Moderate prices
Better facilities
Some services
Increased quality merchandise

12.3 Types of Retailers

OBJECTIVE

Understand how we classify traditional retailers.

The field of retailing covers a lot of ground—from mammoth department stores to **service retailers** like Massage Envy, websites like Amazon.com, and restaurants like Domino's Pizza. Retailers of both goods and services need to understand the possible ways they might offer their products in the market, and they also need a way to benchmark their performance relative to other, similar retailers.

Table 12.1 provides a list of many different retail formats along with information on what they sell and their level of service.

service retailers
Organizations that offer consumers services rather than merchandise. Examples include banks, hospitals, health spas, doctors, legal clinics, entertainment firms, and universities.

Classifying Retailers by What They Sell

To keep this discussion of retailers from being confusing, we need to discuss two different ways we talk about services and service. First, there are retailers whose main products are services—your dry cleaner who cleans your clothes, the salon where you get your hair cut, and the garage that repairs your car. We also use the word *service* to refer to the extras we receive when we buy goods (e.g., the delivery and set-up of your new washer, instructions on how to set your new home security system, and, at the supermarket, bagging your groceries and helping you put them in your car).

In classifying retailers by what they sell, we will first distinguish between retailers who primarily sell goods and those who primarily sell services. For a goods-oriented retailer, one of the most important strategic decisions is *what* to sell—its **merchandise mix**. Service retailers similarly decide what services they will offer consumers. Massage Envy, for example, offers customers specialized massage sessions, personalized stretch sessions, and facials. Canyon Ranch Health Resort in Arizona offers exercise, nutrition instruction, a selection of indoor and outdoor pools complete with underwater treadmills, manicures, pedicures, beauty treatments, and even massages. Athletic apparel retailer Lululemon began offering yoga classes in addition to selling "cool" merchandise.[6] Later in this chapter, we'll talk more about retailers whose main business is to provide consumers with quality services and other intangibles that meet their needs.

Although, as we learned in Chapter 9, a manufacturer's product line consists of product offerings that satisfy a single need, in retailing, a *product line* is a set of related products a retailer offers, such as kitchen appliances or leather goods.

merchandise mix
The total set of all products offered for sale by a retailer, including all product lines sold to all consumer groups.

Table 12.1 | Different Retailers Offer Varying Product Assortments, Levels of Service, Store Sizes, and Prices

Type	Merchandise	Level of Service	Size	Prices	Examples
Convenience stores	Limited number of choices in narrow number of product lines; frequently purchased and emergency items	Self-service	Small	Low-priced items sold at higher-than-average prices	7-Eleven
Supermarkets	Large selection of food items and limited selection of general merchandise	Limited service	Medium	Moderate	Publix, Kroger
Limited assortment supermarkets or extreme-value food retailers	Limited selection of food items; many store brands	Self-service Bag your own purchases	Medium	Low	Aldi
Specialty stores	Large selection of items in one or a few product lines	Full service	Small and medium	Moderate to high	Yankee Candle Co., Alex and Ani
Resale stores (thrift stores and consignment stores)	Used clothing, furniture, household items, and musical instruments	Self-service	Small and medium	Low	Goodwill and Salvation Army stores
Category killers	Large selection of items in one or a few product lines	Full service	Large	Moderate	Home Depot, Best Buy
Leased departments	Limited selection of items in a single product line	Usually full service	Small	Moderate to high	PictureMe portrait studios in Walmart stores
Variety stores	Small selection of items in limited product lines; low-priced items; may have a single price point	Self-service	Small	Low	Dollar General, Dollar Tree
General merchandise discount stores	Large selection of items in a broad assortment of product lines	Limited service	Large	Moderate to low	Walmart, Target
Off-price retailers	Moderate selection of limited product lines; buy surplus merchandise	Limited service	Moderate	Moderate to low	T.J. Maxx, Marshalls
Warehouse clubs	Moderate selection of limited product lines; many items in larger-than-normal sizes	Self-service	Large	Moderate to low	Costco, Sam's Club, BJ's
Outlet stores and factory outlets	Limited selection from a single manufacturer or retailer	Limited service	Small	Moderate to low	Gap Outlet, Nike Outlet, Nordstrom Rack, Off 5th
Department stores	Large selection of many product lines	Full service	Large	Moderate to high	Macy's, Nordstrom, Bloomingdale's
Hypermarkets	Large selection of items in food and a broad assortment of general merchandise product lines	Self-service	Very large	Moderate to low	Carrefour
Pop-up stores, flash retailing	Often a single line or brand; frequently used for seasonal products	Self-service	Very small	Low to moderate	Halloween costume pop-ups
Concept stores	New, inspirational approaches to retailing that seek to sell a lifestyle to a particular target audience through the use of customer interaction, discovery, and experience	Full service	Small	Mostly high	Pandora

As marketers experiment with different retail merchandise mixes, it's getting harder to make direct comparisons between retailers. For example, even though marketers like to distinguish between food and nonfood retailers, in reality, these lines are blurring. **Combination stores** offer consumers food and general merchandise in the same store. **Supercenters**, such as Walmart Supercenters and SuperTargets, are larger stores that combine an economy supermarket with other lower-priced merchandise. Retailers like CVS, RiteAid, and Walgreens drugstores carry limited amounts of food.

combination stores
Retailers that offer consumers food and general merchandise in the same store.

supercenters
Large combination stores that combine economy supermarkets with other lower-priced merchandise.

We can also classify retailers by their **merchandise assortment**, or the selection of products they sell. Merchandise assortment has two dimensions: breadth and depth. **Merchandise breadth**, or variety, is the number of different product lines available. A *narrow assortment*, such as we encounter in convenience stores, means that shoppers will find only a limited selection of product lines, such as candy, cigarettes, and soft drinks. A *broad assortment*, such as what a warehouse store like Costco or Sam's Club offers, means there is a wide range of items from pizzas to new tires for your auto.

merchandise assortment
The range of products a store sells.

merchandise breadth
The number of different product lines available.

Merchandise depth is the variety of choices available within each specific product line. A *shallow assortment* means that the selection within a product category is limited, so a factory outlet store may sell only white and blue men's dress shirts (all made by the same manufacturer, of course) and only in standard sizes. In contrast, a men's specialty store may feature a *deep assortment* of dress shirts (but not much else) in varying shades and in hard-to-find sizes. Figure 12.2 illustrates these assortment differences for one product: science fiction books.

merchandise depth
The variety of choices available for each specific product line.

Classifying Retailers by Level of Service

In addition to classifying goods retailers by the merchandise they sell, we also characterize them by the amount of extra help and assistance—that is, the (other type of) services—they offer customers who buy their merchandise. Firms recognize that there is a trade-off between service and low prices, so they tailor their strategies to the level of service they offer. Customers who demand higher levels of service must be willing to pay for that service, and those who want lower prices must be willing to give up services.

Retailers like Sam's Club that promise cut-rate prices often are self-service operations. When customers shop at *self-service retailers*, they make their product selection without any assistance, they often must bring their own bags or containers to carry

Figure 12-2 *Snapshot* | Classification of Book Retailers by Merchandise Selection

Marketers often classify retail stores on the breadth and depth of their merchandise assortment. In this figure, we use the two dimensions to classify types of bookstores that carry science fiction books.

Depth	Breadth: Narrow	Breadth: Broad
Shallow	Airport Bookstore: A few *Game of Thrones* books	Sam's Club: A few *Game of Thrones* books and a limited assortment of *Game of Thrones* T-shirts and toys
Deep	www.legendaryheroes.com: Internet retailer selling only merchandise for *Game of Thrones, The Highlander, Zena: Warrior Princess, Legendary Swords, Conan,* and *Hercules*	www.Amazon.com: Literally millions of current and out-of-print books plus a long list of other product lines including electronics, toys, apparel, musical instruments, jewelry, motorcycles, and ATVs

Specialty stores are retailers that sell a good selection of only one or a few product lines. Because they sell merchandise that is hard to find in regular retail outlets, they satisfy the needs of targeted customers such as larger and taller men.

their purchases, and they may even handle the checkout process with self-service scanners. From pizzas to autos, retailers went one step further and offered customers contactless delivery service when self-quarantined due to COVID-19.

Contrast that experience to visiting a *full-service retailer*. Department stores like Bloomingdale's and specialty stores like Barnes & Noble provide supporting services, such as gift wrapping, and they offer trained sales associates who can help you select that perfect gift. Nordstrom, an upscale department store, is recognized for its exceptional service. The sales associates, known as "Nordies," have even been known to procure a desired item from another retailer for the shopper if it's not available at a good price in the Nordstrom inventory.

Limited-service retailers fall in between self-service and full-service retailers. Stores like Walmart, Target, Old Navy, and Kohl's offer credit and merchandise return but little else. Customers select merchandise without much assistance, preferring to pay a bit less rather than have more assistance from sales associates.

Before we leave our discussion of retailers classified by level of service, we must mention *vending* machines, which could be called *no-service retailers*. Coin-operated vending machines are a tried-and-true way to sell convenience goods, especially snacks and drinks. These machines are appealing because they require minimal space and personnel to maintain and operate. Some of the most interesting innovations are state-of-the-art vending machines that dispense everything from Legos (but only in Germany!) to nail polish (to update your toes on the go!).[7] Chinese customers can purchase live crabs from vending machines, and in Japan, customers can buy draft beers. In the U.S., vending machines that use touchscreens and accept credit card or mobile payments dispense pricey items like Beats by Dr. Dre headphones and Ray-Ban sunglasses.[8]

Major Brick-and-Mortar Retailing Formats

convenience stores
Neighborhood retailers that carry a limited number of frequently purchased items and cater to consumers willing to pay a premium for the ease of buying close to home.

Now that we've seen how retailers differ in the breadth and depth of their assortments, let's review some of the major forms these retailers take. Table 12.1 provides a list of these types and their characteristics. Some of these have been around for a long time while others are pretty new. First, we'll talk about some of the types of retail formats that are not only succeeding but growing. We'll also talk about those who are falling by the wayside, a victim of e-commerce and the inability to reinvent themselves.

Retail Formats That Continue to Thrive

Convenience Stores

Kohl's, like Target and Walmart, is classified as a discount store with low prices and limited service. Kohl's satisfies the needs of customers who want a broad assortment of items and low prices, and are willing to accept minimal service.

Convenience stores carry a limited number of frequently purchased everyday items, including snacks, soft drinks, candy, over-the-counter drugs, toiletries, and emergency products, such as drain cleaner. Convenience stores typically offer customers speedy checkout so they can quickly be in and out. In 2019, more than 150,000 U.S. convenience stores had total sales of $654.3 billion. The largest U.S. convenience store chain is 7-Eleven Inc. with nearly 8,000 stores.[9] In order to continue to meet the needs of customers, many convenience stores now offer customers beer, wine, a coffee bar, fresh sandwiches, pastries, and other food items.

Limited-Assortment Supermarkets

Limited-assortment supermarkets, or **extreme-value food retailers**, such as German limited-assortment supermarkets Aldi and Lidl, while carrying much the same types of products as larger supermarkets, carry only around 1,500 SKUs. These stores carry only one or two brands of an item instead of the numerous options a regular supermarket is likely to stock.[10] Aldi is able to charge lower prices (the company says 50 percent lower than traditional supermarkets) as it offers significant savings on meat, produce, milk, and other perishables—and no free bags.

limited-assortment supermarkets, or extreme-value food retailers
Stores that carry edibles and related products but in far fewer number, on average around 1,500 SKUs, and at much lower prices than supermarkets.

Supermarkets

Supermarkets are food stores that carry a wide selection of edible and nonedible products. The typical supermarket carries around 30,000 SKUs, half of which are higher-margin perishables: meat, produce, baked goods, and dairy products. Although the large supermarket is a fixture in the U.S., it has not caught on to the same extent in other parts of the world. In many European countries where small, compact towns dominate, for example, consumers walk or bike to small stores near their homes.

The lines between them and other types of retailers are blurring as drugstores, online retailers, and discount stores now offer food and supermarkets increase their offerings of nonfood items. Many supermarkets now carry private label and green (organic, fair trade, natural, or ethnic merchandise) products and offer "make your own" salad bars and other similar take-home meals. Since 1988, traditional supermarkets have lost more than half of their share of the retail food market (from 90 percent to 44 percent) to limited-assortment (whose share went from 2 percent to 44 percent) and convenience stores (whose share went from 8 percent to 16 percent).

supermarkets
Food stores that carry a wide selection of edibles and related products.

Specialty Stores

Specialty stores, including the many specialty apparel stores, do not sell a lot of product lines, but they offer a good selection of brands within the lines they do sell. For a larger, taller man who can't find suits that fit in regular department stores, there are lots of choices in stores that cater to big-and-tall guys. Specialty stores can tailor their assortment to the needs of a targeted consumer, and they often offer a high level of knowledgeable service. Many specialty stores have been located in malls; when department stores leave the malls, the specialty apparel retailers lose their customers. Specialty apparel stores have also been victim to the **Amazon effect**, the consumer trend toward online shopping and shopping with a giant.[11]

specialty stores
Retailers that carry only a few product lines but offer good selection within the lines that they sell.

Amazon effect
The effect of online shopping combined with the consumer trend of shopping with a giant such as Amazon.

Concept Stores

Concept stores are the newest entrant into retail store formats. Marketers use ideas from galleries, magazines, and the hospitality industry in order to sell the idea of a lifestyle. Concept stores may include cafes, talks, and screenings focused on the lifestyle. The use of these elements helps build a community around the lifestyle being "sold."

The overriding goal of the concept store is to create a space where consumers want to hang out, meet with friends, and sit and work. Like magazines in which content is changed each week or month, concept store stock is refreshed and changed on a regular basis in order to encourage frequent visits by customers.

Building this sense of community and physical experience is one way brick-and-mortar stores can focus on the one thing they can offer that e-commerce cannot and thus thrive in the future. Brick-and-mortar stores can act as a place for customers to gather, learn, discover, and enjoy. Creating an alluring experience can attract modern shoppers to engage in real-life experiences with a brand. This also diminishes the idea of a hard sell. Buying feels fun and casual, and customers can feel closer to the brand than ever before.[12]

concept stores
New, inspirational approaches to retailing that seek to sell a lifestyle to a particular target audience through the use of customer interaction, discovery, and experience rather than selling products.

flash retailing, or **pop-up stores and pop-up retailing**
A trend of opening short-term sales stores that close down after only days or weeks. Retail stores, such as Halloween costume stores, that "pop up" one day and then disappear after a period of one day to a few months.

recommerce
The process of selling used products or excess inventory to companies or consumer resale stores.

resale stores
Retail stores that accept and sell used merchandise, including clothing, furniture, household items, and musical instruments.

thrift stores
Resale stores that give their profits to charities.

consignment stores
Resale stores that take used merchandise, resell it, and return a portion of the proceeds to the original owner.

upcycling
A new apparel trend of using discarded products to create a higher-quality, higher-value upcycled product.

dollar and variety stores
Stores that carry a variety of inexpensive items.

general merchandise discount stores
Retailers that offer a broad assortment of items at low prices with minimal service.

off-price retailers
Retailers that buy excess merchandise from well-known manufacturers and pass the savings on to customers.

Flash Retailing, or Pop-Up Stores

Flash retailing, or **pop-up stores and pop-up retailing**, are retail experiences that "pop up" one day and then disappear after a period of one day to a few months. In addition to being a low-cost way to start a business, pop-up stores provide a number of advantages, including building consumer interest, creating buzz, and testing marketing products and locations. Seasonal pop-up stores are frequently opened to sell Halloween costumes, Christmas gifts and decorations, and fireworks.[13]

Recommerce (Resale Stores)

The U.S. **recommerce** industry, driven by a variety of factors including consumers' desire to adopt sustainable practices, generated approximately $17 billion in sales in 2016. Recommerce, or **resale stores**, include **thrift stores**, like Goodwill and Salvation Army stores, not-for-profit thrift stores affiliated with a charity, for-profit thrift stores, used record stores, pawn shop and **consignment stores**, plus a smaller number of antique stores.[14] Resale stores accept used merchandise and sell a wide range of previously owned clothing, furniture, household items, sporting goods, and musical equipment.[15]

A recent innovation in the recommerce industry is the practice of **upcycling**, in which discarded items are used to create a product of higher quality or higher value. While most upcycling is done by startups, traditional retailers like Eileen Fisher ask customers to bring back unwanted items, which they clean and resell as their "Renew" brand, or damaged items, which they upcycle into new pieces. Patagonia resells upcycled items as its "ReCrafted" label.[16]

Dollar and Variety Stores

Dollar and variety stores originated as the five-and-dime or dime stores that began in the late 1800s. In these early variety stores, such as the iconic Woolworth's, all items were sold for a nickel or a dime. Today's dollar and variety stores carry a variety of inexpensive items from kitchen gadgets to toys to candy and candles. It's tough to buy something for a dime today, but many variety stores still stick to a single price point, and some only offer products that don't cost more than a dollar. Some examples of today's variety stores include Dollar General, Family Dollar, and Dollar Tree.[17]

Discount Stores

General merchandise discount stores, such as Target, Kohl's, and Walmart, offer a broad assortment of items at low prices and with minimal service and are the dominant outlet for many products. Discounters are tearing up the retail landscape because they appeal to price-conscious shoppers who want easy access to a lot of merchandise. These stores increasingly carry designer-name clothing at bargain prices, as the companies that make designer brands create new lines just for discount stores.[18] The glow may have faded on some general merchandise stores. Early in 2016, Walmart announced that it would close 269 stores, 154 of them in the U.S., as a result of increased competition from online retailers like Amazon.[19] Since then, Walmart has focused more on its own online business and is now a major competitor of Amazon.

Off-Price Retailers

T.J. Maxx, Tuesday Morning, Marshalls, HomeGoods, Burlington Coat Factory, Big Lots, and Ross Stores are a few of the growing number of **off-price retailers**. Off-price retailers buy merchandise at very low prices when well-known manufacturers produce too many of an item or department stores cancel an order for items that are not "moving." TJX Companies, Inc.—owner of T.J. Maxx, Marshalls, HomeGoods, and Sierra Trading Post—says this on its website: "Our stores are constantly changing as we offer a continual flow of fresh and rapidly changing merchandise." The merchandise in off-price stores provides a form of "retailtainment." Customers visit the stores frequently, just to "see what's new that I can't possibly live without."

Warehouse Clubs

Warehouse clubs, such as Costco and BJ's, are a newer version of the discount store. These establishments do not offer any of the amenities of a full-service store. Customers buy many of the products in larger-than-normal packages and quantities—nothing like laying in a three-year supply of paper towels or five-pound boxes of pretzels, even if you have to build an extra room in your house to store all this stuff! These clubs often charge a membership fee to consumers and small businesses. Consistent with the wheel of retailing, even these stores "trade up" in terms of what they sell today; shoppers can purchase fine jewelry and other luxury items at many warehouse clubs.

Retail Formats That Are Struggling

Why have some retailers struggled while others are growing and new stores are entering the marketplace? There are a number of reasons: markets have shifted; as time went by, new generations of consumers wanted different types of retail options; and cultural changes created new trends. This is the case with department stores. Perhaps even more important, large department stores failed to invest in technology and reinvent themselves.

In other words, they failed to understand the changing consumer signals and adapt to the changing competitive retail environment. Today's consumer is more diverse ethnically, economically, and generationally. Their shopping journey expands across more channels, and their loyalty is virtually non-existent. The bright, shiny new retailer of today could easily be the old, tired retailer of tomorrow if they fail to evolve and remain relevant. Even in the fast-paced world of digital and e-commerce, consumer preference on where to shop may be influenced by something as nebulous as fewer clicks to purchase or consumer perception of price.

Department Stores

Department stores sell a broad range of items and offer a deep selection organized into different sections of the store. Grand department stores dominated urban centers in the early part of the 20th century. In their heyday, these stores sold airplanes and auctioned fine art. Lord & Taylor even offered its customers a mechanical horse to ensure the perfect fit of riding habits. Department stores offer customers a broad variety of products and a deep assortment. They offer services such as credit, and they are organized into distinct departments to effectively display merchandise. The largest U.S. department store chains are Macy's and Nordstrom.

Historically, department stores have sold both **soft goods** (nondurables such as clothing, cosmetics, and bedding) and **hard goods** (durable goods such as appliances, furniture, and electronics).

In many countries, department stores continue to thrive, and they remain consumers' primary place to shop. In Japan, department stores are always crowded with shoppers who buy everything from takeaway sushi dinners to strings of fine pearls. In Spain, a single department store chain, El Corte Inglés, dominates the market. Its stores include huge departments for electronics, books, music, and gourmet foods, and each has a vast supermarket covering one or two floors of the store.

The amenities that attracted customers to grand department stores in their heyday—e.g., a visit with Santa in a snow-covered wonderland or a mechanical bull—don't justify paying higher prices for many shoppers today. A number of large department stores have closed stores and declared bankruptcy after losing business to specialty stores that offer more cutting-edge fashion and to discount stores, catalogs, and online stores that offer the same items at lower prices. This decline of middle-of-the-market retailing and the increasing popularity of both low-end discount/variety stores and upscale specialty retailing is

warehouse clubs
Discount retailers that charge a modest membership fee to consumers who buy a broad assortment of food and nonfood items in bulk and in a warehouse environment.

department stores
Retailers that sell a broad range of items and offer a good selection within each product line.

soft goods
Nondurables such as clothing, cosmetics, and bedding.

hard goods
Durable goods such as appliances, furniture, and electronics.

bifurcated retailing
The decline of middle-of-the-market retailing due to the increasing popularity of both low-end discount stores and upscale specialty retailing.

leased departments
Departments within a larger retail store that an outside firm rents.

factory outlets
Manufacturer-owned brick-and-mortar or online retail stores that sell only a single brand and are almost always located in an outlet mall with other similar stores.

outlet stores
Retailer-owned brick-and-mortar or online stores where excess merchandise or special buys from vendors, not offered in the regular retail stores, are available at lower prices.

category killers, or **category specialists**
Very large specialty stores that carry a vast selection of products in their category.

hypermarkets
Retailers with the characteristics of both warehouse stores and supermarkets; hypermarkets are several times larger than other stores and offer virtually everything from grocery items to electronics.

called **bifurcated retailing**.[20] Indeed, the success of the upscale Nordstrom chain shows that, at least for shoppers with deep pockets who value attentive salespeople, there is a future for department stores—though only the best will survive.

Leased Departments

Leased departments are spaces or departments within a larger retail store (such as a department store) that an outside firm rents. This arrangement allows larger stores to offer a broader variety of products than they would otherwise carry. Some examples of leased departments are in-store banks, photography studios, pet departments, fine jewelry departments, and watch and shoe repair departments.

Factory Outlets and Outlet Stores

Factory outlets began in the 1930s as a means for a manufacturer to salvage some revenue from products produced with imperfections or excess inventory. These "irregulars" or "seconds" were sold to employees first and later to the public in retail stores at the site of, and often within, the manufacturing plant. With manufacturing quality improvement through such programs as TQM and Six Sigma, the amount of merchandise with imperfections has diminished.

Today factory outlets are manufacturer-owned brick-and-mortar or online retail stores that sell only a single brand and are almost always located in an outlet mall with other similar stores. Increasingly, factory outlets sell merchandise that is specifically made for the outlets and is not available in larger retail outlets where higher-priced items are available.

Outlet stores are more often owned by a retailer and offer merchandise that has not sold well or that was purchased from a vendor at a very low price. For example, Saks Fifth Avenue runs Saks Off 5th and Nordstrom operates Nordstrom Rack. Just as the original outlet stores were a place where a manufacturer could gain a little extra revenue from otherwise unacceptable merchandise, today's factory outlets and outlet stores give firms an opportunity to increase revenue or to provide an additional channel.

Category Killers

Category killers, or **category specialists**, are one type of specialty store that has become especially important in recent years. This label describes a very large specialty store that carries a vast selection of products in its category. Some examples of category killers are Home Depot, Best Buy, and Staples. Why the name? By offering a complete assortment in one category, they "kill" a category for other retailers. Most have a general self-service approach, but there is some assistance available for customers who need it. This is especially important at electronics category killers, such as Best Buy.

Because of high levels of competition from the giant online sellers, such as Amazon and Walmart, and their inability to quickly respond to consumers' move to online shopping, category killers are being forced out of business due to shrinking sales and profits. Some of these that have or are expected to file for bankruptcy include Toys "R" Us, Claire's, Sears, Gymboree, David's Bridal, and General Nutrition Centers (GNC).[21]

Hypermarkets

Hypermarkets combine the characteristics of warehouse stores and supermarkets. A European invention, these are huge establishments several times larger than other stores. A supermarket might be 40,000 to 50,000 square feet, whereas a hypermarket takes up 200,000 to 300,000 square feet, or four football fields. They offer one-stop shopping and feature restaurants, beauty salons, and children's play areas. The French company Carrefour has more than 10,000 stores in 33 countries around the globe including about 1,500 hypermarkets; each carries 20,000 to 80,000 food and nonfood items.[22] More recently, Carrefour has expanded to developing countries and now has 236 hypermarkets in China, where a burgeoning population and a lack of large retailers provide hyperopportunities.

12.4 B2C E-Commerce and Other Types of Nonstore Retailers

Stores like Lululemon succeed because they put cool merchandise in the hands of young shoppers who can't get it elsewhere. But competition for shoppers' dollars comes from many sources, from traditional stores to catalogs to websites. Debbie in Dubuque can easily log on to UrbanOutfitters.com at 3:00 a.m. and order the latest belly-baring fashions without leaving home.

As the founder of the Neiman Marcus department store once noted, "If customers don't want to get off their butts and go to your stores, you've got to go to them."[23] Indeed, many products have been available in places other than stores for a long time. The Avon Lady, the Fuller Brush man, and Tupperware parties are all part of the rich history and present reality of retailing. These along with the fast-growing world of e-commerce are part of **nonstore retailing**.

Of course, it's really hard to separate e-commerce from conventional retailers, especially as more merchants aggressively move toward an omnichannel strategy. Most—from upscale specialty stores such as Tiffany's to discounter Walmart to warehouse club Costco—have found it critical to offer nonstore websites for customers who want to buy their merchandise online. For other companies, such as Internet retailer Amazon.com, nonstore retailing is almost their entire business (though the company has moved into brick-and-mortar with its acquisition of Whole Foods). In Chapter 13, we will discuss what direct marketing retailers do through the mail, telephone, and TV. In this section, we'll look at different types of nonstore retailing, shown in Figure 12.3: B2C e-commerce, direct selling, and automatic vending.

B2C E-Commerce

B2C e-commerce is the online exchange between companies and individual consumers. B2C e-commerce in the U.S. totaled $365,207 million in 2019.[24] Consumers are increasingly using their smartphones to make **m-commerce** purchases. Mobile devices, such as phones and tablets, were expected to generate $284 billion, or 45% of the year's total retail e-commerce sales in 2020.[25]

Forrester Research estimates that by 2022, more than half of all U.S. retail sales will involve the Web in some way—that means either a direct purchase of a product online or a **digitally influenced purchase** in which consumers do online research before making a product purchase in a traditional store.[26]

Benefits of B2C E-Commerce

For both consumers and marketers, B2C e-commerce provides a host of benefits and some limitations. Table 12.2 lists some of these.

From the consumer's perspective, electronic marketing increases convenience because it breaks down many of the barriers time and location create. You can shop 24/7 without leaving home, and you can make sure you are getting the best price possible. Consumers in even the smallest of communities can purchase funky shoes or a hot swimsuit from Bloomingdales.com, just like big-city dwellers. At the red-hot WarbyParker.com, one of those D2C retailers we talked about earlier, you can upload your photo and virtually try on different sunglasses before you buy. The company will even send you several pairs if you're undecided; you just return the ones you don't want.

nonstore retailing
Any method used to complete an exchange with a product end user that does not require a customer visit to a store.

B2C e-commerce
Online exchanges between companies and individual consumers.

m-commerce
Promotional and other e-commerce activities transmitted over mobile phones and other mobile devices, such as smartphones and personal digital assistants.

digitally influenced purchases
When consumers do online research before making a product purchase in a traditional store.

Vending machines dispense a lot more than canned beverages and candy bars.

Figure 12-3 *Snapshot* | Types of Nonstore Retailing

Traditional retailers must compete with a variety of nonstore retailers, from automatic vending to dynamic websites.

Direct Selling
• Door to door
• Parties and networks
• Multilevel networks and activities

Automatic Vending	B2C E-Commerce

Table 12.2 | Benefits and Limitations of E-Commerce

Benefits	Limitations
For the Consumer	**For the Consumer**
Shop 24 hours a day	Lack of security
Less traveling	Potential for fraud
Can receive relevant information in seconds from any location	Can't touch or taste items
More product choices	Exact colors may not reproduce on computer monitors
More information for evaluating products	Can be expensive to order and then return
Live chats	Potential breakdown of human relationships
Expanded market presence (don't have to drive across the country to get to a certain store)	
Can check your purchase history and buy or not buy the same item again	
Most sites keep items in your online "cart" so you can wait to make the purchase	
More products available to less developed countries	
Greater price information through shopbots	
Lower prices, so less affluent can purchase	
Participate in virtual auctions on eBay and similar sites	
Fast and often free delivery	
More products are available	
For the Marketer	**For the Marketer**
The world is your marketplace	Lack of security
Decreases costs of doing business	Must maintain site to reap benefits
Very specialized businesses can succeed	Fierce price competition due to total transparency for branded products
Real-time pricing	Conflicts with conventional retailers
	Legal issues not resolved

In less developed countries, the Internet lets consumers purchase products that may not be available at all in local markets. Thus, the Internet can improve the quality of life without the necessity of developing costly infrastructure, such as opening retail stores in remote locations.

Years ago, when giant malls were new to consumers' shopping options, many teens (and their parents) enjoyed spending Saturday wandering around the mall just for entertainment. In the same way, there is a growing number of online experiential shoppers who may spend endless hours "shopping" online even when they have no plans to make any purchases.

virtual experiential marketing
An online marketing strategy that uses enhancements—including colors, graphics, layout and design, interactive videos, contests, games, and giveaways—to engage experiential shoppers online.

Online marketers who wish to attract these customers must design websites that offer surprise, uniqueness, and excitement. Today, marketers provide **virtual experiential marketing** when they offer unique brand experiences using technology like augmented reality, virtual reality, artificial intelligence, and Big Data analytics.[27] Because more than half of all retail customers say that friends influence their purchases, some online retailers have developed groups of "brand friends" who will share the news from the retailer.[28]

Marketers realize equally important benefits from e-commerce. Because an organization can reach such a large number of consumers online, it is possible to develop very specialized businesses that could not be profitable if limited by geographic constraints. The Internet provides an excellent opportunity to bring merchants with excess merchandise and bargain-hunting consumers together.[29] When retailers become concerned that, due to economic downturns or other factors, consumers may not buy enough, they may use online liquidators, such as Overstock.com and Bluefly.com, that offer consumers great bargains on apparel and accessories, items that retailers refer to as "**distressed inventory**." At the same time, the Internet provides consumers with price transparency, making it harder for online retailers to compete at prices that are higher than those of their competitors.

Even high-fashion designers whose retail outlets we associate with Rodeo Drive in Los Angeles, Fifth Avenue in New York, and the Magnificent Mile in Chicago are setting up shop on the Internet to sell $3,000 skirts and $5,000 suits. By 2019, consumers were buying €33.3 billion (about $37 billion) worth of personal luxury goods online globally each year.[30] According to Google, 100 percent of affluent shoppers use technology daily, and 75 percent of them do online research before a purchase.[31] The luxury fashion site Net-a-Porter.com sells designer clothing and accessories from Givenchy, Jimmy Choo, Victoria Beckham, and other top designers.[32] Bottega Veneta bolero jackets sell for $5,600, and Oscar de la Renta lace and tulle gowns sell for $9,290.

As we discussed in Chapter 11, one of the biggest advantages of e-commerce is that it's easy to get price information. Want to buy a new Hellboy action figure, a mountain bike, a virtual reality helmet, or just about anything else you can think of? Instead of plodding from store to store to compare prices, many web surfers use search engines or "shopbots," such as Ask.com, that compile and compare prices from multiple vendors (recall our discussion of shopbots in Chapter 6). With readily available pricing information, shoppers can browse brands, features, reviews, and information on where to buy that particular product.

E-commerce also allows businesses to reduce costs. Compared to traditional brick-and-mortar retailers, e-tailers' costs are minimal—no expensive mall sites to maintain and no sales associates to pay. And, for some products, such as computer software and digitized music, e-commerce provides fast, almost instantaneous delivery. Newer entertainment downloads have gone a step further with sites such as Amazon.com, Netflix, Disney+, and iTunes that offer online shoppers the opportunity to purchase or rent movies. Just download a flick to your new high-definition LED smart TV and pop some corn. You're set for the evening.

Limitations of B2C E-Commerce

But all is not perfect in the virtual world. E-commerce does have its limitations. One drawback compared to shopping in a store is that customers must wait a few days to receive most products, which are often sent via private delivery services. A number of companies are now experimenting with using drones and autonomous robots for faster delivery.

Of course, some e-commerce sites still suffer from poor design that frustrates consumers and leads to **shopping cart abandonment**, where customers leave the site with unpurchased items in their carts. Believe it or not, this happens in almost 7 out of 10 online shopping trips! Why do people get that far and then give up? Some shoppers cite expensive shipping and "just browsing" as the reason, so they don't have to search for items again when they're ready to make a final decision.[33] Customers are less likely to return to sites that are difficult to navigate or that don't provide easy access to customer service personnel, such as the online chats that better sites provide.

Online security is a huge concern to both consumers and marketers. We regularly hear news of yet another retail chain's data system being hacked and information from millions of consumers' credit cards stolen. Although in the U.S. an individual's financial liability in most theft cases is limited because credit card companies usually absorb most or all of the loss, the damage to one's credit rating can last for years. And it's possible for cyberthieves to steal your identity and do all sorts of mischief in your name. Not a pretty picture.

Consumers also are concerned about Internet fraud. Although most of us feel competent to judge a local brick-and-mortar business by its physical presence, by how long it's been around, and from the reports of friends and neighbors who shop there, we have little or no information on the millions of Internet sites offering their products for sale—even though sites like eBay and the Better Business Bureau try to address these concerns when they post extensive information about the reliability of individual vendors. And, as with

distressed inventory
Term used to indicate retailer inventory that may not sell and is sold to online liquidators.

shopping cart abandonment
Occurs when e-commerce customers leave an e-commerce site with unpurchased items in their cart.

catalogs, even though most online companies have liberal return policies, some companies do not pay return shipping costs, so the consumer may get stuck with these charges for items that don't fit or simply aren't the right color.

Developing countries with primarily cash economies pose yet another obstacle to the global success of B2C e-commerce. In these countries, few people use credit cards, so they can't easily pay for items they purchase over the Internet. Furthermore, banks are far less likely to offer consumers protection against fraudulent use of their cards, so a hacked card number can literally wipe you out. For consumers in these countries, there are a growing number of alternatives for safely paying for online purchases. PayPal is a global leader in online payments. Founded in 1998 and acquired by eBay in 2002, PayPal has more than 237 million active customer accounts and services customers in over 200 countries where customers can get paid in more than 100 currencies.[34] As we discussed in Chapter 10, newer digital wallets provide a safe solution and enable consumers in less developed countries to participate in the growing digital marketplace.

As major marketers beef up their presence on the web, they worry that inventory they sell online will *cannibalize* their store sales (we discussed the strategic problem of cannibalization in Chapter 9). This is a big problem for companies like bookseller Barnes & Noble, which has to be careful as it steers customers toward its website and away from its chain of stores bursting with inventory. Barnes & Noble has to deal with competitors such as Amazon (with 300 million worldwide customers and annual sales—for not only books but myriad products from apparel to cell phones—of more than $280 billion in 2019). Amazon sells its books and music exclusively over its 13 global websites, so it doesn't have to worry about this problem.[35] Of course, today, books, including **textbooks** like the awesome one you're reading now, have gone digital and can be purchased and downloaded online. Tablet e-book readers, such as Amazon's Kindle and Apple's iPad, make e-books even more attractive.

Does the growth of B2C e-commerce mean the death of brick-and-mortar stores as we know them? Don't plan any funerals for your local stores prematurely. Although some argue that virtual distribution channels will completely replace traditional ones because of their cost advantages, this is unlikely. For example, although a bank saves 80 percent of its costs when customers do business online from their home computers, Wells Fargo found that it could not force its customers to use PC-based banking services. And for many products, people need "touch-and-feel" information before they buy. For now, clicks will have to coexist with bricks.

However, this doesn't mean that physical retailers can rest easy. Stores as we know them will continue to evolve to lure shoppers away from their computer screens. In the future, the trend will be *destination retail*; that is, consumers will visit retailers not so much to buy a product as for the entertainment they receive from the total experience. As we saw in our discussion of retailtainment, many retailers already offer ways to make the shopping in brick-and-mortar stores an experience rather than just a place to pick up stuff. Bass Pro Shops Mega Outdoor Stores are a store, museum, and art gallery all built into one. Hand-painted murals, 15,000-gallon saltwater aquariums, wildlife exhibits, a full-service restaurant, and a gift and nature center beckon customers to linger. In fact, the average Bass Pro Shops customer spends two and a half hours in the store after driving an average distance of 50-plus miles to get there.[36] This is definitely not your grandfather's bait-and-tackle store!

Direct Sellers

Direct selling occurs when a salesperson presents a product to one individual or a small group, takes orders, and delivers the merchandise. The Direct Selling Association reported that in 2019, 6.8 million individuals were engaged in full-time or part-time direct selling in the U.S. and these activities

textbooks
Books used in the study of a subject; for example, a book containing a presentation of the principles of a subject.

direct selling
An interactive sales process in which a salesperson presents a product to one individual or a small group, takes orders, and delivers the merchandise.

Direct selling continues to grow in popularity as a retailing business model, especially after the pandemic caused many shoppers to prefer to buy in more intimate settings.

generated $35.2 billion in sales.[37] The major product categories for direct sales include home/family care products (such as cleaning products), wellness products (such as weight loss products), personal care products (such as cosmetics), clothing and accessories, and services. Major players in this huge industry include Amway, Mary Kay, Avon, Rodan & Fields, AdvoCare, Scentsy, and Tupperware.

At *home shopping parties*, also called *in-home selling*, a company representative known as a *consultant*, *distributor*, or *adviser* makes a sales presentation to a group of people who have gathered in the home of a friend.[38] One reason that these parties are so effective is that people who attend may get caught up in the "group spirit" and buy things they would not normally purchase if they were alone—even Botox injections to get rid of those persistent wrinkles. We call this sales technique a **party plan system**. Perhaps the most famous home shopping parties were the Tupperware parties popular in the 1950s. Today, though, you're more likely to go to a Thirty-One or Scentsy party.

Another form of direct selling, which the Amway Company epitomizes, is **multilevel** or **network marketing**. In this system, a *master distributor* recruits other people to become distributors. The master distributor sells the company's products to the people he or she entices to join and then receives commissions on all the merchandise sold by the people he or she recruits. Today, Amway has over 3 million independent business owners who distribute personal care, home care, and nutrition and commercial products in more than 100 countries and territories.[39] Amway and other similar network marketers use revival-like techniques to motivate distributors to sell products and find new recruits.[40]

Despite the popularity of this technique, some network systems are illegal. They are really **pyramid schemes**: illegal scams that promise consumers or investors large profits from recruiting others to join the program rather than from any real investment or sale of goods to the public. Often, large numbers of people at the bottom of the pyramid pay money to advance to the top and to profit from others who might join. At recruiting meetings, pyramid promoters create a frenzied, enthusiastic atmosphere complete with promises of easy money. Promoters also use high-pressure tactics to get people to sign up, suggesting that if they don't sign on now, the opportunity won't come around again. Some pyramid schemes are disguised as multilevel marketing—that is, people entering the pyramid do not pay fees to advance, but they are forced to buy large, costly quantities of nonreturnable merchandise.[41] That's one of the crucial differences between pyramid schemes and legitimate network marketers.

party plan system
A sales technique that relies heavily on people getting caught up in the "group spirit," buying things they would not normally buy if they were alone.

multilevel or **network marketing**
A system in which a master distributor recruits other people to become distributors, sells the company's product to the recruits, and receives a commission on all the merchandise sold by the people recruited.

pyramid schemes
An illegal sales technique that promises consumers or investors large profits from recruiting others to join the program rather than from any real investment or sale of goods to the public.

12.5 The Evolution Continues: What's "In Store" for the Future?

OBJECTIVE
Understand the ways that retailing will continue to evolve in the future.

As our world continues to change rapidly, retailers scramble to keep up. A few of the factors that motivate innovative merchants to reinvent the way they do business are the economic environment, changing demographics and consumer preferences, technology, and globalization.

Economic Evolution

Recently, changes in the economic environment have been especially important both to consumers and to retailers. The economic downturn that began in 2007 meant that consumers worldwide were less willing to spend their discretionary income. Retail sales, including the all-important Christmas sales, fell in nearly all retail segments.[42] Sales for most upscale retailers were especially vulnerable, whereas stores such as T.J. Maxx, Marshalls, Dollar General, and online retailer Amazon.com that offer consumers low prices or discounted merchandise

Like other marketers, retailers need to stay on top of cultural trends that affect demand for the merchandise they sell, such as fur-free, vegan, or sustainable products.

experiential shoppers
Shoppers who shop because it satisfies their experiential needs, that is, their desire for fun.

experiential merchandising
A tactic to convert shopping from a passive activity into a more interactive one by engaging the customer in a participatory experience in the store.

retailtainment
The use of retail strategies that enhance the shopping experience and create excitement, impulse purchases, and an emotional connection with the brand.

destination retailer
Store that consumers view as distinctive enough to become loyal to it. Consumers go out of their way to shop there.

point-of-sale (POS) systems
Retail computer systems that collect sales data and are hooked directly into the store's inventory-control system.

perpetual inventory unit control system
Retail computer system that keeps a running total on sales, returns, transfers to other stores, and so on.

thrived. A number of retailers filed for bankruptcy, including Sharper Image, Circuit City, CompUSA, and Waldenbooks.[43]

In 2020, the COVID-19 pandemic again changed the economic environment as state and local governments required consumers to stay at home in order to limit the spread of the virus. This led to the loss of jobs, businesses being shut down, and, some said, the worst economic downturn since the Great Depression. More retailers filed for bankruptcy, including JCPenney, Tuesday Morning, Macy's, JCrew, and Pier 1. Again, the world and the U.S. faced economic uncertainties.

Customer Evolution

As we noted in Chapter 7, keeping up with changes in population characteristics, including demographics and product preferences, is at the heart of many marketing efforts. Here are some of the ways changing consumer demographics and preferences are altering the face of retailing.

- Retailers can no longer afford to stand by and assume that their customer base is the same as it has always been. Costco, for example, built its success on selling to upscale baby boomers and Gen Xers who own their own homes. As that demographic is replaced by Generation Y and millennial consumers who prefer to shop online at Amazon.com, stores like Costco may have to reinvent themselves.[44]

- As more time-challenged consumers (especially women) participate in the workforce, they demand greater convenience. In response, retailers adjust their operating hours and services to meet the needs of working consumers who have less time to shop. Other retailers, including banks, dry cleaners, and pharmacies, add drive-up windows to meet the needs of both working consumers and older consumers. Walmart and a host of other retailers, from large grocery chains to independent wine stores, added the convenience of grocery pick-up, where consumers can order online and schedule a pick-up time. Check in once you arrive, and a store associate will bring your fresh grocery order to the car—and even load it for you![45] Many consumers are flocking to walk-in medical clinics located in strip malls, shopping centers, or pharmacies where retailers not only provide convenience but also save both patients and insurers money on routine care.[46]

- During the COVID-19 pandemic, consumers looked for hygienic experiences. Many stores and service providers created more hygienic environments that offered customers partitions, hand sanitizers, and shopping by appointment only. Traditional services such as a visit to the doctor or therapist or even a physical were replaced by virtual appointments.

- Although members of every ethnic group can usually find local retailers that cater to their specific needs, larger companies must tailor their strategies to the cultural makeup of specific areas. For example, in Texas, California, and Florida, where there are large numbers of customers who speak only Spanish, many retailers make sure that there are sales associates who "habla Español."

- We all love to be entertained (yes, even your marketing professor!). Entertainment cures boredom and satisfies our need for excitement and thrills. Many retailers recognize this aspect of human nature and know that shopping is more than just making a purchase. Now there are **experiential shoppers**, or people who shop because it satisfies their experiential needs, that is, their desire for fun. When the retail experience includes surprise, excitement, and a unique experience, experiential shoppers are more likely to make impulsive purchase decisions.[47] Thus, brick-and-mortar retailers need to provide people with additional reasons to get out of their PJs, turn off the computer, and actually travel to a physical store. They might choose to practice **experiential merchandising**, or a tactic to convert shopping from a passive activity into a more interactive one by engaging the customer in a participatory experience in the store. After all, if you're just picking up an item and throwing it in your cart, why bother to get out of bed when you can get the same thing delivered with a few mouse clicks?

Retailtainment is all about marketing strategies that enhance the shopping experience. Retailers from Disney to Bass Pro Shops have developed instore shopping experiences that create excitement, encourage impulse purchases (that are made spur-of-the-moment), and foster an emotional connection with the brand. When Samsung opened its "Un-Store" (the only thing you could buy was from a café on the top floor), Samsung 837, in the meat-packing district of New York City in 2016, *Forbes* magazine called it "one of the world's top three brand experiences."[48] The 837 experience included multiple hands-on product zones, interactive art, virtual reality, comfortable lounge areas, and a recording studio where customers could record and stream live performances.

This focus on the shopping experience even led some marketers to become a **destination retailer**: a store that consumers would view as distinctive enough to go out of their way to shop there. Luxury fashion designer Hermès, for example, created the Hermès Carré Club,[49] a retailtainment opportunity for customers to enjoy the glamour of Hollywood. Every client is made to feel special while enjoying the exclusivity of the Club. The Hermès Carré Club is designed to be flash retailing, moving from one major city to others around the globe.

The life of the average consumer all around the globe changed radically in early 2020 due to the COVID-19 pandemic. This makes us all wonder what the new "post-COVID" world of retailing will look like. Will patients and medical providers like their telehealth enough for it to continue to be standard medical practioce? Will consumers and retailers continue to see retailtainment as important or will the wheel of retailing go in other new directions? Only time will tell.

Hershey's huge concept store in Times Square is a popular destination for tourists that also makes a strong statement about the brand.

Technological Evolution

As with everything else in our lives, technology is disrupting the way retailers do business—both behind the scenes and as part of the shopping experience. As soon as we learn one new technology, a newer innovation enters business. Retailers have been using recent technological developments including *point-of-sale (POS) systems, perpetual inventory unit control systems, automatic reordering systems,* and *proximity marketing* (also known as *beacon marketing*).

automatic reordering system
Retail reordering system that is automatically activated when inventories reach a certain level.

proximity marketing (also known as **beacon marketing**)
A retail marketing strategy in which beacon devices are placed strategically throughout a store and emit a Bluetooth signal to communicate with shoppers' smartphones as they browse the aisles of the store.

- Advanced electronic **point-of-sale (POS) systems** contain computer brains that collect sales data and connect directly to the store's inventory-control system. Stores may use POS systems to create **perpetual inventory unit control systems** that keep a running total on sales, returns, transfers to other stores, and so on. This technology allows stores to develop computerized **automatic reordering systems** that are activated when inventories decline to a certain level.[50]

- **Proximity marketing**, also known as **beacon marketing**, gives the retailer an opportunity to stimulate a customer while they wander through the store. Beacons, small devices that use Bluetooth technology to transmit information to consumers' smartphones based on location, make it possible for marketers to provide highly targeted promotions that drive impulse purchases and increase store traffic and conversion rates.[51] But wait, it gets scarier. Some retailers including Uniqlo, Lord & Taylor and Saks, have tried a version of beacons that are embedded inside

Smart mirrors in dressing rooms can interact with shoppers while they're trying things on. They can also provide you with a personal trainer and workouts at home.

store mannequins. These supposedly lifeless bodies can talk to you on your phone as you wander through the aisles or pass by a store window and even send you photos of the outfits they are wearing.[52]

- The store of the future will use RFID tags (and other technology) to assist the shopper in ways we haven't even thought of. For example, an RFID tag on a bottle of wine can tip off a nearby plasma screen that will project an ad for Barilla pasta and provide a neat recipe for fettuccine with bell peppers and shrimp. This innovation also increases sales at the restaurant—who can avoid that mouth-watering picture of the eight-layer chocolate cake with peppermint stick ice cream on top?

- As we saw in Chapter 10, digital wallets, which allow you to pay for items without cash or even swiping a credit card, are making it even easier to burn through your paycheck. Already many of us routinely pay for small items with apps like Google Wallet, PayPal, Square, LevelUp, and Venmo. Individual retailers also offer payment opportunities through their own apps. Chick-fil-A allows consumers to load money onto their account and pay with a simple scan of their loyalty app.[53]

omnichannel (omni-channel) marketing
A retail strategy that provides a seamless shopping experience, whether the customer is shopping online from a desktop or mobile device, by telephone, or in a brick-and-mortar store.

- Finally, **omnichannel** (also spelled **omni-channel**) **marketing** is a strategy that provides a seamless shopping experience, whether the customer is shopping online from a desktop or mobile device, by telephone, or in a brick-and-mortar store. New technology enables the sales associate in the store to access the customer's preferences, previous purchases, returns, frequency of shopping, and lots of other data. As the shopper moves from a desktop to a tablet to a smartphone, his or her search history and online shopping "basket" will remain intact, and if they choose, they can then pick up their purchase in the store of their choice the same day as they order it online.[54]

Today the technological evolution has also given retailers these:

extended reality (XR)
The term to describe technologies that can merge the physical and virtual worlds.

- **Extended reality (XR)** provides shoppers with the opportunity both to browse merchandise and to virtually "try them on."
- *Recommendation engines* that we first discussed in Chapter 1 have access to the customer's former shopping behavior in order to make a recommendation for future purposes. Amazon, Netflix, and Spotify already use recommendation engines.

order fulfillment automation
The use of technology and machines to improve the speed and accuracy of order fulfillment, especially for B2C e-commerce.

- Another way retailers seek to compete with the "Amazon effect" is through the use of **order fulfillment automation**, or the use of autonomous mobile robots (AMR) in warehouses to fulfill customers' orders. It is estimated that there will be 580,000 AMRs by the end of 2025.
- Face recognition technology provides retailers with the opportunity to more successfully fight shoplifting and retail crime as well as better serve customers' unique needs.
- *Internet of Things (IoT)* and smart equipment is predicted to transform the shopping experience by providing customers with personalization and information for decision-making. Smart equipment such as sensor-embedded shelves that track inventory will save the retailer money and provide for a better customer experience.[55]

12.6 Ethical Problems in Retailing
Dishonest Behaviors

OBJECTIVE
Understand the problems retailers face with unethical behavior by consumers and employees.

You should now better understand the amount and variety of ways consumers can obtain goods—that important CX (customer experience). Of course nothing is always perfect and the same is true with retailing. In this section, we will talk about some of the ethical problems that retailers and their customers face, including both bricks and clicks.

Retailers must deal with ethical problems that involve both their customers and their employees. Losses resulting from **shrinkage** are a growing problem. *Shrinkage* is the term retailers use to describe stock losses due to shoplifting, employee theft, damage to merchandise, and a variety of errors. Shrinkage cost retailers $61.7 billion in 2019, up from $50.6 billion in 2018.[56] Guess who winds up paying for these "five-finger discounts"? Most shrinkage comes from four different sources: **shoplifting** in which individuals steal goods from a retailer while pretending to be a customer, dishonest employees, return fraud, and administration and paperwork errors.

Shoplifting

In the U.S., shoplifting accounts for 36.5 percent of the total $48.9 billion in shrinkage. The average cost to the retailer for each shoplifting incident in 2016 was $798.48, about double the average in 2015. These thefts in turn drive consumer prices up and hurt the economy, sometimes even causing smaller retailers to go out of business.[57]

Increasingly, shoplifting is an organized criminal activity. Gangs that commit **organized retail crime (ORC)** use store floor plans and foil-lined bags to evade security sensors and get away with thousands of dollars in goods in a single day.[58] A survey of 59 retail-loss prevention executives by the National Retail Federation (NRF) on retail crime found that all of them had experienced ORC in the past year. In 2016, ORC cost retailers $700,259 per $1 billion in sales. ORC is facilitated by **boosters** who steal the merchandise and **fencers** who sell it. While many boosters work alone and steal relatively small amounts of merchandise, others team up with a partner or group of other criminals to operate regionally or even nationally. Smaller fencers directly resell products to consumers and may appear to be a legitimate business, such as a corner market or a booth in a flea market. Larger fencers repackage stolen products (typically in rented houses or storage units) and resell to *diverters* who sell stolen products back to retailers.[59]

The NRF survey also found an increase in **e-fencing**. Instead of selling their stolen watches or t-shirts on street corners, criminals can now join those who sell their legitimate items on online auction sites such as eBay and Etsy. Over half (58 percent) of retailers surveyed by NRF say they were able to identify stolen merchandise on online auction sites. In addition to the online auction sites, thieves sell stolen retail merchandise on Amazon.com, online classified sites such as Craigslist, mobile apps such as LetGo, and the "**deep Web**,"[60] places on the Web that you can't access with most search engines and that provide a means for criminals to connect to buy and sell stolen or illegal items for cryptocurrency, such as Bitcoin.[61]

Employee Theft

A second major source of shrinkage in retail stores is employee theft of both merchandise and cash. In the U.S., it accounted for 30 percent of shrinkage in 2016.[62] The NRF Survey on retail crime found that the average dishonest employee cost the retailer $1,922.80 with a median loss of $962.60 compared to a lower median loss of $622 reported for 2015. Employees not only have access to products but also are familiar with the store's security measures. "Sweethearting" is an employee practice in which a cashier consciously undercharges, gives a cash refund, or allows a friend to walk away without paying for items.[63] Sometimes a dishonest employee simply carries merchandise out the back door to a friend's waiting car.

Retail Return Fraud

Another cause of retail shrinkage is **retail return fraud**. Retail return fraud occurs when someone returns an item that they did not purchase—almost always a stolen item—for a refund. Whether by amateurs or professional criminals, return fraud is a growing concern to retailers. The NRF study on retail crime reported that retail return fraud would cost retailers $1.5 billion in 2017 with an average cost of $1,766.27 and a median of $171. In apparel, the average cost of each incident of return fraud was $968.81 in 2016, almost

shrinkage
Losses experienced by retailers as a result of shoplifting, employee theft, return fraud, and administration and paperwork errors.

shoplifting
Criminal activity in which individuals steal goods from a retailer while pretending to be a customer.

organized retail crime (ORC)
Retail shoplifting by organized gangs of thieves that get away with thousands of dollars in goods in a single day.

boosters
Individuals who facilitate organized retail crime by stealing the merchandise.

fencers
Individuals who facilitate organized retail crime by selling the merchandise to consumers or businesses.

e-fencing
Criminal activity of selling stolen merchandise through online auction sites such as eBay and Etsy.

deep Web
Places on the Web that you can't access with most search engines and that provide a means for criminals to connect to buy and sell stolen or illegal items.

retail return fraud
Criminal activity when someone returns an item they obtained without making a purchase.

as high as shoplifting. The NRF estimates that customers return as much as 11 percent of total retail sales each year and more than 10 percent of those returns are fraudulent. The retail fraud thieves frequently use self-checkouts and have become better at counterfeiting store receipts.

One solution to the retail fraud problem that many retailers have adopted is to require identification for a return, thus enabling the retailer to track individuals who frequently return merchandise. Another tactic is to only give refunds in the form of store credits. Technological advancements such as facial recognition should improve retail fraud prevention.

Retail Borrowing

retail borrowing
The consumer practice of purchasing a product with the intent to return the nondefective merchandise for a refund after it has fulfilled the purpose for which it was purchased.

A similar although not clearly criminal source of shrinkage is an unethical consumer practice the industry calls **retail borrowing**. Merchants over recent decades have developed liberal policies of accepting returns from customers because the product performs unsatisfactorily or even if the customer simply changes her mind. Retail borrowing refers to the return of nondefective merchandise for a refund after it has fulfilled the purpose for which it was purchased.[64] Popular objects for retail borrowing include a dress for a high school prom, a new suit for a job interview, and a large-screen TV for a big football game. For the consumer, the practice provides short-term use of a product for a specific occasion at no cost. For the retailer, the practice results in lower total sales and in damaged merchandise, unsuitable for resale.

Ethical Treatment of Customers

The other side of the retail ethics issue is how retailers and their employees treat customers. Although it may be illegal if a store doesn't provide equal access to consumers of different ethnic groups, behavior that discourages customers who appear economically disadvantaged or socially unacceptable from shopping at a store is not. One study, for example, showed that restaurant servers based their level of service on the customer's perceived ability to pay and leave a good tip.[65]

customer profiling
The act of tailoring the level of customer service based on a customer's perceived ability to pay.

In other **customer profiling** situations, where the level of customer service is tailored based on a customer's perceived ability to pay, some customers were followed around the store by associates and made so uncomfortable that they left before making a purchase, or the customer was ignored altogether to the point he or she left the store disgusted and angry.[66] As a classic scene in the movie *Pretty Woman* starring Julia Roberts depicted, stores that try to maintain an image of elite sophistication may not be helpful to customers who don't look like they belong there.

Many critics argue that retailers have an obligation not to sell products to customers if the products can be harmful. For example, for many years some teens and young adults abused potentially harmful over-the-counter medicines. While government regulations removed many of these drug products from store shelves in recent years, retailers still have to carefully police their distribution. The same is true for products such as alcohol and cigarettes, which by law are limited for sale to adult customers.

Other Ethical Issues in B2C and C2C Retailing

Consumers and legitimate e-sellers all suffer because of the activities of a number of unethical participants in both B2C and C2C e-commerce. A few of the most common areas where unethical activities occur are highlighted in the following list.

- **Deceptive posting:** Deceptive posting of items for sale on C2C retailing sites including eBay, Etsy, Facebook Marketplace, Amazon Marketplace, and Craigslist have provided opportunities for sellers to list items with inadequate information. For example, if a consumer orders from a site showing a picture of a box of 12 pens and using the word *pens*, they may be surprised when one pen arrives. Consumers may also be tempted with C2C listings for items described as *vintage* or *antique*. If the identical item is listed as an antique by 3 or 5 or 10 vendors selling the identical item using an identical photo at different prices, this is a sure sign that it is more likely a reproduction.

- **Intellectual property violations:** Intellectual property violations may be due to ignorance or may be deliberate. Some of the most common violations include use of another company's logos, images, or online content. Copyright infringement is also seen when e-commerce sellers offer to sell movies, music, books, computer software, or other copyrighted content that are illegal copies.

- **Breaches in information security:** One of the most commonly discussed ethical issues in e-commerce is information. Companies that sell goods and services online collect credit card or bank account information along with the name, address, phone number, and email address of buyers. Cybercriminals can hack these companies' computers and gather the information, leaving the consumer subject to theft from their accounts.

- **Misrepresented product quality:** Because you can't view or touch an e-commerce product, customers may unpack an item that is not the quality advertised. If the seller is in another country, there may be no way to solve this problem.

- **Vendor compliance violations:** Some consumer goods are sold only through specified channels in order to protect the value of the brand, but sometimes individuals sell these products via different avenues that are not in compliance with the vendor. For example, during the COVID-19 pandemic, professional brands of hair-care products were readily available on eBay and Amazon.com, having been placed there by individuals looking to profit.

- **Fraud:** Fraudulent activities can be a far more serious problem with e-commerce sites. For example, a consumer may encounter advertisements for nonexistent investment opportunities. Cleverly written communications can lure consumers into sending large amounts of money to purchase these nonexistent investment opportunities. During the COVID-19 pandemic, these offers grew exponentially.

- **Price gouging:** As discussed in Chapter 10, price gouging is all too often seen on C2C e-commerce. Price gouging is not only unethical; it is also illegal by state laws.[67]

Fair Trade: Retailing and Global Social Responsibility

As we learned in Chapter 1, many consumers and marketers have adopted a triple-bottom-line orientation. This means that marketing organizations, including retailers, are concerned about their *social bottom line*—that is, their contribution to communities in which the company operates. This idea is especially relevant when it comes to products produced in developing countries—the same countries that produce most of the clothing and much of the food that we in the U.S. and other developed countries buy. Often workers in these countries must work overtime without extra pay or their employers may even physically punish them for minor infractions. In many of these countries, the minimum wage is less than a living wage; that is, minimum wage doesn't provide enough money for a family to meet basic needs of food and shelter.

Sometimes you will see the phrase "**fair trade** good," "fair trade certified," or something similar on a product label. Fair Trade USA, the organization that provides fair trade certification, defines fair trade as "a global movement made up of a diverse network of producers, companies, shoppers, advocates, and organizations putting people and planet first . . . . The Fair Trade movement promotes greater equity in international trading partnerships, encourages sustainable development, and secures the rights of marginalized producers and workers in developing countries." Because they recognize that many consumers prefer to buy fair trade goods, retailers including Costco, Aldi, Food Lion, Kroger, Sam's Club, Safeway, Target, Sprouts Farmers Market, Walmart, Whole Foods, and Earth Fare, just to name a few, offer customers a selection of these items.[68]

fair trade
Movement made up of a diverse network of producers, companies, shoppers, advocates, and organizations that promotes greater equity in international trading partnerships, encourages sustainable development, and secures the rights of marginalized producers and workers in developing countries.

12.7 Selling What Isn't There:
Services and Other Intangibles

OBJECTIVE

Understand the
marketing of services
and other intangibles.

As we said at the beginning of this chapter, retailing is about selling goods and services to consumers for their personal use. Thus, to understand retailing, we must also understand *services* and how marketers provide consumers with quality services (and other intangibles) that meet their needs.

What do a Rihanna concert, a college education, a Cubs baseball game, and a visit to Walt Disney World have in common? Easy answer—each is a product that combines experiences with physical goods to create an event that the buyer consumes. You can't have a concert without musical instruments (or maybe a pink wig, in Rihanna's case), a college education without textbooks (Thursday night parties don't count), a Cubs game without a hot dog, or a Disney experience without the mouse ears. But these tangibles are secondary to the primary product, which is some act that, in these cases, produces enjoyment, knowledge, or excitement.

In this section, we'll consider some of the challenges and opportunities that face marketers whose primary offerings are **intangibles**: services and other experience-based products that we can't touch. Services are one type of intangible that also happens to be the fastest-growing sector in our economy. As we'll see, all services are intangible, but not all intangibles are services.

Services, as we discussed in Chapter 1, are acts, efforts, or performances exchanged from producer to user without ownership rights. The U.S. Bureau of Labor Statistics reported that the number of people employed in service industries was 130.7 million in the U.S. This accounted for eight out of every 10 individuals employed.[69] If you pursue a marketing career, it's highly likely that you will work somewhere in the services sector of the economy. Got your interest?

intangibles
Experience-based products.

Marketing Services

The service industry includes many consumer-oriented services, ranging from dry cleaning to body piercing. It also encompasses a vast number of services directed toward organizations. Some of the more common *business services* include vehicle leasing, information technology services, insurance, security, legal advice, food services, cleaning, and maintenance. In addition, businesses also purchase some of the same services as consumers, such as electricity, mobile phone service, and natural gas.

intangibility
The characteristic of a service that means customers can't see, touch, or smell good service.

Characteristics of Services

Services come in many forms, from those done *to* you, such as a massage or a teeth cleaning, to those done to *something you own*, such as having your computer tuned or getting a new paint job on your classic 1965 Mustang. Regardless of whether they affect our bodies or our possessions, all services share four characteristics, which Figure 12.4 summarizes: intangibility, perishability, inseparability, and variability. The discussion that follows shows how marketers can address the unique issues related to these characteristics of services that don't pop up when they deal with tangible goods.

Figure 12.4 *Snapshot* | Characteristics of Services

Services have four unique characteristics versus products.

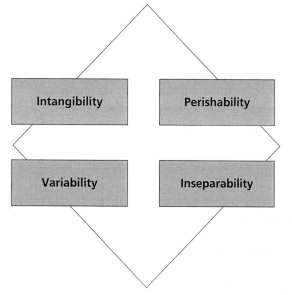

1. Intangibility: Marketing of services might be called "marketing the product that isn't there." The essence is that unlike a bottle of Izze soda or a Samsung 60-inch 4K Ultra HD TV—both of which have physical, tangible properties—services do not assume a tangible form. **Intangibility** means customers can't see, touch, or smell good service. This makes it much more difficult for consumers to evaluate many services.

Because they're buying something that isn't there, customers look for reassuring signs before they purchase, so marketers must ensure that these signs are readily available. That's why they try to overcome the problem of intangibility by providing *physical cues* to reassure the buyer. These cues for a service provider (such as a bank) might be the "look" of the facility—its furnishings, logo, stationery, business cards, the appearance of its employees, or well-designed advertising and websites.

2. **Perishability**: This term refers to the characteristic of a service that makes it impossible to store for later sale or consumption; it's a case of use it or lose it. When rooms go unoccupied at a ski resort, there is no way to make up for the lost opportunity to rent them for the weekend.

   Capacity management is the process by which organizations adjust their services in an attempt to match supply with demand. This strategy may mean adjusting the product, or it may mean adjusting the price. In the summer, for example, the Winter Park ski resort in Colorado combats its perishability problem when it opens its lifts to mountain bikers who tear down the sunny slopes.

3. Variability: A National Football League quarterback may be red hot one Sunday and ice cold the next, and the same is true for most services. **Variability** means that over time, even the same service that the same individual performs for the same customer changes—even if only in minor ways.

   It's difficult to standardize services because service providers and customers vary. Think about your experiences in your college classes. A school can standardize its offerings to some degree—course catalogs, course content, and classrooms are fairly controllable. Professors, however, vary in their training, life experiences, and personalities, so there is little hope of being able to make teaching uniform (not that we'd want to do this anyway).

   The truth is, if you really stop and think about it, we don't necessarily *want* standardization when we purchase a service. Most of us desire a hairstyle that fits our face and personality and a personal trainer who will address our unique physical training needs.

4. **Inseparability**: This means that it is impossible to divide the production of a service from the consumption of that service. Think of the concept of inseparability this way: A firm can manufacture goods at one point in time, distribute them, and then sell them later (likely at a different location than the original manufacturing facility). In contrast, by its nature, a service can take place only at the time the actual service provider performs an act on either the customer or the customer's possession.

The Service Encounter

It's difficult if not impossible to detach the expertise, skill, and personality of a provider or the quality of a firm's employees, facilities, and equipment from the service offering itself. The central role that employees play in making or breaking a service underscores the importance of the **service encounter**, or the interaction between the customer and the service provider.[70] The most expertly cooked meal is just plain mush if a surly or incompetent server brings it to the table.

To minimize the potentially negative effects of bad service encounters and to save on labor costs, some service businesses turn to *disintermediation* that we discussed in Chapter 11. With disintermediation, firms remove the "middleman" from the service encounter, thus eliminating the need for customers to interact with people at all. Examples include self-checkouts at the supermarket or home improvement store, self-service gas pumps, and bank ATMs.

Earlier, we said that a service encounter occurs when the customer comes into contact with the organization—which usually means he or she interacts with one or more employees who represent that organization. The *service encounter* has several dimensions that are important to marketers.[71] First, there is the *social contact dimension*—one person interacting

perishability
The characteristic of a service that makes it impossible to store for later sale or consumption.

capacity management
The process by which organizations adjust their offerings in an attempt to match demand.

variability
The characteristic of a service that means that even the same service performed by the same individual for the same customer can vary.

inseparability
The characteristic of a service that means that it is impossible to separate the production of a service from the consumption of that service.

service encounter
The actual interaction between the customer and the service provider.

with another person. The *physical dimension* is also important; customers often pay close attention to the environment where they receive the service.

Our interactions with service providers can range from the most superficial, such as when we buy a movie ticket, to telling a psychiatrist (or bartender) our most intimate secrets. In each case, though, the quality of the service encounter exerts a big impact on how we feel about the service we receive. In other words, *the quality of a service is only as good as its worst employee.*

However, the customer also plays a part in the type of experience that results from a service encounter. When you visit a doctor, the quality of the health care you receive depends not only on the physician's competence; it's also influenced by your ability to accurately and clearly communicate the symptoms you experience and how well you follow the regimen he or she prescribes to treat you.

As we noted previously, because services are intangible, marketers have to be mindful of the *physical evidence* that goes along with them. An important part of this physical evidence is the **servicescape**: the environment in which the service is delivered and where the firm and the customer interact. Servicescapes include facility exteriors—elements such as a building's architecture, the signage, parking, and even the landscaping. They also include interior elements, such as the design of the office or store, equipment, colors, air quality, temperature, and smells. For hotels, restaurants, banks, airlines, and even schools, the servicescape is quite elaborate. For other services, such as an express mail drop-off, a dry cleaner, or an ATM, the servicescape can be very simple.

Marketers know that carefully designed servicescapes can have a positive influence on customers' purchase decisions, their evaluations of service quality, and their ultimate satisfaction with the service. Thus, for a service such as a pro basketball game, much planning goes into designing not only the actual court but also the exterior design and entrances of the stadium, landscaping, seating, restrooms, concession stands, and ticketing area. Other elements of the servicescape for the basketball fan include the signs that direct people to the stadium, the game tickets, the programs, the team's uniforms, and the hundreds of employees who help to deliver the service.

servicescape
The actual physical facility where the service is performed, delivered, and consumed.

How We Provide Quality Service

If a service experience isn't positive, it can quickly turn into a *disservice* with nasty consequences. Quality service ensures that customers are satisfied with what they have paid for. However, satisfaction is relative because the service recipient compares the current experience to some prior set of expectations. That's what makes delivering quality service tricky. What may seem like excellent service to one customer may be mediocre to another person who has been "spoiled" by earlier encounters with an exceptional service provider. So, marketers must identify customer expectations and then work hard to exceed them.

What can the firm do to maximize the likelihood that a customer will choose its service and become a loyal customer? Because services differ from goods in so many ways, decision makers struggle to market something that isn't there. But, just as in goods marketing, the first step is to develop effective marketing strategies. Table 12.3 illustrates how three different types of service organizations might devise effective marketing strategies.

Of course, no one (not even your marketing professor) is perfect, and mistakes happen. Some failures, such as when your dry cleaner places glaring red spots on your new white sweater, are easy to see at the time the firm performs the service. Others, such as when the dry cleaner shrinks your sweater, are less obvious, and you recognize them only at a later time when you're running late and get a "smaller than expected surprise." But no matter when or how you discover the failure, the important thing is that the firm takes fast action to resolve the problem.

Table 12-3	Marketing Strategies for Service Organizations		
	Dry Cleaner	City Opera Company	A State University
Marketing objective	Increase total revenues by 20 percent within one year by increasing business of existing customers and obtaining new customers	Increase to 1,000 the number of season memberships to opera productions within two years	Increase applications to undergraduate and graduate programs by 10 percent for the coming academic year
Target markets	Young and middle-aged professionals living within a five-mile radius of the business	Clients who attend single performances but do not purchase season memberships	Primary market: prospective undergraduate and graduate students who are residents of the state
		Other local residents who enjoy opera but do not normally attend local opera performances	Secondary market: prospective undergraduate and graduate students living in other states and in foreign countries
Benefits offered	Excellent and safe cleaning of clothes in 24 hours or less	Experiencing professional-quality opera performances while helping ensure the future of the local opera company	High-quality education in a student-centered campus environment
Strategy	Provide an incentive offer to existing customers, such as one suit cleaned for free after 10 suits cleaned at regular price	Correspond with former membership holders and patrons of single performances, encouraging them to purchase new season memberships	Increase number of recruiting visits to local high schools; arrange a special day of events for high school counselors to visit campus
	Use newspaper and direct mail advertising to communicate a limited-time discount offer to all customers	Arrange for opera company personnel and performers to be guests for local TV and radio talk shows	Communicate with alumni, encouraging them to recommend the university to prospective students they know

To make sure that they keep service failures to a minimum and that, when they do blow it, they can recover quickly, managers should first understand the service and the potential points at which failures are most likely to occur so they can plan how to recover ahead of time. That's why it's so important to identify critical incidents. In addition, employees should be trained to listen for complaints and be empowered to take appropriate actions immediately.

In order to consistently provide high-quality service, many service organizations use the **SERVQUAL scale**, a popular instrument to measure customers' perceptions of service quality. SERVQUAL identifies five dimensions, or components, of service quality:

SERVQUAL scale
A popular instrument used to measure customers' perceptions of service quality.

- *Tangibles:* The physical evidence of service quality, such as the physical facilities and equipment, professional appearance of personnel, and the look and functionality of the website
- *Reliability:* The ability to dependably and accurately provide what was promised to the customer
- *Responsiveness:* The willingness to help customers and provide prompt service
- *Assurance:* The knowledge and courtesy of employees that conveys trust and confidence
- *Empathy:* The degree to which the service provider genuinely cares about customers and takes the customer perspective into account when delivering service[72]

The SERVQUAL scale is reliable and valid (concepts discussed in Chapter 4), and service businesses usually administer the scale in a survey format through a written, online, or phone questionnaire to customers.

Marketing People, Places, and Ideas

By now, you understand that services are intangibles that marketers work hard to sell. But as we said previously, services are not the only intangibles that organizations need to market. Intangibles such as people, places, and ideas often need to be "sold" by someone and "bought" by someone else. Let's consider how marketing is relevant to each of these.

Marketing People

As we saw in Chapter 1, people are products too. If you don't believe that, you've never been on a job interview or spent a Saturday night in a singles bar! Many of us find it distasteful to equate people with products. In reality, though, a sizable number of people hire personal image consultants to devise a marketing strategy for them, and others undergo plastic surgery, physical conditioning, or cosmetic makeovers to improve their "market position" or "sell" themselves to potential employers, friends, or lovers.[73] Let's briefly touch on a few prominent categories of *people marketing*.

Sophisticated consultants create and market politicians when they "package" candidates (clients) who then compete for "market share" as measured by votes.

From actors and musicians to athletes and supermodels, the famous and near-famous jockey for market position in popular culture. Agents carefully package celebrities as they connive to get their clients exposure on TV, starring roles in movies, recording contracts, or product endorsements.[74]

In addition to these branding efforts, there are other strategies marketers use to "sell" a celebrity, as Table 12.4 shows. These include the following:

1. *The pure selling approach:* An agent presents a client's qualifications to potential "buyers" until he or she finds one who is willing to act as an intermediary.

2. *The product improvement approach:* An agent works with the client to modify certain characteristics that will increase his or her market value.

Table 12.4	Strategies to Sell a Celebrity

Marketing Approach	Implementation
Pure selling approach	Agent presents a client to the following:
	Record companies
	Movie studios
	TV production companies
	Talk show hosts
	Advertising agencies
	Talent scouts
Product improvement approach	Client is modified:
	New name
	New image
	Voice lessons
	Dancing lessons
	Plastic surgery
	New backup band
	New music genre
Market fulfillment approach	Agent looks for market opening:
	Identify unmet need
	Develop a new product (band or singer) to the specifications of consumer wants

3. *The market fulfillment approach:* An agent scans the market to identify unmet needs. After identifying a need, the agent then finds a person or a group that meets a set of minimum qualifications and develops a new "product."

Marketing Places

Place marketing strategies regard a city, state, country, or other locale as a brand. Marketers use the marketing mix to create a suitable identity so that consumers choose this brand over competing destinations. Because of the huge amount of money tourism generates, the competition to attract visitors is fierce. Marketers invite would-be tourists to come and visit "Pure Michigan." In the commercials, which feature the calm, soothing voice of actor Tim Allen, the state of Michigan shows off its off-the-beaten-path outdoor beauty as well as its big-city adventures. Then, there's the more unfortunate campaign in 2016 to brand the state of Rhode Island. Intense social media criticism forced the state's chief marketing officer to resign after she spent more than $500,000 to develop the slogan: "Cooler & Warmer." Let's just say Rhode Island's residents were cooler rather than warmer to the idea. Of course, it didn't help that some of the footage planned for use in the accompanying tourism ad campaign actually came from Iceland.[75]

place marketing
Marketing activities that seek to attract new businesses, residents, or visitors to a town, state, country, or some other site.

Marketing Ideas

You can see people. You can stand in a city. So how do you market something you can't see, smell, or feel? **Idea marketing** refers to strategies that seek to gain market share for a concept, philosophy, belief, or issue. Even religious organizations market ideas about faith and desirable behavior when they adopt secular marketing techniques to attract young people.

But make no mistake about it; the marketing of ideas can be even more difficult than marketing goods and services. Consumers often do not perceive that the *value* they receive when they recycle garbage or designate a driver or even when they conserve to reduce global warming is worth the *cost*—the extra effort necessary to realize these goals. During the COVID-19 pandemic, sadly many consumers believed that the benefits of social distancing were not worth the costs and cases of the virus spiked.

idea marketing
Marketing activities that seek to gain market share for a concept, philosophy, belief, or issue by using elements of the marketing mix to create or change a target market's attitude or behavior.

The Future of Services

As we look into the future, we recognize that service industries will continue to play a key role in the growth of both the U.S. and the global economy. Figure 12.5 provides several trends for us to consider that will provide both opportunities and challenges for the marketers of services down the road (that means you). In the future, we can expect services we

Figure 12.5 *Snapshot* | Factors That Shape the Future of Services

Changing demographics, globalization, technological advances, and proliferation of information all impact services.

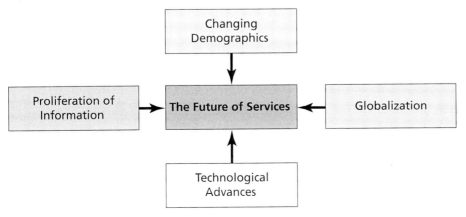

can't even imagine yet. Of course, they will also provide many new and exciting job opportunities for future marketers. These trends include the following:

- *Changing demographics:* As the population ages, service industries that meet the needs of older consumers will see dramatic growth. Companies that offer recreational opportunities, health care, and living assistance for seniors will be in demand.

- *Technology:* Some of the most exciting changes in services relate to the explosion of the sharing economy that uses technology to allow everyday people to provide as well as consume services. A recent major survey reported that 44 percent of U.S. adults (more than 90 million people) have participated in the sharing economy, playing the roles of lenders and borrowers, drivers and riders, hosts and guests.[76] Need to use a car? Go to Zipcar and rent one by the hour. How about a camera, a power drill, or a blender? Go to SnapGoods and rent one of those too. Park your pet with a dogsitter rather than an impersonal kennel at DogVacay. You can even get a low interest loan from other individuals at LendingClub. The sharing economy is revolutionizing industries including taxis (Uber and Lyft), hospitality (Airbnb), used books (BookMooch), and even errand running (TaskRabbit).[77]

- *Globalization:* The globalization of business will increase the need for logistics and distribution services to move goods around the world (discussed in Chapter 11) and for accounting and legal services that facilitate these global exchanges. In addition, global deregulation will affect the delivery of services by banks, brokerages, insurance, and other financial service industries because globalization means greater competition. For example, many "medical tourists" now journey to countries like Thailand and India to obtain common surgical procedures that may cost less than half what they would in the U.S. Meanwhile, hospitals back home often look more like luxury spas as they offer amenities such as adjoining quarters for family members, choice of different ethnic cuisines, and in-room Internet access. In the hotel industry, demand for luxury properties is growing around the world. Hyatt Worldwide is aggressively expanding its Waldorf-Astoria and Conrad brands in China, with at least 16 luxury properties either open or scheduled to open by 2020.[78]

Disruption in Retail

The retail industry has faced a number of highly disruptive forces in the last decade. That leaves many with the question of what they will face in the future. Here are some predictions and some suggestions for retailers.

No Limits!

The Internet not only spawned e-commerce but has also been an equalizing force. The Internet has created a retail environment with no limits on information, access, product choice, convenience, and connection. Retailers are equalized as are their customers.

We No Longer Go Online—We Live Online

Today smartphones have been adopted universally. This has redefined the customer journey. It has also changed thinking about retail locations. No longer do retailers need to be concerned about traffic patterns and retail neighbors. The best location is the smart device. It's where customers shop 24/7, where they find out what their friends and others on social media think, and where they compare retail offerings in design and in price.

The Customer Is in Charge

No customer wants to be average or accept mediocrity. She wants the very best. With the choice and information available today and no scarcity of products, the customer has the power. She's in charge.

Apocalypse? No.

Pundits have announced that retail is dead for nearly a decade and that e-commerce is tolling the death knell. The malls are empty of customers, and there seem to be news of bankruptcy filings weekly. Yes, some retail stores have disappeared and more will follow. But many retailers still have lots of brick-and-mortar locations. As one writer said, the retail industry is not dead, rather it's "experiencing disruption and reinvention." For many retailers, the brick-and-mortar store is essential for the success of their online business. The two types of retailers that are most successful are those that offer strong value and convenience, such as off-price retailers or dollar stores, and those that are upscale retailers, like Lululemon.

The mistake many of the failed retailers made was defending the status quo. Instead of envisioning and trying new retail models, they closed stores and cut costs so they could remain solvent. In the future, innovation and a willingness to embrace a culture of experimentation must be a constant in the retail industry.[79]

12.8 Brand You: Evaluating and Finalizing Your Offer

OBJECTIVE
How to make every interview successful.

Taylor has done a great job of planning his Personal Brand. He has used his strengths and weaknesses to develop his core product. He has been successful in his job interview and has received an offer. Now he needs to learn more about how to evaluate and accept an offer.

This is it! You've impressed your prospective employer and you're about to receive a job offer. But don't get caught up in the excitement and miss something important. You don't want to be disappointed when you start your job.

Salary Discussions

For most people, salary is an important factor in evaluating a job offer, but it shouldn't be the only consideration. Most people are only happy if the job provides personal career satisfaction, flexibility, and the lifestyle they want.

In order to get the best offer, there are two important considerations:

- You need to know what you're worth.
- You need to delay salary discussions as long as possible.

How to know what you're worth.

First, you should calculate your market value. Study typical salaries for the job you're considering. Then think about the job description and how much a qualified person like you can add to the goals of the company and its profitability. You should also consider how prepared you are for the job. If you've gained experience for this job through an internship, you are probably worth more than if the company must train you for the position. It's also important that before you discuss salary, you have a minimum number in mind, one that you're willing to live with.

Why should you delay salary discussions?

The answer to this question is found in how a great salesperson sells a product. When a salesperson wants the customer to buy a high-end product, he or she presents all the features and benefits, making sure the customer is sold on the product. Then and only then, he or she brings up price. In other words, you need to wait to make sure there is a strong interest in hiring you.

Sometimes you simply can't delay salary discussions since you may be asked for your salary expectations in your first screening interview. Remember that you usually can't negotiate up from the lowest figure you name. In this situation you might say something like, "I'm looking for a competitive entry-level compensation package, but I'm most interested in joining the company with the right fit for me." If you are asked for a more specific answer, you can try another time with, "I know I can contribute value to your organization, but I'd like to wait until we're both sure I'm the right person for the job." Or, "I'm comfortable with the salary range you are offering. I'd like to discuss the specifics when I know more about the responsibilities of the job." And, if you continue to be pressed to name an actual figure, respond with a broad range, a range where you'd be satisfied with the lowest figure in your range.

If the interviewer offers the job at the end of the interview, an appropriate response would be, "Thank you for offering me the position. After learning more about your company and the responsibilities of the job, I'm excited about the opportunity to work for the XYZ Company. I'm sure I can make an impact, and I'm ready to consider your best offer."

Whether the salary offer comes in the interview or, as more often happens, later via a call, don't be so grateful for employment that you say yes without giving yourself time to evaluate the offer. This is an important decision for both you and the employer. You want the job, and they want an enthusiastic employee. Employers don't expect you to answer immediately—they won't withdraw the offer if you ask for a few days to consider it. So, take time to evaluate whether this is the right job for you. If the offer comes by phone, you will need to have paper and pen handy so you can take notes (it's okay to ask the person to hold while you get a pen and paper).

When the offer is made, don't be afraid to ask questions about the offer. Some important questions might include

- What is the entire compensation package, including benefits?
- What exactly does the benefits package include?
- What are the opportunities for personal development and promotion?
- When will your salary be reviewed? What do you need to do to earn at a higher level?
- What salary increases can you expect in three to five years?

Regardless of whether you are offered the job in the interview or on the phone, don't accept immediately. Tell the person offering the job, "Thank you for offering me a position with your company. I'd like a little time to consider your offer. Can we talk again later this week?"

Also, it's a good time to gather your questions so you know exactly what information you need to know before you accept the offer.

Evaluating the Offer

One mistake new grads often make is to fail to take into account the benefits that are offered. Even though you may think you'll never get sick, health and life insurance are important and expensive. Health plans and other benefits actually represent a hefty chunk in the equation and can equal as much as 30 percent of your pay. Some other commonly offered benefits include

- **Vacation, sick leave, personal holidays, and time off.**
- **Health insurance.** Most companies pay a percentage of health insurance costs for employees and their families, and the employee pays the rest. Insurance options may include medical savings accounts, HMOs, PPOs, dental, and vision.
- **Life insurance.**
- **401(k) or pension plan.** A 401(k) plan allows you to build a tax-deferred retirement nest egg. Some employers match your contribution or a portion of it. If a pension plan is offered, the employer puts money into a fund for your retirement.

- **Stock options (ESOPs).** This option allows the employee to buy a certain amount of company stock at a discounted price.
- **Signing bonus.** Bonuses have been a popular way to entice employees to join the company. They are commonly offered during good economic times or to high-demand employees.
- **Child care / elder care assistance.** Some companies offer onsite day care for children of employees.
- **Tuition reimbursement.** This is an important benefit if you plan to pursue a graduate degree.
- **Relocation expenses.** If you are relocating to another city to take the job, many companies offer a relocation allowance. The amount varies by company, location, and position.

But Is It the Right Offer for YOU?

Take a few minutes after you determine the value of your job offer and consider the pros and cons of the offer or offers. It's not always the salary that should be the deciding factor in accepting a job offer. Some other elements in addition to compensation are

- Distance and time of the commute to work
- Option to work remotely
- Work environment
- People with whom and for whom you will work
- Culture of the company
- Dress code (casual vs. formal)
- Employee turnover
- Opportunity for personal development and career advancement
- Job function (is it or will it lead you to what you want to do?)
- Social responsibility of the company
- Community involvement of the company
- Reputation of the company
- Stability of the company
- Travel requirements/opportunity
- Relocation requirements/opportunity

Negotiating an Offer

Now that the job has been offered and you've decided you want it, you're ready to negotiate. **You should not officially accept the offer until you have negotiated the offer that you will accept.**

About half of all job seekers accept the first offer that's put on the table, but some employers expect candidates to counteroffer. Remember that the employer won't withdraw the offer just because you counter it. So, go ahead and ask for what you want—you have nothing to lose and perhaps a lot to gain. Prepare a counteroffer, including salary and benefits. You probably won't be able to negotiate on every aspect of the offer, so pick the one or two things that are most important to you. Your pre-negotiation goals are those things that you consider to be "deal breakers"; if you don't get those, you won't accept the offer. Your counteroffer is what you will ask for in each area. Your counteroffer should be for a little more than your pre-negotiation goals in order to allow some room for negotiation.

Keep a positive outlook during the negotiation. Settle the issue of salary first and then move into a discussion of benefits. Sometimes with entry-level positions there isn't much room for negotiation of salary, but a signing bonus, an extra week of vacation time, or an early salary review are all items that may sweeten the deal for you.

Some things for which you might consider negotiating include the following:

- Additional vacation time
- Availability of medical insurance at start date (some companies have a 30–90 day waiting period)
- Waiving of one or two months of health care insurance premiums
- Signing bonus
- Performance bonus
- Stock options

Accepting the Offer

Once you have agreed to a final offer, you should verbally recap all the elements of the offer. Then you should ask for an offer letter. Every internship and full-time job offer should formally be extended with an offer letter. If the company will not provide an offer letter, don't take the job.

An offer letter is a letter of agreement of the terms of the offer. It usually contains the following as appropriate:

- Title of the position which you are being offered
- Person to whom you will report (optional)
- Location of office (optional)
- Starting salary (either hourly or annual)
- Bonus, commission, signing bonus, car allowance or any additional compensation
- Number of stock options, option price, and vesting schedule
- Vacation days (may reference company benefits package)
- Other benefits (may reference company benefits package)
- Start date
- Any offer contingencies such as passing a company-paid drug screening, background or security check, and/or references

You should have an offer letter within one to two days of accepting the offer. It is acceptable if the offer letter is sent via e-mail as long as it is on the company letterhead.

Offer Letter

An offer letter is standard for internships and full-time positions. Be sure you get an offer letter within one to two days of accepting the offer verbally. If you are already working, don't give notice at your current job until you receive your offer letter for your new job.

When you get your offer letter, review it carefully to be sure it includes all the elements to which you agreed. If it doesn't, call the author of the letter immediately to get clarification and resolution on the issue. Some companies require you to sign the offer letter and return it to the company. It's best to make a copy of the signed offer letter before you return it. Keep your offer letter along with all other information from the company in a reference file.

Congratulations! It's time to enjoy your career. Here's to brand YOU.

A Personal Touch

After you accept an offer, it's a good idea to send a handwritten thank-you note to everyone with whom you interviewed. It's a nice touch to thank each person for his or her support and tell him or her how excited you are about joining the company. Each person will appreciate your note and you will start off your new job on the right foot.

Taylor now knows the important aspects of accepting an offer. He recognizes that many great jobs offer both salary and other benefits that are worth a lot to employees. He is also prepared to negotiate in order to make sure he gets as much as he can.

Objective **Summaries** and **Key Terms**

12.1 Objective Summary

Understand marketing's focus on excellent customer experiences in traditional and online retailing and in omnichannel marketing.

Marketers can no longer satisfy customers with only a great product at a reasonable price. Customer satisfaction comes from all of the customer's experiences, from their first contact with a company ad to the safe delivery of the product (hopefully) unbroken and working. *Customer journey mapping* means identifying all of the individual touchpoints customers experience and evaluating each touchpoint. This process allows marketers to keep customers happy and (hopefully) delighted.

Key Terms

retailing
customer journey mapping

12.2 Objective Summary

Define retailing and understand how retailing evolves.

Retailing is the process by which goods and services are sold to consumers for their personal use. The wheel-of-retailing hypothesis suggests that new retailers compete on price and over time become more upscale, leaving room for other new, low-price entrants. Four factors that motivate retailers to evolve are changing economic conditions, demographics, technology, and globalization. Changing demographics has led to the growth of m-commerce, experiential merchandising, and destination retailing, while technology has brought beacon marketing, digital wallets, and omnichannel marketing to retailing. Marketers must also recognize that norms relating to marketing may be different around the globe.

Key Terms

wheel-of-retailing hypothesis
direct-to-consumer (D2C) retail

12.3 Objective Summary

Understand how we classify traditional retailers.

Retailers are classified by NAICS codes based on product lines sold; however, new retail models, such as combination stores, offer consumers more than one product line. Merchandise assortment is described in terms of breadth and depth, which refer to the number of product lines sold and the amount of variety available for each. Retailers may also be classified by the level of service offered (self-service, full-service, and limited-service retailers) and by the merchandise assortment offered. Thus, stores are classified as convenience stores; limited-assortment supermarkets, or extreme-value food retailers; supermarkets; specialty stores; concept stores; pop-up stores; resale stores (thrift and consignment); dollar and variety stores; general merchandise discount stores; off-price retailers; warehouse clubs; department stores; factory outlets and outlet stores; category killers; and hypermarkets.

Key Terms

service retailers
merchandise mix
combination stores
supercenters
merchandise assortment
merchandise breadth
merchandise depth
convenience stores
limited-assortment supermarkets, or extreme-value food
        retailers
supermarkets
specialty stores
Amazon effect
concept stores
flash retailing, or pop-up stores and pop-up retailing
recommerce
resale stores
thrift stores
consignment stores
upcycling
dollar and variety stores
general merchandise discount stores
off-price retailers
warehouse clubs
department stores
soft goods
hard goods
bifurcated retailing
leased departments
factory outlets
outlet stores
category killers, or category specialists
hypermarkets

12.4 Objective Summary

Describe business-to-consumer (B2C) e-commerce and the other common forms of nonstore retailing.

The two more common types of nonstore retailing are B2C e-commerce and direct selling. B2C e-commerce, online exchanges between companies and consumers, is growing rapidly. For consumers, B2C benefits include greater convenience, greater product variety, and increased price information. For marketers, B2C offers a world market, decreased costs of doing business, opportunities for specialized businesses, and real-time pricing. The downside of B2C e-commerce for consumers includes having to wait to receive products, security issues, and the inability to touch and feel products. For Internet-only marketers, success on the Internet may be difficult to achieve, whereas cannibalization may be a problem with traditional retailers' online operations.

In direct selling, a salesperson presents a product to one individual or a small group, takes orders, and delivers the merchandise. Direct selling includes door-to-door sales, party or network sales, and multilevel marketing (network marketing).

Key Terms

nonstore retailing
B2C e-commerce
m-commerce
digitally influenced purchases
virtual experiential marketing
distressed inventory
shopping cart abandonment
textbooks
direct selling
party plan system
multilevel or network marketing
pyramid schemes

12.5 Objective Summary

Understand the ways that retailing will continue to evolve in the future.

Four factors that motivate retailers to evolve are changing economic conditions, demographics, technology, and globalization. Changing demographics has led to the growth of m-commerce, experiential merchandising, and destination retailing while technology has brought proximity (or beacon) marketing, digital wallets, and omnichannel marketing to retailing.

Key Terms

experiential shoppers
experiential merchandising
retailtainment
destination retailer
point-of-sale (POS) systems
perpetual inventory unit control system
automatic reordering system
proximity marketing (also known as **beacon marketing**)
omnichannel (omni-channel) marketing
extended reality (XR)
order fulfillment automation

12.6 Objective Summary

Understand the problems retailers face with unethical behavior by consumers and employees.

One of the ethical issues retailers face is shrinkage as a result of shoplifting, employee theft, and retail borrowing. Much shoplifting is by organized retail crime in which boosters steal

the merchandise and fencers sell it to consumers, businesses including retailers, or via e-fencing through online auction sites.

Retailers and their employees must also be cognizant of the ethical treatment of customers and avoiding customer profiling.

Key Terms

shrinkage
shoplifting
organized retail crime (ORC)
boosters
fencers
e-fencing
deep Web
retail return fraud
retail borrowing
customer profiling
fair trade

12.7 Objective Summary

Understand the marketing of services and other intangibles.

Services are products that are intangible and that are exchanged directly from producer to customer without ownership rights. Generally, services are acts that accomplish some goal and may be directed either toward people or toward an object. Important service characteristics include the following: (1) intangibility, (2) perishability, (3) variability, and (4) inseparability from the producer.

Marketers know that both the social elements of the service encounter (i.e., the employee and the customer) and the physical evidence, including the servicescape, are important to a positive service experience. To measure service quality, marketers use the SERVQUAL scale, which measures five dimensions of service quality: tangibles, reliability, responsiveness, assurance, and empathy. Gap analysis, a related measurement, gauges the difference between a customer's expectation of service quality and what actually occurs.

Managers follow the steps for marketing planning when marketing other intangibles as well. People, especially politicians and celebrities, are often packaged and promoted. Place marketing aims to create or change the market position of a particular locale, whether a city, state, country, resort, or institution. Idea marketing (gaining market share for a concept, philosophy, belief, or issue) seeks to create or change a target market's attitude or behavior. The future of services will be determined by changing demographics, globalization, technological advances, and the proliferation of information.

Key Terms

intangibles
intangibility
perishability
capacity management
variability
inseparability

service encounter

servicescape

SERVQUAL scale

place marketing

idea marketing

12.8 Objective Summary

How to make every interview successful.

After you have the job offer, you still need to engage in a successful interview about the job and the offer. While salary is important, most people are only happy if the job provides personal career satisfaction, flexibility, and the lifestyle they want.

To get the best offer, you need to know what you're worth. By studying typical salaries for the job, how much a qualified person can add to the organization, and how prepared you are for the job, you can develop a good minimum salary estimate.

Salary discussions should be delayed as long as possible. When delaying is no longer possible, respond with a salary range where you'd be satisfied with the lowest figure in your range. If an offer is made, give yourself time to evaluate it and ask questions to make sure it is right for you. You should always negotiate the offer you will accept.

You should have an offer letter that details the terms of the offer before you accept a job. After accepting the offer, send a handwritten thank-you note to everyone with whom you interviewed.

Chapter **Questions** and **Activities**

Concepts: Test Your Knowledge

12-1. What is CX? Why is it such an important part of retailing? Explain how companies measure CX.

12-2. Define *retailing*.

12-3. Describe experiential merchandising, experiential shopping, destination retailing, and omnichannel marketing.

12-4. What is beacon marketing? What are digital wallets?

12-5. Explain retail store shrinkage and the ways shrinkage normally occurs. What is organized retail crime and retail return fraud? What are fencers, boosters and diverters? What is "sweethearting"? What is retail borrowing? What are some of the ethical issues in retailers' treatment of consumers?

12-6. How do marketers classify retail stores? Explain merchandise breadth and depth. What are concept stores? What is recommerce? What is flash retailing?

12-7. Detail the difference between the assortment of merchandise you would typically find in convenience stores, specialty stores, discount stores, and resale stores.

12-8. Explain the different types of direct selling. What is the difference between multilevel marketing and a pyramid scheme?

12-9. What is B2C e-commerce? What is m-commerce? What are some benefits of B2C e-commerce for consumers and for marketers? What are the limitations of B2C e-commerce? What are some ethical problems B2C and C2C retailers face?

12-10. How has e-commerce changed traditional retailing?

12-11. What are intangibles? How do basic marketing concepts apply to the marketing of intangibles?

12-12. What is a service? What are the important characteristics of services that make them different from goods? What are some ways marketers practice capacity management for services?

12-13. What dimensions do consumers and business customers use to evaluate service quality? How should marketers respond to failures in service quality?

12-14. What do we mean by marketing people? Marketing places? Marketing ideas?

Activities: Apply What You've Learned

12-15. *Creative Homework* This activity requires that you go to one of the C2C e-commerce sites, such as eBay, Etsy, or Craigslist. Search the following categories:

1. Hair-care products such as hair color, shampoos, conditioners, and hair thickeners.

2. Vintage and antique tablecloths.

3. Antique furniture.

Your search is for items that you find suspicious, that may be counterfeit, that may have been sold without permission of the distributor, that are overpriced, or that in some other way are suspicious. Present the results of your study to your class.

12-16. *In Class, 10–25 Minutes for Individuals* You have decided to open your own business after graduation—a local coffee shop and bookstore combination in a location near your school. You understand that you have competition in the marketplace and are beginning to think about how to design the atmosphere to attract both college students and other customers from the local community. Develop a detailed plan for how you will use the concept of *retailtainment* to assist in creating the image you desire.

12-17. *Creative Homework/Short Project* In many areas, traditional supermarkets are experiencing increased competition from the limited assortment supermarkets, also called extreme-value food retailers, such as German chains Aldi and Lidl. Develop a list of products that includes at least two items from the meat, dairy, produce, cleaning, paper, and snack categories. Visit a traditional supermarket and an extreme-value food retailer. Make notes on the price, sizes, variety available, and location in the store for each product in both stores. Analyze your notes and prepare a presentation that identifies differences in the two types of stores and the advantages and disadvantages for shoppers in both.

12-18. *For Further Research (Individual)* One problem that traditional retailers face when they open online stores is cannibalization. Select a traditional retailer where you and your fellow students might normally shop that also sells products online. You might, for example, select Best Buy, H&M, Old Navy, Walmart, or Target. Visit the retailer's online store and make notes on the site's product offering, pricing, customer service policies, and so on. (If the store you have chosen offers many different product lines, you might wish to limit your research to one or two different product lines.) Then, visit the store and compare what is offered there with the online offerings. Which of the two provides the best experience and would make you want to return? Develop a report that summarizes your findings and discusses the potential for cannibalization and its implications for the retailer. Also, discuss any changes in either the online or store strategies that you would recommend.

12-19. *In Class, 10–25 Minutes for Teams* You are currently a customer for a college education, an expensive service product. You know that a service organization can create a competitive advantage by focusing on how the service is delivered after it has been purchased—making sure the service is efficiently and comfortably delivered to the customer. Develop a list of recommendations for your school for improving the delivery of its service. Consider both classroom and non-classroom aspects of the educational product.

12-20. *Creative Homework/Short Project* Assume you are working as an intern for the city or town where your college is located. You have been asked to prepare a marketing plan with the objective of making the city/town an important part of the overall college experience for current and future students. First, list the special problems and challenges associated with marketing a place rather than a physical product. Then, outline your ideas for each of the four Ps.

Concepts: Apply Marketing Metrics

Inventory management is an important aspect of retail strategy. For example, it is important to know *when* it is time to reorder and *how much* to order at a time, a metric called the *reorder point*.

As consumers buy a product day after day, the inventory level declines. The question for retailers is how low they should allow the inventory level to decline before they place an order. That is, when is the *optimal* time to reorder? If you order too late, you take a chance of losing sales because you are out of stock. If you order too soon, consumer tastes may change, and you will be stuck with excess and unsellable merchandise. And as we learned in Chapter 11, retailers do not want more inventory on hand than is necessary to avoid stock-outs because inventory ties up cash.

Hence, the decision of when to order and how much to order is critical to a retailer's bottom line. The simplest formula to determine the reorder point is the following:

$$\text{Reorder point} = \text{Daily usage rate} \times \text{Lead time}$$

Usage rate is basically how quickly the inventory sells, and lead time is the length of time from reorder to delivery. Retailers

tend to keep a little extra stock on hand—"safety stock"—just in case their historical data on usage rate and lead time might vary from any one particular reorder experience. Adding in safety stock, the formula becomes the following:

$$\text{Reorder point} = \text{Daily usage rate} \times \text{Lead time} + \text{Safety Stock}$$

Sam's 24-Hour Gas 'n' Sip sells 97 large sodas a day. It takes 5 days to place an order and receive a new shipment of large cups from the company distribution center. But to be prepared for the possibility of extra sales or a late shipment, they need to have a safety stock equal to 3 days of sales.

12-21. What is the reorder point for large cups for Sam's gas station?

Choices: What Do You Think?

12-22. *Critical Thinking* We said at the beginning of this chapter that firms must focus on providing the consumer with an extraordinary CX, or customer experience. What are some suggestions for how the following retailers could provide an extraordinary CX?
   a. A coffee shop
   b. A high-end specialty apparel store
   c. An automobile dealer

12-23. *Ethics* Shrinkage is a huge problem for retailers—they face challenges on the consumer side with shoplifting and retail borrowing, as well as on the employee side with theft. Assume you are the owner of a business—how would you handle each of the situations below?

   a. You have video footage of a frequent customer leaving the store with merchandise he has not paid for in his backpack.
   b. You have an employee who has come to you with an accusation that she witnessed another employee pack up merchandise in a box and take it to her car.
   c. A teenage customer is returning a semi-formal dress a week after a formal dance at her high school, and the clerk has noticed that it smells of perfume.

12-24. *Critical Thinking* Experts predict the future of B2C e-commerce to be very rosy indeed, with exponential increases in Internet sales of some product categories within the next few years. What effect do you think the growth of e-retailing will have on traditional retailing? Do you think we will have a future of empty malls and stores? In what ways will this be good for consumers, and in what ways will it not be so good? What suggestions do you have for brick-and-mortar retailers for competing with e-commerce?

12-25. *Critical Thinking* The majority of consumers have made a purchase online. Retailers are making it easier than ever by accepting digital wallets, such as Apple Pay, PayPal, and other payment methods that help protect your information and make checking out faster and more convenient. So let's say you use a digital wallet. How does having the digital wallet impact your decision to place an order? Do you find yourself ordering more often? Is it important to you to know how retailers are keeping your information secure? Why or why not?

12-26. *Critical Thinking* Many retail stores now use proximity or beacon marketing to communicate with shoppers' smartphones as they browse through a store. Think about service providers such as a restaurant, a spa, or your college. What are some creative ways service providers might use these innovations to improve the customer's experience (CX)?

12-27. *Ethics* Many not-for-profit and religious organizations have found that they can be more successful by marketing their ideas. What are some ways that these organizations market themselves that are similar to and different from the marketing by for-profit businesses? Is it *ethical* for churches and religious organizations to spend donor money on marketing? How about fundraising dollars? Why or why not?

12-28. *Critical Thinking* Many developed countries, including the U.S., have in recent decades become primarily service economies; that is, there is relatively little manufacturing of goods, and most people in the economy are employed by service industries. Why do you think this has occurred? In what ways is this trend a good and/or a bad thing for a country? Do you think this trend will continue?

Miniproject: Learn by Doing

Miniproject 1

Select a good that you, as a consumer, would like to purchase in the next week or so. Shop for this product both online and at a physical retailer.

12-29. As you shop, record the details of both shopping experiences, including the following:

   a. Type of retailer
   b. Clerks available to assist you
   c. Website or physical facilities
   d. Product variety
   e. Product availability
   f. Product price
   g. Store hours
   h. Ease of transaction
   i. Return policy

12-30. Explain why you would be more likely to purchase this product online or at a physical retailer in the future.

Miniproject 2

Theme and entertainment parks like Universal Studios fall in the middle of the goods/services continuum—half goods and half services. To be successful in this highly competitive market, how must a park position its product? Visit the websites of three of the top theme park organizations: Walt Disney World (https://disneyworld.disney.go.com), Six Flags parks (www.sixflags.com), and Universal's Orlando Theme Park (www.universalorlando.com/Theme-Parks/World-Class-Theme-Parks.aspx).

12-31. How is this positioning communicated through the website?

12-32. What changes or improvements would you recommend for each website?

Marketing in Action **Case** Real Choices at Lululemon Athletica

Consumers' use of online retailers to purchase general merchandise continues to increase. As a result, some major retail chains, such as Gap and Macy's, have closed many locations and others, like Pier 1 Imports, Neiman Marcus, JCPenney, and Forever 21, have filed for bankruptcy. When shoppers can find anything they want online and have it delivered directly to their homes, what does it take to get consumers to go to the trouble of making a trip to a physical store? Popular athleisure retailer Lululemon Athletica seems to have found the answer: *experiential retailing*.

Chip Wilson got the idea for Lululemon while he attended his first yoga class at the age of 42. He noticed that while the instructor wore thin and sheer dance clothing, most of the students wore baggy clothes. He realized that sweaty clothes meant clothes that bind, and those baggy clothes also made it harder for the yoga instructor to check students' form. Wilson had developed a stretch fabric for other clothing that he believed would be perfect for yoga enthusiasts. This patented lycra/nylon mix known as "luon" stretches four ways and wicks away moisture. The company's Wunder Under stretchy pants were a big hit, and a new category known as *athleisure* was born.

The Lululemon product line is primarily focused on higher-quality, stylish workout clothes that can stand up to the rigors of a workout. The clothing also comes at a higher price that fans of the brand say is worth the cost. In addition to workout clothing, the company offers water bottles, backpacks, and personal care items. As a vertical retailer, Lululemon controls the entire supply chain and sells the products it creates exclusively at Lululemon stores. As of February 2020, the company had 491 stores that fall into one of four categories: a pop-up store, a 3,000-square-foot store, a 5,500-foot version and its most impressive format, the 25,000-square-foot *experiential* store, with one each in Chicago and at the Mall of America in Minnesota.

At the massive Chicago store, Lululemon customers will find many of the Lululemon products they love and a whole lot more. A restaurant will serve you $12 "power bowls" that contain kale and roasted sweet potatoes. Or, if you prefer, you can order a burger and a beer, or maybe some chocolate covered bacon. Then, to work off those calories (or to think deeply about what you just ate), you can take a class in hip hop yoga or guided meditation, each offered for $25. Classes are also offered in packs of five at a discount; you can choose from 6 to 10 classes offered each day. Forget your workout clothes? No problem. Lululemon will let you try out its gear free of charge. Feel free to use the spacious locker rooms and showers available in the store after your workout.

Lululemon's approach with these experiential stores may at first seem like the "retailtainment" that other retailers and malls use to draw customers into those retail spaces. The Lululemon strategy is differentiated by the level of involvement it offers customers and the customers' level of engagement with the company's products. Rather than just giving customers something to observe, the company facilitates active participation and that participation conveniently includes the use of Lululemon's clothing. A good experience with an expertly-led yoga class will also increase the likelihood of a successful health outcome, continued involvement in exercise, and an ongoing need for quality and stylish Lululemon athleisure products.

The company's approach is also highly focused on community—it brings people together who live what Lululemon calls the "sweatlife." Instead of seeing customers as a group of anonymous buyers, the company considers them as people who buy Lululemon for a reason—sometimes emotional, highly motivational reasons. Lululemon knows that the purchase of workout clothes can mean more than just acquiring a nice pair of yoga pants or gym shorts. These purchases could signify a fresh start or a way to spend time with friends. This community focus is core to the company's marketing strategy and can be seen in promotional materials, its Web and social media presence, and most notably in its brick-and-mortar stores.

While the community focus is central to Lululemon's approach, the company is also hedging its bets with a more personalized approach to fitness. In 2020, Lululemon Athletica purchased Mirror, the company behind the $1,500 device with speakers and a camera that lets home exercisers stream workout classes and allows them to watch both themselves and the workout on the innovative technology. Of course, home athletes need workout clothes, too, and seeing Lululemon fashions worn by the virtual instructors provides a not-so-subtle suggestion for how that need can be met.

During the height of the 2020 pandemic, Lululemon temporarily closed its North American stores, ending its in-store experiences and helping to make at-home exercise options like Mirror a popular alternative for workouts. Post pandemic, the approach to yoga and other workout classes will likely change, but the larger spaces in stores like the experiential Lululemon stores should put the company in a better position than many smaller yoga studios to continue to hold such events. In June of 2020, Lululemon management stated that they were committed to continuing and expanding the experiential approach.

Lululemon's strategy seems to be working. Between 2013 and 2019, revenue for the company nearly doubled, and in 2019, the stock price increased more than 80 percent, considerably more than rivals Nike and Under Armour. Plans for continued growth include international expansion and a major push in their men's clothing line. The experiential store and its ability to foster a community of "Luluheads" will continue to be a key part of the strategy: Lululemon CEO Calvin McDonald says the new format could eventually represent about 10 percent of the company's store base. Emphasizing its importance, McDonald described the experiential store model as "the pinnacle expression of our vision" and added that Lululemon is "an experiential brand that ignites a community of people living the sweat life."[80]

Questions for Discussion

12-33. Lululemon's experiential stores offer customers an opportunity to use its products with other customers. Choose a favorite brand and describe a retail format for that brand that could provide an experience similar to the Lululemon store experience.

12-34. Lululemon's acquisition of Mirror was not without risks. What were the potential benefits and potential risks of the purchase for Lululemon? What are two other strategies Lululemon might consider for future growth? What are the pros and cons of each?

12-35. Lululemon's competitor Nike has tried experiential retail formats, including its Nike Live stores (see https://news.nike.com/news/nike-live-launches-in-long-beach-and-tokyo). Compare the Lululemon and Nike approaches and evaluate the effectiveness of the two approaches. Which strategy best promotes customer engagement with its company's brand?

Chapter **Notes**

1. Micah Solomon, "The Power of the Customer Experience (CX) during the Current Crisis," *Forbes*, May 9, 2020, https://www.forbes.com/sites/micahsolomon/2020/05/09/the-power-of-the-customer-experience-cx-during-the-current-crisis/#e5c7e62323bd (accessed June 20, 2020); Shama Hyder, "Three Principles for Navigating and Mapping the 'Connected' Customer Journey," *Forbes*, April 13, 2018, https://www.forbes.com/sites/shamahyder/2018/04/13/three-principles-for-navigating-and-mapping-the-connected-customer-journey/#23d9a40233b1 (accessed June 16, 2020); Michael R. Solomon, *The New Chameleons: Connecting with Consumers Who Defy Categorization*, London, Kogan Page, 2021.

2. Jessica Young, "US Ecommerce Sales Grow 14.9% in 2019," *Digital Commerce 360*, February 19, 2020, https://www.digitalcommerce360.com/article/us-ecommerce-sales/ (accessed January 2, 2020).

3. Bureau of Labor Statistics, U.S. Department of Labor, "Industries at a Glance," https://www.bls.gov/iag/tgs/iag44-45.htm (accessed April 24, 2018).

4. "History of the Sears Catalog," http://www.searsarchives.com/catalogs/history.htm (accessed January 15, 2021).

5. Stanley C. Hollander, "The Wheel of Retailing," *Journal of Retailing*, July 1960, 41.

6. Benna Crawford, "Lululemon Yoga Classes," https://yoga.lovetoknow.com/yoga-centers/lululemon-yoga-classes (accessed June 5, 2020).

7. Bianca Bahamondes, "The 25 Most Bizarre Things You Can Buy from Vending Machines around the World Slideshow," *The Daily Meal*, June 22, 2017, https://www.thedailymeal.com/travel/most-bizarre-things-you-can-buy-vending-machines-around-world-slideshow/slide-4 (accessed May 8, 2018).

8. Jill Becker, "Vending Machines for All Your Needs," *CNN*, August 16, 2012, https://www.cnn.com/2012/08/16/travel/odd-vending-machines (accessed May 15, 2014).

9. Statista, "Convenience Stores in the U.S. - Statistics & Facts," https://www.statista.com/topics/3869/convenience-stores-in-the-us/ (accessed April 29, 2018); Statista, "All Commodity Volume (ACV) of the Leading Convenience Stores in the United

States in 2017," https://www.statista.com/statistics/763290/acv-convenience-stores/.

10. Nandita Bose, "Exclusive: Aldi Raises Stakes in U.S. Price War with Wal-Mart," *Reuters*, May 11, 2017, https://www.reuters.com/article/us-aldi-walmart-pricing-exclusive-idUSKBN1870EN (accessed April 29, 2018).

11. Barbara Bean-Mellinger, "Analysis of the Retail Apparel Industry," *Chron*, March 8, 2019, https://smallbusiness.chron.com/analysis-retail-apparel-industry-70514.html.

12. "Are Concept Stores the Future of Physical Retail?," *Bouncepad*, https://us.bouncepad.com/blogs/news/are-concept-stores-the-future-of-physical-retail; Melanie Anzidei, "Pandora Unveils New Concept Store in Paramus, the First of Its Kind in U.S.," *NorthJersey*, November 7, 2019, https://www.northjersey.com/story/news/business/2019/11/07/pandora-unveils-concept-store-paramus-nj-1st-kind-us/4158751002/; Jack Stratten, "47 Best New Retail Concept Stores in the World," *BrandKnew*, November 6, 2019, https://www.brandknewmag.com/47-best-new-retail-concept-stores-in-the-world/.

13. Greg Cuccinello, "Flash Retailing: What It Is and Why You Should Care," *In-Store Experience*, March 13, 2019, https://www.instore-experience.com/strategies/flash-retailing-what-is-and-why-you-should-care.

14. NARTS, The Association of Resale Professionals, "Industry Statistics & Trends," https://www.narts.org/i4a/pages/index.cfm?pageid=3285 (accessed April 29, 2018).

15. "Thrift Stores Industry in the US - Market Research Report," IBIS-World, April 4, 2019, https://www.ibisworld.com/united-states/market-research-reports/thrift-stores-industry/.

16. Greg Petro, "Sustainable Retail: How Gen Z Is Leading the Pack," *Forbes*, January 31, 2020, https://www.forbes.com/sites/gregpetro/2020/01/31/sustainable-retail-how-gen-z-is-leading-the-pack/#38f183132ca3; Joan Verdon, "The Rise of the Resale Market," *CO*, https://www.ibisworld.com/united-states/market-research-reports/thrift-stores-industry/; Marcia Kaplan, "Recommerce Surges as Retailers, Brands Get in the Game," *Practical Ecommerce*, August 28, 2019, https://www.practicalecommerce.com/recommerce-surges-as-retailers-brands-get-in-the-game.

17. "Dollar & Variety Stores Industry in the US - Market Research Report," *IBISWorld*, September 24, 2020, https://www.ibisworld.com/united-states/market-research-reports/dollar-variety-stores-industry/.

18. Mark Albright, "Kohl's Debut with Fresh New Look," *St. Petersburg Times*, September 28, 2006, 1D.

19. Tribune Wire Reports, "Wal-Mart to Close 269 Stores, 154 of Them in the U.S.," *Chicago Tribune*, January 16, 2016, https://www.chicagotribune.com/business/ct-walmart-closing-stores-20160115-story.html (accessed April 24, 2016).

20. Barry Berman and Joel R. Evans, *Retail Management: A Strategic Approach*, 12th ed. (Upper Saddle River, NJ: Pearson Education 2013).

21. Jennifer Barbee, "Seven Lessons Brands Can Learn from the Toys R Us Closure," *Forbes*, April 13, 2018, https://www.forbes.com/sites/forbesagencycouncil/2018/04/13/seven-lessons-brands-can-learn-from-the-toys-r-us-closure/#64652df157a0 (accessed April 29, 2018).

22. https://www.forbes.com/sites/forbesagencycouncil/2018/04/13/seven-lessons-brands-can-learn-from-the-toys-r-us-closure/#51c1e0557a06 (accessed October 6, 2020).

23. Quoted in Stratford Sherman, "Will the Information Superhighway Be the Death of Retailing?" *Fortune*, April 18, 1994, 110.

24. J. Clement, "United States: Retail E-Commerce Sales 2017-2024," *Statista*, Feb 6, 2020, https://www.statista.com/statistics/272391/us-retail-e-commerce-sales-forecast/.

25. Andrew Meola, "Rise of M-Commerce: Mobile Ecommerce Shopping Stats & Trends in 2020," Business Insider, December 17, 2019, https://www.businessinsider.com/mobile-commerce-shopping-trends-stats (accessed March 25, 2020).

26. Forrester Research, "Digitally Impacted Retail Sales in 2018: Still Only Half of Retail," Internet Retailer, March 26, 2018, https://www.forrester.com/report/Digitally+Impacted+Retail+Sales+In+2018+Still+Only+Half+Of+Retail/-/E-RES122907 (accessed May 7, 2018).

27. Prasun Kumar, "Virtual Experiences Have Real Impact on Business," Exchange4Media, April 2, 2018, https://www.exchange4media.com/guest-column/guest-column-virtualexperiences-have-real-impact-on-business-mktg-head-magicbricks_89178.html (accessed May 7, 2018).

28. The Network Experiential, "Creating a Storm: Two Retail Trends That Demonstrate the Real Value of Experiential Marketing," February 2, 2014, www.thenetwork-experiential.com/blogview.asp?ID={27BA6D5C-85F0-428C-833C-37D7067AB651} (accessed May 22, 2014).

29. Bob Tedeschi, "A Quicker Resort This Year to Deep Discounting," *New York Times*, December 17, 2007, https://www.nytimes.com/2007/12/17/technology/17ecom.html?scp541&sq5forrester1research&st5nyt (accessed May 1, 2008).

30. Lauren Sherman, "Case Study: Luxury Ecommerce Online Retail," The Business Of Fashion, April 1, 2020, https://www.businessoffashion.com/articles/education/case-study-luxury-ecommerce-online-retail (accessed October 4, 2020).

31. "How Affluent Shoppers Buy Luxury Goods," Google, https://www.thinkwithgoogle.com/_qs/documents/4126/affluent-shoppers-luxury-goods-global_research-studies_xG91wmN.pdf (accessed May 7, 2018).

32. Net-a-Porter, https://www.net-a-porter.com (accessed May 19, 2014).

33. Vinay Koshy, "Shopping Cart Abandonment: 13 Ways to Reduce in 2018," *Automate.io*, March 26, 2018, https://automate.io/blog/reduceshopping-cart-abandonment/ (accessed May 8, 2018).

34. Paypal, "Who We Are," https://www.paypal.com/us/webapps/mpp/about (accessed May 8, 2018).

35. Market.US, "Amazon statistics and Facts," September 11, 2020, https://market.us/statistics/e-commerce-websites/amazon/ (accessed October 5, 2020).

36. OutdoorHub, "Bass Pro Shops Announces New Features of Mega Outdoor Store in Tampa/Hillsborough County, Fla.," April 4, 2014, https://www.outdoorhub.com/pr/2014/04/24/bass-pro-shops-announces-new-features-mega-outdoor-store-tampahillsborough-county-fla/ (accessed May 17, 2014).

37. Direct Selling Association, "Direct Selling in the United States, 2019 Industry Overview," https://www.dsa.org/statistics-insights/overview (accessed October 6, 2020).

38. Ibid.

39. Amway, "Business Opportunity," https://www.amway.com/about-amway/business-opportunity (accessed May 8, 2018).

40. Wikipedia, "Amway," https://en.wikipedia.org/wiki/Amway#:~:text=Amway%20(short%20for%20%22American%20Way,of%20%248.8%20billion%20in%202018. (accessed October 7, 2020).

41. Direct Selling Association, "The Difference between Legitimate Direct Selling Companies and Illegal Pyramid Schemes," https://www.dsa.org/docs/default-source/ethics/legitimatecompanies.pdf (accessed May 19, 2014).

42. Stephanie Rosenbloom and Jack Healy, "Retailers Post Weak Earnings and July Sales," *New York Times*, August 13, 2009, https://www.nytimes.com/2009/08/14/business/14shop.html?scp52&sq5christmas%20sales%20percentage%20of%20annual&st5cse (accessed March 15, 2010).

43. Bruce Lambert, "Once Robust, Retail Scene on the Island Is Smarting," *New York Times*, May 7, 2009, https://www.nytimes.com/2009/05/10/nyregion/long-island/10rooseveltli.html?scp55&sq5retail%20bankruptcies&st5cse (accessed March 15, 2010).

44. Peterson, "12 Things about Costco You Ought to Know."

45. Walmart, https://grocery.walmart.com/ (accessed April 24, 2018).

46. Reed Abelson and Julie Creswell, "The Disappearing Doctor: How Mega-Mergers Are Changing the Business of Medical Care," *New York Times*, April 7, 2018, https://www.nytimes.com/2018/04/07/health/health-care-mergers-doctors.html (accessed April 24, 2018).

47. Nancy D. Albers-Miller and Marla Royne Stafford, "An international analysis of emotional and rational appeals in services vs goods advertising," *Journal of Consumer Marketing*, February 1, 1999, https://scholar.google.com/scholar?q=Nancy+D.+Albers-Miller,+Utilitarian+and+Experiential+Buyers,&hl=en&as_sdt=0&as_vis=1&oi=scholart (accessed October 6, 2020).

48. Jason Schwab, "The Transformation of Experiential Retail," *Retail Spaces*, January 17, 2018, https://info.retailspacesevent.com/blog/the-transformation-of-experiential-retail (accessed April 29, 2018).

49. Greatergroup, "5 Best Experiential Retail Examples," December 25, 2019, https://www.thegreatergroup.com/5-best-experiential-retail-examples/ (accessed March 29, 2020).

50. Barry Berman and Joel R. Evans, Retail Management: A Strategic Approach, 11th ed. (Upper Saddle River, NJ: Pearson Education, 2010).

51. Michelle da Silva, "Proximity Marketing: How to Attract More Shoppers With Beacon Technology," Shopify, Apr 12, 2017, https://www.shopify.com/retail/the-ultimate-guide-to-using-beacontechnology-for-retail-stores (accessed July 18, 2018).

52. David Oragui, "A Beginner's Guide to Beacon Marketing in 2018," The Manifest, August 3, 2018, https://medium.com/@the_manifest/a-beginners-guide-to-beacon-marketing-in-2018-15ac361d4226 (accessed October 7, 2020).

53. Chick-fil-A, https://one.chick-fil-a.com/ (accessed April 24, 2018).

54. Clint Fontanella, "15 Examples of Brands With Brilliant Omni-Channel Experiences," January 16, 2020, *Hubspot*, https://blog.hubspot.com/service/omni-channel-experience (accessed October 4, 2020); http://www.slideshare.net/SonataSoftware/omni-channel-retail-the-new-normal.

55. Bernard Marr, "The Top 10 Technology Trends In Retail: How Tech Will Transform Shopping In 2020," *Forbes*, November 25, 2019, https://www.forbes.com/sites/bernardmarr/2019/11/25/the-top-10-technology-trends-in-retail-how-tech-will-transform-shopping-in-2020/#29f783844e03 (accessed June 7, 2020).

56. J. Craig Shearman, "Retail shrink totaled $61.7 billion in 2019 amid rising employee theft and shoplifting/ORC," National Retail Federation, July 14, 2020, https://nrf.com/media-center/press-releases/retail-shrink-totaled-617-billion-2019-amid-rising-employee-theft-and (accessed October 5, 2020).

57. National Retail Federation, "Organized Retail Crime Survey," October 2016, https://nrf.com/research/2016-organized-retail-crime-survey (accessed April 29, 2018).

58. Joel Griffin, "Study: Retailers' Shrink Reduction Efforts Pay Off," Security Infowatch, June 30, 2015, http://www.securityinfowatch.com/article/12088376/retailers-shrink-reduction-efforts-pay-off-2015-national-retail-security-survey-finds (accessed May 11, 2016).

59. Chris Trlica, "Organized Retail Crime Methods: The Booster-Fence Ecosystem," Loss Prevention Media, April 18, 2018, http://losspreventionmedia.com/insider/shoplifting-organized-retailcrime/organized-retail-crime-methods-booster-fence-ecosystem/ (accessed April 29, 2018).

60. MacKenzie Sigalos, "The Dark Web and How to Access it," *CNBC*, April 14, 2018, https://www.cnbc.com/2018/04/13/the-dark-web-and-how-to-access-it.html (accessed May 14, 2018).

61. Maryville University, "E-Fencing: Who Does It, What It Is and How to Fight It," Maryville University, https://online.maryville.edu/blog/e-fencing-who-does-it-what-it-is-and-how-to-fight-it/ (accessed April 29, 2018).

62. National Retail Federation, "2017 National Retail Security Survey," https://cdn.nrf.com/sites/default/files/2018-10/NRSS-Industry-Research-Survey-2017.pdf (accessed April 29, 2018).

63. Kelly Gates and Dan Alaimo, "Solving Shrink," *Supermarket News*, October 22, 2007, 43.

64. Francis Piron and Murray Young, "Retail Borrowing: Insights and Implications on Returning Used Merchandise," *International Journal of Retail & Distribution Management* 28, no. 1 (2000): 27–36.

65. Barbara Farfan, "Customer Service Research Reveals Profiling and Discrimination as Common Employee Practices—How Nordstrom, Costco, Trader Joe's Replace Customer Profiling with Service," March 31, 2013, http://retailindustry.about.com/b/2013/03/31/customer-service-research-reveals-profiling-and-discrimination-as-common-employee-practices-how-nordstrom-costco-trader-joes-replace-customer-profiling-with-service.htm (accessed May 17, 2014).

66. Brandon A. Perry, "Civil Rights Commission Probes Complaints about Retail Discrimination," *Indianapolis Recorder*, May 16, 2013, www.indianapolisrecorder.com/news/article_87bcda4e-be36-11e2-909e-0019bb2963f4.html (accessed May 17, 2014).

67. Lanie Peterson, "The Ethical Problems in E-Business," *Houston Chronicle*, January 24, 2019, https://smallbusiness.chron.com/ethical-problems-ebusiness-62037.html (accessed May 30, 2020).

68. Fair Trade USA, "Where to Find Fair Trade Products," https://www.fairtradecertified.org/shopping-guide/where-to-find-fair-trade (accessed April 29, 2018).

69. U.S. Bureau of Labor Statistics, "Employment Projections, Employment by Major Industry Sector," September 1, 2020, https://www.bls.gov/emp/tables/employment-by-major-industry-sector.htm (accessed October 5, 2020).

70. John A. Czepiel, Michael R. Solomon, and Carol F. Surprenant, eds., *The Service Encounter: Managing Employee/Customer Interaction in Service Businesses* (Lexington, MA: D. C. Heath, 1985).

71. Cengiz Haksever, Barry Render, Roberta S. Russell, and Robert G. Murdick, Service Management and Operations (Englewood Cliffs, NJ: Prentice Hall, 2000), 25–26.

72. A. Parasuraman, Leonard L. Barry, and Valarie A. Zeithaml, "SERVQUAL: A Multiple-Item Scale for Measuring Consumer Perceptions of Service Quality," Journal of Retailing 64, no. 1 (1988): 12–40; A. Parasuraman, Leonard L. Barry, and Valarie A. Zeithaml, "Refinement and Reassessment of the SERVQUAL Scale," Journal of Retailing 67, no. 4 (1991): 420–50.

73. Michael R. Solomon, "The Wardrobe Consultant: Exploring the Role of a New Retailing Partner," *Journal of Retailing* 63 (Summer 1987): 110–28.

74. Michael R. Solomon, "Celebritization and Commodification in the Interpersonal Marketplace," unpublished manuscript, Rutgers University, 1991.

75. Ted Nesi and Perry Russom, "RI Chief Marketing Officer Resigns After 'Cooler & Warmer' Debacle," WPRI.com, April 1, 2016, https://wpri.com/2016/04/01/ri-chief-marketing-officer-resigns-after-cooler-warmer-debacle/ (accessed April 26, 2016).

76. "German Teens Sell to Friends through Yeay," canvas8, October 2, 2017, https://www.canvas8.com/signals/2017/10/02/yeay.html (accessed January 27, 2018).

77. Adapted from Michael R. Solomon, *Consumer Behavior: Buying, Having and Being* 13th ed, Pearson Education, 2019.

78. George Chen, "Hilton to Open More Waldorf, Conrad Hotels in China, Add 40,000 Jobs," June 12, 2013, https://www.scmp.com/business/companies/article/1258695/hilton-open-more-waldorf-conrad-hotels-china-add-40000-jobs (accessed May 16, 2014).

79. Jess Huang, Sajal Kohli, and Shruti Lal, "Winning in an Era of Unprecedented Disruption: A Perspective on US Retail," *McKinsey & Company*, January 11, 2019, https://www.mckinsey.com/industries/retail/our-insights/winning-in-an-era-of-unprecedented-disruption-a-perspective-on-us-retail (accessed June 2, 2020); Steve Dennis, "Shift Happens: 7 Factors That Defined a Decade of Retail Disruption," *Forbes*, December 23, 2019, https://www.forbes.com/sites/stevendennis/2019/12/23/shift-happens-7-factors-that-defined-a-decade-of-retail-disruption/#615f0d502d2e (accessed June 2, 2020).

80. Based on: Milos Djordjevic, "24 Useful Statistics on Online Shopping vs in Store Shopping," *Save My Cent*, March 26, 2020, https://savemycent.com/blog/statistics-on-online-shopping-vs-in-store-shopping/; Thomas Barrabi and Shawn M. Carter, "Retail Apocalypse: Pier 1 and the Other Retailers Closing, Filing for Bankruptcy," *Fox Business*, September 30, 2019, https://www.foxbusiness.com/retail/features-retail-apocalypse-bankruptcy-stores-closing; Hope Ngo, "The Truth about Lululemon's Founder," *The List*, July 7, 2020, https://www.thelist.com/224085/the-truth-about-lululemons-founder/; Kate Hagan Gallup, "The Bizarre Reason Lululemon Got Its Name," *The List*, May 26, 2020, https://www.thelist.com/212557/the-bizarre-reason-lululemon-got-its-name/; Hope Ngo, "Why Is Lululemon So Expensive?" *The List*, March 8, 2020, https://www.thelist.com/193029/why-is-lululemon-so-expensive/; Sergei Klebnikov, "Here's Why Lululemon Stock Is Up over 80% This Year While the Rest of Retail Struggles," *Forbes*, December 4, 2019, https://www.forbes.com/sites/sergeiklebnikov/2019/12/04/heres-why-lululemon-stock-is-up-over-80-this-year-while-the-rest-of-retail-struggles/#39de7ea1bbb4; Lauren Thomas, "Lululemon Just Opened a Sprawling, 20,000-Square-Foot Store in Chicago with Workout Classes and a Restaurant – Here's What It Looks Like," *CNBC*, July 11, 2019, https://www.cnbc.com/2019/07/10/a-look-inside-lululemons-massive-new-store-in-chicago-with-yoga-food.html; Laura Forman, "Lululemon's Surge Could Have Long Legs," *The Wall Street Journal*, May 14, 2020, https://www.wsj.com/articles/lululemons-surge-could-have-long-legs-11589470142; "Where to Buy and Sell Lululemon," *Agent Athletica*, https://www.agentathletica.com/buy-sell-guide/where-to-buy-and-sell/ (accessed August 12, 2020); Lauren Thomas, "Unlike Most Retailers, Lululemon Is Opening Stores. But It's Not One Size Fits All," *CNBC*, April 24, 2019, https://www.cnbc.com/2019/04/24/lululemon-has-a-new-plan-for-its-real-estate.html; "Lululemon Unveils 'Power of Three' Strategic Plan to Accelerate Growth," Lululemon Athletica Inc. corporate website, https://investor.lululemon.com/news-releases/news-release-details/lululemon-unveils-power-three-strategic-plan-accelerate-growth (accessed August 12, 2020); Russ Macumber, "How Lululemon's Marketing Is Making You Their Next Ambassador," *Impress!ve.*, October 21, 2019, https://www.impressivedigital.com/internet-marketing/how-lululemons-marketing-is-making-you-their-next-ambassador/; Sharon Terlep, "Lululemon Buys Mirror, an At-Home Fitness Startup, for $500 Million," *Wall Street Journal*, June 30, 2020, https://www.wsj.com/articles/lululemon-to-buy-at-home-fitness-company-mirror-for-500-million-11593465981; Lauren Thomas, "Lululemon CEO: Some Retailers Will Be Able to 'Weather' Coronavirus Pandemic. Others Won't," *CNBC*, April 2, 2020, https://www.cnbc.com/2020/04/02/lululemon-ceo-not-all-retailers-will-weather-coronavirus-pandemic.html; Financial Post Staff, "What Lululemon's $500 Million Deal to Buy Mirror Says About the Future of Exercising at Home," *Financial Post*, July 6, 2020, https://financialpost.com/news/retail-marketing/what-lululemons-500-million-deal-to-buy-mirror-says-about-the-future-of-exercising-at-home; Joni Sweet, "7 Big Changes Coming to Yoga Studios When They Reopen," *Forbes*, May 28, 2020, https://www.forbes.com/sites/jonisweet/2020/05/27/7-big-changes-coming-to-yoga-studios-when-they-reopen-after-coronavirus/#6f44f97266dc; Adrianne Pasquarelli, "Lululemon Remains 'Very Committed' to Experiential Stores," *AdAge*, June 11, 2020, https://adage.com/article/cmo-strategy/lululemon-remains-very-committed-experiential-stores/2261766; Jim Tierney, "How Lululemon Is Kicking It Up with Its Experiential Premium Loyalty Program," *Clarus Commerce*, December 17, 2019, https://www.claruscommerce.com/blog/how-lululemon-is-kicking-it-up-with-its-experiential-premium-loyalty-program/; Pamela N. Danziger, "Lululemon Is On Fire Thanks to the Power of Community Retail," *Forbes*, December 12, 2019, https://www.forbes.com/sites/pamdanziger/2019/12/12/lululemon-is-on-fire-thanks-to-the-power-of-community-retail/#5f3ea7755df8; "Nike Live Launches in Long Beach and Tokyo," *Nike News*, October 31, 2019, https://news.nike.com/news/nike-live-launches-in-long-beach-and-tokyo.

13 Promotion I: Planning and Advertising

Used with permission from Sara Bamossy

Meet Sara Bamossy
▼ A Decision Maker at the Pitch Agency

Sara Bamossy is a Strategy Executive with 17+ years of experience driving growth for some of the world's largest brands across a breadth of categories with clients including Toyota, P&G, PepsiCo, Roche, Microsoft, Netflix, Burger King, Konami, and Westfield.

At the time of this case study, Sara was the Chief Strategy Officer of Pitch, a creative agency in Los Angeles. Previously, she spent 10 years at Saatchi & Saatchi Worldwide at the LA, London, Paris, and Sydney offices.

One of Sara's specialties is the relationship between data and creativity. She has been consulted for her expertise by publications such as *Ad Age* and has spoken at the Cannes Festival of Creativity on how creative design can unlock the power of modern data. Sara has been recognized by industry honors including Cannes Lions, Effies, and Chiat Awards, and she's been named one of the Internationalist's Innovators of the Year.

Sara's Info

What I do when I'm not working:
I love travel, as well as coming home again to approach everything with fresh eyes and new ideas.

First job out of school:
In high school, I worked at the Gallup Poll doing market research surveys . . . and the rest is history.

Career high:
As someone who loves my job, it's hard to pick! I still remember the first time I was sent to Japan to test drive prototype cars as a young strategist leading a vehicle launch . . . . It was a pinch-myself-to-make-sure-this-is-real career moment.

A job-related mistake I wish I hadn't made:
Not leaving a specific role that wasn't right for me sooner; I knew in my heart and in my mind it wasn't right after three months, and I muscled on for too long.

Business book I'm reading now:
Strategy Is Your Words by Mark Pollard

My hero:
It would be amazing to be reincarnated as a superhuman combination of Ruth Bader Ginsburg, Gwen Stefani, and Tina Fey.

My motto to live by:
Be an arrow not a brick.

What drives me:
The thrill of solving a complicated problem

My management style:
Chameleon Coach. I prefer a strengths-based management style that best fits each individual's needs.

Don't do this when interviewing with me:
Tell me that you view the role as just a short-term stop on your career path.

My pet peeve:
Wasting time (see also: being unprepared, making excuses, finger pointing)

Here's my problem...

Real **People**, Real **Choices**

After a series of enormously successful business decisions across promotions, operations, and menu innovation, Burger King was posting U.S. sales gains when competitors were failing or stagnant. By mid-2015, Burger King was outperforming McDonald's and Wendy's by significant margins in sales. However, the brand was lagging its main competitors in imagery. In the third quarter, Sara and her team turned their attention to refining their advertising strategy and optimizing communications.

Mass communications for quick-service restaurants (QSRs) must drive traffic quickly, often to promote specific menu items with immediate and ambitious sales gains. Sara needed to find a way to develop and implement long-range brand planning within the business reality of this fast-moving industry. Her role was to create a strategy that would enable Burger King to tell a consistent brand story with the flexibility to support a wide range of new and core menu items across all day parts. BK has always been known and loved for "Have It Your Way," flame-grilling, and the Whopper. As the brand evolved, The King was introduced to bring in a younger audience and was later retired in favor of a broader reaching "Taste Is King" campaign. The question became, what's next for BK marketing?

As CSO (Chief Strategy Officer) of Pitch, Sara partnered with Burger King North America on an action plan to get to the ultimate strategy, with inputs from data mining, consumer research, and competitive analysis. Along the way, Sara and her team reached a key decision point for the Burger King brand: Should they bring back The King or find a new road? Should Burger King's new long-range strategy take advantage of latent equity in a past icon?

Sara considered her **options** 1·2

1
Option

Leave The King in the past where he belongs. The QSR landscape, the economy, and consumer attitudes toward fast food had all evolved since Burger King stopped using The King in 2011. The rise of fast casual dining options (like Chipotle), health macro trends (clean eating, organic), and fast meal behavior changes (i.e., Starbucks and meal replacement bars) all impacted the fast-food industry. Also, even at the height of his popularity, The King was a bit tricky as a company spokesman. When depictions were not carefully crafted, he became "creepy" and relevant to a narrow audience of millennial men. His edgy persona differentiated him among this group because as a brand icon, he was a part of pop culture and a

departure from the typical overly wholesome "mascots" many companies use. Clearly, during the time of his reign, The King was a well-recognized advertising icon, but he was not an automatic traffic driver. Some people thought he had nothing to do with where they were going to eat lunch that day.

On the other hand, it is difficult to create a brand new icon from scratch. If a QSR brand doesn't have highly identifiable brand markers (think Ronald McDonald or Wendy), customers can easily misattribute its mass communications to similar products—so you wind up advertising for the competition. The King was like a giant sponge that sucked up *earned media coverage* (exposure as a result of natural publicity rather than paid advertising) and kept Burger King in the pop-culture spotlight. That kind of exposure is hard to replicate.

2
Option

Bring back The King as an instantly recognizable icon. The King still had high awareness even after several years away from the spotlight. Using The King could boost brand attribution, especially for promotions. As an icon, he had the potential to drive PR and buzz when he authentically and organically fit into pop-culture moments. Using a brand icon is one of the fastest ways to optimize media impact because the icon brings an instant branding kick.

On the other hand, brand spokespeople (even imagined ones) need to be very carefully crafted and follow strictly adhered-to guidelines or they can become gimmicks. By the end of his reign in 2011, The King was no longer directly tied to business and brand needs when he was used in messaging. A perception existed that The King had become overexposed by the time he retired. To take full advantage of The King's earned media potential, the brand must be willing to make and act on decisions *very quickly* in a constantly churning Internet news cycle. That would mean resuscitating a new and improved King who would be able to rule over a kingdom that's shaped by unpredictable social media trends rather than the predictable television campaigns of days past.

Now put yourself in Sara's shoes. Which option would you choose, and why?

You Choose

Which **Option** would you choose, and **why**?
☐ Option 1   ☐ Option 2

13.1 Communication Models in a Digital World That Is "Always On"

OBJECTIVE

Understand the communication process and the traditional promotion mix.

Test your advertising memory:

1. Which pizza restaurant's slogan is "Better Ingredients, Better Pizza"? Papa John's or Little Caesars?
2. Which fast-food restaurant's slogan is "I'm Lovin' It"? McDonald's or Burger King?
3. Which insurance company says "15 minutes can save you 15 percent or more on car insurance"? Progressive or GEICO?

4. Which auto manufacturer calls its car "The Relentless Pursuit of Perfection"? Mercedes or Lexus?*

Did you get them all right? You owe your knowledge about these and a thousand other trivia questions to the efforts of people who specialize in marketing communication. Of course, today, these slogans are "old school" as marketers have followed consumers onto Facebook and Twitter and into virtual worlds to talk with their customers.

So far, we've talked about creating, managing, pricing, and delivering products. But it's not enough just to produce great products—successful marketing plans must also provide effective marketing communication strategies. As we said in Chapter 1, *promotion* is the coordination of marketing communication efforts to influence attitudes or behavior. This function is the last of the famous *four Ps* of the marketing mix, and it plays a vital role—whether the goal is to sell pizza, chicken, insurance, or automobiles.

Suppose you want to market a new autonomous (self-driving) car. Let's think about all the tools you have available. Of course, you have the tried-and-true traditional advertising options: TV, radio, magazines, outdoor billboards, etc. You would need personal salespeople to tell prospective customers about the benefits of your car and answer their questions. In today's Web 2.0 world, you also have the many different types of digital advertising and social media marketing. Add to that a bit of sales promotion, public relations, and direct marketing, and, voila—you're selling lots of cars.

Of course, virtually *everything* an organization says and does is a form of marketing communication. The ads it creates, the packages it designs, and the uniforms its employees wear, contribute to the thoughts and feelings people have about the company and its products. The same is true for what other consumers say about their experiences with the brand on Facebook or in their Amazon.com product reviews. Today, the importance of what both the company and others say in the digital world has grown exponentially as consumers spend less and less time with traditional media.

Just what do we mean by communication? Today, messages assume many forms: quirky TV commercials, innovative websites, viral videos, blogs, Internet advertising, mobile apps, social media sites, sophisticated magazine ads, funky T-shirts, blimps blinking messages over football stadiums—even do-it-yourself, customer-made advertising on social media. Some marketing communications push specific products (like the Apple iPad) or actions (like donating blood), whereas others try to create or reinforce an image that represents the entire organization (like General Electric or the Catholic Church).

Marketing communication in general performs one or more of four roles:

1. It *informs* consumers about new goods and services.
2. It *reminds* consumers to continue using certain brands.
3. It *persuades* consumers to choose one brand over others.
4. It *builds* relationships with customers.

integrated marketing communication (IMC)
A strategic business process that marketers use to plan, develop, execute, and evaluate coordinated, measurable, persuasive brand communication programs over time to targeted audiences.

multichannel promotion strategy
A marketing communication strategy where marketers combine traditional advertising, sales promotion, and public relations activities with online buzz-building activities.

Today, marketing experts believe a successful promotion strategy should coordinate diverse forms of marketing communication to deliver a consistent message. **Integrated marketing communication (IMC)** is the process that marketers use "to plan, develop, execute, and evaluate coordinated, measurable, persuasive brand communication programs over time to targeted audiences."[1] The IMC approach argues that consumers come in contact with a company or a brand in many different ways before, after, and during a purchase. Consumers see these points of contact—a TV commercial, a company website, a photo posted on Facebook, a company app, a coupon, the company's physical facilities, the company delivery trucks, or a display in a store—as a whole, as a single company that speaks to them in different places and different ways.

To achieve their marketing communication goals, marketers must selectively use some or all of these to deliver a consistent message to their customers in a **multichannel promotion strategy**

*Answers: (1) Papa John's (2) McDonald's (3) GEICO (4) Lexus

where they combine traditional marketing communication activities (advertising, sales promotion, public relations, and direct marketing) with social media and other online buzz-building activities. That's a lot different from most traditional marketing communication programs of the past that made little effort to coordinate the varying messages consumers received. When a TV advertising campaign runs independently of a sweepstakes, which in turn has no relation to a NASCAR racing sponsorship or the company website, consumers often get conflicting messages that leave them confused and unsure of the brand's identity. We'll talk more about multichannel strategies later in this chapter.

To better understand marketing communications today, let's look at the three different models of marketing communication, as shown in Figure 13.1. The first, the traditional communication model, is a "one-to-many" view in which a single marketer develops and sends messages to many, perhaps even millions of, consumers at the same time. The one-to-many approach involves traditional forms of marketing communication, such as *advertising*. Advertising includes traditional mass media (TV, radio, magazines, and newspapers); *out-of-home materials*, such as billboards; and digital or Internet assets, such as banners, pop-ups, search engines, and email advertising. This model also benefits from *consumer sales promotions*—such as coupons, samples, rebates, games, or contests—and press releases and special events that *public relations* professionals organize.

We also need to expand our traditional communication model to include the *one-to-one model*, where marketers speak to consumers and business customers individually. The one-to-one forms of marketing communication include *personal selling, trade sales promotion*

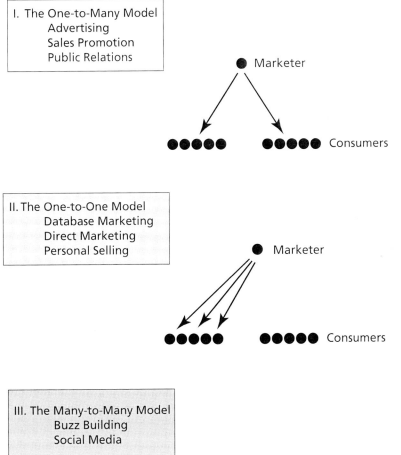

Figure 13.1 *Snapshot* | Three Models of Marketing Communication

Marketers today make use of the traditional one-to-many communication model and the updated many-to-many communication model as well as talking one-to-one with consumers and business customers.

I. The One-to-Many Model
   Advertising
   Sales Promotion
   Public Relations

Marketer

Consumers

II. The One-to-One Model
   Database Marketing
   Direct Marketing
   Personal Selling

Marketer

Consumers

III. The Many-to-Many Model
   Buzz Building
   Social Media

Marketer

Consumers

word-of-mouth communication
When consumers provide information about products to other consumers.

activities used to support personal selling, and a variety of *database marketing* activities that include direct marketing.

In today's "always on" world that we discussed in Chapter 1, the importance of the *updated "many-to-many" model* of marketing communication increases exponentially. This newer perspective recognizes the huge impact of social media and its use in **word-of-mouth communication**, where consumers look to each other for information and recommendations. Many of us are more likely to choose a new restaurant based on users' reviews we read on Yelp than because we saw a cool commercial for the place on TV.

In the updated model, marketers add new tools to their communications toolbox, including *buzz-building* activities that use *viral* and *evangelical marketing techniques* as well as new social media platforms, such as *brand communities, product review sites*, and *social networking sites* where consumers talk to lots of other consumers. The odds are you're using many of these platforms already. After we look at the basic communication process, we'll examine each of these three different ways to communicate with customers more closely.

In this chapter, we focus primarily on advertising, a one-to-many communication model, and also discuss direct marketing, a one-to-one form of communication. In Chapter 14, our second chapter on promotion, we look at social media marketing, consumer and B2B sales promotion, personal selling, and public relations. But first, we need to understand the communication process and Web 2.0 communication.

The Communication Process

communication process
The process whereby meaning is transferred from a source to a receiver.

Of course, promotion strategies can succeed only if we are able to get customers to understand what we're trying to say. The **communication process** shown in Figure 13.2 is a good way to understand the basics of how any kind of message works—from you telling your friends about

Figure 13.2 *Process* | Communication Process

The communication process explains how organizations or individuals create and transmit messages from the marketer (the source) to the consumer (the receiver) who understands what the marketer intends to say (we hope).

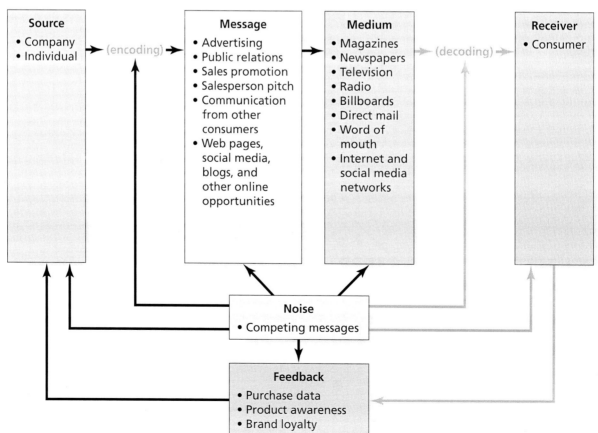

your great spring break in Key West to that little green gecko telling millions of consumers to buy GEICO insurance. In this perspective, a *source* transmits a *message* through some *medium* to a *receiver* who hears, pays attention to, and understands the message (we hope). Marketers need to understand the function and importance of each of the elements of the process.

The Source Encodes

Let's start to explore this basic communication process from a good place: the beginning. First, there is a person or organization—the **source**—that has an idea it wants to communicate to a receiver, such as potential customers. To do this, the source must translate the idea into a physically perceivable form (like a TV commercial) that conveys the desired meaning. This **encoding** process means the source may translate the idea into different forms to convey the desired meaning. We may use words, music, a celebrity (Jennifer Aniston for Aveeno skin care products or Justin Bieber for Calvin Klein), an unknown actor, an actual customer, or even that animated gecko lizard to speak to consumers.

source
An organization or individual that sends a message.

encoding
The process of translating an idea into a form of communication that will convey meaning.

The Message

The **message** is the actual content of that physically perceivable form of communication that goes from the source to a receiver. The message may be in the form of a traditional broadcast or print ad, a public relations press release, a coupon offer, a different sales promotion program, a salesperson's pitch, a direct marketing infomercial, a Facebook post, a video on YouTube, or a customer's comment on a blog. It includes (hopefully) the information necessary to persuade, inform, remind, or build a relationship. The marketer must select the ad elements carefully so that the message connects with end consumers or business customers in its target market.

message
The communication in physical form that goes from a sender to a receiver.

The Medium

No matter how the source encodes the message, it must then transmit that message via a **medium**, a communication vehicle that reaches members of a target audience. For marketers, this vehicle can be TV, radio, a magazine, social media sites such as Facebook or Twitter, a company website, an Internet blog, a billboard, or even a coffee mug that displays a product logo. Marketers face two major challenges when they select a medium: first, that the target market will be exposed to the medium, and second, that the characteristics and image of the product are not in conflict with the medium.

medium
A communication vehicle through which a message is transmitted to a target audience.

The Receiver Decodes

If a tree falls in the forest and no one hears it, did it make a sound? Zen mysteries aside, communication cannot occur unless a **receiver** is there to get the message. The receiver is any individual or organization that intercepts and interprets the message. **Decoding** is the process whereby a receiver assigns meaning to a message; that is, he or she translates the message he or she sees or hears back into an idea that makes sense to him or her.

Marketers hope that the target consumer will decode the message the way they intended, but effective communication occurs only when the source and the receiver have had similar experiences and thus share a mutual frame of reference. Too often, sources and receivers aren't on the same page, a mismatch that is especially likely to happen when the source and the receiver don't share the same cultural background, experiences, values, or language.

receiver
The organization or individual that intercepts and interprets the message.

decoding
The process by which a receiver assigns meaning to the message.

Noise

The communication process also acknowledges that **noise**—anything that interferes with effective communication—can block messages. As the many arrows between noise and the other elements of the communication process in Figure 13.2 indicate, this interference can occur at any stage of communication.

noise
Anything that interferes with effective communication.

Campbell Soup Company's V8 vegetable juice, created in 1933, continues to maintain its loyal following with simple and straightforward messages like this one.

feedback

Receivers' reactions to the message.

Feedback

To complete the communication loop, the source gets **feedback** from receivers. Of course, the best feedback for marketing communication is for consumers to purchase the product. Other types of feedback occur with a phone call or an email to the manufacturer. And it's even better feedback when someone posts the ad on YouTube, Facebook, or Instagram and it goes viral, delivering the message to millions of other consumers. That's why Atticus the hedgehog; Yeti Kong, a monkey; and Ella Bean, a three-pound rescue dog—all animal-clients of The Dog Agency (TDA)—have a combined 1.25 million human followers on Instagram.[2] TDA has secured work for the animals for brands such as Google, Dyson, 20th Century Fox, Barneys New York, Accor Hotels, Purina, and Nikon.[3] More often, though, marketers must actively seek their customers' feedback through marketing research.

Updated Web 2.0 Communication

The communication process we just reviewed still describes the basic process through which many marketers have always connected with their customers. But you'd have to be living under a rock not to recognize that we're living through profound changes in the way we link to companies—and to each other. We can trace these important changes to the advent of Web 2.0, which we discussed in Chapter 1. The continuing evolution of interactive technology (OK, we'll stop and wait while you check your Facebook page) pushes marketers to fundamentally reevaluate how they should reach out and touch consumers. No, we're not going to throw the baby out with the bathwater by claiming that traditional communications are dead. But, we do need to make some important updates that reflect how *you* link to marketers today.

Today, as consumers, we are active participants in the game. We email or post comments on what we see, and many of us post our own original content in the form of YouTube videos, blogs, and perhaps stupid cat photos. As a result, we now live in a 24/7 media environment that is very much a free-for-all in terms of who gets to send and receive messages. In addition, marketers can create messages that reach specific individuals (like when they show you ads on your phone based on the websites you browsed earlier this week), or they can instantaneously beam the same content to literally millions of people with just a click. This fundamental change means that marketers have to revise their thinking in terms of how they can connect with and respond to their customers.

Think this isn't for you? You can be assured that whether you go to work in marketing for a government or not-for-profit agency like a city chamber of commerce, a large retailer like Walmart or a small business like the local pizza restaurant, a manufacturer like Nike or a service provider like a hospital—you will be heavily involved in online marketing communications. It is no longer an option for any organization that seeks to be successful. How does Web 2.0 change the way we look at the communications process? To simplify matters, let's say that it pushes us to take a new look at the three different models of marketing communication that we discussed earlier.

First, as we saw earlier in Figure 13.1, we distinguish among communications in terms of how specific the audience is:

1. The one-to-many model: This model is the traditional form of mass communication whereby a broadcaster sends a message to a very large audience (like a commercial you see while you're watching *Outer Banks*).

2. The one-to-one model: This format describes messages that are up close and personal. This is the oldest way to communicate, but it's still important in many marketing contexts today. Although you may doubt this when you watch a typical couple out on a

date who spend the whole evening texting their friends instead of actually holding a conversation with each other, anytime you work with a salesperson, a wedding consultant, or maybe a financial planner, you're still doing things old school.

3. The many-to-many model: This format describes the social media revolution that allows almost everyone to engage in a constant conversation with almost everyone else! We'll dive into this more deeply in Chapter 14.

Second, we distinguish between communications that originate with the marketers versus those that don't. **Outbound marketing** describes many of the activities we identified in the original one-to-many model: It refers to messages that come from the organization and are intended for those who have agreed to receive them (unless they're spam!). As we'll see later, it's not always clear where these messages actually originate and how accurate they are (think "fake news"), but as a form of promotion, their goal is to inform, remind, persuade, and/or build relationships with receivers.

In contrast, **inbound marketing** refers to linkages that come *to* the organization from others outside. Maybe you're browsing a website, and you click a link to receive an **ethical bribe**, like a free e-book or a product sample; by doing so, you're sending the company feedback on their link. Or, perhaps you're googling a term like "home theaters," and you click a few companies that come up on your search page; again, you're communicating a response to their messages. As we'll see later, virtually all of the millions of dollars that organizations spend to tweak their websites go toward maximizing the likelihood that you will contact them instead of their competitors.

The Promotion Mix

As we said previously, promotion, or marketing communication, is one of the famous four Ps. Marketers use the term **promotion mix** to refer to the communication elements that the marketer controls. The elements of the traditional promotion mix include advertising, sales promotion, public relations, personal selling, and direct marketing. Table 13.1 presents some of the pros and cons of each element of the traditional promotion mix. Because the source creates and manages these, for the most part, they are paid media and owned media. Public relations, on the other hand, focuses more on earned media.

Today, the Internet adds other powerful forms of advertising and marketing communications. Marketers now must add digital and social media to the list of communication elements they can work with. The new promotion mix includes:

- Media advertising
- Sales promotion
- Public relations, including event marketing and sponsorships
- Personal selling
- Direct marketing
- Out-of-home advertising
- Point-of-purchase advertising
- Social media
- Digital/Internet advertising (We'll talk about these digital additions to the marketing mix in Chapter 14.)

Promotion works best when the marketer skillfully combines all of the elements of the promotion mix to deliver a single consistent message about a brand. In addition, the promotion mix must work in harmony with the overall *marketing mix* to combine elements of promotion with place, price, and product to position the firm's offering in people's minds. For example, marketers must design ads for luxury products, such as Rolex watches or Jaguar automobiles, to communicate that same luxury character of the product, and the ads should appear in places that reinforce that upscale image. A chic

outbound marketing
Messages that come from the organization and are intended for those who have agreed to receive them.

inbound marketing
Messages that come *to* the organization from others outside.

ethical bribe
A fancy term for an opt-in incentive to join an email mailing list.

promotion mix
The communication elements that the marketer controls.

Table 13.1 | A Comparison of Elements of the Traditional Promotion Mix

Promotion Element	Pros	Cons
Advertising	• The marketer has control over what the message will say, when it will appear, and who is likely to see it.	• Because of the high cost to produce and distribute, it may not be an efficient means of communicating with some target audiences. • Some ads may have low credibility or be ignored by the audience.
Sales promotion	• Provides incentives to retailers to support one's products. • Builds excitement for retailers and consumers. • Encourages immediate purchase and trial of new products. • Price-oriented promotions cater to price-sensitive consumers.	• Short-term emphasis on immediate sales rather than a focus on building brand loyalty. • The number of competing promotions may make it hard to break through the promotion clutter. • If marketers use too many price-related sales promotion activities, consumers' perception of a fair price for the brand may be lowered.
Public relations	• Relatively low cost. • High credibility.	• Lack of control over the message that is eventually transmitted and no guarantee that the message will ever reach the target. • It is relatively difficult to measure the effectiveness of public relations efforts.
Personal selling	• Direct contact with the customer gives the salesperson the opportunity to be flexible and modify the sales message to coincide with the customer's needs. • The salesperson can get immediate feedback from the customer.	• High cost per contact with customer. • Difficult to ensure consistency of message when it is delivered by many different company representatives. • The credibility of salespeople often depends on the quality of their company's image, which has been created by other promotion strategies.
Direct marketing	• Targets specific groups of potential customers with different offers. • Marketers can easily measure the results. • Provides extensive product information and multiple offers within a single appeal. • Provides a way for a company to collect feedback about the effectiveness of its messages in an internal database.	• Consumers may have a negative opinion of some types of direct marketing. • Costs more per contact than mass appeals.

---

commercial that appears during the commercial breaks of an episode of *Swamp People* just won't cut it.

Marketers have a lot more control over some kinds of marketing communication messages than they do over others. As Figure 13.3 shows, *mass-media advertising* and *sales promotion* are at one end of the continuum, where the marketer has total control over the message he or she delivers. At the other end, is *word-of-mouth (WOM) communication*, where everyday people rather than the company run the show. WOM includes the social media that consumers use today to keep in touch with friends and potentially millions of other consumers. Who knows what they'll post about a product or service? Sandwiched between the ends, we find *personal selling* and *direct marketing*, where marketers have some but not total control over the message they deliver, and *public relations*, where marketers have even less control.

Figure 13.3 *Snapshot* | Control Continuum

The messages that consumers receive about companies and products differ in terms of how much the marketer can control the content.

High	Extent of marketer's control over communication				Low
Advertising	Sales promotion	Personal selling	Direct marketing	Public relations	Word of mouth

Mass Communication: The One-to-Many Model

Some elements of the promotion mix include messages intended to reach many prospective customers at the same time—the one-to-many model of marketing communication. Whether a company offers customers a coupon for 50 cents off or airs a TV commercial to millions, it promotes itself to a mass audience. These are the elements of the promotion mix that use traditional **mass communication**—that is, TV, radio, magazines, and newspapers:

- *Advertising:* Advertising is, for many, the most familiar and visible element of the promotion mix. Advertising reaches large numbers of consumers at one time and can convey rich and dynamic images that establish and reinforce a distinctive brand identity. Advertising also is useful to communicate factual information about the product or to remind consumers to buy their favorite brand. In recent years, Internet advertising has grown exponentially and has become an important part of the one-to-many model as our small screens fill with promotional messages. We'll talk more about Internet advertising and social media later in this chapter and in Chapter 14.

- *Sales promotion:* Consumer sales promotion includes programs such as contests, coupons, or other incentives that marketers design to build interest in or encourage purchase of a product during a specified period. Unlike other forms of promotion, sales promotion intends to stimulate immediate action (often in the form of a purchase) rather than to build long-term loyalty.

- *Public relations:* Public relations describes a variety of communication activities that seek to create and maintain a positive image of an organization and its products among various *publics*, including customers, government officials, and shareholders. Public relations programs also include efforts to present negative company news in the most positive way so that this information will have less damaging consequences.

mass communication
Relates to TV, radio, magazines, and newspapers.

Personal Communication: The One-to-One Model

Sometimes, marketers want to communicate with consumers on a personal, one-to-one level. The most immediate way for a marketer to make contact with customers is simply to tell them how wonderful the product is. This is part of the *personal selling* element of the promotion mix we mentioned previously. It is the direct interaction between a company representative and a customer that can occur in person, by phone, or even over an interactive computer link.

Marketers also use direct mail, telemarketing, and other *direct marketing* activities to create personal appeals. Like personal selling, direct marketing provides direct communication with a consumer or business customer.

We'll talk about advertising and all its forms in this chapter and then continue our understanding of one-to-many communications by discussing sales promotion and public relations in Chapter 14. Also in Chapter 14, we'll provide an overview of one-to-one communication as the very important personal selling function in marketing. We'll also investigate many-to-many communication afforded by social media and buzz marketing.

13.2 An Overview of Promotion Planning

OBJECTIVE

Describe the steps in traditional and multichannel promotion planning.

Now that we've talked about communication and some of the tools marketers can use to deliver messages to their customers, we need to see how to make it all happen. How do we go about the complex task of developing a promotion plan—one that delivers just the right message to a number of different target audiences when and where they want it in the most effective and cost-efficient way?

Figure 13.4 *Process* | Steps to Develop the Promotion Plan

Development of successful promotion plans involves organizing the complex process into a series of five orderly steps.

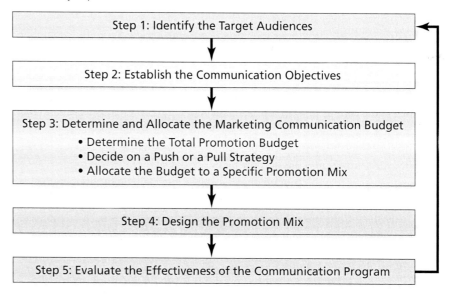

Just as with any other strategic decision-making process, the development of this plan includes several steps, as Figure 13.4 shows. First, we'll go over the steps in promotion planning, and then we'll take a look at how marketers today develop multichannel promotion strategies.

Step 1: Identify the Target Audience(s)

An important part of overall promotion planning is to identify the target audience(s) you want to reach. IMC marketers recognize that we must communicate both with members of our target market and with a variety of stakeholders who influence that target market. After all, we learn about a new product not just from the company that produces it, but also from the news media, from our friends and family, and even from the producers of competitive products. Of course, the intended customer is the most important target audience and the one that marketers focus on the most.

Step 2: Establish the Communication Objectives

As we said, marketers develop communication programs for different target audiences. The whole point of communicating with customers and prospective customers, the most important target audiences, is to let them know in a timely and affordable way that the organization has a product to meet their needs. It's bad enough when a product comes along that people don't want or need. An even bigger marketing sin is to have a product that they *do* want but that you fail to let them know about. Of course, seldom can we deliver a single message to a consumer that magically transforms him or her into a loyal customer. In most cases, it takes a series of messages that moves the consumer through several stages.

We view this process as an uphill climb, such as the one Figure 13.5 depicts. The marketer "pushes" the consumer through a series of steps, or a **hierarchy of effects**, from initial awareness of a product to brand loyalty. At almost any point in time, different members of the target market may have reached each of the stages in the hierarchy. Marketers develop different communication objectives to "push" members of the target market at each level to the next.

hierarchy of effects
A series of steps prospective customers move through, from initial awareness of a product to brand loyalty.

Figure 13.5 *Snapshot* | The Hierarchy of Effects

Communication objectives move consumers through the hierarchy of effects. Marketers have a large number of promotional options to choose from in moving consumers from being unaware of the product to being brand loyal.

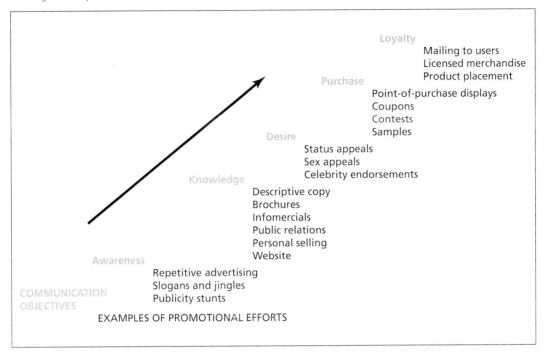

To understand how this process works, imagine how a firm would have to adjust its communication objectives as it tries to establish a presence in the market for Hunk, a new men's cologne. Let's say that the primary target market for the cologne is single men ages 18 to 24 who care about their appearance and who are into health, fitness, working out, and looking ripped. The company would want to focus more on some promotion methods (such as advertising) and less on others (such as personal selling). Next, we'll discuss some communication objectives the company might develop for its Hunk promotion.

Create Awareness

The first step in the hierarchy of effects is to make members of the target market aware that there's a new brand of cologne on the market. The promotion objective might be "To create an 80 percent awareness of Hunk cologne among 18- to 24-year-old men in the first two months."

Note how this objective is worded: Objectives are best when they are quantitative (80 percent), when they specify the target consumer or business group (18- to 24-year-old men), and when they specify the time frame during which the plan is expected to reach the objective (in the first two months). To accomplish this, the fragrance's marketers might place lots of simple advertisements that push the brand name in magazines, on TV, on the radio, and on social media and other Internet sites.

Inform the Market

For those consumers who have heard the name "Hunk" but don't really know anything about it, the challenge is to provide knowledge about the benefits the new product has to offer—to *position* it relative to other colognes (see Chapter 7). The objective at this point might be to "Communicate the connection between Hunk and muscle building so that 60 percent of the target market develops some interest in the product in the first six months of the communication program." To accomplish this, promotion would focus on traditional and online advertising and other communications that emphasize the muscle-building connection.

Create Desire

The next step in the hierarchy is *desire*. The task of marketing communications is to create favorable feelings toward the product and to convince at least some members of this group that they would rather splash on some Hunk than other colognes. The specific objective might be to "Create positive attitudes toward Hunk cologne among 40 percent of the target market and brand preference among 30 percent of the target market in the first year of the campaign." Communication at this stage might include splashy advertising spreads in magazines, perhaps with an endorsement by a well-known celebrity.

Encourage Purchase and Trial

As the expression goes, "How do ya know 'til ya try it?" The company needs to get some of the men who have become interested in the cologne to try it. The specific objective now might be to "Encourage trial of Hunk among 10 percent of 18- to 24-year-old men within the first year." A promotion plan might encourage trial by mailing samples of Hunk to members of the target market, inserting "scratch-and-sniff" samples in bodybuilding magazines, placing elaborate displays in stores that dispense money-saving coupons, or even sponsoring a contest in which the winner gets to have WWE wrestler Braun Strowman as his personal trainer for a day.

Build Loyalty

Loyalty, the final step in the hierarchy of effects, means customers decide to stay with Hunk after they've gone through the first bottle. The objective might be to "Develop and maintain regular usage of Hunk cologne among 5 percent of men from 18 to 24 years old within the first two years of the campaign." Promotion efforts must maintain ongoing communication with current users to reinforce the bond they feel with the product.

Step 3: Determine and Allocate the Marketing Communication Budget

Although setting a budget for marketing communication might seem easy—you just calculate how much you need to accomplish your objectives—in reality, it's not that simple. Figure 13.6 shows the three distinct decisions required to develop the budget.

Budget Decision 1: Determine the Total Marketing Communication Budget

To determine the total amount to spend on marketing communication, most firms rely on one of two types of budgeting techniques: top down and bottom up. With **top-down budgeting techniques**, managers establish the overall amount that the organization will allocate to promotion activities.

The most common top-down technique is the **percentage-of-sales method**, in which the marketing communication budget is based on last year's sales or on estimates for the present year's sales. The advantage of this method is that it ties spending on promotion to sales and profits. Unfortunately, this method can imply that sales cause promotion spending rather than viewing sales as the *outcome* of marketing communication efforts.

The **competitive-parity method** is a fancy way of saying "keep up with the Joneses." In other words, match whatever competitors spend. Another approach is to begin at the beginning: Identify promotion objectives and allocate enough money to accomplish them. That is what **bottom-up budgeting techniques** attempt. This bottom-up logic is at the heart of the **objective-task method**. When it uses this approach, the firm first defines the specific communication goals it hopes to achieve, such as increasing by 20 percent the number of consumers who are aware of the brand. It then tries to figure out how much advertising, sales promotion, buzz marketing, and so on, it will take to meet that goal. Although this is the most rational approach, it is hard to implement because it obliges managers to specify

top-down budgeting techniques
Allocation of the promotion budget based on management's determination of the total amount to be devoted to marketing communication.

percentage-of-sales method
A method for promotion budgeting that is based on a certain percentage of either last year's sales or estimates of the present year's sales.

competitive-parity method
A promotion budgeting method in which an organization matches whatever competitors are spending.

bottom-up budgeting techniques
Allocation of the promotion budget based on identifying promotion goals and allocating enough money to accomplish them.

objective-task method
A promotion budgeting method in which an organization first defines the specific communication goals it hopes to achieve and then tries to calculate what kind of promotion efforts it will take to meet these goals.

Figure 13.6 *Process* | Steps in Developing the Marketing Communication Budget

Budgeting decisions allow marketers to systematically plan IMC spending.

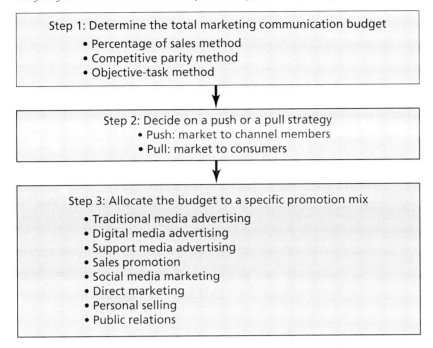

Step 1: Determine the total marketing communication budget
- Percentage of sales method
- Competitive parity method
- Objective-task method

Step 2: Decide on a push or a pull strategy
- Push: market to channel members
- Pull: market to consumers

Step 3: Allocate the budget to a specific promotion mix
- Traditional media advertising
- Digital media advertising
- Support media advertising
- Sales promotion
- Social media marketing
- Direct marketing
- Personal selling
- Public relations

their objectives and attach dollar amounts to them. This method requires careful analysis—and a bit of lucky "guesstimating."

Budget Decision 2: Decide on a Push or a Pull Strategy

The second important decision in marketing communication budgeting is whether the company will use a push or a pull strategy. Push and pull strategies direct decisions about how to divide the market communications budget for different types of promotion activities. A **push strategy** means that the company wants to move its products by convincing channel members to offer them and entice their customers to select these items; it pushes them through the channel. This approach assumes that if consumers see the product on store shelves, they will be motivated to make a trial purchase. In this case, marketers spend the promotion budget on personal selling, trade advertising, and trade sales promotion activities that will "push" the product from producer through the channel of distribution to consumers.

In contrast, a company that relies on a **pull strategy** is counting on creating consumer demand for its products with marketing communication aimed at the consumers. This popularity will then convince retailers to respond by stocking these items. In this case, the bulk of the communication budget goes for traditional and online media advertising and consumer sales promotion to stimulate interest among end consumers who will "pull" the product onto store shelves and then into their shopping carts.

Budget Decision 3: Allocate the Budget to a Specific Promotion Mix

The final step in planning the communication budget is to allocate the total budget among the elements in the promotion mix. In today's dynamic media environment, there are few clear guidelines on how to divide up the promotion pie—though we are witnessing a steady shift away from traditional advertising media and toward so-called "new media," like Facebook and Google. In some cases, managers may simply have a preference for advertising versus sales promotion or other elements of the promotion mix. Also, consumers vary widely in the likelihood that they will respond to various communication

push strategy
The company tries to move its products through the channel by convincing channel members to offer them.

pull strategy
The company tries to move its products through the channel by building desire for the products among consumers, thus convincing retailers to respond to this demand by stocking these items.

elements. College students for example are especially likely to spend most of their time on the Internet (but you knew that).

Although traditional media advertising (TV, newspaper, radio, magazine, and outdoor) used to get the lion's share of the promotion budget, today spending on Internet advertising is almost a third of total advertising spending. Overall U.S. major media advertising spending in 2019, for example, was around $248.9 billion, an increase over 2018 spending of 4.0 percent. Of that, Internet advertising spending increased 18 percent to $108.6 billion, more than total TV spending of $65.7 billion. Spending on other marketing services (sales promotion, telemarketing, direct mail, event sponsorship, directories, and public relations) was $249.1 billion, about a third of which was spent on sales promotion.[4]

Step 4: Design the Promotion Mix

Designing the promotion mix is the most complicated step in marketing communication planning. It includes determining the specific communication tools to use, what message to communicate, and the communication channel(s) that will be used to send the message.

In the "old days" before the Internet (believe it or not, there was such a time!), this was a simple process of primarily deciding on advertising and sales promotion programs. Today the decisions are much more complicated. Do we continue to use traditional mass media advertising? How will we include digital communications? Buzz marketing? Sales promotion? And even more important, how will we make sure these are all integrated to provide our customers with a seamless, consistent experience? Not only are the questions complicated, they are also different for each product and for each target audience.

Step 5: Evaluate the Effectiveness of the Communication Program

As marketers are faced with the need for greater accountability and they often have to document the ROMI (discussed in Chapter 3) of their marketing communications and other marketing activities, evaluating the effectiveness of the communication program is more important than ever. It would be nice if a marketing manager could simply report, "The $3 million campaign for our revolutionary glow-in-the-dark surfboards brought in $15 million in new sales!" It's not so easy. Many random factors in the marketing environment are out of the control of the marketer and can impact sales: a rival's manufacturing problem, a coincidental photograph of a movie star toting one of the boards, or perhaps a surge of renewed interest in surfing sparked by a cult movie hit like *Blue Crush*.

As we discussed in Chapter 4, marketers use a variety of different methods to monitor and evaluate the company's communication efforts. The catch is that it's easier to determine the effectiveness of some forms of communication than others. As a rule, various types of sales promotion are the easiest to evaluate because they occur over a fixed, usually short period, making it easier to link to sales volume. Traditional advertising, on the other hand, has lagged or delayed effects so that an ad people see this month might influence a car purchase next month or even a year from now. Typically, researchers measure brand awareness, recall of product benefits communicated through advertising, and even the image of the brand before and after an advertising campaign. They use similar measures to assess the effectiveness of salespeople and of public relations activities.

Multichannel Promotion Strategies

As we said previously in this chapter, marketers today recognize that the traditional one-to-many communication model in which they spent millions of dollars broadcasting ads to a mass audience is less and less effective. Experts suggest there are two reasons for this. First, advertisers no longer have a captive TV audience, as many consumers have a second screen going while watching TV. Also, other consumers influence purchases via social media. At the same time, it isn't yet clear how effective the new many-to-many model is—or what marketing metrics we should use to measure how well these new media work.

Thus, many marketers opt for multichannel promotion strategies where they combine traditional advertising, sales promotion, public relations, and direct marketing activities with social media or other digital communication activities. The choice to employ multichannel marketing yields important benefits. First, these strategies boost the effectiveness of either online or offline strategies used alone. And multichannel strategies allow marketers to repeat their messages across various channels, strengthening brand awareness and providing more opportunities to convert customers.

Perhaps the best way to really understand how marketers develop multichannel strategies is to look at how some do it and do it well. HBO TV launched the *Game of Thrones* series with what was one of the best multichannel strategies ever. The global campaign included traditional media, TV, billboards, and print. In addition, over-the-top events and newer media including a Tumblr presence, YouTube channel, website, Facebook page, and Twitter account created consumer-generated Internet buzz. The campaigns showed how offline and online activities can work together seamlessly to deliver a single customer experience. Throughout its eight seasons, HBO continued to find innovative ways to keep its *Game of Thrones* consumers engaged at each step of the experience, from generating awareness before the show launched, to maintaining high levels of engagement, and finally, cultivating consumers' loyalty. What's even more remarkable is that HBO continued its very successful multichannel marketing right through the final eighth season of the wildly popular series.

In the final season, all marketing activities were focused on the theme "Capture the Throne." In the South by Southwest "experience" named "Bleed for the Throne," fans were asked to literally bleed for a glimpse at Westeros. This event drew fans from far away to Austin, Texas, to participate in an American Red Cross blood drive. A "Create the Throne" event was a collection of artists' re-imaginings of 18 of the show's props. "Quest for the Throne" was a global scavenger hunt for six hidden Iron Thrones. The prize was a crown and, of course, bragging rights. Other events included NowTV's offer for free *Game of Thrones* tattoos, and dating app OkCupid's offer of a *Game of Thrones* profile badge to allow them to identify other single fans and find dates. To round things out, there were limited-edition Oreos, $100 T-shirts, *Thrones*-themed food trucks in New York City and Los Angeles that earned 120 million digital and social impressions, and a two-page spread of fictional *Thrones* news stories in the *New York Times*.[5]

In the remainder of this chapter and the next, we will look at the various marketing communication activities that marketers may include in the multichannel promotion strategy we discussed already in this chapter. In this chapter, we look at advertising that supports the one-to-many communication model. We begin with traditional advertising that consumers access through traditional media. We also talk about direct marketing in this chapter. In Chapter 14, we discuss some of the fine details of many-to-many social media marketing followed by consumer and business-to-business sales promotion. We continue looking at the remaining communication tools that include personal selling and public relations.

You know from your own daily experience that you interact with brands in many different ways. Maybe you see a TV commercial, check out a T-shirt with a brand logo, look at a billboard on the highway, read a Facebook post where someone in your network rants or raves about a product . . . and that's all before lunch! Today successful marketers know they must use multichannel marketing communication campaigns that provide information and also enhance. The multichannel campaign may include traditional media, social media, mobile applications, email, websites, direct mail, call centers, and the salesforce, maximizing the strengths of each. And it's not just about the information. Multichannel campaigns need to provide a customer experience that will engage the customer and add something of value (in addition to the product) to the customer's life.

13.3 Advertising

OBJECTIVE

Explain what advertising is, describe the major types of advertising, discuss some of the major criticisms of advertising, and describe the process of developing an advertising campaign and how marketers evaluate advertising.

Today it seems everything about marketing is changing—all at one time. Nowhere is that more evident than in advertising. Advertising has been with us a long time. In ancient Greece and Rome, ad messages appeared on walls, were etched on stone tablets, or were shouted by criers, interspersed among announcements of successful military battles, lost slaves, or government proclamations. As the technology that's available to connect us with companies and other consumers continues to evolve, we see that advertising evolves as well. And the differences between advertising and other types of marketing communications have blurred as advertising agencies find new ways to take advantage of all the exciting communications options that are available to them today.

advertising
Nonpersonal communication from an identified sponsor using the mass media.

We traditionally define **advertising** as nonpersonal communication from an identified sponsor using the mass media. Advertising is so much a part of marketing that many people think that advertising *is* marketing (but remember that product, price, and distribution strategies are crucial as well). And, as we saw previously, there are many ways to get a message out to a target audience in addition to advertising. But make no mistake: Traditional advertising is still important, especially because the Internet gives marketers yet another important medium to use when they want to talk to large numbers of customers at once. In 2019, total U.S.-measured-media ad spending for *Advertising Age*'s top 200 advertisers was about $69 billion, or about 40 percent of measured-media ad spending for all advertisers. Of all product categories, retail advertising topped the list with spending for all advertisers on measured advertising (Internet, magazines, newspapers, radio, TV, and cinema) at $15.5 billion.[6]

One thing is sure: As the media landscape continues to change, so will advertising. Sales of Internet-ready smart TVs are booming, as is the number of households with digital video recorders (DVRs) that let viewers skip through the commercials. Watching TV through your mobile devices also is on the rise because many cable and satellite providers now let you use apps to stream your favorite TV episodes. It's so popular that there's even a name for it: **TV Everywhere**, or **authenticated streaming**. TV Everywhere is a term that describes using your Internet-enabled device, like a tablet or smartphone, to stream content from your cable or satellite provider.[7] Digital streaming is growing rapidly; 85 percent of Internet users in the U.S. use streaming services to watch digital content online and 34 percent of U.S. TV viewers use streaming services to watch content on their TV. The revenue for Hulu in 2019 included over $670 million in advertising revenues and $1.27 billion from subscription fees. As more and more consumers subscribe to the streaming services, advertising revenues for traditional cable TV will decline. Advertisers will put more money into streaming services in order to retain their audience.[8]

TV Everywhere, or **authenticated streaming**
The use of an Internet-enabled device, like a tablet or smartphone, to stream content from a cable or satellite provider.

So, with almost everyone spending so much time looking at small screens instead of TVs, billboards, and newspapers, is traditional advertising dead? Don't write any obituaries yet. Mass media communication remains the best way to reach a large audience. For that reason, producers of FMCGs (fast-moving consumer goods that we discussed in Chapter 8), such as P&G and Unilever, will continue to rely on these traditional channels of communication to reach their customers even as they add newer digital communications.

Types of Advertising Based on Marketing Goals

Because they spend so much on advertising, marketers must decide which type of ad will work best to get their money's worth given their organizational and marketing goals. As Figure 13.7 shows, the advertisements an organization runs can take many forms, so let's review the most common kinds.

Product Advertising

When you think about advertising, what comes to mind first? Is it the heartwarming Xfinity commercial where E.T. comes back 37 years later and meets Elliott again? Perhaps it's one of Nike's "Just do it" commercials, or maybe you like the Aflac duck ads best. These are examples of **product advertising**, where the message focuses on a specific good or service.

Institutional Advertising

Rather than a focus on a specific brand, **institutional advertising** promotes the activities, personality, or point of view of an organization or company. The three forms of institutional advertising include the following:

- **Corporate advertising** promotes the company as a whole instead of the firm's individual products. Procter & Gamble's Always brand of feminine hygiene products launched a groundbreaking campaign in 2015 entitled "Like A Girl" to begin a conversation about how people perceive that phrase. The ad debuted during the Super Bowl and featured girls, boys, women, and men acting out what it meant to them to do something "like a girl" with the goal of empowering females. The wildly successful campaign was repurposed in 2018 with a "keep going" message focused on how failure is a part of learning and growing. The aim of the campaign was to celebrate girls as they really are—on a journey, learning how to do what they want to do and having fun doing it. You won't see their products featured—its purpose is to tie the Always brand to positive messaging for girls.[9]

- **Advocacy advertising** seeks to influence public opinion on a specific issue in the interest of the public or a specific group. AT&T's "Close to Home" ad is part of the multiyear "It Can Wait" campaign meant to show consumers that they too can cause fatalities when they use their phones for email, social media, and other activities while they drive. "Close to Home" shows a mother driving with her child in the back seat who quickly checks a social media post on her phone leading to devastating consequences; it is difficult to watch. Data from the Departments of Transportation in Texas, Kentucky, and other states have suggested there is a relationship between the "It Can Wait" campaign and a reduction in crashes.[10] During the spring and summer of 2020, many cities across the U.S. experienced Black Lives Matter protests due to racial prejudice and police killings of people of color. Many firms responded by replacing their product advertising with advocacy ads supporting the victims.

  During the COVID-19 pandemic, offline and online advertising revenues decreased. Companies very quickly recognized that continuing their planned campaigns to sell their goods and services could easily be interpreted as callous and insensitive. Instead of ads selling toilet paper and beer, ads encouraged consumers to stay home, advertised contactless delivery, assured consumers that they were working hard to make more of the things people needed, and promised they were helping those suffering the most due to the pandemic. Then another type of pandemic ad hit the airways. These ads typically included uplifting music and pictures of empty streets or people touching hands through glass while wearing masks, followed by an encouraging voice-over message. For example, in the weeks before St. Patrick's Day, Guinness, the beer company, aired a message about celebrations canceled for safety followed by video of a parade and a voice-over saying, "Don't worry, we'll march again." The message these ads gave was not about products but just to say, "We're a brand and we care."

Figure 13.7 *Snapshot* | Types of Advertising

Advertisements that an organization runs can take many different forms.

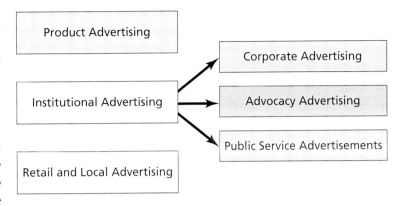

product advertising
Advertising messages that focus on a specific good or service.

institutional advertising
Advertising messages that promote the activities, personality, or point of view of an organization or company.

corporate advertising
Advertising that promotes the company as a whole instead of a firm's individual products.

advocacy advertising
A type of public service advertising where an organization seeks to influence public opinion on an issue because it has some stake in the outcome.

public service advertisements (PSAs)
Advertising run by the media for not-for-profit organizations or to champion a particular cause without charge.

- **Public service advertisements (PSAs)** are messages in the public interest, run by the media at no charge, that seek to change attitudes and behavior toward a social issue. When television was very young, the Federal Communications Commission (FCC), which regulates radio and TV, initiated a variety of "public good" regulations. The Commission felt that since local TV stations were using the public airways for profit, they should do something for their communities in return. For many years, all local television stations in cities and towns were required to air advertisements that related to a social or health issue important to the local community. While this requirement was dropped many years ago, lots of stations still air PSAs.

Retail and Local Advertising

retail and local advertising
Advertising that informs consumers about store hours, location, and products that are available or on sale.

Both major retailers and small, local businesses advertise to encourage customers to shop at a specific store or use a local service. Local advertising informs us about store hours, location, and products that are available or on sale. While historically newspapers have been the medium of choice for **retail and local advertising**, today these ads are more likely to take the form of pop-up ads online or text messages on your mobile device.

Who Creates Advertising?

advertising campaign
A coordinated, comprehensive plan that carries out promotion objectives and results in a series of advertisements placed in media over a period of time.

An **advertising campaign** is a coordinated, comprehensive plan that carries out promotion objectives and results in a series of creatively similar advertisements placed in various media over a period of time. GEICO, for example, has sponsored multiple advertising campaigns over the years, often with several running simultaneously. Five of its more recognized campaigns are (1) the GEICO gecko campaign; (2) the caveman campaign that even spawned a short-lived TV sitcom ("so easy a caveman can do it"); (3) the "money you could be saving" campaign with the googly-eyed dollar bills; (4) the "rhetorical questions" campaign that included ads featuring Elmer Fudd, the Waltons, and Charlie Daniels (Does Charlie Daniels play a mean fiddle?); and (5) the Maxwell the pig campaign. More recently, Geico has aired the "I can't believe it" campaign. Although all of these campaigns promote the same company and its products and all use the same tagline—"15 minutes could save you 15 percent or more on car insurance"—each is creatively distinct. Each includes multiple ads (there have been at least 22 caveman TV commercials), but each obviously is part of its own unique, coordinated advertising campaign.

Although some firms create their own advertising in-house, in most cases firms hire *outside advertising agencies*, like Sara Bamossy's Pitch, to develop an advertising campaign. Agencies that support firms with their advertising include three major types: full-service agencies, limited-service agencies, and in-house agencies.

full-service agency
An agency that provides most or all of the services needed to mount a campaign, including research, creation of ad copy and art, media selection, and production of the final messages.

- A **full-service agency** supplies most or all of the services a campaign requires, including research, creation of ad copy and art, media selection, and production of the final messages.

limited-service agency
An agency that provides one or more specialized services, such as media buying or creative development.

interactive agency, or **digital agency**
A limited-service agency that provides a variety of services for digital marketing, including the creation of websites, design and implementation of SEO strategies, creation of articles for online publications, and creation of online email and social media strategies.

- A **limited-service agency** provides one or more specialized services. The most important ones are interactive agencies, creative boutiques, and media buying agencies. Creative boutiques provide clients with creative services; media buying agencies charge a fee for buying media for their clients. An **interactive agency**, or **digital agency**, is a limited-service agency that provides a variety of services for digital marketing. The growing number of worldwide Internet users and the development of more and more social networks has significantly increased the need for marketers to offer consumers a personalized online experience. The mandate for both advertising agencies and interactive agencies is to support the marketing efforts of a company. An advertising agency can offer traditional print, TV, or radio advertising, while an interactive agency can design and develop websites, design and implement SEO strategies, create articles for online publications, and provide online marketing, email marketing, and social media marketing strategies.

- An **in-house agency** is staffed with company employees and uses an agency model to provide the company with the traditional marketing services of external agencies. In recent years, the use of in-house agencies has skyrocketed as more and more firms have tapped into the benefits of **programmatic advertising**, or **programmatic ad buying**. Programmatic ad buying is the use of algorithms and software to buy digital advertising. In addition, the system will monitor the client's ad spending and look for areas of improvement. The move to in-house agencies and the use of programmatic ad buying give firms greater efficiency, speed, control, and cost savings of around 25 percent. Some top companies that have gone to in-house agencies for their digital advertising include Netflix, Kellogg, Procter & Gamble Co., and Unilever. Programmatic advertising allows firms to have one-to-one conversations with individuals and understand their journey within digital media better.[11]

An advertising campaign has many elements; agencies provide the services of many different people to pull it all together:

- *Account management:* The **account executive**, or account manager, is the "soul" of the operation. This person supervises the day-to-day activities on the account and is the primary liaison between the agency and the client. The account executive must ensure that the client is happy while verifying that people within the agency execute the desired strategy. The **account planner** combines research and account strategy to act as the voice of the consumer in creating effective advertising. It is the job of the account planner to use market data, qualitative research, and product knowledge to become intimately familiar with the consumer and to translate what customers are looking for to the creative teams who create the ads.

- *Creative services:* Creatives are the "heart" of the communication effort. The **creative services** department includes the people who actually dream up and produce the ads. They include the agency's creative director, art director, copywriters, and photographers. Creatives are the artists who breathe life into marketing objectives and craft messages that, it is hoped, will interest consumers.

- *Research and marketing services:* In **research and marketing services**, *researchers* are the "brains" of the campaign. They collect and analyze information that will help the account executive develop a sensible strategy. They assist creatives in getting consumer reactions to different versions of ads or by providing copywriters with details on the target group.

- *Media planning:* The **media planner** is the "legs" of the campaign. He or she helps to determine which communication vehicles are the most effective and recommends the most efficient means to deliver the ad by deciding where, when, and how often it will appear.

Today, more and more agencies practice IMC, in which advertising is only one element of a total communication plan. Client teams composed of people from account services, creative services, media planning, digital and social media marketing, research, public relations, sales promotion, and direct marketing may work together to develop a plan that best meets the communication needs of each client.

User-Generated Advertising Content

One of the most recent and important promotional innovations is to let your customers create your advertising for you. User-generated content (UGC), or consumer-generated media, which we discussed in Chapter 1, includes the millions of online consumer comments, opinions, advice, consumer-to-consumer discussions, reviews, photos, images, videos,

in-house agency
In-house marketing means that marketing activities of a company are handled by employees of the company. Sometimes companies decide to build an in-house marketing team but want to replicate the agency model. They establish so-called "in-house ad agencies."

programmatic advertising, or **programmatic ad buying**
The use of algorithms and software to buy digital advertising, thus providing greater efficiency, control, and cost savings.

account executive
A member of the account management department who supervises the day-to-day activities of the account and is the primary liaison between the agency and the client.

account planner
A member of the account management department who combines research and account strategy to act as the voice of the consumer in creating effective advertising.

creative services
The agency people (creative director, copywriters, and art director) who dream up and produce the ads.

research and marketing services
The advertising agency department that collects and analyzes information that will help the account executive develop a sensible strategy and assist creatives in getting consumer reactions to different versions of ads.

media planners
Agency personnel who determine which communication vehicles are the most effective and efficient to deliver the ad.

TOLBERT PHOTO/Alamy Stock Photo

You may have heard rumors about the strange effects of putting peanuts or other items into bottles of colas. The Diet Coke–Mentos Challenge, was a consumer-created science experiment that became a kind of DIY ad and the basis of major Internet buzz. The experiment had the capability of shooting streams of Diet Coke high in the sky and wound up as performances on and off TV around the world.

do-it-yourself (DIY) ads
Product ads that are created by consumers.

podcasts and webcasts, and product-related stories available to other consumers through digital technology.

Some marketers encourage consumers to contribute their own **do-it-yourself (DIY) ads**. For advertisers, DIY advertising offers several benefits. First, consumer-generated spots cost only one-quarter to one-third as much as professional TV and Internet ads—about $60,000 compared to the $350,000 or more to produce a traditional 30-second spot. This can be especially important for smaller businesses and emerging brands. Equally important, even to large companies with deep pockets, is the feedback on how consumers see the brand and the chance to gather more creative ideas to tell the brand's story.[12]

Marketers need to monitor (and sometimes encourage) UGC for two reasons. First, consumers are more likely to trust messages from fellow consumers than from companies. Second, social media is proliferating everywhere; a person who searches online for a company or product name is certain to access any number of blogs, forums, homegrown commercials, or online complaint sites that the product manufacturer had nothing to do with.

As we saw in Chapter 1, consumers also generate content for firms through a process called *crowdsourcing*. Put simply, this is a way to harness "crowds" to "source" solutions to business problems. Marketers use this technique to come up with new product ideas, brand names, and product redesigns, but in many cases, they look to their customers to create advertising messages for them.

Ethical Issues in Advertising

Advertising, more than any other aspect of marketing, has been sharply criticized as unethical for decades. Much of this criticism may be based less on actual unethical advertising and more on the high visibility of advertising and the negative attitudes of consumers who find ads an intrusion into their lives. The objections to advertising are similar to those some people have to marketing in general, as we discussed in Chapter 2. Here are the main ones:

- *Advertising is manipulative.* Advertising causes people to behave like robots and do things against their will—to make purchases they would not otherwise make were it not for the ads. However, consumers are not robots. In fact, almost all consumers recognize ads when they see them and know the purpose is to convince them to buy whatever the ad is selling. Furthermore, some consumers just don't trust advertisers. Of course, consumers can and often do make bad decisions that advertising may influence, but that is not the same as manipulation.

- *Advertising is deceptive and untruthful.* According to the Federal Trade Commission (FTC), deceptive advertising means that an ad falsely represents the product and that consumers believe the false information and act on it. Indeed, there is a small amount of false or deceptive advertising, but as a whole, advertisers try to present their brands in the best possible light while being truthful.

drip pricing
The illegal practice of advertising one price and then, by the time the sale is completed, presenting a total on which additional hidden fees have "dripped."

Of course, the finding of deceptive advertising is not limited to what false information is communicated. It can also apply to what is not said. Companies, for example, are vulnerable to claims against them for hidden fees, or **drip pricing**. Drip pricing occurs when a company advertises a certain price at the beginning of the purchase process, but by the time the consumers are ready to pay, additional charges or fees have "dripped" onto the total. Thus, the customer is charged a significantly higher price than was advertised. In 2018, several class action suits were filed against companies selling tickets online, including Stub-Hub and Ticketmaster. AT&T was the target of a class-action suit for adding hidden "administrative fees" to customer bills. Other similar suits have been brought against Spirit Airlines (hidden carry-on bag fees), Marriott and Hilton hotels (adding resort fees to hotel rooms), and JustFly Corp. (adding hidden fees to their online flight-booking service).[13]

To protect consumers from being misled, the FTC has specific rules regarding unfair or deceptive advertising. If the FTC finds that an ad is deceptive, it can fine the offending company and the ad agency. In addition, the FTC has the power to require firms to run **corrective advertising**—messages that clarify or qualify previous claims.[14] In 2016, the FTC announced a $2 million settlement with Lumos Labs, whose commercials for Lumosity "brain training" games were deemed deceptive. The FTC said Lumosity "preyed on consumers' fears about age-related cognitive decline suggesting their game would stave off memory loss, dementia, and even Alzheimer's disease."[15]

Other ads, although not illegal, may create a biased impression of products when they use **puffery**—claims of superiority that neither sponsors nor critics of the ads can prove are true or untrue. For example, Tropicana claims it has the "world's best fruit and vegetable juice," Pizza Hut claims that it has "America's best pizza," and Simply Lemonade says it's okay for other people to say it's "the best lemonade ever."

Many consumers today are concerned about **greenwashing**, a practice in which companies promote their products as environmentally friendly when in truth the brand provides little ecological benefit. J.C. Penney, Nordstrom, Bed Bath & Beyond, and Backcountry.com were fined $1.3 million by the FTC for misleading consumers by labeling certain products as "bamboo" fabrics. The problem? The fabrics did not actually include bamboo fibers; they were just exposed to some chemical elements from bamboo when the rayon materials were processed. The FTC ruling showed that it's important for consumers to know that textiles marketed as "green" alternatives may not be as "green" as they were led to believe.[16]

- *Advertising is offensive and in bad taste.* To respond to this criticism, we need to recognize that what is offensive or in bad taste to one person may not be to another. Whereas advertisers seek to go the distance using humor, sex appeals, or fear appeals to get audiences' attention, most shy away from presenting messages that offend the very consumers they want to buy their products.

- *Advertising causes people to buy things they don't really need.* The truth of this criticism depends on how you define a "need." If we believe that all consumers need is the basic functional benefits of products—the transportation a car provides, the nutrition we get from food, and the clean hair we get from shampoo—then advertising may be guilty as charged. If, on the other hand, you think you need a car that projects a cool image, food that tastes fantastic, and a shampoo that makes your hair shine and smell ever so nice, then advertising is just a vehicle that communicates those more intangible benefits.

Develop the Advertising Campaign

The advertising campaign is about much more than creating a cool ad and hoping people notice it. The campaign should be intimately related to the organization's overall communication goals. That means that the firm (and its outside agency if it uses one) must have a good idea of whom it wants to reach, what it will take to appeal to this market, and where and when it should place its messages. Let's examine the steps required to do this, as Figure 13.8 shows.

Step 1: Understand the Target Audience

The best way to communicate with an audience is to understand as much as possible about them and what turns them on and off. An

corrective advertising
Advertising that clarifies or qualifies previous deceptive advertising claims.

puffery
Claims made in advertising of product superiority that cannot be proven true or untrue.

greenwashing
A practice in which companies promote their products as environmentally friendly when in truth the brand provides little ecological benefit.

Figure 13.8 *Process* | Steps to Develop an Advertising Campaign

Developing an advertising campaign includes a series of steps that will ensure that the advertising meets communication objectives.

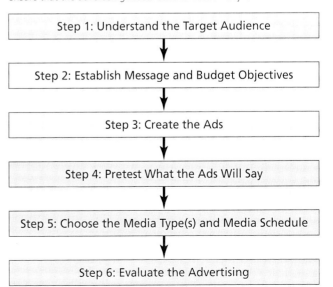

Step 1: Understand the Target Audience

Step 2: Establish Message and Budget Objectives

Step 3: Create the Ads

Step 4: Pretest What the Ads Will Say

Step 5: Choose the Media Type(s) and Media Schedule

Step 6: Evaluate the Advertising

ad that uses the latest teen text slang (e.g., AMOSC, KOTL, or dime) may relate to teenagers but not to their parents, and this strategy may backfire if the ad copy reads like an "ancient" 40-year-old trying to sound like a 20-year-old.

Step 2: Establish Message and Budget Objectives

Advertising objectives should be consistent with the overall communication plan. That means that both the underlying message and the expenditures for delivering that message need to be consistent with what the marketer is trying to say about the product and the overall marketing communication budget. Thus, advertising objectives generally will include objectives for both the message and the budget.

1. *Set message objectives.* As we noted previously, because advertising is the most visible part of marketing, many people assume that marketing *is* advertising. In truth, advertising alone is quite limited in what it can achieve. What advertising *can* do is inform, persuade, and remind. Accordingly, some advertisements aim to make the customer knowledgeable about features of the product or how to use it. At other times, advertising seeks to persuade consumers to like a brand or to prefer one brand over the competition. But many ads simply aim to keep the name of the brand in front of the consumer, reminding consumers that this brand is the one to choose when they look for a soft drink or a laundry detergent.

2. *Set budget objectives.* Advertising is expensive. Comcast Corp., which leads all U.S. companies in advertising expenditures, spent $6.1 billion in 2018, whereas second-, third-, and fourth-place ad spenders AT&T, Amazon, and Procter and Gamble Co. spent more than $6 billion each.[17]

An objective of many firms is to allocate a percentage of the overall communication budget to advertising, depending on how much and what type of advertising the company can afford. The major approaches and techniques to setting overall promotion budgets discussed previously in this chapter, such as the percentage-of-sales and objective-task methods, also set advertising budgets.

Step 3: Create the Ads

creative strategy
The process that turns a concept into an advertisement.

creative brief
A guideline or blueprint for the marketing communication program that guides the creative process.

Using the terminology of the communication process, this is where the sender of a message encodes the idea into a physically perceivable form, the message. The creation of the advertising begins when an agency formulates a **creative strategy**, which gives the advertising creatives the direction and inspiration they need to begin the creative process. The strategy is summarized in a written document known as a **creative brief**, a rough blueprint that guides the creative process. A creative brief provides relevant information and insights about the marketing situation, the advertising objective, the competition, the advertising target, and most important, the message that the advertising must deliver.

It's one thing to know *what* a company wants to say about itself or its products and another to figure out *how* to say it. The role of the creative brief is to provide the spark that helps the ad agency come up with "the big idea," the visual or verbal concept that delivers the message in an attention-getting, memorable, and relevant manner. From this, the creatives develop the ads by combining already-known facts, words, pictures, and ideas in new and unexpected ways. Specifically, to come up with finished ads, they must consider four elements of the ads shown in Figure 13.9: the appeal, the format, the tonality, and the creative tactics and techniques.[18]

Advertising Appeals

advertising appeal
The central idea or theme of an advertising message.

An **advertising appeal** is the central idea of the ad and the basis of the advertising messages. It is the approach used to influence the consumer. Generally, we think of appeals as informational versus emotional. Often, informational appeals are based on

Figure 13.9 *Snapshot* | Creative Elements of Advertising

Creating good ads includes making decisions about the four different ad elements.

Creative Element	Element Options	Description	Example
Appeals: the central idea of the ad	Informational/ Rational	Satisfies customers' practical need for information; emphasizes the features or benefits of the product.	The Unique Selling Proposition (USP) appeal has been a highly successful rational appeal since the 1940s. USP appeals explain the unique benefit(s) of a product that are meaningful to customers and enable it to stand out among competitors. Geico's USP appeal is in its ad slogan, "15 Minutes could save you 15% on car insurance."
	Emotional	Tries to influence our emotions, "pull our heartstrings"	Ads that make us cry might be created by nonprofits who wish us to donate money for abused animals, sick and starving children, or wounded veterans. Even ads for greeting cards can touch our hearts.
	Reminder Advertising	Just keeps the name of the brand in people's minds so they will repurchase	Coke and Pepsi make sure their names are seen in ads on TV programs, in movies, in college and professional sports venues, inside retail stores—just about everywhere.
	Teaser/Mystery Ads	Generates curiosity and interest in a yet-to-be-introduced product	These ads are often used to make consumers eager to see upcoming movies and TV shows.
Execution Formats: the basic structure of the message	Comparison	Explicitly names, shows, or in some way clearly identifies one or more competitors	Peanut butter ads frequently say one brand is better than another. "Jif tastes more like real peanuts."
	Demonstration	Shows the product in action or the results of using the product	Demonstration ads are frequently used for floor cleaning, car polishing, exercise equipment, or diet ads.
	Storytelling	Features a story—for example, a 30-second movie—that involves the product in a more peripheral way	The 90-second Toyota Prius Hybrid ad for Superbowl 50 told the story of two bank robbers who outran police and got away in a Prius.
	Testimonial	Shows a celebrity, expert, or "man on the street" stating the product's benefits	Recent examples of popular celebrity endorsement ads include Taylor Swift for Diet Coke, LeBron James for Nike, Michael Phelps for Under Armour, and Ellen DeGeneres for CoverGirl.
	Slice of Life	Presents a dramatized scene from everyday life showing that "real people" buy and use the product	Coca-Cola has aired slice-of-life commercials, including one in which a father teaches his daughter to dance for her wedding.

(continues)

Figure 13.9 *Snapshot* | Creative Elements of Advertising (*Continued*)

Creative Element	Element Options	Description	Example
	Lifestyle	Shows people who are attractive to the target market in a scene that demonstrates a certain lifestyle	As automobiles have become more like commodities with the same features, Subaru has found success through focusing on its cars meeting the desires of people who have or want a certain lifestyle.
Tonality: the mood or attitude the ad conveys	Straightforward	The many types of straightforward ads include such information as what the product is, how much it costs, and where you can buy it. Some of the most popular types focus on pain solutions, scarcity, and statistics.	Scarcity ads typically include headlines such as "Limited Time Sale," "Don't miss out," "Share the joy Nov. 13-17," and "Holiday savings you won't want to miss."
	Humor	Breaks through the "clutter," as people tend to enjoy humorous ads; however, humor is different for different people, so while one person may find an ad humorous, another may find it offensive or stupid; humor may overpower other elements of the ad so consumers remember the ad in detail but can't remember what brand it was for	Mountain Dew's 50th Super Bowl ad received rave reviews for its puppymonkeybaby.
	Dramatic	Presents a dramatization of a problem and a solution, often in a manner that is exciting and suspenseful	Pantene in Thailand aired a commercial showing a deaf and mute girl who learns to play the violin against all odds and wins the top prize in a music competition.
	Romantic	Presents a romantic situation, effective at getting attention and selling products people associate with dating and mating	Ads for luxury resorts, cruises, and Internet dating sites often use romance and may seem to promise romance if you purchase the product.
	Sex Appeals	Appears like selling sex; effective at getting attention and at selling when there is a connection between sex and the product	Victoria's Secret advertises its lingerie worn by voluptuous models.
	Apprehension/Fear	Highlights the negative consequences of not using a product; can be social disapproval or physical harm	These ads are used by marketers of deodorant, dandruff shampoo, auto insurance, and home security systems.
Creative Tactics and Technology	Animation and Art	Uses art, illustration, or animation to attract attention and give a unique "look" to the ad	GEICO's gecko is an animated character.
	Celebrities	Features celebrities to attract attention and maybe influence people's favorable attitude toward a product	Movie actor, former champion body builder, and former California Governor Arnold Schwarzenegger stars in ads for the game Mobile Strike, "Command Center."
	Music, Jingles, and Slogans	Features original words and/or music that can make an ad memorable; slogans link the brand to a memorable linguistic device	"15 minutes can save you 15 percent or more on car insurance"

a **unique selling proposition (USP)** that gives consumers a clear, single-minded reason why the advertiser's product is better than other products at solving a problem. Because consumers often buy products based on social or psychological needs, advertisers also use emotional appeals that focus on an emotional or social benefit the consumer may receive from the product, such as safety, love, excitement, pleasure, respect, or approval. Of course, not all ads fit into these two appeal categories. Well-established brands like Coca-Cola and Pepsi often use **reminder advertising** just to keep their name in people's minds. Sometimes advertisers use **teaser ads**, or **mystery ads**, to generate curiosity and interest in a to-be-introduced product.

Execution Format

Execution format describes the basic structure of the message. Some of the more common formats include the following:

- *Comparison:* A **comparative advertisement** explicitly names one or more competitors. Comparative ads can be very effective, but there is a risk of turning off consumers who don't like the negative tone. This format is best for brands that have a smaller share of the market and for firms that can focus on a specific feature that makes them superior to a major brand.

- *Demonstration:* A demonstration ad format shows a product "in action" to prove that it performs as claimed: "It slices, it dices!" Demonstration advertising is most useful when consumers are unable to identify important benefits except when they see the product in use.

- *Brand storytelling:* In Chapter 9, we introduced the concept of *brand storytelling*. From an advertising execution perspective, brand storytelling commercials are like 30-second movies with plots that involve the product in a more peripheral way. An example is the Subaru commercial that depicts a loving dad handing his six-year-old daughter the car keys and telling her to be careful. We eventually learn that she is a teenager, but he still sees her as a little girl. The Subaru brand is not even revealed until we see the logo and slogan at the end.

- *Testimonial:* An ad that shows people telling about their experience with a product. The happily married couple giving credit to Christian Mingle for their relationship is a testimonial as is Kim Kardashian talking about her morning sickness and a drug to relieve it.

- *Endorsement:* Ad that includes a celebrity, an expert, or a "man on the street" stating the product's effectiveness. David Beckham selling H&M clothing or Matthew McConaughey driving a Lincoln are both endorsements.

- *Slice of life:* A slice of life format presents a (dramatized) scene from everyday life. **Slice-of-life advertising** can be effective for everyday products, such as peanut butter and headache remedies, that consumers may feel good about if they see that "real" people buy and use them.

- *Lifestyle:* A **lifestyle** format shows a person or persons attractive to the target market in an appealing setting. The advertised product is "part of the scene," implying that the person who buys it

---

unique selling proposition (USP)
An advertising appeal that focuses on one clear reason why a particular product is superior.

reminder advertising
Advertising aimed at keeping the name of a brand in people's minds to be sure consumers purchase the product as necessary.

teaser ads, or **mystery ads**
Ads that generate curiosity and interest in a to-be-introduced product by drawing attention to an upcoming ad campaign without mentioning the product.

execution format
The basic structure of the message, such as comparison, demonstration, testimonial, slice of life, and lifestyle.

comparative advertising
Advertising that compares one brand with a second named brand.

slice-of-life advertising
A slice-of-life ad presents a (dramatized) scene from everyday life.

lifestyle advertising
Lifestyle ads show a person or persons attractive to the target market in an appealing setting with the advertised product as "part of the scene," implying that the person who buys it will attain the lifestyle.

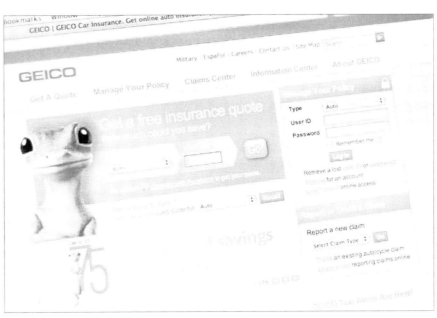

The GEICO gecko is a familiar animated character that personifies the insurance company.

will attain the lifestyle. Perhaps the most successful lifestyle brand ever is energy drink Red Bull. With its unique tagline, "Red Bull gives you wings," Red Bull associates itself with extreme sporting events.

- *Rich media:* Rich media advertising, which we discussed in Chapter 6, provides digital ads that have advanced features such as video, audio, games, or other elements that offer more ways for a consumer to interact and engage with the content and thus generate greater user response. For example, a simple website button ad for an international hotel chain includes the following interaction opportunities: links for different languages; a "roll over and learn more" link; a "view exclusive offers" link; 10 city/country locations links, each with multiple links for different properties in each city; links in each property site to access special discounts; links to book online; and links to sign up for special email offers. There are also many large interior and exterior photos of each property. You can easily spend (or waste) an hour or more with this rich media ad.

Tonality

tonality
The mood or attitude the message conveys (straightforward, humorous, dramatic, romantic, sexy, or apprehensive/fearful).

Tonality refers to the mood or attitude the message conveys. Some common tonalities include the following:

- *Straightforward:* Straightforward ads simply present the information to the audience in a clear manner.
- *Humorous:* Consumers, in general, like humorous, witty, or outrageous ads, so these often provide an effective way to break through advertising clutter. But humor can be tricky because what is funny to one person may be offensive or stupid to another. In addition, humor can overpower the message. It's not unusual for a person to remember a hilarious ad but have no idea what product it advertised.
- *Dramatic:* A dramatization, like a play, presents a problem and a solution in a manner that is often exciting and suspenseful—a fairly difficult challenge in 30 or 60 seconds.
- *Romantic:* Ads that present a romantic situation can be especially effective at getting consumers' attention and at selling products that people associate with dating and mating. That's why fragrance ads often use a romantic format.
  - *Sexy:* Some ads appear to sell sex rather than products. In an ad for the Fiat 500 Abarth, an Italian-speaking woman first angrily slaps a man for looking at her but then turns the tables and begins to seduce him. As the man leans in to kiss her, the camera pans in on the Fiat and "reality" sets in. Although sex appeal ads are known to get an audience's attention, they may or may not be effective in other ways. *Sex appeal* ads are more likely to be effective when there is a connection between the product and sex (or at least romance). For example, sex appeals will work well with a perfume but are less likely to be effective when you're trying to sell a lawn mower.

fear appeals
Advertisements that highlight the negative consequences of *not* using a product by either focusing on physical harm or social disapproval.

Some creative ads use other cultural genres to make a dramatic point, like this one that looks like a movie or propaganda poster.

- *Apprehensive/fearful:* **Fear appeals** highlight the negative consequences of *not* using a product. Some fear appeal ads focus on physical harm, whereas others try to create concern for social harm or disapproval. Mouthwash, deodorant, and dandruff shampoo makers and life insurance companies successfully use fear appeals. So do ads aimed at changing behaviors, such as messages discouraging drug use or smoking. In general, fear appeals can be successful if the audience perceives that the level of intensity in the fear appeal is appropriate for the product being advertised. For example, graphic photos of teens lying on the highway following an auto accident can be quite effective in public service advertisements designed to persuade teens not to text and drive, but they are likely to backfire if an insurance company tries to scare people into buying life insurance.

Figure 13.9 provides more information on and additional examples of various ad appeals, execution formats, tonality options, and creative tactics.

Creative Tactics and Techniques

In addition to ad formats and tonality, the creative process may also include a number of different creative tactics and techniques. Some of these are the following:

The pandemic gave advertisers a unique opportunity to get a bit creative. Face masks with logos are one innovative solution.

- *Animation and art:* Not all ads are executed with film or photography. Sometimes a creative decision is made to use art, illustration, or animation to attract attention or to achieve the desired look for a print ad or TV commercial.
- *Celebrities:* Sometimes celebrities appear in testimonials or for endorsements, such as Jessica Simpson's pitches for Weight Watchers.
- *Jingles:* **Jingles** are original words and music written specifically for advertising executions. Many of us remember classic ad jingles such as "I wish I were an Oscar Mayer Wiener" and "I am stuck on Band-Aid, and Band-Aid's stuck on me." Today, jingles are used less frequently than in the past.
- *Slogans:* **Slogans** link the brand to a simple linguistic device that is memorable but without music. We usually have no trouble reciting successful slogans (sometimes years after the campaign has ended); think of such die-hards as "Finger lickin' good" (KFC), "Got milk?" (the California Milk Processor Board), "Just do it" (Nike), and "Even a caveman can do it" (GEICO insurance).

jingles
Original words and music written specifically for advertising executions.

slogans
Simple, memorable linguistic devices linked to a brand.

Step 4: Pretest What the Ads Will Say

Now that the creatives have performed their magic, how does the agency know if the campaign will work? Advertisers try to minimize mistakes by pretesting the ads—that is, getting reactions to ad messages before they actually place them. Much of this **pretesting** goes on in the early stages of campaign development. It centers on gathering basic information that will help planners to be sure they've accurately defined the product's market, consumers, and competitors. As we saw in Chapter 4, this information often comes from quantitative sources, such as surveys, and qualitative sources, such as focus groups.

pretesting
A research method that seeks to minimize mistakes by getting consumer reactions to ad messages before they appear in the media.

Step 5: Choose the Media Type(s) and Media Schedule

Media planning is a problem-solving process that gets a message to a target audience in the most effective way. In terms of the communication process, it's selecting the medium to deliver the message. Planning decisions include audience selection and where, when, and how frequent the exposure should be. Thus, the first task for a media planner is to find out when and where people in the target market are most likely to be exposed to the communication. Many college students read the campus newspaper in the morning (believe it or not, sometimes even during class!), so advertisers may choose to place ad messages aimed at college students there.

For the advertising campaign to be effective, the media planner must match the profile of the target market with specific media vehicles. For example, many Hispanic American consumers, even those who speak English, are avid users of Spanish-language media. To reach this segment, marketers might allocate a relatively large share of their advertising budget to buying Spanish-language newspapers, magazines, TV, and Spanish webcasts available on the Internet.

media planning
The process of developing media objectives, strategies, and tactics for use in an advertising campaign.

The choice of the right media mix is no simple matter, especially because new options, including videos and DVDs, video games, personal computers, streaming TV and movies via the Internet, social media, hundreds of new TV channels, and even satellite radio, now vie for our attention. In 1965, TV signals came into most consumers' living rooms through wires from the TV to a tall antenna on top of the house or via "rabbit ears" on top of the TV. Consider, however, that advertisers could reach 80 percent of 18- to 49-year-olds in the U.S. with only three 60-second TV spots placed on the three networks available: ABC, CBS, and NBC. That kind of efficiency is just a pipe dream in today's highly fragmented media marketplace. Later, we'll discuss the many media choices marketers have to choose from.

Step 6: Evaluate the Advertising

John Wanamaker, a famous Philadelphia retailer, once complained, "I am certain that half the money I spend on advertising is completely wasted. The trouble is, I don't know which half."[19] Now that we've seen how advertising is created and executed, let's step back and see how we decide if it's working.

There's no doubt that a lot of advertising is ineffective. With so many messages competing for the attention of frazzled customers, it's especially important for firms to evaluate their efforts to increase the impact of their messages. How can they do that?

Posttesting means conducting research on consumers' responses to advertising messages they have seen or heard (as opposed to *pretesting*, which, as we've seen, collects reactions to messages *before* they're actually placed in "the real world"). Ironically, many creative ads that are quirky or even bizarre make an advertising agency look good within the industry (and on the résumé of the creative director) but are ultimately unsuccessful because they don't communicate what the company needs to say about the product itself. Three ways to measure the impact of an advertisement are *unaided recall*, *aided recall*, and *attitudinal measures*:

1. **Unaided recall** tests by telephone survey or personal interview whether a person remembers seeing an ad during a specified period without giving the person the name of the brand.

2. **Aided recall** tests use the name of the brand and sometimes other clues to prompt answers. For example, a researcher might show a group of consumers a list of brands and ask them to choose which items they have seen advertised within the past week.

3. **Attitudinal measures** probe a bit more deeply by testing consumers' beliefs or feelings about a product before and after they are exposed to messages about it. If, for example, Pepsi's messages about "freshness dating" make enough consumers believe that the freshness of soft drinks is important, marketers can consider the advertising campaign successful.

---

posttesting
Research conducted on consumers' responses to actual advertising messages they have seen or heard.

unaided recall
A research technique conducted by telephone survey or personal interview that asks whether a person remembers seeing an ad during a specified period without giving the person the name of the brand.

aided recall
A research technique that uses clues to prompt answers from people about advertisements they might have seen.

attitudinal measures
A research technique that probes a consumer's beliefs or feelings about a product before and after being exposed to messages about it.

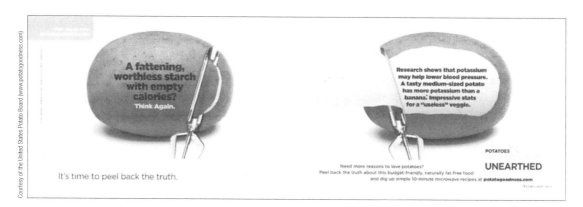

A communication objective may focus on educating consumers about a product such as potatoes. The sponsor can measure the effectiveness of a campaign by assessing people's knowledge before and after the messages have run to determine if they had any impact.

Where to Say It: Traditional Mass Media

What does a professional football game (viewed on your Samsung 85" Class - TU800D Series - 4K UHD LCD TV plasma TV) have in common with the Swimsuit Issue of *Sports Illustrated*? Each is a media vehicle that permits an advertiser to communicate with a potential customer. In this section, we'll take a look at the major categories of traditional mass media, Internet advertising, and some less traditional indirect forms of advertising. Table 13.2 summarizes some of the pros and cons of each type.

Television

Because of TV's ability to reach so many people at once, it's often the medium of choice for regional and national companies. However, advertising on a TV network can be very expensive. The cost to air a 30-second spot one time on a popular prime-time network TV show normally ranges between $75,000 and $200,000, with higher costs for top-rated shows. For the 2019–2020 season, shows with the highest **upfront TV ad pricing** were *This Is Us* ($359,413), *The Masked Singer* ($201,683), *Sunday Night Football* ($665,677), and FOX's *Thursday Night Football* ($540,090). A 30-second Super Bowl ad in 2020 was priced at $5.6 million. Of course, just like consumer buying, some advertisers don't pay the full price because they negotiate better pricing or they wait until after the season has begun and buy their ad space "on sale."[20]

> **upfront TV ad pricing**
> *Upfront* is the term used to describe the practice of buying and selling national TV advertising time for the entire broadcast year, October through September; upfront buying allows advertisers to lock in pricing and get the best time slots.

With such high prices for 30-second television commercials, it makes one question if all ads need to be 30 seconds. In some countries, the standard length of commercials is 20, 40, and 60 seconds. Sixty-second commercials, formerly seen quite often, are very rare in the U.S. market today. One recent research study found that 15-second commercials may be as both rationally and emotionally effective as traditional 30-second ones. Longer commercials do possess a greater ability to elicit emotion and are more useful for communicating complex messages such as those used in launching a new brand. Still it's no wonder that more and more 15-second commercials are used.[21]

Radio

Radio as an advertising medium dates back to 1922, when a New York City apartment manager went on the air to advertise properties for rent. One advantage of radio advertising is flexibility. Marketers can change commercials quickly, often on the spot by an announcer and a recording engineer.[22] Traditional radio advertising has declined in recent years as satellite radio, mostly by subscription only and without ads, has gained in popularity.

Newspapers

The newspaper is one of the oldest communication platforms. Retailers, in particular, relied on newspaper ads since before the turn of the 20th century to inform readers about sales and deliveries of new merchandise. Although most newspapers are local, *USA Today*, the *Wall Street Journal*, and the *New York Times* have national circulations and provide readerships in the millions. In the past 25 years, local newspaper circulation has declined. The decline in newspaper readership began with the introduction of TV and continued with 24-hour-a-day TV news services and then with the availability of online news. As circulations have declined, so have advertising revenues. Newspapers are an excellent medium for local advertising and for events (such as store sales) that require a quick response. Today, most newspapers also offer online versions of their papers to expand their exposure, but most of these do not include the ads we see in the paper versions. Some, such as the *New York Times*, offer online subscribers downloads of the actual newspaper, including all the ads, at a much lower cost than the paper

My good man, you have a face only a mother could love.

Thank you Sir, your mother seems to agree.

For gentlemen of distinction

Print media like magazines can provide vivid messages and images to readers.

Table 13.2	Pros and Cons of Media Vehicles	

Vehicle	Pros	Cons
TV	• TV is extremely creative and flexible. • Network TV is the most cost-effective way to reach a mass audience. • Cable and satellite TV allow the advertiser to reach a selected group at relatively low cost. • A prestigious way to advertise. • Can demonstrate the product in use. • Can provide entertainment and generate excitement. • Messages have high impact because of the use of sight and sound.	• The message is quickly forgotten unless it is repeated often. • The audience is increasingly fragmented. • Although the relative cost of reaching the audience is low, prices are still high on an absolute basis—often too high for smaller companies. A 30-second spot on a prime-time TV sitcom can cost well over $250,000. • Fewer people view network TV. • People switch from station to station and record programs so they can zap commercials. • Rising costs have led to more and shorter ads, causing more clutter.
Radio	• Good for selectively targeting an audience. • Is heard outside the home. • Can reach customers on a personal and intimate level. • Can use local personalities. • Relatively low cost, both for producing a spot and for running it repeatedly. • Because of short lead time, radio ads can be modified quickly to reflect changes in the marketplace. • Use of sound effects and music allows listeners to use their imagination to create a vivid scene.	• Listeners often don't pay full attention to what they hear. • Difficulty in buying radio time, especially for national advertisers. • Not appropriate for products that must be seen or demonstrated to be appreciated. • The small audiences of individual stations mean ads must be placed with many different stations and must be repeated frequently.
Newspapers	• Wide exposure provides extensive market coverage. • Flexible format permits the use of color, different sizes, and targeted editions. • Provides the ability to use detailed copy. • Allows local retailers to tie in with national advertisers. • Readers are in the right mental frame to process advertisements about new products, sales, etc. • Timeliness, that is, short lead time between placing ad and running it.	• Most people don't spend much time reading the newspaper. • Readership is especially low among teens and young adults. • Short life span—people rarely look at a newspaper more than once. • Offers a cluttered ad environment. • The reproduction quality of images is relatively poor. • Not effective to reach specific audiences.
Magazines	• Audiences can be narrowly targeted by specialized magazines. • High credibility and interest level provide a good environment for ads. • Advertising has a long life and is often passed along to other readers. • Visual quality is excellent. • Can provide detailed product information with a sense of authority.	• With the exception of direct mail, it is the most expensive form of advertising. The cost of a full-page, four-color ad in a general-audience magazine typically exceeds $100,000. • Long deadlines reduce flexibility. • The advertiser must generally use several magazines to reach the majority of a target market. • Clutter.
Directories	• Customers actively seek exposure to advertisements. • Advertisers determine the quality of the ad placement because larger ads get preferential placement.	• Limited creative options. • May be a lack of color. • Ads are generally purchased for a full year and cannot be changed.
Out-of-home media	• Most of the population can be reached at low cost. • Good for supplementing other media. • High frequency when signs are located in heavy traffic areas. • Effective for reaching virtually all segments of the population. • Geographic flexibility.	• Hard to communicate complex messages because of short exposure time. • Difficult to measure advertisement's audience. • Controversial and disliked in many communities. • Cannot pinpoint specific market segments.

Table 13.2	Pros and Cons of Media Vehicles (*Continued*)	
Vehicle	**Pros**	**Cons**
Internet websites	• Can target specific audiences and individualize messages. • Web user registration and cookies allow marketers to track user preferences and website activity. • Is interactive—consumers can participate in the ad campaign; can create do-it-yourself ads. • An entertainment medium allowing consumers to play games, download music, etc. • Consumers are active participants in the communication process, controlling what information and the amount and rate of information they receive. • Websites can facilitate both marketing communication and transactions. • Consumers visit websites with the mind-set to obtain information. • Banners can achieve top-of-mind awareness, even without click-throughs.	• Limited to Internet users only. • Banners, pop-ups, unsolicited email, etc., can be unwanted and annoying. • Declining click-through rates for banners. • If web pages take too long to load, consumers will abandon the site. • *Phishing* is email sent by criminals to get consumers to go to phony websites that will seek to gain personal information, such as credit card numbers. • Because advertisers' costs are normally based on the number of click-throughs, competitors may engage in click fraud by clicking a sponsored link. • Difficult to measure effectiveness.
Place-based media	• Effective for certain industries, such as pharmaceutical companies, to reach their target audience. • In retail locations, it can reach customers immediately before purchase; this provides a last opportunity to influence the purchase decision. • In locations such as airports, it receives a high level of attention because of lack of viewer options.	• Limited audience. • Difficult to measure effectiveness.
Branded entertainment	• Brand presented in a positive context. • Brand message presented in a covert fashion. • Less intrusive and thus less likely to be avoided. • Connection with a popular movie plot or TV program and with entertaining characters can help a brand's image. • Can build emotional connection with the audience. • Can create a memorable association that serves to enhance brand recall.	• Little control of how the brand is positioned—is in the hands of the director. • Difficult to measure effectiveness. • Costs of placement can be very high.
Advergaming	• Companies can customize their own games or incorporate brands into existing popular games. • Some game producers now actively pursue tie-ins with brands. • Millions of gamers play an average of 40 hours per game before they tire of it. • Millions of consumers have mobile phones "in their hands."	• Audience limited to gamers.
Mobile phones	• A large variety of different formats using different mobile phone apps.	• Consumers may be unwilling to receive messages through their phones.

Sources: Adapted from J. Craig Andrews; Terence A. Shimp, *Advertising, Promotion and Supplemental Aspects of Integrated Marketing Communications*, 10th ed. (Cengage Learning 2018); Sandra Moriarty; Nancy Mitchell; Charles Wood; William D. Wells, *Advertising & IMC*, 11th ed. (Upper Saddle River, NJ: Pearson 2019)

version. The future of the newspaper industry is not clear because more people choose to get their news online.

Comparing Traditional Media Vehicles

In developing a media schedule, marketers need information about the content of the media vehicles (such as different magazines or TV programs) they are considering. This way, they will be able to determine if the vehicle and the brand image desired are compatible. While a crime show with lots of images of guns and corpses may be OK with ads for tires or trucks, it probably would not be good for advertising baby lotion.

Media planners also use a number of quantitative factors to evaluate different media vehicles and thus develop an optimal media schedule. **Reach**, also referred to as the **rating** for a broadcast (TV or radio) media vehicle, is the percentage of the target market that will be exposed to the vehicle at least one time during a given period, usually four weeks. Reach is expressed as a whole number. For example, if the target market includes 5 million adults age 18 and older, and a specific TV program over a four-week period has an unduplicated audience of 250,000 individuals (the total of all who were exposed to at least one ad during the period), then the program has a reach of 5 percent, or just 5.

Developing a media plan with high reach is particularly important for widely used products when the message needs to get to as many consumers as possible. **Frequency** is simply the average number of times an individual or a household is exposed to the message. Note this is the average number of times. Thus, if 100,000 members of the target audience see a weekly TV show two out of the four weeks in the period, and 100,000 see the show all four weeks, the average frequency is 3 times. High levels of frequency are important for products that are complex or those that are targeted to relatively small markets for which multiple exposures to the message are necessary to make an impact.

Gross rating points (GRPs) are a measure of the quantity of media included in the media plan. Just as we talk about buying 15 gallons of gas or a pound of coffee, media planners talk about a media schedule that includes the purchase of 250 GRPs of radio and 700 GRPs of TV. Marketers calculate GRPs by multiplying a media vehicle's reach by the number of planned ad insertions. If 30 percent of a target audience watches *Thursday Night Football*, and you place 12 ads on the show during a four-week period, you are buying 360 GRPs of that show (30×12).

Although some media vehicles deliver more of your target audience, they may not be cost efficient. More people will see a commercial aired during the Super Bowl than during a 3:00 a.m. rerun of a Tarzan movie. But the advertiser could probably run late-night commercials every night for a year for less than the cost of one 30-second Super Bowl spot. Therefore, media buyers also need to know which vehicles are the "best buys." Here are some of the upfront prices for a 30-second commercial during the 2019–2020 season.

Sunday Night Football	$685,227
Thursday Night Football	$540,090
This Is Us	$359,413
Grey's Anatomy	$286,026
Empire	$171,187

Of course, advertisers were happy to pay even more for a Super Bowl 30-second spot—$5.6 million. That's over $186,000 a second.

To compare the relative cost-effectiveness of different media and of spots run on different vehicles in the same medium, media planners use a measure they call **cost per thousand (CPM)**. This figure reflects the cost to deliver a message to 1,000 people.

Assume that the cost of each 30-second commercial on a popular show like *Young Sheldon* is $400,000, but the number of target audience members the show reaches is 20 million,

---

reach, or **rating**
The percentage of the target market that will be exposed to the media vehicle.

frequency
The average number of times a person in the target group will be exposed to the message.

gross rating points (GRPs)
A measure used for comparing the effectiveness of different media vehicles: average reach × frequency.

cost per thousand (CPM)
A measure used to compare the relative cost-effectiveness of different media vehicles that have different exposure rates; the cost to deliver a message to 1,000 people or homes.

or 20,000 units of 1,000 (in CPM, everything is broken down into units of 1,000). Hence, the CPM of *Young Sheldon* is $400,000/20,000 = $20 CPM.

Compare this to the cost of advertising in *Fortune* magazine: A full-page, four-color ad costs approximately $115,000, and the readership includes approximately 2 million members of our target audience, or 2,000 units of 1,000. Thus, the cost per thousand for *Fortune* is $115,000/2,000 = $57.50 CPM. As a result of this standardization to units of 1,000, you end up comparing "apples to apples," and the comparison reveals that *Young Sheldon*, which has a higher total cost, is a much better buy!

Magazines

Between 2015 and 2020, the global magazine industry declined by 3.9 percent. This decline has paralleled the increased integration of magazines with digital platforms. Newsstand sales have declined while publishers have maintained the numbers of subscriptions with deep discounts. In the future, the number of magazines in developed countries is expected to continue to decline while there will be significant growth in developing countries.

Today, in addition to general interest magazines such as *People*, *Rolling Stone*, and *Vanity Fair*, there are literally thousands of special-interest magazines from *Decanter* to *Garden Railways*. Technology allows *selective binding* whereby publishers can localize their editions with local business advertising.

Print advertising is an ideal medium to convey a point visually. This ad for the Austin Humane Society sends a strong message without resorting to words.

For advertisers, magazines also offer the opportunity for multipage spreads as well as the ability to include special inserts so they can deliver samples of products such as perfumes and other "scratch-and-sniff" treats.[23]

Where to Say It: Branded Entertainment

Today, more and more marketers rely on **product placement**, or **embedded marketing**, and **branded entertainment**, or **branded content**, to grab the attention of consumers who tune out traditional ad messages as fast as they see them. All of these terms refer to paid placement of brands within entertainment venues, including movies, TV shows, videogames, novels, and even retail settings.

While similar, there are significant differences between product placement and branded entertainment. Product placement is the insertion of brands, the logo or the product itself, into entertainment venues such as movies and TV shows. With branded entertainment, the brand is integrated into the storyline of the TV show or movie. Think about it this way: *The Lego Movie* and Marvel productions are just two-hour advertisements in the form of branded entertainment.

Are product placements and branded entertainment solid strategies? The idea is that when consumers see a popular celebrity who uses a specific brand in their favorite movie or TV program, they might develop a more positive attitude toward that brand. Over 350 product placements were in the nine films nominated for the 2020 Best Picture Academy Award. These brands included Apple, the Monopoly game, at least five automobile brands (Lincoln, Ferrari, Chevrolet, Ford, and Cadillac), and Canada Dry soft drink, just to name a few.[24]

Beyond movies and TV shows, what better way to promote to the video generation than through brand placements in video games? The industry calls this technique **advergaming**. If you are a video gamer, watch for placements of real-life brands, such as the Audi R7S Sportback in *Forza Motorsport 5* or the Nissan Leaf electric car in *Gran Turismo*. Auto marketers aren't the only ones that place their products in video games,

product placement, or **embedded marketing**
The placement of brands, logos, or a product itself into entertainment venues.

branded entertainment, or **branded content**
A form of advertising in which marketers integrate products into the storylines of entertainment venues.

advergaming
Brand placements in video games.

however. All told, the in-game advertising industry is worth about $7.8 billion annually. That's almost 100 times more than in 2006![25]

We mentioned previously that increasingly the once-solid line between traditional advertising and other forms of promotion is rapidly blurring. Nowhere is this trend more evident than in the growth of a technique marketers call **native advertising**. This term refers to sponsored messages that mimic or resemble the normal content of the media vehicle where they appear. Basically, the ad looks like part of the TV program or magazine article, as when an article about the Tesla electric car gets inserted in the middle of a magazine feature on new advances in green products.

Native advertising most commonly appears on the Internet, but it also pops up in other types of media, such as print magazines or TV. For example, the actors in a sitcom may also appear in a commercial so that you're not really sure if you're still watching the show or not.

Even though the label "sponsored content" usually appears somewhere in the message, consumers may not notice. Nationwide, for example, a regular sponsor of AMC's *Mad Men* series aired a special commercial designed to resemble programming in which the chief marketing officer (CMO) of Nationwide discusses the company's advertising history. In the commercial, the CMO refers to a 1964 memo that resulted in the Nationwide slogan changing from "In service with the People" to "The man from Nationwide is on your side," later shortened to "Nationwide is on your side."[26]

Content marketing, which we mentioned in Chapter 7, also referred to as *branded content*, is another form of branded entertainment in which a marketer provides information that is educational and useful to the customer. The information is not about the brand, good, or service; it's about the customers and what information has value for them.

Content marketing may include educational articles, e-books, videos, entertainment, and webinars that answer specific questions people have and thus provide something they can't get elsewhere; it creates a more knowledgeable customer.

The result of content marketing is that it sets your product apart from the competition because your product has provided the customer with something of real value. For example, companies that sell pomegranates or avocados often create helpful videos to demonstrate the best way to use these items in a great dessert or guacamole—and how to get that darn seed out. A company that makes baby products might include a blog where new mothers could ask questions and share their solutions. Instead of just being a company selling their product, you become an authoritative resource on topics of value to customers and potential customers, thus earning their loyalty and trust. This leads to a stronger relationship with the customer and increases profits.

One of the best ways to understand content marketing is to look at an example. Creating a resource page made up of helpful links on a given topic is an effective way to create helpful content. Colgate, the oral hygiene company, uses a content marketing strategy that includes a resource page. Often companies already have lots of related content to use. Colgate, for example, has over 2,400 pieces of content related to the broad topic "gum disease." With that much content, it's easy to break it up into useful subcategories, such as gum disease causes, gum disease treatment, and gum disease symptoms, to name a few.[27]

Where to Say It: Support Media

Although marketers (and consumers) typically think of advertising as messages that pop up on television, magazines, and radio, in reality, many of the ads we see today show up in other places as well, such as public venues like restrooms, on coasters we get in restaurants and bars, or on signs that trail behind airplanes. These **support media** reach people who may not have been exposed to mass-media advertising, and these platforms also reinforce the messages traditional media delivers. Here, we'll look at some of the more important support media advertisers use.

native advertising
An execution strategy that mimics the content of the website where the message appears.

support media
Media such as directories or out-of-home media that may be used to reach people who are not reached by mass-media advertising.

Directory Advertising

Directory advertising is the most "down-to-earth," information-focused advertising medium. In 1883, a printer in Wyoming ran out of white paper while printing part of a telephone book, so he substituted yellow paper instead—and so the "yellow pages" were born! In 2018, measured U.S. ad spending in directories was $8 billion.[28] Often consumers look through directories just before they are ready to buy.

Out-of-Home Media

Out-of-home media, as the name implies, includes a large variety of ad locations and formats where consumers are exposed to the advertising messages in public places. The Out of Home Advertising Association of America reports that $8.7 billion was spent on out-of-home advertising in 2019. Of that amount, 63.8% was for **billboards**, 18.6% for **transit advertising**, 11.5% for **place-based media advertising**, and 6.1% for **street furniture** ads.[29]

Billboards are standardized large-format outdoor advertising that can be seen from extended distances, generally more than 50 feet. Billboards range from spectacular displays to the smallest eight-sheet poster.[30]

Street furniture advertising displays are placed close to pedestrians and shoppers and at eye level or at the curbside for viewing by consumer in vehicles. Street furniture advertising is seen on bus shelters, city furniture such as sidewalk benches, and shopping malls.

Transit advertising is found in airports and in bus, subway, and train stations. Transit advertising also includes ads on the outside and on the inside of subway and rail cars, busses, and taxis.

Place-Based Media

Place-based media, like CNN's *Airport Channel*, transmit messages to "captive audiences" in public places, such as airport waiting areas. The channel, which appears at more than 2,000 gates and other viewing areas in 50 major U.S. airports, offers on-the-go news and entertainment.[31] Similar place-based video screens are now in thousands of shops, offices, and health clubs across the country, including stores like Best Buy, Foot Locker, and Target.

Place-based media also includes advertising at arenas and stadiums, aerial advertising (airplanes and blimps), marine advertising on a variety of motor and sail boats, and ads shown on the screen in movie theatres.

In recent years, out-of-home advertising has pushed the technology envelope with **digital signage** that enables the source to change the message at will. Swedish carmaker Volvo placed interactive digital signs for its new V40 model at train and bus stops throughout the United Kingdom. The sign teased, "Do you want to know more about yourself?" and let passersby use the touchscreen to customize their own V40.[32] Of course, many consumers dislike out-of-home media, especially outdoor advertising, because they feel it is unattractive.

Where to Say It: Digital Media

Here's where things get really confusing. We've talked about traditional advertising and about traditional media. But as we said previously, marketers are relying less and less on these traditional forms of marketing communication and moving more of their communications to digital media. Although we can name the traditional media pretty much on one hand, there are many different forms of communication on digital media.

The term **digital media** refers to any media that are digital rather than old-school analog, the technology used for landline telephones and nondigital watches. The more popular types of digital media advertisers use today include email, their own websites, ads placed on other websites and blogs, social media sites such as Facebook, search engines such as Google, and digital video such as YouTube, available via a variety of devices. Marketers also send advertising text messages to consumers via mobile phones.

---

directory advertising
Advertising in printed directories, such as the yellow pages.

out-of-home media
Communication media that reach people in public places.

billboards
Large-format outdoor advertising that can be seen from extended distances.

transit advertising
Advertising in airports and in bus, subway, and train stations, and ads on the outside and on the inside of subway and rail cars, busses, and taxis.

street furniture advertising
Advertising placed close to pedestrians and shoppers at eye level or at the curbside.

place-based media
Advertising media that transmit messages in public places, such as movie theatres and airports, where certain types of people congregate.

digital signage
Out-of-home media that use digital technology to change the message at will.

digital media
Media that are digital rather than analog, including websites, mobile or cellular phones, and digital video, such as YouTube.

Figure 13.10 *Snapshot* | Owned, Paid, and Earned Digital Media

For successful digital communications, marketers understand and use all three: owned media, paid media, and earned media.

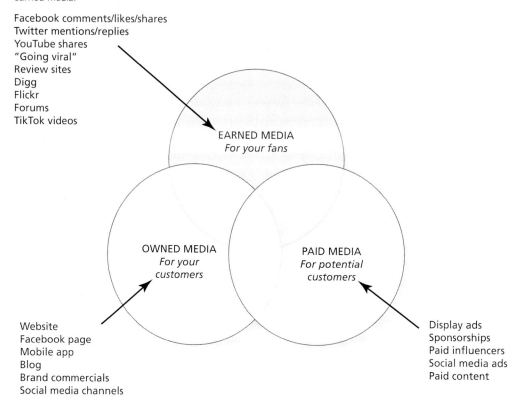

Facebook comments/likes/shares
Twitter mentions/replies
YouTube shares
"Going viral"
Review sites
Digg
Flickr
Forums
TikTok videos

EARNED MEDIA
For your fans

OWNED MEDIA
For your customers

PAID MEDIA
For potential customers

Website
Facebook page
Mobile app
Blog
Brand commercials
Social media channels

Display ads
Sponsorships
Paid influencers
Social media ads
Paid content

Digital media can take many different forms. Some require the marketer to invest a lot of money to create them (hint: others don't). For online marketing communication, we'll make a distinction that divides media into one of three buckets in terms of what the marketer has to do to create the message.[33]

Figure 13.10 summarizes these buckets:

1. Companies can create **owned media**, including their own websites, blogs, Facebook pages, YouTube channels, and Twitter accounts. The advantage of these owned media is that they are effective means for companies to build relationships with their customers while they maintain control of content.

2. **Paid media**, the most similar form to traditional media, includes display ads, sponsorships, and paid key word searches on search engines such as Google. Consumers generally dislike paid ads, reducing their effectiveness.

3. **Earned media** refers to word of mouth or buzz created by consumers themselves on social media. The positive of earned media is that it is the most credible to consumers, just like their friends and families have been most credible pretty much forever. The challenge is that marketers have little control over earned media, where messages may be positive or negative; they can only listen and respond.

owned media
Internet sites, such as websites, blogs, Facebook, and Twitter accounts, that are owned by an advertiser.

paid media
Internet media, such as display ads, sponsorships, and paid key word searches, that are paid for by an advertiser.

earned media
Word-of-mouth or buzz using social media where the advertiser has no control.

Website Advertising

Online advertising no longer is a novelty; companies now spend more than $78 billion a year to communicate via digital media.[34] That's because today Americans spend more time on their mobile devices (just over five hours daily) than they do watching TV (about four and a half hours daily).[35]

Online advertising offers several advantages over other media platforms. First, the Internet provides new ways to finely target customers. Web user registrations and *cookies* allow sites to track user preferences and deliver ads based on previous Internet behavior. In addition, because the website can track how many times an ad is "clicked," advertisers can measure in real time how people respond to specific online messages.

Specific forms of Internet advertising include banners, buttons, pop-up ads, search engines and directories, and email:

Banners, rectangular graphics at the top or bottom of web pages, were the first form of web advertising.

Buttons are small banner-type advertisements that a company can place anywhere on a page.

Pop-up ads are advertisements that appear on the screen while a web page loads or after it has loaded. Many surfers find pop-ups a nuisance, so most Internet access software provides an option that blocks all pop-ups.

Pre-roll ads are video messages that play before the content the user has selected. These ads are typically between 10 and 15 seconds and provide a captive audience for the advertiser. Some are unable to be skipped; others can be bypassed after a certain number of seconds have passed.

Email Advertising

Email advertising that transmits messages to very large numbers of in-boxes is one of the easiest ways to communicate with consumers—it's basically the same price whether you send 10 messages or 10,000. One downside to this platform is the explosion of **spam**, defined as the practice of sending unsolicited email to five or more people not personally known to the sender. Many websites that offer email give surfers the opportunity to allow or refuse email. This **permission marketing** strategy gives the consumer the power to *opt in* or out. Marketers in the U.S. send about 258 billion emails to consumers every year, so they hope that a good portion of these will be opened and read rather than being sent straight to the recycle bin.[36]

Social Media Advertising

Social media advertising is advertising that is executed within the confines of social media channels, such as Facebook, Instagram, and Twitter. Marketers realize that they need to go wherever the clients are—now the clients can be found frequently hanging out in a variety of online social communities. Seven out of every 10 Americans use some form of social media to connect, engage, share, or entertain.[37] Paid ads appear as users scroll through their normal feeds, and they can be targeted based upon demographic and psychographic behavior or upon data the social media has collected on the user. We'll talk more about social media advertising in Chapter 14.

Search Engines

Search engines are Internet programs that search for documents with specified key words. Increasingly, consumers use the Internet to search for information about products. Search engines, sites such as Google (www.google.com) and Bing (www.bing.com), help us locate useful information as they search millions of web pages for key words and return a list of sites that contain those key words.

Of course, the problem for marketers is that consumers seldom follow up on more than a page or two of results they get from these searches; we're all bombarded by way too much information these days to ever look at all of it. This has led marketers to develop sophisticated **search marketing** techniques. With search engine optimization (SEO), which we discussed in Chapter 5, marketers first find what key words consumers use most in their searches. Then, they edit their site's content or HTML to increase its relevance to those key

banners
Internet advertising in the form of rectangular graphics at the top or bottom of web pages.

buttons
Small banner-type advertisements that can be placed anywhere on a web page.

pop-up ads
Advertisements that appear on the screen while a web page loads or after it has loaded.

pre-roll ads
Promotional video messages that play before the content the user has selected.

spam
The use of electronic media to send unsolicited messages in bulk.

permission marketing
Email advertising in which online consumers have the opportunity to accept or refuse the unsolicited email.

social media advertising
Advertising that is executed within the confines of social media channels.

search engines
Internet programs that search for documents with specified key words.

search marketing
Marketing strategies that involve the use of Internet search engines.

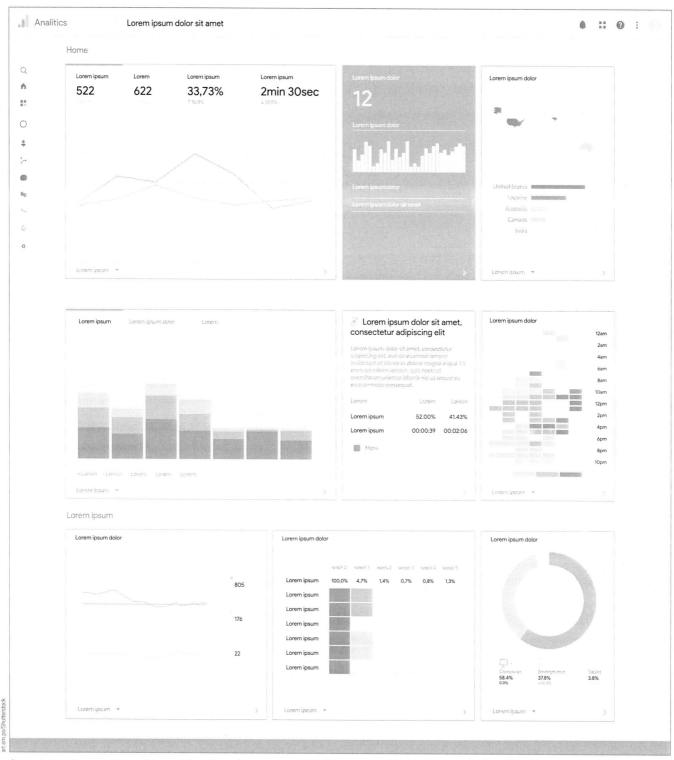

Google Analytics is a valuable tool to track the effectiveness of SEM campaigns. This is a template of a report that Google customizes for any business that chooses to receive it.

search engine marketing (SEM)
Search marketing strategy in which marketers pay for ads or better positioning.

sponsored search ads
Paid ads that appear at the top or beside the Internet search engine results.

words so that they can try to place their site high up in the millions of sites the search might generate. With **search engine marketing (SEM)**, the search engine company charges marketers to display **sponsored search ads** that appear at the top or beside the search results. Google, which has over half of all U.S. web searches,[38] has total global revenues of more than $95 billion.[39] What have you Googled today?

While search engine advertising (SEA) can be a tremendous help to advertisers, it also comes with its own set of challenges. Most businesses dream of having millions of visitors to their site—and fast. Yet increasing the SEA budget only to get a higher volume of clicks and impressions may not offer great results. Companies should focus on getting relevant traffic to their site—all clicks are not valued the same. It's also important to make sure you are using Google Analytics to track your campaigns and accurately track ROI.[40]

Mobile Advertising

The Mobile Marketing Association defines **mobile advertising** as "a form of advertising that is communicated to the consumer via a handset."[41] Mobile marketing offers advertisers a variety of ways to speak to customers (ideally with the customer's permission), including mobile websites, mobile applications or apps, **text message advertising**, and mobile video and TV.

Newer phones with GPS features that pinpoint your location allow additional mobile advertising opportunities. This technology enables smartphone geotargeting, discussed in Chapter 7, which is the ability to identify where customers are and deliver ads that are relevant to that location, increasing the relevancy of the message. Geotargeting is also used with social media apps with location check-in features, such as Swarm, Instagram geotargeting, and Facebook Places, that enable marketers to deliver promotional offers at the right time and place and can also be used to deliver coupons within a store at the point of sale. Restaurants and other retailers can use geotargeting to contact consumers to let them know where the closest outlet is. Within stores, advertisers can send ads to your smartphone as soon as you stand in front of a product.[42]

Most smartphone users prefer free apps and many refuse to pay for any. Therefore, developers of mobile apps must find some way to **monetize** their product. **In-app advertising** is often the best way to do this.

QR code advertising offers another way to engage consumers via their mobile phones. Marketers print QR codes in magazines and other forms of advertising, in stores, and even on "House for Sale" signs in yards. Smartphones are used as QR code scanners and convert the code to a usable form, such as a URL for a website. For the consumer, it is an easier and faster way to access a brand's website. For marketers, because consumers choose to access the website, the *conversion rate* we learned about in Chapter 5 (the chance that a sale will result from the contact) is much higher.

Video Sharing: Check It Out on YouTube

Video sharing describes the strategy of uploading video recordings or **vlogs** (pronounced "vee-logs") to Internet sites. Although YouTube is certainly the most popular video-sharing site, it is not the only one. After YouTube, the top seven video sharing sites include Vimeo, Wistia, Brightcove, Facebook Live, Instagram Live and Stories, Periscope, and Snapchat.[43]

For marketers, YouTube and other video platforms provide vast opportunities to build relationships with consumers. Cuisinart and other appliance makers post videos to show consumers how to use their new products. Nike, in preparation for the World Cup kickoff, released a five-minute World Cup–themed short film featuring animated versions of some of the world's best football (or soccer, for you U.S. fans) players. More than 18.6 million viewers watched the video, titled "Risk Everything," in the first three months.[44] Universities and their students also have gotten into video sharing. Have students in your university created a "happy" video and placed it on YouTube or Facebook?

Ethical Issues in Digital Media Advertising

The Internet is an open source revolution, where everyone can join in creating and sharing unlimited entertainment, news, information, and commerce in ways we've never before imagined. It's almost like a fairy tale—too good to be real. And like any good fairy tale, there's a villain threatening the future of unfettered web usage. The villain's name is **ad fraud**, or **click fraud**, and his sidekick is **ad blocking**.

---

mobile advertising
A form of advertising that is communicated to the consumer via a handset.

text message advertising
Delivering ads to consumers as mobile phone text messages.

monetize
The act of turning an asset into money. Websites and mobile apps monetize their content through advertisers.

in-app advertising
To monetize free mobile phone apps, developers use advertising to create revenue and to engage the consumer.

QR code advertising
QR (quick response) code advertising uses smartphone GPS technology to deliver ads and other information to consumers in stores and in other locations.

video sharing
Uploading video recordings on to Internet sites such as YouTube so that thousands or even millions of other Internet users can see them.

vlogs
Video recordings shared on the Internet.

ad fraud, or **click fraud**
The use of automated browsers to falsify the number of views or click-throughs the advertisers must pay for.

ad blocking
The use of powerful ad-blocking software created to stop ad fraud by stripping ads from the website at the network level.

Advertisers create digital ads to deliver to potential customers who are online reading articles from publications such as the *New York Times*, searching websites for a new pair of shoes, visiting their Facebook page, or using a search engine. Here is where ad fraud rears its ugly head. Advertising online networks, the intermediaries between the advertiser and your phone or tablet, seek to make as much money as they can. Because they are paid per view or click-through, the more connections they can generate, the richer they become. Cybercriminals use *fraud bots*, automated browsers programmed to cause ads to load and then to click them in the background of the device where they will not make contact with real consumers and thus falsify the number of views or click-throughs the advertisers must pay for. One study that looked at this **mobile hijacking** found consumers had unknowingly downloaded "zombie apps" onto 12 million devices over a 10-day period, each of which can run up to 16,000 ads in the background of a phone without the owner ever knowing it. Although it may only cost consumers some battery life, ad fraud is estimated to cost advertisers more than $7 billion a year. Some estimates are much higher—as much as $12–13 billion.[45]

One solution is to use powerful ad-blocking software created to stop ad fraud by stripping ads from the website at the network level. But is this the way to go? In 2019 it was estimated that 30 percent of Internet users worldwide have some type of ad blocking software.[46]

Just like TV commercials are essential to pay for TV programming, online ads power the open Internet so that consumers can enjoy unlimited content for free. Certainly, individuals can block ads from their own devices, but that is their choice. Network ad blocking takes away consumers' ability to control what they see and don't see, the foundation of the World Wide Web. An argument against network ad blocking is that it creates censorship and destroys freedom of the press and will eventually mean that consumers pay more and more for less and less information. In other words, it would be the end of the open and free Web as we know it.

Google now blocks all advertising on websites that deliver particularly annoying ads. Many believe that the scale of Google's business (Chrome has 59.23 percent browser market share across desktop and mobile) gives Google too much power.

Some experts argue that ad and content blocking is inevitable. As the amount of web content grows exponentially every year, consumers will eventually want to block ads and other content.

mobile hijacking
The use of automated browsers to falsify the number of views or click-throughs the advertisers must pay for.

When and How Often to Say It: Media Scheduling

media schedule
The plan that specifies the exact media to use and when to use it.

After he or she chooses the advertising media, the planner then creates a **media schedule** that specifies the specific outlets the campaign will use as well as when and how often the message will appear. Figure 13.11 shows a hypothetical media schedule for the promotion of a new video game. Note that much of the advertising reaches its target audience in the

Figure 13.11 *Snapshot* | Media Schedule for a Video Game

Media planning includes decisions on where, when, and how much advertising to do. A media schedule, such as this one for a video game, shows the plan visually.

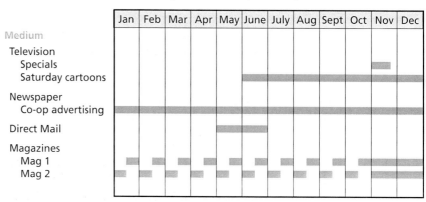

months just before Christmas and that much of the expensive TV budget focuses on advertising during specials just prior to the holiday season.

The media schedule outlines the planner's best estimate of which media (TV or magazines, for example) will be most effective to attain the advertising objective(s) and which specific media vehicles (TV shows such as *The Crown* or *The Mandalorian*) will be the most effective. The media planner considers qualitative factors, such as the match between the demographic and psychographic profile of a target audience and the types of people a media vehicle reaches, the advertising patterns of competitors, and the capability of a medium to adequately convey the desired information. The planner must also consider factors such as the compatibility of the product with editorial content. For example, viewers might not respond well to a serious commercial about preventing animal cruelty that tugs at one's heartstrings while they watch a "fun" show like *Keeping Up with the Kardashians*.

After deciding where and when to advertise, the planner must decide how often he or she wants to send the message. What time of day? And what overall pattern will the advertising follow?

A *continuous schedule* maintains a steady stream of advertising throughout the year. This is most appropriate for products that we buy on a regular basis, such as shampoo or bread. A *pulsing schedule* varies the amount of advertising throughout the year based on when the product is likely to be in demand. A suntan lotion might advertise year-round but more heavily during the summer months. *Flighting* is an extreme form of pulsing, in which advertising appears in short, intense bursts, alternating with periods of little to no activity.

Disruption in Advertising

Disruption of advertising and specifically of the TV ad marketplace over the last nine decades pretty much shows the evolution of not only advertising but our lives. Here are some of the highlights of this journey.

- *Ad Age*, the publication many think of as the must-read source of news in the advertising industry, was born in 1930. On July 1, 1941, Bulova aired the first official FCC-sanctioned TV commercial on New York City's WNBT.

- In 1983, an *Ad Age* headline proclaimed, "Atari founder develops revolutionary tv." This referred to a world where addressable advertising allowed advertisers to aim commercials at homes with specific demographics and psychographics. This would make the traditional measurement of TV audiences obsolete.

- On April 19, 1993, *Ad Age* published the news that NBC, searching for another stream of revenue, planned to sell products directly to consumers, thus becoming a direct marketer.

- On May 24, 1993, *Ad Age* spread the news about Time Warner's electronic superhighway, "the first full-service interactive network" that would bring interactive games, home shopping, movies, and telephone services through cable TV. There was no mention of the term "Internet."

- The COVID-19 pandemic in 2020 offered the opportunity for advertising and TV to change again. With the largest work-at-home/virtual education experiment ever, certainly TV and the entire advertising industry would create new headlines.[47]

13.4 Direct Marketing

OBJECTIVE
Understand the elements of direct marketing.

Are you one of those people who loves to get lots of catalogs in the mail or pore over online catalogs for hours and then order just exactly what you want without leaving home? Maybe you're the one who ordered the Donatella Arpaia Multifunctional Pizza Oven from the Home Shopping Network for two easy payments of only $29.98 or who responded to an infomercial on TV for the DashCam Pro or the Pedi Paws pet nail trimmer. All these are examples of direct marketing, the fastest-growing type of marketing communication.

Direct marketing, a form of one-to-one marketing communication, refers to any direct communication to a consumer or business recipient that is designed to generate a response in the form of an order, a request for further information, or a visit to a store or other place of business for purchase of a product. Spending on direct marketing continues to increase. Direct and digital ad spending in 2019 was $363.4 billion and was expected to grow to $389.5 billion in 2020.[48]

Why do so many marketers love direct marketing? One reason is simple but powerful: You know almost immediately whether your pitch worked. Unlike traditional advertising, every message can link directly to a response (hence the term direct marketing). For this reason, organizations that want to see evidence of a promotion's ROI ("show me the money!") can get very specific feedback about what worked and what didn't.

Let's look at the four most popular types of direct marketing as portrayed in Figure 13.12: mail order (including catalogs and direct mail), telemarketing, direct response advertising, and m-commerce. We'll start with the oldest—buying through the mail—which is still incredibly popular!

Mail Order

In 1872, Aaron Montgomery Ward and two partners put up $1,600 to mail a one-page flyer that listed their merchandise with prices, hoping to sell to farmers through the mail.[49] The mail-order industry was born, and today consumers can buy just about anything through the mail. Mail order comes in two forms: catalogs and direct mail.

A **catalog** is a collection of products offered for sale in book form, usually consisting of product descriptions accompanied by photos of the items. The innovator retailers, Montgomery Ward, Sears, and JCPenney, pioneered catalogs as a way to reach an additional target market, people in remote areas who lacked access to stores.

Today, despite the growth in online shopping, the catalog is still alive and may be making a comeback. For many brands, the catalog drives both online and in-store sales. According to the Data and Marketing Association, approximately 100.7 million Americans made purchases from catalogs in 2016. Of course, many catalogs are available and viewed online, often on mobile devices. Why do retailers think catalogs are still so important? The answer is because they drive sales. When Lands' End reduced the number of catalogs it distributed, the result was a $100 million decrease in sales.

Direct Mail

Unlike a catalog retailer that offers a variety of merchandise through the mail, **direct mail** is a brochure or pamphlet that offers a specific good or service at one point in time. A direct mail offer has an advantage over a catalog because the sender can personalize it. Charities, political groups, and other not-for-profit organizations also use a lot of direct mail.

direct marketing
Any direct communication to a consumer or business recipient designed to generate a response in the form of an order, a request for further information, or a visit to a store or other place of business for purchase of a product.

catalog
A collection of products offered for sale in book form, usually consisting of product descriptions accompanied by photos of the items.

direct mail
A brochure or pamphlet that offers a specific good or service at one point in time.

Figure 13.12 *Snapshot* | Key Forms of Direct Marketing

Key forms of direct marketing are mail order (including catalogs and direct mail), telemarketing, direct-response advertising, and m-commerce.

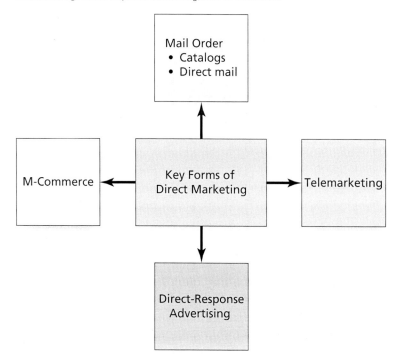

Just as with email spamming, Americans are overwhelmed with direct-mail offers—"junk mail"—that may end up in the trash. Of course, many consumers not only open but also respond with cold cash to their direct mail. Research from the Data and Marketing Association (DMA) found that the direct mail household response rate increased to 5.1% in 2017 and included a 12.4 percent response rate for consumers aged 18–21.[50] The direct-mail industry constantly works on ways to monitor what companies send through the mail, and it allows consumers to "opt out" of at least some mailing lists.

Telemarketing

Telemarketing, which was discussed earlier in Chapter 4, is direct marketing an organization conducts over the telephone (but why do they always have to call during dinner?). It might surprise you to learn that telemarketing actually is more profitable for business markets than for consumer markets. When business-to-business (B2B) marketers use the telephone to keep in contact with smaller customers, it costs far less than a face-to-face sales call yet still lets these clients know they are important to the company.

The Federal Trade Commission (FTC) established the National Do Not Call Registry to allow consumers to limit the number of telemarketing calls they receive. The idea is that telemarketing firms check the registry at least every 31 days and clean their phone lists accordingly. Consumers responded very positively to the regulation, and more than 220 million have posted their home numbers and mobile numbers on the registry.[51] While it may have limited some telemarketing calls, the National Do Not Call Registry unfortunately does not screen out a large majority of the vendors. As we said in Chapter 2, the growth of "robocalls" prompted passage of the Telephone Robocall Abuse Criminal Enforcement and Deterrence Act, or the TRACED Act, in 2019.

Direct-Response Advertising

Direct-response advertising allows the consumer to respond to a message by immediately contacting the provider to ask questions or order the product. Although for many companies the Internet has become the medium of choice for direct marketing, this technique is still alive and well in magazines, in newspapers, and on TV.

direct-response advertising
A direct marketing approach that allows the consumer to respond to a message by immediately contacting the provider to ask questions or order the product.

As early as 1950, the Television Department Stores channel brought the retailing environment into the TV viewer's living room when it offered a limited number of products the viewer could buy when he or she called the advertised company. TV sales picked up in the 1970s when two companies, Ronco Incorporated and K-Tel International, began to peddle products such as the Kitchen Magician, Pocket Fisherman, Mince-O-Matic, and Miracle Broom on TV sets around the world.[52] And who can forget the late Billy Mays's enthusiastic hawking of OxiClean, Jupiter Jack, and nearly 20 other products on TV? Make a simple phone call, and one of these wonders could be yours ("but wait, there's more . . . ").

Direct-response TV (DRTV) includes short commercials of less than 2 minutes, 30-minute or longer infomercials, and the shows that home shopping networks, such as QVC and HSN, broadcast. Top-selling DRTV product categories include exercise equipment, self-improvement products, diet and health products, kitchen appliances, and music. Of course, even home shopping networks have gone online, so if you miss the show, you can still order the product.

direct-response TV (DRTV)
Advertising on TV that seeks a direct response, including short commercials of less than 2 minutes, 30-minute or longer infomercials, and home shopping networks.

The primitive sales pitches of the old days have largely given way to the slick **infomercials** we all know and love (?) today. These half-hour or hour-long commercials resemble a talk show, often with heavy product demonstration and spirited audience participation, but of course they really are sales pitches. Although some infomercials still carry a low-class, sleazy stereotype, over the years, numerous heavyweights from Apple Computer to Volkswagen have used this format.

infomercials
Half-hour or hour-long commercials that resemble a talk show but actually are sales pitches.

M-Commerce

As we learned in Chapter 12, a final type of direct marketing is *m-commerce*. The "m" stands for "mobile," but it could also stand for "massive"—because that's how big the market will be for this platform. M-commerce refers to the promotional and other e-commerce activities transmitted over mobile phones and other mobile devices, such as smartphones and tablets with phone capabilities. With more than 7 billion mobile phones in use worldwide—more and more of them Internet enabled—it makes sense that marketers would want to reach out and touch this large audience, which is just over 85 percent of the world's population. That means there are more mobile phones throughout the world than working toilets![53]

M-commerce through text messages (such as an ad for a concert or a new restaurant) is known as *short message service* (SMS) marketing. In terms of unwanted "junk mail," m-commerce has the same potential dark side as other forms of direct marketing, such as snail mail and email. And the rise of the all-in-one smartphone on which the user engages in 24/7 social networking has created an up-and-coming industry of social networking activity tracking and analytics, such as Google Analytics and similar programs that we discussed in Chapter 5.

13.5 Brand You: Developing a Personal Marketing Communication Plan

Taylor has done a great job of planning his **personal brand.** *He has identified his personal strengths and weaknesses and studied the job environment identifying where the best opportunities for him are. He has made a list of industries and companies that would likely be in the market for an employee with his knowledge and skills and where he believes he would like to work. He has refined the concept of himself as a product (his core, actual, and augmented product) and understands how much he can expect in terms of compensation from a prospective employer.*

Now it is time to develop a **personal brand communication plan** *that will allow Taylor to land a great job. To do this, he knows he must first identify the right "media" to get his résumé to the right people at the right time. He must also identify the important benefits he can offer an employer and develop a brand story that will set him apart. Then, he will be able to deliver effective advertising (a résumé and cover letter) to his preferred prospective employers, obtain an interview, and hopefully get an offer from one or more of his top job choices.*

In the very first chapter, we discussed how a product could be a good, a service, a person, or a place. Just like any other product, successfully marketing a person (in this case, you) requires a great marketing communication plan.

Step 1: Your Job Search: What "Media" to Use

To maximize your chance of getting the internship or full-time job you want, you need to use all the options you have to get the word out about your brand. You need to develop a communication plan that has both high reach and high frequency. That means sending your résumés frequently through multiple media. You should use all media available. These include:

- Networking
- Online job boards and recruiting websites
- Social networking websites
- Company websites
- Direct mail
- Career fairs

Networking

Networking is one of the most effective means of getting an internship or a first job. Never underestimate the importance of networking, not just for getting a good first job but for the rest of your career. In fact, many successful people say that as many as 80 percent of jobs they have had are the result of networking—people who know a person recommend that person to other people. It's like anything else consumers buy—if someone you know recommends a new restaurant or a new gym or even a new brand of socks, you are far more likely to try the product than if you get information from any other source. And most managers find it's far more efficient and effective to ask people they know and trust if they can suggest someone who would be a good candidate for a job than to post a job and go through hundreds of résumés. Indeed, there is nothing more powerful than someone recommending you for a job.

Building and maintaining a successful network is more than just making people you have met your Facebook friends. Networking needs regular cultivation so remember to:

- Keep in touch with people in your network
- Help people in your network when they ask for assistance or when you have information that they might like about a job, even if it's not convenient
- Grow your network by developing relationships with people in your network's network

Whether you know it or not, you already have the foundation of a great network. You have family and friends and friends of your family and families of your friends. And, of course, you have professors, advisors, and career center counselors at your school. It's easy to add to your network when you meet new people, such as speakers in your classes and people you meet at campus events or professional meetings.

Some useful suggestions for networking:

- Join and create a profile on LinkedIn and ask others to join your LinkedIn network.
- Have professional-looking business cards made with your name and contact information.
- Join a professional association that allows student members, often at reduced rates.
- Reach out through Facebook and other social networks to ask people for help with your search.
- Start networking before graduation.
- Consider an internship or volunteering—you'll get to know professionals.
- Always be professional; imagine every day in every situation that there may be someone you meet who will have the perfect job for you. Be sure to clean up any digital dirt you may have on social media, such as inappropriate conversations, pictures, and images.

Online Job Boards and Recruiting Websites

Online job boards and recruiting websites are generally the least likely to respond to your application with an offer for an interview. Many times the job postings are just to satisfy a legal requirement to let the public know about the job when the job has already been filled. Still, job boards as one of many approaches to your marketing communication plan will make sure you have left no stone unturned. Some of the more popular job boards are ZipRecruiter, CareerBuilder, Monster, and Nexxt. National, regional, and local professional organizations in your field may also have job postings.

Social Networking Sites

Many companies use Facebook to recruit for entry-level jobs. Professional social networking websites, such as www.linkedin.com and www.jobster.com can provide contacts in your target industry or at your target companies.

Company Website

Most companies post job openings on their websites, and many of these do not post on job boards or with recruiters. You should visit the websites of companies you have identified as being in your target market. You may wish to check a source of company names, such as a list of the 100 Fastest-Growing Companies. Publications such as *Businessweek* and *Fortune* regularly publish such lists. Check publications and sort out the best ones.

Direct Mail

If you have specific companies that you are interested in, and you should, send them a letter to let them know about you and your value proposition. Just like retailers send you an email or an online catalog to show you what they have to offer, you can send a cover letter and a résumé to let the right person with a company know what you have to offer them, even before a job is posted. This is especially important if you are seeking an internship, as many companies do not advertise their internship programs. A hard-copy letter will make you stand out and break through the email clutter. Because direct mail response rates are very low—i.e., between 1 and 2 percent—you will need to send letters to as many target companies as possible. Also, it will help you stand out from the crowd if you personalize your letters by using mail merge software. You should also send multiple personalized letters to different managers in each company. Some people who you might consider are vice presidents, directors, or managers of departments where you would like to work; vice presidents or directors of human resources; recruiting managers; and internship managers. Again, be sure that you are spelling all words and names correctly and that you don't have any grammatical errors or typos.

Career Fairs

Career fairs can be extremely productive, especially if you develop an action plan. First, check the list of employers who will be attending, and make a list of those you are most interested in talking with. Visit as many companies as possible. Be sure to bring copies of your "advertising"—i.e., your résumé and cover letter. Finally, be sure you dress for success, introduce yourself to each representative from your target companies, and ask for a business card and offer them one of your own.

Step 2: Advertising: Developing Your Marketing Communication Messages

The most important messages in your job search are a résumé and a cover letter that stand out and get the attention of a recruiter or manager. Think of these as your direct mail advertising—what you send out to a prospective buyer to get an interview.

Universities normally have career centers where there is someone who can help you develop the résumé and cover letter. Be sure to get a head start with your work on these; you don't want to wait until the last minute when no one has time to help you.

Here are some suggestions for your résumé:

- Be totally honest. Don't lie or exaggerate on your résumé.
- You need to include more than a simple list of what you have done. To advertise effectively, you need to outline the benefits you can provide to a prospective employer. You need to describe the skills, knowledge, and competencies you have gained from each experience. Even if you've only been a server at a restaurant, that says that you can be customer focused and can multitask.
- You can also include the skills and knowledge you have gained from your classes. Most students have participated in team projects, which has given you experience in teamwork.
- Provide evidence of what you are saying. If you are a high achiever academically, include your GPA and any recognition you have received.
- Include an honest appraisal of your personal characteristics that an employer might want. Are you detail-oriented? Highly motivated? An excellent communicator? Committed to a work ethic? Do you have leadership experience? Community service experience? What software are you proficient with?
- Keep your résumé to one page. The résumé is to get you noticed and moved to the top of the pile of applicants. You can add additional information about yourself during the interview.
- Make sure your résumé includes identifying information (name, address., etc.) and appropriate headings to make it easier for an interviewer to find what she is looking for. Suggested headings are Objective (the first heading), Education, Honors and Scholarship, Work Experience (the most important part of the résumé), Leadership Experience, Athletic Achievements, Extracurricular Activites, and Skills.
- Make sure the résumé looks good; contains no spelling, punctuation, or grammatical errors; and is on white or neutral-colored résumé paper.
- Do not include references in your résumé. They should be supplied only when requested.

Your cover letter provides you with a great opportunity to set yourself apart and is a necessity for a job. It should summarize why you are sending your résumé (a job advertisement?), what makes you unique, and how you would bring value to the company. It should be short, concise, and professional and addressed to a person, not a department. It should also include an inside address. Again, and we can't say it too many times, make sure there are no typos, misspelled words or names, or other errors. Note: If you are sending cover letters to a number of different organizations, check to make sure that you don't use the wrong company name in the body of the letter—that is an easy mistake and it happens a lot.

Of course, there is more to this job hunting thing. In the next chapter, we'll talk about Step 3, your one-to-one communication: personal selling in the interview.

Taylor is well on his way to having a great marketing communication plan. He has begun networking and regular scanning of online job boards, recruiting websites, social networking websites, and company websites. His résumé and cover letter are completed and ready to send with his direct mail and when he responds to various websites or attends a career fair. Taylor is feeling even more confident that he is on the right track for a great job.

Objective **Summaries** and **Key Terms**

13.1 Objective Summary

Understand the communication process and the traditional promotion mix.

Firms use promotion and other forms of marketing communication to inform consumers about new products, remind them of familiar products, persuade them to choose one alternative over another, and build strong customer relationships. Recognizing that consumers come in contact with a brand in many different ways, firms today often practice integrated marketing communications (IMC) to reach consumers through a multichannel promotion strategy. Because marketers understand the impact of word-of-mouth communication, they are likely to supplement the traditional one-to-many communication model with a newer many-to-many model and also to talk one-to-one with consumers.

The traditional communication process includes a message source that creates an idea, encodes the idea into a message, and transmits the message through some medium. The message is delivered to the receiver, who decodes the message and may provide feedback to the source. Anything that interferes with the communication is called "noise."

The promotion mix refers to the marketing communication elements that the marketer controls. Advertising, sales promotion, and public relations use the mass media to reach many consumers at a single time, whereas personal selling and direct marketing allow marketers to communicate with consumers one-on-one.

Key Terms

integrated marketing communication (IMC)
multichannel promotion strategy
word-of-mouth communication
communication process
source
encoding
message
medium
receiver
decoding
noise
feedback
outbound marketing
inbound marketing
ethical bribe
promotion mix
mass communication

13.2 Objective Summary

Describe the steps in traditional and multichannel promotion planning.

Recognizing the importance of communicating with a variety of stakeholders who influence the target market, marketers begin the promotion planning process by identifying the target audience(s). Next, they establish communication objectives. Objectives often are to create awareness, inform the market, create desire, encourage purchase and trial, or build loyalty.

Marketers develop promotion budgets from rules of thumb, such as the percentage-of-sales method, the competitive-parity method, and the objective-task method. They then decide on a push or a pull strategy and allocate monies from the total budget to various elements of the promotion mix.

Next, marketers design the promotion mix by deciding how they can use advertising, sales promotion, personal selling, and public relations most effectively to communicate with different target audiences. The final step in any advertising campaign is to evaluate its effectiveness. Marketers evaluate advertising through posttesting. Posttesting research may include aided or unaided recall tests that examine whether the message had an influence on the target market.

Marketers today often opt for multichannel promotion strategies where they combine traditional advertising, sales promotion, and public relations activities with social media and online buzz-building activities. Multichannel strategies boost the effectiveness of either online or offline strategies used alone and allow marketers to repeat their messages across various channels, thus strengthening brand awareness and providing more opportunities to convert customers.

Key Terms

hierarchy of effects
top-down budgeting techniques
percentage-of-sales method
competitive-parity method
bottom-up budgeting techniques
objective-task method
push strategy
pull strategy

13.3 Objective Summary

Explain what advertising is, describe the major types of advertising, discuss some of the major criticisms of advertising, and describe the process of developing an advertising campaign and how marketers evaluate advertising.

Advertising is nonpersonal communication from an identified sponsor using mass media to persuade or influence an audience. Advertising informs and reminds consumers and creates consumer desire. Product advertising seeks to persuade consumers to choose a specific product or brand. Institutional advertising is used to develop an image for an organization or company (corporate advertising), to express opinions (advocacy advertising), or to support a cause (public service advertising). Retail and local advertising informs customers about where to shop. Most firms rely on the services of advertising agencies to create successful advertising campaigns.

Full-service agencies include account management, creative services, research and marketing services, and media planning, whereas limited-service agencies provide only one or a few services.

User-generated content (UGC), also known as consumer-generated media (CGM), includes online consumer comments, opinions, advice, consumer-to-consumer discussions, reviews, photos, images, videos, podcasts and webcasts, and product-related stories available to other consumers through digital technology. To take advantage of this phenomenon, some marketers encourage consumers to contribute their own do-it-yourself (DIY) ads. Crowdsourcing is a practice in which firms outsource marketing activities (such as selecting an ad) to a community of users—that is, a crowd.

Advertising has been criticized for being manipulative, for being deceitful and untruthful (including puffery and drip pricing), for being offensive and in bad taste, for creating and perpetuating stereotypes, and for causing people to buy things they don't really need. Although some advertising may justify some of these criticisms, most advertisers seek to provide honest ads that don't offend the markets they seek to attract.

Development of an advertising campaign begins with understanding the target audiences and developing objectives for the message and the ad budget. To create the ads, the agency develops a creative strategy that is summarized in a creative brief. To come up with finished ads, they must decide on the appeal, the format, the tonality, and the creative tactics and techniques. Pretesting advertising before placing it in the media prevents costly mistakes.

Media planning gets a message to a target audience in the most effective way. The media planner must decide whether to place ads in traditional mass media or in digital media. Digital media are classified as owned media, paid or bought media, and earned media. Website advertising includes banners, buttons, and pop-up ads. Other types of digital media include email advertising and search engine strategies. Mobile advertising includes text message advertising, in-app advertising, geotargeting, and QR code advertising. Video sharing allows marketers to upload videos to websites such as YouTube. Product placements, a type of branded entertainment, integrate products into movies, TV shows, video games, novels, and even retail settings. Advergaming, native advertising, and content marketing are additional types of branded content. Support media include directories, out-of-home media, and place-based media. A media schedule specifies the exact media the campaign will use and when and how often the message should appear.

The final step in any advertising campaign is to evaluate its effectiveness. Marketers evaluate advertising through posttesting. Posttesting research may include aided or unaided recall tests that examine whether the message had an influence on the target market.

Key Terms

advertising

TV Everywhere, or **authenticated streaming**

product advertising

institutional advertising

corporate advertising

advocacy advertising

public service advertisements (PSAs)

retail and local advertising

advertising campaign

full-service agency

limited-service agency

interactive agency, or **digital agency**

in-house agency

programmatic advertising, or **programmatic ad buying**

account executive

account planner

creative services

research and marketing services

media planners

do-it-yourself (DIY) ads

drip pricing

corrective advertising

puffery

greenwashing

creative strategy

creative brief

advertising appeal

unique selling proposition (USP)

reminder advertising

teaser ads, or **mystery ads**

execution format

comparative advertising

slice-of-life advertising

lifestyle advertising

tonality

fear appeals

jingles

slogans

pretesting

media planning

posttesting

unaided recall

aided recall

attitudinal measures

upfront TV ad pricing

reach, or **rating**

frequency

gross rating points (GRPs)

cost per thousand (CPM)

product placement, or **embedded marketing**

branded entertainment

advergaming

native advertising

support media

directory advertising

out-of-home media

billboards

transit advertising

street furniture advertising

place-based media

digital signage

digital media

owned media

paid media

earned media
banners
buttons
pop-up ads
pre-roll ads
spam
permission marketing
social media advertising
search engines
search marketing
search engine marketing (SEM)
sponsored search ads
mobile advertising
text message advertising
monetize
in-app advertising
QR code advertising
video sharing
vlogs
ad fraud, or click fraud
ad blocking
mobile hijacking
media schedule

13.4 Objective Summary

Understand the elements of direct marketing.

Direct marketing refers to any direct communication designed to generate a response from a consumer or business customer. Some of the types of direct marketing activities are mail order

(catalogs and direct mail), telemarketing, and direct-response advertising, including infomercials and m-commerce.

Key Terms

direct marketing
catalog
direct mail
direct-response advertising
direct-response TV (DRTV)
infomercials

13.5 Objective Summary

Understand how to increase your chances of getting a great job or internship by developing an effective résumé and cover letter, how to get these to the right people, and how you can make yourself stand out among other applicants.

In developing a personal Brand You communication plan, you should create a communication program that provides both high reach and high frequency. This is best accomplished through the use of a multimedia program that includes networking, online job boards and recruiting websites, social networking websites, company websites, direct mail, and career fairs.

The marketing communication messages that you will use in your Brand You marketing strategy are your résumé and cover letter. In order to maximize your chances for success, it is best to develop these early to help you in all of your career-planning activities.

Chapter **Questions** and **Activities**

Concepts: Test Your Knowledge

13-1. What is promotion? What is integrated marketing communication (IMC)? What are multichannel promotion strategies?

13-2. List and describe the elements of the traditional communication model.

13-3. List the elements of the promotion mix and describe how they are used to deliver personal and mass appeals.

13-4. List and explain the steps in promotion planning.

13-5. Explain the hierarchy of effects and how it is used in communication objectives.

13-6. Describe the three steps in developing marketing communication budgets. What is a push strategy? What is a pull strategy?

13-7. What is advertising, and what types of advertising do marketers use most often? What is an advertising campaign?

13-8. Firms may seek the help of full-service or limited-service advertising agencies for their advertising. Describe each. What is an interactive, or digital, agency? What is an in-house agency? Explain what has led to an increase in in-house agencies in recent years.

13-9. What is consumer-generated advertising, and what are its advantages? What is crowdsourcing, and how is it used in advertising? What is native advertising?

13-10. List three pros and three cons for each of the following types of advertising: TV, radio, newspaper, magazine, out-of-home, Internet.

13-11. Describe the steps in developing an advertising campaign. What is a creative brief? What is meant by the appeal, execution format, tonality, and creative tactics and techniques used in an ad campaign?

13-12. What is digital media? What are owned, paid, and earned media? What are the different advertising activities or techniques included in website advertising, mobile advertising, and video sharing?

13-13. What are different types of branded content? How do marketers use branded entertainment and support media, such as directories, out-of-home media, and place-based media, to communicate with consumers?

13-14. How do marketers pretest their ads? How do they posttest ads?

13-15. What is media planning? How do media planners use reach, frequency, gross rating points, and cost per thousand in developing effective media schedules?

13-16. Describe continuous, pulsing, and flighting media schedules.

Activities: Apply What You've Learned

13-17. Spend an hour or two watching network TV with advertising. Make a list of 10 or more ads you see. Tell what brand and product is being advertised and classify each ad according to the following:

1. Appeal
   - USP
   - emotional
   - reminder
   - teaser of mystery ad

2. Execution format
   - comparison
   - demonstration
   - storytelling
   - testimonial
   - slice of life

3. Tonality
   - straightforward
   - humor
   - dramatic
   - romantic
   - sex
   - apprehension/fear
   - romantic appeal

What did you learn from this project?

13-18. *Creative Homework/Short Project* Assume you are the director of marketing for a firm that markets healthy snack foods (i.e., chips, cookies, etc.). You are developing a promotion plan. Develop suggestions for each of the following items and explain your reasons for each.

   a. Marketing communication objectives
   b. The method you will use for determining the communication budget
   c. The use of a push strategy or a pull strategy
   d. Elements of the traditional promotion mix you will use

13-19. *Creative Homework/Short Project* Your company has developed a new high-end lotion designed to reduce the appearance of wrinkles on the face and neck when used twice daily. Using the hierarchy of effects, develop communications objectives for your product for consumers who may be at each stage in the hierarchy. Make sure your objectives are quantitative, specific, and within a time frame.

13-20. *For Further Research (Individual)* More and more firms are engaged in multichannel promotion programs. You can learn about many of these by searching library or Internet sources. Some Internet sources that may be useful are the following:

Brandchannel.com
Adweek.com (*Adweek* magazine)
NYTimes.com (*New York Times*)
Adage.com (*Advertising Age* magazine).

You can also find examples by simply searching for "multichannel promotion program examples."

Gather information on one or more multichannel promotion programs. Develop a report that describes the program(s) and make suggestions for how it or they might be improved.

13-21. *Creative Homework/Short Project* As we discussed in this chapter, many consumers are highly critical of advertising. To better understand this, conduct a short survey of (1) your college classmates and (2) a different group of consumers, such as your parents and their friends. In the survey, ask the respondents about the criticisms of advertising discussed in this chapter—that is, that advertising (1) is manipulative, (2) is deceptive and untruthful, (3) is offensive and in bad taste, (4) creates and perpetuates stereotypes, and (5) causes people to buy things they don't really need. Be sure to ask respondents to give you examples of ads that they feel fall in these categories. Develop a report that summarizes your results and compares the attitudes of the two consumer groups.

Concepts: Apply Marketing Metrics

13-22. You learned that media planners use a variety of metrics to help in making decisions on what TV show or which magazines to include in their media plans. Two of these are *gross rating points (GRPs)* and cost per thousand (CPM).

Assume you are developing a media plan for a new brand of gourmet frozen meals. Your target market includes females ages 25 to 44. The table that follows lists six possible media buys you are considering for the media plan, along with some relevant information about each (note that the numbers are fictitious, created for example purposes only). The plan is based on a four-week period:

   a. Calculate the GRPs for each media buy based on the information given.
   b. Calculate the CPM for each media buy.
   c. Based on the cost of each buy, the reach or rating of each buy, and any qualitative factors (e.g., decision criteria beyond the numbers) that you believe are important, select the top three media buys that you would recommend.
   d. Explain why you would select these three.

Media Vehicle	Rating	Cost per Ad or Insertion	Number of Insertions	CPM	GRPs for This Number of Insertions
Young Sheldon	30	$500,000	4 (one per weekly episode)		
NCIS	20	$400,000	4 (one per weekly episode)		
CBS Evening News	12	$150,000	20 (one per weeknight news program)		
People magazine	5	$ 40,000	4 (one per weekly publication)		
Better Homes and Gardens magazine	12	$ 30,000	1 (one per monthly publication)		
USA Today	4	$ 10,000	12 (three ads per week)		

13-23. You have done some research on your target audience and are convinced that the best outlet for promotional investment in your product is either a commercial during *NCIS* or an ad in the print version of the *Wall Street Journal (WSJ)*. For the purposes of this exercise, assume that *NCIS* reaches 10 million members of the target audience in the U.S., while *WSJ* reaches 5 million members. CBS is quoting you $400,000 per 30-second spot on *NCIS*; *WSJ* charges $225,000 for a full-page, four-color ad.

   a. Calculate the CPM for each option.
   b. Which media buy is the better financial deal?
   c. What other factors besides CPM might impact your decision?

Choices: What Do You Think?

13-24. *Critical Thinking* Ad spend on digital advertising, including websites, apps, mobile gaming, etc., is increasing steadily—digital spend is poised to overtake television as the largest in media spending! What types of products and services do you think benefit the most from digital advertising campaigns? Why do you think so? What type of audience do you think marketers expect to reach when advertising digitally? Do a little research online to see if your expectations match up with the results of studies of digital advertising audiences.

13-25. *Critical Thinking* User-generated advertising content is on the rise. Some marketers encourage consumers to contribute their own ads through social media or website platforms. How do you think this content benefits the marketer? How does it benefit other consumers? Are there any potential downsides to the practice?

13-26. *Critical Thinking* Advertising and other forms of marketing communications have changed radically during the last decade or so as a result of digital technology. List some of these changes. What about each of these changes has benefitted consumers? Harmed consumers? Benefitted marketers? Harmed marketers? What changes would you recommend?

13-27. *Ethics* Firms are increasing their use of search engine marketing in which they pay search engines, such as Google and Bing, for priority position listings. Social media sites such as Twitter generate revenue by offering to sell "search words" to firms so that their posting appears on top. Are such practices ethical? Are consumers being deceived when a firm pays for priority positioning?

13-28. *Ethics* You learned that puffery occurs when an ad makes claims about a product in advertising that cannot be proven true or untrue. Find and describe some examples of puffery in a magazine, online, or in a TV ad. What do you think is the likelihood of the ad causing consumers to buy a brand they would not otherwise buy for each? Discuss whether these types of ads should or should not be made illegal. What is the positive side of such ads? What is the negative side?

Miniproject: Learn by Doing

13-29. This miniproject is designed to help you develop your skills in marketing communication planning. Working with one or more of your classmates, complete the following suggested activities.

   Assume you are developing a multichannel marketing communication program for a firm that produces and sells disposable diapers and other products to care for babies.

   1. What are the objectives of your communication plan?

   2. What are two types of traditional marketing communications you would use? Provide details and be specific. Why are these the best for this product?

   3. You will also be using website advertising, mobile advertising, video sharing, and branded entertainment. Design these specific activities and provide details.

   4. Look over your recommendations and check to see if your plans:
      a. Work together to be one integrated program of communication.
      b. Provide a program that will engage the consumer in interactive activities.
      c. Provide some benefit to improve the life of the consumer.

   5. If they do not, revise your program.

   6. Make a presentation of the plan to your class.

Marketing in Action **Case**   Real Choices at Nestlé

Digital advertising has revolutionized the promotion component of the marketing mix. Digital advertising allows businesses large and small to reach prospects and customers more quickly and personally than advertising that uses old-school media, like print and broadcast. It is also much more complex, with multiple intermediaries, each having a part in the sale of the digital ad space. With that complexity comes the opportunity for inefficiency and ad fraud. Some companies, like food giant Nestlé, are turning to the nascent technology *blockchain* to determine whether ads are actually viewed by people (not "bots") and what amount of the ad spend goes to middlemen.

Digital advertising offers the opportunity to reach specific prospects who are likely to be interested in a company's product and to do so in real time. This requires millisecond communication between the marketer with a message to share (through a digital ad) and the "publisher," such as a particular website, handled through an automated process known as *programmatic ad buying*. Determining which prospects are of interest and then handling a payment for the ad placement involves several parties—trading desks, media agencies, exchanges, and technology platforms, to name a few. Each middleman in the process expects to be paid. With so many moving parts, there is not only cost, but also opportunity for fraudulent reporting of the actual number of consumers who see the ad and determine the cost to the marketer.

Enter blockchain. Best known as the underlying technology of the somewhat mysterious currency bitcoin, blockchain is at a basic level a distributed ledger of transactions. Unlike most systems that facilitate exchanges, there is no central control; the database is instead distributed across many computers, which is key to the integrity of the process. Once a transaction or "block" is recorded in the ledger, it can only be updated when all the computers involved evaluate and confirm it (via algorithms). Once approved, that block can become part of the "chain" of transactions. By eliminating the need for all transactions to pass through a central clearinghouse, transactions can happen much more quickly, and the verification by multiple computers helps to reduce fraud. It's easy to see why these features would be important to those who purchase and exchange bitcoin currency. While purchasing ads does not involve the use of bitcoins, Nestlé and other companies have realized that the underlying blockchain technology can also be used as a tool to streamline the process of purchasing and tracking digital ads.

In the past, about 85 cents per advertising dollar was received by the digital publisher. Largely due to the many middlemen in today's digital advertising environment, that number has dropped to 40 cents. Using blockchain, the many transactions that occur in the digital ad buying process can each be treated as a block and verified through multiple computer systems across which the transaction ledger is distributed. Discrepancies can be flagged and actions taken to correct payment amounts or to spot unauthorized or unnecessary intermediaries that add costs to the process. The technology can also help determine whether ads are running on websites (or pages on those websites) that web surfers actually see and can help uncover situations in which internet "bots" (rather than real human users) are driving up clicks and with them, ad costs.

At Nestlé, blockchain is providing real results. The company has used a blockchain technology (along with other third-party verification providers) to ensure fee transparency and to modify campaigns in real time. This approach helped to flag campaign impressions that the company believed consumers would find objectionable. In one example, 3.7 percent of a campaign's impressions were flagged as potential problems, representing 9.23 percent of the campaign budget. Will Luttrell of Nestlé technology partner Amino Payments said, "Hundreds of thousands of domains being purchased programmatically are reduced down to a much more manageable view of the inventory grouped by sellers: publishers, conglomerates, aggregators, resellers, etc. . . . Viewing the world through the lens of 'who is supplying your inventory' is transformative." Amino Payments claims that advertisers that use its blockchain technology save an average of 10–15 percent in their media spend.

Along with Nestlé, major marketers such as Unilever, McDonald's, Toyota, and Kellogg have piloted blockchain technology to increase transparency in online advertising. Nestlé also uses blockchain to trace—and allow customers to learn—the origin of the coffee beans used in its products. Walmart also uses the technology to trace food products through the supply chain, and Chinese shipper COSCO employs blockchain to speed data flow and goods in ocean transportation.

Some warn that blockchain may not be ready for prime time. Successful use of the technology depends upon the cooperation of the many middlemen in the digital advertising process, some of which may not be so enthusiastic about coming under the authority of a consortium. A universal infrastructure has not yet emerged that is widely accepted by the many parties that are involved in the process. Also, some of the intermediaries may find the *status quo* more profitable. Donny Dovorin of Brave, a blockchain solution, says, "There are companies—I'm not going to name names of specific [demand-side platforms] or whatever—that don't want this technology to succeed."

Companies like Nestlé have the market power to coax reluctant digital ad intermediaries into playing ball. It has created a set of standards that digital media suppliers must meet, including contractual guarantees for quality, scale, and analytics. Sebastien Szczepaniak, the former head of e-business at Nestlé, suggested that contracts could include a requirement to use a blockchain technology solution. The effort to deploy the technology may be worth it. Digital advertising is expected to grow to over $427 billion by 2022, and Juniper Research estimates that advertising losses could reach $100 billion by 2023. In 2019, Nestlé spent 40 percent of its ad budget on digital. Given its heavy use of this medium, Nestlé and other companies will likely continue to use disruptive technologies like blockchain to ensure that its advertising messages actually reach their intended targets and that the company's investment in promotion pays off.[54]

Questions for Discussion

13-30. The success of a blockchain approach is largely dependent upon the cooperation of the many parties in the ad buying process. What arguments could Nestlé and other likeminded companies use to convince reluctant intermediaries to get on board with a blockchain strategy?

13-31. What role, if any, could *consumers* play in encouraging more accountability among the parties in the digital advertising process? What arguments might convince consumers to do this?

13-32. Beyond those mentioned above, what other steps could be taken to reduce both cost and fraud in the digital advertising process? In your answer, consider options such as self-regulation of the industry, government regulation, and organizational governance approaches.

Chapter **Notes**

1. Don E. Schultz and Heidi Schultz, *IMC. The Next Generation. Five Steps for Delivering Value and Measuring Returns Using Marketing Communication* (New York: McGraw-Hill, 2003), 20–21.

2. "This Week on 'Sunday Morning' (April 15)," *CBS News*, April 13, 2018, https://www.cbsnews.com/news/this-week-on-sunday-morning-april-15/ (accessed March 15, 2018).

3. "Facts," *The Dog Agency*, http://www.thedogagency.com/facts/ (accessed March 15, 2018).

4. *Advertising Age 200 Leading National Advertisers 2020 Fact Pack*, Crain Publications, 2020; "Marketing Services Spending in the U.S. 2017–2020 by Category," June 19, 2020, Published by A. Guttmann, June 19, 2020, https://www.statista.com/statistics/987009/marketing-spending-us-category/ (accessed October 11, 2020).

5. Emma Grey Ellis, "*Game of Thrones* Marketing Is Spreading Like Greyscale," *Wired*, April 11, 2019, https://www.wired.com/story/game-of-thrones-marketing/ (accessed July 10, 2020); Mihika Barua, "How HBO Sells Fantasy: The 'Game of Thrones' Customer Journey," *Percolate News*, Jun 26th, 2015, https://blog.percolate.com/2015/06/how-hbo-sells-fantasy-the-game-of-thrones-customer-journey/ (accessed July 10, 2020); Amrita (Amy) Bhattacharyya, "The Marketing Genius Of Game Of Thrones - Part 1," *LinkedIn*, April 17, 2016, https://www.linkedin.com/pulse/marketing-genius-game-thrones-part-1-amrita-amy-bhattacharyya (accessed July 10, 2020).

6. *Advertising Age 200 Leading National Advertisers 2018 Fact Pack*, Crain Publications.

7. Molly Wood, "TV Apps Are Soaring in Popularity, Report Says," *New York Times*, June 4, 2014, http://bits.blogs.nytimes.com/2014/06/04/report-tv-apps-are-soaring-in-popularity/?_php=true&_type=blogs&_r=0 (accessed June 10, 2014).

8. Brad Adgate, "TV Networks Look Toward Ad Supported Streaming To Grow Revenue," Forbes, September 17, 2020, https://www.forbes.com/sites/bradadgate/2020/09/17/tv-networks-look-toward-ad-supported-streaming-to-grow-revenue/#2541a6d1664d (accessed October 11, 2020); Wayne Friedman, "Disney's Hulu Posts Nearly $700M In 2019 Ad Revenue, $1.3B In Subscriber Revenue," Television News Daily, September 17, 2020, https://www.mediapost.com/publications/article/343844/disneys-hulu-posts-nearly-700m-in-2019-ad-revenu.html (accessed October 11, 2020).

9. Jillian Burman, "Why That 'Like A Girl' Super Bowl Ad Was So Groundbreaking," *Huffington Post*, February 3, 2015, https://www.huffingtonpost.com/2015/02/02/always-super-bowlad_n_6598328.html (accessed April 7, 2018); Kristina Monllos, "Don't Be Afraid of Failure, Says Latest Inspiring 'Like a Girl' Manifesto From Always," *AdWeek*, August 18, 2017, http://www.adweek.com/brand-marketing/dont-be-afraid-of-failure-says-latest-inspiring-like-a-girl-manifesto-from-always/ (accessed April 7, 2018).

10. Ann-Christine Diaz, "Best of 2015 #8 TV/Film: A Mom's Social Media Post Shatters Lives in AT&T's Gut-Wrenching Ad," *Ad Age*, July 20, 2015, http://creativity-online.com/work/att-it-can-wait–close-to-home/42768 (accessed May 11, 2016); Ann-Christine Diaz, "The Story Behind AT&T's Disturbing Phone-Safety Ad," *Ad Age*, July 27, 2015, http://adage.com/article/behind-the-work/story-disturbing-mobile-phone-safety-ad/299678/ (accessed May 11, 2016).

11. Kristina Monllos, "Marketers Feel Growing Pains As In-House Agencies Become a Necessity," *Digiday*, October 11, 2019, https://digiday.com/marketing/marketers-feel-growing-pains-house-agencies-become-necessity/ (accessed June 21, 2020); Will Burns, "As In-House Agencies Become the Norm, the Opportunities for Outside Agencies Evolve," *Forbes*, September 12, 2018,

https://www.forbes.com/sites/willburns/2018/09/12/as-in-house-agencies-become-the-norm-the-opportunities-for-outside-agencies-evolve/#6befccf9661c (accessed June 21, 2020); Digital Marketing Institute, "Beginner's Guide to Programmatic Advertising," February 6, 2020, https://digitalmarketinginstitute.com/en-us/blog/the-beginners-guide-to-programmatic-advertising (accessed June 15, 2020).

12. Interactive Advertising Bureau (IAB), "User-Generated Content for Marketing and Advertising," May 15, 2019, https://www.iab.com/insights/user-generated-content-for-marketing-and-advertising-purposes/ (accessed October 11, 2020).

13. Jason Howell, Amanda J. Beane and Jared Bryant, "AGS and consumers fight drip pricing and hidden fee programs," *Consumer Protection Review*, October 16, 2019, https://www.consumerprotectionreview.com/2019/10/ags-and-consumers-fight-drip-pricing-and-hidden-fee-programs/#more-2220 (accessed April 21, 2020).

14. Natasha Singer, "A Birth Control Pill That Promised Too Much," *New York Times*, February 11, 2009, B1.

15. "FTC Calls B.S. on Lumosity's Deceptive 'Brain Training' Advertising," *Ad Age*, January 5, 2016, https://www.adage.com/article/news/ftc-calls-b-s-lumosity-brain-training-company-pay-2m/302006/ (accessed April 28, 2016).

16. "Nordstrom, Bed Bath & Beyond, Backcountry.com, and J.C. Penney to Pay Penalties Totaling $1.3 Million for Falsely Labeling Rayon Textiles as Made of 'Bamboo,'" December 9, 2015, https://www.ftc.gov/news-events/press-releases/2015/12/nordstrom-bed-bath-beyond-backcountrycom-jc-penney-pay-penalties (accessed April 7, 2018).

17. *Advertising Age 200 Leading National Advertisers 2019 Fact Pack*, Crain Publications, 2019.

18. Peter Cornish, personal communication, March 2010.

19. This remark has also been credited to a British businessman named Lord Leverhulme; see Charles Goodrum and Helen Dalrymple, *Advertising in America: The First 200 Years* (New York: Harry N. Abrams, 1990).

20. Anthony Crupi (contributing), "TV's Most Expensive Commercials for the 2019-'20 Season," *Ad Age*, October 7, 2019, https://adage.com/article/media/tvs-most-expensive-commercials-2019-20-season/2202481 (accessed June 28, 2020).

21. Melinda Gaines, "Effectiveness of Fifteen Second TV Advertising," *Smallbusiness Chronicle*, https://smallbusiness.chron.com/effectiveness-fifteen-second-tv-advertising-42772.html (accessed July 3, 2020).

22. Phil Hall, "Make Listeners Your Customers," *Nation's Business*, June 1994, 53R.

23. "Global Magazine Publishing Industry - Market Research Report," *IBISWorld*, January 14, 2020, https://www.ibisworld.com/global/market-research-reports/global-magazine-publishing-industry/ (accessed

24. Concave Brand Tracking, "Product Placement in 2020 Oscars Best Picture Nominees – 92nd Academy Awards," January 22, 2020, https://concavebt.com/product-placement-2020-oscars-best-picture-nominees-92nd-academy-award/ (accessed December 29, 2020).

25. Kevin Dugan, "Company Seeks to Target Players with In-Game Advertising," *New York Post*, November 5, 2017, https://nypost.com/2017/11/05/company-seeks-to-target-players-with-in-game-advertising/ (accessed April 7, 2018).

26. Stuart Elliott, "Nationwide Insurance Teams with 'Mad Men,'" *New York Times*, April 4, 2013, https://www.nytimes.com/2013/04/05/business/media/nationwide-insurance-teams-up-with-mad-men.html (accessed June 27, 2014).

27. Michele Linn, "How to Explain Content Marketing to Anyone," Content Marketing Institute, September 4, 2018, https://content-marketinginstitute.com/2018/09/explain-content-marketing-anyone (accessed June 24, 2020).

28. *Advertising Age 200 Leading National Advertisers 2018 Fact Pack*, Crain Publications, 2018.

29. Out of Home Advertising Association of America, "OOH Revenue By Format 2019," http://www.oaaa.org/portals/0/Public%20PDFs/Facts%20&%20Figures/2019/OOH%20by%20Format%20Pie%20Chart%20-%20YE%202019.pdf (accessed October 10, 2020).

30. Out of Home Advertising Association of America, "Planning for OOH Media," https://oaaa.org/LinkClick.aspx?fileticket=xvYomzPIw6o%3d&portalid=0 (accessed October 11, 2020).

31. "CNN Airport Network Adds New Entertainment and Sports Programming to Lineup," *CNN*, June 18, 2013, https://cnnpressroom.blogs.cnn.com/2013/06/18/cnn-airport-network-adds-new-entertainment-and-sports-programming-to-lineup (accessed June 16, 2014).

32. Digital Signage Universe, "Volvo Gets Personal Using Interactive Digital Signage Advertising Campaign," September 7, 2012, https://digitalsignageuniverse.typepad.com/digital_signage_universe/2012/09/ (accessed October 11, 2020).

33. Sean Corcoran, "Defining Earned, Owned and Paid Media," December 16, 2009, https://go.forrester.com/blogs/09-12-16-defining_earned_owned_and_paid_media/ (accessed April 27, 2010).

34. *Advertising Age 200 Leading National Advertisers 2018 Fact Pack*, Crain Publications, 2018.

35. "Digital Set to Surpass TV in Time Spent with US Media," *eMarketer*, August 1, 2013, https://www.emarketer.com/Article/Digital-Set-Surpass-TV-Time-Spent-with-US-Media/1010096 (accessed June 11, 2014).

36. Mobile Marketing Association, "Mobile Marketing Industry Glossary," https://www.mmaglobal.com/files/glossary.pdf, (accessed April 27, 2010).

37. "Social Media Fact Sheet," Pew Research Center, February 5, 2018, https://www.pewinternet.org/fact-sheet/social-media/ (accessed April 8, 2018).

38. "Share of Search Queries Handled by Leading U.S. Search Engine Providers as of January 2018," *Statista*, 2018, https://www.statista.com/statistics/267161/market-share-of-search-engines-in-theunited-states/ (accessed April 8, 2018).

39. "Google's Ad Revenue from 2001 to 2017 (in billion U.S. dollars)," *Statista*, January 22, 2013, https://www.statista.com/statistics/266249/advertising-revenue-of-google/ (accessed April 8, 2018).

40. "What Are the Challenges Regarding Search Engine Advertising?," *E-Commerce Wiki*, https://www.ecommercewiki.org/Search_Engine_Advertising/Search_Engine_Advertising_Basic/What_are_the_challenges_regarding_Search_Engine_Advertising (accessed April 8, 2018).

41. Kyle Christensen, "Still Running Marketing Campaigns? Chances Are, You're Running Out of Time," https://blogs.oracle.com/marketingcloud/marketing-orchestration-still-running-marketing-campaigns-chances-youre-running-time (accessed June 10, 2014).

42. Joshua Brustein, "If Your Phone Knows What Aisle You're in, Will It Have Deals on Groceries?" *Bloomberg Businessweek*, January 26, 2014, https://www.businessweek.com/articles/2014-01-06/apples-ibeacon-helps-marketer-beam-ads-to-grocery-shoppers-phones (accessed June 16, 2014).

43. Kayla Hollatz, "The 8 Best Video Hosting Sites for Creators," ConvertKit, https://convertkit.com/best-video-hosting-sites (accessed June 22, 2020).

44. Mark J. Miller, "Nike Risks Everything on Soccer Promotions as World Cup Kickoff Nears," June 9, 2014, https://www.brandchannel.com/home/post/2014/06/09/140609-Nike-World-Cup-Risk-Everything.aspx?utm_campaign=140609nikeriskeverything&utm_source=newsletter&utm_medium=email (accessed June 30, 2014).

45. George Slefo, "What the Industry's New Plan to Fight Ad Fraud Gets Wrong—and Right," *Ad Age*, May 24, 2017, https://adage.com/article/digital/iab-ads-txt-ad-fraud-wrong-right/309139/ (accessed July 18, 2018).

46. Irfan Ahmad, "Global Ad Blocking Behavior 2019," *Social Media Today*, April 2, 2019, https://www.socialmediatoday.com/news/global-ad-blocking-behavior-2019-infographic/551716/ (accessed July 7, 2020).

47. Simon Dumenco, "90 Years of Ad Age," *Ad Age*, May 11, 2020, https://adage.com/article/90-years-ad-age/we-interrupt-tvs-disruption-even-more-disruption/2256011 (accessed July 3, 2020).

48. Winterberry Group, Ltd., "Winterberry Group Research Finds U.S. Advertising and Marketing Spend to Grow to Nearly $390 Billion in 2020, Up More Than Seven Percent over 2019," https://www.globenewswire.com/news-release/2020/01/16/1971612/0/en/Winterberry-Group-Research-Finds-U-S-Advertising-and-Marketing-Spend-to-Grow-to-Nearly-390-Billion-in-2020-Up-More-Than-Seven-Percent-Over-2019.html

49. Leslie Kaufman with Claudia H. Deutsch, "Montgomery Ward to Close Its Doors," *New York Times*, December 29, 2000, https://www.nytimes.com/2000/12/29/business/montgomery-ward-to-close-its-doors.html (accessed August 29, 2014).

50. "30 Direct Mail Statistics You Can Use Right Now," Compu-Mail, July 14, 2017, https://www.compu-mail.com/statistics/30-direct-mail-statistics-you-can-use-right-now (accessed July 19, 2018).

51. Alan Farnham, "Fighting Telemarketers: When Do-Not-Call List Fails, These Strategies Work," *ABC News*, January 21, 2014, https://abcnews.go.com/Business/best-ways-turn-tables-telemarketers/story?id=21534413 (accessed June 19, 2014).

52. Alison J. Clarke, "'As Seen on TV': Socialization of the Tele-Visual Consumer," paper presented at the Fifth Interdisciplinary Conference on Research in Consumption, University of Lund, Sweden, August 1995.

53. Yue Wang, "More People Have Cell Phones Than Toilets, U.N. Study Shows," *Time*, March 25, 2013, https://newsfeed.time.com/2013/03/25/more-people-have-cell-phones-than-toilets-un-study-shows/ (accessed June 19, 2014).

54. Based on: Lara O'Reilly, "Big Advertisers Embrace Blockchain to Root Out Digital Spending Waste," *Wall Street Journal*, July 12, 2018, https://www.wsj.com/articles/big-advertisers-embrace-blockchain-to-root-out-digital-spending-waste-1531396800; Richa Pathak, "How Blockchain Will Dominate the Digital Advertising Industry in 2020," *Search Engine Watch*, February 26, 2020, https://www.searchenginewatch.com/2020/02/26/how-blockchain-will-dominate-the-digital-advertising-industry-in-2020/; Steven Norton, "CIO Explainer: What Is Blockchain?" *Wall Street Journal*, February 2, 2016, https://blogs.wsj.com/cio/2016/02/02/cio-explainer-what-is-blockchain/; Daniel Newman, "How Blockchain Is Changing Digital Marketing," *Forbes*, September 18, 2019, https://www.forbes.com/sites/danielnewman/2019/09/18/how-blockchain-is-changing-digital-marketing/#6babeb616ebd; Ivan Guzenko, "How Blockchain Is Affecting the Marketing and Advertising Industry," *Forbes*, September 27, 2019, https://www.forbes.com/sites/forbestechcouncil/2019/09/27/how-blockchain-is-affecting-the-marketing-and-advertising-industry/#27e6e4196366; Ronan Shields, "Nestlé Is Doubling Down on Ad Tech," *Adweek*, November 13, 2019, https://www.adweek.com/programmatic/nestle-is-doubling-down-on-ad-tech/; IAS Team, "Introducing Total Visibility with Amino Payments," *IAS Insider*, https://insider.integralads.com/total-visibility-amino/ (accessed August 12, 2020); Sydney Perelmutter, MJ, "Nestlé Expands Use of Blockchain Technology to Its Coffee Brand," *Xtalks*, April 16, 2020, https://xtalks.com/nestle-expands-use-of-blockchain-technology-to-its-coffee-brand-2209/; Patrick Kulp, "2 Years Ago, Blockchain Was Hyped as a World Changer. So What Happened?" *Adweek*, January 5, 2020, https://www.adweek.com/digital/2-years-ago-blockchain-was-hyped-as-a-world-changer-so-what-happened/; Costas Paris, "Cosco Strikes Blockchain Pact for Ocean Cargo with Alibaba, Ant," *Wall Street Journal*, July 7, 2020, https://www.wsj.com/articles/cosco-strikes-blockchain-pact-for-ocean-cargo-with-alibaba-ant-1594144848.

14 Promotion II: Social Media Platforms and Other Promotion Elements

Courtesy of Andrew Mitchell/Brandmovers

Meet Andrew Mitchell
▼ A Decision Maker at Brandmovers

Dr. Andrew Mitchell has over 20 years of global digital engagement experience with some of the world's leading marketers. He has worked on digital promotions for a diverse portfolio of global clients that includes MasterCard, Disney, PepsiCo, Wrigley's, Marriott, Hilton Hotels & Resorts, and L'Oréal. His areas of expertise span multiple industries, including consumer goods, entertainment, retail, travel, and financial services. Andrew earned his doctorate for studies in identifying and developing digital technology that can be deployed and measured across various digital and social media channels.

Andrew founded Brandmovers in an incubator in 2003 and has since expanded across multiple continents and industries. He is a Chartered Marketer and a graduate of Manchester University and the Harvard Business School.

Andrew's Info

What I do when I'm not working:
Scuba diving, fishing

First job out of school:
Salesman

Career high:
Earning my doctorate

A job-related mistake I wish I hadn't made:
Believing that taking a hands-off management approach was the best strategy to grow the business

Business book I'm reading now:
The Creator's Code: The Six Essential Skills of Extraordinary Entrepreneurs by Amy Wilkinson

My hero:
Andrew Carnegie

My motto to live by:
Understand your "Forrest Gump Genius" and live it

What drives me:
When negative words say it can't be done

My management style:
Collaborative, driven, and empowering

Don't do this when interviewing with me:
Tell me you have never failed

Here's my problem...

Real **People**, Real **Choices**

Andrew built Brandmovers into a major digital sales promotion company. Headquartered in Atlanta, GA, with offices in the U.K. and India, Brandmovers specializes in digital promotions including:

- Contests, sweepstakes, instant wins
- Social/UGC promotions
- Digital rewards and affinity programs
- Product launch campaigns

For example, the agency conducted an innovative campaign for the Manchester United soccer team when it built a social promotion called www.unitedinhistory.com to explore the club's history with a personal timeline. Brandmovers has successfully launched innovative promotions for hundreds of the world's leading brands.

However, after 14 years of successful growth, Andrew and his team realized that the future of the business could not depend on the strategies and tactics they had used in the past. The sales promotion business faced the dilemma of "feast or famine": One month Brandmovers could have more business than resources and the next month more resources than business. In addition, as the digital ecosystem became more complex, the cost of resources increased because digital talent was scarce and in high demand for this rapidly growing marketing channel. At the same time, new competitors at the lower end began to erode margins. The vast majority of the business was project-based. These projects typically ranged from $15K to more than $250K. The complexity of the project dictated what talent and resources would be required to build the program, so it was becoming difficult to plan for long-term growth.

Andy began to question how he could take the business to the next level. In an ideal world, his clients would commit to a budget for a yearly retainer (the same model that most advertising agencies use). This would allow the agency to bill hours spent against approved budgets. In essence, the more hours Brandmovers devoted to a project, the more the agency earned. In addition, the agency could hire new talent against that budget and scale the operations according to the needs of the client.

But it was difficult to find clients that preferred to work that way rather than just hiring an agency like Brandmovers for a specific sales promotion project. Brandmovers had built a substantial technology portfolio that seamlessly delivered captivating online sales promotions. How could the company leverage these insights to expand even more and in the process develop a better match between resources and client demand?

Andrew considered his **options** 1·2·3

Option 1

Explore additional markets that could benefit from digital promotional marketing. For example, Brandmovers had yet to develop a clientele in the financial services industry or partner/joint venture with other companies in potential export markets. The agency had the expertise to cultivate these new possibilities, which gave it a leg up on competitors. On the other hand, it was likely that these efforts could just yield more project work. In that event, the same problem of unpredictability would still be there, even though there would be more projects going on at any given time.

Option 2

Build a digital loyalty marketing platform. Andrew was seeing a lot of activity in the online space centered on cultivating customer loyalty. Digital technologies were evolving that could reward people for repeat purchases. For example, building upon the "frequent flyer" model that American Airlines invented many years ago, airlines and hotel groups were developing more sophisticated programs that offer customers free flights and hotel stays for a variety of purchases. The Brandmovers team certainly could replicate that approach because they already knew how to build promotions that allowed the client to track exactly which individuals or groups bought its products. Essentially, this approach is a lot like designing an online sales promotion campaign because it involves online/mobile registration, integrated transaction monitoring, and digital communication channels. A platform like this could result in a more regular stream of revenue because clients would pay a periodic subscription fee for the service rather than lining up for à la carte projects when a specific need arose. For this reason, it would be less expensive to scale this kind of business model—Andrew could predict the resources he would need down the road and be more efficient when he aligned his staff with clients' needs. On the other hand, it wasn't clear if there was a strong market for this kind of product. Also, as a newcomer to the loyalty space, Andrew wasn't sure about how strong the competition was in this area. He could lose a lot of money if his hunch was wrong.

Option 3

Capitalize on the company's success to date and put Brandmovers up for sale. The agency held a strong position in its niche, and it would probably be very attractive to potential buyers. It had recently run very successful sales promotions for clients, including MasterCard, Nestlé, and Disney, and it had a high profile in the industry. Andrew could cash in while the company still retained major customers and had a very positive cash flow. However, a sale would force Andy to expose his proprietary technology to competitors. This would make it difficult for him to start a new company that built upon the efforts of his team for the last 14 years. And it wasn't clear that the owners would recoup the full value of Brandmovers because it was common in these situations for owners to work for the company as employees until they made back the sales cost over time.

Now, put yourself in Andrew's shoes. Which option would you choose, and why?

You Choose

Which **Option** would you choose, and **why**?

☐ Option 1   ☐ Option 2   ☐ Option 3

14.1 Social Media Marketing

OBJECTIVE

Understand how marketers communicate using an updated communication model that incorporates new social media and buzz marketing activities.

In Chapter 13, we saw how advertising follows the one-to-many marketing communication model. In this chapter, we first look at social media marketing that provides many-to-many marketing communication. Then we examine sales promotion, another one-to-many communication tool. We next discuss one type of one-to-one communication: personal selling. Finally, we will learn about public relations. Public relations is the final element of the promotion mix, and it includes a variety of communication activities.

It seems as if most of us are "on" 24/7 these days, whether we're checking our email while on vacation, walking all over campus playing *Alto's Odyssey* on our smartphone, tweeting about the fabulous new Netflix series we just binged, or watching TikTok videos to practice the latest dance challenge. Authors Charlene Li and Josh Bernoff refer to the changing communication landscape as the **groundswell**: "a social trend in which people use technology to get the things they need from each other, rather than from traditional institutions like corporations."[1] In other words, today's consumers increasingly get their information, news, and entertainment via their social interaction with friends, family, and even strangers.

groundswell
A social trend in which people use technology to get the things they need from each other, rather than from traditional institutions like corporations.

You may not remember a time when social media were not available, but believe it or not, all of this is relatively new to the world. Facebook, the first and the most popular social media platform, was founded in 2004 but was only available to college students and was not made available for the general public until 2006. Now Facebook is the largest single social media platform with 2.5 billion active users worldwide. Twitter, founded in 2006, has over 386 million active users, Instagram, which came online in 2010, has reached 1 billion active users, and Snapchat, not introduced until 2012, has 398 million.[2] Today, people around the globe surf the Web, talk with their friends, watch TV, and purchase products from traditional marketers, Internet-only marketers, and each other on their computers, smartphones, smartwatches, or tablets. All these users have the potential to connect with each other and to share feedback—whether it's about how hard that statistics test was this morning or where they bought a great new case for their smartphone and how much they paid for it.

The new many-to-many communication model has altered the face of marketing. As we mentioned in Chapter 13, marketers no longer are the only ones who talk about their products. Millions of consumers also have the ability—and apparently the desire—to spread the good (or bad) news about the goods and services they buy.

In 2019, U.S. advertisers spent approximately $108 billion on Internet ads, surpassing spending on TV ads by more than $40 billion.[3] And just before the COVID-19 pandemic, *Ad Age* projected that worldwide advertisers would spend over half of their budgets on Internet ads for a total of $326 billion, representing an 11.1 percent growth rate.[4]

Formerly the most popular advertising medium, television is now far from number one with Internet advertising spending expected to exceed $160 billion by 2023—a full $90 billion more than TV. Advertisers are spending less and less on traditional media because they no longer see it as quite as effective when they talk to customers. Consumers, especially younger ones, spend more and more time engaged in **media multitasking**, or **second screening**, and consume multiple forms of media simultaneously.[5] Have you ever hopped on Instagram when a TV commercial comes on? You're a media multitasker!

media multitasking, or **second screening**
Consuming multiple forms of media simultaneously.

Magazine consumption reached 1.64 billion overall as of fall 2018. This includes a 0.6 percent increase over the previous year, as consumers shifted to engaging with more mobile and video content.[6]

Although some of the spending on digital will come from funds advertisers previously spent on TV, most will come from new money they allocate just for this. Between 2019 and 2020, total paid TV subscriptions in the U.S. dropped by 2.7 million. Instead, more and more consumers opt to watch programs and films through paid and free streaming services, such as Hulu, Netflix, Amazon Prime, Disney+, Apple TV+, and Peacock.[7] The abundance of choices and the proliferation of **cord-cutting**—consumers' cancelling of their traditional cable subscriptions and instead relying on streaming services to provide televised entertainment—makes the job of reaching a mass market even more complex and costly.[8] But, make no mistake—traditional TV advertising is not going to disappear any time soon. The 28.4 percent increase in television viewership during the early days of the coronavirus all but guarantees this.[9] TV remains a viable way to reach a large, diverse audience and is one of several tools today's marketer can use to reach consumers.

The online retailers we talked about in Chapter 12 also find that their online business is growing but that the Internet customer is harder to please and less loyal. This is not surprising, because people have easy access to competing prices and to reviews of products and sellers from other online shoppers. The growth of Internet consumer-to-consumer (C2C) shopping sites, such as eBay, Etsy, Pinterest, and Craigslist, means more and more consumers buy from each other rather than (gulp) pay retail prices. To better understand this new communication model and its consequences, we need to first look at how marketers encourage and enable consumers to talk about their products in "buzz-building" activities. Then we'll look at some of the specific new media trending in the marketing communication landscape.

Social Media

Social media are an important part of the *updated communication model*. This term refers to Internet-based platforms that allow users not only to modify existing content but also to create and share their own content with others who access these sites. It's hard to grasp just how much these new formats transform the way we interact with marketers; they "democratize" messages because they give individual consumers a seat at the table where organizations used to shape brand meanings on their own. This makes it much easier for companies to spread the word through their **brand ambassadors**, or **brand evangelists**, loyal customers recruited to communicate with and sell to other consumers. The flip side is that the bad stuff also gets out much quicker and reaches people a lot faster: In one survey, 36 percent of respondents said they had used social media to shame a company for poor customer service.[10]

There's no doubt that social media is the place to be in marketing communications now. Social media advertising spending in the U.S. is expected to grow from $33.7 billion in 2019 to $47.1 billion in 2023.[11] Social media include social networking sites, such as Facebook; blogs; microblogs, such as Twitter; picture- and video-sharing sites, such as Instagram and YouTube; product review sites, such as Yelp; wikis and other collaborative projects, such as Reddit and Wikipedia; and virtual worlds, such as Second Life. Before we highlight how these platforms may be used for social commerce, let's take a brief tour of some of the most important social media platforms for marketers.

Social Networks

Social networks are sites that connect people with other users. Successful networking sites ask users to develop profiles of themselves so that those with similar backgrounds, interests, hobbies, religious beliefs, racial identities, or

cord-cutting
Consumers' cancelling of their traditional cable subscriptions and instead relying on streaming services to provide televised entertainment.

social media
Internet-based platforms that allow users to create their own content and share it with others who access these sites.

brand ambassadors, or **brand evangelists**
Loyal customers recruited to communicate with and sell to other consumers for a brand they care a great deal about.

social networks
Online platforms that allow a user to represent himself or herself via a profile on a website and provide and receive links to other members of the network to share input about common interests.

The number of worldwide mobile phone owners increased from 2.5 to 3.8 billion in the five-year period from 2016 to 2020 and is expected to continue to grow. For marketers, this means the competition for eyeballs is much more intense.

Geoff Smith/Alamy Stock Photo

political views can "meet" online. Social networks such as Facebook and LinkedIn are some of the most popular sites on the Internet, with millions of users from around the globe. Once a user creates a profile, it's easy to connect with old and new users (whom you'll probably never meet in person!).

So, what's in all this social networking for marketers? First, by monitoring social networks, marketers learn what consumers think and what they say to each other about the brand and about the competition. Such information can be invaluable to improve advertising messages or even to correct defects in products.

brand community
A group of social network users who share an attachment to a product or brand, interact with each other, and share information about the brand.

By following and participating in the conversations, marketers can reach influential people, such as journalists and consumers, who are opinion leaders. But even more important is the opportunity social networks provide to create a **brand community**, a group of social network users who share an attachment to a product or brand. Members of the brand community interact with each other, sharing information about the brand or just expressing their affection for it. As a result, the relationships between the consumers and the brand grow even stronger.

cosplay
Costume play; dressing up as characters from brands, movies, video games, books, and more.

Members of the community show their connection in all types of ways. Fans of the Jolly Green Giant might buy the costume from Amazon so they can **cosplay**—or costume play, dressing up as characters from brands, movies, video games, books, and more. Ever thought about what Red and Yellow M&M'S do when they're not filming commercials? You're not alone. Check out takes from other storytellers at FanFiction.net.[12] And let's not forget about how fans of the hit TV program *Scandal* worked together to identify and purchase the lead character's signature wine glass.[13]

Sometimes, brand communities develop spontaneously among consumers, while at other times, the brand's marketers purposely create them—or at least nurture them along. One reason brand communities are successful is because going online becomes a "we" experience rather than us versus them—marketer versus customer. Brand communities allow marketers to really listen to customers and use the information they gain to develop new marketing strategies or even to invent a new product that members ask for.[14]

Sephora, a French chain of cosmetics stores, encourages users of its Beauty Insider brand community to ask questions, share ideas, and get advice from other community members. They can also post photos and videos to share with other community members. Without lifting a finger other than to create the platform, Sephora has gained loyal brand ambassadors who sell the brand for them.[15]

Now that we've discussed brand communities, let's examine a couple of the most popular social media sites.

Facebook

Facebook
A social networking site where users develop profiles and can choose to connect with a "friend."

Facebook is the most popular of all social networking sites with, as we said previously, more than 1.7 billion daily active users worldwide as we write this book—and no doubt tons of new ones even as you're reading it.[16] Users of Facebook first develop a profile that remains private unless they choose to connect with a "friend." Although this social media site was originally created to allow college students to keep in touch with their friends (in those days, you had to have ".edu" in your email address to join), it is no longer just for students. Today, there are many significant user segments, including baby-boomer women and even grandparents, who use the platform to locate long-lost friends (and keep tabs on their grandchildren).[17]

Despite its worldwide popularity, Facebook continues to lose college-aged users. Instead, college-aged users spend more time on other sites such as Instagram, Snapchat and YouTube.[18] And in the summer of 2020, Facebook began to lose advertisers due to a boycott stemming from its handling of hate speech on its site.[19] Another change is how college students access social media sites. Many prefer to use their mobile phones to access social media sites, receive and send email, and otherwise interact on social media.

Instagram

Instagram, a social networking site dedicated to sharing photos and short-form videos, is a favorite among U.S. teenagers. Founded in 2010, Instagram was sold to Facebook in 2012 for $1 billion and reported more than 500 million daily active users worldwide as of June 2018.[20]

Beyond being a place for consumers to follow one another, 47 percent of U.S. Instagrammers use the site for entertainment while 34 percent use it to follow brands and companies.[21] Brands connect with consumers through their own accounts and through those of celebrity influencers via **sponsored posts**—content brands pay celebrities to share through their personal accounts. Celebrities can earn tens of thousands from a single post, with mega celebrities such as Kylie Jenner and Dwayne "The Rock" Johnson earning $1 million per sponsored post in 2019.[22]

In 2016, Instagram introduced its Stories feature, which allows users to post content that disappears after 24 hours—"borrowing" from rival platforms such as Snapchat. The feature currently engages 500 million Instagram users daily.[23] And in 2018, IGTV was introduced. This is Instagram's in-app video feature that allows users to post long-form video. It has yet to take off, however, as users seem to prefer to watch long-form video on YouTube.[24]

YouTube

YouTube is a free online video platform launched in 2005 and acquired by Google in 2006. The platform is used by 1.68 billion users worldwide and features channels from both consumers and businesses. Believe it or not, 500 hours of video are uploaded to YouTube every minute.[25]

YouTube is also a popular place for the product reviews we mentioned earlier in the chapter—particularly unboxing videos. These videos feature a consumer taking a product out of its original packaging or shipping box, and they're hugely popular.[26] This trend saw 57 percent growth from 2013 to 2014, and it's especially prevalent during gift-giving seasons. From kids to adults, consumers turn to unboxing videos to fill their holiday and celebratory wish lists.[27] In fact, Ryan Kaji of Ryan's World (formerly Ryan ToysReview) was YouTube's highest earner in 2018 at $22 million—at the age of 7![28] His YouTube channel mainly features unboxings of toys and had over 25.5 million subscribers and 39 billion views at the time we wrote this.

TikTok

TikTok is a social networking site that hosts short-form videos. These videos may last for 15 seconds and are typically accompanied by music. Following a successful 2016 launch as Douyin in China, TikTok was released in the United States in 2017[29] after its parent company bought the lip-synching app, Musical.ly.[30] After being downloaded 738 million times in 2019, TikTok started 2020 as the world's fastest-growing social network.[31]

With its dance challenges and quickly expanding user base, TikTok has become very attractive to brands and influencers alike. The platform offers a number of branding opportunities, such as in-feed video ads and hashtag challenges—all designed to capture the attention of its 800 million monthly active users.[32] Did you flip your lid competing in the 2019 #LidChallenge sponsored by Chipotle?[33] Or participate in the Renegade dance challenge? The Renegade dance was created by then-14-year old Jalaiah Harmon who later partnered with Warner Brothers to choreograph the #ScoobDance in anticipation of the studio's release of its film *SCOOB!*[34]

And while we're talking about short-form video platforms, let's not forget about TikTok's predecessor, Vine. Active between 2012 and 2016, Vine was re-introduced in 2020 as Byte. During its initial run, Vine allowed its 200 million users to post videos that lasted no more than seven seconds.[35] The platform is credited with pushing users' creativity and

Instagram
A social networking site dedicated to sharing photos and short-form videos.

sponsored posts
Content brands pay celebrities to share through their personal accounts.

YouTube
A free online video platform launched in 2005 and acquired by Google in 2006. Channels for both consumers and businesses are used by 1.68 billion worldwide.

TikTok
A social networking site that hosts short videos lasting for 15 seconds or less, typically accompanied by music.

changing storytelling as we knew it.[36] Despite its popularity, Vine went from the hot new thing to just about nothing. Some analysts attribute Vine's demise to an inability—or unwillingness on some accounts—to monetize. This was an issue not only for brands but also for influencers. And like LeBron James in 2010, these influential powerhouses decided to take their talents elsewhere—namely to rivals such as YouTube.[37]

Snapchat

Snapchat
A social networking site that allows users to share snaps—pictures and videos that are only available for a limited period of time. Lenses and Geofilters allow users to create photos with unique elements.

Released in 2011, **Snapchat** bills itself as the fastest way to share a moment. It is a social networking site that allows users to share snaps—pictures and videos that are only available for a limited period of time. Snaps are deleted once viewed by all recipients but can be added to a user's Snapchat Story and made available for 24 hours. Though the app originally focused on private communication, it has expanded to include video chatting, avatars, and a "Discovery" area featuring content from major brands and media outlets.[38] This area was a key update to the platform as it separated brand and media content from friend and family content, allowing users to access each on different spaces.[39]

The most popular social network among U.S. teenagers, Snapchat includes popular features such as lenses and Geofilters. Users can overlay filters from picture frames to flower-filled headbands onto photos or videos and then share them as snaps. Geofilters allow consumers and brands to create custom filters and make them available depending on the user's geolocation. We'll highlight a couple of Snapchat's other features later on in the chapter as we discuss social media's influence on consumer purchasing. The site continues to see increased usage growing from 100 million daily active users in May 2015 to 229 million daily active users by the first quarter of 2020.[40]

Twitch

Twitch
A social media site that is the most-used streaming platform for broadcasting video games and is used for videos from cooks, artists, vloggers, and musicians.

Twitch is the social networking site for live streaming and is the most used streaming platform for broadcasting video games.[41] Gamers visit Twitch not only to watch competitions but also to tune in so they may see a game being played and decide if they're interested in purchasing the game. Twitch's unique setup allows viewers to watch the game and the gamer via separate video captures. And some Twitch users, such as American science fiction writer and gamer N. K. Jemisin, employ moderators to help manage viewers and maintain order in the space. One of Jemisin's rules? No backseat gaming. Watch her play, but let her figure it out on her own.

Twitch is not just the go-to for gamers. The platform also hosts videos from cooks, artists, vloggers, and musicians who have been able to use some of the platform's features to great effect. In March of 2020, electronic music duo Josh Gabriel and Dave Dresden introduced their very own Club Quarantine via Twitch with some sets lasting over 10 hours. And while DJ D-Nice had to ask his Instagram Live viewers to tune in to other artists when his set was ending, Gabriel and Dresden were simply able to send the viewers from their Twitch channel to another Twitch channel of their choosing using the platform's raid feature—a habit they and their fans adopted in order to boost lesser-known artists.[42]

During the COVID-19 pandemic, the platform saw users seeking out diverse content and welcomed more unique viewers than prime-time television dynamos such as *The Bachelor* and *American Idol*. Twitch reached 500 billion hours watched during the second quarter of 2020—with over 77,000 viewers at any one time.[43]

Twitter

Twitter
A free microblogging service that lets users post short text messages with a maximum of 280 characters.

Twitter is a free microblogging service that lets users post short text messages. People who subscribe to an individual's Twitter feed are called "followers." Users can follow anyone from friends to politicians. And, as of 2019, users are also able to follow topics. Attesting to its popularity, Twitter now has 166 million monetizable daily active users (mDAUs), a 24 percent increase over 2019.[44] In late 2017, Twitter increased its 140-character limit to

280 characters to allow followers more opportunity for expression as they add photos, videos, hashtags, GIFs, and more.[45]

Because of this ongoing activity, it is especially important for marketers to monitor Twitter to understand what consumers say about their products. Unlike some other social media that work only on closed networks, Twitter is a broadcast media vehicle. This means that marketers can send messages to hundreds of thousands of people at a time, and they can encourage users to rally around a cause (or brand) when they include the now familiar # (hashtag). Today, it seems that everyone from athletes to music and movie celebrities uses Twitter. In fact, Twitter seems to be playing an especially important role in the entertainment industry.[46]

In May of 2016, former NFL player Matthew A. Cherry posted his idea for an "Oscar-worthy" animated short film, seeking a 3D animator. In 2017, Cherry announced a Kickstarter campaign for his idea, again via Twitter, eventually raising over $284,000 for "Hair Love." In 2019, the *Hair Love* book was released by Kokila Books/Penguin Random House, and Sony Pictures Animation released an animated short film. In February 2020, the film went on to win the Academy Award for Best Animated Short.

Many consumers love to create Boards on Pinterest that reflect their interests, some of which are more than a little strange, e.g., Sumo wrestling, blue candy, and edible insects. Still, this platform is very valuable to marketers who want to be a part of "some" consumer visions.

Virtual Worlds

Virtual worlds are online, highly engaging digital environments where **avatars**—graphic representations of users—live and interact with other avatars in real time. The blockbuster movie *Avatar* exposed many people to this basic idea as it told the story of a wounded soldier who takes on a new (10 feet tall and blue) identity in the world of Pandora.

In virtual worlds, residents can hang out at virtual clubs, shop for clothing and accessories for their avatars, buy furniture to deck out virtual homes, and, yes, even go to college in virtual universities. These virtual worlds can range in their intricacy. For example, while *Second Life*, launched in 2003, is a 3D virtual world in which users can buy land and create properties, *Online Town*, founded in 2020, is a 2D space that looks more like an 8-bit videogame and bills itself as a free video-calling space. Users, or residents of *Second Life*, can design their own avatars, while users of *Online Town* are limited to a set of pre-built avatars. And let's not forget about multiplayer online role-playing games such as *Fortnite* that are set in virtual worlds.[47] Some people find it hard to believe, but it's common for people to spend real money to buy digital products that don't exist in the real world. Indeed, the **virtual goods** market is booming. Virtual goods represent a $50 billion market that is expected to grow to $250 billion by 2025 between consumers spending in video games and virtual worlds. All this for items that can only be used virtually![48] *IMVU* is advertised as the "#1 avatar-based social experience" available, and it certainly delivers unmatched 3D animation. The central world is a room full of chairs where you wait for other users to join so you can text chat with them. You can restrict who has the ability to approach you and can also use the "Get Matched" area similar to an online dating service. The basic room is free, but you can shop for new outfits, poses, pets, and furniture.[49]

Most virtual goods, whether sold in virtual worlds or through other social media sites, have microprices—from less than $1 to $3; but others, such as dances or emotes within *Fortnite*, may cost $5–$10.[50] So, what's in it for real-world marketers? Some firms enter the market for virtual goods to keep in touch with consumers, improve the brand's image, and

virtual worlds
Online, highly engaging digital environments where avatars live and interact with other avatars in real time.

avatars
Graphic representations of users of virtual worlds.

virtual goods
Digital products consumers buy for use in online contexts.

develop loyal customers. And even micropriced items, such as digital clothing for avatars, start to add up when you sell many thousands of them.

Social Commerce

social commerce

Consumer decision-making activities that occur in, or are influenced by, someone's social network, particularly online.

Social commerce refers to consumer decision-making activities that occur in, or are influenced by, someone's social network—particularly online.[51] The activities in question are those we discussed back in Chapter 6—problem recognition, information search, evaluation of alternatives, product choice, and postpurchase evaluation. Social media's influence on consumer decision making is undeniable. Over 50 percent of global Internet users between the ages of 16 and 24 have searched for product information via social media and 70 percent of consumers say they have purchased something after seeing it in a YouTube video.[52]

From Pinterest's buyable pins to shoppable YouTube ads, social networks continue to update their social commerce offerings in the hopes of encouraging more in-app purchases. For example, in June 2020, Snapchat announced its first shoppable show, "The Drop." Products introduced in the show will become available for purchase right within the episode, allowing viewers to "swipe up to buy."[53] Though consumers were already able to purchase products directly through some posts and ads, in May 2020, Instagram and Facebook made it easier for users to see a product they like in the feed and then complete the entire purchase without ever leaving the platform with the introduction of Shops.[54] Now, consumers can browse, save, and ultimately buy products they find within a business's uploaded catalog. Snapchat has also updated its Augmented Reality Lens with a shoppable option that will allow Snapchat users to try on a product and then purchase it directly from the Lens using a "Shop Now" button.[55]

Product Review Sites

product review sites

Social media sites that enable people to post stories about their experiences with goods and services.

Product review sites are social media sites that enable people to post stories about their experiences with goods and services as part of their postpurchase evaluation. These sites are an aspect of social commerce all their own and serve as resources for consumers who may be in the early stages of their decision-making process. Marketers hope that product review sites create a connection between the consumer and the brand. Product review sites give users both positive and negative information about companies:

- *TripAdvisor* provides unbiased hotel reviews complete with photos and advice. The site gives consumers an opportunity to rate and comment on a hotel that they recently stayed in or to use other consumers' comments to select a hotel for an upcoming trip. Consumers can also rate local attractions.

- *Yelp* is a product review site that provides reviews of local businesses, such as places to eat, shop, drink, or play. Consumers can access *Yelp* through either the Internet or a mobile phone. Businesses can create pages to post photos and send messages to their customers. Whereas *Yelp* focuses on local businesses, *Trustpilot* allows consumers to post reviews of companies big and small. Its goal is to help consumers connect with and influence businesses while giving businesses a place to engage with, listen to, and collaborate with consumers.

- *Angie's List* and *HomeAdvisor* are sites for consumers who are "tired of lousy service." Angie's List members, who cannot remain anonymous, rate service companies in more than 700 categories, and a certified data collection process ensures that companies don't report on themselves or their competitors.[56]

- While sites such as Yelp, TripAdvisor, and Angie's List don't generate money for reviewers, there is a growing bank of sites, such as Swagbucks and ReviewStream, that help consumers find ways to get paid for their reviews.

One of the fastest-growing review sites is *Glassdoor*, a jobs and recruiting site. In addition to offering employers free listings of their jobs, *Glassdoor* has a database of millions of company reviews, executive approval ratings, salary reports, and those dreaded office photos. For a college student like you who will soon be on the job market if not already, *Glassdoor* lets you know what companies are hiring and what it's really like to work there.[57] Looking for an option that's closer to home? Check out *Handshake*, a career-services platform that launched in 2014 and dominates the college market. The platform has partnered with over 800 colleges and is now available to any student with a .edu email address. Not sure if a new opportunity sounds too good to be true? Log into *Handshake* to read reviews and see what others have said about the position and employer. *Handshake* touts the reviews as ways to help students explore careers, get advice, and gain insight.[58]

Location-Based Social Networks and Mobile Apps

Location-based social networks, as we mentioned in Chapter 13, integrate sophisticated GPS technology (like the navigation system you may have in your car). Like Uber and Google Maps, these location-based social networks allow users to engage based upon their current location, enabling users to alert friends of their exact whereabouts via their mobile phones.

In 2016, the **augmented reality (AR)** mobile app game *Pokémon Go* (which also relies on GPS technology in smartphones) took the world by storm, attracting millions of users. Augmented reality is a view of a physical, real world that is enhanced or altered by computer-generated sounds, videos, graphics, or GPS data. And *Pokémon Go* doesn't seem to be going anywhere. Players spent more in *Pokémon Go* at the start of 2020—approximately $445 million—than in any previous year.[59] In 2019, players spent $894 million, making *Pokémon Go* the top location-based game and among the top five among all mobile games.[60] During the coronavirus pandemic, and in the midst of a physically distant world, developers made the game easier to play at home with several tasks and events doable from home.[61] The popularity of games that use augmented reality creates an opportunity for advertisers to reach consumers who are highly engaged in a game.

Foursquare, a social network that uses GPS, was one of the most popular location-based networks when, in May 2014, the Foursquare folks announced they were splitting the app in two: Foursquare for discovering new places and Swarm for checking in at places you visit. Like Foursquare, the Swarm app has the popular Mayor feature, but instead of competing against everyone who uses Swarm for the most check-ins, you compete only against your friends. Despite the controversial split, Foursquare and Swarm still maintain approximately 50 million users within a 60-day period.[62] In 2019, Foursquare introduced a new feature called Hypertrending. This feature allows you to see how people are spreading out in a particular city. Think of it like a heat map that lets you see where people are gathered without identifying any individual person.[63]

Businesses can ride this wave by offering discounts or free services to people who check in to their locations. For example, Boloco, a burrito chain in Boston, used a feature from the *LevelUp* app, which offered customers $5 off a food and drink purchase of $10. To "level up," customers returned to the restaurant for $10 off a $25 purchase and then $14 off a $45 purchase. Boloco saw 26 percent of its customers return for the Level 3 reward.[64]

It's obvious to almost anyone who has a pulse today that the future of marketing communication lies in that magic little device you practically sleep with— your smartphone (the average Gen Zer spends 4 hours and 15 minutes on their phone per day).[65] Combine web-browsing capability with built-in cameras, and the race is on to bring the world to your fingertips. Apple lit up this market when it introduced the iPhone, and now everyone is scrambling to "monetize" the mobile market through sales of ringtones, on-demand video, online

location-based social networks
Networks that integrate sophisticated GPS technology that enables users to alert friends of their exact whereabouts via their mobile phones.

augmented reality (AR)
A view of a physical, real world that is enhanced or altered by computer-generated sounds, videos, graphics, or GPS data.

The *Pokémon Go* craze revived a popular videogame from many years ago—but, more importantly, it was a breakthrough for augmented reality applications as people around the world scrambled to find cartoon characters in all kinds of real-world settings.

New social media platforms emerge periodically. TikTok, which is wildly popular especially among younger consumers, is gaining traction as an advertising medium for companies that want to reach this age segment.

coupons, and apps that entertain or educate. A few to watch include the following:[66]

- *Instacart* allows you to order groceries and everyday essentials from retailers in your area—all from your phone, tablet, or computer. Consumers are able to read nutritional labels while also specifying quantities and acceptable substitutes for out-of-stock items. Instacart users are also able to schedule pickup or delivery for as soon as the same day.

- *Bitmoji* is an emoji lover's dream. The app allows you to customize an avatar down to its outfits and accessories and includes a huge library that allows you to customize and send out personal emojis through messaging or other apps that include a copy/paste feature. You can also link it to Snapchat to jazz up your posts or even create a four-minute cartoon starring your avatar![67]

- *Signal Private Messenger* is available for both mobile and desktop devices and allows users to send and receive encrypted messages and calls. Signal does not track you or your connections and is touted as the most secure and private messenger app around.[68]

The Internet of Things

We would be remiss if we ended our discussion of social media without mentioning the *Internet of Things*, which we mentioned in Chapter 6. This term refers to the network of physical things—watches, vehicles, devices, buildings, and so on—in which designers have embedded sensors, electronics, and network connectivity. With this technology, "things" can collect data and communicate it to each other—the many to many of things.

Many analysts believe the Internet of Things will dominate marketing's future as more and more devices get "smart." Already providers of Internet services are offering to "connect" your home with your phone to turn off your TV, lock your doors, adjust your heat, and on and on. Ask Amazon Alexa to keep track of your shopping list or to convert measurements so you can prepare a new recipe. Just as the Internet has created a revolution in marketing communication, the Internet of Things will change our lives again.

Disruption in Storytelling

All communication—whether an epic novel or the guilty pleasure that is reality television—is based upon a story. Happy, sad. Dramatic, comedic. At the most basic level, the art of **storytelling** typically involves characters, setting, plot, conflict, and resolution. In a television series for example, that resolution might not come until the end of the story arc, the season, or even the series.

As we mentioned in Chapter 13, commercials of 15 seconds are more common than those that last a full minute. Consumers are busy with life and engaged in media multitasking—a concept we introduce here in Chapter 14—to make the most of the time they do dedicate to engaging with broadcast, print, and social media.

For some of us, our first foray into public **short-form storytelling** was the haiku. You remember, don't you? They're those three-line poems composed of just 17 syllables. But for more and more consumers, their first public short-form story is a tweet, a snap, a captionless Instagram post, or a fifteen-second TikTok video.

Storytelling through marketing communications has been disrupted by both consumers' waning attention span and the proliferation of social media. Remember: At their core,

storytelling
The foundation of all communication, usually including characters, setting, plot, conflict, and resolution. Brand storytelling is practiced by marketers.

short-form storytelling
Because consumers today prefer short messages, successful marketing communication often includes 15-second TV commercials, a tweet, a snap, a captionless Instagram post, or a TikTok clip.

disruptive innovations occur when a small company with few resources succeeds in changing the industry. And some would argue that Vine did just that. The compressed time limit of a Vine pushed storytellers to be more creative and efficient—to say more with less. And Vine's successors, such as TikTok and Snapchat, continue to benefit from users' innovativeness in short-form storytelling. GIFs? They're short-form stories, too, and show up across a variety of platforms.

But we won't drone on here. Remember: Keep your marketing communications short and sweet. But don't blink or you just might miss the changing rules about just how short your story ought to be.[69]

14.2 Sales Promotion

OBJECTIVE
Explain what sales promotion is and describe the different types of consumer and B2B sales promotion activities.

Sometimes when you walk through your student union on campus, you might get assaulted by a parade of people eager for you to enter a contest, taste a new candy bar, or take home a free T-shirt with a local bank's name on it. These are examples of **sales promotions**— programs that marketers design to build interest in or encourage purchase of a good or service during a specified period. As we saw from the Brandmovers challenge at the beginning of the chapter, sales promotion activities also encompass new, more sophisticated online initiatives.

sales promotions
Programs designed to build interest in or encourage purchase of a product during a specified period.

How does sales promotion differ from advertising? Great question! Both are paid promotion activities from identifiable sponsors designed to change consumer behavior or attitudes. Often, a traditional advertising medium actually publicizes the sales promotion, as when Applebee's restaurant used TV advertising to tell military personnel and veterans about its free entrée offer for Veterans Day.[70]

But while marketers carefully craft advertising campaigns to create long-term positive feelings about a brand, company, or store, sales promotions are more useful if the firm has an *immediate* objective, such as bolstering sales for a brand quickly or encouraging consumers to try a new product. Indeed, the purpose of many types of sales promotion is to induce action by the consumer or business buyer. For example, a parallel sales promotion by Applebee's might involve distributing coupons to veterans that they can redeem for a free meal during the week where the holiday occurs.

Marketers today place an increasing amount of their total marketing communication budget into sales promotion. Several reasons account for this increase. First, due to the growth of very large grocery store chains and mass merchandisers such as Walmart, there has been a shift in power in the channels. These large chains can pressure manufacturers to provide deals and discounts. A second reason for the growth in sales promotion is declining consumer brand loyalty. This means that consumers are more likely to purchase products based on cost, value, or convenience. A special sales promotion offer is more likely to cause price-conscious customers to switch brands.

Marketers target sales promotion activities either to ultimate consumers or to members of the channel, such as retailers that sell their products. Thus, we divide sales promotion into two major categories: *consumer-oriented sales promotion* and *trade-oriented sales promotion*. We'll talk about the consumer type first, after which we'll discuss trade promotion. You'll see some examples of common consumer-oriented sales promotions in Table 14.1.

Sales Promotion Directed toward Consumers

One of the reasons for an increase in sales promotion is because it works. For consumer sales promotion, the major reason for this is that most promotions temporarily change price/value relationships. A coupon for 50 cents off the price of a bottle of ketchup reduces the price, whereas a special "25 percent more" jar of peanuts increases the value. And if you

Table 14.1	Consumer Sales Promotion Techniques: A Sampler	
Technique	Description	Example
Coupons (newspaper, magazine, in the mail, on product packages, in-store, and on the Internet)	Certificates for money off on selected products, often with an expiration date, are used to encourage product trial.	Crest offers $5 off its Whitestrips.
Price-off packs	Specially marked packages offer a product at a discounted price.	Tide laundry detergent is offered in a specially marked box for 50 cents off.
Rebates/refunds	Purchasers receive a cash reimbursement when they submit proofs of purchase.	Uniroyal offers a $40 mail-in rebate for purchasers of four new Tiger Paw tires.
Continuity/loyalty programs	Consumers are rewarded for repeat purchases through points that lead to reduced price or free merchandise.	Airlines offer frequent fliers free flights for accumulated points; a car wash offers consumers a half-price wash after purchasing 10 washes.
Special/bonus packs	Additional amount of the product is given away with purchase; it rewards users.	Colgate Total Whitening toothpaste provides a free travel-size tube with each purchase.
Sweepstakes/contests	Offers consumers the chance to win cash or merchandise. Sweepstakes winners are determined strictly by chance. Contests require some competitive activity, such as a game of skill.	Publisher's Clearing House announces its zillionth sweepstakes.
Premiums: Free premiums include in-pack, on-pack, near pack, or in-the-mail premiums; consumers pay for self-liquidating premiums	A consumer gets a free gift or low-cost item when a product is bought; reinforces product image and rewards users.	A free makeup kit comes with the purchase of $50 worth of Clinique products.
Samples (delivered by direct mail, in newspapers and magazines, door-to-door, on or in product packages, and in-store)	Delivering an actual or trial-size product to consumers to generate trial usage of a new product.	A free small bottle of Camille Rose Naturals shampoo arrives in the mail.

get a free hairbrush when you buy a bottle of shampoo, this also increases the value. As shown in Figure 14.1, we generally classify consumer sales promotion as either price-based or attention-getting promotions.

Price-Based Consumer Sales Promotion

Many sales promotions target consumers where they live—their wallets. They emphasize *short-term price reductions* or *rebates* that encourage people to choose a brand—at least during the deal period. Price-based consumer promotions, however, have a downside similar to trade promotions that involve a price break. If a company uses them too frequently, this "trains" its

Figure 14.1 *Snapshot* | Types of Consumer Sales Promotions

Consumer sales promotions are generally classified as price-based or attention-getting promotions.

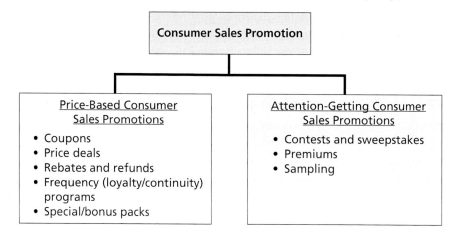

customers to purchase the product at only the lower promotion price. Price-based consumer sales promotion includes the following:

- *Coupons.* Try to pick up any Sunday newspaper without spilling some coupons. These certificates, redeemable for money off a purchase, are the most common price promotion. Indeed, they are the most popular form of sales promotion overall. Companies distributed nearly 300 billion of them in 2017 in newspapers and magazines, in the mail, in stores, by email, and through the Internet.[71] Despite continued growth in mobile couponing and the popularity of sites such as Slickdeals.net, consumers still prefer to receive coupons through postal mail.[72] Even industries such as pharmaceuticals that never tried this approach before now use it in a big way. This industry offers coupons that customers can redeem for free initial supplies of drugs in hopes that patients will ask their physician for the specific brand instead of a competing brand or a more economical generic version.[73]

Some resourceful marketers discovered that the widespread use of face masks during the pandemic created a new format to promote their brands.

- *Price deals, refunds, and rebates.* In addition to coupons, manufacturers often offer a temporary price reduction to stimulate sales. This price deal may be printed on the package itself, or it may be a price-off flag or banner on the store shelf. Alternatively, companies may offer refunds or **rebates** that allow the consumer to recover part of the purchase price via onsite rebates or mail-ins to the manufacturer with redemption rates ranging from 40 to 60 percent.[74]

- *Frequency (loyalty/continuity) programs.* **Frequency programs**, also called *loyalty* or *continuity programs,* offer a consumer a discount or a free product for multiple purchases over time. Mike Gunn, former vice president of marketing at American Airlines, is widely credited with developing this concept in the early 1980s when he coined the phrase "frequent flyer" miles. Of course, all the other airlines were quick to follow suit, as were a host of other firms, including retailers, auto rental companies, hotels, restaurants—you name it, and they have a customer loyalty program.

- *Special/bonus packs.* Another form of price promotion involves giving the shopper more products instead of lowering the price. How nice to go to your local supermarket and find the normal 16-ounce jar of Planters peanuts made larger to contain four ounces or 25 percent more free! A special pack also can be in the form of a unique package, such as a reusable decorative dispenser for hand soap.

rebates
Sales promotions that allow the customer to recover part of the product's cost from the manufacturer.

frequency programs
Consumer sales promotion programs that offer a discount or free product for multiple purchases over time; also referred to as *loyalty* or *continuity programs.*

Attention-Getting Consumer Sales Promotions

Attention-getting consumer promotions stimulate interest in a company's products. Some typical types of attention-getting promotions include the following:

- *Contests and sweepstakes.* According to their legal definitions, a contest is a test of skill, whereas a sweepstakes or giveaway is based on chance.
  - Kellogg's encouraged its Australian customers to "color and win" daily prize packs through its partnership with Crayola. The company released black-and-white versions of its most popular flavors that consumers were able to color in and bring to life via browser-based augmented reality.[75]
  - In an effort to launch the new Axe Apollo brand of men's grooming products and do something that's epic, the Axe Apollo Big Game Sweepstakes was designed to send 22 everyday people up to 64 miles into space where they would be weightless for up to six minutes. All contestants had to do was plead their case about why they wanted to become astronauts. Popular vote would determine the top 100 finalists, and both the brand and the transport company would determine the winners.[76] Giveaways are also used within social media, whereby entrants may be asked to follow an account, repost content, or even tag other users as their form of entry.

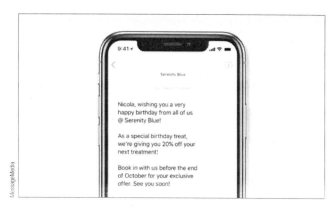

Sales promotions are getting more tech-savvy as well. Some marketers take advantage of SMS technology (via texting) to send personalized offers to a shopper's phone.

premiums
Items offered free to people who have purchased a product.

product sampling
Distributing free trial-size versions of a product to consumers.

trade sales promotions
Promotions that focus on members of the "trade," which include distribution channel members, such as retail salespeople or wholesale distributors, that a firm must work with to sell its products.

- *Premiums.* **Premiums** are items you get free when you buy a product. General Mills Cheerios brand cereal gave away millions of bilingual children's books inside Cheerios boxes during a 12-year period. In 2015, the company switched to offering free e-books that can be downloaded using a code provided in Cheerios boxes.[77]
- *Sampling.* When was the last time you scooped up free food samples at your local grocery store? Some stores, like Publix and Sam's Club, actually promote Saturdays as sampling day in their advertising. **Product sampling** encourages people to try a product by distributing trial-size and sometimes regular-size versions in stores; in other public places, such as student unions; or through the mail. When U.S. grocery stores put in-store sampling on hold due to the coronavirus pandemic, brands had to find other ways to get samples into consumers' hands. Brands such as Coca-Cola began including samples of its new energy drink in online orders, while Pipcorn provided free options via its website.[78]

Trade Sales Promotion: Targeting the B2B Customer

As we said, sales promotions also target the B2B customer—located somewhere within the supply chain. Such entities are traditionally referred to as "the trade." Hence, **trade sales promotions** focus on members of the supply chain, which include distribution channel members that we discussed in Chapter 11.

Trade promotions take one of two forms: (1) those designed as discounts and deals and (2) those designed to increase company visibility. Let's take a look at both types of trade promotions in more detail. To help you follow along, Figure 14.2 portrays several of the most important types of trade sales promotion approaches, and Table 14.2 provides more details about each approach. You will note that some of the techniques, although targeted primarily to the trade, also appeal to consumers.

Discount Promotions

Discount promotions (deals) reduce the cost of the product to the distributor or retailer or help defray its advertising expenses. Firms design these promotions to encourage stores to

Figure 14.2 *Snapshot* | Trade Sales Promotions

Trade sales promotions come in a variety of forms. Some are designed as discounts and deals for channel members, and some are designed to increase industry visibility.

Table 14.2	Characteristics of Trade Sales Promotion Approaches		
Technique	Primary Target	Description	Example
Allowances, discounts, and deals	Trade	Retailers or other organizational customers receive discounts for quantity purchases or for providing special merchandising assistance.	Retailers get a discount for using a special Thanksgiving display unit for Pepperidge Farm Stuffing Mix.
Co-op advertising	Trade and consumers	Manufacturers pay part of the cost of advertising by retailers who feature the manufacturer's product in their ads.	Toro pays half of the cost of Brad's Hardware Store newspaper advertising that features Toro lawn mowers.
Trade shows	Trade	Many manufacturers showcase their products to attendees.	The National Kitchen and Bath Association trade shows allow manufacturers to display their latest wares to owners of kitchen and bath remodeling stores.
Promotional products	Trade and consumers	A company builds awareness and reinforces its image by giving out "premiums" with its name on them.	Coors distributors provide bar owners with highly sought-after "Coors Light" neon signs. Caterpillar gives customers caps with the Caterpillar logo.
Point-of-purchase displays	Trade and consumers	In-store exhibits attract consumers' attention. Many point-of-purchase displays also serve a merchandising function.	The Behr's paint display in Home Depot stores allows consumers to select from more than 1,600 colors, including 160 Disney colors.
Incentive programs	Trade	A prize is offered to employees who meet a prespecified sales goal or who are top performers during a given period.	Mary Kay cosmetics awards distinctive pink cars to its top-selling representatives.
Push money	Trade	A particular type of incentive program in which retailer or distributor salespeople are given a bonus for selling a specific manufacturer's product.	A retail salesperson at a cosmetics counter gets $5 every time she sells a bottle of Glow perfume by JLo.

stock the item and be sure it gets a lot of attention. Marketers offer these discounts for a limited period of time, and they should not be confused with discounts that are part of the pricing strategy and are offered long term.

One form of trade promotion is a short-term *price break*. A manufacturer can reduce a channel partner's costs with a sales promotion that discounts its products. For example, a manufacturer can offer a **merchandising allowance** to reimburse the retailer for in-store support of a product, such as when a store features an off-shelf display for a brand. Another way in which a manufacturer can reduce a channel partner's cost is with a **case allowance** that provides a discount to the retailer or wholesaler during a set period based on the sales volume of a product the retailer or wholesaler orders from the manufacturer.

However, allowances and deals have a downside. As with all sales promotion activities, the manufacturer expects these to be of limited duration, after which the distribution channel partner will again pay full price for the items. Unfortunately, some channel members engage in a practice the industry calls **forward buying**: They purchase large quantities of the product during a discount period, warehouse them, and don't buy them again until the manufacturer offers another discount. Some large retailers and wholesalers take this to an extreme when they engage in **diverting**. This describes an ethically questionable practice where the retailer buys the product at the discounted promotional price and warehouses it. Then, after the promotion has expired, the retailer sells the hoarded inventory to other retailers at a price that is lower than the manufacturer's nondiscounted price but high enough to turn a profit. Obviously, both forward buying and diverting go against the manufacturer's intent in offering the sales promotion.

merchandising allowance
Reimburses the retailer for in-store support of the product.

case allowance
A discount to the retailer or wholesaler based on the volume of product ordered.

forward buying
The questionable retailer practice of purchasing large quantities of a product during a discount period and not buying again until there is another discount.

diverting
The retailer practice of buying a product at a promotional price and selling it after the promotional price has expired.

Co-op Advertising

co-op advertising
A sales promotion where the manufacturer and the retailer share the cost.

Another type of trade allowance is **co-op advertising**. These programs offer to pay a portion, usually 50 percent, of the cost of any retailer advertising that features the manufacturer's product. Co-op advertising is a win-win situation for manufacturers because most local media vehicles offer lower rates to local businesses than to national advertisers. Both the retailer and the manufacturer pay for only part of the advertising, plus the manufacturer gets the lower rate. Normally, the amount available to a retailer for co-op advertising is limited to a percentage of the purchases the retailer makes during a year from the manufacturer. This type of program has also been used in the mortgage industry with mortgage sales representatives and real estate agents partnering to run advertisements.

Sales Promotion to Increase Industry Visibility

Other types of trade sales promotions increase the visibility of a manufacturer's products to channel partners within the industry. Whether it is an elaborate exhibit at a trade show or a coffee mug with the firm's logo that the manufacturer gives away to channel partners, these promotions aim to keep the company's name topmost when distributors and retailers decide which products to stock and push. These forms of sales promotion include the following:

trade shows
Events at which many companies set up elaborate exhibits to show their products, give away samples, distribute product literature, and troll for new business contacts.

- *Trade shows.* The thousands of industry **trade shows** in the U.S. and around the world each year are major vehicles for manufacturers and service providers to show off their product lines to wholesalers and retailers. Usually, large trade shows are held in big convention centers where many companies set up elaborate exhibits to show their products, give away samples, distribute product literature, and troll for new business contacts. Today, we also see more and more online trade shows that allow potential customers to preview a manufacturer's products remotely. And with the COVID-19 pandemic forcing many of these shows online, more and more marketers are realizing the untapped benefits of virtual trade shows. For example, over 9 million people viewed the keynote speech from Apple's June 2020 developer conference—significantly more people than could have fit in the convention center that usually hosts the event.[79]

promotional products
Goodies such as coffee mugs, T-shirts, and magnets given away to build awareness for a sponsor. Some freebies are distributed directly to consumers and business customers; others are intended for channel partners, such as retailers and vendors.

- *Promotional products.* We have all seen them: coffee mugs, visors, T-shirts, ball caps, key chains, and even more expensive items, such as golf bags, beach chairs, and luggage emblazoned with a company's logo. They are examples of **promotional products**. Unlike licensed merchandise we buy in stores, sponsors give away these goodies to build awareness for their organization or specific brands.

point-of-purchase (POP) displays
In-store displays and signs.

- *Point-of-purchase displays.* **Point-of-purchase (POP) displays** include signs, mobiles, banners, shelf ads, floor ads, lights, plastic reproductions of products, permanent and temporary merchandising displays, in-store TV, and shopping card advertisements. Marketers use POP displays because it keeps the name of the brand in front of the consumer, reinforces mass-media advertising, calls attention to other sales promotion offers, and stimulates impulse purchasing. Generally, manufacturers must give retailers a promotion allowance for use of POP materials. For retailers, the POP displays are useful if they encourage sales and increase revenues for the brand. Many are invaluable aids for shoppers.

push money
A bonus paid by a manufacturer to a salesperson, customer, or distributor for selling its product.

- *Incentive programs.* In addition to motivating distributors and customers, some promotions light a fire under the firm's own sales force. These incentives, or **push money**, may come in the form of cash bonuses, trips, or other prizes. Mary Kay Corporation—the in-home party plan cosmetics seller—is famous for giving its more productive distributors pink cars to reward their efforts. Another cosmetics marketer that uses a retail store–selling model, Clinique, provides push money to department store cosmeticians to demonstrate and sell the full line of Clinique products. This type of incentive has the nickname *SPIF* for "sales promotion incentive funds."

14.3 Personal Selling: Adding the Personal Touch to the Promotion Mix

OBJECTIVE

Understand the important role of personal selling, the different types of sales jobs, and the steps in the creative selling process.

Now we turn our attention to one of the most visible—and most expensive—forms of marketing communication: personal selling. Like direct marketing, personal selling is an example of one-to-one marketing communications.

Personal selling occurs when a company representative interacts directly with a customer or prospective customer to communicate about a good or service. This form of promotion is a far more intimate way to talk to customers. Another advantage of personal selling is that salespeople are the firm's eyes and ears in the marketplace. They learn which competitors talk to customers, what they offer, and what new rival goods and services are on the way—all valuable competitive intelligence.

Many organizations rely heavily on personal selling because at times the "personal touch" carries more weight than mass media material. For a B2B market situation, the personal touch translates into developing crucial relationships with clients. Also, many industrial goods and services are too complex or expensive to market effectively in impersonal ways (such as through mass advertising). An axiom in marketing is: The more complex, technical, and intangible the product, the more heavily firms tend to rely on personal selling to promote it.

Personal selling has special importance for students (that's *you*) because many graduates with a marketing background will enter professional sales jobs. The U.S. Bureau of Labor Statistics estimates job growth of about 3 percent for sales representatives across fields between 2016 and 2026.[80] Jobs in selling and sales management often provide high upward mobility if you are successful because firms value employees who understand customers and who can communicate well with them. The old business adage "nothing happens until something is sold" translates into many firms placing quite a bit of emphasis on personal selling in their promotion mixes. And the sales role is even more crucial during tricky economic times, when companies look to their salespeople to drum up new business and to maintain the business they already have.

Sold on selling? All right, then let's take a close look at how personal selling works and how professional salespeople develop long-term relationships with customers.

personal selling
Marketing communication by which a company representative interacts directly with a customer or prospective customer to communicate about a good or service.

The Role of Personal Selling in the Marketing Mix

When a woman calls the 800 number for the MGM Grand Hotel in Las Vegas to book a room for a little vacation trip and comes away with not only a room but also show tickets, a massage booking at the hotel spa, and a reservation for dinner at Emeril's, she deals with a salesperson. When she sits in on a presentation at work by a website consultant who proposes a new content management system for her firm's website, she deals with a salesperson. When she shops in an upscale clothing store for several new outfits to wear at an important business conference, she deals with a salesperson. And when that same woman agrees over lunch at a swanky restaurant to invest some of her savings with a financial manager's recommended mutual fund, she also deals with a salesperson.

For many firms, some element of personal selling is essential to land a commitment to purchase or a contract, so this type of marketing communication is a key to the success of their overall marketing plan. To put the use of personal selling into perspective, Figure 14.3 illustrates some of the factors that make it a more or less important element in an organization's promotion.

Figure 14.3 *Snapshot* | Factors That Influence a Firm's Emphasis on Personal Selling

A variety of factors influence whether personal selling is a more or less important element in an organization's overall promotion mix.

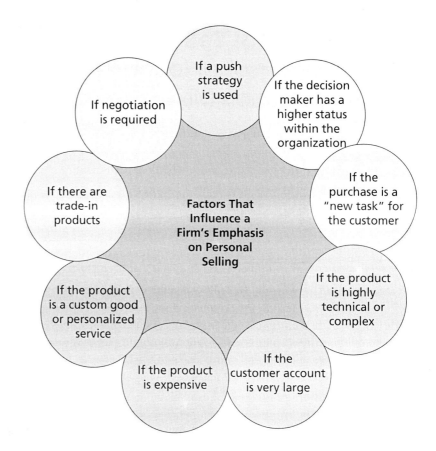

If a push strategy is used

If the decision maker has a higher status within the organization

If negotiation is required

Factors That Influence a Firm's Emphasis on Personal Selling

If the purchase is a "new task" for the customer

If there are trade-in products

If the product is highly technical or complex

If the product is a custom good or personalized service

If the customer account is very large

If the product is expensive

In general, a personal selling emphasis is more important when a firm engages in a *push strategy*, in which the goal is to move or "push" the product down through the channel of distribution so that it is available to consumers. As a vice president at Hallmark Cards once observed, "We're not selling *to* the retailer, we're selling *through* the retailer. We look at the retailer as a pipeline to the hands of consumers."[81]

Personal selling also is likely to be crucial in B2B contexts where the firm must interact directly with a client's management to clinch a big deal—and often when intense negotiations about price and other factors will occur before the customer signs on the dotted line. In consumer contexts, inexperienced customers may need the hands-on assistance that a professional salesperson provides. Firms that sell goods and services that consumers buy infrequently—houses, cars, computers, lawn mowers, and even college educations—often rely heavily on personal selling. (*Hint:* Your school didn't pick just any student at random to conduct campus tours and help those clueless freshmen.) Likewise, firms whose goods or services are complex or very expensive often need a salesperson to explain, justify, and sell them—in both business and consumer markets.

If personal selling is so useful, why don't firms just scrap their advertising and sales promotion budgets and hire more salespeople? There are some drawbacks that limit the role personal selling plays in the marketing communication mix. First, when the dollar amount of individual purchases is low, it doesn't make sense to use personal selling—the average cost per contact with each customer is more than $300, much higher than other forms of promotion. The per-contact cost of a national TV commercial is minuscule by comparison. A 30-second prime-time commercial costs an average of $104,000 (or as we said in Chapter 13, more than $5 million for a 30-second commercial aired during the Super Bowl), but with millions of viewers, the cost per contact may be only $25 or $35 per 1,000 viewers.[82] For low-priced consumer packaged goods such as Doritos or beer, personal selling to end users simply doesn't make good financial sense.

Technology and Personal Selling

Personal selling is supposed to be, well, "personal." By definition, a company uses personal selling for marketing communications in situations when one person (the salesperson) interacts directly with another person (the customer or prospective customer) to communicate about a good or service. All sorts of technologies can enhance the personal selling process, and clearly today the smartphone is the communication hub of the relationship between salesperson and client. However, as anyone making sales calls knows, technology itself cannot and should not *replace* personal selling. Today, a key role of personal selling is to manage customer *relationships*—and remember that relationships occur between people, not between computers (as much as you love your Facebook friends or checking in on Swarm).

However, there's no doubt that a bevy of technological advancements makes it easier for salespeople to do their jobs more effectively. One such technological advance is *customer relationship management (CRM) software*, which we introduced in Chapter 5. For years now, *account management software*, such as ACT and GoldMine, has helped salespeople manage their client and prospect base. These programs are inexpensive and easy to navigate, and they allow salespeople to track all aspects of customer interaction. Currently, many firms turn to *cloud computing* CRM applications, which are more customizable and integrative than ACT or OnContact yet are less expensive than major companywide CRM installations. A market leader in such products is SalesForce.com, which is particularly user friendly for salespeople. A key benefit of cloud computing versions of CRM systems is that firms "rent" them for a flat fee per month (at SalesForce.com, monthly prices are as low as $75 per user), so they avoid major capital outlays.[83]

Carvana turns an entire building into a car "vending machine" to entice buyers.

Michael Ventura/Alamy Stock Photo

Recently, some sales organizations have turned to a new-generation system called **partner relationship management (PRM)**, which links information between selling and buying firms. PRM differs from CRM in that both supplier and buyer firms share at least some of their databases and systems to maximize the usefulness of the data for decision-making purposes. Firms that share information are more likely to work together toward win-win solutions.

Beyond CRM and PRM, numerous other technology applications enhance personal selling, including teleconferencing, videoconferencing, and improved corporate websites that offer frequently asked questions (FAQs) pages to answer customers' queries. Many firms also use intranets and blogs to facilitate access to internal and external communication.

Voice-over Internet protocol (VoIP)—systems that rely on a data network to carry voice calls—get a lot of use in day-to-day correspondence between salespeople and customers. With VoIP, the salesperson on the road can just plug into a fast Internet connection and then start to make and receive calls just as if in the office. Unlike mobile phones, there are no bad reception areas, and unlike hotel phones, there are no hidden charges.

One popular VoIP product is Skype. Thanks to Skype, built-in laptop and tablet web cams, instant messaging, and the like, customers of all types are becoming more comfortable with the concept of doing business with a salesperson who is not actually in the same room. As such, a good portion of the future of face-to-face sales calls may occur on your own computer screen. Since its purchase by Microsoft in 2011, Skype has introduced Skype for Business, which offers the Skype technology for meetings of up to 250 people for a monthly fee.

Zoom is another tool that makes remote communication easier. This cloud-based VoIP solution was founded in 2011—the same year that Microsoft bought Skype—and rose in

partner relationship management (PRM)
Similar to a CRM, the PRM system allows both selling and buying firms to share some of their information.

voice-over Internet protocol (VoIP)
Communication systems that use data networks to carry voice calls.

Zoom-bombing
Uninvited guests showing up for a Zoom meeting.

telecommute
Working with fellow employees from a distant location using Internet communication technology, such as VoIP, sometimes referred to as *WFH* or *work from home*.

virtual office
The use of Internet technology to work and participate from a distant physical office.

social selling
Using social media to engage in the selling process.

popularity during the COVID-19 pandemic of 2020. Zoom's usage soared from 10 million daily meeting participants in December 2019 to 300 million in April 2020—even amidst concerns about privacy and **Zoom-bombing** (uninvited guests showing up for a Zoom meeting). Zoom and Skype are not without competition, however. For example, Apple's FaceTime and Google's Meet are viable options as are the virtual worlds we mentioned earlier in the chapter.[84]

Technology such as VoIP has made a major change in the attractiveness of sales jobs. In the past, salespeople were expected to travel and be away from home as much as four nights a week, entertaining customers with a big expense account. This type of job was hard on families because it left little time for the employee to hang out at home. Today, firms and their salespeople use computer networks, smartphones, email, and video conferencing. These technological advances and changing cultural values that require a balance in life mean that an increasing number of salespeople **telecommute** from a **virtual office**. Telecommuting has long been seen as a win-win opportunity and may become more commonplace in a post-COVID-19 workplace.[85] Companies spend less on office space and travel, and salespeople are able to balance their time between work and home and can respond to family responsibilities.[86]

Consider the following hypothetical transaction related to buying a set of solar panels for your roof—a complex and expensive purchase. The sales consultant calls at an appointed time. You open her email message, click a link to start the presentation, and a picture of your roof appears, courtesy of satellite imaging. Colorful charts show past electricity bills and the savings from a solar-panel system. A series of spreadsheets examine the financing options available—and these are dynamic documents, not static images, so the salesperson can tinker with the figures right before your eyes. Would more panels be justified? A few keystrokes later, new charts display the costs and savings. Could they be shifted to another part of the roof? With a mouse, she moves some black panels from the east side to the west side. How about more cash up front? She scrolls to the spreadsheets, highlights three payment options, and computes the numbers over the next 15 years. In less than an hour, the exchange is over.

Perhaps for a few days or a week, you mull over the choices and study the fine print in the contract, but the sale was essentially closed by the time you hung up the phone. You decided to make a major, complex purchase, worth thousands of dollars, without ever meeting anyone in the flesh and without holding any product in your hands. And unlike many purchases, you had no *buyer's remorse* despite the fact it was done online—or maybe *because* it was online.[87]

Social selling is the practice of using social media to engage in the selling process. From finding to following up with customers, social selling is a practice that may be used to reach customers across generations.[88] For some salespeople, it has replaced cold calling. This practice has been shown to improve conversions and decrease the length of the sales cycle. It is so effective that 78 percent of salespeople engaged in social selling are outselling their peers.[89] Twitter and LinkedIn are among the most popular platforms for social selling. No matter the social network platform used, however, it is important for salespeople to build out their own profiles and join relevant groups while also following and sharing relevant content.

For years now, all of us have been shopping online, taking in the bargains and wide selection, usually for relatively straightforward goods and services and without any human contact unless a problem arises with the ordering technology itself. The brave new world of virtual selling adds another dimension and is yet another example of how the Internet transforms business and remakes job descriptions. These more sophisticated virtual selling capabilities won't replace all face-to-face salesperson–client encounters any more than e-commerce replaced brick-and-mortar retailers. But smart sales organizations can find the right blend of technology and personal touch, tailored to their particular clientele and product offerings, to make the most of building strong customer relationships.

Future Trends in Professional Selling

Professional selling continues to evolve. Huge advances in new technology continue to rock the sales industry. Four trends of note are the influence of artificial intelligence (AI), the rising influence of millennials as both buyers and sellers, account-based selling, and a growing focus on diversity and inclusion.[90]

Artificial intelligence and machine learning are one of the most exciting trends in sales. AI means prioritizing the customers. This tells the salesperson which accounts he or she is most likely to finalize a deal with each day. Another important benefit from AI is what it means to salesperson productivity. By automatically handling time-consuming tasks such as logging emails and generating invoices, AI can spend time doing other things, like anticipating customer needs. The use of chatbots to connect with customers continues to gain in popularity.[91]

A second sales trend is, in a word, *millennials*. Millennials are making giant inroads into professional selling as both buyers and sellers. Millennials feel empowered by technology. They enjoy interacting with customers, but as in other parts of their lives, many are more comfortable doing so online rather than via in-person sales calls. As a result, we can expect to see a lot more sales activity occurring via text, video, etc., and perhaps a decrease in the amount of actual travel to call on clients at their IRL (in-real-life) offices. Soon, however, this focus will shift to Generation Z.[92]

A third trend is **account-based selling**, often used in B2B marketing. Account-based selling does away with the one-size-fits-all mentality and sells from an account-specific perspective. The sales organization evaluates individual accounts based upon their potential to become great customers. Then they choose the best way to develop relationships and sell to these preferred accounts.

A fourth trend is the growing focus on diversity and inclusion. From the greater visibility of LGBTQ+ equality to the increasing diversity of younger generations, including millennials and Gen Z, we are seeing more and more diversity on both the sales and buyer sides.[93]

Types of Sales Jobs

Maybe you aspire to work in sales someday, or perhaps you've already held a sales job at some point. If you see sales in your future, there are several different types of sales jobs from which you can choose, each with its own unique characteristics. Let's look more closely at some of the different types of sales positions. Figure 14.4 summarizes the most important types.

As you might imagine, sales jobs vary considerably. The person who answers the phone at DSW to take your order for a new pair of UGG boots is primarily an **order taker**—a salesperson who processes transactions the customer initiates. Many retail salespeople are order takers, but often wholesalers, dealers, and distributors also employ salespeople to assist their business customers. Because little creative selling is involved in taking orders, this type of sales job typically is the lowest-paid sales position.

In contrast, a **technical specialist** contributes considerable expertise in the form of product demonstrations, recommendations for complex equipment, and setup of machinery. The technical specialist provides *sales support* rather than actually closing the sale. He or she promotes the firm and tries to stimulate demand for a product to make it easier for colleagues to actually seal the deal.

Then there is the **missionary salesperson**, whose job is to stimulate clients to buy. Like technical specialists, missionary

account-based selling
The practice of choosing the best way to sell to B2B individual customers.

order taker
A salesperson whose primary function is to facilitate transactions that the customer initiates.

technical specialist
A sales support person with a high level of technical expertise who assists in product demonstrations.

missionary salesperson
A salesperson who promotes the firm and tries to stimulate demand for a product but does not actually complete a sale.

Figure 14.4 *Snapshot* | Types of Sales Jobs

A wide range of different types of sales jobs are available, each of which has different job requirements and responsibilities.

salespeople promote the firm and encourage demand for its goods and services but don't take orders.[94] Pfizer salespeople do missionary sales work when they call on physicians to influence them to prescribe the latest-and-greatest Pfizer medications instead of competing drugs. However, no sale gets made until doctors or their patients get the prescriptions to pharmacies, which then place orders for the drug through their wholesalers or directly from the maker of the drug.

The **new-business salesperson** is responsible for finding new customers and calls on them to present the company's products. As you might imagine, gaining the business of a new customer usually means that the customer stops doing business with one of the firm's competitors (and they won't give up without a fight). New-business selling requires a high degree of creativity and professionalism, so this type of salesperson is usually very well paid.

Once a new-business salesperson establishes a relationship with a client, he or she often continues to service that client as the primary contact as long as the client continues to buy from the company. In that long-term-relationship-building role, this type of salesperson is an **order getter**. Order getters are usually the people most directly responsible for a particular client's business; they may also hold the title of *account manager*.[95]

More and more, firms find that the selling function works best via **team selling**. A selling team may consist of a salesperson, a technical specialist, someone from engineering and design, and other players who work together to develop products and programs that satisfy the customer's needs. With multiple individuals participating in a selling team, all working with a single account, team selling becomes very expensive. Thus, team selling is usually limited to large customers, or **key accounts**, where potential business justifies the extra human resource commitment.

When the company includes people from a range of areas, it often calls this group a **cross-functional team**.

Two Approaches to Personal Selling

Personal selling is one of the oldest forms of marketing communication. Unfortunately, over the years, smooth-talking pitchmen who will say anything to make a sale have tarnished its image.

Fortunately, personal selling has moved from a transactional, hard-sell approach to an approach based on relationships with customers. Let's see how.

Transactional Selling: Putting on the Hard Sell

Smooth-talking pitchmen practice a high-pressure, hard-sell approach. We've all been exposed to the pushy electronics salesperson who puts down the competition when telling shoppers that if they buy elsewhere, they will be stuck with an inferior home theater system that will fall apart in six months. Or how about the crafty used car salesman who plays the good-cop/bad-cop game, gives you an awesome price, but then sadly informs you that the boss, the sales manager, won't go for such a sweet deal. These hard-sell tactics reflect **transactional selling**, an approach that focuses on making an immediate sale with little concern for developing a long-term relationship with the customer.

As customers, the hard sell makes us feel manipulated and resentful, and it diminishes our satisfaction and loyalty. It's a shortsighted approach to selling. As we said previously in the book, constantly finding new customers is much more expensive than getting repeat business from the customers you already have. And the behaviors transactional selling promotes (i.e., doing anything to get the order) contribute to the negative image many of us have of salespeople as obnoxious and untrustworthy. Such salespeople engage in these behaviors because they don't care if they ever have the chance to sell to you again. This is really bad business!

---

new-business salesperson
The person responsible for finding new customers and calling on them to present the company's products.

order getter
A salesperson who works to develop long-term relationships with particular customers or to generate new sales.

team selling
The sales function when handled by a team that may consist of a salesperson, a technical specialist, and others.

key accounts
Very large customer organizations with the potential for providing significant sales revenue.

cross-functional team
A form of selling team where the team includes individuals from various areas of the firm.

transactional selling
A form of personal selling that focuses on making an immediate sale with little or no attempt to develop a relationship with the customer.

Relationship Selling: Building Long-Term Customers

Relationship selling is the process by which a salesperson secures, develops, and maintains long-term relationships with profitable customers.[96] Today's professional salesperson is more likely to practice relationship selling than transactional selling. This means that the salesperson tries to develop a mutually satisfying, win-win relationship with the customer. Securing a customer relationship means converting an interested prospect into someone who is convinced that the good or service holds value for him or her. Developing a customer relationship means ensuring that you and the customer work together to find more ways to add value to the transaction. Maintaining a customer relationship means building customer satisfaction and loyalty—thus, you can count on the customer to provide future business and stick with you for the long haul. And if doing business with the customer isn't profitable to you, unless you're a charitable organization, you would probably like to see that customer go somewhere else.

The Creative Selling Process

Many people find selling to be a great profession, partly because something different is always going on. Every customer, every sales call, and every salesperson is unique. Some salespeople are successful primarily because they know so much about what they sell. Others are successful because they've built strong relationships with customers so that they're able to add value to both the customer and their own firm—a win-win approach to selling. Successful salespeople understand and engage in a series of activities to make the sales encounter mutually beneficial.

Whether they adopt a transactional or relationship selling approach, a salesperson's chances of success increase when following a systematic series of steps we call the **creative selling process**. These steps require the salesperson to seek out potential customers, analyze their needs, determine how product attributes provide benefits, and then decide how best to communicate this to prospects. As Figure 14.5 shows, there are seven steps in the process. Let's take a look at each.

Step 1: Prospect and Qualify

Prospecting is the process by which a salesperson identifies and develops a list of *prospects* or *sales leads* (potential customers). Leads come from existing customer lists, telephone directories, commercially available databases, social media, and of course, the diligent use of web search engines like Google. Sometimes companies generate sales leads through their advertising or sales promotion when they encourage customers to request more information. As we discussed earlier in this chapter, trade shows also are an important source of sales leads.

Another way to generate leads is through *cold calling*, in which the salesperson simply contacts prospects "cold," without prior introduction or arrangement. It always helps to know the prospect, so salespeople might rely instead on *referrals*. Current clients who are satisfied with their purchase often recommend a salesperson to others—yet another reason to maintain good customer relationships.

However, the mere fact that someone is willing to talk to a salesperson doesn't guarantee a sale. After they identify potential customers, salespeople need to *qualify* these prospects to determine how likely they are to become customers. To do this, they ask questions such as the following:

- Are the prospects likely to be interested in what I'm selling?
- Are they likely to switch their allegiance from another supplier or product?
- Is the potential sales volume large enough to make a relationship profitable?
- Can they afford the purchase?
- If they must borrow money to buy the product, what is their credit history?

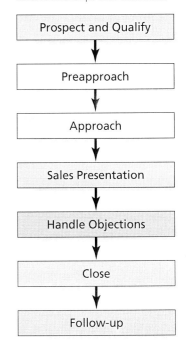

Figure 14.5 *Process* | Steps in the Creative Selling Process

In the creative selling process, salespeople follow a series of steps to build relationships with customers.

relationship selling
A form of personal selling that involves securing, developing, and maintaining long-term relationships with profitable customers.

creative selling process
The process of seeking out potential customers, analyzing needs, determining how product attributes might provide benefits for the customer, and then communicating that information.

prospecting
A part of the selling process that includes identifying and developing a list of potential or prospective customers.

preapproach
A part of the selling process that includes developing information about prospective customers and planning the sales interview.

Step 2: Preapproach

In the **preapproach** stage, you compile background information about prospective customers and plan the sales interview. Firms don't make important purchases lightly, and it's often difficult even to get an appointment to see a prospect. It's foolish for a salesperson to blindly call on a qualified prospect and risk losing the sale because of a lack of preparation. Salespeople try to learn as much as possible about qualified prospects early on. They may probe a prospect's prior purchase history or current needs or, in some cases, may even try to learn about their personal interests. Does the customer like for a salesperson to spend time informally talking about golf or football, or does he or she prefer a salesperson who gets to the point quickly and leaves? And, of course, it's always good to know which football team the customer roots for.

Salespeople can draw information about a prospect from a variety of sources. In the case of larger companies, they can find financial data, names of top executives, and other information about a business from outlets such as *Standard & Poor's 500 Directory* or Dun & Bradstreet's *Million Dollar Directory*. They can also find a great deal of information for the preapproach on customers' websites. And the inside scoop on a prospect often comes from informal sources, such as noncompeting salespeople who have dealt with the prospect before.

Of course, if the salesperson's firm has a CRM system, he or she can use it to see whether the database includes information about the prospect. Say, for example, a salesperson at Mike's Bikes plans to call on a buyer at Greg's Vacation Rentals to see about selling some new bikes for guests to use at Greg's various resort properties. If Mike's has had a CRM system in place for some time, any contacts with customers and potential customers (prospects) are recorded in the database. The salesperson can simply run an inquiry about Greg's Vacation Rentals, and with luck, the CRM database will deliver information on the company, prior purchases from Mike's, when and why customers stopped buying from the company, and perhaps even the preferences of the particular buyer.

approach
The first step of the actual sales presentation in which the salesperson tries to learn more about the customer's needs, create a good impression, and build rapport.

Step 3: Approach

After the salesperson lays the groundwork with the preapproach, it's time to **approach**, or contact, the prospect. During these important first minutes, several key events occur. The salesperson tries to learn even more about the prospect's needs, create a good impression, and build rapport. If the salesperson found prospect Audrey Wright through a referral, he or she will probably say so to Audrey up front: "Al Smith with Prentice Industries suggested I call on you."

During the approach, the customer decides whether the salesperson has something to offer that is of potential value. The old saying "You never get a second chance to make a good first impression" rings true here. A professional appearance tells the prospect that the salesperson means business and is competent to handle the sale. Of course, what is appropriate depends on industry norms. Today, you may be out of place calling on some customers in a suit and tie. Even so, "casual Friday" rarely cuts it in the sales world.

sales presentation
The part of the selling process in which the salesperson directly communicates the value proposition to the customer and invites two-way communication.

Step 4: Sales Presentation

Many sales calls involve a formal **sales presentation**, which lays out the benefits of the product and its advantages over the competition. When possible and appropriate, salespeople should incorporate into their sales presentations a great multimedia presentation via their tablet or laptop to jazz things up. And thanks to tools such as Zoom and Skype, these types of multimedia presentations are possible even if everyone is in different locations! A picture is worth a thousand words, and a video showing how each weld in the grocery carts is triple welded—well, you know.

The focus of the sales presentation should always be on ways the salesperson, the products, and the company can add value to the customer (and in a B2B setting, to the customer's company). It is important for the salesperson to present this value proposition clearly and to invite the customer's involvement in the conversation. Let the customer ask questions, give feedback, and discuss his or her needs. Canned approaches to sales presentations are a poor choice for salespeople who want to build long-term relationships. In fact, sales managers rate *listening* skills, not talking skills, as the single most important attribute they look for when they hire relationship salespeople.[97] In a sales call, it's a good idea to put the *80/20 rule to* work—that is, spend 80 percent of your time listening to the client and assessing his or her needs and only 20 percent talking. (Note: This rule of thumb is a spin-off of the 80/20 rule for market segmentation we discussed in Chapter 7.)

Automation is becoming increasingly common. It picked up speed during the pandemic, when many shoppers were reluctant to be in physical contact with store employees. The age of the robot salesperson may not be far away.

Step 5: Handle Objections

It's rare when a prospect accepts everything the salesperson offers without question. The effective salesperson anticipates *objections*—reasons why the prospect is reluctant to make a commitment—and is prepared to respond with additional information or persuasive arguments. The salesperson should welcome objections because they show that the prospect is at least interested enough to consider the offer and seriously weigh its pros and cons. Handling the objection successfully can move a prospect to the decision stage. For example, the salesperson might say, "Mr. Smith, you've said before that you don't have room to carry our new line of trail bikes, although you mentioned that you may be losing some sales by carrying only one brand with very few different models. If we could come up with an estimate of how much business you're losing, I'll bet you'd consider making room for our line, wouldn't you?"

Step 6: Close the Sale

The win-win nature of relationship selling should take some of the pressure off salespeople to make "the dreaded close." But there still comes a point in the sales call at which one or the other party must move toward gaining commitment to the objectives of the call—presumably a purchase. This is the decision stage, or **close**. Directly asking the customer for his or her business doesn't need to be painful or awkward: If the salesperson has done a great job in the previous five steps of the creative selling process, closing the sale should be a natural progression of the dialogue between the buyer and seller.

close
The stage of the selling process in which the salesperson asks the customer to buy the product.

There are a variety of approaches salespeople use to close the sale:

- A *last objection close* asks customers if they are ready to purchase, providing the salesperson can address any concerns they have about the product: "Are you ready to order if we can prove our delivery time frames meet your expectations?"

- An *assumptive* or *minor points close* mean the salesperson acts as if the purchase is inevitable with only a small detail or two to be settled: "What quantity would you like to order?"

- A *standing-room-only* or *buy-now close* injects some urgency when the salesperson suggests the customer might miss an opportunity if he or she hesitates: "This price is good through Saturday only, so to save 20 percent we should book the order now." When making such closes, salespeople must be sure the basis they state for buying now is truthful, or they'll lose a valuable relationship for the price of a one-time sale!

Step 7: Follow-Up

Understanding that the process doesn't end after the salesperson earns the client's business is basic to a relationship selling perspective that emphasizes the importance of long-term

follow-up
Activities after the sale that provide important services to customers.

satisfaction. The **follow-up** after the sale includes arranging for delivery, payment, and purchase terms. Follow-up may even include a social media post highlighting a successful deal or sharing a testimonial from a satisfied customer. It also means the salesperson makes sure the customer received delivery and is satisfied. Follow-up also allows the salesperson to *bridge* to the next purchase. Once a relationship develops, the selling process is only beginning. Even as one cycle of purchasing draws to a close, a good salesperson already lays the foundation for the next one.

public relations (PR)
Communication function that seeks to build good relationships with an organization's publics, including consumers, stockholders, and legislators.

14.4   Public Relations

OBJECTIVE
Explain the role of public relations and the steps in developing a public relations campaign.

Public relations (PR) is the communication function that seeks to build good relationships with an organization's *publics*; these include consumers, stockholders, legislators, and other stakeholders in the organization. Today marketers use PR activities to influence the attitudes and perceptions of various groups not only toward companies and brands but also toward politicians, celebrities, and not-for-profit organizations.

The old rule of PR was, *Do something good, and then talk about it*. Nowadays, public relations is a more conscious, intentional, ongoing, and day-in, day-out exercise than it used it to be. With 24/7 news cycles and consumers watching every like, comment, and follow on social media, brands must accept the fact that everything they do impacts the relationships they will build with their publics. A company's efforts to get in the limelight—and stay there—can range from humanitarian acts to sponsoring band tours. For example, National Basketball Association (NBA) player Kevin Love (Cleveland Cavaliers) suffered a panic attack during a game in 2018. He opted to take his story public to try to help others, writing a first-person account entitled "Everyone Is Going through Something." His story was picked up in multiple national media outlets, and he has become a spokesperson for anxiety in America.[98] The big advantage of this kind of communication is that when PR messages are placed successfully, they are more credible than if the same information appeared in a paid advertisement. As one marketing executive observed, "There's a big difference between hearing about a product from a pitchman and from your trusted local anchorman."[99]

proactive PR
Public relations activities that are based on the company's marketing objectives.

publicity
Unpaid communication about an organization that appears in the mass media.

crisis management
The process of managing a company's reputation when some negative event threatens the organization's image.

PR strategies are crucial to an organization's ability to establish and maintain a favorable image. **Proactive PR** activities stem from the company's marketing objectives. For example, marketers create and manage **publicity**, unpaid communication about an organization that gets media exposure. It's interesting to note that this aspect of PR is blending into other promotional strategies as social media continue to mushroom. Essentially, buzz marketing is also one form of PR because it tries to motivate consumers to talk up a brand or service to one another (ideally for free).

As many of the other functions of PR blend into buzz-marketing activities, perhaps the most important function it still "owns" is **crisis management**. This refers to the process of managing a company's reputation when some negative and often unplanned event threatens the organization's image. Do you remember the video of the passenger who was violently dragged off an overbooked United Airlines flight? United made the mistake of standing by the action at first and then made a cold apology. Finally, the airline took full responsibility and made a sincere apology—but it was too little, too late. United's consumer perception dropped to a 10-year low following the incident and the company's handling of it.[100]

The goal in such situations is to manage the flow of information to address concerns so that consumers don't panic and distributors don't abandon the product. Although some organizations don't seem to learn this lesson, typically the best strategy is to be honest about the problem and to quickly take responsibility for correcting it. Carnival Cruise Lines learned this lesson all too well when a fire in the engine room on its ship

Triumph caused 3,100 passengers and crew to be stranded at sea for five days without air conditioning or working toilets. Thanks to social media, word of the conditions on the "Poop Cruise" quickly spread. Then Carnival's crisis team jumped into action, launching a Facebook page and using Twitter to send out updates and mobilizing more than 200 Carnival employees to assist disembarking passengers when the ship finally docked. Carnival also gave a full refund to passengers, reimbursement for most of their onboard expenses, a flight home, $500 cash, and a credit toward a future cruise in an effort to make up for the unplanned disaster.[101]

PR professionals know that when a firm handles a crisis well, it can minimize damage and help the company make things right. Thus, a vitally important role of PR is to prepare a *crisis management plan*. This is a document that details what an organization will do *if a* crisis occurs—who will be the spokesperson for the organization, how the organization will deal with the press, and what sort of messages it will deliver to the press and the public.

Plan a PR Campaign

A **public relations campaign** is a coordinated effort to communicate with one or more of the firm's publics. This is a three-step process that develops, executes, and evaluates PR objectives. Let's review each step, and then we'll examine some of the more frequently used objectives and tactics shown in Figure 14.6.

Like an advertising campaign, the organization must first *develop* clear objectives for the PR program that define the message it wants people to hear. For example, the International Apple Institute, a trade group devoted to increasing the consumption of apples, had to decide if a campaign should focus on getting consumers to cook more with apples, drink more apple juice, or simply buy more fresh fruit. Because fresh apples brought a substantially higher price per pound to growers than apples used for applesauce or apple juice, the group decided to push the fresh fruit angle. It used the theme "An apple a day . . . " (sound familiar?) as it mounted a focused campaign to encourage people to eat more apples by placing articles in consumer media extolling the fruit's health benefits.

Marketing communication experts know that PR strategies are best used in concert with advertising, sales promotion, and personal selling to send a consistent message to

public relations campaign
A coordinated effort to communicate with one or more of the firm's publics.

Figure 14.6 *Snapshot* | Objectives and Tactics of Public Relations

Successful PR campaigns include clearly defined objectives and the use of the right PR activities.

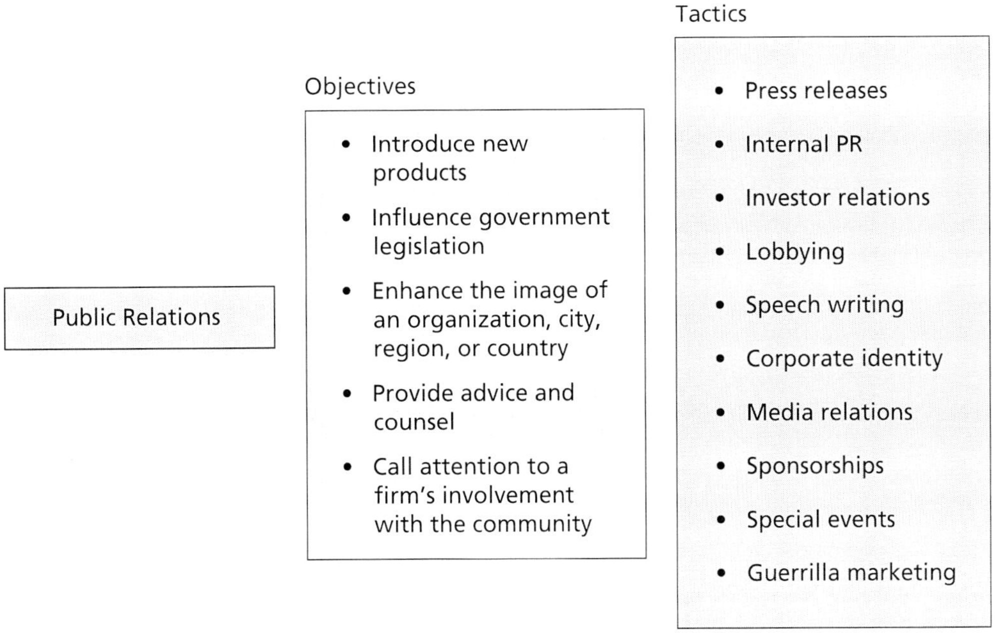

Public Relations

Objectives
- Introduce new products
- Influence government legislation
- Enhance the image of an organization, city, region, or country
- Provide advice and counsel
- Call attention to a firm's involvement with the community

Tactics
- Press releases
- Internal PR
- Investor relations
- Lobbying
- Speech writing
- Corporate identity
- Media relations
- Sponsorships
- Special events
- Guerrilla marketing

customers and other stakeholders. As part of the total marketing communication plan, they often rely on PR to accomplish the following objectives:

- *Introduce new products to retailers and consumers.* Amazon CEO Jeff Bezos created great excitement when he announced the company's work on Prime Air, a new delivery system that would deliver packages to customers in 30 minutes or less using drones. Of course, the excitement calmed down when a few months later the Federal Aviation Administration ruled that Amazon and other firms could not use drones to deliver packages.[102] Fortunately for Amazon, that ruling has since been reversed, and in 2019, the company received FAA clearance for research and testing of its drone delivery service.[103]

- *Influence government legislation.* Airplane maker Boeing spent more than a decade in public relations activities to persuade regulators that jetliners with two engines are as safe as those with three or four engines even for nonstop international flights, some as long as 16 hours.[104]

- *Enhance the image of an organization.* The Women's Professional Golf Association used a variety of public relations and other promotion activities—from product endorsements to player blogs—in its "These Girls Rock" campaign. The program to change the image of women's golf to a hip sport seems to be working, as both tournament attendance and TV audiences have increased.[105]

- *Provide advice and counsel.* Because of their expertise and understanding of the effects of communication on public opinion, PR professionals also provide *advice and counsel* for top management. When a firm needs to shut down a plant or to build a new one, to discontinue a product or add to the product line, to fire a vice president, or to give an award to an employee who spends hundreds of hours a year doing volunteer work in his community, it needs the advice of its PR staff. What is the best way to handle the situation? How should the announcement be made? Who should be told first? What is to be said, and how?

- *Enhance the image of a city, region, or country.* The city of Brooklyn Park, a suburb of Minneapolis, Minnesota, hired a PR firm to revamp its image. Once known as a high-crime area, the city also suffered from "suburban blah." Brooklyn Park hopes its new PR investment can turn around the city's image, making it a place people want to call home.[106]

- *Manage a crisis.* PR specialists handle the crucial but often difficult task of communicating with stakeholders when something goes wrong, such as when BP is involved in a massive oil spill, when GM issues a massive recall of cars with faulty ignition switches, or when Volkswagen is found to be cheating on vehicle emissions tests.

- Organizations respond in many ways, ranging from (unfortunately) complete denial or silence to full disclosure. For example, when a viral YouTube video (https://youtu.be/t4DT3tQqgRM) highlighted the challenges HP's web cam had with following a Black user, the company declined comment and instead directed journalists to a post on its Voodoo Blog.[107]

- *Call attention to a firm's involvement with the community.* Marketers in the U.S. spend about $24.2 billion a year to sponsor sporting events, rock concerts, museum exhibits, and the ballet.[108] PR specialists work behind the scenes to ensure that sponsored events receive ample press coverage and exposure. We'll talk more about sponsorships later in this section.

- *Bring attention to a social issue.* Ben & Jerry's spends as much as 20 percent of its discretionary marketing dollars on its **corporate activism**, or **social marketing**, efforts.[109] These efforts are meant to improve society by influencing consumers to change their behaviors.[110] The company has focused on issues ranging from climate justice and GMO labeling to racial justice and LGBTQ+ equality.

corporate activism, or **social marketing**

Marketing efforts meant to improve society by influencing stakeholders to change their behavior.

PR Tactics

Execution of the campaign means deciding precisely how to communicate the message to the targeted public(s). An organization can get out its positive messages in many ways: news conferences, sponsorship of charity events, and other attention-getting promotions.

To accomplish their objectives, PR professionals choose from a variety of tactics, as shown in Figure 14.4. These activities include press releases, activities aimed at specific internal and external stakeholder groups, speech writing and corporate communications, sponsorships and special events, and guerrilla marketing activities.

Press Release

The most common way for PR specialists to communicate is with a **press release**. This is a report of some event or activity that an organization writes and sends to the media in the hope that it will be published for free. Because fewer consumers are reading newspapers and magazines, the importance of the print press release has diminished. A newer version of this idea is the **video news release (VNR)** that tells the story in a film format instead. Some of the most common types of press releases include the following:

- *Timely topics* deal with topics in the news, such as Levi Strauss's efforts to promote "Casual Fridays" to boost sales of its Dockers and Slates casual dress pants by highlighting how different corporations around the country are adopting a relaxed dress code.
- Universities publish *research project stories* to highlight breakthroughs by faculty researchers.
- *Consumer information releases* provide information to help consumers make product decisions, such as helpful tips from Butterball about how to prepare dishes for Thanksgiving dinner.

> **press release**
> Information that an organization distributes to the media intended to win publicity.

> **video news release (VNR)**
> Similar to a press release, information that an organization sends to the media in a film format.

Internal PR and External Stakeholders

Internal PR activities target employees; they often include company newsletters (often delivered digitally) and closed-circuit TV to keep people informed about company objectives, successes, or even plans to "downsize" the workforce. Often, company newsletters also are distributed outside the firm to suppliers or other important publics.

Investor relations activities focus on communications to those whose financial support is critical; this is especially vital for publicly held companies. It is the responsibility of the PR department to develop and distribute annual and quarterly reports and to provide other essential communications with individual and corporate stockholders, with investment firms, and with capital market organizations.

Lobbying means talking with and providing information to government officials to persuade them to vote a certain way on pending legislation or even to initiate legislation or regulations that would benefit the organization.

> **internal PR**
> PR activities aimed at employees of an organization.

> **investor relations**
> PR activities, such as annual and quarterly reports, aimed at a firm's investors.

> **lobbying**
> Talking with and providing information to government officials to influence their activities relating to an organization.

Speech Writing and Corporate Communications

An important job of a firm's PR department is **speech writing**; specialists provide speeches for company executives to deliver. Although some executives do write their own speeches, it is more common for a speechwriter on the PR staff to develop an initial draft of a speech to which the executive might add her own input. PR specialists also provide input on **corporate identity** materials, such as logos, brochures, building design, and even stationery that communicates a positive image for the firm.

One of the tasks of the PR professional is to develop close **media relations** to ensure that the organization will receive the best media exposure possible for positive news, such as publicizing the achievements of an employee who has done some notable charity work or for a product the company developed that saved someone's life. And as we've seen, good media relations can be even more important when things go wrong. News editors are

> **speech writing**
> Writing a speech on a topic for a company executive to deliver.

> **corporate identity**
> Materials such as logos, brochures, building design, and stationery that communicate an image of the organization.

> **media relations**
> A PR activity aimed at developing close relationships with the media.

less inclined to present a story of a crisis in its most negative way if they have a good relationship with PR people in the organization.

Sponsorships and Special Events

sponsorships
PR activities through which companies provide financial support to help fund an event in return for publicized recognition of the company's contribution.

Sponsorships are PR activities through which companies provide financial support to help fund an event in return for publicized recognition of the company's contribution. Many companies today find that their promotion dollars are well spent to sponsor a golf tournament, a NASCAR driver, a symphony concert, or global events such as the Olympics or the World Cup soccer competition. These sponsorships are particularly effective because they allow marketers to reach customers during their leisure time; people often appreciate these efforts because the financial support makes the events possible in the first place.

AT&T, for example, served as an exclusive "super sponsor" for South by Southwest (SXSW), the insanely popular music, film, and interactive festival held annually in Austin, Texas. For the event, AT&T installed network resources so that fans could stay connected no matter where they went. That meant 215 Wi-Fi spots throughout the Austin area, including a Wi-Fi Hot Zone and charging stations. But that was just the beginning. AT&T also held a competition for the MOFILM community, hosted an AT&T Hackathon for mobile apps developers, and showed attendees the coolest places around Austin via the AT&T Teleporter.[111]

special events
Activities—from a visit by foreign investors to a company picnic—that are planned and implemented by a PR department.

A related task is to plan and implement **special events**. Companies find special events useful for a variety of purposes. For example, a firm might hold a press conference to increase interest and excitement in a new product or other company activity. A city or state may hold an annual event such as the strawberry festivals in Florida and California or the National Cherry Blossom Festival in Washington, D.C., to promote tourism. Companies also hold special events or outings, such as the huge road rallies that Harley-Davidson's Harley Owners' Group (HOGs) sponsors, to reinforce loyalty toward an existing product. Other special events aim simply to create buzz and generate publicity. For New York City shoppers, Unilever created its "All Small & Mighty Clothes Bus," a 40-foot bus it covered in all the shirts, shorts, and socks that one bottle of super-concentrated All laundry detergent can wash. Consumers who spotted the bus during its 12-day campaign could "clean up" if they entered a sweepstakes to win a $5,000 shopping spree or $200 gift cards.[112]

Like their counterparts in other areas, PR departments are employing technology to help them be more efficient and effective. In addition to the CRM software we mentioned earlier in this chapter, PR folks also engage software specific to event management, such as Eventbrite and Cvent. Eventbrite is a web-based event management and ticketing application that planners may use to promote their event, sell tickets, manage attendees, and communicate post event. Users are easily able to connect their Eventbrite and social media accounts to make promotion efforts easier. And since free events don't incur fees, it's a viable option for nonprofits or individuals who are hosting events. Cvent is a cloud-based solution including tools for online event registration, venue research, marketing, and attendee engagement.

Brand Ambassadors and Evangelists

Many marketers recruit loyal customers as *brand ambassadors* or *brand evangelists* to help them spread the word about their products. These zealous consumers can be the best salespeople a company can ever find—and they often work for free. They are heavy users, take a product seriously, care a great deal about it, and want it to succeed.[113] In addition, they know the target audience better than anyone because they are a part of it.

So how do marketers identify and motivate these loyal customers to be brand ambassadors? Sometimes, they seek out customers who already blog about the product and share what they love about the brand. One way to motivate brand ambassadors is to give them special access or privileges to the company and its marketing strategies. Some might be recruited and featured through a brand contest.

Guerrilla Marketing

Organizations with tiny advertising budgets need to develop innovative—and cheap—ways to capture consumers' attention. **Guerrilla marketing** activities are an increasingly popular way to accomplish this objective. No, this term doesn't refer to marketers making monkeys out of themselves (that's "gorilla marketing"). A guerrilla marketing strategy involves "ambushing" consumers with promotional content in places where they don't expect to encounter these messages.

Ambient advertising is a popular type of guerilla marketing. This term describes the placement of messages in nontraditional media. Some examples include the backs of garage and theater receipts, screens attached to the back of supermarket carts, signs on elevator doors, or the ever-popular signs on urinals in bars and restaurants—the possibilities are endless.

Today, big companies buy into guerrilla marketing strategies big time. Consider the "Wallet Drop" campaign in Singapore to help launch Burger King affordables—food so affordable it was like BK was putting money back in your wallet. To attract customers, BK dropped wallets loaded with BK coupons on park benches, under clothes racks, and in other locations throughout Singapore.[114] Now there's something you don't see every day.

Companies use guerrilla marketing to promote new drinks, cars, clothing styles, or even computer systems. Much to the annoyance of city officials in San Francisco and Chicago, IBM painted hundreds of "Peace Love Linux" logos on sidewalks to publicize the company's adoption of the Linux operating system. Even though the company got hit with a hefty bill to pay for cleaning up the "corporate graffiti," one marketing journalist noted that they "got the publicity they were looking for."[115] Given the success of many of these campaigns that operate on a shoestring budget, expect to see even more of these tactics as other companies climb on the guerrilla bandwagon.

Buzz Marketing

Why do the heavy lifting when you can put your customers to work for you? The many-to-many communication model relies on consumers like you to talk to one another about goods, services, and organizations. Marketers think of **buzz** as everyday people helping their marketing efforts when they share their opinions with their friends and neighbors.[116] The idea is nothing new. It's basically the so-called "office water-cooler effect" where coworkers dish about the latest TV sitcom on Monday morning—but on steroids.

In reality, a lot of the online marketing you're exposed to every day in social media posts, TV shows like *Access Hollywood* that breathlessly report about the outrageous gown Cardi B wore to the Met Gala, or even gossip websites like Perez Hilton that dish about the glam nightclub where Lauren Conrad was supposedly spotted twerking with heartthrob Chris Pine (OK, we made that one up) fall under the heading of public relations rather than advertising. The reason: News about a cool new brand is likely to reach you informally from other members of your network, rather than as a message some company paid to send to you. And you're a lot more likely to take that message seriously because it comes from someone you know (at least online) who is not being paid to try to convince you to buy the item (but a warning: see the section on buzz marketing ethics that follows for a wake-up call about that!). That's why the buzz marketing element of PR actually makes public relations a much *more important* part of the promotional mix than it ever used to be.

The trick is to create buzz that works for you, not against you. Specifically, **buzz marketing** refers to specific marketing activities designed to create conversation, excitement, and enthusiasm—that is, buzz—about a brand. How does this happen, or more specifically, how do marketers make sure it happens? Let's take a look at Jaguar Land Rover, maker of Land Rover vehicles. As a publicity stunt to create buzz, the company parked its new £90,000 Range Rover luxury SUV outside Harrods, the popular London department store. On the vehicle were the words "Cheater" and "Hope she was worth it" spray painted in huge red

guerrilla marketing
Marketing activity in which a firm "ambushes" consumers with promotional content in places they are not expecting to encounter this kind of activity.

ambient advertising
Advertising placed where advertising isn't normally or hasn't ever been seen.

buzz
Word-of-mouth communication that customers view as authentic.

buzz marketing
Marketing activities designed to create conversation, excitement, and enthusiasm—that is, buzz—about a brand.

Heinz introduced its new vinegar ketchup with the help of a tryvertising strategy to create buzz for the new flavor.

tryvertising
Advertising by sampling that is designed to create buzz about a product.

f-commerce
E-commerce that takes place on Facebook.

brand polarization
The gap between good buzz and bad buzz.

letters. The result was not only thousands of mentions online, but the stunt also hit the news—even the BBC fell for the stunt and reported the "incident."[117]

Companies today spend millions to create consumer-positive buzz. Firms like Apple specifically hire word of mouth (WOM) marketing managers to track, engage in, and leverage buzz.[118] Techniques to encourage consumers to spread information about companies and their products come under a variety of names, such as *word of mouth marketing, viral marketing, buzz marketing*, and *evangelist marketing*.

Heinz opened a pop-up (temporary) **tryvertising** (advertising by sampling that is designed to create buzz about a product) page using **f-commerce** (Facebook e-commerce, a version of the social commerce we discussed earlier in the chapter) to launch its newest ketchup.[119] The new limited-edition ketchup, one flavored with balsamic vinegar, was made available online to 3,000 of Heinz's biggest fans before the company placed more than a million bottles of the product in traditional stores. The result? Fans were definitely buzzing, and each positive product comment gets syndicated to approximately 130 other Facebook walls, generating even more buzz.

As we've noted, buzz isn't *really* new. In fact, we can point to the fame of none other than the *Mona Lisa* portrait as one of the first examples of buzz marketing. In 1911, the painting was stolen from the Louvre museum in Paris. The theft created buzz around the globe while it catapulted da Vinci's masterpiece into the limelight (note that we're not advocating that you arrange to get your product stolen to build buzz).

What *is* new is the magnifying effect that technology exerts on the spread of buzz: When you think of the effect of consumers talking one-on-one about the *Mona Lisa* theft a century ago, imagine the exponential increase in influence of the individual consumer "connectors" or "e-fluentials" who use Facebook, blogs, and other social media to increase their reach.[120] How many online "friends" do you have? Compared to traditional advertising and public relations activities, these endorsements are far more credible and thus more valuable to the brand.

People like to share their experiences, good or bad, with others. Truly happy customers will share their excitement about a brand. Unfortunately, the unhappy ones will be even more eager to tell their friends about their unpleasant experiences. For some brands, the difference between "good" buzz and "bad" buzz is very large; for others, it is almost the same. For example, when asked about their feelings toward the Amazon brand, 56 percent of consumers were "brand lovers," whereas only 3 percent were "brand haters." In contrast, 33 percent of consumers were "brand lovers" of McDonald's, while 29 percent were "brand haters." **Brand polarization**, the gap between good buzz and bad buzz, isn't always a bad thing, however. Bad buzz spreads faster than good buzz; in addition, it stimulates controversy, causing product lovers to vehemently defend the brand they love so much.[121] Of course, marketers don't necessarily create the buzz around their product anyway; sometimes they just catch a wave that's building and simply ride it home.

Viral Marketing

One popular form of buzz building is viral marketing. This term refers to marketing activities that aim to increase brand awareness or sales because consumers pass a cool message along to others in their networks, and (hopefully) these recipients do the same until many thousands, or even millions, of people are exposed to the content. Thus, if the tactic works, the message "goes viral."

Did you party at DJ D-Nice's #ClubQuarantine during the spring of 2020 amidst the COVID-19 pandemic? If so, you're one of millions who joined in on this viral sensation. What began as Derrick Jones playing a live set for a few hundred followers and fans via Instagram Live, grew to hours-long sessions that drew tens of thousands of viewers. At the height of #ClubQuarantine, D-Nice hosted 105,000 simultaneous party-goers. As celebrities like Oprah Winfrey and news outlets such as CNN caught on to this viral experience, brands ranging from the NBA to Spotify began partnering with Jones.[122]

Apple implements viral marketing when it simply inserts the message "Sent from my iPad/iPhone" into an email. Today, most viral marketing tactics consist of marketers' use of video clips, interactive games, or other activities that consumers will find so interesting or unique that they want to share them with their friends using digital technology.

What's your favorite meme these days? **Memes** are ideas with staying power, moving from person to person and competing for attention along the way.[123] Despite the trickiness of using them correctly, memes are a tactic brands continue to use. IHOb, anyone?[124]

memes
Ideas with staying power that move from person to person competing for attention along the way. Memes are a tactic brands use.

Ethical Problems with Buzz Marketing

Just as firms are discovering there are a myriad of opportunities for buzz marketing, there are equally large opportunities for unethical or at least questionable marketing behavior. Some of these include the following:

- *Activities designed to deceive consumers:* Buzz works best when companies put unpaid consumers in charge of creating their own messages—after all, consumers perceive endorsements from their friends to be more credible. The FTC Guides Concerning Use of Endorsements and TestImonials in Advertising require endorsers to disclose their brand relationships to consumers, including an acknowledgment of any renumeration received, such as payment or free product. This disclosure must be made in each individual Instagram post or Tweet, for example, and cannot be hidden in the endorser's bio.[125]

- *Sock puppeting:* In recent years, we've witnessed a new attempt to manipulate attitudes that some call **sock puppeting**. This term describes a company executive or other biased source that poses as someone else to plug a product in social media. For example, it came to light that the CEO of Whole Foods had posted derogatory comments about rival Wild Oats without revealing his true identity.[126] Another form of sock puppeting is so-called **paid influencer programs** that attempt to start online conversations about brands when they encourage bloggers to write about them. As a typical example, Mercedes gave a blogger use of an SUV for a week in exchange for posts about it. These "sponsored conversations" can be effective, but they are unethical if the blogger doesn't reveal that he or she has actually received payment in the form of cash or free products to promote a sponsor's product.

sock puppeting
A practice where a company executive or other biased source poses as someone else to plug a product in social media.

paid influencer programs
Another form of sock puppeting in which bloggers are paid or rewarded in some way for attempting to start online conversations about a brand.

- *Directing buzz marketing at children or teens:* Some critics say buzz marketing should never do this because these younger consumers are more impressionable and easier to deceive than adults.[127]

- *Buzz marketing activities that damage property:* Puma encouraged consumers to stencil its cat logo all over Paris. Such activities lead to damage or vandalism, which the company will ultimately have to pay for. In addition, individual consumers could find themselves in trouble with the law, a problem that could ultimately backfire and damage the company image.

- *Social marketing that upsets consumers and partners.* While firms choose to engage in social marketing or corporate activism, the practice is not without drawbacks. Firms such as Ben & Jerry's have faced backlash from both consumers and retailers for the stances they've taken. And Wendy's recently faced scrutiny for not following through on its promises.[128]

Evaluation of a PR Campaign

One of the barriers to greater reliance on PR campaigns is *evaluation*; compared to many other forms of marketing communications, it's difficult to devise metrics to gauge their effectiveness. Who can say precisely what impact an appearance by Seth Rogen on *The Tonight Show* to plug his new movie exerts on ticket sales or whether Virgin's sponsorship of the London Marathon boosted purchases of airline tickets? It is possible to tell if a PR campaign gets media exposure, though compared to advertising it's much more difficult to assess bottom-line impact. Table 14.3 describes some of the most common PR measurement techniques.

Table 14.3 | Measuring the Effectiveness of Public Relations (PR) Tactics

Method	Description	Example	Pros	Cons
Personal (subjective) evaluation of PR activities	Evaluation of PR activities by superiors may occur at all levels of the organization.	Items in employee annual reviews relate to the successful fulfillment of PR role.	Simple and inexpensive to complete; ensures that an annual assessment will be completed.	Subjective nature of the evaluation may result in biased appraisal. Employees may focus on the annual review to the exclusion of some important PR goals.
Matching of PR activity accomplishments with activity objectives	Simple counts of actual PR activities accomplished compared with activity goals set for the period.	Goal: To obtain publication of three feature articles in major newspapers in the first quarter of the year. Result: Four articles published.	Focuses attention on the need for quantitative goals for PR activities and achievements. Easy and inexpensive to measure.	Focuses on activity goals rather than image or communication goals. Ignores image perception or attitudes of the firm's publics.
Evaluation of communication objectives through opinion surveys among the firm's publics	Surveys are used to determine if image/communication goals are met within key groups.	Goal: To achieve an improved image of the organization among at least 30 percent of financial community stakeholders.	Causes PR professionals to focus on actual communication results of activities.	May be difficult to measure changes in perceptions among the firm's publics. Factors not under the control of PR practitioners may influence public perceptions. It is relatively expensive. Results may take many months, thus preventing corrective actions in PR activities.
Measurement of coverage in print and broadcast media, especially those generated by PR activities	Systematic measurement of coverage achieved in print media (column inches/pages) and broadcast media (minutes of airtime).	Total number of column inches of newspaper articles resulting from PR releases. Total number of articles including those not from PR releases. Total amount of positive print and broadcast coverage. Total amount of negative print and broadcast coverage. Ratio of negative to positive print and broadcast coverage.	Very objective measurements with little opportunity for bias. Relatively inexpensive.	Does not address perceptions, attitudes, or image issues of the organization.
Impression measurement	Measure the size of the audience for all print and broadcast coverage. Often, assessment includes comparisons in terms of advertising costs for same number of impressions.	Network news coverage during the time period equaled over 15 million gross impressions. This number of impressions through advertising would have cost $4,500,000.	Objective, without any potential bias in measurement; provides a monetary measure to justify the expenditures of the PR office or consultant. Relatively inexpensive.	Does not differentiate between negative and positive news coverage. Does not consider responses of publics to the coverage. Assumes that advertising and PR communication activities are equal.

14.5 Brand You: How Networking Can Help You Achieve Your Career Goals

OBJECTIVE
Understand the importance of networking in managing a successful career.

Taylor has done a great job planning his personal brand. He has used his strengths and weaknesses to develop his core product. He understands his potential value in terms of salary and other compensation to potential employers and the keys to effective interviewing and negotiation. Now it's time to think about networking for now and for his future career.

Networking—How It Works

"The more people you know, the more people who can help you, and the more people they may know that can help you. That's what networking is all about."

—Stephen Facenda, President, ViaMark Advertising

How do you get information about a marketing course? How about a professor's teaching style or a new hamburger joint across town? For most of us, information about most things comes from our friends and family. And that goes for jobs too.

With as many as 80 percent of jobs being filled through networking, you might be wondering why there are so many internship and job postings online. You might assume that's how most jobs are filled. The fact is, most hiring managers hate to post open positions. Posting a job can mean hundreds of candidates with hundreds of résumés to go through. It's far more efficient (and effective) for hiring managers to talk with people they know and trust and ask them if they know someone who would be a good fit for the position. That's where a network comes in. There's nothing more powerful than someone referring you for an internship or a job.

Although you might find the prospect of networking scary, it's a simple method of connecting to people that you already know how to do. You probably have a network at school—people you can call on when you've missed a class or need help understanding an assignment. Networking isn't just about meeting lots of people; it's about building relationships.

In general, there are three "must do's" for effective networking:

1. Keep in touch.
2. Always help people in your network, even when it's not convenient.
3. Develop strong relationships with people in your network and then expand your network via the networks of members of your network.

Networking is a way to share information and help people. Networking is *not* a way to ask for a job.

Where to Start Networking

The first step in developing a professional network is to focus on the people you already know. Start by making a list of people already in your network—your family and friends. Then, list friends of the family as well as friends' family members. Add the people you meet every day, such as guest speakers in your classes and people you meet at professional meetings.

And don't forget about people on your campus. Be sure to include your fellow students, your professors, career counsellors, people you meet in campus clubs, and alumni.

You can enhance your networking efforts in other ways as well:

- Have business cards made with your name and contact information.
- Join a professional association.
- Connect with alumni through your college's career center or alumni office.
- Talk to speakers in class, at conferences, and at professional meetings.
- Email or call authors of articles in trade journals or magazines.

Ask people you know through Facebook or other social networks for people you might contact for help in finding an internship or a job. Of course, you first need to be sure your social networking pages are appropriate for business contacts. The pictures of the spring break trip are probably *not* what you want your prospective employer to see. And, yes, hiring managers do check.

How LinkedIn Can Help You Build Your Network

Professional social networks like LinkedIn can help you connect to professionals in the area in which you would like to work. Over 30 million companies have LinkedIn profiles, and 3 million jobs are posted to the platform monthly in the U.S. alone.[129] Professional social networks are a great partner for your in-person networking for connecting to the right people.

LinkedIn is the largest professional social network. As of March 9, 2020, LinkedIn had 675 million monthly users, a 14 percent increase since the end of 2018.[130] Forty percent of these use the network daily.

The first step is to create a LinkedIn profile. Include all of your relevant work experiences, including internships, volunteer experience, and involvement in campus, athletic, and community service organizations and activities. Then, you can use LinkedIn to search for people or companies at which you may want to work. Try to find people you are connected to at a company you are interested in and ask for an introduction to someone who works there.

People who are hiring for jobs look for people who have been recommended by someone in authority. LinkedIn is a good place to contact people such as your supervisor from your summer or campus job or internship, athletic coach, or volunteer manager and ask them to write a recommendation about your work ethic, skills, and character.

You can also join groups on LinkedIn. For example, if you are interested in public relations, you can find several groups, including Public Relations Society of America (PRSA). Once you are a member of a group, you can get involved in group discussions.

Other Ways to Enhance Networking

Of course LinkedIn isn't the only way to ensure that you are maximizing the potential of networking. Some other suggestions are:

- Have professional-looking business cards made with your name and contact information. They are inexpensive and set you apart from other young professionals and students.
- Join a professional association that allows student members, often at reduced rates. Your professors may have information on these types of organizations.
- Reach out to Facebook and other social networks and ask people for help with your search.
- Start networking before graduation—the earlier, the better.
- Consider an internship or volunteering—you'll get to know professionals. Depending on how well you get to know them, you may be able to ask them if you might call on them later for advice in your career.
- Always be professional; imagine every day in every situation that there may be someone you meet today who will have the perfect job for you.
- Be sure to clean up any digital dirt you may have on social media, such as inappropriate conversations, pictures, and images.

Taylor understands the importance of networking. But he also needs to make sure he uses his network effectively. The challenges aren't over when he gets a job. Throughout his career, Taylor will have more responsibilities, and that means he will need to continue networking throughout his career.

Objective **Summaries** and **Key Terms**

14.1 Objective Summary

Understand how marketers communicate using an updated communication model that incorporates new social media and buzz marketing activities.

Because consumers spend more time online and less time watching TV or reading magazines, traditional advertising has diminished as a way to talk to consumers. Consumers today are increasingly getting their information on products from one another rather than from firms as technology magnifies the spread of consumer buzz.

Social media are Internet-based platforms that allow users to create their own content and share it with others in the many-to-many communication model. Social networking sites or social networks, such as brand communities, Facebook, Instagram, Snapchat, TikTok, YouTube, Twitter, virtual worlds, product review sites, mobile apps, and location-based social networks, connect people with other, similar people. Social networks provide opportunities for the development of brand communities formed by social network users on the basis of attachment to a product or brand. The Internet of Things (IoT) allows many-to-many things communication.

Key Terms

groundswell
media multitasking, or second screening
cord-cutting
social media
brand ambassadors, or brand evangelists
social networks
brand community
cosplay
Facebook
Instagram
sponsored posts
YouTube
TikTok
Snapchat
Twitch
Twitter
virtual worlds
avatars
virtual goods
social commerce
product review sites
location-based social networks
augmented reality (AR)
storytelling
short-form storytelling

14.2 Objective Summary

Explain what sales promotion is and describe the different types of consumer and B2B sales promotion activities.

Sales promotions are programs that marketers design to build interest in or encourage purchase of a good or service during a specified period. Marketers target sales promotion activities either to ultimate consumers or to members of the channel, such as retailers that sell their products. Price-based consumer sales promotions include coupons, price deals, refunds, rebates, frequency (loyalty/continuity) programs, and special/bonus packs. Attention-getting consumer sales promotions include contests and sweepstakes, premiums, and sampling.

Trade sales promotions come in a variety of forms. Some are designed as discounts and deals, including co-op advertising, for channel members, and some are designed to increase industry visibility. Approaches aimed at increasing industry visibility include trade shows, promotional products, point-of-purchase (POP) displays, incentive programs, and push money.

Key Terms

sales promotions
rebates
frequency programs
premiums
product sampling
trade sales promotions
merchandising allowance
case allowance
forward buying
diverting
co-op advertising
trade shows
promotional products
point-of-purchase (POP) displays
push money

14.3 Objective Summary

Understand the important role of personal selling, the different types of sales jobs, and the steps in the creative selling process.

Personal selling occurs when a company representative interacts directly with a prospect or customer to communicate about a good or service. Many organizations rely heavily on this approach because at times the "personal touch" can carry more weight than mass-media material. Generally, a personal selling effort is more important when a firm uses a push strategy in B2B contexts and for firms whose goods or services are complex or very expensive. Personal selling has been enhanced by new technology, including customer relationship management (CRM) and partner relationship management (PRM), software systems, and video conferencing systems, such as Zoom, that allow customers and salespeople to interact over the Internet.

Professional sales jobs are varied and include order takers, technical specialists, missionary salespersons, new-business salespeople, and order getters, as well as team selling opportunities. Transactional selling focuses on making an immediate sale with little concern for developing a long-term relationship with the customer. In contrast, relationship selling involves securing, developing, and maintaining long-term relationships with profitable customers.

The steps in the creative selling process include prospecting and qualifying, preapproach, approach, sales presentation, handling objections, closing the sale, and follow-up.

Key Terms

personal selling
partner relationship management (PRM)
voice-over Internet protocol (VoIP)
Zoom-bombing
telecommute
virtual office
social selling
account-based selling
order taker
technical specialist
missionary salesperson
new-business salesperson
order getter
team selling
key accounts
cross-functional team
transactional selling
relationship selling
creative selling process
prospecting
preapproach
approach
sales presentation
close
follow-up

14.4 Objective Summary

Explain the role of public relations and the steps in developing a public relations campaign.

The purpose of PR is to build good relationships between an organization and its various publics and to establish and maintain a favorable image. Crisis management is the process of managing a company's reputation when some negative and often unplanned event threatens the organization's image.

The steps in PR are setting objectives, creating and executing a campaign strategy, and planning how the PR program will be evaluated. PR is useful to introduce new products; influence legislation; enhance the image of a city, region, or country; polish the image of an organization; provide advice and counsel; and call attention to a firm's community involvement.

PR specialists often use print or video news releases to communicate timely topics, research stories, and consumer information. Internal communications with employees include company newsletters and internal TV programs. Other PR activities include investor relations, lobbying, speech writing, developing corporate identity materials, media relations, arranging sponsorships and special events, and guerrilla marketing activities, including ambient advertising.

Social media is also very important to successful PR campaigns. Marketers use buzz-building activities to encourage consumers to share their opinions about products with friends and neighbors. Buzz marketing can be unethical when marketers use activities designed to deceive consumers, when they direct buzz marketing to children or teens, and when buzz marketing activities encourage people to damage property.

Viral marketing refers to activities that aim to increase brand awareness or sales by consumers passing a message along to other consumers. Marketers may recruit loyal customers who care a great deal about a product and want it to succeed as brand ambassadors or brand evangelists to help create buzz. The importance of public relations is somewhat diminished because of the difficulties in evaluation of its effectiveness.

Key Terms

public relations (PR)
proactive PR
publicity
crisis management
public relations campaign
corporate activism, or social marketing
press release
video news release (VNR)
internal PR
investor relations
lobbying
speech writing
corporate identity
media relations
sponsorships
special events
guerrilla marketing
ambient advertising
buzz
buzz marketing
tryvertising
f-commerce
brand polarization
memes
sock puppeting
paid influencer programs

14.5 Objective Summary

Understand the importance of networking in managing a successful career.

As many as 80 percent of jobs are filled through networking, probably because of the value of someone you know recommending you for a job. Start networking by listing your family and friends; then list friends of family and family of friends.

The three "must do's" for effective networking are:

1. Keep in touch.
2. Always help people in your network, even when it's not convenient.
3. Develop strong relationships with people in your network and then expand your network via the networks of members of your network.

Start networking by making a list of people already in your network, your family and friends. Then, list friends and family of those people, people on campus, and others you meet professionally. Have business cards made with your name and contact information.

Professional social networks like LinkedIn can help you connect to professionals in the area in which you would like to work. People who are hiring for jobs look for people who have been recommended by someone in authority. LinkedIn is a good place to contact people, such as your supervisor from your summer or campus job or internship, athletic coach, or volunteer manager, and ask them to write a recommendation about your work ethic, skills, and character.

Chapter **Questions** and **Activities**

Concepts: Test Your Knowledge

14-1. What is buzz? How do marketers practice buzz building?

14-2. What are some ethical problems in buzz marketing?

14-3. What is viral marketing? How do marketers use brand ambassadors or brand evangelists?

14-4. What is social media? What are social networks? Describe Facebook, Twitter, Instagram, TikTok, Snapchat, YouTube, virtual worlds, product review sites, mobile apps, and location-based social networks.

14-5. What is social commerce?

14-6. What is sales promotion? Explain some of the different types of price-based consumer sales promotions marketers frequently use. Explain some of the different types of attention-getting consumer sales promotions marketers frequently use. Describe some of the types of trade sales promotion frequently used by marketers.

14-7. What role does personal selling play within the marketing function? Describe the various types of sales jobs.

14-8. What is relationship selling? How does it differ from transactional selling?

14-9. Explain these steps in the creative selling process: prospecting, qualifying, the approach, the sales presentation, and the follow-up after the sale. How can you overcome a customer's objections?

14-10. What is the purpose of public relations? How does it differ from advertising? What are some of the traditional activities that are part of PR?

14-11. What is lobbying? Describe media relations and tell why this is such an important part of PR.

Activities: Apply What You've Learned

14-12. *Creative Homework/Short Project* Think about a business or place that you and your classmates might visit. You might, for example, think about (1) an online jewelry and accessories shop, (2) a night spot where you and your friends might hang out on the weekends, or (3) a drive-in movie theater. Assume you have been hired as a marketing consultant by that business. You believe that the business would benefit from nontraditional marketing. Develop several ideas for social media tactics that you feel would be successful for the client. Describe in detail each idea, how it should be implemented, and your reasons for it being a successful communication strategy.

14-13. *In Class, 10–20 Minutes for Teams* A coffee shop near campus is debating between advertising via traditional cable TV or via streaming platforms, such as Peacock and Hulu. Discuss your individual experiences with streaming services. Are there any cord-cutters in your group? What platforms do you use? How do experiences vary between traditional platforms and streaming ones? Develop a brief recommendation for this local advertiser. Should they switch? What are your reasons for your recommendation?

14-14. *In Class, 10–25 Minutes for Teams* Assume that you are a member of the marketing department for a firm that produces several varieties of organic candy bars. Your assignment is to develop recommendations for consumer and trade sales promotion activities for the candy bars. Develop an outline of your recommendations for these sales promotions. In a role-playing situation, present and defend your recommendations to your boss.

14-15. *In Class, 10–25 Minutes for Teams* Timing is an important part of a sales promotion plan. Trade sales promotions must be properly timed to ensure channel members fully maximize the opportunity to sell your product. Assume that the introduction of the candy bars in question 14-14 is planned for August 30. Place the activities you recommended in your answer to question 14-14 onto a 12-month calendar of events. (Hint: The calendar needs to start *before* the product introduction.) In a role-playing situation, present your plan to your boss. Be sure to explain the reasons for your timing of each trade sales promotion element.

14-16. *In Class, 10–25 Minutes for Teams* In this chapter, we learned that marketers are increasing their use of social media in their marketing communication strategies. Why is this happening? What social media does your university use? Make a list of all the different platforms and pages you can find for each. How might these be improved?

14-17. *Creative Homework/Short Project* You work for a local bakery that specializes in cupcakes and cake pops. Your boss is interested in having you set up social media accounts for the bakery. Consider carefully which social media sites would be most effective and why. Devise a short presentation for your boss so that he can weigh the various options you recommend.

14-18. *Creative Homework/Short Project* Assume you work for a local juice shop that specializes in beverages that use ginger. Your assignment is to develop recommendations for using social commerce for the shop. Is social commerce a viable option for the shop? Develop an outline of your recommendations. In a role-playing situation, present and defend your recommendations to your manager.

14-19. *Creative Homework/Short Project* Think of the last time you interacted with a salesperson, whether it was for a new smartphone or a trendy pair of eyeglasses. Identify the type of salesperson you were interacting with and describe what this person did to fulfill that particular role. Also identify whether this salesperson used a transactional selling approach or a relationship selling approach. Was this approach appropriate for the purchase you were considering? Why or why not?

14-20. *Creative Homework/Short Project* Assume a firm that publishes university textbooks (including this marketing textbook) has just hired you as a field salesperson. Your job requires that you call on university faculty members to persuade them to adopt one of your textbooks for their classes. As part of your training, your sales manager has asked you to develop an outline of what you will say in a typical sales presentation. Write that outline, including how you might handle a specific objection, like "But this [a competitor's book] is the textbook we've always used, and it's always worked well for us."

14-21. *Creative Homework/Short Project* Your assignment for this project is to develop recommendations for a local not-for-profit's marketing communication program. First, schedule an appointment with the organization to discuss what they are currently doing in the way of marketing communication. You will probably want to ask them about the following:
a. The target audiences for their communication program
b. The objectives of their communication program
c. The different types of traditional and nontraditional communication methods they use
d. How they evaluate the effectiveness of their communication program(s)
e. Who handles the marketing efforts

Based on your discussions, develop a report that (1) provides a critique of the current communication program and (2) makes recommendations for improvement.

14-22. *In Class, 10–25 Minutes for Teams* Assume that you are the head of PR for a national airline. A passenger has claimed that you forcibly removed him from the plane

for no reason and in the process injured his back, which has resulted in many doctor visits and medical bills. Another passenger videoed the incident and it has now appeared online. As the director of public relations for the airline, what specific recommendations do you have for how the company should handle the crisis?

Concepts: Apply Marketing Metrics

One of the important benefits of social media sites is that they allow marketers to easily learn what consumers are saying about their brand—and about the competition. To better understand that process, you can go to Twitter to conduct a little detective work to see what consumers are saying about a brand.

14-23. Select a product type and particular brand of that product to study. It can be in any product category you choose. If you are doing a marketing plan project for your marketing course, you may use that product for this exercise. If not, choose a product type and brand that you use and like, one that you might use and are curious about, or one that you dislike.

14-24. Search for your selected brand on both Twitter and Instagram and see what is revealed. After you have reviewed the results, provide a summary of the following information:
a. The number of posts within each platform that are positive
b. The major aspects of your brand that people think are positive
c. The number of posts within each platform that are negative
d. The major aspects of your brand that people think are negative
e. The number of TikTok videos within each platform
f. Any obvious trends in the types of photos, videos, and GIFs people are sharing

Choices: What Do You Think?

14-25. *Critical Thinking* Have you ever interacted with a company or a brand on social media—think tweeting them, liking a page on Facebook, tagging them on Instagram, etc.? Why did you choose to do so? If you have ever posted a comment or question, did the company respond to you? How effectively do you think companies in general manage their social media accounts and interact with consumers?

14-26. *Critical Thinking* Companies sometimes teach consumers a "bad lesson" with the overuse of sales promotions. As a result, consumers expect the product always to be "on deal" or have a rebate available. What are some examples of products for which you think marketers have overused discounts and/or rebates, causing customers to buy only "on-deal"? How do you think companies can prevent this?

14-27. *Ethics* Many salespeople earn a commission on what they sell, often meaning that the more the customer buys, the more the salesperson makes. Does this pose any ethical issues for the salesperson? How should a salesperson conduct themselves in this situation? What responsibility does the buyer have in such situations?

14-28. *Critical Thinking* Recently, Snapchat has joined other social media sites by introducing shoppable videos. Do you feel that such revenue-generating activities make these sites less attractive to users? If you know brands are placing videos on a site in order for you to buy directly from the video, are you likely to change your behavior in clicking or using the site? Are there other ways that these websites can generate revenue?

14-29. *Critical Thinking* In general, professional selling has evolved from hard selling to relationship selling. Do some organizations still use the hard-sell style? If so, provide examples and explain. What do you think the future holds for these organizations? Are there examples of businesses where the hard sell will continue to be successful? If so, what kind of businesses?

14-30. *Critical Thinking* A woman sued Taco Bell for deceptive advertising, claiming its tacos had far less beef than advertised. Taco Bell, understanding the potential damage to its brand, immediately went on the defense and filed a countersuit. In addition, Taco Bell's CEO posted a video statement and essentially released its recipe for seasoned beef, which contains 88 percent beef that is 100 percent USDA inspected.[131] Was this enough for Taco Bell to do to avert a PR crisis? What else could they have done?

14-31. *Critical Thinking* There is increasing concern about consumer privacy on social networking sites. Facebook continues to face scrutiny about how it handles user data and to whom it grants permission to access this data. Research Facebook's response to these data privacy PR crises. Do you think they handled the issue correctly? What else could Facebook do to address consumer concerns about privacy? Do you think Facebook will be hurt in the long run based on this data breach? Should the government do more to protect user privacy?

14-32. *Creative Homework/Short Project* Many firms today are using a variety of buzz-building activities to encourage word-of-mouth communication about their products. Think about a business or place that you and your classmates might visit. You might, for example, think about (1) a speciality shoe store, (2) a night spot where you and your friends might hang out on the weekends, or (3) a local restaurant. For your selected product, develop ideas for at least three different buzz-building activities. Outline the details as to exactly how these activities would be carried out and integrated with more traditional marketing communications. Next, rank the activities in the order that you feel would be the best and tell why you feel that way. Develop a report for your class on your ideas.

14-33. *Critical Thinking* Some critics denounce PR specialists, calling them "spin doctors" whose job is to hide the truth about a company's problems. What is the proper role of PR within an organization? Should PR specialists try to put a good face on bad news?

Miniproject: Learn by Doing

Miniproject 1
The purpose of this miniproject is to help you understand the advantages of following the creative selling process:

14-34. With several of your classmates, create a new product in a category that most college students buy regularly (e.g., toothpaste, shampoo, pens, pencils, soft drinks—anything that interests you that might be sold through a drugstore like Walgreens). Make up a new brand name and some creative features and benefits of the new product you come up with.

14-35. Assume you are a salesperson trying to sell your product to an organizational buyer like Walgreens for adding to their product lines. Develop a plan for executing each of the steps in the creative selling process. Make sure that you cover all the bases of how you would go about selling your product.

14-36. Report on your plan to your class and ask the other students for feedback on whether your approach will convince the Walgreens buyer to make a purchase. Alternatively, with a classmate demonstrate your plan in a role-playing exercise.

Miniproject 2
One of the more difficult parts of developing a marketing communication plan that includes a variety of traditional and new media activities is coordination. This project will provide you with an opportunity to explore the difficulties of this.

Assume you are the CMO for the Glam Face Shield Company. You are responsible for developing a marketing communication plan for your firm's new low-profile face shield for people who perform their job in a dangerous work environment where there are safety hazards that can harm any part of their face. You have decided that your program could best be developed if it includes the following:

1. Traditional TV advertising
2. Brand ambassadors and evangelists
3. A mobile app
4. An interactive brand website with a game, information about your product, and one or more other interactive devices
5. Digital advertising on various platforms
6. Consumer sales promotion
7. A TikTok challenge

14-37. Design each of these communication program elements with detailed descriptions, including timing and venues.

14-38. Each of these activities must be tied to the other activities. Now describe all of these connections.

14-39. To be successful today, a firm must do more than just provide consumers with information. Their marketing communication activities must engage the consumer, must provide something of value (in addition to information about the product), and must make the customer's life better. Describe how your communication activities will do these things.

Marketing in Action **Case**   Real Choices at Brud

Many of us look to recommendations from others to help make decisions about which clothes to buy, what skin care products to use, or which technologies will make our lives easier. This need has spawned the social media *influencer marketing* industry. Influencer marketing is a method of advertising products via credible individuals with loyal social media followings whose popularity allows them to influence others on platforms such as Instagram, YouTube, Snapchat, and Facebook. The influencer marketing industry is expected to grow from $8 billion in 2019 to $22 billion by 2022.

Millennials and Gen Z consumers seem to pay particular attention to influencers. In a recent study, 72 percent reported that they follow at least some influencers. Some consumers feel that the advice of a social media influencer may be more authentic than traditional advertising since it comes from a real person. But what if the influencer is not real but instead is a *virtual* influencer? A technology startup known as Brud is one of several companies testing the idea with its computer-generated influencer, Lil Miquela.

Modern influencer marketing has been enabled by the rapid expansion of social media tools and usage, with Instagram being the influencer tool of choice. Seventy-nine percent of brands choose Instagram as the predominant tool for influencer campaigns as compared to Facebook (46 percent) and YouTube (36 percent). The currency of influence in Instagram is "likes"—the more an influencer gets, the more his or her ideas are worth.

One of the top influencers today is Miquela Sousa with over 2.6 million Instagram followers. A 19-year-old model from Downey, California, Lil Miquela (as she is sometimes known) now lives in Los Angeles where she is pursuing a music career but still finds time to hang out with celebrities like Migos and Amanda Stenberg. She is half-Spanish, half-Brazilian and has freckles, brown eyes, and hair often styled in double buns. Modeling keeps her busy: She's done gigs for fashion brands Prada, Lululemon, and Calvin Klein (posing with Bella Hadid) and has appeared in *Vogue*. You can check out her music on Spotify—each month, more than 80,000 people stream her songs.

Miquela shares openly in her Instagram posts, letting followers track her emotional ups and downs, her likes and dislikes, including her love for (and sadly, her recent breakup with) boyfriend Nick (aka "angel boi"). She also talks about saving the environment, a social cause that is important to her. But in 2018, she shared her most dramatic Instagram post in which she stated: "I am not a human being. I'm a robot."

Brud, the mysterious company that created Miquela, describes itself as a "transmedia studio that creates digital character driven story worlds." Its creations fit into the category of CGI—*computer-generated images*. The result is an extremely lifelike still or video image that can be blended with photographs or videos of humans and other real-world images (like products). Miquela may consider herself to be a robot, but in reality (so to speak), she is just a very well-crafted visual image.

If you forgot for a moment that Miquela is not real, you are not alone. One study showed that 42 percent of Gen Zers and millennials have followed a social media influencer that they did not know was a non-human. While much of Miquela's story is fake, her influence and that of similar digital creations is very real. In one study, 55 percent of 18- to 34-year-olds following a virtual influencer said that they have purchased something because of the influencer. The money that major brands pay her (or more precisely, her creators) to wear their fashions is real, too. She even has a real agency managing her—CAA; that's the same one that has represented Tom Hanks, Emma Watson, and Ryan Gosling.

Virtual influencers are an attractive option for some marketers. Real human influencers are subject to real human frailties, such as making insensitive remarks or engaging in illegal or otherwise unsavory behavior. Human endorsers may switch teams. The Verizon "Can Your Hear Me Now?" guy now pitches for Sprint. Human influencers may be reluctant to deliver a specific brand message that may not be consistent with their values or their personal brand. A virtual influencer is totally under the control of the company's storytellers, graphic designers, and programmers. The specific messages the company (or its sponsors) wants the virtual influencer to deliver can simply be programmed in, word for word. A dream spokesperson, right?

While these CGI influencers may offer marketing benefits the ability of a virtual influencer to impact consumers' decisions raises questions about the very nature of influencer marketing. While Miquela cannot be "known" because she is not human, how well do consumers "know" the human influencers who recommend products to them? Defenders of the virtual approach to influence point out that the images of human influencers are often digitally improved so that the images are less than "real." However, CGI images can produce a level of perfection that can never be attained, a real concern in an era in which body positivity is being encouraged.

Miquela is the top virtual influencer among several other digitized peers that include Shudu, Bermuda, and Blawko22. Investors in Brud believe there are opportunities for these characters to star in movies or their own Netflix shows, reminiscent of BET's show *Cita's World*, the first show to feature a virtual reality black character (named Cita) as the host. The show included a series of videos between which Cita would answer viewer mail and give her opinions on a variety of people and events. As the technology improves and images become more lifelike, real human influencers may also have a digital version of themselves that becomes an additional source of influencer marketing revenue. Whether these virtual influencers continue to grow in popularity will depend on the skills of their creators but even more on whether their followers continue to find the virtual stories they tell—and the images they project—interesting and "authentic" enough to continue to follow them.[132]

Questions for Discussion

14-40. What potential ethical issues should be considered with the use of virtual influencers? Given the young age of some of those who follow influencers such as Miquela, should sponsors be required to disclose the fact that she is not a human?

14-41. Compare the use of human influencers, virtual influencers, and traditional advertising from the standpoint of their effectiveness as promotion tools. What advantages does each uniquely offer? What are some potential risks of using each?

14-42. Many brands use non-human characters as a component of a brand promotion strategy (e.g., Mr. Clean or the GEICO gecko). How are virtual influencers the same as and/or different from these other virtual creations?

14-43. For many consumers, there is an expectation that social media posts are created by real people who identify themselves truthfully, but this is not always the case. While any company employee might be embarrassed if caught sock puppeting, if that employee is a CEO, it is illegal and can lead to prison. Should there be more guidelines for honesty in online posts? Should such guidelines be applicable to virtual influencers? Explain your answers.

Chapter **Notes**

1. Charlene Li and Josh Bernoff, *Groundswell: Winning in a World Transformed by Social Technologies* (Boston: Harvard Business School Publishing, 2008), 9.
2. "Most Popular Social Networks Worldwide as of April 2020, Ranked by Number of Active Users *(in millions)*," *Statista*, https://www.statista.com/statistics/272014/global-social-networks-ranked-by-number-of-users/ (accessed June 25, 2020).
3. *Ad Age Leading National Advertisers 2020 Fact Pack* (July 13, 2020), page 18.
4. Bradley Johnson, "In a New Milestone, the Internet Will Account for Half of Ad Spending in 2020," *Ad Age*, December 23, 2019, https://adage.com/article/datacenter/new-milestone-internet-will-account-half-ad-spending-2020/2223511 (accessed June 26, 2020).
5. S. Adam Brasel and James Gips, "Media Multitasking Behavior: Concurrent Television and Computer Usage," *Cyberpsychology, Behavior, and Social Networking* 14, no. 9 (2011): 527–534 (accessed June 24, 2020).
6. "2019 Magazine Media Factbook," The Association of Magazine Media, https://www.magazine.org/MPA/Research/MPA_Factbook/Magazine/Research_Pages/MPA_Factbook.aspx?hkey=1d597851-dd8b-455a-9dcf-4caad7688ff2 (accessed June 25, 2020).
7. Jared Newman, "Look How Far Cable TV Has Fallen," *Fast Company*, February 21, 2020, https://www.fastcompany.com/90466112/look-how-far-cable-tv-has-fallen (accessed June 26, 2020).
8. Alec Tefertiller, "Media Substitution in Cable Cord-Cutting: The Adoption of Web-Streaming Television," *Journal of Broadcasting & Electronic Media* 62, no. 3 (2018): 390–407 (accessed June 28, 2020).
9. "Coronavirus and TV viewing: Increase in Broadcast Network Viewership in the United States between the Weeks of February 17 to 21 and March 16 to 20, 2020, by Daypart," *Statista*, https://www.statista.com/statistics/1107040/broadcast-tv-viewer-increase-coronavirus-us/ (accessed June 28, 2020).
10. "90 Percent of Social Media Users Reach Out to Retailers. Why Social Media Is Your Secret Weapon," https://www.v12data.com/blog/90-percent-social-media-users-reach-out-retailers-why-social-media-your-secret-weapon/ (accessed May 16, 2018).
11. "Social Media Advertising Spending in the United States from 2017 to 2023 (in million U.S. dollars)," *Statista*, https://www.statista.com/statistics/459609/social-media-advertising-revenue-digital-market-outlook-usa/ (accessed June 28, 2020).
12. "TV Commercials," https://www.fanfiction.net/tv/TV-Commercials/ (accessed on June 26, 2020).
13. "The Most Popular Wine Glass in the Country Has Scandal to Thank," VinePair, February 26, 2015, https://vinepair.com/booze-news/popular-wine-glass-country-scandal-thank/ (accessed June 26, 2020).
14. Michael Brenner, "5 Examples of Brilliant Brand Communities That Are Shaping the Online World," *Marketing Insider Group*, May 1, 2017, https://marketinginsidergroup.com/contentmarketing/5-examples-brilliant-brand-communities-shaping-online-world/ (accessed May 12, 2018).
15. Ibid.; https://www.sephora.com/community?icid2=meganav_community_top_explorenow_110217_image.
16. "Number of Daily Active Facebook Users Worldwide as of 1st Quarter 2020 (in Millions)," *Statista*, https://www.statista.com/statistics/346167/facebook-global-dau/ (accessed June 25, 2020).
17. Garett Sloane, "Facebook Sees Its Gen Z Slipping Away to Snapchat," *Ad Age*, February 12, 2018, https://adage.com/article/digital/facebook-sees-gen-z-audience-slipping-snapchat/312330 (accessed May 17, 2018).
18. "Why Do Different Generations Use Social Media?," Marketing Charts, October 21, 2019, https://www.marketingcharts.com/digital/social-media-110652 (accessed June 29, 2020).
19. Mike Isaac and Tiffany Hsu, "Facebook Fails to Appease Organizers of Ad Boycott," *New York Times*, July 7, 2020, https://www.nytimes.com/2020/07/07/technology/facebook-ad-boycott-civil-rights.html (accessed July 15, 2020).
20. Mansoor Iqbal, "Instagram Revenue and Statistics (2020)," *Business of Apps*, June 23, 2020, https://www.businessofapps.com/data/instagram-statistics/ (accessed July 2, 2020); "Instagram – Statistics and Facts," *Statista*, May 14, 2020, https://www.statista.com/topics/1882/instagram/ (accessed June 20, 2020).
21. "Leading Instagram Usage Reasons According to Users in the United States as of 3rd Quarter 2019," *Statista*, October 9, 2019, https://www.statista.com/statistics/259484/instagram-usage-reasons-us/ (accessed July 2, 2020).
22. Margaret Abrams, "Dwayne 'The Rock' Johnson Tops the Instagram Rich List over Kylie Jenner with Estimated $1 Million for a Single Post," *Evening Standard*, July 1, 2020, https://www.standard.co.uk/insider/alist/dwayne-the-rock-johnson-tops-the-instagram-rich-list-over-kylie-jenner-a4485756.html (accessed July 2, 2020).
23. Sarah Perez, "Instagram's Latest Test Puts all Stories on One Page," *Tech Crunch*, July 1, 2020, https://techcrunch.com/2020/07/01/instagrams-latest-test-puts-all-stories-on-one-page/ (accessed July 2, 2020).
24. Mansoor Iqbal, "Instagram Revenue and Statistics (2020)," *Business of Apps*, June 23, 2020, https://www.businessofapps.com/data/instagram-statistics/ (accessed July 2, 2020).
25. J. Clement, "YouTube – Stats and Facts," *Statista*, April 8, 2020, https://www.statista.com/topics/2019/youtube/ (accessed June 29, 2020); "Unboxing," *Technopedia*, https://www.techopedia.com/definition/25549/unboxing (accessed February 14, 2020).
26. Phil Kemish, "Unboxing: The Trend Anyone Launching a Product Needs to Know . . . ," *Medium*, February 4, 2019, https://medium.com/brandtrepreneur/unboxing-the-trend-anyone-launching-a-product-needs-to-know-f0c15e1df04c (accessed June 29, 2020).
27. "The Magic Behind Unboxing on YouTube," *Think with Google*, November 2014, https://www.thinkwithgoogle.com/consumer-insights/youtube-insights-stats-data-trends-vol7/ (accessed June 29, 2020); Kalhan Rosenblatt, "It's Holiday Season, which Means Kids Are Flocking to Unboxing Videos on YouTube," *NBC News*, December 22, 2018, https://www.nbcnews.com/tech/

tech-news/it-s-holiday-season-which-means-kids-are-flocking-unboxing-n950521 (accessed February 12, 2020).

28. Natalie Robehmed and Madeline Berg, "Highest-Paid YouTube Stars 2018: Markiplier, Jake Paul, PewDiePie and More," *Forbes*, December 3, 2018, https://www.forbes.com/sites/natalierobehmed/2018/12/03/highest-paid-youtube-stars-2018-markiplier-jake-paul-pewdiepie-and-more/#5cb976e9909a (accessed June 29, 2020).

29. Sarah Perez, "44% of TikTok's All-Time Downloads Were in 2019, but App Hasn't Figured Out Monetization," *Tech Crunch*, January 16, 2020, https://techcrunch.com/2020/01/16/44-of-tiktoks-all-time-downloads-were-in-2019-but-app-hasnt-figured-out-monetization/ (accessed July 5, 2020).

30. MJ Widomska, "Want Your Brand to Be Present on TikTok? Here are Your Options," *The Drum Network*, January 20, 2020, https://www.thedrum.com/opinion/2020/01/20/want-your-brand-be-present-tiktok-here-are-your-options (accessed July 2, 2020).

31. Mansoor Iqbal, "TikTok Revenue and Usage Statistics (2020)," *Business of Apps*, June 23, 2020, https://www.businessofapps.com/data/tik-tok-statistics/ (accessed July 2, 2020); MJ Widomska, "Want Your Brand to Be Present on TikTok? Here are Your Options," *The Drum Network*, January 20, 2020, https://www.thedrum.com/opinion/2020/01/20/want-your-brand-be-present-tiktok-here-are-your-options (accessed July 2, 2020).

32. Mansoor Iqbal, "TikTok Revenue and Usage Statistics (2020)," *Business of Apps*, June 23, 2020, https://www.businessofapps.com/data/tik-tok-statistics/ (accessed July 2, 2020).

33. MJ Widomska, "Want Your Brand to Be Present on TikTok? Here are Your Options," *The Drum Network*, January 20, 2020, https://www.thedrum.com/opinion/2020/01/20/want-your-brand-be-present-tiktok-here-are-your-options (accessed July 2, 2020).

34. Warner Brothers, "Scooby Dooby Doo, Where Are You? . . . On TikTok!," May 4, 2020, https://www.warnerbros.com/news/articles/2020/05/04/scooby-dooby-doo-where-are-youon-tiktok (accessed July 5, 2020).

35. Andrew Hutchinson, "Vine Returns as 'Byte' – But Is It Too Late for a Comeback?," *Social Media Today*, April 13, 2019, https://www.socialmediatoday.com/news/vine-returns-as-byte-but-is-it-too-late-for-a-comeback/553214/ (accessed July 2, 2020).

36. Casey Newton, "Why Vine Died," *The Verge*, October 28, 2016, https://www.theverge.com/2016/10/28/13456208/why-vine-died-twitter-shutdown (accessed July 2, 2020).

37. Steven Rosenbaum, "Death of Vine Should Be a Lesson to Other Social Media Platforms," *Forbes*, November 2, 2016, https://www.forbes.com/sites/stevenrosenbaum/2016/11/02/death-vine-lesson-social-media/#4b346f339b1e (accessed July 2, 2020).

38. Maggie Tillman, "How Does Snapchat Work and What's the Point?," *Pocket-lint*, April 6, 2020, https://www.pocket-lint.com/apps/news/snapchat/131313-what-is-snapchat-how-does-it-work-and-what-is-it-used-for (accessed June 25, 2020).

39. Christina Newberry, "How to Use Snapchat: A Guide for Beginners," *Hootsuite*, January 9, 2018, https://blog.hootsuite.com/how-to-use-snapchat-beginners-guide/ (accessed June 26, 2020).

40. J. Clement, "Snapchat – Statistics & Facts," *Statista*, February 7, 2020 https://www.statista.com/topics/2882/snapchat/ (accessed June 25, 2020).

41. Joseph Yaden, "What is Twitch?," *Digital Trends*, May 6, 2020, https://www.digitaltrends.com/gaming/what-is-twitch/ (accessed July 2, 2020).

42. Corey Massey, "Gabriel and Dresden Dominate Twitch with Club Quarantine Amid COVID-19 Lockdown," *EDM Identity*, May 20, 2020, https://edmidentity.com/2020/05/20/gabriel-dresden-club-quarantine/ (accessed July 6, 2020).

43. Kim Key, "Why Twitch Is Giving Network TV Real Competition," *Screenrant*, July 1, 2020, https://screenrant.com/twitch-stream-viewer-numbers-television-ratings-higher-2020/ (accessed July 2, 2020).

44. Michael Grothaus, "Twitter Q1 2020 Earnings: mDAU Growth Explodes Thanks to 'Global Conversation Related to the COVID-19 Pandemic'," *Fast Company*, April 30, 2020, https://www.fastcompany.com/90499289/twitter-q1-2020-earnings-mdau-growth-explodes-thanks-to-global-conversation-related-to-the-covid-19-pandemic (accessed June 29, 2020).

45. Selena Larson, "Welcome to a World with 280-Character Tweets," *CNN Money*, November 7, 2017, https://money.cnn.com/2017/11/07/technology/twitter-280-character-limit/index.html (accessed May 16, 2018).

46. Stephanie Ogbogu, "How Social Media Helped Land 'Hair Love' Creator Matthew Cherry His First Oscar," *Afro Tech*, March 27, 2020, https://afrotech.com/social-media-hair-love-oscar (accessed June 29, 2020).

47. Louise Matsakis, "Zoom Not Cutting It for You? Try Exploring a Virtual World," *Wired*, May 3, 2020, https://www.wired.com/story/zoom-not-cutting-it-virtual-world-online-town/ (accessed July 6, 2020); Jack Morse, "Online Town Solves the Most Annoying Thing about Zoom Parties," *Mashable*, April 14, 2020, https://mashable.com/article/online-town-video-chat-for-groups/ (accessed July 6, 2020).

48. "Virtual Goods Are the Next Big Thing for Brands," *Vrroom*, January 10, 2020, https://vrroom.buzz/vr-news/business/virtual-goods-are-next-big-thing-brands (accessed July 6, 2020).

49. Anne Freier, "VR and AR spending up 78% in 2020," Business of Apps, December 3, 2019, https://www.businessofapps.com/news/vr-and-ar-spending-up-78-in-2020/#:~:text=Spending%20on%20virtual%20reality%20(VR,increase%20of%2078.5%25%20from%202019 (accessed October 10, 2020).

50. Nick Statt, "Fornite Keeps Stealing Dances — and No One Knows If It's Illegal," *The Verge*, December 20, 2018, https://www.theverge.com/2018/12/20/18149869/fortnite-dance-emote-lawsuit-milly-rock-floss-carlton (accessed July 6, 2020).

51. Manjit S. Yadav, Kristine De Valck, Thorsten Hennig-Thurau, Donna L. Hoffman, and Martin Spann, "Social Commerce: A Contingency Framework for Assessing Marketing Potential," *Journal of Interactive Marketing* 27, no. 4 (2013): 311–323.

52. "Social Commerce Activities According to Internet Users Worldwide as of 1st Quarter 2019, by Age Group," *Statista*, August 6, 2019, https://www.statista.com/statistics/1031962/global-social-commerce-activities-age/ (accessed June 20, 2020); Sarah Perez, "YouTube Announces a New Shoppable Ad Format," *Tech Crunch*, June 18, 2020, https://techcrunch.com/2020/06/18/youtube-announces-a-new-shoppable-ad-format/ (accessed July 2, 2020).

53. Todd Spangler, "Snapchat Announces First Shoppable Show, 'The Drop,' to Sell Limited-Edition Streetwear," *Variety*, June 23, 2020, https://variety.com/2020/digital/news/snapchat-the-drop-shoppable-show-peter-naylor-newfronts-1234644788/amp/ (accessed July 2, 2020).

54. Anthony Ha, "Facebook and Instagram Roll Out Shops, Turning Business Profiles into Storefronts," *Tech Crunch*, May 19, 2020, https://techcrunch.com/2020/05/19/facebook-shops/ (accessed July 6, 2020).

55. Andrew Hutchinson, "Snapchat Launches New Shoppable AR 'Try-On' Campaign with Gucci Shoes," *Social Media Today*, June 29, 2020, https://www.socialmediatoday.com/news/snapchat-launches-new-shoppable-ar-try-on-campaign-with-gucci-shoes/580762/ (accessed July 2, 2020).

56. Angie's List, "How It Works," https://www.angieslist.com/how-it-works.htm (accessed May 24, 2018).

57. Glassdoor, "About Us," https://www.glassdoor.com/about-us/ (accessed May 17, 2018).

58. Jeremy Bauer-Wolf, "Handshake for All," *Inside Higher Ed*, August 21, 2019, https://www.insidehighered.com/news/2019/08/21/handshake-popular-career-services-platform-now-open-all-students (accessed July 7, 2020); Tawnya, "Reviews in Handshake," Handshake Help Center, April 2020, https://support.joinhandshake.com/hc/en-us/articles/360000323168-Reviews-in-Handshake (accessed July 7, 2020).

59. Patricia Hernandez, "Pokémon Go Is Breaking Records Despite Coronavirus Limitations," *Polygon*, July 6, 2020, https://www.

polygon.com/2020/7/6/21314911/pokemon-go-coronavirus-record-player-spending-niantic-raids-fest-microtransactions-passes (accessed July 6, 2020).

60. Craig Chapple, "Pokémon GO Has Best Year Ever in 2019, Catching Nearly $900 Million in Player Spending," *Sensor Tower*, January 9, 2020, https://sensortower.com/blog/pokemon-go-has-best-year-ever-in-2019-catching-nearly-900m-usd-in-player-spending (accessed July 6, 2020).

61. Patricia Hernandez, "Pokémon Go Is Breaking Records Despite Coronavirus Limitations," *Polygon*, July 6, 2020, https://www.polygon.com/2020/7/6/21314911/pokemon-go-coronavirus-record-player-spending-niantic-raids-fest-microtransactions-passes (accessed July 6, 2020).

62. Harry McCracken, "Foursquare's First Decade, from Viral Hit to Real Business and Beyond," *Fast Company*, March 11, 2019, https://www.fastcompany.com/90318329/foursquares-first-decade-from-viral-hit-to-real-business-and-beyond (accessed June 20, 2020).

63. Karissa Bell, "Foursquare Introduces Experimental 'Hypertrending' Feature for SXSW," *Mashable*, March 8, 2019, https://mashable.com/article/foursquare-launches-hypertrending-sxsw/ (accessed June 20, 2020).

64. Todd Wasserman, "5 Creative Location-Based Campaigns for Small Businesses to Learn From," *Mashable*, https://mashable.com/2011/06/21/small-business-foursquare-scvngr (accessed May 24, 2018).

65. Anne Freier, "A Look at Gen Z Mobile Behaviors – 64% of Mobile Users Are Always Connected," *Business of Apps*, June 19, 2019, https://www.businessofapps.com/news/a-look-at-gen-z-mobile-behaviours-64-of-mobile-users-are-always-connected/ (accessed June 29, 2020).

66. Brenda Stolyar, "The Best iPhone Apps Available Right Now," *Digital Trends*, May 10, 2018, https://www.digitaltrends.com/mobile/best-iphone-apps/5/ (accessed May 24, 2018).

67. Josh Constine, "Snapchat Launches Bitmoji TV: Zany 4-Min Cartoons of Your Avatar," *Tech Crunch*, January 30, 2020, https://techcrunch.com/2020/01/30/bitmoji-tv/ (accessed July 7, 2020).

68. Michael Grothaus, "If You Value Your Privacy, Switch to Signal as Your Messaging App Now," *Fast Company*, April 19, 2019, https://www.fastcompany.com/90335034/if-you-value-your-privacy-switch-to-signal-as-your-messaging-app-now (accessed July 7, 2020).

69. Education Help, "What Are the Different Events of Story?" *Medium*, September 16, 2016, https://medium.com/@english_grammar/what-are-the-different-elements-of-story-e16bddae98d6 (accessed July 7, 2020); James Gilmore, "Short Form Storytelling, Part 1: One Story, One Idea," *Story Science*, October 25, 2013, https://storysci.com/2013/10/25/short-form-storytelling-part-1-one-story-one-idea/ (accessed July 7, 2020); Matthew Woodget, "Mastering the Art of Short-Form Storytelling," *Go Narrative*, November 5, 2019, https://www.gonarrative.com/blog/2019/11/5/mastering-the-art-of-short-form-storytelling (accessed July 7, 2020); Paula Kupfer, "Perspective: The Art of Short Form Storytelling: Vine, Snapchat, To.be & Gifs | #ICPMeetup," *ICP*, January 20, 2016, https://www.icp.org/perspective/the-art-of-short-form-storytelling-vine-snapchat-tobe-gifs-icpmeetup (accessed July 2, 2020).

70. Applebee's, "For the 12th Consecutive Year, Applebee's Honors Veterans and Active-Duty Military with Free Entrée," November 4, 2019, https://www.businesswire.com/news/home/20191104005030/en/Applebees%C2%AE-Restaurants-Nationwide-to-Serve-Free-Meals-in-Honor-of-Veterans-Day (accessed October 10, 2020).

71. "2K17 Valassis Coupon Intelligence Report," http://intelligence.valassis.com/rs/275-QRU-089/images/PDF-Coupon-Intelligence-Report.pdf (accessed July 18, 2018).

72. "Consumers' Preferred Sources of Coupons and Discounts in the United States in 2019," *Statista*, https://www.statista.com/statistics/995532/consumers-preferred-sources-coupons-discounts-us/ (accessed June 28, 2020).

73. Michael Fielding, "C'est Délicieux," *Marketing News*, September 15, 2010, 10.

74. Bobbi Dempsey, "How Mail-In Rebates Rip You Off," *Investopedia*, June 25, 2019, https://www.investopedia.com/financial-edge/0810/how-mail-in-rebates-rip-you-off.aspx (accessed July 6, 2020).

75. James Herring, "Kellogg's Turns Packaging Black and White to Make Breakfast More Creative," *Famous Campaigns*, July 11, 2019, https://www.famouscampaigns.com/2019/07/kelloggs-turns-packaging-black-and-white-to-make-breakfast-more-creative/ (accessed July 6, 2020).

76. Dale Buss, "Super Bowl Ad Watch: With Space Trips, Axe Strives for 'Something That's Epic,'" January 23, 2013, www.brandchannel.com/home/post/2013/01/23/SuperBowl-ApolloUpdate.aspx (accessed June 27, 2014).

77. General Mills, "Cheerios Serves Spoonfuls of Stories for the 11th Year to Get Books into the Hands of Children," PR Newswire, April 25, 2013, https://www.prnewswire.com/news-releases/cheerios-serves-spoonfuls-of-stories-for-the-11th-year-to-get-books-into-the-hands-of-children-204701591.html (accessed October 10, 2020).

78. "Get Creative with In-Store Sampling," *NACS*, May 13, 2020, https://www.convenience.org/Media/Daily/2020/May/13/3-Get-Creative-With-In-Store-Sampling_Marketing (accessed July 7, 2020).

79. Eric J. Savitz, "Big Trade Shows Have All Been Canceled. Why They May Never Come Back," *Barron's*, June 26, 2020, https://www.barrons.com/articles/apple-dazzled-with-wwdc-event-why-virtual-trade-shows-could-be-the-future-51593210508 (accessed June 29, 2020).

80. U.S. Bureau of Labor Statistics, *Occupational Outlook Handbook*, December 17, 2015, https://www.bls.gov/ooh/home.htm (accessed May 24, 2018).

81. Quoted in Jaclyn Fierman, "The Death and Rebirth of the Salesman," *Fortune*, July 25, 1994, 88.

82. "Average Cost of a 30-Second Commercial on TV in the United States from 2014 to 2019 (in U.S. Dollars)," *Statista*, https://www.statista.com/statistics/302200/primetime-tv-cost-commercial-usa/ (accessed June 29, 2020).

83. Salesforce, https://www.salesforce.com (accessed May 24, 2018).

84. Mansoor Iqbal, "Zoom Revenue and Usage Statistics (2020)," *Business of Apps*, June 23, 2020, https://www.businessofapps.com/data/zoom-statistics/ (accessed June 29, 2020).

85. Olga Khazan, "Work from Home Is Here to Stay," *The Atlantic*, May 4, 2020, https://www.theatlantic.com/health/archive/2020/05/work-from-home-pandemic/611098/ (accessed July 6, 2020).

86. Mark W. Johnston and Greg W. Marshall, *Sales Force Management, Leadership, Innovation, Technology*, 12th ed. (New York: Routledge, Taylor & Francis, 2016).

87. Adapted from Mitchell Schnurman, "The Game-Changing Reality of Virtual Sales Pitches," *Star-Telegram*, April 9, 2010, www.startelegram.com/2010/04/09/2103717_p2/the-game-changing-reality-ofvirtual.html (accessed May 1, 2010).

88. Regis Crawford, "What Is Social Selling and How Does it Work?" *Salesforce Blog*, April 2, 2019, https://www.salesforce.com/blog/2017/08/guide-to-social-selling.html (accessed July 6, 2020).

89. Christina Newberry, "Social Selling: What It Is, Why You Should Care, and How to Do It Right," *Hootsuite*, April 23, 2019, https://blog.hootsuite.com/what-is-social-selling/ (accessed July 2, 2020). Emma Brudner, "The Sales Playbook to Social Selling," *Hubspot*, October 29, 2019, https://blog.hubspot.com/sales/sales-professionals-guide-to-social-selling (accessed July 2, 2020).

90. Lynne Zaledonts, "3 Sales Trends to Watch in 2018," *Salesforce Blog*, January 31. 2018, https://www.salesforce.com/blog/2018/01/sales-trends-for-2018.html (accessed May 25, 2018).

91. Jana, "4 Sales Trends of 2020 and How They'll Shape the Market," *Medium*, December 25, 2019, https://medium.com/salesrocksblog/4-sales-trends-of-2020-and-how-theyll-shape-the-market-8b18c36d714d (accessed June 29, 2020).

92. Lilach Bullock, "4 Sales Trends That You Need to Know About in 2019," *Forbes*, December 3, 2018, https://www.forbes.com/sites/lilachbullock/2018/12/03/4-sales-trends-that-you-need-to-know-about-in-2019/#f771cd428573 (accessed June 29, 2020).

93. Max Altschuler, "10 Sales Trends & Predictions for the Future of Sales in 2020," *Sales Hacker*, December 18, 2019, https://www.saleshacker.com/sales-trends-predictions-2020/ (accessed June 29, 2020).

94. Dan C. Weilbaker, "The Identification of Selling Abilities Needed for Missionary Type Sales," *Journal of Personal Selling & Sales Management* 10 (Summer 1990): 45–58.

95. Derek A. Newton, *Sales Force Performance and Turnover* (Cambridge, MA: Marketing Science Institute, 1973), 3.

96. Mark W. Johnston and Greg W. Marshall, *Relationship Selling*, 3rd ed. (Boston: McGraw-Hill, 2010).

97. Greg W. Marshall, Daniel J. Goebel, and William C. Moncrief, "Hiring for Success at the Buyer-Seller Interface," *Journal of Business Research* 56 (April 2003): 247–255.

98. David Aldridge, "NBA, NBPA Taking Steps to Further Address Mental Wellness Issues for Players," *NBA*, March 12, 2018, https://www.nba.com/article/2018/03/12/morning-tip-nba-nbpa-addressing-mental-wellness-issues (accessed May 24, 2018).

99. Kate Fitzgerald, "Homemade Bikini Contest Hits Bars, Beach for 10th Year," *Advertising Age*, April 13, 1998, 18.

100. Ronn Torossian, "The Biggest PR Crises Of 2017," *Forbes*, May 23, 2017, https://www.forbes.com/sites/forbesagencycouncil/2017/05/23/the-biggest-pr-crises-of-2017/#5b0f301c50a8 (accessed May 24, 2018).

101. Rich Thomaselli, "PR Response Has Been Swift and Active, but Test Will Come When Ship Finally Docks," *Ad Age*, February 14, 2013, https://adage.com/article/news/carnival-cruises-pr-response-triumph-crisis/239819 (accessed June 20, 2014).

102. Mark Prigg, "Amazon's Drone Dreams Come Crashing Down, U.S. Regulators Ban Package Delivery Services Using 'Model Aircraft,'" *Daily Mail*, June 24, 2014, https://www.dailymail.co.uk/sciencetech/article-2668411/Amazons-drone-dreams-comecrashing-USregulators-ban-package-delivery-services-usingmodel-aircraft.html#ixzz35rMKW4VF (accessed June 30, 2014).

103. Jillian D'Onfro, "Amazon's New Delivery Drone Will Start Shipping Packages 'in a Matter of Months,'" *Forbes*, June 5, 2019, https://www.forbes.com/sites/jilliandonfro/2019/06/05/amazon-new-delivery-drone-remars-warehouse-robots-alexa-prediction/#57094cc4145f (accessed July 6, 2020).

104. Andy Pasztor, "FAA Ruling on Long-Haul Routes Would Boost Boeing's Designs," *Wall Street Journal*, June 5, 2006, A3.

105. Amy Chozick, "Star Power: The LPGA Is Counting on a New Marketing Push to Take Women's Golf to the Next Level," *Wall Street Journal*, June 12, 2006, R6.

106. Shannon Prather, "Identity Crisis: Brooklyn Park Hires PR Firm to Improve Its Reputation," *Star Tribune*, April 8, 2014, https://www.startribune.com/local/north/254292091.html#FLeReIJRQyImAWVq.97 (accessed June 24, 2014).

107. K.T. Bradford, "HP Face Tracking Software Not Racist, Just Contrast Challenged," *LaptopMag*, December 21, 2009, https://www.laptopmag.com/articles/hp-webcam (accessed June 24, 2020)

108. ESP Sponsorship Report, "Signs Point to Healthy Sponsorship Spending in 2018," January 8, 2018, http://www.sponsorship.com/Report/2018/01/08/Signs-Point-To-Healthy-Sponsorship-Spending-In-201.aspx (accessed May 24, 2018).

109. John D. Stoll, "Corporate Activism Gets Its Day. Ben & Jerry's Has Been at It for Decades," *Wall Street Journal*, June 5, 2020, https://www.wsj.com/articles/corporate-activism-gets-its-day-ben-jerrys-has-been-at-it-for-decades-11591365921 (accessed June 24, 2020); Ben & Jerry's, "Issues We Care About," https://www.benjerry.com/values/issues-we-care-about (accessed June 24, 2020).

110. Allan R. Andreasen, "Social Marketing: Its Definition and Domain," *Journal of Public Policy & Marketing* 13, 1 (March 1994): 108–114.

111. "SXSW 2014: Sponsors Going All In," FleishmanHillard, February 25, 2014, https://fleishmanhillard.com/2014/02/social-innovation/sxsw-2014-sponsors-go-all-in/ (accessed October 10, 2020).

112. Jeremy Gutsche, "The Dirty Clothes Bus," May 17, 2006, Trend Hunter, https://www.trendhunter.com/trends/the-dirty-clothes-bus (accessed October 10, 2020).

113. Tamar Weinbert, *The New Community Rules: Marketing on the Social Web* (Sebastopol, CA: O'Reilly Media, 2009).

114. Campaign Asia, "Case Study: Burger King's Wallet Drop Stunt Creates Online Buzz in Singapore," July 22, 2010, www.campaignasia.com/agencyportfolio/CaseStudyCampaign/220642,casestudyburger-kings-wallet-drop-guerilla-stunt-creates-onlinebuzz-insingapore.aspx#.U6jGlKhKvDk (accessed June 23, 2014).

115. Quoted in Michelle Kessler, "IBM Graffiti Ads Gain Notoriety," February 6, 2002, http://usatoday30.usatoday.com/tech/news/2001-04-25-ibm-linux-graffiti.htm (accessed May 24, 2018).

116. Lois Geller, "Wow—What a Buzz," *Target Marketing*, June 2005, 21.

117. Natasha Salmon, "Revealed: Watch the TRUTH behind Viral 'Cheater' Spray Painted Range Rover Left Outside Harrods," Mirror.com (*Daily Mirror*), May 15, 2016, http://www.mirror.co.uk/news/uk-news/revealed-watch-truth-behind-viral-7972090 (accessed May 16, 2016).

118. Matthew Creamer, "In Era of Consumer Control, Marketers Crave the Potency of Word-of-Mouth," *Advertising Age*, November 28, 2005, 32.

119. Paul Marsden, "F-Commerce: Heinz Innovates with New 'Tryvertising' F-Store," *Digital Wellbeing*, March 8, 2011, https://digitalwellbeing.org/f-commerce-heinz-innovate-with-new-tryvertising-f-store-screenshots/ (accessed June 23, 2014).

120. Todd Wasserman, "Blogs Cause Word-of-Mouth Business to Spread Quickly," *Brandweek*, October 3, 2005, 9.

121. Pano Mourdoukoutas, "Good Buzz, Bad Buzz Brand Management: A Social Media Strategy That Pays Off," *Forbes*, November 7, 2013, www.forbes.com/sites/panosmourdoukoutas/2013/11/07/good-buzz-bad-buzz-brand-management-a-social-media-strategy-that-pays-off (accessed June 18, 2014).

122. Tamantha Gunn, "NBA to Host #ClubQuarantine with DJ D-Nice on Instagram Live," *Revolt*, March 27, 2020, https://www.revolt.tv/2020/3/27/21197456/nba-host-club-quarantine-dj-d-nice-instagram-live (accessed June 24, 2020); Martin Berrios, "Club Quarantine: DJ D-Nice Launches Homeschool Playlist on Spotify," *Hip Hop Wired*, March 26, 2020, https://hiphopwired.com/848446/dj-d-nice-homeschool-spotify/ (accessed June 24, 2020).

123. James Gleick, "What Defines a Meme?," *Smithsonian Magazine*, May 2011, https://www.smithsonianmag.com/arts-culture/what-defines-a-meme-1904778/ (accessed June 29, 2020).

124. Michelle Greenwald, "How Memes Help and Hurt Brands: Maximizing the Upside and Minimizing the Downside," *Forbes*, March 14, 2019, https://www.forbes.com/sites/michellegreenwald/2019/03/14/how-memes-are-helping-and-hurting-brands-maximizing-the-upside-and-minimize-the-downside/#71a4b0162a1a (accessed June 29, 2020); Kevan Lee, "The Meme-ification of Instagram," *Buffer*, June 13, 2019, https://buffer.com/resources/the-meme-ification-of-instagram/ (accessed June 29, 2020); Ben Tobin, "IHOP Changes Name Back from IHOb," *USA Today*, July 9, 2018, https://www.usatoday.com/story/money/2018/07/09/ihop-changes-name-back-ihob/769310002/ (accessed June 29, 2020).

125. Janée N. Burkhalter, Natalie T. Wood, and Stephanie A. Tryce, "Clear, Conspicuous, and Concise: Disclosures and Twitter Word-of-Mouth," *Business Horizons* (May 2014), 57(3):319–28.

126. Stephanie Strom, "Nonprofit Punishes a 2nd Founder for Ruse," *New York Times*, January 15, 2008, https://www.nytimes.com/2008/01/15/us/15givewell.html (accessed January 15, 2008); Ross D. Petty and J. Craig Andrews, "Covert Marketing Unmasked: A Legal and Regulatory Guide for Practices That Mask Marketing Messages," *Journal of Public Policy & Marketing* (Spring 2008): 7–18; Brian Morrissey, "'Influencer Programs' Likely to Spread," *Adweek*, March 2, 2009, http://www.adweek.

com/news/advertising-branding/influencer-programs-likely-spread-98542 (accessed March 2, 2009); Katie Hafner, "Seeing Corporate Fingerprints in Wikipedia Edits," *New York Times*, August 19, 2007, https://www.nytimes.com/2007/08/19/technology/19wikipedia.html (accessed August 19, 2007); Brian Bergstein, "New Tool Mines: Wikipedia Trustworthiness Software Analyzes Reputations of the Contributors Responsible for Entries," *NBC News*, September 5, 2007, http://www.nbcnews.com/id/20604175/ns/technology_and_science-tech_and_gadgets/t/new-tool-mines-wikipedia-trustworthiness/#.X32ETZNKh0s (accessed September 5, 2007).

127. Todd Wasserman, "Word Games," *Brandweek*, April 24, 2006, 24.

128. Mary Emily O'Hara, "Wendy's Promised to 'Amplify Black Voices' on Twitter Then Ghosted. What Went Wrong?" *Adweek*, June 17, 2020, https://www.adweek.com/brand-marketing/wendys-promised-to-amplify-black-voices-on-twitter-then-ghosted-what-went-wrong/ (accessed June 24, 2020).

129. Mansoor Iqbal, "LinkedIn Usage and Revenue Statistics (2020)," *Business of Apps*, June 23, 2020, https://www.businessofapps.com/data/linkedin-statistics/ (accessed June 29, 2020).

130. Paige Cooper, "20 LinkedIn Statistics That Matter to Marketers in 2020," *Hootsuite*, March 9, 2020, https://blog.hootsuite.com/linkedin-statistics-business/ (accessed June 29, 2020).

131. Paula Forbes, "Taco Bell Says Their Meat Is 88% Beef, Not 36%", *Eater*, https://www.eater.com/2011/1/27/6699949/taco-bell-says-their-meat-is-88-beef-not-36 (accessed November 24, 2020).

132. Based on: Calum Chace, "The Impact of Artificial Intelligence on Influencer Marketing," *Forbes*, June 22, 2020, https://www.forbes.com/sites/cognitiveworld/2020/06/22/the-impact-of-artificial-intelligence-on-influencer-marketing/#35abc53317a2; Amine Rahal, "Is Influencer Marketing Worth It in 2020?" *Forbes*, January 10, 2020, https://www.forbes.com/sites/theyec/2020/01/10/is-influencer-marketing-worth-it-in-2020/#464031c531c5 (accessed August 19, 2020); Morning Consult, "The Influencer Report: Engaging Gen Z and Millennials," https://morningconsult.com/wp-content/uploads/2019/11/The-Influencer-Report-Engaging-Gen-Z-and-Millennials.pdf (accessed August 15, 2020); Audrey Schomer, "Influencer Marketing: State of the Social Media Influencer Market in 2020," *Business Insider*, December 17, 2019, https://www.businessinsider.com/influencer-marketing-report; Laura Forman and Lauren Silva Laughlin, "Instagram's Changes Could Leave Influencers Heartbroken," *Wall Street Journal*, August 16, 2019, https://www.wsj.com/articles/instagrams-changes-could-leave-influencers-heartbroken-11565947801; lilmiquela, Instagram, https://www.instagram.com/lilmiquela/?hl=en (accessed August 15, 2020); Time Staff, "The 25 Most Influential People on the Internet," *Time*, June 20, 2018, https://time.com/5324130/most-influential-internet/; Anne Steland, "Top 20 Virtual Influencers – Understanding the Latest Trend and 10 Great Examples," *Influencer Marketing Cloud*, September 23, 2019, https://influencerdb.com/blog/top-10-virtual-influencers/; Kaya Yurieff, "Instagram Star Isn't What She Seems. But Brands Are Buying In," *CNN*, June 25, 2018, https://money.cnn.com/2018/06/25/technology/lil-miquela-social-media-influencer-cgi/index.html; Sheryl Garratt, "Don't Envy This Instagram Influencer," *Medium*, October 24, 2019, https://medium.com/creative-living/influencer-miquela-sousa-has-1-6-million-followers-on-instagram-8ecfb2584fb6; Tiffany Hsu, "These Influencers Aren't Flesh and Blood, Yet Millions Follow Them," *New York Times*, June 17, 2019, https://www.nytimes.com/2019/06/17/business/media/miquela-virtual-influencer.html; Brud, Brud Corporate Website, http://www.brud.fyi/ (accessed August 15, 2020); Colin and Samir, "The Curious Case of Lil Miquela," *YouTube*, November 13, 2019, https://www.youtube.com/watch?v=i4rwlQ7IA1U (accessed August 15, 2020); Mukta Chowdhary, "Bot or Not? Exploring the Rise of CGI Influencers," *Fullscreen*, January 30, 2019, https://fullscreen.com/2019/01/30/bot-or-not-exploring-the-rise-of-cgi-influencers/; Alex Dudok de Wit, "From the Uncanny Valley to Hollywood: Miquela is CAA's First Virtual Being Client," *Cartoon Brew*, May 7, 2020, https://www.cartoonbrew.com/business/from-the-uncanny-valley-to-hollywood-miquela-is-caas-first-cartoon-client-191055.html; Annlee Ellingson, "CAA Clients Like Vin Diesel and Jennifer Aniston Dominate Highest-Paid Actors List," *L. A. Biz*, August 23, 2017, https://www.bizjournals.com/losangeles/news/2017/08/23/caa-clients-like-vin-disel-and-emma-stone-dominate.html; Ruth Reader, "Cult Beauty Brand SK-II's New Spokesperson Is a Total Fake," *Fast Company*, June 18, 2019, https://www.fastcompany.com/90364120/cult-skincare-line-sk-iis-new-spokesperson-yumi-is-so-fake?utm_source=postup&utm_medium=email&utm_campaign=tech-forecast&position=8&partner=newsletter&campaign_date=12212019; Sarah Penny, "Virtual Influencers Might Be Easier to Mould But They're Not Necessarily a Safer Option," *Xeim*, March 27, 2019, https://www.marketingweek.com/virtual-influencers/; Kaitlyn Tiffany, "Lil Miquela and the Virtual Influencer Hype, Explained," *Vox*, June 3, 2019, https://www.vox.com/the-goods/2019/6/3/18647626/instagram-virtual-influencers-lil-miquela-ai-startups;[1] Yoree Koh and Georgia Wells, "The Making of a Computer-Generated Influencer," *Wall Street Journal*, December 13, 2018, https://www.wsj.com/articles/the-making-of-a-computer-generated-influencer-11544702401; Miranda Katz, "CGI 'Influencers' Like Lil Miquela Are About to Flood Your Feeds," *Wired*, May 1, 2018, https://www.wired.com/story/lil-miquela-digital-humans/.

Marketing Plan: The S&S Smoothie Company

This sample marketing plan includes the typical content you should include in all marketing plans. The Executive Summary comes first (highlighted here in gray), followed by the various sections of the plan, beginning with the Situation Analysis. Note that in the margins, there are a number of notes to provide guidance as you develop your own marketing plan. Also, the relevant book part for each section is referenced.

Executive Summary

Situation Analysis

S&S Smoothie Company is a relatively young business that produces fruit-and-yogurt–based beverages that offer superior flavor and nutritional content and are enhanced with unique packaging. Within the United States, S&S has targeted a consumer market of younger, health-conscious, upscale consumers who frequent gyms and health clubs and two broad reseller markets: (1) gyms and health clubs and (2) smaller upscale food markets. S&S distributes its products through manufacturers' agents in the United States, Canada, and the United Kingdom and through Internet sales. An analysis of the internal and external environments indicates the firm enjoys important strengths in its product, employees, and reputation, while weaknesses are apparent in its limited size, financial resources, and product capabilities. S&S faces a supportive external environment, highlighted by a growing interest in healthy living and limited threats, primarily from potential competitive growth.

Marketing Objectives

The S&S marketing objectives are

1. To increase awareness of S&S Smoothies from 20 percent of the target market to 50 percent within the next 12 months

2. To grow the percentage of the target market who have tried the product from 10 percent to 15 percent within the next 12 months

3. To increase gross sales of S&S Smoothies by 40 percent within the next 12 months

4. To increase channels of distribution to include three new organizational customer segments

5. To introduce two new product lines over the next three years, including:

   - A line of smoothies with unique gourmet flavors
   - A line of low-carb smoothies

Marketing Strategies

To accomplish its growth goals, S&S will direct its marketing activities toward the following strategies:

1. *Target Market Strategy:* S&S will continue to target its existing consumer markets while expanding its organizational markets to include hotels and resorts, golf and tennis clubs, and university campuses.

2. *Positioning Strategy:* S&S will continue to position its products as great-tasting fun beverages that are designed for the modern, health-conscious consumer.

3. *Product Strategy:* S&S will introduce two new product lines, each identifiable through unique packaging and labeling:
   a. *S&S Smoothie Gold:* A product similar to the original S&S Smoothie beverages but in six unique, fun flavors identified with quirky names that create smiles.
   b. *Low-Carb S&S Smoothie:* A product made with kale (the superfood), yogurt, and fruit that has 50 percent fewer grams of carbohydrates. This product is expected to be popular with people who follow the very popular ketogenic diet.

4. *Pricing Strategy:* S&S will maintain the current pricing strategy for existing and new products.

5. *Promotion Strategy:* S&S will augment current personal selling efforts with a strong emphasis on digital, social media, and mobile advertising strategies. Targeted television and magazine advertising will be carefully planned for maximum impact. S&S will also sponsor marathons in major cities accompanied by a sampling program. In order to take maximum advantage of the introduction of the new S&S products, consumers will be invited to participate in a product/flavor-naming contest using social media belonging to S&S.

6. *Supply Chain Strategy:* S&S will expand its distribution network to include the organizational markets targeted. In addition, to encourage a high level of inventory in larger health clubs, S&S Smoothie will offer free refrigerated display units.

Implementation and Control

The Action Plan details how the marketing strategies will be implemented, including the individual(s) responsible, the timing, and the budget necessary for each activity. The measurement and control strategies provide a means of measuring the success of the plan.

PART ONE

S&S Smoothie Marketing Plan

Situation Analysis

The S&S Smoothie Company* was founded in September 2015 in New York with distribution of the product beginning in early 2016. The company's goal is to create and market healthy smoothie beverages to health-conscious consumers. S&S Smoothie expects to take advantage of an increasing desire for healthy foods both in the United States and internationally—and to ride the wave of consumer interest in low-carb alternatives. Although there are other companies both large and small that compete in this market, S&S Smoothie feels it has the expertise to create and market superior products that will appeal to its target market.

If you are developing a marketing plan for your class project, you may have the options of using a real company; an imaginary company that has been in business for a while, such as S&S Smoothie; or an imaginary new business that has never been in the market. Depending on which you choose, your marketing plan will have some differences. For example, if you use an existing firm, you will have to find accurate information about the company for the situation analysis. If you have a fictitious company, you will have to create that information based on logical thinking. In this case, we have chosen to create an imaginary business.

* S&S Smoothie Company is a fictitious company created to illustrate a sample marketing plan.

Internal Environment

Mission Statement

The S&S Smoothie Company's mission drives its strategic direction and actions:

> S&S Smoothie seeks to meet the needs of discriminating, health-conscious consumers for high-quality, superior-tasting smoothie beverages and other similar products.

Organizational Structure

As an entrepreneurial company, S&S Smoothie has a simple organizational structure. Key personnel include the following:

- Patrick Haynes, founder and co-president. Haynes is responsible for the creation, design, packaging, and production management of all S&S Smoothie products.

- William "Bill" Sartens, founder and co-president. Sartens is responsible for international and domestic distribution and marketing.

- Allyson Humphries, chief financial officer. Humphries develops financial strategy and keeps the company's books.

- Alex Johnson, national sales manager. Johnson is responsible for maintaining the sales force of independent sales reps. He also advises on product development.

- Bob LeMay, Pam Sartens, and Paul Sartens, shareholders. Next to Patrick Haynes and William Sartens, Bob, Pam, and Paul own the largest number of shares. They consult and sit on the company's board of directors. Bob is a lawyer and also provides legal services.

Corporate Culture

S&S Smoothie is an entrepreneurial organization. Thus, a key element of the internal environment is a culture that encourages innovation, risk taking, and individual creativity. The company's beginning was based on a desire to provide a unique, superior product, and company decisions have consistently emphasized this mission.

Current Products

The original S&S Smoothie product, introduced in early 2016, is a fruit-and-yogurt–based beverage that contains only natural ingredients (no additives) and is high in essential nutrients. Because of the company's patented production process, S&S Smoothie beverages do not have to be refrigerated and have a shelf life of more than a year. Therefore, the product can be shipped and delivered via nonrefrigerated carriers. As a producer of dairy-based beverages, S&S Smoothie's North American Industry Classification System (NAICS) classification is 311511, Fluid Milk Manufacturers.

At present, the single product line is the S&S Smoothie fruit-and-yogurt beverage. This healthy beverage product has a flavor and nutritional content that makes it superior to competing products. The present product comes in five flavors: strawberry, blueberry, banana, peach, and cherry. S&S offers each in a 12-ounce and a 20-ounce size. S&S packages the product in a unique hourglass-shaped, frosted glass bottle with a screw-off cap. The bottle design makes the product easy to hold, even with sweaty hands after workouts. The frosted glass allows the color of the beverage to be seen, but at the same time it communicates an upscale image. The labeling and lid visually denote the flavor with an appropriate color. Labeling includes complete nutritional information. In the future, S&S Smoothie plans to expand its line of products to grow its market share in the health drink market.

Current Markets

The consumer market for S&S Smoothie products is made up of anyone who is interested in healthy food and a healthy lifestyle. Although according to published research, nearly 70 percent of American consumers say they are interested in living a healthy lifestyle, the

For our imaginary young firm, we have decided that the company is already producing a single product. If you have a new firm, there would be no new products, so this section including the discussion of current products, pricing, sales, and distribution would not exist. You will probably want to include a statement to this effect. If you are using a "real" firm, you will need to find accurate information about that firm. (Be sure to cite your sources for that information.)

number of those who actually work to achieve that goal is much smaller. It is estimated that approximately 80 million Americans actually engage in exercise or follow nutritional plans that would be described as healthy. As experts expect the trend toward healthier living to grow globally, the domestic market and the international market for S&S Smoothie products are expected to expand for some time.

Pricing

The suggested retail prices for S&S Smoothie beverages are $4.00 for the 12-ounce size and $6.00 for the 20-ounce container. S&S's prices to distributors are $1.20 and $1.80, respectively. At present, S&S Smoothie outsources actual production of the product. Still, the company takes care to oversee the entire production process to ensure consistent quality of its unique product. With this method of production, variable costs for the 12-ounce S&S Smoothie beverages are $0.63, and variable costs for the 20-ounce size are $0.71.

Customers/Sales

Sales of S&S Smoothie products showed increasing growth through 2019 because of improving U.S. and world economic conditions. Actual sales figures for 2016 through 2020 are shown in Table A.1. Sales for 2020 were significantly lower than predicted sales of $2.8 million for the year due to the economic and social problems created by the COVID-19 pandemic.

Even if you are using an existing firm in your project, sales figures may not be available. Check with your instructor and ask if he or she would like for you to create sales records based on some logical assumptions.

These sales figures plus S&S customer research show a strong and growing loyal customer base. This customer asset is important to the future of S&S. Nevertheless, research indicates that only about 20 percent of all consumers in the target market are aware of the S&S brand.

Within the U.S. consumer market, S&S Smoothie targets upscale consumers who frequent gyms and health clubs. Based on research conducted by S&S Smoothie, these consumers are primarily younger; however, there is also an older segment that seeks to be physically fit and that also patronizes health clubs.

Table A.1	Company Sales Performance
Year	Gross Sales
2016	$187,850
2017	$572,146
2018	$911,445
2019	$1,686,228
2020	$1,415,120

Distribution

To reach its target market, S&S Smoothie places primary distribution emphasis on gyms, health clubs, other physical fitness facilities, and upscale specialty food markets. The company began developing channel relationships with these outlets through individual contacts by company personnel. As sales developed, the company solicited the services of manufacturers' agents and specialty food distributors. Manufacturers' agents are individuals who sell products for a number of different noncompeting manufacturers. By contracting with these agents in various geographic regions, the company can expand its product distribution to a significant portion of the United States and Canada. Similar arrangements with agents in the United Kingdom have allowed it to begin distribution in that country.

The company handles large accounts, such as Gold's Gym and World Gyms directly. Although total sales to these chains are fairly substantial, when considering the large number of facilities within each chain, the sales are very small with much room for growth. It has been suggested that S&S might consider expanding distribution to additional new channels based on the success of the current expansion. Under consideration are supermarkets that have special gourmet and healthy food sections.

The Internet is a secondary channel for S&S Smoothie. While online sales accounted for only about 5 percent of S&S Smoothie sales through 2019, in 2020, that portion increased to 25 percent due to the pandemic. Although this channel is useful for individuals who wish to purchase S&S Smoothie products in larger quantities, S&S does not expect that online sales will become a significant part of the business in the near future.

External Environment

Competitive Environment

S&S Smoothie faces several different levels of competition. Direct competitors are companies that also market smoothie-type beverages and include the following:

1. Franchise smoothie retail operations

2. Online-only smoothie outlets

3. Other smaller manufacturers

4. Larger companies, such as Nestlé, that produce similar products

   Indirect competition comes from the following:

1. Homemade smoothie drinks made from powders sold in retail outlets and over the Internet

2. Homemade smoothie drinks made using a multitude of available recipes

3. Other healthy beverages, such as juices

4. A growing number of energy drinks that are especially popular with younger consumers

Economic Environment

S&S Smoothie first introduced its products to the market early in 2016. The recession of 2007 was officially over in 2009. By 2015, economists saw the strongest economy since 2005 suggesting there were strong growth opportunities for a variety of sectors of the economy.

Technological Environment

Because S&S Smoothie produces a simple food product, technological advances have minimal impact on the firm's operations. Nevertheless, the use of current technology enables and enhances many of the company's activities. For example, S&S Smoothie uses the Internet to enhance its operations in two ways. As noted previously, the Internet provides an additional venue for sales. In addition, manufacturers' agents and channel members can keep in contact with the company, allowing for fewer problems with deliveries, orders, and so on. Finally, in recent years, the company has established a presence on social media sites such as Facebook and Twitter through which it can communicate with consumers in a more personal way while monitoring consumers' feedback communication. Digital and social media advertising is a growing part of the company's marketing communication program.

Political and Legal Environment

Because they are advertised as nutritional products, all S&S Smoothie products must be approved by the Food and Drug Administration (FDA). Labeling must include ingredients and nutritional information, also regulated by the FDA. In addition, S&S Smoothie products are regulated by the U.S. Department of Agriculture.

Although there are no specific regulations about labeling or advertising products as low-carb, there is potential for such regulations to come into play in the future. In addition, there are numerous regulations that are country-specific in current and prospective global markets of which the company must constantly remain aware. Any future advertising campaigns developed by S&S Smoothie will have to conform to regulatory guidelines both in the United States and internationally.

For most of the discussion of the external environment, you should use accurate data that you normally can find on the Web. (Be sure to cite your sources for that information.) For other parts of this discussion, you may not be able to find real data and will need to create the section based on some logical assumptions.

Sociocultural Environment

S&S Smoothies uses marketing research to monitor the consumer environment. This research shows that changing cultural values and norms continue to provide an important opportunity for S&S Smoothie. The trend toward healthy foods and a healthier lifestyle has grown dramatically for the past decade or longer. In response to this, the number of health clubs across the country and the number of independent resorts and spas that offer patrons a healthy vacation experience have grown. In addition, many travelers demand that hotels offer health club facilities.

During the past decade, consumers around the globe have become aware of the advantages of a low-carbohydrate diet. Low-carb menu items abound in restaurants, including fast-food chains such as McDonald's. A vast number of low-carb foods, including low-carb candy, fill supermarket shelves.

There are approximately 125 million American adults aged 15 to 44. Demographers project that this age group will remain stable for the foreseeable future, with an increase of less than 8 percent projected to 2025. Similarly, incomes should neither decrease nor increase significantly in the near future in this segment of the population.

SWOT Analysis

The SWOT analysis provides a summary of the strengths, weaknesses, opportunities, and threats identified by S&S Smoothie through the analysis of its internal and external environments.

Many but not all experts recommend that the SWOT analysis should be a summary of the material covered in the discussions of the various internal and external environments. Strengths and weaknesses come from the facts presented in the discussion of the internal environment, whereas opportunities and threats are based on discussions about the external environments. Be sure you check with your instructor on his or her perspective on the SWOT analysis.

Strengths

The following are the strengths S&S Smoothie identified:

- A creative and skilled employee team

- A high-quality product recipe that provides exceptional flavor with high levels of nutrition

- Because of its entrepreneurial spirit, the ability to remain flexible and to adapt quickly to environmental changes

- A strong network of manufacturers' agents and distributors

- The growth of a reputation for a high-quality product among health clubs, other retail outlets, and targeted consumer groups

Weaknesses

The following are the weaknesses S&S Smoothie identified:

- Limited financial resources for growth and for advertising and other marketing communications

- Little flexibility in terms of personnel because of size of the firm

- Reliance on external production to maintain quality standards and to meet any unanticipated surges in demand for the product

Opportunities

The following are the opportunities S&S Smoothie identified:

- A strong and growing interest in healthy living among both young, upscale consumers and older consumers

- Continuing consumer interest in low-carb alternatives that offers opportunities for additional product lines

Threats

The following are the threats S&S Smoothie identified:

- The potential for competitors, especially those with large financial resources who can invest more in promotion, to develop products that consumers may find equal or superior to the S&S Smoothie products

- Fizzling of the low-carb craze if other forms of dieting gain in popularity

- Increase in popularity of energy drinks like Rockstar, etc.

Marketing Objectives

Remember that you will need to measure the success of your marketing strategies against your objectives. Therefore, your objectives should be quantitative, realistic, and measurable.

The following are the marketing objectives set by S&S Smoothie:

- To increase awareness of S&S Smoothies from 20 percent of the target market to 50 percent within the next 12 months

- To grow the percentage of the target market who have tried the product to 30 percent within the next 12 months

- To increase gross sales of S&S Smoothies by 40 percent within the next 12 months

- To increase channels of distribution to include three new organizational customer segments:

  - Hotels and resorts

  - Golf and tennis clubs

  - University campuses

- To introduce two new product lines over the next three years, including:

  - A line of smoothies with unique gourmet flavors

  - A line of low-carb smoothies

Marketing Strategies

PART TWO

Target Markets

S&S Smoothie has identified a number of consumer and organizational markets for its products.

Consumer Markets

Because the S&S Smoothie Company has an existing product that was discussed in the Internal Environment section, we were able to say we were continuing some of those same strategies in our Marketing Strategies sections. If you have determined that your marketing plan is for a new business without any marketing history, you will have to provide complete details on the target market, product, price, promotion, and distribution.

S&S Smoothies will continue to target its existing consumer markets. Company research shows that the primary consumer target market for S&S Smoothie beverages can be described as follows:

Demographics

- Male and female teens and young adults

- Ages: 15–39

- Household income: $50,000 and higher

- Education of head of household: College degree or higher

- Primarily located in midsize to large urban areas or college towns

Psychographics

- Health-conscious; interested in living a healthy lifestyle

- Spend much time and money taking care of their bodies

- Enjoy holidays that include physical activities

- Live very busy lives and need to use time wisely to enjoy all they want to do

- Enjoy spending time with friends

Media Habits

- Individuals in the target market use the Internet as their primary source of news and entertainment. When they watch television, it is usually on a computer or more often on a tablet or smartphone. Many simply avoid the news altogether and only get secondhand news through Facebook or other social media.

- When they do watch television programming, these consumers prefer watching edgier shows, such as *The Walking Dead*, *Breaking Bad*, *Schitt's Creek*, and *Tiger King*.

- They are likely to have satellite radio installed in their automobiles.

- They are heavy users of social media, spending between two and three hours a day on sites including Facebook, Twitter, LinkedIn, and Foursquare.

- They frequently read magazines such as *Men's Health*, *BusinessWeek*, *Sports Illustrated*, and *The New Yorker*.

Organizational Markets

In the past, S&S Smoothie has targeted two categories of reseller markets: (1) health clubs and gyms, and (2) small, upscale specialty food markets. To increase distribution and sales of its products, S&S Smoothie will target the following in the future:

1. Hotels and resorts in the United States and in selected international markets

2. Golf and tennis clubs

3. College and university campuses

Upscale young professionals frequently visit hotels and resorts, and they demand that even business travel should include quality accommodations and first-rate health club facilities. The membership of golf and tennis clubs, although including many older consumers, also is an excellent means of providing products conveniently for the targeted groups. College and university students, probably more than any other consumer group, are interested in health and in their bodies. In fact, many universities have built large, elaborate health and recreational facilities as a means of attracting students. Thus, providing S&S Smoothie beverages on college campuses is an excellent means of meeting the health beverage needs of this group.

Positioning the Product

S&S Smoothie seeks to position its products as the first-choice smoothie beverage for the serious health-conscious consumer, including those who are seeking to lower their carbohydrate intake. The justification for this positioning is as follows: Many smoothie beverages are available. The S&S Smoothie formula provides superior flavor and nutrition in a shelf-stable form. S&S Smoothie has developed its product, packaging, pricing, and promotion to communicate a superior, prestige image. This positioning is thus supported by all of the S&S marketing strategies.

PART THREE

Product Strategies

To increase its leverage in the market and to meet its sales objectives, S&S Smoothie needs additional products. Two new product lines are planned:

1. *S&S Smoothie Gold:* This product will be similar to the original S&S Smoothie beverage but will come in six unique flavors:

   a. Piña ramada colada

   b. Chocolate banananana

   c. Apricot nectarine madness

   d. Pineapple berry crush

   e. Tropical tofu cherry surprise

   f. Peaches and dreams come true

The nutritional content, critical to the success of the new products, will be similar to that of the original S&S Smoothie beverages. Nutritional information is shown in Table A.2.

Table A.2	Nutritional Information: S&S Smoothie Beverage			
	S&S Smoothie Gold		Low-Carb S&S Smoothie	
	Amount per Serving	% Daily Value	Amount per Serving	% Daily Value
Calories	140		130	
Calories from fat	6		7	
Total fat	<0.5	1%	<0.5	1%
Saturated fat	<0.5	2%	<0.5	2%
Cholesterol	6 mg	2%	6 mg	2%
Sodium	70 mg	3%	70 mg	3%
Potassium	100 mg	3%	100 mg	3%
Total carbs	20 g	8%	10 g	4%
Dietary fiber	5 g	20%	5 g	20%
Protein	25 g	50%	25 g	50%
Vitamin A		50%		50%
Vitamin C		50%		50%
Calcium		20%		20%
Iron		30%		30%
Vitamin D		40%		40%
Vitamin E		50%		50%
Thiamin		50%		50%
Riboflavin		50%		50%
Niacin		50%		50%
Vitamin B6		50%		50%
Vitamin B12		50%		50%
Biotin		50%		50%
Pantothenic acid		50%		50%
Phosphorus		10%		10%
Iodine		50%		50%
Chromium		50%		50%
Zinc		50%		50%
Folic acid		50%		50%

Serving Size: 12 ounces
For 20-ounce sizes, multiply the amounts by 1.67.

The packaging for the new S&S Smoothie product will also be similar to that used for the original product, utilizing the unique, easy-to-hold, hourglass-shaped, frosted glass bottle and providing the new beverage with the same upscale image. To set the product apart from the original-flavor Smoothie beverages in store refrigerator cases, labels will include the name of the beverage and the logo in gold lettering. The bottle cap will also be gold.

2. *Low-Carb S&S Smoothie:* As shown in Table A.2, the Low-Carb S&S Smoothie beverage will have approximately 50 percent fewer grams of carbohydrates than the original Smoothie beverage or the S&S Smoothie Gold. Low-Carb S&S Smoothie will come in the following four flavors:

   a. Strawberry

   b. Blueberry

   c. Banana

   d. Peach

Packaging for the Low-Carb S&S Smoothie will be similar to other S&S Smoothie beverages but will include the term "Low-Carb" in large type. The label will state that the beverage has 50 percent fewer carbs than regular smoothies. The bottle cap will be black.

Pricing Strategies

The current pricing strategy will be maintained for existing and new products. This pricing is appropriate for communicating a high-quality product image for all S&S Smoothie products. The company feels that creating different pricing for the new beverages would be confusing and create negative attitudes among consumers. Thus, there is no justification for increasing the price of the new products.

Pricing through the channel including margins is shown in Table A.3.

S&S Smoothie will continue to outsource actual production of the new offerings as it does with its existing product. As noted previously, with this method of production, variable costs for the 12-ounce S&S Smoothie beverages are $0.63 and variable costs for the 20-ounce size are $0.71. Anticipated annual fixed costs for S&S Smoothie office space, management salaries, and expenses related to sales, advertising, and other marketing communications are as follows:

Salaries and employee benefits	$525,000
Office rental, equipment, and supplies	$124,600
Expenses related to sales (travel, etc.)	$132,000
Advertising and other marketing communications	$450,000
Total fixed costs	$1,231,600

Sales of the two sizes of all S&S products are expected to be approximately equal; that is, half of sales will be for the 12-ounce size and half will be for the 20-ounce size. Thus, there will be an average contribution margin of $0.83 per bottle. Based on this, to achieve breakeven in units, S&S Smoothie must sell the following:

$$\frac{\$1,231,600}{.83} = 1,483,856 \text{ bottles}$$

Again, assuming equal sales of the two sizes of products, the breakeven point in dollars is $2,225,784.

Promotion Strategies

In the past, S&S Smoothie has used mainly personal selling to promote its products to the trade channel. To support this effort, signage has been provided for the resellers to promote the product at the point of purchase. Posters and standalone table cards show appealing

Even if you are using an existing firm in your project, fixed and variable costs may not be available. Check with your instructor and ask if he or she would like for you to estimate these figures based on some logical assumptions.

Table A.3	Pricing of S&S Smoothie Beverages	
	12 Ounces	20 Ounces
Suggested retail price	$4.00	$6.00
Retailer margin	50% / $2.00	50% / $3.00
Price to retail outlets (health clubs, etc.)	$2.00	$3.00
Distributor/sales agent margin	40% / $0.80	40% / $1.20
Price to distributor/discount to sales agent	$1.20	$1.80
Variable costs	$0.63	$0.71
S&S contribution	$0.57	$1.09

photographs of the product in the different flavors and communicate the brand name and the health benefits of the product. Similar signage will be developed for use by resellers who choose to stock the S&S Smoothie Gold and the Low-Carb Smoothies.

Selling has previously been handled by a team of more than 75 manufacturers' agents who sell to resellers. In addition, in some geographic areas, an independent distributor does the selling. To support this personal selling approach, S&S Smoothie plans for additional promotional activities to introduce its new products and meet its other marketing objectives. These include the following:

1. *Television advertising:* The major objectives of television advertising are to increase awareness and knowledge of S&S Smoothies' superior product quality and to introduce the two new lines of Smoothies. Television advertising will be limited to programming related to healthy athletes, such as the Olympics, major tennis matches, and golf tournaments. Ads will project health and happiness among young people who live a healthy lifestyle.

2. *Magazine and newspaper advertising:* Because consumers in the target market are not avid magazine readers, magazine advertising will be limited and will supplement other promotion activities. During the next year, S&S Smoothie will experiment with limited magazine advertising in such titles as *Men's Health.* The company will also investigate the potential of advertising in university newspapers.

3. *Sponsorships:* S&S Smoothie will attempt to sponsor several marathons in major cities. The advantage of sponsorships is that they provide visibility for the product while at the same time showing that the company supports activities of interest to the target market.

4. *Digital, social media, and mobile marketing:* S&S Smoothie will increase its use of digital and social media marketing to leverage its popularity among members of the target market. The objectives of these activities will be (1) to engage consumers with the company and the product, (2) to provide a benefit (i.e., something of value to the consumers delivered through the communication), (3) to better understand and, when possible, respond to the positive and negative comments about the S&S products by monitoring consumer postings on social media sites, and (4) to enhance the awareness and knowledge of the S&S products through the company website, YouTube videos, and entries on related blogs.

The key to successful digital and social media marketing is to provide more than just information. As noted, the challenge is to provide content that engages the consumer and that provides a benefit. For example, S&S could offer through its website and YouTube videos content such as how to make healthy dishes or meals, new exercise techniques, evaluation of different exercise equipment, and stories about amateur athletes—their victories, their techniques, and so on. Inviting consumers to add to this information with their own videos would be one of many ways to encourage consumer engagement. The specifics of these activities should be developed as soon as possible. One of S&S's greatest assets is its loyal customer base, so a priority will be to turn avid users into ambassadors for the brand who will help to promote positive word of mouth on social media platforms.

5. *Sampling:* Sampling of S&S Smoothie beverages at select venues will provide an opportunity for prospective customers to become aware of the product and to taste the great flavors. Sampling will include only the two new products being introduced. Venues for sampling will include the following:

   a. Marathons

   b. Weightlifting competitions

   c. Gymnastics meets

   d. Student unions located on select college campuses

6. *Sales promotion:* In order to create interest in the new S&S Smoothie Gold products and to generate buzz about their introduction to the target market, S&S will hold a product/flavor-naming contest. During each week of the contest, consumers will submit fun names for a designated new flavor in the new S&S Smoothie Gold line. Five weekly winners will receive a case of the new product. At the end of the six weeks, a grand prize will be awarded to the best overall name; the grand prize will be a cash award. Consumers can participate in the contest via the company website and other social media sites.

Supply Chain Strategies

PART FOUR

As noted previously, S&S Smoothie distributes its beverages primarily through health clubs, gyms, and small, upscale specialty food stores. S&S Smoothie plans to expand its target reseller market to include the following:

1. Hotels and resorts in the United States and in targeted international markets

2. Golf and tennis clubs

3. College campuses

   To increase leverage in larger health clubs, S&S Smoothie will offer free refrigerated display units that feature a prominent product logo. This will encourage the facility to maintain a high level of inventory of S&S Smoothie beverages.

Implementation

PART ONE

The action plan details the activities necessary to implement all marketing strategies. In addition, the action plan includes the timing for each item, the individual(s) responsible, and the budgetary requirements. Table A.4 shows an example of one objective (to increase distribution venues) and the action items S&S Smoothie will use to accomplish it.

Measurement and Control Strategies

PART TWO

A variety of activities will ensure effective measurement of the success of the marketing plan and allow the firm to make adjustments as necessary. These include targeted market research and trend analysis. It is also important to maintain the stats on consumer access of digital media and social media marketing.

Table A.4 | Action Items to Accomplish Marketing Objective Regarding Supply Chain

Objective: Increase Distribution Venues

Action Items	Beginning Date	Ending Date	Responsible Party	Cost	Remarks
1. Identify key hotels and resorts, golf clubs, and tennis clubs where S&S Smoothies might be sold.	July 1	September 1	Bill Sartens (consulting firm will be engaged to assist in this effort)	$25,000	Key to this strategy is to selectively choose resellers so that maximum results are obtained from sales activities. Because health club use is greater during the months of January to May, efforts will be timed to have product in stock no later than January 15.
2. Identify 25 key universities where S&S Smoothies might be sold.	July 1	August 1	Bill Sartens	0	Information about colleges and universities and their health club facilities should be available on the university web pages.
3. Make initial contact with larger hotel and resort chains.	September 1	November 1	Bill Sartens	Travel: $10,000	
4. Make initial contact with larger individual (nonchain) facilities.	September 1	November 1	Bill Sartens	Travel: $5,000	
5. Make initial contact with universities.	August 15	September 15	Manufacturers' agents	0	Agents will be assigned to the 25 universities and required to make an initial contact and report back to Bill Sartens on promising prospects.
6. Follow up initial contacts with all potential resellers and obtain contracts for coming six months.	September 15	Ongoing	Bill Sartens, manufacturers' agents	$10,000	$10,000 is budgeted for this item, although actual expenditures will be on an as-needed basis, as follow-up travel cannot be preplanned.

Research

Firms need to regularly engage in marketing research activities to understand brand aware-ness and brand attitudes among their target markets. S&S Smoothie will therefore continue its program of focus group research and descriptive studies of its target consumer and re-seller markets.

Trend Analysis

S&S Smoothie will do a monthly trend analysis to examine sales by reseller type, geographic area, chain, agent, and distributor. These analyses will allow S&S Smoothie to take corrective action when necessary.

Glossary

80/20 rule   A marketing rule of thumb that 20 percent of purchasers account for 80 percent of a product's sales.

A

A/B test   A method to test the effectiveness of altering one characteristic of a marketing asset (e.g., a web page, a banner advertisement, or an email).

ABC Theory of Attitudes   A term for referring to attitudes that brings to mind the three components of attitudes.

account executive   A member of the account management department who supervises the day-to-day activities of the account and is the primary liaison between the agency and the client.

account planner   A member of the account management department who combines research and account strategy to act as the voice of the consumer in creating effective advertising.

accountability   A process of determining just how much value an organization's marketing activities create and their impact on the bottom line.

account-based selling   The practice of choosing the best way to sell to B2B individual customers.

action plans   Individual support plans included in a marketing plan that provide guidance for implementation and control of the various marketing strategies within the plan. Action plans are sometimes referred to as *marketing programs*.

activities, interests, and opinions (AIOs)   Measures of consumer activities, interests, and opinions used to place consumers into dimensions.

activity metrics   Metrics focused on measuring and tracking specific activities taken within a firm that are part of different marketing processes.

actual product   The physical good or the delivered service that supplies the desired benefit.

ad blocking   The use of powerful ad-blocking software created to stop ad fraud by stripping ads from the website at the network level.

ad fraud, or click fraud   The use of automated browsers to falsify the number of views or click-throughs the advertisers must pay for.

administered VMS   A vertical marketing system in which channel members remain independent but voluntarily work together because of the power of a single channel member.

adoption pyramid   Reflects how a person goes from being unaware of an innovation through stages from the bottom up of awareness, interest, evaluation, trial, adoption, and confirmation.

advergaming   Brand placements in video games.

advertising   Nonpersonal communication from an identified sponsor using the mass media.

advertising appeal   The central idea or theme of an advertising message.

advertising campaign   A coordinated, comprehensive plan that carries out promotion objectives and results in a series of advertisements placed in media over a period of time.

advocacy advertising   A type of public service advertising where an organization seeks to influence public opinion on an issue because it has some stake in the outcome.

affect   The feeling component of attitudes; refers to the overall emotional response a person has to a product.

Affordable Care Act   Provides access to health care for all Americans.

agile marketing   Using data and analytics to continuously source promising opportunities or solutions to problems in real time, deploying tests quickly, evaluating the results, and rapidly iterating (doing it over and over).

agility   The ability to be nimble, or to move quickly and easily.

aided recall   A research technique that uses clues to prompt answers from people about advertisements they might have seen.

Airbnb   A sharing service for consumers to lease or rent short-term lodging, including holiday cottages, apartments, homestays, hostel beds, and hotel rooms.

Amazon effect   The effect of online shopping combined with the consumer trend of shopping with a giant such as Amazon.

ambient advertising   Advertising placed where advertising isn't normally or hasn't ever been seen.

androgyny   The possession of both masculine and feminine traits.

anonymity   Is a condition in which the identity of individual subjects is not known to researchers.

anticipatory shipping   A system of delivering products to customers before they place an order, utilizing predictive analytics to determine what customers want and then shipping the products automatically.

anticonsumption   The deliberate defacement of products.

approach   The first step of the actual sales presentation in which the salesperson tries to learn more about the customer's needs, create a good impression, and build rapport.

Arab Spring   A series of anti-government protests and uprisings in a number of Arab countries facilitated by new social media tools available to people in the region.

artificial intelligence (AI)   The broad concept of machines being able to carry out tasks in a way that humans would consider "smart."

attention   The extent to which a person devotes mental processing to a particular stimulus.

attitude   A learned predisposition to respond favorably or unfavorably to stimuli on the basis of relatively enduring evaluations of people, objects, and issues.

attitudinal measures   A research technique that probes a consumer's beliefs or feelings about a product before and after being exposed to messages about it.

attributes   Include features, functions, and uses of a product. Marketers view products as a bundle of attributes that includes the packaging, brand name, benefits, and supporting features in addition to a physical good.

augmented intelligence   The application of AI to help people make better decisions.

augmented product   The actual product plus other supporting features, such as a warranty, credit, delivery, installation, and repair service after the sale.

augmented reality (AR)   A view of a physical, real world that is enhanced or altered by computer-generated sounds, videos, graphics, or GPS data.

automatic reordering system   Retail reordering system that is automatically activated when inventories reach a certain level.

avatars   Graphic representations of users of virtual worlds.

average fixed cost   The fixed cost per unit produced.

B

B2C e-commerce   Online exchanges between companies and individual consumers.

baby boomers   The group of consumers born between 1946 and 1964.

back-translation   The process of translating material to a foreign language and then back to the original language.

backward invention   Product strategy in which a firm develops a less advanced product to serve the needs of people living in countries without electricity or other elements of a developed infrastructure.

badge   A milestone or reward earned for progressing through a video game.

bait-and-switch   An illegal marketing practice in which an advertised price special is used as bait to get customers into the store with the intention of switching them to a higher-priced item.

balance of payments   A statement of how much trade a country has going out compared to how much it has coming in. If a country is buying more than it is selling, it will have a negative balance of payments.

banners   Internet advertising in the form of rectangular graphics at the top or bottom of web pages.

BCG growth–market share matrix   A portfolio analysis model developed by the Boston Consulting Group that assesses the potential of successful products to generate cash that a firm can then use to invest in new products.

behavior   The doing component of attitudes; involves a consumer's intention to do something, such as the intention to purchase or use a certain product.

behavioral learning theories   Theories of learning that focus on how consumer behavior is changed by external events or stimuli.

behavioral segmentation   A technique that divides consumers into segments on the basis of how they act toward, feel about, or use a good or service.

benefit   The outcome sought by a customer that motivates buying behavior that satisfies a need or want.

beta test   Limited release of a product, especially an innovative technology, to allow usage and feedback from a small number of customers who are willing to test the product under normal, everyday conditions of use.

bifurcated retailing   The decline of middle-of-the-market retailing due to the increasing popularity of both low-end discount stores and upscale specialty retailing.

Big Data   A popular term to describe the exponential growth of data—both structured and unstructured—in massive amounts that are hard or impossible to process using traditional database techniques.

billboards   Large-format outdoor advertising that can be seen from extended distances.

Bitcoin   The most popular and fastest-growing cryptocurrency.

bleeding-edge technology   An innovative technology that is not yet ready for release to the market as a whole, potentially because of issues related to reliability and stability, but is in a suitable state to be offered for beta testing to evaluate consumer perceptions of its performance and identify any potential issues in its usage.

blockchain   A time-stamped series of immutable records of data that is managed by a cluster of computers not owned by any single entity.

boosters   Individuals who facilitate organized retail crime by stealing the merchandise.

bottom of the pyramid (BOP)   The collective name for the group of consumers throughout the world who live on less than $2 a day.

bottom-of-the-pyramid pricing   Innovative pricing strategy in which brands that wish to get a foothold in bottom-of-the-pyramid countries appeal to consumers with the lowest incomes.

bottom-up budgeting techniques   Allocation of the promotion budget based on identifying promotion goals and allocating enough money to accomplish them.

brand   A name, term, symbol, or any other unique element of a product that identifies one firm's product(s) and sets it apart from the competition.

brand ambassadors, or **brand evangelists**   Loyal customers recruited to communicate with and sell to other consumers for a brand they care a great deal about.

brand anthropomorphism   The assignment of human characteristics and qualities to a brand.

brand community   A group of social network users who share an attachment to a product or brand, interact with each other, and share information about the brand.

brand competition   When firms offering similar goods or services compete on the basis of their brand's reputation or perceived benefits.

brand dilution   A reduction in the value of a brand typically driven by the introduction of a brand extension that possesses attributes that adversely contrast with the current attributes consumers associate with the brand.

brand equity   The value of a brand to an organization.

brand extensions   A new product sold with the same brand name as a strong existing brand.

brand loyalty   A pattern of repeat product purchases, accompanied by an underlying positive attitude toward the brand, based on the belief that the brand makes products superior to those of its competition.

brand manager   An individual who is responsible for developing and implementing the marketing plan for a single brand.

brand meaning   The beliefs and associations that a consumer has about the brand.

brand personality   A distinctive image that captures the character and benefits of a good or service.

brand polarization   The gap between good buzz and bad buzz.

brand storytelling   Compelling stories told by marketers about brands to engage consumers.

branded content   Marketing communication developed by a brand to provide educational or entertainment value rather than to sell the brand in order to develop a relationship with consumers; may indicate the brand is the sponsor.

branded entertainment, or **branded content**   A form of advertising in which marketers integrate products into the storylines of entertainment venues.

brandfests   Events that companies host to thank customers for their loyalty.

break-even analysis   A method for determining the number of units that a firm must produce and sell at a given price to cover all its costs.

break-even point   The point at which the total revenue and total costs are equal and above which the company makes a profit; below that point, the firm will suffer a loss.

breaking bulk   Dividing larger quantities of goods into smaller lots in order to meet the needs of buyers.

Brexit   Term used to refer to the U.K.'s (**Br**itain's) **exit** from the European Union.

bribery   When someone voluntarily offers payment to get an illegal advantage.

BRICS countries   Also referred to as the BRICS, Brazil, Russia, India, China, and South Africa are the fastest growing of the developing countries. With more than 3 billion people, they represent over 41 percent of the world's population and about 22 percent of the gross world product.

business analysis The step in the product development process in which marketers assess a product's commercial viability.

business cycle The overall patterns of change in the economy—including periods of prosperity, recession, depression, and recovery—that affect consumer and business purchasing power.

business ethics Basic values that guide a firm's behavior.

business performance metrics Metrics that directly assess outcomes related to the profitability of a company.

business plan A plan that includes the decisions that guide the entire organization.

business planning An ongoing process of making decisions that guides the firm both in the short term and in the long term.

business portfolio The group of different products or brands owned by an organization and characterized by different income-generating and growth capabilities.

business-to-business (B2B) e-commerce Online exchanges between two or more businesses or organizations.

business-to-business (B2B) markets The group of customers that includes manufacturers, wholesalers, retailers, and other organizations.

business-to-business marketing The marketing of goods and services from one organization to another.

buttons Small banner-type advertisements that can be placed anywhere on a web page.

buyclass One of three classifications of business buying situations that characterizes the degree of time and effort required to make a decision.

buyer's remorse The anxiety or regret a consumer may feel after choosing from among several similar attractive choices.

buying center The group of people in an organization who participate in a purchasing decision.

buying power A concept in segmentation that can help marketers to determine how to better match different products and versions of products to different consumer groups based on an understanding of what discretionary and nondiscretionary allocations of funds they are able to make.

buy-now-pay-later (BNPL) Services that allow consumers to get a product now and pay for it over three or four months.

buzz Word-of-mouth communication that customers view as authentic.

buzz marketing Marketing activities designed to create conversation, excitement, and enthusiasm—that is, buzz—about a brand.

C

cannibalization The loss of sales of an existing brand when a new item in a product line or product family is introduced.

capacity management The process by which organizations adjust their offerings in an attempt to match demand.

captive pricing A pricing tactic for two items that must be used together; one item is priced very low, and the firm makes its profit on another, high-margin item essential to the operation of the first item.

case allowance A discount to the retailer or wholesaler based on the volume of product ordered.

case study A comprehensive examination of a particular firm or organization.

cash cows SBUs with dominant market shares in low-growth-potential markets.

cash discounts A discount offered to a customer to entice them to pay their bill quickly.

cashless society An economic state where financial transactions are executed through the transfer of digital information—usually in the form of a credit card, debit card, mobile wallet, or digital currency such as Bitcoin—rather than with banknotes.

catalog A collection of products offered for sale in book form, usually consisting of product descriptions accompanied by photos of the items.

category killers, or **category specialists** Very large specialty stores that carry a vast selection of products in their category.

catfish Someone who pretends to be someone else online.

causal research A technique that attempts to understand cause-and-effect relationships.

channel conflict Incompatible goals, poor communication, and disagreement over roles, responsibilities, and functions among firms at different levels of the same distribution channel that may threaten a manufacturer's distribution strategy.

channel cooperation Occurs when producers, wholesalers, and retailers depend on one another for success.

channel intermediaries Firms or individuals, such as wholesalers, agents, brokers, or retailers, who help move a product from the producer to the consumer or business user. An older term for intermediaries is *middlemen*.

channel leader, or **channel captain** The dominant firm that controls the channel.

channel levels The number of distinct categories of intermediaries that make up a channel of distribution.

channel of distribution The series of firms or individuals that facilitates the movement of a product from the producer to the final customer.

channel partner model A relationship between channel partners in which a two-way exchange of information between purchasing organizations and their respective vendors is facilitated through shared or integrated IT systems.

channel power The ability of one channel member to influence, control, and lead the entire channel based on one or more sources of power.

chatbots A computer program that uses either voice or text to allow consumers to talk with the computer's AI capability.

chief customer officer (CCO) An increasingly popular C-suite role, the CCO is positioned as a firm's leading force of all things customer related.

classical conditioning The learning that occurs when a stimulus eliciting a response is paired with another stimulus that initially does not elicit a response on its own but will cause a similar response over time because of its association with the first stimulus.

clearance sale A closeout or clearance sale is a discount sale of inventory either by retailer or wholesaler. Clearances are meant to help sell unwanted inventory that may be seasonal or outdated in order to make room for new merchandise and minimize the financial impact of products that were not popular.

click-through rate (CTR) A metric that indicates the percentage of website users who have decided to click on an advertisement to visit the website or Web page associated with it.

climate change A significant change in the measures of climate, including major changes in temperature, precipitation, or wind patterns, that occurs over several decades or longer.

close The stage of the selling process in which the salesperson asks the customer to buy the product.

cobranding An agreement between two brands to work together to market a product.

code of ethics Written standards of behavior to which everyone in the organization must subscribe.

cognition The knowing component of attitudes; refers to the beliefs or knowledge a person has about a product and its important characteristics.

cognitive learning theory Theory of learning that stresses the importance of internal mental processes and that views people as problem solvers who actively use information from the world around them to master their environment.

collaborative savings and consumption A savings plan where members are placed into small groups and make monthly payments. One member is selected randomly every 30 days to withdraw the entire monthly contributions.

collectivist cultures Cultures in which people subordinate their personal goals to those of a stable community.

combination stores Retailers that offer consumers food and general merchandise in the same store.

commercial success Indicates that a product concept is feasible from the standpoint of whether the firm developing the product believes there is or will be sufficient consumer demand to warrant its development and entry into the market.

commercialization The final step in the product development process in which a new product is launched into the market.

common good approach Ethical philosophy that advocates the decision that contributes to the good of all in the community.

communication and transaction functions Happens when channel members develop and execute both promotional and other types of communication among members of the channel.

communication process The process whereby meaning is transferred from a source to a receiver.

comparative advertising Advertising that compares one brand with a second named brand.

comparison-shopping agents (shopbots) Web applications that help online shoppers find what they are looking for at the lowest price and provide customer reviews and ratings of products and sellers.

compatibility The extent to which a new product is consistent with existing cultural values, customs, and practices.

compensatory decision rules The methods for making decisions that allow information about attributes of competing products to be averaged in some way.

competitive advantage A firm's edge over its competitors that allows it to have higher sales, higher profits, and more customers and enjoy greater success year after year.

competitive intelligence (CI) The process of gathering and analyzing publicly available information about rivals.

competitive-effect pricing, or market-based pricing Pricing a product based on (above, below, or the same as) the competition's pricing.

competitive-parity method A promotion budgeting method in which an organization matches whatever competitors are spending.

complexity The degree to which consumers find a new product or its use difficult to understand.

component parts Manufactured goods or subassemblies of finished items that organizations need to complete their own products.

concentrated targeting strategy Focusing a firm's efforts on offering one or more products to a single segment.

concept stores New, inspirational approaches to retailing that seek to sell a lifestyle to a particular target audience through the use of customer interaction, discovery, and experience rather than selling products.

confidentiality Refers to a condition in which the researcher knows the identity of a research subject, but takes steps to protect that identity from being discovered by others.

congestion pricing Pricing strategy of charging a high fee for operating cars during peak traffic times to reduce congestion.

conscientious consumerism A continuation of the consumerism movement in which consumers are much more mindful of environmental issues in their daily purchases and marketers support consumerism issues in their advertising.

consideration set The alternative brands a consumer seriously considers when making a decision.

consignment stores Resale stores that take used merchandise, resell it, and return a portion of the proceeds to the original owner.

consumer The ultimate user of a good or service.

consumer addiction A physiological or psychological dependency on goods or services, including alcohol, drugs, cigarettes, shopping, and use of the Internet.

consumer behavior The process involved when individuals or groups select, purchase, use, and dispose of goods, services, ideas, or experiences to satisfy their needs and desires.

consumer ethnocentrism Consumers' feeling that products from their own country are superior or that it is wrong to buy products produced in another country.

consumer goods The goods individual consumers purchase for personal or family use.

consumer packaged good (CPG), or fast-moving consumer good (FMCG) A low-cost good that is consumed quickly and replaced frequently.

consumer satisfaction/dissatisfaction The overall feelings or attitude a person has about a product after purchasing it.

consumer xenocentrism Consumer belief that products produced in other countries are superior to those produced at home.

consumerism A social movement that attempts to protect consumers from harmful business practices.

content marketing The strategy of establishing thought leadership in the form of bylines, blogs, commenting opportunities, videos, sharable social images, and infographics.

contingency planning Planning that assesses the risk of a variety of possible, mostly external, environmental factors and their potential level of impact on the firm's ability to add value and serve its market through its offerings.

continuous innovation A modification of an existing product that sets one brand apart from its competitors.

contractual VMS A vertical marketing system in which cooperation is enforced by contracts (legal agreements) that spell out each member's rights and responsibilities and how they will cooperate.

contribution per unit The difference between the price the firm charges for a product and the variable costs.

control A process that entails measuring actual performance, comparing this performance to the established marketing objectives, and then making adjustments to the strategies or objectives on the basis of this analysis.

convenience product A consumer good or service that is usually low priced, widely available, and purchased frequently with a minimum of comparison and effort.

convenience sample A nonprobability sample composed of individuals who just happen to be available when and where the data are being collected.

convenience stores Neighborhood retailers that carry a limited number of frequently purchased items and cater to consumers willing to pay a premium for the ease of buying close to home.

conventional marketing system A multiple-level distribution channel in which channel members work independently of one another.

convergence The coming together of two or more technologies to create a new system with greater benefits than its separate parts.

convergent thinking After successful divergent thinking, convergent thinking moves toward analyzing the different ideas in order to come to a decision on the best choice.

conversion rate The number of sales leads converted into customers from various channels such as search marketing, personal selling, email marketing, and mobile marketing.

cookies Text files inserted by a website sponsor into a web surfer's hard drive that allow the site to track the surfer's moves.

co-op advertising A sales promotion where the manufacturer and the retailer share the cost.

copycat packaging Packaging designed to mimic the look of a similar or functionally identical national branded product often meant to lead the consumer to perceive the two products as comparable.

copyright infringement The use of works protected by copyright law without the permission of the copyright holder.

cord-cutting Consumers' cancelling of their traditional cable subscriptions and instead relying on streaming services to provide televised entertainment.

core product All the benefits the product will provide for consumers or business customers.

corporate activism, or **social marketing** Marketing efforts meant to improve society by influencing stakeholders to change their behavior.

corporate advertising Advertising that promotes the company as a whole instead of a firm's individual products.

corporate citizenship, or **corporate social responsibility** Refers to a firm's responsibility to the community in which they operate and to society in general.

corporate identity Materials such as logos, brochures, building design, and stationery that communicate an image of the organization.

corporate VMS A vertical marketing system in which a single firm owns manufacturing, wholesaling, and retailing operations.

corrective advertising Advertising that clarifies or qualifies previous deceptive advertising claims.

cosplay Costume play; dressing up as characters from brands, movies, video games, books, and more.

cost per thousand (CPM) A measure used to compare the relative cost-effectiveness of different media vehicles that have different exposure rates; the cost to deliver a message to 1,000 people or homes.

cost-per-click An online ad purchase in which the cost of the advertisement is charged only each time an individual clicks the advertisement and is directed to the web page that the marketer placed within the advertisement.

cost-per-impression An online ad purchase in which the cost of the advertisement is charged each time the advertisement shows up on a page that the user views.

cost-plus pricing A method of setting prices in which the seller totals all the costs for the product and then adds an amount to arrive at the selling price.

countertrade A type of trade in which goods are paid for with other items instead of with cash.

create assortments To provide a variety of products in one location to meet the needs of buyers.

creative brief A guideline or blueprint for the marketing communication program that guides the creative process.

creative selling process The process of seeking out potential customers, analyzing needs, determining how product attributes might provide benefits for the customer, and then communicating that information.

creative services The agency people (creative director, copywriters, and art director) who dream up and produce the ads.

creative strategy The process that turns a concept into an advertisement.

creativity A phenomenon in which something new and somehow valuable is created.

Credit Card Responsibility and Disclosure Act Limits credit card rates and other fees.

crisis management The process of managing a company's reputation when some negative event threatens the organization's image.

cross-browser digital fingerprinting An approach to identifying fake responses to online questionnaires by correlating specific computers used with multiple browsers.

cross-docking A supply chain efficiency technique in which products are transferred off a supplier's truck directly onto a buyer's truck bound for the next distribution point, such as a retail store.

cross-elasticity of demand When changes in the price of one product affect the demand for another item.

cross-functional team A form of selling team where the team includes individuals from various areas of the firm.

cross-sectional design A type of descriptive technique that involves the systematic collection of quantitative information.

crowdfunding Online platforms that allow thousands of individuals to each contribute small amounts of money to fund a new product from a start-up company.

crowdsourcing A practice where firms outsource marketing activities (such as selecting an ad) to a community of users.

cryptocurrency A digital currency that uses cryptography for security.

C-suite A popular term for a firm's top executive team, so-called because of the "chief" titles of each officer, such as chief executive officer (CEO).

cultural diversity A management practice that actively seeks to include people of different sexes, races, ethnic groups, and religions in an organization's employees, customers, suppliers, and distribution channel partners.

cultural values A society's deeply held beliefs about right and wrong ways to live.

culture The values, beliefs, customs, and tastes a group of people produces or practices.

custom research Research conducted for a single firm to provide specific information its managers need.

customer acquisition cost (CAC) The cost of convincing a potential customer to buy a product or service.

customer churn rate The percentage of a company's customers (for a given span of time) who by the end of that time span can no longer be considered customers of the company (e.g., because they have cancelled their contract for a service or they have stopped shopping at the related retail location).

customer co-creation The process when a company and their customers work together to create a product.

customer experience (CX or **CEX)** A customer's overall assessment of every interaction the customer has experienced with a business, from navigating the company website to talking to customer service to the packaging the product arrives in.

customer insights The collection, deployment, and interpretation of information that allows a business to acquire, develop, and retain its customers.

customer journey mapping The process of identifying customer touchpoints and tracking the experiences customers have when they interact with a brand or a store as they become aware of, consider and evaluate, and decide to purchase a product in order to improve the customer experience.

customer lifetime value (CLV)   Represents how much profit a firm expects to make from a particular customer, including each and every purchase he or she will make from them now and in the future.

customer loyalty   A customer's low likelihood of switching to a competitor's offering, especially because of being highly engaged and connected with their current brand.

customer orientation   A business approach that prioritizes the satisfaction of customers' needs and wants.

customer perception metrics   Metrics, such as satisfaction, that are concerned with the extent to which customer experiences are enhanced as a result of CRM.

customer profiling   The act of tailoring the level of customer service based on a customer's perceived ability to pay.

customer reference program   A formalized process by which customers formally share success stories and actively recommend products to other potential clients, usually facilitated through an online community.

customer relationship management (CRM)   A systematic tracking of consumers' preferences and behaviors over time to tailor the value proposition as closely as possible to each individual's unique wants and needs.

customer stickiness   Highly cultivated customers who are likely to follow through on an intended purchase, buy the product repeatedly, and recommend it to others.

customized marketing strategy   An approach that tailors specific products and the messages about them to individual customers.

cyberattack   An attempt to gain illegal access to a computer or computer system for the purpose of causing damage or harm.

cybersecurity   A strong commitment by firms to protect digital data, such as those in an electronic database, from destructive forces and from the unwanted actions of unauthorized users.

D

data   Raw, unorganized facts that need to be processed.

data analytics   The process of examining raw data to discover trends, answer questions, and gain insights in order to make evidence-based decisions.

data breach   The intentional or unintentional release of secure or private/confidential information to an untrusted environment.

data mining   A process in which analysts sift through Big Data (often measured in zettabytes—much larger than gigabytes or even terabytes) to identify unique patterns of behavior among different customer groups.

data privacy   Refers to the ability an organization or individual has to determine what data collected can be shared with third parties.

data scientist   An individual who uses skills in mathematics, computer science, and trend analysis to explore multiple, disparate data sources to discover hidden insights that will provide a competitive advantage.

data security   Firms must protect information collected from consumers from unauthorized access, use, disclosure, disruption, modification, or destruction in order to provide confidentiality, integrity, and ultimately trust by the consumer in the firm.

data warehouse   A system to store and process the data that result from data mining.

database   An organized collection (often electronic) of data that can be searched and queried to provide information about contacts, products, customers, inventory, and more.

data-driven disruptive marketing   Relationship-oriented marketing where the use of data and the content of marketing is used to build trust.

decline stage   The final stage in the product life cycle, during which sales decrease as customer needs change.

decoding   The process by which a receiver assigns meaning to the message.

decoy pricing   A pricing strategy where a seller offers at least three similar products; two have comparable but more expensive prices and one of these two is less attractive to buyers, thus causing more buyers to buy the higher-priced, more attractive item.

deep learning   A subset of machine learning that allows machines to solve complex problems even when using a dataset that is very diverse, unstructured, and interconnected.

deep Web   Places on the Web that you can't access with most search engines and that provide a means for criminals to connect to buy and sell stolen or illegal items.

deepfake   A realistic-looking photo or video of people doing or saying things they did not actually do or say.

demand   Customers' desires for products coupled with the resources needed to obtain them.

demand-based pricing   A price-setting method based on estimates of demand at different prices.

demographics   Statistics that measure observable aspects of a population, including size, age, gender, ethnic group, income, education, occupation, and family structure.

department stores   Retailers that sell a broad range of items and offer a good selection within each product line.

derived demand   Demand for business or organizational products caused by demand for consumer goods or services.

descriptive research   A tool that probes more systematically into the problem and bases its conclusions on large numbers of observations.

design thinking   A process that draws upon logic, imagination, intuition, and systemic reasoning to explore possibilities of what could be—and to create desired outcomes that benefit the end user (the consumer). Design thinking is also referred to as *human-centered design*.

destination retailer   Store that consumers view as distinctive enough to become loyal to it. Consumers go out of their way to shop there.

determinant attributes   The features most important to differentiate and compare among the product choices.

developed country   A country that boasts sophisticated marketing systems, strong private enterprise, and bountiful market potential for many goods and services.

developing countries   Countries in which the economy is shifting its emphasis from agriculture to industry.

differential benefit   Properties of products that set them apart from competitors' products by providing unique customer benefits.

differentiated targeting strategy   Developing one or more products for each of several distinct customer groups and making sure these offerings are kept separate in the marketplace.

diffusion   The process by which the use of a product spreads throughout a population.

digital disruption   The effect of digital technologies and digital business models on an organization's value proposition and its resulting position in the markets in which it competes.

digital marketing channels   The paths of distribution through which a company's digital marketing communications can be delivered to reach their respective audiences.

digital media   Media that are digital rather than analog, including websites, mobile or cellular phones, and digital video, such as YouTube.

digital natives   Individuals who spend a big chunk of their time online, so they expect brands to engage them in two-way digital conversations.

digital signage Out-of-home media that use digital technology to change the message at will.

digital vortex The inexorable movement of industries toward a "digital center" in which business models, offerings, and value chains are all digitized to the maximum extent possible.

digital wallet A financial account used to store funds, make transactions, and track payments.

digitally influenced purchases When consumers do online research before making a product purchase in a traditional store.

direct channel A channel of distribution in which a manufacturer of a product or creator of a service distributes directly to the end customer.

direct competitors Competitors whose offerings are very similar to yours.

direct mail A brochure or pamphlet that offers a specific good or service at one point in time.

direct marketing Any direct communication to a consumer or business recipient designed to generate a response in the form of an order, a request for further information, or a visit to a store or other place of business for purchase of a product.

direct selling An interactive sales process in which a salesperson presents a product to one individual or a small group, takes orders, and delivers the merchandise.

directory advertising Advertising in printed directories, such as the yellow pages.

direct-response advertising A direct marketing approach that allows the consumer to respond to a message by immediately contacting the provider to ask questions or order the product.

direct-response TV (DRTV) Advertising on TV that seeks a direct response, including short commercials of less than 2 minutes, 30-minute or longer infomercials, and home shopping networks.

direct-to-consumer (D2C) retail E-commerce companies that manufacture, sell, and ship their products without middlemen.

discontinuous innovation A totally new product that creates major changes in the way we live.

discretionary income The portion of income people have left over after paying for necessities such as housing, utilities, food, and clothing.

disintermediation The elimination of some layers of the channel of distribution to cut costs and improve the efficiency of the channel.

disruptive innovation An innovation that creates a new market and value chain and eventually disrupts an existing market and value chain, displacing established market-leading firms, products, and alliances.

disruptive marketing A process whereby marketers, by understanding customer needs and identifying what is missing, step "outside the box" to displace something well established, such as filling a need with a totally new product.

distinctive competency A superior capability of a firm in comparison to its direct competitors.

distressed inventory Term used to indicate retailer inventory that may not sell and is sold to online liquidators.

distribution center A warehouse that stores goods for short periods of time and that provides other functions, such as breaking bulk.

distribution intensity The number of intermediaries at each level of the channel.

distribution planning The process of developing distribution objectives, evaluating internal and external environmental influences on distribution, and choosing a distribution strategy.

divergent thinking Coming up with as many new ideas as possible and exploring new "out-of-the-box" alternatives.

diversification strategies Growth strategies that emphasize both new products and new markets.

diverter An entity that facilitates the distribution of a product through one or more channels not authorized for use by the manufacturer of the product.

diverting The retailer practice of buying a product at a promotional price and selling it after the promotional price has expired.

dogs SBUs with small shares of slow-growth markets. They are businesses that offer specialized products in limited markets that are not likely to grow quickly.

do-it-yourself (DIY) ads Product ads that are created by consumers.

dollar and variety stores Stores that carry a variety of inexpensive items.

downward product line stretch A product line extension strategy that adds new items toward the lower-priced end of the market.

drip pricing The illegal practice of advertising one price and then, by the time the sale is completed, presenting a total on which additional hidden fees have "dripped."

dual or **multiple distribution systems** A system where producers, dealers, wholesalers, retailers, and customers participate in more than one type of channel.

dumping A company tries to get a toehold in a foreign market by pricing its products lower than it offers them at home.

durable goods Consumer products that provide benefits over a long period of time, such as cars, furniture, and appliances.

dynamic pricing A pricing strategy in which the price can easily be adjusted to meet changes in the marketplace.

dynamically continuous innovation A change in an existing product that requires a moderate amount of learning or behavior change.

E

early adopters Those who adopt an innovation early in the diffusion process but after the innovators.

early majority Those whose adoption of a new product signals a general acceptance of the innovation.

earned media Word-of-mouth or buzz using social media where the advertiser has no control.

e-commerce The buying or selling of goods and services electronically, usually over the Internet.

economic communities Groups of countries that band together to promote trade among themselves and to make it easier for member nations to compete elsewhere.

economic infrastructure The quality of a country's distribution, financial, and communications systems.

edge computing The practice of processing data near the edge of the network where the data is being generated, instead of in a centralized data processing warehouse.

e-fencing Criminal activity of selling stolen merchandise through online auction sites such as eBay and Etsy.

elastic demand Demand in which changes in price have large effects on the amount demanded.

elevator pitch A statement that details your value proposition in about 30 seconds, the average time it takes for an elevator ride.

embargo A quota completely prohibiting specified goods from entering or leaving a country.

emergency products   Products we purchase when we're in dire need.

emotion analysis   A sophisticated process for identifying and categorizing the emotions a follower possesses in relation to a product or brand by assessing the content of that communication.

encoding   The process of translating an idea into a form of communication that will convey meaning.

encryption   The process of scrambling a message so that only another individual (or computer) with the right "key" can unscramble it.

enterprise resource planning (ERP) systems   A software system that integrates information from across the entire company, including finance, order fulfillment, manufacturing, and transportation, and then facilitates sharing of the data throughout the firm.

equipment   Expensive goods that an organization uses in its daily operations that last for a long time.

ethical bribe   A fancy term for an opt-in incentive to join an email mailing list.

ethical relativism   Suggests that what is ethical in one culture is not necessarily the same as in another culture.

ethnocentric pricing   A pricing strategy where the firm sets a single price for a product around the globe.

ethnography   An approach to research based on observations of people in their own homes or communities.

evaluative criteria   The dimensions consumers use to compare competing product alternatives.

evidence-based decision making   A marketer's capability to utilize all of the relevant information available in order to make the best possible marketing decisions.

evoked set   All of the alternative brands a consumer is aware of when making a decision.

exchange   The process by which some transfer of value occurs between a buyer and a seller.

exclusive distribution   Selling a product only through a single outlet in a particular region.

execution format   The basic structure of the message, such as comparison, demonstration, testimonial, slice of life, and lifestyle.

experiential loyalty   Customer loyalty that results not just in increased purchases but also in an enhanced broader experience for the customer.

experiential merchandising   A tactic to convert shopping from a passive activity into a more interactive one by engaging the customer in a participatory experience in the store.

experiential shoppers   Shoppers who shop because it satisfies their experiential needs, that is, their desire for fun.

experiments   A technique that tests predicted relationships among variables in a controlled environment.

exploratory research   A technique that marketers use to generate insights for future, more rigorous studies.

export merchants   Intermediaries a firm uses to represent it in other countries.

exposure   The extent to which a person's sensory receptors are capable of registering a stimulus.

expropriation   When a government or state seizes a foreign-owned asset, normally with some compensation for company owners or individuals (but often not for the full value).

extended reality (XR)   The term to describe technologies that can merge the physical and virtual worlds.

external environment   The uncontrollable elements outside an organization that may affect its performance either positively or negatively.

external validity   The extent to which the results of a research study can be generalized to the population its sample was intended to represent, providing a higher level of confidence that the findings can be applied outside of the setting where the research was conducted.

extortion   When someone in authority extracts payment under duress.

extranet   A private, corporate computer network that links company departments, employees, and databases to suppliers, customers, and others outside the organization.

eye tracking technology   A type of mechanical observation technology that uses sensors and sophisticated software to track the position and movement of an individual's eyes in order to gain context-specific insights into how individuals interact with and respond to different visual elements and stimuli.

F

Facebook   A social networking site where users develop profiles and can choose to connect with a "friend."

facilitating functions   Functions of channel intermediaries that make the purchase process easier for customers and manufacturers.

factory outlets   Manufacturer-owned brick-and-mortar or online retail stores that sell only a single brand and are almost always located in an outlet mall with other similar stores.

fair trade   Movement made up of a diverse network of producers, companies, shoppers, advocates, and organizations that promotes greater equity in international trading partnerships, encourages sustainable development, and secures the rights of marginalized producers and workers in developing countries.

fair trade suppliers   Companies that pledge to pay a fair price to producers in developing countries, to ensure that the workers who produce the goods receive a fair wage, and to ensure that these manufacturers rely where possible on environmentally sustainable production practices.

fairness or **justice approach**   Ethical philosophy that advocates the decision that treats all human beings equally.

family brand   A brand that a group of individual products or individual brands share.

family life cycle   A means of characterizing consumers within a family structure on the basis of different stages through which people pass as they grow older.

f-commerce   E-commerce that takes place on Facebook.

fear appeals   Advertisements that highlight the negative consequences of *not* using a product by either focusing on physical harm or social disapproval.

feedback   Receivers' reactions to the message.

fencers   Individuals who facilitate organized retail crime by selling the merchandise to consumers or businesses.

filling-out product strategy   A strategy to add sizes or styles not previously available in a product category.

firewall   A combination of hardware and software that ensures that only authorized individuals gain entry into a computer system.

first-mover advantage   Being the first firm to enter a market with a new product, perhaps as a disruptive innovator.

fixed costs   Costs of production that do not change with the number of units produced.

flash retailing, or **pop-up stores and pop-up retailing**   A trend of opening short-term sales stores that close down after only days or weeks. Retail stores, such as Halloween costume stores, that "pop up" one day and then disappear after a period of one day to a few months.

flawsome   Flawsome is a new term that combines two words, *flaws* and *awesome*. Flawsome describes a person who accepts themselves despite their flaws and knows that they are awesome regardless. It would not be wrong to say that it is the word which best describes a person and every minutiae associated with them.

F.O.B. delivered pricing A pricing tactic in which the cost of loading and transporting the product to the customer is included in the selling price and is paid by the manufacturer.

F.O.B. factory pricing, or F.O.B. origin pricing A pricing tactic in which the cost of transporting the product from the factory to the customer's location is the responsibility of the customer.

focus group A product-oriented discussion among a small group of consumers led by a trained moderator.

folksonomy A classification system that relies on users rather than preestablished systems to sort contents.

follow-up Activities after the sale that provide important services to customers.

food porn Social media posts featuring consumers' photos of their meals.

foreign exchange rate (forex rate) The price of a nation's currency in terms of another currency.

forward buying The questionable retailer practice of purchasing large quantities of a product during a discount period and not buying again until there is another discount.

four Ps Product, price, promotion, and place.

franchise organizations A contractual vertical marketing system that includes a *franchiser* (a manufacturer or a service provider) who allows an entrepreneur (the *franchisee*) to use the franchise name and marketing plan for a fee.

franchising A form of licensing involving the right to adapt an entire system of doing business.

free trade zones Designated areas where foreign companies can warehouse goods without paying taxes or customs duties until they move the goods into the marketplace.

freemium pricing A business strategy in which a product in its most basic version is provided free of charge but the company charges money (the premium) for upgraded versions of the product with more features, greater functionality, or greater capacity.

freight absorption pricing A pricing tactic in which the seller absorbs the total cost of transportation.

frequency The average number of times a person in the target group will be exposed to the message.

frequency programs Consumer sales promotion programs that offer a discount or free product for multiple purchases over time; also referred to as *loyalty* or *continuity programs*.

full-line product strategy A product line strategy that targets many customer segments to boost sales potential.

full-service agency An agency that provides most or all of the services needed to mount a campaign, including research, creation of ad copy and art, media selection, and production of the final messages.

full-service merchant wholesalers Wholesalers that provide a wide range of services for their customers, including delivery, credit, product-use assistance, repairs, advertising, and other promotional support.

functional planning A decision process that concentrates on developing detailed plans for strategies and tactics for the short term, supporting an organization's long-term strategic plan.

G

gamer segment A consumer segment that combines a psychographic/lifestyle component with a heavy dose of generational marketing.

gamification A strategy in which marketers apply game design techniques, like awarding points, badges, or levels, to nongame experiences in order to engage consumers.

gender identity The personal sense of one's own gender that may or may not correlate with a person's assigned sex at birth.

gender roles Society's expectations regarding the appropriate attitudes, behaviors, and appearance for men and women.

gender-bending products Traditionally sex-typed items adapted to the opposite gender.

General Agreement on Tariffs and Trade (GATT) International treaty to reduce import tax levels and trade restrictions.

general merchandise discount stores Retailers that offer a broad assorment of items at low prices with minimal service.

Generation X The group of consumers born between 1965 and 1978.

Generation Y (millennials) The group of consumers born between 1979 and 1994.

Generation Z (iGen) The group of consumers born after 1994.

generational marketing Marketing to members of a generation, who tend to share the same outlook, values, and priorities.

generic branding A strategy in which products are not branded and are sold at the lowest price possible.

geocentric pricing A pricing strategy that establishes a global price floor for a product but recognizes local conditions in setting the price in each market.

geodemography A segmentation technique that combines geography with demographics.

geofencing marketing The use of GPS or RFID technology to create a virtual geographic boundary, enabling software to trigger a response when a mobile device enters or leaves a particular area.

geographic information system (GIS) A system that combines a geographic map with digitally stored data about the consumers in a particular geographic area.

geographic segmentation An approach in which marketers tailor their offerings to specific geographic areas because people's preferences often vary depending on where they live.

geotargeting Marketing to a set of specific users based on their current real-time location.

GIGO Garbage in, garbage out.

good A tangible product that we can see, touch, smell, hear, or taste.

government markets The federal, state, county, and local governments that buy goods and services to carry out public objectives and to support their operations.

gray market A distribution channel in which a product's sale to a customer may be technically legal but is at a minimum considered inappropriate by the manufacturer of the related product. Gray markets often emerge around high-end luxury goods sold through exclusive distribution.

gray market goods Items manufactured outside a country and then imported without the consent of the trademark holder.

green customers Those consumers who are most likely to actively look for and buy products that are eco-friendly.

green marketing A marketing strategy that supports environmental stewardship, thus creating a differential benefit in the minds of consumers.

Greenhouse Effect The turning of our atmosphere into a kind of greenhouse as a result of the addition of carbon dioxide and other greenhouse gases.

greenwashing A practice in which companies promote their products as environmentally friendly when in truth the brand provides little ecological benefit.

gross domestic product (GDP) The total dollar value of goods and services produced by a nation within its borders in a year.

gross margin The markup amount added to the cost of a product to cover the fixed costs of the retailer or wholesaler and leave an amount for a profit.

gross rating points (GRPs) A measure used for comparing the effectiveness of different media vehicles: average reach x frequency.

groundswell A social trend in which people use technology to get the things they need from each other, rather than from traditional institutions like corporations.

Group of 7 (G7) An informal forum of the seven most economically developed countries that meets annually to discuss major economic and political issues facing the international community. Formerly the G8, Russia was excluded from the group as a result of its invasion of Crimea in 2014.

growth stage The second stage in the product life cycle, during which consumers accept the product and sales rapidly increase.

guerrilla marketing Marketing activity in which a firm "ambushes" consumers with promotional content in places they are not expecting to encounter this kind of activity.

H

hacker A person who illegally gains access and sometimes tampers with information in a computer system.

hard goods Durable goods such as appliances, furniture, and electronics.

haul videos Videos consumers post on YouTube that detail the latest stuff they bought.

heuristics A mental rule of thumb that leads to a speedy decision by simplifying the process.

hierarchy of effects A series of steps prospective customers move through, from initial awareness of a product to brand loyalty.

hierarchy of needs An approach that categorizes motives according to five levels of importance, the more basic needs being on the bottom of the hierarchy and the higher needs at the top.

high/low pricing, or **promo pricing** A retail pricing strategy in which the retailer prices merchandise at list price but runs frequent, often weekly, promotions that heavily discount some products.

HoloLens Microsoft's mixed reality headset that is a combination of hardware, mixed reality, and artificial intelligence (AI).

horizontal marketing system An arrangement within a channel of distribution in which two or more firms at the same channel level work together for a common purpose.

hybrid marketing system A marketing system that uses a number of different channels and communication methods to serve a target market.

hyperchoice A term used to describe the condition in which consumers have too many choices, leading them to make poorer decisions and experience greater frustration.

hypermarkets Retailers with the characteristics of both warehouse stores and supermarkets; hypermarkets are several times larger than other stores and offer virtually everything from grocery items to electronics.

I

idea marketing Marketing activities that seek to gain market share for a concept, philosophy, belief, or issue by using elements of the marketing mix to create or change a target market's attitude or behavior.

ideation Idea generation through a process characterized by the alternation of divergent and convergent thinking, typical of the design-thinking process.

import quotas Limitations set by a government on the amount of a product allowed to enter a country.

impulse products A product people often buy on the spur of the moment.

impulse purchase A purchase made without any planning or search effort.

in-app advertising To monetize free mobile phone apps, developers use advertising to create revenue and to engage the consumer.

inbound marketing Messages that come *to* the organization from others outside.

independent intermediaries Channel intermediaries that are not controlled by any manufacturer but instead do business with many different manufacturers and many different customers.

in-depth interview A relatively unstructured personal interview with a single respondent, conducted by a highly skilled interviewer.

indirect channel A channel of distribution in which firms sell their products through third parties.

indirect competitors Competitors whose offerings are different from yours but potentially could provide the same benefits and satisfy the same customer needs as your offerings do.

individualist cultures Cultures in which people tend to attach more importance to personal goals than to those of the larger community.

industrial goods Goods that individuals or organizations buy for further processing or for their own use when they do business.

inelastic demand Demand in which changes in price have little or no effect on the amount demanded.

infomercials Half-hour or hour-long commercials that resemble a talk show but actually are sales pitches.

information Interpreted data.

information overload A state in which the marketer is buried in so much data that it becomes nearly paralyzing to decide which of the data provide useful information and which do not.

information search The process whereby a consumer searches for appropriate information to make a reasonable decision.

ingredient branding A type of branding in which branded materials become "component parts" of other branded products.

in-homing A pattern of living in which almost all activities are done in the home.

in-house agency In-house marketing means that marketing activities of a company are handled by employees of the company. Sometimes companies decide to build an in-house marketing team but want to replicate the agency model. They establish so-called "in-house ad agencies."

innovation A product that consumers perceive to be new and different from existing products.

innovators The first segment (roughly 2.5 percent) of a population to adopt a new product.

inseparability The characteristic of a service that means that it is impossible to separate the production of a service from the consumption of that service.

insourcing A practice in which a company contracts with a specialist firm to handle all or part of its supply chain operations.

Instagram A social networking site dedicated to sharing photos and short-form videos.

institutional advertising Advertising messages that promote the activities, personality, or point of view of an organization or company.

intangibility The characteristic of a service that means customers can't see, touch, or smell good service.

intangibles Experience-based products.

integrated marketing communication (IMC) A strategic business process that marketers use to plan, develop, execute, and evaluate coordinated, measurable, persuasive brand communication programs over time to targeted audiences.

intensive distribution Selling a product through all suitable wholesalers or retailers that are willing to stock and sell the product.

interactive agency, or digital agency A limited-service agency that provides a variety of services for digital marketing, including the creation of websites, design and implementation of SEO strategies, creation of articles for online publications, and creation of online email and social media strategies.

intercept research A study in which researchers recruit shoppers in malls or other public areas.

internal customer mindset An organizational culture in which all organization members treat each other as valued customers.

internal customers Coworkers who interact and harbor the attitude and belief that all activities ultimately impact external customers.

internal environment The controllable elements inside an organization, including its people, its facilities, and how it does things that influence the operations of the organization.

internal PR PR activities aimed at employees of an organization.

internal reference price A set price or a price range in consumers' minds that they refer to in evaluating a product's price.

internal validity The extent to which the results of a research study accurately measure what the study intended to measure by ensuring proper research design, including efforts to ensure that any potentially confounding factors were not included or introduced at any point during the execution of the research study.

International Monetary Fund (IMF) An international organization that seeks to ensure the stability of the international monetary exchange by controlling fluctuations in exchange rates.

Internet of Things (IoT) Describes a system in which everyday objects are connected to the Internet and in turn are able to communicate information throughout an interconnected system.

Internet price discrimination An Internet pricing strategy that charges different prices to different buyers for the same product based on order size or geographic location.

interpretation The process of assigning meaning to a stimulus based on prior associations a person has with it and assumptions he or she makes about it.

intranet An internal corporate communication network that uses Internet technology to link company departments, employees, and databases.

introduction stage The first stage of the product life cycle, in which slow growth follows the introduction of a new product in the marketplace.

inventory control Activities to ensure that goods are always available to meet customers' demands.

inventory turnover, or inventory turns The number of times a firm's inventory completely cycles through during a defined time frame.

investor relations PR activities, such as annual and quarterly reports, aimed at a firm's investors.

involvement The relative importance of perceived consequences of the purchase to a consumer.

ISO 9000 Criteria developed by the International Organization for Standardization to regulate product quality in Europe.

J

jingles Original words and music written specifically for advertising executions.

joint demand Demand for two or more goods that are used together to create a product.

joint venture A strategic alliance in which a new entity owned by two or more firms allows the partners to pool their resources for common goals.

just-in-time (JIT) Inventory management and purchasing processes that manufacturers and resellers use to reduce inventory to very low levels and ensure that deliveries from suppliers arrive only when needed.

K

key accounts Very large customer organizations with the potential for providing significant sales revenue.

key performance indicators (KPIs) The critical indicators of progress toward an intended result.

keystoning A retail pricing strategy in which the retailer doubles the cost of the item (100 percent markup) to determine the price.

knockoff A new product that copies, with slight modification, the design of an original product.

knowledge management A comprehensive approach to collecting, organizing, storing, and retrieving a firm's information assets.

L

laggards The last consumers to adopt an innovation.

lagging indicators Performance indicators that provide insight into the performance of an action plan based on outcomes realized.

landing page A single page on a website that is built for a particular direct marketing opportunity.

late majority The adopters who are willing to try new products when there is little or no risk associated with the purchase, when the purchase becomes an economic necessity, or when there is social pressure to purchase.

lead An individual or firm with a potential interest in buying something you sell.

lead nurturing The automated process of sending personalized and relevant content to the prospect to build their trust, making it more likely that they will eventually make a purchase.

leading indicators Performance indicators that provide insight into the performance of *current efforts* in a way that allows a marketer to adjust relevant marketing activities, (hopefully) resulting in performance improvements against the current action plan.

learning A relatively permanent change in behavior caused by acquired information or experience.

leased departments Departments within a larger retail store that an outside firm rents.

least developed country (LDC) A country at the lowest stage of economic development.

level loading A manufacturing approach intended to balance the inventory holding capabilities and production capacity constraints of a manufacturer for a particular product through the implementation of a consistent production schedule, employed both during and beyond periods of peak demand.

level of economic development The broader economic picture of a country.

licensing An agreement in which one firm sells another firm the right to use a brand name for a specific purpose and for a specific period of time.

licensing agreement An agreement in which one firm gives another firm the right to produce and market its product in a specific country or region in return for royalties.

lifestyle The pattern of living that determines how people choose to spend their time, money, and energy and that reflects their values, tastes, and preferences.

lifestyle advertising Lifestyle ads show a person or persons attractive to the target market in an appealing setting with the advertised product as "part of the scene," implying that the person who buys it will attain the lifestyle.

lifestyle brands Brands that seek to inspire, guide, and motivate people with the goal of contributing to the consumer's way of life.

limited-assortment supermarkets, or extreme-value food retailers Stores that carry edibles and related products but in far fewer number, on average around 1,500 SKUs, and at much lower prices than supermarkets.

limited-line product strategy A product line strategy that has fewer product variations in order to send a signal of exclusivity or specialization to the market.

limited-service agency An agency that provides one or more specialized services, such as media buying or creative development.

limited-service merchant wholesalers Wholesalers that provide fewer services for their customers.

list price, or manufacturer's suggested retail price (MSRP) The price that the manufacturer sets as the appropriate price for the end consumer to pay.

lobbying Talking with and providing information to government officials to influence their activities relating to an organization.

local content rules A form of protectionism stipulating that a certain proportion of a product must consist of components supplied by industries in the host country or economic community.

location-based social networks Networks that integrate sophisticated GPS technology that enables users to alert friends of their exact whereabouts via their mobile phones.

locavorism The trend for shoppers to actively look for products that come from farms within 50–100 miles of where they live.

logistics The process of designing, managing, and improving the movement of products through the supply chain. Logistics includes purchasing, manufacturing, storage, and transport.

long tail A new approach to segmentation based on the idea that companies can make money by selling small amounts of items that only a few people want, provided they sell enough different items.

longitudinal design A technique that tracks the responses of the same sample of respondents over time.

loss-leader pricing The pricing policy of setting prices very low or even below cost to attract customers into a store.

M

machine learning The application of AI based on the idea that machines can and should have access to data and engage in learning for themselves.

maintenance, repair, and operating (MRO) products Goods that a business customer consumes in a relatively short time.

malware Software designed specifically to damage or disrupt computer systems.

market All the customers and potential customers who share a common need that can be satisfied by a specific product, who have the resources to exchange for it, who are willing to make the exchange, and who have the authority to make the exchange.

market development strategies Growth strategies that introduce existing products to new markets.

market fragmentation The creation of many consumer groups due to a diversity of distinct needs and wants in modern society.

market intelligence system A method by which marketers get information about what's going on in the world that is relevant to their business.

market manager An individual who is responsible for developing and implementing the marketing plans for products sold to a particular customer group.

market penetration strategies Growth strategies designed to increase sales of existing products to current customers, nonusers, and users of competitive brands in served markets.

market planning The functional planning marketers do. Market planning typically includes both a broad three- to five-year marketing plan to support the firm's strategic plan and a detailed annual plan for the coming year.

market research The process of collecting, analyzing, and interpreting data about customers, competitors, and the business environment in order to improve marketing effectiveness.

market research ethics Taking an ethical and aboveboard approach to conducting market research that does no harm to the participant in the process of conducting the research.

market research online community (MROC) A privately assembled group of people, usually by a market research firm or department, utilized to gain insight into customer sentiments and tendencies.

market segment A distinct group of customers within a larger market who are similar to one another in some way and whose needs differ from other customers in the larger market.

market share The percentage of a market (defined in terms of either sales units or revenue) accounted for by a specific firm, product line(s), or brand(s).

market test, or test market Testing the complete marketing plan in a small geographic area that is similar to the larger market the firm hopes to enter.

marketing Marketing is the activity, set of institutions, and processes for creating, communicating, delivering, and exchanging offerings that have value for customers, clients, partners, and society at large.

marketing analytics A group of technologies and processes that enable marketers to collect, measure, analyze, and assess the effectiveness of marketing efforts.

marketing automation A group of systems and technologies that can be used to establish a set of rules for handling different marketing-related processes without human intervention.

marketing concept A management orientation that focuses on identifying and satisfying consumer needs to ensure the organization's long-term profitability.

marketing dashboard A comprehensive display and access system providing company personnel with up-to-the-minute information necessary to make decisions.

marketing decision support system (MDSS) The data, analysis software, and interactive software that allow managers to conduct analyses and find the information they need.

marketing information system (MIS) A process that first determines what information marketing managers need and then gathers, sorts, analyzes, stores, and distributes relevant and timely marketing information to system users.

marketing metrics Specific measures that help marketers watch the performance of their marketing campaigns, initiatives, and channels, and when appropriate, serve as a control mechanism.

marketing mix A combination of the product itself, the price of the product, the promotional activities that introduce it, and the places where it is made available that together create a desired response among a set of predefined consumers.

marketing plan A document that describes the marketing environment, outlines the marketing objectives and strategy, and identifies how the company will implement and control the strategies embedded in the plan.

marketing-generated lead An inbound sales lead in which a potential customer contacts a company with an interest in their goods or services, resulting from their marketing efforts.

marketplace Any location or medium used to conduct an exchange.

markup An amount added to the cost of a product to create the price at which a channel member will sell the product.

MarTech Short for "marketing technology," this term is commonly used to denote the fusion of marketing and technology. A particular focus is placed on the application of marketing through digital technologies.

mass class The hundreds of millions of global consumers who now enjoy a level of purchasing power that's sufficient to let them afford high-quality products.

mass communication Relates to TV, radio, magazines, and newspapers.

mass customization An approach that modifies a basic good or service to meet the needs of an individual.

mass market All possible customers in a market, regardless of the differences in their specific needs and wants.

materials handling The moving of products into, within, and out of warehouses.

maturity stage The third and longest stage in the product life cycle, during which sales peak and profit margins narrow.

m-commerce Promotional and other e-commerce activities transmitted over mobile phones and other mobile devices, such as smartphones and personal digital assistants.

Me Too movement A movement against sexual harassment and sexual abuse of women that went viral on social media with the hashtag #MeToo.

mechanical observation A method of primary data collection that relies on machines to capture human behavior in a form that allows for future analysis and interpretation.

media blitz A massive advertising campaign that occurs over a relatively short time frame.

media multitasking, or **second screening** Consuming multiple forms of media simultaneously.

media planners Agency personnel who determine which communication vehicles are the most effective and efficient to deliver the ad.

media planning The process of developing media objectives, strategies, and tactics for use in an advertising campaign.

media relations A PR activity aimed at developing close relationships with the media.

media schedule The plan that specifies the exact media to use and when to use it.

medium A communication vehicle through which a message is transmitted to a target audience.

memes Ideas with staying power that move from person to person competing for attention along the way. Memes are a tactic brands use.

merchandise agents and brokers Channel intermediaries that provide services in exchange for commissions but never take title to the product.

merchandise assortment The range of products a store sells.

merchandise breadth The number of different product lines available.

merchandise depth The variety of choices available for each specific product line.

merchandise mix The total set of all products offered for sale by a retailer, including all product lines sold to all consumer groups.

merchandising allowance Reimburses the retailer for in-store support of the product.

merchant wholesalers Intermediaries that buy goods from manufacturers (take title to them) and sell to retailers and other B2B customers.

message The communication in physical form that goes from a sender to a receiver.

microcultures Groups of consumers who identify with a specific activity or art form.

micromarketing The ability to identify and target very small geographic segments that sometimes amount to individuals.

mission (or purpose) A firm's core reason for being.

mission statement A formal statement in an organization's strategic plan that describes the overall purpose of the organization and what it intends to achieve in terms of its customers, products, and resources.

missionary salesperson A salesperson who promotes the firm and tries to stimulate demand for a product but does not actually complete a sale.

mobile advertising A form of advertising that is communicated to the consumer via a handset.

mobile hijacking The use of automated browsers to falsify the number of views or click-throughs the advertisers must pay for.

mobile wallet A smartphone app that stores credit card and other information in order to make purchases/payments.

modified rebuy A buying situation classification used by business buyers to categorize a previously made purchase that involves some change and that requires limited decision making.

monetize The act of turning an asset into money. Websites and mobile apps monetize their content through advertisers.

monopolistic competition A market structure in which many firms, each having slightly different products, offer unique consumer benefits.

monopoly A market situation in which one firm, the only supplier of a particular product, is able to control the price, quality, and supply of that product.

motivation An internal state that drives us to satisfy needs by activating goal-oriented behavior.

multichannel promotion strategy A marketing communication strategy where marketers combine traditional advertising, sales promotion, and public relations activities with online buzz-building activities.

multilevel or **network marketing** A system in which a master distributor recruits other people to become distributors, sells the company's product to the recruits, and receives a commission on all the merchandise sold by the people recruited.

multiple sourcing The business practice of buying a particular product from several different suppliers.

multitasking Moving back and forth between various activities, such as checking emails, watching TV shows, sending instant messages, and so on.

mystery shoppers Individuals employed by retailers and other service providers to experience and report back on the way actual customers are handled.

N

national or **manufacturer brands** Brands that the product manufacturer owns.

nationalization When a government or state seizes a business enterprise, natural resource, or other asset and justifies this action as being in the best interest of the country or state. Reimbursement is typically not required.

native advertising An execution strategy that mimics the content of the website where the message appears.

need The recognition of any difference between a consumer's actual state and some ideal or desired state.

neglected segment An unserved or underserved market segment for which opportunity may exist for a new product entry.

net promoter score (NPS) A quick and effective tool to assess customer satisfaction.

netnography A form of qualitative research that tracks the consumption patterns and conversations of online consumers.

neuromarketing　A type of brain research that uses technologies such as functional magnetic resonance imaging (fMRI) to measure brain activity in order to better understand why consumers make the decisions they do.

new product development (NPD)　The phases by which firms develop new products, including idea generation, product concept development and screening, marketing strategy development, business analysis, technical development, test marketing, and commercialization.

new-business salesperson　The person responsible for finding new customers and calling on them to present the company's products.

new-task buy　A new business-to-business purchase that is complex or risky and that requires extensive decision making.

nimble organization　A firm with the culture, leadership, and operational capability to change very rapidly as external conditions demand.

noise　Anything that interferes with effective communication.

nondurable goods　Consumer products that provide benefits for a short time because they are consumed, such as food, or are no longer useful, such as newspapers.

nonprobability sample　A sample in which personal judgment is used to select respondents.

nonstore retailing　Any method used to complete an exchange with a product end user that does not require a customer visit to a store.

North American Industry Classification System (NAICS)　The numerical coding system that the United States, Canada, and Mexico use to classify firms into detailed categories according to their business activities.

not-for-profit organizations, or **nongovernmental organizations (NGOs)**　Organizations with charitable, educational, community, and other public service goals that buy goods and services to support their functions and to attract and serve their members.

O

objective-task method　A promotion budgeting method in which an organization first defines the specific communication goals it hopes to achieve and then tries to calculate what kind of promotion efforts it will take to meet these goals.

observability　How visible a new product and its benefits are to others who might adopt it.

observational learning　Learning that occurs when people watch the actions of others and note what happens to them as a result.

offering　A generic term often used by marketers to denote the broad range of possibilities of product attributes and sources of product value.

off-price retailers　Retailers that buy excess merchandise from well-known manufacturers and pass the savings on to customers.

offshoring　A process by which U.S. companies contract with companies or individuals in remote places like China or India to perform work they used to do at home.

oligopoly　A market structure in which a relatively small number of sellers, each holding a substantial share of the market, compete in a market with many buyers.

omnichannel (omni-channel) marketing　A retail strategy that provides a seamless shopping experience, whether the customer is shopping online from a desktop or mobile device, by telephone, or in a brick-and-mortar store.

one-to-one marketing　Facilitated by CRM, one-to-one marketing allows the organization to customize some aspect of the goods or services it offers to each customer.

online auctions　E-commerce that allows shoppers to purchase products through online bidding.

online distribution piracy　The theft and unauthorized repurposing of intellectual property via the Internet.

operant conditioning　Learning that occurs as the result of rewards or punishments.

operational planning　A decision process that focuses on developing detailed plans for day-to-day activities that carry out an organization's functional plans.

operational plans　Plans that focus on the day-to-day execution of the marketing plan. Operational plans include detailed directions for the specific activities to be carried out, who will be responsible for them, and timelines to accomplish the tasks.

opinion leader　A person who is frequently able to influence others' attitudes or behaviors by virtue of his or her active interest and expertise in one or more product categories.

order fulfillment automation　The use of technology and machines to improve the speed and accuracy of order fulfillment, especially for B2C e-commerce.

order getter　A salesperson who works to develop long-term relationships with particular customers or to generate new sales.

order processing　The series of activities that occurs between the time an order comes into the organization and the time a product goes out the door.

order taker　A salesperson whose primary function is to facilitate transactions that the customer initiates.

organizational demographics　Organization-specific dimensions that can be used to describe, classify, and organize different organizations for the purpose of segmenting business-to-business markets.

organizational markets　Another name for business-to-business markets.

organizational values　The core attributes valued by the firm that most closely reflect the firm's culture.

organized retail crime (ORC)　Retail shoplifting by organized gangs of thieves that get away with thousands of dollars in goods in a single day.

outbound marketing　Messages that come from the organization and are intended for those who have agreed to receive them.

outcome metrics　Metrics focused on measuring and tracking specific events identified as key business outcomes that result from marketing processes.

outlet stores　Retailer-owned brick-and-mortar or online stores where excess merchandise or special buys from vendors, not offered in the regular retail stores, are available at lower prices.

out-of-home media　Communication media that reach people in public places.

outsourcing　The business buying process of obtaining outside vendors to provide goods or services that otherwise might be supplied in house.

oversegmentation　A marketing malady that occurs when consumers may become confused if an organization offers too many choices.

owned media　Internet sites, such as websites, blogs, Facebook, and Twitter accounts, that are owned by an advertiser.

P

package　The covering or container for a product that provides product protection, facilitates product use and storage, and supplies important marketing communication.

paid influencer programs　Another form of sock puppeting in which bloggers are paid or rewarded in some way for attempting to start online conversations about a brand.

paid media　Internet media, such as display ads, sponsorships, and paid key word searches, that are paid for by an advertiser.

partner relationship management (PRM)　Similar to a CRM, the PRM system allows both selling and buying firms to share some of their information.

party plan system   A sales technique that relies heavily on people getting caught up in the "group spirit," buying things they would not normally buy if they were alone.

patent   A legal mechanism to prevent competitors from producing or selling an invention, aimed at reducing or eliminating competition in a market for a period of time.

payment pricing   A pricing tactic that breaks up the total price into smaller amounts payable over time.

peak load pricing   A pricing plan that sets prices higher during periods with higher demand.

peer-to-peer (P2P) lending, or social lending   Allows individuals to borrow money from other individuals giving the lender higher rates and the borrower lower rates than banks.

penetration pricing   A pricing strategy in which a firm introduces a new product at a very low price to encourage more customers to purchase it.

perceived risk   The belief that choice of a product has potentially negative consequences, whether financial, physical, or social.

percentage-of-sales method   A method for promotion budgeting that is based on a certain percentage of either last year's sales or estimates of the present year's sales.

perception   The process by which people select, organize, and interpret information from the outside world.

perceptual map   A technique to visually describe where brands are "located" in consumers' minds relative to competing brands.

perfect competition   A market structure in which many small sellers, all of whom offer similar products, are unable to have an impact on the quality, price, or supply of a product.

perishability   The characteristic of a service that makes it impossible to store for later sale or consumption.

permission marketing   Email advertising in which online consumers have the opportunity to accept or refuse the unsolicited email.

perpetual inventory unit control system   Retail computer system that keeps a running total on sales, returns, transfers to other stores, and so on.

personal selling   Marketing communication by which a company representative interacts directly with a customer or prospective customer to communicate about a good or service.

personality   The set of unique psychological characteristics that consistently influences the way a person responds to situations in the environment.

personas   Fictional characters created by marketers that represent different key potential user types for an offering.

physical distribution   The activities that move finished goods from manufacturers to final customers, including order processing, warehousing, materials handling, transportation, and inventory control.

place   The availability of the product to the customer at the desired time and location.

place marketing   Marketing activities that seek to attract new businesses, residents, or visitors to a town, state, country, or some other site.

place-based media   Advertising media that transmit messages in public places, such as movie theatres and airports, where certain types of people congregate.

point-of-purchase (POP) displays   In-store displays and signs.

point-of-sale (POS) systems   Retail computer systems that collect sales data and are hooked directly into the store's inventory-control system.

polycentric pricing   A pricing strategy where the local partners set the prices for the product in each global market.

pop-up ads   Advertisements that appear on the screen while a web page loads or after it has loaded.

portfolio analysis   A management tool for evaluating a firm's business mix and assessing the potential of an organization's strategic business units.

positioning   Developing a marketing strategy to influence how a particular market segment perceives a good or service in comparison to the competition.

positioning statement   An expression of a product's positioning that is internally developed and maintained in order to support the development of marketing communication that articulates the specific *value* offered by a product.

posttesting   Research conducted on consumers' responses to actual advertising messages they have seen or heard.

preapproach   A part of the selling process that includes developing information about prospective customers and planning the sales interview.

predatory pricing   An illegal pricing strategy in which a company sets a very low price for the purpose of driving competitors out of business.

predictive analytics   Uses large quantities of data within variables that have identified relationships to more accurately predict specific future outcomes.

predictive technology   Analysis techniques that use shopping patterns of large numbers of people to determine which products are likely to be purchased if others are.

premiums   Items offered free to people who have purchased a product.

pre-roll ads   Promotional video messages that play before the content the user has selected.

press release   Information that an organization distributes to the media intended to win publicity.

prestige pricing, or premium pricing   A pricing strategy used by luxury goods marketers in which they keep the price artificially high to maintain a favorable image of the product.

prestige products   Products that have a high price and that appeal to status-conscious consumers.

pretesting   A research method that seeks to minimize mistakes by getting consumer reactions to ad messages before they appear in the media.

price   The assignment of value, or the amount the consumer must exchange to receive the offering.

price bundling   Selling two or more goods or services as a single package for one price.

price elasticity of demand   The percentage change in unit sales that results from a percentage change in price.

price gouging   An illegal act in which a seller seeks to take advantage of an emergency or extreme need to charge exorbitant prices for items.

price leadership   A pricing strategy in which one firm first sets its price and other firms in the industry follow with the same or similar prices.

price lining   The practice of setting a limited number of different specific prices, called *price points*, for items in a product line.

price segmentation   The practice of charging different prices to different market segments for the same product.

price-fixing   The collaboration of two or more firms in setting prices, usually to keep prices high.

primary data   Data from research conducted to help make a specific decision.

private-label brands   Brands that a certain retailer or distributor owns and sells.

proactive PR   Public relations activities that are based on the company's marketing objectives.

probability sample   A sample in which each member of the population has some known chance of being included.

problem recognition   The process that occurs whenever the consumer sees a significant difference between his or her current state of affairs and some desired or ideal state; this recognition initiates the decision-making process.

processed materials   Products created when firms transform raw materials from their original state.

producers   The individuals or organizations that purchase products for use in the production of other goods and services.

product   A tangible good, service, idea, or some combination of these that satisfies consumer or business customer needs through the exchange process; a bundle of attributes including features, functions, benefits, and uses.

product adaptation strategy   Product strategy in which a firm offers a similar but modified product in foreign markets.

product adoption   The process by which a consumer or business customer begins to buy and use a new good, service, or idea.

product advertising   Advertising messages that focus on a specific good or service.

product category manager   An individual who is responsible for developing and implementing the marketing plan for all the brands and products within a product category.

product competition   When firms offering different products compete to satisfy the same consumer needs and wants.

product concept development and screening   The second step of product development in which marketers test product ideas for technical and commercial success.

product development strategies   Growth strategies that focus on selling new products in existing markets.

product diversion   The distribution of a product through one or more channels not authorized for use by the manufacturer of the product.

product invention strategy   Product strategy in which a firm develops a new product for foreign markets.

product life cycle (PLC)   A concept that explains how products go through four distinct stages from birth to death: introduction, growth, maturity, and decline.

product line   A firm's total product offering designed to satisfy a single need or desire of target customers.

product line extension   A strategy to expand an existing product line by adding more brands or models.

product line length   Determined by the number of separate items within the same category.

product management   The systematic and usually team-based approach to coordinating all aspects of a product's strategy development and execution.

product mix   The total set of all products a firm offers for sale.

product mix width   The number of different product lines the firm produces.

product objectives   The direction and focus that marketers establish for their products, which ultimately support the broader marketing objectives of the business unit and are consistent with the firm's overall mission.

product placement, or embedded marketing   The placement of brands, logos, or a product itself into entertainment venues.

product quality   The overall ability of the product to satisfy customer expectations.

product relaunch   Using principles of segmentation, target marketing, and positioning to reposition an existing product for reintroduction into the product life cycle.

product review sites   Social media sites that enable people to post stories about their experiences with goods and services.

product sampling   Distributing free trial-size versions of a product to consumers.

product specifications   A written description of the quality, size, weight, and other details required of a product purchase.

production orientation   A management philosophy that emphasizes the most efficient ways to produce and distribute products.

programmatic advertising, or programmatic ad buying   The use of algorithms and software to buy digital advertising, thus providing greater efficiency, control, and cost savings.

promotion   The coordination of a marketer's communication efforts to influence attitudes or behavior.

promotion mix   The communication elements that the marketer controls.

promotional products   Goodies such as coffee mugs, T-shirts, and magnets given away to build awareness for a sponsor. Some freebies are distributed directly to consumers and business customers; others are intended for channel partners, such as retailers and vendors.

prospecting   A part of the selling process that includes identifying and developing a list of potential or prospective customers.

protectionism   A policy adopted by a government to give domestic companies an advantage.

prototypes   Test versions of a proposed product.

proximity marketing (also known as beacon marketing)   A retail marketing strategy in which beacon devices are placed strategically throughout a store and emit a Bluetooth signal to communicate with shoppers' smartphones as they browse the aisles of the store.

psychographics   The use of psychological, sociological, and anthropological factors to construct market segments.

public relations campaign   A coordinated effort to communicate with one or more of the firm's publics.

public relations (PR)   Communication function that seeks to build good relationships with an organization's publics, including consumers, stockholders, and legislators.

public service advertisements (PSAs)   Advertising run by the media for not-for-profit organizations or to champion a particular cause without charge.

publicity   Unpaid communication about an organization that appears in the mass media.

puffery   Claims made in advertising of product superiority that cannot be proven true or untrue.

pull strategy   The company tries to move its products through the channel by building desire for the products among consumers, thus convincing retailers to respond to this demand by stocking these items.

purchase journey   The process or roadmap a customer follows to become aware of, consider and evaluate, and decide to purchase a product or service.

push money   A bonus paid by a manufacturer to a salesperson, customer, or distributor for selling its product.

push strategy   The company tries to move its products through the channel by convincing channel members to offer them.

pyramid schemes   An illegal sales technique that promises consumers or investors large profits from recruiting others to join the program rather than from any real investment or sale of goods to the public.

Q

QR code advertising   QR (quick response) code advertising uses smartphone GPS technology to deliver ads and other information to consumers in stores and in other locations.

qualitative research Research with results that provide detailed verbal or visual information about consumers' attitudes, feelings, and buying behaviors rather than offering numeric data.

quantitative research Research that produces numeric results that can be analyzed using a variety of statistical programs.

quantity discounts A pricing tactic of charging reduced prices for purchases of larger quantities of a product.

question marks SBUs with low market shares in fast-growth markets.

questionnaire A survey research instrument (either on paper or electronic) consisting of a series of questions for the purpose of gathering information from respondents.

R

radio frequency identification (RFID) Product tags with tiny chips containing information about the item's content, origin, and destination.

raw materials Products of the fishing, lumber, agricultural, and mining industries that organizational customers purchase to use in their finished products.

reach, or **rating** The percentage of the target market that will be exposed to the media vehicle.

rebates Sales promotions that allow the customer to recover part of the product's cost from the manufacturer.

rebranding Taking an established brand and intentionally and strategically creating a new name, concept, symbol, design, imagery, and messaging in order to develop a new, differentiated identity in the minds of consumers and other stakeholders.

receiver The organization or individual that intercepts and interprets the message.

reciprocity A trading partnership in which two firms agree to buy from one another.

recommendation engine Computer system that has access to customers' former shopping behavior in order to make a recommendation for future purposes.

recommerce The process of selling used products or excess inventory to companies or consumer resale stores.

reference group An actual or imaginary individual or group that has a significant effect on an individual's evaluations, aspirations, or behavior.

relationship selling A form of personal selling that involves securing, developing, and maintaining long-term relationships with profitable customers.

relative advantage The degree to which a consumer perceives that a new product provides superior benefits.

reliability The extent to which research measurement techniques are free of errors.

reminder advertising Advertising aimed at keeping the name of a brand in people's minds to be sure consumers purchase the product as necessary.

rent-to-own A buyer rents an item and at a set end of the rental period, the buyer owns the merchandise.

repositioning Redoing a product's position to respond to marketplace changes.

representativeness The extent to which consumers in a study are similar to a larger group in which the organization has an interest.

resale stores Retail stores that accept and sell used merchandise, including clothing, furniture, household items, and musical instruments.

research and development (R&D) A well-defined and systematic approach to how innovation is done within the firm.

research and marketing services The advertising agency department that collects and analyzes information that will help the account executive develop a sensible strategy and assist creatives in getting consumer reactions to different versions of ads.

research design A plan that specifies what information marketers will collect and what type of study they will do.

resellers The individuals or organizations that buy finished goods for the purpose of reselling, renting, or leasing to others to make a profit and to maintain their business operations.

retail and local advertising Advertising that informs consumers about store hours, location, and products that are available or on sale.

retail borrowing The consumer practice of purchasing a product with the intent to return the nondefective merchandise for a refund after it has fulfilled the purpose for which it was purchased.

retail return fraud Criminal activity when someone returns an item they obtained without making a purchase.

retailer cooperative A group of retailers that establishes a wholesaling operation to help them compete more effectively with the large chains.

retailer margin The margin added to the cost of a product by a retailer.

retailing The final stop in the distribution channel in which organizations sell goods and services to consumers for their personal use.

retailtainment The use of retail strategies that enhance the shopping experience and create excitement, impulse purchases, and an emotional connection with the brand.

retro brands A once-popular brand that has been revived to experience a popularity comeback, often by riding a wave of nostalgia.

return on experience (ROX) A metric used to measure the real value of personalized customer experiences.

return on investment (ROI) The direct financial impact of a firm's expenditure of a resource, such as time or money.

return on marketing investment (ROMI) Quantifying just how an investment in marketing has an impact on the firm's success, financially and otherwise.

reverse engineering The process of physically deconstructing a competitor's product to determine how it's put together.

reverse logistics Includes product returns, recycling and material reuse, and waste disposal.

reverse marketing A business practice in which a buyer firm attempts to identify suppliers who will produce products according to the buyer firm's specifications.

rich media A digital advertising term for an ad that includes advanced features, like video and audio elements, that encourage viewers to interact and engage with the content.

rights approach Ethical philosophy that advocates the decision that does the best job of protecting the moral rights of all.

risk management Refers to the practice of identifying potential risks in advance, analyzing them, and taking precautionary steps to reduce/curb the risk.

risk-taking functions The chance retailers take when they buy a product from a manufacturer, as the product might just sit on the shelf if no customers want it.

robocall An unsolicited phone call—most often from an unscrupulous source—that uses a computerized autodialer to deliver a pre-recorded message, as if from a robot.

S

sachet Affordable one-use packages of cleaning products, fabric softeners, shampoo, and other items for sale to consumers in least developed and developing countries.

sadvertising Advertising designed to arouse negative emotions in order to get our attention and create a bond with the brand's products.

sales cycle The series of events that takes place from the moment a salesperson first engages with a prospect up until the moment when the sale is made.

sales funnel The process through which a company finds, qualifies, and sells its products to buyers.

sales presentation The part of the selling process in which the salesperson directly communicates the value proposition to the customer and invites two-way communication.

sales promotions Programs designed to build interest in or encourage purchase of a product during a specified period.

sampling The process of selecting respondents for a study.

save-now-buy-later (SNBL) A payment process whereby payments are automatically drafted from a customer's bank account; when the agreed-upon amount is saved, the customer can order the item.

scanner data Data derived from items that are scanned at the cash register when you check out with your loyalty card.

scenarios The multiple strategic paths a firm develops in contingency planning.

Scrum A popular methodology for executing agile marketing.

search engine marketing (SEM) Search marketing strategy in which marketers pay for ads or better positioning.

search engine optimization (SEO) A systematic process to ensure that your firm comes up at or near the top of lists of typical search phrases related to your business.

search engines Internet programs that search for documents with specified key words.

search marketing Marketing strategies that involve the use of Internet search engines.

seasonal discounts Price reductions offered only during certain times of the year.

secondary data Data that have been collected for some purpose other than the problem at hand.

segment of one Tracking the activity and preferences of a single potential customer and then tailoring products or ads for that individual according to their behaviors.

segment profile A description of the "typical" customer in a segment.

segmentation The process of dividing a larger market into smaller pieces based on one or more meaningfully shared characteristics.

segmentation variables Dimensions that divide the total market into fairly homogeneous groups, each with different needs and preferences.

selective distribution Distribution using fewer outlets than intensive distribution but more than exclusive distribution.

self-concept An individual's self-image that is composed of a mixture of beliefs, observations, and feelings about personal attributes.

self-driving (autonomous) vehicle A self-driving or autonomous car (also known as a *driverless car* or *robotic car*) and unmanned ground vehicle is a vehicle that is capable of sensing its environment and navigating without human input.

selling orientation A managerial view of marketing as a sales function, or a way to move products out of warehouses to reduce inventory.

sensory branding The use of distinct sensory experiences not only to appeal to customers but also to enhance a brand.

sensory marketing Marketing techniques that link distinct sensory experiences, such as a unique fragrance, with a product or service.

sentiment analysis The process of identifying a follower's attitude (e.g., positive, negative, or neutral) toward a product or brand by assessing the context or emotion of his or her comments.

service encounter The actual interaction between the customer and the service provider.

service retailers Organizations that offer consumers services rather than merchandise. Examples include banks, hospitals, health spas, doctors, legal clinics, entertainment firms, and universities.

service-dominant logic A firm's mindset for understanding the exchange process, acknowledging that all firms are service firms and that a firm has more opportunities with the service-dominant logic.

services Intangible products that are exchanged directly between the producer and the customer.

servicescape The actual physical facility where the service is performed, delivered, and consumed.

SERVQUAL scale A popular instrument used to measure customers' perceptions of service quality.

share of wallet The percentage of an individual customer's purchase of a product that is a single brand.

sharing economy A consumer activity where consumers share goods and services that is facilitated by an online platform.

shoplifting Criminal activity in which individuals steal goods from a retailer while pretending to be a customer.

shopping cart abandonment Occurs when e-commerce customers leave an e-commerce site with unpurchased items in their cart.

shopping for control Consumers, facing a world with terrorism and political unrest, value products and services that provide some degree of control, such as smart home technology or gated communities.

shopping products Goods or services for which consumers spend considerable time and effort gathering information and comparing alternatives before making a purchase.

short-form storytelling Because consumers today prefer short messages, successful marketing communication often includes 15-second TV commercials, a tweet, a snap, a captionless Instagram post, or a TikTok clip.

showrooming Consumers browsing products on their mobile devices while in a brick-and-mortar store.

shrinkage Losses experienced by retailers as a result of shoplifting, employee theft, return fraud, and administration and paperwork errors.

simulated market test Application of special computer software to imitate the introduction of a product into the marketplace, allowing the company to see the likely impact of price cuts and new packaging—or even to determine where in the store it should try to place the product.

single sourcing The business practice of buying a particular product from only one supplier.

situation analysis An assessment of a firm's internal and external environments.

Six Sigma A process whereby firms work to limit product defects to 3.4 per million or fewer.

skimming price A very high, premium price that a firm charges for its new, highly desirable product.

slice-of-life advertising A slice-of-life ad presents a (dramatized) scene from everyday life.

slogans Simple, memorable linguistic devices linked to a brand.

slotting allowance A fee paid in exchange for agreeing to place a manufacturer's products on a retailer's valuable shelf space.

SMART goals Goals that meet the criteria of being specific, measurable, achievable, relevant, and timely.

Snapchat A social networking site that allows users to share snaps—pictures and videos that are only available for a limited period of time. Lenses and Geofilters allow users to create photos with unique elements.

social class The overall rank or social standing of groups of people within a society according to the value assigned to factors such as family background, education, occupation, and income.

social commerce Consumer decision-making activities that occur in, or are influenced by, someone's social network, particularly online.

social graph A graph that represents social relations between people or other entities. A social graph is a representation of a social network. The social graph has been referred to as "the global mapping of everybody and how they are related."

social media Internet-based platforms that allow users to create their own content and share it with others who access these sites.

social media advertising Advertising that is executed within the confines of social media channels.

social networking platforms Online platforms that allow a user to represent himself or herself via a profile on a website and provide and receive links to other members of the network to share input about common interests.

social networks Online platforms that allow a user to represent himself or herself via a profile on a website and provide and receive links to other members of the network to share input about common interests.

social norms Specific rules dictating what is right or wrong, acceptable or unacceptable.

social selling Using social media to engage in the selling process.

societal marketing concept A management philosophy that marketers must satisfy customers' needs in ways that also benefit society and deliver profit to the firm.

sock puppeting A practice where a company executive or other biased source poses as someone else to plug a product in social media.

soft goods Nondurables such as clothing, cosmetics, and bedding.

source An organization or individual that sends a message.

spam The use of electronic media to send unsolicited messages in bulk.

special events Activities—from a visit by foreign investors to a company picnic—that are planned and implemented by a PR department.

specialized services Services that are essential to the operation of an organization but are not part of the production of a product.

specialty products Goods or services that have unique characteristics and are important to the buyer and for which he or she will devote significant effort to acquire.

specialty stores Retailers that carry only a few product lines but offer good selection within the lines that they sell.

speech writing Writing a speech on a topic for a company executive to deliver.

sponsored posts Content brands pay celebrities to share through their personal accounts.

sponsored search ads Paid ads that appear at the top or beside the Internet search engine results.

sponsorships PR activities through which companies provide financial support to help fund an event in return for publicized recognition of the company's contribution.

spoofed numbers Numbers used that look familiar to the intended receiver but are actually fake.

spyware Software that covertly gathers information from an individual's or an organization's computer.

stakeholders Buyers, sellers, or investors in a company; community residents; and even citizens of the nations where goods and services are made or sold—in other words, any person or organization that has a "stake" in the outcome.

standard of living An indicator of the average quality and quantity of goods and services consumed in a country.

staple products Basic or necessary items that are available almost everywhere.

stars SBUs with products that have dominant market shares in high-growth markets.

status symbols Visible markers that provide a way for people to flaunt their membership in higher social classes (or at least to make others believe they are members).

stock-keeping unit (SKU) A unique identifier for each distinct product.

stock-outs Zero-inventory situations resulting in lost sales and customer dissatisfaction.

storytelling The foundation of all communication, usually including characters, setting, plot, conflict, and resolution. Brand storytelling is practiced by marketers.

straight extension strategy Product strategy in which a firm offers the same product in both domestic and foreign markets.

straight rebuy A buying situation in which business buyers make routine purchases that require minimal decision making.

strategic alliance Relationship developed between a firm seeking a deeper commitment to a foreign market and a domestic firm in the target country.

strategic business units (SBUs) Individual units within the firm that operate like separate businesses, with each having its own mission, business objectives, resources, managers, and competitors.

strategic pivot The operationalization of a rapid demand to change a firm's business model, business direction, product line, or market focus, including the ability to rapidly increase output, to satisfy unexpected new and/or different demand.

strategic planning A managerial decision process that matches an organization's resources and capabilities to its market opportunities for long-term growth.

strategy The execution of the elements of a plan based on goals and objectives to bring about a desired future.

street furniture advertising Advertising placed close to pedestrians and shoppers at eye level or at the curbside.

structured data Data that (1) are typically numeric or categorical; (2) can be organized and formatted in a way that is easy for computers to read, organize, and understand; and (3) can be inserted into a database in a seamless fashion.

sub-branding Creating a secondary brand within a main brand that can help differentiate a product line to a desired target group.

subculture A group within a society whose members share a distinctive set of beliefs, characteristics, or common experiences.

subliminal advertising Supposedly hidden messages in marketers' communications.

subscription boxes A new business model for distribution that supplies surprises by sending out a box each month filled with items you never knew you wanted but you just have to have.

subscription pricing Pricing tactic where customers pay on a periodic basis, normally monthly or yearly, for access to a product.

supercenters Large combination stores that combine economy supermarkets with other lower-priced merchandise.

supermarkets   Food stores that carry a wide selection of edibles and related products.

supply chain   All the activities necessary to turn raw materials into a good or service and put it in the hands of the consumer or business customer.

supply chain management   The management of flows among firms in the supply chain to maximize total profitability.

support media   Media such as directories or out-of-home media that may be used to reach people who are not reached by mass-media advertising.

surge pricing   A pricing plan that raises prices of a product as demand goes up and lowers it as demand slides.

survey research   The collection of information from respondents via their answers to questions.

sustainability   A design and manufacturing focus that meets present needs without compromising the ability of future generations to meet their needs.

sustainable packaging   Packaging that involves one or more of the following: elements that can be produced from previously used materials, elements that use materials in their development that can be repurposed after use, materials that require fewer resources to cultivate, and materials and processes that are generally less harmful to the environment.

SWOT analysis   An analysis of an organization's strengths and weaknesses and the opportunities and threats in its external environment.

syndicated research   Research by firms that collect data on a regular basis and sell the reports to multiple firms.

T

take title   To accept legal ownership of a product and assume the accompanying rights and responsibilities of ownership.

target costing   A process in which firms identify the quality and functionality needed to satisfy customers and what price they are willing to pay before the product is designed; the product is manufactured only if the firm can control costs to meet the required price.

target market   The market segments on which an organization focuses its marketing plan and toward which it directs its marketing efforts.

target marketing strategy   Dividing the total market into different segments on the basis of customer characteristics, selecting one or more segments, and developing products to meet the needs of those specific segments.

targeting   A strategy in which marketers evaluate the attractiveness of each potential segment and decide in which of these groups they will invest resources to try to turn them into customers.

tariffs   Taxes on imported goods.

team selling   The sales function when handled by a team that may consist of a salesperson, a technical specialist, and others.

teaser ads, or **mystery ads**   Ads that generate curiosity and interest in a to-be-introduced product by drawing attention to an upcoming ad campaign without mentioning the product.

technical development   The step in the product development process in which company engineers refine and perfect a new product.

technical specialist   A sales support person with a high level of technical expertise who assists in product demonstrations.

technical success   Indicates that a product concept is feasible purely from the standpoint of whether or not it is possible to physically develop it, regardless of whether it is perceived to be commercially viable.

telecommute   Working with fellow employees from a distant location using Internet communication technology, such as VoIP, sometimes referred to as *WFH* or *work from home.*

telemarketing   The use of the telephone to sell directly to consumers and business customers.

text message advertising   Delivering ads to consumers as mobile phone text messages.

textbooks   Books used in the study of a subject; for example, a book containing a presentation of the principles of a subject.

The Tax Cuts and Jobs Act of 2017 (TCJA of 2017)   A major overhaul of personal and corporate taxes enacted by Congress in 2017.

thrift stores   Resale stores that give their profits to charities.

TikTok   A social networking site that hosts short videos lasting for 15 seconds or less, typically accompanied by music.

time poverty   Consumers' belief that they are more pressed for time than ever before.

tipping point   In the context of product diffusion, the point when a product's sales spike from a slow climb to an unprecedented new level.

tonality   The mood or attitude the message conveys (straightforward, humorous, dramatic, romantic, sexy, or apprehensive/fearful).

top-down budgeting techniques   Allocation of the promotion budget based on management's determination of the total amount to be devoted to marketing communication.

total costs   The total of the fixed costs and the variable costs for a set number of units produced.

total quality management (TQM)   A management philosophy that focuses on satisfying customers through empowering employees to be an active part of continuous quality improvement.

touchpoint   Any point of direct interface between customers and a company (online, by phone, or in person).

trade discounts   Discounts off list price of products to members of the channel of distribution who perform various marketing functions.

trade sales promotions   Promotions that focus on members of the "trade," which include distribution channel members, such as retail salespeople or wholesale distributors, that a firm must work with to sell its products.

trade shows   Events at which many companies set up elaborate exhibits to show their products, give away samples, distribute product literature, and troll for new business contacts.

trademark   The legal term for a brand name, brand mark, or trade character; trademarks legally registered by a government obtain protection for exclusive use in that country.

transactional selling   A form of personal selling that focuses on making an immediate sale with little or no attempt to develop a relationship with the customer.

transit advertising   Advertising in airports and in bus, subway, and train stations, and ads on the outside and on the inside of subway and rail cars, busses, and taxis.

transportation   The mode by which products move among channel members.

transportation and storage   Occurs when retailers and other channel members move the goods from the production point to other locations where they can hold them until consumers want them.

trial pricing   Pricing a new product low for a limited period of time to lower the risk for a customer.

trialability   The ease of sampling a new product and its benefits.

triple-bottom-line orientation   A business orientation that looks at financial profits, the community in which the organization operates, and creating sustainable business practices.

tryvertising   Advertising by sampling that is designed to create buzz about a product.

TV Everywhere, or **authenticated streaming**   The use of an Internet-enabled device, like a tablet or smartphone, to stream content from a cable or satellite provider.

Twitch   A social media site that is the most-used streaming platform for broadcasting video games and is used for videos from cooks, artists, vloggers, and musicians.

Twitter   A free microblogging service that lets users post short text messages with a maximum of 280 characters.

two-part pricing   Pricing that requires two separate types of payments to purchase the product.

two-way product line stretch   A product line extension strategy that simultaneously expands new items both toward the higher and lower ends of the market.

U

Uber   A peer-to-peer sharing service offering shared rides, food delivery, and transportation worldwide via websites and mobile apps.

unaided recall   A research technique conducted by telephone survey or personal interview that asks whether a person remembers seeing an ad during a specified period without giving the person the name of the brand.

undifferentiated targeting strategy   Appealing to a broad spectrum of people.

unfair sales acts   State laws that prohibit suppliers from selling products below cost to protect small businesses from larger competitors.

uniform delivered pricing   A pricing tactic in which a firm adds a standard shipping charge to the price for all customers regardless of location.

unique selling proposition (USP)   An advertising appeal that focuses on one clear reason why a particular product is superior.

Universal Product Code (UPC)   A set of black bars or lines printed on the side or bottom of most items sold in grocery stores and other mass-merchandising outlets that correspond to a unique 10-digit number.

unobtrusive measures   Measuring traces of physical evidence that remain after some action has been taken.

unsought products   Goods or services for which a consumer has little awareness or interest until the product or a need for the product is brought to his or her attention.

unstructured data   Nonnumeric information that is typically formatted in a way that is meant for human eyes and not easily understood by computers.

upcycling   A new apparel trend of using discarded products to create a higher-quality, higher-value upcycled product.

upfront TV ad pricing   *Upfront* is the term used to describe the practice of buying and selling national TV advertising time for the entire broadcast year, October through September; upfront buying allows advertisers to lock in pricing and get the best time slots.

upward product line stretch   A product line extension strategy that adds new items toward the higher-priced end of the market.

U.S. Generalized System of Preferences (GSP)   A program to promote economic growth in developing countries by allowing duty-free entry of goods into the United States.

usage occasions   An indicator used in behavioral market segmentation based on when consumers use a product most.

usage rate   A measurement that reflects the quantity purchased or frequency of use among consumers of a particular product or service.

user adoption metrics   Metrics focused on the extent to which employees are using the CRM system as intended, including various IT metrics, such as number of logins and data completeness.

user-generated content, or **consumer-generated content**   Marketing content and activities created by consumers and users of a brand such as advertisements, online reviews, blogs, social media, input to new product development, or serving as wholesalers or retailers.

utilitarian approach   Ethical philosophy that advocates a decision that provides the most good or the least harm.

utility   The usefulness or benefit that consumers receive from a product.

V

validity   The extent to which research actually measures what it was intended to measure.

VALS™   A psychographic segmentation system that divides U.S. adults into eight groups according to what drives them psychologically as well as by their economic resources.

value chain   A series of activities involved in designing, producing, marketing, delivering, and supporting any product. Each link in the chain has the potential to either add or remove value from the product the customer eventually buys.

value co-creation   The process by which benefits-based value is created through collaborative participation by customers and other stakeholders in the new product development process.

value pricing, or **everyday low pricing (EDLP)**   A pricing strategy in which a firm sets prices that provide ultimate value to customers.

value proposition   A marketplace offering that fairly and accurately sums up the value that will be realized if the good or service is purchased.

variability   The characteristic of a service that means that even the same service performed by the same individual for the same customer can vary.

variable costs   The costs of production (raw and processed materials, parts, and labor) that are tied to and vary by the number of units produced.

venture teams   Groups of people within an organization who work together to focus exclusively on the development of a new product.

vertical marketing system (VMS)   A channel of distribution in which there is formal cooperation among members at the manufacturing, wholesaling, and retailing levels.

video news release (VNR)   Similar to a press release, information that an organization sends to the media in a film format.

video sharing   Uploading video recordings on to Internet sites such as YouTube so that thousands or even millions of other Internet users can see them.

virtual experiential marketing   An online marketing strategy that uses enhancements—including colors, graphics, layout and design, interactive videos, contests, games, and giveaways—to engage experiential shoppers online.

virtual goods   Digital products consumers buy for use in online contexts.

virtual office   The use of Internet technology to work and participate from a distant physical office.

virtual worlds   Online, highly engaging digital environments where avatars live and interact with other avatars in real time.

virtue approach   Ethical philosophy that advocates the decision that is in agreement with certain ideal values.

vision   What a firm aspires to do or be in the future.

vision statement   A firm's articulation of its vision.

vlogs   Video recordings shared on the Internet.

voice-over Internet protocol (VoIP)   Communication systems that use data networks to carry voice calls.

W

want   The desire to satisfy needs in specific ways that are culturally and socially influenced.

warehouse clubs   Discount retailers that charge a modest membership fee to consumers who buy a broad assortment of food and nonfood items in bulk and in a warehouse environment.

warehousing Storing goods in anticipation of sale or transfer to another member of the channel of distribution.

Web 1.0 The beginning phase of the Internet that offered static content provided by the owner of the site.

Web 2.0 The second generation of the World Wide Web that incorporated social networking and user interactivity via two-way communication.

web scraping The process of using computer software to extract large amounts of data from websites.

webrooming Consumers comparing prices of products online.

wheel-of-retailing hypothesis A theory that explains how retail firms change, becoming more upscale as they go through their life cycle.

wholesaler margin The amount added to the cost of a product by a wholesaler.

wholesaling intermediaries Firms that handle the flow of products from the manufacturer to the retailer or business user.

wisdom of crowds Under the right circumstances, groups are smarter than the smartest people in them, meaning that large numbers of consumers can predict successful products.

word-of-mouth communication When consumers provide information about products to other consumers.

World Bank An international lending institution that seeks to reduce poverty and better people's lives by improving economies and promoting sustainable development.

world trade The flow of goods and services among different countries—the value of all the exports and imports of the world's nations.

World Trade Organization (WTO) An organization that replaced GATT; the WTO sets trade rules for its member nations and mediates disputes between nations.

Y

yield management pricing A practice of charging different prices to different customers to manage capacity while maximizing revenues.

YouTube A free online video platform launched in 2005 and acquired by Google in 2006. Channels for both consumers and businesses are used by 1.68 billion worldwide.

Z

ZMOT Google's term for the *zero moment of truth* when the consumer decides to make a purchase, often on a smartphone, tablet, or laptop.

Zoom-bombing Uninvited guests showing up for a Zoom meeting.

Name Index

Subject Index